Dedicated to those from whom we have learned much—our families, the clients with whom we have worked, the students we have known, and our professional colleagues.

SOCIAL WORK PROCESSES

Fifth Edition

SOCIAL WORK PROCESSES

Beulah R. Compton
University of Southern Mississippi

Burt Galaway
University of Manitoba

Brooks/Cole Publishing Company
Pacific Grove, California

ITP ™ The trademark ITP is used under license.

A CLAIREMONT BOOK

Brooks/Cole Publishing Company
A Division of Wadsworth, Inc.

Printed in the United States of America
10 9 8 7 6 5 4 3 2 1

Library of Congress Cataloging-in-Publication Data

Compton, Beulah Roberts.
  Social work processes / Beulah R. Compton, Burt Galaway.
    p.   cm.
  5th ed.—Pref.
  Includes bibliographical references and index.
  ISBN 0-534-17364-0
  1. Social service. 2. Social case work. 3. Social service—
United States. 4. Social case work—United States. I. Galaway,
Burt. II. Title.
  HV37.C62 1994   93-49529
  362.3'2'0973—dc20   CIP

Sponsoring Editor: Claire Verduin
Editorial Associate: Gay C. Bond
Production Service: Graphic World Publishing Services
Production Coordinator: Laurel Jackson
Permissions Editor: Catherine Gingras/Lillian Campobasso
Interior Design: Rita Naughton
Cover Design: Roy R. Neuhaus
Cover Artist: Judith Larzelere
Cover Photo: Jan Bindas Studio, Boston
Typesetting: Graphic World, Inc.
Printing and Binding: Malloy Lithographing, Inc.

Contributors

Benavides, Eustolio. Executive Director, Neighborhood House Association, St. Paul, Minnesota.

Boland, Mary. Director, Pediatric AIDS Program, Children's Hospital of New Jersey, Newark.

Brentnall, Peter. Social Worker, Social Service Department, Walsall, England.

Compher, John Victor. Social Work Supervisor, Philadelphia County Children and Youth Agency, Philadelphia, Pennsylvania.

Compton, Beulah Roberts. Professor Emeritus, School of Social Work, University of Southern Mississippi.

Cournoyer, Barry. Associate Professor and Clinical Social Worker, Indiana University School of Social Work, Indianapolis.

Evans, Patricia. Director of Professional Services, Children's Hospice of New Jersey, Union.

Fein, Edith. General Partner, Connecticut Planning Associates, West Hartford, Connecticut.

Gilgun, Jane F. Associate Professor, School of Social Work, University of Minnesota, Minneapolis.

Goldstein, Howard. Professor Emeritus, Mandel School of Applied Social Sciences, Case Western Reserve University, Cleveland, Ohio.

Hagen, Jan L. Professor, School of Social Welfare, State University of New York, Albany.

Hardman, Dale G. Professor Emeritus, University of Wisconsin, Oshkosh.

Harrison, W. David. Professor, School of Social Work, University of Alabama, Tuscaloosa.

Hartman, Ann. Elizabeth Marting Treuhaft Professor and Dean, School of Social Work, Smith College, Northampton, Massachusetts.

Hess, Howard J. Professor, Fordham University Graduate School of Social Service, New York, New York.

Hess, Peg McCartt. Associate Professor, Columbia University School of Social Work, New York, New York.

Ho, Man Keung. Professor, School of Social Work, University of Oklahoma, Norman.

Hoshino, George. Professor Emeritus, School of Social Work, University of Minnesota, Minneapolis.

Huber, Marg. Program Coordinator, Center for Conflict Resolution, Justice Institute of British Columbia, Vancouver.

Johnson, Miriam. Instructor and doctoral student, School of Social Work, University of Alabama, Tuscaloosa.

Keresztes, Judith. Ambulatory Care Coordinator, Children's Hospital of New Jersey, Newark.

Lewis, Ronald G. Professor, School of Social Work, Eastern Michigan University, Ypsilanti, Michigan.

Lockhart, R.A. (Sandy). Professor and Chair of Sociology, Catharine Parr Traill College, Trent University, Peterborough, Ontario.

Longclaws, Lyle. Social Worker, Child Protection Center, Children's Hospital, Winnipeg, Manitoba.

Maluccio, Anthony N. Professor of Graduate School of Social Work, Boston College, Chestnut Hall, Massachusetts.

McKnight, John. Professor, Speech Communication Studies and Center for Urban Affairs and Policy Research, Northwestern University, Evanston, Illinois.

Morris, Addie. Assistant Director, Arkansas Mental Health Services, Little Rock.

Narayan, Uma. Associate Professor, Department of Philosophy, Vassar College, Poughkeepsie, New York.

Pawlak, Edward J. Professor, School of Social Work, Western Michigan University, Kalamazoo.

Solomon, Barbara. Vice Provost for Graduate & Professional Studies and Dean of Graduate Studies, University of Southern California, Los Angeles.

Specht, Harry. Professor and Dean, School of Social Welfare, University of California, Berkeley.

Staff, Ilene. Research Associate, Casey Family Services, Hartford, Connecticut.

Tasker, Mary. Social Worker/Consultant, Institute for Family-Centered Care, Bethesda, Maryland.

Tebb, Susan. Assistant Professor and Director of BSW Program, School of Social Science, St. Louis University, St. Louis, Missouri.

Velasquez, Joan. Research Director, Ramsey County Human Services, St. Paul, Minnesota.

Vigil, Marilyn E. Associate Professor, Department of Human Services, Metropolitan State University, St. Paul, Minnesota.

Walsh, M. Ellen.   Social Worker, Employee Assistance Program, Boeing Company, Seattle, Washington.

Weinbach, Robert.   Professor, College of Social Work, University of South Carolina, Columbia.

Woehle, Ralph.   Professor, Department of Social Work, Southwest State University, Marshall, Minnesota.

Contents

Preface

In this fifth edition, we continue our commitment to the problem-solving model for *Social Work Processes*. This focus has stood the test of time since initial formulation by Helen Harris Perlman in the 1950s, and has served as the dominant paradigm for social work practice since our first edition in the mid-1970s. This fifth edition continues the process of clarifying our earlier notions and enriching the concepts presented in the first four editions. We have persevered in our effort to strengthen our material from the situation side of the person-situation paradigm. We have done so by utilizing theories to guide assessment that can take into consideration the situation of individuals and approaches to intervention that include environment and situation change. In this respect, we have introduced new material on the influence of the environment and the culture in which the individual is embedded and ways social workers may utilize these forces: the process of social care planning, the empowerment of families, and understanding of various cultures of our clients.

Social Work Processes, intended as a primary text for foundation courses, provides a conceptual and theoretical framework for social work practice in a diversity of settings and client systems with which social workers interact. The conceptual framework presented will support, encourage, and provide an organizing frame as a foundation for social work practice in the variety of settings in which social workers find themselves. Published in 1975, the first edition grew out of our extensive social work practice and teaching experiences. The ideas for this conceptual framework have been refined, modified, and expanded as a result of our continued teaching and practice experiences. We have had the opportunity to work with hundreds of students and practitioners as they apply these concepts in practice. Equally important, we continue to be engaged in practice, giving us direct experience with this framework, which has continued to demonstrate an ability to combine classic foundation with the newest research.

Social Work Processes is based on our understanding of the Council on Social Work Education's (C.S.W.E.) position on the desired thrust of the foundation courses. We both have extensive practice experience in public agencies, continue to work in these settings, and believe this book supports the C.S.W.E. position that schools should emphasize practice in public welfare. Foundation courses need to offer students a central model of practice that is related to an identified theoretical knowledge base that serves social work practice actions. Students should finish the foundation courses with a mastery of practice principles and the underlying theoretical knowledge. To discuss specialized modalities and the theories underlying them at a level that ensures mastery, and enough competence to protect the client, would require space beyond the scope of this volume. The introduction of specialized methods should wait until the second MSW year as spelled out in the *Standards of Accreditation*.

We want to express our debt to those individuals who have made comments about each edition of the text, especially the teachers whose suggestions came from the use of the book in their classes. Such comments have been invaluable to us over the years. In the fourth edition, in response to readers' desire for more case material, we included seven cases at the end of Chapter 1, hoping they would be useful throughout the text. However, many teachers seemed to dislike this position, so we have now placed these cases at the end of the book. We hope they are more useful there as problems of application of the material in each chapter. The cases have been selected to offer a variety of clients and their problems so that students may apply common knowledge to a variety of situations. We have also tried to introduce discussion of these examples throughout the text. In addition, we have added more vignettes in the chapters.

We have received many comments, both pro and con, about our selection of readings. The selection has been a difficult task for us, and we have increasingly moved from using reprints from journals to using original papers written, at our suggestion, by practitioners and educators whom we respect. We have valued the readings as a way of introducing the student to a number of different writers, so that the book does not become simply our work. Believing in the importance of students' familiarity with their own professional history and literature, we have included classic articles. In addition, we have sought articles that deal with the newer problems of social work practice. We have tried to select articles that are generic, linking theory to practice, rather than more specialized articles focused on specific techniques.

We appreciate the thoughtful, helpful comments on this manuscript provided by Robert Evans, University of Illinois at Chicago; Cynthia Franklin, University of Texas at Austin; John Goldmeier, University of Maryland at Baltimore; Karen Harper, West Virginia University; Alice Lieberman, University of Kansas; Irene Queiro-Tajalli, Indiana University; Jack Richman, University of North Carolina at Chapel Hill; and Carolyn Weaver, Tulane University. While we are grateful to those who have commented and to our students who have questioned us, we must assume sole responsibility for this text.

—*Beulah R. Compton*
Burt Galaway

SOCIAL WORK PROCESSES

The Context for Deciding What to Do

Purpose of Social Work

What do social workers do? Where and how do they intervene? For most of us these are perplexing questions—questions made more perplexing by our lack of contact with social workers and the variety of social work practice. Most of us, from our life experiences, have little difficulty identifying the job of the doctor as healing the body—mediating between the physical organism and environmental influences that threaten health. The doctor's job becomes less clear and less well understood, however, when it moves out of the area of physical illness and into the treatment of mental illness. Likewise, the lawyer's job as mediator between the individual and the legal institutions that have been developed to ensure a reasonably orderly society is usually understood. And few of us have any difficulty identifying the job of the teacher in transmitting the accumulated knowledge of the culture. But what about social workers? What is their job? William Schwartz (1961, pp. 150–151) has noted that "Every profession has a particular function to perform in society; it has received a certain job assignment for which it is held accountable." To Schwartz the social work job assignment is to "mediate the process through which the individual and . . . society reach out for each other through a mutual need for self-fulfilment." The Schwartz mediating model rests on the assumption that the interests of the individual and the interests of society are essentially the same but that in a complex and changing society the individual's desire to belong as a full and productive member and the society's ability to integrate and enrich its people are sometimes blocked. Social work intervention is directed toward these blockages and toward freeing the "individual's impetus toward health, growth, and belonging; and the organized efforts of society to integrate its parts into a productive and dynamic whole," according to Schwartz.

What Schwartz calls blockage between the individual's impetus toward growth and the organized efforts of society will be experienced by individuals, families, groups, or organizations as problems. The problems may be varied—finding a job, caring for a child, maintaining communications in a marriage, getting along with others, dealing with threats of mugging in the street, boredom because of inactivity, lack of adequate housing, discrimination, and so on. We speak of social work as a problem-solving process; problem solving is the way social workers and clients put Schwartz's concept of mediation into action. Thus we think of problem solving as mediating between the person and resources of the environment, or person-in-situation (the immediate environment). In this first chapter we develop further the nature of social work as mediating the person-situation interaction.

We present a model of social work practice built on three key concepts—the ecological perspective, the client and worker partnership, and the problem-solving process. All three concepts have well-established traditions in social work practice and provide a framework for practice in all settings and with diverse populations. We will briefly introduce you to these concepts in this chapter. You will also find them as recurring themes throughout the book. We will also introduce some key contextual matters necessary to understanding the nature of social work practice. These include the differences between social work, social welfare, and social science; social work and case management; social work and therapy; the definition of client; prevention versus intervention; generalists and specialists; and the practitioner as researcher.

At this early stage, we must emphasize a crucial distinction between practice, process, and intervention; these are often confused by social workers. Social work practice is the totality of what social workers do. It encompasses both a process (we call this the problem-solving process) and planned-change actions that we consider methods of intervention. Although methods of intervention are often called social work practice, they are only one piece of practice. We see intervention as one part of the problem-solving process. The focus of this book is on the problem-solving process, which must be understood and mastered before one turns to ways of intervening to bring about change.

Ecological Perspective

Person-in-Situation   Alex Gitterman and Carel Germain (1980, pp. 10–13) offer a life model that "integrates the treatment and reform traditions, by conceptualizing and emphasizing the dysfunctional transactions between people and their social and physical environments." Social workers focus on problems in living that fall into three areas: (1) problems and needs associated with tasks involved in life transitions; (2) problems and needs associated with tasks in using and influencing elements of the environment; and (3) problems and needs associated with interpersonal obstacles that impede the work of a family or a group as it deals with transitional and/or environmental tasks. Ecological models such as Gitterman and Germain's have been developed in social work over several years (Peterson, 1979; Baer & Federico, 1978; Germain, 1973; Meyer, 1970; Pincus & Minahan, 1973). These models focus on the transactions of individuals and their environments with both individuals and environments in a constant state of reciprocity, each shaping the other. Social work interventions are directed toward the interface of the individual and environment or at problems of living generated from the person-in-situation interaction.

The ecological focus views individual human beings as living in constant reciprocity with their communities. The individual influences community and vice versa. Problems are experienced when there is not a good fit between the needs and wants of the individual and the resources made available by the community; resolving these problems requires a simultaneous focus on individuals and the communities and societies in which they live. This has often been referred to as the person-in-situation focus; this dual focus on person and situation is one of the consistent themes to have emerged over time as social workers have struggled with defining the nature of the social work profession.

Martin Rein (1970, p. 15) has suggested that one of the obstacles to the development of a professional social work creed has been the difficulty in defining the social work profession. Nevertheless, efforts have been made to define both the target and the nature of social work practice. The Commission on Social Work Practice of the National Association of Social Workers (1958, p. 56) published a working definition that defined social work practice as a "constellation of value, purpose, sanction, knowledge, and method." The working definition identified three purposes of social work practice:

1. To assist individuals and groups to identify and resolve or minimize problems arising out of disequilibrium between themselves and the environment.
2. To identify potential areas of disequilibrium between individuals or groups and the environment in order to prevent the occurrence of disequilibrium.
3. In addition to these curative and preventive aims, to seek out, identify, and strengthen the maximum potential in individuals, groups, and communities.

Werner Boehm (1958, p. 18) has also published a widely used definition of social work.

> Social work seeks to enhance the social functioning of individuals, singularly and in groups, by activities focused upon their social relationships which constitute interaction between individuals and their environments. These activities can be grouped into three functions: restoration of impaired capacity, provision of individual and social resources, and prevention of social dysfunction.

The West Virginia Undergraduate Social Work Curriculum Development Project conceptualized social work as concerned and involved with the interactions between people and the institutions of society that affect the ability of people to accomplish life tasks, realize aspirations and values, and alleviate distress. These interactions between people and social institutions occur within the context of the larger societal good. Therefore, three major purposes of social work may be identified:

1. To enhance the problem-solving, coping, and developmental capacities of people.
2. To promote the effective and humane operation of the systems that provide people with resources and services.
3. To link people with systems that provide them with resources, services, and opportunities. (Baer & Federico, 1978, p. 68)

All these definitions place the focus of social work intervention on the interaction between individuals and their environments. They are consistent with Schwartz's mediating approach, since social work is considered as intervening or mediating between people and their social environments, and with the ecological approaches formulated by Gitterman and Germain.

Harriett Bartlett (1970, p. 116) wrote of a social work focus on social functioning, which she defines as the "relation between the coping activity of people and the demand from the environment." For Bartlett the concept of social functioning did not refer to the functioning of individuals or groups, which she found characteristic of earlier definitions. Instead she directed attention to what goes on between people and environment through the exchange between them. A dual focus ties them together. Thus person and situation, people and environment, are encompassed in a single concept, which requires that they be constantly reviewed together.

William Gordon (1969, p. 6), with whom Bartlett was in agreement, found that "the central focus of social work traditionally seems to have been on people in their life situation complex—a simultaneous dual focus on individuals and environment." Gordon further noted that emphasis is on individualizing the person-situation complex to achieve the best match between each person and the environment, in which either person-behavior or environmental situation may deviate widely from the typical or normative. He writes, "We conclude, therefore, that the central target of technical social work practice is matching something in person and situation—that is, intervening by whatever methods and means necessary to help people be in situations where their capabilities are sufficiently matched with the demands of the situations to make a go of it."

The focus of social work intervention is on the interaction between humans and their environments. In Schwartz's terms social workers mediate; in Gordon's terms social workers match something in the environment to something in the individual; in Bartlett's terms social workers seek to strike a balance between coping ability and environmental demands; and in Baer and Federico's terms social workers link people with resource-providing systems. But do mediating, matching, striking a balance, and linking mean changing the individual or changing the environment? This is an old issue in social work that was enunciated at an early date by Porter Lee (1929) in his distinction between social work as cause and social work as function. Social workers do both, and the debate about whether the profession should focus primarily on individual change or on environmental change results largely from an incorrect formulation of the focus of social work intervention and failure to understand the ecological perspective. The parties to this debate tend to polarize social workers as focusing either on the individual or on the environment and miss the central focus as on the interaction of the two. Gisela Konopka (1963, Chapter 9) has pointed out the inappropriateness of this dichotomous thinking in social work, and Martin Rein (1970, p. 19) noted that both individual and social change approaches can be used either to support or to challenge contemporary standards of behavior. Research by Merlin A. Taber and Anthony J. Vattano (1970) found no sharp distinction between clinical and social orientations among practicing social workers and suggested that most social workers are able to integrate both functions. Rein's concept of radical casework is particularly well suited to a social work focus on person-situation interaction. For Rein (1970, p. 19), "a radical casework approach would mean not merely obtaining for clients social services to which they are entitled or helping them adjust to the environment, but also trying to deal with the relevant people and institutions in the clients' environment that are contributing to their difficulties." Social workers may direct change strategies toward individuals, toward environments, and toward the interaction of individuals and environments. But in all cases these strategies are toward modifying the person-situation interaction.

The concept of social functioning and dual focus on both person and situation holds profound implications for social work practice. Some social workers have considered themselves as caseworkers, group workers, or community organizers. Francis Purcell and Harry Specht in a classic social work case (Appendix, A-7) illustrate the need to move beyond this tripartite division of practice when responding to a housing problem presented by a low-income client. Thinking traditionally as a caseworker, a group worker, or a community organizer tends to obscure the range of problem definitions and change strategies that might be considered by encouraging a focus on one side or the other of the person-situation interaction. A recent study of 226 children seen at a child guidance clinic found a high frequency of family and social problems (Proctor, Vosler, & Sirles, 1993); the authors write that "these findings provide support for a traditional social work concept—the person-in-environment perspective. A focus on only the individual yields an incomplete picture: social workers need to provide a sufficiently comprehensive assessment to detect problems in the broader social context." Schwartz (1961, p. 148) notes the inappropriateness of basing a definition of method on the number of persons with whom the worker interacts and suggests that the terms casework, group work, and community organization refer to the relational system in which the worker implements method. For Schwartz, method is "a systematic process of ordering one's activity in the performance of a function. Method is function in action." The method becomes a systematic way in which social workers carry out their function—that is, the systematic way in which they mediate between the individual and the social environment.

Martin Rein (1970, p. 19) notes that the association of social change with community organization and of individual change with social casework may oversimplify social work, inasmuch as work with individuals can be directed toward change in social standards and work with groups or communities can be directed toward helping people adapt to their current situations. We agree with the Rein formulation but think that this distinction has been largely missed in social work—the expectation remains that the community organizer works at community change, the caseworker works to produce individual change, and the group worker may do either, depending on the nature of the group. This expectation diverts the focus of social work from the person-situation interaction to either the person or the situation, depending on the particular method in which the practitioner has been steeped.

Models focusing on the person-situation intervention have the potential for bridging the unfortunate dichotomy of social change versus individual change that has developed in our profession by removing blinders that limit the vision of some social workers, who focus on individuals, and other social workers, who focus on social conditions. We present here a practice model that will involve you, as a social worker, in activities directed toward resolution of problems that develop in the interactions of individuals and their environments. Through your social work education, you will develop skills of problem definition as well as commitment and ability to use a range of change strategies.

Knowledge for Practice   You will require social work knowledge to maintain this focus. Thinking of social work as mediating the person-situation interaction to assist clients in the resolution of problems suggests the types of knowledge you will require. First, of course, is knowledge about the person—individual behavior and patterns of adaptation and all that impacts on these. Then, of course, is knowledge about the situation—the community, its institutions, and the various resource structures. Third, we require what Carel Germain (1981, p. 325) calls the transactional concept to help explain and understand "transactions between people and environments that, on one hand promote or inhibit growth, development, and the release of human potential and, on the other hand, promote or inhibit the capacity of environment to support

EXHIBIT 1-1
Reference
Tools for
Social Work
Literature
Research

These tools will assist you to conduct searches of the social work literature.

Publication Manual (3rd ed.). (1983). Washington, D.C.: American Psychological Association.

This is the manual of style used by most social work journals and is widely used by publishers of other social and behavioral science materials.

Social Work Research and Abstracts. Silver Spring, MD: National Association of Social Workers.

Published four times a year; the winter (December) issue contains a cumulative index for the year. Available in data bases, including CD-ROM. Check your library to determine if the CD-ROM version is available.

Barker, R. L. (1987). *The Social Work Dictionary.* Silver Spring, MD: National Association of Social Workers.

First social work dictionary, containing definitions of over 3,000 terms commonly used in social work.

Beebe, L. (1987). *Users Guide to Social Work Abstracts.* New York: National Association of Social Workers.

Instructions for using the *Abstracts;* information on the on-line data base. Includes descriptors and access terms in use as of July 1987.

Minehan, A. (Ed.). (1987). *Encyclopedia of Social Work* (18th ed.). Washington, DC: National Association of Social Workers.

Edwards, R. (Ed.). (in press). *Encyclopedia of Social Work* (19th ed). Washington, D.C.: National Association of Social Workers.

Two volumes of articles on topics related to social work and social welfare.

the diversity of human potential." Fourth, we require knowledge of the problem-solving process. This involves problem definition and assessment as well as knowledge of intervention models. You will be expected, as a professional, to understand the knowledge base of your profession and to keep informed about new developments. You will be doing regular literature searches to learn from what others have done and to make knowledge available to your clients. Exhibit 1-1 provides an introduction to the tools you will be using to remain current with the social work literature.

To a very large extent our profession borrows knowledge of person and knowledge of situation from supporting social sciences. In Chapters 3 and 4, we discuss some of the types of knowledge and theories useful for social work practice and offer guidelines for selecting knowledge. Knowledge of the problem-solving process and of social work assessment and intervention is the responsibility of social work. Social work practice is clearly the responsibility of our profession. While we may occasionally borrow and integrate practice concepts from other professions, the responsibility for developing, testing, and transmitting knowledge about social work practice—both the process and the models of intervention—must remain a central responsibility of social work. We think that all social workers have a responsibility as researchers to be doing evaluations and studies of their own practice and to be contributing to the profession's knowledge base. The NASW (National Association of Social Workers) Code of Ethics makes development of knowledge an ethical duty for us: "the social worker should contribute to the knowledge base of social work and share research knowledge and perspective wisdom with colleagues" (Reading 7-1, section V.0.3). This is a theme to which we will return in Chapter 16.

Knowledge can be used in two very different ways. For some, knowledge can be used as a justification for power; the possession of knowledge not commonly held can be used to advance one's claim to exercise power over persons who do not have the knowledge. This is the power of the expert. But knowledge can also be used by an expert as a resource to be made available to persons and organizations for consideration in their own decision making. This occurs when experts offer information to clients for their use. The worker-client partnership, which we think is central to social work practice, suggests that you avoid using your expertise as a way of justifying your power and instead make your knowledge available to clients to assist them in their own decision making and planning.

Problem Solving Let us turn to the broad brush strokes of the practice model developed in this book. We are reminded of the professor who regularly met her freshman classes by writing

$$\frac{3}{2}$$

in large bold print on the blackboard. She then turned and smiled expectantly at her class. A few braver souls responded 5, to which the professor shook her head negatively, and then a few more would indicate 1, to which there was also a negative head shake. Then, in a veritable chorus, the class shouted out 6, to which the professor commented, "But you see, you have given the answer before you knew the problem." Having answers before we know the problem is a common temptation to which many inexperienced and even some experienced social workers succumb.

Process for Practice Abraham Kaplan (1964, p. 23) has referred to a law of the instrument: "Give a small boy a hammer, and he will find that everything that he encounters needs to be pounded. It comes as no particular surprise to discover that scientists formulate problems in ways which require for their solution just those techniques in which they themselves are especially skilled." The same problem has characterized much of social work practice, especially when practice is thought about as models of intervention. What is necessary is the ability to define problems independent of intervention models and then to select the most appropriate model for intervention.

One way to reduce this risk is to be very clear about the difference between social work process and social work intervention. Intervention, by which we mean a conscious planned effort to produce change, is but one component of social work process. Before intervening you must be clear about the nature of the problem you are attempting to resolve as well as the goals and purposes of intervention; social work process is a broader concept than intervention and encompasses all of the elements of practice including intervention. A clear understanding regarding social work process and skills at managing this process are prerequisites to intervention. This is primarily a book about social work process, with intervention treated as one component of social work process. It is not, therefore, a book on models of intervention.

Herbert Bisno (1969, p. 9) and John Kidneigh (1969, p. 159) have both suggested that two sets of skills are necessary for social work—skills in knowing what change strategies to use and skills in actual use of change strategies. Kidneigh believes that social workers must possess the capability both of "deciding what to do" and "of doing the decided." The Kidneigh and Bisno division of skills provides a helpful guide to refining the more global Schwartz model of the mediating function of the profession. Operationalizing the mediating function involves arriving at decisions about how to intervene and how to implement these decisions.

Social workers, in carrying out their mediating function, are engaged in problem-solving behavior to assist in the resolution of problems of interaction between persons and their situations. Thus mediation is a problem-solving process. An overview of the problem-solving model is presented in Chapter 2 and the various components of the model presented in more detail in Chapters 10 through 16. Problem solving is a rational process including actions to define the problem, actions to collect information on which to base decisions, actions to engage the client in goal setting and decision making, actions to produce change, and actions to evaluate progress.

Describing a change process as a problem-solving model is quite different from characterizing it as a problem-focus model. Social workers do start with a problem—some sense of distress or discomfort in the relationship between the individual and his or her broader community or environment. The process of working out a solution to that problem will involve the use of strengths brought by the client, the worker, and the environment. Thus the model might well be called problem solving but strength-focused; the identification of strengths becomes a very important part of the assessment process; planning for use of these strengths becomes a part of the process of developing an intervention plan.

Intervention Models for Practice   Intervention refers to deliberate planned actions undertaken by the client and worker to resolve a problem. Thus intervention occurs after a problem has been defined and after the desired resolution (we will call this the *goal*) has been identified. An intervention model is an organized set of procedures that, based on research including our practice experience, are thought to be useful for bringing about a resolution of the specific problem confronting the client and worker.

We have already noted that intervention is a part, but not the totality, of social work practice. We have also established that the purpose of this book is to present a model for social work practice and not to present models of intervention (that comes later, after the practice model is understood and mastered). We do want to alert you, however, to two errors commonly made by social workers, especially inexperienced ones. One is to assume that practice is only intervention. A second equally serious error is to gobble up, hook, line, and sinker, an intervention model, frequently external to social work, which is then indiscriminately applied without regard for the definition of the problem or client goals. We have known of social workers, for example, who have indiscriminately adopted transactional analysis, reality therapy, Adlerian psychology, behavioral modification, or another system of thought that has then been haphazardly applied under the pretext of doing social work. The fish analogy may be appropriate. Grabbing for a tender morsel may be easier than the hard work of developing social work models, including a wide range of interventive strategies for use in mediating the person-situation interaction. This may be especially true if the morsel is attractive and the lure faddish.

Sanctions for Practice   At the beginning of this chapter, we noted that Schwartz (1961, pp. 150–151) emphasizes that every profession has an assigned function in society for which the profession is accountable. Social work is no exception. The community and client systems need assurance that the interventions of the practitioner with the various systems of practice are within the recognized and approved parameters of society's assignment to the profession. Social work practice is sanctioned through three structures—the profession, licensing, and the social welfare institutions within which most social workers are employed. Chapter 6 will deal with the meaning of these sanctioning structures to practice actions.

Worker and Client as Partners

Values for Practice   Values guide and direct practice. Values for social work practice are discussed more extensively in Chapter 7, but two aspects of the value orientation should be clarified at the outset. Social workers have long held a commitment to increasing opportunities for choices available to clients as well as assisting clients in making use of available sources. Note, for example, the work of the social worker in "The House on Sixth Street" (Appendix, A-7) both to make use of available resources and to increase the availability of housing. Harold Lewis (1972, p. 411) asserts that "institutionalized restrictions which limit opportunities, as well as the personal shortcomings of the client which may curtail options, are legitimate targets for change." We refer to these changes as increasing client self-determination by increasing opportunities for choice and by assisting clients with decision making. Self-determination is a hollow concept if the environment does not provide opportunities or if the client is unable to use opportunities. In carrying out the mediating function you will be working to increase opportunities for choice and in so doing to increase client self-determination.

Social work is a partnership arrangement. We think the client and social worker function together as partners throughout the problem-solving process. This means the client is fully involved and participating in all of the decisions and that the social worker is working with the client rather than doing things to the client. We frequently see students wishing to come into the social work profession because they want to reform or change people. If this is your interest, we suggest that you carefully rethink your reasons. Unless you can change your point of view, you are likely to find social work a very frustrating experience. Our function as social workers is not to reform or to change people; rather we engage people in a problem-solving process by which they resolve their own problems. Note, as you review the cases in the appendix, how the workers involved clients in the decision making. (You might also watch for examples of times the worker may have missed an opportunity to involve clients in decision making.) The involvement of clients in decision making is very clear in "The House on Sixth Street." The focus of the work was assisting clients to strengthen their own ability to deal with city government and public bureaucracies rather than taking over and attempting to solve the problems for this group of tenants. An unusual application of the partnership concept is reported in Reading 1-3, in which an agency shows responsibility for keeping an adolescent in foster care by involving the adolescent as a partner in this process. This was done by permitting the adolescent the option of changing placement upon serving a 28-day notice. The youth would then be involved in planning for an alternative placement, with the social worker and foster parent serving as partners in this process; much of the responsibility for the

EXHIBIT 1-2
Governments
as Community
Economic
Development
Partners

Populations are generally aware of factors affecting their fragile economy but the citizens usually do not engage actively in altering the conditions which cause the economies of their communities to be forever insecure and reliant upon extraordinary measures. They view such work as belonging to government. Thus, announcements of plans from above are the perennial expectation of a population which has learned to be helpless. Governments as partners in CED must take into account the current state of learned helplessness and follow processes to enable the population to see and take hold of ways to transform their community through its economy.

Development of communities, and especially less-advantaged communities, must follow a strategy which places responsibility for formulating and realizing change firmly in the hands of the people of the community who, in turn, learn to grasp and deal with that responsibility. Ideally, this approach involves all levels of the nation's governmental and corporate forces. First and foremost, it requires citizens to understand the facts of their economic circumstances and the causes of their underdevelopment. It then requires them to identify, choose, and act on their development options. To place responsibility more squarely in the hands of citizens does not mean that governments must abandon their responsibility for economic development. Rather, government is situated as a stage-setter, as an enabler, and as the sponsor of a process which will transform a community according to the choice and determination of its population. Government is the force to handle those functions and activities which are otherwise impossible for citizens to handle themselves. The role of specialists is shifted from being decision makers who specify development policy to being the major source of support for citizens who would determine the direction of development in their local economy. This is a formidable role shift.

SOURCE: MacNeil, Teresa. (1994). Governments as partners in community economic development. In B. Galaway and J. Hudson (Eds.), *Community economic development: Perspectives on Canadian research and policy.* Toronto: Thompson Educational Publishing.

work, however, must be carried by the young person. In this sense, social work may well differ from the other professions. We are here to assist clients to participate in a problem-solving process, not to solve problems for others.

The concept of partnership is becoming relatively well developed in the field of community economic development. This particularly exciting area for social work practice has been evolving partially from our community organization and community development roots. It attempts to merge practices of community development, social development, and economic development to assist whole communities, often underdeveloped and marginalized, to control their own resources and destinies. Community economic development often involves the need for partners that are external to the communities. In Exhibit 1-2 Teresa MacNeil describes the role and some of the pitfalls when the external partner is a government agency. Alexander (Sandy) Lockhart, in Reading 1-2, discusses the dialectical nature of the partnership between an insider and outsider working toward a community economic development plan for a Canadian Aboriginal community.[1] Each partner brings resources and information on work to be done; while the contributions of each partner are different, they are of equal importance to accomplishing the tasks. The

---

[1] Canadian indigenous peoples prefer the titles Aboriginal, Native, or First Nations, and generally prefer not to be referred to as Indians. Lockhart uses the term *outside consultant* rather than *social worker* and *tribal council* or *insiders* rather than *clients*.

notion of partnership comes through in terms of the importance of information exchanged and assessment: "if a current fashionable term 'social impact assessment' is to mean anything beyond a cheap strategy to usurp the ability of a community to determine what kinds of development are most consistent with its own sense of being, then such assessment must ensure that community insiders learn as much about themselves from the process as do any outsiders who may be involved."

We will be returning to this concept of assessment as joint learning and joint decision making in Chapters 10 and 11. At this point we want simply to alert you of all aspects of social work processes involving worker and client partnership and note that none are the exclusive jurisdiction of the worker. This concept of worker and client partnership, of joint decision making, is quite different from the concept of the professional as the expert who knows or should know what needs to be done. The concept of joining a partnership with a client may even be at variance with your own image of professional practice. So we invite you to consider seriously the possibilities of partnership, to think about this notion and discuss it with your colleagues, and we hope that you will find this a journey of discovery.

Some Matters of Context

The model of social work practice that we will be developing with you is based on the three central concepts of an ecological perspective, a problem-solving process, and a worker and client partnership. Before proceeding to develop these themes, however, we want to address seven matters of context that will have quite a bearing on your ability to practice social work in ecological, problem-solving, and partnership perspectives. These matters have to do with social work, social welfare, and social science; social work and case management; social work and therapy; definition of *client;* prevention and intervention; generalists and specialists; and research and practice.

Social Work, Social Welfare, and Social Science We want to be clear about the concepts of social welfare, social work, and social sciences. The term *social welfare* refers to an organized set of norms and institutions through which we put into effect our collective responsibility to care for one another. In complex societies our responsibility is often carried out through formal organizations to which we attach labels, such as child welfare services, family services, criminal justice services, and so forth. But social welfare can also be a set of norms (commonly held expectations of each other) that define our mutual responsibilities. In cultures whose extended family and clan systems are intact, shared norms often require extended family system members to provide care for dependent children or aging persons. The Lee case of a Laotian refugee family (Appendix, A5) provides an illustration of this type of social welfare; the continued presence of the extended family system provides norms and expectations of self-help among members. John McKnight (Reading 16-2) suggests that formal social services may deter the work of informal helping systems. When we talk about social welfare policy, we are referring to opinions or positions regarding the goals of our collective responsibility as well as a set of arrangements or services for carrying out the collective responsibility.

We often refer to social welfare policy as public social welfare policy, meaning a set of laws and administrative rules that define the purposes of public social welfare and that establish and authorize organizations to work toward accomplishment of those purposes. Thus we have laws providing income for dependent children and establishing a set of organizations to provide this income. Likewise we have laws that provide for protection of dependent populations such as children and the aged and that authorize agencies to provide protective services. Social welfare policy addresses a number of fundamental questions: What is the nature of our collective responsibility to each other? What structures and arrangements enable us to carry out this collective responsibility? To what extent is the collective responsibility to be carried out through formal organizations and to what extent through informal norms of self-help? What is the relationship between formal institutions and informal help giving? How and to what extent can public agencies, private nonprofit agencies, and for-profit agencies be involved in the formal social welfare delivery system? Becoming conversant with and developing views on these social welfare questions are part of becoming a liberally educated person in late 20th century society. As a social worker, you will be practicing within the social welfare system and will be expected to provide informed leadership and direction to that system and to social policy.

But this book is not a book about social welfare; that knowledge will come in other courses. This is a book about social work and specifically about social work practice. Social work is a profession involving knowledge, values, and skills; it is the central and dominant but not the only profession involved in staffing the formal social welfare system. The distinction between social work and the social welfare system is like the distinction between teachers and the educational system or doctors and nurses and the health care system. One is the set of organizations and norms designed to accomplish policy goals; the other is the profession on which the organizations rely. This book will introduce you to a model for social work practice that will guide your work as a professional within the social welfare system. We refer to it as the problem-solving model.

We speak of social welfare as the set of goals and institutions and social work as a profession, but what about the social sciences? The social sciences—such as sociology, psychology, political science, economics, and anthropology—are disciplines that provide knowledge regarding the nature of society and the human condition. Knowledge generated by the social sciences informs social welfare as social welfare has become formalized in law and formal institutions. Likewise, social sciences provide necessary but not sufficient knowledge to guide the social work profession as we work jointly with people to find solutions to problems they are experiencing in their environments. As social workers, we will draw knowledge from the social sciences to help us understand the nature of human beings, the nature of societies, and the nature of interaction between social institutions and human beings. To this, however, we must contribute our own knowledge regarding the nature of assessment (how we view and define problems) and the nature of interventions used in social work. Thus, we borrow knowledge from the social sciences, translate that knowledge into forms useful to us in our practice, and contribute knowledge from our own profession regarding assessment and intervention. But is social work a social science? We think not. Social work is a profession, using knowledge developed by social sciences for furthering the goals of social welfare. This formulation does not permit us to escape the responsibility to be scientific, to be rigorous, and to engage in research. In Chapters 3 and 16, we will discuss our responsibility to generate knowledge and as a profession to use knowledge borrowed from the social sciences as well as knowledge generated by our profession. Application of the problem-solving model requires discipline and rigor; we view the social worker as a practitioner-researcher.

Social Work and Case Management   The term case management has different meanings. To some it means assisting clients to access resources, that is, to manage the resources of their communities (Rose, 1992). To others it means managing the client and often carries the connotation of rationing or controlling access to resources, usually formally organized resources, of the community. The first definition, assisting clients to access and utilize the resources of their communities, is central to social work practice. In Chapter 12, we talk about the social broker role, which involves a set of activities by which social workers link clients to community resources. In Reading 12-1 W. David Harrison and Miriam Johnson use a case example to illustrate the practice of community care that plays a central place in social work practice in the United Kingdom. This is a good example of social work practice as case management.

Social work practice is case management that involves helping people link to the resources of their community. Linking, however, will be to neighbors, extended family members, clubs and organizations, churches and other religious groups, recreational and mutual aid groups, and so forth as well as to formally organized service providers. This linking function, especially to the informal systems, is very consistent with the ecological perspective, which addresses the interdependent nature of humans and their communities. One of the shortcomings of much case management is that it fails to recognize the importance of assisting clients to access, use, develop, and manage informal sources of social support and overemphasizes the connections to formal social service delivery systems. John McKnight, in Reading 16-2, discusses possible unintended consequences of formalizing human services and suggests that one of these may be the breakdown of informal sources of support and help. This will occur, for example, when professionals encourage clients to talk just to professionals and not to share matters of concern more informally with neighbors and family members. Social work practice is, in our view, case management directed toward assisting people to participate in community life.

Social Work and Therapy   Harry Specht, in Reading 4-1, traces the relationship of social work to psychiatry, humanistic psychology, and what he calls the popular psychotherapies. Specht believes that the major function of social work is with developmental socialization and suggests that we have been seduced by the popular psychotherapies:

> . . . that the psychotherapies have diverted social work from its original vision, a vision of the perfectibility of society, the building of the "city beautiful," the "new society," and the "new frontier." There is a yet unfulfilled mission for social work that might be resuscitated. It is a mission to deal with the enormous social problems under which our society staggers. The social isolation of our aged, the anomie experienced by our youths, the neglect and abuse of children, homelessness, drug addiction, and AIDS. Psychotherapy is not useful in dealing with these great problems. . . .
>
> Our mission must be to build a meaning, a purpose, and a sense of obligation for the community, not one by one. It is only by creating a community that we establish a basis

for commitment, obligation, and social support. We must build communities that are excited about their child care systems, that find it exhilarating to care for the mentally ill and the frail aged. Psychotherapy will not enable us to do that, and the further down the psychotherapeutic path we go, the less effective we will be in achieving our true mission.

We agree with Specht that the mission of social work must be in building community, but we disagree with his view that building community cannot occur on a one-by-one, individual-by-individual basis. There is an important role for community development and community economic-development activities in which communities are defined as client. Social work needs to be much more active in these activities. We hope that many of you will see yourself as becoming community-development workers and will find the ecological perspective, problem-solving process, and partnership concepts that we are developing in this text useful in your work with communities. Work with individual clients, however, can also contribute to building communities to the extent that this work is focused on assisting persons to become community participants, to access informal networks, and to make contributions to the overall welfare of their communities. This is our vision of social work, and is historically the mainstream of social work. And it is not therapy.

Does the fact that our primary mission and vision is one of building communities and assisting persons to participate in communities mean there is no role at all for social work in therapy? There is a place for some social workers doing therapy; but within the profession it is a relatively minor role. Social work therapists are like heart surgeons. Clearly there is a role in medicine for highly skilled doctors to perform heart surgery, but within all of medicine this is a relatively minor role, and a relatively small number of highly skilled specialists are needed as heart surgeons. It would be disastrous to the public health if heart surgery became the model for all of medicine. Likewise we believe that therapy can be considered a specialty within social work, one that requires considerable advanced training and one that requires a relatively small proportion of the total numbers of social workers. We also believe it will be a disaster for community and social development if therapy becomes the model of training of all social workers.

Where can social workers do the kind of social work we're talking about— building community, linking persons to resources, assisting persons in mobilizing informal support networks, helping persons contribute to the well-being of their communities? The best opportunities are still to be found in the areas of greatest need—child welfare work, probation services, and work with community centers, either those serving geographic communities or those serving communities of interest such as aged persons, chronic mentally ill in nonresidential settings, homeless, and so forth. Many of these agencies are under public auspices; we believe there are unusually good opportunities to practice social work in public child and family service agencies. The auspices of the agencies, however, are probably less important than the nature of the work itself; there are innovative private agencies that provide excellent opportunities for social work focused on developing social networks, socialization, and normalization. Exhibit 1-3, for example, illustrates a response by a private child welfare agency to an effort by the Foster Family Base Treatment Association to define

EXHIBIT 1-3
The Nature
of Treatment
Foster Family
Care

This agency strongly supports the view, consistently expressed in the position paper, that treatment foster care is "... an alternative to group home or facility-based residential treatment programs. ..." We agree that treatment foster care programs are to focus on reducing the use of institutional programs, and their harmful effects; thus, the population to be serviced by treatment foster care programs are persons who are, or otherwise would be, institutionalized. We are troubled, however, by two unnecessary dichotomies which consistently run through the position paper and which we believe will be divisive in their effects by isolating treatment foster care from sister programs.

One dichotomy is the effort to separate and distance treatment foster care from traditional foster care. This dichotomy goes so far as stating that treatment foster care is not a variant of traditional foster care. Such a sharp distinction ignores the historic record and potentially isolates treatment foster care programs from the long social service tradition of foster family care. The child welfare service of foster family care is one of the major roots of treatment foster care programs. While this root may be traced in various ways, one clear development was payment of difficulty of care rates authorized by the 1961 amendments to the U.S. Social Security Act. This possibility resulted in many foster parents receiving additional rates to care for challenging children and adolescents and, over time, developing skills necessary to provide stable, consistent, growth producing environments for these young people. These care providers did not become organized into a program until the 1970's but this development is clearly a forerunner of treatment foster care. Further, foster family care has, over the last one hundred years, been developed and promoted as an alternative to institutional care. Treatment foster care takes this development one step further. With an increased level of support and assistance, family care providers are able to develop the ability to care for more difficult young persons, to respond appropriately to the behaviours of these young people, and to create an environment in which the young people may grow and accomplish developmental tasks appropriate for their ages. Thus, treatment foster care is a variation of foster family care. It is a very significant step forward but is, none the less, a part of a long and distinguished tradition of providing foster family care as an alternative to institutional care for children and youths.

Second, drawing a sharp distinction between care and protection and structured treatment programs is ill advised. Limiting the definition of treatment foster care to programs that provide structured treatment interventions will result in focusing on the child or youth as the source of the problem, will lead to stigmatization, and fails to recognize the power of family and community environments both as a source of problems and a mechanism for healing. Care and nurturing environments in which children are reacted to appropriately by supportive family care providers and from which they are assisted to develop supportive social networks and to engage in age appropriate activities are probably more powerful ways of healing than any formal "Treatment" technologies. Indeed the argument usually made regarding the harmful effects of institutional programming is that the institutional environment itself encourages the development of maladaptive behaviours; thus a family and community environment will be a powerful source of support for age appropriate behaviors.

We are not arguing against structured interventions. We are, however, arguing against a restricted definition of treatment foster care that limits the definition to programs that provide these structured interventions. Programs which help produce change through use of supportive, growth producing environments involving connections to broader social networks are just as legitimately considered treatment foster care as those based on the use of narrow treatment technologies. Ultimately, the former may be more effective and cost efficient.

SOURCE: Board of Directors, Alberta Family and Community Alternatives, Edmonton, Alberta, Canada. Statement submitted to the Foster Family-based Treatment Association, New York.

treatment foster family care narrowly in terms of treatment technologies, developed by professionals external to the foster family care system, and directed towards the youth care.

Who Is a Client?   Included in the Appendix are several cases that illustrate markedly differing conditions under which the social worker initiated services to persons who are identified as clients. In "Pain Clinic Evaluation" Mr. Z and his family approached the social worker for assistance in managing pain. We can think of other examples of services initiated under this type of circumstance: a couple comes to a family service agency for assistance in resolving difficulties in their marriage; parents approach an agency for assistance in managing a rebellious adolescent; a young adult comes in for assistance in handling symptoms of depression. In all of these situations the person, whom we often call a client, has initiated a request for service.

Contrast this with the way the services were initiated in the Lee case, the Debbie Smith case, the case of Mrs. Z, and "The House on Sixth Street." In all of these situations the worker is reaching out to establish contact and offer services to a person or group who have not requested the services. In the Lee case the request came from an American sponsor of the Laotian family being resettled in the United States; based on this referral the worker first made a telephone contact with the family and then reached out for a home visit. Who would you consider the client at the beginning of this case—the Lee family or the sponsor who made the referral and requested the service? In the case of Debbie Smith, the worker, representing a child welfare agency, initiated contact by calling on Debbie Smith at her home because of concerns about possible child neglect. There is no indication at all that Debbie Smith requested the services. Who is the client here—Debbie Smith or the agency that is carrying out a public mandate and requested that the worker reach out to Debbie Smith? Likewise, in "The House on Sixth Street," the worker is reaching out to a group of tenants to organize them to solve a problem in the quality of housing provided by their building management. Reaching out is a way in which workers often offer services to persons who are not actively seeking services. And often, as in the case of Debbie Smith, the reaching out goes well beyond making contact and attempting to offer services and into the realm of marketing the services. The person or persons who are the object of this reaching-out effort are interacting with the social worker under very different circumstances from those of the person who comes to the worker or agency and requests service.

Of course, there is a third set of circumstances under which we may initiate services to people. Often, as with offenders, drug abusers, situations of child neglect, and some types of mental illness, the person is told, under pressure of outside authority, that he or she must see the social worker. The Debbie Smith case may well have been an example of this type of involvement, although the record does indicate more of a reaching out on the part of the worker than use of coercion. But look at the situation of Joe described in Exhibit 1-4. Joe is being held against his will under a 72-hour hold. Hospital officials believe that commitment proceedings are necessary to protect Joe. The social worker has been asked to discover if the parents would be willing to do so. Who in this case is the client? Is it Joe? Is it the physician? Is it the hospital? Or is it society at large acting through the social worker to protect Joe?

EXHIBIT 1-4
Joe, a Potential
Suicide

Joe, an 18-year-old, single, white male was admitted to the hospital on a 72-hour medical hold. Joe had attempted to end his life by slashing his wrists two nights prior to this hospitalization. Tonight Joe made an additional attempt to take his life and, in addition, had self-inflicted wounds some two to three inches on his right arm, three- to four-inch cuts on the left side of his abdomen, as well as long scratches on his sternal chest area. He explains that he recently has broken up with his girlfriend (Karen), that he had attended a party that evening at which the girlfriend was present with a new boyfriend. Karen, according to Joe, is pregnant with his child. Seeing her proved very difficult for him. Thus he left the party, broke into Karen's home, and obtained a paring knife from the kitchen to inflict his injuries. I was asked by the attending physician to learn if Joe's parents would be willing to petition to have him committed for inpatient treatment. It is the physician's belief that Joe is not stable enough psychologically to refrain from harming himself if released. Since he is refusing the recommended help, and the physician believes that he is dangerous to himself, commitment is the only alternative to pursue within the 72-hour hold.

These cases illustrate very different circumstances under which you may be initiating contacts with persons often called clients. But there is also another dimension to consider. The nature of the interactions and the role relationships between a social worker and persons called clients will differ according to the phase of the work. For example, the role relations and responsibilities will be quite different during a period in which you are exploring with the person, family, group, or organization whether a problem exists from the role relations and your interactions after this determination has been made and you are working in the intervention phase. Several years ago Helen Harris Perlman (1962), the grandmother of the problem-solving model, identified this difference and referred to *applicants* and *clients*. According to Perlman, an applicant became a client after there was a problem identified and an agreement to work with the worker toward a resolution of the problem. Several scholars in our field have identified a need to make this distinction as well as a distinction among the varying circumstances in which initial contacts occur (Gambrill, 1983, pp. 13–14; Reid, 1978, pp. 39–41; Germain and Gitterman, 1980, pp. 39–45).

The term *client,* however, continues to be very loosely used in the profession and is generally applied to any person, family, group, or organization with which the social worker interacts for purposes of either defining a problem or producing change. Such use of the term shows little regard for the differing sources of authority for the interaction, the differing circumstances under which the interactions occur, the differing levels of client desire for the interactions, and the difference between interactions for purposes of problem definition and interactions for purposes of intervention. We believe the profession must develop a more precise nomenclature as a step toward clarifying our thinking and acting.

We will be using the term *client* in a restricted sense to mean any individual, group, family, or organization with whom the social worker has an explicit agreement regarding the nature of the problem to be resolved and an intervention plan. Thus, clienthood, or client status, comes into existence based on a clear agreement regarding the problem to be solved and the steps to be carried out to solve the problem. But obviously we interact with individuals, groups, families, and organizations to develop this clear agreement. What terms shall be used for these earlier phases of the work? We will be using the term *applicant* to refer to the person who voluntarily seeks out the services of the social worker, the term *contact*[2] to refer to persons to whom the social worker is reaching out, and the term *respondent* to refer to the person who is required to interact with the social worker. The term *respondent* in this context indicates that the person is responding to external pressure. Under these terms Mr. H of the pain clinic case is an applicant; Mr. Lee and Mrs. Z are contacts; Debbie Smith is either a contact or a respondent, depending on whether she is legally mandated to permit the social worker to interact with her; and Joe is a respondent.

Many applicants will enter into agreements with you and become clients, but others may not. Also, contacts and respondents may find a basis for work with a social worker and become clients. Ron Rooney (1988, 1992) has been developing a framework for work with what he calls *involuntary clients* (this term is of course not consistent with our nomenclature, as we would use the term *respondents*) in which he is suggesting ways that the social worker may go about converting respondents to clients.

Making these distinctions creates a language problem. As we discuss the stages of the problem-solving process up to the establishment of client status through the development of a service agreement, we are left with a choice either to develop a term that can collectively refer to applicants, contacts, and respondents or to be cumbersome and use all three of these terms. We could use the term *potential clients,* as of course all of these are, or we could develop a cute acronym such as ARC or RAC, or we could arbitrarily select one term and ask that you read the triple meaning into it. We are going to use this last choice and adopt the convention of using the term *applicant* unless the context or illustration clearly suggests that *contact* or *respondent* would be more appropriate. Therefore, as you go through this book, please read the term *applicant* in context; if the context does not suggest that the term should be limited to a voluntary approach to the social worker, then read it to mean *applicant, contact,* or *respondent.* We have the same problem in referring to the size of the applicant or client system. We have already indicated that an applicant or client may be an individual, family, group, or organization. We have considered using the term *system*, which would be an acceptable and correct term, to represent any of these possibilities, but we have decided that this may be a bit too impersonal and will be using the term *person.* Again, we ask when you read the term *person* in relation to an applicant or client to try to read into this *person, group, family,* or *organization.*

Prevention and Intervention?   The focus of social work on the person-situation interaction and conceptualizing the function of social work as using a problem-solving process to resolve problems in the person-situation interaction will reduce the dichotomy between individual change and social change that has been so divisive through the history of our profession. The model demands that social workers maintain both orientations and possess interventive skills in both areas. The social worker in "The House on Sixth Street" case required skills at organizing the tenants to work toward better housing. In a different circumstance or with a different set of

---

[2] This term was suggested by John Helget, an M.S.W. student at the University of Minnesota.

facts, however, the same worker might well have focused the intervention efforts to assist a family to secure adequate housing or to assist a family to develop the skills and ability to improve existing housing.

A closely related dichotomy is the argument between rehabilitation and prevention in social work. Arguments are advanced that social workers may spend too much time with the casualties of our society instead of attacking root problems in efforts at prevention. This is also an unacceptable dichotomy for two reasons. First, to a large extent, it is a renewed manifestation of the issue of work with the community versus work with individuals. Prevention is frequently assumed to require social change, with rehabilitation perceived as helping individuals to cope with immediate situations. We consider all social work activity as both preventive and rehabilitative. Helping a mentally ill person is rehabilitative but also prevents future distress. Efforts to provide deprived children with adequate nutrition, clothing, and in some cases substitute living arrangements are both rehabilitative and preventive.

A second objection relates to the matter of timing and readiness. The social worker, as an agent of the client, does not intervene until the client (individual, family, group, or community) perceives a problem and is ready to engage in a process of problem solving; for the social worker to act otherwise increases the danger of doing to or for rather than with. A social worker may at times be called on to serve as an agent of society—for example in dealing with child abuse or delinquency. In such instances it is highly unlikely that either prevention or rehabilitation will occur until a respondent and worker discover a mutually acceptable area for joint problem solving. Rehabilitation is preventive, and prevention may be rehabilitative; ideally neither occurs until an applicant has perceived a problem, after which client and worker engage in a mutual problem-solving undertaking.

Generalists and Specialists We have argued that social work skills can be classified in two broad areas—skills necessary for assessment or for deciding what to do and skills necessary for intervention or doing the decided. Does this imply that all social workers must be able to do all things for all people? We think the model provides a sound basis for thinking of general social work practice and for the development of specialists in relation to highly technical and complex models of intervention.

In this approach a social worker in general practice is a person who is skillful in deciding what to do. These practitioners will not be limited in their vision by any preferred relational system (individual, family, small group, and so on) or prior commitment to any particular change strategy. Thus they will be able to focus attention on the totality of the person-situation interaction. In the process of deciding what to do, the practitioner is free to examine variables in the person, in the situation, and in the interaction of the two. Skills in engaging the applicant in data collection and assessment are essential for such a practitioner both to define the problem and to arrive at a practical and workable decision about what needs to be done.

The profession must provide clients with a wide range of interventive strategies for doing the decided. Some of these models may require skilled specialists. In some situations the generalist practitioner will possess skills in the necessary interventive strategies and may implement the intervention plan, but in other situations the generalist may call in a specialist for assistance. As you read "The House on Sixth Street," note that this social work practitioner relied on specialists—a city planner and an attorney—to assist in implementing the plan. At least one of these specialists, the attorney, brought to the situation knowledge and skill that were significantly different from those of the social worker. Some plans may well involve the social work generalist in making use of specialists from outside the profession, while other plans will involve the social work generalist in the use of specialists from within the profession. In some instances the specialist may carry most of the responsibility for implementing the service plans; for others, more of doing the decided will be the responsibility of the generalist, who will work as a team member with the specialist in meeting the objectives of the service plan. We will be discussing the matter of teamwork in Chapter 14.

While we find much that is objectionable in the use of the medical model in social work, we find the relationship between the work of the general practitioner or family doctor and specialists a useful analogy. A specialist is to back up and support the work of the general practitioner, who will retain overall responsibility for the case. In making referrals to a specialist, the generalist is guided by the nature of the problem, the nature of the intervention plan, his or her own skills, and availability of the necessary specialist.

Research and Practice   Often a sharp distinction is made between research and practice that we believe is incorrect. Social work practice is research, and social work practitioners are researchers. Social work practice involves the systematic definition of a problem, collection of data both defining the problem and working toward a solution, a clear statement of goals, development of an intervention plan, and systematically carrying out that plan of intervention. These are precisely the same things done in research, although unfortunately, different language is used to describe the processes, which only creates confusion and furthers the erroneous view that the two are quite separate. Defining a research problem is essentially the same as defining a problem for practice. What in research you are taught to call dependent variables in social work practice are the goals or objectives to be accomplished with the intervention plan. The intervention itself is analogous to the independent variables; we expect the intervention to lead to the accomplishment of the goal. The research plan is a description of how you will carry out the research project and is essentially the same as the intervention plan, a description of how you will carry out the intervention. There is a wide range of approaches to research, just as there is a wide range of approaches to intervention. When practice is disciplined and systematic, it is research and you are a practitioner-researcher.

Recapitulation

By now you have been introduced to the central ideas found in this book—the themes that will be recurring in subsequent chapters. The focus of social work intervention is on the person-situation interaction. Thus a focus solely on the individual or on the situation is inappropriate. The long debate in the social work profession about individual services versus social reform detracts from this focus. The function of social workers is to assist clients to resolve problems in person-situation interactions. Social work involves a partnership arrangement with clients to engage in problem solving. Social workers are case managers in the sense that their primary mission is to help link persons to the resources of their environments, including informal social networks and support systems. An overemphasis on therapy in the education of social workers and in practice will detract from the profession's responsibility for carrying out its mission of community building. A distinction must be made between social work practice and models of intervention. Social work practice encompasses all components of the problem-solving process, including deciding what to do and doing the decided. Models of intervention relate to doing the decided or carrying out a plan designed to produce change. The structure of the profession provides for both social work generalists and social work specialists who are available when intervention plans call for particularly complex and technical skills.

A Look Forward   In Chapter 2 we outline the problem-solving model in more detail, but do keep in mind the distinction between problem-solving and problem-focused models. This is a problem-solving model, one that uses strengths to solve problems; it cannot be called a problem-focused model. Chapters 3 through 9 provide an overview of the types of knowledge you will need to work within an ecological perspective on how this knowledge might be used. These chapters include information on the knowledge base, theoretical perspectives, practice across cultures, sanctions, values, relationship, and communication. Then follow Chapters 10 through 16 to provide further elaboration on the problem solving process. We introduce content regarding initial contact with applicants, moving from initial contact through assessment, developing a service contract, understanding both intervention roles and intervention methods, teamwork, terminating, and evaluation of practice.

We encourage you to study the three readings reprinted with this chapter and the Harry Specht reading (4-1) reprinted with Chapter 4. Specht traces the relationship between social work and psychiatry, humanistic psychology, and the popular psychotherapies. He argues that overemphasis on the popular psychotherapies has detracted from the primary vision and mission of social work. Lyle Longclaws presents a summary of the ecological approach. He then analyzes traditional healing practices of the Ojibway Anishinabe peoples. The medicine wheel framework calls attention to the importance of a holistic approach, including attention to spirituality. Longclaws also attempts to develop a model of practice derived from these traditions that he contrasts with what he calls the ecological model. His description of social work practice is at odds with what he perceives to be the type of practice necessary for working with Aboriginal people. The model of practice Longclaws has constructed from his own reading and experiences with social work, however, is quite different from the model we are presenting in this text. The model we present is very similar to Longclaw's conceptualization of social work from Anishinabe traditions; thus we believe we are more compatible with his vision than with his interpretation of current social work. Alexander (Sandy) Lockhart presents a community economic development case study to illustrate the importance and nature of insider-outsider partnerships for the economic development of communities. He does not use social work terms. We recommend that you carefully analyze the article in terms of the nature of the partnership being described, which we believe parallels the type of client and worker partnership we will be further developing in the text. Finally, a very short reading by Peter Brentnall illustrates use of the partnership concept in work with adolescent youths in foster family care.

We are including several cases in the appendix to give you a flavor of social work practice under different circumstances. We invite you to turn to the appendix and to read through the cases included there. You may well want to use them as a basis for discussion with your colleagues and instructors. As you study these cases, consider how the person-in-situation or ecological forms discussed in this chapter may help you understand the problems being encountered by these persons. We'll be referring to these cases throughout the book; they will become a part of your work to understand social work practice.

We have found social work hard yet rewarding, and we hope you will find this book both challenging and rewarding. You will be challenged to search the literature further (see Exhibit 1-1). We hope you will be rewarded by finding a framework for practice that will be useful in your own career.

Reading 1-1 *Social Work and the Medicine Wheel Framework*

Lyle Longclaws

INTRODUCTION

The ecological, or person-in-situation, approach is used by social workers to understand the person and environment better. This approach cannot be appreciated in isolation of cultural factors, specifically Anishinabe. This paper describes cultural factors existing within the Anishinabe (Ojibway-Saulteaux Indians) medicine wheel and compares principles central to the ecological and medicine-wheel models.

ECOLOGICAL MODEL AND SOCIAL WORK

Social work has always been interested in the person and environment, despite the emphasis on one or the other throughout the development of the profession. Several decades ago, social workers may have been viewed as being more psychologists than sociologists, with peoples' relationships with environments as secondary and defined as indirect work. However, since the late 1960s, a definite reciprocal interest in environment has emerged. Brower (1988) realizes that the ecological model, often defined as the social environmental approach, developed from the profession's dual commitment to the person and environment. The ecological perspective, which grew directly from the profes-

sion's roots, views other models of understanding behavior and environment used in social work practice as largely dependent on current concepts found within the allied social and behavioral sciences, while Germain and Gitterman (1980) promote the ecological perspective and view social work as being at the interface between people and the environment. They see a reciprocal relationship between the person and environment, with each shaping the other, and advocate treatment of the person within the context of the environment. Bryant (1980) applies an ecological formula to treatment of inner-city families, and Compher (1982) limits his analysis to the educational environment. Both suggest the possibility for social workers to intervene effectively in order to ensure appropriate relationships and productivity within such settings.

The ecological perspective provides a framework that assists in organizing information about people and environments. One main characteristic explores the reciprocal relationship between the person and the environment in order to understand the interconnectedness. Another characteristic involves the adaptiveness and evolutionary view of human beings as in constant interchange with all elements of their environment. This approach recognizes that human needs and problems are

Paper prepared for this edition.

generated by the transactions between people and their environments. Additionally, like all living systems, people need to maintain a notion of fit in order to match human needs to the environment better.

The ecological perspective views stress as the cognitive appraisal of imbalance between perceived demand and perceived capability. Stress is due to external or internal demands. Stress occurs in a cyclical form in which one stressful event leads to another. This way of thinking regards stress as part of any transaction; social workers may intervene in the cycle to help mobilize the client's ability to deal with the perceived demand. Social workers may also reframe the situation and deal with demand or provide supportive interventions.

The concept of coping examines personality attributes and situational elements—such as the incentive system, societal preparation, and societal support—for coping. The social work profession is part of the social environment and is a mediator with the outward environment. Social workers offer emotional support by providing problem-solving skills and may be responsible for advocating at case level while working with the person. Further, social workers may advocate on behalf of a class, such as single mothers, and in areas of policy.

Germain and Gitterman emphasize that people go through specific life transitions. The notion of life transitions includes human development in stages, changing of occupations, moving from rural to urban settings, and other transitions common to people's lives. They are concerned with the extent to which the environment can assist or hinder life transitions. Germain and Gitterman place an emphasis on culture because it determines patterns of interaction and gives meaning to events. One can think of different layers in the environment. The first two layers include the natural world, the built world, and their effects on people's behavior. The third layer, which consists of three sublayers, is a social world that deals with people in terms of organizations. Examples of the first sublayer include neighbors and self-help groups, and the second sublayer includes service organizations such as school systems. The last sublayer is composed of

culture broadly shared across families and organizations and includes values and political systems commonly referred to as an environment of law and policy. The attention of social work has been on the third layer. Meanwhile, the built and social worlds are in continual interaction among these layers and the individual.

The profession of social work is interested in qualities of both person and environment. Social workers interpret the ecological perspective as needing to understand the person, the environment, and transactional concepts. Transactional concepts can help focus assessment and intervention on the nature of the transaction between person and environment. Social workers must recognize that labeling results in a deficit view of person and therefore need terms to describe this focus. Transactional ideas view adaptation as a process of shaping physical and social environments, with people in turn shaped by the environment. Thus the intent is to intervene in transactions in order to release adaptive capacities and also to improve environment. Social workers are interested in transactions that promote or inhibit growth and development in order to determine the problem associated with behavior. Transactional concepts demand that social workers understand adaptation prior to the examination of the qualities of person and environment in order to detect how behavior can be changed. This means social workers must understand that individuals possess a biological process of adaptation in addition to a psychological, social, and cultural process.

In summary, social workers are attempting to assess the nature of interaction and thus intervene in the transactions. Interventions in transactional processes generally involve stress-oriented and coping-oriented interventions. Increasing the size of the social network often adds to the life space to improve transactions in order to establish firmer or looser boundaries. This practice strategy is normally determined after the completion of a social-setting analysis, which can ensure that boundaries regulate tension. Network intervention tries to increase mutual aid among those within the social network. Structuring of specific oriented situations supports the development of self-esteem, personal autonomy, sovereignty and other such experiences that will increase the well-being of people. An adaptation evaluation will incorporate emotional and situational stress in order to help people discover their inner resources and assist them in enhancing their self-esteem and confidence.

The ecological approach is conceptually appealing to social workers of Anishinabe ancestry because it may provide for culturally appropriate treatment being provided to Indian people within their environments. Red Horse, Lewis, Feit, and Decker (1978) challenge the profession to apply ecological standards to Indian families, who are vanishing like the buffalo. However, the Anishinabe social worker hesitates to accept the ecological model, as one cannot afford to be drawn to yet another mirage just because the need to quench one's thirst is real when one is walking in the desert.

THE ANISHINABE MEDICINE-WHEEL TEACHINGS

Anishinabe elders from Waywayseecappo First Nation, who possess a strong midewewin base, orally pass down the medicine-wheel teachings. Waywayseecappo elders teach that there were four laws, or ceremonies, given to the Anishinabe in order for them to obtain balance and harmony. These are the midewewin, aniba-qwayshimoong, anishinabe-nee-mide-wing, and ape-tong (see Glossary). Of the four, the midewewin is most frequently practiced by Anishinabe. The other three have been modified; the council dance, for example, is held for peaceful purposes and not for war as in traditional tribal times. These elders continue to practice ceremonies in which the four laws are handed down. These age-old practices continue their direct influence on the medicine wheel and its teachings. Thus, in order to appreciate and participate fully in the four major ceremonies, or laws, Anishinabe must travel the medicine-wheel journey. Figure 1 is a diagram of the medicine wheel that serves as a framework and process of learning the significance of ceremonies and rituals.

The medicine-wheel approach views the universe and determining a person's position in it as critical to understanding the meaning of a good life. The elders define *worldview* as the interconnection among all beings and forces existing on physical and spiritual worlds. The medicine-wheel framework has teachings for Anishinabe that are critical for the physical world while recognizing the direct link to oda aki (centeredness). This centeredness is the goal hoped to be achieved within the medicine wheel circle. That is the achievement of balance, or peace and harmony with oneself and all other living things. Each individual travels within his or her own medicine wheel but is guided by the teachings given to all Anishinabe. One's life affects all others in the circle of life in both the present and the future. All living things are born with a spirit, but it is the human beings who must find harmony within the circle, because all other living things, such as the plants, animals, and elements, are already in balance with the universe. Therefore, for harmony and balance in the medicine wheel the philosophy of interdependence is paramount. The medicine wheel demonstrates the absence of a hierarchy, as it has no top or bottom and all living things have their place and responsibility in the natural order of life within the wheel. To achieve balance, people and nature were viewed as interdependent and connected. Whatever happened to one happened to all. Thus, utmost respect and reciprocity were practiced with all others in the medicine-wheel circle.

The purpose of the medicine wheel, given the worldview, is to provide a process or framework for ensuring the balance and harmony of Anishinabe within the circle of life. Those who did not follow the ways proposed experienced imbalance and disharmony with all around them. The framework includes a way of living that emphasizes responsibilities, values, and ethics that ensure achieving balance and harmony. Ceremonies assist individuals in centering themselves and give them strength to participate in a lifelong learning process. It was believed that people were born good but that throughout life the teachings of the medicine wheel provided guidance and therefore protection from evil forces present in the universe that could lead people astray and off the good, or red, road. These evil forces were found in the spiritual realm as well as the physical realm. The evil forces of the spiritual world were manifested in the physical world through the use of bad medicine and were found all

FIGURE 1–1
The Anishinabe
Medicine
Wheel

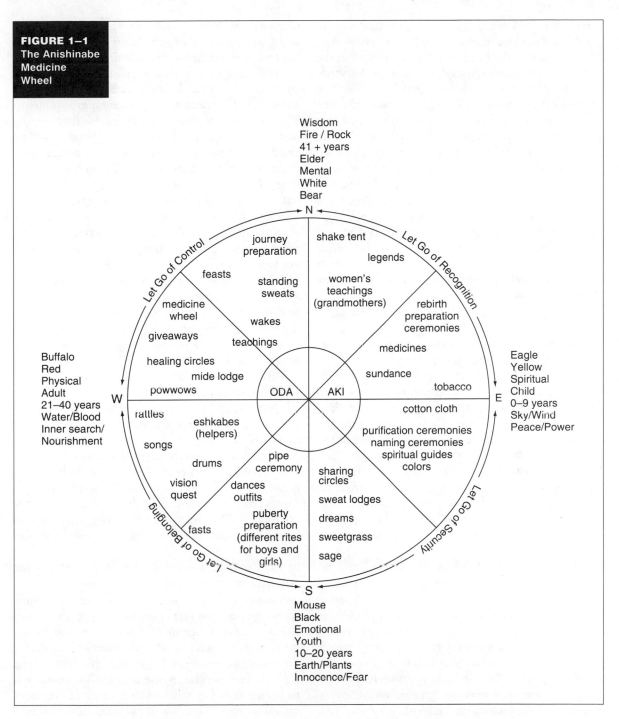

Wisdom
Fire / Rock
41 + years
Elder
Mental
White
Bear

Let Go of Control

journey
preparation

shake tent

legends

Let Go of Recognition

feasts

standing
sweats

women's
teachings
(grandmothers)

rebirth
preparation
ceremonies

medicine
wheel

wakes

medicines

giveaways

teachings

healing circles

mide lodge

sundance

Buffalo
Red
Physical
Adult
21–40 years
Water/Blood
Inner search/
Nourishment

powwows

ODA   AKI

tobacco

cotton cloth

Eagle
Yellow
Spiritual
Child
0–9 years
Sky/Wind
Peace/Power

rattles

eshkabes
(helpers)

purification ceremonies
naming ceremonies
spiritual guides
colors

songs

drums

pipe
ceremony

sharing
circles

vision
quest

dances
outfits

sweat lodges

dreams

Let Go of Security

fasts

puberty
preparation
(different rites
for boys and
girls)

sweetgrass

sage

Let Go of Belonging

Mouse
Black
Emotional
Youth
10–20 years
Earth/Plants
Innocence/Fear

across Turtle Island, mother earth, and Indian country. They were also found in physical substances such as alcohol and drugs as well as in the values of materialism, greed, jealousy, and dishonesty. Anishinabe were discouraged from adopting these values, which were viewed as encouraging the evil forces dominating one's personal medicine wheel and would prevent the individual from reaching a personal centeredness. People who were involved with these evil forces were thought to be lost not only to themselves but to the nation. Therefore, given this direct connection to the spirit world, Anishinabe were careful not to offend any of their relations, living or dead, through their actions or thoughts, lest they be the recipient of that spirit's wrath. The worldview then reinforces and determines ethics and values of the Anishinabe, as the spiritual world is the context from within which most aspects or life are seen, defined, and given significance.

Traditional ethics are a way of avoiding antagonizing those in the spirit world as well as determining acceptable and appropriate behavior. Central life principles that determine behavior of Anishinabe include respect, kindness, caring, sharing, honor, and the attainment of wisdom, strength, and truth. These ethics and values are operationalized within extended family groups or clans. Roles and responsibilities are outlined within the extended family groups or clans, such as the bear clan, that are responsible for protection within the nation or tribe. Responsibility for the extended family groups is inherent and based on the survival of the family.

There are defined ethics for use within the extended family groupings in addition to different ethics for use within the tribe and with other nations. Anishinabe are either part of an extended family or actual members of a clan. This reality creates a unique life experience of participating in the circle of life that has different phases and responsibilities. The circle is a powerful symbol that demonstrates how all phases are interconnected and dependent on each other.

Parents make a gift of tobacco and cotton cloth to an elder with the specific role of naming young boys or girls. A child enters the circle at birth and is given an Indian name so that Manitou will recognize the child's spirit. Later in life the child's prayers will be heard by Manitou, as the child identifies his or her Indian name before praying, and the traditional belief is that the prayers are answered. This ceremony is a strong group identification activity that demonstrates that family members accept their responsibility to raise the child in a prescribed way. Part of the ceremony includes the burial of the child's umbilical cord, signifying that the child is forever a member of the nation. The child is recognized as not being the property of the parents; the name reinforces the deep connection to all of mother earth and enables the child to grow in spirit. The name provides guidance. As the child understands the name more fully, the child will be able to distinguish individual gifts. Frequently the child receives personal colors, and the meaning of the colors is expanded upon through traveling through the circle. Colors are related to the name and are believed to give strength when worn by the child.

After the receiving of traditional gifts, the elder will instruct and prepare for the ceremony. When the time is right to share the naming celebration, a pipe ceremony is conducted at sunrise with family members, and prayers of gratitude are expressed. The name is given to the child by the spirits through the dreams of the elder. The name signifies the belief that the child will have a spirit guide to protect and direct the child over the course of the life journey. As part of the ceremony, a feast is held by the extended family to celebrate their commitment to the child.

Clan members continue traveling through the circle of life, growing in ways of knowledge, spirit, and wisdom. The four directions of the medicine wheel possess the teachings to assist in the acquisition of knowledge and wisdom. Anishinabe believe that the east is the direction to look for illumination, peace, and spiritual influence. These gifts are represented by the eagle, who flies closest to Manitou and is believed to have great vision, or farsightedness. This is also the direction in which the sun rises to begin a new day; therefore this is the direction of the child and also the color, yellow to signify the sun's rays. Recent interpretations have denoted the eastern color of yellow to signify the yellow race. The eastern direction is also represented by the elements such as wind and is the domain of the sky.

Moving in the direction that the sun travels as it crosses the sky, the next direction is south. The south is represented by the mouse, and the gifts received there include innocence and fear. This direction is viewed as the realm of the emotional and is signified within the circle of life as the time in a person's life between the ages of 10 and 20 years. The south represents the worlds of plants; mother earth is represented by the color black, signifying a time of letting go of security and belonging, which can be a dark or unknown time. Ceremonies such as the sweat lodges, pipe ceremonies, vision quests, and puberty rites are introduced at this time to assist youth. These ceremonies are enriched with the right to conduct sharing circles, songs, chants, and dancing. The young Anishinabe person may be given the right to hold sharing circles, in which sweetgrass, sage, and other medicines are used, depending on their ability to respect these gifts. The south begins making contact with the center of the circle known as oda aki and experiences of being in harmony and being balanced are consciously felt. The more frequent this experience, the greater the development of the ability to visit the spiritual world and the more the assurance of having a meaningful journey.

The next direction in the medicine wheel is that of the west, represented by the buffalo, the leader of the hoof clan, and represents the gifts of nourishment and introspection. This direction represents the age cycle of people 21 to 40 years of age and is the physical domain of the circle. The red represents the setting sun and the blood or water of the physical world. People in this phase of life are like the buffalo, which protects and provides nourishment for its young as well as protecting the weak and old. This phase is also a time in many people's lives when the opportunity for searching inwardly occurs and provides the strength for letting go of control, which is necessary in order to continue the process of balance and harmony with all living things. During this phase, the vision received in youth is given meaning and strengthened by participating as an eshkabe (helper) to an elder or medicine person. Gifts of songs, drums, and rattles reinforce the teachings in greater depth and provide greater insight. The medicine wheel teachings at this phase enable greater influence in healing circles and ensure a place of credibility in the midewewin lodge. Giveaways are a necessary part of benefiting from the spiritual nourishment provided in this direction. Songs and dances at social gatherings such as powwows are expressed in a different style.

The fourth direction is the north, which is represented by the bear. The gifts of this direction are knowledge, guidance, and wisdom. This phase is the mental sphere in the circle of life, when Anishinabe have lived over 40 years and are the teacher elders of the young and old alike. This direction is represented by the color white to denote the blanket of wisdom found in the winter of an Anishinabe's life cycle. The elements of fire and rock signify the powerful symbols of completing the foundation within the medicine wheel. The rocks, because of the recognition as being the oldest substance on mother earth, are referred to as grandfathers and are used in the sacred sweat lodge ceremony. The rocks, or grandfathers, are placed in a fire, where they are heated and then placed with great reverence in the center of the sweat lodge; when the water is sprinkled on the rocks with medicines, the spirits of the grandfather rocks are released to heal the individuals participating in the sweat lodge ceremony. When Anishinabe has reached this phase in life and has practiced the ways of the people as outlined in the medicine wheel teachings, the elder will be prepared to assume leadership in the conducting of certain ceremonies. Therefore, elder Anishinabe are those who conduct the sweat lodge, pipe ceremonies, standing sweats, sundance, shake tents, council dance, naming ceremonies, burial rites, and feasts, as well as the passing on of teachings through stories. Elders are those who have knowledge of the medicines available from the plant world and are the healers of the Anishinabe. Because of elders' wisdom and life experience, Anishinabe are very respectful of the elders and look forward to this role in the clan with anticipation. Elders have let go of control and recognition so that they live life for their Manitou and all creation. In addition, elders are seen as returning to the beginning of the circle, which is the spiritual world; they are becoming a child once again, particularly toward the end of their life in the physical world.

The last three directions within the Anishinabe medicine wheel are the vertical, which represents Kitche Manitou; the horizontal, which represents mother earth; and the inward, which represents the heart or center. One may travel on the medicine-wheel circle in a chronological sense but will not necessarily attain the gifts and teachings of each direction. For example, contrary people will do everything backward, and others may travel vertically or horizontally within the circle or start at a certain direction and work their way around the circle. The process is not linear but cyclical, in that the time must be right. Anishinabe may be born in one direction, learn those teachings, but never progress throughout their lifetime; these people are referred to as warriors. A chief or clan mother would travel through two phases and receive the teachings and gifts. An elder would travel and obtain the gifts and teachings of three phases, and the medicine person will have completed or trav-

eled through all four phases and be knowledgeable of the teachings and gifts. Medicine people supervise others in their journey through the medicine wheel.

ECOLOGICAL PRACTICE AND ANISHINABE HEALING PRINCIPLES

The descriptions of the ecological and medicine wheel frameworks are presented as independent models. However, they may overlap in some areas. An example is in respect of person and environment for people who require treatment within the context of their environment (Figure 2). Another similarity is engagement of an expert who is recognized within his or her own environment. This action demonstrates that when people require assistance, they involve another party. In reality, they are entering into a process essential for benefiting from the assistance. As part of the process, all experts identify problems in relationship to the environment as they understand it. General principles relevant to each model can be identified. These principles are contrasted in Table 1-1. These differing principles are key to any discussion that may lead to the integration of the ecological and medicine wheel models.

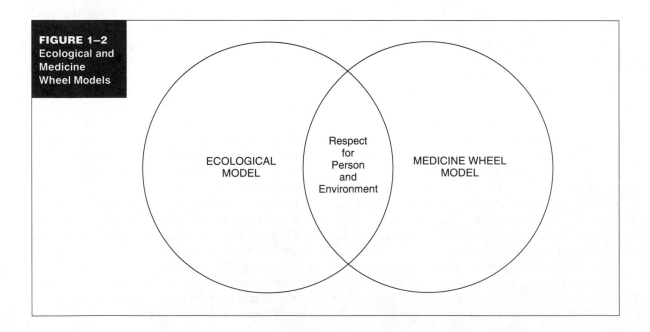

FIGURE 1–2
Ecological and Medicine Wheel Models

ECOLOGICAL MODEL

Respect for Person and Environment

MEDICINE WHEEL MODEL

Table 1—1 **Principles of Social Work Practice and Anishinabe Principles of Healing**	ECOLOGICAL PRACTICE PRINCIPLES[1]	ANISHINABE HEALING PRINCIPLES[2]
	Respect, rights, dignity	Respect, relationship, reciprocity
	Expertise	Age respect
	Expertise is valued	Self as principal resource
	Others as resource are of principal value	Extended family supports
	Secular	Spiritual
	Objective	Connected and personal
	Labelled client	Referred to as family
	Problem or task oriented	Person oriented
	Definitive short-term intervention	Sacred offering to request indefinite healing
	Independence viewed as progress	Interdependence viewed as healthy
	Goal or plan for client change	Free will
	Goal is to do or with client	Restore balance/harmony by centering family
	Worker role or use of environment set by goal	Teacher elder as mediator
	Worker assesses problem	Sacred offerings to interpret solution
	Workers accountable for progress	Teacher-elder responsible for person's life or spirit
	Client change desirable or possible	Balance, harmony, centering viewed as healing

[1]Adapted from Germain and Gitterman, 1980.
[2]Adapted from Waywayseecappo Elders.

A major principle derived from the ecological model is respecting the fundamental rights of individuals within their environments to dignity, regardless of circumstances. But ecological practice principles may be operationalized through experts who have authority and who are expected to exercise authority. Obtaining this authority requires levels of qualifications or academic preparation that emphasize intellectual ways of helping clients. This type of training is highly valued by the profession and society in general and is viewed as preparing people with specific skills and knowledge to assist individuals who need help. In addition, experts often look to experts in other fields such as medicine, psychology, education, and so forth as resources when dealing with individuals seeking help. These experts often operate within a spiritual anomie and consider spiritual values as taboo. Help is secular in nature, which is due to the influence of dominant society's principles, thereby resulting in a deliberate non-acceptance of spiritual assistance. Practice may

not encourage clients to go beyond the healing that the experts themselves have personally experienced.

Professional principles hold that experts must be objective and professional in order to be effective. Emotional and personal involvement with people requiring assistance is discouraged in the belief that this will cloud the judgment of the expert and prevent correct diagnosis or treatment. Labeling of individuals is rationalized as objective, acceptable, and necessary to help client or patient; unfortunately, labeling often creates a deficit view of the person. Clients' problems are examined, diagnosed, and treated in isolation from other aspects of their lives. Similarly, diagnosis and treatment of individuals occur within a time span that is part of the goal setting as determined by the expert. The expert not only becomes responsible for the assessment of a person's problem but also accepts accountability for the outcome of planned goals.

This process is all part of a plan with definite

goals determined by an expert based on academic training and proven success in other cases. Goals are often presented to clients as the answer to the situation supported by the authority given to the expert; often the goals are not questioned by clients, who embark on the process hoping for change. The expert determines the role of environment in the goal setting and interprets the definition of environment from their perspective as opposed to the clients' perspective.

In comparison, the Anishinabe healing principles recognize the inherent rights of the individual but simultaneously believe in the interconnectedness of all so that the healing of the individual is necessary not only for the person but for family and clan. Holistic values, with ceremonial supports, contribute balance to the spiritual dimensions of life. The Anishinabe experts base their qualifications on life experience and giftedness. The key is to respect the family and clan in order to establish a relationship so that reciprocity can occur. Reciprocity is necessary for the person to become centered so that balance and harmony can be restored both to the person and to those affected, such as family and clan, thereby strengthening relationships within the environment.

Anishinabe revere age, believing that elders have gained the wisdom to understand the family's reality and can use the dynamics of that reality to guide people to healthier lives. Therefore, elders serve as mentors in guiding unhealthy families beyond their trapped reality. This guidance, provided within the medicine-wheel framework, suggests that behavior is determined by environment. In other words, to change behavior requires that the environment be changed. Yet crucial to this is the principle that a centered self (includes one who is in harmony with spirituality) will effectively balance the realities of the physical world or environment.

The centering of oneself is an empowering process; less emphasis is placed on expertise while acknowledging self as the principal resource. Utilization of extended family is encouraged to support this self-empowering process and contributes to the overall healing of the person within the context of the environment. The process may also include isolating parts of the person that do not permit self-to provide leadership. Ceremonial activities support the person in reaching an agreement with all parts of the self. These healing practices are driven by spiritual principles in which secular values are not considered. Holistic principles are rooted in ancient wisdom, are humanistic in nature, and do not permit the isolation of person or problem from environment.

The interconnectedness of all cannot be overemphasized, but assistance is personalized in order to provide meaning and mutual healing. Person is not viewed as client but referred to as family. This is in direct contrast to labeling people as clients or patients, with the emphasis to remain problem or task oriented. Instead there exists a person-oriented focus throughout an indefinite treatment time span. Unlike short-term intervention, in which independence is viewed as progress, the Anishinabe healing principles emphasize restoring balance and harmony, which can only occur if there is interdependence.

After acceptance of a sacred offering, the elder's role is to identify the source of imbalance in the person requesting healing. Throughout the healing process and within the corresponding ceremonial supports the elder accepts responsibility as a mediator in the healing of the person's spirit. Additionally, throughout the entire process, there is acceptance and encouragement of the person's free will to influence self and environment. Centering of the person is encouraged by elders through the use of extended family and ceremonial supports. These important components are part of the process needed by people to achieve the balance and harmony necessary to function within the realities of their environments.

CONCLUSION

This description of social work from an ecological perspective and Anishinabe healing principles suggests that in the most general sense there are similarities. But closer examination reveals definite differences. A major area that requires further examination is the area of spiritual versus secular. Elders identify problems in terms of the spiritual relationship to environment. Although Anishinabe healing deals with one's environment, the healing of person occurs primarily from the inside out (spiritual) and not outside in (environment). Can this idea find common ground with social work from an ecological perspective?

Involvement of extended family is central to Anishinabe healing. The extended family is also a part of the ecological system of all people. How can extended family involvement be made a more central part of social work practice?

Encouragement of other professional resources that may provide arm's-length treatment will discourage voluntary requests for assistance from most Anishinabe people. Additionally, an authoritarian attitude that the expert will solve the problems of the client and knows what is best for the person does not result in the independence of client hoped for by professionals. Can the integration of a personal and connected relationship evolve if the person seeking assistance is viewed as an individual as opposed to another client in one's overflowing caseload? Is it reasonable to expect such a professional to ignore the academic training that encouraged objectivity and authority in order to practice beliefs held by Anishinabe people when helping people in need of healing?

The Anishinabe medicine wheel is not a model of social work, but the teachings can be tools for social work. Perhaps the most useful approach for social workers with Aboriginal clients is to recognize the importance of elders, ceremonies, spirituality, and family in the ecological systems of these clients. Supporting participation in one's culture, and not getting in the way of these practices, may be the most useful way of restoring balance and harmony of the person and environment.

Glossary

Aniba-qwayshimoong: one of the four lodges, or laws, of the Anishinabe

Anishinabe: literally, *the original people* in the Ojibway-Saulteaux language

Anishinabe-nee-mide-wing: one of the four lodges, or laws, of the Anishinabe

Ape-tong: one of the four lodges, or laws, of the Anishinabe

Bad medicine: a term used among Anishinabe to refer to the destructive use of medicine and knowledge to harm an individual

Council dance: ceremony performed in traditional times during time of war but in recent times has been changed to promote peace and goodwill

Eshkabe: a term in the Ojibway-Saulteaux language to refer to an individual who assists a teacher-elder during ceremonies. This individual may also be an apprentice who is learning the teachings

Giveaway: traditional custom held among the Anishinabe for various reasons, at which time personal possessions are distributed to those attending ceremony

Indian Country: common term that describes land traditionally held by First Nations

Kitche Manitou or Manitou: literally, *the great mystery*

Medicine wheel: a pattern or framework that refers to a way of thinking about existing in the universe that organizes, clarifies and is dynamic in nature

Midewewin: one of four lodges, or laws, of the Anishinabe and most frequently practiced in contemporary times

Mother earth: the earth as giver and sustainer of life

Naming ceremony: a ceremony held among the Anishinabe during which a child or adult is given his or her spiritual or Indian name

Oda aki: literally, in Ojibway-Saulteaux, *heart of the earth,* or *center*

Ojibway: common English term used to refer to Anishinabe

Saulteaux: common French term used to refer to Anishinabe, specifically those who historically were found living at present day Saulte Ste. Marie and who later migrated to present-day Manitoba and Saskatchewan

Shake tent: sacred ceremony practiced for specific purposes and only on rare occasions

Sundance: ceremony held for four days every June commencing on the longest day of the year in which the general purpose is to strengthen the commitment of participants in the ways of the medicine wheel teachings

Sweat lodge: purification and healing ceremony

Sweetgrass: one of four sacred cleansing medicines used by the Anishinabe

Turtle Island: term used by indigenous peoples when referring to North America

Reading 1-2

The Insider-Outsider Dialectic in Native Socioeconomic Development: A Case Study in Process Understanding

Alexander Lockhart

INTRODUCTION

The purpose of this paper is to document that which is often most crucial to the success of a project, but which because of its intrinsically elusive character seldom appears in the formal documentation. I speak specifically of the organizational processes, as distinct from the substantive outcomes, that lie behind those pathfinding initiatives that attempt to overcome some chronic problem in an area of critical concern.

The pathfinding initiative I wish to discuss is that of the North Coast Tribal Council's[1] effort to become an effective socio-economic development agent for its seven constituent band communities. The chronic problem addressed by this effort is that which Beaver so eloquently identifies in the Report of the National Indian Socio-Economic Development Committee, i.e., how are native development organizations going to avoid replicating the bureaucratic centralism and/or paternalistic approaches of their past masters, given that this past has left such a massive residue of community level distrust and skepticism over any development planning? The area of critical concern is specifically how native administered socio-economic development initiatives are to overcome the inherent conflict between the need to access wider economic opportunities while at the same time guarding and enhancing their own social traditions and cultural identities.

There are several reasons why I feel this particular effort is noteworthy. Most manifestly is my own sense that it is perhaps, just perhaps, a critical learning experience in overcoming the accumulation of pessimism and disillusionment that has so notably attended native efforts to gain control over their own destinies. If so, then the experience should be more widely recognized and understood, for like all fundamental departures, it is a fragile thing and easily destroyed, not out of malice, but from ignorance of what it represents. More subtly, though no less importantly, is the hint which this experience offers as to how the broader native/mainstream cultural relations might be restructured in the context of the major change forces that are impinging on both.

In rendering this account I have made no attempt to include any more of the substantive outcome material—what might be called the product of the exercise—than is required to render the underlying processes comprehensible. As a consequence, some of what I say may appear out of proportion to those who viewed the same events from other vantage points. This is as it should be, for my purpose is to project into "figure" that which normally remains "field" in order that innovative background processes may be seen to play the crucial role that they do in achieving substantive results.

So far as is possible, I have attempted to avoid the more obvious pitfalls of participant observation methods and the perspective distortions of my own cultural heritage. I hope that my social scientific training has aided the former and that my long association with the North and its native and non-native communities has tempered the latter. However, the reader should remain as conscious as I have tried to be of the inevitable limitations of participant and cross-cultural reporting.[2]

BACKGROUND

It is no news to anyone familiar with Canada's northern and rural development scene that the past decade has seen a massive increase in the efforts of

NOTE: From "The Insider-Outsider Dialectic in Native Socio-Economic Development: A Case Study in Process Understanding" by A. Lockhart, 1982, *The Canadian Journal of Native Studies, 2*(1), pp. 159–168. Reprinted by permission.

native Canadians to regain control over their own social and economic destiny. Because it is so fundamental, most of this effort has been directed toward the restoration of resources and the recognition of rights. This is as it should be. But to succeed, it is also necessary to develop two kinds of knowledge without which the attainment of resources and rights may fail to achieve the kind of future to which most native Canadians aspire, i.e., the establishment of economic opportunities within the context of their own cultural traditions.

The first knowledge requisite is an *insiders* understanding of the particular community process dynamics that pre-date the development initiative. While such community process knowledge is desirable in designing new developments anywhere, it is especially crucial to the native situation precisely because native culture, unlike that of the predominantly atomized white society, has always recognized the centrality of community in the life of the individual. Thus any new development which is not predicated upon a detailed *insiders* knowledge of the particular social, economic and political process dynamics of the participating community is predestined to failure. Indeed, the case study accounts of many past development efforts—native initiated no less than paternalistically imposed—are littered with derelict projects that foundered because they failed to incorporate the community's particular sense of need or appropriateness.

But if an intimate *inside* knowledge of community process is crucial for achieving native development goals, so too is a knowledge of the *outside* opportunity structure. By outside opportunity structure I mean the full range of mainstream organizational and technical structures through which social, political and economic options are made available and rendered functional within the wider context of regional, national and international relationships. Given the power and pervasiveness of these *outside* forces, no local, community based development initiative is likely to succeed if it does not take into account the relevant elements of this ambience. But since these *outside* structures are overwhelmingly predicated upon values and assumptions that are profoundly alien

and hence threatening to those found *inside* native communities, many of the problems associated with the new wave of native self-initiated development may be understood in terms of the difficulty of finding ways and means of combining these *inside* and *outside* knowledge components so as to affirm rather than negate native cultural identity.

Since most new native development initiatives will require some broader base of organizational and technical support than can be found within the community they are designed to support, native development initiatives are not likely to be able to encompass fully all the required inside and outside knowledge frames. Some means of obtaining, rationalizing and controlling both the internal community process information and the external knowledge requisites thus becomes a crucial prerequisite to any native development scheme.

For those engaged in development initiatives who are themselves native, the acquisition of inside community process knowledge may seem the lesser of the two problems. To be sure, there can be no substitute for cultural belonging. But as all native people know, there is a great deal of sub-cultural variety to be found within the native world, and even deep personal familiarity with the target community may not be a sufficient basis for development decision-making. This is because it is characteristic of all community knowledge that it contains a good deal of folklore, including not a few distortions of reality. There is nothing wrong with this at the functional level. Indeed, a certain amount of mystification is required before any social system can operate. But it is important to be able to separate the essential process characteristics from colourful interpretations if they are to serve as a basis for development decision-making. Also, these process understandings need to be organized in a form that ensures compatibility with the other knowledge requirements that go into forecasting the developmental impact effects. All of which suggests that while only community members can provide the crucial *insider* information, there is a need for somewhat more formal instruments for the collecting, inter-relating and evaluation of community process knowledge than can be achieved by personal familiarity alone.

It was the recognition of the lack of such an instrument that caused several concerned social scientists, including myself, to gain assistance from the Department of Indian and Northern Affairs for some basic research into remote community life. The goal was to develop a community process model capable of identifying and evaluating by means of social indicators the critical variables through which a community attains, or fails to attain, its "social vitality", "economic viability" and "political efficacy". The utility of such a community process model was specifically articulated in terms of its applicability as a diagnostic research and evaluation instrument of value to local community groups wishing to assess their own situation with respect to proposed development impacts, whether these proposals came from outside agents, their own initiative, or some combination of the two.

While the outcomes of this model building enterprise might be usefully discussed here, space hardly permits such a digression. What are relevant to our current purpose, however, are the following coincidental observations. The model development culminated in a field test pilot study that was conducted in a number of relatively isolated northern British Columbia communities. Two of these communities just happened to be numbered among the North Coast Tribal Council's constituency. The pilot study results were published (Blishen et al.) just prior to the North Coast Tribal Council's decision to reorganize. And finally, the authors of the model asked the Socio-Tech consulting group at B.C. Research to evaluate the model in terms of its applicability potential to their own well-established "action research" approach to assisting community development.

The relevance of these observations becomes apparent when a year after the completion of the pilot study the North Coast Tribal Council contracted B.C. Research's Socio-Tech group to act as outside consultants to their reorganizational efforts. I was then asked by B.C. Research to assist them in applying the community process model and to act as an independent observer of the whole reorganizational process.

THE TERMS

In essence, the terms of reference of the contract between North Coast Tribal Council and their outside consultants were that the latter should assist the NCTC first in attaining a clear understanding of the range of socio-economic development needs and aspirations within the seven constituent Band communities, and second, by helping the Council design the most effective organizational structure through which it could facilitate such development. Latent within these terms was an understanding of the need for a great deal of sensitivity to the complex, often opaque and currently fluid nature of the political and administrative interfaces that exist between individual Bands, the Tribal Council and the external public and private sector agency environment within which socio-economic development, or the lack of it, takes place.

These terms were themselves the product of a great deal of preliminary discussion between the Band leaders, the Tribal Council executive and the consultants. In the process, three prime tasks were identified. First, it was recognized that the above mentioned community process model was a viable basis for undertaking community evaluation research, but that the detailed design would require extensive local level relevance and acceptability testing. Second, each of the seven Bands would select their own researchers from within their communities. These researchers would then undergo a common training program to be administered by the Tribal Council and their consultants, with the Band managers in attendance. And third, the critical action research issue of the determination of the "ownership" of the research process and results would be pursued as an on-going part of the information gathering and decision-making process which the consulting arrangements were intended to aid.

This last concern for establishing an effective and workable distribution of future development responsibilities between the Band, the Tribal Council and the outside agency levels as part of the research and reorganizational process was somewhat complicated by the fact that the relevant outside agencies wished to maintain a "hands off" policy with respect to the internal review process. While this policy was no doubt motivated by a laudable desire to avoid past "paternalistic" practices, it was also problematic from the perspective of working out an innovative and integrated set of mutually accepted and respected responsibility jurisdictions for the future. It was therefore understood that various ways and means of bringing the principal outside agencies into the review and evaluation process would have to be developed as part of the consultative exercise.

Thus the whole consulting/client relationship, as well as the hoped for relationship with key external agencies, was suffused with an intentional *insider/ outsider dialectic*. This dialectic required raising to a manifest level the tensions which lie latent within virtually all native/mainstream societal relationships. Such a dialectical approach was seen as a necessary and important component of the consulting process if this process was to facilitate the development of mechanisms and structures through which the Tribal Council could act as an effective interface agency between its constituent Bands and the larger society.

The early identification of these task priorities and *modus operandi* was a crucial outcome of the consultants' early meetings with the Tribal and Band Councils and clearly established the basis of all subsequent client/consultant relationships. These relations may be summarized as follows: the consultants were to aid the client in developing a *process* rather than delivering a *product;* this process would involve continuous learning and evaluation on the part of both the *outside* consultants and the *inside* client constituencies; the clients would at all times maintain control over this process through their complete participation and on-going rejection/acceptance decisions; and the consultants would take a fresh look at their mandate at each of these in-process decision points with a view to what these decisions implied with respect to the consultants' most useful contributions to the next stage of the process.

It is worth pointing out that such terms and working relations between client and consultants are in marked contrast to the usual "employment" of *outside* expertise in the service of *inside* problem solving. In particular, these arrangements had the following effects:

1. The definition of the "problem" was not frozen into the consultants' terms of reference. It is the nature of real problems that they are as difficult to define adequately at the point of early recognition as is the early determination of solutions. Solutions are therefore not "products" to be delivered by outsiders, but rather "processes" which engage *on equal footing* the complementary components of *inside* knowledge and *outside* expertise.

2. This differential but equal knowledge recognition between client and consultant effectively precludes the unintentional substitution of the consultant's interest agenda for the client's need agenda. It also short-circuits any tendency for the client to surrender the ownership of the problem, and hence the ultimate responsibility for its solution, by progressively contracting out more and more to those who may justifiably claim "special" knowledge of solutions, but who should not—in any event, cannot—maintain a lasting jurisdiction over the problem.

3. Finally, by treating the abstract, technical and universalistic knowledge frames of the consultants and the concrete, experiential and particular knowledge frames of the clients as equally valid to the understanding and solution of problems, the all-too-common tendency to withhold or perhaps reject vital information on each side is undercut. Thus the client/consultant relationship was carefully constructed and effectively practiced in such a way as to minimize either the "paternalism of expertise" on the part of the consultants or the reverse "paternalism of jurisdiction" on the part of the client. In so doing, both sides were more completely bonded to a mutual learning and accepting approach than is typical in most consulting arrangements. This is a particularly important understanding when it is recognized, as indeed it was recognized, that although the Tribal Council was the formal contractual "client", it was absolutely essential to the task at hand that all the member Bands as well as the principal outside

agencies begin to recognize themselves as co-proprietors of the initiative.

THE PROCESS

The research phase of the project was to serve two functions. The most obvious was the "information out" function, i.e., the determination of the socio-economic development needs and priorities of each of the Band communities. In essence, this was to be achieved by using the community process model as a basis for developing a framework that would identify the existing socio-economic profile of the community at the objective level and the ideally desired profile at the subjective level. The difference between these two profiles would then define the direction and extent of future development needs and priorities for each Band community and, to the extent that this identification produced common themes, for the whole tribal group.

But the research exercise was also intended to serve an "information input" function. By virtue of its pervasive presence within each community, the research project would alert the community to the fact that the Tribal Council was attempting to establish a pan-Band planning and development capability. However, it was also important to indicate that this capability must be from the outset community centred, community controlled and ultimately community dependent if it were to succeed. In other words, the research had to be designed in such a way as to ensure that the "respondents" were not left with the impression that they could simply turn over development project initiative and responsibility to the Tribal Council and then blame them later for failures. Thus the importance of determining distribution of problem ownership and solution responsibility was given early and widespread expression within the research method itself.

The research was also designed in such a way as to communicate its conceptual base back to the community. This was seen to be important precisely because the pilot studies upon which the community process model had been predicated in the first place had revealed the existence of some self-destructive processes within those communi-

ties that most clearly needed some social and/or economic development initiative. Thus the first step in motivating and achieving such an initiative would be a community recognition of process problems. The pilot studies had also revealed that in the past many communities had unwittingly initiated or cooperated with development projects that had subsequently proved to be highly disruptive of positive community processes. Since the purpose of both the community process model and the current community research was to cast the community in the role of "planner", it was obviously desirable to include within the research design the kind of feed-back loops that would allow the whole community to develop an understanding of the likely effect of a given development choice upon a reflective assessment of their own established structures and processes.

Needless to say, the design and development of a research project that was at once required to satisfy the subjective requirements of the *inside* knowledge system and the objective requirements of the *outside* knowledge frame, while at the same time ensuring an appropriate distribution of responsibility, was not achieved in the usual abstract and academic way. Similarly, the training sessions in which the locally selected community researchers and the consultants struggled together to find the most appropriate methods bore no resemblance to the typically didactic exercises in which those with more formal research expertise tutor those with less on the niceties of how to ask questions. In the process, problems which are seldom recognized in traditional research approaches were discovered and dealt with. For example, while conventional measures of reliability could be applied to the "information out" data, how were the extent and effect of the "information in" data to be measured? And given that the research design anticipated that the subjective "information in" and the objective "information out" functions would be interactive (i.e., as the former was acquired the latter would change), when, how and how often were the two levels of data to be analyzed relative to each other? While the original community process model had gone some distance in developing formal measures of the relationship between subjective process variables and objective indicators, this first application test was highly dependent on the informal understandings of those closest to the actual realities for answers to these and many other questions. Of course, to admit this kind of informality into the highly prescribed realm of methodological purity was bound to do some injury to those universal measures of research accuracy upon which expert reputations rest. But if it is the widest possible understanding, rather than the narrowest possible margin of uncertainty, that is most required for the success of a project, then the beloved formalism of the *outside* knowledge experts must be tempered by the informality of the *inside* knowledge system if a successful outcome is to be achieved.

And, after all was said and done, the project did satisfy both the inside and outside criteria of success. For those outsiders who require objective evidence before cooperation may be secured, the project provided a well documented set of accustomed "products." Included here were such tangible objects as the clear identification of specific development needs, preferences and capabilities, the emergence of an appropriate development plan and a restructured Tribal Council whose outward facing posture included all the necessary capabilities to meet the mainstream culture's competence criteria. But there also developed an inward facing posture that could not be measured in terms of products but rather took shape as a consequence of the process through which inside understandings were consolidated, solidified and recognized by all. This process also included a growth in understanding of the outside knowledge system and the sense that it could be controlled and brought to bear in ways that need not be destructive to culture, community and self and which might well help resolve some of the chronic inside problems that seemed unyielding to purely internal effort. This same process also brought many formerly intransigent outsiders into contact with the inside knowledge system in a way that engendered various degrees of understanding, but in all cases a new respect and tolerance—a small beginning to be sure, but still a beginning.

CONCLUSIONS

Clearly, there are some salient lessons to be gleaned from this experience. First, there is the recognition that while any development initiative requires some "information out" objects, *community* development also requires a knowledge exchange process that includes strong "information in" subjects. For without such an exchange there can be no collective growth in understanding the relationship of what is to what should be and what might be in the context of any given development option. Indeed, if the currently fashionable term "social impact assessment" is to mean anything beyond a cheap strategy to usurp the ability of a community to determine what kinds of development are most consistent with its own sense of being, then such assessment must ensure that community insiders learn as much about themselves from the process as do any outsiders who may be involved. This is only to reiterate what Hayden Roberts (1979) argued as lying at the heart of all community development, the collective learning process:

> An important feature of community development is its assumption that man must take a hand, that he is a necessary and capable partner in the shaping of his life and the life of the society he lives in. In other words, it assumes a capacity for the process of learning . . . on the part of the people in the [inside] group and, *if possible,* on the part of other [outside] groups. . . .
>
> (Roberts, 1979:34-35; emphasis added)

The second lesson which emerges speaks to what in the above quotation appears as only a tentative "possibility", i.e., what I described earlier as the "insider/outsider dialectic". This is a concept of learning which places the very different knowledge frames possessed by outside consultants and the inside clients on an equal footing and that eschews pretense and risks conflict in the belief that deep insights leading to new possibilities will eventually emerge in the context of growing trust and mutual appreciation. While there were no guarantees this would work, the results did justify the risks, and this may give some inspiration to others. At a minimum, it offers a role model for non-native consultants who have tended to be either overly confident or excessively insecure with respect to the applicability of their kind of knowledge to the problems which native clients are trying to resolve.

And finally, the exercise underscores the importance of engaging in a predevelopmental process that recognizes that serious problems have a variety of proprietors and hence their solutions require some careful working out of the most appropriate distribution of responsibility. In this particular example, there was a real danger that an interface organization like the North Coast Tribal Council would be assigned the job of mediating the initially incompatible expectations of their inside constituents and the outside agents, thus incurring the blame for the failure that must inevitably result from such buffer arrangements. But by engaging in the dialectical process that forced both the outsiders and the insiders to recognize their own ownership of a piece of the problem, the probability of achieving a viable distribution of solution responsibility is greatly enhanced.

In presenting this account of one aspect of a much broader and still ongoing initiative, my intention has not been to offer yet another packaged prescription for others to emulate unquestioningly. Indeed, if there is an ultimate lesson in any of this, it is that there has been far too much focusing on pre-packaged products rather than on discovery processes in the pursuit of social and economic development projects. If past history is any guide, the solution of pervasive societal level problems will not be achieved by "break-through" innovations, but rather as the consequence of many different resolution attempts resulting in the mergence of a whole new collective consciousness of what causes problems and what represents solutions. The experience described here would appear to be one such step along this road.

NOTES

1. The North Coast Tribal Council constituency is spread along the remote fjords and islands of north coastal British Columbia. Its offices are located at 718 Fraser Street, Prince Rupert, B.C.

2. While none can be held responsible for what appears here, I would like to acknowledge my indebtedness to Frenchy Louis, Clarence Martin and Frank Parnell of the North Coast Tribal Council; Bert Painter, Bill Warren and Allan Sutton of B.C. Research; Dr. Katie Cook and her staff at the Department of Indian and Northern Affairs; and to the Skeena Manpower Development Committee for generously supporting my own participation in the project.

| Reading 1-3 | *Teenagers Take Control* |

Peter Brentnall

Here, at the Walsall Adolescent Placement Team (A.P.T.), we have been placing teenagers with families since 1987. Our practice is based on the celebrated work of the Kent Family Placement Scheme. We use contracts, we train families and we prepare youngsters from 12 to 17 years for short- to medium-term, task-centred, time-limited placements. Our aim is to either return young people home or help them into independent accommodation at the appropriate time. Along the way of course, we hope that the young people make personal changes to aspects of their behaviour which cause them difficulty and which clearly hold them back from their full potential. Recently, we have developed an approach which is bringing about real change for troubled young people in these sensitive areas of their lives.

EVALUATION

In 1990, during an evaluation of our work, three important facts emerged which were to focus our minds on a fundamental change in approach.

The first was that families were still investing time, effort and resources into helping young

From "Teenagers Take Control" by P. Brentnall, September 1992, *Social Work Today*, pp. 14–15. Reprinted by permission.

people straighten out their lives and this was an exhausting process.

The second was that placements continued to 'disrupt'. Particularly disappointing was the number of young people who, beyond 18, continued in the same destructive patterns of behaviour.

Lastly, there was a comment from a probation officer, "You can always tell young people who have been in care because they can't do a thing for themselves."

EFFORT
In order to get to grips with this and to find possible solutions, we started with the notion that for a placement to succeed, 100% effort had to be made, and we asked the question, who was making most of the effort? Certainly it was easy to see that placement workers were under strain, particularly when young people were in periods of acting out, eg. not going to school, absconding, in trouble with the police, etc. We reflected on our numerous meetings when placements were breaking down and remembered how hard social workers and placement workers worked to keep placements going. We then began to understand how young people experience that it may be *more* important to these adults than to themselves that the placement succeeds.

During the period of evaluation, we assessed that placement workers and social workers were doing anything from 70 to 90% of the work and that they were happy to do this as long as the placement continued. This solved *their* problem of keeping the young person in placement, but it did not promote the self-learning needed in adolescence. At this realisation, we began to understand the experience and comment of the probation officer working with young people who had most of the effort made for them.

PERSONAL RESPONSIBILITY
Alongside this understanding, we zoomed in on the personal responsibility for change through 'contracts', still evident in so many counselling and therapy arrangements, and decided to match the two together. What we ended up with was an approach designed to separate out responsibility for specific areas of behaviour and practical arrangements.

Particularly useful in this process was the time-honoured 28 days notice which could be handed in by anybody wishing to withdraw from the agreement. Traditionally, this had been used by placement workers who were too exhausted to carry on, or the social worker who took pity on them because of the behaviour of the young person. But if it was the young person's behaviour that was putting the pressure on, how do we make them responsible? Well, the answer was amazingly simple—accept *their* 28 days notice.

Immediately, there is a chorus of disapproval from social workers, who see young people as 'victims'. The discounting of these young persons' ability to solve their own problems, lies at the heart of the failure of our work. Our job is not to solve young persons' problems, but to give young people feedback on choices, information about outcomes and support through the process of making the wrong decisions. This is the valuable experience that they take with them into their adult life. In fact, we have been surprised and delighted with their ability to make good choices and learn effectively through mistakes when the process is managed effectively.

RESULTS
With this fundamental shift in approach, we no longer have placement disruptions. In our agreements, young people can hand in 28 days notice if they break any part of their agreement. If (and when) they break their agreement, their notice is accepted and they are informed of their leaving date and told to contact their social worker to make arrangements. If the young people want to stay, they make arrangements for a meeting to give them an opportunity to re-negotiate.

If they do not move and if they do not even bother to re-negotiate, they move before their 28 days is up. We have had many young people who move, but we take the line they didn't want to stay, *not* that they couldn't re-negotiate. We always offer another family to give the young person an opportunity to learn from their move. In addition, we try to encourage their attendance at a disruption meeting to ensure they take full learning with them.

We have been supported in this with the introduction of the 1989 Children Act, which, we believe, is based on personal and family responsibility. There is more room now, particularly when young people are accommodated, to move away from substitute care and make young people and their families more responsible for their actions, and to encourage young people to learn while they have the support of the organization around them.

For Further Reading

Alcabes, A., & Jones, T. A. (1985). Structural determinants of clienthood. *Social Work, 30,* 49–53.

Aponte, H. J. (1986). If I don't get simple, I cry. *Family Process, 25,* 531–548.

Belcher, J.R., & Ephross, P.H. (1989). Toward an effective practice model for the homeless mentally ill. *Social Casework, 70,* 421–427.

Brilliant, E. L. (1986). Community planning and community problem solving: Past, present, and future. *Social Service Review, 60,* 568–589.

Brody, R. (1982). *Problem solving: Concepts and methods for community organizations.* New York: Human Sciences Press.

Brower, A. (1988). Can the ecological model guide social work practice? *Social Service Review, 62,* 411–429.

Cowen, E. (1985). Person-centered approaches to primary prevention in mental health: Situation-focused and competence-enhancement. *American Journal of Community Psychology, 13*(1), 31–48.

Doel, M., & Lawson, B. (1986). Open records: The client's right to partnership. *British Journal of Social Work, 16,* 407–430.

Galaway, B., & Hudson, J. (Eds.). (1994). *Community Economic Development: Social and Economic Perspectives in Research and Policy.* Toronto: Thompson Educational Publishing.

Goldstein, H. (1986). Toward the integration of theory and practice: A humanistic approach. *Social Work, 31,* 352–357.

Lewis, W. W. (1984). Ecological change: A necessary condition for residential treatment. *Child Care Quarterly, 13*(I), 21–29.

Libassi, M. (1988). The chronically mentally ill: A practice approach. *Social Casework, 69,* 88–96.

Martin, M.A., & Nayowith, S.A. (1988). Creating community: Groupwork to develop social support networks with homeless mentally ill. *Social Work with Groups, 11.*

Milner, J. (1987). An ecological perspective on duration of foster care. *Child Welfare, 66,* 113–123.

O'Regan, P., & O'Connor, T. (1989). *Community: Give it a go.* Wellington, New Zealand: Allen & Unwin.

Parsons, R. F., Hernandez, S. H., & Jorgenson, F. D. (1988). Integrated practice: A framework for problem solving. *Social Work, 33,* 417–421.

Paster, O. S. (1986). A social action model of intervention for difficult to reach populations. *American Journal of Orthopsychiatry, 56,* 625–629.

Proctor, E., Vosler, N., & Sirles, E. (1993). The social-environmental context of child clients: An empirical exploration. *Social Work, 38,* 256–261.

Raynor, P. (1985). *Social work, justice, and control.* Oxford: Basil Blackwell.

Reamer, F. (1993). *The philosophical foundations of social work.* New York: Columbia University Press.

Rein, M. (1970). Social work in search of a radical profession. *Social Work, 15,* 13–33.

Rose, S. (ed.) (1992). *Case Management and Social Work Practice.* White Plains, N.Y.: Longman.

Scott, D. C. (1989). Meaning construction and social work practice. *Social Service Review, 63*(1), 39–51.

Schwartz, W. (1961). Social worker in the group. In National Conference on Social Welfare (Ed.), *Social welfare forum.* New York: Columbia University Press.

Thyer, B. A. (1987). Contingency analysis: Toward a unified theory for social work practice. *Social Work, 32*(2), 150–158.

Weick, A. (1983). Issues in overturning a model of social work practice. *Social Work, 28*(6), 467–471.

Weick, A., Ropp, C., Sullivan, W., & Kishardt, W. (1989). A strengths perspective for social work practice. *Social Work, 31,* 332–337.

Whittaker, J. K., Schinke, S. P., & Gilchrist, L. D. (1986). The ecological paradigm in child, youth, and family services: Implications for policy and practice. *Social Service Review, 60,* 483–503.

Chapter 2

Problem Solving: A Process for Social Work Practice

In the first chapter of this book we briefly discussed six elements that we identified as components of social work practice. In this chapter we will begin with an overall introduction to the problem-solving process. The individual phases of the process will be discussed in more detail in other chapters, as will the other five elements.

The problem-solving process may be understood as a series of interactions between the client system and the practitioner, involving integration of feeling, thinking, and doing, guided by a purpose and directed toward achieving an agreed-upon goal. It is the work of process that brings about the solution of the problem, although for process to be effective it must involve an interaction supported and guided by appropriate knowledge. It must be conducted within the values and sanctions of the profession, and a relationship appropriate to working together must develop between or among worker and client systems.

Relationship and understanding do not develop just because two bodies, one called the worker and the other the client, find themselves in a common enclosed space. (We will discuss the development and use of the relationship in detail in Chapter 8). Relationship is the medium of emotions and attitudes that acts to sustain the problem-solving process as practitioner and client systems work together toward some purpose. Thus, considered in relation to the practitioner's interaction with the client system, the problem-solving process can be thought of as operating through a partnership resting on the ability of each partner to relate and communicate with the other. The clients (or client system) have available information about (1) what brings them in contact with the social work practitioner, (2) the emotions, fears, and conflicts generated by the problem, and (3) what they expect of this contact and the social worker. The social worker has at hand (1) a body of knowledge about a variety of problems, (2) access to resources that may be available to bring to bear on the problem, (3) certain methods and skills of helping, and (4) an orderly way of proceeding (a pattern of thinking, if you will) that move client and worker toward a problem solution. This partnership increases the probability of appropriate selection and use of what the client brings to the situation and the practitioner's knowledge and information geared to improving the client's ability to cope effectively with the problem.

Our notion of process as a problem-solving activity rests on the principle that troubles in living stem from difficulties in effective coping with specific situations that we encounter in daily life. Difficulties in coping may stem from a combination of deficiencies in (1) motivation, which may be conceptualized as an imbalance of hope and discomfort relative to goal achievement, (2) capacity (needed knowledge, social skills, rational skills, interaction and relationship with external reality, and some interplay of current and past biopsychosocial factors in development) and (3) opportunity (access to support systems, needed resources, and helping relationships). We believe that for anyone, or for any social system, effective movement toward altering something one wishes to alter rests on the motivation and coping capacity of the person, or system, with whatever help is available, to engage in a problem-solving process.

The problem-solving process involves a series of phases, such as problem definition, goal-setting, and data collection, that must proceed in order. Each stage involves a particular kind of work aimed at the particular goal of that stage. The way the work on this phase is done will determine the effectiveness with which work on the next stage can go forward. Since this is the process by which each person attempts to solve the inevitable problems of life or reach the necessary decisions about alternative solutions to be selected, the worker who follows this model is following a life model of human growth and development. This means that the worker is not involved in treating an illness or in bringing about a cure for client troubles but rather is joining the forward motion of the client system and along with helping the client is strengthening the client's capacity to cope more effectively with life.

Problems as a Part of Life

There are some particularly pervasive misunderstandings and assumptions that always seem to surround the introduction of the process of social work practice as a problem-solving effort. One assumption seems to relate to a common culturally supported notion that competent people do not have problems or that there is something wrong or bad or weak implied when one speaks of problem solving. This position seems to stem from a totally unrealistic assumption that people should not have problems. It implies an unrealistic judgment of ourselves and others, a rejection of the growth process in all life. We all need to accept ourselves and our life struggles. This is impossible if we think that problems in living represent mistakes or weaknesses rather than a part of growth and change.

Some social workers seem to prefer to define the purpose of social work as the meeting of need. They seem to believe that to speak of a client's need is less assaultive on the client's sense of self or competence than to speak of a problem in living. We do not believe this to be true, although we recognize that the notion of "fulfilling the client's need" may support the worker's sense of omnipotence more than does the notion of helping the client solve a problem. Further, we find the notion of need to be vague and poorly defined. It can mean whatever the worker wants it to mean. Thus we feel that the determination of what the client needs tends to be the decision of the professional and comes close to the medical model of practice. We prefer to think of clients' wants rather than needs. When we use the word *need,* we are usually speaking of something that the client lacks, but when we use the word *want,* we are usually thinking of something the client desires or wishes for. When we listen for client wants, we are hearing the client's desires and goals rather than busying ourselves in trying to assess need, which is usually our judgment related to something we think the client lacks. The following example may help clarify the distinction between want and need. Mr. K's wife had to be hospitalized, leaving him with no care for three preschool children. Mr. K was referred to a child-care agency to plan for child care, a need defined by the court. The assigned worker in the child-care agency accepted the referral information that Mr. K's need was child care. However, Mr. K was struggling primarily with concern and worry about his wife's illness. He wanted desperately to understand the cause and the course of the illness, to know when she could come home. The worker's attempt to meet client need as she saw it was not related to the help Mr. K wanted. She ignored questions about the meaning of his wife's illness. Since the worker's attempt to meet the client need as she defined it was not related to the client's basic problem, the understanding of his wife's illness, her work actually resulted in Mr. K's level of functioning looking more and more pathological in her eyes. Also, Mr. K continued to struggle with his problem a year later, while the worker was still struggling with Mr. K's need for child care. Thus, neither the worker nor the client had achieved their goals because there was not a common understanding of Mr. K's problem or goals. The concept of meeting the client's need is an old one in social work, used in the early days of the friendly visitor and still being used without an analysis of what the concept means to the client, the worker, and the process of working together.

These assumptions do violence to our notion of the place of problem solving in the life process of all people. Life itself is a problem-solving process. Reid (1978, p. 26) says it well when he says that "a want . . . experienced without satisfaction becomes a problem." Since human wants are endless and when one is satisfied another immediately takes its place, we all are constantly involved in problem solving; although some of us, because we do not understand how one solves problems effectively, make a great mess of it. Everything we do in our daily life represents a response to a problem of wants, even though few of us are conscious of it in this way. Perhaps that is why we find it so hard to help others problem-solve effectively—so difficult to follow the steps of the process. Those who are good problem solvers do it so automatically that they do not understand the process, concentrating only on the result. For example, when we awake in the morning, we are immediately confronted with a problem: Do we get up, and if so, when? We quickly and sometimes quite unconsciously collect data about this problem. What do we anticipate accomplishing today? How important is it to us? (Goals?) What will be the reaction of meaningful people to our decision? Will those around us impose certain sanctions on us because we have not done this? As we perceive and integrate the data, we come to a decision and (hopefully) take action. We will have further difficulties and a growing set of problems developing around this simple problem if we incorrectly perceive the implications of the problem for what we want to accomplish. For example, we may try to get up when physically we cannot or should not. Or we may decide to remain in bed when getting up and taking certain actions are critically important to our well-being. It is not that those who are successful in life are without problems. It is that they solve problems well.

Problem Solving as a Life Process   To solve problems in living competently there are certain steps we all must take, and these steps are the same as those that social workers use to help the client. First, one must perceive a want and define the problem that must be solved to satisfy this want. Wants often arise out of our goals for ourselves, and a satisfactory solution must relate to these goals. Actually, a careful discussion of client goals is a part of the beginning phase of client engagement. Problem definition and tentative goal setting are a part of the process of framing the problem, of deciding what we will pay attention to in the process of helping the client. It is also critical to remember that motivation is what a client wants and how much he or she wants it. Thus the client's engagement with the problem-solving process will be determined by a tentative selection of a goal that the client, at the time of the initial contact, seeks or believes is a reasonable answer to his or her want. This problem and goal formulation may well change over the period of exploration and data collection, but client and worker must have some agreement on a tentative goal to begin working together. Without this agreement the worker should not be surprised if the client does not seem motivated. This emphasis on clarifying tentative goals when client and worker first come together is critical both to building a partnership and to the client's motivation to work on the problem. The problem, the goal, and the situation will set the parameters of what we will pay attention to in data collection. Without this, data collection is often unfocused and strays into unrelated areas of the client's life.

Given our goals, we start to gather data related to the situation. It is impossible at this point to list in detail all the data one would want to collect relative to any one presenting problem, but the data collected in general involve the internal emotional response, the feelings one has; the feelings of others who are important to one, their wishes; the possible responses, sanctions, and opportunities of the environment; and one's abilities and skills to carry through on the action proposed. It is usually the worker's responsibility to consider and guide the consideration of the plan to achieve the goal sought. The greater the number of alternative responses or solutions one is able to consider as possible goals, the more satisfactory the final action will be, provided that one is able to take action to achieve the solution. It can be devastating if one constantly gets tangled in so many alternatives that one cannot act, or if one selects a solution totally beyond one's ability to achieve.

As we consider solutions, we need to consider again the data we have acquired. Given the data, we must plan for possible action to reach our goal. Action is then taken to carry out the decision and to evaluate the results of the action so we can learn from the process. This evaluation is an attempt to assess whether the action taken moved us toward the goals we selected. If our evaluation of a step taken is negative, we often go back and try to assess what step in the problem-solving process was not well done. We say, "If only we had known . . . " When we say this, we are usually saying that we either perceived or defined the problem incorrectly, or we did not have the knowledge (data) necessary to an appropriate decision. Sometimes it may mean that our method of action was not effective. There are those of us who may suffer a great deal at this point in the problem-solving process, because we hold ourselves totally responsible for a negative outcome. Actually the only 20/20 vision in life is hindsight. We all approach all problems in living with incomplete knowledge. We can never be sure of the solution. Our only security is the process.

The process of working toward the solution of problems in living always contains emotions or feelings, always involves the knowledge base that we have available to us, always involves our perception of the world around us as well as our internal state, a way of organizing data, skills in action, our values and basic philosophies and attitudes (which often determine our goals), and a way of thinking that involves an orderly approach. These elements interact in a most complex way, and it is with this tangled interaction that most social workers are asked to help. Certainly, if one has a problem that one recognizes one cannot solve by oneself, or that is perceived as representing a serious threat to the goals one holds, or seriously threatens the needs and wants of those close to one, one may find oneself in a very painful situation. This pain, the high feeling generated by the problem, and one's judgment of self as one recognizes one's inability to solve it, usually obscures parts of the problem. It interferes with data collection and consideration of alternative solutions as well as blocking the effective actions toward solution. In many situations the client system is quite able to solve the problem, given the help of the social worker to deal with and dissipate the feeling. Thus, if the client has the appropriate knowledge, skills, and resources, it may be that the problem-solving activities concentrate primarily on the dissipation of feeling or understanding and acceptance of self. However, for most of our clients dissipation of feeling is not enough. They may need additional knowledge either about the problem, what data is needed, or appropriate solutions, and most important, they may need the appropriate resources to enable them to take the necessary action.

Interaction of Emotion, Knowledge, and Relationship   An example of the interaction of emotion, knowledge, and relationship is well illustrated by the following statement made by the mother of a retarded child when she was asked to evaluate the service given her by the social worker. This mother had gone from physician to physician seeking someone to tell her that her son would eventually be "normal" in intelligence. She had endured the comments of neighbors and her own in-laws that implied that she had done something wrong during the pregnancy. She had become exhausted and near collapse from trying to care for her retarded baby and her family with no knowledge of how to care for him or what the course of his development might be. She came to the social worker at very low ebb indeed, seeking help with the problem of understanding and caring for her son. As you read the case example, you see how dealing with feeling, supplying knowledge, and the use of a supportive relationship helped this mother.

> Miss B helped immeasurably at this point. She gave us a place to start. We were actually relieved to hear, for the first time in Tony's life, our suspicions confirmed and to find that there were still many things that Tony could do; and that with our understanding and help Tony had a chance to find a fairly satisfactory life. This did not come overnight. It took many meetings, going over and over the subject, before it began to take hold. It is a shock to find out that your child isn't as bright as normal and that his retardation will probably be more apparent as the years go by. At first you feel hopeless, but after many conferences you begin to realize that there are still many accomplishments of your child that you have a right to be proud of. You also realize that it really isn't too important what your relatives and neighbors think. You realize that it is your problem to work out, and most important, you can be happy doing it. You are helped to see the retarded child's rightful place in the home, that he needn't be the hub around which the entire family revolves.
>
> When I started working with Miss B I was at a very low ebb. I did not think that I would ever be able to handle Tony, and my lack of confidence with him was beginning to tell on the other children. She made me feel that I had done a fine job under very difficult circumstances, and even if it developed that we could not keep Tony at home, that it would not be a particular failure on my part. She helped me sort out my ideas and feelings so that I could see the total picture more clearly. She helped me get over the feelings of guilt I had. I realize now that one of her most important functions was not telling me what to do but

asking a pertinent question at just the right moment. Sometimes when a parent is trying to solve these things alone, I believe, they begin thinking in a circle that they can't escape without aid from someone who understands but who is not emotionally bound up in the problem. Many times I have come home from the clinic with a perfectly obvious answer that occurred to me only after a question from the social worker stimulated my thinking.

All effective clinical processes involve feelings on the part of both practitioner and client. These feelings become a part of the content of problem solving—a necessary and vital part—as well as providing a climate in which helping takes place. Because the steps in problem solving in clinical practice resemble the steps of the research process, it is possible for those inexperienced in its use to see it as essentially a cognitive process engaging only the intellectual capacities of the client. Actually the best of research is, in the last analysis, an orderly process of problem solving. Thus, we may say that the processes of research and social work practice are similar. The difference between the two efforts lies in their purpose, their content, and the emotional climate. The purpose of research is to build knowledge; the purpose of problem solving with clients is to help them in their forward progress in living. The content of problem solving in research efforts depends on the questions asked or the hypotheses developed. The content of problem solving in clinical practice depends on how the client defines the problem and goals. The climate of the work in research is cool and rational, but the climate of the work in problem solving is determined by what the client brings to the relationship.

Dewey and Problem Solving

The ancestor to problem solving is typically identified to be *How We Think,* by John Dewey in 1933, in which he attempted to describe the thought processes of a human being when confronted with a problem. In doing so, Dewey was interested in clarifying reflective or rational thinking, goal-directed thinking, or problem solving. According to Dewey, problem-solving behavior is based on reflective thought that begins with a feeling of perplexity, doubt, or confusion. The person wants to eliminate the difficulty or solve the puzzle, but to do this effectively one must follow a rational procedure. If one fails to do so, one can act uncritically or impulsively, leaping to inappropriate conclusions, mistaking the nature of the problem, becoming involved in searching for the answer to the wrong problem, or making a number of other errors. Any one of these behaviors may very well compromise the capacity to cope with the situation and undoubtedly makes it likely that the problem will remain unsolved.

Dewey held that effective problem solving demands the active pursuit of a set of procedural steps in a well-defined and orderly sequence. Dewey referred to these steps as the "five phases of reflective thinking." They include (1) recognizing the difficulty, (2) defining or specifying the difficulty, (3) raising suggestions for possible solutions and rationally exploring the suggestions, which include data collection, (4) selecting an optimal solution from among many proposals, and (5) carrying out the solution. Since Dewey, many persons working in various areas of endeavor have come to recognize that when one engages in investigation and problem solving, there is a preferred model for orderly thought and action that can be laid out in progressive steps and pointed toward the reaching of a solution and that the conscientious implementation of such a model materially increases the likelihood that one's objectives can be achieved.

It has been recognized that Dewey's list of five successive phases can be broken down into finer incremental steps and that orderly precision follows when this is done. Further, it has been recognized that Dewey's list failed to include the terminal aspects of problem solving—the evaluation of the effectiveness of the attempted solution and the use of feedback loops (see Chapter 4) into the process, by which modifications can be made in the procedures employed even as one is engaged in employing them. In social work literature, one will find a number of models that divide the activities of a social worker into sequential phases, each phase characterized by some broad goal of its own that must be accomplished before the worker moves on to complete the next phase.

In the early 1940s, a mathematics professor, George Polya (1957), developed a model to help mathematics instructors teach mathematical problem solving, but his aim really went beyond that. He intended that the book should be used as a guide by all problem solvers. He presented a four-phase model: (1) understanding the problem, including understanding the problem situation, the goal of the problem solver, and the conditions for solving the problem; (2) devising a plan by which the goal could be attained; (3) carrying out the plan; and (4) evaluating the plan, its implementation, and the results.

The scientific method itself may also be considered a model of problem solving, and other frameworks have been developed by other authors in the behavioral sciences. Notable among these efforts is the work of Bennis, Benne, and Chin (1969) in their development of strategies of effecting change in human systems. These authors, however, see the problem-solving process as a normative reeducative approach to change. It is our position that the formulation is broader than that.

Problem Solving in Social Work

We are neither the first nor the only people in social work to have conceptualized social work practice within this type of framework. In social work Helen Harris Perlman must be considered the originator of the problem-solving framework. Her principal work, *Social Casework: A Problem-Solving Process,* was published in 1957 and has had tremendous impact on social work thinking. Both Perlman and we have based our formulations on constructs from ego psychology and on Dewey's work on principles of problem solving. One of the principal differences in the knowledge base used by Perlman from that used by us is the use of systems theory as a foundation in the present text. This results in our extending the problem-solving process to groups, organizations, and communities and in our broadening our model to include more emphasis than one finds in Perlman's work on transactions with and change in other social systems. While Perlman presents problem solving as a casework process, we see the problem-solving process developed in this book as the base for generalist practice.

Also, Perlman puts particular emphasis on the professional practitioner's primary responsibility for thinking about the facts and for the other activities of diagnosis and planning. While we believe with Perlman that the worker carries responsibility to do this hard responsible head work and to see that the process moves forward, we also believe that the worker must test out such thinking with the client and that there is a shared responsibility between worker and client for every phase of problem-solving work, including especially the assessment and decision-making phase. Perlman basically sees problem solving as both a process and a method of helping. We see it as a process that may lead to the selection of an appropriate interventive method, but it is not itself a method of intervention. We see the worker engaging in a broader array of helper roles than does Perlman. She primarily emphasizes the enabler role of the worker and does not distinguish as sharply as we do between the various stages of the process. She says that treatment begins with the first glance between worker and client, although she puts considerable emphasis on the fact that the work between worker and client cannot proceed until the client has moved from role of the applicant to that of client. In this respect our notions coincide with hers.

In social work literature a number of other authors who write about problem solving divide the activities of a social worker into sequential phases, each phase characterized by some broad goal of its own and requiring specific social work skills, which must be accomplished before moving on to complete the next phase. In general such models demand that the worker be successively involved with (1) recognition or definition of the problem and engagement with the client system, (2) data collection, (3) assessment of the situation, (4) goal setting and the planning of action, (5) intervention, or the carrying out of action, (6) evaluation, and (7) termination. However, our model of the process is the only one that has two stages of goal setting. We add a stage, called goal setting, immediately following or concurrent with problem identification. The goal set this early in the exploration of the problem is a statement of what the client wants. Such a goal will probably need to be changed later, but if we accept the fact that motivation is what one wants and how much one wants it, then we need to recognize the push toward problem solving that is found in the early goal setting with the client. This early clarification of goals also moves the relationship toward a partnership and results in active client engagement. In addition to this early goal setting we place a reconsideration and finalization of goals setting just after or concurrent with assessment and just before treatment planning. It is at this point that we have collected enough data that we, in partnership with the client, can reach a decision about the goal that will direct the treatment plan.

Problem Solving and the Practitioner's Responsibility

While we believe that the problem-solving process is orderly, that it is sequential, and that any one phase depends on the successful completion of the preceding phase, we also feel that any linear sequencing of tasks is an oversimplification of the process. In any given situation the worker may be operating in more than one phase at a time. In spite of the fact that the phases follow each other in some rough order, one phase does not wait upon the completion of another before it begins. Problem solving in social work probably proceeds not linearly but by a kind of spiral process in which action does not always wait upon the completion of assessment and assessment often begins before data collection is complete. In fact, one often becomes aware that one has not collected enough facts, or the proper facts, only after one begins the process of trying to put all one knows together in some sort of summing-up process. Also, when the worker and the client system begin to take action toward some solution of the problem, it may well be discovered that they have selected an unworkable course or are proceeding on the wrong problem and must start all over again. However, in this case one begins again with the distinct advantage of having some knowledge and some observations and some working relationships that one did not have before.

We can well understand Perlman's statement about treatment beginning with the first glance between client and worker. However, we phrase it somewhat differently. We say that the beginning of the relationship comes with that first glance and that this beginning climate has meaning for the problem identification, analysis, and solution. As the problem-solving work progresses through the various phases, this beginning relationship will also change, perhaps in a progressive developmental way and perhaps radically and abruptly. At the moment of meeting the beginning of work together on an identified problem still is to come, but it will be inevitably affected by that first glance. Thus it is important as we move through the sequence of the phases of the model to remember that it is not a simple linear process.

The fact that the problem-solving process is a squirming, wriggling, alive business that may be grasped as an intellectual concept concerning what goes on in the worker's head—but also vitally concerning the social reality between the worker, the client, and all the interrelated systems of which the worker and the client are a part—makes it a difficult model to carry out in practice. All parts of the model may be present at any one time in a way that may obscure for the ordinary viewer, and often for the worker as well, the fact that there is rhyme and reason in what is being done. But it is the worker's business to know in general what phase is the primary focus of coming together with the client, and it is the worker's business to check constantly to see that all phases are dealt with. As many failures in helping stem from the worker's impulsive leap to some action from what is seen at the moment as the problem, with no pause for thought and consultation in between as from the worker's inability to engage in a helping relationship. In fact, these two parts of the helping process (the capacity to relate to and communicate with others and problem-solving efforts) are so firmly interwoven that we often do not pause to see them as separate things.

The problem-solving process in and of itself is the process by which worker and client decide (1) what the problem or question is that they wish to work on; (2) what the desired outcome of this work is; (3) how to conceptualize what it is that results in the persistence of the problem in spite of the fact that the client wants something changed or altered; (4) what procedures should be undertaken to change the situation; (5) what specific actions are to be undertaken to implement the procedures; and (6) how the actions have worked out.

For the worker the use of the process involves considerable skill and the cultivated capacity to keep both a clear head and an understanding heart. However, the problem-solving framework gives the worker no specific guides to specific procedures. It does not promise that if one does this type of thinking and exploring one will come out with *the* (or with *this*) answer. It promises rather that one must do this type of thinking and exploring, consciously and knowingly, in about this order, if one wants to increase the probability of coming out with an *effective answer* that is in the direction of the client's goals. What the answer is specifically will depend on (1) what the question is specifically, (2) what the client wants specifically, and (3) what the worker and the client can bring to the process in knowledge, understanding, resources, and capacity for joint action.

Thus there are some very significant requirements that relate to workers' use of the model and to workers' approach to clients. There may be a tendency to think that since the model requires a lot of rational headwork on the part of the worker, it is appropriate only for clients who come with a well-developed ability to weigh and measure alternative courses of action. Nothing could be further from the truth. This burden of rational headwork lies with the practitioner, not the client. In fact, we have used this way of working successfully with families who had been judged by other community helping facilities—schools, mental health clinics, and social agencies—to be totally unreachable and beyond help by any professional. It is so helpful to these clients because one of the reasons for their difficulties is that they do not possess these skills to the extent demanded by their living situation.

Beginning Where the Client Is   The key to the use of this treatment model with clients who appear to have no coping skills, or no ability to trust others, is to begin, just as the model indicates, with the problem as seen by the client at whatever level the client may present it. Workers run into great difficulty when they are so focused on their own definition of the problem or their concern with client capacity or with the real problem or cause of the problem that they cannot hear the client. Also, workers often appear totally unaware of how they differ with the client about the understanding of the problem. Not only can there be no use of this model at all, there can be no helpful use of any model without the active engagement of the client, and that engagement must be around concerns congruent with clients' expectations and problem definition (see the discussion on basic role theory in Chapter 4). Also, workers often find it difficult to accept the pace of the clients' early movement and the problems that often are involved in human change.

People who have little ability to weigh and measure alternative courses of action and who have no reason to trust the help that the worker offers will neither express their problems in the worker's terms nor express their goals in terms of learning to live a more productive life. Rather, they express their problems in terms of basic survival needs. What is more important? The worker who understands the problem-solving process in terms of the model will see such expression of concrete needs as the place to begin. Such workers can then join with the client in setting the goals at this level—to secure necessary repairs on the refrigerator or to find a way to get a new stove. These are worthy goals in that they do help to make the client's life more satisfying, or at least less hard, and they are the client's goals. Such problems and goals are the stuff of the beginning engagement. But for the worker there may also be the concern of using this problem and its solution as a way of building some trust and sense of success that can be used to move on to other problems and other goals, if there are others. The problem many people have in using the model is that they assume that the problem has to be a basic problem in living rather than something else that the client identifies as an important want. One also needs to remember that beginning where the client is does not mean that one stays there.

Causes, Problems, and Symptoms   Wendell Johnson (1951, pp. 176–177) discusses these symptoms and basic causes. Perhaps if the reader could substitute *presenting problem,* meaning "the problem the client brings" for Johnson's word *symptom,* it would be possible to understand why workers often have difficulty with the problem-solving model, which says in essence that they must start with where the client is—which is usually not with "cause" but with relief of the symptom. Johnson writes:

> Let us make this very absurd. What I am trying to say is that one of the things we do which tends to keep us from understanding handicapped children and adults better is that we do not spend enough time trying to appreciate the symptoms, as we call them. To them, they are not symptoms so much as they are causes of frustration and misery. They want to have

everything possible done to alleviate or remove the symptoms. They want to work on the so-called causes, too, of course. But in the meantime, they are in pain or distress.

Now, as I suggested, let us make the situation very absurd. Suppose that we were out in the woods and we came upon a man who had accidentally got his foot caught in a bear trap. There he is, howling and carrying on frightfully, weeping and straining in a most profane fashion. Then two psychologists come by and one of them wants to give the man the Rorschach test and an intelligence test and take a case history. The other psychologist, however, has undergone a different kind of training; and he says, "No let's start intensive psychoanalysis right now." So, they talk it over. They have their differences, of course, but they agree eventually that what this man in the bear trap needs is obviously psychotherapy. If he would just be trained to be a more mature individual; if he could have the release therapy he needs; if he would undergo the needed catharsis, achieve the necessary insight, and work through the essential abreaction, he would develop more maturity, he would understand the difficulty he is having, and he would then be able to solve his problem himself. Obviously, the psychologists agree, that is the only sound way to deal with the poor fellow. Suddenly, however, a farmer comes by and lets the man out of the bear trap. To the utter amazement of the psychologists, the man's behavior changes greatly and quickly. Besides, he seems to take a great liking to the farmer, and goes off with him, evidently to have a cup of coffee.

The basic principle illustrated by this absurd example is that psychotherapy is most beneficial when it is carried on under optimal conditions. And one way to prepare optimal conditions for psychotherapy, or for classroom teaching, for that matter, or for any kind of special instruction, is to do everything possible first—or as you go along—to relieve any distressing symptoms that may be distracting the individual you are trying to help. If the symptoms make a difference to the individual, if they are producing impaired social relationships, impaired self-evaluations, impaired parent-child relationships, or tantrums, or anxiety, then clearly anything that can be done directly, by means of literal or figurative aspirin, to relieve the symptoms will be all to the good in helping to bring about favorable conditions for therapy.

In the problem-solving process, any symptoms or needs or wants become problems to be solved. In problem solving, practitioner and client may work on a whole array of these problems one at a time. Generally, in carrying out the action plan with client systems, the worker will be involved in four primary activities: (1) provision of needed resources, which may involve roles of broker and advocate (among others) and will undoubtedly require work with a target system that is different from the client system and a broad action system; (2) change in transactions between client system and other systems, that in addition to the roles and systems mentioned earlier may involve the worker in the role of enabler and teacher with the client system; (3) the problem-solving work, which will involve the worker primarily in teaching and enabling a client system to work in this way; and (4) the use of the therapeutic relationship for change in the internal interaction of the client system, which calls for roles of enabler, teacher, and therapist.

Values in Using the Problem-Solving Process   Although there are other frameworks for social work practice, we like the problem-solving framework for a number of reasons:

1. No assumptions about the cause, nature, location, or meaning of the problem are built into the model itself. Thus the framework allows the problem to be

defined as lying within the client system, as lying within the other systems with which the client system has transactions, as lying in some lack in social resources that should be supplied by the environment, or as lying in transactions among these factors. The problem itself carries no implication of impaired functioning or personality malfunctioning.

2. The framework is based on a belief in the growth potential for all human systems and thus both fits social work's belief in human struggles toward growth and rests on the knowledge borrowed from systems theory and ego psychology.

3. At the level of foundation knowledge, the framework is based on selected constructs from ego psychology, systems theory, role theory, communication theory, and group dynamics, all of which depart from the personal deficit theory and put emphasis on social transaction. At the level of practice theory, the model is not based on any one theoretical orientation and thus allows the worker and client to agree on any method of help appropriate to the problem, the problem location, the goals, the client system, and the worker's competence and resources.

4. The framework gives a prominent spot to consideration of client goals, or goals of other social systems with which one is working. This is congruent with social work values of the importance of the individual, of individuals' differences, and of self-determination and with systems theory, role theory, and ego psychology.

5. The way the problem is defined and the goal is established determines which data are relevant and where the emphasis and direction of inquiry will lie. This allows for data collection that is relevant, salient, and individualized. It further requires that intervention in the client's life be kept at a minimum.

6. The framework is congruent with the function and purpose of the social work profession in that it supports the client's right to personal definition of the problem and in case the worker has a different view demands that some negotiation be undertaken in defining the problem to be worked (which simply means that worker and client must agree on what they are going to undertake together). The framework also recognizes the importance of the purposes of the client system.

7. In addition to supplying a process applicable to a wide variety of situations and settings in which social work is practiced and to different sizes and types of systems, the problem-solving framework demands that the tasks and activities of the social worker be stated at a very specific level and related to client goals. This seems to us to be a distinct advantage over frameworks that allow for a more abstract treatment plan.

The Client System and Problem Solving

It is difficult to speak of what is required of the client apart from the workers' activities. As in any system, including the helping system of worker and client, the behavior of one element has tremendous impact on the actions of other elements. Thus we must start our discussion of what is required of the client by pointing out that we begin with what is required of the worker. To speak of the clients' requirements without recognizing that these requirements rest on the assumption that the worker is concerned and caring, able to communicate a desire to understand, and willing to start with the client's presenting the problem has little meaning. In our experience, individuals, families, or groups who were often held by earlier helping systems to be unreachable and beyond help could participate as partners in the problem-solving process once they understood that we (having learned to listen) really wanted to know them as people and were willing to help them pursue their own goals. They could tell us something about goals they had for themselves that were impossible to achieve because changes were needed that they alone could not effect. And it was here that the problem-solving process began. In other words, this process demands the following of clients: (1) that they be able to share with the worker information about something that they would like to have changed; (2) that they achieve something that is of value to them; (3) that as the worker is able to demonstrate concern and competence to help with the exploration of this problem, clients are able to trust this concern enough; and (4) that they allow the worker to continue to meet with them around this purpose. That is all that is demanded of the client system.

Basic Assumptions of the Model

This model does not in any way deny people's irrational and instinctive characteristics, but it accepts the findings of social scientists who have studied the social milieu of the mental hospital that even the most regressed psychotic patients are at least as responsive to changes in external reality as to their internal fantasies, that altering their external reality alters their ways of coping, and that "given a chance to participate in making decisions that affected their lives, inmates generally did so in a responsible manner and with constructive results for all concerned—professionals as well as themselves" (Lerner, 1972, p. 161). This model further accepts the view that social work processes are not a set of techniques by which experts who understand what "is really wrong" seek in their wisdom to improve, enlighten, plan for, or manipulate the client system. Rather, it sees social work processes as an attempt "by one human being with specialized knowledge, training, and a way of working to establish a genuinely meaningful, democratic, and collaborative relationship with another person or persons in order to put one's special knowledge and skills at the second person's (or group's) disposal for such use as can be made of it" (Lerner, 1972, p. 11). It recognizes that decisions about what individuals and groups of individuals should be, have, want, and do are cognitive decisions that involve rational and nonrational processes, perceptions of the describer, the possible, and values, an area in which "every person is a legitimate expert for oneself and no person is a legitimate expert for others" (Lerner, 1972, p. 161). The model rests on the assumption that the given in each human being is a desire to be active in one's life—to exercise meaningful control of oneself for one's own purposes. Systems theory states that living systems are purposive, and we believe that practitioners are more effective when they start with the client's purposes and the obstacles to their achievement. We further believe that the push toward change comes from the discomfort of unfulfilled wants but the pull toward change comes from hope that with certain efforts one can achieve these wants. This does not mean that one is naive about unconscious and irrational factors. It simply means that one starts with the rational, with consciously expressed problems and goals. Such goals may appear to the practitioner as totally irrational and impossible, but the model demands that they be respected and seen as a valuable statement of client wants.

Presentation of the Phases of the Problem Solving Process

The phases of the problem-solving process and the skills demanded of the worker will be developed further in succeeding chapters. However, the process and skills may be briefly outlined as follows.

I. Contact (or engagement) phase
   A. Activities
      1. Engagement and problem definition
      2. Definition of the problem for work
      3. Goal identification
      4. Negotiation of preliminary contract
      5. Exploration, investigation, data collection
      6. Assessment
   B. Skills needed
      1. Ability to use self in the interests of the client system or potential client system based on self-awareness and understanding of resources and possible target and action systems
      2. Listening, which includes not only listening with ears to words and with eyes to body language but a total kind of perceptiveness that is best described as listening with the third ear, attending carefully both physically and psychologically to client
      3. Communication of empathy, genuineness, trustworthiness, respect, and support
      4. Use of such techniques as paraphrasing, clarifying, perception checking, focusing, questioning, reflecting, informing, confronting, interpreting, assuring, and reassuring
      5. Skill in use of a range of data collection methods, including not only interviewing skills listed earlier but also the use of records, test data, other written materials, interviews or conferences with other than the client, observations, and documentary evidence
      6. Skill in using a theoretical knowledge base to guide the collection of salient and relevant information
      7. Skill in determining meaning of data
II. Contract phase
   A. Activities
      1. Assessment and evaluation
      2. Formulation of an action plan
      3. Prognosis
   B. Skills needed
      1. All of skills listed in contact phase
      2. Ability to use a basic theory of the growth, development, functioning, malfunctioning, interactions, and transactions of human systems to assign meaning and to analyze the data collected
      3. Ability based on above, plus knowledge of problems, goals available, to prioritize and organize data in such a way as to suggest useful action
      4. Ability to generate a range of alternative plans with associated predictions as to probable success and cost

5. Ability to use own judgment and client participation to select among alternatives
6. Ability to put all of the above together in a statement of actions to be taken, when and by or with what systems, within what time frame

III. Action phase
A. Activities
1. Carrying out plan
2. Termination
3. Evaluation
B. Skills needed
1. All skills listed in contact and contract phrases
2. Skills in use of a range of social work methods as appropriate to roles necessary to carrying out the plan (see Chapters 5, 12–16)
3. Skills in a range of evaluative skills (see Chapter 16)
4. Skills in ending and disengagement (see Chapter 15)

Recapitulation

In this chapter we have introduced the problem-solving model of social work practice as we have developed it. This model is based on five selected theories of human development, growth, and transactions between and among human systems: systems theory, communications theory, role theory, ego psychology, and notions of human diversity and difference. From these theories we have developed the following basic assumptions that are the base of our approach to problem solving: (1) people want to control their own lives and to feel competent to master the tasks they see as important; (2) motivation for change rests on some integration between a system's goals and its hope-discomfort balance; (3) the social worker is always engaged in attempting to change some interactions or transactions within or among systems; (4) systems are open and the input across their boundaries is critical for their growth and change; (5) while a system must have a steady state for its functioning, it is constantly in flux; and (6) all human systems are purposive and goal seeking.

This model is constructed on the notion that the change process has three basic phases, each of which has its own stages and list of activities. Each stage demands some different skills as well as requiring some similar ones. These phases are so wound together that they are hard to disentangle for study, but it is important that workers be aware of the primary phase of the work in which they are engaged. We take the position that this model demands three primary things of the worker: (1) the headwork involved in trying to understand the situation and make an orderly approach to the process; (2) the ability to engage the client and other systems to understand and negotiate the problem and the goals; and (3) the ability to develop and sustain a working partnership. It further requires that workers be aware of the six systems with which they may be involved and have the skills necessary to use any system or attempt to change any system. The initial demand on the clients is that they be able to share their view of their trouble with the worker and that they allow the worker to maintain some contact with them long enough to demonstrate the worker's intentions toward them.

One final caution! The following problem-solving outline has been developed to be used selectively by the worker.

A Look
Forward
We are going to suggest three activities that should help to connect this chapter to the next three chapters. First, following this discussion, you will find two outlines of the problem-solving model. We have not included these outlines in the text because inevitably they become the focus of consideration before persons have read the whole chapter. We want you to finish the chapter, then study the outlines. We are offering two outlines because we want to give an example of a complete, long outline, and demonstrate how it can be shortened. Neither of these outlines is presented as cast in concrete. We offer them as guides. We hope they raise questions for what you need to consider in assessing a situation. We do not expect you to include every point in your assessment. Include only the points that relate to the situation with which you are involved.

Mary Richmond (1917), in preparing the first text on social diagnosis ever written, included long lists of things to guide workers in making a complete study of a situation. Much to her horror, she found that workers were actually trying to find out and act on everything she had included in the list. She is supposed to have exclaimed, "I didn't mean for them to do it all" (Pumphrey 1981, p. 223). We do not intend for you to do it all.

Second, we would like you to read carefully the two articles that follow the outlines. The author of the first article critiques some models of problem solving, highlighting the aspects that we have tried to keep at the center of our model. The next article relates to recording of work together.

To consider how you can record the problem-solving effort from problem definition through assessment to plan, we suggest that you look again at the cases in the Appendix. The outline of the work with Mr. H (Appendix, A-3) closely follows the outlines below. Perhaps reading this case ("Pain Clinic Evaluation") and reviewing the outlines will help you to understand how to use the points in the outline selectively.

In "Pain Clinic Evaluation" (A-3), "The Lee Family" (A-5), the "House on Sixth Street" (A-7), and the case of Mrs. Manley (A-2), those concerned approach the agency as clients seeking the help of the social worker in relation to specific problems. In the H case and the Lee case the client's definition of the problem seems to fit the usual problems the agency is ready and able to deal with and to constitute an appropriate problem for work, so there is little confusion or conflict in the relationship or problem definition between client system and worker in assessing the problem and planning alternatives that appear appropriate for its solution. In the "House on Sixth Street" the worker sees the problem as involving more than worker, individual client, and the family system. The worker suggests, with the client's approval, that the problem be explored further before it is defined and brought to closure. The result is a somewhat different definition of the problem from what the client brought, but in the exploration and definition client and worker were in agreement. All individuals facing similar difficulties were willing to become clients, and the attempt to deal with the situation was considerably different than if the problem had remained solely that of one individual client. In the Manley case we find that the worker is conflicted over the way Mrs. Manley and her doctor have defined the situation. The worker sees the problem as one of the family system but feels constrained from accepting the definition that she believes has been agreed on by the doctor and the client. When she discovers that her assumption is not correct, she discusses a broader definition of the problem, and the client accepts an intervention plan that follows from such a definition.

The Z case (A-4), the Stover case (A-6), and the Smith case (A-1) reach the worker by a different route. In these cases the worker is required by an agency or institution to contact the client for problems identified by the referral source, and in the Z and Stover cases there is considerable resistance. Mrs. Stover seems to have perfected an avoidance technique for dealing with social workers. However, in spite of her problems with practitioners, she is willing to accept a client role when she needs certain resources that she knows the agency can provide. There is no evidence in the record of a conscious agreement on the problem that brought worker and Mrs. Stover together. However, as the worker demonstrates her willingness to accept without question Mrs. Stover's definition of the immediate problem of financial and medical needs and her desire to be of help, Mrs. Stover seems to accept the role of client and to raise issues that as they were discussed, move her toward the solutions of the problems that led to the referral of the situation. It is interesting to note that this situation had been assessed by professional authorities in the community as totally untreatable and unreachable, yet the worker was able to assist Mrs. Stover in learning to manage her life. Is it because the worker began with work on the problems as identified by Mrs. Stover? Certainly Mrs. Stover's case history presented considerable evidence of pathology, but as this was not a problem identified by Mrs. Stover, the worker did not present this as a problem for work.

By contrast, Mrs. Z never becomes a client, and she and the worker never reach a definition of a problem for work. Perhaps this is because the worker never appropriately explained her purpose in seeing Mrs. Z and did not ask Mrs. Z if she could identify things with which the worker could help her. Mrs. Z kept insisting that she could care for herself. Was this in part because she was fearful that the worker would take over the management of her life? If Mrs. Z needed something done, the worker took over and did it without involving her in the planning. Getting the ice water is a good example. The worker went to get the water and then was irritated at Mrs. Z's instructions about how the glass should be filled and where it should be placed so that Mrs. Z could reach it. Would that problem have been better resolved if the worker had asked her how much ice and how much water she wanted and where the worker should place it so it would be convenient? In the following chapters we are going to continue to discuss the problem-solving model, dealing with the process from the initial contact through assessment.

Outline of Problem Solving Model— Short Form

I. Contact phase
   A. Problem identification and definition
      1. Problem as client system sees it
      2. Problem as defined by significant systems with which client system is in interaction (family, school, community, others)
      3. Problem as worker sees it
      4. Problem for work (place of beginning together)
   B. Goal identification
      1. How does client see (or want) the problem to be worked out?
         a. Short-term goals
         b. Long-term goals

    2. What does the client system think is needed for a solution of the problem?

    3. What does client system seek and/or expect from the agency as a means to a solution?

    4. What are worker's goals as to problem outcome?

    5. What does worker believe the service system can or should offer the client to reach these goals?

C. Preliminary contract

    1. Clarification of the realities and boundaries of service

    2. Disclosure of the nature of further work together

    3. Emergence of commitment or contract to proceed further in exploration and assessment in a manner that confirms the rights, expectations, and autonomy of the client system and grants the practitioner the right to intervene

D. Exploration and investigation

    1. Motivation

       a. Discomfort

       b. Hope

    2. Opportunity

    3. Capacity of the client system

II. Contract phase

A. Assessment and evaluation

    1. If and how identified problems are related to needs of client system

    2. Analysis of the situation to identify the major factors operating in it

    3. Consideration of significant factors that contribute to the continuity of the need, lack, or difficulty

    4. Identification of the factors that appear most critical, definition of their interrelationships, and selection of those that can be worked with

    5. Identification of available resources, strengths, and motivations

    6. Selection and use of appropriate generalizations, principles, and concepts from the social work profession's body of knowledge

    7. Facts organized by ideas—ideas springing from knowledge and experience and subject to the governing aim of resolving the problem—professional judgment

B. Formulation of a plan of action—a mutual guide to intervention

    1. Consideration and setting of a feasible goal

    2. Consideration of alternatives—likely costs, possible outcomes.

    3. Determination of appropriate service modality

    4. Focus of change efforts

    5. Role of the worker

    6. Consideration of forces either within or outside the client system that may impede the plan

    7. Consideration of the worker's knowledge and skill and of the time needed to implement the plan

C. Prognosis—what confidence does the worker have in the success of the plan?

III. Action phase

A. Carrying out of the plan—specific as to point of intervention and assignment of tasks, resources and services to be used, methods by which they are to be used, who is to do what and when

B. Termination
1. Evaluation with client system of task accomplishment and meaning of process
2. Coping with ending and disengagement
3. Maintenance of gains
C. Evaluation
1. Continuous process
2. Was purpose accomplished?
3. Were methods used appropriate?

Outline of Problem Solving Model— Long Form

I. Contact phase
A. Problem identification and definition
1. Problem as the client system sees it
   a. Nature and location of need, lack, or difficulty
   b. Significance and meaning assigned by the client system to the need, lack, or difficulty
   c. Length of existence, previous occurrences, precipitating factors
   d. Conditions that bring client system and worker into interaction at this time
   e. Significance and meaning assigned by the client system to this interaction
2. Problem as defined by significant systems with which the client system is in interaction (family, school, community, others, including referral system)
   a. Nature and location of need, lack, or difficulty as seen by these systems
   b. Significance and meaning assigned by these systems to this need, lack, or difficulty
   c. Significance and meaning assigned by these systems to client's interaction with interventive agent
3. Problem as the worker sees it
   a. Nature and location of need, lack, or difficulty
   b. Precipitating factors that the client system knows about and believes to be related and that the worker knows about and believes to be related
   c. Significance of conditions that bring client system and worker into interaction
   d. Nature and degree of effort that client system has put into coping with problem and client system's feeling about such efforts
4. Problem-for-work (place of beginning together)
   a. Problem or part of problem that the client system feels is most important or a good beginning place
   b. Problem or part of problem that in the worker's judgment is most critical
   c. Problem or part of problem that in the worker's judgment can most readily yield to help
   d. Problem or part of problem that falls within the action parameters of the helping system
B. Goal identification
1. How does the client system see (or want) the problem to be worked out?
   a. Short-term goals
   b. Long-term goals

2. What does the client system think is needed for a solution of the problem?
   a. Concrete resources
   b. Specific assistance
   c. Advice, guidance, or counseling
3. What does the client system seek and/or expect from the agency as a means to a solution?
   a. Specific assistance (concrete service to enable the client system to do something)
   b. Specific resources (concrete things)
   c. Change in the environment or other social systems
   d. Change in specific individuals
   e. Advice or instruction
   f. Support or reassurance
   g. Change in self
   h. Change in interaction between client system and others
4. What are the worker's goals as to problem outcome?
   a. Long-term goals—are they different from client system's goals?
   b. Short-term goals—are they different from client system's goals?
   c. Does worker believe client system's goals to be realistic and acceptable?
   d. What facilitating and intermediate goals can be identified?
   e. Level of agreement between workers and client system on goals
5. What does the worker believe the service system can or should offer the client to reach these goals?
   a. Specific assistance
   b. Specific resources
   c. Change in the environment or other social systems
   d. Advice or instruction
   e. Support or reassurance
   f. Change in self
   g. Change in interaction between client system and others

C. Preliminary contract
   1. Clarification of the realities and boundaries of service
   2. Disclosure of the nature of further work together
   3. Emergence of commitment or contract to proceed further in exploration and assessment in a manner that confirms the rights, expectations, and autonomy of the client system and grants the practitioner the right to intervene

D. Exploration and investigation
   1. Motivation
      a. Discomfort
         (1) Quantity and quality of discomfort
         (2) Is discomfort generalized to total life situation?
         (3) Is it attached to present situation?
         (4) Is it focused on presenting problem?
         (5) How much discomfort is attached to help-seeking or help-taking role?

    b. Hope

        (1) Quality and quantity of hope

        (2) Is there a generalized quality of optimism based on evaluation of past successes in coping?

        (3) Are past experiences separated from present situation with realistic perception of the differences involved?

        (4) Does client system perceive means of dealing with problems that are acceptable and does client system perceive ways of access to such means?

        (5) Gratifications from efforts toward solution including relationship to worker, other critical systems, and resources

2. Opportunity

    a. What opportunities have there been for client system to experience success in coping?

    b. What feedback has been available to client system as to value of these successes?

    c. What opportunities have there been for client system to acquire knowledge and skills needed for coping with present problem?

    d. What part of present problem is a departure from average level of opportunity made available to individuals, families, and groups in present society?

    e. What opportunities for solution of problem does the worker see in the present situation?

        (1) Socioeconomic

        (2) Within individual, family, or group as primary system

        (3) Within family, group, or community as secondary sources

        (4) In worker's skill, service system, and community or outside resources

        (5) Other

3. Capacity of the client system*

    a. Factors in the study and evaluation of the individual in any system—family, small group, organization, or community

        (1) Physical and intellectual

            (*a*) Presence of physical illness and/or disability

            (*b*) Appearance and energy level

            (*c*) Current and potential levels of intellectual functioning

            (*d*) How one sees one's world, translates surrounding events—perceptual abilities

            (*e*) Cause and effect reasoning—ability to focus

        (2) Socioeconomic factors

            (*a*) Economic factors—income level, adequacy of subsistence, and way this affects lifestyle, sense of adequacy, and self-worth

            (*b*) Employment and attitudes about it

---

* This outline of the capacity of the client system is indebted to that suggested in Howard Goldstein's *Social Work Practice: A Unitary Approach,* University of South Carolina Press, 1973.

        (*c*) Racial, cultural, and ethnic identification sense of identity and belonging

        (*d*) Religious identification and linkages to significant value systems, norms, and practices

    (3) Personal values and goals

        (*a*) Presence or absence of congruence between values and their expression in action—meaning to individual

        (*b*) Congruence between individual's values and goals and the immediate systems with which the individual interacts

        (*c*) Congruence between individual's values and practitioners— meaning of this for interventive process

    (4) Adaptive functioning and the response to present involvement

        (*a*) Manner in which individual presents self to others— grooming—appearance—posture

        (*b*) Emotional tone and changing levels

        (*c*) Communication style—verbal and nonverbal—level of ability to express appropriate emotion—to follow train of thought— factors of dissonance, confusion, and uncertainty

        (*d*) Symptoms or symptomatic behavior

        (*e*) Quality of relationship individual seeks to establish— direction—purposes and uses of such relationships for individual

        (*f*) Perception of self; social roles that are assumed or ascribed— competence with which these roles are fulfilled; relational behavior

          (i) Capacity for intimacy

          (ii) Dependency-independency balance

          (iii) Power and control conflicts

          (iv) Exploitative

          (v) Openness

    (5) Developmental factors

        (*a*) Role performance equated with life stage

        (*b*) How developmental experiences have been interpreted and used

        (*c*) How individual has dealt with past conflicts, tasks, and problems

        (*d*) Uniqueness of present problem in life experience

b. Factors in the study and evaluation of the family

    (1) Family as a social system

        (*a*) The family as a responsive and contributing unit within the social network of other units

          (i) Family boundaries—permeability of rigidity

          (ii) Nature of input from other social units

          (iii) Extent to which family fits into cultural mold and expectations of larger system

          (iv) Degree to which family is considered deviant

        (*b*) Roles of family members

          (i) Formal roles and role performance (father, child, and so on)

        (ii) Informal roles and role performance (scapegoat, controller, follower, decision maker)

        (iii) Degree of family agreement on assignment of roles and their performance

        (iv) Interrelationship of various roles—degree of fit within total family

    (c) Family rules

        (i) Family rules that foster stability and maintenance

        (ii) Family rules that foster maladaptation

        (iii) Conformation of rules to family's lifestyle

        (iv) How rules are modified—respect for difference

    (d) Communication network

        (i) Way family communicates and provides information to members

        (ii) Channels of communication—who speaks to whom

        (iii) Quality of messages—clarity or ambiguity

(2) Developmental stage of the family

    (a) Chronological stage of family

    (b) Problems and adaptations of transition

    (c) Shifts in role responsibility over time

    (d) Ways and means of problem solving at earlier stages

(3) Subsystems operating within the family

    (a) Function of family alliances in family stability

    (b) Conflict or support of other family subsystems and family as a whole

(4) Physical and emotional needs

    (a) At what level does family meet essential physical needs?

    (b) At what level does family meet social and emotional needs?

    (c) Resources within family to meet physical and emotional needs

    (d) Disparities between individual needs and family's willingness or ability to meet them

(5) Goals, values, and aspirations

    (a) Extent to which family values are articulated and understood by all members

    (b) Do family values reflect resignation or compromise?

    (c) Extent to which family will permit pursuit of individual goals and values

(6) Socioeconomic factors; see list under D, 3, *a*, (2)

c. Factors in the study and evaluation of small groups

(1) Functional characteristics

    (a) How group came to be

        (i) Natural group

        (ii) Group formed by outside intervention

    (b) Group's objectives

        (i) Affiliative, friendship, and social groups—mutuality and satisfaction derived from positive social interaction—tendency to avoid conflict and to stress identification

           (ii) Task-oriented groups—created to achieve specific ends or resolve specific problems—emphasis on substantive rather than affective content

           (iii) Personal change groups—emphasis on psychological and social content—dynamics of interpersonal behavior

           (iv) Role enhancement and developmental groups—recreational, educational, and interest clusters—emphasis on rewards and on gratifications of participation, observation, learning, and improved performance

        (c) How group relates to contiguous groups—how it perceives itself and is perceived as conforming to or departing from outside values

    (2) Structural factors

        (a) How the members were selected and how new members gain entry

        (b) Personality of individual members

           (i) Needs, motivations, personality patterns

           (ii) Homogeneity-heterogeneity

           (iii) Age of members

           (iv) Factors of sex, social status, and culture (see appropriate entries under D, 3, *a* and D, 3, b that relate to functions and purposes

           (v) Subgroups, their reasons for being, and purposes

           (vi) Nature and locus of authority and control

               (A) How leadership roles develop

               (B) How decisions are made

    (3) Interactional factors

        (a) Norms, values, beliefs, and guiding values

        (b) Quality, depth, and nature of relationships

           (i) Formal or informal

           (ii) Cooperative or competitive

           (iii) Freedom or constraint

        (c) Degree to which members experience a sense of interdependence as expressed in individual commitments to the group's purposes, norms, and goals

  d. Factors in the study and evaluation of organizations

    (1) Organization as a system with a mandate

        (a) Organization's task—its mission within the social structure

           (i) Clarity with which task is stated

           (ii) How task is perceived by organization's members

        (b) Individual and group roles relevant to the task

           (i) Which persons have the responsibility for carrying out the mandate of the organization?

           (ii) Elements and parameters of their roles

           (iii) Congruence between expected role behaviors and how these roles are seen by role bearers and others

           (iv) Are roles assumed, delegated, earned, or appointed?

       (*c*) Location of organization within system of organizations
          (i) Population group organization is designed to serve
          (ii) Kind of problem for which it is accountable
          (iii) Organization's isolation from or cohesion with other organizations
          (iv) Quality of interorganizational communication
          (v) Way organization manages input from other systems
  (2) Culture of the organization
       (*a*) Style with which organization operates
          (i) Governing beliefs of members
          (ii) Expectations and attitudes of members
          (iii) Theories that govern and guide organizational action
       (*b*) Modes of interaction and external groups or within organization itself
          (i) Formal or informal
          (ii) Deference to authority—hierarchical
          (iii) Ritual
          (iv) Channels of communication
       (*c*) Organization's technologies—resources, methods, and procedures in implementation of organization's task
          (i) Jargon
          (ii) Routine and protocol
          (iii) Accepted and approved modes of communication
  (3) Competence of the organization
       (*a*) Availability and adequacy of funds, physical plant, equipment
       (*b*) Scope of authority vis-à-vis the community
       (*c*) Special status, force, and control in relation to larger community
       (*d*) Merit of guiding policies, flexibility, and responsiveness
       (*e*) Efficiency of internal decision-making process
       (*f*) Level of morale, spirit of commitment of members
       (*g*) Degree to which above factors combine to make the organization more than the sum of its parts
e. Factors in the study and evaluation of a community
  (1) Community as a social system
       (*a*) Organizations, institutions, and groups of the community that affect existing condition and how they are linked
       (*b*) Location of the problem and community units related to it
       (*c*) Units that can be engaged to deal with the problem—their stake in change—their accessibility
       (*d*) How will change in any one unit affect other units?
  (2) Community as an organic entity
       (*a*) Attitudes toward social control and conformity
       (*b*) Opportunities for social mobility
       (*c*) How the community defines success and failure
       (*d*) Beginning appraisal of the community power structure and how it exercises controls
       (*e*) How power is achieved in the community

    (*f*) How prevailing problems are identified and by whom

    (*g*) Beliefs about causes of social problems

    (*h*) How the community labels the victims of social problems

    (*i*) Problem-solving capacity and resources

   (3) Intercommunity structures and processes

    (*a*) Relationships and regulations within governmental and non-governmental sectors

II. Contract phase

 A. Assessment and evaluation

  1. If and how identified problems are related to needs of client system

  2. Analysis of the situation to identify the major factors operating in it

  3. Consideration of significant factors that contribute to the continuity of the need, lack, or difficulty

  4. Identification of the factors that appear most critical, definition of their interrelationships, and selection of those that can be worked with

  5. Identification of available resources and motivations

  6. Selection and use of appropriate generalizations, principles, and concepts from the social work profession's body of knowledge

  7. Facts organized by ideas—ideas springing from knowledge and experience and subject to the governing aim of resolving the problem—professional judgment

 B. Formulation of a plan of action—a mutual guide to intervention

  1. Consideration and setting of a feasible goal

   a. Goal is set as the direct result of and during the process of problem definition and analysis

   b. Goal should be mutually agreed upon and within a set time limit

   c. Goal should be within the commitment and the capacity of client system and worker to achieve, given the opportunities the environment can offer, the worker's resources and skills, and what the client system can bring to bear

  2. Consideration of alternatives—likely costs—possible outcomes

  3. Determination of appropriate modality of service

  4. Focus of change efforts

   a. Client system (what particular aspect of functioning?)

   b. Family system (what aspect?)

   c. Significant others in the client system network

   d. Agencies and other institutions in the community

   e. Worker's own service system

  5. Role worker

   a. Advocate: when legitimate resources are resistive or resources must be created

   b. Broker or mediator: locates resources for client system, interprets client system's needs to others, attempts to modify others' behavior toward client system, mediates between client system and others

   c. Teacher: provides information, explanations, and expressions of opinions and attitudes; models effective behavior

   d. Enabler: attempts to help the client system to find within the system itself and the system's situation the necessary answers and resources by communication of interest, sympathy, understanding, and the desire to help; encourages exploration or ventilation of content concerning the nature and interactions of the client system and the client system's situation; encourages the reflective consideration, awareness, and understanding of the present person-situation-problem gestalt; plans with the client system and encourages the client system to act independently

  e. Therapist: makes communications that contribute to or encourage reflective consideration, awareness, and understanding of the psychological patterns and dynamics of the client system's behavior; or aspects of the client system's earlier experiences that are thought to be relevant to such present behavior; or aspects of the person-situation gestalt that lie in the past

 6. Consideration of forces in or outside of the client system that may impede the plan

 7. Consideration of the worker's knowledge and skill and of the time needed to implement the plan

 C. Prognosis—what confidence does the worker have in the success of the plan?

III. Action phase

 A. Carrying out of the plan—specific as to point of intervention and assignment of tasks; resources and services to be used; methods by which they are to be used; who is to do what and when

 B. Termination

  1. Evaluation with client system of task accomplishment and meaning of process

  2. Coping with ending and disengagement

  3. Maintenance of gains

 C. Evaluation

  1. Continuous process

  2. Was purpose accomplished?

  3. Were methods used appropriate?

Reading 2-1

Variations on a Theme: Implications for the Problem-Solving Model

Ralph Woehle

In her introduction to the book *Social Casework,* Perlman (1957) wrote that describing casework itself is a problem-solving task, the subject matter being complex and in motion. It is necessary, she

said, to carve out some parts that are essential qualities of the whole and view them as parts in a continuum. The content of this paper will concur with Perlman and go further. This paper will see parts in a process in the context of a system. The process is not seen as being as smooth as Perlman

An original paper for this edition.

saw it, and the system is seen as more complex than a continuum.

On the other hand, this is a limited paper. The problem-solving model is the basis of this paper. It will not consider social-work methods for clients who are not able to articulate problems, such as the task-centered model including open endedness and unstructured approaches (Kanter, 1983). And except for analogical, the approaches indicated by Siporin (1985), metaphorical, symbolic, tacit and parallel models, which are prominent in therapeutic practice, will not be considered here. Finally, marked movement from the problem-solving model, even though it may be suggested by some of the literature reviewed here, will not be undertaken.

Rather, this analysis will draw on existing literature to indicate variations in problem solving that may be useful to social work practitioners.

The literature includes social work literature on problem solving as well as literature from other fields, particularly where it has implications for the assumptions regarding rationality that underlie the problem-solving model. Most significant here is the "mixed scanning" of Etzioni (1986).

The variations on problem solving are of two types. First several generalizations are drawn from the literature and discussed in relation to problem solving. Then variations on the task processes suggested by the literature are presented.

PROBLEM SOLVING

Originally, Perlman (1957) saw three components in the problem-solving process. These were study or fact finding, organizing the facts into a goal-oriented explanation, and implementing the conclusions as action on the problem. She recognized that these three steps did not differ radically from the three steps of the diagnostic schools that preceded problem solving. Rather, the major difference was in the fact that the problem-solving approach was a cooperative process with the client. Therefore, problem solving had to abandon the Freudian preoccupation with the unconscious, and instead conscious rationality was emphasized.

Compton and Galaway (1984) also see problem solving as three major phases, contact, contracting,

and action. The contact phase consists of problem identification and definition, goal identification, preliminary contracting, and exploration and investigation. Contracting consists of assessment and evaluation, formulation of an action plan, and prognosis. The action phase consists of carrying out the plan, termination, and evaluation. Similarly, Epstein (1988) divided the task-centered approach into five steps. The first step is a start-up phase for clients who have been referred by another agency. For such clients goal negotiation with the agency may be necessary. For clients who apply independently and voluntarily, this phase will not be necessary. In Epstein's next phase client target problems are identified. Then a contract step follows. Problem solving, the next step, consists of specification of the target problem, generation of alternatives, negotiation of support, and implementation. Finally Epstein identifies a termination step. Sheafor, Horejsi, and Horejsi (1988) summarize Compton and Galaway, Epstein, and the problem solving approach of Pincus and Minahan (1973) and other authors as having five basically similar stages. They are (1) intake and engagement, (2) data collection and assessment, (3) planning and contracting, (4) intervention and monitoring, and (5) evaluation and termination.

Epstein (1988), along with Reid (1978), has integrated client tasks and time limits into the problem-solving framework. Task achievement and problem reduction are the essential stages of the task-centered model (Epstein, 1988). They include restatement of a particular problem, additional assessment, generation of alternatives, negotiation of support from collaborative agencies, and implementation of the strategy. Implementation of the strategy includes further development of the tasks, support of task performance, and verification and monitoring of tasks, effects, and problem reduction. Finally, termination may lead to extension if the client wants and is committed to further services, or monitoring as authority requires, or simply ending the services.

ROOT AND BRANCH

As Macht and Quam (1986) have indicated, problem solving and planned change are now accepted as the key commonalities in social work. Clearly these elements draw rational thought and constitute an abstract model that is essentially rational. However, few social-work writers have made this rational base explicit. Exceptions include policy analysts who draw on a rich literature in political science and sociology. For example, Denito and Dye (1983) identify six conditions necessary for rational change. They are (1) the identification of problems and agreement of relevant parties on the need to solve these problems, (2) all relevant values being known and weighted, (3) the consequences of each planned action being known and weighted, (4) the consequences of each alternative being understood in terms of both costs and benefits for the present and the future and for clients and others, (5) the possible calculation of the ratio of cost and benefits for each alternative, and (6) choosing the alternatives that maximize net values—that is, the greatest benefit for the least cost. Clearly two major assumptions underlying rational problem solving are that social science provides comprehensive and specific knowledge for decision making and that parties in decision-making processes can agree on the values that prescribe use of that knowledge.

If we reverse each of the assumptions of purely rational approaches, we have the assumptions of the incremental approach to social change. As Denito and Dye (1983) indicate, our social science abilities fall far short of the requirements of rationality. We cannot specify all of the alternatives in advance, and actions are not easily related to effects. And as Fox (1987) points out, goals can vary in type—goals as ultimate ends are only one type of the three he identifies. Facilitative, or incremental, goals may be easier to see in advance and to relate to specific actions. Or the functional or normative goals he identifies may be more consistent with systems theory. And decision-making parties often disagree. As Barker (1987) indicates, incremental social change is an effort to take into account a variety of political and pluralistic influences. In brief, the major assumptions of rationality are not fully met, and a more incrementalist approach seems compatible with realistic assumptions.

Linblom (1977, 1980), whose work spanned the ideological spectrum, also spanned the range of thought on rationality and incrementalism. He referred to the first as the "root" approach and to the latter as the "branch" approach. Originally he preferred the branch approach, which he called "muddling through." In his *magnum opus* (1977), however, he came to praise the possibilities of both approaches and their traditions. On a practical level, Etzioni (1986) integrated the two approaches in his "mixed scanning."

SYSTEMS THEORY IN SOCIAL WORK

Social work theory has considered the limitations of rational thought via systems theory. Systems theory takes account of the environment and usually adds a feedback loop to the problem-solving model. This is displayed as input to throughput to output, feeding back, along with inputs from the environment (Fordor, 1976). But some social-work writers using the systems approach have not altered the problem-solving model significantly. Pincus and Minahan (1973), in the first major practice development of the systems model, do not move beyond traditional problem solving. Others adopt a more complex cybernetic model (Fordor, 1976). This is the traditional problem-solving model, expanded to include feedback loops. Such views are consistent with systems theory but avoid major issues raised by systems theory. They leave rational and scientific reductionist assumptions in place even if they are multicausal (Auerswald, 1987). The causes are simply additive rather than an ecology whose whole is greater than the sum of its parts.

The ecological issues raised by systems theory are its greatest contribution. In fact, Auerswald (1987) says this is a new epistemology. Unlike the old epistemology, which saw things as true or false based on the scientific method, this epistemology sees truth as heuristic. Science and rationality are also heuristic devices in this new epistemology and are therefore acceptable ways of understanding, but they no longer represent an underlying truth. And there are also other ways of understanding that are adequate. Analogy is one such device. If we consider rationality as analogy, our use of rationality will change significantly. We will recognize that problem solving is *like* rationality in some ways but that the comparison can only be taken so far. Thus, systems theory is important because it takes us from a static view of rationality as a reflection of the underlying truth to rationality as an abstraction of the far more complex reality, which cannot be captured by our abstraction.

Systems theory is also important because it points to the environmental factors in the functioning of systems. In this respect it has had great impact on social work. Pincus and Minahan (1973) moved social work boldly into the social environment with their practice model. Similarly, Etzioni (1968) points to the importance of structural factors in decision making in his mixed-scanning model. But he later indicates that considerations of the mixed scanning approach have largely ignored such factors. By combining the contributions of systems theory to problem solving and the contributions of mixed scanning to the rationality-incrementalism debate, it is possible to generate variations of the problem-solving model that are compatible with practice as social workers have always found it.

SYSTEMS, SCANNING, AND PROBLEM SOLVING

Lantz (1986) makes a significant addition to problem solving in family therapy by adding reflexive feedback loops to the model. He sees ten stages. The first six are conventional problem solving. Then Lantz adds a problem-escalation stage, which follows task preparation and which limits the ability to resolve the problem. Escalation may follow task preparation and lead back to assessment, or task preparation may be followed by resistance, reflection, and insight. The therapist must respect the resistance and explore the family's "catastrophic expectations" about the dangers of change. Insight can then reveal the nature of the family's resistance, and the therapist and family can move back to the task preparation stage. In brief, Lantz adds feedback loops within the client system, a significant addition to the problem-solving process.

Auerswald (1987) drew on systems theory to describe an approach to family therapy that is very similar to problem solving, especially to the task-centered approach. But he adds problem-solving sequences that go outside the client system. While he recognizes that work may be directed at the client's larger environment and he claims to be drawing on a revolutionary development, he does not go as far as he might. His work model is still primarily reductionist, sequential problem solving.

Etzioni (1986) offers a significant addition to the rational-incremental discussion. He called this process, which might be called a politically adaptive rationality, mixed scanning. After nearly 20 years of discussion by himself and others, Etzioni summarized and modified the mixed-scanning approach. While he had policy-making processes in mind, his model indicates that scanning might also be used in personal decisions about careers, marriage, health, and financial security.

Etzioni (1986) sees mixed scanning as a hierarchical mode of decision making. Fundamental decisions are of a high order, and nested within them are lower-order, more incremental decisions. Scanning, according to Etzioni, refers to the gathering, evaluation of, and use of information to come to conclusions. In social work terms, then, scanning is assessment. But the hierarchical nature of the decision making offers something more. It recognizes that most decisions are made in the larger context, a context partly consisting of larger decisions and organizational structures. When we become aware of the limitations of that context, the rational consideration of all alternatives is less productive because many alternatives are not possible in that context. Scanning (Etzioni, 1986) is therefore less demanding than the full rational search for solutions, but it is more strategic than pure incrementalism. Rational approaches demand an evaluation of all possible solutions, and incrementalism deals with just the trouble spots. Scanning strikes some middle ground.

Etzioni (1986) lists four major steps that make the mixed scanning approach operational. First, he indicates that all relevant *known* alternatives should be listed on strategic occasions (options explored?). Second, the implementation should be fragmented (partialized?) into several sequential steps. Third, steps should be reviewed as they are implemented (continued assessment?). And fourth, a rule for the allocation of time and assets among the various levels of scanning should be formulated (review policies?). Etzioni also looks at the substeps of each of these major steps.

The purpose of scanning the alternatives is to allow the elimination of those that will not be pursued. Etzioni (1986) suggests three criteria for elimination. These are (1) utilitarian (the lack of means to pursue the alternatives), (2) normative (the violation of basic values of the decision makers), and (3) political (the violation of values or interests of the actors whose support seems necessary for making a decision and implementing it). For alternatives not so rejected, examination in greater detail is in order. Basically this involves repetition of the scanning process in ever greater detail until only one (or some other small number?) remains.

Before implementing the isolated alternative, it should be broken down into parts in three ways (Etzioni, 1986). First, for administrative clarity, it is broken down into sequential parts. Second, for political purposes, commitment to implement is made in serial steps. Resources are committed a piece at a time while maintaining a strategic reserve. Furthermore, arranging commitments so that the most costly ones can be made later will make the process reversible and less costly. Finally, scanning should continue on scheduled occasions and as the need arises. At important turning points scanning at higher levels is desirable.

As each subset of increments is completed, scanning at the level of that set should be undertaken (Etzioni, 1986). Even if things seem to be working, scanning should continue, though less intensively. Trouble requires more intensive scanning. Alternative strategies may appear more desirable in light of experience with the present alternative. Or if the goal has been achieved or become undesirable, the effort may be discontinued.

Finally, the allocation of time and resources to the various levels of scanning is required (Etzioni 1986). All of the above levels of scanning need time, and time should be reserved for occasions when its use is triggered by set intervals rather than a crisis. And the allocation of time and resources for the review of the allocations themselves should be made.

The theme running throughout the scanning process is that of limited foresight. Each step is a hypothesis that needs evaluation, or more practically, each step is a trial that may be more or less successful. Likewise, each set of steps, which constitute larger steps, are trials. When a course of action is failing, scanning is a way of learning about the reasons and considering alternative courses of action.

From the literature reviewed here, several generalizations and task processes that modify problem solving are suggested.

GENERALIZATIONS

The generalizations emerging from the literature include the continual use of assessment and the recognition of high-order decisions in which task decisions are nested. Also included is the generation, elimination, and prioritization of alternative tasks. Lastly, the commitment of resources and the provision of support are important parts of the processes. Each of these generalizations will now be discussed in greater detail.

Assessment

Assessment is present in every part of the social-work process. Everything that happens reveals things to the worker and client. Participants in the process do not adhere strictly to a particular task process, even when they have agreed to do so. Therefore assessment continues naturally. But there is a need to maintain order in the assessment process if the work is to maintain some direction. Clients and workers can strategically guide the assessment process by emphasizing it at certain times and deemphasizing it at other times. There are at least three occasions when assessment should be the primary work of the process. The first is the assessment process that is associated with problem and task identification in each task process. This is assessment as described traditionally in problem-solving and task-centered approaches to social work.

The second strategic use of assessment occurs on specified occasions. Often these occasions are specified by the policies of the agency or larger governing bodies. For example, these occasions may be established in advance by state policy for review of cases or by the supervisor who directs a case review at specified time intervals. Or the need for further assessment may emerge from the process itself. For example, a task process may develop a problem that requires the ongoing task process to be modified. This may call for the worker and client to shift the work to assessment of the emerging problem.

Finally, assessment occurs at the end of each task process. This has usually been referred to as evaluation, but given the connection of one task process to another, which will be described below, evaluation will often be assessment leading to another task.

Nested Decisions

A second generalization important in the modification of the traditional problem-solving process is the recognition that decisions in the work process are nested in higher-order decisions. Generally this means that work occurs within the context of decisions made in larger social structures. Such structures include the agency and the larger public bureaucracy in which the agency is typically located. Also included are professional associations, client interest groups, and communities, with their particular cultural values.

The decisions at higher levels guide particular decisions, but they also suggest two kinds of processes used in social-work decisions. First, since higher-order decisions guide work decisions, the higher-order decisions may themselves emerge as work issues. In this case the work will move out of the client system to some external system. For example, changing agency policy may be a proper work task if a particular policy limits desirable work tasks at the client level.

A second, more indirect implication involves decisions affected by relationships between more or less equal social units that are somehow nested in the higher-level decisions or social groups. The professional social work value for client participation and self determination, for example, nests all client-worker efforts within the professional asso-

ciation, which guides the process of decision making. Both considerations point to the political nature of work decisions, suggesting that decisions will often be political compromises rather than rational conclusions. The political nature of decisions limits the use of purely rational decision making. But if rationality is the model we use to limit pure muddling, then it must also guide decision making. The compromise between these two approaches is to make relatively limited commitments to tasks that we are quite certain we will be able to complete.

A third implication of nested decisions is related to assessment, discussed above. Since the problems may lie in the higher-order decisions, assessment may at times be directed at systems responsible for the higher-order systems. It is therefore necessary to assess such issues, not just when they emerge in relation to an individual case, but on scheduled occasions or when it becomes obviously necessary.

Generating Feasible Alternatives

Epstein (1988) recommends the generation of alternatives, but the generalizations presented here are primarily those of Etzioni (1986). First Etzioni suggests the generation of known alternatives on strategic occasions. This follows assessment, which was discussed above. Basically this is a matter of working with the client to identify as many options as time and knowledge allow. So even in the process of initial assessment, we recognize that our job is limited by present resources of knowledge and time.

Second Etzioni (1986) recommends the elimination of alternatives by tests of feasibility. He would have us look at resources and at the values of participating parties. In social work this involves the values of clients, workers, and sanctioning bodies such as agencies and professional associations. Epstein's (1988) suggestion that tasks be prioritized in terms of clients, workers, and referral-source priorities is closely related to this generalization, since a low-priority task will probably be eliminated from the work. While we undertake feasible, highly prioritized tasks, we do not necessarily continue with them. As assessment and work continue, priorities may change or new tasks of high priority may emerge.

Resource Commitment

Commitment to tasks may change if the availability of resources to complete tasks changes. Available resources in social-service agencies are subject to fluctuation because society's commitment is politically unstable and demands for services fluctuate. So long-term tasks always face uncertainties with regard to resources. Furthermore, our ability to judge resource requirements in advance is limited. So it is generally not rational to commit to a task at any cost.

Etzioni (1986) suggests a fragmented commitment of resources to task completion. Basically, this means limiting the commitment at present to small amounts, pending the accomplishment of small tasks. He also suggests leaving the biggest commitments to last where possible. The short-term tasks of Reid (1978) and Epstein (1988) obviously help to meet this requirement. But just as we should not assume that resources will be available, we should not assume that they cannot be found. Workers should be prepared to work with clients to seek support for task completion from the larger social environment, inside or outside of the agency's network, as Epstein suggests.

TASK PROCESSES

Given the generalization identified here, various modifications of the task process can be suggested. While the number of such potential modifications is probably very large, some compromise in the number must be made for the sake of clarity. Therefore, six obvious modifications are suggested. They are the extended sequential task processes, three task processes with feedback loops, the terminated task process, and simultaneous task processes.

Sequential Task Processes

As Epstein (1988) recognizes, the work with the client does not necessarily end when a specific set of tasks is completed. If the worker, client, and other involved parties agree, additional tasks may be undertaken. If this work begins after the completion of a task cycle as indicated above, then the next set of tasks is a repetition of the original process, with different goals, tasks, and so on. In brief, this variation is merely the sequential continuation of repetitions of the problem-solving process.

Processes with Feedback

Variations of the task-centered approach with internal feedback loops have been identified by Lantz (1986). Lantz indicates that two types of feedback loops involving work with the family may emerge. One such loop may occur when tasks are being identified. If family members resist at this stage, exploration of that resistance can lead to reflection, insight, and return to the prescribed tasks. Or if problem escalation occurs as tasks are being undertaken, it may be necessary to return to the assessment stage to redefine tasks. Lantz sees these loops as reflexive, and both involve work within the family system.

Auerswald (1987) did not describe the diagram suggested by his approach. He would, in fact, disagree with an attempt to reduce it to a diagram. While I have earlier described his approach as sequential, it can also be diagrammed as feedback loops that spiral into the social environment or into subsystems. Auerswald looks at family systems but recognizes that the problem may not exist in the family system. Thus, when problem solving undertaken in the family does not work, it may be because the problem is not in the family system. Return to assessment may indicate that the problem may lie in an individual or in the larger environment—the school, for example. If such problems are identified, the worker then takes up the problem-solving process in that environment.

The Terminated Process

Because feasibility is continually being evaluated, the process may be discontinued at any stage. Indeed, the process may end almost as soon as it begins. For example, if an agency refers a client with goals for certain services but the services are not authorized by some overriding authority, then the start-up suggested by Epstein (1988) may lead to discontinuation of services. Or services may be discontinued at any time the ongoing assessment or unavailability of resources suggest that feasibility is being diminished.

The Simultaneous Task Variation

This type of variation occurs when an initial task process is undertaken but can proceed only if another is undertaken. For example, if a family has a child with behavior problems, the parents may undertake consistent discipline as a task. But the child also has control of his or her behavior. A task for the child may include working on positive behavior.

Thus, simultaneous work on discipline and the behavior of the child may be undertaken.

CONCLUSION

This paper does not go beyond rational problem solving to (for example) creative approaches (Heus & Pincus, 1986). So it does not utilize the even greater potential of the ecosystems paradigm. The new paradigm suggests that rational problem-solving processes are an analogy for the social-work process. Rationality is *like* the work process, not the underlying "truth" of the process. Thus, it is possible to say the work process is like some other formulation.

Rather than rejecting traditional social work by saying that social work is like rationality, this paper suggests that there is much to be said for the traditional approaches to social work, even while the underlying assumptions of scientific rationality should not be taken too seriously.

So this paper is a small step. Recognizing the limitations of the assumptions of rationality that seem to underlie the abstraction of social work as a linear process implies nonlinear approaches. This paper has identified several generalizations about such processes that suggest modifications of traditional problem solving. The generalizations include (1) the liberal use of assessment that is both continuous and used on special occasions; (2) the nestedness of decisions in higher-order decisions, which carries work to other levels on occasion and unites decisions at similar levels in political processes; (3) the need to generate limited alternatives in terms of feasibility; and (4) the need to fragment commitment to selected alternatives. Task processes may be modified from the traditional problem-solving model by (1) making them sequential, (2) adding feedback loops at various system levels, (3) terminating them at any point, and (4) operating them simultaneously.

As a small step, this paper leaves many larger steps to be taken. Two such steps seem obvious at this point. First, any or all of the above task processes may be used in a given case. So case diagrams may be permutations and combinations of the above. Second, the release from scientific rationality as underlying truth has much greater implication, suggesting a variety of nonrational approaches. But both of these, as well as other undertakings, must wait for another day.

Reading 2-2   ## Client-Focused Recording: Linking Theory and Practice

Susan Tebb

ABSTRACT: *The current use and teaching of recording is explored. The development of the use of records for worker accountability and the loss of recording as part of the social work process is traced historically. An alternative to the medical model (problem-oriented record) is proposed based on a client-focused model that espouses social work values.*

Note. From "Client-Focused Recording: Linking Theory and Practice," by Susan Tebb, September 1991, *Families in Society: The Journal of Contemporary Human Services*, pp. 425–431. Copyright © 1991 by Family Service America. Reprinted by permission.

At a time when most social workers writing

about recording are concerned only with client outcomes, cost effectiveness, and work accountability, several professionals (Davis, 1985; Imre, 1985; Pieper, 1985; Goldstein, 1986; Weick, 1987; Saleebey, 1990) are asking social workers again to look at the values and client-worker relationships upon which the profession was founded. In the process of developing a client record reflecting effective outcomes and work accountability, a basic tenet of social work, client-centered values such as self-determination have been lost. This article examines the present use of social work recording, the history of recording within the profession, criticisms of the popular medical model of recording, and an alternative recording model based upon the mutual involvement of client and worker.

The history of recording social work interventions has been an indelible part of the social work profession. Recording has served to capture values in practice as well as provide detailed knowledge on the art of practice. Today, however, textbooks and the literature have very little discussion about the use, method, or purpose of recording. Most of the articles on social work recording in the past ten years have addressed the use of records for worker accountability (Challis & Chesterman, 1985; Mutschler & Hasenfeld, 1986; Wilson, 1980), structured case recording (Edwards & Reid, 1989; Streat, 1987; Videka-Sherman & Reid, 1985), and confidentiality of records (Doel & Lawson, 1986; Foster, 1979; Freed, 1978; Schrier, 1980; Zeilinger, 1979).

Currently the discussion and teaching of social work recording, its purpose, method, and use, is left up to the field practicum instructors and agency supervisors. Although an important link in the process between theory and practice, recording is not usually taught in social work schools. In looking at two of the more popular textbooks (Compton & Galaway, 1984; Germain & Gitterman, 1980) used in social work practice classes, recording is not in the index or referred to in either text. The apparent lack of value that academia places on recording and its importance in social work practice is representative of how the profession presently views practice wisdom (Imre, 1985).

The social work profession holds the assumption "that effective or 'good' practice must be rooted in a sound and established theoretical foundation" (Goldstein, 1986, p. 2) and must somehow be subject to measurement and evaluation. Goldstein (1986) points out that social work professionals have accepted the belief that the nature of knowledge is static, objective, and therefore can be investigated, producing hypotheses about cause and effect. These hypotheses, if proved, support theories that workers apply and test in practice with clients. However, theory is not derived only from the rigors of quantitative analysis. Theory in practice goes beyond the scope of academic inquiry. To look only at theory derived from scientific inquiry limits its utility and applicability. "There is a danger that complex diagnostic systems, even if valid and reliable, might evolve in the course of time to be mere exercises on paper that are often praised but seldom practiced" (Jampala, Sierles, & Taylor, 1986). *Practice wisdom,* of which recording is a small part, is often used to describe what occurs in social work practice that cannot be quantified. It is the intuitive and subjective knowledge that is used in context of the client-worker relationship and subsequently recorded in the social work record (Imre, 1985).

A look at the history of recording and its place in the profession today indicates why this assumption about knowledge acquisition is being questioned by numerous social workers (Davis, 1985; Goldstein, 1986; Imre, 1985; Saleebey, 1990; Weick, 1987). It is imperative that we examine social work recording and determine whether it is being used as a viable part of the client-worker relationship.

HISTORICAL PERSPECTIVES

Recording has served many diverse purposes and uses over the years. Social work recording had considerable importance in earlier social work literature. Richmond (1917) concluded that social casework would have to depend upon recording for advancing standards and new discoveries within the profession. The first textbook on social work recording, *The Social Case History—Its Construction and Content* (Sheffield, 1920), viewed recording as "a body of personal information conserved with a view to the three ends of social casework . . ."

1. the immediate purpose of furthering effective treatment of individual clients,
2. the ultimate purpose of general social betterment,
3. the incidental purpose of establishing the caseworker herself in critical thinking (pp. 5–6).

Sheffield also encouraged the worker to be critical of his or her work with the client, including examining the meaning of facts and searching for confirmation or disproof of the meaning.

Bristol (1936) saw four main purposes for recording:

1. facilitating treatment,
2. study and research of social problems as a basis for social reform,
3. training of students, as well as for teaching purposes generally,
4. educating the community as to its social needs and the place of social casework in filling some of these needs (p. 5).

In the intervening years it was assumed that good recording meant good practice, which may explain why recording is often seen today as a way of checking on the accountability of the worker (Timms, 1972).

Timms (1972) did a thorough search of the social work literature and found that recording had gone through four phases in its history. The first phase, which occurred in the early to mid-1800s, used *register-type records,* wherein singleline entries noted the name of the client, address of the client, and the friendly visitor's brief description of the problem (large family, age, widow, drunk, etc.). The register was used to document resources that were distributed to the poor. No judgment was involved in this type of record except for the friendly visitor's short remark regarding the problem; it was simply a record of fact as seen by the visitor.

During the second phase, from the latter 1800s to the early 1900s, the worker recorded more detail about the client's own statement of his or her problem as well as verified facts and problems subjectively observed by the worker. Recorded as a diary entry, this account listed the person(s) to whom resources were distributed, described the resources distributed and stated why they had been selected, and noted the worker's view of the effect the distribution had on the client(s). Thus, the record began to log workers' judgments, creating a *narrative record* that began to justify services.

The third phase, the process record, gained widespread use in the 1930s due to the invention of the typewriter and the popularity of psychoanalytic theory. Burgess (1928) argued that process recording or verbatim accounts would show "the person as he really is to himself" (p. 527). Process recording was the social worker's account of the interaction between the worker and client as it unfolds during the course of the interview. The record, presented from the worker's perspective, reflected both sides of the interaction. Workers used this method of recording to study their work critically and thus improve their practice techniques. This method is still used today as an educational tool.

The fourth phase, *differential diagnostic summary recording,* evolved after World War II as a synthesis of elements drawn from the previous phases. With this method, the worker or the agency organize and select what is recorded. Generally, a narrative summary of the social work process as applied to the client and seen by the worker is recorded. This type of recording emerged because process recording became too time consuming; process recording is now used only in the supervision and education of social work students.

Hamilton (1946) described the differential diagnostic summary style. Hamilton saw recording as a part of the social work process; the record provided a vehicle whereby the situation and client could be looked at uniquely. Social work treatment could be examined critically as it evolved over time. Kagle (1988) noted that Hamilton did not view recording as a skill to be learned by following a "cookbook" type of outline, but rather as the ability to record information out of the worker's knowledge and understanding of the client. Skill in recording evolved as one's diagnostic judgment and competence improved. Hamilton believed that only a trained social worker could find significance or meaning in the client's various experiences. This meaning or significance was selected by the worker and recorded in summary form at timely interludes. The function of the interaction and type of client determined the differential diagnostic recording's structure and content. This method of recording emerged when practice was not complicated and was used mainly for supervision purposes. Today, it is too expensive, unsystematic, and subjective for agency use (Kagle, 1988), although many social workers still use this method.

Eliot (1928) was concerned about the subjective selection of process recording: "Can one be simultaneously scientific and sympathetic? Can one simultaneously experience and reflect? Can one preserve objectivity in a subjective experience?" (p. 542). Over the years, social workers have persistently raised such questions about recording and practice. As early as 1928, Swift raised a question that is being asked again today: Should not the ultimate purpose of the record be the treatment of the client? Despite these questions, process recording and differential diagnostic summary recording are primarily used today for educational supervision in many agencies.

Bristol (1936) noted that the major problem in recording was making it objective and brief. She pointed out that one of the most effective methods of shortening the narrative was the careful selection of that which was recorded. However, the major dilemma in shortening the recording was that vital information had to be eliminated. Consequently, objective material was reduced to subjective accounts. Bristol suggested using a carefully defined terminology in a diagnostic record of the unique social work interaction (Kagle, 1984b). Hamilton (1946) recommended that records be written to meet the individual case needs and not written to fit a particular theory. The record was the practitioner's expression of meaning with regard to the case. Workers needed to be taught how to select information for the diagnostic record. This need for training resulted

in the use of recording by the supervisor to check whether the worker understood and used appropriate diagnostic skills.

During the 1950s and '60s, the purpose of recording turned from the treatment relationship to the supervision of the worker. In theory, the record became a retrospective account of what occurred in treatment rather than a prospective tool. It is easy to see how recording, as used in supervision in the 1960s, has become a means for social worker accountability in the '70s and '80s. The demands to cut costs, availability of computer technology, complex funding arrangements for service, and concern for client record confidentiality have supported the use of recording to determine worker accountability.

This climate fostered the profession's adoption of the problem-oriented medical record, first proposed by Weed (1969) and later described and adapted in the social work literature (Beinecke, 1984; Hartman & Wickey, 1978; Johnson, 1978; Kagle, 1984b; Kane, 1974; Wilczynski, 1981).

In 1968, Weed's medical model record was introduced into the medical field to reform awkward and ineffective medical records. This model provided a simple, organized framework that allowed medical records to be used to develop planning and goals. Four components made up the medical model record: (1) data base—initial patient information obtained from medical examination and tests; (2) a problem list derived from the data base; (3) plans for each problem listed; and (4) progress of the plans for each problem monitored. The monitoring is guided by the four categories in the acronym SOAP (Subjective data, Objective data, Assessment synthesizing subjective and objective data, and Plan).

The medical model record breaks down problems so that they can be dealt with separately. According to Bloom and Fischer (1982), clinicians often confront problems that are not related to one another, and it may be wise not to work on all the problems simultaneously, but to select one problem that seems most representative or most important to record. This selection is a subjective judgment on the part of the worker.

The medical model record is often criticized for its subjectivity. The worker is responsible for selecting the problem(s); he or she gathers objective and subjective information, then makes an assessment and devises a treatment plan. With this process, the client's view of the complexity and meaning of his or her life situation may be neglected. Several variations of the medical model record have been adapted to include the client's perception of the problem (Beinecke, 1984; Hartman & Wickey, 1978; Kagle, 1984b).

Another criticism of the medical model record is that it does not work with or address the interrelatedness of client problems. Rather, problems are fragmented and detached from the client, thus causing the client to be viewed as an object instead of a knowing and feeling person. In other words, the client is viewed by his or her weaknesses and deficits as opposed to his or her strengths. Problems are perceived as being outside the individual's control.

A third criticism is that the worker assumes total responsibility for assessing and implementing a plan of action for a client and determining when a problem has been resolved. However, this process violates client self-determination and client-focused values. The medical model record does not show the ongoing process that occurs between the client and the worker. It is concerned with the professional's control of the client's problem(s).

CHALLENGING THE EXPERIMENTAL PARADIGM IN
SOCIAL WORK PRACTICE

In recent decades, social work has operated in the shadow of the experimental model, which was developed out of Newtonian physics and since been adopted or employed by an increasing number of fields of study. When applied to social work, the scientific model assumes that the worker observes and remains apart from the client and the environment. The worker serves as an objective observer of the client and assesses the client according to quantifiable standards of measure. However, the scientific model, although useful in many fields, is not a complete guide to reality. Since Heisenberg, even physics has had to include the observer as well as the observed in experimental study and understanding. When employed as a paradigm in social work, the experimental model gives rise to what Wilber calls a "category error" (Weick, 1987); that is, researchers mistakenly believe that data can be objectively maintained when in fact such data are always subject to the researcher's perceptive and cognitive processes. There are no "pristine" data.

Social work research and, certainly, the social work academy tend to support use of quantification and the positivistic empirical methodology, thus ensuring the popularity of problem-oriented, single-subject, or goal-attainment scaling records. The demand for scientific rigor has encouraged the adoption of "objective" recording methods, and consequently the client, the main knowledge source, is overlooked. The validity of the information provided by the client is best expressed by Anne Morrow Lindbergh (1975): "Validity need have no relation to time, to duration, to continuity. It is on another plane, judged by other standards. It relates to the actual moment in time and place. And what is actual is actual only for one time and only for one place" (p. 76).

A survey of 94 social work agencies and departments confirmed that the purpose of recording is no longer seen as providing educational supervision but as providing "case continuity, service documentation, evaluation of service effects, and interprofessional communication" (Kagle, 1984b, p. 10). No single method of recording can meet all the needs of social work practice. Recording is and should be as diverse as social work knowledge acquisition, while organized to provide structure for communicating social work interactions. Kagle (1984a) stated that the current recording practices that offer the best potential for use by social workers are those that "facilitate communication between worker and client about the content and meaning of the record [and the process]" (p. 50).

Recording is not emphasized or used advantageously in practice because popular recording methods do not recognize the nature of process or the knowledge and responsibility the client has in the social work interaction. Records often contain a lot of data about a client's history and diagnosis but not much about the plans for change or the steps taken to initiate change. The record does not project a clear picture of what happens in the social work relationship, nor does it assist the worker in the process and planning.

CLIENT-FOCUSED RECORD, THE RECORD OF CHANGE

The client-focused record is an alternative to the experimental paradigm. Goldstein (1988) suggests that using a method that emphasizes a person's capability and potential "encourages clients to discover their own abilities to explore every possibility to discover the richness of choice and the cornucopia of opportunity" (pp. 16–17). This effort to explore and discover gives meaning and security to clients during chaotic, messy, and unpredictable times (Goldstein, 1988). The worker, with the client, needs to construct an understanding of the situation and reframe it.

In reframing the situation, the worker and client are concerned with the uniqueness, uncertainty, and instability of the situation and, as Schon (1983) suggests, aim at developing themes or meaning. A client's reality forms an everchanging pattern of meanings constructed from experience, heritage, and future options (Holbrook, 1983); it is not an objective, worker-understood or -defined entity recorded for posterity. Client reality is jointly and subjectively arrived at in the quest for meaning and the reframing of a situation.

Written material is too often perceived as the objective formulation of a client's reality. Unless workers are conscious of the symbolic effects of the written word and its social and political connotations, they will violate basic beliefs deeply ingrained in the social work process (Holbrook, 1983). These basic beliefs, handed down over the years, are sound principles underlying the social work profession:

• That people have the inherent capacity to develop in more fully human ways
• That this development occurs within complex, interactive social and physical environments

• That positive change in both individual and social spheres can occur through the professional relationship (Weick, 1987).

Currently, many professionals do not seem to support these beliefs.

Change, as the norm, is the core of social work process. Weick's (1987) questions about change were used as the basis for developing a recording method that deals with the client as a viable and knowledgeable part of the social work process.

• How such change might occur
• What factors seem to be contributing
• What forces constitute resistance
• In what ways can change be fostered

These questions can help the worker and client examine the process of change, allowing both the client and the worker to become an integral part of the recording process.

In finding a replacement for the medical model record (SOAP) that is congruent with social work values, we need to incorporate the medical model's strong points: simplicity, organization, and rememberability. One client-focused alternative, CREW, embraces the mutuality expressed in the social work value of client determination. The word *crew* comes from the middle French *creue,* based on the verb *creistre,* which means "to grow" (*Webster's New Collegiate Dictionary,* 1991). A crew is a group of people banded together to work toward a goal. In using this acronym as a guide in recording, the following questions are asked:

Contributors: What factors contribute to the need for change?
Restraints: What constitute the restraints or barriers to change(s)?
Enablers: What factors seem to be enabling or contributing to change(s)?
Ways: How can change be fostered?

The medical model record (SOAP) frames problems as being within the purview of the individual or system to be cured or remedied by the professional. The client-focused record (CREW) focuses

Table 2-1 Comparison of Medical Model Recording with Client-Focused Recording		SOAP (MEDICAL/PROBLEM RECORD)	CREW (CLIENT-FOCUSED RECORD)
	View of problem, need for change	1. Professional defines the problem through careful observation 2. Problem externally caused and separate from client	1. Client defines the need for change and shares it with the professional 2. Client sees self as an active player in the problem and need for change
	Client-professional relationship	1. Client relies on professional's expert knowledge 2. Client is passive; professional is the leader and expert 3. Specialized expert knowledge separates professional from client	1. Professional relies on client's personal knowledge 2. Professional supports client with expert knowledge as a consultant and enabler for change 3. Professional's knowledge and relationship strengthens client's ability for change
	Nature/process of change	1. Professional is the change agent 2. Professional is given power to create client's meaning of problem and change 3. Change is initiated by the professional and client follows professional's plans	1. Client, with the support of the professional, is the change agent 2. Client, with the professional, defines personal meaning of problem and change 3. Client designs plans for change with professional's input 4. Change is a naturally occurring process directed by client with support of professional

upon the situation and how the client and worker mutually view this situation. In her study of client involvement in the recording process, Badding (1989) found that mutual involvement and responsibility on the part of both client and worker gave the client opportunity for self-determination, thus making the client-worker relationship more compatible with social work values (see Table 2-1).

The client-focused recording method allows persons to review the process and meaning of change on an ongoing basis and to agree upon the next step(s). It removes the burden of change from the client and places him or her within a particular situation. Weick's (1987) questions allow clients to become actively involved in the case-recording

process, while recognizing that the client is a knowledge source.

Since the enactment of the Privacy Act of 1974, several professionals (Badding, 1989; Doel & Lawson, 1986; Houghkirk, 1977; Schrier, 1980; Wilczynski, 1981) have used the recording process as an integral part of intervention with their clients. This law permits individuals to be informed about all records maintained on them by government agencies and allows them to have access to these records. Workers who have used records as part of the social work intervention have found it to be a positive experience. Wilczynski (1981) states, "The client's active participation in establishing and achieving the goal is as therapeutically valid as the actual achievement" (p. 315). Houghkirk (1977) concluded her study of client involvement in recording by questioning who has the best knowledge and who has a better right to this knowledge other than the client.

AGENCY RECORDING IN PERSPECTIVE

Recording is currently viewed by most social workers as a necessary evil instead of an aid to practice. Given the lack of attention to teaching recording in schools, agencies have had to assume, by default, full responsibility for teaching recording. Basic recording should be taught in the practice classroom. Social workers who have not learned basic recording do not have a framework within which they can place theory, practice, and policy in their proper context. Workers who have been exposed to only one method of recording have difficulty applying other job-required recording methods. They do not understand the connection between actual practice and the recording process. When workers learn recording in the agency rather than in the classroom, they perceive its origin and meaning as being rooted in agency practice. As such, they may not see recording's larger connection with the profession's values and practices (Kagle, 1984b). Education for social work recording should occur in the classroom, during field instruction, and at the workplace. A generic introduction to recording should be part of the curriculum in every school of social work, thus exposing students to the link recording provides between practice, theory, and policy.

The selection of material to be recorded is currently based upon a worker's judgment. The importance of values and ethical decisions made by workers as reflected in records needs to be examined and discussed in the agency and classroom setting. Records are often used in decisions that involve elements of social control. For example, who gets welfare? Should parents continue to have custody of a child? The agency's social control function more often than not shapes the record and the interaction process (Holbrook, 1983). Language reveals a worker's underlying values. Factors that influence recording judgments and decisions need to be studied and discussed by everyone who writes and uses records. Opening records to the client and making the client part of the recording process require that the worker examine the consequences this may have on the client-worker relationship and the social work process.

Sytz (1949) argued that recording was separated from the social work process. This separation continues today. Recording is not considered to be part of the social work process. Practitioners need to understand that recording fosters critical thinking on the part of both client and worker about the growth and change process.

Client-focused recording (CREW), one of many methods of recording, is based on beliefs that underlie social work practice. We speak often of "the social work process." Recording allows the practitioner to communicate the process of growth. Client-focused recording allows the worker and client to look critically at meanings. Holbrook (1983) asks: "Who has more at stake or is in a better position to understand process and recommend solutions than social workers themselves" (p. 657)? Recording can be an important bridge connecting social work values with social work practice.

Suggested Readings

Brown, L. B., & Levitt, J.L. (1979). A methodology for problem-solving identification. *Social Casework, 60,* 408–415.

Golan, N. (1969). How caseworkers decide. *Social Services Review, 43,* 286–296.

Hofstein, S. (1964). The nature of process: Its implications for social work. *Journal of Social Work Process, 14,* 3–53.

Johnson, W. (1951). Being understanding and understood: or how to find a wandered horse. *ETC., 8,* 171–179.

Perlman, H. H. (1972). The problem-solving model in social casework. In R. W. Roberts and R. H. Nee (Eds.), *Theories of Social Casework.* Chicago: University of Chicago Press.

Spitzer, K., & Welsh, B. (1969). A problem-focused method of practice. *Social Casework, 50,* 323–329.

Sucato, V. (1978). The problem-solving process in short-term and long-term service. *Social Service Review, 52,* 244–264.

Chapter 3
Knowledge for Social Work Practice

In this chapter we will discuss the knowledge base of practice, which is made up of three elements: theories, collections of clinical observations or findings of research studies, which we will call facts, and models of practice. We will focus on the distinction between knowledge and values and the role of the knowledge base in social work practice. We will use the readings found at the conclusion of Chapter 1, as well as those found at the end of Chapters 2, and 3 to help differentiate between the elements of the knowledge base and values as well as to illustrate the use social work makes of its knowledge base and the role of values.

Purpose of Knowledge Base

The central and distinguishing mark of a profession is the ability of the professional person, through an active thinking process, to convert knowledge into professional services that are tailored to the unique requirements of the client. Students and social work practitioners often think first of "doing"—of a model of action—rather than of knowledge as a base of decision making that directs that action. Yet, as was stated in Chapter 1, to concentrate on the application of interventive techniques alone is to fail as a professional. To develop a high level of methodological skill, no matter how demanding and complex, and to apply it to all situations regardless of problem, goal, or capacity of the system, is to miss the crucial distinction of a profession. A profession demands that interventive skills be used selectively and differentially as determined by a body of knowledge and theory, the process of deciding, and the purpose and values of the profession. Social work confronts those who would practice in its name with tasks that are complex, constantly changing, and nonroutine. These unique tasks do not yield to means that can be mastered and communicated in the form of specific techniques.

Differentiation of Knowledge and Value

Before we go further in the discussion of the elements of knowledge, it may be wise to discuss the difference between knowledge and value in professional practice. Values and knowledge are often confused because all value dimensions of human life and living influence the knowledge base of practice one way or another. Values are what we hold as desirable. We express values when we use the term *ought*. When we describe what "is," we are using knowledge. Values imply a preference for certain "means, ends and conditions of life, often accompanied by strong feeling" (Pumphrey, 1959, p. 23). Knowledge, on the other hand, is information about the world and its qualities, about people and their interrelationships. When we consider knowledge, we are concerned about truth; when we consider values, we are concerned about what is right. In our search for the distinction between values and knowledge, we found a statement by Gordon (1965) very helpful. He states:

> Knowledge refers to what, in fact, seems to be established by the highest standards of objectivity and rationality of which people are capable. Value refers to what people prefer or would want to be . . . it becomes clear that the heart of continuity and professional utility lies in what social work wants for people (values) and what it knows about them (knowledge).
>
> Values . . . refers to what is regarded as good and desirable. These are qualitative judgments; they are not empirically demonstrable. They are invested with emotion and represent a purpose or goal toward which the social worker's action will be directed. Knowledge propositions, on the other hand, refer to verifiable experience and appear in the form of rigorous statements that are made as objective as possible. Value statements refer to what is preferred; knowledge statements to what is confirmable. (p. 34)

Bartlett (1970) also points out that the statement "There is interdependence between individuals in this society" has often been included under values in social work literature, although it is a demonstrable fact and thus should be classified as knowledge:

> At any stage in the development of scientific knowledge there are some propositions that do not appear confirmable and thus must be regarded as value assumptions. In some instances, however, statements that are identical in form can be taken as either part of knowledge or as values. The idea that home is the best place for a child is an example; it can be taken as preferred or as a hypothesis for investigation. Here it is the intention regarding the proposition, rather than the actual substance, that makes the difference. There is also a long-range shift that will take place between a profession's body of knowledge and values. As scientific knowledge increases, some propositions that were at first preferred assumptions will become established as confirmed knowledge.
>
> . . . Knowledge and value play distinctly different roles, both of which are needed. . . . Proper use of knowledge and value rests not only on distinguishing those propositions that belong in different categories but also in recognizing that the user's intent—whether as a preferred or confirmable statement—also makes a difference as to how they should be classified. According to this approach, propositions regarded as verifiable by science and research—and that are intended to be verified—are considered knowledge. (pp. 63–64)

Simply put, values answer the question of whether a proposition is right or wrong, while knowledge answers the question of whether something is true or false. This becomes very important to social work, from the perspective of both the worker and the client. If we believe we have tested evidence that a particular proposition is true and also believe that it is right, there will be no desire to change it. In fact, there will be strong opposition to any proposal to change it. Some of our greatest conflicts in social work are found at the point where knowledge conflicts with value. For example, there are significant research findings that children who are treated violently often grow up to be adults who act violently toward others. However, there are people who believe that parents have a right to discipline children in any manner they please to control their behavior. A value cannot be challenged with another value, but it can be challenged with knowledge. Thus, one can ask that parents who believe differently about child care look at the evidence. Another important conflict that concerns social workers centers on treatment of the poor. There is significant evidence that living in abject poverty with too little food for adequate nourishment can be severely damaging to children both physically and psychologically, but we often confront a value system that says that people should "stand on their own two feet" and not take help from anyone "no matter what." In a democratic society all individuals have a right within limits to their own value system. These values can be challenged only by empirical evidence that shows them to be damaging to human beings. We cannot demand that people change their values to conform to ours, but if tested knowledge showing a proposition to be true is available, people can be asked to consider this evidence.

Another example of the possible confusion between knowledge and value concerns the social work value of self-determination—the notion that people be allowed as far as possible to determine their own lifestyles (this concept will be discussed further in Chapter 7). If, in working with children, this value is not tempered with the knowledge that children need both freedom and firm, consistent limits to grow and develop, we may be destructive to our child clients and/or to their families that come for help. Another important example of the confusion of value and knowledge is the way in which the knowledge that "clients will change with greater ease and less pain if they are actively involved in the process of deciding about change" is confused with the value that "clients as human beings have the right to make their own decisions about what they will do." In this instance, knowledge and value support each other, but it is necessary to be clear in discussing work with the client whether one's actions are primarily based on knowledge, value, or both in some combination.

In earlier quotations, Gordon (1962, 1965) discussed two kinds of knowledge: (1) knowledge that has been confirmed by empirical testing and/or observation and (2) knowledge that is accepted and acted on as though it were true but has not yet been confirmed, although the intent is to confirm it eventually. This might be called *assumptive knowledge.* The important fact to note is that assumptive knowledge is open to efforts to test whether it is right or wrong. The only concern is that the person who engages in such testing follows the accepted guidelines of research design. If there is resistance to the effort to test a notion, it may be that a value is being dealt with and not a piece of assumptive knowledge. In the human services, much knowledge is assumptive knowledge, notions that, given what tested base is available, seem to follow logically. The important thing for us as professional people is not so much the extent of the assumptive knowledge that is presently accepted as our willingness to expose it to exploration and the commitment to active attempts to test what are held as truths.

In our actual practice experience, the three principal value issues for us as we seek to determine a plan for intervention are these: (1) What solution does the client seek? (2) What is our notion of the outcome to be sought or how the client should deal with the problem? (3) Do we have a duty to protect the interests of others against the client's wishes or the client's actions (Reid & Epstein, 1972, p. 16)?

The Model   In much of social work literature and in the cited quotations, one finds knowledge used as though it were a large undifferentiated collection of statements. However, as stated above, the knowledge base of practice is made up of the elements of theory, model, and observations. It is common to find these elements of the knowledge base used as though they were interchangeable, but they are really quite different and serve quite different functions for the practitioner. Therefore, it is important for us to concentrate on the task of understanding these differences. We will begin with a discussion of models.

A model may be defined as a set of directives that states how a given kind of intervention is to be carried out. It is basically definitional and descriptive, stating what the practitioner is expected to do or what practitioners customarily do under given circumstances. For example, this book presents a model of a process—that of problem solving. Models are made up of principles, methods, and techniques (Reid & Epstein, 1972, p. 7) that fit together in an organized hierarchy. A principle is a general statement of a law or a rule concerning a natural phenomenon. There is a principle in social work that when we have a problem, we generally feel better and become less anxious if someone gives us encouragement, approval, praise, or concrete aids. A method is a collection of related procedures and techniques by which we translate a principle into action. Thus, in social work, we consider support a method, a collection of related techniques, that we use to offer people encouragement, approval, praise, or aid. Techniques are sets of systematic procedures through which we accomplish the tasks of encouragement, approval, or aid giving. The specific ways we go about offering a client encouragement or approval are techniques.

Models may differ along a number of dimensions. Different models aim their interventive efforts at different targets. Some models may be aimed at particular populations; others may be developed for specific problems or may promise to be effective only in bringing about specific change. In our model of the problem-solving process, our aim is to provide a set of directives about how the practitioner and the client may go about selecting a model of intervention that is effective in achieving the change sought. In later chapters in this book, we do develop some very general notions of a model of intervention that are congruent with our process model. Thus this book presents two models. The primary model is that of the problem-solving process, which is aimed at the selection of an appropriate model of intervention. We also deal in very broad outlines with some elements of one model of intervention that we find congruent with our process model. In summary, when you are dealing with material that seeks to answer the questions What does one do? and How does one do it? to achieve a defined aim, you are dealing with a model.

Theories and Facts

Theory, on the other hand, is not concerned with the doing but seeks to answer the questions Why? and Under what conditions? A theory is a coherent group of general propositions or concepts used as principles of explanation for a class of phenomena—a more or less verified, established, or accepted explanation accounting for confirmed or confirmable phenomena and their interrelationships. It attempts to explain why phenomena behave the way they do. What is the genesis of human growth and effective social functioning? What is the genesis of human problems? Why do people keep suffering from problematic interaction that they want to change? What new and different elements interjected into a situation promise change, and in what direction? Basically, interventive theory consists of formulations about the etiology or causes of a phenomenon (be it human development or social problems) and the effects of different kinds of experience on the course of the phenomenon. While the directives found in models usually are built on and related to a body of supporting theory, theory carries absolutely no directives about action to be taken.

Theories are usually built from observations of the happenings around us and are ways to explain these happenings. These observations (or bits of knowledge) are, or claim to be, statements of events that have taken place. They differ from theoretical statements in that they offer no explanations of the why of the phenomenon observed, and unlike a model, they provide no directions about what to do. They are a statement of what is. (Reid & Epstein, 1972, pp. 7–10). One way of understanding these two concepts is to think of observations as discrete facts or events, like a pile of bricks, and to think of theory as a wall of bricks. In a theory the observations of the real world are ordered and put together in a certain way and are held together by certain assumptions and hypotheses as bricks in a wall are held together by cement. The cement holds the bricks in place and allows their arrangement in certain patterned ways. A list of unrelated facts, no matter how well verified by empirical observations, never tells us their meaning; data do not have meaning until they are interpreted. It is theory, constructed of known facts and phenomena held together by certain conceptual notions, that speaks to the meaning of facts. We use these concepts of why and how the elements in the situation interact the way they do and which operations of which elements bring which change in which directions as a guide or a base for our models of action that tell us what to do about a situation.

Later in this book we will discuss our notion of what a worker should do to engage with the client in the problem-solving process. In setting forth these directives, we are presenting the reader with a model of the problem-solving process. But the model does not tell you why we think its directives constitute an effective way for you and your client to go about solving problems in social functioning. The theory base from which we draw to support our model gives you that answer. This is why the first chapters in this book are very important if you want to understand fully the model presented. These first chapters present the theory and the value base from which we have drawn to develop our model and its directions for action.

Human service professions generally rely on two levels of theory: (1) general theories of the nature of humanity, including the necessary supports for normal growth and development, the genesis of human problems, and general theories of human interrelationships, including theories of society and its development, culture, and families and their roles in society, and (2) the profession's practice theory, which consists of formulations about the etiology and causes of the problems to which the practice is addressed and the effects of different kinds of interventive actions. Practice theory usually rests on the general theory and embodies certain value positions.

Borrowed Knowledge

In social work, as in all other professions, we often borrow theories that are constructed by others but that seem to provide us with helpful explanations for our purposes. All professions rely on borrowed knowledge generated and tested in the basic disciplines. And all human service professions borrow from each other. This is partly because practicing professionals, social workers included, are more interested in the application of present knowledge than in the creation of new knowledge and partly because social workers, in discussing their practice knowledge in the journals of the profession, often write only of unique individual situations without making appropriate attempts to generalize their experiences and to connect them with what is already known and set forth in the literature.

In discussing the problem of the generation of new knowledge vis-à-vis the application of borrowed knowledge, Sidney Berkowitz (1969), a practicing social worker and agency executive, points out that the present-day heroes in the field of medicine are the surgeons who are engaged in organ transplants. Yet these men are, strictly speaking, technicians who are largely dependent on borrowed knowledge supplied by research biologists, biochemists, geneticists, physiologists, and other scientists. Berkowitz reminds the reader that the majority of professional social work practitioners are largely concerned with practical and emotional motives rather than with intellectual drives; that although they may have contributed little to theory building in the basic social, behavioral, or biological sciences, they have contributed much to the knowledge of the development and refinement of various social work methods and techniques. In addition they have developed and passed on to others a kind of wisdom about human behavior that can come only from skilled clinical practice over time. This statement is as true today as it was in 1969.

It would appear that if social work is to expand its tested knowledge, its practitioners must actively engage in scientific inquiry. Social work practitioners must be active in raising the important questions and pursuing the answers.

In his inquiry into behavioral science, Abraham Kaplan (1964, pp. 304–305), a philosopher of science, points out that "knowledge grows not only by accretion and replacement of dubious elements by more sound ones but also by digestion, by remaking of the old cognitive materials into the substance of a new theory." Although the growth of scientific knowledge is marked by the replacement of poor theories by better ones, if knowledge is to advance, each new theory must take account of the theory it seeks to replace. Each new theory must reshape and integrate the old so that there is continuity of knowledge development, even in the most revolutionary of times.

Kaplan says that the problem in the behavioral sciences is that this is not done, that individuals do not steep themselves in the theories available before taking off on a charge of their own. He is concerned that the lag in the behavioral sciences comes because researchers and theoreticians are busily drawing their own "new" blueprints. The social and behavioral sciences are replete with low-level empirical findings, but these remain empirical bricks, unusable until someone can find the connection to hold them together. It is frustrating and troubling to read a piece of research in social work that would never have been undertaken if the researcher had done the proper literature search. To use precious time and money to test something that has already been tested because of ignorance of past efforts is almost criminal given the great needs in this field. Thus, the first principle of attempting to develop new knowledge is thorough knowledge of the old and the work that went into developing it so that we can build our present efforts on this foundation.

Actually, as pointed out by Kadushin (1959), there is an embarrassingly rich literature that details what the social worker needs to know, do, and feel. But that knowledge is not organized in a manner that lets one readily specify what one will need to know about what. Thus, nowhere will you find a book on all knowledge necessary for social work practice.

There have been any number of attempts to select and organize knowledge in a manner that would constitute an adequate base for social work practice. In his review of the history of social work knowledge, Kadushin (1959) points out that between

1929 and 1959 there were two major reviews of social work education throughout the world and five major studies of social work education in the United States. Since then there have been other attempts to specify the knowledge base of social work. Perhaps the most comprehensive and exhaustive attempt yet made is the Curriculum Study of the Council on Social Work Education (Boehm, 1959). This 12-volume study can hardly be summarized in the space available in this text or used by students in a discrete course. The most recent example of an attempt to set forth a knowledge base of social work practice is the Undergraduate Social Work Curriculum Development Project (Baer & Federico, 1978). It was undertaken for the purpose of further developing both the educational objectives and the curriculum content essential for the bachelor of social work degree. Kahn (1954), who has studied the knowledge base of social work, gives us some notion of the possible range of data with which social work may be concerned:

> Social work knowledge is, at the present time, in fact, an amalgam of several different things: (1) propositions borrowed from or markedly like those of psychiatry and some branches of psychology; (2) propositions fewer than in (1), borrowed from, or markedly like those of, sociology, social anthropology, and a scattering from other fields; (3) apparently original propositions about how to do certain things in casework, group work, and community organizations; (4) methods, techniques, and attitudes, clearly derived from the fields of administration, statistics, and social research; (5) propositions about how to do things apparently derived from, or markedly like, those of progressive education. (p. 197)

It is interesting that points 1 and 2 in Kahn's quotation appear to deal with borrowed theory and 4 and 5 have to do with borrowed models or elements of models, and 3 has to do with models originating from social work itself. But as we stated earlier, the problem is not that we borrow knowledge but that we need a way to select, organize, and limit the knowledge available to that which is necessary or desirable for the practice of social work. We also need to be able to identify clearly the gaps in our knowledge, places where knowledge needs to be developed if we are to perform our professional tasks and get on with the business of knowledge development.

Function as a Guide to Knowledge Building

Perhaps the major obstacle in the attempt to develop a knowledge base of social work practice is the problem of defining our professional responsibility our societal charge. Although social workers have struggled with this problem over the years, it is still an unresolved issue. Meyer (1973, p. 38) speaks to the issue of the function of knowledge in social work practice: "Reliance upon empirical data has not been a hallmark of professional social work practice, partly because of our tools and objectives of research, but also, perhaps, because we have not yet agreed upon the goals and boundaries of social work practice."

In the professions, in contrast to the basic sciences, knowledge is sought for use rather than for its own sake. What the social worker is supposed to be about dictates and "defines the boundaries of relevant knowledge as well as stimulating the search for new knowledge. Part of what makes a given profession distinctive is the nature of action or practice evolving from placing knowledge within a particular frame of reference" (Kamerman, Dolgoff, Getzel, & Nelson, 1973, p. 97).

This frame of reference is dictated by the purposes and values of the profession. Thus, a profession does not seek to build knowledge outside of or beyond its purposes. However, knowledge and purpose have an interactive relationship in that as purposes change, new knowledge is sought to deal with the new purposes, but also, as knowledge expands within a given purpose, it is sometimes found that the purpose itself is changed by the new knowledge (often more slowly than one would wish). For example, when the polio vaccine was developed, its wide use resulted in significant reduction in the numbers of children crippled by polio. As a result, a large world-famous center devoted to the rehabilitation of polio patients found the demand for its services so reduced that it had to reconsider its mission. To make use of its highly trained specialists, it changed its purpose to the offering of rehabilitative services to persons with spinal cord injuries or brain damage. Thus new knowledge changed purpose. However, when polio was widespread and many children were being left crippled by its ravages, the center was established to develop new knowledge about how to treat such crippling.

Thus it appears that the major reason for the problem in selecting and organizing knowledge is the inability to define with any precision the areas of expertise necessary for social workers. We refer you to Schwartz's (1961, p. 150) statement that "Every profession has a particular function to perform in society: it has received a certain job assignment for which it is held accountable." In Chapter 1 we discussed the focus of social work intervention and quoted the working definition of social work published by the National Association of Social Work. According to this definition, the purpose of the profession is to assist persons who either in their own eyes or in the judgment of others are unable to carry on the business of satisfactory living in their own environment because of some disequilibrium between their own resources, skills, abilities, and knowledge and the situations in which they find themselves. A secondary purpose of social work is to offer protection to people and society by engaging in activities aimed at preventing such disequilibrium. If we have accurately stated the purpose of social work, the principal focus for knowledge building should be the development of theories to account for such disequilibrium in various situations and of models composed of directives for helpful intervention in such situations.

Given the above, we can classify the knowledge we need as follows: (1) knowledge that contributes to the understanding of the complex interactions in which the client is involved and of the meaning the client assigns these interactions; (2) knowledge that contributes to the understanding of the individual and the impact of environmental factors on the psychological, social, and physical development and functioning of the person; (3) knowledge that contributes to the understanding of the interrelatedness of person and situation (environment) as a continuously emerging and ever-changing process over time; (4) knowledge that contributes to our understanding of what is involved in assessment and its relationship to planning and carrying out intervention; and (5) knowledge that contributes to our understanding of what is involved in effective social work intervention. If the statements above overwhelm you with their breadth and complexity, perhaps they also help you to understand the problems of building a knowledge base for social work practice.

One of the major problems with social work's borrowing of knowledge is that we have borrowed rather indiscriminately, so that, as one might gather from the Kahn quotation in the last section, we have huge lumps of knowledge from various disciplines, but we do not have any way to bring them together and integrate them into a coherent base.

When we borrow knowledge, we need to ask how that knowledge fits into and furthers the understanding of one of the classifications listed above. How does it contribute to our ability to further the purposes of the profession? Was the knowledge developed from the perspective of human behavior as a part of an ongoing bidirectional person-situation interrelatedness in which the individual is an active agent? Is the knowledge based on characteristics of the person, viewed as developed through experience and held to be stable and resistant to change? Or are characteristics of the environment seen as the crucial issue in explaining behavior? Are human beings simply reactive organisms whose functioning represents only a response to environmental stimuli? The problem with borrowed knowledge is that so much of such knowledge is derived from the perspective either that personality is the overriding influence in social functioning or that environment is the overriding influence. The basic problem in building social work knowledge is not the extent to which individual personality and environment contribute to the development of the person's social functioning but rather how these factors, independently and in interaction over time, influence our social functioning. However, there are few research findings or theoretical concepts available that deal with developmental and adaptational interrelatedness of personality and environment. Social workers over the years have recognized this problem, but in their search for appropriate theory they have tended to accept the view of the environment and the individual as interrelated but separate entities. This focus has largely resulted in creating a mental image of the person and the environment in which each piece of the equation affects the other in much the way billiard balls do—by striking one another. In this transaction only the course of each ball is changed, leaving the essential nature of each unaffected.

To carry out society's charge, we must have a theory that helps us to be constantly aware that the structure and culture of society and transactions with others are reflected in the self and that the life structure of each individual and the way each individual copes with his or her life affects all the rest of us. Yet this theory must also recognize that a person's life is individual and unique—a reflection of self and choices, that all human beings have their own particular world that presents them with opportunities, meanings, feelings, identities, and myths that each person individually and selectively uses and internalizes (Levinson, 1978, pp. 1–40). See Exhibits 3-1 and 3-2 for some diagrams showing the complexity of this interpenetration, inter-action, and transaction. Studying the diagrams will help you to begin to grasp the complexity of understanding the individual in interaction and transaction with the environment. Yet complex as Exhibit 3-1 appears, it deals principally with only a selected aspect of the environment—the social. However, it does deal with several levels of the social environment of people—the individual, the group, the family, the community and class, and the culture. In addition to the social, with its various sizes of systems, the environment includes another large division—the physical. The physical environment may be further divided into the natural physical environment, such as climate, and the constructed environment, such as the shelters we build to protect us from the various natural phenomena of environment, and various unforeseen climatic events of nature. The third large division of the environment we have chosen to label *temporal,* meaning time and space. Because human life is finite

EXHIBIT 3–1
We, As Individuals, Are. . .

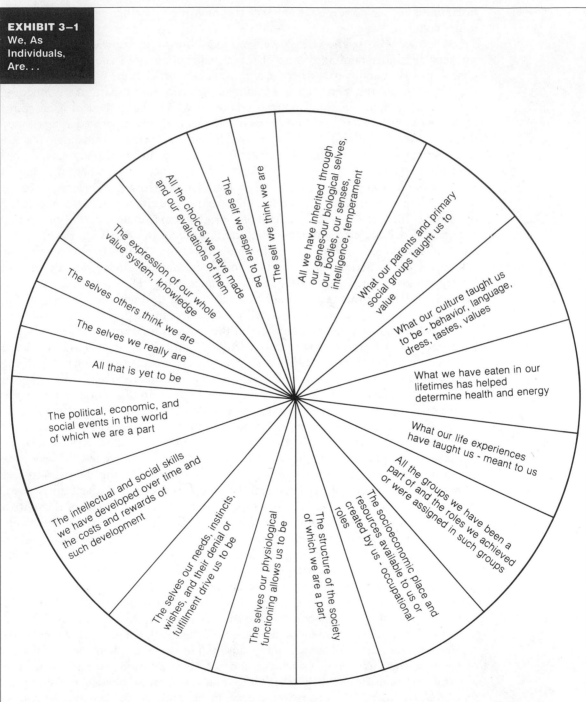

- The self we think we are
- All we have inherited through our genes—our biological selves, our bodies, our senses, intelligence, temperament
- The self we aspire to be
- All the choices we have made and our evaluations of them
- The expression of our whole value system, knowledge
- The selves others think we are
- The selves we really are
- All that is yet to be
- The political, economic, and social events in the world of which we are a part
- The intellectual and social skills we have developed over time and the costs and rewards of such development
- The selves our needs, instincts, wishes, and their denial or fulfillment drive us to be
- The selves our physiological functioning allows us to be
- The structure of the society of which we are a part
- The socioeconomic place and resources available to us or created by us - occupational roles
- All the groups we have been a part of and the roles we achieved or were assigned in such groups
- What our life experiences have taught us - meant to us
- What we have eaten in our lifetimes has helped determine health and energy
- What our culture taught us to be - behavior, language, dress, tastes, values
- What our parents and primary social groups taught us to value

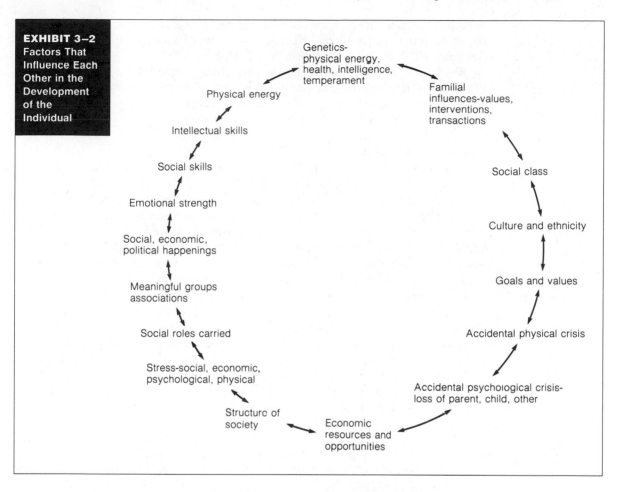

EXHIBIT 3–2
Factors That Influence Each Other in the Development of the Individual

Genetics-physical energy, health, intelligence, temperament

Physical energy

Intellectual skills

Social skills

Emotional strength

Social, economic, political happenings

Meaningful groups associations

Social roles carried

Stress-social, economic, psychological, physical

Structure of society

Economic resources and opportunities

Accidental psychological crisis-loss of parent, child, other

Accidental physical crisis

Goals and values

Culture and ethnicity

Social class

Familial influences-values, interventions, transactions

and is lived within certain defined spaces, time and space are critical environmental qualities.

Time and space can be further divided into two subclasses: general and personal. Most human beings construct shelters to protect them from the environment, but in so doing they also construct a personal and/or family space that gives them a certain privacy from the group. While this construction of shelter and marking of private space may be different from culture to culture, such effort is generally found in all cultures. Most Americans see their shelter in relation to both time and space. We need to have the shelter readily accessible to our place of employment or education. Being our private world, it also must meet certain other criteria such as having certain electrical appliances, heat, and perhaps air conditioning, as well as a certain attractiveness according to our definition. In evaluation of our private space, we are able to create or demand (through money or other resources) that which then interacts with our feelings about ourselves.

Given the above, for social work practice, environment may be defined as a combination of people and their interactions and transactions in a particular geographic, socially defined, and constructed space over a particular period of time both in the individual and family's life and in the life of the social and cultural system (Germain, 1979; Pincus & Minahan, 1973; Siporin, 1975).

We cannot regard environment as something outside ourselves—as another billiard ball with which we collide once in a while. Rather, environment is of us and we are of it. From the moment of our birth it becomes an intimate part of us and presents us with the material from which we construct our lives through the choices we make and the social transactions in which we engage in response to the opportunities and deprivations presented us.

To give an example, John and Richard are both eighteen-year-old American white men who have just graduated in the upper 10% of their respective classes. They look very much alike and are both attractive and in good health. John's family was an established professional family with a more than adequate financial base. From birth, John had little exposure to other than a professional life, and a university education following high school was expected in his environment. Thus John attended the university his father attended and became in his turn a professional man. His choice of this pattern of life was highly approved and came naturally in this environment. To make another choice would have been extremely difficult.

Richard, however, was the oldest son of a family of five siblings. His father was a farmer, but during his long terminal illness the family sold the farm and exhausted its assets to pay for his care. His mother and the children now lived in a small rural community where his mother ran a small grocery store. Money was extremely tight for the family, which was without Social Security support because Richard's father was not covered. Richard was extremely bright and very much interested in farming. He would have liked to attend the university and major in agribusiness. However, the university was 100 miles away, and Richard could see no way to finance his education. In addition, his mother needed both his financial and his emotional support. There was a job in a local creamery that was open, and Richard took it. After ten years he became manager of the creamery. It was a good, steady, and adequately paying job. It meant that Richard had daily contact with the farm life he loved, but it was far short of the contribution he could have made and of the life he had dreamed of.

Both these men constructed their lives from the choices the environment offered them as they saw them. Starting their adult life with very similar internal resources, they became very different through the opportunities the environment offered and the choices they made.

It is not only our individual lives that are shaped by the choices we make given the environmental opportunities presented us. By our choices and our activities we in turn shape the environment. Interested as he was in the land, Richard was concerned with how certain practices of the farmers were destroying the topsoil and depriving birds and small animals of their habitat. These farmers had forced the land to adapt to their poor practices. Richard organized a group of concerned farmers who were able to arrange for a representative of the local university to come and help them to understand better land use. The farmers learned to cooperate with the needs of their environment and grew more prosperous for it. So not only did the farmer adapt to the land, but he forced the land to adapt to his practices. Through our interactions and our transactions, we shape both our future and the future of our environment. A great deal of social work practice is devoted to helping clients analyze the impact of the environment on their problems and making a planned effort to change undesirable conditions. "The House on Sixth Street" (Appendix, A-7) is an example of a worker helping clients to change some very difficult living conditions.

In considering the transactions between any level of human system and the larger level within which it is embedded, we need to be familiar with the concept of adaptation. In common usage adaptation is often seen as meaning the way the smaller system capitulates to the power of the larger environment. Thus, adaptation is often interpreted as submission and is instinctively rejected as coercion. However, submission is only one method of adaptation, and even so it affects the environment. Adaptation should be seen as an active concept, meaning the transactional processes by which people shape their environment, physical and social, and in turn are shaped themselves.

Attempting to define the environment of any social system is complex. Think of the environment as a set of boxes, each of a slightly larger size so that they nest inside each other. Stack them so that they fit together in order of size. Pick any one of the boxes. The environment is not only the next larger box but all the boxes that are larger. Yet each larger box will have its own characteristics that are different from, yet shaped by, the still larger boxes that constitute its environment. However, the impact and meaning of the largest box for the smallest box are usually mediated through the different-sized boxes that come between the largest and the smallest. Thus, for most of us as individuals, the meaning of the community as an environment is mediated through the next larger box, which is usually the family or some other small group.

As there does not exist any generally accepted set of boundaries demarcating in an obvious way different levels in the environment, we find it helpful to distinguish four levels: the situation in which the individual finds himself or herself at a particular point in time, the micro level, the meso level, and the macro level. Each level is embedded in the higher levels, and the functioning of each level is determined in large part by its interaction with the higher level (Magnusson & Allen, 1983; Bronfenbrenner, 1979). The situation is the part of the environment that is accessible to the individual's perception at any given moment. Situations play an important role because "it is in actual situations that we encounter and form our conceptions about the world and develop specific kinds of behavior for dealing with it." Situations present "the information that we process, and they offer the feedback necessary for building valid conceptions of the outer world. Knowledge about the actual situations that an individual has encountered, along with the accompanying physical, social, and cultural microenvironments, will help us understand behavior at different stages of development" (Magnusson & Allen, 1983, p. 11).

The micro level of environment has been defined by Magnusson and Allen as "that part of the total physical and social environment that an individual is in contact with and can interact with directly in daily life during a certain period of time" (1983, p. 11). This level of environment includes the individual's experiences in his or her family, experiences at school, at work, during leisure time, and so forth and is to a large extent specific to the individual in that no other person experiences the same environment the same way. The microenvironment is very important in the development of an individual in that it determines the type of situations an individual will encounter.

The meso level of environment is "that part of the total environment that in some way or another influences and determines the character and functioning of the microenvironment" (Magnusson & Allen, 1983, p. 11). It includes relationships between major groups, organizations, and institutions that the individual's daily life touches, such as school, work, church, recreation, and community resources.

The macro level of environment is common to most members of the groups living in it and involves the physical, social, cultural, economic, and political structure of the larger society in which individuals grow up, including technology, language, housing, laws, customs and regulations, and the like. What we have here (remember our illustration of the different-sized boxes) are five systems of different sizes, from individual to macrosystem, in which each system is part of a larger whole and itself is a suprasystem to other systems. The whole is reflected or contained in each of its parts, and all parts are complementary aspects of the whole. Thus language, an element of the larger macrosystem, is also a critical part of each individual. Since the macro level of environment is a part of each individual system, it is easy for social workers to overlook the meaning of the macroenvironment to the smaller individual system. This kind of oversight may be called to our attention when we are confronted by a problem in a relationship with a client from a different macrosystem.

There are some factors in the environment that operate at all levels. Perhaps the most important of these is the extent to which the environment sets limits on the behavior of individuals and offers opportunities for their development. The actual environment does have an impact on behavior and development, but it is through the individual's perception and interpretation of the environment and the meaning assigned to these perceptions and interpretations that the environment has the most influence. Thus, social workers must be concerned about three environments: the actual environment, the environment as perceived by the client, and the environment as perceived by the practitioner. It is very easy and very seductive for us as practitioners to conclude that our perception of the actual environment is more accurate than the client's. However, it is dangerous for us to act on this belief. Not only may our perception be more distorted than the client's, but such an assumption will probably result in an inability to understand the meaning that the client assigns to her or his perception. Reading 9-3, "Point of View," at the end of chapter nine is an excellent illustration of how a happening in the environment is perceived differently by different people, and how each interpreted it according to her or his own perception.

We will carry this discussion of person-environment interaction farther in Chapter 4, which deals with theoretical perspectives. Because we conceptualize the person and environment as being an ecological system, we believe that further discussion will be better understood following the presentation of systems theory.

For now let us return to the problem of how we build knowledge for social work practice. We have established that it is acceptable to borrow knowledge but that we must be concerned about the congruency of the underlying assumptions of such knowledge and the perspective from which the knowledge was developed with the purposes and values of social work. Knowledge developed to serve a profession whose function in society is different from that of social work may not serve us well without considerable adaptation. For example, social work has found much that is useful in knowledge of human growth and development originating in the fields of psychiatry and medicine. However, in borrowing this knowledge, social work did not consider the difference in the function of the two professions. In borrowing a conceptual framework from medicine and psychiatry, social work—and especially social work involving individual clients—also accepted the goals of psychiatry and borrowed approaches and methods focused on the cure of illness rather than on solving problems of social functioning. Thus the client's problems have become the client's pathology.

Criteria for Selecting and Organizing Knowledge

Knowledge developed from a different perspective may have to be carefully considered in light of the function and values of social work. This may be illustrated by a quotation from an article by Harriet Trader (1977) in which she identifies five areas of concern and develops some questions that may be used as criteria in borrowing theories and models for use in social work practice:

1. Pathology-health balance. Do the basic concepts on which the theory is developed focus either on illness rather than on well-being or on deficits rather than strengths? Are the definitions of pathology and health based solely on the expectations of the dominant group in society? Do standards for health include a range of potentials that allows for minority-group differences? Are class differences implied or stated in the models for either normality or abnormality?

2. Practitioner-client control balance. Does the theory suggest that the worker carries more responsibility than the client in the process of changing the client's situation? Are clients perceived even subtly as being inferior to practitioners? Are practitioners seen as being obliged to use their knowledge and skills to increase clients' coping abilities? Does the theory view human beings as primarily dependent, interdependent, or independent? Can the theory allow for shared control? From what source does the practice derive its legitimacy?

3. Personal-societal impact balance. In assigning causation for problems, does the theory embody a personal-deficit model rather than a societal model? Does the theory take into account historical as well as current societal conditions? Can the theory account for political-economic influences on behavior? Does the theory assign importance to variations in socialization experiences among oppressed minorities? Does the theory allow for linking of the personal to the social and environmental aspects of behavior?

4. Internal-external change balance. Does the theory emphasize internal, psychic change in preference to changes that occur in society? Does the theory assume that the nature of society is primarily punitive rather than supportive? Are the definitions for change based essentially on the dominant societal patterns, or do they allow for a variety of patterns? To what extent is the view of change synonymous with adjustment?

5. Rigidity-flexibility balance. Does the theory allow for the adjustment of concepts to the needs of particular groups? Do the abstract principles lend themselves to creative and differential application in practice? Can the theory accommodate new information about oppressed minorities? Does the theory relate to a view of the class structure of society? Does the theory demand an uncritical adherence to its postulates? Are there built-in criteria for continual assessment of the utility of the theory? (pp. 10–13)

We consider that Trader's questions are the type we should ask of borrowed theory. Trader asks that we examine the borrowed knowledge from the perspective of social work's function in society: to be concerned with the problems of people in their situation. Her questions reflect concern with the congruency between the purposes and values of social work and the theory base used to guide practice.

Other authors have also tried to develop criteria for selecting and ordering social work knowledge. Briar and Miller (1971) have developed the following criteria. Note that they, too, are concerned with goals and assumptions about what needs to be changed. They write:

> An adequate theory must be explicit about the question of goals. It should be clear what is to be changed. . . . And an adequate theory must deal with the issue of who sets the goals of intervention and how this should be done.
>
> Second, an intervention theory can be evaluated according to its assumptions about what can be changed. . . . The optimistic view has the practical virtue of orienting the practitioner to the potentials for change and to searching for more effective and powerful ways to bring it about.
>
> Third, it should be clear what effective application of the theory would require of the client.
>
> Fourth, an adequate theory should specify, in behavioral terms, what the practitioner needs to do in order to bring about the desired changes.
>
> Fifth . . . an intervention theory should indicate what the practitioner needs to do in order to make sure that changes that occur within the treatment situation are carried over into the client's real life.
>
> Finally, the theory should tell the practitioner how to assess the outcome of . . . intervention efforts. (p. 180)

In addition to using borrowed knowledge, social workers should develop their own theories and their own models of practice through a commitment to an orderly discovery process. Earlier in the chapter we referred to Berkowitz (1969), who speaks of the wisdom that social workers acquire in and through practice and then pass on to others, including both practice methods and knowledge of human behavior. Certainly from our earliest history social workers have been concerned with understanding clients' problems from the clients' perspective and learning more about how to help them.

We spoke earlier of the way that theory grows through the collecting of observations and the developing and testing of assumptions about the meaning of these observations. The literature of social work is indeed rich with important observations of our practice, but these observations of the interactions between client and practitioner and of the ways people lived, thought, and felt as they struggled with their problems of living have tended to remain as idiosyncratic accounts of professional experiences. Perhaps one reason for this is to be found in the growth of a particular view of how one arrives at acceptable knowledge—a view of knowledge that resulted in selective inattention to practical competence and professional artistry.

Social work began to grow and develop at about the time that industrialism, technology, and the scientific movement also began to have tremendous impact on the professions. Increasingly, people began to adopt the notion that the only significant knowledge about the world was based on empirical observations and that "all disagreements about the world could be resolved, in principle, by reference to observable facts. Propositions which were neither analytically nor empirically testable were held to have no meaning at all. They were dismissed as emotive utterance, poetry, or mere nonsense" (Schon, 1983, pp. 32–33). Empirical science was not just a form of knowledge; it was the only source of positive knowledge in the world. "According to the positivist epistemology of practice, craft and artistry had no lasting place in rigorous practical knowledge" (Schon, 1983, p. 34).

Social work also adopted the logical positivism approach to research, and many social work researchers became less concerned about determining the questions that needed answering and more concerned with the technique of how to examine and test a phenomenon. They became methodologists enamored of their methodology and blind to the questions that social work needed to answer. In their concentration on methodology and their view that if one could not measure a phenomenon, it did not exist, researchers failed to examine the phenomena that were central to the everyday experience of the practitioner. As a result, practitioners found research publications of little or no help in responding to people in trouble. And in the process there developed a divisive split between research and practice in which practitioners accused researchers of not producing either useful knowledge or knowledge that took into account the critical elements of practice. In turn, researchers accused practitioners of not being interested in "hard knowledge" and of lacking discipline and intellectual rigor. Involved in the messy but crucially important problems of human life, practitioners spoke of experience, trial and error, intuition, and even of muddling through. Researchers, however, tended to be people who were devoted to technical rigor and solid competence and who, perhaps, were afraid to enter the messy, slippery situations that confront practitioners. As one would expect, research and practice lost their connectedness, and given the strong belief that real knowledge lay in the techniques of a particular research methodology, researchers assumed an elitist and patronizing attitude toward practitioners. They knew and practitioners only felt.

We believe that this dominance of logical positivism is retreating. Although the elitist attitude of researchers and the view of social work as a "soft" rather than a "hard" science still lurks in the corners of the profession, we now have both the opportunity and the obligation to look at methodological issues involved in social work research in a much broader perspective. One approach that has been a part of methodological quarrels for a long time seems to be gaining new respectability. That is the phenomenological approach, which focuses on the experience of living as the person lives, on making a commitment to understanding through seeing and sensing the world as the other person sees and senses it. This approach has great appeal for many social workers, for whom the demand to understand the client's feelings is a comfortable one that they have mastered in practice.

Crisis always brings in its wake the possibility for change. Perhaps given the chaos we are now experiencing, it is time for us to think seriously about the possibility of incorporating the practitioner into research. It appears that those who decide what professional issues are to be explored are by this process defining what is important to the profession. Should practitioners be the persons asking such questions? Should they be the central part of this process? Haworth, in an article on research and practice, says that "knowledge as to the utility and meaning of the behaviors must be gained from involvement in the ongoing lives of human beings. The practitioner is in the ideal position to be a researcher. A new paradigm would relieve the need to apologize for the 'unscientific' anecdotal nature of the data, for it is in that direction that the most appropriate understanding of human processes can be found" (Haworth, 1984, p. 355). We find ourselves in agreement with Haworth about the nature of the knowledge that is of greatest use to the practitioner.

It is our position that scientific inquiry and practice can be integrated through the use of the problem-solving process, a process familiar to and used by both practitioners and researchers. The best of scientific inquiry is an attempt to solve a problem, and the best of practice is an attempt to join a client in problem solving. The process in general is similar. In each a problem must be defined; a hypothesis must be stated with greater or lesser confidence (assessment in practice terms); data must be collected; a methodology must be stated (plan of intervention in practice terms); and an outcome must be evaluated.

We have discussed the importance of developing knowledge needed to fulfill social work's assigned purpose and the difficulty created by borrowing knowledge developed to serve a different purpose. In an article in *Social Work Research and Abstracts,* Mullen (1985) supports this position of the importance of knowledge being developed to serve purpose. He feels that the tension between research and practice has resulted in a situation in which both researchers and practitioners are losing their focus on purpose and becoming narrowly preoccupied with method "out of context with purpose."

> A refocus on purpose directs attention to the type of knowledge needed to facilitate the profession's mission. The knowledge that is required is the type that would facilitate problem solving and be close to the context of practice. There are various approaches to problem solving, ranging from the traditional to the modern and cutting across both familiar and novel situations. The profession needs practice and research approaches that are responsive to these problem-solving alternatives. (Mullen, 1985, p. 18)

We must remember that in knowledge building there is no one single scientific method. When we speak of scientific inquiry, we are not speaking of a research method. People down through the ages have argued the questions How do we know what we know? and What is knowledge? It would seem to us that social work could well examine this statement: "The scientific method, as far as it is a method, is nothing more than doing one's damnedest with one's mind, no holds barred" (Bridgman, 1945, p. 450).

Is Knowledge Necessary?

Given all the effort to identify the knowledge base of social work, and given the fact that it keeps eluding our grasp with such persistence, it may be asked whether knowledge and theory are necessary. We hold that they are. Although it has proven impossible to come up with a definitive statement of the knowledge base of the profession, all statements issued over the years are in remarkable substantive agreement at a generalized level. Thus there must be more grasp of a common knowledge base by social work practitioners than one might think. In addition, the idea that one can operate without theory and knowledge is naive. Briar and Miller (1971) discuss this point:

> The choice for the practitioner is not whether to have a theory but what theoretical assumptions to hold. All persons acquire assumptions or views on the basis of which they construe and interpret events and behavior, including their own. These assumptions frequently are not explicit but are more what has been called "implicit theories of personality." Thus, the appeal for practitioners to be atheoretical amounts simply to an argument that theory ought to be implicit and hidden, not explicit and self-conscious.

It is difficult, however, to defend an argument favoring implicit theory that, by definition, is not susceptible to scrutiny and objective validation and therefore cannot be distinguished from idiosyncratic bias. The weaknesses of implicit theory are particularly serious for a profession in which a significant portion of the practitioner's activity consists in forming judgments and impressions about persons on the basis of which decisions are made affecting their lives in critical ways. . . .

Whether implicit or explicit, social workers' particular assumptions about human behavior can be expected to influence their professional actions, and therefore, to have important consequences for their clients. (pp. 53–54)

As an example of their point, Briar and Miller (1971, p. 30) indicate that the assumptions social workers hold about the possibilities of change in human nature will probably affect the degree of optimism with which they approach their clients and their problems and that the premises about what can be changed will largely determine what one attempts to change. Perhaps the important thing to keep in mind is that the interventive repertoire (what one does) of social workers grows out of and is dependent on knowledge-based theory (what one assumes is the nature of the phenomenon and what one assumes will be of help) and values (what social workers see as desired ends) in interaction with the problems clients bring and the solution sought. The social worker's input into work with any client system depends on social work purposes and values, on how the worker understands the situation through the use of social work knowledge and theory, and on "where" one thinks the client is with the problem presented, based on what the practitioner hears the client say and how that is interpreted.

It is the social worker's responsibility to analyze and understand the situation before taking action. An essential of all professional practice is that it requires the rapid, continuous, expert selection and use of generalizations from the profession's body of knowledge, while remaining open to feedback from the client system that may force the abandonment of the first premise and the selection of another. Social workers put their professional knowledge to its first important use through their ability to "know where the client is," so that client and worker may be actively and appropriately involved in assessing the situation with which they are dealing.

To summarize, social workers, particularly educators, are continually trying to identify the knowledge base on which the profession rests. However, the problems in such identification are almost overwhelming in that (1) the primary knowledge of the profession, empirically acquired, is drawn from the immense range of human problems as they are revealed by individuals in their situations and as they emerge in their cumulative aspects; (2) knowledge needed for many of the problem-solving activities of the profession has to be drawn from allied disciplines, with all the problems that this poses for selection, translation, and use; (3) the relevant knowledge is changing constantly and advancing rapidly; and (4) the profession is engaged in multiple functions and is uncertain as to what it should be expert about. For example, as the focus shifts from concern with the internal state of individuals and their adaptive functioning to a broader, and certainly more complex, view of individuals as participants in the interactional field of psychological and social forces, the knowledge base of social work begins to be organized differently than it was in earlier years, and an expanded range of approaches and techniques will have to be used. Helen Perlman (1957, p. 27) recognizes this point when she says, "Knowledge, no sooner grasped, leaps forward again to excite new pursuit, and this is both the gratification and the frustration of trying to work on problems-in-change."

It is reassuring to realize, however, that all the statements of the Council on Social Work Education, all the minutes of conferences, and all the books and articles on social work knowledge, which if laid end to end might well circle the world several times, are in general agreement on the four broad areas of knowledge important to the social worker: (1) people in interaction with environment, (2) policy and programs, (3) research, and (4) practice actions. However, as already stated, the problem lies not in the task of finding a consensus on the broad areas of knowledge but in the task of selecting the critical concepts for use by the social work practitioner from this immense range of knowledge and in the task of relating these concepts to one another.

Dealing With Incomplete Knowledge

The practitioner-to-be in the here-and-now is faced with a great deal of knowledge to master—knowledge that is not very well related or integrated. Some of this knowledge is supported by empirical evidence, and some of it is assumptive and supported, if at all, by only the roughest of evidence. Sometimes knowledge and value are all mixed up, and yet there never seem to be the appropriate interrelationships between bits of knowledge. The fact is that the amount of knowledge needed is so great and some of it is so uncertain that social workers are faced with the uncomfortable fact that they are constantly intervening in people's lives based on incomplete knowledge (as are all other practitioners in the human services). This, however, raises some hard questions. How can we help people to feel some confidence in us as helpers while we remain tentative and often uncertain about what we know? How can we doubt our effectiveness and still be effective? How can we act as experts and yet be so constantly aware of our own ignorance?

The stress of acting on incomplete knowledge confronts all professionals in the human services, but it may bear most heavily on social workers because of their commitment to individuals and their worth. Some social workers handle it by trying to forget what they do not know, and they become very dogmatic people, certain of their own knowledge but unable to grow because one cannot learn if one already knows. Some social workers try to handle it by emphasizing what they do not know and how helpless they are. They often run around looking for authorities while their client suffers from the lack of a secure helper. Some practitioners try to handle it by blaming the profession for their discomfort. They then find themselves in the bind of representing a profession in which they have no confidence and with which they have no identification. That must be one of the most uncomfortable binds of all. Such workers have neither read nor considered enough literature of other professions to understand that all professions are woefully lacking in knowledge of human beings and their interaction. These workers never come to grips with their need to know.

The demand that we act on uncertain knowledge goes along with being a helping person in complex and ever-changing situations. The best way of living with this is to commit ourselves (1) to becoming active learners all the time and (2) to the scientific method as a part of our equipment. We need to pledge to ourselves each and every day:

I will try everything I know to help the client with whom I am involved. In some aspects I may be too ignorant to know what way is best, but I will think carefully about my procedures, and I will be willing to assume the responsibility for my actions. I will neither be blinded by preconceptions nor impulsively follow a fleeting impulse or an easy answer. I will draw thoughtfully and responsibly upon every bit of knowledge that is available, and I will constantly and actively seek for more. I will be an insistent questioner rather than a passive taker, remaining identified with the profession while I vigorously question it. This is my solemn vow to my client. Thus, if my knowledge proves inadequate to the situation and the client's problem, my client and I will know that everything possible, given the present state of knowledge, has been done.

This book will offer some practice knowledge that we believe, from our study, our own questioning, and our own experience as both practitioners and teachers, will be helpful to people who are interested in beginning the challenging journey of becoming a truly competent social worker—a journey that no one ever completes. We believe that any other author, or even two, can offer only partial knowledge. For example, only a little knowledge about the social services network and the human condition per se will be offered here. We have chosen to offer knowledge about professional social work practice itself, believing that the other necessary knowledge (at least for now) can be acquired from other sources within the curriculum of the university and the social work major. We also believe that the knowledge given here will be the most valuable and the most immediately needed in fieldwork or on a first job. In some ways we are building the structure and trusting that you will be able to construct the basement from other sources. This may mean that for the time being your building is setting somewhat uncertainly on jacks without the underpinnings that will gradually have to be put in place.

Recapitulation

In this chapter we have looked at social work knowledge and the problems involved in the selection and organization of knowledge for professional practice. We have pointed out that the functions of a profession determine the parameters of the knowledge that helps in the delivery of services, the maintenance of organizations, and the effecting of change. We need to know more about the process of human and social change, the design of services responsive to the human systems that seek to use our help, and the final evaluation of what we do.

We have attempted to set forth some guidelines for the selection of theory and have offered some ways of dealing with our feelings when we are aware of the need to act on incomplete knowledge. We further remind you that all knowledge of human systems and their change is now and may be forever incomplete.

A Look Forward

We have now reached the end of this chapter. However, we have not reached the end of our discussion of the knowledge base of practice. You will want to study carefully the article by Goldstein on the knowledge base of social work practice. In the next chapter we will discuss some selected theories of human growth and social functioning that we believe support the problem-solving model of practice that we have developed. There are many differing notions of how people grow, develop, and function. No one theory can claim that it is the absolute truth. It may not be so important that a theory be true as that it be useful, that it be congruent with the purpose of the profession, and that it not have been disproved by scientific inquiry. It is our belief that social work is best served by a dynamic model of human beings that views people as being inherently active rather than inactive; as acting on the environment rather than being passive recipients of external stimuli; and as being organized configurations of parts with all parts interrelated in some way, with each element related to other elements in both a cause and effect relationship, and with the whole being greater than the sum of its parts. The next chapter will present some theories that are congruent with this view of people.

The Knowledge Base of Social Work Practice: Theory, Wisdom, Analogue, or Art?

Howard Goldstein

Almost seventy years ago, in March 1920, the premier issue of the parent of *Families in Society*, called *The Family*, was published by the American Association for Organizing Family Social Work. The lead article, quite fittingly, was written by Mary Richmond (1920a), the dominant figure in social casework. The purpose of the new journal was to gather and disseminate knowledge. In reaching out to social workers in the field, Richmond's article asked, "What Are You Thinking?"

Here was a profession in the making, shaped, in large part, by the rational and organized principles of the charity organization societies. Although social work was certain about its mission, a strong need existed for systematized knowledge to make these principles operative. Richmond hoped that the "pooled thinking" of the readers of the journal about their work with families and children might help develop what she called "a new way of serving humanity."

Consider the term "serving humanity," because it bears on the discussion that follows. This term was neither a rhetorical nor an editorial device used merely for effect. Rather, variations on this theme were quite familiar. In 1907, Jane Addams (1964) expressed a similar view when she elucidated the meaning of *social ethics*. Emphasizing the profession's social obligations, Addams said that social

ethics are not attained by traveling alone "but by mixing on the thronged and common road where all must turn out for one another, and at least see the size of one another's burdens" (pp. 6–7). In this, the profession's concern with the family, the community, and the environment as well as with social reform, the mission of the profession was firmly cast in a way that distinguished it from other allied professions.

At its origins, and to the extent that these values have persisted over time, social work might well have been called "social humanism." Addams's "social ethics" and Richmond's "serving humanity" are, in effect, natural extensions of the humanitarian commitments (both religious and secular) to charity, philanthropy, and caring that social work inherited when philanthropy became organized. The "social" in social work is the expression of this heritage. Implicit in these commitments is the recognition that we are, at the root of things, social beings existing with one another in a state of symbiosis, interdependence, and community. On reflection, this philosophical and also practical understanding of the social context of the human state might have served as the substratum or wellspring of the profession's knowledge structure.

A review of these beginnings is necessary in considering the transformations of and deviations from these first principles that have occurred in the ensuing decades. Following this course will help us understand how we arrived at the current state of the art, the implications of this state, and possibilities for future directions. In this regard, the title of the present article raises the question as to whether the knowledge base of social work comprises theory, wisdom, analogues, or art. More specifically, it asks whether a comprehensive conceptual foundation is readily translatable into direct practice. Or does our work with human problems depend on a certain wisdom—a body of knowledge that derives from the experience of doing social work? Perhaps we are deluding ourselves if what we call our knowledge base is actually a random collection of analogues or metaphoric simulations of the theories, models, or systems that we have borrowed or collected over time—that is, "an eclectic approach." Or should we admit that social work practice is basically an art that expresses the intuitive, creative, and imaginative talents of the practitioner? Or is social work practice some unique combination of all of the above?

These questions will be probed in this article in an effort to assess the current state of knowledge and practice and to consider other alternatives. The historical path is necessarily arbitrary: First, it is selective and interpretive in terms of the conditions that had bearing on knowledge development over the years; second, space limitations constrain this study to casework or direct practice, the major modality of social work throughout its history.

A BRIEF HISTORY OF PRACTICE THEORY

An ironic turn of events occurred around the time in which Richmond's article appeared in *The Family*. Social work was maturing into a legitimate profession via the establishment of university-affiliated educational programs. Up to this point, social work practice had been a practical, common-sense endeavor that, when it was not moralistic or policing, rested on tenets of social interdependence and obligation. In her appeal for "pooled thinking," Richmond respected practitioners' wisdom and expertise about family, community, and social problems.

The ironic turn happened when, with the need for educational content in the growing number of university programs, an intellectual or theoretical template was required to overlay and organize social work practice. Not surprisingly, within a society that was enthralled with the aura and the remarkable benefits of the new sciences and technologies, certain leaders (among them, Richmond) departed from the profession's humanistic roots and elected to define social casework as a science. This choice was also influenced by the prominent educator, Abraham Flexner (1915), who informed social work that it could not be a profession until it, too, possessed its own foundation of scientific knowledge and educationally communicable techniques. In contrast, the settlement house movement and its leaders, Addams and Florence Kelley, abstained from such a scientific pursuit; social reform, women's participation in Progressivism, and grassroots community education were their down-to-earth, humanistic causes (Sklar, 1985).

The split between mission and method (also referred to as "cause and function") was magnified by the fact that science at that time was rooted in a positivistic philosophy. By adopting this perspective, intuition and common-sense ways of understanding were discredited. Emphasizing the rigor of detached objectivity, positivism held little regard for subjective constructs such as morality, spirituality, and cultural or personal belief systems. Not the least, a positivistic preoccupation with instrumental means tended to overlook the profession's commitments to certain social ends.

A peculiar paradox that has been insistent over time is that, in adopting a scientific character, social work has not entirely discarded its humanistic and social ideals, nor has it lacked for advocates, as we will see, for a return to common-sense humanism and the "social" in social work. Thus, from the beginning social work moved forward on two distinct tracks that rarely crossed. One carried the cargo of its humanist traditions. The other twisted its searching way through vastly different theoretical territories—for example, Freudian psychology, the empiricism of behavioral psychology, and the objectivity of the scientific methods of the social sciences—pausing at times to collect still other ideologies, fads, techniques, models, and theories.

Richmond's book *Social Diagnosis* (1917) mollified some of Flexner's concerns. It became the standard text for professional education. Although

Richmond did not lose sight of the humanistic texture of casework, her book conveyed *legalistic* and *medical* metaphors, emphasizing the importance of collecting accurate evidence about families and clients as a basis for making rational decisions about service. To the fledgling profession in search of a respectable theory, other kinds of metaphors also were freely given: Healy (1917) called for social work to adopt the scientific spirit of applied psychology, and Southard (1919) proposed that social problems be approached from the point of view of medical analysis.

One perspective, apparently ignored because it was so far ahead of its time, was that of Bernard Bosanquet, chairman of the council of the London Charity Organization Society. Anticipating what we are just now beginning to understand about the working mind of the practitioner and the reflective flow and process of practice (Schön, 1983), Bosanquet (1916) referred to this process as the use of common sense informed by available knowledge. In his view, theory does not guide practice; rather, it is "trained judgment," a disciplined and reflective creative reasoning, that makes effective practice possible. Theory comes into play when a novel problem is encountered. The value of any theory, however, depends on the extent to which it enhances common-sense understanding of that novel problem. Thus the kind of thinking that advances practice is more like the product of the mind of a speculative, imaginative philosopher than it is like the controlled, analytic, and logical mind of the prototypical scientist.

Bosanquet's ideas remain an odd historical footnote. Probably more typical of education than of practice in the field, the hope persisted that a guiding theory might be found that would serve as a blueprint for social work practice. Following Flexner's directive, "communicable techniques" were required to shape the curricula of the 17 educational programs that were in place by the end of World War I. Moreover, the profession had already turned its attention away from the poor and dependent toward the more complex problems of the middle class. New specializations such as medical and psychiatric social work and child

welfare also increased the need for a dependable knowledge base.

Not surprisingly, Freudian thought was eagerly adopted in the 1920s and 1930s. In an opportune way, it provided not only a fascinating and coherent theory but techniques for implementing the theory as well. At the same time, social work practice could not, for obvious reasons, take on the many embellishments of psychoanalytic treatment; the unavoidable result was a diluted rendition of or a vague analogy to the grand theory. Speaking of his days as a student at the New York School of Social Work in the 1930s, Perry Gangloff recalls that "teachers were as much absorbed in the potential of their new theories as were the students. Indeed, an atmosphere of warm collegiality existed, but it was fraught with danger. No one . . . paid any attention to the weaknesses of that original presentation of Freudian-influenced concepts and it was allowed to go unchallenged" (P. Gangloff, personal communication, March 1989).

Over the following years, the deterministic principles of Freudian psychology shaped the conventions and form of the profession's knowledge base and came to be known as the diagnostic school. Among others, Bertha Reynolds (1932) was troubled that the profession was losing sight of its commitments to the whole person, to the community, and to reform. These vestiges of the profession's original mission were, for the time being, put to rest. As Grace Marcus (1939) advised:

> To a group who have so frequently been concerned to reform and rescue, it came hard to admit that the nature of man's mind, like that of his body, is determined . . . how difficult it is to accept this harsh truth is revealed by our distortion of it into the facile concept of "self-determination" (p. 130).

The rush toward theoretical respectability and sophistication was tempered by the Great Depression of the 1930s. With the depletion of funds and the closing of agencies, psychiatric social workers who had been treating middle-class clients returned to serving the poor and unemployed (Goldstein, 1973). During this period, a new metaphor for practice materialized—the functional school of social work—as a result of the efforts of Jesse Taft (1935) and Virginia Robinson (1930, 1944). It offered a dialectic contrast to the diagnostic school by substituting humanism for scientism and employing the ideas of theorists as varied as Otto Rank, George Mead, and John Dewey. The immediate, real-life nature of the helping relationship was given priority; the idea that behavior was determined was replaced by regard for the client's will; the medical metaphors of causality, diagnosis, and pathology were rejected; and the concepts of growth and change replaced that of cure. The profession could now claim two distinct (and contradictory) identities; depending on the practitioner's orientation, any one client's problem might be defined and treated in either of two radically different forms.

The separation of methods and schools was short lived. By the end of World War II, the crisp borders between the functional and diagnostic schools began to soften, doctrinaire Freudian psychology was easing into a more secular ego psychology, and the growing number of schools of social work were juggling and combining various approaches. As was the case in my own education, it became necessary to resolve a kind of professional schizophrenia in the attempt to integrate the diagnostic content I was taught in class with the functionalist mentoring I was given in the field.

In the optimistic glow of the postwar years, science achieved even greater stature. In this bright light, the maturing social sciences offered hope that long-troubling social problems might finally be remedied through the use of sophisticated scientific methods. Social work eagerly grasped this hope and added a yet more polished scientific metaphor to its store and to its identity. Although it now may appear naive, Hamilton (1949), a leading figure in social casework, represented a popular outlook in her belief that problems such as delinquency could at least be controlled if not entirely prevented.

A few other thinkers were not entirely convinced about the promise of the social sciences and continued to plead the cause of humanism. Lindeman (1949) argued that science can furnish means but not ends, instruments but not goals, facts but not values. Stressing the importance of social ethics, he observed that the social worker must achieve something more than technical proficiency. Stroup (1960) concurred, observing that reliance on the superficialities of science and its methods rather than on an adequate understanding of the human condition would result in the loss of the profession's vitality. Unheeded, these injunctions also became footnotes.

The 1950s witnessed many efforts to augment the structure of the profession (for example, the standardization of education and the formation of the National Association of Social Workers) and to burnish its scientific image. Yet it was apparent, even to outside observers, that "social work was a profession chasing its tail" (Sanders, 1957, p. 56). Satirizing the profession's eagerness for dignity and status, she depicted a fictional day after the bomb fell. While other professions were grappling with effects of the holocaust, the two remaining social workers "held a conference on Interpersonal Relationships in a Time of Intensified Anxiety States" (p. 56). She added:

> social workers—though specialists in good deeds—seem to have lost track of what particular good needs doing by them. Preoccupied with a strange game of musical chairs called the search for professional status, they have yet to settle in a seat that suits their current hopes and capacities (p. 57).

These few critiques had little effect, especially because social work was on the verge of entering into the tumult of the 1960s. Practitioners in the field and academics in the universities tried to juggle a mélange of metaphors, frameworks, and models. The profession was peppered with all kinds of demands from within and outside its own ranks. The War on Poverty called for training and knowledge to prepare social workers for new approaches in the form of outreach, grass-roots, and community services. At the same time, the effusion of the new therapeutic systems (for example, Rogerian, transactional analysis, gestalt, and reality therapies) were exceedingly tempting rations for a profession hungry for richer and even more sophisticated techniques. And now even the humanists were prescribing new-fashioned approaches to practice in existential, artistic, and value-based terms as countermeasures for the profession's deference to the scientific method (Stretch, 1967; Teicher, 1967; Salomon, 1967).

The social science model persisted even though evidence showed that its theories were unevenly and inconsistently used in practice (Taber & Shapiro, 1965). The answer, according to some of its proponents, was to do more of the same. An increase in scientific research was seen as the only hope of gaining truth and knowledge about casework practice (Herstein, 1969).

In her review of social work methods of the preceding decade, Perlman (1965) did not agree. She acknowledged that social science concepts such as role, class, and reference groups added to diagnostic understanding. She was less certain, however, whether this understanding added anything substantial to the development of skills and techniques. Perlman was even more troubled about social workers' dogged belief that somewhere out there were keys that might at least unlock the doors to human behavior. First, it was sociology, then psychoanalysis, and then the social sciences. Not at all sure of what social science consisted or whether it was even a science, she offered the following summation:

> The caveat we must hold before ourselves is against letting the need blind us. Words seem to hold magic, and the use of words like . . . "client-system" and "role network" may infuse us with a heady sense of having something to conjure with. . . . Unless we plumb these words for their particular meaning, for what phenomena they express, and then for what their implications for action are, we will find ourselves disappointed again (p. 71).

Words apparently did not lose their magic. The variegated mix of fragments of techniques, models, schools, fads, and theories that were appropriated in a wholesale fashion readily turned the language of the profession into a word salad—a collection of elegant metaphors unrelated both to the human event they described and to the demands of practice. The practitioner could (and still can) refer to the dysfunctional communication patterns within an enmeshed family in which role allocations are diffused by the weak ego of a chronically depressed father who has poor object relations.

The influence of several authors and the availability of systems theories (and, no doubt, the changing ethos of society) brought about in the early 1970s an apparent reaffirmation of the profession's earlier concern with social functioning. Bartlett (1970) focused this concern on the "relation between the coping activity of people and the demand from the environment" (p. 116).

Almost spontaneously, the social systems analogue was widely adopted by educators as a scheme or structure for conceptualizing the complexities of person-environment relations. This analogue, in turn, spawned a new version of the social worker as generalist (Goldstein, 1973; Pincus & Minahan, 1973; Siporin, 1975). Many graduate programs revised the traditional separation of methods (casework, group work, and community organization) in favor of an "integrated" approach or a "macromicro" orientation.

Although this framework was extremely useful as a lens for viewing and comprehending the relationships and linkages among the members of a system, like other theories that had been adopted it offered little in the way of prescriptions about how one might translate these perceptions into action. At the same time, little agreement existed about how the abstract notion of the generalist ought to take shape in practice. The generalist was variously defined as one who employed all of the traditional methods; as one who could fill a variety of roles (for example, adviser, therapist, consultant, caretaker); as a case manager; a problem solver; or human services worker (Goldstein, 1981b). In addition, questions remained about whether the tasks of the generalist were rudimentary and to be performed by the baccalaureate social worker or whether they demanded the competencies of the master's-level graduate.

More important, few opportunities were available to practice as a generalist in agencies (at least in the United States), which persisted in being highly specialized and focused on specific client groups, problems, or fields of service. Although the subsequent "life model" of social work practice (Germain & Gitterman, 1980) substantially modified the social systems analogue, the value of this approach was also blunted by the constraints of agency specialization.

Despairing of the resistance of various "vested interests" in the profession to a generic, common-base model of practice, Siporin (1978) observed that the state of the art in social work mirrored the fragmentation and the individualistic pursuits of our culture. In some ways, the history of ideas covered in the preceding pages confirms Siporin's impression. Over a large part of this century, the profession succeeded in accumulating a remarkable grab bag of diverse (and, in many instances, incompatible) theories, methods, techniques, models, schools, and specializations. For example, Turner's first survey (1974) of practice models covered 14 approaches; his most recent (1986) included 22. Other methods have not been touched upon in this discussion, including the many forms of practice with groups or communities and the swarm of family therapies that have burst forth over the years.

The result of this serial importation of ideas is not a coherent knowledge base that supports the profession's objectives, but something resembling a variety-store warehouse. Even this inventory is not dependable, because the stored items are merely analogues, metaphors, or simulations of the borrowed models or techniques. The lack of fit between many of the models and the purposes and intent of social work means that, at best, the typical social worker can only simulate in practice the training and expertise needed to apply, say, the principles of psychoanalysis, the medical model, or the scientific method. It is safe to say that the use of the euphemism "eclectic" serves to justify this kind of fragmentation and incoherence.

IMPLICATIONS FOR PRACTICE

The profession's quest for communicable techniques and knowledge is one story. A second and far more salient issue that needs examination is whether the knowledge and techniques that have been acquired are indeed communicable. In other words, we must ask whether knowledge is transferred or generalized from education to practice. Are the actions of social workers actually influenced or prescribed by the theories they learn in professional education?

Not much evidence substantiates that this transfer occurs. A group of recent studies (Sheldon, 1978; Sainsbury, 1980; Kolevzon & Maykranz, 1982; Carew, 1979) found little connection between theoretical knowing and practical doing. These researchers variously expressed concern that practice may be random, muddled, and unpredictable and that theory building is merely an "academic exercise."

Is this actually the state of the art? Have social workers over time merely deceived themselves? Are they hoodwinking the society they are supposed to be serving? Or are we asking the wrong kind of questions in an attempt to understand the nature and quality of practice? What would we find if we asked not *whether practitioners are guided* by certain theoretical principles or strategies but *how they are guided* and by *what kind* of principles? In other words, is the experiential form of social work practice based on something other than intellectual and abstract systems of thought? Surveys of exhaustive research on this question offer some interesting answers.

A major review of many years and types of research on a broad range of therapist variables (Beutler, Crago, & Arizmendi, 1986) concluded that the outcomes of psychotherapy have very little to do with therapists' theoretical orientation. The variables that appear to effect a positive outcome have more to do with the natural qualities of the therapist, including personal well-being, social influence ability, expectations, competence, and democratic attitude. These findings were supported and enlarged by another review of research on the process and outcome of therapy (Orlinsky & Howard, 1986), which underscored the central importance of the relationship or the therapeutic alliance. The optimal therapeutic relationship is one that is marked by collaboration, the sharing of initiative and responsibility, and the avoidance of dependency and authority. Concern with feelings, the therapist's self-investment, affirmations, genuineness, and empathy also contribute to the quality of the helping relationship.

Social work research yields comparable findings. Beck's (1988) study of counselor characteristics and outcomes pointed not only to the dominant influence of the counseling relationship but also to the finding that the counselor's education was not associated with outcome. In fact, counselors with less education were, in some instances, more effective. Other studies seem to confirm the primary importance of practice wisdom and common-sense understanding. DeMartini and Whitbeck (1987) sought to determine the sources of knowledge used by social workers. They found that in a way that could not be explained, practitioners used *contextual knowledge,* that is, a synthesis of knowledge from a variety of sources, including life experience, for the purpose of understanding their clients' circumstances. Reminiscent of Bosanquet's foresights, Harrison's (1987) study cast light on the practitioner's reflective modes of thinking as a means of gaining understanding. Workers creatively attempted to deduce new applications of what they knew, asked themselves a succession of "what if" questions, and often relied on a personal ideology to provide structure for their practice. When, in Kunin's (1985) study, clients were asked, "What made a difference in your counseling?" they consistently offered the perception that the helpful counselor was one who showed a consistent regard for and appreciation of the client's worth and ability to change.

The ironies commented on earlier in this essay seem to persist. Despite the insistent pursuit of a scientific image for social work, the experiential and subjective characteristics of direct practice continue to call for a humanistic identity. Unfortunately, as Imre (1982) observes, these characteristics have been discounted as merely "intuitive" and unsubstantial, lacking in the desired scientific objectivity and validity. As a result, we have not exploited or developed the grounded and seasoned source of practice knowledge.

A second irony follows from the first. The social sciences are undergoing change and revision. While scientific stalwarts in social work have been following the straight line leading to coveted scientific purity, many thinkers in the social sciences have turned the post-positivistic corner, recognizing that human science is inevitably *interpretive* in nature (Feyerabend, 1975; Gadamer, 1981; Gergen, 1982; Hahn et al., 1983). Rabinow and Sullivan (1987) describe the "interpretive turn" this way:

> . . . human life is characterized as an open system. It cannot be shielded from external interference and studied in a vacuum or a scientifically controlled and delimited environment. From this it follows that the exactitude that is open to the human sciences is quite different from that available to the natural sciences. Our capacity to understand is rooted in our own self-definitions, hence in what we are. We are fundamentally self-interpreting and self-defining, living always in a cultural environment, inside a web of signification that we ourselves have spun. There is no outside, detached standpoint from which we gather and present brute data. When we try to understand the cultural world, we are dealing with interpretations and interpretations of interpretations (p. 7).

The moss-grown aphorism "start where the client is" is not, after all, a piece of hollow rhetoric, but a sound and instructive principle. Ethically and practically, it advises us that effective practice begins and continues within the ground of the client's own interpreted reality (Goldstein, 1983).

If this is indeed the case, then the profession's historic track of social humanism and practice wisdom proves to be the one we should be riding to resolve these ironies. As is yet to be shown, the modern versions of the social sciences (and to some extent, the humanities) now permit us to give more serious attention to and have more regard for the subjective domain of our clients' moral, theological, and cultural beliefs, which, along with other beliefs, give meaning to the experiences of individuals and families (England, 1986).

HUMANISTIC ALTERNATIVES

Not only the practice research already cited but also case recordings and conversations with social workers suggest that effective practice is less a technical enterprise than it is a creative, reflective, and, to a considerable extent, an artistic and dramatic event. Social workers, if they are not self-consciously involved in devising strategies and interventions, will hear their clients recount a story—a narrative of how they believe things came to be, how they ought to be, perhaps how things might yet be. Entering into the context of the client's life is not far removed from witnessing (and respectfully becoming part of) a drama replete with plot, protagonists, antagonists, crises, and critical choices. In assuming his or her role, the social worker surely is an expert about many things that need to be known or provided; the client, however, remains the expert about his or her reality, which includes the beliefs, values, culture, goals, and other subjective factors that give life meaning and purpose. In effect, these "experts" (literally, client and worker; metaphorically, author and editor or actor and director) join in a collaborative endeavor within a life in process to unravel awareness and the means of confronting certain problems of living.

Theories or frames of reference are necessary for this purpose, as Bosanquet (1916) implied, to inform and enhance our innate sensitivities, intuitions, and hunches. The ideal frame of reference would therefore be of the kind that encourages reflective and penetrating questions that deepen understanding. Such questions direct us, first of all, to the nature of human purpose. They preserve rather than simplify the complexity of the human event. Rather than categorizing, they take into account the variability of human situations. Paradox and uncertainty are seen as reasonable. And not the least, these questions respect feeling, intuition, and imagery as being as important as is logic (Kiefer, 1988).

This frame of reference is in accord with Saleebey's (1988) conception of *generative theory*. Modifying the work of Gergen (1982) for social work, Saleebey makes a useful distinction between theories that "generate" critical thought and questions and the more familiar forms of *normative theory*. The former is pliable, inductive, open-ended, and therefore responsive to new informa-

tion; the latter is deductive, abstract, and serves as a structure within which the human event may be shaped, arranged, and explained. Saleebey observes that normative theories have not readily lent themselves to translation into practice, nor have they helped in translating practice into theory. In addition, normative theories are essentially conservative insofar as they support and rationalize the existing moral, social, and political order; accept conventional wisdom; and denude the elegance of modern practice. Generative theories, in contrast, challenge guiding assumptions of our culture, raise fundamental questions about social life, and generate fresh alternatives for personal and social action.

The generative concept, as it applies to the profession's knowledge base, helps us identify a new range of theories that have made their appearance in the profession's literature as alternatives to the normative or positivistic orientations. A sampling of these theories follows.

Narrative Theory

As a major expression of the interpretive social sciences, the narrative form of understanding is the conceptual scaffold within which the subsequent theories may be organized. In addition, it most closely captures the nature of the human exchange that characterizes the social work relationship.

In this view, one's conception of self, relationships, and life experience is not a collection of facts; rather it is a story—a basic means of communication—that is shaped to offer self and others a quality of meaning and purpose. Whan (1979) states, "These individual tales reflect our culture, not only its folklore, religion and literature, but also its philosophies. . . . Story helps create an awareness of time and history." By revealing the meaning-laden character of social behavior and its interpersonal and environmental contexts (Polkinghorn, 1988), the narrative form not only operationalizes the precept "start where the client is," but offers a sound basis for ongoing dialogue and relationship.

Social Constructionism

Building on the ideas of Gergen, Witkin (1989) refines narrative theory by defining the social processes that influence the way people construct their stories and, thus, their versions of reality. He outlines the four assumptions of this theory: (1) How we understand the world is not primarily based on fact or observation but on the language we inherit and the cultural assumptions and historical precedents that shape our language; (2) as a result, the concepts we employ to describe ourselves and our world are products of the period and the culture in which we live; (3) therefore, how and what we understand depends on the existing sociocultural rules, values, and goals; and (4) this socially shaped understanding justifies how we behave and treat others.

This approach, Witkin states, is consistent with the aims and practice of social work for a number of reasons. By stressing historical, cultural, and linguistic factors, the conception of person-in-environment and the linkages between the two are enriched. Constructionism induces one to examine the values, morals, and beliefs that guide not only the client's but also the professional's intentions and behaviors. Not the least, this orientation offers the profession a practical, common-sense frame of reference for research and practice.

Cognitive Theory

Moving from the social to the personal construction of reality, the theories now emerging from the frontier of the cognitive sciences provide pathways of understanding how the mind works to create meaning and personal truths. Whereas the narrative approach illuminates the themes and plots of living and social constructionism directs us to queries about the contextual sources of meaning, cognitive theories allow us to inquire about individual and shared frames of reference, styles of thinking, and, in general, the way people process their perceptions.

This new knowledge casts serious doubts on the traditional efforts of psychology and psychiatry to classify behavior, traits, motives, and drives as well as on the methods used to change them (Ornstein, 1986). Moreover, brain and mind research confirm the thesis that to understand behavior we must first understand the way that experiences of living are interpreted (Gazzaniga, 1988). Werner (1986) shows that long before the emergence of the cognitive sciences, many cognitive principles guided practice (for example, in functional casework). He goes on to cite many examples of modern translations of this theory for application to present-day practice (for example, Berlin, 1982; Goldstein, 1981a, 1983, 1984; Werner, 1982; Witkin, 1982).

Moral Theory

As long as human behavior was viewed in categorical or deterministic terms, one had little reason to question or pay heed to the moral, ethical, and value-laden beliefs that guide choices and actions. Once we attend to the client's story, however, we begin to appreciate the compelling force of these beliefs. In many ways, we, as helpers, become an audience to the dramatic quality of even the prosaic or somber life, because moral dilemmas are marked by anguish and the absence of easy solutions.

In recent years, some social work theorists have had a rebirth of interest in the moral and valuing realms of being. Siporin (1983) for example, outlines some of the misconceptions of morality and ethics and points to the absence of moral discourse in the profession. This absence, he suggests, not only handicaps social workers in their work with their clients' moral dilemmas, but also creates the false impression that social workers themselves are amoral. In this regard, Imre (1989) outlines the moral responsibilities of social workers and develops the perspective of caring as a guide to moral decisions in practice. In addition, a number of useful texts have appeared in recent years that increase the probability of our developing the kind of moral discourse Siporin believes is necessary (Loewenberg & Dolgoff, 1982; Rhodes, 1986). Rhodes's work is particularly enlightening in that it addresses the neglected elements of power and politics in the helping relationship, which is ordinarily seen as benign and free of coercion.

Faith and Spirituality

Not a theory as such, but nonetheless a motive

force in human belief systems, formal religious commitments as well as spirituality in its broadest sense have regained a measure of professional concern. Despite (or perhaps because of) social work's early religious roots, the ingredient of spirituality or a moral conscience has, until recently, been purposively avoided in theory and practice. Other than recognizing the religious dimension as one variable among many other human variables, the scientific method cannot account for these beliefs.

Again, it is the unforeseen content of the client's narrative that reveals the nature and meaning of his or her faith. Examples of the emerging literature offering conceptual support for openness to these forms of faith include Imre's (1971) theological view of casework, Canda's (1988) scheme for conceptualizing spirituality, and Joseph's study (1988) revealing the need for religious content in education for practice. In more comprehensive terms, Holland (1989) reaffirms the moral and spiritual heritage of social work and contends that the principles derived from this heritage need to be reintegrated into the identity, vocabulary, and practice of our profession.

Feminist Theory

In its own right, feminist theory in social work expresses and sums up many of the theses outlined in this essay. Laird and Allen (1989) refer to the work of feminist social scientists and therapists who have criticized the gendered nature of epistemology that is also evident in social work's development. In accord with the social constructionist view outlined above, they argue that prevailing definitions of gender and mental health are themselves vestiges of a male-dominated, positivistic epistemology. The power of the personal narrative challenges this outlook and provides a basis for creating a feminist frame of reference.

In harmony with the argument stated at the outset, Collins (1986) asserts that "a feminist perspective enables social work to examine itself with new insight, yet in a manner consistent with its tradition and values (p. 218)." Likewise, Wetzel (1986) observes that social work and feminism

share the same values. However, feminists insist on applying their values and ethics, whereas social workers have succumbed to the thrall of status offered by the "objective" systems of positivism, psychoanalysis, and psychodynamics. As a result, their values "lie fallow, disconnected from the people and problems affected by them (p. 167).

The personal narrative has been the traditional means by which women have attempted (often privately and without recognition) to find meaning in their lives. The use of this method is most instructive for social work practice because it reveals how personal and social change may be spurred by the kind of consciousness raising that occurs when people explore their own stories or the stories of others in troubling circumstances. As Jelinek (1980) states,

> Men tend to idealize their lives or to cast them into heroic molds to project their universal import. . . . This is contrary to the self-image projected in women's autobiographies. What their life stories reveal is a self-consciousness and a need to sift through their lives for explanation and understanding. The autobiographical intention is often powered by the motive to convince readers of their self-worth, to clarify, to affirm, and to authenticate their self-image (pp. 14–15).

The Humanities

Defecting from the models of positivism, the scientific method, and technology, which have been the cherished pilots of the profession's search for method and identity, may seem perilous. Like the good mentor or parent, these models promise security of a sort: they lead one to expect that our work with human problems is subject to control, measurement, prediction, systematization, and expertise, promoting the illusion that plans, answers, and solutions exist. Practice experience hardly confirms this hope. Upon entering our clients' lives and worlds, we quickly discover that we are dealing with uniquely personal and often opaque personal constructs and stories, with lives that are fluidly in process, with a culture that is in some ways alien to us, with odd metaphors and uncommon moral overtones, with beliefs in myths, legends, and faiths. Few of these symbolic sets can be explained without distortion by rational-scientific systems of thought.

The kinds of creative, imaginative, and reflective thought that are required to grasp the world as it is interpreted by the client can be stirred by the humanities. In art, literature, drama, philosophy, religion, and history, we discover that our own and our clients' triumphs and struggles have been played out in a multitude of ways in an effort to make sense of living and find meaning within it. The humanities do not profess to offer answers; rather, they encourage the kind of disciplined questioning and reflection that are fundamental to what effective practice may be. Not to be overlooked, the humanities enable us to understand the life of the sciences we depend on, because the various social sciences are human inventions that imply a certain view of human nature, have ethical and political overtones, and specify their own social purposes.

CONCLUSION

In response to the question posed in the title of this essay, social work practice is an everchanging and complex blend of theory, analogue, wisdom, and art. In one respect, this mosaic is a natural consequence of the heterogeneous demands of practice with diverse problems of living. In another, it is the penalty resulting from the doubtful pursuit of scientific respectability. Overlooked in this pursuit was the opportunity to develop and exploit our mission and the unique strengths and competencies that are integral to social work as it is typically practiced.

These competencies fall under the rubric of "practice wisdom." This accretion of knowledge, insights, skills, and values derive from at least three sources. One source is the unique ethos of our profession that is expressed in our concern not only with the whole person and his or her social and physical contexts, but more important, the transactional and symbiotic bond that unites the two. The second involves not only the kinds of problems and conditions that are familiar to social work but the inclusive way (involving family, community, and society) in which we construe them. The third source of practice wisdom, oddly enough, includes not only the knowledge and theories that we import from other disciplines but that which we learn from the lives of our clients and from the experiences we share with them.

The analogic, metaphoric, or eclectic character of practice will persist as long as grand theories, technologies, and systems of practice are adopted in a wholesale, untranslated fashion from other disciplines and traditions of thought. Greater reliance on the generative theories of the interpretive social sciences will help forestall this possibility and enable us to achieve a deeper and more accurate grasp of the subjective realities as well as the beliefs and values of our clients.

In this regard, active social work practice is far more an art than an applied science. Reflectively, creatively, and imaginatively, the mind of the practitioner strives to blend and incorporate fragments of theory, information, intuitions, sensations, and other perceptions into something ambiguously called "understanding." To this end, we might also turn to the humanities for vision and guidance.

In closing, it is worth recalling Richmond's (1920) plea for "pooled thinking" as advice to the profession to turn inward to its own practice wisdom and artistry as dependable sources of knowledge. Reminding us of what we might have achieved, her appeal remains instructive for what we might yet achieve:

> Here you are with more than forty years of striving for social welfare to your credit. You . . . have been the parents of over a baker's dozen of social movements; and, what's more, . . . you have now shaped a way of serving humanity, which bids fair to reorganize every branch of public administration and private endeavor that deals directly with human relations. Only one more decade of earnest practice and discovery at the rate of gain of the last decade and you . . . will have developed a way of studying and adjusting human relations that cannot fail to penetrate our courts, our schools, our industries, and even our municipal departments . . . what, then, are you thinking (p. 1)?

For Further Reading

Bartlett, H. M. (1970). *The common base of social work practice*. New York: National Association of Social Workers.

Gordon, W. E. (1981). A natural classification system for social work literature and knowledge. *Social Work, 262*, 134–138.

Haworth, G. O. (1984). Social work research, practice and paradigms. *Social Service Review, 583*, 343–357.

Imre, R. W. (1984). The nature of knowledge in social work. *Social Work, 291*, 41–45.

Kamerman, S. B., Dolgoff, R., Getzel, G., & Nelsen, J. (1973). Knowledge for practice: Social science in social work. In A. Kahn (Ed.), *Shaping the new social work*. New York: Columbia University Press.

Meyer, C. (1973). Direct services in new and old contexts. In A. Kahn (Ed.), *Shaping the new social work*. New York: Columbia University Press.

Lewis, H. (1982). *The intellectual base of social work practice*. New York: Haworth Press.

Reid, W. J. (1981). Mapping the knowledge base of social work. *Social Work, 262*, 124–132.

Schriver, J. M. (1987). Harry Lurie's critique: Person and environment in early casework practice. *Social Service Review, 613*, 514–532.

Weissman, H. H. (1983). Knowledge base of clinical social work. In D. Waldfogel & A. Rosenblatt, (Eds.), *Handbook of clinical social work*. San Francisco: Jossey-Bass.

Chapter 4

Theoretical Perspectives for Social Work Practice

In this chapter we are going to discuss very briefly some of the theories that we believe support our development of the problem-solving model for social work practice. Only the bare bones of each theory will be presented, as our principal task in this book is to develop a practice model. It is important to recognize that no attempt to state briefly the central issues of a complex set of propositions, even if not misleading in its simplicity, does justice to the totality of the theory. Thus you may wish to consult other sources to clarify any theory presented here.

Ecological Systems Theory

Given the purpose of the profession, it is essential that the theories used as a base of social work practice inform us about the nature of the person-environment interrelatedness and the person-situation transactions. We believe ecological systems theory meets this requirement. It offers a conceptual framework that shifts attention from the cause-and-effect relationship between paired variables (does the environment cause the person to behave in a certain way, or does the person affect the environment in a certain way?) to the person and situation as an interrelated whole. The person is observed as a part of his or her total life situation; person and situation are a whole in which each part is related to all other parts in a complex way through a complex process in which each element is both cause and effect. These dynamic interactions, transactions, and organizational patterns, which are critical to the functioning of both the individual and the situation, are observable only when we study the whole system. Thus the whole is always more than the sum of its parts. In attempting to understand a problem in social functioning, you cannot achieve understanding by adding together, as separate entities, the assessment of the individual and the assessment of the environment. Rather you must strive for a full understanding of the complex interactions between client and all levels of social systems as well as the meaning the client assigns to these interactions. For social workers to carry out their professional purpose as discussed in earlier chapters, their basic theory must allow for problems of dysfunctioning to be lodged in the transactions, lack of fit, opportunities and limitations among the individual and the various levels of environment that make up his or her social system rather than in individual pathology.

It has only been within the past 20 years that social workers have had a systems framework available for use. We are only now becoming comfortable with it because it is so different in perspective from the pattern of earlier thinking that saw the individual as a unit and the environment as another unit without a conceptual framework that allowed for understanding their interrelatedness. Their relationship was perceived as that of the billiard balls in our earlier illustration. In addition, the language of systems is often different from what social workers are accustomed to finding in their literature. However, it is becoming increasingly familiar as we find certain models of practice, such as those found in Hartman's, Germain's, and Minuchin's work, being built on concepts derived from systems theory.

A system is usually defined as a whole, a unit, composed of people and their interactions, including their relationships. Each person in the system is related to at least some others in the system in a more or less stable way within a particular time and space. Although a system should be viewed as a constantly changing whole that is always in process of movement toward its goals, its parts are assumed to interact in a more or less patterned way within a more or less stable structure at any particular point in time. Within a system something is always going on, and that something is not random; it is an effort to achieve the system's goals. Kaplan (1986, p. 16) has suggested that it is possible to compare a system to a tuning fork: "When you strike one end, the other end reverberates." An individual within a social system cannot *not* interact. The absence of overt interaction is in itself an interaction. Systems theory serves social work well in that it offers a conceptual framework that supports the purpose of the profession by shifting our attention from either the person or the environment to problems in the interaction.

As a theory the ecological systems perspective does not present us with directives or prescriptions for action. However, it does give us a theory base on which we can develop a model of a much-expanded repertoire of interventive actions. Systems theory holds that an intervention at any point in the system will affect the entire system. If you want the other end of the tuning fork to reverberate, you may either strike that end directly or you may strike the fork at any place along its length. Thus, as a social worker, you must consider alternative actions that lead to the change sought. An important part of your service to clients involves the careful and creative use of alternatives in planning with your client.

One of the most important concepts in systems theory for social work practitioners is the concept of the open system. According to systems theory, closed systems do not interact with any other systems; they neither accept input from them nor convey output to them. When systems are closed, they are said to have a quality called entropy. What this means is that closed systems over time tend toward less differentiation of their elements (all elements begin to be alike), and thus they lose organization and effective function. All social systems must be open to input from other systems with which they interact if they are to grow and develop. A striking example of this is the problems that social workers find in children of families that have rigid, closed boundaries and do not permit input from other systems in the community. Another example is found in the problems of effectively and humanely governing our prisons, given the fact that they are relatively closed systems in which there is only guarded input across their boundaries.

The individual may be considered a system nested within a person-situation system, but the person as a system is composed of a set of subsystems that operate at another level of organization, such as the physical-biological system, the cognitive system, the emotional system, and the action and reaction system. Beyond the level of the person-situation interaction are larger systems. Thus, open systems exist both above and below the level of the person-situation. Think of this person system as being embedded within a hierarchal arrangement of systems that is characteristic of all living entities. Not only is each system a part of a larger whole, but it is also a suprasystem to other systems. A critical principle for consideration by social workers is that the smaller systems incorporate and assimilate the whole of the larger system into themselves. This principle is reflected in the familiar stance of social work that we need to consider the individual and the environment. Actually the principle probably should read that we should consider the environment as found in the individual. The importance of culture is not only that it is a larger system that surrounds the individual but that culture is also a part of the individual. Simon (1952, pp. 130-139) has called this arrangement "layering," pointing out that the individual, primary groups, organizations, and so on can best be considered as "nests of Chinese blocks" in which any activity taking place in one system at one of these layers will be operating simultaneously in at least one other system (the larger or smaller block) at another level. Another way of conceptualizing this is by use of the system's term *holon,* which means that each level in a system faces both ways, toward the smaller systems of which it is composed and toward the larger system of which it is a part. This concept leads to the principle that any action that a practitioner takes with any piece of the system may affect the whole system and may spread like ripples on the water out into the larger system as well as affect smaller divisions of the system. Thus, your action with an individual is going to affect the family or intimate group of which he or she is a part and will spread from there out into the larger social groups and organizations of which the group is a part. In the same way, actions taken with the individual will affect all systems of that individual, physical, psychological, cognitive, and so on.

Two very important implications of this arrangement are that activity within a particular system relies on the performance of all systems at lower levels and that activity of a system at any given level is a part of and may be controlled by systems at higher levels. New properties emerge at each successively higher level (Magnusson & Allen, 1983a, p. 9). A common example of this principle in operation is the family system. The family as a larger system relies on each individual member to play his or her part if it is to function successfully as an entity in the community. A member of the family who cannot fill his or her function in the family will require that the family make some adjustment to this fact and may, depending on the extent of the failure, severely handicap that family's ability to function. If a parent loses his or her job, each member of the family will suffer individually, and the family as a system will be highly stressed. The parent will seek to find a new job within the larger social system, and if the family is to continue to function at previous levels of behavior, the larger system must provide the parent the resource (work) that is sought. Even if the parent can find no job and his or her children are hungry, the community will take action against him or her if he or she is caught stealing. Or the community may take legal action against the parent if the children are allowed to go hungry. It is assumed that if the children are hungry, the parent should appeal to the public welfare resources of the community. Thus, we see that the community expects the parents of the family to find appropriate ways to feed the children of the family. Two possible ways of doing this are through use of the institutions of the mesosystem—work and welfare. The community will take action against parents who attempt to feed their children through theft or who allow children to go hungry to the point of malnourishment.

We can conceptualize the ability to limit behavior and to offer opportunities for growth on the part of any larger system in its relationships to the smaller systems as power. It has been suggested that power may be the key concept in linking the various levels of systems (Ullman, 1969, pp. 253-266). Certainly this notion is critical for social workers, forcing us to consider the relationship between power, powerlessness, and the processes of human growth and development. We must be aware of how power blocks within the larger social systems may deprive the smaller system of adequate and effective social solutions to problems of growth and development and thus may act to decrease, in the case of the individual, the individual's power to select appropriate alternative solutions to problems of social functioning. Thus an individual may have the personal qualities and resources required to cope effectively with life but may not be able to do so because the larger social system deprives the person of adequate access to appropriate means to do this. It is particularly important that social workers who work with minority clients or concerns be aware of this concept of power and its impact on the smaller social system that is embedded in the larger one.

The discussion of open and closed systems and the layering of systems leads us to the consideration of boundaries.

Boundaries A boundary may be defined as a closed circle around selected variables, where there is less interchange of energy or communication across the circle than there is within the circle. Open systems have, by definition, semipermeable boundaries. However, the relative openness or closedness of those boundaries will vary with the system. All of us are probably familiar with certain communities that are very conscious of themselves, of their entity, and are extremely unwilling to admit strangers or new behavior. Such communities have relatively closed boundaries and in time may well suffer some of the effects of entropy.

We all have met families with such boundaries, boundaries well guarded by careful parents, and we may also know other families in which boundaries seem too open and unguarded to preserve the unit, in which social workers are allowed to intrude at will, with no challenge to their business there. In the beginning of the contact between worker and client system, it is most helpful for the practitioner to observe the qualities of the boundaries of the systems they contact. All healthy systems have well-defined semipermeable boundaries and have ways of maintaining these boundaries. If you, a social worker, visit a family because a child is in trouble with the school or community and a parent greets you at the door with the statement that they need none of your interference, that they can take care of their own children, thank you, you have two pieces of important data. You know that this parent is probably the person in the family charged with boundary maintenance, and you know that the boundaries around this family appear at first contact to be tightly closed. Given closed boundaries, you may expect that the system itself will be in trouble because of lack of input of new information and energy. You also will have questions about what is involved for you in being admitted inside the boundaries. Are the boundaries closed to you only because of the organization you represent or the mission on which you came? Or is this the family's usual way of functioning? If it's the usual pattern of functioning, is it a desperate attempt to protect the integrity of the system or is it a cultural pattern of the family in relating to outsiders? Regardless of the cause of the closed boundaries, you know that they must become more flexible and open for the health of the system. There are other families in which, no matter how serious your message, you are invited in and find yourself sitting in the midst of chaos with no sense that this is any more than a collection of individuals, a collection of people with no meaningful interaction. These families are in serious trouble, and your first clue may be the lack of boundary maintenance. To understand the boundary of a family is simple, but the concept of boundary itself is complex.

The foregoing discussion deals with the empirical boundaries of an actual social system. Social workers are concerned with a second level of boundaries, conceptual boundaries that social worker and client system establish to limit the range of the systems and phenomena that given the problem and goals, are within their range of concern. We might call this the boundary of the system of concern. Social workers confronted with a problem involving the functioning of an individual, a family, or a social group will find that the definition of the problem and the definition of the boundaries of the social systems with which they will work are inextricably related. For example, when an individual brings a problem to a social worker, does the worker define the problem and the boundaries of the social system in such a way that the problem is seen as lying within the boundaries of the individual as a complete social system? Or does the worker define the problem in such a way that the family system becomes the focus of concern and the individual is seen only as a component of the system? Or does the worker believe that the problem falls within the sphere of another institution? The boundaries of a system of concern are established by the practitioner, and it becomes the worker's task to determine what transactions are central to the solution of the problem (Klenk & Ryan, 1974, p. 21).

Tension Tension in human beings or in their organizations can be viewed as a pathological or disturbing factor that occurs only occasionally or residually. In contrast to this notion, systems theory conceives of tension as characteristic of, and necessary to, complex adaptive systems, though there is recognition that tension may manifest itself in either destructive or constructive ways. Thus, systems theory does not attribute a positive or a negative value to tension per se, or even to conflict. Rather, such elements are seen as attributes of all systems simply because they are alive and open to transactions across their boundaries. It is the identification and analysis of how and to what purpose tensions operate within a system and between systems that are of major importance for social work practitioners. Rather than consider "inertia" as a given, or sought for, quality of complex, adaptive systems, with tension occurring as a "disturbing factor, some level of tension must be seen as characteristic of and vital to such systems although it may manifest itself as now destructive, now constructive" (Buckley, 1967, p. 53).

Feedback and Purposive Systems A basic characteristic underlying purposive, goal-seeking mechanisms is that of feedback. By *feedback* is meant "a communications network which produces action in response to an input of information and includes the results of its own action in the new information by which it modifies its subsequent behavior" (Deutsch, 1968, p. 390).

Feedback-controlled systems (and all human systems are thus controlled) are goal directed, "since it is the deviations from the goal state itself that direct the behavior of the system" (Buckley, 1967, p. 53). The goal-directed feedback loop underlying the self-directing human and social systems involves a receptor that accepts information from the outside, an element that imputes meaning to the information, a selector that establishes priorities of information processed, and a mechanism that measures or compares the feedback input against a goal and passes the information on to a control center, which has the capacity of activating appropriate behavior to bring the system in line with its goal (p. 69). The meaning of the feedback is not something in it, or something in the system, but concerns in the interaction between the system and its environment. In the complex adaptive system, there are "multistaged mediating processes" (p. 55) between the reception of feedback and the "output."

The question for the social worker is under what conditions the information carried on the feedback loop promotes change and under what conditions it inhibits change. Two kinds of feedback have been identified. It is generally held that negative feedback carries information that the system is behaving in such a way as to make it difficult to achieve its goal and that such feedback results in behavioral correction in line with goals. Positive feedback is generally held to indicate that the system is behaving correctly in relation to its goal and that more behavior of the same quality is called for. Negative feedback is seen as deviation correcting, since it results in behavioral change back to the goal. Positive feedback, since it calls for more of the same, is seen as moving toward ever greater deviation from the previous state. The important thing here is the goal of the system. It is critical that social workers understand the system as goal directed and that they accept the principle that the system will evaluate the usefulness of the social worker's input into it against its goals. Thus to be optimally helpful the worker needs to know the goals of the system. This is a critical part of meeting clients where they are and addressing oneself to their central concern. In much of social work practice, goals of the client may be ignored, and the helping effort may wander along with no direction, or the worker may see it as within the helper's province to set goals. While the goals of work together may be negotiated, it is critical to the understanding of the client system that you understand how that system wants the problem solved and the place of this desired solution in the life goals of the system.

Change and Stability Because of the openness of human systems and the interaction of elements within their boundaries, it is impossible to conceive of such systems as static. They are constantly in the process of change and movement. And such movements in a human system represent the system's attempt to take purposive goal-directed action. Human systems strive for the enhancement and elaboration of internal order and for the ordering and selection of outside stimuli accepted across the system boundary in such a way that purposive movement toward a selected goal is maintained. At the same time that a system is constantly in a state of change, it must also maintain a dynamic equilibrium. This notion is expressed in the notion of a steady state. Thus although the movement of systems toward some goal is essential to their continued existence, systems also have a need for a certain amount of order and a certain stability. All views of human growth and behavior have some central notion to account for the need for stability and pattern in human life. However, different theories give this notion a more critical place than we do by seeing it as an overwhelming force that needs to be the central concern of the practitioner. Some theories maintain that once a pattern is established, it cannot be changed by the system alone. Because of this force, the system cannot change without help. These theories usually label this concept *homeostatis* and take as their model a thermostatically controlled heating system. What this position ignores is that a system cannot not change. A system is an emergent entity. This way of viewing social systems means that while one recognizes the forces of stability and their utility, one sees the change forces as inevitable. Such forces are generally used by the system to achieve goals, provided that they are not blocked by environmental forces. Thus, instead of being concerned with opposing and changing a force within the client system, the worker is concerned with finding ways to ally worker strength with system strength to deal with the obstacles that lie in the way of growth or positive push in the system. If the direction of the movement of the system appears to be destructive, the worker must first examine and perhaps negotiate system goals so that the innate push of the system toward change can be allied with worker strength.

Equifinality and *multifinality* are two concepts relative to the change and stability of systems that are important to social workers. Equifinality is the capacity to achieve identical results from different initial conditions. If a system is open, it can be shown that the final state will not depend on those conditions. Such a system will have a goal of its own, and the end state will depend on the interactions of the elements of the system and the transactions of the system with other systems in relation to that purpose. The concept of multifinality suggests an opposite principle: similar conditions may lead to dissimilar end states. Thus, similar initial conditions in any living system may or may not be relevant to or causally important in the establishment of the end state.

All systems, over time, develop patterns of recurring interactions. These patterns result in certain routine interactive behaviors between various subsystems. Patterns can be either rigid or flexible. Next time you are a member of a class, observe the seats that members take at the first and following class meetings. People tend to take the same seats each class meeting, although no overt rule has been made about where people should sit. This is an example of the patterned behavior that occurs in a system. Systems function better and meet the needs of both the system and the subsystems when they have a flexible pattern of action and are able to use many patterns and adapt to a variety of situations as opposed to when they use a rigid pattern with few responses available. You can test the rigidity of the seating pattern in a class by taking a seat usually occupied by someone else and observing the behavior of that person. There may be an overt objection to your change of seats. Is the objection brief or is it obviously upsetting to some members to have you change the pattern? If you try to explain that you were testing the rules of the system, is there general acknowledgment of what happened, or do some members give you good reasons why the pattern is important? Such patterns usually operate below the conscious level of the people in the system, particularly in family systems, and people are surprised when the pattern is identified and called to their attention.

All attempts to change a system are based on an identification of such patterns. An example that social workers often see occurs in a family interview in which every time the practitioner asks the adolescent a question, the mother answers. In such a case, the pattern in the family denies the adolescent a certain autonomy, especially when he or she is interacting with someone who is outside the boundaries of the family system.

We may now be dealing with a rule of family behavior. When any outsider enters the family, the mother may answer for all members in the family. Thus each pattern of interaction in a system is based on rules or injunctions about behavior within that system, and the violation of these rules has consequences, as the system has power to limit individual expression. Rules are "implicit and unwritten; indirectly expressed and inferred; recurring over time; self-perpetuating"; and a parsimonious way of dealing with the complexity of interaction (Kaplan, 1986, p. 18). There are two types of system rules. One type of rule is related to behavior; the other type is about how to make rules. We often meet families in which there is an ongoing quarrel over how often the adolescent may date during the week or when she or he must come home. These quarrels may not be over these problems at all but may be the adolescent demanding that the rules about how rules are made be changed to give her or him some participation in making rules. Kaplan gives us a good example of these two types of rules:

> Within the Jackson family, everyone knows that one should not talk while someone else is talking. Although unspoken this rule is understood by each family member. It remains with the family over time, is self-perpetuating, and is learned by watching other family members. Typically, family members bring rules they have learned in their own families into their marriages. The fact that there are rules about how to make rules is illustrated by a mother deciding that her daughter will take out the garbage once a week. This rule tells you that the mother has the power to make rules in the family. Two rules, not one, are evident. (1986, p. 17)

The quotation above illustrates another way rules operate when we move from one system to another. The fact that these rules are unconscious leads to acceptance of the rules as reality—as the way things work. Thus when two people marry and begin their own family system, they may bring conflicting rules into the new relationship. Since each assumes his or her rule is the way things are or should be, there can be many conflicts over which rule is "right," when neither represents a "correct" view of reality, but is simply a residue from an earlier system. This is also an important concept when we move into another culture or when we are working with people from another culture. Neither our way of doing things nor their way of doing things represents the truth, but unless we understand the way larger systems' rules become a part of our reality and a part of ourselves, we will fail in our helping role.

Concept of Role

Another concept that helps us to enrich and expand our understanding and use of systems theory is that of role. This concept can be applied to interaction within the system, but it also serves as a transactional, or bridging, concept between the individuals and the larger social systems in which they are embedded. *Roles* are concerned with the expected behavior of a person occupying a particular social status or position in a social system. Some informal roles are only of importance to persons within a system, such as the role of family joker or the scapegoat. But the formal roles within a smaller system (such as the family) carry important implications for both the individual (the subsystem in this case) and the family because the larger social system (society) has established rules, patterns, and expectations for this particular role within the smaller system.

Remember what we said earlier about the dependence of larger systems on smaller systems and about the larger systems' power to give or withhold opportunities for growth. For example, a person who occupies the role of parent within a family and who violates society's standards for the performance of that role may be punished by the larger system even though the smaller system, the family, has no complaint about how the role is being enacted. We spoke earlier of the fact that there are certain factors of the environment that impact systems of all sizes. We identified the most important of these factors as the extent to which the environment sets limits on the behavior of individuals and the way the environment offers opportunities for their development. It is, in part, through its power to define acceptable role performance that each larger system offers opportunities and imposes limitations on smaller systems and subsystems of smaller systems. Thus role, in combination with power, is a bridging concept that gives us a linkage between larger and smaller systems, because both the larger system and the smaller system have socially constructed notions of what the behavior should be and what it means to fulfill the role. The concept of role gives us one of the ties that is important in assessing a systems network in that it is never a notion that is limited to one system but always involves the system that is expected to operate in the role and the system in relation to which the role is performed. It usually involves the larger society and the culture in that the roots of role performance standards and expectations usually lie in this larger system, and the larger system often has tremendous investment in the carrying out of certain roles in prescribed ways (Biddle & Thomas, 1966).

Social norms for a position provide guides for the attitudes, feelings, and behavior that are permitted, expected, or prohibited for the individual filling that role. These norms will differ from culture to culture. In other words, the cultural environment in which the system finds itself will set different norms and expectations for role occupants. For example, all cultures have prescribed specific role behavior for a woman filling the role and status of mother within the family system. However, these prescribed attitudes and behaviors may differ significantly according to the cultural environment of the particular family system. This fact has great importance for the activities of the social worker in problem definition, data collection, assessment, and interventions.

Three related concepts associated with role are the notions of *role set, role complementarity,* and *role conflict.* Important to the notion of role complementarity and reciprocity is the fact that role positions, or statuses, are usually paired. For every parent there is a child; for every wife there is a husband. If the position of husband is no longer filled in the family system, the role of wife changes to the role of widow, divorced person, or separated or abandoned woman. If a system is to enjoy some stability and integration, there must be some reciprocity of expectations between role partners. If an industrial organization is to be free to pursue its goals, there must be some agreement between persons occupying management and policy-making roles and those occupying labor roles. If a husband and wife are to create a family system with some stability, there must be some agreement between them about how their varying roles will be performed.

The patterns of expected role behavior grow from the need of social systems, as discussed earlier, to have a steady state—to have the stability that comes from being able to predict within some acceptable limits the behavior of elements within the system. These patterns of expectation grow from two types of interaction. First, the opportunities, the deprivations, and the needs in the interactions between elements internal to the system will establish role expectations related to system maintenance and growth. For example, children need protection and nurture if they are to grow and make their contribution to life. The system must answer as to what position, or positions, within the system will be given that job and what behavior from that element will ensure effective care of the child. The second source of the expectations is found within the transactions the system has with other systems and environments. These come from the same sources as discussed earlier. For example, all individuals need food, clothing, and shelter, and depending on the geographic and climatic environment within which people find themselves, patterns of securing these needs will develop. When individuals group themselves into larger systems, certain differentiation of functions that are essential to the functioning of the system will develop. This differentiation will then result in assigning roles to system elements, and expected role patterns will develop. When other systems and environments change, there will be problems within the system as the various elements of the system continue previously patterned behavior. Thus, today one sees conflict between parents and children—the aged and youth—that is largely a conflict between expected role patterns and the changing environment that appears to make certain of these patterns dysfunctional. This will be discussed further under role incongruity.

While there is always room in role expectation for certain individual interpretations and behaviors, when a role is either ascribed or achieved, it is often found that certain aspects of the self are developed and brought out and certain aspects are neglected and often very consciously repressed. This is true of all choices of life. However, the more rigid and circumscribed the notion of role behavior, and the more certain characteristics of the person are tied to role position, the more stress individuals may feel in being placed in, or even in selecting, that role. At the moment many women in our society are very active in trying to change the woman's role. However, this is most difficult, since all members of our society have been conditioned so strongly in sex-role differentiation. Consciousness may be raised, but conditioning is hard to deal with.

The construct of role set or role clusters, which is an array of roles that any one person may be filling at any particular time (Merton, 1957), is an important notion for social workers. Conflict between the various roles in any role set may be particularly painful for the individual or the system involved. For example, employers sometimes defend themselves against charges of discrimination against women by the statement that women are not as much interested in advancement as men and will not fulfill certain prescribed behavior for management roles, such as accepting night work or travel assignments. For the women involved, this type of demand may conflict in particularly difficult ways with the roles of wife and mother that may also be within their cluster of roles. What happens in this situation is that the woman suffers from role conflict. She is involved in two different role sets in two different systems, and the expected behavior of the roles is defined so that the two roles cannot be simultaneously filled satisfactorily by one person.

The role expectations may conflict in at least three ways. The social system of which the system is a part may provide no acceptable alternative for a different solution. The woman's own internalized notions about acceptable behavior within the role may limit her alternatives. And the other occupant of the role pair may hold role expectations that clash with the woman's wishes and generate conflicted interaction between these two primary elements of the system involved.

Role Incongruity   Another construct in role theory has been defined as a situation in which one's own perception of one's role is defined differently from the expectations of significant others in the system or the environment. The concept of the behavior expected of women who occupy the role of mother that has been held by our culture over the years has resulted in denying to women the resources of child care that would allow mothers to occupy with some comfort the role of employee in occupational systems.

Another example of role incongruity is often found in the differing expectations for the behavior of the client system held by social worker and the client system, or conversely, the difference between the client's notion of the role of the worker and that held by the worker. Studies have shown that there is often conflict between the client's expectations that the worker will tell him or her what to do and what actually happens in the interview, which is directed by the social worker's notion of what is helpful. In correctional systems the worker may conceive of the role as that of helper, while the client may conceive of it as one of surveillance and control (Perlman 1961). There may be unrecognized but very painful and difficult problems when a social worker from one culture attempts to deal with role performances of an individual from another culture unless the worker understands the importance of role incongruity. The two cultures may hold very different and conflicting prescriptions about the attitudes and behavior that are appropriate to the role.

For example, an Indian social work student was working with an Indian woman who desperately needed medical care but was too frightened to go to the clinic. In an attempt to act as a broker for her troubled client, the student went to talk to the doctor at the clinic. The student felt very angry and upset because she felt that the doctor had been rude, suspicious, and rejecting. When she shared her perception with her field instructor, it was revealed that she came to this conclusion because the doctor began immediately to question her about the client and continued to ask many very direct questions. This behavior was incongruent with her norms about the way strangers should behave with each other.

In this example the social worker (change agent), coming from a culturally defined role expectation about the way strangers should interact, misinterpreted the meaning of the behavior of an element of an action system she was trying to construct for the client system. Incidentally, a very important principle here is that if the worker misinterpreted the doctor's behavior, how do you think the doctor would have related to the client's expectations?

Even the social scientists who originated the concept of role disagree on its definition and some of the basic constructs and propositions that surround it. However, since the authorities from which it is borrowed disagree, and since borrowed knowledge always has to be reshaped to fit the function of the profession, this discussion on role will be pulled together with some notions of our own

(Compton & Galaway) and some notions taken from the work of another social worker, Helen Harris Perlman (1961, 1962).

Social roles are elements of all social systems and are generally assigned or achieved on the basis of the positions within the various social systems in which we all find ourselves. These expectations involve not only our overt behavior but what we are expected to be and feel like in interaction with what the other is expected to be, to act like, and to feel like (Perlman, 1961, p. 379). In open systems there are two further principles that apply: (1) role prescriptions are very general and allow for certain changes in our behavior, and (2) changes in the way system elements fill their role (acting, feeling, and being) may result in significant system changes (see the discussion in Chapter 6 of the way the change agent may change the change agent system). Thus, change in a system may be brought about by some change in the feeling, acting, or being of an element within the system or by a change in the system's role behavior that affects the transactions of relating systems within larger social systems.

Perlman (1961, p. 375) writes as follows regarding the use of role in social work practice:

> We know it to be true of ourselves that, when we find ourselves in a social situation in which behavioral expectations (role) are not clear, we fumble in trial and error adaptation. When we are clear what the requirements are but find they run counter to our drives and needs, we feel conflicted. When our interpretation of requirements is different from the interpretation made by the person with whom we interact, both conflict and confusion may result. When requirements themselves are ill-defined or inadequately defined, we may feel and act in diffuse and inept ways.

To summarize, the following concepts from role theory are important to social workers:

1. Certain behaviors are prescribed (by us and by other elements of our social system) relative to our position within that system.
2. Every role involves both our own expectations and abilities and those of one or more other people.
3. The notion of role expectation implies that there are certain social norms that set the outside limits for congruent, nonconflicted interactions and transactions between positions within the system and between systems.
4. There are emotionally charged value judgments to how people carry out their roles both on the part of the person occupying the role position and others.
5. Social functioning may be seen as the sum of the roles performed by a human system (Boehm, 1959a, pp. 95-97).
6. The concept of role, role functioning, role expectations, and role transactions may be used to increase the knowledge base used for the assessment of the problem situation. Role failure and/or role conflict will tend to follow:
    a. When resources necessary to a system's ability to perform a role well are lost or absent.
    b. When systems are thrust into new roles without knowing the role expectations.
    c. When there is a conflict in role expectation on the part of interacting systems.

    d. When there is a conflict of role expectations within the cluster of roles carried by one system.

    e. When there is ambiguity on the part of other systems about role expectations.

    f. When the individual as a system, or as a member of a social system, is deficient or handicapped in physical, intellectual, or social capacities demanded by the role.

    g. When high feeling or crisis suddenly and without warning disrupts previously effective role patterns (Perlman, 1962, pp. 17–31).

Potential Values of Systems Theory

Some potential values of systems theory as an organizing framework for social work knowledge are as follows:

1. Systems theory allows one to deal with far more data than does the analytical model, enabling one to bring order into a massive amount of information from all the different disciplines on which social work must draw. It is the collection and ordering of the data that give structure to all else in the social work process, as all else is operational.

2. The concepts relating to systems and their development, function, and structure are equally applicable to the range of clients served by social workers, from the individual to society.

3. Systems theory provides a framework for gaining an appreciation of the entire range of elements that bear on social problems, including the social units involved, their interrelationships, and the implications of change in one as it affects all.

4. Systems theory shifts attention from the characteristics possessed by individuals or their environments to the transactions between systems, changing the vantage point of the data collector and focusing on interfaces and the communication process that takes place there. Social work has long been struggling to see individuals and their environments as complete units.

5. Systems theory sees people as active personality systems capable of self-initiated behavior and thus able to contribute to and alter their environment's behavior or even to create new environments. Adaptation of the environment is as much a property of human systems as is the tendency to be affected by or adapt to the environment. These concepts negate the tendency to see disturbances as pathology and move the worker into the present life of the system.

6. The concept of systems as purposive, combined with the concepts of equifinality and multifinality, radically changes the view of both causation and the possibilities for change. It supports the worker's concern with self-determination and with the client's participation in the change process, and it emphasizes the necessity of knowing and considering client goals in assessment and planning of intervention.

7. The use of systems theory brings the purpose of the system into the center of the worker's consideration, engendering further concern with self-determination and the necessity of relating professional feedback to client purpose.

8. If a living open system requires constant transaction with other systems and its environment for its progressive development, a major function of social workers must be the provision and maintenance of such interchange opportunities for all populations.

9. Given what systems theory tells us about closed systems, social workers must be increasingly concerned with populations and systems heading toward isolation, with the strains in our society that result in isolation, and with our now isolated populations.

10. If change and tension are inherent in open systems, social workers must direct their attention to why suggested changes may be resisted and why such changes become unbearable for a system. This further emphasizes the principle of meeting clients where they are and with self-determination. It removes the notion that tension or conflict is pathology.

11. The concept of system boundary gives us a new way to observe the systems with which we work. It tells us to expect certain caution and testing from healthy systems and to be concerned with the health of systems that are too open or too closed. It speaks to social workers' concerns with clients' rights and recognizes that social workers should be concerned with the ways they and their services move across the boundary of a social system.

12. The recognition that change in one part of a system can often greatly affect the whole means that one must be increasingly aware of the impact of intervention in the broader transactions of clients. In addition, it speaks to the fact that it is not necessary to change a whole system to bring meaningful change but that the point of intervention must be chosen with care. It broadens the concept of the points at which a system can be entered, provides one with more ways of entering effectively, and may make the intervention simpler.

13. The systems perspective also places the agency as a social system and the worker and client in the same transactional field. Social workers are a social system and are involved as components of a social system network.

In summary, we see the person-situation interaction as an open system with all the qualities we have discussed about open systems. The person-situation system exists within a hierarchical arrangement of systems that extends from the individual as a very small system of interacting variables to the macro level of society and culture. The precise nature of an individual's social functioning will depend on a variety of factors present in the interaction of person, situation, and environment.

Basic Conceptual Systems in Social Work Practice

At this point there will be a brief departure from the development of basic knowledge to insert some material related to a conceptual practice framework. We are inserting this material here because it has to do with systems theory and it will be referred to from time to time as the material in the next few chapters is developed. The notions to be discussed were developed originally by Allen Pincus and Anne Minahan (1973, pp. 54–74) as a model for teaching social work practice.

According to the discussion of systems theory, most of the examples used so far have involved what could be called client systems. However, social workers do some of their most important, time-consuming, and demanding work with people other than those traditionally viewed as clients. In "The House on Sixth Street" (Appendix, A-7) the change efforts were primarily focused on other than the client system, although client skills in problem solving were improved. Social workers often find that if they are to help clients solve problems in social living, their primary focus may involve work with other systems. If the practitioner works in protective services for children, there will also be the necessity to work with court services, medical services, neighbors, police, attorneys, and perhaps the school system and foster parents or other child-care services. As a practitioner in a child-care agency, the worker may be involved with the children and their families, medical resources, the school, foster parents, and perhaps community centers and organized groups outside of the agency boundaries. If the agency has a residential center, the worker will be involved with others who have contact with their clients—the maintenance staff, child-care staff, teachers, and perhaps nurses inside the agency. In addition to the people they see outside of the agency, the workers are always a part of an organized structure in which they do their work. Even in private practice they will usually have a secretary and someone to answer the telephone with whom they interact as a system. Workers usually think first of their clients, who they feel are the people they are there to help, but they may want to consider seriously who really benefits from their change efforts. Who is the client in the case of child abuse—the child, the parents, or the community that asked the worker to get involved? Who gives the worker the right to interfere in other people's lives? Who sanctions what the worker does? In daily transactions between themselves and others, workers find that they are working with many different people about different things and for different reasons to achieve some overall goal.

Pincus and Minahan (1973, pp. 54–74) suggest that the people with whom the worker interacts in practice actions can be classified into four types of social systems: the change agent system, the client system, the target system, and the action system. To this could be added two more systems: the professional system and the referral-respondent system. The decision of the worker about the purpose and the relationships that should be a part of each encounter will determine the definition of the system. The systems that make up social work practice may be described in the following ways.

The Change Agent System   Social workers may be viewed as change agents, specifically employed for the purpose of planning and working with the six systems toward the planned change. The agency or organization that employs them or of which they are a part can be thought of as the *change agent system*. Obviously, the agent system heavily influences the worker's behavior through various policies and resources that represent sanctions, constraints, and resources. These will be discussed in greater detail in the Chapter 6 section on sanctions.

The Client System   People may be considered to be a part of the client system when (1) they have either asked for or sanctioned the worker's services; (2) they are expected to benefit from these services; (3) they have entered into an explicit or implicit contract with the worker (See the discussion on contracts in Chapter 11). This definition leads to a brief consideration of the nature of the first coming together of client and worker. There are clients who come to the agency voluntarily seeking the help of the worker, but there are large numbers of situations in which the worker approaches the client because the agency function calls for it to assume this type of responsibility in behalf of the community (which should be considered the client at this point); for example, corrections, child welfare, protection for the aged and incompetent, and so on. Also, a neighborhood center staff (a change agent system) may identify what they see as a neighborhood need and ask a staff member to form an organization to deal with it. In all these instances the community or the change agent system itself may more appropriately be considered the client than the people the worker approaches "to help." The people identified as targets of the worker's efforts are more appropriately regarded as potential clients or respondents until some sort of agreement is reached in which potential clients sanction the worker's intervention in their lives and transactions. This principle will be discussed further in several parts of the text, as it is a crucial one that is often not understood. An interesting example is found in "The Stover Family" (Appendix, A-6). The worker attempted for several months to engage Mrs. Stover concerning care of her children, only to have the woman become a client when she needed financial help.

The Target System The people that the change agents "need to change or influence in order to accomplish their goals" are the target system (Pincus & Minahan 1973, p. 58). The target system and the client system often overlap when it is the client or the client's part in an intersystem transaction that needs to change. However, much of social work practice involves the social worker working with the client system toward some desired change in some other system (a target system).

The term *action system* is used to describe those with whom the social worker interacts in a cooperative way to accomplish the purposes of the change effort. There are an endless number of different action systems in which the worker may be engaged. Chapter 14 will deal with the skills of teamwork; this is essentially a discussion of the ways of working with action systems made up of professional or paraprofessional people. However, action systems may be a neighborhood group, a family group, or others that the worker works with toward bringing about a change helpful to the client. You will find an interesting example of workers' efforts to develop an action system in the case of "Pain Clinic Evaluation" (Appendix, A-3). The worker suggests using a number of resources to help the client deal with pain.

Professional System This system is made up of the professional association of social workers, the educational system by which workers are prepared, and the values and sanctions of a professional practice. The values and the culture of the professional system strongly influence both the required and the permitted actions of the worker as change agent. In working to change their own agency or in acting as an advocate of social change, practitioners often use the professional system.

Referral-Respondent System We discussed this system earlier to differentiate it from the client system. We believe it is important to recognize that unless intervention is clearly in the interests of the client and with his or her agreement, a system cannot be considered a client system. If you approach a client at the request of someone else, or a client comes to you because he or she is ordered to do so, the client system is truly the person who brought you together. To differentiate this system from the usual client system, we have chosen to call it a **referral** system and call the person who is sent or comes under duress a **respondent.** When the person who comes because of the influence or orders of another person accepts the fact that you can help him or her and expresses a wish for help, he or she becomes a client.

Ego Psychology as Foundation Knowledge

The most complete theory of human development is psychoanalytic theory as first developed by Sigmund Freud and further refined and expanded by countless disciples. There are several problems involved in any attempt to treat psychoanalytic theory briefly. First, there is the need to differentiate between the concept of human development found within psychoanalytic theory, the notion of how people get in trouble and how they change that is a part of this theory, and the method of treating human psychological disorders that was based on this theory. Because of the complexity and volume of psychoanalytic theory, we will not try to present any coherent summary in this chapter. We suggest instead that students of social work may want to seek other sources of such understanding. The theory is introduced here only because certain concepts from ego psychology rest on a psychoanalytic base about the development and functioning of the human personality, and thus understanding psychoanalytic theory is important to knowing and using ego psychology.

Psychoanalytic Constructs Psychoanalytic theory conceives of the human being as a dynamic energy system consisting of basic drives and instincts that in interaction with the environment serve to organize and develop the personality through a series of developmental stages. Individuals are pushed from birth by these largely unconscious and irrational drives toward satisfaction of desires that are largely unconscious and irrational. Because of the operation of an unconscious defense system and the structure of the mind, people go through life largely unaware of these irrational forces, which have tremendous effect on their behavior and on the way they relate to others. The behavior that others observe and our own knowledge of our behavior and our purposes are actually a very incomplete view of what we are as individuals and what drives us. Most of the motivating forces of personality are thus beneath the surface and are available to our conscious and rational understanding and direction only through a careful exploration of these buried regions. Thus an individual's personality is seen primarily as an elaboration of the unconscious irrational drives with which each of us is born and the early vicissitudes that lay down a foundation of personality in early childhood. The personality system is viewed as primarily a semiclosed energy system that operates primarily to conserve energy by resisting stimulus and change. Because individuals are seen as being driven by these unconscious forces that tend primarily to struggle to maintain a homeostatic balance, real change in behavior after childhood can come only through an experience that is able to reach the deepest levels of one's personality. The environment and happenings in the world around us have an impact on us as individuals and on our behavior only through the meanings we assign such events as a result of our unconscious needs and defenses.

Freud held that the personality was structured into three divisions: "The id comprises the psychic representatives of the drives, the ego consists of those functions which have to do with the individual's relation to his environment, and the superego comprises the moral precepts of our minds as well as our ideal aspirations" (as related in Brenner 1955, p. 45). The ego is expected to act as the executive officer of the personality, dealing with impulses from the id and with moral signals of the superego as well as with the realities of the environment.

It is our position that classical psychoanalytic theory, taken in its entirety, does not serve social workers well because of the basic assumptions on which it rests. The theory assumes that people primarily seek freedom from discomfort, choosing comfort and peace rather than growth. The theory is deterministic in that the human personality is seen as a semiclosed rather than an open system. As a semiclosed system analogous to such mechanical devices as the thermostat, people strive to conserve energy and to return to their previous state, homeostasis. The need of the system is primarily for stability rather than for some balance between stability and change. Thus there is always great resistance to change. The primary motivating factor is freedom from internal conflict, and people can be pushed into change only by unendurable discomfort. The notion of goals and the importance of hope in motivation are not a part of this theory. People change only to avoid a greater discomfort. Thus the notion of motivation rests only on discomfort or anxiety.

Over the years various individuals working with the concepts of psychoanalytic theory and observing human behavior began to focus primarily on the development of the rational conscious processes in personality. They are called ego psychologists, because coming from a base in psychoanalytic theory, they have differed in that they have given the central place in human functioning not to the irrational and instinctual forces of the id but to the rational processes of the ego. They hold that the individual comes into this world with rational as well as irrational instincts and that the personality develops and becomes differentiated in relation to the environmental interactions, concerns, goals, and unconscious needs rather than being almost entirely an elaboration of inner instinctual drives. Ego psychologists believe that rather than being fixed early in life, personality is constantly developing.

Ego Psychology Constructs Eric Erikson, one of the earliest ego psychologists, held that although early experience was significant, the personality system all through life was open to meaningful interaction with both the inner and outer life experiences. The notion that throughout life new tasks and new biopsychosocial demands bring human beings new opportunities for growth and change was an important departure from the older psychoanalytic beliefs. However, the manner in which these opportunities are used will be reflective of the individual's success and failure in dealing with earlier life tasks (Hartman, 1970).

Ego psychologists began to challenge the earlier psychoanalytic view of the conservation of energy and the notion of a semiclosed system. They argued for the construct of an open personality system, as they believed there was empirical evidence that human beings were born with an ego need to seek both difference and stimulus from the environment. Thus in ego psychology personality development is seen as the result of interaction with the environment that is actively sought by the individual. Another earlier concept that was challenged was the notion of the personality's push toward static homeostasis. This concept was replaced by the notion that while the personality needs certain stability, people also seek and must have for appropriate growth and development new experiences and new transactions from the environment. In this notion systems theory is in agreement with and supported by ego psychology.

Competence and Mastery   Robert White's works (1959, 1963) further developed the notion that individuals are motivated from childhood on to interact actively with the environment, not merely as a result of drives such as hunger, thirst, and sex but because of a need to explore the world and to import new experiences and stimuli into the system. White has called this motive **effectance,** by which he means a kind of general push from the ego to master the environment. When individuals master a new experience in line with their standards and with the approval of the real world (called **competence** by White), they are innately motivated to try new and more complex tasks. White called this motivational force a push toward mastery. This notion is discussed further by Trader (1977) in her article on the theories that form the base of effective work with minorities, discussed in Chapter 5.

White holds that as a result of experiences of competency, individuals grow to feel a sense of mastery—a belief that one can change one's environment by obtaining knowledge of how to change it and by the use of effective skills that one has developed. The concept of learned helplessness (explained later in this chapter) supports this notion by discussing what happens when persons are deprived of ways of controlling their environment. These concepts have tremendous significance for social workers in that they support the notion that given a relatively benign environment, individuals actively seek control of their lives and welcome new experiences. Resistance to change and apathy are seen as states resulting from environmental lacks and hurtful interactions and transactions over time. Thus the forces of growth and change are seen as stronger than the resistance to change, provided the individual's transactions with the environment and other systems have offered experiences of effectance and mastery leading to a sense of competence.

In ego psychology, the ego is seen to be the part of the personality that takes action in life situations—it is the executive officer of the personality. In the process of coping, the ego develops both protective-defensive operations and seeking-discovering-learning operations. "The main categories of ego functions are its clusters of cognitive, affective, motoric, executive, and integrative operations" (Perlman, 1975, p. 214). Cognitive functions are the thought processes that consist of facts, notions, concepts, memories, and beliefs and the way this material is acquired, stored, retrieved, organized, and reorganized. The affective functions of the ego have to do with our feeling processes: anger, guilt, hate, love, caring, and excitement. The executive function of the ego involves decision making and action. Decision making rests on the ability to perceive one's natural and external environment accurately, to think logically and analyze, to integrate thinking, feeling, and a sense of mastery, and on the possession of action skills with which to carry through with some satisfaction on the decisions.

All these functions of the ego are interrelated, and each affects the others. Feeling affects thought; thought affects feeling. Action can bring significant change in both thinking and feeling. The feedback that a system receives from the environment about its actions affects thinking, feeling, and future actions. Since these things are true, it is equally true that individuals can intervene to change the total functioning of any system by approaching any one of the three functions. Thus, we may begin work with thinking, feeling, or action. Where we will begin depends on how we assess the client system, the problem, the goal, and the situation and what the client wants. It is important to the selection of helping actions to remember that coping skills of the individual can be increased by starting with whichever function seems appropriate as our activity in one area will affect all functions.

Motivation From these concepts of ego, competence, and mastery there has developed some important work on motivation. A feeling of mastery, or control over one's internal reactions and relevant external events, appears to be a significant force in motivating human behavior (Liberman, 1978, p. 35). A number of laboratory investigations in the area of the importance of control is summarized by Lefcourt (1966, p. 188) as follows: "When individuals are involved in situations where personal competence can effect . . . outcomes, they tend to perform more actively and adequately than when . . . situations appear less controllable." Thus "insofar as individuals believe that their actions and inactions affect their well-being, the achievement of a sense of mastery becomes a major goal throughout their lives" (Liberman, 1978, p. 36). Liberman further points out that for an individual to acquire a sense of mastery, there must be a framework that links a person's performance to self-esteem. The link between performance and self-esteem is governed among other things by the person's background and current situation, task relevance, task difficulty, attribution of performance, and the attitudes of significant others.

The faculty of the School of Social Work of the University of Chicago, interested in determining what factors influenced the client's effective use of social service, decided to investigate whether client motivation, capacity, or opportunity was most central to problem resolution. They defined motivation as what a person wants and how much he or she wants it. In congruence with the principles of ego psychology discussed earlier, they discovered that the forces of motivation were hope that one can achieve the goals one seeks and discomfort because one has not achieved those goals as yet (French, 1952). They also discovered that what the worker did about the hope factor in the first interview was the most important factor in involving persons in effective problem solving. (Ripple, Alexander & Polemis, 1964). These concepts may be summarized as follows: People will not move toward change unless they see that change will aid them in achieving their (not the worker's) goals and they have a significant commitment to achieving that goal. The commitment to the goal will be determined by the balance between hope that they can achieve the goal and discomfort with not having achieved it as yet. These principles were further tested by a research and demonstration project that sought to discover whether clients labeled "untreatable" could actually be reached and helped by practice based on and guided by these concepts. This project found that these concepts, expanded by a more complex notion of discomfort, were a key to helping people (Compton, 1979). In order for discomfort to serve as a force for problem solving, it must be at a manageable level and focused on the problem to be solved. Clients whose experience has resulted in failure in all aspects of living develop an enveloping, all-pervasive sense of discomfort that results in a deterioration of goal-directed efforts. Thus a sense of discomfort that pervades all areas of one's life results in a sense of helplessness and apathy. This is supported by the work done by many others on the development of a sense of frustration and helplessness that is discussed later.

The pull toward goal-directed effort is provided by hope. Hope increases the amount of pressure that can be withstood before the disintegration of goal-directed efforts begins. When one is hopeful that one can effectively move toward what one wants, one becomes willing to forego other satisfactions and withstand other pressures from other needs and wants to realize the greater goal or want. This is why we feel it is important to establish a tentative goal in the first interview. It supports and expands the client's hope of achieving a desired outcome and thus generates motivation. Based on the work of Perlman (1957), Towle (1948, 1950), French (1952), White (1960, 1963) and Ripple (1956, 1964) and our own experience, we believe a sense of hope is based on (1) a sense of trust that there is some relationship between one's needs and the intentions of the world around one; (2) a sense that one has meaning for others, that one's actions are important; (3) a sense of who one is; (4) a sense of competence built on evaluation of past efforts (past successes as one evaluates them); (5) perception of the opportunities in the environment around one; (6) one's experience with frustration in the past; (7) a generalized sense of mastery; and (8) relationship between one's perception of one's competence and one's perception of the skills needed to reach the goal.

Thus, one's capacity to use the want and discomfort of motivation to change in a goal-directed way depends first on hope and second on how much one knows of how to achieve a purpose. This includes the ability to see the totality of the situation, including the results of choices made in the process, the time factors, and the possible obstacles; reassurance from the real world; and experiences with the real world, including the pleasure in functional activity, substitute gratifications, and appropriate evaluation of achievement of subgoals or small steps.

In discussing motivation it is important to mention frustration. It is possible to avoid frustration by avoiding a commitment to a goal. Severe and repeated frustration will move an individual in this direction. Frustration is the realization that the goal to which one is committed is unattainable. The intensity of frustration is proportional to the degree of previous commitment to the purpose being thwarted. If goal-directed striving is frustrated after a particular quantum of pressure is committed to it, perhaps it is possible to find substitute goals so that the pressure can be rechanneled. If substitute goals are not found, it is possible that the pressure and desire may be discharged in destructive forms such as rage. If one has been pursuing a goal with confidence and the goal becomes unattainable, hope is destroyed and overt rage is produced. The experience of frustration over time is destructive of an individual's sense of competence and mastery. Frustration ends with the disintegration of goal-directed striving. The end phase of loss of hope is apathy and learned helplessness.

The research by Ripple, Alexander and Polemis (1964) attempted to assess the importance of the three constructs for the client's effective use of social work services: motivation, capacity, and opportunity. Their findings were that the client's level of hope plus the opportunities available were the critical factors in use of services. In spite of a belief that the personality functioning of the client and the type of problem are important, these factors did not appear to have a critical impact on the use of help. As a result of her research Ripple recommended that in the initial explorations of the client's problem the worker make a careful assessment of the hope-discomfort balance. Ripple further recommended that workers should be concerned with the impact of their activities on this critical balance during the beginning stages of client-worker interaction.

The Concept of Learned Helplessness

The concept of learned helplessness, while not formally a part of ego psychology, fits neatly with White's concepts of competence and aids in the understanding of unmotivated and apathetic clients. We believe it is critical that social workers understand this concept. We are troubled when we hear social workers say that they cannot help people who are unmotivated and apathetic. Apathy and lack of motivation should be seen as an individual's response to the extent to which the environment offered opportunities in the individual's struggle to be competent and the extent to which the environment limited the individual's effort to cope with life. If the individual is to develop competence and autonomy in social functioning, she or he must be able to make valid predictions about the response of the environment to individual action. Thus the environment that the individual experiences must be patterned and consistent, and certain interventions into certain problematic situational conditions must generally lead to certain outcomes, so that it is possible for the individual to make valid predictions about the outer world and the effect of individual action. The individual must have some confidence that as in the past, what seems to be a problem is reasonably responsive to his or her efforts.

These are critical concepts for social workers because we so often deal with people whose lives consist of prolonged crisis in which they repeatedly experience the inability to have any impact on the arbitrary and bewildering responses they receive from the environment. Social workers often speak of unmotivated or apathetic clients, assigning the client these qualities with no consideration of how such apathy develops. But for people to take action and engage in the processes of changing their lives, they must be convinced that they can correctly predict the effects of their actions. Seligman writes: "Helplessness is a psychological state that frequently results when events are uncontrollable" (1975, p. 9). In this state people believe that nothing they do makes any difference in their lives. "Learned helplessness produces a cognitive set in which people believe that success and failure is independent of their own skilled actions" (Seligman 1975). We believe, along with Seligman, that if people are to develop competence, initiative, and autonomy, the response of the environment to their efforts and their actions must be comprehensible, ordered, and consistent. When we encounter people who have met defeat regardless of the coping strategies they have used or who have constantly experienced inconsistent responses to the same coping strategies, we should not be surprised when they appear helpless.

Before assigning the properties of apathy and lack of motivation to clients, we must examine what has happened and is happening in their lives. What kind of control do they have over life events? How does the situation respond, if at all, to the client's efforts? If the situation constantly responds to the client's efforts in a negative or inconsistent way, the client will be in a bad way indeed if he or she does not learn by experience to stop his or her efforts to act in that situation. In an article in *Social Work* Hooker (1976) writes, "Learned helplessness may develop when individuals believe they have no control over events—even when those events could actually be affected by their behavior."

The significance of a person's beliefs about his or her control over life events can be gleaned from the work of Greer, Davison, and Gatchel (1970, pp. 731–738). Their study of the relationship between stress and perceived control revealed that individuals who believed they had control over the aversive stimuli in the experiment found these conditions much less stressful than did those who believed they had no control over them. Geer, Davison, and Gatchel postulated that the subjects who experienced less stress did so because their belief in their ability to control the aversive stimuli allowed them to label the condition as one in which they were not helpless.

To recapitulate, the experimental evidence indicates that learned helplessness develops when one objectively is or believes oneself to be unable to control the outcome of events. This cognitive disturbance gives rise to the motivational and emotional aspects of learned helplessness. A person who believes himself or herself to be unable to control the outcome of life events and fails to see that his or her actions make a difference is less motivated to try. Based on the observation that helpless subjects quit responding and passively endured trauma—even under controllable conditions—Seligman et al. (Seligman, 1974, pp. 83–107; 1975, pp. 54–55) contended that the emotional manifestation of learned helplessness is reactive depression. (1975, p. 195)

Significant Contributions of Ego Psychology to Social Work Knowledge

1. The concept of the ego as having its own needs and drives and as being autonomous, coupled with the belief in the human personality as emergent and developing over a life cycle, gives importance to helping efforts directed to present life experiences.
2. The concept of the personality as an open system gives great weight to the importance of the day-by-day input from transactions with the environment. It joins with systems theory to support the importance of the active involvement of the client system with a benign environment.
3. The construct of the individual's need for competence and mastery offers social work an optimistic view of the possibilities of human growth and change while demanding that social workers be constantly concerned with input from networks of other social systems and environment.
4. Concepts from ego psychology focus on individuals as active conscious participants in their own destiny rather than as reactors to stimuli or to needs beyond their control. This leads to the concept of the relationship between the worker and the client system as a partnership.
5. The constructs of competence and mastery from ego psychology support the view of human beings as seeking active experiences and control of their own destiny. This gives guidance in assessment, demands that client systems be active participants in planning and change, and supports social work values of self-determination and respect for the individual.
6. The notion that motivation is what the client system wants and how much it wants it joins with the concept of goal in systems theory to remind social workers of the importance of both client system goals and the value of self-determination.
7. The importance of hope as a stimulus for active problem solving gives social workers a totally new view of the meaning of apathy and challenges many of the other concepts of what produces dependency.

Concepts of
Stress,
Coping, and
Crisis

Understanding of the concepts of stress, coping, and crisis is an important part of the knowledge base of social work practice. Much of social work practice involves engagement with the client system at some point between the system's (or some other concerned system's) identification of a stress situation as threatening and either the point at which the individual's coping devices have been exhausted and the situation remains threatening (crisis) or the point at which the system is depressed and apathetic because of the belief that resolution of troubles is impossible. The notions of stress, crisis, and coping are important to social work practice in that they, like role, give us some further linking concepts between the microsystem and the environment. In working for policy and administrative change in larger social systems, we are essentially working toward making changes in the larger system that makes the resources of social institutions more easily available as a part of the normal coping repertoire of the smaller systems.

There is an extensive literature on stress, including considerable work on the connection between major events in life and physical illness. There is considerable controversy about how stress should be defined. For our purposes here we define stress as the tension that arises in a system—individual, family, group, and so on—from the perception of an event as involving uncertainty and risk. For many systems stress may precipitate appropriate problem-solving activities leading to effective choice of alternatives, appropriate choice-directed action, and a satisfying solution. Thus for many of us the feeling of stress is at least semipleasurable. We gear ourselves up to meet a challenge, the risk and the uncertainty imparting an excitement to our efforts to solve a problem effectively. However, we may interpret other life events differently and may perceive them as a loss or a threat. There are other people who interpret all such events as beyond their capacity to influence and therefore as disasters before they make any attempt to problem-solve.

In the literature stress and coping are usually linked as related phenomena. Certainly for social workers the understanding of the coping patterns of the client is critical. You must understand the generalized coping resources of the client and how these resources are generally used. You must also determine the client's ability or inability to mobilize or successfully use these mechanisms. Generalized coping resources can be divided into several categories that you must assess in working with client systems. Perhaps the first and most basic category is that of beliefs and attitudes toward life. In keeping with the notion of motivation being composed of hope and discomfort, someone who does not believe that effort will produce results will not be motivated to marshal coping resources. And in keeping with the concept of learned helplessness, someone who does not see that he or she has any input into what happens or its outcome will be apathetic. Antonovsky, a medical sociologist who has done significant studies on stress and illness throughout the major countries of the world, maintains that people who believe that life is an orderly, purposive process in which processes can be understood and outcomes are generally for the best suffer less debilitating illness than their cohorts, no matter how severe the level of stress. While we may often neglect to explore this aspect of our clients' lives, it would appear that perhaps the most powerful coping mechanism is a belief in life.

The second large group of coping mechanisms includes the range of one's knowledge and successful experiences with life tasks and one's cognitive capacities and ability to reason from cause to effect. The ability to control and use emotional and affective responses to the stress is an important coping ability. The fourth important class is that of the environmental resources available to one. Perhaps one of the most important resources we possess in our society is money. Money aids us in coping by giving us the means to purchase services or things we may need (a satisfying environment), and its power serves to assure us that we are worthwhile and capable of controlling our own destiny. The second large subgroup of resources is the network of supporting social systems that may be available to us. The last important group of coping mechanisms is the skills to carry out planned action. Such skills usually come from past successful experiences (Antonovsky, 1980, pp. 98–182).

Concepts of Diversity and Difference

We also need a theory that supports the importance of difference in the development of human societies, that recognizes that human organizations grow and develop through the expression of individual differences, and that demands respect for diversity. Such foundation theories mean that our standards of health and/or normality have to include a range of coping behaviors and value positions that allow for individual diversity and for minority or ethnic group differences. Such theories are congruent not only with social work functions in society but with the core values of social work practice that demand respect for the individual and the unique ways people deal with their life situations. Exhibit 3-1 offers a very simple example of human difference. What do you see as you look at it? Do you see a vase or two faces? Both perceptions are correct, but could you imagine an argument between two people who see it differently over which view is "normal" or "correct" and therefore evidence of mental health or intelligence?

This notion of equal but different is very difficult to understand because of the human tendency to assume that if two objects are different, one must be of innately

EXHIBIT 4–1
Do You See a Vase? Or Is It a Picture of Two People Facing Each Other?

more worth than the other or one must be right and the other wrong. It is easy to confuse the concept of same with the concept of equal.

Often in discussing equal rights of men and women, someone will protest that this is impossible, as men and women are obviously different, thus confusing sameness and equality. Yet to offer the same education or the same opportunities to two different people with different wants and needs may be a violation of the notion of equality. It appears that no society in the world exists without some oppression of the different by those who by reason of possession of valued resources have oppressive power. Such resources may be money, cattle, physical strength, knowledge, or education. Those who have the power to impose their will on other groups that are different tend to assign the highest value to the qualities they possess and less desirable qualities to the others. For example, in our society, women, blacks, and children tend to be assigned similar qualities. These groups are seen by many as careless, carefree, emotional, excelling in song and dance, impulsive, and have great difficulty with logical abstract reasoning. Once certain qualities are assigned members of a group, it is commonly assumed all members are alike in the possession of these qualities.

It is often difficult for any one of us to see a person as an individual with individual differences because of the nature of human learning. We learn by categorizing people, objects, and experiences and assuming a certain commonness to whatever falls within the category. We use such categories to communicate with others. For example, when we speak of a tree to another English-speaking person, we are understood by the other person to be speaking of a certain group of growing things. However, if the person we addressed was an expert in forestry, he or she would want to know a great deal more about the tree. As a specialist in trees, he or she must know much more than the broad classification, and each piece of knowledge leads increasingly to the individualization of a particular tree. Thus we, as specialists in human interaction, cannot be satisfied with putting people in broad categories based on certain innate characteristics such as sexual organs or skin color. Neither can we see all people who are of a common ethnic origin or who subscribe to certain common ways of life as alike. We must know enough about each individual to see him or her as distinctly different from other individuals.

At another level of conceptualization, systems theory and ego psychology point to the importance of diversity in the ongoing development of human systems. Without the stimulation of difference, human systems would not develop. However, the notion of patterned expectations and the feelings and values attached to them from role theory, the construct of "steady state" from systems theory, and the formulation of homeostasis from psychoanalytic theory all post a certain resistance to change, diversity, and difference.

Human systems need stability, the security of knowing that at least in some dimensions of human life their expectations of the behavior of others and transactions with others will be fulfilled and that the meanings they attach to that behavior will be accurate. This allows systems to shape and control their own actions through being able to predict both (1) the reactions of others to a contemplated action and (2) what they may expect from others in the ordinary course of their transactions.

A part of the need for stability of behaviors and meanings, if workers are to make any predictive judgments about behavior and transactions with others, results from the intolerance of difference on the part of human systems and their elements, and part arises from the definition of "normal" behavior. As stated earlier, role expectations become internalized as value systems. Thus there is a tendency in human systems to view difference in role behaviors as right or wrong rather than to consider whether they are essential (given social work's present knowledge base from which to make judgments) to the existence and ongoing development of the system. This tends to be particularly true of the family system, so some examples from the operation of that system will be used to illustrate this point. But first it must be recognized that the importance of the family system stems from the fact that society cannot exist without some form of reproduction of the elements of society (children) and their protection and socialization. There is considerable evidence that children need certain protections, which are usually furnished within the family system. However, family systems in different cultures will have different notions about which member of the family system performs this role and which behaviors are necessary to such safeguarding of children. In white middle-class America, this role is usually assigned to the position of mother, but it could be assigned just as effectively to an aunt, grandmother, uncle, father, or even to another system outside the family, such as a nursery. The tendency, however, for human systems that assign this behavior to the role of mother is for members of that system to view the assignment of such tasks to any other position in the system, or particularly outside the system, as wrong or abnormal and needing change. In fact, in contemporary society the grandmother, uncle, or another member of the extended family may be considered as properly belonging within another system. It is extremely important for social workers not to mix up their own internalized value expectations of role performance with their knowledge of the basic needs of human systems and what systems transactions are truly damaging to humanity.

The definitions of pathology and health seem to have developed solely from the expectations of the dominant groups in society about role behaviors and the feelings and meanings attached to these behaviors. While it may be necessary to recognize that there is such a thing as health and well-being, definitions are also needed for pathology and health that are based on knowledge of the minimum required needs of individuals and systems and of the maximum allowable transactional behavior. It is also necessary to include a range of behaviors and feelings that allows for difference in the performance of necessary systems roles, particularly when that difference itself may stem from different cultural notions of expected role performance and different interpretations of the meanings of such performance. It is necessary to question the concepts of normality and pathology in relation to knowledge of what constitutes damaging deprivations and transactions and not to measure them against the expected role patterns of the dominant society. It is also necessary to recognize that problems in system functioning often stem from a conflict in role expectations, which then leads to failure and conflict in role performance. Thus social workers must become sensitive to the damage done to minority groups and other groups who live differently when they are constantly confronted with role expectations through their necessary transactions with systems of the dominant groups in society that conflict with their own notions of expected role performance.

It is important that social workers have a broad knowledge of how cultures develop, of how opportunities and deprivation over time shape the culture of a people, and of how a given culture becomes a part of the human systems that transact with it.

Recapitulation   In this chapter we have presented some brief outlines of theories that we have found useful in developing our model of problem solving. The theories presented include ecological systems theory and related theories of role, power, and learned helplessness. We have also presented ego psychology and its concepts of motivation and have discussed the importance of a recognition of diversity and difference. We believe these theories serve social workers well in that they see human beings and their organizations as emergent or developing over time and hold an optimistic view of human potential for growth and change. The theories we have presented do not focus on a personal deficit model but allow for problems of dysfunctioning to be lodged in the transactions and lack of fit between the individual and the various social systems of which he or she is a part.

A Look
Forward   We are suggesting that to develop a better understanding of the theories you have studied in this chapter, you may want to put the theories to use. Hartman's article (Reading 4-2) presents the use of an assessment tool she calls an eco-map. Go to the cases in the appendix and draw an ecomap of each case situation using the instructions found in Reading 4-2. Label each system as being a microsystem, a mesosystem, or a macrosystem. After you have completed the ecomap, list at the bottom of your paper the opportunities and the sanctions that the larger system has offered the individual or family system over time as you can identify them from the cases. This exercise should help you as you continue in this book.

In Chapter 7 we are going to deal with another of the basic variables of social work practice—values and ethics and their function in practice.

| **Reading 4-1** | *Social Work and the Popular Psychotherapies* |

Harry Specht

The profession of social work is on the verge of being engulfed by the popular psychotherapies. Origins of popular psychotherapies lie in early nineteenth-century American social movements

Note: From "Social Work and the Popular Pychotherapies" by H. Specht, September 1990, *Social Service Review,* pp. 345–356. Copyright 1990 by University of Chicago. Reprinted by permission.

I would like to express my appreciation for helpful comments and criticisms from colleagues William Smelser, Neil Gilbert, Bart Grossman, Ed Nathan, William McKinley Runyan, and Al Kalmanoff; and thanks to the School of Social Work at California State University, Fresno, and Region C, California chapter of the National Association of Social Workers for opportunities to discuss this material.

and not in Freudian psychoanalysis as is commonly believed. A good grasp of the historical development of social work's engagement with the popular psychotherapies will help the profession clarify its mission in a modern community. This mission requires social work to separate itself from the popular psychotherapies.

INTRODUCTION

The relation between social work and popular psychotherapy is the most significant issue facing the profession today. As things currently stand, there is good reason to expect that the profession will be entirely engulfed by psychotherapy within the next 20 years, and social work's function in the public social services will become negligible.

The proportion of social work professionals in private practice has increased enormously over the last 20 years. Currently, it is estimated that as many as 25 percent of the members of the National Association of Social Workers are in private practice for at least part of their work week (Barker, 1987). Most of these people engage in what I shall refer to as the "popular psychotherapies."

Popular psychotherapy deals primarily with the aloneness of modern life; the absence of purpose and meaning in our life; the difficulty of knowing who you are, how you should behave, what you deserve, and what your obligations are to others.[1] Some psychotherapists deal with people who cannot carry out normative social and personal responsibilities such as keeping themselves housed, clothed, and fed, and fulfilling parental obligations, but many—perhaps a majority—of those seen by psychotherapists are "the worried well," white middle class, 20–40-year-olds who are unhappy, unfulfilled, and unsatisfied.[2] Some licensed clinical social workers and some social workers in private practice maintain a clear focus on the person in the environment. But the evidence is that most of them do not (Borenzweig, 1981).

The function of helping people find a purpose and meaning to life was, until early in this century, carried by the church. However, throughout the twentieth century the church and clergy have lost their capacity to carry out this function. Ministers and priests have come to look and act more and more like psychotherapists, just as psychotherapists have come to look and act more and more like priests. In fact, psychotherapists are modern-day "secular priests," and psychotherapy is our modern-day "church of individual repair." The major difference between the traditional church and psychotherapy is that the former provided a set of morals, values, and beliefs for the community. The secular priests of the church of individual repair go one by one. Essentially, the psychotherapist helps each individual construct his or her own personal church.

The public social services are staffed increasingly by personnel in lower civil service grades (Teare, 1983; Pecora & Austin, 1983). These services provide social care for dependent children, the mentally ill, the developmentally disabled, and older adults, a large proportion of whom are poor and minorities. At the same time, more and more higher-level supervisory and administrative jobs in the public services now require a clinical social work license so that the agencies can meet statutory requirements for diagnostic and treatment services. The clinical license (e.g., the Licensed Clinical Social Worker [LCSW] in California) requirement for many of these positions is questionable because the particular specialized knowledge and skill represented by the license are of dubious value for many of the tasks of professionals in the public social services (Goode, 1969). The requirement of a clinical license for supervision in the public social services is one indication of a general trend, evident even in the public social services, of the psychotherapizing of social work practice.

Another indication of this trend is the well-known secret in social work education that a vast proportion—possibly even the majority—of graduate students are preparing themselves for careers as psychotherapists (Rubin & Johnson, 1984). Many fill their applications to graduate schools with fabrications about their devotion to serving the poor and oppressed while secretly aspiring to hang out a private-practice shingle as soon as they graduate and complete the licensing requirements. The continuing drift toward the psychotherapeutic is one of the reasons that many schools of social work cannot enroll full classes in their programs for community organization, community development, administration, and social planning.

The profession's continuing growth of interest in psychotherapy as the practice modality of choice is, in large part, a reflection of the psychotherapy market. Apparently, a growing proportion of Americans seeks and is able to pay for psychotherapy. In their study of a random sample of the American population, Joseph Veroff, Richard Kulka, and Elizabeth Douvan found that, in 1976, 26 percent of Americans had used professional psychotherapeutic help of some kind, compared to only 14 percent in 1957. This represents an 85.7 percent increase in the 20-year period, and that is the reason why I refer to the psychotherapy enterprise as "popular" (Veroff, Kulka & Douvan, 1976). It is interesting to note that a larger proportion of the 1976 population was likely to have sought help for non-work-related problems than the 1957 population (Veroff, Kulka & Douvan, 1976). We do not know whether the psychotherapy market continued to grow after 1976, but the increases in numbers of licensed therapists over that period suggest that it has. These figures illustrate a phenomenal growth of public interest and belief in the utility of psychotherapy.

However, large numbers of social workers and psychologists have been involved in popular psychotherapy for only about 45 years, a relatively short period of time. The significant growth began at the end of World War II.

Americans' interest in self-improvement movements has waxed and waned since the beginning of the nineteenth century. Some of these movements lasted for almost a century and are now all but forgotten. In the first three sections of this article, I discuss social work's engagement with psychiatry, which began in the 1920s; the origins of popular psychotherapy, which began in the 1830s; and the emergence of humanistic psychology in the 1950s. In the fourth section I describe how social work emerged as a force in popular psychotherapy in the 1950s, and in the concluding section I present what I perceive to be social work's mission in a modern community.

SOCIAL WORK AND PSYCHIATRY

Social work discovered psychiatry in 1919. World War I had just ended, and there were many shell-shock victims to be treated. Sexual hygiene, child guidance, and mental hygiene were new social movements and provided new areas for social work practice. Psychiatry in 1919 was not psychoanalytic. The psychiatry that social workers took to at that time was based on theories of modern psychiatry that had been developing for 50 years in Europe. Social workers learned about and practiced this psychiatry under the tutelage of physicians

such as Adolf Meyer, A. A. Brill, Richard Cabot, Lawson Lowry, and Marion Kenworthy.

Until the mid-nineteenth century, mental illness was perceived to be primarily the result of sin and demons, or brain lesions and neurological malfunctions (Grob, 1985). "Lunatics" of all types and ages, with both functional and organic disorders (e.g., psychotics, epileptics, the feebleminded and senile, and cases of general paresis) for the most part were cared for indiscriminately in almshouses, lunatic asylums, and jails. By the latter part of the nineteenth century, the mentally ill in the United States were being cared for primarily in state hospitals. The development of this institutional system, which resulted from the work of social reformers like Dorothea Dix, represented a great advance in its day.

Psychiatry, which is a relatively young profession, evolved primarily from the nineteenth-century physicians who administered these hospitals.[3] The great reforms in caring for the mentally ill (e.g., "moral treatment," "no restraint," and the "open door") were introduced by these psychiatrists, who constituted a significant part of what Albert Deutsch referred to as "the culture of curability" (Redlich & Freedman, 1966).

A number of new ideas about the relation of mental illness to unconscious mental processes and sexual drives, which had been developing in Europe from the work of Mesmer, Galton, Charcot, Janet, and Freud, were absorbed only gradually by American psychiatry. The bulk of clinical psychiatrists were either apathetic about or hostile to the theories of Freud and his followers until after World War II (Grob, 1985). The somatic therapies (e.g., insulin and shock therapy, and prefrontal lobotomy) were introduced more readily in the state hospitals. In the United States, psychiatric social work developed first as an adjunct to psychiatry in the care of the mentally ill in state hospitals where a majority of patients suffered from somatic conditions (Grob, 1985). This created a clear condition for proscribing the involvement of social workers and clinical psychologists in psychotherapy, a condition that continued until the middle of the twentieth century.

The 1919 shift to psychiatry was the significant intellectual choice of the century for social work as a profession. Up to 1919, if one had tried to predict what the knowledge base of social work would be, sociology would have seemed a more likely choice than psychology. Jane Addams, the most famous of all social workers in the early twentieth century, was well connected with the world-renowned department of sociology at the University of Chicago, and there was no other intellectual force on the scene for social work comparable to sociology. At that time, psychology was concerned mostly with experiments, testing, and measurements. There was no clinical psychology. Social workers used bits of biology, economics, and eugenics, but nothing to compete with sociology.

Why then the shift to psychiatry? Very simply because social workers had nothing better they could do in the way of intervention. You cannot *do* sociology. How many community studies can you have? Sociology offered little in respect to managing face-to-face interaction with clients; and that is where psychiatry could be applied. Moreover, there were no others besides physicians who were ready, willing, and able to practice applied psychiatry.

Mary Richmond, who had formulated the first systematic description of social casework in her book, *Social Diagnosis,* knew this to be so. She was rather unhappy about the psychiatric deluge. In 1920, Richmond said that after the investigation (i.e., the social diagnosis) "the treatment seems to drop to a lower level almost as suddenly as though it went over a cliff" (Richmond, 1920). That is, there was nothing to do after the diagnosis. Though Richmond had read Freud and Jung, she was dubious about psychiatry being social work's theory of choice. She thought there was much promise in small-group psychology. What was needed, she said, were "expert observations of the normal reactions of two or more persons to one another. . . . Halfway between individual psychology and studies of neighborhoods . . . there is a field almost as yet unexplored." And, she added sadly, "I have neither the time nor the equipment for such an excursion" (Richmond, 1920). She was, of course, reaching for a theory that we today call "social

psychology," but that did not begin to crystallize until the 1940s: too late for Richmond, and too late for social work.

Social workers were ecstatic at having found something so significant to do. One can get a sense of the exhilaration over the discovery of psychiatry from the writings of social workers in the 1920s. Jessie Taft, writing in 1922, is a good example.

> What gives the case worker the right to take on so unlimited a responsibility? [i.e. to use psychiatric knowledge in dealing with children in placement]. . . . What right has case work to go on experimenting *with life itself?* . . . There is as yet no justification in conscious knowledge or technique; but the work is there to be done. There is no other profession to do it. . . . The position of the case worker is at once the most thrilling and the most terrifying in the whole gamut of scientific or semi-scientific undertakings which seek to gain social control in terms of the behavior of the human organism (Taft, 1920; italics added).

Thus, social workers took as their primary method what Jerome Wakefield (1988a, 1988b) has aptly described as "a derivative function."

In the 1930s, psychoanalytic treatment was adopted by some physicians practicing privately. Unlike treatment in mental hospitals, which involved primarily physiological, neurological, and pharmacological technologies, psychoanalytic therapy was a "talking cure" that could be employed by nonphysicians and, hence, was attractive to nonmedical health professionals such as social workers and psychologists. As it turned out, in the United States, psychoanalysis came to exercise influence on concepts of mental health and explanations of behavior disorders far beyond that of any other theoretical framework. The adoption of the Freudian paradigm, then, was instrumental in strengthening the capacities of social workers and clinical psychologists to engage in psychotherapy (Redlich & Freedman, 1966).

Psychiatry and psychoanalysis remained central to social work and social work education through the 1940s. The Depression and World War II drew the profession back momentarily to social concerns and provided a social context for the emergence of social group work and community organization as social work specializations. But those changes were episodic; psychiatry maintained its hold.

THE ORIGIN OF THE POPULAR PSYCHOTHERAPIES

Popular psychotherapy, as distinct from psychoanalytically oriented therapy, does not date back to Freud. Rather, its historical roots lie in great social movements of early-nineteenth-century America, beginning in approximately the 1830s. That is, psychotherapy today (both the serious and the "flaky") is primarily not Freudian. Its origins are more American than Austrian; currently it is more humanistically oriented than it is psychoanalytic.

The story is simple. Although the popular psychotherapies have been bubbling along in American life for over 150 years, social work did not incorporate them until after 1950. On the way, social work connected with modern psychiatry in the 1920s, psychoanalysis in the 1930s, and humanistic psychology in the 1950s.

Popular psychotherapy had its beginnings in nineteenth-century "mind cure" movements like phrenology, mesmerism, spiritualism, hydropathy, Christian Science, and electrotherapy (Wrobel, 1987). At first, these movements were concerned primarily with developing means by which individuals could use their own intellectual, emotional, and spiritual resources to cure themselves of physical illnesses. Through the nineteenth century, the objectives of the mind cures expanded to include attainment by the individual of perfection in both mind and body. Each of these mind cure movements developed extensive pseudoscientific bodies of knowledge.

The power of the mind cures subsided by the end of the century. However, the ideology has continued to the present day. Some of it was absorbed by the medical profession, and other parts were continued and elaborated in the work of the "positive thinkers" (Meyer, 1988). There is a direct line of descent from the work of the mind curists to that of the positive thinkers, but the latter's work is somewhat more familiar to many of us. The positive thinkers were less concerned with physical cures and more with the "power of positive thinking" to help the individual achieve "peace of mind" and success. Readers will, of course, recognize here the words of Norman Vincent Peale and Joshua Leibman (Peale, 1952; Liebman, 1946). Even more significant was Dale Carnegie (1936), whose book, *How to Win Friends and Influence People,* has sold in the tens of millions. The great intellectual positive thinkers were William James (1942), Harry Emerson Fosdick (1926), and George Beard (1881). Beard published a book in 1881 called *American Nervousness,* a best seller in its day. He is responsible for bringing the phrase "nervous breakdown" to our vocabulary.

Both of these movements—mind cure and positive thinking—were powerful in their time and constitute the basis of popular psychotherapy in our day.

HUMANISTICALLY ORIENTED PSYCHOLOGY

Following World War II, a great change took place in psychology, which until then had been concerned almost exclusively with experiments and testing. The great figure here is, of course, Carl Rogers (1951), who introduced "client-centered therapy." It is remarkable that, today, psychotherapeutically oriented clinical psychologists dominate the field of psychology. When Rogers began his work, the universities did not teach clinical psychology at all. They disdained Rogers and psychotherapy. The story of Rogers's assault on and victory in the academy is an interesting one. Suffice it to say that he lost the battle, but won the war. He did not survive in the university, but his system of psychotherapy did (Rogers, 1967, 1974).

Rogers (1951) opened the way for nonmedically based psychotherapy. It is not surprising that psychotherapeutically oriented social workers adored Rogers. He laid the foundation for what is today called humanistically oriented psychology. Unlike Freudian psychoanalytic theory and other biologically based and behavioral theories, there is very little that is theoretical or empirically based in the humanistically oriented psychologies of Rogers, Maslow, Perls, Pollack, and a host of others. ("Theory" is used here in the sense of testable and tested propositions that enable one to predict.) However, there is, in humanistically oriented psychology, a very powerful attitude and belief system about how to build and reconstruct the self: "you can do it, you're wonderful and good, there is richness in you, if it feels good on you it's okay." These are the fundamental beliefs of those secular priests mentioned earlier, and these ideas are the extension of the early 1800s belief in the perfectibility of the individual and the later 1800s optimistic beliefs of the positive thinkers.

From client-oriented psychotherapy based on humanistic psychology, it is only a short hop to the popular psychotherapies. There are not great differences among the positive thinking of Norman Vincent Peale and Dale Carnegie, the humanistic thinking of Rogers and Maslow, the channeling of Shirley MacLaine, transcendental meditation, Rolfing, hypnosis, massage, and the scores of other therapies now available. You find them all advertised together, along with the LCSWs, in monthly free issues of *Open Exchange* and *Common Ground,* your local newspaper, and the *NASW News.*

SOCIAL WORK AND THE POPULAR PSYCHOTHERAPIES
It is interesting that, although mind cure and positive thinking were significant and powerful ideologies, social workers had nothing to do with either. That is, until the 1950s, social work was not involved in the mainstream of popular psychotherapy.

Social work began in the 1890s as an outgrowth of another great social movement of that time known as "charities and corrections." The charities and corrections movement was based on a very powerful belief in the perfectibility of society; a belief that has dwindled and atrophied over the course of a century. It is difficult to envision the passion and fervor of that movement. The charities and corrections people were concerned about every corner of darkness, despair, and deprivation on earth: the "feebleminded," the insane, criminals, drunks, the tubercular, the poor, children, sanitation, playgrounds, disaster relief, and so forth. They were ruled by a fierce morality and determined to uplift every fallen sparrow they came upon. Darwinism, eugenics, and social mechanics were their intellectual tools.

The first National Conference of Charities and Correction was held in 1874. The conference (as an organization) continued until 1983.[4] Given their interest in social change, uplift, and improvement of the individual, the question why this group had no interest in the popular psychotherapies is intriguing. Whatever occasional mention there is of them in conference proceedings is negative.

The major reason for the movements remaining separate was that the charities and corrections movement was dominated by people who had three overlapping characteristics: they were primarily males, physicians, and clergymen. The ideologies of the mind curists and the positive thinkers were anathema to all three of these groups. First, these ideologies helped people, especially women, to experience greater control over their own lives; second, they offered alternatives to established medical practice; and third, these ideologies were anticlerical because they elevated self-development and self-reliance above divine guidance.

But social work was an important career choice and route to upward mobility for women. Social work's potential for providing a significant career for women remained latent for quite a long while. For example, it was only in 1910 (at its thirty-seventh annual meeting) that the conference chose a woman as its president. And she was not an ordinary woman; it took a powerhouse like Jane Addams to make the gender breakthrough in the recognized leadership of the emerging profession of social work.

As I have indicated, from the 1920s to the 1950s, social workers' involvement in psychiatry was kept squarely under the control of physicians. Freud's "talking cure" provided a technology that could be used by social workers, but in the United States the practice of psychoanalysis had been preempted by physicians so that they continued to control the conditions under which social workers could practice psychotherapy until the 1950s. Until then, professional discussions of the issue began with the assumption that psychiatric and psychoanalytic theory was the central core of social work knowledge. With that assumption, there remained only the task of dividing up the territory between social workers and psychiatrists. Today, those discussions sound like so much hairsplitting. The following are examples. Helen Ross and Adelaide M.

Johnson wrote in 1946 that "there is no qualitative difference [between casework and psychiatric therapy]. . . . The differences are quantitative. . . . The transference is probably handled more intensively by the psychoanalyst . . . than by the social worker." Robert Waelder wrote in 1944 that "the psychoanalytic therapy . . . works with interpretations" while nonanalytic psychotherapies do not. And in 1941, Gordon Hamilton wrote, "While never *treating* unconscious material, the caseworker must be aware of how unconscious factors operate."

This hairsplitting was meaningful in the context of the 1940s and 1950s because physicians did not relinquish willingly authority over psychotherapy. For example, in 1948, Menninger, one of the most socially oriented of psychiatrists, said of psychiatric social workers, "[Their] therapy is directed toward helping the individual accept the situation, modifying external factors insofar as this is possible. . . . The social worker rarely attempts to change the structure of personality; rather does he help the individual to live with his personality."

At the time Menninger was writing, humanistic psychology was just emerging and provided the intellectual base from which social work and clinical psychology would undermine the hegemony of medicine over the psychotherapies. The gender conflict underlying this struggle was obvious; the members of the American Association of Psychiatric Social Workers were almost exclusively female, while psychiatry was a male-dominated profession (Grob, 1985). It was with the advent of humanistically oriented (i.e., non-medically based) psychotherapy that social workers became free to practice the popular psychotherapies.

Thus, the journey of the profession over this century appears likely to end here as social workers become part of the institution of popular psychotherapy, one of the major battalions in the armies of the secular priesthood to carry forth the tenets of the church of individual repair. Why not? The pay is good. The clients are nice. There is more prestige in it than working with welfare clients, and a lot of it makes you feel good—as though you matter to someone.

SOCIAL WORK'S MISSION

Is there a difference between social work and psychotherapy? Does social work have a mission of its own that distinguishes our profession from the psychotherapies?

Generally, as I have noted elsewhere, the major function of social work is concerned with developmental socialization, while psychotherapy is concerned with resocialization and restoration (Specht, 1988). The concern of developmental socialization is with helping people perform in their appropriate social roles by providing information and knowledge, social support, social skills, and social opportunities. It is also concerned with helping people deal with interference and abuse from other individuals and groups, physical and mental disabilities, and overburdening responsibilities they have for others (Specht, 1988). The concern of resocialization is with helping people deal with feelings, perceptions, and emotions that prevent them from performing their social roles adequately because of impairment or insufficient development of emotional and cognitive functions intimately related to the self (Specht, 1988).

Professional social workers will recognize the close relation between—and the overlapping of—these two social functions. However, to say that social work is similar to and overlaps with the work of other professions (e.g., law, medicine, education, and psychotherapy) is not to say that all these professions are identical. We must, if we desire to give direction to our profession, take on the difficult task of drawing boundaries between ourselves and other professions. The drawing of boundaries can be difficult and painful because it may lead us to establish priorities and require us to exclude some functions and practices that, no matter how socially desirable, are diversionary and subversive to our mission.

The central point of this article is that the psychotherapies have diverted social work from its original vision, a vision of the perfectibility of society, the building of the "city beautiful," the "new society," and the "new frontier." There is a yet-unfulfilled mission for social work that might be resuscitated. It is a mission to deal with the enormous social problems under which our society staggers: the social isolation of our aged, the anomie experienced by our youths, the neglect and abuse of children, homelessness, drug addiction, and AIDS. Psychotherapy is not useful in dealing with these great problems.

Let us not be confused over the fact that there is some overlapping knowledge about human growth and development that social workers and psychotherapists share, or the fact that we both make focused use of interpersonal relationships, or that there are some small similarities we share in respect to practice. All human services professions share similar knowledge, but the uses they make of that knowledge are determined by their respective missions.

Our mission must be to build a meaning, a purpose, and a sense of obligation for the community, not one by one. It is only by creating a community that we establish a basis for commitment, obligation, and social support. We must build communities that are excited about their child care systems, that find it exhilarating to care for the mentally ill and the frail aged. Psychotherapy will not enable us to do that, and the farther down the psychotherapeutic path we go, the less effective we will be in achieving our true mission. There are models for doing this: the Civilian Conservation Corps of the 1930s, the War on Poverty of the 1960s, Alcoholics Anonymous, the civil rights movement, the Peace Corps, and the National Service Corps now being discussed in Congress are all models by which we can build communities that change people, communities that give a purpose and meaning to people's lives and, most important, communities that enable us to care about and love one another. To take that as our professional mission requires us to make a great change in our way of thinking and practicing.

This is a task that is tantamount to the cleaning of the Augean stables. We have, all of us, been socialized to think and act in psychotherapeutic terms and to prize one-on-one interventions. We educate our students to follow suit, and it is therefore not surprising that they, too, prize the psychotherapeutic role. Social services, whether public, voluntary, or for profit, are organized to

make individualized psychotherapeutic forms of helping the most significant we have to offer. Whether we are dealing with child abuse and neglect, addictions, loneliness, anxiety, economic dependency, or other physical and mental disabilities, it is psychotherapeutically oriented work with individuals that is considered to be the key.

Use of groups, community associations, and voluntary associations are usually considered to be secondary means for change. At best, they provide significant "social support" and "helping networks"; somewhat less important, they are good informational resources, recreational experiences, and they provide respite for caregivers and backups and reenforcement for individual treatment. Rarely are they perceived by professionals to be the primary and most desirable means for change. There are occasional episodes—usually at times of national crises—when we rediscover the group and the community. This occurred during the two world wars, the Depression, and the civil rights revolution. When there are cuts in allocations for social programs, agencies retreat unhappily to offering group treatment in place of psychotherapy. But when the crises subside, we quickly return to individualized therapy as our major means for dealing with social problems. For the most part, all nonpsychotherapeutic interventions are perceived by professionals to be inferior.

We have these perceptions of social treatments because, as Americans, our belief in the individual's capacity for change is strong, and our faith in the power of the group and community is weak, evidence to the contrary notwithstanding. It would, indeed, require a very great change in the profession, in professional education, in the organization of our service systems, and, most of all, in our systems of belief for social work to provide the community with a social program to deal with social problems.

It may be too late. We have been socialized for 70 years to believe that psychiatry, psychoanalysis, and humanistic psychology are appropriate means for dealing with social problems. We are about to be engulfed by popular psychotherapy. We must differentiate between these two practices and stop deluding ourselves that they are not different. The difference between them is vast. We should not be secular priests in the church of individual repair; we should be the conscience of the community. We should not ask, "Does it feel good?" We should help communities create good. We must have a vision of social work that enables us to direct our energies to the creation of healthy communities. That is how we make healthy people.

NOTES

1. See, e.g., the following critiques of psychotherapy: Paul Halmos, *The Faith of the Counselors* (New York: Schocken, 1966); Perry London, *The Modes and Morals of Psychotherapy,* 2d ed. (New York: Hemisphere, 1986); O. Hobart Mowrer, *The Crisis in Psychiatry and Religion* (Princeton, N.J.: Van Nostrand, 1961); and Philip

Rieff, *The Triumph of the Therapeutic: Uses of Faith after Freud* (New York: Harper & Row, 1966).

2. The distinction made here between individuals' strivings for happiness vs. societal concerns for helping persons meet normative expectations is drawn from Hans H. Strupp and Suzanne Hadley, "A Tripartite Model of Mental Health and Therapeutic Outcomes," *American Psychologist* 32 (March 1977): 187–96.

3. Psychiatry was recognized as a medical specialization only in 1934 (Grob, 1985, p. 232).

4. *Proceedings of the First Conference of Charities and Correction* (Boston: Press of George H. Ellis, 1875). It became the *National Conference of Social Work* in 1917, and the *National Conference on Social Welfare* in 1956.

Reading 4-2   *Diagrammatic Assessment of Family Relationships*

Ann Hartman

Integrating new knowledge and conceptual frameworks from the many sources that inform and support social work practice is a long and arduous process. General systems theory, which was introduced to social workers over 20 years ago (Lutz, 1956), has been particularly difficult to assimilate because it is so abstract. The distance is great between the lofty principles enunciated by systems theorists and the practical knowledge and skill that guide the practitioner's work with people day by day. The field has made some progress in utilizing systems concepts in developing middle-range theory, in organizing practice models (Hearn, 1969), in extending and clarifying the boundaries of the unit of attention (Germain, 1968), and in prescribing general directions for action (Hartman, 1974). Professionals in the field are now at the point of attempting to translate concepts from this middle-range theory into specific and testable prescriptions for practice.

Particularly interesting is the potential a systems orientation has for altering cognitive styles and enabling practitioners to organize and process increasingly complex systems of variables (Hartman, 1970). The attempt here is to derive from systems framework new conceptual models that can enhance the practitioner's and the client's perceptions of reality, thereby contributing to competence and creative adaptation in therapy.

Social workers, in attempting to understand their traditional unit of attention—the person in the total life space over time—are faced with an overwhelming amount of data. These data must be ordered, selected, and arranged to reduce confusion and overload. Edward Tolman has likened this mediating process to a map room where intervening cognitive charts shape data, lending meaning and manageability to the influx of information (Bruner, Goodnow, & Austin, 1962). These cognitive patterns have tremendous influence on how reality is perceived but are not readily observed or easily changed. They are an ongoing and familiar part of the self, and, as Frederick Duhl (1969) has pointed out, "that which is constantly experienced is neutral to awareness, being so immersed in the identity, so 'egosyntonic,' that it is rarely open to observation or challenge." As social workers interact with their environment, these mediating cognitive processes so strongly imprint a particular view of reality that they may well be just as crucial as knowledge and values in determining professional decision-making.

In dealing with almost continual information overload, cognitive processes tend to operate analytically: to partialize, to abstract parts from wholes, to reduce, and to simplify. Although this makes data more manageable, it does damage to the complexity inherent in reality. Ways of conceptualizing causation have tended to be particularly reductionist as reality is arranged in chains of simple cause and effect reactions. Such linear views reflect the limitations of thought and language rather than the nature of the real world, where human events are the result of transactions among multiple variables.

An emphasis on identifying the roots of problematic conditions in tremendously complex situations has frequently pushed social workers into supporting simplistic explanations and into arguments over what is the cause and hence the cure. Since 19th century scientism found expression in Mary E. Richmond's *Social Diagnosis* (1917), the profession has struggled with the temptation to deal with this "radically untidy universe" through reductionist solutions growing out of reductionist assessments.[1]

If social workers are to avoid reductionism and scientism, if they are to translate a systems orientation into practice, they must learn to "think systems," or to develop within their own cognitive map rooms new and more complex ways of imprinting reality. They must then devise ways of using this view in specific interventive techniques and strategies.

As one learns to "think systems," one tends to move to the use of metaphor and to the use of visual models in order to get beyond the constraints of linear thought and language. Social workers have always been frustrated in writing psychosocial summaries—they find it not unlike the attempt to describe the action in a football game over the radio. In attempting to describe the complex system of transacting variables, the meaning and the nature of the integration of the variables, and the totality of the events and action is lost. The use of metaphor in poetry and of two- and three-dimensional simulations in painting and sculpture demonstrate the integrative power of such approaches. Similar artistry can be used to expand the social worker's understanding of the nature of reality. Of many possibilities, two simple paper-and-pencil simulations have proved to be particularly useful, not only as assessment tools, but in interviewing, planning, and intervention.

One simulation is the ecological map or "eco-map," which was originally developed three years ago as an assessment tool to help workers in public child welfare practice examine the needs of families.[2] This tool pictures the family or the individual in the life space and has since been tested in a variety of settings with a wide range of clients. The second simulation is the genogram, which has been used by systems-oriented family therapists to chart intergenerational family history.[3] This tool has also been found to be highly adaptable for use with individuals or families in many different settings where it is important to understand the development of the family system through time.

THE ECOLOGICAL METAPHOR

The task of making general systems concepts operational and humane, of giving them flesh and

---

[1] For a discussion of casework's relationship with science and scientism, see Germain (1971).

[2] The eco-map was developed in 1975 by the author as a part of the Child Welfare Learning Laboratory, a project of the University of Michigan School of Social Work Program for Continuing Education in the Human Services. The project was supported in part by a grant from Region V, Social and Rehabilitation Service, U.S. Department of Health, Education, and Welfare, Section 426, Title IV, Part B of the Social Security Act. The author is grateful to Lynn Nybell, Coordinator of the Family Assessment Module, for her ideas, criticisms, and encouragement.

[3] The genogram has been used extensively by systems-oriented family therapists. For example, see Guerin and Pendagast (1976).

blood meaning, presents a difficult challenge. Although "input," "throughput," "moving steady state," and "deviation amplifying feedback loops" are precise and useful concepts, they mean little to social workers if they are unrelated to a human context. Recently, there has been a growing effort to utilize the science of ecology as a metaphorical way of humanizing and integrating system concepts (Germain, 1973). The science of ecology studies the delicate balance that exists between living things and their environments and the ways in which this mutuality may be enhanced and maintained.

In utilizing the ecological metaphor, it is clear that the salient human environment includes far more than air, water, food, spatial arrangements, and other aspects of the physical environment. Human environments also include networks of intimate human relationships. Further, over the centuries, human beings have erected elaborate social, economic, and political structures that they must sustain and through which their needs are met. People must maintain an adaptive mutuality with these intricate systems which are required for growth and self-realization.

An ecological metaphor can lead social workers to see the client not as an isolated entity for study but as a part of a complex ecological system. Such a view helps them to focus on the sources of nurturance, stimulation, and support that must be available in the intimate and extended environment to make possible growth and survival. It also leads to a consideration of the social, relational, and instrumental skills individuals must have to use possibilities in their environment and to cope with its demands.

THE ECO-MAP

The eco-map is a simple paper-and-pencil simulation that has been developed as an assessment, planning, and interventive tool. It maps in a dynamic way the ecological system, the boundaries of which encompass the person or family in the life space. Included in the map are the major systems that are a part of the family's life and the nature of the family's relationship with the various systems. The eco-map portrays an overview of the family in their situation; it pictures the important nurturant or conflict-laden connections between the family and the world. It demonstrates the flow of resources, or the lacks and deprivations. This mapping procedure highlights the nature of the interfaces and points to conflicts to be mediated, bridges to be built, and resources to be sought and mobilized. Although all one needs is a piece of paper and a pencil, it saves time to have "empty" maps available. These maps can be worked on by an individual or a family (see Figure 4-2).

Instructions for Drawing an Eco-Map

First the nuclear family system or household is drawn in a large circle at the map's center. It has been common practice in mapping families to use squares to depict males and circles to depict females. Relationships are indicated as in the traditional family tree or genetic chart. It is useful to put the person's age in the center of the circle or square. Thus, a circle with "80" in the center would represent an elderly woman.

Figure 4-1 represents a household consisting of a father, a mother, three children, and the wife's mother. The usefulness of this is demonstrated when one considers the number of words it would take to portray the facts thus represented. (The mapping of more complex nuclear family systems will be demonstrated in the discussion of genograms.)

After drawing the household in the large circle in the middle, add the connections between the family and the different parts of the environment. In the empty map (see Figure 4-2), some of the most common systems in the lives of most families have been labeled, such as work, extended family, recreation, health care, school, and so on. Other circles have been left undesignated so that the map can be individualized for different families.

Connections between the family and the various systems are indicated by drawing lines between the family and those systems (see Figure 4-3). The nature of the connection can be expressed in the type of line drawn: A solid or thick line represents an important or strong connection and a dotted line a tenuous connection; jagged marks across the line represent a stressful or conflicted relationship. It is

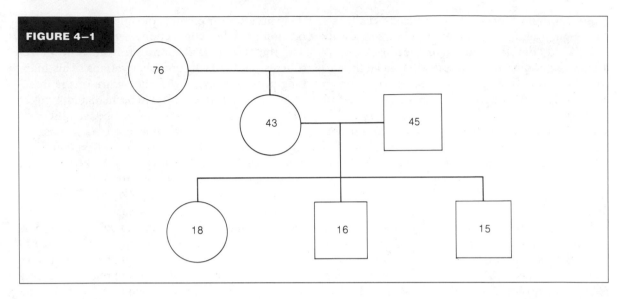

FIGURE 4–1

useful to indicate the direction of the flow of resources, energy, or interest by drawing arrows along the connecting lines:

In testing the eco-map, it has been found that the use of the three kinds of lines for conflicted, strong, and tenuous relationships is an efficient shorthand when the worker uses the eco-mapping procedure, without the family, as an analytic tool. However, when using the map as an interviewing tool, this code has often been felt to be too constraining. Workers have preferred to ask clients to describe the nature of the connection and will then qualify that connection by writing a brief description along the connecting line.

Connections can be drawn to the family as a whole if they are intended to portray the total family systems relationship with some system in the environment. Other connections can be drawn between a particular individual in the family and an outside system when that person is the only one involved or different family members are involved with an outside system in different ways. This enables the map to highlight the contrasts in the way various family members are connected to the world.

It is easy to learn to plot the eco-map, and it is important to become comfortable with the tool before using it with clients. A simple way to learn is to sketch one's own eco-map. It is also useful to practice with friends. By then, one is generally ready to use it with clients.

Uses of the Eco-Map

No matter how the eco-map is used, its primary value is in its visual impact and its ability to organize and present concurrently not only a great deal of factual information but also the relationships between variables in a situation. Visual examination of the map has considerable impact on the way the worker and the client perceive the situation. The connections, the themes, and the quality of the family's life seem to jump off the page, and this leads to a more holistic and integrative perception. The integrative value of visual experience was aptly expressed by one 12-year-old client when he said, "Gee, I never saw myself like that before!"

Initially, the eco-map was developed as a thinking tool for the worker. It was helpful in organizing material and in making an assessment. Sketching out an eco-map in the early stages of contact brought out salient areas of the family's life space that had not as yet been explored and suggested

FIGURE 4–2

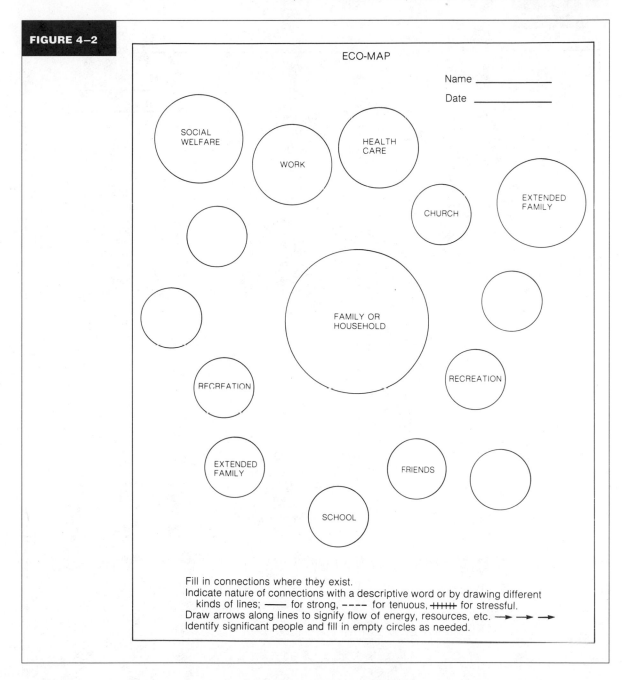

ECO-MAP

Name _____

Date _____

SOCIAL
WELFARE

WORK

HEALTH
CARE

CHURCH

EXTENDED
FAMILY

FAMILY OR
HOUSEHOLD

RECREATION

RECREATION

EXTENDED
FAMILY

FRIENDS

SCHOOL

Fill in connections where they exist.
Indicate nature of connections with a descriptive word or by drawing different
   kinds of lines; —— for strong, – – – – for tenuous, ++++++ for stressful.
Draw arrows along lines to signify flow of energy, resources, etc. → → →
Identify significant people and fill in empty circles as needed.

hypotheses for treatment. Before long, it became apparent that the eco-map would make a useful interviewing tool. Client and worker cooperated in picturing the client's life space. This led to much more active participation on the part of the client in the information-gathering and assessment process. The growing collaborative relationship between worker and client was often expressed in a

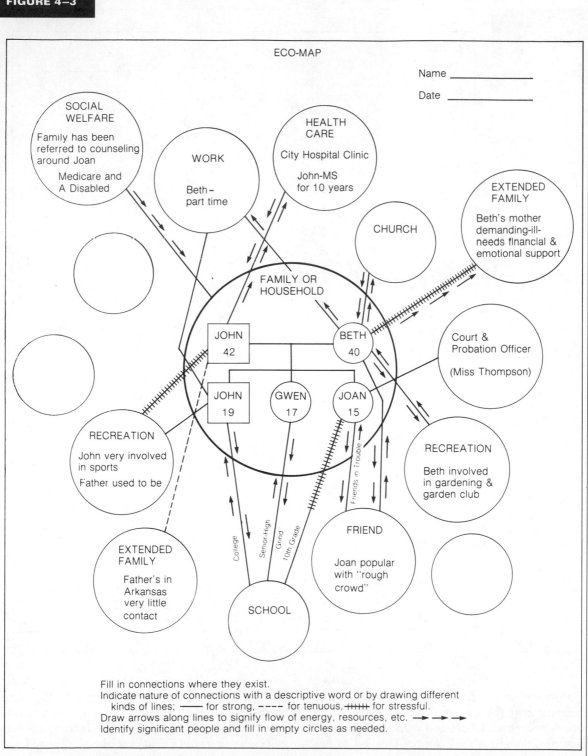

FIGURE 4–3

ECO-MAP

Name _____

Date _____

SOCIAL WELFARE

Family has been referred to counseling around Joan

Medicare and A Disabled

WORK

Beth – part time

HEALTH CARE

City Hospital Clinic

John-MS for 10 years

EXTENDED FAMILY

Beth's mother demanding-ill- needs financial & emotional support

CHURCH

FAMILY OR HOUSEHOLD

JOHN 42

BETH 40

JOHN 19

GWEN 17

JOAN 15

Court & Probation Officer

(Miss Thompson)

RECREATION

John very involved in sports

Father used to be

RECREATION

Beth involved in gardening & garden club

EXTENDED FAMILY

Father's in Arkansas very little contact

College

Senior-High

"Grind"

10th Grade

Friends in Trouble

FRIEND

Joan popular with "rough crowd"

SCHOOL

Fill in connections where they exist.
Indicate nature of connections with a descriptive word or by drawing different kinds of lines; ——— for strong, - - - - for tenuous, ++++++ for stressful.
Draw arrows along lines to signify flow of energy, resources, etc. → → →
Identify significant people and fill in empty circles as needed.

change in seating arrangements as the two tended to sit shoulder-to-shoulder, working together on the joint project.

Sharing the eco-mapping process also led to increased understanding and acceptance of the self on the part of the client. For example, an almost empty eco-map helps the client objectify and share loneliness and isolation. An eco-map full of stressful relationships showing all of the arrows pointing away from the family may lead a father to say, "No wonder I feel drained, everything is going out and nothing is coming in!" The eco-map has been extensively tested with natural parents working toward the return of their placed children through the Temporary Foster Care Project of the Michigan Department of Social Services (Thomas, 1978). Foster care workers noted that parents who were generally angry and self-protective following placement of their children because of abuse or neglect were almost without exception engaged through the use of the map. Workers were aware of a dramatic decrease in defensiveness. The ecological perspective made it clear to parents that the worker was not searching for their inner defects but rather was interested in finding out what it was like to be in the client's space, to walk in their shoes.

In working with the eco-map, clients have responded in some unanticipated ways. Although it was expected that they would gain a new perception by being able to step outside and look at themselves and their world, the emotional importance of the maps to the clients was a surprise. One mother demonstrated this early in the project by putting the eco-map up on her kitchen wall. In responding to clients' attachments to the maps, workers have regularly arranged to have them photocopied or have used pencil carbon so that clients may have a copy.

Contracting and Intervention

The eco-map has also been a useful tool in planning and has had considerable impact on intervention. Because it focuses attention on the client's relationship with the life space, interventions tend to be targeted on the interface, with both worker and client becoming active in initiating changes in the life space. Problematic conditions tend to be characterized as transactional and as a function of the many variables that combine to affect the quality of the individual's or the family's life.

In the Temporary Foster Care Project mentioned earlier, the worker and client moved quite naturally from the eco-map to a task-oriented contract.[4] They talked together about the changes that would be needed in the eco-map before the family could be reunited. They identified problem areas, resources needed, and potential strengths and planned what actions were needed to bring about change. Further, they established priorities and developed a contract describing the tasks to be undertaken by the worker and by the client.

The uses of the eco-map have multiplied in the hands of creative practitioners. For example, it has been used to portray the past and the future: In a rehabilitation program in a medical setting a social worker used eco-maps with clients to picture their world before their accident or illness; this helped clients to objectify what changes would be made in their lives following hospitalization. It helped them to mourn interests and activities that would have to be relinquished and also to recognize sources of support and gratification that would continue to be available. The mapping encouraged anticipatory planning and preparation for a new life, consideration of appropriate replacements for lost activities, and possible new resources to be tapped, all of which could expand the client's horizons. This technique was not only useful with the patient alone but was very helpful in conjoint work with disabled persons and their families.

Retrospective use of the map tends to highlight changes in a client's life space that could have precipitated current difficulties. When families and individuals seek help, a major question is always "Why has the client sought help now?" A review of the changes that have taken place in the previous months may well bring to light shifts of which the client was quite unaware.

---

[4] The work of William Reid and Laura Epstein (1977) and their collaborators has been useful in this area.

Recordkeeping and Measurements of Change

A complete eco-map deposited in a case record is a useful tool to present and record a case situation. Not only does it tend to keep the total situation clear for the worker, it can also serve as a means of communication to others should a staff member have to respond to a client in the absence of the regular worker. A crisis walk-in center where case responsibility is shared by a team to provide extended coverage uses the eco-map this way.

Finally, eco-maps can be used to evaluate outcomes and measure change. For example, a 10-year-old boy on a return visit to a school social worker asked for the map. He had made a new friend and wanted to put him on the map. The mother who had hung the map in the kitchen called her worker after two months of considerable activity on both their parts. She wanted to come into the office to plot another map so that she and the worker could look together at the changes. A comparison of eco-maps done at outset and at termination can help clients and workers measure the changes that have taken place. As such the maps can become an important device in maintaining accountability.

THE GENOGRAM

Families not only exist in space but also through time, and thus a second kind of simulation is needed to picture the development of this powerful relationship system. Not only is each individual immersed in the complex here-and-now life space, but each individual is also a part of a family saga, in an infinitely complicated human system which has developed over many generations and has transmitted powerful commands, role assignments, events, and patterns of living and relating down through the years. Each individual and each family is deeply implicated in this intergenerational family history.

Just as the eco-map can begin to portray and objectify the family in space, so can the genogram picture the family system through time, enabling an individual to step out of the system, examine it, and begin to gain a greater understanding of complex family dynamics as they have developed and as they affect the current situation.

Instructions for Drawing a Genogram

A genogram is simply a family tree that includes more social data. It is a map of three, four, or more generations of a family which records genealogical relationships, major family events, occupations, losses, family migrations and dispersal, identifications and role assignments, and information about alignments and communication patterns. Again, all that is needed is paper and pencil. For most genograms, a rather large piece of paper is usually required. It is important for the genogram to be uncrowded and clear to make visual examination possible.

The skeleton of the genogram tends to follow the conventions of genetic and genealogical charts. As in the eco-map, a male is indicated by a square, a female by a circle, and if the sex of a person is unknown, by a triangle. The latter symbol tends to be used, for example, when the client says, "I think there were seven children in my grandfather's family but I have no idea whether they were males or females." Or, "My mother lost a full-term baby five years before I was born, but I don't know what sex it was."

A marital pair is indicated by a line drawn from a square to a circle; it is useful to add the marital date, on the line. A married couple with offspring is shown as illustrated in Figure 4-4. Offspring are generally entered according to age, starting with the oldest on the left. The family diagrammed in Figure 4-4 has an older son followed by a set of twins. A divorce is generally portrayed by a dotted line, and again, it is useful to include dates (see Figure 4-5). A family member no longer living is generally indicated by drawing an "X" through the figure and giving the year of death. Thus, a complex, but not untypical, reconstituted family may be drawn as shown in Figure 4-5.

It is useful to draw a dotted line around the family members who compose the household. Incidentally, such a family chart enables the worker to grasp who is who quickly in complicated reconstituted families.

With these basic building blocks, expanded horizontally to depict the contemporary generation of siblings and cousins and vertically to chart the generations through time, it is possible to chart any

FIGURE 4–4

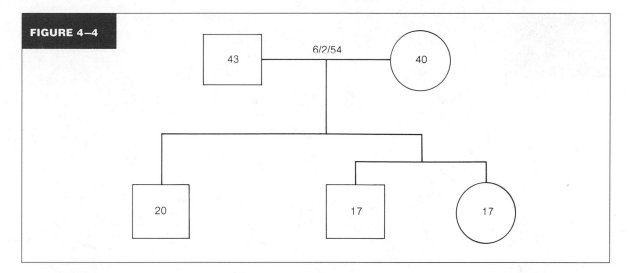

FIGURE 4–5

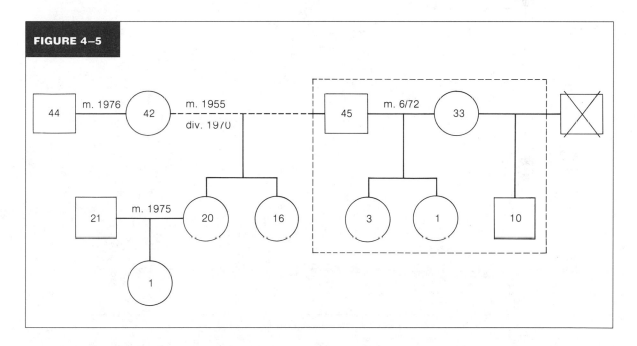

family, given sufficient paper, patience, and information (see Figure 4-6). As one charts the skeletal structure of the family, it is also important to fill this out with the rich and varied data which portray the saga of the particular family being studied.

Many different kinds of information may be gathered. First and middle given names identify family members, indicate naming patterns, and bring identifications to the surface. In understanding where a client may fit into the family and what expectations and displacements may have affected the sense of self, a first step is to discover who, if anyone, the client was named after. Once this person is identified, it is important to discover what

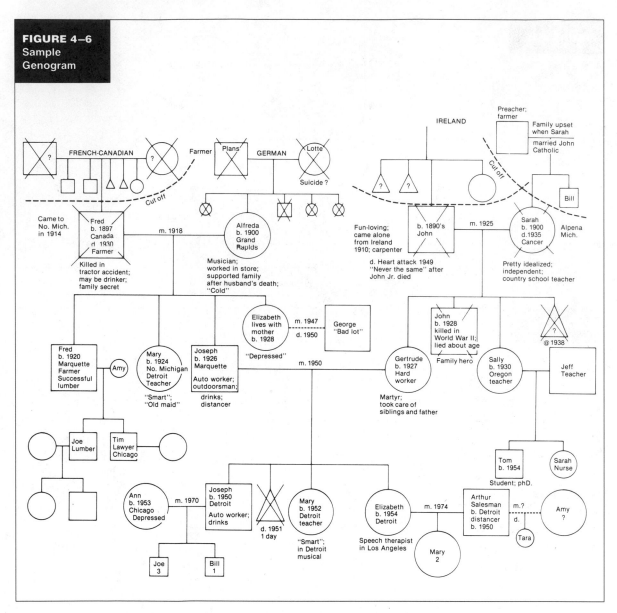

FIGURE 4–6
Sample Genogram

he or she was like, what roles he or she carried, and, perhaps most salient, what the nature of the relationship was between the client's parents and this relative.

Sometimes meanings and connections are not obvious and emerge only through careful exploration. For example, in charting a genogram with a young man who was struggling with identity issues

and a complex tie with his mother, naming patterns were being discussed. The client's name was Tony; his American soldier father had met his mother abroad and, immediately after their marriage, the couple had moved to the United States. The move and subsequent political events resulted in the wife's being completely cut off from her family. The client, their firstborn child, was born a year after the marriage. When asked whom he was named after, he replied, "I wasn't named after anyone in the family—I was named after St. Anthony—the patron of lost objects." The symbolic meaning of Anthony's name to his mother became dramatically apparent: Tony was named after everyone in his mother's family!

Dates of birth and dates of death record when members joined the family, their longevity, and family losses. Birth dates indicate the age of family members when important events occurred. They indicate how early or late in a marriage a child came and the age of the parents at the birth. In a sense, birth, marriage, and death dates mark the movement of the family through time. In working with a client's genogram, it is helpful to discover all of the events that took place around the birth. Major losses experienced in the family around that time can be of particular significance. The tendency to use newborn family members as replacements for lost members seems almost universal and has even been institutionalized in some culturally proscribed naming patterns.

Birth dates also identify each individual's place in the sibship. This brings to the surface such potential roles as "older responsible," "firstborn son," or "baby." It is also relevant to discover who else in the family has occupied the same sibling position. Sibling position can be a powerful source of intergenerational identifications.

Place of birth and current place of residence mark the movement of the family through space. Such information charts the family's patterns of dispersal, bringing into focus major immigrations or migrations and periods of loss, change, and upheaval. Such information may also point to the fact that generations of a family have stayed within a fairly small radius except, perhaps, for a particular individual in each generation who moves away. If a client happens to be this generation's "wanderer," that could be a valuable piece of information.

Picturing the family's movement through space may communicate a good deal about family boundaries and norms concerning mobility. Is this a family that holds on or lets go? Further, the impact of world history on families often becomes evident as responses to war, persecution, westward migra-

tion, depression, industrialization, and even climatic or ecological changes are often seen in relocations.

Occupations of family members acquaint one with the interests and talents, the successes and failures, and the varied socioeconomic statuses that are found in most families. Occupational patterns may also point to identifications and can often portray family proscriptions and expectations.

Finally, facts about members' health and causes of death provide overall family health history and also may say something about the way clients see their own future. These predictions may well have some power of self-fulfillment.

This demographic data can take a worker a long way toward understanding the family system. However, gathering associations about family members can add to the richness of the portrayal. One can ask, "What word or two or what picture comes to mind when you think about this person?" These associations tend to tap another level of information about the family as the myths, role assignments, characterizations, or caricatures of family members come into the client's mind. Characterizations such as lazy, bossy, martyr, beautiful, caretaker, are likely to be offered, bringing forth reminiscences or stories that have become a part of the family biography and mythology.

Finally, certain aspects of the family's communication structure can be indicated. Parts of the family that have been cut off become quite obvious because the client generally has very little information about them. Cutoffs can be portrayed by drawing a fence where the cutoff exists whereas tight communication bonds can be demonstrated by drawing a line around portions of the family that form close linkages. It helps to keep things clear if a colored pencil is used to indicate communication linkages and cutoffs so as not to confuse these with the basic genealogical structure. Cutoffs are of particular significance as they are usually indicative of conflict, loss, and family secrets. Cutoffs generally develop to protect family members from pain and conflict, but they are usually indicators of unfinished business and may leave the person out of touch with important aspects of family and perhaps of self.

It is often found that a client doing a genogram will have considerable information about one section of the family, for example, the maternal grandmother's family, and almost none about other relatives. This uneven distribution of knowledge is significant in assessing communication and relationship patterns.

Uses of the Genogram

The genogram is a classic tool for gathering and utilizing family data in any family oriented practice. No matter what the setting, if the individual is to be understood in the context of the total family system, the genogram can portray that system and move worker and client toward an understanding of the impact of that system and its relevance to the issues at hand. In counseling regarding marital and parent-child conflict, the routes or prototypes of these conflicts may well emerge. The use of the genogram in conjoint marital counseling can increase empathy between the marital pair and help each to identify the old family issues that have been displaced in the marriage.

In working with the aging, the genogram is an invaluable tool in life review. Elderly people can reminisce and organize memories but also, in working with the genogram, can experience themselves as a central link between the past and the future. This process expresses continuity and the generative process and illustrates that, although the individual's life span may be brief, the family's life reaches back into the past and on into the future. One residence for the aging encourages staff to meet with family members to teach them how to build genograms and help their aged relatives reconnect with their family saga. This sharing of the genogram has been an important experience for both the aged person and the younger family members.

Genograms have also been used in child welfare agencies. As part of an adoptive home study, for example, the genogram may clarify why a couple experiences their family as incomplete and also brings to the surface considerations and plans concerning who an adopted child is intended to be. Charting a genogram with natural parents ensures that, should family ties be legally severed, there will be a full family history available to the child in the future. One child-care agency that regularly makes use of the genogram in adoption practice has found that often the experience of doing the genogram has been very meaningful to natural parents who see the process as giving something of themselves to the child. The issue of open adoption has yet to be settled but, in the interim, the genogram can gather and keep available the kind of information adopted children often want.

In a hospital setting, a genogram can be used to gather an expanded health history. Such a history provides information about patterns of illness and health in a family: for instance, a paternal grandmother may have died of heart disease at 38 while the maternal grandmother lived an active life to age 94. Further, patterns of illness as well as attitudes toward illness and ill people may appear.

SUMMARY

The eco-map and the genogram are paper-and-pencil simulations that can organize and objectify a tremendous amount of data about the family system in space and through time. Such objectivity and visual portrayal can lead to new insights and to altered perceptions, of the complexity of human systems. Such altered perceptions may point to new ways of bringing about change, ways that relate to the complexity of human existence.

For Further Reading

Anderson, R., & Carter, I. (1974). *Human behavior in the social environment: A systems approach.* Chicago: Aldine.

Auerswald, E. H. (1968). Interdisciplinary vs. ecological approach. *Family Process, 7,* 202–215.

Beavers, R. W. (1977). *Psychotherapy and growth—a family systems perspective.* New York: Brunner/Mazel.

Bertalanffy, L. V. (1968). *General systems theory: Foundations, development, and applications.* New York: George Braziller.

Block, J. H. (1984). *Sex role identity and ego development.* San Francisco: Jossey Bass.

Brenner, C. (1973). *An elementary textbook of psychoanalysis* (2nd ed.). Garden City, NY: Anchor Press/Doubleday.

Buckley, W. (1967). *Sociology and modern systems theory.* Englewood Cliffs, NJ: Prentice Hall.

De Hoyos, G., De Hoyos, A., & Anderson, C. B. (1986). Sociocultural dislocation: Beyond the dual perspective. *Social Work, 311,* 61–67.

Devore, W., & Schlesinger, E. C. (1981). *Ethnic-sensitive social work practice.* St. Louis: C. V. Mosby.

Lum, D. (1982). Toward a framework for social work practice with minorities. *Social Work, 263,* 244–249.

Ganter, G., & Yeakel, M. (1980). *Human behavior and the social environment: A perspective for social work practice.* New York: Columbia University Press.

Green, J. W. (1982). *Cultural awareness in the human services.* Englewood Cliffs, NJ: Prentice-Hall.

Maas, H. S. (1984). *People and contexts: Social development from birth to old age.* Englewood Cliffs, NJ: Prentice-Hall.

Morell, C. (1987). Cause is function: Toward a feminist model of integration for social work. *Social Service Review, 611,* 144–155.

Perlman, H. H. (1968). *Persona: Social role and personality.* Chicago: University of Chicago Press.

Polansky, N. A. (1982). *Integrated ego psychology.* New York: Aldine.

White, R. W. (1963). Ego and reality in psychoanalytic theory: A proposal regarding independent ego energies. *Psychological Issues, 33,* Monograph 11.

Practice Across Difference

Working relationships between people who differ in terms of important factors such as class, race, ethnicity, gender, sexual preference, etc., are often hard to initiate or sustain, despite the need of the clients and the desire of the professional to be of help. Therefore it seems important to include a chapter in this book that draws out some of the implications of a cross-cultural perspective for social services. We need to note at the beginning of this discussion that there is no way to easily acquire cross-cultural sensitivity.

We need to consider the importance of difference in the development of individuals and human societies. When we are confronted with difference there is a tendency to consider which position is "correct." The notion that two positions can be different but of equal value is difficult for us. It is easy to confuse the concept of same with the concept of equal. This is evident when we consider the difficulty we have in accepting that men and women are equal. Our tendency is to deny that they are equal as human beings when they are biologically different. In human societies there is the tendency for the group that possesses the most power to label their qualities as most desirable and the roles performed as "right." Social workers must become sensitive to minority groups when they are constantly confronted with role expectations that conflict with their own notions of expected role performance. Culture and cultural norms are powerful forces that are inevitably part of our unconscious so deeply buried and accepted as part of us that we express them in all areas of life without any awareness. We need to quit denying that we have such attitudes, accept them as part of ourselves, and work at identifying them and how we express them in order to change.

Cross, Bazron, Dennis and Isacs (1989) outline five elements that contribute to dealing with cultural problems: acknowledging and valuing diversity; being aware of one's own culture and how it shapes beliefs and behavior, both personal and professional; recognizing and understanding the dynamics of difference; acquiring cultural knowledge; and adapting to diversity. Cultures differ in the way decision-making is structured, in the life events that are emphasized, in how the developmental cycle of household and family units are ordered, and how individuals and households relate to crises and external interference.

There are two primary explanatory models for ethnicity. One model treats ethnicity as a categorical phenomenon. In this model differences are explained by listing the qualities that make group A different from group B. The other model deals with group boundaries and the interaction across these boundaries. This model is compatible with social work's use of systems theory.

We strongly suggest that students study the readings at the end of this chapter, particularly Readings 5-2 and 5-3, to gain a sense of the importance of the emotional costs of working across difference.

As social workers we need to pledge our allegiance to the following principles:

1. We will acknowledge that social inequalities and oppression exist.
2. We will acknowledge that we have been misinformed about groups, especially if we are members of devalued groups. This is true for both majority and minority group members.
3. We will realize that we cannot be blamed for the misinformation we have acquired, but we will be responsible for correcting inaccuracies or informational gaps.
4. We will not blame victims for their oppression.
5. We will assume that people always do the best they can.
6. We will actively pursue information about our group and other groups with members of the class and we will never demean or in any way "put down" people for their experience.

Reading 5-1 | # Social Work with Native Americans*

Ronald G. Lewis and Man Keung Ho

In the past, the social work profession has failed to serve effectively an important segment of the population—the Native Americans. Although social workers are in sympathy with the social problems and injustices long associated with the Native American people, they have been unable to assist them with their problems. This lack of success on the part of social workers can be attributed to a multitude of reasons, but it stems, in general, from the following: (1) lack of understanding of the Native American culture, (2) retention of stereotyped images of Native Americans, (3) use of standard techniques and approaches.

Currently, the majority of social workers attempting to treat Native Americans are whites who have never been exposed to their clients' culture. Even when the social worker is a Native American, if his education and training have been in an environment that has completely neglected the Native American culture, there is still the possibility that he has drifted away from his people's thinking. Social workers with no understanding of the culture may have little or no sympathy for their Native American clients who fail to respond quickly to treatment.

Furthermore, Native Americans continue to be stereotyped by the current news media and often by the educational system. In all likelihood, the social worker will rely on these mistaken stereotypes rather than on facts. As Deloria explained, "People can tell just by looking at us what we want, what should be done to help us, how we feel, and what a 'real' Indian is like." If a worker wishes to make progress in helping a Native American, he must begin by learning the facts and discarding stereotypes.

The ineffectiveness of social workers in dealing with Native Americans can often be attributed directly to the methods and techniques they use. Naturally, social workers must work with the tools

*Copyright 1975, National Association of Social Workers, Inc. Reprinted with permission, from *Social Work*, vol. 20, no. 5 (September 1975), pp. 379–382.

they have acquired, but these may have a detrimental effect on a Native American. For example, the concept of "social work intervention" may be consistent with much of the white man's culture, but it diametrically opposes the Native American's cultural concept of noninterference. There is a great need for social workers to examine carefully those techniques they plan to use in treating their Native American clients. If the worker discovers any that might be in conflict with the cultural concepts of the Native American, he should search carefully for an alternative approach. To do this, of course, the social worker must be aware of common Native American cultural traits.

Although there is no monolithic Native American culture—because each tribe's culture is unique to that individual tribe, and no social worker could be expected to be familiar with the cultures of some two hundred tribes—the worker should familiarize himself with those customs that are generally characteristic of all Native Americans. Only after a worker has gained at least an elementary knowledge of Native American customs and culture can he proceed to evaluate the various approaches and techniques and choose the most effective ones.

NATIVE AMERICAN TRAITS

The concept of sharing is deeply ingrained among Native Americans, who hold it in greater esteem than the white American ethic of saving. Since one's worth is measured by one's willingness and ability to share, the accumulation of material goods for social status is alien to the Native American. Sharing, therefore, is neither a superimposed nor an artificial value, but a genuine and routine way of life.

In contrast to the general belief that they have no concept of time, Native Americans are indeed time conscious. They deal, however, with natural phenomena—mornings, days, nights, months (in terms of moons), and years (in terms of seasons or winters). If a Native American is on his way to a meeting or appointment and meets a friend, that conversation will naturally take precedence over being punctual for the appointment. In his culture, sharing is more important than punctuality.

Nature is the Native American's school, and he is taught to endure all natural happenings that he will encounter during his life. He learns as well to be an independent individual who respects others. The Native American believes that to attain maturity—which is learning to live with life, its evil as well as its good—one must face genuine suffering. The resilience of the Native American way of life is attested to by the fact that the culture has survived and continues to flourish despite the intense onslaught of the white man.

One of the strongest criticisms of the Native American has been that he is pessimistic; he is presented as downtrodden, low-spirited, unhappy, and without hope for the future. However, as one looks deeper into his personality, another perspective is visible. In the midst of abject poverty comes "the courage to be"—to face life as it is, while maintaining a tremendous sense of humor. There exists a thin line between pathos and humor.

The Native American realizes that the world is made up of both good and bad. There are always some people or things that are bad and deceitful. He believes, however, that in the end good people will triumph just because they are good. This belief is seen repeatedly in Native American folktales about Iktomi the spider. He is the tricky fellow who is out to fool, cheat, and take advantage of good people. But Iktomi usually loses in the end, reflecting the Native American view that the good person succeeds while the bad person loses. Therefore, the pessimism of Native Americans should instead be regarded as "optimistic toughness."

Those who are unfamiliar with the culture might mistakenly interpret the quiet Native American as being stoical, unemotional, and vulnerable. He is alone, not only to others but also to himself. He controls his emotions, allowing himself no passionate outbursts over small matters. His habitual mien is one of poise, self-containment, and aloofness, which may result from a fear and mistrust of non-Native Americans. Another facet of Native American thought is the belief that no matter where any individual stands, he is an integral part of the universe. Because every person is fulfilling a purpose, no one should have the power to impose values. For this reason, each man is to be respected, and he can expect the same respect and reverence from others. Hence, the security of this inner fulfillment provides him with an essential serenity that is often mistaken for stoicism.

Native American patience, however, can easily be mistaken for inactivity. For instance, the Kiowa, like other Native American tribes, teach their young people to be patient. Today, when the young Native American has to go out and compete in another society, this quality is often interpreted as laziness. The white man's world is a competitive, aggressive society that bypasses the patient man who stands back and lets the next person go first.

The foregoing are only a few of the cultural traits that are common to most Native American tribes, but they represent important characteristics about which the effective social worker must be informed. The concepts of sharing, of time, acceptance of suffering, and optimism differ significantly from the white man's concepts. In dealing with a Native American client, the social worker must realize this and proceed accordingly. He must be familiar with the Native American view that good will triumph over evil and must recognize that Native Americans are taught to be patient and respectful. If the worker fails to do this, he is liable to make false assumptions, thus weakening his ability to serve his client effectively.

CLIENT-WORKER RELATIONS

A social worker's ability to establish a working relationship with a Native American will depend on his genuine respect for his client's cultural background and attributes. A worker should never think that the Native American is primitive or that his culture and background are inferior.

In the beginning, the Native American client might distrust the worker who is from a different race and culture. He might even view the worker as a figure of authority, and as such, the representative of a coercive institution. It is unlikely that he will be impressed with the worker's educational degrees or his professional title. However, this uncompromising attitude should not be interpreted as pugnacity. On the contrary, the Native American is gregarious and benevolent. His willingness and capacity to share depend on mutual consideration, respect, and noncoercion.

Because their culture strongly opposes and precludes interference with another's affairs, Native Americans have tended to regard social work intervention with disfavor. Social workers usually are forced to use culturally biased techniques and skills that are insensitive to the Native American culture and, therefore, are either detrimental to these clients or, at best, ineffective.

In an effort to communicate more fully, a social worker is likely to seat himself facing the client, look him straight in the eye, and insist that the client do likewise. A Native American considers such behavior—covert or overt—to be rude and intimidating; contrary to the white man, he shows respect by not staring directly at others. Similarly, a worker who is excessively concerned with facilitating the display of inner feelings on the part of the client should be aware of another trait. A Native American client will not immediately wish to discuss other members of his family or talk about topics that he finds sensitive or distressing. Before arriving at his immediate concern (the real reason he came to the worker in the first place), the client—particularly the Native American—will test the worker by bringing up peripheral matters. He does this in the hope of getting a better picture of how sincere, interested, and trustworthy the worker actually is. If the worker impatiently confronts the client with accusations, the client will be "turned off."

Techniques of communication that focus on the client—that is, techniques based on restating, clarifying, summarizing, reflecting, and empathizing—may help a worker relate to the client who sometimes needs a new perspective to resolve his problem. It is important that the worker provide him with such information but not coerce him to accept it. The worker's advice should be objective and flexible enough so that its adoption does not become the central issue of a particular interview.

For the Native American, personal matters and emotional breakdown are traditionally handled within the family or extended family system. For this reason, the client will not wish to "burden" the worker with detailed personal information. If the client is estranged from his family and cultural group, he may indirectly share such personal information with the worker. To determine the appropriate techniques for helping a Native American client deal with personal and psychological problems, the worker should carefully observe the client's cultural framework and his degree of defensiveness. The techniques of confrontation traditionally associated with the psychoanalytic approach and the introspective and integrative techniques used by the transactional analysts tend to disregard differences in culture and background between a client and worker.

FAMILY COUNSELING

In view of the close-knit family structure of Native Americans, along with the cultural emphasis to keep family matters inside the family, it is doubtful that many social workers will have the opportunity to render family counseling services. In the event that a Native American family does seek the worker's help, the family worker should be reminded that his traditional role of active and manipulative go-between must be tempered so that family members can deal with their problems at their own pace. Equally important is the worker's awareness of and respect for the resilience of Native American families, bolstered in crisis by the extended family system. The example of the Redthunder family serves as illustration.

> The Redthunder family was brought to the school social worker's attention when teachers reported that both children had been tardy and absent frequently in the past weeks. Since the worker lived near Mr. Redthunder's neighborhood, she volunteered to transport the children back and forth to school. Through this regular but informal arrangement, the worker became acquainted with the entire family, especially with Mrs. Redthunder who expressed her gratitude to the worker by sharing her homegrown vegetables.
>
> The worker sensed that there was much family discomfort and that a tumultuous relationship existed between Mr. and Mrs. Redthunder. Instead of probing into their personal and marital affairs, the worker let Mrs. Redthunder know that she was willing to listen should the woman need someone to

talk to. After a few gifts of homegrown vegetables and Native American handicrafts, Mrs. Redthunder broke into tears one day and told the worker about her husband's problem of alcoholism and their deteriorating marital relationship.

> Realizing Mr. Redthunder's position of respect in the family and his resistance to outside interference, the social worker advised Mrs. Redthunder to take her family to visit the minister, a man whom Mr. Redthunder admired. The Littleaxe family, who were mutual friends of the worker and the Redthunder family, agreed to take the initiative in visiting the Redthunders more often. Through such frequent but informal family visits, Mr. Redthunder finally obtained a job, with the recommendation of Mr. Littleaxe, as recordkeeper in a storeroom. Mr. Redthunder enjoyed his work so much that he drank less and spent more time with his family.

Obviously, treating a family more pathogenic than the Redthunders might necessitate that the social worker go beyond the role of mediator. Nevertheless, since Native Americans traditionally favor noninterference, the social worker will not find it feasible to assume the active manipulative role that he might in working with white middle-class families. The social work profession needs new and innovative approaches to family counseling that take into account social and family networks and are sensitive and responsive to the cultural orientation of Native American families.

GROUP WORK

Groups should be a natural and effective medium for Native Americans who esteem the concept of sharing and apply it in their daily lives. Through the group process, members can share their joy, intimacy, problems, and sorrows, and find a means of improving their lives. Today's society tends to foster alienation, anomie, disenfranchisement, dissociation, loneliness, and schizoid coolness. People wish for intimacy but at the same time fear it. The new humanistic approaches to counseling and psychotherapy have developed a wide variety of powerful techniques for facilitating human growth, self-discovery, and interpersonal relations. The effectiveness of these approaches in cutting through resistance, breaking down defenses, releasing creative forces, and promoting the healing process has been amply demonstrated. However, such approaches are highly insensitive to the cultural orientation of Native Americans. These people consider such group behavior to be false; it looks and sounds real but lacks genuineness, depth, and real commitment.

As the worker uses his skills in forming the group, diagnosing the problems, and facilitating group goals, he may inevitably retain certain elements of manipulation. However, if he is committed to recognizing individual potential and to capitalizing on the group model of mutual assistance, he should come close to meeting the needs of Native Americans who value respect and consideration for oneself as well as for others.

To avoid manipulation and coercion, a group worker needs to utilize indirect and extra-group means of influence that will in turn influence the members. Thus the worker may act upon and through the group as a mediating structure, or through program activities, for the benefit of his clients. This success of the worker's influences and activities is related to his knowledge and acceptance of Native American culture, its formal and informal systems and norms.

Regardless of whether the purpose of the group is for effecting interpersonal change or social action, such Native American virtues as mutual respect and consideration should be the essential components of the group process. Using the group to pressure members who are late or silent will not only jeopardize and shorten the group's existence, but will cause alienation and withdrawal from future group activities.

In view of the vast cultural difference between Native Americans and other ethnic groups, especially whites, it is doubtful that a heterogeneous grouping of members will produce good results. Similarly, group activities that are action oriented may be contradictory to Native Americans who view the compulsion to reduce or ignore suffering as immaturity.

COMMUNITY WORK

Because of the Native Americans' experience of oppression and exploitation—along with their emphasis on noninterference and resolute acceptance of suffering—it is doubtful that a social worker, regardless of his racial identity, could bring about any major change in community policies and programs. The only exception might be the social worker who is accepted and "adopted" by the community and who agrees to confine himself to the existing system and norms. A worker's adoption by the Native American community will depend on his sincerity, respect, and genuine concern for the people. This concern can best be displayed through patience in daily contact with the community as well as through his efforts to find positive solutions to problems.

A worker who uses the strategy of trying to resolve conflict as a means of bringing about social change will undoubtedly encounter native resistance and rejection. On the other hand, a worker who shows respect for the system, values, and norms of the Native American eventually places himself in a position of trust and credibility. Only through mutual respect, and not through his professional title and academic degree, can the worker produce meaningful social change.

Obviously, social work with Native Americans requires a new orientation and focus on attitudes and approaches. The term Native American encompasses many tribes, and within these there are intratribal differences; furthermore, individuals within each subtribe may react differently to problems or crises. Therefore, it is impossible for a social worker always to know precisely how to respond to a Native American client or group. The worker must be willing to admit his limitations, to listen carefully, to be less ready to draw conclusions, and to anticipate that his presuppositions will be corrected by the client. The worker must genuinely want to know what the problem or the situation is and be receptive to being taught. Such an unassuming and unobtrusive humanistic attitude is the key to working with Native American people.

The social worker who can deal most effectively with Native Americans will be genuine, respectful of their culture, and empathic with the welfare of the people. By no means does the Native American social worker have a monopoly on this type of attitude. In fact, the Native American social worker who has assimilated the white man's culture to the extent that he no longer values his own culture could do more harm than good.

Recognizing the distinct cultural differences of the Native American people, those who plan social work curricula and training programs must expand them to include specific preparation for workers who will be dealing with Native American clients. Literature on the subject is almost nonexistent, and researchers and educators would do well to devote more study to how social workers can serve Native Americans. More Native Americans should be recruited as students, faculty, and practitioners in the field of social work. All persons, regardless of race, should be encouraged to develop a sensitivity toward Native Americans whom they may have the opportunity to serve. Social work agencies that deal primarily with Native American clients should intensify and refocus their in-service training programs.

A worker has the responsibility of acquiring knowledge that is relevant to the Native American culture so that he is capable of providing this effective treatment. A joint effort on the part of all those involved is required to give the service to Native Americans that they justly deserve.

Reading 5-2 *A Framework for Establishing Social Work Relationships Across Racial/Ethnic Lines**

Joan Velasquez, Marilyn E. Vigil, and Eustolio Benavides

It is well documented that disproportionately large numbers of social work clients, particularly in public agencies, are racial/ethnic minority group members. When we examine the use of social work services by these clients, we find a substantially higher rate of discontinuance than among majority group clients (Miranda, 1976). It is our assumption that many of these clients "drop out" of service because they do not perceive what they are offered as helpful and that the partnership which ideally evolves from engaging a client in a positive, purposeful relationship does not develop.

Our purpose here is to explore the development of the social work relationship across racial/ethnic lines based on a framework of biculturalism. Although this framework has evolved primarily from social work with Latinos, we believe it applies to work with any ethnic or racial minority group.

Defining culture as a relatively unified set of shared values, ideas, beliefs, and standards of action held by an identified people, numerous cultural groups can be identified within this country. The dominant culture integrated the values and norms of European immigrant groups as each was encouraged to drop its language and become assimilated by the majority. Minority groups with recognizable physical characteristics have also been pushed to accept the dominant culture as their own, yet have been responded to as separate and inferior groups and thus not allowed to participate fully in it. Due to this exclusion and to a desire on the part of some to retain their original culture, distinct groups continue to exist. We view the retention of one's culture of origin as desirable and see the perspective of biculturalism as one which encourages acceptance of difference and the capacity to work with it.

*An original article prepared especially for this volume by the authors, two of whom have been instructors, and one a student, in a student unit of the University of Minnesota School of Social Work serving Latino clients in Remsey County Mental Health Center, St. Paul, Minnesota.

Let us diagram a cultural continuum to reflect this perspective.

Relationship

Dominant Anglo/ White culture	Minority group culture
Values, norms, role expectations	Values, norms, role expectations

Each group's cultural system is based on a set of values manifested in norms and role expectations which are distinct from those of the majority cultural system. Though a wide range of individual differences exists within each group and parts of one group's system may be similar to that of others, recognizable boundaries exist and must be bridged if relationships are to be developed across them.

At either end of the continuum are located those who function within the boundaries of that cultural system. They identify and interact primarily with other members of the same group, govern their behavior according to its values and norms, and often speak a common language. Movement across the continuum in either direction indicates exposure to another cultural system and generally occurs as one interacts with members of the other group. At least one participant in a relationship which crosses racial/ethnic lines must move toward the other in order to develop common ground for communication. If movement does not occur, interaction remains on a superficial level. As noted earlier, such movement in society has generally been from right to left on this continuum, with differences viewed as negative characteristics in need of alteration. Alfred White's *The Apperceptive Mass of Foreigners as Applied to Americanization* (1971) exemplifies the concerted, largely unquestioned, effort made throughout much of our history to resocialize minority group members to abandon their heritage and become as much like members of the dominant group as possible. Majority group members have traditionally ex-

pected others to move toward them to understand their cultural system and modify their behavior accordingly. We maintain that the preferred alternative is for the social worker to develop the capacity to move across the continuum to wherever the client is located on it.

Let us consider the implications of this perspective for social work practice. Movement across the continuum essentially requires that one understand the values and norms of another cultural system, of one's own system, be aware of where differences lie, and accept both as legitimate. The Anglo/white worker, then, must acquire a substantial knowledge base including the values, expected role behaviors, historical experiences, and language of the group to which the client belongs as a basis for their work together. It is essential that the worker accept both self and other before this knowledge can be integrated and applied effectively. Workers, as they offer service to the client, then draw from this understanding and acceptance to assess where the particular individuals involved are located on the continuum.

Social workers who are members of a racial/ ethnic minority group have, when working with other members of the same group, the advantage of having learned through life experience what is expected and appropriate within its boundaries. They also have the advantage of being identified by physical characteristics as people with common experiences, more likely to be trusted than Anglo/ white workers who must overcome this immediate barrier if service is to be used. Minority workers in addition to understanding their own system, however, must develop the capacity to interact effectively within the Anglo/white system as well since its members predominantly control needed services and resources. When working with members of the other minority groups, the minority worker moves across two continua, developing his/her capacity to interact within both the dominant and other minority cultures.

Worker movement across the bicultural continuum is diagrammed in the examples on the next page. The arrows indicate that workers move from wherever they are located both to where the

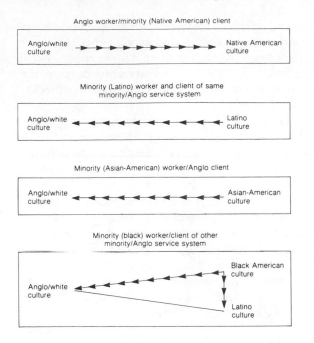

client is and toward competence in interacting with the Anglo/white system.

In order to establish helpful, purposeful relationships across racial/ethnic lines, workers of all groups must be able to move along each continuum to interact within the cultural context which has meaning for the client.

The purpose of the social work relationship is to assist clients to become the kind of people they want to become, or to do something they have chosen to do in terms of overcoming barriers in dealing more effectively with the stresses of life. The magnitude of this task for the client will not be understood by the worker if the worker lacks empathy—"the capacity to enter into the feelings and experiences of another—knowing what the other feels and experiences—without losing oneself in the process" (Compton & Galaway, see p. 291).

Unless workers have some knowledge of the values, norms, and expectations of the culture of the client and of this particular client, they will not be able to understand either the client's goals or the barriers impeding progress toward these goals. The worker will thus be unable to fulfill the purpose of

the social work relationship. It is easier for each of us as workers to work with clients who share the same cultural values, norms, expectations and world view since it is easier to be appropriately empathic with such clients. A more conscious effort is required of workers to work effectively with clients of another culture who have a different frame of reference, particularly in regard to perceptions of the importance of activity, the nature of relationships, and human nature.

Empathy, which requires openness to the reality of another person's feelings, experiences, and perceptions, facilitates the conscious efforts of workers in establishing relationships with clients of a different culture. Work with clients of a culture different from that of the workers requires, in addition, an openness on the part of workers to values, norms, and world views that their own culture may not share. This requires of the workers the capacity to understand and respect their own culture and the role it has played in their development, and to feel free to respect the culture of the other. It demands from workers a belief that no culture is inherently better than or superior to another, but that each is merely different. Such an attitude will allow workers to attempt to perceive situations from the point of view of the minority client.

We have chosen three dimensions of the Latino culture in order to illustrate factors that must be taken into account in the development of the social work relationship across racial/ethnic lines. The Latino culture is selected for illustration because it is the one with which we are most familiar. The dimensions of language, locus of control, and world view are not the only, or perhaps even the most important, dimensions of the Latino culture. However, they provide examples of how the bicultural framework can be applied in client-worker situations and illustrate points of possible incongruities between the perceptions of the worker and those of a Latino client.

Although these incongruities may not exist if either the Latino client or the worker has ease of movement on a bicultural continuum, nevertheless the onus of movement on the bicultural continuum is on the worker if he/she is to meet the client wherever the client is and if there is going to be any possibility of establishing a working relationship. This fact again emphasizes the necessity for empathy on the part of the worker.

Verbal and nonverbal communications express a person's feelings, ideas, and world view developed in a particular cultural context. The meanings assigned to verbal and nonverbal communication can result in incongruities between worker and client.

A nonverbal gesture, such as lowering of the eyes or not looking at someone directly, is interpreted by some persons as a sign of respect and deference to authorities and elders, while it is interpreted by other groups as a sign of the lack of veracity in a person. Nonverbal communication is much more open to misinterpretation than is verbal communication. However, verbal communication can also be misinterpreted when one language does not allow for the full expression of the nuances and concepts behind another language. This is especially true in regard to Spanish and English.

In Spanish there are two means of addressing another person depending on their status in terms of both age and social role. *Tu* is the personal pronoun used for addressing peers or persons who are younger, whereas *Usted* is used to address elders and persons in positions of authority. To address an authority or an elder by using *tu*, the familiar form, is not seen as a misuse of language but rather as a lack of respect due to that individual. This is not a cause for embarrassment, for there is no such term in Spanish. Rather it is a cause for shame, since disrespect is never seen as a matter to be taken lightly.

The use of *you*, the familiar pronoun in English, is appropriate at all times, since English usage does not distinguish its salutation either according to function or age. The general trend in the usage of English in this country is to do away with distinctions and to become acquainted with another on a first-name basis. To do the opposite in English is sometimes viewed as an attempt to create an artificial distance between the two parties.

In dealing with persons who are of Spanish heritage, the emphasis is not on creating an artificial distance but rather in acknowledging that which is already so, namely that some people have more power by virtue of position and some have more experience by virtue of age. To address another who is older or in authority on a first name basis is not viewed as an attempt to get closer to the other but rather as an attempt to challenge authority or to discount experience. A person who would do this would be viewed as being ill-bred or, at a minimum, ill-mannered and disrespectful.

Respect, then, becomes the key for dealing with authority. Respect, however, is not the same as *respeto*. In English one can respect another while violently opposing the opinions that that person holds. In English *respect* does not contain the element of acceptance of another's view as one's own. *Respeto*, on the other hand, means that one must not challenge the opinions of others. It means that if one chooses not to adopt the opinions of another as one's own, one must at least pay deference to the other person's views by not saying anything. Thus, the locus of control for Hispanic people tends to be much more external than internal, whether the locus is God, fate, nature, authority, or age, and this condition is constantly reinforced by means of language.

Because the respect for authority is essential to the highly structured and hierarchical world view of Hispanic people, relationships do not occur as often between equals as they do in the dominant culture. Relationships are perceived as occurring between one who is in authority and one who is not. A social worker is seen as a person who is an authority. The purpose of the social work relationship—the conscious and deliberate use of self for the benefit of the client—remains the same. The way that the purpose is viewed by Hispanic clients may be different from the way it is viewed by the majority clients.

As the Latino client enters into a social work relationship, he/she views the relationship as unequal. The worker is assigned a sense of authority and *respeto*. The client may disagree with the worker but remain silent rather than appear disrespectful. A worker, unaware of this culturally determined approach, may view the silence as resistance. Errors in assessment resulting from culture-based misinterpretations lead to antagonistic relationships and selection of inappropriate methods of intervention. Consider the discordant perceptions which may result from differences on the dimensions of locus of control and world view. Latinos tend to see many aspects of their lives in which the control is external. Anglos consider more aspects of their lives to be under internal control. The fostering of independence and self-reliance, if taken at face value, can be viewed by the Latinos as a lack of concern for others and as a pompous and unrealistic attitude on the part of the proponent. This logically follows from a Latino world view in which there is a balance of pain and pleasure and where the natural order is controlled by God. The white/Anglo world view is one in which the individual is the powerful force. Individuals are in charge of themselves and can change what they want to change about themselves or their world. Latinos view themselves as much more interdependent and not as solely in charge of themselves. What they as individuals can do is more dependent on others and the external environment.

Such contrasting views impede working toward common goals if not recognized and addressed. In working with adolescents, for example, the worker may decide to deal with that adolescent on a one-to-one basis. However, the Latino mother may view this as inappropriate since she sees herself as in control of her child. Failure to recognize and acknowledge the mother's position is likely to result in discontinuance from service. The reason might never be shared with the worker because of the authority element in the relationship.

In empathizing with a Latino client, a worker may want to move too quickly from recognizing the difficulty the client is experiencing to what could be done to help. For the client, it may be more helpful to dwell on the difficulty longer to the point where the worker might interpret this as resistance or that the client does not have the capacity to use the service. From the Latino client's point of view, the dwelling on the difficulty could be viewed as helpful since he/she knows that pain is balanced by pleasure. The worker could acknowledge that cultural element and use it with the client to prepare for the more pleasant phase of life, thus resulting in a more useful service for the client.

We have presented a framework for viewing transracial/ethnic social work relationships as developing across a bicultural continuum. The dimensions of language, locus of control, and world view illustrate points of possible incongruities between the perceptions of an Anglo worker and a Latino client which, in turn, create difficulties in establishing effective working (social work) relationships. Empathy is required if workers of one culture are to move on a bicultural continuum toward clients of a different culture. We believe that recognizing the necessity of, and developing the capacity for, such movement will increase the likelihood of engaging clients of a different culture in positive, purposeful, and effective relationships. From this perspective the worker's capacity to both move across the continuum and to assess where the client is located on it are considered essential elements in the delivery of social services to minority clients.

| Reading 5-3 | *Working Together Across Differences**

Uma Narayan

TAKING EMOTIONS SERIOUSLY

Communication and working relationships between people who differ in terms of important factors like class, race, ethnicity, gender, sexual preference, etc., are often hard to initiate or sustain, despite the presence of common interests and shared goals. I think it would be a helpful practice for individuals with different backgrounds and groups with heterogenous components to reflect on the ways in which communication between people who share, and people who do not share, the experience of oppression can be damaged. The emotions, and hence the sense of self, of the members of the oppressed group are *unintentionally* violated by nonmembers of the oppressed group who participate in the dialogue.

I have tried to analyze a number of ways in which this can happen. I think the cases I have considered are common enough to be easily recognized, and I hope they will provide a starting point for people to talk together about and work through problems in dialogue they may have had or can envision having. The cases I have considered are by no means exhaustive, and I am sure that people who focus on these problems will discover many more. I think that such an examination of the problems of communicating across our differences is a prerequisite for any individuals or groups who sincerely intend to, and need to, keep working together across and despite differences.

Such problems in communication can occur between heterogenous members of political groups, in the course of professional relationships, for instance, between social workers and the people they work with and assist, and also between friends from heterogenous backgrounds. Working across differences is a morally and socially important enterprise in every context. Both in political and

professional contexts, and in the context of friendship, such differences in elements of background and identity can be enriching resources, epistemologically, socially and personally. Learning to understand and respect these differences can make more complex our understanding of our selves and our societies, can broaden the range of our politics and enrich the variety of connections we have as persons. But such efforts are not without costs; I shall focus on these costs.

I shall, for the sake of convenience, use the term insider to refer to a member of an oppressed group and the term outsider to refer to nonmembers. These terms have a disadvantage in that they lack an explicit sense of hierarchy, but have the advantage of reversing conventional ideas of what is central and what is marginal. People are insiders or outsiders only with respect to specific forms of oppressive social structures—racism, sexism, compulsory heterosexuality, and so forth. An individual who is an insider with respect to one form of oppression (say, by being a woman) may be an outsider with respect to another form of oppression (say, by being white).

These problems in communication may have different implications when they occur in the context of political and professional relationships than they do when they occur between friends. The intimacy that characterizes friendships may permit such problems easier articulation. They may also arouse less hostility because insiders may be more willing to make allowances for outsiders who are friends than they do for outsiders who they relate to only in professional or impersonal contexts. Outsiders may be more concerned about having caused offense to insiders who are friends and hence, more willing to try and understand the nature of the problems that arise. However, working across differences is an unavoidable and valuable project in all these contexts. Hence, understanding the costs of communicating across differences and trying to minimize costs is something we must work towards.

---

*Revision of paper originally published in *Hypathia*. Revised by author for this book.

My focus on the role of the emotions in problems of communication follows the injunction of several strands of feminist theory that insist that the emotions must be taken seriously and not regarded as mere epiphenomenal baggage. Thus, although I shall be addressing problems that have to do with communicating across all sorts of difference, and not gender differences alone, my project is still primarily inspired by the feminist commitment to take emotions seriously.

Much feminist writing about the importance of taking emotions seriously has focused on the positive contributions that emotions make to knowledge and communication. This is both understandable and appropriate, since feminist theory is trying to oppose perspectives where the emotions have been regarded as totally opposed to reason and always as impediments to knowledge.

One of the most attractive features of feminist thinking is its commitment to contextualizing its claims. It would tend to be skeptical of claims that regard emotions as always a hindrance to knowledge as well as to claims that emotions always make a positive contribution to knowledge. It would prefer to examine the specific roles emotions could play in particular contexts and critically examine their contributions in such concrete contexts. In keeping with this commitment, feminist theory, in opposing perspectives that are contemptuous and/or dismissive of the emotions, would fail to live up to its own standards if it countered with another absolutist perspective on the emotions—one that said that emotions *always* had a positive contribution to make in the domain of knowledge and communication.

Therefore, I shall not apologize if at least some of my focus on the emotions is in some ways negative, in that I see them as capable of creating problems for communication across differences. However, even where my focus is thus negative, I am still committed to taking emotions seriously and to understanding their validity in the contexts in which they arise.

Differences that arise from class, race, gender, sexual preference, etc., contribute to making insiders and outsiders often significantly different in their opportunities, values, and social experiences.

Factors like race, class, and gender have historically been a significant part of deep and divisive social structures, which have engendered conflict, tension, hostility, and mistrust between insiders and outsiders. Communication and relationships between insiders and outsiders are in constant danger of breaking down if people do not learn to trust one another across divisive social differences and if people do not learn how to sustain working relationships in contexts of sometimes powerful distrust and disagreement. Even when people are working together for powerfully binding and common social, political, professional, or personal goals, communication cannot be sustained unless the prejudices and problems which arise between insiders and outsiders are examined and addressed.

So, working together continuously across our differences seems to be a project we cannot avoid or get away from. We are condemned to either ignoring and annihilating differences at the cost of conflict and mistrust, or to working tenuously across them to form always risky bonds of understanding.

EPISTEMIC PRIVILEGE AND THE POLITICS OF DIFFERENCE

My starting premise about what it takes to work together across differences is that goodwill is not enough. What I mean is that a simple resolution on the part of individuals or groups that they will try to understand the experiences of more disadvantaged persons or groups, whose oppression they do not share, and a resolve to try and empathize with their interests, although a useful thing to have, is not going to solve or resolve the thousands of problems that are going to crop up in discussion and communication. Too often, even the most resolute possessors of goodwill will find themselves baffled and angered by failures of communication.

The possession of such resolute goodwill on the part of members of more advantaged groups (men, white people, straight folk, westerners, etc.) towards members of more disadvantaged groups (women, people of color, gay people, members of Third World cultures, etc.) may be an important foundation for the beginning of trust-building experiences between them. But the advantaged outsiders would be wrong to expect this to be sufficient to cause strong, historically constituted networks of distrust to simply evaporate into thin air. If anything, such goodwill must help sustain communication through situations, issues and discussions which inevitably cause resurgences of mistrust.

Annette Baier says:

> One leaves others an opportunity to harm one when one trusts, and also shows one's confidence that they will not take it. Reasonable trust will require good grounds for such confidence in another's good will, or at least the absence of good grounds for expecting their ill will or indifference. Trust then, on this first approximation, is accepted vulnerability to another's possible but not expected ill will (or lack of good will) toward one. (1986, p. 235)

The situations I am concerned about differ in significant ways from the sort of situation of trust that Baier seems to have in mind, since they are characterized by the presence of historically constituted relations of power, privilege and lack of understanding on the part of members of advantaged groups, and reasonable grounds for mistrust on the part of members of disadvantaged groups. Members of disadvantaged groups may be willing to set aside their mistrust of members of advantaged groups with whom they work or relate, to the extent of accepting the existence of goodwill on the part of these advantaged outsiders. But they cannot fail to be aware that the presence of goodwill on the part of the outsiders is not enough to overcome assumptions and attitudes born out of centuries of power and privilege.

Insiders cannot fail to realize that being hurt by the insensitivity of outsiders they endeavor to work with and care about is often more difficult to deal with emotionally than being hurt by the deliberate malice of outsiders they expect no better of. Here, insiders render themselves more vulnerable because they accept the existence of goodwill on the part of outsiders, and they have good reason to expect that they will be hurt, goodwill notwithstanding.

I shall try to examine where some of the difficulties in communicating across differences may lie. I shall start by examining the claim that members of oppressed groups may have epistemic privilege (Harding, 1982; Hartsock, 1983; Jaggar,

1985). The claim of epistemic privilege amounts to claiming that members of an oppressed group have a more immediate, subtle and critical knowledge about the nature of their oppression than people who are nonmembers of the oppressed group. I shall try to flesh out what I understand by the notion of the epistemic privilege of the oppressed while simultaneously trying to state what this claim does not imply.

The claim of epistemic privilege for the oppressed need not imply that the insiders have a clearer or better knowledge of the *causes* of their oppression. Since oppression is often partly constituted by the oppressed being denied access to education and hence to the means of theory production (which would include detailed knowledge of the history of their oppression, conceptual tools with which to analyze its mechanisms, etc.), the oppressed may not have a detailed causal/structural analysis of how their specific form of oppression originated, how it has been maintained, and of all the systemic purposes it serves. Explanatory theories and conceptual tools such as class structure and patriarchy that help us understand the specificities of a certain form of oppression and its links with other forms are often developed by people who are not members of the oppressed group and whose relative privilege in that regard has given them greater access to the means of theoretical reflection and production.

So, what is it about the nature of their oppression that the oppressed can be said to have epistemic privilege about? I think they have epistemic privilege when it comes to immediate knowledge of everyday life under oppression—all the details of the ways in which their oppression is experienced, seen to be inflicted, and of the ways in which the oppression affects the major and minor details of their social and psychic lives. They know firsthand the detailed and concrete ways in which oppression defines the spaces in which they live and how it affects their lives. I think that the emotions play an important role in the knowledge that is part of the epistemic privilege of the oppressed. I shall return to this shortly. I do not wish to suggest a rigid distinction between description (which the oppressed insiders do better) and explanation (which the outsiders may do better), between questions (which the insiders may raise) and answers (that outsiders may have theoretical tools to provide). No explanation of a form of oppression can be adequate that totally fails to account for the way it is experienced and described by the oppressed; questions that the oppressed raise have assumptions and are theory-laden and may serve to shatter the neat explanatory paradigms of outsiders.

Second, the claim to epistemic privilege for the oppressed does not mean, as far as I am concerned, that people who are not members of the oppressed group can *never* come to understand the experiences of the oppressed or share in their insights or knowledge. Such a claim would have very undesirable political consequences. It could be taken as a license to excuse all those who are not members of any oppressed group from any concern with that oppression. After all, if outsiders can never understand many or most significant aspects of a form of oppression, how could they meaningfully take an interest in it or help fight against it? Taken this way, the claim to epistemic privilege would make communication between insiders and even sympathetic outsiders close to useless. Besides, such an unconveyability of insights thesis is simply untrue. Many of us would claim to know, say, a few men who are sympathetic to and understand a good deal about feminist concerns, or white people who are concerned with and understand a good deal about issues of race.

But I think that the claim to the epistemic privilege of the oppressed does imply that people who are not members of the oppressed group will have to make a great deal of effort to come to grips with the details of lived oppression. Having insiders as friends and colleagues, sharing in aspects of their life-style, fighting alongside them on issues that concern them, and sustaining a continuous dialogue with them can all help outsiders develop a more sophisticated understanding of what oppression involves. But outsiders who do none of the above, but simply have an abstract sort of goodwill towards insiders, are unlikely to have a clear or detailed awareness of the forms in which an oppression is experienced.

Outsiders should not yield to the temptation to use the thesis of the epistemic privilege of the insider as an excuse for the view that they can learn nothing about oppression unless educated about it by insiders. If insiders have epistemic privilege about their oppression, outsiders cannot educate themselves satisfactorily about the situation of insiders except by listening to or reading about their experience of their situation. But concerned outsiders must recognize that their concern carries with it a responsibility to actively seek out and acquire such knowledge, rather than see it as the insider's responsibility to bring such knowledge to their attention because the oppression is the insider's problem. Such an attitude on the part of outsiders would merely add a pedagogic burden to all the other burdens of the insider. Sympathetic outsiders must recognize that their concern for a form of oppression must be reflected in their willingness to actively educate themselves about it.

Third, the claim that the oppressed have epistemic privilege does not amount to a claim that the knowledge they have of their oppression is in any way incorrigible. Members of an oppressed group, like human subjects in general, can always be mistaken about the nature of their experience. Other insiders may differ in the way they perceive or interpret certain incidents or even certain general types of incidents. It may well be the case that not all of them can be right, and at times, it may even be that all of them are wrong. The operations of ideology may sometimes convince insiders that their situation is other than it is, and an outsider may occasionally be able to more clearly see and articulate what is going on. It is certainly not my intention to rule out such possibilities a priori.

But the thesis that the oppressed have epistemic privilege does have some implications for outsiders who want to argue that the understanding of an insider is wrong. The outsider must undertake the attempt with what I shall call methodological humility and methodological caution. By the requirement of methodological humility I mean that the outsider must always sincerely conduct herself under the assumption that, as an outsider, she may be missing something, and that what appears to her to be a mistake on the part of the insider may make more sense if she had a fuller understanding of the context. By the requirement of methodological caution, I mean that the outsider should sincerely attempt to carry out her attempted criticism of the insider's perceptions in such a way that it does not amount to, or even seem to amount to, an attempt to denigrate or dismiss entirely the validity of the insider's point of view.

Fourth, the claim to epistemic privilege for the oppressed should not be *identified* with the claim that the oppressed should speak for themselves and represent their own interests. That the oppressed should speak for themselves may be a thesis to which we may have a moral and political commitment quite regardless of the view that the oppressed have epistemic privilege. Even if insiders had no epistemic privilege whatsoever, there are several other good and important reasons why they should speak for themselves. Historically, those in power have always spoken in ways that have suggested that their point of view is universal and represents the values, interests, and experiences of everyone. Today, many critiques of political, moral and social theory are directed at showing how these allegedly universal points of view are partial and skewed and represent the viewpoints of the powerful and the privileged (Young, 1986). Insiders will, therefore, be quite warranted in being skeptical about the possibility of outsiders adequately speaking for them.

Besides, the right and power to speak for oneself is closely tied to the oppressed group's sense of autonomy, identity, and self-respect. That it will foster and safeguard this sense of autonomy and self-respect is a good enough reason to say that the oppressed should speak for themselves, questions of epistemic privilege apart. However, if the thesis of the epistemic privilege of the oppressed is true, it would provide yet another reason for arguing that oppressed groups should speak for themselves. If insiders do have epistemic privilege, they can understand their problems and represent their own interests better than outsiders could.

EPISTEMIC PRIVILEGE AND THE EMOTIONS

I would like to argue that a very important component of what constitutes the epistemic privilege of the oppressed has to do with knowledge that is at least partly constituted by and conferred by the emotional responses of the oppressed to their oppression. Unlike concerned outsiders whose knowledge of the experience of oppression is always more or less abstract and theoretical, the knowledge of insiders is enriched by the emotional reactions that the lived experience of oppression confers.

In what ways does an insider's emotional responses to lived oppression enrich knowledge of the nature of that oppression in ways that are much more difficult for an outsider to achieve? I can think of at least three ways.

1. *Minimizing the Emotional Costs of Oppression.* Sympathetic outsiders can and do react not only intellectually, but emotionally to incidents of racism, sexism, and so forth, even though they are not and may never be the targets of such oppression. But outsiders may often fail to realize that the insiders' emotional responses to the oppression may be much more complex than their own. Such failure may lead their understanding of the emotional costs of the oppression to be more sketchy than that of insiders. Sympathetic outsiders, when told about or present at an incident that is racist or sexist often do feel anger at the perpetrator and sympathy with the victim. The insider victim, however, may feel a complex and jumbled array of emotions: anger at the perpetrator, a deep sense of humiliation, a sense of being soiled by the incident, momentary hatred for the whole group of which the perpetrator is a part, rage at the sort of history that has produced and sustains such attitudes, anger and shame at one's powerlessness to retaliate, a strong sense of solidarity with those who face the same problems, and maybe even pity for the stupidity of the perpetrator. Outsiders, not having been at the receiving end of the oppression, may fail to wholly grasp its effects on its victims and their understanding may, therefore, fail to do justice to the costs of that experience.

2. *Missing the Subtler Manifestations of Oppression.* Outsiders who have not experienced an

oppression firsthand and have only learned about it secondhand are likely to understand only the *general* and *commonplace* ways in which the oppression is manifested. For instance, if a professor uses openly racist or sexist examples or is openly hostile to minority or female students, sympathetic white male students may be able to spot his attitudes quite as well as the victims of the attitudes. But if his attitudes are expressed more covertly, through dismissing their queries, not taking their contributions seriously, undervaluing their work, or lack of cordiality, outsiders may fail to see what is happening to the insiders.

An insider who is sensitized to such prejudiced attitudes will often pick up cues ranging from facial expressions to body language that an outsider may simply fail to spot and will often also be alerted by her own feelings of unease about the person or situation. As a consequence, the insider is far more likely than the outsider to know the extent to which a form of oppression permeates a society and affects the lives of its victims and the very subtle forms in which it can operate.

3. *Not Making Connections or Failing to See Oppression in New Contexts.* Outsiders usually know about the more widespread and commonplace contexts in which an oppression is manifested and may fail to carry over what they know from one context when they encounter the same sort of phenomena in new or unusual contexts. Or, they may fail to make the connection between what they know in theory and what is actually taking place in a given situation. For instance, men who have been sensitized to the silencing of women in public or professional forums may fail to see the phenomenon taking place in informal gatherings or between friends. Insiders are more likely to make these connections and to carry over what they have learned to new contexts, because they become more vigilant in their attitudes the more they are exposed to the oppression.

EMOTIONAL COSTS OF WORKING
ACROSS DIFFERENCE

Although being an insider to a form of oppression may confer epistemic privilege, it certainly constitutes a burden. Insiders live burdened by all the forms an oppression takes, from everyday and trivial manifestations to violent and life-threatening ones. Insiders pay a heavy social and psychological price that no outsider pays. For insiders to work together with outsiders is a project that is often fraught with difficulty, for, in any communication, the two groups are not equally vulnerable. Maria Lugones and Elizabeth Spelman explain the nature of this unequal vulnerability thus:

> And yet, we have had to be in your world and learn its ways. We have to participate in it, make a living in it, live in it, be mistreated in it, be ignored in it, and rarely, be appreciated in it. In learning to do these things or in learning to suffer them or in learning to enjoy what is to be enjoyed or in learning to understand your conception of us, we have had to learn your culture and thus your language and self-conceptions. But there is nothing that necessitates that you understand our world; understand, that is, not as an observer understands things, but as a participant, as someone who has a stake in them understands them. So your being ill at ease in our world lacks the features of our being ill at ease in yours precisely because you can leave and you can always tell yourselves that you will soon be out of there and because the wholeness of your selves is never touched by us, we have no tendency to remake you in our image. (Lugones & Spelman, 1983, p. 576)

It is the insider who pays the price of oppression and even sympathetic outsiders, since they are prone to blind spots and clumsiness, can offend and hurt the insider more often than they imagine. Insiders can neither simply walk away from the problems and issues that permeate their lives, as the outsider always can, nor can they ever inadvertently hurt outsiders in quite the same way that outsiders can hurt them. Thus, since the brunt of possible hurt is most often on the insider, the burden of taking care not to cause offense can fairly be laid on the outsider. Outsiders often assume, wrongly, that goodwill on their part is a guarantee against causing offense to insiders; when insiders are offended and express their anger, the outsiders often react with honest bafflement and anger since they cannot understand how someone as sympathetic to a form of oppression could conceivably be seen as having offensive views or attitudes.

I shall try to list and analyze a number of ways in which outsiders may reveal lack of understanding and cause affront and grief to insiders. The list is in no way exhaustive. Understanding these ways in which communicating across differences may falter and go wrong may help outsiders avoid these problems and may help insiders to try and understand why the outsider is going wrong.

These failures have in common the inability of outsiders to fully understand and respect the emotional responses of insiders. In some cases, the responses of outsiders violates insiders' sense of self-identity, self-worth or self-respect. In other cases, the responses of outsiders violate insiders' sense of identity, respect, and solidarity with their group.

Case 1: Overt Denial of the Validity of the Insider's Understanding and/or Response. Given the way differences work, it is hardly surprising that insiders and outsiders may often have very different understandings of what is involved in a situation or issue. For instance, men and women often have very different understandings concerning what is involved and where responsibility lies in cases of sexual harassment. Men often think women are responsible for attracting unwanted attention because of the way they dress or conduct themselves. Women often see this sort of view as a selfexculpating explanation that absolves men of their real responsibility. When, for instance, men totally blame women for the sexual harassment from which they suffer, they wholly deny the validity of the insiders' understanding of such harassment as something inflicted on them. The insider will most often respond emotionally to such attempts to negate her understanding—with anger, tears, etc. The issue, to the insiders, is not a purely theoretical one, and their anger and pain at what they have to endure becomes exacerbated by the seeming inability of even well-intentioned outsiders to see their point of view.

The situation is complicated by the fact that most outsiders and insiders have been socialized differently and understand and display emotions in

very different ways. For instance, public (or even private) displays of emotion by women, which are experienced as natural and authentic by the women, often seem excessive and artificial to men.

Outsiders often react to insiders' emotional responses over a disagreement in two ways. The outsider may dismiss the emotional response as just one of those silly and irrational responses to which insiders are prone and/or the outsider may accuse the insider of using the emotional response as a manipulative measure. The insider may be told that since she could not muster arguments that were cogent enough to convince the outsider, she is now resorting to emotional tactics to win the argument.

If the outsider takes both tacks, the insider is in a strange double-bind over her emotions. If her response is authentic and natural, it is also pathetic and a symptom of her weakness, irrationality, and lack of self-control. If her response is not a symptom of weakness and irrationality, it is a calculated, manipulative and unauthentic strategic move on her part. To an insider, who already feels that she has rendered herself vulnerable by displaying her emotions, such dismissals or accusations of manipulation add insult to injury. The outsider must realize that such denial of the validity of the insiders' responses will almost certainly cause a serious breach in the dialogue, since they deeply violate the insider's self-respect.

Case 2: Accusations of Paranoia. Outsiders often consider the reactions of insiders to be paranoid and accuse them of paranoia. They mean that they think that the insiders are imagining the existence of racist or sexist attitudes, say, in too many cases where outsiders fail to see it and where they therefore consider these attitudes to be absent. (This is another way in which the outsider can deny the validity of the insider's response, but I think it is common and important enough to treat separately). I have already examined reasons why even sympathetic outsiders may fail to pick up on subtle forms of prejudice and discrimination. An accusation of paranoia is a particularly dangerous reaction from outsiders, especially since, in many cases, insiders are never totally sure that their judgments are accurate. Often, subtle instances of racism or sexism are such as to be open to interpretation. Insiders are often aware of this and are often anxious and uncertain about their own perceptions. They are often extremely ambivalent about whether to make an issue of it, especially since the incident or remark can be explained away; and once such explaining away occurs, the insider who raised the issue ends up being made to feel nasty and suspicious for having raised the issue in the first place.

But insiders are more often correct than mistaken in their suspicions. Sometimes less subtle manifestations follow that give the show away, or else the insider meets other insiders who have the same feelings of unease and suspect similar prejudices on the part of the same outsider. For instance, women students and students of color seem to have quite a lot of agreement in their individual judgments as to which of their professors are sexist or racist, often in the subtlest of ways.

Outsiders should refrain as far as possible from such accusations of paranoia, since outsiders are more likely than not to be wrong, and since such accusations undermine insiders' trust in their own perceptions. This may reduce their capacity for vigilance, something that those who are on the receiving end of oppression can ill afford.

Case 3: Insensitive Reactions to an Insider's Response. Outsiders can be offensively insensitive to the reactions of insiders without necessarily overtly dismissing them as irrational, manipulative, or paranoid. I shall illustrate this sort of insensitivity with an incident. A group of people, who were interested in various sorts of oppression, were discussing the question of whether it was important that women (rather than men) taught courses in feminist theory, and whether it was important that black professors (rather than white ones) taught courses in black literature, philosophy, and history.

A black male participant talked about an awful pedagogic experience with a white teacher who taught Richard Wright with little sensitivity to the context of black culture and experience, and who constantly dismissed what his black students had to say. He was, presumably, arguing that there was a reason for black writings to be taught by black professors. A white participant responded to this by saying that it was better that such works got included on syllabi, regardless of who taught them, rather than their not being included because there were no teachers from appropriate backgrounds to teach them. This reaction was experienced as an insensitive one because the insider's account of his unhappy pedagogic experience was brushed aside and not addressed and because the same basic point could have been made very differently. For instance, the outsider could have said, "I can understand what you are talking about. Such experiences must be awful. But don't you think that, perhaps, it may be a good thing to push for black writings to be included on syllabi, regardless of who is there to teach them?" In this case, the outsider was white, a woman, and a feminist. This becomes not only a case of an insensitive response, but a case of an insensitive failure to analogize. If a woman had talked about how awful it was to do Virginia Woolf with a sexist male teacher, and if a man, whatever his race, had dismissed it similarly, any feminist would have perceived it as a sexist response.

If working together across difference is to be possible, we must all learn to analogize from situations of oppression in which we have been insiders to those in which we are outsiders. It is sad, but seems unfortunately true, that experience and understanding of one form of oppression does not necessarily sensitize one to other forms. But if we make the effort to analogize, it may give us some clues as to how to avoid insensitive responses in areas in which we are outsiders.

Case 4: Failure by Outsiders to Avoid Crude and Stereotypic Generalizations about Insiders. Sometimes, even the best-intentioned outsiders cannot seem to get away from cliches and stereotypic generalizations about insiders. I am not talking about cliches at the level of all blacks are lazy or all women are irrational, which are self-evidently offensive, but much more insidious and difficult to see cliches and generalizations. For instance, outsiders may see complexly culturally mediated attitudes to birth control, family size, work and so forth as results of simple ignorance or backwardness on the part of insiders. Outsiders should carefully scrutinize their explanations for the ways insiders think and act for such cliches that are insulting to insiders.

Case 5: Failure to See Why Something That Is Not Explicitly Insulting to a Person or Group May Be Implicitly So. Outsiders are often taken aback by the sharp reactions of insiders to statements that the outsider cannot see as having anything to do with the insider, let alone be insulting. For instance, women in a group may react sharply to a man's statements that are frequently insulting to *particular* women, who may not be present or even be members of the group. The women may suspect, with perhaps some justification, that the man's statements reflect the man's attitudes to women in general. If the outsider is to avoid that sort of reaction, he must be very careful to specify what his criticism of a particular insider is and try to show why it is not an expression of a general negative attitude to insiders in general.

Outsiders often fail to understand why, for instance, an Indian may react negatively to implicitly derogatory remarks about say Chinese or African cultures. Outsiders fail to see that the insider may quite legitimately suspect similar derogatory attitudes on the outsider's part towards her own culture, because she suspects the derogatory attitudes stem from a negative view of nonwestern cultures in general. It may be very difficult, but outsiders will have to try and focus on the more general implications that statements they make may have for insiders, or else they are likely to insult them unintentionally.

Case 6: Inappropriate Judgments about What Insiders Ought to Do or Feel. Outsiders often think that their relationship with insiders warrants their making judgments about what insiders ought to do or feel. These judgments, almost inevitably, turn out to be insulting to the insider. For instance, women philosophers and philosophers of color who are interested in areas like mathematical logic are offended by implications that someone like them should be devoting themselves to political philosophy and/or feminist theory. Outsiders who imply this fail to see why, for someone like them, it may be a matter of pride to excel in an unconventional (for people like them) and difficult field like mathematical logic. Similarly, many western femi-

nists imply that they find some nonwestern feminists too harsh and critical about their own cultures. They may fail to see how women who have fought against some of the most oppressive aspects of those cultures cannot afford the more rose-tinted view of it that outsiders can. Good advice to outsiders is that they should try and learn from the perceptions of insiders, rather than tell insiders what they ought to do or feel, especially about contexts and issues that they ought to suspect they know less about than insiders.

There are, no doubt, several other ways in which communicating across difference can create problems for the participants. For instance, outsiders may fail to understand why their desire for praise or acknowledgment for their interest in an issue that does not directly affect them, could be met with resentment on the part of insiders. Or, outsiders may fail to understand why, at moments of crisis, even insiders whom they are close to may prefer to sort their feelings out with and discuss their problems with other insiders.

I think these problems of communicating across difference will be easier to handle if both insiders and outsiders take the idea of the epistemic privilege of the oppressed seriously. Outsiders must try to understand that goodwill on their part is not sufficient to guarantee that their perceptions and comments are inoffensive to insiders. They must sensitize themselves to the fact that insiders may have more subtle and complex understanding of the ways in which oppression operates and is experienced. They must realize that insiders are specially vulnerable to insensitivities from outsiders whose goodwill they have accepted and who they have begun to trust. Awareness of these features that impinge on dialogue with insiders would convince outsiders that they have good reason to proceed with what I have called methodological humility and methodological caution and focus more careful attention on the implications of what they say.

Outsiders may, rightly, feel that the exercise of methodological humility and methodological caution may cramp the spontaneity of their reactions and the ease with which they communicate. However, this loss of ease and spontaneity seems a necessary and small price to pay to avoid causing offense to insiders and causing serious breaches in communication. If it is not only possible that insiders have epistemic privilege, but if it is also true that insiders are specially vulnerable to insensitivities from outsiders they trust and work with, it seems both unavoidable and only fair that outsiders bear the burden of exercising caution and of taking care not to offend.

Is there anything insiders can do to help in working across differences? Perhaps, taking the idea of the epistemic privilege of the oppressed seriously can make a difference to insiders as well. Realizing that outsiders do not have the subtle understanding of oppression that insiders have, may help insiders deal with insensitive perceptions or comments by outsiders with greater charity. It may help insiders realize that such insensitivities are not necessarily a symptom of lack of goodwill on the part of outsiders. By realizing the difficulties outsiders may have in understanding the subtleties of oppression, insiders may see their insensitivities as less culpable.

This is not to say that such insensitivities must be simply overlooked or forgiven instead of being confronted or dealt with. But the manner in which the confrontation takes place may be different. For instance, instead of reacting with understandable anger that inevitably makes the outsider defensive, the insider could try instead to point out why the outsider's remarks or perceptions were experienced as hurtful or offensive.

I shall not pretend that this is an easy thing to do, or that this is asking no more of insiders than exercising methodological humility and methodological caution asks of outsiders. It is very hard for insiders not to react with anger to such insensitivities, for each such insensitivity evokes memories of countless others. Besides, anger is a necessary emotion for those who must constantly exercise vigilance and retain their self-respect in the face of systematic social prejudice and discrimination. Insensitivities from outsiders one trusts make insiders especially bitter and pessimistic about hopes for change, and anger is often an inevitable corollary.

Besides, revealing one's anger makes one less vulnerable than revealing one's hurt. In revealing one's anger, one seems to react from a position of strength, while revealing one's hurt lacks this quality and seems to open up possibilities of the outsider reacting with either pity or guilt, neither of which the insider can find very palatable. Moreover, insiders are often fed up with the burden of constantly having to explain themselves and their perceptions to outsiders, and bitter about the fact that, while they must unavoidably live and function in the outsider's world, the outsider has no such imperative to understand their world and their experience. However, perhaps insiders must try, whenever possible, to raise issues of insensitivity from outsiders, with some rein on their anger. And outsiders, in their turn, must try to understand the nature and sources of the insider's anger.

I am sure that serious examination of the project of communicating across differences will reveal several other kinds of problems. What is important is that these problems are seriously examined, analyzed, and addressed, leading to more sensitive perceptions on the part of outsiders and more easy dialogue and interaction between insiders and outsiders.

For Further Reading

Acosta, F. (1980). Self-described reasons for premature termination of psychotherapy by Mexican American, Black American, and Anglo-American patients. *Psychological Reports, 47,* 435-443.

Bernal, G., & Flores-Ortiz, Y. (1982). Latino families in therapy: engagement and evaluation. *Journal of Marital and Family therapy.*

Bookin, D., & Dunkle, R. (1985). Elder abuse: Issues for the practitioners. *Social Casework,* 3-12.

Burgest, D. (1973). Racism in everyday speech and social work jargon. *Social Work,* 18(4), 20-25.

Cafferty, P. (1976). Bilingualism in America. In P. Cafferty & Chestang (Eds.), *The Diverse Society.* NASW.

Cain, R. (1991). Stigma management and gay identity development. *Social Work*, 36, 67-73.

Cowger, C. (1992). Assessment of client strengths. In D. Saleebey (Ed.), *The strengths perspective in social work practice*. New York: Longman.

Dahrendorf, R. (1968). On the origin of inqeuality among men. *Essays in the theory of society*. Stanford University Press.

Davis, L. (1985). Female and male voices in social work. *Social Work*, 106-113.

Davis, L., & Proctor, E. (1989). *Race, gender and class: guidelines for practice with individuals, families and groups*. Englewood Cliffs, New Jersey: Prentice-Hall.

Devore, W., & Schlesinger, E. (1983). Adaptation of skills for ethnic-sensitive practice. In *Ethnic-sensitive social work practice*. St. Louis: C.V. Mosby.

Dobelstein, A., & Johnson, A. (1985). Understanding older people. In Serving older adults. Englewood Cliffs, N.J.: Prentice-Hall.

Dowd, J., & Bengton, V. (1978). Aging in minority populations: An examination of the double jeopardy hypothesis. *Journal of Gerontology*, 33, 427-36.

Dressel, P. (1988). Gender, race, and class: Beyond the feminization of poverty in later life. *The Gerontologist*, 28, 177-180.

Dung, T. (1984). Understanding Asian familics: Viet-namese perspective. *Social Work*, 13, 10-12.

Gonzales, J. (1990). The nature of prejudice and discrimination. In *Racial and ethnic groups in America*. Dubuque, Iowa: Kendall/Hunt.

Goodluck, C., & Short D. (1980). Working with American Indian parents: A cultural approach. *Social Casework*, 16, 472-467.

Green, J. (1982). Help seeking behavior. In *Cultural awareness in the human services. Englewood Cliffs, New Jersey: Prentice-Hall*.

Green, J. (1982). *Cultural awareness in the human services*. Englewood Cliffs, New Jersey: Prentice Hall, 3-27.

Gutierrez, L. (1990). Working with women of color: An empowerment perspective. *Social Work*, 149-153.

Hirshman, C. (1983). America melting pot reconsidered. *Annual Review of Sociology*.

Hogan, P., & Siu, S. (1988). Minority children and the child welfare system: An historical perspective. *Social Work*, 493-498.

Holzberg, C. (1982). Ethnicity and aging: anthropological perspectives on more than just the minority elderly. *The Gerontologist*, 22, 249-257.

Hooyman, N., & Lustbader, A. Taking care of the caregivers. In *Taking care: Supporting older people and their families*. New York: Free Press.

Horse, J. (1984). Family Structure and value orientation in American Indians. *Social Casework*, 16, 472-475.

Johnson, B. (1982). American Indian jurisdiction as a policy issue. *Social Work*, 31-37.

Kadushin, A. (1972). Cross-cultural interviewing. In *The social work interview* (3rd ed.) New York: Columbia Press.

Logan, S. (1990). Black families: Race, ethnicity, culture, social class, and gender issues. *Social work practice with black families*. New York: Longman.

Longress, J. (1974). Racism and its effects on Puerto Rican continental. *Social Casework*, 67-75.

Lukes, C., & Land, H. (1990). Biculturality and homo-sexuality. *Social Work*, 151-161.

McGoldrick, M. (1982). Ethnicity and family therapy: An overview. in McGoldrick, Pearce & Giordano (Eds.), *Ethnicity and Family Therapy*. New York: The Guildford Press.

McIntosh, P. (1989). White privilege. Unpacking the invisible knapsack. *Peace and Freedom*.

Miller, J.B. (1976). Domination-subordination. *Toward a new psychology of women*. Bacon Press.

Morales, A. (1981). Social work with third-world people. *Social Work*, 45-51.

Nes, J., & Iadicola, P. (1989). Toward a definition of feminist social work: A comparison of liberal, radical, and socialist models. *Social Work*, 12-21.

Norton, D. (1978). *The dual perspective*. New York: CSWE.

Pinderhughes, E. (1983). Empowerment for our clients and for ourselves. *Social Casework*, 331-338.

Robinson, J. (1989). Clinical treatment of black families: Issues and strategies. *Social Work*, 34, 323-329.

Rogler, L. et al. (1987). What do culturally sensitive mental health services mean? The case of hispanics. *American Psychologist*.

Roth, S. (1989). Psychotherapy with lesbian couples: Individual issues, female socialization, and the social context. In M. McGoldrick, C. Anderson, & F. Walsh, *Women in families: A framework for family therapy*. New York: W.W. Norton & Co.

Sanders, D. *A psychotherapeutic approach to homosexual men*

Schaefer, R. (1990). Ethnicity and religion in american life. In *Racial and ethnic groups*. Glenview, Illinois: Scott, Foresman and Company.

Sidel, R. *Women and children last: The plight of poor women in affulent america*. Penguin Books. Chapter 4. Welfare: How to Keep a Good Woman Down.

Solomon, B. (1976). *Black empowerment: Social work in oppressed communities*. New York: Columbia Press. Chapter 10. Characteristics of the nonracist practitioner.

Sue, S., & Zane, N. (1987). The role of culture and cultural techniques in psychotherapy. *American Psychologist*.

Torres-Gil, F. (1986). An examination of factor affecting future cohorts of elderly hispanics. *The Gerontologist*, 26, 140-146.

Valentich, M. (1986). Feminism and social work practice. In F. Turner, (ed.), *Social Work Treatment* (3rd ed.) New York: Free Press.

Velasquez, J., Vigil, M., & Benavides. (1989). A framework for establishing social work relationships across racial/ethnic lines. In Compton and Galaway. *Social Work Processes* (4th ed.). Belmont, CA: Wadsworth.

Walsh, F., & Scheinkman, M. (1989). (Fe)male: The hidden gender dimension in models of family therapy. In M. McGoldrick, C. Anderson, & F. Walsh. *Women in families: A framework for family therapy*. New York: W.W. Norton & Co.

Walter, R. (1982). Race, resources, conflict. *Social Work*, 24-30.

Chapter 6

Sanctions for Social Work Practice

In the preceding chapters we have discussed knowledge and values as important components of social work practice. In this chapter we will discuss the accountability of the practitioner to client, community, profession, and agency and the sanctions within which social workers are expected to function. We will also discuss our responsibility to work within policy and agency limitations as creatively and fully as possible and to advocate changes in law, policy, and procedures that appear to limit our services to our clients.

Professional Account- ability

A profession develops when society identifies a complex problem of social importance whose solution demands knowledge and skill that are greater than those possessed by the average member of society. The solution of the problem is seen as requiring specialized knowledge and skill involving nonroutine decision making and tasks that cannot be standardized. The knowledge and skill demanded are usually such that persons desiring to practice in the name of the profession must invest considerable time in their development and must demonstrate a satisfactory level of competence.

The knowledge and skill possessed by professionals give them powerful control over persons and things. Because of the specialized knowledge involved, the persons using the services of the professional may not have the expertise to judge the adequacy of the services they are receiving. Professionals usually demand an autonomy that allows them to make judgments and take actions independent of lay control; they often consider themselves accountable only to their peers. Society provides the professional the opportunity to secure this power. It is therefore important that it be used primarily in the community interest and not to advance professionals at the cost of those who support their acquisition of such knowledge. Thus the community usually has some organized way of sanctioning the persons who may claim the status and practice in the name of the profession. Also, the profession itself, to safeguard against the self-aggrandizement of its members and ensure that its function in society is fulfilled, supports the underlying value of community service.

In all professions the community sanctions the individual's right to practice through some combination of the following elements: (1) completion of a certain prescribed course of education; (2) proof of a certain level of competency through an examination process administered by the profession; (3) licensing and regulation of the practitioner through a license, registration, or certification administered by the state (usually through a board with professionals as members); and (4) employment by an organization authorized by the state to offer certain services. Thus there exists licensing of teachers and doctors and the registration of nurses.

Early social workers were volunteers. As the responsibilities of social workers grew, paid staff began to replace the volunteer. As is true in the beginning of most professions, paid staff were trained on the job by senior and experienced people. Later there came the demand for formal education as preparation for professional positions, and schools of social work were established.

Licensure of Social Work Since the beginning of professional schools, there has been pressure within the profession to license social workers and to require certain qualifications as well as a passing grade on a licensing examination to practice as a social worker. Since licensing has come slowly to social work, the National Association of Social Workers (NASW) attempted some time ago to set some standards through the establishment of a restricted title. The title, Certified Social Worker, has been registered with the federal government and can be used only by persons certified by the professional association, the National Association of Social Workers. To use this title, social workers have to possess an M.S.W. degree (a master's degree in social work), have worked two years in practice under supervision following the earning of the M.S.W., supply appropriate references, be a member in good standing of the NASW, and pass a professional examination. A person who meets these requirements may use the title Certified Social Worker and use the letters ACSW (Academy of Certified Social Workers) after his or her name. The profession recommends that no one who is not a member of the academy engage in private practice.

Licensing as a restriction of who may practice in the name of the profession is a legal procedure that requires legislation in each state. Social work, what social workers do, the responsibilities they assume, and the demands for knowledge and skill are poorly understood both by the public and by the legislators. Consequently, the passage of licensing bills has been slow and the process of advocating for them has been difficult. But progress is being made. Most states now require licenses or certification. As licensing is mandated by the state, the requirements for licensing are different from state to state, although many states allow reciprocity for social workers licensed in another state. Many states have different levels of licenses that depend on the qualifications and experience of the candidate. Most states require social workers to participate in various ongoing educational experiences to keep their license current.

All professions are organized into some kind of professional association. These professional organizations serve three purposes: (1) increasing the adequacy of the performance of the individual practitioner; (2) policing the ranks of its membership to ensure competent performance of the individual members; and (3) protecting the members' exclusive right to practice their profession. In social work the professional association is the National Association of Social Workers, a national association operating through regional chapters in each state. It accepts for full membership those persons who have a B.S.W. (Bachelor of Social Work) degree in social welfare or social work.

The admission of the B.S.W. worker to membership in the professional association followed the setting up of professional undergraduate courses in social work in universities and the implementation of an accreditation program of B.S.W. work by the Council on Social Work Education, the organization that accredits professional social work programs in higher education.

Social work, as an emergent profession without licensing of practitioners, has never had complete control of who could call oneself a social worker and who could do the job in the field. Generally, the social agencies were the ones that effectively decided who could be social workers in that the persons they hired to fill social work positions were entitled to call themselves social workers. Thus, the education, knowledge, and skill of agency employees who have filled social work positions and have been known to the public and clients as social workers have varied widely. In general the private agencies that serve the middle class have insisted on M.S.W. degrees for employment, and the public services have required only a B.A. (or less). In an effort to deal with this, NASW has developed a statement of levels of social work practice complete with professional qualifications for each level.

Levels of Practice   Today the National Association of Social Workers has identified six levels of social work practice. There are two levels—the *social service aide* and the *social service technician*—that require less than a college degree in social work. To carry the title *social worker,* the person must have a bachelor's degree in social work. To be a *graduate social worker* the person needs a master's degree in social work from an accredited professional school. This usually requires two academic years beyond the B.A. degree, although it may require less time if the person has a B.S.W. degree. To be a *certified social worker* one must possess an M.S.W., have two years of practice beyond the degree under careful supervision, and must pass an ACSW examination. To be a *social work fellow,* one must possess a Ph.D. in social work or D.S.W. (Doctor of Social Work) and have either two years' experience in specialization or have passed the ACSW examination plus two further years of specialized practice. At the present time the NASW is working on qualifications and license examinations for special advanced levels of competence.

It has long been held that the requisite knowledge to judge professional performance is available only to those who have themselves been trained in applying such knowledge. The knowledge and skill of the professional person are so different from general knowledge and skill that no one outside the profession can judge the professional. This is usually discussed under the rubric of professional autonomy. Thus, every profession has some means of the self-regulation of practice.

Generally, these "shoulds" of professional practice are stated in a formal code of ethics. However, as certain professionals may engage in unethical or incompetent behavior, and as the community becomes more and more dependent on professional knowledge, the community is increasingly demanding that the people served by the profession should have the right to judge professionals by the outcome of their service as the public perceives it. They are questioning whether it is possible for the operation to be a success if the patient dies. This stance may well mark some unrealistic perceptions of the capacity of professionals on the part of the community, but it also marks a realistic concern with the notion that clients do not have the capacity to know when they have been well served—that only professionals have the ability to judge the outcome of their actions.

Professional Autonomy Another element in this notion of autonomy is that professionals are supposed to be self-directing in their work. As used here, the word autonomy refers to the professional's control of the content and terms of the work. However, autonomy is not a simple criterion of who is to be considered professional—at least most people have never been willing to designate those wives and mothers who run their own households as being professional. This introduces the notion that when we speak of professionals, what we are really talking about is some kind of organized autonomy—not the autonomy of the individual practitioner. Thus, the more that a profession as a profession is able to exercise autonomy, the more it represents, and its members are controlled by, a hierarchy of institutionalized expertise (Friedson, 1970, pp. 71–92). The question of the professionalization of social work has been raised by many authors on the basis that social welfare organizations are usually considered bureaucratic, not professional organizations. Thus there are professionals operating in organizations marked by the fact that the authority is that of the administrative office held. This conflicts with the notion that in a profession the authority is that of expertise. This will be discussed later under "Bureaucracy," but it should be noted that perhaps one of the problems of all professions is that the rigidity and conservatism in the professions are also enforced by the concept of autonomy.

Each profession has its own culture. The interactions of social and professional roles required by the professional activities and professional groups generate particular ways of thinking and acting and a particular language unique to the profession. This may be called a professional culture. The value system of the profession in interaction with the value system of the bureaucracy is an important part of the culture of social work. A critical aspect of all professional education and in-service training is the attempt to socialize the workers to the agency and profession. By this is generally meant the internalization of the values and culture of the profession so that the professional person is constrained to work in certain ways and to take certain positions.

One of the problems in the achievement of greater autonomy of the profession is found in the fact that when agencies hire people who have less than the recognized professional training, these workers do not have a well-integrated identification with their profession that will allow them to stand outside bureaucratic expectation. Instead, they tend to be socialized to the culture of the agency rather than the culture of the profession. Thus they may first see themselves as public welfare employees rather than first identifying themselves as social workers. As these workers often cannot easily go elsewhere and find employment as social workers, they are tied to their position in the agency rather than to their identification as a professional.

Sound internalization of professional values is critically important as protection to the client system, since in the helping process workers must use themselves and their judgments. There is seldom any way that another can interfere in the process of action to protect the client in advance of the worker's action. Therefore, the only assurance people have that a professional person can be trusted with professional tasks is that the person acts according to deeply internalized feelings and judgments that stem from professional values and knowledge. This value system and the feelings and actions that derive from it become a part of the culture of the profession. The ambiguous position of social work within society in its multiple functions and purposes also contributes greatly to shaping the culture of social work.

Lydia Rapoport (1959) says that "no other profession is as self-examining and critically self-conscious as social work." While she relates some problems of the profession to its youth, she also attributes much stress to the profession's ambiguous position in society and to its multiple purposes and functions. Social work, concerned with the social functioning of people and the adequacy of the social institutions that affect human functioning, "seeks to embrace and implement some principles and values which may be essentially unpopular and uncongenial to the dominant social order." This particular role of the profession, as has been observed, results in its being seen as a minority group that is both tolerated and feared. From this come outright attacks and deprecation by the society that sanctions social work. In addition, the social views of the profession tend to isolate individual workers from other professional groups.

One problem of social work is that the tasks it is expected to perform are unclear and the responsibilities for which it is held to account are often contradictory. For example, many people expect the social worker to control every expenditure of the welfare client but at the same time to further independent behavior on the part of welfare recipients. Both expectations cannot be satisfied; one or the other must be chosen. Social work is supposed to be working to produce social change, but the society of which social work is a part is totally unable to reach agreement about the kinds of social change it will support.

Rapoport (1959) points out other sources of strain for social workers, some of which have been touched on earlier in this text. Among them are the following:

1. Being constantly confronted with the problems of human need, pain, and injustice.
2. The capacity for self-awareness and self-control required for the purposeful use of the social work relationship and the need "to harmonize personal capacity and inclination with professional behavior and values."
3. The institutional framework within which the social worker practices.
4. The opposing demands for "the maintenance of nearness and distance, of involvement and detachment, of rapport and objectivity."
5. The requirement for the tolerance of uncertainty, given our limited knowledge about human development and our difficulty in attempting to use what we do know.

As discussed in the first chapter of the text, social work practice is sanctioned through both the accountability of the profession and the accountability to the community of the agency within which the worker practices. Social work began, grew, and developed to its present stage as a professional practice within a bureaucratic structure. Many social workers over the years have been very unhappy with the notion of working within an agency structure. However, while the private practice of social work is growing (and private practice may not free one from the problems of a bureaucratic structure), practice within an agency is a reality of professional life for most social workers today. Thus we need to understand agency and professional sanctions as an important element of social work practice. In addition to furnishing salaries, office space, utilities, and so on to workers, the agencies of the community are organized to offer the resources that may be needed to help in the solution of the client's problem. Agencies also specify the policy under which resources are available. And the necessity of meeting the requirements, or conforming to policies through which resources are available, may pose tremendous barriers to client access and use. Thus as social workers we should be aware that our relationship with our client system involves more than just us and the client alone together. The agency, with its purposes and policies, is always a vital part of our interaction with our clients. Thus skill in the effective use of agency resources, an understanding of the network of agencies of the community and their access routes, and a working relationship with the agency of employment are necessary to effective practice.

No practitioner should ever forget that the policies and practices of an agency are communicated to the client through our words and actions with our client system. We suggest that you turn to "Four Pennies to My Name" (Reading 8-1) and consider how the various agency representatives that came in contact with Mrs. Morgan could have acted to be more helpful. How could they have communicated a different climate in the agency without any change in the policy or procedures of the agency? Too often we forget that it is the way we handle ourselves as concerned professional people that is critically important to clients when they have to face and deal with less than adequate resources. Workers so often see the agency as a monolithic organization that is a given. We need to recognize that bureaucracies are also systems and as social systems are amenable to change. Workers need to learn the ways of changing agency policy and be alert to using these means. In this chapter we will discuss this point in considerable detail. It is especially important that we recognize that no policy dictates how it is to be used. We are responsible for how we interpret policy, for being creative in the ways we find to make resources available. In addition, all policy, all procedures, all rules have some slippage, some room for maneuver, and workers must be alert about how these may be used to help clients or to expand worker autonomy in decision making. This matter is also discussed further in the chapter.

Perhaps the primary danger in offering service to clients within a bureaucratic structure is the impact of the policy and programs of the agency on the definition of the client's problem. Often it becomes almost second nature to assume that the client's problem falls within the agency's purpose. A worker within a child-placing agency may tend to define all problems concerning children as problems for which placement is a good solution or to define all problems as problems of placement. We can do great harm to our clients if we define initial problems in terms of known agency resources. This narrow focus severely limits the alternatives we see for solution of the client's problem. It is as we plan alternatives for solutions that the agency and its resources become critical. This is not to say that one can serve all types of problems within one agency; but if the problem is not one your agency is capable of serving, then you must be willing to make a referral, or at least consider alternative solutions. And, finally, we must recognize that it is possible for clients to be a powerful force in changing policy that does not serve them well. Do you think Mrs. Morgan, in "Four Pennies to My Name," might be able to organize and lead an organization of former welfare clients in an effort to humanize the welfare agency? Clients can organize to help in the push toward change and may even have an impact through individual letters or written positions dealing with troublesome policies. Enough individual letters to a governor or legislator can sometimes have an important impact. We do not often enough think of our clients as our allies in policy change. While we do not want clients to endanger themselves by social action or to relieve us of our responsibility for advocacy, we must recognize that one way clients may act to help themselves is to push for policy changes in areas that affect their lives. Too often we tend to see clients as helpless victims of circumstance and ourselves as knights in shining armor defending them. One of the ways of respecting and helping clients is to recognize their strength, to assume they can also act for themselves in working at life's difficulties. We will now examine some of the realities of sanctions and accountability that impact social work practitioners and their clients.

The Interstitial Profession?

In the first chapter of this text, we spoke of social workers as concerned with the interactions between the individual and society. We now return to a consideration of social work as an interstitial profession that serves both the client in need and society at large. This issue is complex. The individual social worker's function is defined and the worker's salary paid by an agency (public or voluntary, traditional or nontraditional) that receives its sanction from and is accountable to the community or to some community group whose members differ from, although they may include, the members of the client system. This point is of fundamental importance, since the parameters of the service any particular professional can offer are determined by the parameters of the agency's societal charge. Social workers use two types of tools in their work. The first type is internalized knowledge and skill, which, while they cannot be used up and in fact may be increased and sharpened by practice, are costly because they are what social workers (or any other professional) sell to obtain the money they need to maintain their physical existence in society. Most professionals (lawyers, doctors, and so on) sell their services directly to their clients or patients. In the case of social work, however, services to the client usually are paid for by the community and may be, at least in theory, available to all members of the community, many of whom cannot afford to pay for them themselves. In addition to knowledge and skill, social workers frequently dispense external resources such as money. Now, money, whether it is used to pay for the knowledge and skill of the worker or for concrete resources or is given directly to the client, is usually scarce. And money to support social work efforts is not the social worker's property but belongs to some identified community. The community that allocates its scarce resources to the support of social work services wants to assure itself that these resources are used responsibly.

Clients who go to a lawyer for service or patients who go to a doctor for treatment may look elsewhere for help if they think the service they receive is not adequate. Thus they express their evaluation of that professional's competence by depriving the professional of income. If professionals want to support themselves and their dependents, they must practice in a way that satisfies the users of the services by which they support themselves. However, since most client systems do not pay the full cost for social work services, their withdrawal in disappointment and disgust from the inadequate social work practitioner seldom directly penalizes that practitioner. Social workers (and their agencies) are thus well protected from their client's evaluations. However, they are open to the evaluation of their supporting community. The supporting community, however, neither pays nor evaluates workers directly. Rather, it gives its money to an organization, usually called an agency, that hires the professional practitioners. It is usually the agency in interaction with its supporting community through certain representative groups that both sets the parameters of practice within which workers must operate and evaluates their performance within the parameters.

The Bureaucratic Organization

In the modern world most formal organizations are structured in a particular way. This particular type of administrative organization, known as a *bureaucracy,* has triumphed in modern society because it is thought to operate with an efficiency superior to that of any other form of secondary group social structure thus far devised. The classical criteria for a bureaucracy were originally set forth by Max Weber (1947, pp. 333–334) as follows:

1. [The employees] are personally free and subject to authority only with respect to their impersonal official [work] obligations.
2. [The employees] are organized in a clearly defined hierarchy of offices.
3. Each office has a clearly defined sphere of competence.
4. The office is filled by a free contractual relationship. (Thus, in principle, each person makes a free selection, or choice, as to whether the person will accept the office and its terms.)
5. Candidates [for offices in the bureaucracy] are selected on the basis of technical qualifications. In the most rational case, this is tested by examination or guaranteed by diplomas certifying technical training, or both. They are appointed, not elected.
6. [The employees] are remunerated by fixed salaries in money, for the most part with a right to pensions. . . . The salary scale is primarily graded according to rank in the hierarchy.
7. The [position] is treated as the sole, or at least the primary, occupation of the incumbent.
8. It constitutes a career. There is a system of "promotion" according to seniority or to achievement, or both. Promotion is dependent on the judgment of superiors.
9. The official works entirely separated from ownership of the means of administration and without appropriation of his position.
10. The worker is subject to strict and systematic discipline and control in the conduct of the office.

Weber (p. 334) says that the Roman Catholic Church, the modern army, and large-scale capitalistic enterprises, along with certain "charitable organization[s], or any number of other types of private enterprises, servicing ideal or material ends are bureaucratic organizations."

Although bureaucracy is usually seen in terms of pragmatic necessity as the most efficient way to organize any large group of people to get any big job done, inherent in its very being are certain dysfunctional characteristics that vitally affect its operations. Social workers are often forced to conclude that the relationship between bureaucracy and efficiency is complex, questionable, and perhaps, at its worst, inverse.

Wilensky and Lebeaux (1958, p. 243) describe the limitations of social work bureaucracy as follows:

Along with its gains—efficiency, reliability, precision, fairness—come what many students have called its pathologies: timidity, delay, officiousness, red tape, exaggeration of routine, limited adaptability. The agency as a means, a mechanism—for carrying out welfare policy becomes an end in itself. Between the altruist with the desire to help and the client with the need lies the machine, with its own "needs." These needs can result in an emphasis on technique and method, on organizational routines and records, rather than on people and service.

Barbara Lerner (1972, pp. 169–170), a psychologist, is concerned with this last limitation of bureaucracy when she writes:

> Bureaucratic means are intrinsically unsuited to the achievement of ultimate mental health ends because they are standardized means—the whole point of breaking up tasks into component parts and component parts into subcomponents is to standardize procedures—and standardized procedures are rational only if one is striving to produce a standard product. . . .
>
> Each human being is a unique entity and wants to remain so. People who voluntarily seek treatment may do so because they want to achieve an ultimate end, such as the realization of something like their full share of the universal human potential for adequate psychosocial functioning, but people want to achieve their own unique version of that end in their own unique way. . . .
>
> Thus clients who come seeking aid come as unique individuals seeking aid which is individually tailored to the totality of their needs by a person who is in close enough contact with them to apprehend them and who has the freedom and flexibility to respond to them in a unique way.

Lerner (p. 171) goes on to say that the bureaucratically organized agency is organized around "abstract, standard parts: specific programs organized around specific problems that are dealt with by specific procedures," rather than around clients as unique personalities or around the concern of practitioners for their clients. She complains that clients are "then defined in terms of the particular problems around which programs are organized" and are "processed to and through those programs and subjected to the various procedures and techniques which constitute them" rather than seen in terms of their own goals and expectations.

Listening to Lerner, one becomes aware that the problems of professionals in bureaucracies are not restricted to social work. These problems occur in any organization staffed by personnel who spend a considerable number of years in developing a particular expertise. Weissman (1973, p. viii) points out:

> Professionals share a desire for and expect a large degree of autonomy from organizational control; they want maximum discretion in carrying out their professional activities, free from organizational interference or confining procedures. In addition, professionals tend to look to other professionals to gain some measure of self-esteem, are not likely to be devoted to any one organization, and accept a value system that puts great emphasis on the client's interest.
>
> Bureaucrats are different from professionals. They perform specialized and routine activities under the supervision of a hierarchy of officials. Their loyalty and career are tied up with their organization. Therefore, conflict results when professionals are required to perform like bureaucrats.

We would differ with the conclusion of this last quotation and might repeat that famous quotation, "We have met the enemy and they is us." Professionals and bureaucrats are not two different sets of people. There are bureaucrats who are not professionals, but increasingly in our society, given the advancement of group practices in medicine and law, there are few professionals who are not also bureaucrats. With regard to social work, we need to recognize that bureaucratic forms of organization are useful in social services, not because society is unmindful of what is wrong with this form or because society is basically evil, but because there simply are not at this time any feasible, superior organization models that have properties as well suited to carrying out the very complex functions required of social services involving the cooperative contributions of large numbers of specialized individuals (Pruger, 1978).

For the foreseeable future individual social workers will find it necessary to work within a bureaucratic structure. Thus it will not help either the worker or the client for the worker to see the bureaucracy as something bad that should be condemned at every turn. Rather, it must be understood as a reality—a complex system in which both worker and client are subsystems. Given this important fact of life, we need to learn to work within, to use, and to change bureaucracy rather than simply make ourselves feel good by seeing bureaucracy as bad (Pruger, 1978).

Conflicts Between the Bureaucracy and the Professional

Practicing social workers have been confronted with the harsh reality of the conflict between their judgment about the ideal interventive actions needed to move toward the client's goal and what is possible given the resources and parameters of the agency within which both they and the client are operating. Often the most sensitive and concerned workers find themselves discouraged and angered by the many unavoidable compromises they must make between their client's needs and those of their agency in particular and of society in general. Perhaps some of this frustration could be avoided, and workers could be more effective in bringing about change in agency functioning, if they understood better the bureaucracy within which they of necessity operate. Actually, as we said earlier, social work has been a bureaucratic profession from its very beginning, and social workers employed in agencies are not only professionals but bureaucrats. Thus, while social work has struggled to synthesize bureaucratic and professional norms, it has not always recognized that a profession and a bureaucracy possess a number of norms that are opposed in principle.

Weissman (1973, p. vii) points out that one of the crucial problems of professionals who are working to change the bureaucratic structure is their lack of recognition of the difference between nonprofit and profit-making organizations: "Money serves as an alarm system in private enterprise: Ford sooner or later must respond to the tension caused by lack of Edsel sales." In nonprofit organizations the connection between the product produced and the revenues is indirect. Thus the alarm system that should bring change is severely flawed. Both professionals and agency executives may prefer to be judged by effort expended rather than by the success or failure of the effort. Weissman (p. 3) says that without an effective accountability system social agencies cannot solve their problems, and administration has little need seriously to consider the views and ideas of lower-level staff, since it will not be penalized if it does not. However, today agencies are depending more and more on third-party payments. This causes some very difficult problems as the bureaucracy struggles to find sound measures of accountability. In this struggle the views of lower-level staff are often ignored in favor of outside notions of efficient service.

In an earlier chapter the importance of evaluation was discussed. This has been a long-standing problem in all professions. Who is to evaluate the professional? Against what standard is the professional's work to be judged? The present struggle of the physician against some kind of publicly supported health care is an example of the problem. Physicians have successfully maintained up until now that only they (or in some cases, a jury of their peers) can be allowed to judge their work. Incidentally, this stance probably explains the growing number of malpractice suits, since patients are no longer content, when the results of treatment are negative, to accept the professional's judgment that the process of treatment was correct. So, too, in the social work bureaucracy the question of who shall evaluate the effectiveness of the work is a difficult one. Is it to be the worker, the supervisor, the executive, the board, the general public, or the client? We have said that to achieve contracted goals is the appropriate outcome of service. It follows that we hold individual goal setting to be a decision of client and worker, not of the agency. Yet the agency has a vital stake in both what the goals are and how they are reached. Agencies may define four or five broad classes of goals appropriate to their function. However, these broad goal classifications usually must be operationalized and individualized for the individual system. Thus the agency policy often becomes an important part of goal setting. It often takes a great deal of skill for the worker to negotiate agency policy and client desires so that a realistic desired goal is set and effective alternative means to goal achievement developed for choice.

Weber (1947, pp. 333–334) held that what is central to bureaucracy is the specialization and standardization of tasks and the rational allocation or assignment of these tasks in accordance with an overall plan. Collective tasks may thus be broken down into component tasks that are means to a collective end. Two assumptions underlie this concept. The first is that there is something approaching a clear, consistent, complete, and generally agreed-upon definition of the ultimate end toward which the organization is working, and the second is that the end is achievable through standardized means (Lerner, 1972, p. 167). When a social agency defines its function, it usually states the ends it intends to pursue in general terms. However, these ends are usually expressed in such general terms (for example, the support of healthy family life) that the extent to which they have been achieved cannot be measured; or the ends are expressed in programmatic terms—such as crisis intervention, aftercare program, family therapy program, drug program—which often result in defining the client's problems in terms of programs rather than of the client's goals. And most of us would agree that we do not have standardized means to apply even if the client could fit within a standardized goal. We are simply not able to say in working with individual human beings, "If this, then that." There are too many variables in the situation of the unique human system. A profession works by applying principles and methods to resolve problems determined by unique client input and professional judgment rather than by employing standardized procedures toward some predetermined goal established by a hierarchical authority. This means that the individual goal of any client system must fit within the agency's generalized goal but be specific to the client system. In certain public welfare agencies there is a mandatory goal of increased self-care for all clients. This broadly stated, generalized goal applies to all cases, but it really means very little to worker and client. In these agencies, almost without exception, clients come seeking increased ability to care for themselves. However, for each client the specific skills and tasks of self-care will be different. Thus, the client-worker goal should be a specific statement about what must be achieved for this particular client, in this particular situation, to achieve self-care. Self-care becomes the overall general parameter within which individual goals must be developed. Most generalized agency goals easily lend themselves to the development of particular client goals if the worker understands the purpose and function of goals in the helping process. The important point is that any overall goals of the agency must be individualized for client's use.

Another conflict between the bureaucratic structure and the professional is found in the orientation toward authority. The professional regards authority as residing in professional competence; the bureaucrat sees authority as residing in the office held. An important difference is found in the orientation toward the client, in that professionals orient themselves toward serving the best interests of the client, and the bureaucrat seeks to serve the best interests of the organization. Professionals usually identify with their professional colleagues. They should find their identification from their professional association. Bureaucrats identify with their particular social stratum within the bureaucratic hierarchy. And last, there is a different orientation toward the method of exercising power. "The professional norm is to influence clients and peers by modes which are oriented toward the pole of free exchange while the bureaucratic norm is oriented toward the pole of coercion" supported by the invoking of sanctions (Morgan, 1962, p. 115).

Types of Bureaucrats

In an empirical study of social work performance in large public agencies, Ralph Morgan (1962, pp. 116–125) identified and developed an anchoring description of four ideal types of role conceptions of social workers in a bureaucratic setting. His work is summarized below.

Functional Bureaucrats These are professionals "who just happen to be working in a social agency." They seek interaction with and recognition from their professional peers both inside and outside the agency. "Such individuals by their skill, good judgment, and technical efficiency often provide a type of service" that is recognized by the agency as being highly effective. As a result the agency overlooks certain violations of agency norms as the price it must pay for having such a competent professional on its staff.

Service Bureaucrats These are social workers who are oriented toward helping their clients but who recognize that they are a part of a bureaucracy. They integrate themselves "into the bureaucratic group while maintaining professional peer group ties." While they are still "ambivalent about their identification with their agency, they see in it the best means of attaining their goals of practicing" their profession and as helping resources rather than as antagonists of their clients and themselves.

Specialist Bureaucrats This classification, Morgan says, encompasses the largest group of social workers. This worker is interested in reconciling the "bureaucracy to humans and humans to the bureaucracy." Specialist bureaucrats use the rules and regulations of the agency to guide their professional judgments. "While they recognize that agency directives are in general necessary, they also recognize the richness of the human situation that can never be fully encompassed by specific rules and regulations." They see the agency as authorizing them to use their professional discretion to protect the interests both of the agency and of its clients. They realize that the agency is a bureaucracy and therefore heir to all the dysfunctional characteristics of this form of human organization. They usually have the professional "courage to sacrifice bureaucratic norms when they interfere with their professional function." They have successfully, through understanding and professional judgment, adapted in practice to norms that in theory are essentially irreconcilable. In fact, they may see this constantly shifting adaptation as the very stuff of professional life.

Executive Bureaucrats   These people like "to manage people, money, and materials. While functional bureaucrats are oriented toward their profession, service bureaucrats toward those they serve, specialist bureaucrats toward the profession and the bureaucracy, executive bureaucrats seem oriented primarily toward the exercise of power. While executive bureaucrats are innovators and do not consider themselves bound by a rigid application of rules and regulations [in fact, they may be daring bureaucratic infighters and risk takers], they tend not to appreciate innovations by their own subordinates." They lean toward enforcement of bureaucratic norms for others and run a disciplined agency.

Job Bureaucrats   These are people, professional workers, who "have a substantial career investment in the bureaucracy. At the center of their attention is the security of their own career, and they seek to safeguard and advance it through a meticulous application of regulations and adherence to the norms of the organization." Effective job bureaucrats achieve their greatest success in supervisory or administrative positions. While they hold themselves firmly to official policies of the organization, they realize that the other professionals in their sections have a different orientation, and while they tend to supervise closely, they exercise sufficient "selective nonattention" to the less rigid way in which their subordinate professionals operate that through the proper amount of social slippage the social work job gets done. The ineffective job bureaucrat is characterized by a rigid overcompliance with regulation and norms. Directives that originally were issued to accomplish a mission become ends in themselves, and the mission of social work, even of the agency itself, become secondary considerations.

Agency Bureaucracy and the Worker

No one ever meets a pure type in real life, so perhaps it is understandable that we are not willing to put ourselves in any one of the classes listed. But we suppose that we are probably somewhere between the service bureaucrat and the specialist bureaucrat. We do not believe that a worker who accepts a position as a member of an agency staff, who accepts a salary from the agency, and who uses agency resources, no matter how unsatisfactory they may be, for helping clients can act as though the worker were a private practitioner or without concern for agency policies and procedures. As a staff member, the worker is bound by the agency policies. If these policies are unacceptable, you must either work to change them while remaining bound by them or leave the agency and work for change outside it.

The first principle for workers who would give their clients maximum service is to understand the organization for which they work and to know how its structure and function were and are determined. If you are going to be actively involved in change, you need to know what the possible points of intervention are. Three major factors affect the organization of agencies: their source of support; the source of their sanction, or right to operate; and the areas of their concern. Agencies obviously cannot operate without a source of funds. As a rule an agency's funds come either from public tax funds or from private voluntary contributions, although agencies supported primarily by private contributions may use tax funds through various contracts and grants. Any agency's policy and structure, procedures, and flexibility will be determined by the source and adequacy of its funding. As a general rule the funds are not adequate to the demands that workers wish to meet, so difficult choices among real needs must usually be made.

The public tax-supported agency will usually operate within legislation and will be dependent on some legislative body (for example, county commissioners) for its broad policy and for the appropriation of public funds for its support. In some cases the board or commission of a public service may be appointed by an elected executive officer (that is, governor). Such agencies are usually administered by individuals who may be required to prove their competence by passing various tests. These administrators will determine procedures and more detailed policy issues within the broad legislation that established and maintains the agency.

Private agencies usually operate under the general policy directives of a board of directors. Such a board has three primary functions: it establishes the right of the agency to carry on its program and sanctions the agency's activities; it is responsible for the agency's overall policy; and it is responsible for fund raising. Until very recently almost all boards were composed of an elite group of members with little understanding of the realities of the lives of those for whom they developed programs. Boards almost always operate by consensus. Because the board members of private agencies are volunteers, the members who are constantly on the losing side of an issue soon drop out unless they have a deep commitment. In most situations the board hires the executive of the agency, and it often happens that the executive sees the job as keeping the board happy on the one hand and running the agency the executive's own way on the other. The executive usually controls staff access to the board and the flow of information to the board about the agency's work. So the worker's attempts to represent clients and their interests in policy and program matters are often unheard.

Some social work departments (such as the social service department of a school system, a hospital, a court, and so on) operate as part of a larger host agency. In this situation the financial support and policy-making processes will be determined by those of the host agency, which generally operates under a similar structure.

Agencies have both a function and a program. The program is the ways and means that an agency uses to carry out its function as defined by the community. For the practitioner this distinction has some importance in that although an agency's function may remain constant, its program ought to be responsive to the changing needs of the times. Thus an agency whose function is the care and treatment of children may initially have cared largely for orphaned or dependent children but now may be concerned primarily with disturbed children or with day care.

Each agency has an organizational (bureaucratic) structure by which it delegates its responsibilities and tasks and stabilizes and systematizes its operations. The executive is the primary administrative officer. Officers have direct responsibility for the day-to-day functioning of the agency. Because they are usually responsible for getting the money to run the agency, this responsibility may occupy most of their time and thought. They are responsible for relationships with the board of directors or a public body. They are usually responsible for working with other agencies toward community social work goals and for the public relations functions of the agency.

Below the executive on the organization table of a large agency one may find a bewildering array of division directors, unit supervisors, consultants, and line supervisors. A small agency may have only three levels of hierarchy: the executive, the supervisors, and the workers. Line workers are more conscious of their relationship to their direct supervisor—a professional person who is usually held responsible for two functions that at some times and to some people seem contradictory: (1) helping workers to improve their skills both in the interests of getting the present job done at the best level possible and for the worker's and client's future benefit, and (2) administratively holding workers responsible for doing the job to certain standards and evaluating their performance relative to those standards.

Many articles in social work literature deal with the supervisory process and its problems. Supervisors, like workers, differ, and some may be more interested in their job security and tenure than in the client's needs for service or the worker's need for both support and learning opportunities. All beginning workers can use considerable help in increasing their awareness of themselves and their way of working and in adding to their fund of knowledge about people, resources, and helping processes. And in a large agency with considerable work pressure and a constant scarcity of resources, all line workers need considerable support of their supervisors in dealing with the constant frustrations of the day-to-day job.

Harry Wasserman (1970) examined the work of professional social workers in a large public agency. He found that structural constraints rather than social work knowledge and skills dictated what the worker was able to offer in the client's life situations. In this instance eight of the 12 workers studied had left the agency after two years. Wasserman (p. 99) concluded that "the two principal feelings expressed by the 12 new professional social workers during the two-year period were frustration and fatigue" and that "they were exhausted by having day after day to face critical human situations with insufficient material, intellectual and emotional resources and support." Certainly supervisors cannot wave a magic wand and undo the effects of structural constraints on the worker's capacity to help, but a supervisor who cares about the worker's capacity to help and the worker's mental health can, through support and the offer of intellectual and emotional resources, make a great deal of difference in what the worker is able to do and in how the worker grows on the job.

Because of the constant strains and problems of the supervisor's job, there has been some push in certain agencies to do away with supervision. Perhaps social work could develop a better form than the supervisory process, but one cannot do away with the supervisory function. Doing away with authority relationships does not necessarily change either people or structural constraints or result in more effective work. As long as personal needs, attitudes, and differing levels of commitment and skill are brought to a job, there is a need for leadership. As Weissman (1973, p. 131) points out:

> The planning and management of an organization requires specific expertise. . . . There is an ongoing need to reconcile the dilemmas and strains of organizational life. . . . As long as there is concern for the effectiveness of an organization, there will be considerable strain

between the needs of the individuals for self-actualization and the needs of organizations for achievement and efficiency.

Somehow these strains must be reconciled and resolved if clients are to be effectively served. The question concerning the supervisor that is of critical importance for the worker is the supervisor's position on the list of roles that Morgan developed.

Perhaps the primary problem with supervision is not that it is not valuable or necessary but that it has been used in such a way that agencies have avoided consideration of their effectiveness by focusing on the effectiveness of their employees. In most agencies workers receive yearly evaluations on the anniversary of their joining the staff. Perhaps what is needed are set dates on which both the workers and the agency are evaluated. In other words, the agency needs to look at itself at the same time that it is looking at its workers. As Weissman (1973, p. 58) writes:

> The environment in which the agency operates—physical, social, financial—affects the worker's efforts. To tell workers to refine their skills or work harder in order to be successful is to ignore the impact of environment. The caseload or lack of cooperation from other agencies, not diagnostic or therapeutic skills, may be at fault.
>
> Evaluating individuals at different times during the year solely in terms of their individual therapeutic skills makes it less likely that the agency will have to react as a system to the results of evaluation. The problems of each worker can be viewed idiosyncratically.
>
> ... Through consultation with experienced workers, agencies should establish the areas of skill needing improvement and the basis upon which to judge improvement—recordings, observations, client queries, and the like. The worker should choose how to get help, whether through conferences with the supervisor, through taking courses, through peer supervision, or through consultation. Letting the worker decide reduces the dependency feelings which develop through forced supervision.
>
> A degree of arbitrariness will always exist unless an agency has some method of appraising success with clients. Without agency standards of success and an evaluation of the worker's record, workers and supervisors are dependent on secondary data. Case presentation becomes more important than the people treated. The way one writes or speaks about a case becomes more important than the results achieved.

Weissman (1973, p. 59) then goes on to discuss the accountability of the agency for evaluation of its job. (This is another side of our earlier argument about the need for evaluative research and ways of evaluating services.) He says:

> The key to increasing the influence of lower level staff vis-à-vis their superiors lies in a board (or other body) that can hold the agency accountable. Where there is real accountability, the ideas and experience of all levels of staff become valuable, and the incompetence of individuals becomes a matter of serious concern. If a board discovers that 80% of the agency's clients feel they have not been helped by the agency, the incompetent supervisors have something to worry about.

Client, Worker, and Bureaucracy

The procedures of bureaucracy as well as the limitations of policy may be frustrating to both the client and the worker. It is well to recognize that red tape was and is developed to ensure that people with equal troubles receive equal help and resources. But often it really operates to reduce the client's access to services or to make an already complex situation more difficult and confusing. It is the worker's responsibility to act as the client's broker and advocate in dealing with the policies and procedures of the bureaucracy. These roles will be discussed later, but we will introduce the idea here.

If workers are to help the client cope with the problems of access to services in the most helpful way possible, it is critically important that they know with accuracy and understanding the policies and procedures of their agency and the way they operate. Workers are not always as careful and disciplined as they might be in getting a really workable grasp of this knowledge. Paperwork can be a very naughty word in the worker's language, but the capacity to handle paperwork efficiently, accurately, and with concern for deadlines and the client's time is an absolute requirement of the worker who would be a skilled advocate and broker. We have worked in agencies where certain chief clerks made more important decisions about who got what than some workers because the clerks had mastered the paper flow and the workers were too impatient to do so. While paperwork can be irritating, the worker needs to understand that it is an attempt to establish procedures by which clients are ensured equal service.

One of the authors of this book worked in public welfare before the Social Security Act took effect, when it was the responsibility of the local township to aid people in need of money. At that time paperwork was considerably lighter than it became after the agency was able to secure federal funds if it established certain procedures to ensure people equal service and the right of appeal if they felt that they had been capriciously denied. Before Social Security, people were able to secure aid only if they were able to convince the worker and/or the supervisor that they were "worthy of aid." Sometimes this meant that they had supported the proper political candidate with the proper enthusiasm. This decision could not be challenged—there were no procedures to assure this, no paper on which the basis of the decision was recorded. But back to the present.

The worker must thoroughly understand the parameters of the policy of the agency and the authority available for interpretation. A policy is a broad statement. It has to be interpreted by some individual before it can be applied in the interests of another individual. Far too often a worker will either ask the worker at the next desk what the agency does about such and such or give the supervisor a quick call.

Our position is that the worker starts with what the client and the worker have decided is needed. Next the worker is responsible for finding out exactly what the written statement of the policy says. Then the worker sits down and thinks long and hard about what that policy actually means and what are all the different possible ways to interpret and apply it. Next the plan made with the client is used to test the various interpretations. The interpretation that will best enable the worker to help the client with what is needed for problem solving is selected. Workers then write down that interpretation of the policy and the way they would apply it to the client situation. If necessary, this statement may be submitted to the supervisor for approval, but in any case it has to be made a part of the record of service to the client. Our view is that taking the quick and easy route of asking colleagues or supervisors about policy is not the proper way to perform one's role as an independent professional person; and our experience has been that following that course increases the likelihood of receiving a directive that limits what one can do. Others do not always want to do the hard headwork either, and when one is in doubt about a policy the easiest thing is to say no. It is out of this way of functioning—the use of the traditional messages about policy that circulate on the office grapevine—that old patterns get stabilized and become harder and harder to change. Far too often workers accept routine word-of-mouth statements about agency resources as givens. They may gripe about them, but they do not question them. By really knowing policy and by using creative interpretations of policy, the worker can help keep the agency active as an ever-changing bureaucracy.

Several years ago one of us conducted a study to find out (1) whether clients were receiving aid they needed and (2) why or why not. In the agency under study, workers reported great discouragement with the limitations of agency policies and felt that these policies prevented them from really helping their clients. The study revealed that the average client of that agency was receiving less than half of the amount of services and resources to which the client was legally entitled under its policies. In other words, it was not the agency policies that were limiting client access to services but rather the narrow and traditional way that workers and supervisors were interpreting the policies. In the year following the study, as workers were helped to assume active responsibility for broadly interpreting policy, the aid to their clients more than doubled in cost, yet no one in the agency or on its board reached out to stop this more expensive way of operating. The point is that service to the client is not limited to what one does when one sits with the client. Some of the most important work, and sometimes the work that is most difficult and requires the most self-discipline and commitment, is the work involved when the worker takes on the role of broker with the agency's programs and its bureaucracy. Social workers are often the kind of people who prefer to deal with people rather than with paper—yet dealing with paper is a part of everyone's life in today's world. So workers can often fail the client in real and hurtful ways if they do not have expert skills in dealing with paper. Operating contrary to traditional grapevine interpretations of policy may often involve the worker in uncomfortable confrontations with the agency colleagues and the supervisor. And it is not easy for an individual worker as part of a system to move contrary to the patterns and relationships in the system. However, if workers' interpretations conform to written policy, they can usually prevail in the client's interests, which is what social work is all about.

But there are times when policy does not permit adequate service to clients. The first rule of policy change is that "griping does not do it"; neither does making eloquent broad statements of one's feeling. To bring about change, one must first define the problem concisely and assume the responsibility to document this definition in some detail. The contention that there needs to be change must be documented by organized and verifying data. This is a beginning in the change effort. We will discuss the other tactics of change in the following section.

Changing the Bureaucracy

Reading 6-1 is an article by Edward J. Pawlak, "Organizational Tinkering." More important than its title indicates, it really relates to what is being discussed in this section; the focus is on tactics for "tinkering" with the organizational structures, rules, and policies to bring about bureaucratic change. Another author who has written some excellent articles on the social worker's activities within the bureaucratic structure is Robert Pruger (1973). We have borrowed some of Pruger's ideas to combine with our own thoughts in putting together this section.

The first suggestion for change is to be clear about what needs to be changed, about the difficulties that can be anticipated in bringing about the solution, and about the cost of both the problem and its solution (problem definition, goals, and plan). Too often people not experienced in the complexity and the balances of the bureaucratic setting will take a drastic step to change the situation and will be completely overwhelmed by the unexpected repercussions that follow. Let us consider, for example, the worker who feels that clients are being poorly served by a policy. Unable to change anything, the worker resigns in anger and frustration. A newspaper reporter hears of the problem and asks the worker about it. Seeing an opportunity to use the power of public opinion and certain of the virtue of the cause, the worker tells the reporter of the problems. However, many people in the community do not see the story as an attempt to provide better service. They interpret it as an example of how poorly social workers administer public funds, and a strong community pressure develops to cut the funds of the agency, to set up more stringent rules and regulations for the social workers to follow, and to replace the social work director with a business manager who will see that rules are followed.

The second principle is to determine what factors and forces inside and outside the organization are keeping the problem alive. What the worker did not know in this example was that the executive and the board were as deeply concerned as the staff with certain policies but that given the power position of certain people in the community, they had made a decision that any attempt to change things would result in costly backlash. This is not to say that one does not take on an open fight in spite of the threat of backlash. It is to say that one should know the approximate force of that movement and decide in advance how it should be met. The freedom fighters in the civil rights movement are an example of this. They knew in advance something of the expected response to their activities, and they not only seriously considered them but drilled themselves in advance so they would not be taken unawares by sudden actions of the opposition.

The next point follows logically from the above. You should anticipate the difficulties of the solution. Almost any solution to a social problem brings other problems in its implementation. Be sure that the solution is not worse than the problem and know some ways of dealing with anticipated difficulties of the solution. Find out whether those who have the responsibility of deciding about the problem are simply unaware of it or are strongly invested in present policy or opposed to any movement because a clash of interests and values is involved.

This leads to point four, which is to determine where in the organization the responsibility for formal decision making in respect to the problem lies. Who formally makes the decision and who or what can influence this decision?

Timing one's efforts can be crucial. Agencies are most often open to change (as are individuals) when they are in periods of crisis—for example, when budgets are increasing or decreasing, when there are great decreases or increases in the number of clients served, when their performance reports are being questioned, or when new methods of dealing with the problem are being widely acclaimed.

The process by which change takes place must be understood, and it must be recognized that the initiation of change often requires a different approach than does the implementation of change. We have often seen workers fight a hard and bruising battle for the initiation of change, only to lose the war because they were unwilling or unable to be an active part of its implementation. It is the changes in the way things are done that are the test of how the client will be served differently.

Consider whether change can be achieved more effectively in this situation by advocacy strategy, by collaborative strategy, or by both. Advocacy strategy employs an impressive array of tools, including the use of citizen groups, unions, and professional organizations to engage with the practitioner in litigation, picketing, bargaining, building pressure alliances, contriving for crises to occur, bringing sanctions to bear through external authorities, and, perhaps encouraging noncompliance with policy by workers and clients. Collaborative strategy may employ some of the techniques outlined by Patti and Resnick (1972). Here the change agent may provide facts about the nature of the problem, present alternative ways of doing things, try to develop an experimental project that involves different ways of doing things and get permission to implement it, seek to establish a committee to study the situation and make recommendations for change, attempt to improve the working climate of the agency so that individuals feel trusted and safe and thus can look beyond securing their own position to the task to be done, attempt to bring professional values and ethics to bear, use a logical argument to persuade, and point out what is really happening under the present policy. This last approach will require documentation of the results of present policy.

Pruger (1973) deals with the strategic concerns of the "good bureaucrat" in some ways similar to the above discussion and adds some additional factors. We have summarized his material as follows:

1. "One important property of a good bureaucrat is staying power." This means a recognition that things happen slowly in complex organizations but that whatever changes workers have in mind cannot be implemented if they do not stay in and with the organization.
2. "The good bureaucrat must somehow maintain a vitality of action and independence of thought." Organizational life tends to suppress vitality of action and independence of thought. Workers must resist such pressure.
3. "There is always room for insights and tactics that help the individuals preserve and enlarge the discretionary aspect of their activity and, by extension, their sense of personal responsibility."

These are tactics the good bureaucrat will employ:

1. "Understand legitimate authority and organizational enforcement." The inescapable degree of generality found in the regulatory policies and codes of the organization allows for considerable autonomy of the individuals if they just recognize it and use it. The organization's power to control is less than many realize, but if the limits of legitimate authority are recognized, the individuals may expand their discretionary limits.
2. "Conserve energy." Change agents should not thrash around and feel discouraged and unappreciated because they do not receive in a large organization the kind of support they receive from their friends. Also, as stated earlier, master the paper flow of the organization. This will not only help the client but will also remove from your shoulders the weight of resentment and emotional turmoil you may feel as you look at the uncompleted statistical

forms on the desk. Workers should describe what can be changed and work on it rather than spend valuable hours bemoaning what cannot be dealt with.

3. "Acquire a competence needed by the organization."

4. "Don't yield unnecessarily to the requirements of administrative convenience. Keep in mind the difference between that which serves the organizational mission and that which serves the organization." Rules, standards, and directives as to the way things should be done are meant to be means that serve ends. In organizations means tend to become ends, so that a worker may be more concerned about turning in the mileage report than about the results of the visit to a client. Ends and means should be kept clear.

5. Workers should remember that "the good bureaucrat is not necessarily the most beloved one."

We would like to stress that these skills in changing the bureaucracy or acting as an advocate for client groups involve the following knowledge and abilities: the knowledge of how individual human beings and social systems develop, grow, exist, change, and cope with problems; the knowledge of how individuals interact within small social systems such as the family or primary groups (knowledge of family development and interaction, knowledge of group process); the knowledge of transactions within larger social systems (organizational behavior); and the knowledge of common human needs and the way culture affects how these needs are expressed. These are all critical knowledge bases necessary for effective planning for advocacy and institutional change. In addition, to carry through such plans the workers will need self-awareness, especially in certain areas such as innate pushes toward the expression of competition and aggression, their own level of anger and the favorite ways of using it; they will need the capacity to use self in a disciplined way within the parameters of the plan; and they will need a high level of communication skills and ability to use effectively the various skills outlined in Chapter 12.

Legal Sanctions

As we discussed earlier, licensing is a legal process. There are several other forms of legal sanctions within which a social worker must work: sanctions for professional misconduct; licensing laws that define the parameters of social work practice in certain broad terms; laws and practices that operate to protect the client's legal rights and control professional or official discretion; and the various legislative actions and administrative procedures that define the limitations of the agency's services.

Some of the areas in which social workers need specialized legal knowledge are the rights of parents and child, the rights of family members, the protections and limits of the rights of confidentiality, client consent to social work intervention, the role of the case record in legal proceedings, and testifying in court actions as an expert witness.

We have discussed the importance of decision making in professional practice. The exercise of decision making carries with it the implication that there is a responsibility to decide correctly. Thus, social workers, like other professionals, are exposed to liability for their actions. However, the social worker has an obligation to supply the services his or her agency is mandated to give. To do nothing or to withhold services may also have legal consequences. To serve their clients well, social workers must be aware of the legal consequences of both action and inaction.

Social workers who wish to engage in advocacy for the client and his or her social environment need an understanding of legislative and administrative processes. Social workers need to know how laws are made and how they are changed. The ability to read a statute with some understanding can greatly increase the worker's ability to challenge persons who seek to subvert the right or privileges of persons under that law.

Recapitulation

In this chapter we have discussed the sanctions by which social work practitioners are held accountable by society. Sanctions are necessary because community and client systems need assurance that the interventions of the social work practitioner are within the recognized and approved parameters of society's assignment to the profession. Each practitioner and each agency must operate within the legal structure of society. These mandates inform all aspects of social work practice, from the requirements that agencies verify responsible use of funds within legal and policy requirements to the licensing of the individual worker. Social workers are also sanctioned through the profession and their employing agency.

A Look Forward

We urge a careful reading of "Organizational Tinkering," at the end of this chapter. Consider how you might use some of the ways of changing the agency that Pawlak outlines. Think carefully about the responsibility of those who call themselves social workers in their interaction with a client such as Mrs. Morgan.

Now go back to the seven cases in the Appendix. Try to identify which agencies were involved with these clients and why these agencies were used. All workers in the situations were social workers. How does the agency structure influence the worker's use of self in each case? What are the general knowledge and skill that every worker needs to serve these clients? What are the specific knowledge and skill that clients may expect workers to have because they represent the particular agency in which they are employed? Can you identify some agency policies that may limit the help the client might receive? If you had unlimited resources at your command, what would you want to make available to each client?

Reading 6-1   *Organizational Tinkering**

Edward J. Pawlak

To tinker means to work at something in an experimental or makeshift way. Although clinicians' positions and roles in many social welfare organizations preclude them from pursuing ambitious organizational change, they still may be able to work at change in modest, makeshift ways. And,

despite the fact that clinical social work is usually practiced in an organizational and policy context, many clinicians are uninterested in acquiring the knowledge and skills that might facilitate intraorganizational tinkering on behalf of their practice or their clients. Others are overwhelmed, cynical, or disillusioned by their dealings with bureaucracy (Briar, 1968; Gottlieb, 1974, p. 34; Hanlan, 1971; Piliavin, 1968; Podell & Miller, 1974; Specht, 1968, pp. 42–43). Some front-line practitioners,

* *Note.* From "Organizational Tinkering" by E. J. Pawlak, 1976, *Social Work, 21*, pp. 376–380. Copyright 1976 by National Association of Social Workers. Reprinted by permission.

however, have learned to tinker effectively (Hyman & Schreiber, 1974; Maher, 1974; Senna, 1974).

To help clinicians improve their talent in dealing with organizations, this article identifies tactics they can use to tinker with organizational structure, modes of operation, rules, conventions, policy, and programs. The specific tactics discussed are tinkering with bureaucratic succession and rules, the white paper or position paper, demonstration projects, modification of board composition, bypassing, influencing grant reviews, leaking information, and protest by resignation.

Although the author takes a partisan stand on behalf of clinicians, it does not follow that managers are necessarily the villains. However, some of the tactics identified here are directed toward those administrators who cause clinicians to harbor severe misgivings about the organization.

This article stems not only from the author's observation of and experience with organizational tinkering, but also from the contributions of others who have addressed similar themes (Bennis, 1969; Brager, 1968; Martin, 1971; Patti & Resnick, 1972; Specht, 1968, pp. 42–52; Weissman, 1973, pp. 57–131). It warns clinicians to bear in mind the pitfalls and dilemmas of organizational tinkering—that it takes place in a political climate and in a structure of authority, norms, and sanctions (Epstein, 1968; Green, 1966; Nader, Petkas, & Blackwell, 1972; Patti, 1974; Weisband & Franck, 1975).

BUREAUCRATIC SUCCESSION
Bureaucratic succession usually refers to a change in leadership at the highest levels of an organization. Here, however, the author uses the broader concept that includes changes in leadership at all levels in the hierarchy (Gouldner, 1954, pp. 59–104; Levenson, 1961). Bureaucratic succession must be called to the attention of clinicians because it is an opportunity to influence intraorganizational change. For clinicians to exert influence during this phase of organizational transition, it is essential that they understand certain features of organizational life that frequently accompany succession.

Prior to an administrator's departure, organizations usually go into a period of inaction. Most staff

members are aware of the lame-duck character of this phase of organizational life, when any major change is avoided until the new administrator takes office. There are, however, ways in which clinicians take advantage of this period. They can, for example, (1) suggest criteria for the selection of a successor, (2) seek membership on the search committee, (3) prepare a position paper for the new administrator, (4) propose a revision in the governance structure to enhance participatory management, (5) organize fellow subordinates to propose changes that had been unacceptable to the outgoing administrator, or (6) propose the formulation of a task force to facilitate transition.

The "first one hundred days" is another critical phase of bureaucratic succession that should be examined for the opportunities it offers. Although new administrators tend to be conservative about implementing changes until they are more familiar with the organization, they still are interested in developing and in making their own mark. This three-month period, therefore, provides opportunities to orient and shape the perceptions of new administrators who, until they acquire their own intelligence about the organization, are both vulnerable and receptive to influence.

The following case illustrates how practitioners can tinker with organizational hierarchy by taking advantage of a resignation.

> The resignation of a clinician who had served as director of staff development in a child welfare agency provided the staff with an opportunity to influence the transformation of the position into that of administrative assistant. The agency had recently undergone rapid growth in staff size, resources, and diversity, without an accompanying increase in the administrative staff. Thus, the clinician's resignation became the occasion for examining whether the position should be modified to serve such administrative staff functions as program development and grant management.

Bureaucratic succession, therefore, provides an opportunity for an organization to take pause; to examine its mission, structure, policies, practices, accomplishments, and problems; and to decide what it wants to become. It is incumbent upon practitioners to participate in these processes and to take advantage of the structure of influence during that vulnerable phase.

RULES

Rules are features of organizations that, by their nature, invite tinkering. They act as mechanisms of social control and standardization, provide guidelines for decision-making, limit discretion, and structure relationships between persons and units within the organizational structure and between separate organizations (Perrow, 1972, pp. 23–32). There are two types of rules—formal and informal. Formal rules are derived from law or are determined administratively or collectively. Informal rules—which may be as binding as formal ones—are practices that have been routinized so that they have become organizational conventions or traditions. Rules vary in specificity, in their inherent demand for compliance, in the manner in which compliance is monitored, and in their sanctions for a lack of compliance.

Clinicians can tinker with rules either by the kind of interpretations they apply to them or by using their discretion, as is permitted with an ambiguous or general rule. Rules do not necessarily eliminate discretion, but they may eliminate alternatives that might otherwise be considered (Thompson, 1967, p. 120). Gottlieb (1974, p. 8) describes them as follows:

> Rules are not necessarily static. They appear to be a controlling force working impersonally and equally, but they vary both in adherence and enforceability and are used variously by staff in their adaptation to the "welfare bind."

Hanlan (1967, p. 93) suggests that "in public welfare there exists an informal system that operates without invoking the formal administrative machinery of rules." The author overheard the director of a community action program encourage new workers "to err on the side of generosity in determining eligibility for programs." A vocational rehabilitation counselor reported that he had had many teeth fixed by liberally interpreting a rule that provided dental care for only those clients whose appearance and dental problems would otherwise

have prevented them from being considered for employment involving public contact. This shows that one can tinker with the manner in which rules are interpreted and enforced.

Another way of tinkering with rules is to avoid what Gottlieb (1974, p. 8) calls "rule interpretations by agents of the system alone." She goes on to report that welfare workers encouraged clients to seek help in interpreting rules enforced by the National Welfare Rights Organization (NWRO). It is generally known that legal-aid clinics have been called on to give a legal interpretation of welfare rules and rules governing commitment to mental hospitals.

A supervisor for public assistance eligibility once reported that a thorough knowledge of all the rules enables the welfare worker to invoke one rule over another in order to help clients get what they need. This observation is supported by Gottlieb (1974, p. 32), who points out that rules allow for exceptions and that many NWRO members know the rules better than the workers and thus can challenge their interpretations. In his study of regulatory agencies, Nader (Nader et al., 1972) suggests that rules not only are opportunities for action but are potential obstacles as well and that major effort is frequently required to persuade the agency to follow its own rules.

Another way of dealing with rules is to avoid asking for an interpretation. One agency administrator has suggested that personnel should not routinely ask for rulings and urges them to use their own discretion. He commented: "If you invoke authority, you put me in a position where I must exercise it. If I make a decision around here, it becomes a rule."

These ways of tinkering with rules suggest that clinicians should examine the function of rules, discern the latitude they are allowed in interpreting them, and exercise discretion. Although the foregoing examples are primarily taken from welfare settings, the principles outlined can be applied to traditional clinical settings.

INDIRECT INFLUENCE

Too often, clinicians rely on the anecdotal or case approach to influence change in an organization.

Such an approach is too easily countered by the rejoinder that exceptional cases do not require a change in policy but should be handled as exceptions. The white paper, or position paper, is a much ignored means of tinkering with organizations.

A white paper is a report on a specific subject that emanates from a recent investigation. A position paper is a statement that sets forth a policy or a perspective. The first is usually more carefully reasoned and documented; the second may be argued instead of reasoned. Both white papers and position papers provide opportunities for social documentation and for formulating a compelling case. Such statements strive for logic and are characterized by their use of both quantitative and qualitative data. As the following example shows, by virtue of their character and quality, both position papers and white papers demand a specific response.

> A student social worker wrote a position paper identifying the number of teenage pregnancies, the number of associated medical problems, and the high rate of venereal disease among adolescents. She argued for the redirection of the original planned parenthood proposal from the main office to satellite clinics in public housing developments and schools. The paper was well received and spurred the executive to obtain funding from the housing authority.

Lindblom (1970) has characterized decision-making in organizations as "disjointed incrementalism." Simon (1957) indicates that organizations "satisfice"—that is, they make decisions that are good enough. Uncertainties in the environment, the inability to scan all alternatives, and the unknown utility of a solution or decision all preclude optimal decision-making. If organizations were to try to comprehend all the information and contingencies necessary before making a rational decision, the complexity would be overwhelming. Thus, organizations are reluctant to make changes on a large scale because this could lead to large-scale and unpredictable consequences. Resistance to change, therefore, may often be attributed to structure rather than to a malevolent or unsympathetic administrator. This calls attention to orga-

nizational structure and processes, but does not mean that the values and roles of administrators are to be ignored.[1]

Given this perspective of organizational behavior, clinicians may consider approaching innovation incrementally and on a small scale by first gaining authorization for a demonstration project.[2] A demonstration project may be bounded by the duration of time or the proportion of the budget or staff time that is devoted to it. The problem with demonstration projects is that the people for whom the demonstration is being carried out are not always specified, nor are they always kept abreast of developments. Often there is a failure to articulate the ramifications and consequences of a successful or unsuccessful demonstration. Practitioners must develop a strategy of demonstration—a means of diffusing innovation throughout the organization or into other organizations and of obtaining commitments from the administration when the demonstration is complete. The following is an example of the commitment one social worker obtained.

> A social worker met with a group of suspended or expelled junior high school students after class to discuss their problems. Realizing that she needed to have a chance to intervene directly in their school behavior, she persuaded the agency supervisor, the principal, and the classroom teacher to develop a pilot project—"the opportunity class"—to be used as a last resort before expulsion. When the project was organized, the social worker remained in the classroom for several periods at least two days each week. She handled the acting-out behavior problems while the teacher continued classroom instruction. Eventually the teacher acquired skill in handling students who were acting out. The class continued without the social worker's presence, and some students returned to a regular classroom while others were expelled.

Agency board committees are typically composed of elected members and the executive director of the agency. In addition, in some

---

[1] For a useful discussion on organizational resistance to change, see Patti (1974).

[2] For a negative view of demonstration grants, see Pratt (1974).

agencies, one or two staff members may also serve on the committee or occasionally attend meetings to make reports. One strategy of tinkering with the composition of the committee and the kind of information and influence it receives is to promote the idea that nonboard and nonstaff members with certain expertise be included on the committee. For example, a psychiatrist and a local expert on group treatment with children might be recruited to join a case services committee in order to provide legitimation to innovations that board members were grudgingly resisting.

Bypassing refers to a process whereby practitioners avoid taking proposals for change or grievances to their immediate superiors but seek instead a hearing or decision from a higher level in the hierarchy. In an enlightened organization, this form of bypassing is acceptable and even encouraged; government workers, in fact, are entitled to it as part of "due process." Bypassing is risky, however, in that it can discredit the judgment of the complainants if the matter is trivial or if it appears that it could have been resolved at a lower level in the hierarchy. Bypassing also places the administration in a vulnerable situation because if the tactic is justified, it reflects poorly on the judgment of the superior and the administrators who hired them. This may lead to questions of nonretention or spur a desired resignation. A successful instance of bypassing is described in the following example:

> When a clinician's complaints concerning the physical plant and security of a youth home went unheeded by the director, he demanded to meet with the executive committee of the board. The director admitted that his own sense of urgency differed from that of his staff, but arranged for the meeting. The executive committee approved some of the recommendations for change and authorized that they be implemented as soon as possible.

Agencies often write grant applications for funds to support their programs. A critical phase of the application process occurs at a public review of the grant application when the funding agency invites comment or a letter of support from the agency or from interested parties. If clinicians are dissatisfied with a particular program, and if it is an important matter, they can provide the agency issuing the grant with dissenting information, testify at the review of the grant application, or respond from the standpoint of an "expert witness." In any event, the grant-review process may be an opportunity to voice concern about an agency's program and to influence the advisory group to give conditional approval or disapproval. As is shown in the following example, clinicians may attempt to influence the review process indirectly—by encouraging an expert third party to raise questions about the grant application—or directly.

> A social worker was asked to serve as a technical reviewer for a volunteer program for young offenders in a regional planning advisory group. The program was modeled after an existing program in another part of the state. The documents supporting the application contained a manual that described the role of the volunteer. It suggested that a volunteer should report any violations of parole to the corrections authority but should not reveal this action to the offender. In seeming contradiction, it emphasized that the volunteer should be a "friend" of the offender. The social worker informed the advisory group of this provision and of his strenuous objection to it. The director of the program had failed to read the manual thoroughly and was unaware of the statement. The advisory group approved the program on the condition that the volunteer not serve as an informer and demanded that the staff codify the conditions under which it may be morally imperative for the volunteer to reveal the offender's behavior.

Social workers are often asked and frequently do endorse a program or a grant application perfunctorily, without having read the proposal. In other instances, programs and grants are endorsed in spite of strong reservations. Notwithstanding the pressures toward reciprocity that exist among agencies, such exchanges of professional courtesy are questionable.

Social workers should take advantage of requests for endorsement or participation in the grant-review process, particularly if they believe that certain aspects of a proposal or program are questionable. The desire for professional endorsement also underlies agency efforts to recruit clinicians for board membership or as paid consultants. Refusal of such offers is a way of "making a statement" about a program.

RADICAL TACTICS

Leaking information, or the covert release of information about an organization, is a tactic that should be used only in grave matters after all other remedies within the organization have been exhausted. The third party to whom the informant gives the information has to verify it and the credibility of the informant, since this person is not willing to put one's character and job on the line. However, until "blowing the whistle" becomes an accepted institutionalized value, and until protections are legislated, it is likely that members of organizations will continue to act like "guerillas in a bureaucracy" (Nader et al., 1972, pp. 15, 25–33; Needleman & Needleman, 1974).

Clinicians who anticipate the need to leak information would be well advised to seek counsel, for discovery could result in liability damages. They are obliged to have a thorough, accurate, and verifiable account of the objectionable situation. As the ethics of leaking information have not been well formulated, clinicians need to consider carefully the professional, moral, and legal standards that support such action (Nader et al., 1972, pp. vii, 1–8, 29–30, 225–230). One way in which the clinician may choose to attack the problem is shown as follows.

> The clinician in a foregoing example who was concerned about the physical plant and security of a youth home notified the state monitor about the condition of the home. At the next site visit, the monitor raised questions about the residents' access to balconies and the roof and about the staff-client ratio on weekends.

Resignation in protest, or public defection, is another tactic that should be used only when a clinician experiences unbearable misgivings and finds it both morally and professionally imperative to reveal them publicly. The major problem is that the organization has the financial and operational resources to counter the protest, but the employee has none. Also, with few exceptions, resignation in protest has a history of aversive consequences for the protester (Weisband & Franck, 1975).

A resignation in protest may also discredit the agency. Therefore, prospective protesters must be prepared to have their observations and conclusions verified and their judgment subjected to public review and scrutiny. In addition, the protester must realize that future employers will wonder whether such history of protestation will continue. An example follows.

> When his concerns went unheeded by the board, a clinician resigned in protest. Moreover, he informed the board and the director that he would discourage any professional worker from accepting employment at the agency. He was effective in discouraging local professionals from accepting employment at the agency unless firm commitments were made to modify policies and practices that were detrimental to clients.

The theory of escalation urges protesters to begin by using conventional and formal means to express grievances and influence change. Only after these have been exhausted, and traditional means have encountered failure and resistance, should they engage in a series of escalations to such unconventional or radical forms of protest as boycotting, "palace revolts," picketing, leaking information, and the like. The essential point of this strategy is that protesters should not begin by engaging in the most radical and abrasive strategy. To document the intransigence of the bureaucracy, change must be approached incrementally. If this is not done, the bureaucracy may point to the failure to follow administrative due process. The protester's etiquette and failure to go through channels then become the bone of contention, and the protester becomes the object of protest (Nader et al., 1972, pp. 16–25; Needleman & Needleman, 1974, pp. 285–289, 335–339; Weisband & Franck, 1975, pp. 55–94).

As a condition of employment and as a professional right and responsibility, clinicians should have the opportunity to bring their insights into the plans and programs of the organization they work for. Such participation requires that clinicians acquire skill in dealing with organizations.

It is hoped that the participation of clinicians in organizational activity will promote responsive service delivery systems and satisfactory work climates.

For Further Reading

Albert, R. (1986). *Law and social work practice.* New York: Springer.

Austin, C. (1981). Client assessment in context. *Social Work Research and Abstracts, 17,* 4–12.

Barton, W. E., & Sanborn, C. J. (1978). *Law and mental health professions.* New York: International Universities Press.

Flynn, J. P. (1985). *Social agency policy.* Chicago: Nelson-Hall.

Korr, W. (1987). The APA model law and three legal issues in mental health. *Social Work, 124,* 259–266.

Maluccio, A. (1979). *Learning from clients: Interpersonal helping as viewed by clients and social workers.* New York: The Free Press.

Schroeder, L. (1982). *The legal environment of social work.* Englewood Cliffs, NJ: Prentice-Hall.

Stein, T. J. (1987). The vulnerability of child-welfare agencies to class-action suits. *Social Service Review, 614,* 636–654.

Weissman, H., Epstein, I., & Savage, A. (1983). *Agency-based social work: Neglected aspects of clinical practice.* Philadelphia: Temple University Press.

PART

II

Tools for Deciding What to Do

Chapter 7

Values and Social Work Practice

In Chapters 3 through 6 we discussed knowledge and theory for social work practice and identified our responsibilities as social workers to make knowledge available to the applicant-client and worker problem-solving partnership. We considered the various types of knowledge, indicated that social work both borrows knowledge from other disciplines and generates knowledge for its own use, and suggested criteria to be considered in selecting knowledge for use in problem solving with your clients. We noted that some knowledge is in the form of confirmed propositions—knowledge that we accept and act on as true because science has been unable to reject the propositions. We also spoke of confirmable or assumptive knowledge. This is knowledge that can be confirmed (or rejected), has not been subject to rigorous testing, and is often in the form of the practice wisdom of the profession transmitted from generation to generation of social workers. While assumptive knowledge may have been confirmed in the practice experience of social workers, we in the profession have a responsibility rigorously to test this knowledge through systematic research.

But you will bring more than knowledge—both confirmed and assumptive—to your partnership work with applicants and clients. You will bring a set of values and ethics that guide and direct your practice. In this chapter we will attempt to define the concept of value, will identify two fundamental value premises for social work practice, will consider the role of values in practice, and will discuss the matter of ethical dilemmas.

What Is a Value?

No issue can be more troublesome for social work than that of values. Efforts to make definitive statements about social work values stir heated controversy. Is there a value base that all social work practitioners must accept? Does social work possess a set of values that are in some way unique in our culture? Are there interventive methodologies that social workers should not use because they may be inconsistent with what the profession believes about the nature of humanity? Henry Miller (1968) has noted some of the value dilemmas encountered by social work practitioners and suggests the withdrawal of social work from settings in which treatment is imposed or coerced. Elizabeth Salomon (1967) suggested the possibility of inherent conflict between the humanistic stance of social work and scientific methodology. Scott Briar and Henry Miller (1971, p. 42) advance the intriguing suggestion that one of the profession's traditional values—client self-determination—might be conceptualized as a treatment technique rather than a value. They suggest that clients in one-to-one relational systems make faster progress when they are extended maximum opportunities for self-determination. Thus self-determination can be viewed as a treatment technique geared toward facilitating client progress rather than as a human value that the profession promotes (p. 40).

Webster's Ninth New Collegiate Dictionary defines value as "something . . . intrinsically valuable or desirable" (definition 7). William Gordon (1965) has noted that *value* refers to things that are preferred, whereas *knowledge* refers to things that are known or knowable. Charles Levy (1973) has developed this idea and indicates that values can be classified as preferred conceptions of people, preferred outcomes for people, and preferred instrumentalities for dealing with people. Values can be thought of as beliefs that a profession holds about people and about appropriate ways of dealing with people. Paul Halmos (1966), an English sociologist, completed an extensive review of the literature of the helping professions and concluded that they operate from tenets of faith concerning the nature of people. This faith, Halmos argued, is accepted without proof and provides guidance and direction for the helping professions. Thus values can be considered as unproved (probably unprovable) beliefs that a profession holds about the nature of people. These beliefs are reflected in the day-to-day work of the practitioner and provide direction and guidance to professional practice.

But are a profession's values uniquely its own? Does a profession find its uniqueness and distinctiveness in the value premises underlying its work? We think not. The social work profession exists within a larger cultural context; it identifies and operationalizes value premises already existing in society and not held exclusively by the profession. Schwartz's concept of the sources of limitations on professional social work practice relates to this point. Schwartz identifies three sources of limitations— the norms of the overall society, the function of the agency, and the service contract with the particular client system (Schwartz, 1961, pp. 146–171). The social work profession exists within a culture whose value premises provide a source of limitation to the profession. A complex culture, however, is characterized by diverse value premises, some of which may be in conflict with each other. Like other professions, social work selects from this diversity the premises it will support in practice. The profession may achieve a degree of uniqueness in the particular way in which it operationalizes value premises, but the premises themselves are shared with other components of the culture.

One way of thinking of values is to picture an inverted triangle (see Exhibit 7-1). The top of the triangle represents values in a remote, general, or abstract sense. Near the point of the triangle the values become more proximate, specific, and concrete. The challenge, if values are to guide practice, is to take abstract concepts such as client self-determination and the innate dignity of the individual and to apply these concepts in specific situations. When asking how-to-do-it questions, movement is from the general to the specific; conversely, in asking a why question to seek justification or explanation of actions, movement is from the specific to the abstract. In thinking of values at these two levels—abstract and concrete—we must recognize that agreement generally increases with abstractness. For example, agreement with the abstract principle of client self-determination is readily secured; but at the specific level, say, of working with a 15-year-old who is bent on stealing cars, there may be considerable controversy over how to make this principle concrete. Our next task is to discuss two abstract principles—client self-determination and the innate dignity of the

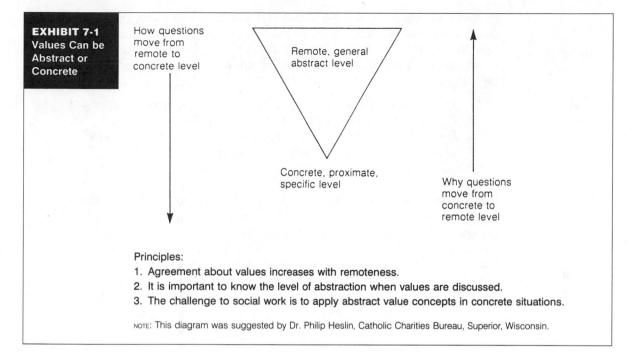

**EXHIBIT 7-1
Values Can be
Abstract or
Concrete**

How questions
move from
remote to
concrete level

Remote, general
abstract level

Concrete, proximate,
specific level

Why questions
move from
concrete to
remote level

Principles:
1. Agreement about values increases with remoteness.
2. It is important to know the level of abstraction when values are discussed.
3. The challenge to social work is to apply abstract value concepts in concrete situations.

NOTE: This diagram was suggested by Dr. Philip Heslin, Catholic Charities Bureau, Superior, Wisconsin.

individual—and to identify ways in which they can be operationalized by the social work practitioner.

In summary, values can be construed as unproven beliefs that guide and direct the work of a professional. These beliefs are not uniquely the possession of the profession. They are elements of the overall culture and are shared with others in the culture. However, they may achieve a degree of uniqueness in the way they are operationalized by particular groups. What are the value premises with which the social work profession identifies, and how are these premises operationalized? Two essential value premises underlie the practice of social work: (1) belief in the uniqueness and inherent dignity of the individual, and (2) belief in client self-determination.

**Respect
for the
Dignity and
Uniqueness
of the
Individual**

One of the central premises accepted and supported by the social work profession is that each person is a unique individual with inherent dignity that is to be respected. People are sufficient ends in themselves and are not to be treated as objects or as means to other ends. Diversity and variety among individuals are to be welcomed and encouraged. Paul Tillich (1962), a theologian who has directed attention to the philosophy of social work, referred to the uniqueness of every individual and situation as people's existential nature. William Gordon (1969) derived his matching concept of the social work function (referred to in Chapter 1) from the same notion. Gordon (1969, p. 6) has suggested that the social work profession does not attempt to move either the environment or the person toward some ideal model but rather strives to establish linkages between individuals and their environment, allowing for the widest possible diversity of both people and environments.

What are some of the implications of this principle for social work practice? This is the how question. How can the premise that every individual is unique and has the right to be treated with respect and dignity be applied in concrete social work situations? We have found five fundamental ways social workers can operationalize this value in practice:

1. Treat people as individuals; avoid use of classifications.
2. Provide and encourage participation in problem solving.
3. Discover and make use of strengths.
4. Expect and hold people, including yourself, accountable.
5. Carefully consider what your communications convey about dignity.

Dignity through Individualization   A thorny problem that will confront you as you work to operationalize the value of individual uniqueness and dignity is to strike a balance between classification and the responsibility to respond to persons as individuals. Classification refers to the need to generalize beyond individuals and to organize phenomena by common characteristics. This process is necessary to make sense out of a mass of raw data and, as discussed in Chapter 3, is an essential part of the process of knowledge building. When the phenomena being dealt with are people, however, classification may result in social workers responding to people as objects placed in a particular category rather than as individuals. The pitfalls of this process have been documented in a body of literature from sociologists studying deviance from a labeling perspective (Rubington & Weinberg, 1968; Simmons, 1969; Tannenbaum, 1951; Becker, 1963; Schur, 1973; Platt, 1977; Lemert, 1967). Not only does labeling, or classification, lead to distortion of individual differences, but as labeling theorists and their supporting research have noted, when a person is labeled deviant, those doing the labeling and the surrounding audience frequently respond to the person according to the label rather than individual characteristics. This creates conditions for the development of a self-fulfilling prophecy, in which the person becomes what he or she has been labeled (Merton, 1957, pp. 421–436). Two social work scholars in a review of cohort and other studies (Shireman & Reamer, 1986, pp. 67–68) have raised the possibility that the juvenile justice system itself may be crimogenic. Hans Toch (1970, p. 15) states the problem succinctly:

> Playing the classification game in the abstract, as is done in universities, is a joyful, exhilarating experience, harmless and inconsequential. Classifying people in life is a grim business which channels destinies and determines fate. A person becomes a category, is processed as a category, plays the assigned role, lives up to the implications. Labeled irrational, the person acts crazy; catalogued dangerous, the person becomes dangerous or stays behind bars.

One system of classification that you are likely to encounter is DSM-III, the *Diagnostic and Statistical Manual of Mental Disorders* of the American Psychiatric Association. While some social workers (Williams, 1981, pp. 101–106; Jahn, 1986, pp. 91–99) find DSM-III useful for social work, we think its use raises fundamental ethical questions and agree with the analysis of Kutchins and Kirk (1987, pp. 205–211) that the use of DSM-III by social workers raises important malpractice considerations. Kirk and Kutchins (1992) have also studied the development of

DSM-III and conclude that it emerged largely as a political document to lend an air of credibility to psychiatrist's claim to be scientific. At the time a first version of DSM was adopted, Karl Menninger (1968, pp. 117–118), a noted psychiatrist, had a similar concern and reacted with strong words:

> A committee of our worldly national body has just published a manual containing a full description of all the bewitchments to which all human flesh is err, with the proper names for each one, the minute suborder and subspecies listed and a code number for the computer. The colleagues who prepared this witch's hammer manual are worthy fellows—earnest, honest, hard-working, simplistic; they were taught to believe that these horrible things exist, these things with Greek names and Arabic numerals. And if patients show the stigmata, should they not be given the label and the number? To me this is not only the revival of medieval nonsense and superstition; it is a piece of social immorality.

We think there are two fundamental issues here. One is the inappropriateness of relating to people according to a diagnostic label that has been imposed. Equally problematic is the use by social work of a typology or classification scheme developed to guide the work of another profession. DSM-III may be useful for psychiatry, but social workers are not psychiatrists and have no business using terms and labels developed for a sister profession. We may need to understand DSM-III to be able to communicate with our psychiatric colleagues, but we do not need to use it as a guide to our own practice.

But isn't classification necessary? Or are we to agree with Salomon (1967) that there is an inherent conflict between the needs of science to order and classify and the humanism of social work? Toch (1970, p. 15) suggests that "the point of concern rests in any labels that lead to sorting or disposition." Toch takes the position that labeling is necessary for thinking or theory building but is not particularly helpful in making dispositional decisions about people. Concern should occur when decisions about what is going to happen to people are based on the individual having previously been placed in a particular category. And yet it is precisely at this point that classification appears to be most useful. Generally classifications come into play when professionals are attempting to assess or diagnose a situation as a guide for selecting appropriate procedures for dealing with the problem. Our point of view on this will be more completely developed in Chapter 10, in which assessment procedures will be discussed in terms both of the participation of worker and applicant in developing an understanding of the problem and of a service plan based on an analysis of the person-situation interaction being experienced by the applicant. We will propose assessment procedures that provide for individuality and minimize the need for categorization yet maintain scientific rigor in dealing with valid and reliable data, vigorously pursue facts, and conscientiously seek alternative explanations.

Dignity through Strength Our focus on problems and work with disadvantaged populations creates the occupational hazard that workers will focus too much on client weakness and problems and fail to identify strengths. In Chapter 1 we noted that a problem-solving approach does not have to be problem-focused. The focus is on using strengths to solve problems. Failure to identify strengths is likely to occur in work with minority groups by a worker unfamiliar with the culture, who may fail to recognize the cultural supports and traditions available to a client. Anthony

Maluccio's (1979, p. 399) study of social worker and client perceptions of treatment outcome and client functioning found some striking differences of view:

> In general, clients presented themselves as pro-active, autonomous human beings who are able to enhance their functioning and competence through the use of counselling service along with the resources operant in themselves and their social networks. Workers, on the other hand, tended to view clients as reactive organisms with continuing problems, weakness, and limited potentialities.

Consider, in light of Maluccio's research, this excerpt from a letter of reference written on behalf of an applicant for admission to a school of social work: "His main weakness is his tendency to prefer to believe the positive in clients, and he may therefore minimize pathology. With increased formal training in the social work program, I would anticipate significant improvement in this area."

Do you agree with the referee that a preference to believe the positive about applicants and clients is a weakness to be corrected by social work education? We think social work assessment and intervention are best based on the strengths brought by applicants and clients to their situations. Working with strengths is not the same, of course, as overidentifying with applicants, which implies a denial of weaknesses or pathology. We can and should be aware of weakness and pathology, but the focus of our work will be on how to mobilize and use strengths brought by the applicant, the worker, and the environment to resolve problems in the person-situation interaction.

Maluccio (1979, p. 401) concludes that "there is a need to shift the focus in social work education and practice from problems or pathology to strengths, resources, and potentialities in human beings and their environments. If this shift occurs, practitioners would be more likely to view clients as capable of organizing their own lives." We concur with this suggestion and consider a focus on strengths as in keeping with respect for individual dignity. Think about how different your reactions are when your strengths rather than weaknesses are mentioned. This is not to deny that there are problems to be addressed and weaknesses to be considered; but most of us are more willing and able to address weaknesses when strengths can also be brought into play.

Dignity through Participation Participation in decision making, planning, and action on one's own behalf is essential to the maintenance of human dignity. Think of the impact on dignity and individualism of entering an institution such as a hospital, where you have little or no control regarding decisions about what happens to you. We emphasize joint decision making on the part of worker and client and your responsibility to enable client participation because we see this as essential to the maintenance of human dignity. A. Weick and L. Pope (1988) suggest that social work, as a corrective to the tendency to emphasize professional expertise as the principle source of knowledge necessitates an approach to practice that places the client's own knowledge at the center of social work practice. Recognizing and developing a client's wisdom contributes to both self-determination and the establishment of a caring partnership. Both of these are keys to good social work practice. People's dignity is respected and preserved to the extent that they are involved in decisions and actions affecting them.

In this respect we suspect that social work may differ from other professions. In most dealings with professionals in our culture, the decision-making authority of the client is largely overshadowed by the expertise of the professional and to a large extent limited to decisions of whether to accept the professional's advice. Not so with the social work profession. Expertise of the social worker lies less in the substantive area of knowing what is best for the client than in the process area of assisting clients to develop alternatives for themselves, make decisions among the alternatives, and implement decisions. To assume that one knows what is best for the client both robs the client of dignity and runs the very grave risk of developing what Matthew Dumont (1968, p. 6) has referred to as a rescue fantasy:

> The most destructive thing in psychotherapy is a "rescue fantasy" in the therapist—a feeling that the therapist is the divinely sent agent to pull tormented souls from the pit of suffering and adversity and put them back on the road to happiness and glory. A major reason this fantasy is so destructive is that it carries the conviction that the patient will be saved only through and by the therapist. When such a conviction is communicated to patients, verbally or otherwise, they have no choice other than to rebel and leave or become even more helpless, dependent, and sick.

Exhibit 7-2 is an example of an attempt to impose a treatment plan on a youth without providing him an opportunity to participate in the decision making. This comes close to Dumont's rescue fantasy. How do you think this matter could have been approached differently to provide J. J. with an opportunity to participate in the decision making?

One way to begin providing for applicant and client participation is to shift our focus from needs to wants. The social work literature is replete with references to the needs of people. However, speaking of needs frequently translates as someone's (usually a professional's) view of what is good for someone else. In Exhibit 7-3

EXHIBIT 7-2 A Small Group for J. J.?	J. J., a white, 14-year-old ninth-grader, was discussed at a suburban junior high school case conference involving the principal, teacher, attendance clerk, and social worker. His teachers and principal have identified him as an aggressive youth who is failing in the classroom, lacks motivation, and displays poor attendance and social skills. J. J. did not have a history of problems prior to this year and was able to achieve satisfactory grades until the current school year. The staff have used various methods to promote acquiescence within the school setting including detention, suspension, and tutoring, but all attempts have failed. Contact with the mother has been frequent. She is described as verbally supportive but has been unable to impact J. J.'s current behavior. She has refused referral to outside assistance due to a negative past experience which resulted in loss of her job. The consensus was that J. J., if his behavior continued to decline, was in danger of failing ninth grade and being summoned before the juvenile court on a truancy petition. The staff was hesitant to adopt drastic action at this time because they believed the situation was salvageable and J. J. could be retracked toward appropriate behavior. He is of above-average intelligence, has athletic prowess, and is personable. Negative sanctions or stigmatization through the court might increase his level of frustration and prove harmful in the long run. Thus he was temporarily assigned to a small group of delinquent, acting-out students in an attempt to discover whether J. J. would be willing to discuss and work through various problems in a group of students in similar situations.

EXHIBIT 7-3 Wants as a Focus for Social Work	A want is close to (though not synonymous with) a "need" when the latter is an expression of a person's wishes, as in "I need a job," but not when "need" is used to express an outsider's evaluation of what a person should have, as in "he needs help." This distinction is particularly important given the traditional emphasis in social work on the second meaning of "need." Historically, social work programs have been based on professional and agency conceptions of the needs of different classes of people—the poor, mentally ill, delinquents, troubled families, and so on. In the process, not enough attention, in my judgment, has been paid to what people want. It is hoped the central position given to wants in the present framework will help to serve as a corrective to one of the primary occupational hazards of social work—acting on the basis of what we think is good for clients.

A focus on wants rather than needs may give us a different perspective on unmotivated client. Usually, he is unmotivated to be what social workers or others believe he ought to be. He lacks "motivation" to be a better spouse or parent, or to be more law abiding. To our dismay we see vast numbers of people who do not have motives for self-betterment, as we define it. While many clients lack motivation in these terms, few lack wants. If the client's wants are our concern, then the essential questions become: What does the person want? Can we help him get it? Should we do so? Should we try to create wants he does not have? If so, by what means? These questions are not easily answered, but they may help clarify our position and thinking about the many people who are less than enthusiastic about our efforts to help them.

NOTE: From *The Task Centered System* (pp. 25–26) by W. Reid, 1978, New York: Columbia University Press. Copyright 1978 by Columbia University Press. Reprinted by permission.

William Reid (1978, pp. 25–29) suggests *wants* as a better concept. A want is a "cognitive affective event consisting of an idea that something is desirable and a feeling of tension associated with not having it." Further, "when a want is experienced without means of satisfaction at hand or in sight, one has the sensation of having a problem." We agree with Reid's analysis that a person's wants provide a more useful frame of reference for social work than needs.

Placing emphasis on what the client wants should deter zeal to do things for people—ostensibly to meet their needs—that they do not want done. Even if well motivated, efforts to meet people's needs are properly attacked because many of these efforts may violate the liberty of people (Gaylin, Glasser, Marcus, & Rothman, 1978). A number of rights movements—children's rights, students' rights, patients' rights, inmates' rights, gay rights, and so forth—have emerged partially in response to unbridled discretion in the name of doing good. There may be a serious conflict between efforts to meet people's needs and efforts to protect people's rights; the notion that large bureaucracies can be consistently benevolent and act in the best interest of individuals is open to a very serious challenge. The concept of wants as needs experienced by the individual rather than perceived by some external organization provides a focus for social work that respects individual liberty and the dignity of the persons being served.

Sometimes the new or even the experienced worker feels frustration at coming to grips with the reality that the social worker cannot be the fountainhead of all wisdom, the person who can masterfully assume and resolve the applicant's problems. A certain humility is necessary to recognize that the applicant and the client are the chief problem solvers. This is not to deny that the worker plays a major part in assisting the client through the process and may at times serve rather forcefully as the client's agent. Opportunities for participation will be missed unless you are willing to maintain expectations for applicant and client participation, engagement in problem-solving activities, and belief that the problem can be solved. Oxley (1966, pp. 432–437) discusses the importance of worker's expectations for applicant and client motivation and suggests

> . . . that the worker should learn to expect a little bit more than the client expects of himself. Social workers are very well versed in beginning where the client is but perhaps too often tend to stay where the client is. If they instead assume the responsibility for leadership and imparting realistic hope, they may more effectively strengthen a client's ego and help him to reach to achieve his full potential and assume social responsibility.

Schwartz (1961, p. 269) refers to this as lending a vision and identifies it as one of the worker's tasks. Lending a vision by expecting, permitting, and encouraging applicant or client participation will emphasize and strengthen human dignity.

Dignity through Accountability We have been discussing enhancing applicant and client dignity by basing work on an individualized problem statement, focusing on strengths, and structuring our work in such a way as to encourage and expect applicant and client participation. Accountability is a fourth dimension of dignity that is often overlooked. People's dignity is enhanced when they are treated as responsible persons—persons responsible for their thoughts, their decisions, and their behaviors. To treat people as not responsible is to deny their strengths and is an open invitation to worker behavior similar to what Dumont refers to as the rescue fantasy.

What is meant by holding applicants and clients accountable? First we will discuss what accountability does not mean. Accountability does not mean imposing consequences. In some fields, such as juvenile and criminal justice, the concept of accountability has been distorted and used as a justification for imposing harsh punishments. In other disciplines consequences may be systematically controlled by professional staff as an effort to mold behavior desired by the staff. Neither the concept of accountability as consequences systematically controlled by the professional nor the concept of accountability as a justification for harsh penalties is appropriate for social work.

On the other hand, this does not mean that the social worker should fall into the trap of protecting the applicant or client from the consequences or results that may flow from the social situation of the client. From systems theory we know that any behavior will result in a reaction from the environment or social systems in which the applicant and client function. Further, we agree with the cognitive behavioralists that behavior is profoundly impacted by cognition, or thought processes. Thus an analysis of the likely consequences of a course of action for consideration by applicants and clients in decision making is very appropriate social work activity. What is not appropriate is for you to attempt either to protect the client from these consequences (unless there is a clear legal mandate to do so, a topic to which we'll return in our discussion of self-determination) or to manipulate the consequences to secure a behavior you desire.

How, then, will you enhance dignity through accountability? The partnership arrangement that characterizes the relationship between the applicant or client and the social worker implies that the parties to the relationship have legitimate expectations of each other. When one person's behavior is not consistent with expectations, that person can be properly held accountable for the behavior. This will occur within a social worker–client relationship when you discuss the fact that the client did not do what was agreed on, explore what was back of that, and establish the firm expectation that this will change and that the client will follow through on commitments.

We can illustrate this with an example. Let's assume that the J. J. case, which we introduced in Exhibit 7-2 as a failure to provide for dignity through participation, was handled differently. The principal and teacher called the attendance, performance, and behavioral problems to the attention of the school social worker, who instead of going to a meeting in which a plan was put together for J. J., reached out to make contact with J. J. Under this set of circumstances J. J. would, as we discussed in Chapter 1, be a contact. He would become a client if he accepted services and developed a plan with the worker. Let us further assume for the sake of illustration that the worker and J. J. explored the problem areas and that J. J. did agree to participate in the group as a means of assisting him to deal with his behavior, attendance, and performance problems. But then J. J. did not show up for the group meeting. Under this scenario, dignity through accountability would require the worker to contact J. J., to note that he has not followed through on what he has agreed to do, to discuss what was back of this, to discover what J. J. plans to do about it, and to reinforce and maintain the expectation that J. J. will follow through on what he has agreed to do because he has the strength to do so. This concept of accountability does not require imposing consequences or punishments on J. J. for failure to attend. In this context exploring what was back of failure to attend the group means discussing with J. J. what happened that he missed the group meeting; it does not mean asking him why he did not attend. We are not interested in justifications and rationalizations for failure to follow through on one's agreements and commitments. Asking the why question is likely to produce this. We are, however, interested in learning what prevented J. J. from doing what he said he was going to do, and what he plans to do about that in the future.

Maintaining accountability will involve you in developing skills at confrontation that we will discuss more in Chapter 16. Confrontation is sometimes perceived as a harsh attacking activity that we think is inappropriate, just as we think accountability as a consequence-oriented activity is inappropriate. Confrontation, in our view, means that you gently but nonetheless firmly discuss with people the fact that they have not lived up to their agreements and reinforce your expectations that they will do so. Confrontation grows out of your desire to assist people to become responsible, not out of your anger that they have been irresponsible. If you are experiencing anger when a client fails to follow through, this is a matter that you need to take up with your supervisor and begin working on in terms of your own professional competence. Anger leads to desire for harsh consequences and rejection; desire to assist people to be responsible leads to a factual discussion of the behavior and a reinforcement of expectations. And failure even to discuss irresponsible behavior is a rejection of the inherent dignity of the individual.

Remember that the issue of accountability goes both ways. The client has as much right to expect you to be accountable as you have to expect the client to be accountable. Failure to make telephone calls, to secure information you have promised, to be available when you have agreed to be available, or to follow through on other things you have agreed to do is also irresponsible. Some clients are able to confront workers when this happens, but most are uncomfortable doing so. Thus the responsibility will fall on you to acknowledge your own irresponsibility, to apologize for your failures, and to be forthright with your client about what you plan to do. No person, client, or worker is infallible; thus we will all at times fail to do what we have promised. When this happens to us, we can model a nondefensive way of handling our own fallibility by accepting accountability, apologizing, and moving ahead to correct the problems in our own performance.

We have tried to establish that accountability is an important component of enhancing client dignity because it derives from the fundamental notion of the client as a responsible person. To make any other value assumption is to place applicants or clients in a dependency position in which they must sacrifice their dignity to some other caretaker, often a professional person. We have suggested that accountability does not mean manipulation of consequences and is not a justification for harsh punishment. Accountability may, however, involve experiencing the consequences that may flow from one's environment. Analyzing these potential consequences as an aid to decision making is an important client–social worker activity. We have also suggested that client and worker are accountable to each other for carrying through on what they have agreed to do. When this fails to happen, we think there should be a confrontation between worker and client, which we perceive as a gentle but firm discussion of the failure to follow through, what was back of that, and what will be done in the future. Confrontation grows out of desire to assist people to become responsible, out of a desire to support the inherent dignity of the individual, and not out of the anger or frustration that a worker may be experiencing.

Communicating Dignity We have identified the social work value premise that the individual is unique and should be treated with respect and dignity. And we have argued that this value premise can be operationalized as you individualize each applicant and client situation to avoid classification, help clients to discover and assist them in making use of their strengths, expect and provide for client participation in problem solving, and maintain accountability of both client and worker.

These dimensions of dignity—individualization, strength, participation, and accountability—are, of course, manifest in our communications with applicants and clients. Thus we have an obligation to be constantly reviewing and aware of what we are communicating about human dignity. Social psychologists have established that people's images of themselves develop largely out of their communication with others (Rose, 1962). People build and incorporate their self-image from the messages they receive from other people about themselves. Further, people who feel good about themselves, see themselves as persons of worth, and have a sense of their own strength and capability tend to be happier and have the ability to deal constructively and appropriately with their environment.

Social workers and other professionals intervening in the lives of people are well advised to be constantly sensitive to the messages they are extending to others about their worth. Do you, in the little things you do, communicate to other people that they are unique individuals to be highly prized? What, for example, is the message communicated when you safeguard an hour and provide a client with a specific time to be seen as opposed to acting on a catch-as-catch-can basis? Do appointments in advance communicate to the client a higher sense of respect than unannounced visits or hurriedly arranged telephone appointments? Speaking of telephoning, how about the all too frequently overlooked return call? What message does a person get when you do not have the courtesy or good sense to return a telephone call promptly? How about the ability to listen to a person, to secure an account of his or her situation, and to avoid prejudgments?

Does not privacy, both in how you conduct the interview and how you treat the material gained from interviews, communicate something to people about the esteem in which they are held? Emily Jean McFadden (1992) considers therapy with children who have been victims of sexual assault as both an invasion of their privacy and a painful undertaking. She suggests that communicating and respecting the dignity of the child requires that we not engage in therapeutic interventions that invade privacy without the permission of the young person. When attempting to operationalize the premise of individual uniqueness and dignity, you may find it useful repeatedly to inquire, "What does this action on my part communicate to this person about my perception of him or her?"

In Chapter 8 we include an article by Addie Morris describing her experiences as a client of a large public welfare agency. We suggest that you take a few minutes now and read "Four Pennies to My Name: What It's Like on Welfare" (Reading 8-1) and think of yourself as a worker in that agency. How might you have responded differently to show more respect for the dignity of Addie Morris and her children? Either now or when you read Chapter 8, think about your responsibility as a social worker for what agency procedures and policies communicate to clients. How do agency procedures and their use express values?

Self-Determination

Self-determination implies that persons be permitted to make decisions for themselves. This carries with it the clear assumption that most of the time those decisions will be responsible—responsible in that people in their decision making will for the most part make decisions that are consistent with the welfare of the community. The social work stance has generally been to couple the concept of client self-determination with that of responsibility for the total community and to attempt to work out a balance between the two. S. Freedberg (1989) has reviewed self-determination within the history of social work and suggests that the practice implication of self-determination is that social workers confront a basic contradiction in their roles as client advocates and as agents of a society in which clients are disenfranchised; social workers are encouraged, however, to apply self-determination to empower clients. Barring some clear-cut indication of danger to others, the social worker in day-to-day contact with clients will generally attempt to maximize opportunities for client self-determination.

Self-Determination as Alternatives   Inherent in the concept of client self-determination is the idea of alternatives. Self-determination implies decisions, or the making of choices between one course of action as contrasted with other courses of action. It is fraudulent to think of self-determination without alternatives. If there is only one course of action, how can there be self-determination? The person has no choice and thus no opportunity for self-determining. Much of social work activity with applicants and clients consists of a quest for alternatives to expand the opportunities for self-determination. The quest for alternatives may take various forms—helping the person develop new alternatives and resources within the environment or helping him or her find and develop new ways to respond to environmental demands.

You may often encounter applicants or clients with learned helplessness. In an extreme example they are persons who believe they cannot avoid victimization. When people believe there is nothing they can do to control events or there are no decisions they can make that will impact on their situation, their self-determination is constrained—if not denied. Self-determination comes as these views can be modified and as people can be helped to exercise choice. You have read "The House on Sixth Street" in the Appendix. In this case self-determination was limited by the lack of adequate housing; efforts to permit greater choice regarding housing helped increase self-determination. Self-determination may be increased by activity focused on removing blockages within the environment that are limiting opportunities as well as by helping people remove blockages within themselves that limit their abilities to see and use alternative courses of action. Internal blockages may include cognitive structures that prohibit the applicant or client from considering other alternatives, including alternative ways they can think and behave, as well as patterned emotional responses to the social situation of the applicant or client. People whose range of response to their environment is limited by their own stereotyped and patterned cognitions, feelings, and behavior are as much lacking in opportunity for self-determination as the ghetto client confronted with the lack of environmental opportunities.

Self-Determination and Client Values The value premises of both human dignity and self-determination imply respect for and support of a wide diversity of applicant and client value orientations. But these values also raise many issues for the social worker. For example, if we believe in the self-determination of all people, what do we do when one of our clients coerces another or interferes seriously with the rights of a vulnerable person? Another issue in self-determination is inherent in the nature of choice itself. What is the meaning of self-determination if alternatives are so seriously limited as to be no choice at all? Can one really exercise self-determination if one does not understand the consequences of the choice or if one does not have adequate facts on which to base a decision? Certain laws to protect consumers and laws relating to warranties and truth in lending are examples of society's actions to protect those who must make certain decisions. If we believe that each person has a right to total self-determination with no limits, we must support the notion that the race is always for the strong and the uncaring. Some of the most difficult jobs of the social worker are those involving conflicts between those who would exercise self-determination in ways that are destructive to themselves and others and those they damage. Does the principle of client self-determination require the social worker to support such value orientations among cultural groups in which they are dominant? It is our position that when client behavior results in damage to another individual or another group, damage that our knowledge of the needs of others tells us is severe, workers cannot support the hurtful action. However, this principle that workers do not support the action says nothing about what our response should be.

Charles Levy (1972, pp. 488–493) identifies a number of areas in which social workers favoring planned change have value conflicts with applicants. There may be times when a social worker's conception of how to operationalize the notion of human dignity and client self-determination is inconsistent with value orientations held by applicants; when this occurs, these differences become a matter for discussion and negotiation between the worker and applicant. The differences must be clarified and a workable resolution achieved before intervention efforts occur. Applicant values may also serve as a barrier to alternatives and a limit to self-determination.

Hardman, in Reading 7-3, suggests that when the values of a respondent or client conflict with the welfare of others or with the person achieving the agreed-upon goals, the values themselves become an appropriate target for change. He confronts the question whether social work is always bound to support the self-determined actions of the respondent or client. Hardman's unexamined belief in the right to self-determination had left him uneasy but essentially uninvolved with values of a parolee regarding sexual activity that were likely to lead to illegal behavior and to damage the dignity and feelings of another. The rights of another only became a real problem for him when he realized that the person being damaged could be his daughter. Suddenly the rights of the other became critical. Thus Hardman was confronted with an issue not only of his own value system and its difference from the respondent's but with the issue of the responsibility of a professional person to be concerned with the rights of all people. Another intriguing example is the problem of spouse abuse, which seems to be related to a value orientation present in some groups of our society; this orientation holds that the proper role of women is subservience to the husband. And what about certain groups in our society that believe that to spare the rod spoils the child?

It is our position that social workers are not engaged in the process of forcing people to change behavior. Therefore, any work to change an applicant's values or behavior in the interests of increasing life satisfactions of applicants or of others involved with applicants has to come from the engagement of client and worker in an agreed-upon plan. Applicant or client values may be such that actions that follow from them may hurt others, and certain values may also serve to limit the adequate choices of the applicant. However, effort toward change must involve the applicant. Thus when the values of a person conflict with the rights of others or get in the way of the client achieving agreed-upon goals, the values themselves become a topic for discussion and for consideration as an appropriate target for change.

The principle of self-determination will lead you in the direction of engaging persons in three actions: (1) consideration of how values may restrict progress toward the goals desired by the applicant, (2) consideration of possible alternatives and their consequences for goal achievement, and (3) consideration of the rights and needs of others. The principle of self-determination is misunderstood if it is taken to suggest that the worker does nothing but put the total responsibility for considering choice on the applicant with no offer of alternatives or consideration of the outcomes of choice.

The applicant and client exercising decision making are a key component in this formulation. The concept of self-determination as operationalized in social work calls for increasing opportunities for people to make decisions for and about themselves. This is an area in which the social work profession may differ markedly from other professions. People generally go to other professionals for expert advice; that is, they expect to be told what in the view of the professional is best for them. Patients expect the doctor to diagnose an ailment and to recommend a specific course of treatment, and clients expect the lawyer to advise them about what action should be taken in dealing with a legal problem. In both of these situations there is, of course, an element of self-determination, inasmuch as the patient or client must ultimately decide whether to follow the expert's advice. But the social worker is not an expert in what's best for the applicant and is not primarily a giver of advice. Rather we manage a process that involves applicants or clients in the solution of their own problems, including modifying their values if these contribute to the problem.

Does this mean the social worker does not offer an opinion or make a suggestion? Emphatically not. Just as the extreme of taking over and making decisions for applicants is to be avoided, so is the extreme of never sharing a viewpoint. Such action denies applicants or clients the benefit of your judgment and may effectively deny people alternatives they may wish to consider in their own decision making. As Charlotte Towle (1965, p. 26) noted 50 years ago, "The social worker's devotion to the idea that every individual has a right to be self-determining does not rule out valid concern with directing people's attention to the most desirable alternative." Workers have obligations to share their own thinking, perhaps their own experiences, with clients and applicants. Sharing information is not a way of directing lives but rather is an additional source of information and input for the others to consider in their own decision making. Your input is to be recognized as information to be considered, not as an edict to be followed. Schwartz (1961) offers some helpful suggestions in this regard. He notes that the worker has a responsibility to contribute data to the client and that the data may include facts, ideas, and value concepts. In contributing data, the worker should inform the client that the worker is offering only part of the total available social experience and is not the source of all knowledge. Moreover, the data contributed should be clearly related to the purpose of work with the client. Opinions, while important data, should be clearly labeled as opinions and not represented as facts. Self-determination does not imply worker nonparticipation. A mark of successful practitioners is their ability to share knowledge and thinking without imposing a judgment, thus leaving others free to accept or reject their views.

Worker Self-Determination Another aspect of self-determination requires emphasis. Some workers confuse applicant and client self-determination with worker self-determination. We are not arguing for the latter. As you take on a professional responsibility, you agree to limit your own self-determination in the interest of others. The various social work codes of ethics, including that of The National Association of Social Workers, reprinted with this chapter, clearly limit worker self-determination. If your communication style or dress style arouses the antagonism of applicants and clients or others who may influence clients, your professional responsibility calls for the forfeiting of your own self-determination in the other's behalf. Exhibit 7-4 is an excerpt from an interview with a social worker functioning in a community organization capacity. Does this worker have an obligation to set aside

**EXHIBIT 7-4
The Excitement
of Organizing?**

I remarked that it certainly must be satisfying to organize and be part of such an event. I was surprised when Alice shook her head slowly and said in a much more somber tone of voice, "No, 99% of the time there is very little glamour to organizing." I asked her to explain further, and she went on to say that it is hard, hard work and that one of the most discouraging things for her to realize is that oftentimes the people you are organizing aren't necessarily looking for a change in the system but rather to become a part of that system. Usually that means playing the same games that those in power play. She talked further about the frustration she deals with constantly. I, too, began to feel that organizing was not the glamorous, romantic job I had pictured it to be.

her own goals of changing the system and work with clients who want to be successful within the system rather than produce more revolutionary change? We think she does.

Self-Determination Summary In this section on client self-determination, we have attempted to establish this concept as one of the value premises underlying social work. Five points have been made: (1) Self-determination will commit you and clients to a quest for alternatives. Without alternatives there is no opportunity to make decisions and no opportunity to engage in self-determination. (2) As a social worker, you are responsible for increasing applicants' and clients' opportunities for decision making. We are not experts in what is substantively best for people and thus should avoid making decisions for applicants, but social workers are expert in assisting people in a process of joint decision making. (3) You have an obligation to offer your own viewpoints and suggestions to applicants and clients. These are offered as alternatives and input to be considered, and not as an edict or a right answer for the person. (4) Efforts to modify client values are not inconsistent with the concept of self-determination, provided the values interfere with efforts to attain goals or with the welfare of others and that clients concur with efforts to produce value change. (5) A differentiation must be made between client self-determination and worker self-determination. In assuming professional responsibility, you sharply limit your own self-determination and become responsible for conducting yourself in ways that best meet the interests of applicants and clients and increase opportunities.

**Legal
Authority
and Self-
Determination**

Fields of practice in which you possess legal authority that may be used to coerce respondents present some special questions in regard to the matter of self-determination. Coercion is typically mandated for two different types of respondents and for different reasons. One group is perceived as being in need of protection because of dependency status, and coercion is justified as necessary to protect the respondent. Dependent children, developmentally disabled persons, and the aged are often perceived as in need of protection. A second use of coercion is to force rehabilitation for those who have violated the norms of society; persons in this group include juvenile and adult offenders, chemically dependent persons, and mentally ill persons. The stance of a profession, such as social work, with a high commitment to the principle of self-determination may vary in regard to the use of coercion depending on whether the coercion is used for protection or forced rehabilitation purposes.

Use of Authority to Protect   William Reid and Laura Epstein (1977) make a distinction between the protective and helping functions of the social worker. They suggest that the practitioner must not only recognize these differences but also must make sure the respondent understands them. We have argued that available knowledge should direct our interventions (see Chapter 3). Our knowledge base confirms that dependent children, developmentally disabled persons, and aged persons may be victimized and harm themselves; responsible action requires some limitations on their self-determination in the interest of providing protection. Even within the limits imposed as necessary to protect the respondent, you will have responsibility to develop as many practical alternatives as possible for decision making, thus increasing self-determination.

For example, children who must be removed from their homes because of neglect or abuse may be provided considerable involvement in the decision making regarding the alternative living arrangements. Involving the children in this decision making may open up resources such as relatives, neighbors, and others previously unknown to the social worker. Exhibit 7-5 provides an illustration; we do not provide the entire case summary, but Arthur was placed with the Jelnecks, a family he suggested after social workers failed to find a foster home. Likewise, our knowledge may indicate that a physically ill or aged person may no longer be able to live alone at home despite his or her wish to do so. A need for protection may limit self-determination in regard to this choice, but the astute worker may well be able to engage the respondent in decision making regarding the type of alternative living arrangement to be followed. B. Nicholson and G. Matross (1989) analyze several cases to illustrate how social workers can enhance client self-determination in persons—such as the elderly and individuals with advanced AIDS—who live beyond their ability to make autonomous decisions; one set of approaches to enhance self-determination are advance directives—for example durable power of attorney, living will, and oral communication—whereby clients can give instructions regarding their care after their decision-making ability has been impaired because of disease or frailty.

We think that when coercive authority is being used and justified on the basis of protecting a respondent, it is essential for you to be clear about the knowledge base that justifies the use of authority as well as the source and extent of the authority; further, these matters must be clearly communicated to the respondent. The source and extent of authority are an example of agency function, Schwartz's (1961) second source of limitation on the worker's activity. Because of possibilities of abusing protective authority, respondents are entitled to opportunities to request appeal and review of your decisions. The involvement of courts and guardians independent of you is an appropriate check and balance against abuses. We and the profession have an obligation continually to reassess whether coercive authority is necessary to protect the respondent or is being used unnecessarily to impose a particular standard on a person. In Exhibit 7-6, Marvin Silverman (1977, p. 177) addresses this issue in relation to coercion of children.

Use of Authority to Force Participation in Treatment Programs   The use of authority to force rehabilitation efforts on the respondent creates a serious dilemma for the profession. There are at least two distinct directions in which this dilemma may be resolved. One option is to attempt to integrate the authority and service roles and

EXHIBIT 7-5
Finding a
Foster Home
for Arthur

As a new probation officer, I had just been assigned to Arthur. I had not met him prior to this trip to the State Training School. The case record was fairly sketchy but he was sixteen and a half years old and was the oldest of six siblings from an impoverished family of tenant farmers who lived in what were described as squalid conditions. Arthur was described as of average intelligence although he did not do well in school and was frequently truant; he was apparently dependable and good at farm labour when work was available. Records contained references to possible sexual abuse within the family but none of this had been substantiated. He had been sent to the training school by the court after a series of break-ins in neighboring farm homes as well as in the town which served as a business centre for the area. He also had another previous court finding for truancy, for incorrigibility, and for a run away from home which also involved the unauthorized use of a motor vehicle. Two and a half months ago the placement committee at the Training School had decided that Arthur was ready for release to a community setting. Both the institutional staff and Arthur's previous probation officer were adamant that he could not go home but would require a foster home placement. The previous probation officer had been very diligent in attempting to locate a placement and had made contact with every agency providing foster family care services in the area. But there were no homes available for a sixteen and a half year old delinquent. In the meantime, Arthur was becoming somewhat impatient at being held at the institution while fruitless efforts were under way to find a placement.

I met Arthur and spent some time reviewing his progress at the institution; he seems to be enjoying school. Arthur seems accepting of the fact that he will not be going home. His parents have not been able to visit in the now nearly a year that he spent in the institution; it is unclear as to whether the failure to visit is lack of interest or lack of resources to make the 150 mile one-way trip to the institution which is located in a relatively remote area not readily accessible by public transportation. Arthur did express some unhappiness about the fact that his institutional stay is being extended because we are unable to find a placement.

I asked him if he had any ideas—any relatives or other persons that we might talk with about a possible placement. He seemed a bit hesitant, said he didn't really think he had any relatives that would be willing to let him live with them. But there was this neighbor; apparently he had lived with for short periods of time and worked for a neighbor during previous summers. I explored this as much as I could; Arthur believed he got along well with the neighbor but didn't have an opinion as to whether the couple would be interested in letting him live with them. After some further discussion, he agreed that the matter could at least be looked into. We spent some time discussing how to approach the neighbor. Arthur agreed to write a letter indicating that I would be in touch with them to discuss this parole planning and agreed to prepare the letter tonight so that it could be mailed tomorrow. I let him remain vague as to whether he would raise in the letter the possibility of living with the neighbor, and have no idea whether he did or did not raise this possibility.

I waited about a week and then called the Jelnecks; Mrs. Jelneck indicated that they had received a letter from Arthur and agreed to let me come out and talk with she and her husband about parole planning. They live on a modest farm home on a piece of land which they owned and farmed; they had raised three children the youngest of which completed high school last spring and has gone off to the state university. We talked at length about their past contact with Arthur which, by and large, they perceived as positive; I indicated that we did not believe it would be appropriate for Arthur to return home and that he agreed with this; I wondered if they would be in a position to consider letting Arthur live with them. They didn't seem to be particularly surprised by the request, perhaps Arthur had raised it in the letter, and agreed to consider and discuss the possibilities.

EXHIBIT 7-6 Children's Rights	If children's rights became a reality, there would clearly be a change in the nature of many social workers' professional relationships. These would become largely voluntary—the kind of relationship most consistent with the traditions of social work. There would also be changes in specific roles. At the present time, there are large and expensive professional and bureaucratic structures which are organized to maintain children in nonvoluntary associations and to work with the problems such associations generate. They would no longer be needed. If schools were populated by willing students, there would be far less need for school social workers, school psychologists, guidance personnel, and administrators who deal mainly with discipline problems. There are children in residential treatment centres not because of family problems but because of inability to function in school. Police, courts, and probation officers spend a great deal of energy in dealing with truancy, status offenses, incorrigibility, and runaways. With increased children's rights, social work roles would flow directly from children's needs rather than being filtered through structures which, to some extent, at least, are organized around social control. Similarly, teachers could concentrate on improving the educational program, and police could concentrate on true crime—juvenile and adult.

NOTE: From *"Children's Rights and Social Work"* by M. Silverman, 1977, *Social Service Review, 51,* p. 177. Copyright 1977 by University of Chicago Press. Reprinted by permission.

within the limitations imposed by the setting try to expand opportunities for self-determination. A second alternative is for social work to withdraw from the coercive efforts to rehabilitate.

Typically, social workers have attempted to integrate their authority and service functions (Hardman, 1960; Hatcher, 1978; Klockars, 1972; Overton, 1965; Rooney, 1992). The presence of legal authority limits self-determination but leaves other areas available for the exercise of self-determination. These include determining how the authority will be exercised as well as noting areas in addition to the legal requirements in which self-determination may be emphasized. A probation officer may enforce the legal requirement that the probationer must report; this is not a matter for self-determination. But the sensitive probation officer can allow for considerable self-determination in the frequency of reporting, the length of the interviews, the time of reporting, and the content to be discussed during the interviews. Respondents in correctional settings can be extended considerable self-determination in how they use workers, including, if they choose, only using them for the minimum mandated by the probation orders.

Three recent social work scholars, struggling with this dilemma that is a part of the history of the profession, have arrived at positions consistent with the use of authority and expanding opportunities for self-determination position. Shireman and Reamer (1986), in an analysis of juvenile justice policy, reached the conclusion that the concept of just desserts might be used to limit what public authority can coerce, but within these limits rehabilitative programs can be required and the social worker will find an opportunity to work with respondents. Ron Rooney (1988, 1992) has developed a conceptual framework for social work practice in which one possibility may simply be complying with the minimum requirements of the court order (the limits that Shireman and Reamer believe may be derived from the concept of just desserts) but in which there is also an effort to convert the respondent to a client through negotiation of a mutually acceptable service plan. Rooney suggests that many persons who start seeing a worker as respondents may, with creative and good social work practice, find an area in which they can voluntarily agree to work and thus become clients. Rooney also notes that respondents who are initially required to receive services in the interest of protection may also shift from respondent to client status. Latitude exists in situations involving legal authority for respondents to exercise self-determination. Skillful workers can use these opportunities with the respondent. At the very least, of course, the respondents have the option of determining whether they are going to do anything more than the legal minimum, as well as the option of ignoring the requirements of the authority and accepting the consequences.

You will still see many persons in coercive settings who will be unwilling to negotiate a service plan and who will continue in the role of respondent. They will continue seeing you only because they are under external coercion to do so. This raises the possibility, which we introduced in Chapter 1, that in these situations we might reconceptualize the notion of client and think of the state, through its formal institutions (courts, hospitals, correctional institutions, and so forth) as the client. Bradley Googins and Bruce Davidson (1993) suggest that the organization may be the client for social workers practicing in employee assistance programs—a setting in which coercion is present but probably more subtle than in corrections or some chemical dependency services. The social worker's authority to intervene in these settings derives from a contract with the organization or with the state, representing all of us collectively, with the goals of that service being to reduce behavior that collectively we find undesirable. Under this concept the person the social worker is seeing becomes the target of change. The notion of the state as client is one that may be troublesome to many social workers because it clearly identifies the social control function of the profession. But a straightforward identification of this relationship between the worker, the state, and the respondent will make it much easier forthrightly and honestly to address the key issues of under what conditions you, representing the state, can forcibly intervene in the life of the respondent. What are the limits to what you may do under these circumstances? What are both the rights and obligations of the respondent?

Another possible response to the dilemma of self-determination vis-à-vis coercive services is the withdrawal of social work from these roles (Miller, 1968; Galaway, 1981). Withdrawal of social work from coerced rehabilitative roles does not, of course, mean that social services should not be provided to offenders and others who are subjected to forced rehabilitation efforts. The services of social workers should certainly be provided to these populations, but structures that permit the provision of these services on a voluntary basis can be developed. In Exhibit 7-7 Gerald O'Connor offers an insightful position on the question of self-determination in prisons.

Peter Rayner (1985) projects two contrasting scenarios for probation work. One scenario is derived from the model of coerced treatment, in which he perceives probation as becoming more and more repressive, with social work having relatively little involvement except to provide an ideological justification for repression. The second scenario perceives the probation officer working in partnership with

EXHIBIT 7-7
Self-
Determination
in Prison

The principle of self-determination, the freedom to choose one's own destiny, is based on an assumption of individual dignity. . . . The recognition of people's right to free choice guarantees that they may choose to run their life as they see fit. This choice may run counter to society's welfare and even their own, yet essentially it is their choice and their prerogative. Society may censure, but it cannot take from them the right; nor should society strip them of personal dignity by a censure. The criminal then has a right to say "crime is my choice and I am willing to pay the price. If you send me to prison, I am paying my debt to society and refuse to submit to your attempts to reform me." The principle of self-determination makes it incumbent upon society to honor such a plea. There are large numbers of inmates in correctional institutions who recognize a need for rehabilitation and are willing to become involved in programs for that end. An inmate's voluntary recognition of a need for assistance does not, in turn, give officials a free rein in outlining the inmate's rehabilitation program. It is reasonable that the offender have input into the definition of the offender's own problem and have this included in the official assessment. The inmate should have the opportunity to say what type of program would be of assistance and who should provide the services. Further, it seems appropriate that the inmates have a right, in part, to determine the conditions under which the services are delivered.

NOTE: From *"Toward a New Policy in Adult Corrections"* by G. O'Connor, 1972, *Social Service Review, 46,* p. 582. Copyright 1972 by University of Chicago Press. Reprinted by permission.

offenders. Probation terms are negotiated, and much of the change effort will be directed toward developing social support networks and mobilizing the resources of the community to meet needs and wants identified by the offender.

The matter of whether offenders and other persons who are required to receive coerced services are respondents or clients, and thus the extent to which their self-determination is respected, may hinge largely on the type of services offered and the manner in which they are made available. Many offenders are likely to enter into agreements to work jointly with social workers to resolve problems the offender is experiencing in personal situations and interactions. Silverman (1977) makes the same assertion for children.

This issue is complex and will be debated within the profession for quite some time: our inclination, however, is to begin challenging the appropriateness of social work activity in coerced rehabilitative settings and to begin developing structures, policies, and programs to permit a more voluntary association and partnership between offender and social worker. Such a process is consistent with the principle of client self-determination. This does not, of course, exempt persons who are found guilty of violating laws from being negatively sanctioned or punished by the society. We do, of course, have a professional obligation to be concerned about what penalties are used. Are they fair and humane? Do we rely too much on high-cost penalties such as jail and prison, which sap resources that might otherwise be available for social welfare and educational services? Are penalties restorative and healing or alienating and separating in their effects (Galaway, 1981; Galaway & Hudson, 1990; Zehr, 1990)? Most important, are we using the criminal law where more informal sanctions might be equally or more effective?

Values, Ethics, and Ethical Dilemmas

We have defined values as unprovable assumptions or tenets of faith that guide social work practice and have mentioned Levy's (1973) typology of values as preferred conceptions of people, preferred outcomes for people, and preferred instrumentalities for dealing with people. Our discussion of the values of innate human dignity and self-determination might suggest that these values fall in the classification of preferred instrumentalities for dealing with people, as we have focused on ways in which you can put these values into effect in day-to-day social work practice. These values, however, also address the preferred conceptions of people, as they assume people are capable of making decisions, of participating, are respected for individual differences and diversity, and are self-determining. We have said little about the preferred outcomes for people, except to indicate that the outcomes must be consistent with the value premises; to a large extent the outcomes of service provisions for people are subject to the values themselves and thus are negotiated individually with clients.

Ethical Dilemmas or Bad Practice?   Linked to the notion of values and derived from them is the concept of professional ethics. Professional ethics refer to the obligations of a professional person in his or her relationship with other persons, including clients, other professionals, and the general public. Professional ethics are usually codified and represent a set of obligations that we accept as a part of assuming the role and status of a professional. You will find a large number of codes of ethics in social work. The various state licensing boards, social work professional associations, and other professional associations to which social workers often belong have all formulated codes which are binding on members. R. Barker (1988) reviewed these various codes and has concluded that they are so similar as to be indistinguishable and should be given equal consideration. Reading 7-1 is the Code of Ethics of the U.S. National Association of Social Workers. This code includes statements regarding ethical responsibility to clients, to social work colleagues, to employing organizations, to the social work profession, and to the society at large.

Social workers are in a role set in which we have simultaneous ethical obligations to several people. This raises the possibility of a conflict among these obligations and thus an ethical dilemma. An ethical dilemma occurs when you cannot simultaneously meet your obligations to two different parties in the role set without violating your ethical commitment to one or the other. Most students of ethics suggest that ethical dilemmas can be resolved only by establishing a hierarchy of values or principles. The more important provisions take precedence in resolving ethical dilemmas (Reamer, 1982b; Loewenberg & Dolgoff, 1988, pp. 120–123) and guidelines for resolving these dilemmas.

Loewenberg and Dolgoff (1985) suggest that the concept of ethical dilemmas, or ethical problems, may not be quite correct; they prefer to think of ethical aspects of practice. We understand that ethical dilemmas do exist and that individual social workers as well as the profession as a whole must struggle to resolve these complex problems. We are concerned, however, that what may initially be described as an ethical dilemma on closer examination may not be an ethical dilemma at all but simply an example of bad practice. Exhibit 7-8 is an example of a situation represented as an ethical dilemma. We do not see an ethical dilemma in Exhibit 7-8 but do see the very strong likelihood of serious practice errors. It appears that Mr. Corrado did not

EXHIBIT 7-8 **An Ethical** **Dilemma?**	Warren Duffy, a 15-year-old six footer, was charged with armed robbery. In a juvenile court hearing Warren denied this charge. He claimed complete innocence and suggested that this might be a case of mistaken identity. He was remanded to Youth House while the charge was investigated. Orlando Corrado was assigned to be his social worker. While Mr. Corrado was evaluating his background, Warren admitted that he committed the crime with which he was charged. Corrado suggested that it might be best if Warren himself informed the judge of this. Warren refused to do so and added that what he had told the social worker was said in strictest confidence.

NOTE: From *"Ethical Issues for Social Work Practice,"* 3rd ed. (p. 57), by F. Loewenberg and R. Dolgoff, 1988, Itasca, IL: F. E. Peacock. Copyright 1988 by F. E. Peacock. Reprinted by permission.

EXHIBIT 7-9 **Who Tells** **Debbie's** **Parents?**	Debbie Roberts, a 12-year-old sixth grader, is ten weeks pregnant. She has been a good student. Her teacher reported that she never has had any trouble with her. Until now she has not been known to the school social worker. She was sent to the worker only because she refused to talk to the school nurse about her condition. In her conversation with Debbie, the social worker learned that Debbie did not want to have an abortion, but wanted the social worker to help her make arrangements so that she could carry to full term. She stressed that she did not want her parents to know that she was pregnant.

NOTE: From *"Ethical Issues for Social Work Practice,"* 3rd ed. (p. 30), by F. Loewenberg and R. Dolgoff, 1988, Itasca, IL: F. E. Peacock. Copyright 1988 by F.E. Peacock. Reprinted by permission.

inform Warren of whom he represented. Further, there was no clarity about the purpose of their meeting and what use would be made of the information shared. Our view is that Corrado failed to recognize that he was dealing with a respondent (not a client) and may have had a distorted view of the issue of confidentiality.

Exhibit 7-9 provides another example that is sometimes cited as an ethical dilemma regarding breaking confidentiality and sharing information with parents. We fail to see how this could possibly be considered an ethical dilemma except by a very distorted application of the idea of confidentiality. In our view, good practice dictates that this worker engage Debbie, either as a contact or a respondent, in a plan about how she will discuss this matter with her parents, and without much delay. This girl and her parents need to be moving rather quickly to assess their choices, including the health risk of a 12-year-old carrying a pregnancy to full term. Our knowledge base tells us that this is not a matter for a 12-year-old to be left dealing with alone (even with a friendly social worker and school nurse) and that we should direct our efforts immediately toward assisting this young girl to use any support systems available to her, including her parents, to work through the tensions in those systems and to engage in some planning regarding the pregnancy. To delay this, based on confidentiality, would be bad practice; clearly, of course, good practice would require the worker to attempt to involve Debbie in all of the decision making and to keep Debbie fully informed of actions the worker is taking.

There are at least three contributing factors to the tendency to label or justify bad practice an ethical dilemma. First, there may be confusion about who the client is. In Exhibits 7-8 and 7-9, Debbie is a contact and Warren is a respondent; in both cases the social worker has been asked to intervene by another party. Good practice necessitates that we share this fact with the people with whom we are talking (in either case there's no indication that this occurred) and then be guided by our knowledge in regard to appropriate practice decisions. But would this situation have been any different had Debbie voluntarily approached the social worker and requested services rather than having the request come from the nurse? We think not, for a second reason. Confusion also stems from failure to understand the use and application of knowledge in social work practice. The social worker's knowledge about the handling of stress and the thought processes of a 12-year-old, the risks of pregnancy to a 12-year-old, and the expected and normal tensions between an early adolescent and her family all should have been brought to bear on this situation. The worker should have focused the discussion with Debbie in the direction of developing a plan to share the matter with the parents. We've already noted the nature of partnership in practice and will be further stressing that this involves input from the worker as well as the respondent or applicant. One of the key things that the social worker brings to the interaction is knowledge. Operating based on the respondent's or applicant's initial request without making our knowledge base available to that planning is bad practice. But what happens, even after this interaction, if the 12-year-old adamantly maintains that she does not want her parents told? We think that at that point good practice dictates that the parents be told anyway, and that if there is need for protective services, the social worker assist in making these arrangements. The worker will, of course, discuss with Debbie the actions that are to be taken.

Rethinking Confidentiality A third contributing factor to the identification of bad practice as an ethical dilemma is the overemphasis on confidentiality. Many authors treat confidentiality as a value for social work practice; we have not done so because we believe there are some fundamental problems with this concept. Confidentiality may be very important for some limited areas of social work practice, such as psychotherapy, which is a relatively small part of social work practice. One reason confidentiality is important in psychotherapy is that people are revealing past feelings and not current actions. Even in a psychotherapeutic relationship, if a client reveals a plan to hurt others, the therapist has the duty to warn.

The duty to warn and the duty to report have created a very large number of situations in which confidentiality, if extended, must be breached. All states and provinces require reporting of child abuse and neglect, and many have statutory requirements for reporting of abuse of vulnerable adults. These reporting requirements may create dilemmas for family counselors (Butz, 1985; Watkins, 1989), as confidentiality must nonetheless be breached and a report made. A series of court decisions as well as some state statutes impose a duty on social workers to warn potential victims if a client reveals intention to harm someone, even if this is done in the context of a confidential relationship (Schwartz, 1989). AIDS creates a significant duty-to-warn challenge for the social worker (Reamer, 1991). If you are working with an HIV-positive client, do you have a duty to warn partners of that client? Susan Landers, in Exhibit 7-10, suggests that you first attempt to get the client to warn

EXHIBIT 7-10	Most social workers will be able to convince HIV-positive clients to warn their sexual partners about
Helping HIV-Positive Clients Warn	possible exposure to the AIDS virus. "Use your clinical skills," urges Rhode Island College social work professor Frederic G. Reamer.

According to social worker Beth Dillon, who oversees the Centers for Disease Control's national counselling and testing program, key issues to be addressed with clients involve their:

- concern about the possibility of being abandoned by their partners;
- anger that partners may, in fact, have infected them; and
- fear that partners might tell others about the clients' HIV status.

Help clients choose the right time and place to tell their partners, Dillon suggests. For example, Friday night might not be the best time, because many counseling centres are closed during weekends. A good time might be right before clients' regular therapy appointments.

Many people, including counselors, often become fearful when discussing AIDS issues, she says. Dillon urges social workers to take care not to transfer their fear to their clients.

Role playing could help clients prepare for possible twists and turns in the actual disclosure, Reamer suggests. Social workers could also offer to sit-in when partners are told. In addition, local AIDS support and service projects might provide resources to help clients through the event.

If all efforts to persuade clients to notify their partners should fail, says NASW national staff member James Brennan, clients should be told that as a last resort, the social workers will have to make sure the partners are warned. While steps should be taken to preserve the therapeutic relationship, Brennan adds, that probably won't be possible, and the clients should be referred to other therapists.

NOTE: From *"Helping HIV-Positive Clients Warn"* by S Landers, January 1993, *NASW News,* p. 3. Copyright 1988 by National Association of Social Workers. Reprinted by permission.

partners, but if this is not successful, that you must do so. Exhibit 7-8 illustrates the problem of offering confidentiality in a host setting where you must report to a team involving other disciplines. Confidentiality has been found to be particularly problematic for social workers practicing in police settings (Curtis and Lutkus, 1985) and in schools (Berman-Rossi and Rossi, 1990). A New Jersey survey found social workers more likely than psychiatrists and psychologists to report that they would breach confidentiality; the groups were presented with a series of vignettes relating to duty to warn and duty to protect matters (Lindenthal, Jordan, Lentz, and Thomas, 1988). There are so many limitations on confidentiality that social workers might seriously reconsider even offering it. We believe you do have an obligation, however, clearly to discuss with the client what you will be sharing, to whom you will be sharing the information, and the reasons. Exhibit 7-10 illustrates a very sound approach to practice; try to get the client involved in the decision in carrying out the necessary action, but if he or she refuses, the information must still be shared. This is the same position that we took in relation to handling the matter of the 12-year-old pregnant girl as presented in Exhibit 7-9.

There are additional reasons seriously to reconsider the importance of confidentiality. First, the concept may deprive applicants and clients of the opportunity and obligation to take responsibility for their own oral statements. Warren, for example, has now shared information with Mr. Corrado for which we think he should accept responsibility; he must struggle with how to share this information with the court. To deny him this opportunity would be to treat Warren as dependent and irresponsible and would be a threat to his dignity. But what do you do if a person such as Warren, or any other respondent with whom you may be interacting, says, "I would like to tell you something but I want you to keep it secret"? Our view is that you do not make these promises in advance. You may say that you can determine how to use the information only after it is shared, that the respondent or applicant should be aware of this in the decision about sharing, and that you will discuss with the person how and in what way the information will be used.

A third problem with confidentiality is that it may reduce the options available to the worker and client. In a partnership, we don't think these options should be arbitrarily reduced by one side of the partnership. Worker and applicant, respondent, contact, or client constitute a system. In Chapter 4 we discussed some of the problems and dangers of closed systems. Confidentiality will result in a closed worker-client system and may deprive the system of opportunities for growth and change that can be brought to bear by outside influence. Zealous adherence to confidentiality may be inconsistent with such important service approaches as working with social networks and support systems. Confidentiality tends to isolate worker and client, whereas the focus of much of our intervention is likely to be in larger support systems.

We are not arguing for an abandonment of the concept of confidentiality, but only a serious consideration of its limitations. Clearly, the best practice will be directed toward jointly deciding who is going to share what in what way and proceeding on the basis of a jointly developed service plan. Confidentiality is a resource that a social worker may offer, but it should not be used as a justification for failure to act, a justification for protecting people from taking responsibility for their own moral behavior, or a justification for failure to assist clients in building support systems and mutual support groups in which sharing is essential to developing the necessary support. Perhaps confidentiality can be considered as one of the negotiated conditions of the service—not a value.

Recapitulation

This section has presented our views concerning social work values. Values were defined as things that a profession prefers but that cannot be proven to be true. Values are not unique to a profession but are adapted from the overall culture. The uniqueness and innate dignity of the individual and self-determination are two value premises underlying social work practice. Respecting the dignity of the individual occurs when we respond to people as individuals and avoid classification including diagnostic labels, focus on strengths in the problem-solving process, provide for maximum client participation, maintain joint accountability with the client, and carefully consider how we are communicating respect in all of our behaviors. Self-determination occurs as we work with the client to create options and choices. This will include examining characteristics the client brings, including values, which may limit choices as well as considering lack of opportunities in the environment. The process of operationalizing these values, especially self-determination, provides an opportunity for social work to find its distinctiveness among the professions.

Several principles implicit in the preceding discussion should be more explicitly stated: (1) Values are guides to action; they are principles that whenever possible are to be maximized. However, values are not straitjackets. They are to be used selectively and creatively, although the primary focus will be on maximizing them. (2) In situations where the value premise and knowledge are in conflict, opt for knowledge. In Chapter 3 a potential conflict was noted between self-determination and a child's need for protection and stability to meet developmental needs; a lower priority was attached to the value of self-determination because of knowledge of the child's needs. (3) When knowledge is lacking, the value premises should become the prevailing standards. (4) Values limit the uses to which the profession's methodology can be placed. Group processes, for example, may be used to subvert individualism or to stir up fear and hysteria, which threaten diversity and self-determination. This use of group strategies is inappropriate because it is inconsistent with the value premises of the profession. Change strategies and methodology can be used for a variety of ends. Social work practitioners must be sure that their strategies are used to support the uniqueness of the individual and the client's right to self-determination. (5) Social work ethics are derived from values and are a codification of professional obligations. What are sometimes called ethical dilemmas, however, are to be carefully analyzed to distinguish between ethical dilemmas and bad practice. The failure to make this distinction may stem from global concepts of client, failure to recognize the role of knowledge in decision making, and treatment of confidentiality as a value rather than as one aspect of service to be discussed and negotiated by worker and applicant.

A Look Forward The Code of Ethics of the U.S. National Association of Social Workers, a brief piece by George Hoshino, and an article by Dale Hardman are reproduced as Readings 7-1, 7-2, and 7-3. Hardman focuses on the intriguing issue of whether social workers should attempt to change client values. His answer will provide considerable opportunity for discussion and debate. The National Association of Social Workers Code of Ethics provides a statement at an abstract level of the present values of the profession. We would like you to think about the Hoshino piece in light of our discussion of ethical dilemmas. Does this illustrate an ethical dilemma, or do you think the obligations of the social worker are clear?

The pages ahead will present an approach to social work practice that is both humanistic and scientific. Classification is minimized, clients are involved in a partnership undertaking with workers, and individuality is maximized. In Chapter 8 the concept of relationship—the medium through which much of the problem-solving work may occur—is introduced. A discussion of communication and interviewing as essential skills is found in Chapter 9. The problem-solving process was outlined in Chapter 2; Chapters 10 through 16 provide a detailed description of the phases of the problem-solving model.

Reading 7-1	*The NASW Code of Ethics**

National Association of Social Workers

Preamble

This code is intended to serve as a guide to the everyday conduct of members of the social work profession and as a basis for the adjudication of issues in ethics when the conduct of social workers is alleged to deviate from the standards expressed or implied in this code. It represents standards of ethical behavior for social workers in professional relationships with those served, with colleagues, with employers, with other individuals and professions, and with the community and society as a whole. It also embodies standards of ethical behavior governing individual conduct to the extent that such conduct is associated with an individual's status and identity as a social worker.

This code is based on the fundamental values of the social work profession that include the worth, dignity, and uniqueness of all persons as well as their rights and opportunities. It is also based on the nature of social work, which fosters conditions that promote these values.

In subscribing to and abiding by this code, the social worker is expected to view ethical responsibility in as inclusive a context as each situation demands and within which ethical judgment is required. The social worker is expected to take into consideration all the principles in this code that have a bearing upon any situation in which ethical judgment is to be exercised and professional intervention or conduct is planned. The course of action is to be consistent with the spirit as well as the letter of this code.

In itself, this code does not represent a set of rules that will prescribe all the behaviors of social workers in all the complexities of professional life. Rather, it offers general principles to guide conduct, and the judicious appraisal of conduct, in situations that have ethical implications. It provides

Reprinted with permission, from "Code of Ethics of the National Association of Social Workers" as adopted by the 1979 NASW Delegate Assembly, effective July 1, 1980, revised in 1990.

the basis for making judgments about ethical actions before and after they occur. Frequently, the particular situation determines the ethical principles that apply and the manner of their application. In such cases, not only the particular ethical principles are taken into immediate consideration, but also the entire code and its spirit. Specific applications of ethical principles must be judged within the context in which they are being considered. Ethical behavior in a given situation must satisfy not only the judgment of the individual social worker but also the judgment of an unbiased jury of professional peers.

This code should not be used as an instrument to deprive any social worker of the opportunity or freedom to practice with complete professional integrity; nor should any disciplinary action be taken on the basis of this code without maximum provision for safeguarding the rights of the social worker affected.

The ethical behavior of social workers results not from edict, but from a personal commitment of the individual. This code is offered to affirm the will and zeal of all social workers to be ethical and to act ethically in all that they do as social workers.

The following codified ethical principles should guide social workers in the various roles and relationships and at the various levels of responsibility in which they function professionally. These principles also serve as a basis for the adjudication by the National Association of Social Workers of issues in ethics.

In subscribing to this code, social workers are required to cooperate in its implementation and abide by any disciplinary rulings based on it. They should also take adequate measures to discourage, prevent, expose, and correct the unethical conduct of colleagues. Finally, social workers should be equally ready to defend and assist colleagues unjustly charged with unethical conduct.

I. *The Social Worker's Conduct and Comportment as a Social Worker*

A. Propriety—The social worker should maintain high standards of personal conduct in the capacity or identity as social worker.

  1. The private conduct of the social worker is a personal matter to the same degree as is any other person's, except when such conduct compromises the fulfillment of professional responsibilities.

  2. The social worker should not participate in, condone, or be associated with dishonesty, fraud, deceit, or misrepresentation.

  3. The social worker should distinguish clearly between statements and actions made as a private individual and as a representative of the social work profession or an organization or group.

B. Competence and Professional Development—The social worker should strive to become and remain proficient in professional practice and the performance of professional functions.

  1. The social worker should accept responsibility or employment only on the basis of existing competence or the intention to acquire the necessary competence.

  2. The social worker should not misrepresent professional qualifications, education, experience, or affiliations.

C. Service—The social worker should regard as primary the service obligation of the social work profession.

  1. The social worker should retain ultimate responsibility for the quality and extent of the service that individual assumes, assigns, or performs.

  2. The social worker should act to prevent practices that are inhumane or discriminatory against any person or group of persons.

D. Integrity—The social worker should act in accordance with the highest standards of professional integrity and impartiality.

  1. The social worker should be alert to and resist the influences and pressures that interfere with the exercise of professional discretion and impartial judgment required for the performance of professional functons.

  2. The social worker should not exploit professional relationships for personal gain.

E. Scholarship and Research—The social worker engaged in study and research should be guided by the conventions of scholarly inquiry.

  1. The social worker engaged in research should consider carefully its possible consequences for human beings.

  2. The social worker engaged in research should ascertain that the consent of participants in the research is voluntary and informed, without any implied deprivation or penalty for refusal to participate, and with due regard for participants' privacy and dignity.

  3. The social worker engaged in research should protect participants from unwarranted physical or mental discomfort, distress, harm, danger, or deprivation.

  4. The social worker who engages in the evaluation of services or cases should discuss them only for professional purposes and only with persons directly and professionally concerned with them.

  5. Information obtained about participants in research should be treated as confidential.

  6. The social worker should take credit only for work actually done in connection with scholarly and research endeavors and credit contributions made by others.

II. *The Social Worker's Ethical Responsibility to Clients*

F. Primacy of Clients' Interests—The social worker's primary responsibility is to clients.

1. The social worker should serve clients with devotion, loyalty, determination, and the maximum application of professional skill and competence.
2. The social worker should not exploit relationships with clients for personal advantage.
3. The social worker should not practice, condone, facilitate, or collaborate with any form of discrimination on the basis of race, color, sex, sexual orientation, age, religion, national origin, marital status, political belief, mental or physical handicap, or any other preference or personal characteristic, condition or status.
4. The social worker should avoid relationships or commitments that conflict with the interests of clients.
5. The social worker should under no circumstances engage in sexual activities with clients.
6. The social worker should provide clients with accurate and complete information regarding the extent and nature of the services available to them.
7. The social worker should apprise clients of their risks, rights, opportunities, and obligations associated with social service to them.
8. The social worker should seek advice and counsel of colleagues and supervisors whenever such consultation is in the best interest of clients.
9. The social worker should terminate service to clients, and professional relationships with them, when such service and relationships are no longer required or no longer serve the clients' needs or interests.
10. The social worker should withdraw services precipitously only under unusual circumstances, giving careful consideration to all factors in the situation and taking care to minimize possible adverse effects.
11. The social worker who anticipates the termination or interruption of service to clients should notify clients promptly and seek the transfer, referral, or continuation of service in relation to the clients' needs and preferences.

G. Rights and Prerogatives of Clients—The social worker should make every effort to foster maximum self-determination on the part of clients.

1. When the social worker must act on behalf of a client who has been adjudged legally incompetent, the social worker should safeguard the interests and rights of the client.
2. When another individual has been legally authorized to act in behalf of a client, the social worker should deal with that person always with the client's best interest in mind.
3. The social worker should not engage in any action that violates or diminishes the civil or legal rights of clients.

H. Confidentiality and Privacy—The social worker should respect the privacy of clients and hold in confidence all information obtained in the course of professional service.

1. The social worker should share with others confidences revealed by clients, without their consent, only for compelling professional reasons.
2. The social worker should inform clients fully about the limits of confidentiality in a given situation, the purposes for which information is obtained, and how it may be used.
3. The social worker should afford clients reasonable access to any official social work records concerning them.
4. When providing clients with access to records, the social worker should take due care to protect the confidences of others contained in those records.
5. The social worker should obtain informed consent of clients before tap-

ing, recording, or permitting third party observation of their activities.

I. Fees—When setting fees, the social worker should ensure that they are fair, reasonable, considerate and commensurate with the service performed and with due regard for the client's ability to pay.

1. The social worker should not accept anything of value for making a referral.

III. *The Social Worker's Ethical Responsibility to Colleagues*

J. Respect, Fairness, and Courtesy—The social worker should treat colleagues with respect, courtesy, fairness, and good faith.

1. The social worker should cooperate with colleagues to promote professional interests and concerns.

2. The social worker should respect confidences shared by colleagues in the course of their professional relationships and transactions.

3. The social worker should create and maintain conditions of practice that facilitate ethical and competent professional performance by colleagues.

4. The social worker should treat with respect, and represent accurately and fairly, the qualifications, views, and findings of colleagues and use appropriate channels to express judgments on these matters.

5. The social worker who replaces or is replaced by a colleague in professional practice should act with consideration for the interest, character, and reputation of that colleague.

6. The social worker should not exploit a dispute between a colleague and employers to obtain a position or otherwise advance the social worker's interest.

7. The social worker should seek arbitration or mediation when conflicts with colleagues require resolution for compelling professional reasons.

8. The social worker should extend to colleagues of other professions the same respect and cooperation that is extended to social work colleagues.

9. The social worker who serves as an employer, supervisor, or mentor to colleagues should make orderly and explicit arrangements regarding the conditions of their continuing professional relationship.

10. The social worker who has the responsibility for employing and evaluating the performance of other staff members should fulfill such responsibility in a fair, considerate, and equitable manner, on the basis of clearly enunciated criteria.

11. The social worker who has the responsibility for evaluating the performance of employees, supervisors, or students should share evaluations with them.

K. Dealing with Colleagues' Clients—The social worker has the responsibility to relate to the clients of colleagues with full professional consideration.

1. The social worker should not solicit the clients of colleagues.

2. The social worker who serves the clients of colleagues, during a temporary absence or emergency, should serve those clients with the same consideration as that afforded any client.

IV. *The Social Worker's Ethical Responsibility to Employers and Employing Organizations*

L. Commitment to Employing Organization—The social worker should adhere to commitments made to the employing organization.

1. The social worker should work to improve the employing agency's policies and procedures, and the efficiency and effectiveness of its services.

2. The social worker should not accept employment or arrange student field placements in an organization which is currently under public sanction by

NASW for violating personnel standards or imposing limitations on or penalties for professional actions on behalf of clients.

M. The social worker should act to prevent and eliminate discrimination in the employing organization's work assignments and in its employment policies and practice.

N. The social worker should use with scrupulous regard, and only for purpose for which they are intended, the resources of the employing organization.

V. *The Social Worker's Ethical Responsibility to the Social Work Profession*

O. Maintaining the Integrity of the Profession—The social worker should uphold and advance the values, ethics, knowledge, and mission of the profession.

1. The social worker should protect and enhance the dignity and integrity of the profession and should be responsible and vigorous in discussion and criticism of the profession.

2. The social worker should take action through appropriate channels against unethical conduct by any other member of the profession.

3. The social worker should act to prevent the unauthorized and unqualified practice of social work.

4. The social worker should make no misrepresentation in advertising as to qualifications, competence, service, or results to be achieved.

P. Community Service—The social worker should assist the profession in making social services available to the general public.

1. The social worker should contribute time and professional expertise to activities that promote respect for the utility, the integrity, and the competence of the social work profession.

2. The social worker should support the formulation, development, enactment and implementation of social policies of concern to the profession.

O. Development of Knowledge—The social worker should take responsibility for identifying, developing, and fully utilizing knowledge for professional practice.

1. The social worker should base practice upon recognized knowledge relevant to social work.

2. The social worker should critically examine, and keep current with, emerging knowledge relevant to social work.

3. The social worker should contribute to the knowledge base of social work and share research knowledge and practice wisdom with colleagues.

VI. *The Social Worker's Ethical Responsibility to Society*

P. Promoting the General Welfare—The social worker should promote the general welfare of society.

1. The social worker should act to prevent and eliminate discrimination against any person or group on the basis of race, color, sex, sexual orientation, age, religion, national origin, marital status, political belief, mental or physical handicap, or any other preference or personal characteristic, condition, or status.

2. The social worker should act to ensure that all persons have access to the resources, services, and opportunities which they require.

3. The social worker should act to expand choice and opportunity for all persons, with special regard for disadvantaged or oppressed groups and persons.

4. The social worker should promote conditions that encourage respect for the diversity of cultures which constitute American society.

5. The social worker should provide appropriate professional services in public emergencies.

6. The social worker should advocate changes in policy and legislation to improve social conditions and to promote social justice.

7. The social worker should encourage informed participation by the public in shaping social policies and institutions.

Reading 7-2 ## The Means Test: A Source of Dilemmas in Social Work Practice

George Hoshino

A very interesting discussion came up the other day in a session in which I was explaining the means test, by using the AFDC (Aid to Families with Dependent Children) means test as an example. Among other things I told the students that they should know something about income maintenance whether they worked in an income maintenance agency or not, because most of their clients probably would be recipients of some form of maintenance, whether universal and not means tested, like Social Security, or means-tested like AFDC, General Assistance (GA), Supplemental Security Income (SSI), food stamps, Medicaid, public housing, housing assistance, or the like. Because of the misunderstandings about the means test, I usually spend quite a bit of time explaining exactly what the means test is: its three elements (standard of requirements, definition of resources, and procedures); its disincentive characteristics; its inherently demeaning nature; and its effects on individuals and families. I try to make a point of emphasizing the implications and consequences of the means test for social work practice and to use them to illustrate the informal organization—the unwritten personal rules, practices and relationships that arise in any formal organization alongside the explicit written official rules and relationships. The discussion always is enlivened by the presence in the class of students who are current or past welfare recipients and who bring a personal and vivid element to the discussions. Invariably, also, several students will have been on the other

side of the desk, as public assistance eligibility workers. This brings a personal and vivid element to the discussions, especially when they reach the point of examining the consequences for the worker-recipient relationship and the social worker–client relationship. Thus the means test, as in AFDC, results in a cat-and-mouse worker-recipient relationship that encourages coercion, duplicity, and collusion.

The session the other day was typical. When I gave the example of a professional social worker in a family service agency counseling a client who was an AFDC recipient and learning in the confidential relationship that the AFDC mother was working and earning a weekly income from baby-sitting, how would or should the worker handle the situation? One student, who said he had been an eligiblity worker, said he used to tell his clients, in effect, "Don't tell me anything I shouldn't know." Another student fell back on the confidentiality rule; what went on between the worker and the client in the interview room was strictly confidential; else how could the client relate to the worker? It was pointed out that there is a difference between confidentiality in the professional meaning and privileged communication in the legal meaning, which applies to the attorney-client, doctor-patient, priest-confessor, and certain other relationships such as husband-wife. But even those are not absolutes; for example, doctors must report suspected child abuse.

Assuming that social workers know what the general public assistance policies are, which includes the responsibility of the recipient to report

An original paper prepared for this volume.

any changes that affect eligibility, in particular, income, how should social workers behave? This behavior obviously takes into account the knowledge that in a means-test program, income and assets operate to reduce the amount of the grant or disqualify the recipient entirely. One student even mentioned that he had lived with a woman who was a recipient; the question was whether his presence and any support he provided the woman and her children constituted income or resources and therefore would affect the grant.

As the discussion proceeded, it was clear that the students tended to resort to various subterfuges to get around the effects of the means test: it is the recipient's responsibility to report, it is not a concern of the worker. If the worker becomes aware of income or assets during the course of his or her professional relationship with the client, he or she has a responsibility to inform the client of this requirement. If the client refuses to notify the public assistance agency and so advises the worker, what then? Our county, for example, has a general policy that all staff who learn of unreported income must report that information to the public assis-

tance unit whether or not the client does. Some students stated that if they informed the client that they were reporting the income to the AFDC agency, the client would terminate service immediately; thus the dilemma was maintaining the relationship with the client and at the same time ensuring that the laws were obeyed. What happens when the worker, while encouraging the client to find work and get off assistance, is told by the client that this would mean not only termination of assistance but loss of Medicaid protection for herself and children? Most jobs that AFDC recipients can get are not covered by health insurance. To advise them to get work would be seen as insane by some recipients, since they also would have the added cost of day care, which few could afford.

Thus dilemmas for social work practice are created by the means test. As usual, I fudged the matter by suggesting that these issues were also practice issues and might be brought up in their practice classes. I'd be interested in how practice teachers handle such questions when they arise in their classes. Whom do they pass the buck to?

Reading 7-3 *Not with My Daughter You Don't*

Dale G. Hardman

It was a balmy spring afternoon at the Blintz County workhouse. The interviewing room was only half separated from the cell corridors. The inmate looked out the dirt-specked window for some time, then returned his gaze to the social worker. "Twelve more days. I could do 12 days on a bed of spikes. You're the reason I got 55 days knocked off my six months. I wouldn'ta got it without you went to bat for me."

Oscar De Curia only nodded, but inwardly he beamed because expressions of gratitude were infrequent among workhouse clients. "I would

like," he said, "to get some idea of your plans when you get out. Most guys need some help getting into a job or school or...."

"Nah. I work for my old man, putting up siding. I always got a job waiting."

"Good. What about school?"

"Can't work and go to school too."

"Some guys do." De Curia bit his lip; he knew as soon as he said it. There he was, imposing his middle-class norms on a lower-class client.

"I quit when I was 15. Nine years ago—too late to go back now."

De Curia had an impulse to suggest some Voc-Ed courses, but instead he just nodded and said, "Okay then, what about your social life?"

"That's all I been thinking about since I got my commutation."

De Curia brightened a bit. At least here he didn't have to worry about imposing his own norms. Here he could relax, be more natural, more human.

"Chicks," said the inmate. He leaned back and clasped his fingers behind his thick black curly hair. "Chicks is my specialty. Take the average guy in here—for him sex is just quick service stuff: roll in the hay, be on your way. No art to it. No class."

"You're most artistic, then."

"That's it. I'm an artist. Most guys in here wouldn't know the difference."

"But you do. How would you go about it that's any different from anybody else?"

"Well see, same as me they've been locked up for six months to a year. Anything would look good to them, and they'll try to make up for the whole year in the first ten minutes they're out. First broad they see. But not me. Like the soup commercial says: 'To make the best you gotta begin with the best. Then prepare it tenderly . . . carefully . . . slowly.' So I begin with the best. Nothing but fresh meat for me—very fresh. A virgin."

"I see. Well, since there's not a lot of those around. . . ."

"Well, ya gotta know where to look. For one thing you gotta start young—maybe 14 or 15—so you find where they hang out."

"Hmm." De Curia opened his mouth to point out that a sex act with an adolescent would constitute a new violation, but he again bit his tongue and admonished himself that he must not be a moralist. And certainly this client was canny enough to know the law on this point.

"They hang out a lot around Whiffy Dip, especially on weekends. Skating rinks and bowling alleys is good hunting grounds. Always full of teeny chicks."

"Hmm." In truth, De Curia felt a bit more uncomfortable with each self-revelation of his client. But he knew that disapproval on his part would only serve to turn off his client's verbal spigot, and certainly the man needed to talk after four months in lock-up.

"There was one little chick I met at the Rollerama just before I got busted. A virgin, I'll bet my shirt. About 14. Real good skater."

"Hmm." De Curia resolved to be nondirective if it killed him, but his discomfort continued to rise.

"I only saw her two, three times before I got sent up. Skated with her each time. I know she likes me. I think she's the one I'll start with."

"I see." De Curia shifted uneasily as his tension mounted.

"Like I say, begin with the best. And she's the best. Long slender legs. Willowy. Little round bazoobs like ripe peaches. Long auburn hair, always in a pony-tail. Her name was Irma Jean something."

Every man has a sort of safety plug in his boiler; it melts at a lower temperature than the boiler and serves to prevent the boiler from rupturing. And here De Curia blew his plug. Out spewed his professional role, his persona, in a great gust and blast, and he stood before his client a very angry human being. "Hey, wait a minute! That's my daughter you're talking about, you lecherous bastard!"

OSCAR'S CONFLICT

It was several hours later that Oscar De Curia sat in his office, pondering his misdirected interview at the workhouse. In ten years of practice he had held doggedly to the dictum of nondirection: the nonmoralistic listener, eschewing judgments, never imposing his own norms, never playing God, never setting himself up as an ethical model for his clients' emulation. For ten years, he had adhered to these fundamental premises, drilled into his skull in classrooms, in texts and journals, and in interaction with other social workers. He was, he believed, the epitome of Powers and Witmer's delineation (1951): "Modern casework is distinguished . . . by the fact that its practitioners seldom give advice, cite ethical precepts or the consequence of antisocial behavior, or urge particular courses of action." True, he constantly had to remind himself in those pesky situations that clashed against his own middle-class value system. He had come, in fact, to feel a bit apologetic for being middle class or subscribing to its norms. He felt as though he had been called a dirty name when he was referred to as middle class. But now, suddenly, when these norms were violated close to home, his carefully cultivated professional posture had disintegrated and he had blown his cool, the interview, and the case.

Although De Curia was not given to extensive self-contemplation, he was, in those brief and unaccustomed moments of introspection, essentially honest with himself. Perhaps these two facts were related: in introspection he usually came out a loser, due to a basic trait of honesty, so he indulged in it rarely.

Oscar had experienced similar interviews in the past, listening with composure to expressions of sexual exploitation, tales of assaults on persons or property, and threats of vengeance or power or violence. He had often felt a rising discomfort and a need to protest, and always, until today, he had successfully repressed such unprofessional impulses. But now, with his treasured, auburn-haired teenager as the proposed object. . . .

At this juncture a new thought trekked across Oscar's synapses: suppose the name his client had dropped had not been Irma Jean; suppose instead it had been Sandra or Millie. Wasn't it conceivable that the fathers of other pony-tailed, knobby-kneed damsels might harbor feelings for them as tender as his? De Curia was struck by this thought much as Goliath encountered David's stony projectile: such a thing had never before entered his head. It jolted him in his tracks. A host of balding and paunchy middle-aged fathers arose in his mind's eye, like a legion of Banquo's ghosts, to ask: In how many hundred cases, have you said "Mm hmm" or "I see" and thereby given tacit acquiescence to illegal, immoral, or violent acts? It was well beyond closing time when the janitor found De Curia still at his desk pondering his conflict.

Upon his return home, De Curia was unusually attentive to his daughter, but otherwise his manner was, for him, exceptionally quiet and subdued. His wife reckoned that he had either been fired or out philandering but that in either case he would shortly tell her so. He hadn't and he didn't.

GENERALIZING THE PROBLEM

During the ensuing week, Oscar De Curia resolved that he would, at whatever cost, resolve his newly mounted conflict. One of his first acts was to request that his supervisor transfer the client who had torpedoed his cool. As has been noted, Mr. De Curia was not a profoundly thoughtful man, but an honest one. His supervisor, on the other hand, was not a profoundly honest man, but a thoughtful one, and so he asked the reason for his subordinate's request. And within the next half hour De Curia had upended the whole wretched can of worms.

The supervisor had indeed encountered this knotty question before; he had mulled it over at considerable length and then shelved it. But Oscar would not be shelved. He was a persistent clod, and he insisted on answers. And answered he was. The supervisor said: "Mm hmm."

"Well, it's true, ain't it?" De Curia waxed ungrammatical only when he became emotional. "From the time we enter graduate school we're admonished against imposing our own values on people. So I don't and look what happens! My own daughter is up for grabs!"

"Mm," said the supervisor, thoughtfully.

"Tell me honestly, Jake," (the supervisor encouraged this bit of familiarity) "What would you do? You must have encountered this kind of incongruity before. How did you handle it?"

Jake could not admit that he had resolved the question by shelving it. So he said, "Hmm." Thoughtfully, that is.

"That doesn't exactly answer my question, you know," De Curia persisted.

Jake squirmed considerably, inwardly at least. Outwardly he was all concern and empathy, as a supervisor should be.

"Well, the problem is really much larger than you are recognizing here, Oscar. What you are saying applies to a lot of lower-class values besides sex behavior."

"So?" said Oscar De Curia.

"You have already mentioned one: you tried to get the guy back into school. Walter Miller (1958, 1959) says that dropping out at about age 16 is the norm for lower-class culture. Riessman (1962) calls it anti-intellectualism—actual hostility toward egg-headedness. Yet the poverty experts had a truism: 'In the poverty battle, all roads lead to the schoolhouse.' How are we ever going to get kids—or young adults—back into the schoolhouse without changing their basic values?"

"That doesn't answer my question. Anyway, maybe we middle class do overvalue education. There are still thousands of blue-collar jobs, some with pretty good pay, that don't require literacy, much less a high school diploma."

"Oh, yes. But high school represents something else to an employer. I once went to a foundry to line up a job for a male parolee. The foreman's first question was: 'Has he finished high school?' I asked why a guy needed a high school diploma to tamp sand into a casting mold. His answer was a good one: 'To us, completion of high school means a guy has stick-to-it-iveness, that he'll stick with a job until it's finished, that he's more likely to be here all day every day than a guy who hasn't finished school.' You can't argue with that reasoning."

"Yeah. Now about my question."

"Patience. At least half our welfare bill can be traced directly to family breakdown. Yet it seems pretty clear that the lower class doesn't take family ties as seriously as does the middle class (Goode, 1964; Hollingshead, 1950; Udry, 1966). How are we ever going to crack the poverty cycle without family stability? And how do you get family stability without changing the cultural norms regarding families?"

"You're not giving me answers, you're giving me more questions. I need more questions like Noah needed more rain."

"Let me finish, please." Jake was merely stalling for time, of course. But sometimes if you talk long enough, a problem will go away—or the client will, which is functionally the same. "Sexual exploitation," continued Jake, "is only one corner of lower-class attitudes toward female status (Rainwater, 1960; Riessman, 1962). A general subordination of females is the norm. If you're an advocate of women's rights, or even if you subscribe to the social work Code of Ethics regarding sex discrimination, you're going to run afoul of a major lower-class value."

"There is also an item in the Code of Ethics that says I will subordinate my personal interests to my professional responsibility. Like I have a profes-

sional responsibility not to impose middle-class values. Well, I'll be damned if I'm gonna subordinate my daughter's chastity to that or any other code of ethics."

"Of course. But I want you to look at the whole perspective, the whole panorama of lower-class norms."

"To hell with all that. Let's answer the question about my daughter first." Persistent as dysentery.

"But we can't answer for your daughter until we answer some of these broader questions first. They all gotta be answered." Jake immediately cursed himself for this slip. An entire shelf full of unresolved questions, like the contents of Fibber McGee's closet, tumbled down upon him in an avalanche of evaded issues. Damn my big flapping mouth, he thought.

"Okay, then let's answer them," said Oscar De Curia.

"I think we are never going to make a dent in the poverty problem until the anti-intellectual attitudes of the poor are changed. And their male chauvinism too."

"Okay, let's change them."

"But these attitudes are dependent on, related to, and interfunctional with a dozen other lower-class norms—maybe all of them, tied up together like a spider web."

"For instance."

"Masculinity, for instance. The poor emphasize masculinity much more than we do (Walter Miller, 1958). And action—getting things done as opposed to theory and abstraction. Therefore, school is considered sissy-prissy and largely female-dominated."

"You think it would help to hire a few football players and prize fighters for teachers?"

"It would be a step toward the schoolhouse. But it would also reinforce their ideas of masculinity and chauvinism. Further, the poor crave excitement more than do the middle and upper classes (Rainwater, 1960; Reissman, 1962). Schools aren't noteworthy for excitement, you know."

"Judging from the slum schools I've been in, about half the teacher's time and energy is spent in trying to keep a lid on the excitement the kids generate. I think if they took the lid off for a minute the average slum classroom would erupt into bedlam."

"Right. And this leads into teaching methods. Student-centered education is based on the same assumptions as client-centered counseling: the students or clients must carry the ball, must be responsible for their own decisions, must set their own goals and limits, and so on. There is a mountain of research indicating that these student-centered teaching methods produce about the same level of retention of class material as do lecture-recitation methods. But when it comes to measuring such intangible traits as self-confidence, initiative, creativity, and leadership, the student-centered methods will win by ten lengths" (Blair, Jones, & Simpson, 1954; Cronbach, 1954).

"Seems like the answer is pretty obvious: use more student-centered teaching in slum schools."

"It would be nice if life were so simple. A guy in California ran off an experimental group project in a boys' club (Maas, 1963). He found that middle-class kids adapted quite readily to group-centered methods. But lower-class kids resisted them to beat hell. They'd stand around with their thumbs in their bums and say: 'Why don't somebody tell us what we're supposed to do?'"

"Mmm," said Oscar De Curia.

"So let me point out, there is nothing the poor need more than self-confidence, creativity, and leadership (Goff, 1954; Keller, 1963). Yet they consistently resist the methods that develop it."

"Hmm."

"And this leads directly to another point. The same guy who did the California study also found that the great majority of correctional workers prefer nondirective methods, even though most of their clients are of the lower class and don't dig them" (Maas, 1954).

"Hmm," said De Curia. "Maybe this is why most counseling agencies have better success with middle-class clients. We've always blamed the lower-class failures on the stratification gap; you know, middle-class social workers can't communicate with lower-class clients."

"Yes. And there's still more to this story. This same guy studied parents bringing kids into guidance clinics (Maas, 1955). He asked specifically about their expectations at the clinic. How long did they think it would take? How much would they, the parents, have to participate? How much would the parents have to change their ways? He found that middle-class parents had much more realistic expectations concerning both time and involvement. The poor usually expected that the treatment would take perhaps a few weeks and that the clinic would straighten the kid out without much parental responsibility."

"So maybe middle-class parents are better risks for therapy regardless of the therapist's socioeconomic background."

"At least you can stop your self-flagellation for being a middle-class caseworker."

"Okay, you have absolved my middle-class guilt. You have also given me a dozen more questions, when all I really wanted was one answer. So how about an answer: Do we or don't we impose middle-class norms on people?"

IMPOSING VALUES

Jake knew when he had talked himself into a corner. He glanced at the desk phone, hoping that perhaps a call might spare him a confrontation with his untenable position. It didn't. He glanced out his window, hoping perhaps to see a tidal wave rolling across the midwestern prairie. There was not so much as a ripple. He glanced out his door, perchance to spot a client in need of his attention. A swatch of blue and a hank of white hair caught his eye. "Hey Dave!" yelled Jake, much as a man might yell when stranded on a sandbar by high tide.

Dave had been retired from the agency for several years now, but occasionally popped in "to see how things were going." These visits by the old warhorse at pasture were usually welcome and especially so today.

"Come in, Dave, and shoot the bull a spell," said Jake with an outward show of camaraderie and an inward sigh of relief. "Oscar and I were just talking about lower-class norms. How they often impede therapy or movement or progress, or whatever you wanna call it, but how we're not supposed to tamper with them."

"So what did you tell him to do?" asked Dave. "Huh?"

"I imagine he asked you whether he should or shouldn't impose his own value system. What did you tell him?"

I'm stabbed in the back, thought Jake. He was desperate now. "First I'd like to hear your opinion. You must have run into this question in your 20-odd years here?"

"That's the biggest understatement since Genghis Khan was called unneighborly," said Dave. "Not a day went by that that question didn't pop up."

"Ever have a client make a pass at your daughter?" asked Oscar. "Your 13-year-old daughter?"

"That's how we got started," added Jake.

"So what did you tell him?" asked Dave persistently. But Jake was a skilled infighter. He would try a show of honesty to disarm them. When all else fails, a guy should consider being honest. Well, partially. "I really haven't answered it yet," said Jake. "We were just generalizing the problem, sort of."

"That's what I figured," said Dave. "So you want me to get you off the hook."

Jake grinned like a nauseated sailor demonstrating his seaworthiness, but he said nothing. He resolved never again to resort to honesty.

"My friend," said Dave, "there is nothing in social service more frequently encountered than interclass conflict regarding values. Every social worker I know runs into it daily, and most of them, like you, never really come to grips with the realities of the problem. And every social worker I know, consciously or unconsciously, overtly or covertly, imposes his norms on the poor every day of his working life."

"But you're different," said Jake, with a noticeable edge to his voice.

"Only that I'm honest about it," said Dave. "I do it intentionally. Deliberately. In cold blood. Further, a half dozen studies indicate that the more moralistic, value-imposing workers have better success with their clients" (Parloff, Iflund, & Goldstein, 1957; Powers & Witmer, 1951; Rosenthal, 1955).

"Then what about the advice of the experts? You can't pick up a journal today without some author jollyragging us about understanding the poor instead of trying to change them to our nasty middle-class way of life."

"Slop and hogwash," said Dave. "I suggest that the more you understand the poor, the more you will see the need for them to make some basic changes."

Oscar De Curia brightened noticeably. "For instance?" he said.

"For instance, take the time orientation of the Chicanos and Puerto Ricans (Clapp, 1966; Lewis, 1966). Half of them don't own a clock. A street-gang worker I know says a lot of his Chicano teen-agers can't even tell time. You say, 'Let's be ready to go at ten,' and they'll show up maybe at twelve-thirty. While you're at lunch, likely."

"Understandable, though," said Jake. "They come from an agrarian background where you get up when it's morning and go to bed when it's dark. So who needs a clock?"

"General Motors needs one. Bell Telephone and General Electric need one. And there ain't no way that Chicanos are ever going to adapt to an industrial society without getting clock wise. I've never heard of a factory that will let one guy come to work at eight, another at nine-thirty, and another at ten-fifteen. We either impose our middle-class time consciousness or let them remain forever in unemployment."

"Ah, ha!" Jake burst in. "Now you are blaming the victim."

"Ryan's point (1971), I believe. But Alinsky (1946) said it 25 years earlier."

"Well, were they wrong, both of them?"

"Let's pick one—Alinsky, since he had nothing good to say about middle-class values."

"Right."

"Alinsky would have screamed like a ruptured panther if he heard me say this, but I'll say it to you. I suggest that Alinsky made his living precisely by imposing middle-class norms on the poor. A better living, incidentally, than the three of us combined."

"Please go on."

"The poor have always been more comfortable in primary group relations: first names, informal buddy relations, that sort of thing (Barber, 1961; Brager, 1963; Guttentag, 1970; Riessman, 1962).

They always shy away from formalized secondary groups, like titled officers, by-laws, committees, *Robert's Rules of Order*. Now, in themselves, a million people are powerless; they are nothing unless they are organized, whether in the military or in power politics. You can't cite an example in history of a primary group wielding any political clout. The major reason that the middle class carries a bigger stick is not their numbers but their organization. And Alinsky made his living teaching the poor to organize for power, to form secondary groups—a middle-class norm."

"Mm hmm," said Jake. Oscar merely said, "Hmm."

FATALISM AND POVERTY

"Let me point up another lower-class norm that, in my mind, constitutes one of the biggest hang-ups the poor have to carry, maybe the biggest."

"What's that?"

"Fatalism. *Que sera sera*. A belief that what happens to you has already been decided by some capricious Fate (Lewis, 1966; Walter Miller, 1958; Reissman, 1962). A conviction that it is not only a waste of time, but actually hazardous to take arms against a perverse and incontrovertible Fate, because she may stomp on you to straighten you out."

"For example?"

"For example, a hundred studies plus common sense confirm that the poor have too many kids. But to date no birth control program among the poor is even moderately successful as compared to middle-class family planning."

"Why?"

"Fatalism. Rainwater found that the number one cause of birth control failures among the poor is a belief that 'you're just gonna have the kids you're s'posed to have and you can't do nothin' to change it'" (Riessman, 1962).

"Seems kinda extreme."

"Not at all. My brother Gus was driving a truck for a mining company in Wyoming. He picked up a couple of hitchhikers and put them in back. 'Now for hell's sake don't you guys smoke,' he told them. 'I've got seven tons of dynamite on here.' They both agreed, but when he stopped for gas an hour later, there they both sat, smoking on top of a box

of dynamite. Gus blew his stack and kicked their cans off his truck. As they went stomping off down the highway he heard one mumble, 'Well, the way I figure, if it's gonna blow it's gonna blow.' Now there's extreme."

"But an isolated case."

"Okay, think back. In the years you've been handling offenders, how many times have you heard expressions like 'my luck ran out,' 'my number was up,' 'the dice were loaded against me,' 'it wasn't in the cards for me,' 'the Bear (bad luck) was after me,' 'I was fighting a stacked deck,' 'it wasn't my day,' and so on and on."

"Or, 'I'm a born loser,'" said Oscar. "Or, 'when my ship comes in.' Or 'Dame Fortune smiles on me.' Or 'some guy was born with a silver spoon in his mouth.' Or 'there's no oil on my dipstick.' Or 'I lucked out or crapped out.'"

"Right. Nobody in the hoosegow ever got there by goofing off. Always he fell. Or his foot slipped. Or, he 'landed behind the eight ball.' Or 'the old wheel came up on black.' Some day I'm gonna write a book. There must be a thousand such expressions."

"I think," said Oscar, "that these are defense mechanisms to rationalize getting busted. Like 'if I'm so damn smart, how come I'm locked up? Bad luck, that's why.'"

"Okay, but in no way is this limited to offenders. You find these same expressions among the poor everywhere. And for the same reason: it gets them off the hook for being poor. Fate is to blame."

"Well," said Jake, "without these defenses what do the poor bastards have? Isn't it better to leave them their defenses at least?"

"I suggest that a valid social service is to help them find or develop more realistic defenses—defenses that don't perpetuate the cycle of poverty."

"How do you mean?"

"The culture of poverty is self-perpetuating (Lewis, 1966; D. R. Miller, 1963). It forms a vicious circle that repeats over and over. Like kids believe that school grades are mostly a matter of luck. Incidentally, I think true-false exams reinforce this crap-game concept of grades. So they flunk out or drop out of school. They're unqualified for employment and grow up in poverty. The surrounding culture constantly reinforces their belief in fatalism, which they and the other poor pass on to their kids. And they in turn enter school expecting Luck or Fate or Chance to determine their outcome. Sure enough, it does, and the cycle repeats. And there are a number of others. McClelland (1961, 1969) says that father dominance—a lower-class norm—has gotta be decreased and that a number of other child-rearing practices of the poor have to be changed too. He also says we gotta push for the good old Protestant ethic and urge more creative and expressive fantasy production. Less traditionalism. All these things, mind you, require changes in lower-class values."

"So you think the place to break this poverty cycle is at the level of norms and values."

"It's all one place. Myrdal (1948) says that it's not so important where we begin as that we begin somewhere. Consider this one. Mobilization for Youth workers found kids who would say: 'Why go down to the employment office? I'll be here; let the job find me.' At first they thought it was the kids' perversity. But it wasn't; the kids were dead serious. Being employed or unemployed, they believed, was a matter of being touched by the fickle finger of Fate. Hustling for a job may only make Fate mad at you. It seems to me this is a good place to make a dent in the poverty cycle."

De Curia pondered this a bit. "It seems to me this is the only place to make a dent."

"I think Hyman (1953) would agree. He says that 'the variable which keeps the poor poor is a system of beliefs and values . . . which reduce the very *voluntary* actions which would ameliorate their low position.' My own view is that this is the best place to make a dent. But there are others: They gotta get back to high school, vocational school, college, on-the-job training. There's delinquency, medical and housing problems, discrimination, exploitation. You name it and it's a good starting place. But working on any one of these will inevitably necessitate some value changes. If not—if no values are changed—we may as well take the poverty funds and dump them in the street for grabs, because volitional behavior doesn't change if attitudes, values, and norms don't change.

In fact, I think dumping our funds in the ghetto streets would be at least as effective as some programs I know of."

"Touché!" Oscar De Curia said, but without a smile. "However, you and Jake both mentioned the road to the schoolhouse. Harrison (1972) cites some pretty convincing figures that additional years of school won't affect the ghetto kid's lifetime income as much as dropping school and working a couple of extra years."

"Ah, yes, years of school. But he only gives passing acknowledgment that there may be a difference in quality of lower- and middle-class education. If this goes unrecognized, then the whole area of educational enrichment is meaningless. Yes, a kid can graduate from a ghetto school but be unable to write a purchase order, add up a grocery list, or understand directions on a can of spray paint. About a third of the kids on my caseload couldn't travel across town and find an address because they couldn't read street signs from a bus. Try listening to one of them giving directions to another. They memorize routes, not addresses. Half of them couldn't look up a number in a phone book. They were limited to the numbers they memorized or wrote down because they didn't dig alphabetical listing. And not one in a hundred could write an intelligible letter if the kid's life depended on it, even if they had a high school diploma. They were graduated, not educated. Now who's going to give one of them a job at anything better than tamping sand in a rathole?"

"To me the solution seems obvious—improve slum schools," Oscar said.

"My friend, I suggest that Jesus himself could not teach these kids as long as they retain their self-defeating attitudes. Yes, schools must change, but student attitudes must change also."

SCAPEGOATING
"Dave old boy, you claim to be honest with yourself," Jake put in. "Aren't you really blaming the victim when the real blame lies elsewhere? In social injustice, unequal opportunity, exploitation, discrimination? You've said yourself that the criminal justice system screens out the poor predominantly."

"Right. And all social workers should redouble their efforts to correct all these inequities. But let's say they've all been corrected, no discriminating employers and so on. It's still a competitive job market, and the better trained, the aggressive job hustlers, and the pushers are the ones who'll get the jobs."

"Okay, you will easily find a hundred authors who assert that once these injustices are corrected and people begin to move upward into middle-class society, their cultural norms will change accordingly."

"I think it's true that whenever people are placed in another subculture, whether above or below their own, in time some of that culture will rub off on them. But the preponderance of evidence indicates that the social strivers, the upwardly mobile, change their values *before* they begin their upward mobility. Mobility is much more often a result than a cause of value change" (Berelson & Steiner, 1964; Hyman, 1953; McClelland, 1969).

Jake shook his head. "It still seems to me that by putting the onus on the poor, we lift the blame from the guilty ones."

Dave pondered this one for a few minutes. Finally: "Jake, if there's anything I've learned in 40 years of social work, it's that scapegoating— hunting up someone to blame for a social problem—is not only a gross waste of time, but it actually inhibits the solution of problems." Dave ran his finger across Jake's bookshelf. "Do you have any idea how many tons of pulpwood trees have been butchered in the past decade to make publications that are essentially given over to scapegoating."

He hadn't, and Dave proceeded. "I have never heard of a social problem that was attributable to a single cause. There are always multiple causes if you bother to scratch the surface, so finding a suitable scapegoat merely focuses attention on one factor and ignores the others. As for me, I'm not going to burn up good mental energy either in blaming the poor for being poor or blaming the middle class for being middle class."

But Jake recalled another problem. "Did I misunderstand you when you admitted that you superimpose your own values?"

"That's right, deliberately."

"Then aren't you saying, in effect, that your values are better than those of the lower class?"

"Ah, now comes the stinger. I impose *some* middle-class values. There are quite a number of lower-class values that I prefer to middle-class ones."

"For instance?"

"Comradeship. Closer, more intimate interpersonal relations. More egalitarian views; more emphasis on person than on status. More interpersonal good humor. More freedom of expression. More open expression of affection" (Riessman, 1962).

"Affection?"

"Yes. Take one example: When I was a kid I worked on a string of blue-collar jobs: ranches, mines, factories, railroads, construction. It wasn't uncommon to see two guys who were buddies standing around the fire at night or around the bar or bunkhouse, with an arm slung over the friend's shoulder. No one thought anything of it. Now suppose that on some white-collar job—let's say in an insurance office—you spot two guys at the water cooler with their arms around each other. You'd nudge your neighbor and say, 'Hey, Fred! Lookit!' What a helluva culture when two people can't express honest affection without being considered gay."

"Maybe there are more gays in the lower class."

"Fewer (Kinsey, 1948). I'll tell you another trait of the poor that I'd consider keeping. When a husband and wife are at loggerheads, they are much more likely to have a good old hell-raising, whooping and hollering knock-down-drag-out battle. But in 20 minutes it's over and out of their systems. You and me, when we're on the outs with the old woman, we turn on the deep freeze for about a month. We never speak or look at each other for weeks on end. Now I ask you, honestly, which is better for mental health? And for kids?"

"Hmm."

"And I'll tell you another. I think there's more real honesty in the lower class."

"Aw, come off it, Dave. Nine-tenths of our correctional clients come from the lower class."

"I wasn't thinking of law violations specifically. However, since you've raised the point: a dozen studies of self-reported offenses show no significant class difference in crime and delinquency. Our legal machinery simply screens out more of the poor for processing" (Akers, 1964; Empey & Erickson, 1966; Meyerhoff & Meyerhoff, 1964; Short & Nye, 1957; Voss, 1966).

"Then what do you mean by 'honesty?'"

"Interpersonal honesty. If a lower-class guy doesn't like you, he will say so. Or maybe punch your nose. But we middle class will rationalize it with some kind of mealy-mouthed double-talk. I invite you, for instance, to sit in on a college promotions committee if you want to observe some fancy verbal footwork. Like 'Now understand, I've got nothing personal against old Charlie. But . . .' A blue-collar worker would say, much more honestly, 'I can't stand the damn creep.'"

"Not footwork. Tonguework."

"Okay, I recall one college department of about 25 faculty. There were some faculty cuts coming up, so two sections of the department formed a coalition and voted to abolish the third section in order to save their jobs. I have never heard of this kind of job cannibalism among the blue-collar workers."

FUNCTIONAL NORMS

"Dave, you're not being consistent," Jake said waving his hand. "A minute ago you were the champion of good old middle-class values. Now you've changed sides. You can't play both sides at once. What *do* you want?"

Dave pondered this one briefly: "First, I want social workers to be honest about it when they impose norms, whether middle- or lower-class. Second, I want them to forget the infantile quibble about norms to one class being better than those of another. I want. . . ."

"How do you decide which norms you are going to support, then? You gonna play God?"

"Functionality is how. First we gotta decide on objectives, social workers and clients in dialogue together. And this holds true whether it's one client and one caseworker or a project involving 50 workers and 10,000 clients. We can agree that employment is a goal, or marriage stability or family planning or whatever, but we have to thrash it out and arrive at some consensus regarding our objective. Once the objective is agreed upon, my job is clear. If a certain cultural norm is functional, if it aids in achieving the agreed-upon objective, I will support it. If it's dysfunctional, if it's thwarting our objectives, then it's gotta go, and I'll do my damndest to see that it goes. And I couldn't care less whether the norm comes from the lower, middle, or upper class."

"Meehl and McClosky" (1947), said Jake, "consider that our job definition is to help the client achieve the client's end. Period. That doesn't leave room for negotiation about objectives."

"I'll be damned if I'm gonna help that sonofabitch achieve my daughter's end," said Oscar De Curia hotly.

"And I'll venture no social worker worth his salt would," replied Dave. "In fact, I think they'd draw the line on about half the goals of our correctional clients. Plus a number of others. For instance, I won't help a client toward suicide, if that's his goal. Or to obtain heroin, or to bust out of jail or a hospital. Or to defraud the welfare office or desert his family or go AWOL. Or, in my case, to obtain an abortion. This is why I said we must first agree on objectives."

"And if you and the client can't agree?"

"My personal guideline is this: I will never help clients accomplish something that I consider morally wrong, harmful to them or to me or to others. And I won't help a client to rendezvous with any teenager, not your daughter or anyone else's."

"Okay, let's say we agree on a number of objectives in a certain poverty project," said Jake. "And we find certain lower-class norms that inhibit the achieving of these goals. Dysfunctional, you called them. Now how do you go about changing those norms?"

"That, my friend, is another can of worms. But it can be done and has been done."

"How?"

"Another time, Jake, another time. We've emptied enough worms for today."

For Further Reading

Aponte, H. J. (1985). The negotiation of values in therapy. *Family Process, 24,* 323–338.

Barker, R. (1988). Just whose code of ethics should the independent practitioner follow? *Journal of Independent Social Work, 2(4),* 1–5.

Berman-Rossi, T., & Rossi, P. (1990). Confidentiality and informed consent in school social work. *Social Work in Education, 12,* 195–207.

Biestek, F., & Gehrig, C. (1978). *Client self-determination in social work: A fifty year history.* Chicago: Loyola University Press.

Bogo, M., & Herington, W. (1986). The universality of western social work's knowledge base in the international context: Myth or reality? *Social Development Issues, 10(2),* 56–65.

Butz, R. (1985). Reporting child abuse and confidentiality in counselling. *Social Casework, 66(2),* 83–90.

Constable, R. C. (1983). Values, religion, and social work practice. *Social Thought, 9(4),* 29–41.

Curtis, P., & Lutkus, A. (1985). Client confidentiality in police social work settings. *Social Work, 30(4),* 355–360.

Epstein, W. M. (1986). Science and social work. *Social Service Review, 60,* 145–160.

Freedberg, S. (1989). Self-determination: Historical perspectives and effects on current practice. *Social Work, 34,* 33–38.

Gaylin, W., Glasser, I., Marcus, S., & Rothman, D. J. (1978). *Doing good: The limits of benevolence.* New York: Pantheon Books.

Goldstein, H. (1987). The neglected moral link in social work practice. *Social Work, 32,* 181–186.

Googins, B., & Davidson, B. (1993). The organization as client: Broadening the concept of employee assistance programs. *Social Work, 38,* 477–484.

Kirk, S., & Kutchins, H. (1992). *Selling of DSW-III: The rhetoric of science in psychiatry.* Hawthorne, NY: Aldine de Gruyter.

Kutchins, H., & Kirk, S. (1987). DSW-111 and social work malpractice. *Social Work, 32,* 205–211.

Lewis, H. (1984). Self-determination: The aged client's autonomy in service encounters. *Journal of Gerontological Social Work, 7(3),* 41–63.

Lindenthal, J., Jordan, T., Lentz, J., & Thomas, C. (1988). Social workers management of confidentiality. *Social Work, 33,* 157–159.

McDermott, F. E. (Ed.). (1975). *Self-determination in social work.* London: Routledge & Kegan Paul.

McFadden, Emily Jean. (1992). The inner world of children and youth in care. *Community Alternatives: International Journal of Family Care, 4(1),* 1–17.

Nicholson, B., & Matross, G. (1989). Facing reduced decision-making capacity in health care: Method for maintaining client self-determination. *Social Work, 25,* 234–238.

Reamer, F. (1982). *Ethical dilemmas in social service.* New York: Columbia University Press.

Reamer, F. (1991). AIDS, social work, and the duty to protect. *Social Work, 36,* 56–59.

Reamer, F. (1993). AIDS and social work: The ethics and civil liberties agenda. *Social Work, 38,* 412–419.

Saltzman, A. (1986). Reporting child abusers and protecting substance abusers. *Social Work, 31,* 474–475.

Sancier, B. (Ed.). (1984). Ethics and values [Special issue]. *Practice Digest, 6(4).*

Schwartz, G. (1989). Confidentiality revisited. *Social Work, 34,* 223–226.

Siporin, M. (1983). Morality and immorality in working with clients. *Social Thought, 9(4),* 10–18.

Watkins, S. (1989). Confidentiality and privileged communications: Legal dilemma for family therapists. *Social Work, 34,* 133–136.

Weick, A., & Pope, L. (1988). Knowing what's best: A new look at self-determination. *Social Casework: The Journal of Contemporary Social Work, 69(1),* 10–16.

Chapter 8

Relationship in Social Work Practice

This chapter will focus on the social work relationship and will center primarily on the helping relationship that develops between practitioner and the client system. We remind you that in this type of statement, client may be read "client system" and worker may be read "change agent." The terms *client* and *worker* are used because they lend themselves well to communicating the attitudes being discussed. Readers should always be aware that every social work system is either an individual or composed of individuals.

Chapter 4 focused on systems theory and discussed the need of human systems, individuals, and human groups (all open systems), for input from the world around them if they are to grow and develop and to continue to cope with life tasks. As stated earlier, every human system needs input from relationships with others, although not all systems find it easy to accept the thought that they do. Each of us has experienced the connectedness of emotion and intimacy with others that is called the human relationship. When we cannot find these connections with other people, we often name and personalize trees and animals, or perhaps our car. Then we draw comfort from acting as if another human being were present. In fact, though individuals may rarely be conscious of what these relationships mean and what powers they contain (except at certain points in life when people are suddenly bereft of a meaningful relationship or are in the process of becoming involved in a new one), the most significant characteristic of our humanity is that we live our lives within relationships to other people. Thus "relationships" do not originate for any of us within the social work process or the professional helping effort (and therein may lie the rub, as shall be discussed later). Nor can social workers claim to have been the lone discoverer of this attribute of humanity or the only group interested in pursuing its investigation. Psychology and psychiatry, among other professions, have been very active in attempting to research the helping relationship (Perlman, 1957).

However, social work can take pride in the fact that from its earliest beginnings it recognized the importance of human interaction and attempted to employ the concept of relationship in a conscious and deliberate way for the benefit of the people it served. In the early formulations describing social work activity, the relationship between worker and client was given a special importance—and no concept appears more frequently in the literature of the profession. Although the goals toward which this early activity was directed were those the worker thought desirable for society and personally redemptive for the client, there was a beginning of the principle of self-help and a very clear conviction of the power of personal influence in the

263

stimulation of this process (Pumphrey & Pumphrey, 1961; Reynolds, 1963; Richmond, 1899).

Perhaps the outstanding author and teacher in the field of social casework at the beginning of the 20th century was Mary Richmond. Her writings contain considerable material about the social work relationship. She asserted that social casework stands for the "intensive study and use of social relationships." Richmond (1917, pp. 211–215) defined the focus of casework activity in terms of "skill in discovering the social relationships by which a given personality has been shaped; an ability to get at the central core of the difficulty in these relationships; power to utilize the direct action of mind upon mind in their adjustment." The importance of the effect of "mind upon mind" was recognized in the development of "friendly visitors" in early social work.

In spite of the early recognition of relationship as a basic concept in social work theory and in spite of the years of concern with the development and use of relationship in practice, a clearly defined concept of the social work relationship has yet to be articulated. There is great unanimity about the importance of human relationships in the promotion of growth and change, but there is little common understanding about just how these relationships promote such development. In the professional literature, many authors merely describe qualities of the relationship that they consider important, or they record very specific instances of their use of relationship in the helping process.

Being convinced that the concept of relationship is central to all of social work practice, this chapter will consider some attempts of selected social work authors to express the nature of social work relationships and to examine some of the notions, implicit or explicit, in such statements. We shall consider the roles that social workers carry and how those roles affect and shape social work relationships and the qualities of social workers who would work effectively with others.

A Review of the Literature

Felix Biestek (1957, p. 11) collected a number of excerpts illustrating the attempts of social workers to express the nature of the relationship. He points out that relationship has been compared to an atmosphere, to flesh and blood, to a bridge, and to an open table:

> The essence of the relationship has been called an interplay, a mutual emotional exchange, an attitude, a dynamic interaction, a medium, a connection between two persons, a professional meeting, a mutual process. The concept "interaction" seems to be the most generic and it was most commonly described as "dynamic."
>
> The purpose of the relationship was described as creating an atmosphere, the development of personality, a better solution of the client's problem, the means for carrying out function, stating and focusing reality and emotional problems, and helping the client make a more acceptable adjustment to a personal problem.

Biestek (p. 4) sees the relationship between caseworker and client as the medium through which the knowledge of human nature and the individual is used. "The relationship is also the channel of the entire casework process; through it flow the skills in intervention, study, diagnosis and treatment." Biestek (1951, p. 12) defines the casework relationship as "the dynamic interactions of attitudes and emotions between the caseworker and the client, with the purpose of helping clients achieve better adjustments between themselves and their environments."

In a book on social casework Helen Harris Perlman (1957, pp. 65–66) says of relationship that

> It is a condition in which two persons with some common interest between them, long term or temporary, interact with feeling. . . . Relationship leaps from one person to the other at the moment when some kind of emotion moves between them. They may both express or invest the same kind of emotion; they may express or invest different or even opposing emotions or . . . one may express or invest emotion and the other will receive it and be responsive to it. In any case, a charge or current of feeling must be experienced between two persons. Whether this interaction creates a sense of union or of antagonism, the two persons are for the time "connected" or "related" to each other.

Perlman (1957, pp. 64–68) goes on to say that the identifying mark of a professional relationship "is in its conscious purposiveness growing out of the knowledge of what must go into achieving its goal"; that "all growth-producing relationships, of which the casework relationship is one, contain elements of acceptance and expectation, support and stimulation." She also identifies authority as an element of the professional relationship and clearly differentiates between the relationship and other aspects of the helping process. Perlman sees the caseworker as helping people to deal with their problems through (1) the provision of resources, (2) the problem-solving work, and (3) the therapeutic relationship, which she defines in another work (1971, p. 58) as the "climate and the bond" between workers and clients that "acts to sustain and free clients to work on their problems."

Social workers who attempted to help people through the use of groups were also concerned with the development and use of relationships. Grace Coyle (1948, p. 91), who was very influential in the early development of group work, defined relationship as "a discernible process by which people are connected to each other, and around which the group takes its shape and form." Gisela Konopka (1963, pp. 107–118), an international authority in group work theory, does not define the relationship in her writings. She does discuss it as one of the major helping media available to the social group worker and sets forth its elements as purpose, warmth, and understanding.

In her book *Social Work with Groups,* Helen Northen (1969, pp. 53–58) says that relationship has been described as consisting "primarily of emotional responses which ebb and flow from person to person as human behavior evokes different affective reactions." The social worker in a group situation develops a unique relationship with each member, based on an understanding of the individual.

Writing about the giving and taking of help, Alan Keith-Lucas (1972, p. 47) defines the helping relationship as "the medium which is offered to people in trouble through which they are given the opportunity to make choices, both about taking help and the use they will make of it." Keith-Lucas (1972, pp. 47–65) identifies the qualities of the relationships as (1) mutuality, (2) reality, (3) feeling, (4) knowledge, (5) concern for the other person, (6) purpose, (7) taking place in the here and now, (8) offering something new, and (9) nonjudgmental.

A number of years ago Pincus and Minahan (1973, pp. 69–73) wrote that a relationship "can be thought of as an affective bond between workers" and other systems with which they may be involved and that relationships may involve an "atmosphere of collaboration, bargaining or conflict." They classify all social work into three types: collaborative, cooperative, and conflicted. These authors go on to identify the common elements of all social work relationships as (1) purpose, (2) commitment to the needs to the client system, and (3) objectivity and self-awareness on the part of the worker.

Social Work Roles and Relationship

In studying this brief review of definitions of relationship, one will readily note that except by Pincus and Minahan the concept of the professional relationship has been most thought about, and most written about, by persons concerned with the one-to-one or one-to-group relationship. However, as Pincus and Minahan point out, in addition to the direct helping relationship, social workers carry many other types of relationships. They may be involved with landlords, teachers, employers, and even boards of directors and executives of other agencies on behalf of their clients. Or workers, noting that a number of the parents with whom they work are concerned about drug problems, may help their agency develop a special seminar for workers on the subject of drug use. Another worker may be helping agency representatives develop plans for increased agency coordination on the assumption that this will be helpful to clients. A third may be lobbying for a law requiring that all group insurance carried by employers for employees must cover the pregnancies of unmarried as well as married employees and the pregnancies of minor daughters of employees. In all of the above situations the workers are involved in relationships with others. However, these relationships neither are with clients nor are helping relationships per se, in that the worker offers no services to the other persons in the relationship and carries no professional responsibility to help them with their personal problems or development.

Social workers engaged in administration, policy, planning, and organization activities often carry a client relationship with the system in which they are involved, but the responsibilities they assume within this relationship are quite different from those of the direct services helping relationship. In these relationships, too, they carry no responsibility to help the other system with personal problems or to provide personal growth experiences for any individual member or the group as a unit. Rather, they are involved in helping the client system to change another (target) system in regard to certain professional policies and programs.

It is our position that all social work relationships carry certain common elements but that the mix and importance of the elements are different in different types of relationships. Relationships may be classified along two axes: (1) the role of the worker within the change agent system—for example, as helper, administrator, policymaker, and/or researcher—and (2) the type of system with which the change agent is involved, for example, the action system, the target system, or the change agent system, as well as different compositions and purposes of the client system. However, although relationships may differ with the interaction of elements along these axes, all social work relationships have purposes that have some common aspects because they embody the normative purposes and values of the profession, although not necessarily the operational and the unique aspects. All social work relationships involve elements of power and authority, but these elements may be lodged in persons other than the social worker, especially in situations involving policy-making or organizational change.

All professional relationships involve self-discipline and self-knowledge paired with the capacity for free, genuine, and congruent use of self. However, different types of relationships may involve different qualities of awareness and the use of different elements of the self. Some relationships, particularly those in planning, policy-making, and administration, may call for self-awareness in problems dealing with power and status, competitive feelings, and impatience with colleagues; others, particularly those with individual clients or groups, may call for awareness of one's fear of dependency or the need to do for others. One can deal with other persons and systems better if one has some sensitivity to their situation and goals and some empathy for them. However, the content of the empathic understandings will vary greatly. All social work relationships are emergent and are affected by time and place. In all professional relationships social workers are representing something beyond themselves, either their agency or their profession, and all practitioners share a commitment to client welfare as a base for their professional activities. There are seven essential elements that are a part of social work relationships: (1) concern for others, (2) commitment and obligation, (3) acceptance and expectation, (4) empathy, (5) genuineness, (6) authority and power, and (7) overriding and shaping all the rest, purpose. To carry their professional relationships with professional skill, workers must make the following qualities a part of their professional selves: maturing, creativity, the capacity to observe self, the desire to help, courage, sensitivity, and the ability to endure ambiguity.

Although it is our belief that all social workers need a grasp of the elements discussed in this chapter, we also believe that these elements of the professional social work relationship are used differentially and that the variables affecting their use may be expressed in the following model (Fraley, 1969, pp. 145–154):

1. The purpose of the relationship.
2. The position of the practitioner in the change agent system.
3. The role of the worker and the role of the other in interaction (remember the description of the differing perceptions of role and their importance in Chapter 3).
4. The role and position of the other in the larger social systems of which both worker and other are a part (the community, church, social groups).
5. The goal toward which the social worker is directing change activities.
6. The goal toward which the other systems are directing their activities. Note that in the relationship between client system and change agent system, it is assumed that the goal is to develop a relationship that allows for working together. However, relationships between the change agent and individuals in the target system or the action system may involve relationships of cooperation, negotiation, or conflict.
7. The form of communication. In the direct helping relationship between an individual client and the practitioner as the change agent, communication is usually verbal. However, in the relationship between practitioners and their own change agent system, or between the change agent and action or target systems, many other forms of communication such as letters and reports may be used. It is important that the practitioner be skilled in the use of all methods of communication.

8. The skill of the worker in decision making and the use of appropriate intervention methods.
9. The type of system with which the worker interacts—the practitioner may work toward change in a client system that consists of an individual, group, organization, or community; or workers may work with individuals or groups representing other than client systems.

As an example of these points, Gisela Konopka (1963, pp. 107–116) has written that the relationship between the social worker and the small helping group differs from that of the social worker involved with an individual in the following ways: (1) members support each other and are not alone with authority, (2) there is greater informality, (3) members are surrounded by others in the same boat and there is a feeling of identification impossible in casework, (4) members are not bound to accept other members, (5) the worker is shared, and (6) there is a lack of confidentiality within the group.

Purpose as an Element of Relationship

As we pointed out at the beginning of this chapter, all human beings have experienced connections with other human beings that we call relationships. Most of us are capable of and most of the time are involved in many sets of simultaneous relationships. In social intercourse many of us drift into relationships with others without being aware of just how or why they developed. However, few of us continue relationships with others without some reason; there is something that brings us into contact with them and some reason why the interaction is continued. When one becomes involved with another person, the nature of one's purpose, goals, or intent, together with one's perception of the other individual's purpose, goals, or intent, will determine how one behaves toward that individual and how the relationship will develop.

If purpose is a part of all relationships, why should it be discussed as a special part of professional relationships? And how does purpose in professional relationships differ from that of personal relationships? That the relationship is purposive and goal directed does not give the social work relationship its special mark. What makes the social work relationship special is that its purpose and goal are conscious and deliberate and come within the overall purpose and value system of the profession.

Chapter 1 centers on the purpose of social work practice—the changing or altering of something in the interaction of people and their environment so as to improve the capacity of individuals to cope with their life tasks in a way reasonably satisfying to themselves and to others, thus enhancing their ability to realize their aspirations and values. In Chapter 7 the main points deal with how professional values limit and shape what we do as social workers. These two factors, the overall purpose of the profession and its value system, limit and focus the purpose of the social work relationship so that influence is not used capriciously. This is called the normative limit of purpose in the social work relationship—the normative purpose of all social work relationships is some kind of change in or development of a human or social system to the end that the capacity of individuals to cope with their life tasks and to realize their aspirations and values is improved.

In addition to being shaped by the normative purpose, each social work relationship will be deliberately and consciously shaped in part by the purpose of the given type of encounter. For example, the helping relationship is distinguished by a particular type of purpose—an increase in the coping capacity of the client system. However, a social worker may attempt to convince a legislative committee of the necessity for increasing state aid to school systems so that special education classes or open schools for dropouts may be established. The different purpose of this interaction will be critical to the way the relationship develops and is utilized. This aspect of purpose can be termed the *operational purpose* of the relationship. One of the critical differences among types of social work relationships is that they are governed by different operational purposes even though they share a normative purpose. Within the overall limits set by the normative purpose, the operational purpose determines the outer parameters of a relationship.

Besides the normative and operational purpose, each social work relationship will have a unique individual purpose. These unique purposes will be affected by time: the immediate unique purpose of this particular interaction will differ from the long-range purpose of a series of interactions. Thus Mrs. Jones may have become involved in a helping relationship because she wants to have an enduring and happy marriage (a long-term purpose), but when she comes in today, she may want help about the way she responded this morning to her husband's criticism of her housekeeping (an immediate goal that is a step to the long-term goal). The outreach worker at a community center may be involved with a street group in discussions about using the center for its meetings. The worker's immediate purpose is to provide the group with a better meeting place, while the long-term purpose may be to help the group develop less destructive activities.

It is our position that while the normative and operational purposes of any social work relationship may be implicit, the social worker must be able to formulate clearly the unique immediate purposes of professional contacts with others and to describe such purposes to them. (With some clients who have little acquaintance with the talking therapies, it may be helpful to discuss the normative and operational purposes as well.) A study by Mayer and Timms (1970) shows that one difficulty in establishing a helping relationship with certain clients is their lack of understanding of the purposes and values of the professional person. Ideally, in the helping relationship the unique purpose should come out of mutual consideration of what the client wants; but be that as it may, it is the worker's obligation to see that purpose is established. A professional relationship is formed for a purpose consciously recognized by all participants and ends when that purpose has been achieved or is judged to be unachievable. This understanding or perception of purpose sets certain norms for how persons will behave toward one another in the relationship and how the relationship will develop.

In working with individuals, families, or groups, it is important to clarify the operational purpose of the relationship, because the worker's primary role may not be that of helping. Rather, the court, the community, or other institution may require that the worker investigate a situation in which the worker may be expected to control, attenuate, or in some way modify the behavior of an individual that is harmful to others and that is causing the community distress. In such a situation it is essential that the worker be able to state clearly and honestly the purpose that brought him or her to the family's door. The statement of purpose usually leads the worker into a discussion of the authority and power the worker carries in the situation. The worker must explain carefully and clearly to the family why he or she is there, what his or her responsibility to agency or institution or community is, and what the limits of the authority are. Purpose affects two other related issues: the worker as helper and confidentiality. Workers must not pretend to themselves or the family that their only motivation in entering the situation uninvited is to help the family from its own perspective. The family realizes that this is patently untrue and that the worker has other responsibilities; the worker is perceived as dishonest, which may be taken as giving the family permission to be dishonest in turn. It is certainly possible within the limitation of purpose for the worker to maintain an honest identification as someone who wants to help, but he or she must communicate that he or she is entering the situation for other than helping purposes. For many families who have had difficult experiences with persons who labeled themselves helping professionals, the word *help* is perceived as dishonest and perhaps dangerous. Certainly, help can mean very different things to client and worker. When we use the word *help* in working with an offender in the criminal justice system, do we mean help the offender achieve what he or she wants (which may be to be left alone) or do we mean help from our own perspective (which may mean changing the offender's behavior so that he or she can have a "better" life from our perspective)?

The worker's purpose in entering the situation also affects the approach to confidentiality. The ethics of confidentiality in social work require that the worker inform the clients at the very beginning of the work together what information may be shared with people outside the client-worker relationship, how it will be shared, with whom it will be shared, the form in which it will be shared, and whether the client will be informed when it is shared. Contrary to what may be expected, most families respond favorably to such an approach. The family senses that such honesty and directness respects its right to share information as its members see fit, removes their nagging sense of uncertainty about what happens to information it shares, and results in a more appropriately open response. Workers should avoid all attempts to push the family to trust them. Rather, families should be told that they will have to decide the worker's trustworthiness for themselves based on their experiences with the worker.

However, when a worker explains the purpose of entering the situation unasked by the family, he or she must be prepared for a reaction of anger, distrust, and rejection and must be able to discipline personal feelings and responses. The worker's ability to understand and appropriately use all the elements of the relationship discussed in this chapter are critically important if a working relationship is to develop in such situations.

Development of Relationship

This brings us to a critical point. Relationship in a social work helping process does not emerge spontaneously and whole out of some mysterious chemistry of individuals in interaction but develops out of purposive interaction, out of the business with which the worker and the client (or other system) concern themselves. It cannot be not presumed that the client is looking for a helping relationship when entering the social work situation but rather that the client comes out of concern about a problem in which the professional relationship is instrumental in working toward a solution. This means that we do not speak of the worker's "establishing a relationship" or "offering a relationship"; neither do we speak of needing a good relationship before difficulties can be discussed. The relationship comes out of the communication about difficulties. It grows and develops out of purposive work. The professional relationship as an affective experimental interaction should develop as necessary to the task. It is not necessarily pleasant or friendly; sometimes the problem is worked out in reaction and anger, in conflict as well as in collaboration or bargaining. A wise social worker writes that "the attempt to keep the relationship on a pleasant level is the greatest source of ineffectual helping known to people" (Keith-Lucas, 1972, p. 18). Seek relationship as a goal, "and it will generally elude one." But in a helping situation a relationship will grow wherever people demonstrate to others by their actions and words that they respect the other, that they have concern for them and care what happens to them, and that they are willing both to listen and to act helpfully (Keith-Lucas, 1972, pp. 48–49).

The fact that the relationship develops out of purposive work means that it has motion and direction and emergent characteristics. It grows, develops, and changes; and when the purpose has been achieved, it comes to an end. The time structure is another variable that directly affects the nature and rate of the development of the relationship. Whether time limits are imposed on the process arbitrarily by outside forces or are imposed as necessary for task accomplishment, they have a deep effect on the emergent quality of the relationship. It is generally known that the frequency of meetings and the amount of time the participants spend together affects the climate of the relationship and the speed with which it develops. We believe that the imposition of individualized time limits consonant with a shared unique purpose will increase the effectiveness of the joint purposive work. The setting in which the worker and the other system find themselves will also affect relationship, since the setting interacts with time and purpose. In every instance the operational purpose will be affected by the setting and the worker's position within it; and in most instances the limits of the purpose will also be imposed by the setting and the worker's position within it. This is to be expected, since the unique purpose of the relationship must fall within the parameters of the operational purpose.

Relationship is subject to differentiation and differential use. The kind of relationship that develops between social workers and the system with which they are interacting will depend on the particular combination of a number of variables. The overriding variable is purpose, but other variables combine with purpose to form the relationship: the setting in which the worker and the system come together; the time limits of the process; the individuals or groups involved and the interests they represent; the capacities, motivations, expectations, and purposes of those involved; the problem that brings practitioner and system together and the goals each has for its resolution; the qualities of the workers and what they bring of themselves, their knowledge, and their skills; and the actual behaviors of the members of the relational system in transactions over time.

In the helping process the relationship may be used in one of two ways. The worker may use the relationship to sustain the clients as they and the practitioner work on the problem, or the consideration of the relationship itself may become the task, and the client and worker may focus on the way the client uses this as a prototype of the problems they may have in other meaningful relationships and interactions. Certain problem-focused groups, too, may consist of individuals whose interpersonal transactions with each other are the problem to be worked or whose relationship with the worker or between various members may become the focus of the group's attention. In work with task groups the relationship between worker and group and the relationships between the members is used to sustain the members as they work on a problem common to all of them but external to their relationships with one another.

It is now time to turn to the workers and what they as professional helping people are expected to bring to the helping relationship. Both the worker and the client (or the other system, if this is not a helping relationship) bring to the relationship irrational elements (bits and pieces from past relationships and experiences that do not fit the present), nonrational elements (emotion, feeling, affect), and rational elements (intellectual and cognitive qualities). In the case of both the worker and the other system, these elements come from (1) past experiences that have affected and developed the ability of the individuals to relate to others; (2) the here-and-now physical and emotional state of those involved; (3) the here-and-now thoughts or mental images of each individual about himself or herself, the process, and the problem; (4) each person's anxiety about the present situation and about the person in it; (5) each person's expectations of how one should behave and what should come out of the interaction; (6) each person's perception of the other, or others, involved; (7) the values and ideals shared in common by the participants in the process; and (8) the influence of other social and environmental factors (Goldstein, 1973, pp. 139–150). However, since workers present themselves as the professional people in the relationship and because of this are often allowed to share in the most private and sensitive aspects of vulnerable people, they carry special responsibilities for what they bring to the helping process.

If you reexamine the attempts of earlier authors to explain or describe what the worker should bring to the helping relationship, you will find that most of these attempts deal with the communication of certain affective attitudes. While through the years social workers have used different words to express what they saw as the nature of the helping relationship, the notions of what kind of worker behavior is necessary to what particular relationship have changed relatively little. They have simply been better elaborated and differentiated over the years. The literature of other human service professions also discloses that their professional helping persons have developed very similar concepts. Some of these concepts have been broken down into smaller units and have been the object of experimental study, and some are very well established because they are based on the clinical observations of many professional helping people over many years with many clients (Truax & Mitchell, 1971). Thus most human service professionals use similar words to describe the emotional quality of the helping relationship. It is generally agreed among professional people in the human service professions that certain qualities are necessary within a human relationship for growth and change to take place.

We believe that all these various qualities can be classified into six groups of essential elements of all professional relationships: (1) concern for the other, (2) commitment and obligation, (3) acceptance and expectation, (4) empathy, (5) authority and power, and (6) genuineness and congruence. These elements will be used according to the purpose and type of relationship.

Elements of the Relationship

Concern for the Other   To put this as simply as possible, concern for the other means that the worker sincerely cares about what happens to the client and is able to communicate this feeling. In the helping relationship, concern for the other involves "the sense of responsibility, care, respect, knowledge of other human beings and the wish to further their lives" (Fromm, 1956, p. 47). It is an unconditional affirmation of the client's life and needs—wanting clients to be all they can be and to do all they want to do *for their own sake.* Those last four words are critical.

This demand may be particularly difficult for a worker who enters a situation at the request of a court, a community, or an agency. The family or the individual that the worker confronts in such a situation is not a client, will not be a client until a contract can be agreed on, and will often be an angry, hostile person or group whose lifestyle is offensive to the worker. It is essential in these situations that workers be aware of their feelings and their judgments, that they accept the fact that they do not have to like a person or the way the person acts. They need to be able to acknowledge these feelings so that they do not act in ways that unconsciously communicate anger and rejection.

It is obvious that if we want to help others, we must become deeply involved with them and want for them what they would want for themselves as we would want for ourselves what we want for ourselves. However, there is a danger in this, as the closer our emotional relationship with an individual, the more likely we are to become overinvolved out of a desire to see the trouble removed or the problem solved. When we feel that someone else's problem is our own problem, when we are unable to tolerate the thought of our own pain and need to have the client succeed because that is what we want, rather than offering what the client wants or needs, then we are too much involved.

True concern for another in the helping relationship means that we offer our skills, our knowledge, ourselves, and our caring to the client to be used (or not used, as the case may be) in the client's movement toward desired goals. It means that (within certain limits of purpose, time, and place) we respond as the client needs us to rather than as our need to help demands, that we care enough for the other to leave him or her free to fail. For most of us it is so much easier and more satisfying "to do" than to stand and wait (but "he also serves who only stands and waits") that we convince ourselves that concern is expressed through "doing" rather than through "active waiting." To be truly concerned means that we are willing to be the "agent of a process rather than the creator of it" (Keith-Lucas, 1972, p. 104).

Keith-Lucas (1972, p. 103) gives us an excellent summary of this notion when he writes that concern means the willingness to let the helped person decide to what extent and under what conditions he is willing to be helped. It does not mean necessarily agreeing to help under these circumstances or even refraining from pointing out that help is not possible under them. Nor does it mean refraining from offering what help is available, or even, if the need is desperate, intervening in an attempt to get help started. But it does mean, ever and always, treating the helped person as the subject of the sentence; serving his or her interest, allowing him or her all possible freedom.

Sometimes workers equate this business of concern for others with liking. It is our position that notions of liking and disliking are misleading and that to ask workers to like everyone often results in the denial or repression of feeling rather than a change in it. What we are speaking of in the use of the concept of concern is a sense of so caring for the other (as the subject of our interactions together) that personal feelings of liking or disliking (which are, after all, related to the person as the object of the response) no longer have any meaning. Again according to Keith-Lucas (1972, p. 106), "What the helping person develops is a feeling to which liking and disliking are wholly irrelevant. This is what is meant by concern. It means to care what happens to another person quite apart from whether one finds the person attractive or unattractive."

Under the rubric of the concept of concern we place many descriptive words used by other authors in discussing the helping relationship, words such as warmth, liking, support, nonjudgmental respect, expectation, and understanding. Some of these words are descriptive of emotions and attitudes that also fall partially under other concepts; for example, nonjudgmental respect is also a part of acceptance and will be discussed in some detail when that concept is taken up.

Understanding may also be a part of other attitudes, but it should be pointed out here that it is an important part of this concept that workers seek understanding out of concern for the other person and out of desire to help in a way that can be used, not out of their own need to know, or understand, for their purposes. It is always disturbing to hear a social worker use the amount and extent of the material that the client "felt free to share with me" as the test of a helping relationship or the success of an interview. Sharing oneself with a helping person is never an easy or an unmitigatedly positive experience. Knowing this and being concerned for the privacy and rights of the client, workers seek knowledge about a person, or understanding of the person, only because they are concerned to help. Workers seek only so much understanding as is necessary for the process of helping. To seek knowledge for the sake of knowing or to demonstrate skill at interviewing to others is again to make the client the object rather than the subject of our efforts.

We communicate this attitude of concern and respect in any type of relationship to the people with whom we are working by among other things being on time for interviews and conferences; by making appointments before visiting the home or office (which says that the worker respects them and their privacy and wants them to have the opportunity to present themselves as they wish to); by seeing that interviewing or conference space is as attractive as it can be made; by dressing in the way that their culture says is "appropriate to a helping person offering service to a valued client;" and by concerned listening.

For the worker concerned listening is not a passive "hearing." It is an active search for the meaning in and an active understanding of the client's communication. One may well disagree with what is being said, but one must value the sharing that is going on. In a helping relationship particularly, the worker values the client's offering of feelings, thoughts, and ideas. The high feeling in a situation heavy with conflict should not obscure the worker's need to hear accurately. In the helping relationship the worker must in one way or another convey recognition of the value of the client's communication and the worker's desire to understand it. Responding to the content of the client's communication with relevant questions or comments in the search for understanding is one indication of responsive caring; an expressed desire to understand often conveys concern better than a statement of already achieved understanding.

Concern for the other means that workers view clients as uniquely valuable human beings, and in a helping relationship this means that in addition workers transcend their own needs and view of the problem and lend themselves to the serving of the clients' interests and purposes of getting together.

While concern for other may be difficult to determine from written material, we would like you to try to assess this quality in some of the cases in the Appendix. In what situations did the worker convey nonjudgmental caring? What clients seem especially to need a nonjudgmental caring emotional climate to enable them to trust and work with the practitioner? Why?

Commitment and Obligation   Persons cannot enter into relationships with others in a meaningful way without assuming the responsibilities that are linked to such interactions. These responsibilities may best be expressed in the concept of commitment and in its corollary, obligation in the helping relationship. Both client and worker must be bound by commitments and obligations if the purposes of the relationship are to be achieved. A commitment to the conditions and purposes of the relationship and to an interdependent interaction built on involvement and investment allows the client to feel safe and thus to reduce the testing behavior and trial-and-error searching that usually mark the beginning of a relationship. This allows clients to turn their attention and energy to the task at hand rather than to self-protection. Once a commitment to the relationship has been established and the limits of time, place, and purpose have been accepted, each participant is able to depend on the predictability of the other's behavior, attitudes, and involvement.

The earlier writings on the helping relationship seldom mention commitment and obligation, but recently there has been more and more social work literature that speaks of the helping contract. Usually this phrase means that the expectations and terms of the commitments and obligations of both client and worker are explicitly shared. This defining of commitment and obligation, along with the clarification of purpose, time, and setting, is an important process and will be discussed in greater detail in Chapters 9 and 10. However, whether commitments and obligations are explicitly defined, they are an important and inescapable part of every professional relationship involving the giving and taking of help.

Any person asking for help from another is acutely, if unconsciously, aware of the necessity for commitments and the taking on of obligations; and it is often the fear of what may be involved in the expectations and obligations of the commitments that keeps the person from seeking help. The general obligations that clients are usually expected to assume are an open and honest presentation of the problem, of their situation, and of their ways of coping that relate to the problem and an accommodation to the minimum procedural conditions of the helping relationship, such as coming to a certain place at a certain time for an interview and working as they can on the selected problem. Clients are expected to assume these obligations as they can, and their commitments can be renegotiated without penalty.

The worker assumes more binding commitments and obligations and cannot renegotiate the contract without the consent and participation of the client. The worker's obligations include the responsibility to meet the essential procedural conditions of the relationship in the fullest way—being present at prearranged times and places and in certain emergency situations as well; keeping the focus of the work together on the client's problem; offering a relationship that is conducive to sharing, growth, and change. If these commitments to the contract are violated without adequate reason and adequate explanation to the clients, it is certain that clients will question the worker's desire to help. Perhaps worse, clients may interpret such a violation as a message that we do not consider them important. Being present when we are needed carries a connotation that we think the client important, and being absent or late when we are obligated to be present carries a connotation of rejection.

Thus far the helping relationship has been the focus of discussion. However, in summary we broaden our comments to define *commitment* as an involvement with a client, a client system, or any other system that is unqualified by our idiosyncratic personal needs. Commitment is a freely determined wish to further the purpose of the relationship without the expectation of returns that support a sense of worth, add to our self-esteem, or preserve our status. This commitment is communicated through a resolute consistency, constancy, responsible follow-through, and the preservation of the other's dignity and individuality. This preservation demands more than an awareness of the other's dignity and individuality; it involves actions based on sensitive and thoughtful understanding of the other and the other's position. Commitment requires that the worker assume a simultaneous responsibility and accountability for what he or she says and does to the client, the client system, and other systems; to the professional system that sanctions the right to offer help; and to the self (Goldstein, 1973, p. 74).

When workers enter a situation at the request of a referral source, they can hardly expect that the families they enter have any sense of obligation or commitment to them. However, in these situations it is extremely critical that workers be aware of the commitment they make to the families and that they totally fulfill any obligations they assume. Many of these families have had extremely poor experiences with professional people, and they are prepared to examine every promise in great detail. Any variation in a plan can support their impulse to distrust. They also need to test over and over again whether they can trust. It is not easy or comfortable to be mistrusted. As practitioners, we all feel that we are people who are trustworthy. However, we must be aware that most of the individuals or families that we contact in the referral situation have had experiences that may well justify the negative way they regard us initially. We must earn trust, not expect it to be granted just because we appear at their door.

Acceptance and Expectation In most discussions of acceptance in helping relationships, one finds notions to the effect that this means the communication of a nonjudgmental attitude as well as efforts to help workers differentiate between accepting the person and accepting the person's actions. We prefer that workers regard acceptance as more than a refusal to judge and that they try not to distinguish between a person and the person's actions. We would like them to consider acceptance as an active verb, *accept,* meaning to receive as adequate or satisfactory, to regard as true, to believe in, to receive what the other offers. To accept others means to receive what they offer of themselves, with respect for their capacity and worth, with belief in their capacity to grow and mature, and with awareness that their behaviors can be understood as attempts at survival and coping. Acceptance means acting in the recognition that the essence of being human is having problems, making choices (good and bad, wise and foolish), and participating in the shaping of one's destiny with the resources at one's command. Therefore, a better meaning than "to refuse to judge" would be "actively to seek to understand."

The basic elements in acceptance are perhaps knowing, individualization, and trust or expectation. Knowing relates to one's efforts to take in and understand other people's reality and experience, their values, needs, and purposes, and to acquire some idea of where other people come from, of their life and frame of reference. *Individualization* means the capacity to see the person as a unique human being with distinctive feelings, thoughts, and experiences. The individual must be differentiated from all others, including ourselves. Assumptions about others must not be based on generalized notions about a group, a class, or a race, although there is a need to appreciate and understand the manner in which race, class, and sex influence client-worker transactions. *Trust* or *expectation* means that workers have a belief and faith in the capacity of individuals for self-determination and self-direction—that they consider it the right and responsibility of each individual to exercise maximum self-determination in the person's own life with due regard for the welfare of others.

Acceptance of the client does not just occur. It grows from the roots of a fundamental belief and faith that the inherent processes of individual development will lead a person toward greater maturity when such processes are fostered and matured, and it develops as one seeks to understand the feelings, thoughts, and experiences, resources and lack of resources, opportunities and deprivations that have led the individual to make certain choices. In fact, it is our conviction that one finds it almost impossible to be judgmental when one is fully engaged in a cooperative journey to the understanding of another. One cannot understand if one is observing another through the lenses of what is right or wrong, good or bad. Most human behavior is purposive, and if one can understand the purpose of behavior, it becomes understandable rather than right or wrong.

Acceptance does not mean that we always agree with the other person. It does not mean that we forgo our own values to agree with or support the client's values. It does not mean that clients are excused from the world in which they must live. It means rather that workers may present the importance of and the belief in the importance of behaving in socially appropriate ways in keeping with established laws and regulations at the same time that they seek to understand the intense anger that drives clients to act impulsively against certain limits and regulations and that workers can empathize with their need to strike out. True acceptance carries with it an assumption that people act as they must in the complexity of their particular human situation and that they are what their nature and their environment, coupled with their vision, permit them to be.

Thus it can be seen that self-determination, nonjudgmental respect, sensitivity, individualization, expectation of growth, and understanding are all part of the general notion of acceptance. One of the most effective ways to communicate acceptance is to try to understand the position and feelings of clients. This can be done by commenting on their communication in ways that indicate a desire to understand or further to understand what they are saying or by asking questions that are related to the content they are trying to communicate and thus to reveal that you heard and are interested in understanding them.

"A unique characteristic of human beings is that their mental representations of the future powerfully affect their state of well-being in the present" (Frank, 1978, p.

1). Not only does the type of expectations of the future affect the state of well-being in the present, but it also affects behavior in the present, which in turn affects present and future sense of well-being and future behavior. Freud wrote, "Expectation colored by hope and faith is an effective force with which we have to reckon . . . in all our attempts at treatment" (Frank, 1978, p. 1). Expectation is a potent force with which social workers have to reckon in all their transactions with other human systems. There are at least three elements of expectation that are important for social workers to consider: (1) how they feel about the system's ability or desire or willingness to change and their ability to contribute effectively to the change in the situation of the client or target system, (2) the expectation of the social worker held by the system involved, and (3) the system, particularly the client system's expectation of the effect of the helping process.

There has been considerable research in support of the notion that the change agent's expectation that the client system is capable of growth and change, learning and problem solving has a powerful effect on that growth and change. Teachers given a class of students that had a history of learning problems were told that the class was very bright and capable. Not only did the class achieve far beyond what anyone knowing their history would have predicted, but at the end of the year IQ tests showed a 20-point improvement. Psychology students, told that a group of experimental rats had been specially bred to run mazes, discovered that indeed this group of rats were unusually able in such behavior. The fact of the matter was that this particular group of rats was randomly selected from the shipment of rats that had arrived at the laboratory that day. The key to the difference in the performance of the rats lay in the students' expectations of their exceptional performance and the way the students communicated their regard and expectation to these animals by their handling of their subjects.

In medical practice there have been numerous double-blind studies in which patients improve whether they are given placebos or medication. These improvements are powerful indicators of the importance of the attitude of the attending doctors. Because the physician believed that the placebo was a powerful medication, the physician expected improvement and showed increased interest in the patient's progress in treatment. Both these attitudes had tremendous impact on the patient's improvement. In social work, Ripple, Alexander, and Polemis (1964, pp. 199–203) found that when the worker was strongly encouraging and optimistic about outcome, the client tended to continue with the worker, while a bland or neutral attitude of the worker was associated with discontinuance.

This evidence supports the principle in our relationships to all social systems, to all human beings encountered in the professional life, that social workers need to be very much aware of their inner feelings about the system with which they work. The social workers who are most effective in the helping process (or other change) will be those who expect that their clients (or other systems) can and will change in their own way given appropriate help and support. To go back to the concepts from ego psychology, social workers must be convinced of the power of the push toward growth in all of us if they are to be effective change agents.

The second element of expectation with which we must be concerned is the client's (or other system with which we are working) expectation of what we will do to help. Over and over again studies of the effectiveness of social work help point to the importance of the client's expectation of social workers' behavior. To quote a cogent example from Mayer and Timms (1969, p. 1):

> "My husband's gambling was driving me around the bend and I thought maybe the Welfare could help me do something about it. But all the lady wanted to do was talk—what was he like when he gambled, did we quarrel and silly things like that. She was trying to help and it made me feel good knowing someone cared. But you can't solve a problem by talking about it. Something's got to be done."

While this woman received some help through her contacts with the social worker, she was "dismayed and perplexed by the worker's approach and . . . failed to return after several sessions," as she could not see that anything was being accomplished. Clients will probably not be helped by social work unless their expectations are in accord with what actually happens in their transactions with the practitioner. This principle can be stated another way by drawing from our earlier development of role theory: The more congruent are the notions of client and worker about what will be going on between them in their work together, the more effective that work will be. If the expectations of the worker's behavior are highly discrepant with what actually occurs, the client will rapidly withdraw from involvement in the relationship.

This business of expectation and its effect on successful problem solving is critical in situations in which the workers intervene at the request of referral sources. In this situation the family or individuals may expect nothing but trouble from contact with the worker, and the problem may be made worse if the worker harbors a belief that the family is hopeless. In such a situation we have a total impasse in that both parties have negative expectations that can only reinforce each other. A worker can attempt to change the family's expectation of what they bring to the situation in two ways.

The first is through careful exploration of the family's expectations and attempts to discuss inaccurate perceptions. It is not usually helpful to attempt to correct such perceptions and expectations by explaining to the respondent that you are a helpful person who is different from others. You must begin the effort to find a common meeting ground by examining your ideas and feelings about the family, by realizing that the family has valid reasons for its position, and by setting aside your own judgments and conclusions and focusing on understanding the family. You must make a strong effort to avoid becoming defensive. The family is not angry at you. It is reacting to the situation of being invaded out of its past experience with such invasion. Ask the family members how they feel about your coming into their home and respond to their comments with understanding. As an example, let's look at the following exchange with Mr. D, an angry father.

Mr. D:	Oh excuse me Mr. R, I didn't know you were coming or I'd have cleaned myself up.
Mrs. D:	Oh, Frank! Why do you always gotta borrow trouble? You know darn well he always comes this time.
Caseworker:	(with smile) Maybe he's trying to get my goat.
Mr. D:	(angrily) I ain't trying to get anybody's goat, especially yours. You mean nothing to me. You're just doing your job like you're told.
Caseworker:	What's my job as you see it?

> *Mr. D:* To see I get a job and get our case closed. So I might as well tell you now, I ain't been out for work for quite a while. There's nuthin around; everybody is out of work now, not just me.
>
> *Caseworker:* Boy, I can see you were waiting to let me have it with that. I guess you must get pretty sick of the whole merry-go-round. Reporting here and reporting there and going through the motions and nothing coming out of it.
>
> *Mr. D:* Aw, I get sick of the whole mess. And you people always think it's my fault. Every time I turn around someone's on my back.
>
> *Caseworker:* At times it must seem like we are going out of our way to give you and your wife a hard time because of the kids. But actually it seemed that things were getting in pretty rough shape with them, and as part of our duty we tried—perhaps sometimes not in the best way—to help untangle things.
>
> *Mr. D:* Well, you know, sometimes you caseworkers seem to come around always when things were bad enough as they were. And you know, often I might have a few under my belt. I used to drink a lot, you know.

The other way involves challenging the family's inaccurate perception of the worker's behavior by asking the family to examine the behavior against their expectations of the worker. For example, a social worker was interviewing a young American Indian prisoner, hoping to interest the young man in enrolling in some of the prison's vocational training groups. The man refused to consider such plans. The following conversation ensued.

> *Client:* There's no need to try to do anything with you people. You are all alike.
>
> *Worker:* What do you mean, we are all alike?
>
> *Client:* You all lie to us. You never do anything that you promise to do. We can't trust you.
>
> *Worker:* When have I lied to you? When have I failed to follow through on a promise?
>
> *Client:* You haven't, but everybody else around here does.
>
> *Worker:* But I am not everybody. I am me. If I haven't lied to you or failed you, then I think you should try trusting me until I do. When I do fail, I want you to tell me about it so I can change. But until that time....

It is essential to the family's decision to become a client and accept the worker's professional services that there be a common set of expectations developed and stated between worker and family.

This discussion points out the importance of exploring with the client in the initial contact what it is that the client (or any other system) expects. Is this expectation congruent with what can be done in the given situation? If it is not, what can be done? What is the worker prepared to do? What is seen as what ought to be done? At this point it becomes critically important to both the helping process and the helping relationship that the matter be discussed. Through this discussion either the other system's or the worker's behavior must be altered in such a way that they are congruent if workers are to be helpful.

The third important element in expectation is the client's (or other system's) belief that good results will follow from their interaction with the social worker. Expectations of the future that are critical to the change process are found in client attitudes of trust and faith. In trusting social workers, the clients (or other systems) must perceive them not only as competent and helpful at the present moment but also as competent and helpful over time. For example, in a group of clients seen for approximately six weeks in a mental health clinic, hope scores before treatment showed a positive correlation with improvement after their case was closed (Gottschalk, 1973). There are many examples of this from medicine, such as the finding that patients' scores on an acceptance scale before open heart surgery were considerably better predictors of poor postoperative recovery or death than the actual severity of their disease (Frank, 1978, pp. 3–5).

Empathy All the authors cited in the first section of this chapter agree that empathy is a necessary quality of the helping relationship. Empathy is the capacity to enter into the feelings and experiences of another—knowing what the other feels and experiences—without losing oneself in the process. The helping person makes an active effort to enter into the perceptual frame of the other person without losing personal perspective but rather using that understanding to help the other person. In "Being Understanding and Understood: Or How to Find a Wandered Horse," Wendell Johnson (1951) tells how an experienced cowboy demonstrated an uncanny ability to find a lost horse.

> I understand that he did this by working at the job of trying to feel like a horse. He asked himself, "Now what kind of reason would I have for wandering away if I were a horse? With such a reason where would I go?" Apparently, it is possible for a cowboy to empathize with a horse—to feel like a horse to a surprising degree.
>
> At any rate, the cowboy would imagine that he was a horse, that he had the horse's reason for going, and then he would go to the place he would go if he were a horse—and usually he would find the horse.

The cowboy found the horse because he was able to feel as if he was the horse—to feel and think as the horse might feel and think. However, since he was not a horse, having found the horse, he brought it home.

Carl Rogers (1966, p. 409) defines empathy as "the perceiving of the internal frame of reference of another with accuracy, and with the emotional components which pertain thereto, as if one were the other person but without ever losing the 'as if' condition." Keith-Lucas (1972, pp. 80–81) points out that empathy is the worker's understanding of the feelings the other has about the situation, knowing inside oneself how uncomfortable and desperate these feelings may be for the client, but never claiming these feelings for oneself as the helping person. He goes on to differentiate between pity, sympathy, and empathy with a very cogent illustration:

> Consider three reactions to someone who has told us that he strongly dislikes his wife. The sympathetic man would say, "Oh, I know exactly how you feel. I can't bear mine, either." The two of them would comfort each other but nothing would come of it. The pitying man would commiserate but add that he himself was most happily married. Why didn't the other come to dinner sometime and see what married life could be like? This, in most cases, would only increase the frustration of the unhappy husband and help him to put his

problem further outside himself, onto his wife or his lack of good fortune. The empathetic person might say something like, "That must be terribly difficult for you. What do you think might possibly help?" And only the empathetic person, of the three, would have said anything that would lead to some change in the situation.

Empathy requires what may seem to many beginning workers to be antithetical qualities—the capacity to feel an emotion deeply and yet to remain separate enough from it to be able to use knowledge. Methods of reasoning are necessary if one is to make an objective analysis of the problem and the possibilities of solution. Even as workers let the full awareness of clients' emotions wash over them, they are aware that they are feeling not as clients feel but as if they were the client. They must remember that the clients came to them not to have someone share their feelings (although this is relieving) but to enlist aid in coping with a situation that feeling alone cannot resolve. If it could, clients would not need help, for they have feeling enough invested, and undoubtedly they have hard thinking and trying invested, too. They need a worker who in standing apart can bring some difference in feeling and thinking and who is able with a clear head to manipulate or secure resources that were unavailable to the clients' influence, were unknown to clients, or were not thought of by them.

In learning to be empathic, workers have to develop the capacity for imaginative consideration of others and to give up any fixed mental image that may lead one to change reality to fit any preconceived expectation. In this workers are handicapped by two factors: (1) the set of stereotypes carried with them, which are useful in them quickly to grasp the meaning of encounters in daily life but that block greater discernment; and (2) the limited symbols—words, gestures, and reports—available to them to convey another's reality. Thus the accuracy of interpretation is dependent on sensitivity and intuition; the ability to put this together in a dynamic way with all that is known about the clients (their experiences, behavior, problems, and associations); the conception of their potential and what is known about what they want and hope for; all the theoretical knowledge about helping experiences; and all the other experiences with similar kinds of people and situations, real or fantasized. Then, when workers have this mental representation of the other, they must hold it lightly, recognizing that there is always something unknown and unfelt about the other that makes any mental representation tentative, no matter how hard they have struggled to attain it and no matter how much understanding is brought to it.

In speaking of work with handicapped children, Johnson (1951, pp. 178–179) writes:

> You simply ask yourself, "Now what are the possible reasons for behaving as this child does? If I were the child, what would be my reason for doing what I do? Just what would I be trying to achieve? What would I be trying to avoid?'
>
> You can go from there to a lot of questions, such as "How could I achieve my purposes differently? What other motives could I have? What other effects could I try to achieve, and by what other means? What changes would I have to achieve before I would be able to use other procedures, or work toward other goals?"And so forth. . . .
>
> You never see the child as a whole. You see only what you are prepared to see. You can understand only what you are prepared to understand. It does not matter what books you have read, either—at least, it does not matter as much as we think it does. You had a childhood in which conditions determined and limited what you are now going to do with the books you have read. The child will look different to you from the way he will

look to any other worker. The net result is that the child somehow feels that he or she is being understood or evaluated only by one individual, and that he or she is not being evaluated in anything like a complete sense.

There is another reason why we do not understand these children better than we do, a very obvious reason. It is that we do not have their handicaps. . . . I wonder, however, whether it is possible for an individual who has never had a problem—if there are any individuals like that—to have any significant insight into the difficulties of individuals who do have serious problems. The point is that if you have not had a handicap, then all you can ever have in the way of knowledge of the individual that you are attempting to help is the kind of knowledge that is verbal.

Full knowledge of another being is something forever beyond attainment by anyone; it can only be approached, never achieved. It is questionable whether any client wants to be fully and totally known. There is something very frightening about someone's knowing everything about us as an individual, for in knowledge lies control; so in the ordinary course of living people reveal their intimate selves only to those they trust. Without the pain of the problem and the hope that the worker can offer some help with it, few clients would be willing to share themselves with an unknown other person.

The facts that workers can never fully know another except in a limited way and that if workers felt like the client, workers would be unable to introduce the differences in thinking and feeling that bring change require that workers maintain a certain detachment. This demand is often more difficult for the beginning worker than the demand to feel. Each worker maintains this balance differently. This is an area in which supervision can be of great help. By comments and questions the effective supervisor helps practitioners observe themselves and be aware of their contribution to the relationships they form with others. Thus self-awareness— an essential quality of all social work relationships—grows.

While some degree of empathy is needed at the beginning of a relationship (and without this quality a relationship cannot be formed), it is a quality of the relationship and thus is not something that workers construct by themselves. It comes, grows, and develops from the process of interaction of client and worker in which the client can be encouraged to express personal feelings more and more specifically, fully, and precisely, and the worker grows in capacity to feel with the client and in understanding of what is expressed. What clients seek, especially at the beginning of the relationship, is not full understanding but rather a relationship with a helping person in which they sense that their feelings and thoughts are acceptable and that what they express is understandable as a possible human response to their situation.

Johnson (1951) describes his notion of how workers better understand a client:

And how can we do that? Well, I think we do it mainly in two ways. One is by never being dogmatic when it comes to how the other individual feels. We do not know for sure how another feels, and I think we ought frankly to face that. The other thing we tend to do, I think, if we have this point of view, is to be more ready to ask the child what she/he thinks about the problem and about our approaches to it.

Those who have attempted to help me have always wanted to ask me a good deal about how I felt about my speech problem, and about my mother and father, and so on, but seldom, if ever, have clinical workers asked me how I felt about them, how I felt about what they were doing, how I felt about their ideas. There was always a feeling that the expert was attempting somehow to force on me a point of view, an interpretation, a kind of understanding. And almost always when I would ask questions, or say perhaps, "No, no you don't quite understand . . . ," there was a tendency on the part of the clinical worker to take that to be evidence of what the psychoanalysts call "resistance." It is a rare clinician who listens really effectively to what "the case" tries to share. It could be that as clinicians we are wrong and that "the case" has something to tell us, that they are not resisting at all. They may be trying to teach us something. Some of our methods, for example, sound very good to us and they are backed up by great authorities, but when applied to a particular individual, they do not work. Some of the children and adults on the other side of the desk might be trying to tell us why they do not work.

I had a very strong feeling, most of the time, when I was on the other side of the desk, that the clinician working with me was interested in the work. I hardly ever had the feeling that the interest was directed exclusively at me, and I think I have noticed that sort of thing in other cases. In my own clinical work I feel quite sure that I, too, have a tendency to get interested in the theory and the techniques and somehow to lose sight of the child. It is actually hard to stay interested in [the person].

Acceptance and empathy are seldom discussed in social work literature dealing with the social worker's relationship with other than client systems. However, it seems that such elements can be of help in either cooperative or conflicted relationships that involve purposive change in nonclient target systems. Resistance to change and conflict will be prevented to the degree that the practitioner is able to help the target system develop its own understanding of the need for change as well as an awareness of how members of the target system feel about change and what change will mean to the target system. If conflict is the chosen method of bringing change, the practitioner's ability to empathize with the feelings of the other will facilitate choosing the most effective way to become engaged in the conflict. The practitioner who is able to accept the members of a client or target system as individuals with both rational and nonrational positions and who can empathize with those positions will, other things being equal, be more productive than the practitioner who does not possess these skills. The way the worker uses these skills will differ in different situations. In the helping relationship the worker may communicate empathy directly. In other types of relationships workers may use it to shape other communications.

Authority and Power The two remaining elements of a helping relationship to be discussed are (1) authority and power and (2) genuineness and congruence. Not only are these perhaps the most difficult concepts to understand, but the misunderstanding of the element of authority and power in helping relationships often affects a worker's genuineness with clients. Among other things, authority may be defined as a power delegated to the practitioner by client and agency in which the practitioner is seen as having the power to influence or persuade resulting from possession of certain knowledge and experience and from occupying a certain position. Thus there are two aspects of authority in the helping relationship. The first might be called the institutional aspect in that it comes from the social workers' position and function within the agency's purpose and program. The second aspect is psychological in that clients give workers the power to influence or persuade because they accept them as sources of information and advice—as experts in their field. A person in need of help seeks someone who has the authority of knowledge and skill to be of help. If workers accept the clients' assumptions that they carry this authority, the relationship may become infused with a sense of safety and security when the client's own powers of self-dependence fail them.

The primary characteristic of the concepts of power and authority in the helping relationship is that they are neither good nor bad in themselves. Some aspects of these elements are always present, and the attempt of social workers to abdicate their role and pretend that they carry no authority only leaves clients troubled by suspicions and doubts about why workers are unwilling to admit what they, the clients, are so well aware of. This incongruence between what the client feels and what the worker says makes an authentic relationship impossible. The crucial significance of power and authority lies in how they are used for help.

Social workers have had a hard time with the concepts of authority and power. There has been too little examination of authority and power as factors that enter into all human relationships—all human relationships develop laws about acceptable behavior of the people involved within those relationships (Haley, 1963, pp. 1–68). This is one of the problems that workers often face in using professional relationships for purposes other than the direct helping process. The clients of the community organization worker, the research worker, and the consultant are in a different power relationship to the worker than are the clients in the helping relationship. If what this factor means for the workers and those with whom they work is unexamined (or worse, even denied), they lack the needed knowledge to guide them. Social workers need to be able to deal with power and authority both when they exercise it and when others exercise it in relation to them.

In his discussion of authority in social work relationships, Goldstein (1973, pp. 84–86) points out that when persons require what another has to offer "that cannot be obtained elsewhere—whether one is seeking the adoption of a child, financial assistance, help with a personal problem, or professional services to assist in a social action enterprise—the relationship cannot be equalized." As the social worker's needs have no relevance to the task, "the seeker cannot reciprocate or supply the provider with any reward that can restore the balance. The fact that the seeker has limited alternatives to meet personal needs is further heightened by the fact that workers are seen as having competence and knowledge." When social workers say, "We will meet once a week on a Monday if that is convenient for you," or when they decide to include another family member in treatment, they are setting the conditions of the relationship. Or they may refer clients elsewhere. These are all examples of power and authority.

Questions of power and authority are particularly evident when the worker is required to enter a situation by court order or agency decision. Many of the family's negative expectations and much of its lack of trust and fear of commitment may well relate to the experiences it has had with professional people's misuse of power and authority or with its misunderstanding of the purpose of the professional person's intervention. In situations in which we intervene in people's lives at the request of others, we must be prepared to explain very clearly, and perhaps to explain over again with each action, what authority and power we carry, what the limits of our authority and power are, and how we use it. This is often difficult because of our feelings about authority.

Our own life experiences and our own anger at finding our desires thwarted by someone with more power and authority than we possess often result in our dislike of or distancing ourselves from people who can exercise power over us in our own lives. We often try to manipulate people who have the ability to exercise power and authority over us. Thus it is easy for us to project our fears, our angers, and our dislike of authority onto families we approach and to expect them to regard us with these very feelings. We expect the people we approach to dislike us, so we attempt to deny that we have power to influence what happens to their lives. This denial of our authority, this dislike of power, this expectation that people will not like us if we are honest about having these qualities may very well get in the way of our being honest with families and individuals about our charge in this area. Nothing so convinces a family that we are dishonest and untrustworthy as our denial of our power and authority. Nothing is so important to engagement with a family as being clear and honest.

Genuineness and Congruence In the research that has been done on helping relationships (Truax & Carkhuff, 1967, pp. 1–2; Truax & Mitchell, 1971), it has been found that in an effective helping relationship the helping person needs to communicate four things: empathy, acceptance, unconditional positive regard (we have called this quality "concern for the other," as we find this phrase more expressive of the essential notion), and congruence. Congruence means that workers bring to the relationship a consistent and honest openness and realness and that behavior and the content of communications with and in regard to the client must at all times match each other (be congruent) and must match the underlying value system and the essential self as a professional person. (The qualities needed for helping people will be discussed later in this chapter.)

To be congruent and genuine we must seek three things: (1) an honest knowledge of ourselves, of who and what we really are; (2) a clear knowledge of agency procedures and policies and of the professional role, both in their meaning to the worker and in their meaning to the clients; and (3) an internalization of the first two and our concern for the other, acceptance of clients, commitment to their welfare and to the authority aspects of the workers' role and position, so that these qualities are so much a part of us that we no longer need to be consciously aware of them and can turn our full attention to clients and their situation.

People who are real, genuine, and congruent in a helping relationship are ones who know themselves and are unafraid of what they see in themselves or what they are. They can enter a helping relationship without anything of themselves to prove or protect, so they are unafraid of the emotions of others. For example, unwillingness to be honest with clients about authority in a relationship or about what will be done with the information they share may be a consequence of negative experiences with authority in one's own life. Therefore, we try to deny (to lie about) what the client sees so clearly is really there. To be congruent we must have faced and examined our own feelings about many central life experiences that clients share with us, so that we know which feelings are ours and which are the client's. What are our feelings about the lies we encounter? We are angry about them, and so we must be different? We want the client to see we are different and that we understand better than anyone else? Do we really? Can we free ourselves of certain behaviors and feelings we dislike? Will our being free of them help our client? Or is it better to admit that they are there so that the two of us can examine what they mean for the client? What are we afraid of, or what do we want, in denying to clients the facts about certain agency restrictions on service and about our capacity to skew these so that they do not bear so heavily on them?

This brings up the second half of the worker's awareness, the meaning of the agency role and position to the worker and to the client. Not how workers want the client to see them, but how the client does see them—as representatives of a particular agency or service. Workers and clients come together, as a rule, within some kind of bureaucratic structure. The client usually does not pay for the costs of service, or at least does not pay the full costs. So the worker is paid by someone other than the client. What do the structure of the agency, its position in the community, and the source of the funds to support its services mean to the client? Workers who have not honestly examined these questions and who have not faced what they mean both to themselves and to their clients will often appear to the client to be somewhat divorced from the reality of the client's life. So being honest and real means that workers have examined their roles and tasks in relation to agency, client, and target systems and that they can assume them fully and honestly with an openness about all their parts and about their impact on the client.

Our popular culture tends to place emphasis on irrationality in caring relationships with others, to hold that true caring ought to be something impulsive and instinctive, from the heart as it may be as of this moment, uninhibited, and "natural." There is a belief that to think about a feeling distorts it and makes it less an expression of what people are—as though the head were not a genuine part of the body; or as though only the heart were good, and the head must perforce be evil. This stance neglects the common theme of much of the literature of human emotion, in which the heart is held to be fickle and inconsistent, unwilling to be committed to another. Actually, congruent people need a warm and nurturing heart, an objective, open, aware, and disciplined mind, and an open channel of communication between head and heart so that they appear all of one piece to others.

There is a tendency to view professionalism and objectivity as though these qualities mean coldness, cautiousness, and an impersonal, restricted reaction to the expressed feeling of others. Actually these ways of presenting oneself in a relationship are totally unprofessional and are related to one's own need to be self-protective or to one's fear of oneself and thus of others. Both this impersonal way of operating with others and the undisciplined personal expression of one's impulses of the moment are self-serving modes of behavior that are destructive of the capacity to communicate congruence and genuineness in the helping relationship, which requires that the client be kept squarely in the center of concern.

Perhaps an example will illustrate this point. When a really competent figure skater performs a free skating program, the viewers do not feel that she is incongruent or unreal or dishonest. Instead they feel the spontaneity and creative force with which she puts her whole self into the performance. But the performance required years of slow and painful learning—it required more than a little self-discipline and persistence and hard slow growth and change in the use of self. The creative free movements of this skater are quite unnatural to the untrained beginner on ice skates. They are not in any way the "natural" movements of the skater the first time she put on skates and tried the ice. Yet the skater does not think of each movement or gesture. In fact, if she does, she will not give a free performance. Her performance has the effect it does because she has so internalized the demands of the task that she can give herself to it entirely and can respond freely and spontaneously to what is in herself and in the here and now. As viewers watch her, they are aware that she gets great satisfaction from the use of her competence in a disciplined yet free way. She knows herself and her capacity, and there is a joy in what she does. Workers, too, should enter all professional relationships with a clear knowledge of what can and cannot be done, a sense of competence and a belief in what workers are doing. Satisfaction can be received in helping others. How can workers believe that the creative use of self in helping others demands less time, work, and discipline, and knowledge of self and of the limits of action than does the performance of a figure skater?

Rational and Irrational Elements in the Helping Relationship Obviously there are cognitive elements in the professional relationship. Both workers and those with whom they interact think as well as feel in a helping transaction. Both bring knowledge and values to their association. In all professional relationships social workers need to be actively cognitive—relating what is said and done to their knowledge—and making sense out of the interchange of feelings. Much of the rest of the text will be devoted, as are the first five chapters, to setting forth the values and knowledge that the worker needs to master. It is enough to mention here that cognition is an important element of the relationship.

The irrational elements of the relationship are those elements—feelings and attitudes, inherent patterns of behavior—that are not called forth by the present situation but are brought to it, relatively unchanged by the here and now and by reality, from earlier relational experiences. They are irrational in that they are usually unconscious (and thus not available to present awareness) and in that in the form in which they appear they are inappropriate to the present situation.

As an example of the power of the irrational: One of the authors was once involved in a helping relationship with a family that had been referred by the school social worker because a son was emotionally disturbed. Bob and his brother were one of two sets of twins. Besides the twins there was one other child in the family. None of the other children showed any unusual difficulty in school. After some observation of the mother's relationship to her children, it became obvious that she treated Bob differently from the others. She indulged him more than his brothers and sisters and was totally unable to limit him. When confronted with examples of the different way in which she reacted to Bob, she burst into tears and said she could not deny him because he was just like her. It seems that she had always felt picked on as a child, and she was sure Bob felt the same way. She had been the younger and smaller of a set of twins, as Bob was, and she was sure he felt just as she did, so she was trying to help him feel better. In reality she had no evidence that Bob felt the way she assumed he did. Nor had she ever faced the fact that she and Bob were two very different persons with two very different childhood situations. Her response to Bob was an irrational one with roots in her own painful childhood.

A further and also important example of the effects of the irrational in all our lives is found in the attempt to create a congruent honest working relationship across racial, cultural, or social class barriers. Individuals may master all the knowledge about the history and culture of another race; they may plan rationally how to use themselves in the relationship; but too often, when they actually come together with a member of another race, they find rising inside them feelings and thoughts that may be quite contrary to what they want to feel and think. They condemn themselves for these forbidden feelings and deny them both to themselves and to others, yet the feelings persist. They persist because they are irrational responses that are learned as a part of culture. All individuals live and grow up in a racist society, so they all absorb, to a greater or a lesser extent, the irrational attitudes of that society in regard to race. These attitudes become a part of all persons and are all the more difficult to understand and eradicate because of the very fact that they are irrational.

It is important that workers recognize that such irrational elements are a part of the helping relationship (indeed, of all relationships), because such realization enhances their capacity to understand and accept the expressions of clients and because it helps them to accept the importance of their own self-awareness. The presence of irrational elements in the most knowledgeable and thoughtful of individuals makes the demand for self-awareness a constant one. All people need to exercise all the care of which they are capable to keep such elements in themselves from intruding inappropriately into the helping relationship.

In the development and use of the professional relationship in the service of another there is the demand that workers know themselves. It is necessary to speak of the conscious use of self that carries within it the demand for self-awareness. As one considers the differences in the development and use of the relationship with different size systems and for different purposes, it appears that these differences are significant enough to demand a differing self-awareness on the part of the worker.

It appears that in work with client, target, or action groups one must be self-aware not only in relation to the group as a whole but also to each individual in the group, who, relating differently, may call up different responses. Favoritism, rejection, avoidance, demands for special attention—all present the group worker with special demands in self-awareness. In the one-to-group helping process, because group relationships are concurrent with the worker-to-group relationships, workers must be aware of their push to react in areas of power and status problems, sibling rivalries, competitions, and aggressions. Considerable self-awareness and self-discipline are necessary to maintain focus and purpose while weaving the many strands of individual needs and competitions into a meaningful process. The ability to keep focused on the needs of others in the face of the group's questioning of the worker's operations or authority is a difficult discipline to achieve. Workers with groups must develop an understanding and a discipline of their own status needs, their needs to preserve face before a group, and their innate responses to open conflict.

In the one-to-one relationship, workers can depend less on immediate feedback from clients in relation to inappropriate operations, so there is a greater demand to be aware of feelings and responses that are aroused in the transactions with the client that will affect the helping process. Workers must be particularly aware of their own dependency needs and how these needs affect their reactions to the dependency needs of others and of their feelings about authority. Workers must be conscious of any feelings of omnipotence and the need for client approval. They must be aware of any need to take too much responsibility or assume too little with their clients and of self-expectations and the ways these affect client relationships, both in subtle demands for change, growth, and performance and in the bearing this has on the psychic self-determination of the client. Workers must be aware of the points at which the client's needs and problems touch off feelings in them that may not be helpful in work with the client and must have the kinds of self-discipline that are effective to control such feelings.

Because of their great overriding importance in all social work practice, we want to introduce once again the problems caused in the effective use of relationship by a lack of self-awareness about feeling, thinking about, and attitudes toward racial, ethnic, and sex difference. A study of work with women clients revealed that the theoretical position one espoused had little to do with the social worker's stereotyped reaction to women clients (Davenport & Reims, 1978, p. 306). The theories could be used flexibly. The critical variable that resulted in rigid and stereotyped reactions on the part of social workers came from the individual's biased belief systems. It is absolutely basic to social work practice that workers be aware of their belief systems and the impact of such systems on their use of self and that they find ways to deal with themselves so that they can work without bias with all people.

The Helping Person

It is difficult to discuss "the helping person" because there are almost as many kinds of helpers as there are people who need help. There is probably no one person who is effective in creating helping relationships with all people. And there is probably no one person who is an ideal helping person, so each of us probably lacks some of the qualities a helping person should have. There are, however, certain qualities, attitudes, and approaches toward life that are found to an uncommon degree among helping people—and thus among social workers. There are six qualities that are seen as central to effective social work functioning. Someone once wrote that "helping relationships are created by helping people, not by helping techniques." This means that social work practitioners bring about system change through their use of self—of what they are—of what they have made a part of themselves, including their beings, their thoughts, their feelings, their belief systems, their knowledge. In other words, what they do must be congruent with what they are seeking to become as persons.

There are many people who do not have the capacity to help others—just as there are many people who do not have the capacity to design computers or perform surgery. None of these jobs is simply a matter of knowledge. All require certain kinds of people with certain kinds of talents. Among the kinds of people who are not good helpers are those who are interested in knowing about people rather than in serving them (coldly objective students of humanity); those who are impelled by strong personal needs to control, to feel superior, or to be liked; those who have solved problems similar to the problems of the people in need of help but have forgotten what it cost them to do so; and those who are primarily interested in retributive justice and moralizing (Keith-Lucas, 1972, pp. 89–108).

Maturing People The most effective helping people usually experience themselves as living, growing, developing people who are deeply involved in the process of becoming. They do not exclude themselves from the human condition but view all people, including themselves, as engaged in problem solving. Not only are they unafraid of life, but they frankly enjoy the process of being alive with all the struggle that this may involve. They find change and growth exciting rather than threatening.

Their anxiety and tension are at an optimum level, so they are free to take on new experiences. Thus they do not need to be "right" to defend where they are. Perhaps most of the other qualities to be discussed will stem from this quality.

Creativity When we speak of creativity, we usually are thinking of qualities of originality, expressiveness, and imagination. These qualities are critical to social workers because the most effective practice usually involves the search for alternative ways to define a problem, and once it is defined, the proposal of new and unthought-of ways of attempting to solve it. Clients come to us because they are stuck in the ways they define the problem and in the solutions they see. We are no help if we propose only pedestrian definitions and solutions. We must create something new. Creativity involves an unusual amount of openness to all experiences of life, the ability to hold knowledge in suspension, never-satisfied curiosity, and lack of identification with conformist opinion.

Helping people must be nonconformist in that they hold most solutions to the problems of life as tentative. Conformity involves accepting prevailing opinion as fact, and this stymies openness to other solutions. However, it is necessary to distinguish nonconformity from counterconformity, a term that characterizes a person who is always against authority or accepted ways of doing. Such a person is not truly independent but is motivated by a need to defend personal identity and by hostile and/or aggressive attitudes. Intellectual openness and receptivity suggest a state of freedom to detach oneself from certain theoretical positions or systems of thought. Creative people can allow themselves to be dominated by the problem with which they are grappling rather than search for a known solution. It is not that creative people are not knowledgeable, that they have not given a great deal of themselves to learning what is known, but that they are able in spite of the heavy investment they have made to hold this knowledge tentatively. This seems paradoxical to many people, and it is indeed a heavy demand, for when people invest heavily in things they tend to hold them dearly.

This brings up another paradoxical quality of creative people. Although they are often deeply committed to a problem, they are at the same time detached from it. Creative people like complexity. They do not seek premature closure but can maintain an openness and joy in the contradictory or obscure and have a tolerance for conflict.

Capacity to Observe Self Capacity to observe self is usually discussed in social work literature under the rubric of self-awareness, and it has already been discussed as an element of genuineness and congruence. It is an important capacity for the social worker and is discussed in most material that deals with the helping relationship. Perhaps the two previously discussed qualities are an important part of this capacity, which really means to be sensitive to one's own internal workings, to be involved with oneself and one's needs, thoughts, commitments, and values, yet to stand back enough from oneself to question the meaning of what is going on. This means that the helping person must take a helping attitude toward oneself as well as toward others.

We have chosen not to use the term self-awareness for this quality because we think it is more than self-knowledge. There have to be other qualities. Self-love and love of others, self-respect and respect for others, self-confidence and confidence in others, acceptance of self and acceptance of others, faith in self and faith in others develop together or not at all. So the capacity to observe self probably requires the ability to care deeply about oneself and one's goals, to respect and to believe in oneself, and yet to be able to stand back and observe oneself as an important piece of the complex activity of helping.

This way of regarding self leads to flexibility, a sense of humor, readiness to learn, acceptance of one's limitations, and openness—all of which are important qualities of the helping person. And most of all, the capacity to observe self demands courage—we need to be unafraid of what we will find. All of us, to some extent, distort in one way or another feelings that we do not want to acknowledge, but the more this is true, the less we can help others. It is the need for self-protection, the fear for self, that gets in the way of sincerity, openness, genuineness, and honesty.

Like all other human beings, social workers cannot make themselves over simply because they wish to do so. Like all other human beings, they are the product of their intellectual, emotional, and physical attributes, they are shaped by the range, expansiveness, and richness of their life experiences, including their educational experiences, and by how they have used those experiences in developing their basic beliefs, values, and attitudes. However, even if we cannot remake ourselves at will, it is important in observing ourselves that we have the capacity to see ourselves as growing and developing people.

Desire to Help A deep desire to increase the ability of people to choose for themselves and to control their own lives is an absolutely essential quality of a helping person. Effective helping relationships or other social work relationships simply cannot be created and sustained without this desire. Basically, the desire is a commitment to oneself rather than to others because it must be our desire, be related to us, and be a commitment to ourselves. It is this commitment that gives one the courage to know oneself and the willingness to risk oneself in the service of others.

Courage It takes great courage—not the courage of the unaware and insensitive but the courage of the person who is thoroughly aware yet does what must be done—to take the risks with oneself and others that social work relationships inevitably demand. Workers must be willing to assume the risks of failing to help, of becoming involved in difficult, emotionally charged situations that they do not know how to handle, of having their comfortable world and ways of operating upset, of being blamed and abused, of being constantly involved in the unpredictable, and perhaps of being physically threatened. "It is only the person who can be afraid and not be afraid of this fear who is in a position to help" (Keith-Lucas, 1972, p. 100).

It takes great courage to be able to think about ourselves and others as we are. Even more, it takes great courage and strength to face clients directly with the reality of their problems when this reality appears threatening and hurtful. And it takes courage to engage in honest thinking about others and yet to be basically for people—to be skeptical and inquiring in one's thinking yet trusting in one's attitude toward others.

Sensitivity Our methods of sharing ourselves with others are awkward and imperfect even when we are committed to that sharing. For troubled people the ability to share themselves and their situation is incredibly more difficult because of all their feelings about their problems and about themselves as people with problems, and because of the threat of the unknown in the helping process. Therefore, the worker who would help needs a capacity for feeling and sensing—for knowing in internal ways—the inner state of others without specific clues. This quality probably depends on one's ability to observe even small movements and changes in others and to make almost instantaneous inferences from them, to put oneself into the feeling and thinking of others, and to avoid stereotypes. It is probably closely related to one's capacity to be open to the new and to one's readiness for change.

Difference and the Social Work Relationship We cannot leave a discussion of the professional relationship without some mention of the impact of difference in gender, sexual preference, race, age, class, and culture on the development and use of the professional transaction. It is particularly fitting that this discussion should follow the sections on rational and irrational elements in the helping relationship and on the helping person. Culture and cultural norms related to the above differences are powerful forces that are inevitably and irretrievably part of our unconscious, so deeply buried and accepted as a part of us that we express them in all areas of life every day without any awareness of what we are communicating. They seem right to us. We should not deny that they are a part of us because such attitudes are so deeply embedded in American society that it is impossible for any of us to have escaped their impact on our conscious and unconscious selves and on the ways we relate and the ways clients relate to us. We should quit denying that we have such attitudes and accept them as a part of us, work at identifying them, be aware of how we express them, and then try to change them.

Sexual mores and role expectations are some of the stronger and more troublesome forces. Our attitudes toward homosexuality are probably some of the most powerful culturally based unconscious forces. We cannot discuss here in any detail all the differences about which any one of us may hold negative stereotypes. We will discuss two. The first relates to our feelings about gender difference. The majority of social work clients are women. They may be black women, lesbians, poor and uneducated, or white, heterosexual, or rich, but they are women. Yet a review of the social work literature over an eight-year period found that the sex of the client and the worker was ignored as an important factor in intervention. In fact, race, class, and ethnicity were seen as being much more important than gender (Quam & Austin, 1984, p. 361). In studying recent social work literature, one is struck by the absence of literature relating specifically to nonsexist theories and practice techniques. Most social work practice models are derived from male-centered theories; they are products of men's thinking that take men as the norm and fail to acknowledge women's subordinate place in the social structure. "Psychological concepts mask political realities as women are seen as passive, lacking confidence, discriminating against themselves, self-sacrificing, manipulative, and so on. Implicit in an approach that ignores gender politics is the notion that it is the woman herself who impedes change. What is disregarded are the external constraints that inhibit women's risk-taking activity" (Morrell, 1987, p. 144).

We must seriously explore how we feel when a middle-aged woman comes to us over and over again with tales of husband abuse and brutality but refuses to take steps to leave the situation. Do we recognize social, economic, and moral constraints that may hold her in place in spite of a strong desire to do something about her problem? A group of men and women were invited to a special conference related to a matter of social work concern. They were all selected because of their national expertise. All the men had doctorates. One woman had a doctorate, and a number of others were professors at respected schools of social work. The chair, a man, followed by the rest of the group, men and women alike, called all the men "Dr. Lastname." However, all the women were called by their given names. Finally, the woman with a doctorate pointed out to them what they were doing and asked that she be addressed as "Dr." and the rest of the women as "professor." The group immediately started calling all members by their given name. The chair also delivered a long speech about how tired he was of the sensitivity of women. What is your response to this example? Do you think that the chair was "blaming the victim" or that his response was appropriate?

Just as it is easy to underestimate the extent of the impact of sexist attitudes on all of us, it is easy to underestimate the extent of the impact of racist attitudes on individuals of all races because of the multivarious sources that subject all individuals to both explicit and implicit negative stereotypes. Implicit negative messages are more insidious, hence more devastating and difficult to deal with, yet they affect every one and all relationships.

Shirley Cooper (1978, p. 78) expresses it well when she says: "Clearly racism bites deeply into the psyche. It marks all its victims—blacks and whites—with deep hurt, anger, fear, confusion, and guilt."

Cooper urges that workers examine their thinking with special care, as "efforts to acknowledge and deal with racial factors are affected by highly emotional attitudes." She points out that white people "influenced by a culture rampant with racism and unfamiliar with the intricacies and nuances of the lives of ethnic people may, even with the best of intentions, fail to recognize when social and cultural factors predominate" in their professional attitudes. Cooper (1978, p. 78) notes that "ethnic therapists are vulnerable to the opposite form of clinical error. Because they are so centrally involved, they may exaggerate the importance or impact of ethnic factors." She goes on to say that in color blindness individuals tend to lose their particular richness and complexity and that there is a danger of no longer relating to individuals as they are but rather of relating to individuals as though they were "only culture carriers" (1978, p. 78).

Cooper (1978, p. 78) discusses the unavoidable guilt experienced by white practitioners who live in a privileged and segregated society and says that in their struggle with this guilt they may deal with it through "unrealistic rescue fantasies and activities—a form of paternalism." When white guilt remains unconscious, it can lead to overcompensation, denial, reaction formation, an intense drive to identify with the oppressed, and a need to offer the victim special privileges and relaxed standards of behavior no more acceptable to minorities than to the general population.

In the black practitioner oppression produces its own personality and distortion. It may lead to costly overachievement at the expense of normal development. Whether one achieves or does not achieve, there is the anxiety that hard-won gains or battles lost are not in fact the consequence of one's performance but rather the result of considerations based on race. With the actuality of one's own productivity in doubt, there are anxieties about self-worth and competence and there is no real way to measure one's own behavior (Cooper, 1978, p. 78).

In speaking of the white-black encounter within the professional relationship, Gitterman and Schaeffer (1972, pp. 280–291) say:

> One direct consequence of the institutionalized racial positions of blacks and whites is social distance. . . . As a result of these conditions, there emerge two separate and distinct experiences, each somewhat unknown and alien to the other. It is this very quality of mutual strangeness which characterizes the initial black-white encounter. It may be camouflaged, denied, or rationalized. The void may be filled by stereotyped "knowledge" and preconceptions, but the essential unknownness remains. Not only are the two different, but, not having lived or known each other's differences, they can only speculate about them. They see each other and the world, and are in turn viewed . . . by the world, in different ways. . . .
>
> Thus separated . . . white . . . and . . . black . . . come together . . . face each other and are confronted with the necessity of doing something together. . . . First, there is suspiciousness and fear between them. . . .
>
> There is also anger between them. Once again, much has been written, especially in recent years, of the rage that is felt by black people. White workers also feel anger of which they may or may not be aware. They may be angry at the black client for being so troubled, or helpless, or dependent, or hard to reach. They may be angry at themselves for their inability to do very much to really help their clients, or they may be angry at the clients for being angry at them. The anger is there on some level. It is most likely that the client perceives it even if workers do not.
>
> There is also pain between them. This pain is one of the most complex dynamics because it stems from so many different sources . . . pain and suffering connected with whatever presenting problems caused the client to seek service . . . pain at being black in America . . . pain felt by the worker in response to the client's pains . . . pain from the guilt felt by each party. . . . Most profoundly, there is guilt caused by repressed anger and other negative feelings experienced by both.

Gitterman and Schaeffer (p. 281) recommend some ways of dealing with the racial gap between worker and client. Essentially their recommendations reflect the factors in the relationship that were discussed earlier in this chapter. They point out that the helping process is a mutual endeavor between active participants, that it takes both participants to do the job, and that they must listen to each other. They emphasize that the white worker cannot ignore or minimize the social factors that contribute to the plight of the racially different client.

Perhaps the best way to end this too-brief discussion of race is to quote from the preface of the volume in which Gitterman and Schaeffer's contribution appears. Here the editor (Goodman, 1974, p. xiii) says:

> The profession of social work cannot afford to sustain practices that would diminish the humanity of any group. It must deny that only blacks can treat blacks, or only whites can treat blacks, or only people of the same culture can understand each other well enough to provide help.
>
> Social work must teach that different is not "better," nor is it "worse," it is different and its technology must be developed, in every sense, to propagate a multiracial set of identities that will continue and extend the search for a common basis in humanity.

Recapitulation   In this chapter the professional relationship has been discussed. The chapter is long and complex, but even so it does not fully express the richness and complexity of the professional relationship as it is known by workers and the other systems with which they interact in the daily struggle with human problems. We have attempted to summarize the development in social work literature of the concept of relationship, to identify the various components of relationship, to deal briefly with some of the differences in the use of these components in various types of relationships, to discuss workers themselves and their capacities, and to deal with the issue of difference in professional relationships.

A Look Forward   Let's look again at the cases found in the Appendix and attempt to apply some of the material on relationship found in this chapter to those cases. As you finish reading each case, consider how you feel about the clients (or potential clients) in the situation. Why do you think you feel this way? Is it the problem the client faces, is it the way the client has tried to deal with the problem, or is it the way the client relates to the worker? Can you determine from each case how the worker seems to feel about the client? How would you assess the relationship? How important do you feel the relationship is to work on the problem?

Let's look at the Z case as an example of some of the problems in building a working relationship. One has tremendous respect for the worker in this case for her honesty in evaluating her feelings and her search for what was going wrong between her and Mrs. Z. Can you summarize the feelings of the worker? One problem that we see in the situation is that the worker persisted in treating Mrs. Z as a client when she was not a client and was violently resisting being a client. The worker wrote that she had explained her role to Mrs. Z several times but such explanation did not seem to help. However, there is no record of her having asked Mrs. Z at the beginning of their contact how Mrs. Z thought the worker could help her, or how things were going with Mrs. Z and the hospital routine. The worker was careful to ask her how she felt, meaning how she felt physically. But the worker did not ask if there were things about being in the hospital that were really sending her up the wall. The worker seemed to keep coming back to offer help to Mrs. Z, but the help that was offered seemed to come from the worker's concept of help. There was no contract between them.

The worker saw her own charge as "to initiate a relationship which may or may not be reciprocated." She did not understand that a relationship has to involve at least two people's feelings. The worker kept trying to build what she evidently saw as a "good, helping relationship," and she was feeling very much a failure because she could not persuade Mrs. Z to accept the help the worker felt she was charged to give and could give. The central question that was not dealt with was what kind of help Mrs. Z wanted, if any. Did the worker fail if Mrs. Z said she did not want any help? What was Mrs. Z's right to make her own decisions about her situation? The worker discussed her perception of Mrs. Z as having a strong need to control, yet the worker persisted in trying to pursue what she saw Mrs. Z as needing rather than trying to learn how Mrs. Z wanted to use her. If Mrs. Z was an angry woman, we wonder how the nurses' and the worker's elaborate pleasantness and understanding helped. Could it be that Mrs. Z saw them as humoring her as one would a disobedient child, or a dying person, and not taking her anger seriously? If they really took her anger seriously, would they have responded with anger, or at least with some suggestion that she limit such behavior? Instead, so to speak, they patted her on the head and told her to be a nice girl. Would it have helped if they had told her that her behavior was at times very annoying? Do you suppose that Mrs. Z really was trying to find what the limits of her behavior were? How do you think Mrs. Z might have responded to limits? Do you think the staff's response to Mrs. Z was different from what it would have been had she been a man? What would have been the difference?

Let's look at another case in which the worker set some limits for the client. In the Debbie Smith case, in which the worker's purpose was protection of the children from Miss Smith's neglect, when the worker felt that the condition of the Smith living quarters represented an intolerable threat to the welfare of the children, she confronted Miss Smith with the problem. It is important to note that the worker did not criticize, disparage, or in any way lecture Miss Smith about her failure as a mother or her terrible housekeeping. To do so would only have repeated the kind of response that Miss Smith had been used to. Instead the worker pointed out that such living conditions did not fulfill Miss Smith's own goals of taking good care of her children. A routine and essential part of interaction with clients whose behavior is problematic is a careful assessment with the client of the net gains and losses of such behavior for the client. No attempt is made to discuss behavior in terms of right and wrong, neurotic or normal, good or bad. The question to be dealt with is, does the behavior get clients what they want out of the situation?

When Mrs. Z discussed staying with her cousin, the worker asked if her cousin knew what to expect. What do you think would have happened if the worker had asked Mrs. Z to tell her about her cousin, if the worker had asked her how she and her cousin had decided on this arrangement, and so on?

Do you think the worker felt empathy or pity or concern for Mrs. Z? How do you think this affected Mrs. Z's response to her? Would it have been helpful if the worker could have changed her goal from getting Mrs. Z to change her behavior to helping Mrs. Z explain her thinking and feeling? Look back at the cases again. What kinds of commitments did the workers in the various cases make to their clients? How do the commitments made by the workers correspond with the problems identified for work?

In the next chapter we will discuss skills of communication. Without question, communication is central to social work practice. Most of our attempts to help involve the skilled use of communication, whether with clients, colleagues, referral sources, sources of information, and others. Thus the next chapter deals with a skill that you will work at improving all your professional life, regardless of task or setting.

Four Pennies to My Name: What It's Like on Welfare

Addie Morris

I had to get up at 3:30 A.M. and start getting the kids dressed. Sally was five and the oldest, so I started with her. Then I dressed Sam; he was three. I did the baby last. All I had to do was change her diaper and wash her face because I had dressed her before putting her to bed.

It was cool that morning and I didn't have a coat for Sam. He never had a chance to go any place in the winter anyway, so there had been no reason to buy him one. I decided to use Sally's coat that Aunt Jean had given her two years ago. He wouldn't know the difference, and I could care less about what people would say.

I wrapped the baby snugly and the four of us started off for the bus stop. At 4:45 a bus finally came and the four of us boarded. I put forty-five cents in the box and we took a seat in the rear. But I hadn't settled down before the driver called, "Lady, you owe me another fare." I had only forty-five cents left and if I gave that to him, I wouldn't have any money to return home. I approached the front of the bus with the baby in my arms. By this time, I had tears in my eyes. Couldn't this black man understand what was happening to me? Didn't he realize that if I had the money I would have gladly put it in the box?

I stood holding on to the rail beside the driver, unable to say anything. Every time I tried to speak the words choked in my throat. Finally, I got the words out tearfully, "Mister, I am on my way to the social service office. I don't have but forty-five cents to my name. I will need that to return home on."

A lady that was sitting a couple of seats behind the driver said, "Aw, let the woman go. Can't you see what she's going through?"

The driver looked straight ahead and mumbled, "Go on and sit down, lady." That is exactly what

I did. I returned to my seat too ashamed to look at anyone.

I sat in my seat silently with tears streaming down my cheeks. Sally put her arms around my neck and asked, "What's wrong, Mama? Do you need my shoulder?" I reached over Sam and gave Sally a big hug.

"No, darling, I don't need your shoulder," I replied.

I heard someone in back of me whisper, "Wasn't that sweet?"

It was a thirty-minute drive to the social service department. My kids and I went out the side door of the bus. I couldn't bear to face all of the people by walking out the front door. I felt relieved that only one other lady got off at the bus stop. She walked so fast ahead of us I thought she must be going to some place important. I had to take my time walking because I was carrying the baby and Sam couldn't walk too fast.

When we arrived at the social service office, it was 5:05. The door of the office was still locked, and people were standing around waiting for it to open. After standing for a few minutes, I decided it would be better if I sat on the steps for awhile. It was then that I noticed the lady who got off the bus with us. She quickly turned her head when she saw me looking at her. The door finally opened at 5:30. Everyone rushed in and took a number or crowded half in line around the desk. I didn't know what to do so I took a number, too. Then I went to the front desk. I waited in line for at least ten minutes before my turn came to talk to the receptionist.

I came straight to the point, saying, "I'd like to see someone about getting food, clothes, and shelter for me and my children." The receptionist told me I would have to wait and talk to an intake worker but they didn't just hand out money like that. Then she took my name and said someone would call me later. I felt a little sick to my

Note. From "Four Pennies to My Name," by Addie Morris, 1979, *Public Welfare, 37(2),* pp. 13–22. Copyright 1979 by American Public Welfare Association. Reprinted by permission.

stomach that she thought I was looking for a handout.

Around 9:00 the kids became restless. I kept getting up to give them a drink of water, but the water wasn't relieving their hunger. There was a snack bar next to the information desk and some people were buying things to eat. Naturally this made the kids want food even more. But the only money I had I needed for carfare to get home. Finally, Sam stood up and said, "Mom, can I have one piece of candy?" I was embarrassed and I couldn't think normal. I slapped Sam hard. He began to cry loudly—maybe because he was hurt but also because he was hungry. I told him he better stop crying right away. And of course, not wanting another slap, he did.

By 11:00 the waiting room was crowded. Some people had to stand. However, when noon came everyone that worked there went out to lunch. By this time, my insides felt like they were melting together. I knew how Sally and Sam must feel. But I wasn't thinking much about them because I was too busy feeling sorry for myself.

All of the employees came back to work at 1:00 o'clock. I approached the receptionist again to find out why I hadn't been called. She told me flatly, "Everyone has to wait their turn; they will call you when they get to your name." I tried to explain that my two older children hadn't had breakfast or lunch and I couldn't afford to purchase them anything from the snack bar. She looked up from her scratch pad and said, "What do you expect me to do? I hear this kind of thing all day long." I quickly took my seat hoping too many people hadn't heard our conversation.

Finally, at 1:15 a lady came out and called, "Mrs. Morgan." My name never sounded so beautiful. I hurried to the front desk. A woman instructed me to follow her to a small room I assumed was her office. She began by saying, "I am Mrs. Jenkins and you are Mrs. Morgan."

"Yes," I replied.

She said, "What can I do for you?"

I began, "My husband left me because he was constantly being laid off. He said we could make it better without him."

"Do you know where your husband is?"

"No, ma'am," I replied.

Giving me an application blank, she said, "Fill this out and bring it in tomorrow by 5:30."

It seemed Mrs. Jenkins had finished, but I continued to sit there. After a few seconds, she said, "You may go now."

"But . . . but Mrs. Jenkins, I don't have any food for my two older children. I do have some milk for my baby. Plus I don't have bus fare to return tomorrow." She went into another room and returned with two bus tickets. I said, "I brought two walking children with me that are sitting in the waiting room." She went out again and returned with two more tickets. Then she told me that she would be unable to provide me with a food order; my application would have to be approved first.

As I left the room I thought to myself, "Anyone who thinks being on welfare is fun has to be mentally unstable." The wait alone is enough to make you go out of your mind. Then after the long wait, what did I get? Four bus tickets. Well, at least the bus driver wouldn't be able to embarrass me.

I walked slowly to where Sally and Sam sat. I was thinking hard. I could tell they were glad to see me—it showed in their eyes. But they were afraid to show me because I had been acting so strange and they thought I might lash out at them again.

Someone was sitting in the chair that I was in earlier, so I asked Sam to stand so I could sit down and compose myself. I decided that since I didn't have to use forty-five cents for bus fare, I could buy a snack. I gave the baby to Sally and went to the snack bar. I bought one pack of potato chips and two candy bars. Now, all I had was four pennies to my name.

When I returned with the candy and potato chips, I could see the joy in Sally and Sam's eyes. I gave them each a candy bar and the three of us shared the potato chips. Afterwards, we filled up with water at the fountain.

As we left the building, I was thinking we might go to Aunt Jean's instead of going home. After all, she didn't live too far away. Maybe she would ask us to spend the night and then it would be easier to return to the social service office the next morning. Besides, we didn't have any food at home and she might offer us a little something to eat.

We took a bus going west toward Aunt Jean's house. I was pleased to have two tickets to put in the box when we boarded the bus. It wasn't long before we had arrived at our stop. We got off and started walking to Aunt Jean's home. Sally and Sam realized where we were going and started skipping instead of walking. I was sure they realized that they would get a meal there. Aunt Jean always gave us food.

Aunt Jean was happy to see us. She was even happier that John had finally decided to leave. I didn't bother to explain how desperate I was. It would have only encouraged her to remind me how bad John was. Right then, I could do without hearing that. I tried to make it appear that I was paying her one of those long awaited visits. She was really pleased and indicated that she knew that John was the reason I could never visit before.

Aunt Jean was full of southern hospitality and offered us food immediately. It wasn't long before Sally, Sam, and I were sitting down to a hot meal. It wasn't the greatest, but it was food: salmon, biscuits, syrup, and grapefruitade to drink. I washed the dishes for Aunt Jean.

Then we sat down to talk and watch television. It wasn't long before Aunt Jean started to encourage me to spend the night. Of course, this was what I had been waiting for, but I didn't want to let on. "I am going to fool you this time," I said. "We are going to spend the night." She was happy with this. The children were pleased, too. And I was glad at the way Sally and Sam had been conducting themselves.

The next morning we were able to get up a little later because we were closer to social services. I didn't have to start dressing the children until 4:30. Either Aunt Jean didn't hear our noise or she didn't want to be bothered. I was hoping she would get up and offer us breakfast. At the last minute, she got up and fixed us coffee with a lot of cream. We enjoyed this because we love coffee with lots of cream.

As I boarded the bus, I thanked the Lord again that I was able to put two tickets in the box. I was also thankful that my insides were not clinging together from hunger.

We arrived just as the door of the social services office was opening. People rushed in to take a number. Others formed lines at the receptionist's desk. I rushed to take a number, too. Then I remembered that I had taken one the day before and hadn't returned it. The next number was fifteen. My number from the day before was six. Naturally, I kept the number six. Then I wondered if that was a wise decision. The worker I get with the number fifteen might help me more than the one I would get with the number six.

We waited in the waiting room the same as we did the previous day. People walked back and forth to buy snacks. I know that Sam and Sally were hungry, but neither of them asked for anything. They were probably afraid. In my heart I wanted to be able to buy goodies for my children just like everyone else. I knew this was why I lashed out at them for every little thing. I realized that I wasn't making things any better by doing this, so I promised myself that I would do better.

I was daydreaming about being able to afford things for my children when I heard my name over the paging system, "Mrs. Morgan, front desk." I rushed up to the front desk and identified myself.

A lady said, "This way, please."

She offered me a chair and identified herself as Mrs. Jones. I handed her my application and she began to look it over. She didn't say a word with her mouth, but she said a lot with her facial expressions. I would have felt better if she had spoken. I began perspiring until my hands felt slippery. My knees began to tremble so that it appeared I was shaking my baby. I wondered whether Mrs. Jones was enjoying my extreme anxiety. She certainly wasn't trying to alleviate it by breaking the silence.

I suppose it took Mrs. Jones ten minutes to read my application. To me it seemed like ten years. She finally looked up at me and said, "Mrs. Morgan, do you know where your husband is now?" I told her that I didn't have any idea of where he could be. Then she proceeded to tear apart each of my answers on the application. She asked, "Do all three of your children have the same father?" I suppose I was partly to blame on this one. I didn't indicate their last names on the form because I assumed anyone would know their last name was Morgan. Mrs. Jones wanted to know about the length of time I had lived at our address. She threw one question after another at me: "Why don't you have . . . ?" "What have you been doing up to now for . . . ?" "How come you haven't . . . ?" Either Mrs. Jones was asking the questions in a downgrading manner, or I had a complex and was taking all of her questions the wrong way. But I was meek as a lamb answering all of her questions.

My father always said, "Take it easy when you have your head in a lion's mouth." This was certainly true now, and I needed this woman for my survival.

As she continued to question me, I became choked up. When I began to answer her question on what I had been doing for food, I broke down. Here I was a grown woman crying. Mrs. Jones did or said nothing to comfort me. She just sat there. When I managed to control myself, she said, "Maybe I should tell you a little about what we can do for you. We are not intended to be an agency for people to live off. We are designed to help you out with aid until you are able to manage alone. We only take care of things that are essentials or necessities . . ." She rambled on and on but still wasn't saying anything that I wanted to hear. I wanted to know what they were going to give me.

Finally she told me she would work out a budget for me and tell me how much it was when she got back. She left and was gone for thirty minutes. I was relieved because I knew that at least I would be getting some help. I wasn't even angry when I saw her joking and laughing with her friends instead of working on my budget.

She came back with the budget that the department allowed for me. It included the following:

Rent	$100
Lights	15
Gas	20
Food, clothes	120
Total	$255

I was currently paying $130 for rent, but she said the department only allowed $100. She further explained that my checks would arrive on the first and sixteenth of each month. Each check would be for $127.50. She told me about the food stamp program that I was eligible for. The way I understood it I could pay $10 and get enough stamps to buy $15 worth of food.

I was very thankful. In fact, I was so happy I walked right out of her office without asking for bus tickets to get home or a food order to keep us until the following week. I turned around and went back into the office, stumbling over the chair I had been sitting in. "I don't have any food for my two older children," I told her. "I also don't have any money or bus tickets to get home."

"I see your kind every day," she said. "Want everything you can get. Have a seat outside and they will call your name to pick up the tickets and food order."

I was so thrilled. I went back outside, sat down next to my kids, and hummed "Thank You, Jesus." Suddenly, things had begun to look up for me. I could really pray to God now. Before, I was too depressed to pray as I should.

They didn't call my name until 3:00. When I went up to the front desk, Mrs. Jones gave me a $20 food order and $2 worth of bus tickets. I was so hungry and weak, I just thanked her, got the children, and left.

On the way to the bus stop I decided what I was going to do. I would take a bus to the supermarket that was six blocks from my house. We got off the bus and walked proudly to the supermarket. We were going to be able to buy some groceries.

I was careful to add up every item I put into the basket. I knew I couldn't go over $20. I bought potatoes, eggs, milk, bread, sugar, corn flakes, beans, spinach, beef neck bones, chicken livers, and other items that were reasonable and would stretch a long way. After I had finished, I only had a little over $18 worth of groceries. I told Sally and Sam they could go and pick one thing they wanted. I've never seen two happier kids. Sam got a box of six Baby Ruth candy bars; Sally picked a box of vanilla wafer cookies. I was so full of pleasure with their joy that tears rose in my eyes.

When the cashier finished, I had two bags full of groceries. I realized I couldn't carry the groceries and my baby, too. There were drivers by the door calling, "Transportation. Transportation." I sure needed transportation, but I couldn't afford it.

I pushed my groceries outside and decided to give one of the bags to Sally to carry. I carried the other bag and the baby. But I hadn't gone very far when my load became unbearable. I absolutely couldn't go any farther. I managed to get my bag to the ground before it burst.

For about five minutes, I was out of breath. Sally and Sam seemed to sense what was happening to me because they stood there silently with me. I was trying to stuff some of the groceries into Sally's bag when a car pulled to the curb and stopped.

It was one of the men who was at the supermarket calling, "Transportation." He said, "Lady, do you need a ride?" I told him yes but I didn't have any money. "Get in," he said. Sally, Sam, and I crowded in as he held the seat forward. I told him where we lived. To make conversation, I talked about the weather. I offered him some of my groceries for pay but he refused.

The dinner I prepared that evening was a tasty one. I fried the chicken livers with onions and we had rice, spinach, and corn bread. We felt like saying grace before eating for a change. During our meal, I explained my success of the day. "Now we will be able to eat a meal three times a day. And I won't be so worried and upset."

Sam asked, "Is three times a day a lot of times?" I laughed and assured him that it was enough times that he wouldn't be hungry.

We had never been able to afford story books or television in our home. So I decided I must think of something to entertain the kids. As the three of us sat on the floor, I told them stories. I started with "The Three Little Pigs," continued with "Snow White," and ended up with "The Four Little Rabbits." When I finished, Sally said, "Mom, I didn't know you could tell stories."

The following week was beautiful: three meals each day, peace of mind, and most of all giving love and receiving my children's love.

Saturday was the sixteenth of the month and my check was due. My groceries were getting thin. However, I knew I could make it a few more days. I waited for the postman. He finally came around 1 p.m. He left something in my mailbox. I was so excited. I rushed downstairs and found a sample of Ultra Sheen.

I refused to let my disappointment get the best of me and told myself the check was delayed because of the weekend and would definitely be there on Monday. Meanwhile, things would be all right. I must admit that the weekend wasn't a pleasant one. In fact, it was the longest weekend I've known. I wasn't harsh with kids, though. I just wasn't motivated to talk, clean house, or do anything but the necessities.

Finally, Monday came. The postman always came earlier during the week. But today he didn't stop. My heart was beating so hard, I thought it was going to come through my skin. Without thinking, I ran outside after the postman with only my robe and slippers on. He stopped and went through his bag of mail again but didn't find anything for me.

I ran back inside and fumbled through my purse until I found Mrs. Jones' telephone number. I hurried out to the corner telephone booth with my last dime. I dialed the number but every time the line was busy. At twelve noon, I finally got through but no one answered. Then I realized everyone was out to lunch. But I was determined not to hang up until someone answered.

Around 1:00 someone finally answered the phone. I asked to speak to Mrs. Jones. When she came to the phone she asked, "Was that you letting the phone ring for a whole hour?" She hadn't identified herself.

"Yes," I said, "I'd been calling all morning, and the line was busy. I was determined to reach you." I identified myself and told her about my check not coming in the mail. She said that sometimes it takes two to three weeks for checks to get started. She told me to be down at the office at 8 A.M., and she would have a check for me.

Our food was more than thin at this point. We had been eating generously because we thought we'd be getting more food in two weeks. Anyway, I felt at ease because I would be getting a check the next day.

Tuesday morning I was up bright and early. But it suddenly dawned on me that I didn't have any money to take the bus. I decided I would have to walk. I awakened Sally and told her about feeding the baby and where she could find bread to toast for Sam and herself. I told her to give the baby one bottle in the morning and the other when she wakes from her nap. She agreed to do this faithfully and off I went.

It was a long walk. Although I wasn't wearing a watch, I could tell it was already much later than 8:00. I was so tired I thought my legs would fall from under me. But I couldn't stop. I had to get my check so I could buy food for my children.

Finally, I arrived. I was so exhausted that I had to lean on the receptionist's desk to ask to see Mrs. Jones. She told me to have a seat and Mrs. Jones would call me. There were no vacant seats in the waiting room so I went over to a large ash tray in the corner and sat on it. I was absolutely too tired to stand any longer. As I sat there catching my breath, I looked at the clock on the wall and it said 10:10. Gee whiz, it had taken me more than four hours to walk from home.

Mrs. Jones came out and called different people but not me. Some of the people she called I thought had come in after I had. But I didn't have any proof. And even if I had proof, there was nothing I could do about it.

Just before noon Mrs. Jones came out and called me. As soon as I approached the desk, she handed me a check and two bus tickets. I reached out and tried to shake her hand but she refused. I said, "Thank you so very, very much!" I left humming an old spiritual, "Yes, God Is Real."

What a thrill it was to have a check of my own for $127.50. I had never had a check this large in my whole life. All I could do was sing and pray a thankful prayer all the way to the bus stop.

I got off the bus near the supermarket. Going inside, I asked them to cash my check. Of course, they asked, "Do you have any identification?" All I had was my marriage certificate that I had forgotten to take out of my purse after I'd taken it to the social service office two weeks before. I gave my marriage license to the clerk and told her that was the only identification I had. She smiled and initialed my check and told me that the cashier would cash it after I had made a purchase. Then she asked me whether I would like an identification card so I could cash all of my checks there. Of course, I was pleased and thanked the clerk. She gave me a wallet-size card.

I was so happy walking around the store picking up my groceries. I began to feel as though I was a princess.

After I finished getting my groceries, I still had $90 left. I felt great. The same men were across from the checkout counter saying, "Transportation. Transportation." I walked across and asked the one that had given the children and me a ride two weeks before.

After he had helped me take my groceries in, I asked him would $1 be enough. He said, "Whatever you want to give." So I gave him a dollar and he thanked me.

Then I noticed something different about my house. My children had attempted to clean the house while I was gone. They jumped up and down with joy when they realized that I was bringing food home. I jumped right along with them for the good job they had done. Then Sam and Sally happily assisted me in putting the groceries away.

After I cooked dinner, we sat down to eat. Everyone was quiet. I thought I would break the silence by asking whether anyone had anything they would like to talk about. Sam spoke up, "Mama, aren't you glad Daddy is gone?"

I quickly replied, "No! Why?"

He began to stammer a bit and continued, "We can eat good food all the time since he's away. I hope he stay gone."

"Oh, don't talk like that," I said. I was sorry I had broken the silence. And I had spoken in such a defensive manner. I knew I wasn't letting my children open up and tell me what was on their minds. Yet, I couldn't seem to help myself.

The rest of the week went fine. I told the children stories and even played games with them—games like guessing who has the penny, or who is knocking at my door. All our games had to be things that didn't require a game set. I decided to do exercises and play running games, too. The house had very little furniture—only the necessities: stove, refrigerator, one bed, a mattress on the floor for Sally and Sam to sleep on, and a cradle. So, there was plenty of space available for running.

On Friday, Mr. Perry came over for the rent. I didn't want to give him all of the money that I had.

And, even if I did give him all of the money I had, I would still have a balance due to him. The rent was $130 and I had a little more than $88. I decided to give Mr. Perry $65 of the rent and promised to mail him the balance in two weeks. He wasn't pleased because he'd had trouble with my husband in the past. But he agreed. And I felt more secure with the $23 I kept in case of an emergency.

I kept pretty much to myself the following two weeks and enjoyed my children and having decent food to eat. Before I expected it, my check arrived. It was the first of the month, but somehow I expected it to be late. I now had $150. Happy, I mean I was happy. I only owed a $15 gas bill and a $10 light bill.

I left my children alone, instructing them to keep the door closed and not open it for anyone. First I walked to the grocery store. This way I could get my check cashed. I decided not to get groceries until I was on my way home. After getting my check cashed, I took a bus to the post office and bought three stamped envelopes and three money orders to pay my light, gas, and rent balance.

Then I returned to the supermarket. I spent $30 for groceries. I also paid the driver $1 to take my groceries home. So I had $29 left—not a lot of money, but some in case of an emergency.

The money I received from social services could pay the rent, utilities, and buy some food. However, the food would have to be mostly second rate such as neck bones, chicken livers, or bacon ends. But I couldn't complain because I could at least live.

The time came for Sally to start school and I began to wonder what we would do for clothes. I started looking for a night job, but I couldn't find work doing anything. I would even have taken a job sweeping the street. I knew there had to be more to life than this. I was barely surviving.

The day before school, I made starch out of flour and ironed Sally's best dress which wasn't much. It was old plus it was up to her butt because she had gotten it two years before. I bought her a pair of gym shoes and socks at the supermarket.

The first day of school I dressed Sally along with Sam, the baby, and myself. Of course, today was Sally's day and the rest of us didn't matter that much. But as we waited in line to register, I noticed the way the other children were dressed.

After being in school for several weeks, Sally began to act strangely. One afternoon she came home and asked, "Mama, why do all of the children laugh at me?" I didn't want to tell her it was because I couldn't afford to buy her nice clothes like the others had. She seemed to sense that I didn't want to talk about it, so she never mentioned it again. But she began to withdraw and talk less and less. That winter she had a mental breakdown and was hospitalized for two weeks. When the doctor told me he thought this had happened because of the way she had been treated by her peers at school, I became even more determined to get a job so I could buy us some clothes.

I soon found the Lord was looking out for me. The day Sally was discharged from the hospital, her doctor told me about a job at a nursing home working nights as a nurse's aide. He said the man that was the administrator was a friend of his. He told him about me and the administrator had agreed to give me a try. I felt all I needed was a chance like this. I was so elated I had tears in my eyes when I thanked the doctor. He told me to take good care of my children.

I was due to start to work on Sunday night. I knew I couldn't afford to hire anyone to look after the children when I was at work. So I took time and explained to Sally what I was going to do. I told her in order to get money to buy a few toys and clothes like other people, I had to work. I would need her help with Sam and the baby. I assured her they would be asleep most of the time anyway.

I bought a white uniform with my light bill money and used the rest of my emergency savings to catch the bus to and from work.

It was three weeks before my first pay check, but it was well worth the wait. I cleared $120 and had some money to buy clothes. I went to K-Mart and bought Sam a suit, Sally a dress, shoes and socks, and the baby a new dress, socks, and shoes because she had never had any shoes before.

That Sunday when I got home from work, I dressed everyone; and we all went to church. I was sleepy that night at work, but I was pleased we went. The kids enjoyed it and my heart felt all good inside.

From that time forward Sally kept the kids for me while I worked at night. We had better food and clothes—and I even started saving a little. We went to church every Sunday and sometimes during the week. Sally and Sam began to love Sunday school and looked forward to going.

Sometimes I felt a little guilty for accepting money from social services and working, too. But I rationalized to myself that I couldn't survive on either one alone. So I took the better of two evils and risked going to jail if I got caught.

One night at work an inservice instructor gave a class on "Treating the Patient As a Human Being Through Reality Orientation." I dearly enjoyed the class. Afterwards, I went to the instructor and asked her about continuing my education. She was happy about my interest, especially since I wanted to be a nurse. (I had been thinking about this for some time.) She agreed to bring me literature and an application to a junior college. Of course, I was happy about her promise, but I never expected her to fulfill it. So often people had made promises and never kept them.

The next evening when I arrived at work, I was surprised to find a catalog about a nearby community college and an application. During my lunch break that night I read as much as I could of the catalog and filled out the application.

I wrote a letter to my high school for my transcript. I felt like I was really doing something worthwhile. But in the back of my mind I kept reminding myself that I might not be accepted. Maybe my southern education hadn't been adequate. But I was optimistic. I talked about going back to school with my co-workers and they made fun of me. Even the licensed practical nurse in charge made sarcastic remarks. But this made me keep my head up and try harder.

In less than a month I received a letter from the school to come down for an interview. I became apprehensive, but I decided to go. Surely it couldn't be any worse than my first few visits to social services. Besides, all they can tell me is "yes" or "no."

The interview wasn't as difficult as I expected. The director of nursing was black—although she talked and tried to act like she was white. She was blunt and direct. She informed me that with my academic background I would need one year of liberal arts before entering the nursing program.

I registered early in the summer for the fall semester. I planned to take four courses: English 1, Chemistry 1, Humanities 200, and Speech 200. My classes began at 8:00 A.M. and were over at 11:00. Two were on Monday and Wednesday, and the other two were on Tuesday and Thursday. This meant I would be home by 12:30 every day so Sally could go to school in the afternoon.

Soon summer was over and it was time for Sally and me to start to school. I sat down and explained my plans to Sally. I told her she would be caring for Sam and the baby (now a year and a half old) in the morning while I attended classes. She already knew how to prepare cereal for them. That would be all they would need until I returned home at 11:30. Then I would prepare lunch and dress Sally for school. (Sally was better now and able to return to school.)

This plan worked out well. During that first year, I made two A's in chemistry, four B's in my other courses, and two C's in English. I managed to pay my own way through school in addition to buying our clothing. (I enjoyed dressing Sally each morning after I arrived home from work. I continued to thank the Lord for decent clothes to dress her in.)

In April, I received a letter from the Nursing Evaluation Committee to come for an interview for the nursing program. I was put through the third degree at that interview. I managed to answer their questions and remain calm on the outside. But sometimes two of them would ask a question at the same time. I would answer one. Then, when the opportunity presented itself, I answered the other. At the end of the interview, the director of the program told me that I was accepted to the nursing program and was to begin classes in September. I couldn't have been happier.

The next week I made an appointment to see Mrs. Jones at social services. I told her of my acceptance in the nursing program. She questioned me about my getting into the program without prior preparation. I told her about attending classes for the past eight months. Then she asked me, "What do you want me to do?" I told her the first thing I would need was money for a babysitter. To this she replied, "You didn't seem to have any trouble getting a babysitter for the past eight months." At this point my hands became sweaty. Couldn't this lady see the sacrifices I had made? I composed myself and told her of the arrangement I had made with Sally.

But Mrs. Jones continued the questioning. She asked how I got the money to attend college. Silently I said, "Lord, forgive me for this lie," before I told her that my boyfriend had paid for my schooling. I added that we had broken up now and I wouldn't be receiving any more help from him. At last, she told me that social services could allow me $30 a week for child care but nothing for tuition. She told me to try the financial aid office at the school.

I did exactly as Mrs. Jones said and went to the financial aid office at the college. I was able to get a loan and a grant to cover my entire tuition. But I decided to continue to work. I planned to save the loan money in case I had to stop working. However, if I didn't use the loan money I could pay the loan back upon completion of the program.

So I continued to work at the nursing home. The jokes and remarks about my going to school became less frequent as I progressed in the nursing program. At the request of the nursing director, I even took charge when the supervisor was unable to come in.

At times, working along with going to school and taking care of my children would get the best of me. Sometimes I would catch myself nodding in class, and once I fell asleep. Everyone was leaving the classroom when I awakened. I was so embarrassed. I immediately went up and explained to my instructor that I was working nights.

Finally I graduated. It was a small graduation, but an extremely happy occasion for me and my children. As I walked across the stage for my associate degree in nursing, my baby Nell stood up in her seat in the rear of the auditorium and said, "That's my mama!" The audience turned to her and cheered and clapped.

I am now off AFDC and I am very thankful to God that he helped me through those years. I am very proud to be a nurse, and it feels great to be able to go to the supermarket and pay for my groceries with cash rather than food stamps. I always felt people were watching me when I paid with food stamps. It doesn't mean that I have that much more money now, but I do have more dignity which seems to make the money go further. Bank tellers and checkout clerks seemed to sneer at me when I cashed my welfare check. With a check I've earned, these people respect me and I feel that I am not a burden to society. I feel good about having earned that money.

I can see now that children act in the same way their parent acts. When I was on welfare and barely able to make ends meet from one month to the next, my kids were sad and struck out at each other. Now that I am more content, they are nice to each other. Another factor that has changed their attitude is that they can do things other children do and have things other children have. Now I am able to buy Sam a truck for his birthday. I can afford to take the kids to the zoo or on a picnic in the park. Sally has pajamas so she can spend the night with a friend. Our life is very different from before.

It's a great feeling to be off welfare.

For Further Reading

Gitterman, A. (1983). Uses of resistance: A transactional view. *Social Work, 28,* 127–131.

Hutchison, E. D. (1987). Use of authority in direct social work practice with mandated clients. *Social Service Review, 61,* 581–598.

McNeely, R. L., & Badami, M. K. (1984). Interracial communication in schools, *Social Work, 29,* 22–27.

Palmer, S. E. (1983). Authority: An essential part of practice. *Social Work, 28,* 120–125.

Perlman, H. H. (1979). *Relationship: The heart of helping people.* Chicago: University of Chicago Press.

Proctor, E. K. (1982). Defining the worker-client relationship. *Social Work, 27,* 430–435.

Rubenstein, H., & Bloch, M. H. (1982). *Things that matter: Influences on helping relationships.* New York: Macmillan.

Stewart, R. P. (1984). Building an alliance between the family and the institution. *Social Work, 29,* 386–390.

Chapter 9

Communication and Interviewing for Social Work Practice

Interviewing is a fundamental social work activity. The interview is the major tool used by the social worker to collect data from which to make intervention decisions. While other data collection tools are available to the worker (these will be discussed further in Chapter 10), the interview remains the primary tool and the applicant or client the primary source of data. Many social work interventive strategies are also dependent on interviewing, with the interview used as the modality through which strategies directed toward change are applied. The ubiquitousness of interviewing in social work practice requires some brief consideration of interviewing and communication in any book presenting a practice model. Excellent books are available regarding the social work interview (Gordon, 1992; Benjamin, 1987; de Schweinitz & de Schweinitz, 1962; Epstein, 1985; Evans, Hearn, Uhlemann & Ivey, 1984; Garrett, 1972; Kadushin, 1972; Rich, 1968; Schubert, 1982), and social work educational programs usually devote considerable time to the development of interviewing skills. We do not intend either to provide a comprehensive treatment of interviewing or to offer you a bag of tricks. Rather, this chapter will introduce the use of social work interviewing as a central tool of social work practice, identify some barriers to communication, offer ideas concerning the role of the social work interviewer, and briefly present some techniques we have found useful in the data collection interview. Your interviewing skills will continue to be refined and developed throughout your social work career. Social work communication is done in writing as well as orally. We will also offer some brief thoughts on the importance of your continuing to improve your written as well as your oral communication.

Communication and Interviewing

The Communication Process Communication is an interactional process that gives, receives, and checks out meaning and that occurs when people interact with each other (see Exhibit 9-1). Communication theory concepts of encoding, transmitting, receiving, decoding, and noise provide a useful framework for understanding problems that may arise in the social work interview. *Encoding* refers to the process of putting the message to be sent into symbol form in preparation for transmission. *Transmitting* refers to the process of sending the encoded message; *receiving,* to the process of interpreting the stimuli received; and *noise,* to extraneous influences that may have distorted the message when it was on its way from the transmitter to the receiver. Checkout, or feedback, provides a way of overcoming problems created by noise as well as by inadequate encoding or decoding or faulty transmission or reception.

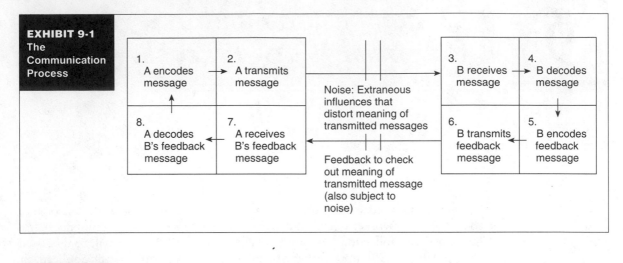

EXHIBIT 9-1
The Communication Process

1. A encodes message → 2. A transmits message → Noise: Extraneous influences that distort meaning of transmitted messages → 3. B receives message → 4. B decodes message

8. A decodes B's feedback message ← 7. A receives B's feedback message ← Feedback to check out meaning of transmitted message (also subject to noise) ← 6. B transmits feedback message ← 5. B encodes feedback message

EXHIBIT 9-2
An Example of Feedback

Worker: But you are very preoccupied with the amount you sleep, and watching the clock, is that correct? At least that's what I've picked up from what you've said about keeping track of times and all.

Mr. H: You could be right there. I just can't relax.

Worker: Is part of the problem knowing how you'll feel when you wake up? You said that was when it was most painful.

Mr. H: Exactly. I'm worried about failing asleep because of the anticipation of the pain I'll experience in the morning. It's absolutely horrible.

The checkout phase, which is essential to the communication process, is discussed as an interviewing technique by Robert Brown (1973). A, for example, sends a message to B, which B receives. But how does B know that he or she has received the message A intended to send? Perhaps B's receptors were faulty; perhaps A's transmitter was faulty; or perhaps there was noise or interference between A and B that distorted the message. B checks out the message with A by indicating what has been received to confirm that the message B received was the message A intended to send. Exhibit 9-2 is an example of feedback from "Pain Clinic Evaluation" in the Appendix.

John Cormican (1978) identifies several potential communication problems in social work practice. When he speaks of language differences and communication problems resulting from the use of various dialects, he is making reference to communication problems with the use of symbols—the symbols encoded and transmitted by one party may be received by the other party but are not decodable. Or the message may be decoded in such a manner that the message sent is not correctly interpreted. Lewis and Ho, in the article included with Chapter 5 (Reading 5-1), give an example of a problem in nonverbal communication between social workers and American Indian clients:

In an effort to communicate more fully, the social worker is likely to seat himself facing the client, look him straight in the eye, and insist that the client do likewise. A native

EXHIBIT 9-3 Feedback as a Communication Problem	The client in treatment struggles to express a feeling or thought that troubles her. She finally manages to say something that perhaps approximates what is on her mind. The social worker's response is, "I really appreciate where you are coming from." What does the social worker's response mean? What does it reveal and what does it conceal? What contribution, positive and negative, does this remark make toward furthering the treatment of the client and fostering a therapeutic relationship? This phrase is a duplicitous expression of confusion, concealment, and lack of understanding and empathy. If one were to ask the therapist what he intended to convey to the client by using the phrase, he would presumably say something like, "I mean that I understand what the client is feeling." But his every word proves otherwise. First, nobody can truly understand what another person is feeling. One can come close, and such approximations of empathy are surely what social workers strive toward in their work, but understanding inevitably remains an approximation. The therapist's use of the word *really* reveals an underlying uncertainty about what the client feels.

Note: From "Social Work and the English Language," by A. Bloom, 1980, *Social Casework, 60,* p. 333. Copyright 1980 by Family Service Association of America. Reprinted by permission.

American considers such behavior to be rude and intimidating; contrary to the white man, he shows respect by not staring directly at others.

Cormican asserts that labels such as borderline state, depressive, behavior disorder, actor-outer, and personality disorder create barriers to communication. These labels, when held by the worker, may distort the decoding process because the message sent by a client may be interpreted in relation to the worker's understanding of the meaning of these labels rather than in relation to what the client intended. Feedback is used to check out whether the receiver got the message the sender intended. Barry Cournoyer, in Reading 9-1, identifies empathic communication skills that are reflective on the part of the worker. Empathic communications derive from your conception of an applicant's or client's frame of reference and reflect content, feeling, thinking, and meaning. Cournoyer discusses reflective skills for work with groups, but these skills can be used with any size client system to check out the messages received. Checkout, or feedback, is also a form of communication and is subject to the same problems as the original message-sending process. Exhibit 9-3 offers an illustration of this problem.

Total communication, in that one can completely understand what another is saying, thinking, and feeling, is impossible. We need to recognize this and not delude ourselves into thinking that we fully understand, but we also need to work to improve clarity and understanding in our communications. We must strive, of course, to understand the client, but we also must strive to be sure our own communications to clients are as clear as possible. We agree with Bloom's (1980, p. 337) advice that "communications to clients ought to be simple, clear, accurate, and direct. Social workers should choose words that are precise and cannot be misunderstood, words that are not evasive and vague."

Communications occur simultaneously on many levels. We speak of verbal and nonverbal communications, overt and covert communications, of denotative and metacommunication levels of messages. The *denotative level* refers to the literal content of the symbols used (usually words). *Metacommunications* are messages about the message; a metacommunication includes such things as voice inflection, gestures, manner of speaking, and so on, all of which provide clues beyond the denotative level of what was intended by the communication. The ability to communicate several messages simultaneously provides opportunity for the famous double bind—the simultaneous transmission of contradictory messages leaving the receiver in a "be damned if I do, be damned if I don't" position (Bateson, Jackson, Haley, & Weekland, 1963).

Interviewing in Social Work Interviewing is a particular kind of communication. Robert Kahn and Charles Connell (1957, p. 16) have offered a classic and often-cited definition of an interview as a

> specialized pattern of verbal interaction—initiated for a specific purpose, focused on some specific content area, with consequent elimination of extraneous material. Moreover, the interview is a pattern of interaction in which the role relationship of interviewer and respondent is highly specialized, its specific characteristics depending somewhat on the purpose and character of the interview.

But what is the meaning of all of this to interviewing in social work? The social work interview is a set of communications with four special characteristics: (1) has a context or setting; (2) is purposeful and directed; (3) is limited and contractual; and (4) involves specialized role relationships. The context or setting for the interview will often be that of an agency offering defined services to applicants bringing specified problems, but it may also be the applicant's home or the offices of other agencies. The context, of course, provides a limit to the communications and becomes a basis for the elimination of extraneous material that is not related to the particular context. Social work interviews are purposeful and directed in that they are conducted to accomplish specific goals (a legitimate purpose may be the definition of the goals or furthering worker-applicant communications). Conversely, interviews are not casual exchanges of information or informal conversations. The purpose of an interview provides a basis for limiting communications and eliminating extraneous material. Interviews are limited and contractual in that the social worker and applicant come together in a specific context for defined purposes; their communications are limited to meeting those purposes. Finally, social worker and applicant occupy specialized roles and interact with each other according to those roles. This again is a limiting factor, inasmuch as applicant and worker interactions will usually be confined to the expected behaviors of the specialized roles.

MacDonald (1988) offers several suggestions that we believe will help improve the social work interview as a communication process with all applicants and clients. She suggests the importance of reviewing our value complex in regard to the attitudes we hold toward women's potential—and, we would argue—toward the potential of all clients. The worker will play a relatively active role in the interview, is committed to an egalitarian relationship between worker and client, will assist the client in developing a new definition of self, will focus on the here and now, and will place the client's experiences within a political context.

Interview as Data Collection To summarize, communication can be viewed as an interactional process involving the giving, receiving, and checking out of meaning;

communication occurs on many levels and may not always be congruent. Interviewing is a specialized form of communication that is contextual, purposeful, and limited and that involves specialized role relationships. This chapter focuses on interviewing to secure information that applicant and worker will use jointly in decision making about the nature of the problem and intervention. The primary source of data is the applicant; interviewing techniques are used to encourage the applicant to share data for use.

Since the data are to be used in decision making about intervention, the social worker must be concerned about the reliability and validity of data collection procedures. You have been introduced to the concepts of reliability and validity in your research courses. These concepts are defined for social work practice as they are in other scientific and research activity. *Reliability* refers to the extent to which data collection tools (in this case, the interview) produce consistent information. If different messages are received from an applicant at different times, you must be reasonably certain that the differences reflect actual changes in the person and are not a consequence of your interviewing style; otherwise a reliability problem exists. *Validity* refers to the extent to which the information being obtained reflects the actual perceptions, thoughts, feelings, and behaviors of the applicant. If the person is not sharing actual perceptions, thoughts, feelings, and behaviors, a validity problem exists, and you should adjust the interviewing techniques to secure more accurate information. Interviewing children suspected of being victims of sexual abuse is an example of an area where concerns about validity and reliability of data collection techniques have surfaced. Separation of a child from familiar settings and support systems, repeated interviewing, and leading questions may result in reports to please the interviewer rather than accurate accounts of what took place. One responsibility of the social worker is to create a climate in which the applicant is able to share valid and reliable information.

Discipline and Spontaneity We regard interviewing as a disciplined art. But does discipline interfere with spontaneity? Will learning interviewing techniques make you mechanical and inhuman? We think not. Learning interviewing techniques will increase your spontaneity for two reasons. First, in the process of learning about interviewing, you become aware of and able to deal with barriers to communication in your usual responses to people. Second, interviewing techniques expand the repertoire of responses available to you. The increased repertoire permits increased spontaneity because you are not locked into an earlier limited set of responses. Alfred Kadushin (1972, p. 2) expresses this point eloquently:

> The interviewer should, of course, be the master of the techniques rather than the obedient servant bound by rules. Technical skill is not antithetical to spontaneity. In fact, it permits a higher form of spontaneity; the skilled interviewer can deliberately violate the techniques as the occasion demands. Technical skill frees the interviewer in responding as a human being to the interviewee. Errors in relation to technique lie with rigid, and therefore inappropriate, application. A good knowledge of techniques makes the interviewer aware of a greater variety of alternatives. Awareness and command of technical knowledge also has another advantage. To know is to be prepared; to be prepared is to experience reduced anxiety; to reduce anxiety is to increase the interviewer's freedom to be fully responsive to the interviewee.

In Chapter 8 we noted that the graceful figure skater could not become spontaneous and free without many hours of disciplined practice. So it is with interviewing. Spontaneity and freedom do not come naturally but with discipline, with practice, and with learning.

The next section considers some potential barriers to communication—barriers that will affect the validity and reliability of data. In subsequent sections the role of the interviewer will be analyzed and suggestions offered that will help you to increase the probability of securing valid and reliable data.

Barriers to Communication

Barriers to communication may occur at any phase in the communication process—encoding, transmitting, receiving, decoding, and checkout. Many of these barriers are obvious—inability to conceptualize and use symbols (encoding problems); speech impediments, hearing or receptor impediments, failure to understand the concepts received (decoding problems), and environmental influences (noise that interferes with the messages or prevents them from traveling clearly from the transmitter to the receiver). These barriers are real and are of concern to you as you collect reliable and valid data on which to base decisions. But these barriers are also reasonably obvious sources of error in communications. In this section we will consider a series of subtler, less obvious, but equally serious barriers to communication that will affect the validity and reliability of the data on which intervention decisions are based. Five worker barriers in addition to the barrier of client resistance will be considered. Approaches on the part of the worker that may serve as barriers to the collection of valid and reliable data include anticipation of the other, the assumption of meaning, confusion of purpose, the urge to change, and inattentiveness.

Anticipating the Other   Carl Rogers (1968) describes how he dislikes himself when he anticipates the other:

> But what I really dislike in myself is when I can't hear the other person because I'm so sure in advance what the other is going to say that I don't listen because it is afterwards that I realize I have only heard what I have already decided the other is saying. I have failed really to listen at those times when I can't hear because what the other is saying is too threatening, because it might make me change my ideas and my behavior.

Cormican (1978) is referring to the same problem when he speaks of diagnostic labels or categories interfering with communication. These labels may result in preconceived notions of what a client is like; preconceived ideas may result in anticipating the client rather than listening and observing carefully. Stereotyping can be very subtle. After experience with several similar applicants, you may note similarities on the basis of which you begin to develop a stereotype of that particular kind of person. The stereotype then interferes with your perception of new applicants and may serve to block out communications inconsistent with the stereotype. Anticipation of the other occurs when one permits an existing stereotype to shape and distort the current communication. And these are not just the stereotypes we all carry into our practices. We may develop stereotypes from our own practice experience or that of our agencies.

Consider that you have recently begun work with an agency and have been asked to provide service to the family whose agency record contains the summary found in

EXHIBIT 9-4 Stereotypes and a Case Summary	The family has been known to the agency for the past 15 years on the basis of 13 applications, mainly because of nonsupport of husband or his jailing. Family consists of Mr. Shasta (age 32), Mrs. Shasta (age 27), and six children. Mr. Shasta has been in and out of court since young boy due to delinquent and antisocial behavior. He received a dishonorable discharge from army. In last few years his drinking has increased to near alcoholism. Mrs. Shasta came from family also long known to agency. She married Mr. Shasta at age 17 to escape an alcoholic father. Recurring pregnancies, health trouble, and abuse by her husband have left her in poor shape to cope with him, let alone child rearing and managing the home. The case is looked on by staff as one of the most unpleasant in the agency because of several incidents of fraud, continued misuse of funds, and Mr. Shasta's refusal to seek and keep work. Mr. Shasta is avoided by workers as much as possible due to his violent temper and drinking. Returning him to employment is seen as hopeless; he has quit or been fired from at least 20 jobs. Mr. Shasta's behavior after drinking seems to affect his disposition toward looking for work and toward his wife and children. Adequacy of child care is a concern with reports that the mother neglects her children. Neighbors have reported that the father beats children when drunk while Mrs. Shasta tries to protect them. Health problems of mother and children are an ongoing issue, but the family is indifferent to need for medical care.

Exhibit 9-4. This summary creates powerful images that will affect interpretation of communications received from the Shasta family. The fact that background information may affect your perception does not mean that you should not consider background information or receive transfer summaries within an agency. We want you to be aware, however, that this information may influence your perception. Thus you must compensate by consciously listening to the client or applicant and work at avoiding anticipation of what he or she may be saying. The summary is only a description of certain discrete behaviors of Mr. and Mrs. Shasta; without additional data you will not know enough about the situation to make inferences about the meaning of the behavior for the Shastas.

Assumption of Meaning The assumption of meaning, a second worker barrier to communication, occurs when you receive an ambiguous message, fail to check out meaning with the applicant, and proceed according to a meaning that you have read into the message. The words themselves may be ambiguous, the way in which they are uttered may convey unclear feelings or thoughts, or the applicant's behavior may be communicating messages inconsistent with the words. In all of these situations checkout of the meaning with the applicant may prevent you from making erroneous assumptions and using invalid and unreliable data. An example of assumption of meaning occurs in this brief excerpt from an interview with a respondent—a 16-year-old boy on parole.

> I asked how things had gone this past week. He looked at me with a grin and said, "Fine." He added that he had not done anything. During this time he kept leafing through the magazine and pointed out someone's picture to me. At this point I told him that we were here to talk and that he should put the magazine away. It is very obvious that this boy knows very little or at least practices few of the common courtesies of everyday living.

This worker assumed from the boy's grin and his leafing through the magazine that he was trying to avoid entering into conversation. The worker, however, erroneously acted on this assumption without first checking it out with the youngster. A few minutes taken to ask the boy what it was about the magazine that interested him or to make a more direct checkout—"I get the message that you are not too interested in talking with me now"—might have clarified the situation and produced a more reliable and valid basis on which to act.

Failure to Make Purpose Explicit   Failure on the part of the worker to make explicit the purpose of an interview may lead to a condition in which the worker and client hold differing, perhaps contradictory, purposes. Given such confusion of purpose, both client and worker will then interpret their own and each other's communications in light of their particular understanding of the objective of the interview. As these subtle distortions continue, the client and the worker will be going in two entirely different directions. Exhibit 9-5 is an example of what happens when purpose is not clarified. Had the social worker started with the purpose of determining how the hospital bill would be met and then moved to the resource most people have—health insurance—the interview could have proceeded without the many uncomfortable feelings that were raised by the indirect questions.

Exhibit 9-6 provides another example of this problem. The client says clearly that he has come to pay his taxes, but the practitioner is concerned about his health. It takes several questions before the worker understands the importance of responding to the client's concerns.

Prematurely Engaging Applicants in Change Activities   One of the more serious barriers to communication arises from prematurely engaging clients in change activities. This is a very easy pitfall for the social worker. Change is a common word in the profession; we are committed to being change agents, both to improve the conditions of the community and to assist individuals to use the resources of the community more effectively. Difficulties occur, however, when change efforts are attempted without sufficient data on which to base an assessment of the problem. Although change may occur through any human interaction, effecting change is not the primary purpose of the data collection interview. Change efforts should be based on valid and reliable data and on a considered decision of the applicant and worker to engage in such efforts. The purpose of the data collection interview is to gather the information on which decisions about intervention can be based. To urge change at this early stage may create a barrier to communication—a barrier that limits the availability of important information that could influence decision making. A secondary problem is that change efforts in these early contacts frequently take the form of directive approaches—such as persuasion and advising—that are seldom effective until a high degree of trust has been developed. When used prematurely, directive approaches create barriers to continuing communication. And it is the process of continuing communication that provides opportunities for the development of increased trust.

Worker Inattentiveness   A potent barrier to communication is inattentiveness. If your mind wanders during an interview or if you are thinking about other clients or planning future activities, you create a barrier for continued applicant-worker communication. Applicants can reasonably expect you to give undivided attention to their present communications; you have the responsibility for establishing a time

EXHIBIT 9-5
Failure to Make
the Purpose for
the Interview
Explicit

Mr. Johnson approached my desk with a worried expression on his face and told me the nurse had said that I wanted to see him. I asked him his name and to be seated. A quick glance at my list of admissions helped me determine that this was Mr. Johnson's first experience of being interviewed at our hospital. He was very worried about his wife's illness and his apprehensiveness of the interview was apparent in his remark that he was "on the stand." I tried to put him at ease and had no difficulty with simple matters such as names, address, and occupation. The interview was frequently interrupted by numerous phone calls. It was apparent Mr. Johnson was becoming restless. He began to fidget uncomfortably and asked for permission to smoke, which unfortunately I had to deny because the office is in a posted area. This incident was unluckily timed with one of the main purposes of the interview, which was to secure financial information to aid in classifying the patient. From a previous question about the patient's address, I had learned that Mr. Johnson was a farmer. I had a regular form to follow in taking the necessary information, but because of Mr. Johnson's previous attitude toward the interview, I decided to change the order of the questions and try to keep him in a better mood. I asked Mr. Johnson how many acres he was farming. He answered 420, but he only owned 160 and rented the rest. I told Mr. Johnson that this was about the size of the farm on which I had spent my youth. Mr. Johnson seemed to become a little more friendly after this. Instead of asking him what he thought his net income for one year usually averaged, I asked him what he usually raised on his farm. He replied, "corn, usual small grain, beans, some pigs and sheep and quite a few milk cows." I asked if he sold much cream, he answered, "It depends. If the cows are dry, I don't make anything, but when they come in I usually get several hundred a month from cream." We were beginning to become more accustomed to each other, so I asked if he kept a checking account. "Yes," he replied, "at the State Bank at home." I asked if he also kept a savings account at the same bank. He replied, "No." I then asked if he could tell me approximately how much he kept in his checking account. He answered, "Several hundred." I was not succeeding in getting a direct figure so I found it necessary to ask what he thought his net income for one year averaged. He replied, "Between six and seven thousand." I asked if he had a mortgage on the farm. He replied, "No, it's clear." The discrepancy in figures confused me, so I asked if he was saving money in another form other than using a savings account. He said he did not believe in banking money except for the convenience of paying bills. He had lost some money when the banks closed during the Depression and now he was putting his money in bonds and had bought some houses in town. It was becoming clear that Mr. Johnson would not need any help in financing his wife's hospital bill. For the matter of records, I completed the financial interview. Mr. Johnson was not too pleased with answering the question as to what kind of car he drove. After some hesitation he finally said, "a new Buick." I asked if he carried any life insurance. "Enough to bury me," he replied. "How about bills?" I asked. "You have any?" Mr. Johnson beamed and he proudly answered, "Not a one, I pay cash." I asked what his additional income other than the farm averaged. "A couple hundred a month from rent of the houses in town. Guess that's about it." He brightened as he suddenly remembered something and proudly announced that he had taken out hospital insurance through the Farm Bureau and was glad that they had to pay him for a change, but that it was too bad that somebody had to get sick before you could use it. I explained the advantages of the insurance to him and told him that because of it we would not require a deposit against his wife's hospital bill. Instead, we wanted him to sign over the insurance to the hospital and when they had paid us after his wife's discharge, we would bill him for the remaining bill, if there was any. He thought this was very fair and signed the necessary papers.

EXHIBIT 9-6
Failure to
Respond to
Clients'
Concerns

Miss C, the medical welfare consultant from State Office, was here studying records for material to use in teaching a class of medical students at the university medical school. She saw Mr. Allen waiting in the reception room and asked worker about the growth on his head. I was surprised, having seen Mr. Allen a few months ago and there was nothing wrong with his head at that time. When Mr. Allen came into the office, worker was completely surprised at the growth. Actually, Mr. Allen gave the appearance of having two heads, one on top of the other. I asked about it and Mr. Allen said that it had just started, but that wasn't what he had come to see worker about. He came because he wanted to pay his taxes. He said he had saved some money out of his grant, and with the extra $5 this month, he had settled with the tax offices. He declared Mrs. Allen still wouldn't pay taxes, but he was going to. Worker told him we would budget the entire tax bill in his grant, and that he would receive a $4 raise or a total of $37. Worker again asked about his head. He had been told that when he was a baby he had fallen off the bed, and has had a small knot since. He said he wanted to keep his taxes current, and would never again be talked out of paying them. Worker assured him his taxes would be included in the future in his grant alone because I knew of Mrs. Allen's attitude. Worker wanted to know when this knot had started growing. Mr. Allen said it suddenly started getting bigger about two months ago. Before getting a breath he started talking about taxes again. He must have had a hard time saving enough money to pay up. He said they settled for $18, and he had a "clean slate." He told of how he had done without his newspaper, hadn't been running his fans much nor watering his flowers as he should. I remarked I wished he had come to us sooner, but now that the taxes were paid, and the future ones budgeted, suppose we talk about his head. What had he done for it? He replied he had not done anything, and again changed the subject to taxes. I told him I noticed each time I mentioned his head, he changed the subject to taxes. It made me wonder if he didn't want to talk about his head, or if there was some connection with his head and taxes. He looked surprised, and then slowly, as if explaining to a child, said, "Long ago the doctors told me if this ever started growing in a hurry I would have to have it cut off. I am 77 years old and may or may not get out of that operating room. If I die, my wife can live on her old age pension if she has a home; if not, she can't. So, I have to get those taxes paid before I go to a hospital or even see a doctor."

frame that will enable you to attend to other matters that require attention without diverting attention from the interview of the moment. But even the most experienced workers will have moments when thoughts wander and attentiveness wanes. M. Ellen Walsh, in Reading 13-4, recommends owning up to these lapses:

> Should a client's storytelling send a therapist into a couple of minutes of personal reflection, it is recommended that he or she admit this interruption to the client. For example, "Excuse me, Frank. What you were saying made me think of something else that's going on, and I haven't been paying close attention for a minute, here. Can you go over that again? I was with you up to the point where you said Jan had no business interfering with the kids." Despite most therapists' fears of revealing such incidents, rural clients are probably aware of these lapses anyhow, and the admission wins respect for its honesty and may relieve the client to some degree.

The likelihood of securing reasonably valid and reliable information will be considerably enhanced as you learn to avoid anticipating what the applicant will say, to check out the meanings of the communications received, clarify purposes, avoid attempts at change until the necessary data are available and change decisions can be made jointly, and give all applicants and clients opportunities for undivided attention.

Applicant Resistance   Applicants may also create barriers to communication. These barriers may be thought of as forms of resistance on their part to entering into a problem-solving process. Resistance may be considered as a specialized kind of defense used by the applicant to ward off the worker and to protect the applicant from any discomfort involved in participating in a problem-solving process. Three sources of resistance can be distinguished. First, resistance may stem from the usual discomfort of dealing with a strange person and situation. This is the normal anxiety and discomfort with which many of us approach new situations. Second, resistance may stem from cultural and subcultural norms regarding involvement with service agencies and asking for help. Norman Johnston (1956), for example, identifies a number of variables in the prison milieu that contribute to distortion and deception in the communications between inmates and prison counselors. Because of cultural norms some persons may find it particularly difficult to admit the existence of a problem and to seek a solution. Agencies may exacerbate cultural differences by establishing procedures that intensify the discomfort of persons of some cultural backgrounds. An agency emphasis on scheduled appointments and office visits, for example, may aggravate the resistance of clients from lower socioeconomic groups and hamper their ability to use more traditional social service agencies. Renate Frankenstein (1982) notes that what is often recorded as resistance on the part of families should also be examined in terms of agency practices and worker expectations that may inhibit establishing communication with troubled families. Third, some applicants may be securing a degree of gratification from their problems. This type of involvement with a problem is a serious source of resistance, interferes with the client's ability to communicate, reduces self-determination, and makes seeking a solution more difficult.

What is your responsibility in relation to applicant resistance? To facilitate communication, you may have to help the applicant identify and deal with any of these obstacles to communication. Dealing with obstacles to communication will become a necessary preliminary goal before you and the applicant can move into any other problem-solving work. Dealing with resistance is one manifestation of the second task conceptualized by Schwartz: "detecting and challenging the obstacles which obscure the common ground" (Schwartz, 1961, p. 157).

Worker Responsibilities   **Creating a Productive Climate**   Your responsibilities for the data collection interview can be considered in three interrelated areas. First, you are responsible for creating a productive climate in which the applicant can comfortably share thoughts, feelings, and perceptions necessary for intervention decisions. The climate will help you secure valid and reliable data. The creation of such a climate involves your skill in avoiding the barriers to communication noted earlier and in helping applicants to deal with the obstacles to communication presented by their own resistances. Jane Gilgun, in Reading 9-2, suggests some techniques available to researchers to create a noncoercive climate in which both victims and perpetrators of child sexual assault will be able to share sensitive data with a researcher. You and the applicant are also engaged in research as you collect data for assessment and intervention planning; the suggestions offered by Gilgun will be useful to you in your practice.

The creation of a productive climate for participation may be construed as the development of a helping relationship. In Chapter 8 we referred to relationship as a climate or an atmosphere and noted that relationship is not the end of service but a stepping-stone toward the provision of problem solving service for the client. One way to operationalize the concept of relationship is as a climate or milieu that is characterized by open and oral communications. Thus the presence of relationship may be inferred from the extent to which communications are open and oral. Creating this kind of climate is a responsibility of the worker.

Creating a productive climate means asking questions in a manner that motivates and encourages applicant or client participation. Your own participation may be at a minimum. We've noted that failure to make the purpose explicit may be a barrier to communication, but purpose can also be stated in a way that inhibits communication. Consider whether this example of the beginning of the first interview conducted by a social work parole officer with a boy at a state institution was likely to encourage or inhibit participation by the respondent.

> I introduced myself to David, and he shyly acknowledged the introduction. I asked him to sit down and I sat across from him, where I proceeded to interpret my role and my interest in working with him and his family. I told him that I knew what the reason was for his being at the training school and that I was there to begin planning with him for his return home. I also indicated to David that I would be talking to him and his parents to help them with any problems that they may have. I also related to David that I had seen his mother and that I planned to see both his mother and father as soon as possible. At the beginning he had come into the office looking very apprehensive and seemed to maintain an air of cockiness about him. I also had the impression that David viewed me with suspicion.

This lengthy explanation probably didn't allay the suspicion! Short, straightforward statements can set the purpose and also invite participation. In this example, something like "I'm Mr. Smith, the parole officer who will be working with you to develop a parole plan. What ideas do you have about that?" would have been a better way to create a climate in which the youth would be comfortable participating.

Providing a Focus   A second responsibility of the worker is to provide a focus for the interview. This occurs when the worker establishes a purpose for the interview very early and focuses the interactions in relation to the purpose. Tangents should be avoided; questions that lead into extraneous areas are not helpful. When pursuing what the applicant has said, you should pick up on areas related to the interview's central focus. Focusing the interview does not mean dictating the purpose, nor does it mean cutting off the applicant. It does mean jointly establishing with the applicant a particular purpose for an interview and fulfilling the responsibility of maintaining that focus. Material brought out in a particular interview may suggest a purpose and focus for subsequent interviews. You may deliberately not respond to this material initially but may bring it up later. Aaron Rosen and Dina Lieberman (1972, p. 398) report on an experimental study of the extent to which workers' responses are content relevant—"the extent to which the content of an interactive response is perceived by a participant to be relevant and in agreement with the participant's own definition and expectations of the content to be dealt with in the treatment relationship." With compliant clients, workers with more training did significantly better at maintaining content relevance. Workers with less training had more content-relevant responses with aggressive clients; however, many of the responses were harsh and retaliatory and ineffective in promoting communications. Rosen and Lieberman (1972, pp. 410–411) suggest that their findings point to the need for clear worker and client orientation about the purpose of the interview.

Separating the Levels of Responses   A third responsibility of the worker is to separate and identify the applicant's levels of response. Responses are typically on one of four levels—perceptual, cognitive, affective, and behavioral. The *perceptual level* of response refers to interactions and communications around what the applicant perceives or has perceived. What was seen and heard? The *cognitive level* refers to interactions and communications around what the applicant thinks. What meaning is ascribed to what was seen and heard? The *feeling,* or *affective, level* refers to interactions and communications around the feelings that were generated in applicants by either their perceptions or their cognitions. How does the applicant feel about what was thought or about what was seen and heard? And the *behavioral level* refers to interactions and communications around the client's past or anticipated behavior. How did the client behave and how might the client behave in relation to what was and will be seen and heard? You may interact with applicants at all these levels. For data collection, however, a thorough exploration of the perceptual and cognitive levels is necessary before moving into the feeling and behavioral levels.

Perhaps an example will clarify this responsibility. Put yourself in the position of the worker who is interviewing a 16-year-old boy who has frequent arguments with his father and who angrily left the house following an argument and drove off in a neighbor's car. In discussing the situation the youth will probably initiate the conversation on the cognitive level with some comment to the effect that he and his dad do not get along, that his dad does not understand him, or that his dad is unfair. These are all cognitive statements; they reflect a meaning or interpretation that the youth has placed on perceived events. A frequent interviewing error is simply to accept the meaning that the applicant has reported and to move immediately into the areas of feelings and behavior. A careful exploration with this boy of his perceptions of the events that led to the interpretation that he and his father do not get along will be very useful. What took place? What did the boy see and hear? What did his father say? What did the boy say? What happened then? After exploring the incident in detail, the boy and the worker are both prepared to consider alternative interpretations of the events. After moving back to the perceptual level (What did you see and hear?) and reconsidering the cognitive level (What meanings do you ascribe to what you saw and heard?), the youth and worker may move to the question of feelings: What did you feel when this was occurring? Do I detect a note of anger still in your voice? As you look back on it now, what kinds of reactions are you having? From the feeling level, the next logical step is to behavior: What did you do when this happened? As you look back, what might have been other ways of handling yourself? In view of such experiences, if you and your father have future arguments, what are ways in which you think you might behave? Before moving into a consideration of the applicant's feelings and behavior, considerable effort is expended to collect an account of the incidents that occurred and the interpretation of those incidents. Failure to explore the perceptual and cognitive levels in detail may lead to very incomplete data with which to engage the applicant in problem-solving plans.

To sum up, you have three primary responsibilities in the interview—creating a productive climate, focusing the interview, and separating and clarifying levels of response. While the purpose of this chapter is not to offer a bag of tricks or to deal at any length with interviewing techniques, a few suggestions may help you to make a start in building a repertoire of interviewing skills for creating a productive climate, focusing the interview, and separating levels of response.

Some Ideas about Technique

Open-ended Questions Open-ended questions are useful, especially in early phases of an interview. An open-ended question is one that cannot be answered yes or no; rather, it is one that requires an essay-type answer. Questions such as "Tell me a little about yourself" and "What would you like us to do?" are open ended. Open-ended questions are good questions to start with because they allow applicants considerable leeway in beginning where they wish. If an applicant fumbles, you can come back with a more focused question. An interview can be thought of as a funnel—starting with broad, open-ended questions that become much more specific and focused as you and the applicant narrow in on specific areas of concern. Consider the difficulty encountered by a student who was interviewing a social worker to learn what the worker found to be the difficult parts of social work.

> Following a brief statement by me concerning the purpose of the interview and an agreement by both of us concerning a time limit, I asked my first real question. "Do you view your work as 'social work?'"
>
> In response, Joan asked, "What is your definition of social work?" I replied that rather than define social work at this point I would prefer to learn more about the work that she is doing and perhaps at some time in another interview we could approach the topic of social work as it relates to her work. At this point in the interview I felt briefly that our roles in the interview situation had been reversed.

How might you have started this interview with an open-ended question that would both have invited participation and focused in relation to the purpose?

Probing You will become adept at probing for additional information as you work to secure data on which to base interventive decisions. Probing may be an unfortunate word—the intent is not to indicate an abrasiveness or harshness but rather an invitation to pursue a particular area. Questions such as "Can you tell me more about that?" and "I'd like to hear a little more in this area" are both open ended and probing inasmuch as they are related to something the applicant has said and are asking for more information. Exhibit 9-7 provides a number of probing questions that are nonabrasive and that invite applicants to continue to express themselves while enabling you to give direction to the interview.

Avoid Biasing Questions The data collection interview requires that the worker maintain neutrality and carefully avoid biasing questions. While people may joke about the "You do love your wife, don't you?" kind of question, biases creep in in subtler ways. Barry Cournoyer, in Reading 9-1, cautions:

> When asking questions, be aware that some questions reflect an implied suggestion or judgment. For example, you might seek expression from a group member by asking, "John, have you told your mother yet?" Such a question may be intended as a simple

EXHIBIT 9-7
Interviewing
Responses

The hypothetical situation I will use is one you will meet many times as a counselor. A client will say, "I don't get along with my parents." Here are numerous responses which can be used to fulfill the two important requirements of interviewing: (1) allowing the client to express feelings, and (2) helping you to direct the interview.

You don't get along with your parents.
Your parents?
What do you mean when you say . . .
I don't understand what you mean when you say . . .
Help me understand what you mean . . .
Give me an example of how you . . .
Tell me more about this.
Uh-huh. -and -For instance? -Go on. Oh? -but -I see.
When did you first notice that . . .
How do you feel about this? (Perhaps the most important question one could ask.)
What are some of the things you and your parents disagree about?
What are some problems kids like you have—not just you but all kids in general?
What are your parents like? What is your dad like? What is your mom like? (General questions.)
You seem to be very upset about this.
You look worried (or you look unhappy).
(Avoid asking a question which calls for a yes or no answer.)
(Just be silent. A word about silence: In patients and particularly in adolescents, silence tends to provoke anxiety. Silence generally loses its effect if too prolonged.)
You say you have trouble getting along with your parents. What are some of your troubles?
Perhaps you could share some of your ideas about what has caused these problems. (It probably never helps to ask the question why. If they knew why they were having trouble with their parents, they wouldn't be seeing you.)
Maybe it would help to talk about this.
Compared to you, what type of people are your parents?
If your parents were here, what would *they say about this problem?*

SOURCE: Dr. Richard J. Bealka, psychiatrist, Mental Health Institute, Independence, Iowa.

request for information. However, for John it may represent a suggestion that he should tell his mother and that if he doesn't you will be critical or disappointed.

One must be cautious about both the wording of questions and the way in which they are asked. Tone of voice and nonverbal communications can betray bias as easily as can a loaded question. The requirement of neutrality does not negate earlier remarks about worker input. The purpose of the data collection interview, however, is to secure reliable and valid information about the applicant's perceptions and interpretations of experiences; your input at this stage would have a biasing effect and should be avoided. First learn the applicant's position and thinking, and then you may consider offering your own experience to the applicant. The sharing of your input comes when various intervention strategies are under consideration.

Feedback Throughout this chapter frequent references have been made to checkout, or feedback. Checkout requires the use of feedback in which you consciously and deliberately reflect to the applicant what you are perceiving to determine whether the communication is correct. "This is what I hear you saying." "I seem to be hearing this." "I see you're doing this." "Am I understanding what you are saying is this?" These are all feedback probes and are an effort to refer to the applicant what you are hearing to allow for correction of errors in meaning. Feedback is a useful and necessary technique for clarifying communications. This type of active listening may sometimes seem awkward because this technique is seldom used in everyday conversation. But reflecting to the applicant what is seen and heard can avoid both pitfalls and misunderstandings and also serves the function of encouraging the applicant to pursue conversation in a particular area. Rosen and Lieberman (1972, p. 398) examined the use of feedback among workers with different levels of training. They used the concept of stimulus-response-congruence—"the extent to which a response by one participant in the relationship provides feedback to the other participant that the message sent was actually received." Rosen and Lieberman found that trained workers maintained a higher rate of congruent responses than untrained workers (p. 409). This finding suggests that the use of feedback is a skill acquired by training and thus helps explain awkwardness with its initial use.

Avoid Asking Why   One final suggestion for enhancing communications is to avoid asking why. Why is a frequently used word in our language. But the why question is defense producing—it is a question that asks a person to explain her or his own behavior. You will not usually be interested in asking people to explain their behavior. Rather, you will want to ask them to describe the situation in which they are behaving and to explore alternative ways of interpreting and reacting to that situation. Such questions as What was happening then? What seemed to be going on? Can you tell me what you were doing? and What seemed to be the nature of the situation? are more productive than asking why when attempting to elicit material that can be used constructively with the applicant and client in problem solving.

Written Communications

This chapter has been focused on the use of oral communications in an interview setting for data collection purposes. You will make extensive use of this type of communication. But we must not negate the importance of written communication skills. The ability to express ideas clearly and accurately in written form is just as essential to social work practice as interviewing. Your practice will probably require at least four different types of professional writing. You will correspond with clients and other persons you serve, will prepare client records, will prepare reports for colleagues and other agencies, and will carry out your professional ethical obligation to contribute to knowledge building by preparing papers for professional conferences and for publication. Each of these requires you to be able to express your ideas clearly and logically and to avoid the use of jargon.

Correspondence   Typically letters will be mailed to applicants or clients to initiate a contact, reschedule a meeting, or to provide information. Remember in your correspondence that you are working in a partnership arrangement. We suggest that these letters be informal and written in the first and second person, as is this text, in an effort to establish a relatively informal level of communication between reader and writer. Try to avoid jargon and official society phrases. Exhibit 9-8 presents an

EXHIBIT 9-8 A Letter on Behalf of a Client	Here are two versions of a letter written by a social worker to an attorney. Both the social worker and attorney serve the same client. Which version do you prefer? For what reasons? Version 1 Dear Ms. Trojan:

RE: Nesti, James

As per discussion on April 30, 1993, please be advised that the writer has interviewed said youth on Tuesday, May 4, between 10:00 a.m. and 12:30 p.m. at the Youth Center. Another interview was undertaken on the same date from 2:00 p.m. to 3:00 p.m. at 100 Horseshoe Avenue with the parents. All parties have agreed to holding a family group conference and the first available date is Sunday, May 16, 1993 from 2:30 p.m. to 5:30 p.m.

A concern is that the aforementioned conference cannot be held at the parties' first choice, which is their residence, because once bail is denied there is no provision for writer to escort the youth from the Youth Center to the location proposed for the family group conference. Therefore, arrangements for the family group conference will have to be made for same date and time at the Youth Center. There are no foreseen difficulties with such arrangements.

The people who have agreed to participate in the family group conference are parents, siblings, sister-in-law, other extended family members, previous teacher and a counsellor, Aboriginal Community Elders, and possibly victims (in either case victim impact reports will be available).

The agenda for the family group conference is as follows:

a) open circle session with pipe ceremony
b) the youth disclosing circumstances with the offence; and
c) family group conference members determining recommendations for disposition.

Trusting this is in order, and please confirm whether as Counsel you are able to attend.

Sincerely,

Social Worker

(continued)

example of a letter sent to a person by a social worker; the formal tone of this letter, which may reflect the nature of the agency, is officious and does not contribute much to developing a cooperative working relationship. Exhibit 9-8 also contains another version of the letter. We suggest that you compare and contrast these two styles and try to move your own correspondence toward the style of the alternate version.

Maintaining Case Records   A number of approaches to case recording have developed, including client-focused recording described by Tebb in Reading 2-2.

Case recording is done for a number of reasons—to provide a record of services, to document progress toward accomplishing service goals, and for use in supervision and consultation. The format to be used for case recording will vary from agency to agency, and you will very early become familiar with the format used in your agency.

**EXHIBIT 9-8
(continued)**

Version 2

Dear Ms. Trojan:

RE: Nesti, James

I interviewed James on Tuesday, May 4 at the Youth Center, and later that day also visited his parents at their home. James and his parents have agreed to a family group conference and one is scheduled for May 16, from 2:30 p.m. to 5:30 p.m.

We are concerned that the conference cannot be held at the Nesti home because there is no provision for me to escort James from the Youth Center to his home.

We expect participants in the family group conference to include James, both parents, siblings, a sister-in-law, other extended family members, a previous teacher and counsellor, Aboriginal Community Elders, and possibly victims (in either case victim impact reports will be available).

The agenda for the family group conference is:

a) open circle session with pipe ceremony
b) James disclosing circumstances with the offence; and
c) family group conference members determining recommendations for disposition.

Please also confirm whether you are able to attend.

Sincerely,

Social Worker

John Goldmier provides a helpful summary of social work recording in Exhibit 9-9. We want to offer these few additional suggestions regarding recording.

1. Retain a record of dates and types of contacts.
2. Keep the record focused on the purpose for the contacts and intervention and avoid extraneous materials.
3. Record facts and observations and avoid generalizations, especially unsupported generalizations.
4. Assessment material in which you and your client provide meaning to the facts and observations you have been collecting should be clearly labeled as such.
5. Avoid the problem of just recording negatives and be sure that the positive observations and facts are also included.

Reports You will also be expected to write reports about your clients. These may be to provide referral information to other agencies, to provide a transfer or closing summary, or simply to provide periodic summaries of the case records as required by your agency policy. We also encourage you to write reports in a way that avoids jargon, presents factual information without undue generalization, and clearly labels opinions as such. B. Cohen (1986) argues that the traditional chronological record is not consistent with modern practice and that content should be organized topically, presented in the present tense, using a systematic presentation of observations, being

EXHIBIT 9-9 Social Work Recording	**WHY RECORD?** In all contacts with clients, their families and community resources, it is necessary to record what took place so that (1) the worker remembers what happened; (2) other people may know; (3) service program and goals may be reviewed; and (4) teaching and learning may occur. Thus, records are for use. **WHAT GOES INTO A RECORD?** A case record, or the account of what the social worker did in a particular case situation, should fit the needs of the case. The purpose of the recording should determine its length and scope. Also, what is written should be geared to those who read it. Good recording is based on factual reporting, good thinking, and sound evaluative judgment. The social worker is not a journalist, but it is pertinent to be guided by the journalistic principals of (1) What? (2) Who? (3) Where? (4) When? (5) How? and (6) Why? Most difficult of these questions to answer is the question why. Here it is wise to heed the researcher's dictum not to go beyond data, that is, to support one's speculations with at least some facts that lend support to one's thinking. **THE FORMS OF RECORDING** There are three major forms of recording: (1) narrative, (2) summary, and (3) assessment and evaluative. **Narrative** Narrative recording, also sometimes known as process recording, is used when it is necessary to report as many facts as one can remember. For example, the worker may need to record particular situations or transactions that were so important that others, including a supervisor, psychiatrist, or the worker, need all the information possible to evaluate a situation. A narrative recording may also be used when it is important to understand the process or content of the interview in order to make sense of the interaction and better to understand the dynamics of the situation. Narrative recordings are useful tools for learning, especially early in the worker's career. They may, however, also be wasteful of the worker's time, the secretary's time, and the supervisor's time if done routinely, mechanically, and without a specific purpose. Thus narrative recording in social work practice should be used sparingly. Workers sometimes find it helpful to record an interview in narrative form so as to help them become more aware of the interaction. For most ongoing treatment situations summary recording may be the preferred tool. **Summary** There are several types of summary recordings, including intake summaries, discharge summaries, transfer or closing summaries, and block summaries.

(continued)

honest about uncertainty in sources of information, and being clear about the purpose for the report.

Conference Papers and Writing for Publication   We hope that you will take seriously your ethical obligation to contribute to the knowledge base of the profession by presenting materials at professional conferences and submitting materials for publication. Writing for publication is quite different from the other types of professional writing you will do. Generally it will be more formal and in the third person, will involve a review of the literature presented in summary form, will include presenta-

**EXHIBIT 9-9
(continued)**

1. Intake summaries are to capture the essence of what brought the client to the agency. They should be clear about the nature of the presenting problem and what is asked of the agency. Agencies usually find it advantageous to use an outline to guide the worker in this phase. It is not possible and necessary to have a complete biography or family chronology in the first interview. However, a foundation for future work with the client should be laid, with focus on the problem and what can be done about it.

2. Discharge summaries put the discharge plan in writing. This is done so that there can be no misunderstanding about the situation upon discharge and what interventions are planned for the future. The discharge summary should be geared to the prospects of the case and should spell out at least some of the factors that led to the discharge plan.

3. Transfer or closing summaries state why a case was closed or transferred, review briefly what was accomplished, and say what remains to be done by the client with or without further help. The nature of the closing contract, that is, how it was fulfilled and what the client's understanding is, should be specified. In all discharge, transfer, and closing summaries it is necessary to summarize what went on during the social work contact, why the case was closed, and what the closing or transfer arrangements were.

4. A block summary is a means for the worker to capture the essence of contacts over time and encapsulate it in one summarized recording. How often such block summaries should be done, especially when there may have been little contact or when a situation has changed little over the months, depends on the nature of the case. A worker who has contacts with a client but allows months to go by without recording may erroneously create the impression that a case situation has been completely dormant during that time. Block recording is a useful way to avoid time-consuming narrative recordings. Block recordings can be interspersed with narratives of particularly important transactions.

Assessment and Evaluative Statements

In a sense all recordings contain elements of judgment, perception, and applications of knowledge. All recordings, except transcriptions from tapes, are therefore impressionistic in one way or another. When the worker uses adjectives and adverbs, he or she is making evaluative comments. This is all to the good. What is asked, however, is that the worker provide evidence for the thinking. Often it is helpful to include a brief paragraph entirely devoted to an impressionistic assessment at the end of a particular recording. It is not necessary to offer a clinical diagnosis, although if the worker is knowledgeable, there is no reason to forgo stating an opinion. Basically, recordings, whatever their form, should at some point encapsulate the worker's impression of how the client looks, feels, thinks, and acts. Inclusion of the worker's own reaction vis-à-vis the client is also appropriate.

SOURCE: John Goldmeier, Professor, School of Social Work and Community Planning, University of Maryland.

tion of case material or other data, and will involve your own analysis or interpretation of the material you present. You will write professionally to share your material and your interpretation of its meaning, not to regurgitate what others have said.

Williams and Hopps (1988) have been encouraging greater involvement in research and publishing by those involved in the day-to-day practice of social work. They believe this necessary to enhance the quality of social work knowledge, and we agree. They offer several suggestions to assist you in the process of getting your work published. There are also other useful guides, including the publication manual of the American Psychological Association which in Chapter 1 we encourage you to secure and use (see Exhibit 1-1).

EXHIBIT 9-10
Some Hints about Preparing Abstracts

An abstract is to provide readers with sufficient information to make decisions about whether or not the publication will be of use in their work or in the case of a conference committee to decide whether or not to invite the writer to prepare a paper. Abstracts are to be both short and specific. Try to avoid general terms which do not convey clear meaning, use as few words as possible, and do not be repetitive.

Here is an example of a poorly written abstract:

> There are a number of dimensions that are common to professions. The author examines the concept of a profession through exploration of literature sources and interviews with persons who consider themselves to be professionals. A group of five particular dimensions are noted. The article discusses five dimensions and arrives at an operational definition of a profession. The author then explores the operability of this definition by applying it to the practice of social work.

Here is another abstract for the same paper:

> A definition of profession is developed by examining five dimensions of the concept—body of knowledge, particular skills and techniques, delivery of service to clients, common culture, and public sanction. Elements of all five dimensions are found in social work, although body of knowledge and skills and techniques may be less apparent than the other dimensions.

How does the second abstract differ from the first? In what way is it more helpful in decision making about reading the entire paper or inviting the author to make a conference presentation?

Developing the skill at preparing abstracts will be important as you think about conference presentations and writing for publication. Unfortunately, this is often overlooked in writing courses. Many students progress through university without having to write abstracts. Typically conference program committees make selections based on abstracts submitted by aspiring authors, and preparing a paper for a conference presentation is quite often the first step toward getting your work ready for publication submission. Exhibit 9-10 presents some material on abstract writing. We suggest you start practicing by preparing abstracts for all of the course papers you are now doing.

Recapitulation   In this chapter we have tried to make a number of points. Interviewing for data collection purposes can be regarded as a set of communications that you use to secure valid and reliable data from an applicant concerning the applicant's perceptions, thinking, feelings, and behavior. The process involves giving, receiving, and checking out meanings. The applicant or client is the primary source of the data from which decisions concerning problem solving are based. Thus, social work interviewing techniques must be considered in terms of whether they contribute to the climate in which an applicant can share reliable and valid data. The reliability and validity of data may be impaired by five worker barriers to communication: (1) anticipation of what the other is going to say, (2) assumptions of meaning about communications from the other, (3) inexplicit purposes for the interview, (4) premature efforts to produce change, and (5) inattentiveness. The quality of the data may also be affected by applicants' resistances stemming from their hesitancy to enter into strange situations, cultural norms affecting the ability to enter into problem solving, and involvement with the problem. We include the "Pain Clinic Evaluation" case in the Appendix. The first part of this reading is an interview between a worker and Mr. H and members of his family. We suggest that you reread the interview, paying particular attention to the worker's questions. How did she create a climate in which Mr. H could participate productively, keep the interview on focus, and secure data on the perceptual and cognitive as well as the affective and behavioral levels? Note also the worker's use of open-ended questions, probing, neutrality, feedback, and her avoidance of why questions.

We have made little explicit mention of problems encountered with communication across cultural or racial barriers. Interracial and intercultural communication places even greater responsibility on you to ensure that messages are being clearly received and transmitted, to be sensitive to cultural differences both in communication patterns and in perceptions of your role, and to become disciplined enough to avoid the worker barriers to communication that have been identified.

A Look Forward

Reading 9-1, by Barry Cournoyer, identifies communication skills for work with groups. When interacting with groups, you will be concerned about your communications with group members as well as the communications among group members. Cournoyer identifies two general forms of communication—empathic and expressive. Empathic communications draw from the client's frame of reference and are attempts to communicate your understanding of the client's expressions. Expressive communications draw from the worker's frame of reference and are efforts to share knowledge, experience, ideas, feelings, and so forth. Cournoyer's analysis and examples are from work with groups. We think his ideas are equally useful for communication with individuals.

Reading 9-2, by Jane Gilgun, presents noncoercive interviewing techniques that she uses in research data collection interviews with victims and perpetrators of child sexual assault. These techniques are useful for interviewing to secure data for practice decisions as well as for research.

In the next chapter we begin a more detailed examination of the problem-solving process that was introduced in Chapter 2. We start by discussing initial contact, data collection, and assessment. You will find interviewing skills necessary for all phases of the problem-solving process.

Reading 9-1   *Basic Communications Skills for Work with Groups**

Barry R. Cournoyer

A well-developed competence in communications skills is essential for all social work practice. When you work directly with client systems of a size larger than one person, proficiency in communications skills is indispensable. Communication with a dyad, a family, or a small group for the purpose of problem solving is an enormously more complex interactional process than communication with an individual client alone. In the group setting you must not only attend to the communications between you and each group member, you must also pay close attention to the communications

* An original article prepared for this text.

between each member and every other member and to communications between you and the group as a whole.

As Schwartz (Shulman, 1984, p. 172) and others have so significantly suggested, the group worker has two clients, the individual and the group. You will be continually shifting focus and redirecting communications from the group to the individual and back again to the group. Accurate reception of so many messages conveyed from so many sources requires an intense observational and listening effort. Similarly, the transmission of messages to the several potential recipients requires that you have well-developed skill in direct and clear communication.

Two general forms of communications have relevance for social work with dyads, families, and small groups. The first form of communication includes skills that may be called empathic. The second form includes skills we may term expressive. The major distinction between the two forms of communications, and it is a distinction of remarkable significance for both the sender and receiver of messages, is that empathic communications from the worker to a client (be it individual or group) derive from the client's frame of reference rather than from the worker's. You attempt to communicate to the client an understanding of the client's expressions. You do not introduce your own thoughts or feelings but rather paraphrase as accurately as possible the client's own message. Expressive communications are significantly different. They derive from the worker's frame of reference and only indirectly, if at all, from the client's. Expressive skills enable you to share knowledge, ideas, experience, feelings, and expectations for the purpose of helping clients "go beyond" where they are likely to progress on their own.

EMPATHIC COMMUNICATION SKILLS

The social work profession has from the time of its inception recognized the importance of empathy. The frequently used phrase "starting where the client is" and the concept of client self-determination reflect an emphasis upon understanding, appreciating, and respecting clients'

feelings, thoughts, and experiences from their own point of view. As Hammond, Hepworth, and Smith (1977, p. 3) have suggested, ". . . empathy is an understanding *with* the client, rather than a diagnostic or evaluative understanding *of* the client."

"It is not an expression of 'feeling for' or 'feeling toward,' as in pity or romantic love. Rather it is a conscious and intentional joining with others in their subjective experience" (Cournoyer, 1991, p. 5). Empathy is probably the single most important quality you must regularly demonstrate in your work with client systems of any size.

Empathic communication skills are responsive or reflective. The content of empathic responses may originate with the nonverbal as well as the verbal expressions of the client. The use of these skills leads clients to feel understood and respected. They tend to encourage clients to explore and express further thoughts, feelings, and experiences that are meaningful to them. They also support the development of the interpersonal rapport so essential to the social work relationship.

Consistent with the group work notion of having two clients, the individual and the group, empathic communications may be directed toward an individual member, one or more subgroups, or the group as a whole. For example, when you observe or hear an individual group member's nonverbal or verbal expression of sadness and say, "Bill, you feel awfully down today," you are utilizing an empathic skill in response to an individual's expression. Of course, even though the empathic communication was directed toward one person, it has an effect upon others in the group and upon the group as a whole.

You can also empathically communicate understanding of the expressions of subgroups or the whole group. You may observe for example, that when Joan begins to talk, most other members cross their arms or legs, change facial expressions, or tilt their heads and eyes downward. You may utilize an empathic communication with the group by saying, "The group seems to be impatient with Joan just now."

Empathic communication occurs through several different specific skills. Each requires that the worker: (1) nonverbally attend, observe, listen, and remember, and (2) communicate accurately what the client expressed.

Nonverbal attending involves assumption of a comfortable open body position, which usually does not include tightly closed hands or crossed arms but does include regular eye contact with the client. In group settings you will periodically make regular eye contact with each member, whether or not they are talking at that moment. Head nods and facial expressions that are congruent with the other's expressions represent further aspects of nonverbal attending. A pleasant, accepting tone of voice that is not too loud or soft is also important. In meetings with groups or families be well aware that disproportionate nonverbal attending to one or more persons is likely to be perceived by the others as taking sides or having favorites. Attending will also involve you in observing the nonverbal behavior of each member as well as listening closely and remembering the verbal expressions of the clients. Observing, listening, and remembering are essential if you are to engage in accurate reflections of what group members have expressed. You may convey your understanding of clients' expressions through the use of these empathic communication skills:

Reflection of content
Reflection of feelings
Reflection of thinking and meaning
Combined reflection
Summarization

Reflection of Content

Reflection of content involves communicating your understanding of the clients' expressions about problems, circumstances, or other aspects of their lives (Carkhuff & Anthony, 1979, pp. 69–72). Frequently you begin by inviting group members to talk about their problems and situations. After someone makes a few statements, you may reflect your understanding of the content. You do this by paraphrasing the message. For example, a group member might share a problem by saying, "I didn't see it coming. She just packed her bags and left without a word. Two weeks ago I received a notification that she is filing for divorce."

Your reflection of the content of the message could be, "She left suddenly without telling you and now she wants to end the marriage."

You may also reflect content expressed by subgroups or the group as a whole. Such a response may begin with, "So the group is saying..." followed by a statement that demonstrates your understanding of a group problem or situation. For example, several members of a group may express their difficulties with meeting at the time and on the days scheduled. You may reflect the content by saying, "The group seems to be saying that meeting at this time on this day of the week presents a real problem."

Reflection of Feeling

Reflection of feeling (Carkhuff & Anthony, 1979, pp. 74–78) involves communicating understanding of the client's verbal and nonverbal expressions of feelings about the problem or situation, other group members, or the worker. A typical reflection of feeling might begin by saying, "You feel..." or, "You're feeling..." followed by a restatement of the feelings expressed by the client. If the reflection is directed toward a particular subgroup or the group as a whole, you may begin by saying, "Johnny and Sue feel..." or, "The group seems to feel..."

For example, following another group member's comments concerning marital infidelity, Jack says, "I'm very ashamed about the affairs I've had throughout my marriage. I don't know how I can make it up to my wife."

You could reflect the feelings by saying, "You're feeling guilty and despondent about the affairs you've had."

Should you observe downcast eyes, slouched body positions, and yawns on the part of a large number of the group members, you might reflect their probable feelings by stating, "The group seems to be tired and perhaps a little bored just now." Frequently feelings expressed by an individual or the group relate to you as a worker. When you reflect these feelings accurately, you enhance the possibility of more complete expression by the group members and a greater level of cohesion and intimacy. When a worker rightly excused a member of a teenage group from a meeting because the youth was obviously intoxicated, the remaining members became silent. They furtively looked at one another and at the worker. The worker reflected the group's feelings by suggesting, "The group seems to be feeling kind of stunned right now. Are you surprised that I would ask one of you to leave?"

Reflection of Thinking and Meaning

Reflection of thinking or meaning (Carkhuff & Anthony, 1979, pp. 72–73) commonly involves communicating an understanding of the thoughts or the meaning that an experience has for a client. A group member might share a beginning description of the problem and situation and perhaps express some of the associated feelings. You may encourage the client to proceed and to explore the thoughts about these experiences by saying, "You think . . ." and then reflect the message as implicitly or explicitly sent by the client. When reflecting messages from the group you may begin with, "Are you (the group members) thinking . . .?" or, "The group seems to mean . . ."

For example, a group member may describe concerns and share feelings such as, "I am really mad at my folks. They want me to get all *A's* in school, to help out at home, and to work part-time too."

This thinking and meaning can be reflected by suggesting, "You think that your parents expect too much of you, that their demands are unreasonable."

In one meeting, following several group sessions in which one person had taken up a disproportionate share of the group's time, other group members began to express their disapproval. This worker may reflect their probable thinking by asking, "Are you thinking it might be time to explore the issue of time-sharing? By time-sharing I'm referring to the process by which we as a group assure that each member has a fair opportunity to speak. Am I on target here? Is that what you're thinking about just now?"

Combined Reflections

Combined reflection involves responding to the client's direct or indirect expression of a mixture of content, feelings, thought, and meaning. Such expressions may reflect the client's view that two or more experiences seem to relate to one another, to occur together, but are not necessarily linked in a causal way. At other times the client may see one experience as the result of or caused by another. When the relationship is associational rather than causal, you may connect the two or more empathic reflections with the word *and, but,* or *yet.* When the relationship is seen by the client as causal, the connecting word changes to *because.* You may, for example, respond to a client's expression by utilizing any of the following combined reflections:

> You have just lost your job *and* you feel devastated, like the world just caved in.
> You feel devastated *because* you lost your job.
> You feel devastated *because* right now you think you will never get another decent job.
> You just lost your job, *and* you think you'll never get another one.

In a group you may, for example, utilize combined reflection by responding to members' expressions in the following ways:

> The group feels annoyed with me just now *because* I carried out my promise to report to the judge any of you who fail the drug screening tests.
> Jean, you're angry with Judy *because* she told you that you should grow up.
> You all feel proud that Julio has progressed so far, *but* since it means that he will be leaving the group, you also feel sad.

Summarization

Summarization (Bertcher, 1979, pp. 105–114) is a reflection by a worker of a number of expressions communicated by one or more of the group members over time. It may involve a single empathic skill such as reflection of content or feeling or reflection of thinking and meaning, but more often it occurs in the form of a combined reflection. A summarization might begin with a statement such as, "You've shared a number of important things here today. Let's see if I can summarize the major ones." You then go on to outline the major expressions. For example, you might summarize a group meeting in the following way:

"We have explored a number of personal experiences and concerns today. Let's see if I have understood the major ones accurately, and maybe I can pull some of them together. Joseph and William are going through divorces and are experiencing feelings of guilt, anger, and loss. Maria's husband has recently died, and this has left her feeling uncertain about the future. She wonders whether she'll be able to make it on her own. Wanda has lost her job and thinks she may never find another one. It seems like all of you in this group are trying to cope with some major changes in your lives, and it's really a struggle to see any bright spots, any hope."

Summarization can contribute to the identification of concerns, issues, and themes that the group members may explore. Especially when used to highlight commonalities among clients' experiences, summarization can aid in the development of group cohesiveness, an important ingredient in successful groups (Yalom, 1985).

EXPRESSIVE COMMUNICATION SKILLS

Expressive communication skills differ from empathic skills in that they involve the worker communicating from his or her own rather than from the client's frame of reference. You will introduce new or extend client-initiated material beyond what the client has actually contributed. When you share knowledge, feelings, perceptions, expectations, judgments, or hypotheses, you are using expressive skills. Use of expressive skills is guided by professional values, knowledge, and experience. In groups a worker most often utilizes group theory, communication theory, role theory, and the values and ethics of the social work profession to guide the use of expressive skills. Expressive skills are worker rather than client generated and as such must be used with sensitivity, care, and respect for the persons for whom they are intended.

The use of expressive communication skills is likely to increase the client's understanding of your view of your role, the purpose of the working relationship, and your expectations of the client.

They are likely to encourage the client to become aware of additional resources and to consider new ways of thinking, feeling, and behaving. They are likely to promote and enhance the interaction between group members. And they tend to equalize the relationship between the client and you as the client learns to perceive you as a genuine human being. The expressive communication skills commonly used in work with groups are these:

Exploration and clarification of roles, purpose, and expectations

Seeking expression from others (probing)

Sharing feelings and experiences (self-disclosure)

Sharing information, knowledge, and opinions (educating)

Focusing

Confrontation

Exploration and Clarification of Roles, Purpose, and Expectations

Perhaps the most fundamentally important of all the expressive skills is the exploration and clarification of roles, purpose, and expectations (Shulman, 1984, pp. 38–39). It is usually the first communication skill demonstrated by social workers, whether the client be an individual or a group. It represents the initial contract for work. In group settings new members typically experience a great deal of ambivalence and anxiety. Members may be asking themselves questions such as, What will this be like? What will the worker do or think of me? Who are these other people? Will they understand my concerns? Will they reject me?

You can alleviate many of these concerns by clearly and directly expressing your view of the general purpose for the group, by clarifying your role in regard to the group's work, and by outlining the expectations you have for the group members. For example, a social worker beginning a group for battered women might initiate the exploration and clarification of roles, purpose and expectations by stating:

Now that we are seated, I'd like to introduce myself and share my view about how we might use these times together. My name is Sue Walker and I'm a social worker here at the counseling center. As I see it, the general purpose for this group is to provide people such as yourselves, who are dealing with aggression and violence in the home, an opportunity to share your problems and concerns with others who are in the same boat. I don't see myself as an expert who listens to your problems and then tells you what you should do. Rather, I see my role as helping you help each other. I'll kind of get things started each time we meet and try to make sure that everybody gets a chance to be heard, and maybe I'll identify some topics or share some of the information that I have about family violence. What I'd like each of you to do in the group is to share your own concerns and experiences with the other members, listen to others express theirs, and then we'll all try to help each other resolve the problems that are presented. How does that sound to you?

Of course, the use of the exploration and clarification skills varies by the particular purpose for each group, the role that the social worker assumes in regard to the group, and the characteristics of group members. Typically clarification of role, purpose, and expectations takes more time with groups than with individuals because these comments may help lessen the greater levels of anxiety and ambivalence that occur in groups. With clients who are more or less forced to participate, the clarification of roles and expectations should be extensive and detailed.

Seeking Expression of Thoughts, Feelings, and Experiences

The communication skill of seeking expression (Bertcher, 1979, pp. 43–53), or probing (Cournoyer, 1991, pp. 146–152), typically occurs through the worker asking questions or making comments that are in effect questions. The regular use of the empathic skills, however, tends to reduce the need to ask questions. After a group has been together for a while, it will usually be possible for you to reduce the number of your questions as group members begin to seek expression from one another. Questions may be open or closed end. Open-end questions tend to lead clients to express themselves in a more lengthy fashion. These are examples of such questions: How did that occur? What were your thoughts? How do you feel? What

did that mean to you? How do you explain that? Closed-end questions lead to short, sometimes even yes or no responses and are likely to yield a great deal of information in a short period of time: How many children do you have? Are you married? When did you move there? Have you ever received counseling services before?

When asking questions, be aware that some questions reflect an implied suggestion or a judgment. For example, you may probe a group member by asking, "John, have you told your mother yet?" Such a question may be intended as a simple request for information. However, for John it may represent a suggestion that he *should* tell his mother and that if he does not you will be disappointed in him.

The seeking expression or probing skill is often routinely used after social workers have used other expressive skills, such as clarifying roles and sharing information. You may seek feedback through such questions as, How does that sound? Does that make sense? I'm wondering what you think and feel about what I've just said.

In problem-solving groups, probes are used not only to encourage members to share personal experiences but also as a means of facilitating group interaction. For example, one group member, Diane, may have been talking about her disappointing experience with men. You may seek expression from another member by asking, "Bill, I wonder if you'd care to share with Diane some of your experiences with women." Other examples of the worker using the seeking expression include "Mary, I'd be interested in your reaction to that," and "Jack, would you like feedback from the group as to how we see you?"

As the group proceeds, you can sometimes become even more directive in promoting interaction. For example, "Jack, would you move over next to Mary and speak directly with her about this?" You can also facilitate interaction by seeking expression from the group as a whole. For example, "I'd like to hear how the group feels toward Jan just now." Usually, as the group develops, you need to facilitate interaction less and less as the members begin to seek and share expressions directly with one another.

Sharing Feelings and Experiences

When you as a social worker appropriately disclose your own feelings and experiences (Hammond, Hepworth, & Smith, 1977, pp. 204–227), you are more likely to be perceived by clients as a genuine, nonmechanical human being. You contribute to interpersonal rapport and mutual understanding when you share your feelings and experiences in nonblaming ways. In so doing, you also model effective interpersonal communication. However, you should be careful not to share so many feelings and experiences that meetings become contexts to work on your own problems. It is difficult for clients to deal with their concerns when they feel a need to take care of you. As a guideline for the sharing of feelings and experiences, you should ask yourself, "Will my self-disclosure support the group's work in relation to its purpose and goals?" If the answer is yes, then you may disclose personal feelings and experiences. However, even when it is determined that the nature of the self-disclosure is professionally advisable, you should express yourself so that you maintain responsibility for your own feelings. Other persons, particularly clients, should not be suggested to be the cause of your feelings. For example, if you were to say to a group member, "You make me feel sad (or angry or protective, and so on)," then you are indicating that the client is responsible for or the cause of your feelings. You are blaming the client for your own feelings. Such a communication is neither personally nor professionally wise. A better expression is, "When I listen to your feelings of loss and sadness, I feel like crying right along with you."

Here are some examples of shared social worker feelings and experiences:

Jim, your feelings about your Vietnam experience really hit home with me. I too was in Nam, and when I came back, I felt more like a foreigner than an American.

I'm feeling uneasy about what just happened here. Judy was talking about her disappointment in us as a support group, and we just seemed to skip over her feelings by going on to a new subject. Judy, when you expressed your feelings, I felt somewhat defensive, you know, like the group isn't meeting your needs and it might be partly my fault. I felt

guilty. I wonder if other group members might have felt guilty too?

Jack, when your voice becomes loud and you point your finger at me, I begin to think that you're angry at me, and then I get mad too.

Yes, I do feel a bit annoyed when you arrive late for the group meetings, and I'd like it better if you were here on time. However, I'd be much more disappointed if you didn't come at all.

Sharing Information, Knowledge, and Opinions

The skill of sharing information (Shulman, 1984, pp. 91–96), or educating (Cournoyer, 1991, pp. 292–297), is a vital one in social work practice. Social workers frequently share information about community programs and services that may represent resources for clients. Social workers provide details about the time and location of meetings, fees, and other information needed by clients. When conducting in-service training or leading educationally oriented groups, social workers regularly share large amounts of information that relate to their teaching function. However, social workers leading problem-solving groups sometimes feel that members must discover certain information on their own. While it is desirable that the group members share information with and learn from one another, often they do not have relevant, accurate, or complete information. If the information is relevant to the purpose for the group and the current work of the group, then you may appropriately provide such data. In fact, in most cases you have a professional responsibility to provide relevant data to clients seeking or needing such information.

In sharing information, however, you should clearly distinguish between fact and opinion, and you should convey the information in such a way that it allows the client to accept or reject the information. When sharing opinions you should qualify your expressions through the use of such phrases as in my opinion or it's my view . . . . You should clearly communicate that the client has every freedom to use or not use and to agree or disagree with the shared information. Here are some examples:

You folks are talking about something here that I know about. The fees for that program are based on a family's ability to pay. The more income a family has, the more services cost, up to a highest fee of $35 per visit.

It's my view that parents are usually wise gradually to loosen the rules that they have and their methods of discipline as their children grow. Generally speaking, I think that the adolescent of 13 should be treated differently by parents than the young adult of 17. What do you think?

Focusing

Focusing (Bertcher, 1979, pp. 95–103) is an expressive communication skill through which social workers highlight or call attention to something that is, or could be, of importance to the group's work. Frequently in their discussions groups wander away from their agreed-upon purpose, and you may have to redirect the discussion back toward the work to be done. Also, there are often interpersonal dynamics or processes that you wish to highlight for the group. For example, a social worker leading a group for persons with personal problems may say, "I noticed that when Sheila said she sometimes thinks of doing away with herself, the rest of us suddenly got quiet and then went on to some other topic. I'd like to back up a little and really respond to what Sheila was saying."

Following is another example of a worker using the focusing skill with a group member who has expressed a desire to improve interpersonal relationships: "Sue, you've said that you have experienced the men in your life as irresponsible and undependable. Since I'm a man and there are other men in the group, I wonder if you'd share what reactions you have had to us."

Confronting

The use of confrontation (Cournoyer, 1991, pp. 317–319) involves directly pointing out to a client a discrepancy or an inconsistency between statements and actions. The social worker in effect requests that the client examine an apparent contradiction or inconsistency in the client's thoughts, feelings, and behavior. You may even suggest that the client consider making a change toward greater congruence between words and deeds. This skill should be used with considerable caution, since clients can experience intense emotional reactions when confronted. Typically confrontation is used infrequently in groups, and when it is, it is communicated with warmth, understanding, and concern for the client. It is good practice to utilize empathic communications before and after confrontations.

Confrontations should be delivered in such a way that you assume responsibility for their accuracy and recognize that others may see things differently. Here are a few examples of confrontations communicated by social workers working with groups:

> Julie, you say that you want to get good grades, but you also tell us that you don't do a whole lot of studying. Are you able to get good grades without putting in time with the books?
>
> George, you've identified a number of goals that you want to work on in the group, but I wonder whether some of them are truly achievable. Are you setting up goals that are impossible to reach?
>
> Everybody here is in this group because the judge gave you a choice between coming here to work on the drinking problem and going to jail. You've all been coming each time, but it seems to me that you're not really interested in trying to get a handle on the drinking problem. Could it be that you're just going through the motions?

SUMMARY

Successful work with groups requires that you maintain a dual focus at all times. Attention must be given to both the individual members and to the group as a whole. Empathic communication skills reflect the client's frame of reference and are the relationship-building tools for work with groups. Their sensitive and consistent use leads to the development of a cohesive, interactive group whose thoughts, feelings, and experiences are freely shared. Expressive communication skills reflect your social work frame of reference and build upon an empathic foundation by assisting clients as they proceed into uncharted territory, exploring and experimenting with new information, new experiences, and new perspectives.

Freedom of Choice and Research Interviewing in Child Sexual Abuse*

Jane F. Gilgun

A significant point of view in the development of knowledge about child sexual abuse is that of persons who have been affected directly. These persons include victims, perpetrators, mothers, fathers, siblings, and other members of the family. This paper is a report on a method of research interviewing used to collect data on child sexual abuse from the point of view of female victims, perpetrators, and the wives of perpetrators. The method is intended to create conditions under which subjects feel free to share or not share their thoughts and feelings.

The chief characteristic of the method is its non-coerciveness. Coercion is defined as pushing or leading the subject to provide data which the subject feels compelled to provide but which the subject does not choose freely to provide. Non-coercion is its opposite: the subject chooses freely to provide data, and the researcher provides a setting in which free choice is possible.

The non-coercive nature of the method is a direct response to subjects' experience with the abuse. Members of families where sexual abuse has occurred typically have extreme difficulty discussing the abuse. Reasons for this difficulty include guilt, shame, fear of being blamed and stigmatized, and the subsequent need to deny the abuse took place, taboos on discussing sex and the lack of appropriate language to do so, and the reluctance to relive traumatic events. Part of the trauma is the self-blame each of the family members frequently takes for the abuse.

In addition, it is assumed that each person in the family already has experienced coercion in three

possible ways: by being a victim of sexual abuse which by its nature is coercive, through the subsequent investigation of the abuse which often is experienced by family members as coercive, or, in the case of adults, through experiences of abuse during childhood or adolescence. Sometimes treatment itself is experienced as coercive. Each family member, therefore, is conceptualized as damaged in some significant way, either because of the abuse itself and/or through a series of developmental insults which have occurred over the life course. Coercing individuals to discuss such highly emotive topics appears to be a violation of self-determination. Coercion also seems to risk causing further harm to individuals.

Coercion potentially can harm the subject's ability to take charge of his or her own life, can undermine the subject's sense of self-worth, and can take away the right to self-determination. The method, in sum, is intended not to perpetuate harm to family members. In fact, it is hoped that the effect of participation in the research will be either therapeutic or neutral for subjects.

The method is based on the value *self-determination*. Synonyms for self-determination are autonomy and freedom of choice. A common definition is the right to make choices which affect the self (Levy, 1983). Self-determination is a core value in social work, and respecting subject self-determination can reduce bias in social research data. Respect for self-determination, therefore, has ethical as well as practical repercussions. Levy considers self-determination to be a "therapeutic and developmental necessity" (p. 908), while Seagull and Noll (1982) wrote that providing a setting where the client can experience a sense of mastery over the content of the interview enhances the efficacy of treatment. Social learning theory shows that when control is perceived as extrinsic to the person, motivation can be reduced and, in some cases, can lead to profound resistance (Seagull &

*This paper was prepared for this volume and is a revised version of a paper presented at the Third National Family Violence Research Conference, University of New Hampshire, Durham, NH, July 6–9, 1987. Support for this research was provided by the Saint Paul Foundation, St. Paul, MN; the Minnesota Agricultural Experiment Station; and the Research and Graduate Affairs Committee, College for Human Development, Syracuse University.

Noll, 1982). The principles of self-determination articulated for therapeutic work were applied to the present research method.

Self-determination also is a concern within social research, both from an ethical stance and from the point of view of the reliability and validity of data. A power differential often exists between subject and researcher. Woodruff and Wicklund (1982) cited many studies which demonstrate the potential of the researcher to lead the subject. The ethical issue is whether the researcher should use power to lead or push subjects.

Bias becomes a possibility either through compliance and/or resistance. Under coercive conditions, the subject could comply and give the researcher what the subject thinks the researcher wants to know, or the subject could resist and either withhold information or purposefully provide distorted information. Compliance to the letter of what the researcher asks could also be a form of resistance. Therefore, when the research is experienced by the subject as coercive, the risks are high. Subjects are not likely to provide researchers with fresh insights, and the data they do provide may be distorted.

This method is not a criticism of court-ordered treatment and legal investigations which sometimes have elements of coercion. The legal system serves a significant social purpose: that of setting limits on behaviors which are harmful to others. Sometimes people have to be coerced into not harming others. Individual self-determination is respected in legal investigations, through the right not to self-incriminate and often through advising persons before they give evidence how the evidence will be used. In court-ordered treatment, self-determination can be respected, within the limits set by the court. When judges order treatment, the individual usually has a choice between treatment and incarceration. When the individual chooses treatment and then chooses not to become engaged in treatment, then she or he is referred back to the court. Within well-defined parameters, then, court-ordered treatment and legal investigations provide some degree of self-determination.

The non-coercive research interviewing described in this paper owes a fundamental debt to the Rogers school of psychotherapy (Meador & Rogers, 1984; Rogers, 1951, 1961). The Rogerian concepts of non-directiveness, empathy, unconditional positive regard, and congruence are part of the interview method. The method also assumes a self-actualizing tendency of all persons. Self-actualization is the assumption the person has an innate developmental elan which, under supportive environmental conditions, leads the person to develop his or her capacities. Unconditional positive regard develops from the belief in the inner wisdom of the self-actualizing person. The assumption is that the person, again under supportive environmental conditions, will find for him or herself the resources which support self-actualization.

The idea of giving as much control as possible to subjects is important in the non-coercive research method. It is based on the assumption that control is an issue for persons who have been affected by child sexual abuse. Providing subjects with control over the direction of the interview, a context which could be quite threatening, might empower the subject in some general way, but it also could provide the subject with security enough to be able to share some painful details of the life history.

Congruence is the ability to be in touch with and know inner feelings, thoughts, and fantasies. With the present method, the researcher makes decisions about when and how to reveal his or her inner experience to the research subject. The researcher also uses his/her inner experiences to understand the experiences the subject is sharing. The researcher allows the self to be open to the feelings, emotions, and other experiences of the subject while at the same time maintaining a sense of self. Being in tune with yet separate from the subject is a task of boundary maintenance and very important in the interview method. If the researcher becomes enmeshed with the subject, the possibility of losing an analytic stance arises. Empathy as defined by Rogers is similar to this boundary maintenance task.

The purpose of this paper is to describe the process of conducting non-coercive research interviews. Excerpts from the transcripts of interviews are provided in order to illustrate the principles discussed above. This paper is not a description of qualitative hypothesis development and testing, nor is it focused on specific techniques of conducting interviews, such as open-ended questions, probes, and asking for clarification and specificity. Rather, the paper attempts to answer the question, How can a researcher create conditions in the research interview where subject self-determination is possible?

METHOD

The method was used with 40 subjects. Twenty of the subjects were girls between the ages of 10 and 15 and who had been sexually abused. Eight were adult male incest perpetrators, 2 were males who abused children outside of their families, 3 were women perpetrators, and 7 were wives of the male perpetrators. Four of the men and one of the women perpetrators were in prison during the interview, 3 men had been incarcerated and were on probation, 1 man had received a suspended sentence, and 2 men and 2 women had never been charged. The girls were interviewed during 1982 and 1983 (Gilgun, 1984a, 1984b, 1984c, 1986, 1987). The adults were interviewed from 1985 to the present (Connor & Gilgun, 1987; Gilgun & Connor, 1987a, 1987b). The interviews were conducted by the author.

The purposes of the interviews were to collect life histories and to develop theory on child sexual abuse. Each subject was interviewed an average of 5 times each, with each interview lasting from one to 3 hours. About 10 hours of interviewing per subject were done. For the research with the girls, the researcher took notes during the interviews. The notes were transcribed and content analyzed. For the adults, the interviews were tape recorded and transcribed. The transcripts were content analyzed and the data were managed using the computer program ETHNOGRAPH (Seidel, Kjolseth, & Clark, 1985). The research method was based on the grounded theory method of Glaser and Strauss (1967) and further developed by Bogdan and Biklen (1982).

An interview guide covering five main areas was used. For the adults, these areas were family history, sexual development and history, history of abuse and neglect, history of friendships, and experience with children. The research with the girls covered the first four areas, but the fifth area was expectations for the future. The interviews were conducted like conversations. When the subject appeared ready to move on to another topic, then a question based on the subject's previous statements was posed. A standardized set of questions asked in sequence was not used. The sensitive nature of the research suggested that each question needed to be individualized to fit the experience of each subject. The same general areas were covered in each life history.

Subjects were told they didn't have to talk about anything they didn't want to; if they started to talk about something and changed their minds, then it was okay to stop; and if the researcher thought they were uncomfortable in discussing a topic, she would ask them if they would like to stop. These statements were made to the subject before the subject consented to participate in the research. They were repeated throughout the research process.

APPLICATION OF THE NON-COERCIVE METHOD

This section presents applications of the points discussed above. Topics include subjects' comfort level, encouraging subjects not to talk, asking subjects' permission, the subject takes the lead, non-coercion as confusing, pushing and confrontation, the expression of empathy, and congruence. The data reported are taken from the transcripts of interviews of the perpetrators and spouses.

Subjects' Comfort Level

The purpose of the non-coercive method is to create a setting where discussion of painful topics is possible. This purpose presupposes that the experience of pain might block a person's motivation to talk. Thus, the interviewer attempted to stay tuned to the subject's level of comfort. Routinely, the researcher opened and closed each interview with an inquiry into how the interviews were going for the subject. The following demonstrates how this was done.

R: How was this today? Was it all right or uncomfortable?

S: It was a little bit hard.

R: Yeah.

S: It's, like I say, it's kind of hard to talk about your past at times.

R: Yeah. I can imagine. It can be real hard.

S: I mean, some people have got, most people have got happy things they think about their childhoods, but I really don't have that much. I don't really have too much that was happy.

The researcher regularly checked out whether the subject would have felt free to stop and emphasized that it was ok to stop.

S: I had no problem today.

R: If you had felt uncomfortable about talking about something, would you have stopped?

S: Oh, yeah.

R: Because I really do want you to do that.

Another quote shows how strongly the researcher sometimes emphasized the goal of not coercing subjects. She told the subject she could tell the researcher less this week than last if she wanted to. The subject explained why she was putting herself in the awkward position of talking about painful issues.

R: Did you feel ok after talking to me the last time or did you feel funny?

S: Yeah. I felt ok.

R: You didn't feel like here I'm telling a stranger all this stuff?

S: Yeah, I felt a little bit like that. But I feel that it might be important to talk about what happened in my childhood.

R: OK. You can tell me less this week if you want, because I want you to do it so it's comfortable for you. I don't want you to feel uncomfortable about it.

S: M-hum.

R: I'd rather you tell me when you feel uncomfortable. I don't want to put somebody in a position where they feel they've got to tell me all these things that they're not really comfortable telling me.

The researcher frequently checked with subjects throughout the interviews on how they were doing. The following is one example.

R: Is this hard for you to talk about now?

S: Oh, not too bad. You know, I've pretty well talked about most of it already.

Sometimes, of course, it is hard to know if the subject is telling the truth about how she or he is feeling, or, if the subject knows at the point they are asked. That is why it's important to encourage subjects to change topics. They might need some encouragement to share or not share.

Encouraging Subjects Not to Talk

Encouraging subjects not to talk is a centerpiece of the non-coercive method. Sometimes the subjects chose not to pursue a topic. Most of the time the subjects wanted to continue.

The invitation not to talk typically came from the researcher when the researcher observed subject anxiety or hesitancy. The following is an example of a subject deciding not to discuss something.

R: What kinds of things did you say to the kids to keep them from telling about the abuse? [The subject hesitated and looked uncomfortable.] You don't have to tell me if you don't want to.

S: I don't think I will.

R: Could you tell me why?

S: I'm too ashamed.

Getting a one-word descriptor of why the subject would prefer not to discuss a topic provided some insight into the subject's inner thoughts and feelings.

The most common response to the researcher's invitation to change topics or stop talking about a topic was for the subject to choose to continue. Sometimes the subject had to persuade the researcher that she or he really wanted to continue. The following is an example. This subject had been discussing sexual fantasies he had about his 5 and 6 year-old girl cousins when he was 9 or 10 years old. He said this was the first time he had told anyone about the fantasies. The researcher encouraged the subject to change topics, and the subject appeared to be putting up an argument.

R: We can get off the subject now if you want. Do you want to?
S: No, that's OK.

The researcher was not convinced that the subject was feeling safe enough to continue the discussion. She said

R: I don't want to push you. Because if this is new, then it's probably better to leave it now. Maybe we can get back to it later if you want to, or we don't have to get back to it at all.
S: It's probably something that's important. I mean if you've got me thinking about it, why I didn't sexually abuse back then. I think, when I abused my daughter being the father figure I was in a position of authority. It was easier to manipulate my daughter than it would've been to abuse my cousins.

The subject then continued for several minutes to talk about the similarities and differences between his fantasies about younger cousins when he was 9 or 10 years old and his abuse of his daughter which began more than a decade later.

Asking Subjects' Permission
The non-coercive method suggests that the research be done with the subject's continual permission. The following are three examples of permission given over time.

R: You don't have to tell me this, obviously, but could you tell me what kinds of things you used to do with the children sexually?

The subject responded with a long and detailed narration on sodomy, fellatio, and fondling. A second example is the following.

R: I did ask you why you didn't take steps to stop the incest, and you've been spending some time thinking about why you went forward with it. Would you mind talking about that? What you've been thinking about; why you went forward with it?

S: Well, as close a conclusion as I've been able to come to so far is just all the, a lot of little things combined. It wasn't just one thing.

Frequently, the researcher would pick up on a point the subject had made in passing in previous parts of the interview. Picking up on such a topic was done with the subject's permission.

R: One thing that I'd like to go back to, again with your permission, if you don't want to it's fine. You said very quickly, maybe 15 minutes ago, that you really didn't want to be close to people in high school. Could you talk about that a little more?

The Subject Takes the Lead
Sometimes subjects expected the researcher to pursue certain topics, and when the researcher didn't, subjects would ask about it. The following is an example.

S: When all this first happened, are we going to talk about that? How I felt about that?
R: Yeah. Probably not today. [It was the end of the interview time.] But I really do want to talk to you about that. Do you want to talk about it next time? Would you be up for it?
S: I suppose.
R: Don't if you don't want to.

The non-directive nature of the interview, then, sometimes moved subjects to take the lead.

Non-Coerciveness as Confusing
In general, the subjects appeared to understand the non-coercive nature of the interview. One perpetrator, who was a resident of a maximum security prison and who saw himself as rebelling against rules, said he was confused by not having to discuss topics if he didn't want to. The subject had been assuming that "being honest" took precedence over speaking out of his own free will. The researcher explained the importance of speaking when the subject felt ready.

R: This research won't work if you're not [*subject interrupts*]
S: Being honest.

R: No, no, not that at all. It won't work if you don't feel free not to talk. It's a funny thing how it works . . . . I think that's true. I really think that is the key. Whatever good is going to come out of this, that you share you feel free sharing and if you don't feel comfortable about sharing something, then you don't.

S: That's kind of confusing because you know what they tell me here: share everything whether you like . . . whether you feel comfortable about it or not.

R: That's right, but you see, I'm doing research, I'm not doing therapy, and as a researcher, I can't, I don't want, I couldn't, feel that I'm putting you in a position where you're forced to do something. It's totally against my principles.

S: That's what I feel in here sometimes. They have a plan for you, a treatment plan.

The goal of respecting subject self-determination overrides the goal of keeping the subject "honest."

Pushing and Confrontation

The method does not preclude pushing the client for clarification or additional detail. It simply enjoins the researcher to be careful that the pushing is not coercive. To ensure this, pushing is done with the subject's permission and was done only after the researcher felt reasonably confident that the research-subject relationship could sustain some pushing. The following conversation took place during the third interview. The researcher was struggling with putting together incongruent pieces of the subject's story. The subject appeared to have joined the researcher in the struggle to understand. Because it appeared that the subject had joined the researcher, the researcher was able to confront the subject with what the researcher believed to be the subject's blind spot regarding his daughter's well-being. The purpose of the confrontation, however, was for research purposes; that is, for the researcher to understand the subject's thinking. If there were a therapeutic outcome for the subject through the confrontation, this was not the primary purpose of the confrontation.

R: I can't get some of the pieces together myself, and maybe I won't be able to because I think there's something about the human mind—there's a mystery there that none of us may ever really understand. I think it's true, I don't have any reason to doubt that you really cared about M [the victim]. But I also, and you correct me, I also see there had to be an enormous blind spot in how you were seeing things with M. . . . Where did it come from? How could you, S, miss that maybe some of this was harmful? How did that happen?

S: Well, at that time, it's a real selfish act. And at that time I was really self-centered.

R: But you loved her. That's what I keep trying to understand. I keep pushing you. You can tell me to stop pushing you if you want to.

S: No.

R: I'm trying to understand this, you know. How can a man, and I believe you, this is your favorite daughter. You were close to her. You cuddled her. You changed her diapers. She waited on you. She loved you. Yet there was this blind spot right in the middle of this whole thing, and I don't get it. I mean you were selfish you are saying and you were self-centered. OK. I can probably buy that, too, but a lot of people are self-centered and selfish.

The subject then continued to struggle with understanding how he could abuse someone he loved.

Another subject was talking about why he was not able to tell anybody about his sexual behavior with his four-year-old son and five year-old daughter. He stated he had no idea what would have happened if he had told. The researcher gently challenged him on that. The dialogue went as follows:

S: I think one of the reasons for not stopping it is the fact that I didn't dare talk to anybody about it. I'm not sure what A's [his wife] reaction would've been if I'd have come to her and said, "Hey, I'm having these feelings." I don't know what. I have no idea what would have happened.

R: I think you have some idea.

S: She, well, now says "Well, if you'd have come beforehand and said you had those feelings we could've dealt with it." But I think she'd have just blown up. I really do.

The gentle confrontation resulted in the subject stating what might be closer to some of what he really feared if he did tell his wife about sexual feelings for his children.

The Expression of Empathy

Empathy often arose out of the researcher's genuine respect for the subject's struggle to share his or her life. Toward the end of the above dialogue about the incongruence of using sexually a child you love, the researcher said

R: I really appreciate your effort. I really do. I think these are extremely difficult areas. I can't imagine anything more painful than talking about this and living it. I just think that has to be among the most painful experiences that a person can have.

The subject apparently felt understood. His response to this empathic statement was a continuation of trying to understand what allowed him to use his daughter. Thus, the expression of empathy appeared to have moved the dialogue along.

Congruence

Congruence has at least two sides. One is the researcher being in touch with her own inner thoughts and feelings, and the other is deciding when to share these thoughts and feelings with the subject. Most of the time, the researcher did not share her thoughts and feelings. The purpose of the interviews was to understand child sexual abuse, not to understand a researcher's reactions to the life histories of persons who have been deeply affected by child sexual abuse.

When the researcher shared her feelings and thoughts, it was brief. When the researcher verbalized her reactions, it was either in the form of fieldnotes or in discussing the research with her associates. Sometimes the researcher allowed her reactions to show through body language. The

ways the researcher handled her congruence are illustrated below.

R: What you're saying makes so much sense. I mean it really fits. So, I think that's why I jumped forward like that. Because what you said just really hit a chord, and I thought, "My God, she's really on to something."
S: I noticed that you jumped forward. [*Laughing*] Thank you very much.

Congruence sometimes came through as the researcher was attempting to clarify something the subject said, and often within the context of an empathic statement.

R: So that's what you're telling me, that you really wanted to be a good father, but for some reason you crossed the boundary. Is that what you said? The boundary?
S: I crossed the kids' boundary.
R: That must be hard. It's hard for me to hear you say that. It must be hard for you to accept that.
S: It is.

The difficulty in using researcher congruence is the danger of leading the subject, which the researcher might've done here. The researcher did, however, see the pain on the subject's face and heard it in his voice before stating how hard this might be.

Most often, however, the researcher did not verbalize her inner thoughts and feelings. The reason was to provide the subject with the psychological space to continue the narration. Sometimes the researcher felt incredulous, shocked, and angry. One instance was when the subject went into graphic detail about the sodomy, fellatio, and fondling into which he had coerced his two children. The following example is part of the dialogue, which took place after the subject gave the researcher permission to push. The subject is discussing sodomizing his daughter.

S: I was concerned enough that I didn't want to physically hurt her. But at the same time, you know, I was after more of what I wanted for me, rather than anything for her.
R: So, if she would say "ouch" or something, would that register?

S: Oh, yeah, to a point. It did to a point.

R: When she would say, "Ow, Daddy," or something, then what would you think?

S: Well, I knew that if she said "ouch" it was hurting.

R: Ummm.

S: But what I would do is I would say, "OK, we'll wait a minute and we'll try again." And just continue like that until I got what I wanted.

R: Ummm.

S: Kind of getting her used to it at the same time. It was somewhat considerate of her feelings. I wasn't just gonna "boom," you know, ram her all at once.

The researcher's "umm's" were code for wanting to scream something like, "Jesus Christ. How the hell could you do that to a six year-old? You seem to think that you were being a nice guy for stopping for a minute." It's pretty obvious that to be congruent at that point in those terms might not have facilitated anything but harm to the subject and the end of the interview.

Another time, the researcher was asking this same subject about how he thought of his motivation to abuse his children. He had just called his sexual pull toward his daughter a driving force.

R: Do you understand that yet? What was going on that you had that driving force?

S: Not in terms that society would understand, no.

R: How do you think of it, though?

S: Oh, it was Satan himself.

R: OK. Can you tell me more about that?

The "Can you tell me more about that?" was code for, "I am really hearing this. Here is a guy who says he believes Satan is responsible for his sexually abusive behavior." The researcher chose not to challenge the subject, but to hear him out. The subject explained in some detail the control Satan has over our lives. Since the purpose of the interviews was to understand child sexual abuse from the subject's point of view, challenging his world view would have defeated that purpose.

Sometimes after the interviews, the researcher would record her reactions. The notes from which these excerpts are taken begin with "I'm sort of half paralyzed." In the interview, the subject appeared to be denying the intensity of his pain over letters of extreme rejection and blaming his wife and daughter had sent him that day. He was due to leave prison in two weeks, and up until that point he and his ex-wife were planning on his rejoining the family. He let the researcher read the letters, but he requested that the tape recorder be shut off. The notes read

> I tried to restrain myself while the tape was off not to speak and feel for him, but it was hard not to. Because he was just sitting there sort of half-smiling, or, at least sitting there. It was a tough time for me. I don't know, but it was pretty clear to me the degree to which he can, as he says it, stuff his feelings since he was still doing it.

Thus, the non-coercive method of research interviewing in child sexual abuse puts a heavy burden on the researcher, who sits and listens to graphic stories of human suffering and insensitivity. Understanding and being able to apply the concept of congruence is an important part of the non-coercion.

DISCUSSION

The non-coercive method of research interviewing appears at first glance to be a passive approach to data gathering. A close analysis of how the method works in practice, however, shows that the researcher is actively engaged with the subject. With permission of the subject, the researcher can push, probe, and confront. The researcher also can share his or her own reactions to the subject's story, with the guideline of providing the subject with a setting where the subject's point of view can be heard. The researcher probably is wise to share only a small part of his or her reactions. It does seem important, though, for the researcher to be in touch continually with his or her own reactions to the subject's stories.

The method owes a great debt to the Rogers school of psychotherapy. Clinical skills appear to be the basic skills in using this method. The method, however, is not therapy. The researcher does not have the injunction to facilitate the subject's coming to terms with himself or herself. The injunction of this method is to provide a setting where the subject can choose freely to share or not share his or her life story. The injunction is to do no harm. If there are therapeutic consequences to being a subject in this study, then this is a consequence and not a goal.

Asking people to bare their souls as this method does, however, suggests that subjects would have to have an incentive to participate in the research. The incentives for subjects appears to be 1) to help in the prevention of child sexual abuse and 2) to work through some of their issues around the abuse. The girl interviewees were pleased with the idea that their experience could be used to help other children. Their parents said that the research has been good for their children. The adults, too, felt strongly about being part of a prevention effort. They wanted something good to come out of the pain of their own lives. Each subject also said that they thought the research would help them. Throughout the interview process, the subjects stated that they were putting things together for themselves in new ways. The adults became engaged in the research process, and the researcher and the subjects struggled together to try to understand child sexual abuse.

Reading 9-3 *Point of View*

A. Averchenko

"Men are comic," she said, smiling dreamily. Not knowing whether this indicated praise or blame, I answered noncommittally: "Quite true."

"Really, my husband's a regular Othello. Sometimes I'm sorry I married him."

I looked helplessly at her. "Until you explain—" I began.

"Oh, I forgot that you haven't heard. About three weeks ago, I was walking home with my husband through the square. I had a large black hat on, which suits me awfully well, and my cheeks were quite pink from walking. As we passed under a streetlight, a pale, dark-haired fellow standing nearby glanced at me and suddenly took my husband by his sleeve.

"Would you oblige me with a light," he says. Alexander pulled his arm away, stooped down, and quicker than lightening, banged him on the head with a brick. He fell like a log. Awful!"

"Why, what on earth made your husband get jealous all of a sudden?" She shrugged her shoulders. "I told you men are very comic."

Bidding her farewell, I went out, and at the corner came across her husband.

"Hello, old chap," I said. "They tell me you've been breaking people's heads."

He burst out laughing. "So you've been talking to my wife. It was jolly lucky that brick came so pat into my hand. Otherwise, just think: I had about fifteen hundred rubles in my pocket, and my wife was wearing her diamond earrings."

"Do you think he wanted to rob you?"

"A man accosts you in a deserted spot, asks for a light, and gets hold of your arm. What more do you want?"

Perplexed, I left him and walked on.

"There's no catching you today," I heard a voice say from behind.

I looked around and saw a friend I hadn't set eyes upon for three weeks.

"Lord!" I exclaimed. "What on earth has happened to you?"

He smiled faintly and asked in turn: "Do you know whether any lunatics have been at large lately? I was attacked by one three weeks ago. I left the hospital only today."

With sudden interest, I asked: "Three weeks ago? Were you sitting in the square?"

"Yes, I was. The most absurd thing. I was sitting in the square, dying for a smoke. No matches! After ten minutes or so, a gentleman passed with some old hag. He was smoking. I go up to him, touch him on the sleeve and ask in my most polite manner: "Can you oblige me with a light?" And what do you think? The madman stoops down, picks something up, and the next moment I am lying on the ground with a broken head, unconscious. You probably read about it in the newspapers."

I looked at him and asked earnestly: "Do you really believe you met up with a lunatic?"

"I am sure of it."

Anyhow, afterwards I was eagerly digging in old back numbers of the local paper. At last I found what I was looking for: A short note in the accident column.

Under the Influence of Drink

Yesterday morning, the keepers of the square found on a bench a young man whose papers show him to be of good family. He had evidently fallen to the ground while in a state of extreme intoxication, and had broken his head on a nearby brick. The distress of the prodigal's parents is indescribable.

For Further Reading

Benjamin, A. (1987). *The helping interview: With case illustrations.* Boston: Houghton Mifflin.

Bloom, A. (1980). Social work and the English language. *Social Casework, 60,* 332–338.

Cohen, B. Z. (1986). Written communication in social work: The report. *Child Welfare, 65,* 399–407.

Cormican, J. D. (1978). Linguistic issues in interviewing. *Social Casework, 59,* 145–152.

Epstein, L. (1985). *Talking and listening: A guide to the helping interview.* St. Louis: Times Mirror/Meghy.

Evans, D. R., Heam, M. T., Uhlemann, M. R., & Ivey, A. E. (1993). *Essential interviewing: A programmed approach to effective communication* (4th ed.). Monterey, CA: Brooks/Cole.

Goldstein, H. (1983). Starting where the client is. *Social Casework: The Journal of Contemporary Social Work, (64),* 267–275.

Gordon, R. C. (1992). *Basic interviewing skills.* Itasca, IL: F.E. Peacock.

Kadushin, A. (1972). *The social work interview.* New York: Columbia University Press.

Manor, O. (1986). The preliminary interview in social group work: Finding the spiral steps. *Social Work with Groups, 9,* 21–39.

McDonald, C. C. (1988). Social work interviewing and feminism. *Australian Journal of Social Work, 41,* 13–16.

Sands, R. G. (1988). Sociolinguistic analysis of a mental health interview. *Social Work, 33,* 149–154.

Weber, T., McKeever, J. E., & McDaniel, S. H. (1985). A beginner's guide to the problem-oriented first family interview. *Family Process, 24,* 357–364.

Williams, L., & Hopps, J. (1988a). On the nature of professional communication: Publication for practitioners. *Social Work, 33,* 453–459.

Chapter 10

From Initial Contact Through Assessment

As discussed in Chapter 2, the problem-solving process may be divided into three major phases, each with its own tasks. This chapter will deal with the beginning phase, which extends from the initial contact through assessment to the initial treatment planning. We will continue to discuss the conditions under which the worker and the potential client (we use the term respondent) come together and explore the situation until they arrive at the definition of the problem; the development and meaning of the beginning relationship within which the respondent makes a decision about becoming a client; and the collection of appropriate data and assessment of the meaning of data for planning the problem-solving activities. Discussion of the last topic will be continued in the next chapter.

As we said earlier, the social worker and the respondent usually come together in one of two different ways: (1) the individual, family, or group may reach out for help with a problem they have identified as being beyond their means of solution; or (2) a community source may identify an individual, a family, or a group as having a serious problem threatening the welfare of themselves or others (a vulnerable person or group) and request that the social worker intervene to solve that problem. In many such instances the worker goes out to the family at the request of the community source, but there are situations in which the individual or family reports to the agency under duress by the referral source. As an example, a judge may suspend a jail sentence on condition that the offender report to a social worker for treatment. In such situations we often label the family, individual, or group an involuntary client. However, it seems to us to be much more appropriate to call these referrals potential clients, or respondents, since we consider a client to be someone who seeks professional services to resolve a problem in which he or she is involved. Persons who come in contact with a worker under duress rather than as a help seeker, can be considered clients only when they become help seekers.

As discussed earlier, the person or the group that originally recognized a problem and asked the worker to intervene may be seen as a client, having sought professional services, even though for others. However, we seldom regard such sources of problem recognition as clients. Although they fit the definition of the client, as they are seeking professional services, they are usually called referral sources. In these situations, before making first contact with the respondent, you should give considerable thought to the relationship between the referral source and the respondent. One of the most common problems occurs when the worker accepts the problem definition or the outcome goals of the referral source as appropriate to the work with the respondents without examining the meaning of the referral for the clients themselves. However, it is always the responsibility of the social worker, when accepting a referral, to determine why the potential client is being referred and what the referral source's perception of the situation is. In fact, you probably should go through a brief problem-solving process with the referral source. This can identify what the referral sees as the problem, how he or she identifies it as a problem, what the facts are that bear on the problem, how he or she sees the possibility for change, and what outcome he or she seeks. Above all, you should complete your contact with the referral source by letting him or her know whether contact was made with the respondent system and whether you and the respondent have agreed to work together. Exercise caution in reporting to the referral source in the two areas. First, do not share information about the respondent with the referral source unless this sharing was first discussed with the respondent and either was approved by him or her or is required by law or court order. Second, exercise caution in giving the referral source any assurance that you will work toward the goals he or she may have in mind in making the referral. In fact, in many situations professional knowledge indicates that the goals are inappropriate or impossible, and you may have to discuss this with the referral source before you agree to intervene. An example of a goal that we could not agree to would be the demand by the referral source that we remove six children from a neighbor who appears to be neglecting them and place them in a foster home before the end of the day.

Of course, you must also explore the potential client's view of the reason for referral and the way that person sees the situation. To accept someone else's view without making your own professional assessment and without understanding the meaning of the referral to the respondent is to court disaster.

If you think that you cannot help or that there is no problem or that the respondent is unwilling to become a client, consider with the referral source how this will be dealt with. It may be that in this process the client recognition system will become the client system in the full sense of the term. For example, there are parents who come to the agency to report a child's problem. Quite often they become the clients, and the child may or may not be seen. Or a neighborhood group may be incensed and upset over the behavior of a new family in the neighborhood. A visit by the social worker reveals that the new family is functioning quite well but very differently from the neighbors. Perhaps the neighborhood becomes the client for purposes of examining the meaning of their problem in being unable to accept this different behavior. Or on contacting the respondent system, you may find that it really does need and want help with some difficulties, but the help to be given does not fall within the defined parameters of sanctioned service. You may then want to suggest to the referral source that it seek help elsewhere. Above all, never ignore the referral source's position in the situation. You must engage in a problem-solving process with it and must bring the contact with it to an orderly termination. This is critical, even though this whole process just described may take place in one telephone call. These notions will be discussed in more detail in the paragraphs on referral found in Chapter 15.

Giving and Taking Help

What is meant by the term *giving help* to someone? Help must be understood as far more than something that one person gives to another. What someone else does on our behalf only becomes help when we can make use of it. Keith-Lucas (1972, p. 15) defines *help* as something tangible or intangible offered by one person or group to another person or group *in such a way that the helped person or group can use it to achieve some solution* of the issue at hand. Help thus has two important elements: (1) *what* is given and (2) *how* it is given and used. To be helpful, what is given must be something of value and of use to the recipients, and it must be given in such a way as to leave the recipients free to use it in their own way without paying the penalty of loss of self-esteem or a loss of control of their own lives. Potential clients, whether self-initiated applicants or other identified clients, move from being potential to actual clients when they decide that it is possible to accept the help offered.

In our culture asking for or taking help (at least from others beyond one's intimate circle of associates) is often a severe blow to one's sense of adequacy. The person who accepts help has to face the fact that (1) there is something in one's situation that one wants changed but that one cannot change by oneself; (2) one must be willing to discuss the problem with another person; (3) one must accord that other at least a limited right to tell one what to do or to do things for one; and (4) one must be willing to change oneself or one's situation or at the very least to go along with changes that others make in one's situation (Keith-Lucas, 1972, p. 20). How difficult these steps are depends on several things. The difficulty in asking for help is greatly increased if the problem is one that is generally seen in our culture as being a fault in the person who has it. When we assume that problems in living are signs of personality malfunction or devalued personal qualities, we erect some difficult barriers between our client and work on problem solution. If people have been taken advantage of much or if their confidence has been abused when in the past they revealed their situation to another, or if their previous attempts to live in a supposedly better way have always resulted in defeat, the business of asking for help may be excruciatingly painful and difficult. On the other hand, some parents support a group work agency financially so that their children can have positive developmental group associations. In that case the enrollment of their children in various helping programs, while a recognition that they need help offering their children growth experiences, is usually seen as a positive and normal thing to do. Or the neighborhood group that seeks the worker's help in advocating change in another system, such as the school or the housing project, may also see this quest for help as a positive step toward controlling its own situation. However, since the social problems of poverty and unemployment are often viewed as the result of individual pathology, the family faced with them may feel inadequate and fearful of asking for help.

Anyone who has driven through miles of confused streets before stopping to ask someone for directions may well ask why he or she had to waste time, gas, and energy before admitting to being lost. And how many persons have said to themselves that there was little point in asking because few natives are ever able to give adequate directions? This attitude is a way of preserving a sense of adequacy, if not superiority, while asking for help.

If something that one gives to another becomes helpful only when the other can use it, it follows that social workers can be helpful to their clients only when they understand what problems the client would like to be able to cope with or to change. Thus, in the beginning phase of their work together, practitioner and client have to clarify what difficulty they are going to work on. (Such clarification is the end product of the considerations outlined in Section I of the problem-solving model in Chapter

2.) They have to determine the expectations and goals that the client holds for the work together. They have to understand the realities and boundaries of the practitioner's abilities and the service system's resources (see Section III A of the model). The client has to have some realistic understanding of what the work together is going to require. As a result of the execution of these tasks, a preliminary contract to proceed with the necessary exploration and data collection is formulated. The mutual decision about problem, goals, and expectations will determine the focus of the data collection. It is not necessary to know all there is to know about a client, but rather to understand what knowledge is necessary to solve the problem and achieve the outcomes sought.

Getting Started

Regardless of the size or type of client system, in the accomplishment of these tasks you will be involved in two major forms of human association that are typical of social work practice: the interview and the group meeting. The following discussion relates to principles that are important in either instance. (In this discussion the reference will be to the clients rather than to the client system simply because this allows the use of the pronoun *they*—a human term—rather than the mechanistic *it* that is grammatically necessary in references to the client system.) The first task you face is that of preparation for the initial contact. Because it is impossible to divide individuals, groups, or human interactions into discrete and entirely orderly parts, this first meeting will undoubtedly involve some elements that bear on all the tasks outlined in the preceding paragraph. However, the primary focus of the beginning will concern Section 1 A through Section 1 C in the model—the problem as it is seen by the client system, by systems with which the client system is in interaction, and by the worker. Certainly these aspects will have to be clarified before the problem for work (Section I D) can be settled, and focused work on data collection (as apart from incidental data collection) cannot begin until this point has been established.

In preparation for the initial contact, you will want to collect and review any pertinent data you have about the client system and the purposes of the coming encounter. In addition, you may want to discuss with others in the setting the kinds of help that the service system can offer. Because beginnings are important in establishing the pattern of ongoing relationships and because you wish to demonstrate respect and concern for the clients, you will want to do everything possible to reduce unnecessary obstacles to complete and free communication. An understanding about the time and place is essential, as are arrangements to ensure that the meeting will be comfortable, private, and as free from interruptions as possible. You may also want to give some thought to contact with other elements of the client system or other systems whose interest and/or participation may impinge on the change endeavor, such as the family of a referred adolescent or the school that suggested that a certain neighborhood group might find a home in a nearby community center. Thought should be given to contact with referral sources—very serious thought, because this action will have many implications for both the practitioner and the clients as they begin work together.

There are no universally applicable rules for information collection that can be set forth before you meet with the clients, but some principles of data collection for the practitioner's consideration can be discussed. The key principles of data collection in social work are these: (1) The clients should be the *primary* source of information, although not necessarily the only source. (2) The data you collect should be related to the problem at issue. (3) You should not acquire information that you would be unwilling to share with the clients. In addition, you should be willing to share with the clients the process by which the information was secured and to explain why it was secured in the way it was. (4) Further, it is our conviction that if you have information about a particular aspect of the problem, this information should be shared with the clients before you ask how the clients feel and think about that particular point. In this way you scrupulously avoid trapping the clients and give the clients the opportunity, before taking a position, to reconcile what you know with what the clients think and feel. (5) If you must seek information in advance of the initial contact with the clients, you should limit that data to the situation that brings clients and you together—nothing more. Amassing large amounts of information unrelated to the problem at hand may well get in the way of your really hearing what the clients are saying about the here and now. (6) In general it is our position that if information should be sought from other sources than the clients and the files of the worker's agency, this can be done after the first meeting, when the practitioner and the clients have established the need for such information and the purposes it serves. Thus, most data collection will take place after you and the clients have agreed to work together and have defined the problem on which you will work and the ends that will be sought.

Perhaps it is time to clarify the earlier discussion in its relationship to two types of clients: (1) the voluntary client, who comes of free will with a problem that has been identified, and (2) the respondent, who comes either because someone in a power position has demanded this or because you have been asked to see the client and have initiated the transaction. At the first meeting this individual or family may or may not be willing to share what they see as the problem, but usually advance information about the problem has been supplied by the individual or agency that took the initiative in forcing the client and you to come together. It is our position that the principles of data collection outlined earlier apply to contacts with both the voluntary and the referred client.

The respondent may not (and usually will not) have given permission for information to be shared with you or have knowledge of what information was shared. This makes it very important that at the very beginning you share the advance information and if possible the source of that information with the client. Sometimes you cannot reveal the source of information—for example, in cases involving the neglect and abuse of children in which the informant asks not to be identified. In the interest of protecting the children such requests are granted. For example, let us suppose that I as a court intake worker have on my desk the police report of the theft of a car. The offender accused of stealing the vehicle is sitting in my office. I prefer to begin the interview by showing the police report to the offender and asking him to comment on it. Does he agree with it? Are there statements that should be corrected? If his story differs markedly from that of the arresting officer, I may suggest that this will have to be cleared up during the court hearing, when both the offender and the officer will be under oath. It is not my function as a social worker to catch people in lies or distortions. Rather, if I am to be helpful, I must try to establish an honest and open relationship, which can be difficult if I trap the client in an untruth.

If I am assigned to a family whose members have had numerous serious troubles that have required my agency's intervention for many years, I prefer to read the case and begin the interview by offering the clients a brief summary of what I know. I then ask for the client's comments or for corrections they want to make in my summary rather than asking the clients to tell me their problems. I will never forget the situation in which I asked a client to tell me what she saw as her problem. She heaved a long sigh and said, "You are the fifth worker I have had, and you all ask me to start over. Don't you people down there ever write anything down?"

There was also a client who told me as we were terminating our successful work together, "The most important thing is that you cared, and I knew that you did because the first time I saw you, you told me you had read our record and you still came out to help. We had been in such a mess for so long that I was surprised to know that anyone who knew about us would think we were worth coming to see."

In referral situations it may be necessary, to protect the rights of others or the client's own interest, for you to collect certain information without the client's permission. This does not relieve you of the responsibility to inform the client of the intention to take such action and to report to the client the content of the information collected. In fact, to give the client as much control of the involuntary relationship as possible, the sharing of intent is essential. If the client cannot decide the action taken, knowing the action and the reasons for it gives some sense of being in at least partial control.

As previously mentioned, there are two types of beginnings: in the first, clients have decided that they need to explore what can be done about some want, felt need, lack, or difficulty and have asked for help. In the second, someone other than the client has been concerned about this matter, and the worker has initiated the contact with the client at that other person's request. When the client has asked to see you, the most sensible thing to do is to let him or her state why he or she has come. But the first contact starts on a different note when you initiate it. Then you must be prepared to explain why you have taken this action, being careful to allow the client time to respond to your statement of purpose and concern.

When you intervene in people's lives at someone else's request, you inevitably stir up a lot of anxiety and perhaps anger. It is difficult for the family or the individual to engage with you until they have answered for themselves their questions about why you have come, what you know about them, and what you are trying to do to them. To ask them to share themselves with you or answer your questions with any comfort, you must first share yourself and, as we said in the last chapter, your purpose with them. There must not be any hidden agenda. Often when we are asked to intervene, we find people who have had a long history of contacts with social agencies or other institutions of society in which they have felt rejected, judged as inadequate, or betrayed. Thus, you may enter a situation in which the individual's or the family's initial response is not to you and why you have come but to their image of you created from this past experience or from their notion of social workers and what they are doing in people's lives.

There are three important principles worth repeating at this point. First, remember that you have walked uninvited into the situation. Thus the clients have the right to their anger. They have the right to challenge you. In fact, appropriate anger and challenge to your right to be in their home observing them are probably signs of good ego strength. These reactions demonstrate appropriate system boundaries. On the other hand, the client who threatens you with physical violence and the client who welcomes you and hands you the problem both have poor boundary structures. You should not placate the client, not try to do away with anger by talking about your "helping" role, but deal openly, realistically, and compassionately with the problem as you understand it. You want to be able to say, "This is what I understand that brought me here. I know the trouble my coming may have brought into your life. But if we can agree on the reality of the problem and what you want done about it, I think maybe together we can work through to some better way of operating."

The second principle concerns feelings about this role. Confronting the client with the situation as we understand may be difficult for us because we have been brought up to be polite, not to confront people with what appear to be negative observations about them. So we have very little experience in being direct with people about negatives unless we are angry with them. Yet in the professional situation we need to learn to share negative facts with compassion and caring. While our words may impart hard and difficult information, our voice must carry a feeling of concern. You may have to practice before you are able to share negatives simply as facts, with a figurative arm around the client's shoulders. We are not trying to change people; we are trying to come to a common understanding of the problem so that we can work together to change it if the client so chooses. We do not like to share negatives with clients because we want to be liked and know that often the communication of negative things results in an angry and rejecting response. Thus, our own feelings often result in our sharing in such a way that we receive the response we are expecting. The things we have to share are often things that bear so closely on our own lives and our own struggles that we prefer not to discuss them; we would rather avoid them.

The third principle to remember about sharing negative facts and evaluations is to share them as if they are a problem to be solved. Tell the client that this is your information. Do not say it is the truth and do not accept the client's word that it is false. The fact that you have this information creates a problem for both you and the client. What do you do with the information? Also, in trying to impart information about the importance of changing his or her behavior, do not tell the client that he or she ought to behave in this way or that you know this. Rather, say something like this: "I have studied this problem in great depth and most of the things I read say that kids get along better and are more satisfying to be with if their parents do not use physical punishment as the only method of discipline. Have you heard this? Have you ever tried to use other ways of correcting your kids? What did you do and how did it work?" This approach avoids setting you up as the authority so that in rejecting your suggestions the client also is rejecting you. It also involves the client by presenting a problem.

In Chapter 7 on values, it was emphasized that client self-determination is important if the client is to solve the problem in a way that contributes to progress in living. It is through exercising choice that we all learn to make better and more productive choices. And we cannot make choices if we do not comprehend the problem. Thus, our primary task is to establish a joint understanding of the facts or an agreement to disagree on the facts. We are not in the situation to make the client like us but to help with choices about the problem to be solved, the goals to be achieved, and the way the client feels they can be achieved.

Crossing System Boundaries

If you are to help people solve their problems, you must cross the boundaries of the client system, and what you do and say in that process will affect the course of your relationship and your ability to be of help. This requires that you always be sensitive to the meaning of boundaries to the client system and for the meaning to the client system of the interactions of the system members within its boundaries. This becomes critically important when you are involved with systems that may have different notions about boundaries. (where they are, how one crosses them, and the pattern of transactions necessary to show respect for the boundaries) and different patterns of interaction within the boundaries, as in working with minority groups and families. "The Lee Family" (Appendix, A-5) is a good example of the worker's sensitivity to cultural norms upon entering the family. Because of the position of the father in the family, the worker addressed most of the questions to him. The worker also asked the husband's permission to interview the wife alone and asked the husband to explain to his wife the role of the worker vis-à-vis the family. Because the worker was a man, a private meeting (a crossing of the boundary of the spouse system) with Mrs. Lee would have to be approved and sanctioned by the husband to conform to the traditional rules governing behavior between a man's wife and another man not related by kinship.

Defining the Problem

So you begin with a consideration of the problem that the client sees as the starting place. For many individuals and groups, needs and wants come in bulk size. But you cannot do everything at once, so the first job you have is to engage with the client in the business of deciding where to start. The client's selection of a starting point is where you ordinarily hope to begin. But if the client's choice is dangerous to self or others or if it promises more trouble and failure, you have the responsibility of pointing out the risks. A social worker cannot be a party to planning that is destructive, but you must be very sure of your ground before rejecting out of hand the client's chosen starting place.

This indicates that you must use the skills of interviewing, communication, and relationship discussed in previous chapters to help in arriving at some understanding of the client's perception of the problem. This does not mean that any worker needs to be, or can be, an instant expert on problems. The primary job at this point is to seek to understand what it is that brings the client to ask for help. One of the primary tools of understanding comes from the ability to empathize with the feeling the client brings (see Chapter 8). This means that you must put all other considerations aside for a moment and fully hear what the client is saying, the words used, the feeling carried by the words, and the unspoken messages sent by the body language. While you must focus an interview and there is certain information you may need, to rush too quickly to understanding through information collection may be to lose the very thing you seek. If the client is able to share, it is better to listen than to question. It is better to make brief comments or ask simple questions related to what the client just said, to encourage the client to continue, than to proceed on your own agenda. Let the clients tell their own story in their own way and time while you seek to understand their pain and the meaning of the way they share it. The critical issue at this point is to understand the clients' view of what brings you together, not to be busy formulating your own judgment or collecting information for your purposes. Not understanding is not necessarily an indication of inadequacy, a cause for despair. You can share with clients your difficulty in knowing what they are saying and ask if they can share more. In working with a problem beyond your understanding or a system very different from your own, it is important that you not burden either yourself or the client with unrealistic expectations of immediate mutual understanding. This is particularly true when you are talking with someone whose life experiences are very different from your own. You can attempt to understand if you can reach into yourself and your own experience to remember a time when you felt something similar to what the client is feeling. This does not mean the experience was similar, but the emotion may be very similar to the feeling the client expresses. One of the reasons we can understand another human being is the commonness of human emotions and the generality of experience. You may not have lost a husband, as the client did, but surely you have suffered some loss sometime—a loss that left you in despair. The depth of feeling, the meaning of it, may be different, but the feeling has certain similarities that help you to understand. The other side of this coin is the danger to understanding the client if you have had a similar experience or are at a similar life stage (as are the worker and Mrs. Manley in the Appendix, Reading A-2). Here it is tempting to feel you understand the client because you had a similar experience or suffered a similar loss or to assume that since you were successful in dealing with a similar problem, the client should be advised to do the same thing. It is critical to remember that no two people experience the same event in the same way. The principle to remember is that to help, you must start where the client is, which means understanding his or her view of what brings you together.

The second piece of knowledge and understanding that goes into problem definition is related to what the client wants from the contact with you. What does the client hope will happen as a result of your coming together? It is through knowing the hopes of the client that you may understand what it is that the client wants changed. Arriving at a notion of the problem is no more an instant process than is arriving at an understanding. It may well take several meetings. The client's perception of the problem and yours may not be the same. Frequently they are not. Then it becomes necessary for you and the client to enter into a series of negotiations and discussions directed toward arriving at a definition of the problem on which you are to begin work. An example of this is found in "The House on Sixth Street" (Appendix, A-7).

The house on Sixth Street came to the attention of the social agency when Mrs. Smith came to an MFY Neighborhood Service Center to complain that there had been no gas, electricity, heat, or hot water in her apartment house for more than four weeks. She asked the agency for help. Mrs. Smith was 23 years old, African-American, and the mother of four children, three of whom had been born out of wedlock. At the time she was unmarried and receiving Aid to Families with Dependent Children. She came to the center in desperation because she was unable to run her household without utilities. Her financial resources were exhausted—but not her courage. The Neighborhood Service Center worker decided that in this case the building—the tenants, the landlord, and circumstances affecting their relationships—was of central concern.

Thus the worker who listened to Mrs. Smith's troubles saw the problem as broader than one person. The worker visited the tenement and found conditions as described. All families were suffering from lack of adequate facilities in their apartments. The worker then defined the problem as one belonging to all the tenants of the house and secured the tenants' agreement to this definition. Thus all the tenants of the apartment became the client system and the problem became helping them to organize their demands for services and utilities to which they were legally entitled. The target was the landlord, and an attempt was made to form an action system of the seven different public agencies responsible for housing code enforcement and other agencies responsible for supplying benefits and services to tenants.

One of the greatest difficulties in identifying the problem occurs when workers are so focused on their definition of the problem that they do not hear what their clients are communicating about how they see and feel the difficulty. Workers often define the goal without discussion of outcome with the client. The workers then continue on their course without being aware of the incongruity between what they are about and what the client wants. Given the lack of a common goal, things do not go well, and it is easy to see the lack of progress as the result of the psychopathology of the client.

As an example of such a situation, the work with Mr. Keene over a 14-month period is summarized below. Mr. Keene was referred to a private family agency by the court following the hospitalization of his wife for mental illness, because the court believed that Mr. Keene would need help in caring for the three children, ages 4, 2, and 1. It appeared that Mrs. Keene had been the family manager and had taken care of Mr. Keene and the children. In this situation both the worker and the court defined the problem as securing care for the children without hearing the pain, guilt, and confusion of Mr. Keene. As a result, at the end of the recording the worker is again asking Mr. Keene how he wants to solve the problem she identified. However, it appears to us that Mr. Keene probably sees the primary problem as the absence of his wife. Second is his lack of comprehension of mental illness, and third is the guilt he carries about what has happened. It can be expected that there will continue to be problems with child care as long as the worker does not recognize Mr. Keene's feelings and begin with Mr. Keene's problem. This case is a good example of how, if we want to be of help, we must start with where the client hurts. If we cannot start there, as in emergency situations involving child care, we can at least recognize with the client what the situation is about and how the views differ. We can at least assure clients that we heard them and that their view of the problem is understood.

Mr. Keene had need of and sought a great deal of help in financial management. He looked to the worker as to a parent to decide on specific expenditures. For several months in weekly contacts the worker helped him manage through putting money for monthly budget items in envelopes each payday. Gradually he became able to figure expenditures himself and to regulate some of his erratic spending. His major problems in financial management were an uncontrollable impulse to overspend on useless gifts to his wife and an inability to deny the children toys, sweets, and recreation jaunts. He would agree with the worker when she carefully figured out with him what would be reasonable and appropriate spending on these items, but he would persistently overspend. At times he would laugh at himself for taking his wife something she was not permitted to have and then would justify it by saying someday she could use it. He talked persistently about his wife, about the fact that he had not known she was ill, about not knowing the cause of her illness, about his concern as to when she would come home. The worker did not respond directly to these concerns but concentrated on the children's needs. In 12 months, however, he was able to afford a housekeeper.

His relationship to the children was characterized by anxious fretting over them, indulging them, and demanding the utmost in care of them from the housekeeper. Momentary sternness with them would be quickly replaced by petting and indulgence. Any illness or behavior deviations caused extreme worry. Though alarmed at Patrick's temper tantrums, he would give in to them. The restlessness, hyperactivity, and food fads of Mary, age 2½ years, worried him. Certain comments indicated that he connected the children's symptoms with their mother's behavior. He persisted in taking the children to visit their mother even though the worker advised against it and he himself would agree that the visit meant little to his wife and were exhausting and disturbing to the children. The worker's efforts to help him largely involved giving recognition to his desire to be a good parent and using his concern for the children's welfare to argue for consideration of their health and emotional comfort. Mr. Keene always presented problems to the worker with an earnest request for advice, and the worker gave sound child guidance advice freely. However, Mr. Keene was able to use the advice only fragmentarily.

The worker observed repeatedly in the record that Mr. Keene was very devoted to his wife. He visited regularly and excessively, taking gifts and writing letters. He talked repeatedly of her eventual return. He would react to any slight improvement in her condition with great optimism and with urgent demands for her discharge. Recently he brought her home against medical advice. She became disturbed, and after she disrupted a smoothly running home, he was forced to return her to the hospital. It was recorded that he often referred to his wife's competence prior to her illness, adding, "And I didn't know she was ill." This statement was not explored.

Mr. Keene's relationship to the housekeepers had been problematic. The first housekeeper probably was incompetent, but this was not clear because of Mr. Keene's nagging and his constant comparisons of her activities with those of his wife. He fired this woman because she was unkind to the children.

The second housekeeper, a competent person who got along fairly well with the children, quit because she could not endure his demands or his competitive undermining of her efforts with them. Mr. Keene was remorseful about this, recognizing too late that she was a good housekeeper and mother substitute. This woman complained to the worker that she was expected to do the man's chores and to coax Mr. Keene to get up every morning. The worker's efforts in helping Mr. Keene with his housekeeper problems were to try to get him to see their side of the situation and to face the errors of his ways. He readily would admit his wrongdoing and declare his intention to do better next time.

The third housekeeper was a competent, motherly woman who got along smoothly with Mr. Keene through joking with him, mothering him, and bossing him. She mended his clothes and packed his lunches. She allowed the children to play without restraint, and they became more quiet and contented. Mr. Keene assumed more responsibility with chores and reported enthusiastically to the worker that now his problems were solved and he would not be needing help much longer. Impulsively, without consulting the worker or the housekeeper, he brought his wife home from the hospital with grudging medical consent but on the basis of his reports of favorable conditions for her care at home. Later he justified his action through saying that he had been unhappy that his wife was not at home to enjoy everything with them. The housekeeper could not put up with the wife's very disturbed behavior and threatened to leave. Mr. Keene turned to the worker, who helped him face the fact that his wife was not ready to live outside a hospital. In returning her, Mr. Keene had to call plainclothes police and win her cooperation through deception.

Subsequently he was very disturbed about this and about his wife's reproachful remarks to him for betraying her.

The Present Situation

Now, following this episode, Mr. Keene is anxious and undecided as to future plans. He thinks he probably can mend matters with the housekeeper, but she is still angry and fearful and on the verge of leaving. How will he ever bring his wife home if no one will give her a trial? Will she ever get well? He cannot always be changing housekeepers. It is bad for the children. This is a good housekeeper, and perhaps he should urge her to stay. He may never find her equal. Certain comments show some anger with her for not putting up with his wife, even though Mrs. Keene was irrational and clearly unable to assume responsibility or to permit anyone else to do so in her home. He cannot endure the thought of separation from the children. Foster home care was discussed, but he thought he could not face not seeing his children every day. The pros and cons of the two plans—foster care and a continuation of the present plan—were reviewed. Mr. Keene left the interview undecided but leaning toward another trial of the housekeeper service.

One of the problems with a situation such as the one discussed above is that the client gradually begins to develop a sense of failure. Mr. Keene must feel that he is not being a "good client." The worker is doing so much for him, but he cannot seem to carry through as she expects him to. In our view he cannot and will not be able to carry through until the worker understands what is the central issue in the situation for him. Just one further comment on the situation. This is not a chapter on interventive roles, but it seems to us that the worker should have involved the hospital and its staff in the action system for Mr. Keene and used the roles of broker and advocate for Mr. Keene with the hospital around his understanding of his wife's illness.

We cannot possibly overemphasize the point that *effective work depends on appropriate problem identification.* The way you define the problem will define what data are collected and will dictate what are seen as appropriate answers. *This step must be right or all else fails.* There can be no engagement between client and worker without a common understanding of what they are about together from the client's frame of reference. This does not mean that you should set aside your definition of the problem. It means that you and the client must spell out both definitions and agree on ordering the problems for work.

Another important difficulty often found in problem definition is that workers get the problem and the cause all mixed up. Suppose you are presented with a case of a 13-year-old boy, James C, who (1) has just stolen a car, (2) comes from a home in which the father has just died in an automobile accident, and (3) has a mother who says that she may overprotect her son. Most students, acting as probation officers and just introduced to the notion of problem definition, will write that the problem is the mother's overprotection and the lack of a father. *The central problem at the moment is that the boy has just been apprehended by the police while driving a stolen car.* There may be some relationship between his and his mother's interaction or their situation and the problem. However, consideration of the meaning of the home situation falls under assessment and follows considerably more data collection. The mother recognizes this difference in that she does not say that the problem is her overprotection, but that *the cause of the behavior stems from this type of relationship with her son.*

If you see the problem as the mother's overprotection, you have shifted the problem from the son's behavior to the mother's. In addition, you may be terribly wrong even in settling on this explanation. For example, if the boy is asked to tell what happened, he may contribute the information that he was a candidate for gang membership and initiation rites required that he steal a car. If this type of explanation is received, assessment requires that the two possible explanations (those of mother and son) be put together in an attempt to plan what can be of help in preventing a recurrence of the delinquency. It may be that in the course of the exploration and assessment the client system and you will redefine the problem for work as the mother's overprotection. However, that awaits the problem definition, the goal setting, the data collection, and the assessment of what this all means and what is to be done about it.

Let us return to Mr. Keene. In that case, as in this, the worker has a goal identified by a referral system: Mr. Keene's children must have care. Obviously that will have to be one problem for work between worker and client, but there must be recognition of Mr. Keene's definition of the problem. In the boy's case, there must be recognition of the mother's definition of the cause and that may well become the primary problem for work. But it is important to recognize that everyone involved saw stealing the car as the primary problem.

Sometimes the development of a common ground for work can be established quickly; sometimes a series of interviews is necessary; and sometimes a common ground cannot be found. However, without a common place to begin, you and the client cannot proceed. When common ground cannot be reached, you and the client may find it necessary to acknowledge this fact and for the present at least, discontinue your efforts. In an authority-related setting, in which you have a legal mandate to provide supervision and the client has a legal mandate to report his or her activities, there are two possibilities. You may return to the court and acknowledge that there is nothing that can be accomplished between the client and you and ask that the court decide the next steps. This may be a wise course of action if the situation involves, for example, the court's charge that you work with a mother who has been abusing her child and you are concerned about the danger of such behavior to the physical well-being of the child. Or you may agree with the client that you will attempt to meet only the responsibilities mandated by law. In either of these situations, however, the possibility of reaching a common ground at a future date should be kept alive by leaving the door open for future negotiations.

Partialization is an important aspect of problem definition. *Partialization* refers to the process of separating from the universe of problems of the client the specific problem or problems that are to become the focus of worker-client attention. No one can deal with a whole range of problems at one time, even when they are closely related. An attempt to do so may lead to floundering, lack of focus, and an overwhelming sense of despair as you and the client recognize the multiplicity of the client's stress experience. These difficulties can be avoided by partializing from the universe of problems a specifically defined problem (the problem-to-be-worked). One of us first heard this phrase used by Helen Harris Perlman in a lecture. It seemed so expressive of the concept discussed here that we adopted it. It carries, for us at least, the connotation of worker activity with the client toward solution of the problem as the beginning point. Later other problems may be tackled. Partialization also provides greater opportunities for finding a common ground—client and worker do not have to agree on all problems to find a beginning place. They must simply agree on a starting place.

Another word of caution. At this stage in the exploration process you must be careful not to assume that the problem lies with the person who first approaches the agency. Although the problem may be very troublesome for this person, it may be rooted in another system. The target of change may not be the client. This is a significant difference between social work and psychology and psychiatry. Social work approaches the total system in which the client is involved to determine where to address change efforts. If the client does not have any suggestions about where to start (as was true for the mother who said to the worker that she did not know which problem was the largest one: "All I know is that we are in a mess for sure"), you may introduce suggestions about a starting place. Sometimes you and the client may find that where to begin can very well turn into the immediate problem to be worked. In other words, it is perfectly possible that the problem for work is to define the problem. If this sounds like double-talk, it is not. To work on something, you have to decide where you should begin and where you are going. The inability of various interests involved in a situation to perceive the problem in the same way—to define it in a congruent way that allows work to be done on it—may well be a central problem. Consider the following example:

> Miss B, a 29-year-old schoolteacher, was admitted to a rehabilitation service following a massive stroke. She has been diabetic since she was 5 years old, and despite constant medical attention and rigid personal self-discipline in diet and medication, the disease was becoming progressively worse. During the past five years she has been losing her sight, and now she is considered legally blind. The stroke, which was also related to the diabetic condition, resulted in paralysis of her right side. Miss B has always been a very goal-directed person, and in spite of an ever more handicapping illness, has an advanced degree in the education of handicapped children. She sees her problem as one of getting well quickly so she can return to her classroom, and she has a somewhat unrealistic notion of what is involved in such an accomplishment, denying the hard and difficult work of learning to walk with a cane and of learning to read by braille. She is angry with the nurses and often refuses to cooperate with them because she feels that they are trying to keep her dependent. Her prognosis (which has been shared over and over again with her) is that she is in the last stages of an irreversible terminal condition and that she can never return to teaching. From their view the problem is that Miss B is unwilling to accept the prognosis and behave properly. The staff feels that the problem is that the patient won't accept the massive damage that she has and will not participate with them in the small, painful, and difficult tasks necessary to achieving minimal self-care. A social worker sees the problem as getting Miss B to apply for welfare because her own funds are almost exhausted and to engage Miss B in planning for a move to a nursing home, as the rehabilitation facility cannot keep her much longer.
>
> In this situation the problem for work probably has to be attempting to resolve the incongruence among the various views of the problem and of finding a beginning that can permit the client and the various other necessary systems to interact to some productive purpose for the client.

Goal Setting This case situation leads us to another consideration that interacts closely and constantly with the definition of the problem to be worked. That is the question of how the client system or other system sees the problem as working out. Not only did each of the significant participants in Miss B's case have a personal view of the problem, but each view of the problem encompassed an objective or a solution. Professional people involved with Miss B wanted her to accept both the inevitability of her physical deterioration and a realistic plan for care—although they differed on the plan. Miss B wanted to return to teaching.

We often find that persons involved in a problem present us with the solution rather than with the problem. The client comes to request help in implementing an already decided solution rather than in examining alternatives to action. This makes eminently good sense, in that the search for some desired end is a constant thrust of all of us when confronted with a problem. Goal seeking is what gives the problem-solving process its thrust and purpose, and the consideration of client goals is an important part of each phase of the problem-solving model. The way workers recognize goals and the way they work with goals will differ in each phase, but client goals must never be ignored. In the beginning contact, it is important that you separate the problem from the goal so that each may be considered separately. When a mother comes to your child welfare agency saying that she needs to place her child, she may well be presenting you with her goal in the shape of a problem. This may be her answer to any one of a whole range of problems, but while it is the only answer she can see, it may be an answer that will cause her great pain and despair. You must become involved in the question to which placing the child is the client's answer. You and the client may or may not find a better answer, but in any case you should not confuse question and answer. However, in the process of defining and exploring the client's problem, you must never lose sight of the fact that the client's original goal was placement, and it is essential to understand the meaning of this goal for the client. Do not dismiss client goals lightly—simply seek to separate goal and problem for more effective work.

Let us return to Miss B, a real person whom I knew. How does one reconcile the disparate views of the goals in this situation? Miss B, desperately needing to deny the prognosis, is determined that she will get well and return to teaching. All she wants is recognition of this goal and help in achieving it. The medical staff is certain that she can never return to teaching, that the illness is progressing rapidly, that her only hope is to stay its progress somewhat by certain attempts at self-care, and they want her to accept these conclusions. A social worker, concerned over the limits of hospital care and Miss B's finances, wants Miss B to plan for other care.

There are different types and dimensions of goals to be recognized and discussed at this point. You may be concerned with an optimal goal—or an ultimate goal—that is the final desired outcome to which the effort is directed. Or you may be concerned with interim goals—objectives that are significant steps on the journey toward the optimal goal. Usually, before the ultimate objective can be realized, a series of intermediate objectives must be met. Often these intermediate objectives can be a way of testing whether the ultimate goal is sound. There are usually several layers, or levels, of interim goals. The first goal achieved becomes an aid to the achieving of more complex or more advanced interim goals. Just as you have to determine a problem for work with which to begin, you will often find that the initial steps have to do with facilitative or interim goals as a way of collecting data and making decisions on the feasibility of the ultimate goal.

If you examine the different levels of goals stated at the time the social worker entered Miss B's case, you will find that the interim goals are not different for the various systems involved. The struggle is over ultimate goals. All the professional people involved in the situation want Miss B to participate in rehabilitative efforts that will keep her functioning as well as possible for as long as possible. These same efforts are necessary if Miss B is to achieve her ultimate goal of returning to teaching.

The worker's efforts may appropriately be directed to sharing with Miss B (1) that the medical staff and Miss B see the problem differently, (2) that they are in strong disagreement over the ultimate goals, (3) that the worker questions whether Miss B can return to full-time teaching, but (4) that perhaps the place to start is with the problem of her ability to work on certain interim goals that are necessary to either ultimate goal. If she wants to return to the classroom, she must struggle to walk again, to read braille, and to care for herself in certain physical matters while collecting data about her progress and planning for the future. Eventually there came a time when the worker and Miss B had to put the results of their efforts together and make an ultimate plan. There appeared to be two choices. Either she returns to the community as an independently functioning person or she accepts some alternate goal for at least partially sheltered care. The time of assessment and renegotiation of goals and of planning for the longer future will come, but for now they can explore the problem and the feasibility of certain long-term goals by starting with interim goals that become the facilitative goals because all can agree on them and they allow further data collection before assessment and final decision making. Miss B soon discovered through trying to cope with self-care that she would be unable to return to the classroom. She decided that part-time work in a nursing home was a realistic goal. I did not have to force a change in goal. She made her own decision.

To begin with the interim goals as the desired outcome for the exploratory (initial) contract is desirable for several reasons. We discussed earlier the importance of hope as a factor of motivation. If you tell clients their goals are unrealistic, you should not be surprised if they do not engage with you. You have destroyed hope. If you can begin with interim goals, the client will usually abandon unrealistic goals as they are tested through work on interim goals.

We believe that both ultimate goals and the means of change are obtained from objective study, evaluation, and planning. These procedures are essential to the effective use of the problem-solving model. But all too often workers see cause, truth, and knowledge as absolutes. Sure of themselves and their understanding, they manipulate data into firm conclusions or use the information to arrive at a psychosocial explanation that seems reasonable and set off on a course of action toward their immediate goals—goals that may not be shared with clients or take account of their expectations. Instead, the contact phase of the problem-solving process demands that you begin with an exploration of the common definition of a problem to be worked and a common understanding of and acceptance of goals that at this stage may only be (and probably should only be) facilitative. These goals serve to engage the client systems and you in jointly unearthing the ongoing knowledge that will eventually establish (in the contract phase) firmer means and ends around the central issues that this assessment will identify. The problem-solving model, as we use it, demands that the client's purposes and expectations in joining the worker in interaction be explored, understood, and kept in the center of concern. It is our firm conviction that lack of initial exploration of expectations and goals and lack of careful selection of the starting place in the contact phase of the worker-client interaction account for a large percentage of the failures of the helping process (Mayer & Timms, 1969).

As an example of the difficulties that can arise if clients are not involved from the beginning in problem definition and exploration of goals and expectations, we have reproduced an actual situation for your consideration.

Restive Campers

This case describes a problem encountered when 200 young people arrived at a summer camp in a developing country. The young people were from four different districts of the country; each district sent 50 youths.

> The national 10-day summer work camps commenced on the morning of August 11. Youth camp managers were responsible for identification of campsites and other facilities. Districts were responsible for transporting their participants to campsites. Accompanying campers brought summer camp entry forms and fees as well as three voluntary leaders. The national coordinator was responsible for organizing food that was transported to the campsite.
>
> At 1 p.m. the first group of campers arrived from district A. They were welcomed by the camp director, registered, refreshed, shown their change room, and assigned sleeping facilities. At approximately 2 p.m. the second group arrived, and they were also hospitably received, as were the third and fourth groups.
>
> The orientation program began at 7 p.m. Campers were introduced to camp staff and other volunteers assigned to the camp. The aims and objective of the camp were outlined. The objective to be reached was to establish a half-acre vegetable garden on the campsite.
>
> At this announcement the campers from district C began to become restive. Staff believed tiredness was the cause of the behavior, but soon district B campers also started to react in the same fashion. The staff became suspicious and tried to find the cause of the change in behavior. The campers said that they were not informed at district level of the type of activities they would be engaged in while at camp, were not prepared for such hard work, and requested to be sent home immediately. This request could not be granted, as the transport that brought the groups had left for the return journey, and it was now 10:30 p.m.
>
> The group of campers began behaving outrageously, which caused the director of the camp to summon the nearby police. On the arrival of the police the groups were involved in various forms of vandalism and destruction of property. This led to the arrest of 25 participants. The police had to spend the rest of the night to maintain law and order.

Preliminary Contract

In arriving at the preliminary contract, which is in essence an agreement between the worker and the client on the problem to be worked and the facilitative goals, there are some other absolutes that must be clarified with the client. You must clarify the realities and boundaries of what can be offered and must behave in such a way as to help the client understand the nature of further work together. To make a brief comment on the first point: this requires that you be able to convey to the client the limits of the service that can be offered while at the same time conveying your belief in the ability to help within those limits and interest in helping the client find another resource if the service that can be offered be too limited. In other words, you must not promise more than you can deliver and so trap the client by false hopes, but neither do you want to operate in such a way as to imply hopelessness to the client. The client may come to you out of pain, despair, or anger but will only become involved in action with you when this feeling of discomfort is joined to a hope that something can be done.

It is usual to find clients confused about how the helping process will work. As was pointed out in Chapter 1, people find it difficult to grasp the nature of the social work job. There are seldom visible technologies or artifacts that will give others some notion of what the process is all about. Your actions in the beginning phase can give the client a sample of the social work method. That is one reason the beginning is so important. Another reason is the pattern-setting nature of communication between elements of a system or among systems.

At the end of the beginning phase of problem identification and goal determination, the client and you decide whether you wish to continue together. If you both do, you are free to begin to collect the information on which assessment and planning will be based. We caution again that nothing is more sterile than information collecting for the purpose of information collecting. Information is collected for the purpose of taking effective action, and all efforts must be directed to that end. The kind and amount of information collected will be dictated by the defined problem for work and the preliminary goal that is established.

Areas of Data Collection

It is difficult to deal with areas of data collection concretely because the specific areas to be explored depend on the situation. However, there are some principles that should be considered:

1. It is a joint process, and the client should be involved in helping to determine the areas to be explored.

2. The client should be aware of the sources being used for data collection (note: clients are not always asked for their permission).

3. There should be a connection between the problems identified and the data collected. The client should be aware of this connection.

4. It is critical to explore all areas that the clients see as connected as well as helping them to understand the areas you seek to explore.

5. Data collection goes on all the time, but it is critical to the problem identification, goal setting, and assessment stages of work.

6. The primary areas of data collection are all points listed under the contact phase of the model presented in Chapter 2.

7. It is important to note that under exploration and investigation the type of client system will determine the areas of data collection to some extent. Please give some attention to these differences.

8. It is crucial that you understand the clients' view of all areas of data collection—their thinking about the meaning of the items, their feelings in those areas, and any actions they may have taken.

It is important for you to note that there are three areas of data collection that are the same for all systems and all problems. They are the areas of hope, discomfort, and opportunity. You may want to go back and read the discussion about the importance of these areas in human growth, development, and functioning, found in Chapter 4 in the section on foundation knowledge. In our thinking these are the most important areas in this stage of work, both in terms of the worker's collection of data and in terms of the worker's actions with the client.

What causes people to act? As was stated earlier, for action to take place, discomfort with things as they are must be felt, but this is not enough. If a person is to act, the hope of being able to reach a goal that is seen as the answer to wants must be added to discomfort, mild or severe. In addition there must be some ability to consider what has gone wrong and some opportunity for change in the situation. Productive engagement in the social work process is dependent on the client's hope-discomfort balance and on the extent to which the practitioner is able to engage that pressure by the hope and clearly defined opportunity offered. Before work can begin on a problem, the client must be uncomfortable about the present state of affairs and hope that something can be done about it, and you must be able to communicate understanding (empathy, if you will) of the client's discomfort. Even more important, you must engage yourself with the client's hope. As was once said, when hope is weak, the practitioners must find a way of "hitching their motor to the client's wagon." For this reason, we urge that you always be concerned with the level of clients' hope-discomfort balance and with your early activity with clients in this area. It is important to note how clients engage themselves with you and with any opportunities you present for problem solving.

Sources and Methods of Data Collection

We would now like to make some general observations about the sources from which you and the client will collect the information that is needed to make an assessment. The first and most important principle is that the client system must be aware of the resources you are using and why they are being used. If at all possible (as was noted earlier in the chapter), the client's permission should be secured before any particular source of information beyond the client system is used. However, whether or not permission is secured, the client must know about the sources used, the information sought, and why the information is believed to be appropriate to the task at hand. If commitment is to the clients' participation in decision making that will lead to action toward their goals, you must share with them all the information on which decisions may be based. Otherwise, you deprive them of an opportunity for representative participation in the discussion about themselves.

In general, modes of data collection can be divided into five groups: (1) the clients' accounts as they tell them; (2) accounts of others; (3) questions and tests, either verbal or written; (4) observation; and (5) records of other professional or institutional systems. Perhaps the most widely used tool for data collection is the interview or group meeting with the client system, in which questioning and observation are used to gain information. The interview or the meeting requires a knowledge of the principles of relationship and communication, which have been discussed in previous chapters. In the use of the face-to-face meeting, you must decide its purpose, the information to be obtained from it, and how you want to structure it. At one extreme is the nondirective interview or meeting in which you follow the feeling and thinking of the interviewee or allow the group to reveal itself as it will. At the other extreme is the completely structured interview or meeting, in which you have a scheduled set of questions from which there will be no departure. However, you are also giving some structure to the interview and determining what data may be collected when you decide where and when it will be held, when you establish ground rules and norms for content and participation, and even when you arrange the chairs of the persons involved. Careful thought should be given to the place of the first meeting: is it to be on the client's turf or yours?

The nondirective interview, which allows clients to tell their own story in their own way and at their own pace, is an important source of information that usually cannot be gained by direct questions. By listening carefully and observing body language, you can gain an understanding of the stress the problem has brought to the client and something of the resources the client has tried to use or has found helpful. You begin to understand the client's cognitive pattern—the way the client relates cause and effect—the kind of reasoning the client uses. You can collect knowledge about the coping strategies of the client and the strengths that have served well. In addition, you can gain considerable knowledge about the client's relationships with others as well as the client's relationship to the helping person, since much of the client's account may concern interactions with meaningful people. The client's understanding of the world around him or her and of social relationships and their utility can be estimated from his or her account of the problem, the way it came about, and what has been done to change it.

Obviously, the interview may be used to collect information from sources other than the client system. In using these other systems, you will want to consider carefully the kinds of information you think they can provide and the need you have for this information. You will have to give thought to the fact that certain information sources may expect the interview to involve a sharing of information. If you are to share information, you should discuss it with the client system. If you are unwilling to share information, you must make this known to the source when the interview is requested.

Many kinds of written questioning techniques are in use. Clients are often asked to fill out application or information forms when they approach an agency. There are various questionnaires that may be used with various client systems for various purposes. If a group is trying to decide a focus for future meetings and members seem reluctant to share their views openly with other members, an anonymous written questionnaire may be helpful. It allows members to express an opinion without penalty. Written exercises are sometimes used in work with families to allow members to express themselves without feeling that they have directly attacked other members of the family. In certain community organization projects, the use of a survey based on a written questionnaire is a valuable technique. Obviously, you do not want to use a written questionnaire with clients who do not express themselves well in writing or clients who may see it as a dehumanizing device or clients to whom it may imply that they are merely being classified into one of a similar group of persons.

In speaking of both verbal and written questioning as data collection tools, we should mention the use of other persons to collect information for you. In certain situations someone close to the client system and knowledgeable about the situation may conduct an interview for you. An indigenous Spanish-speaking community worker may be asked to talk to a Chicano woman who has just suffered the loss of her husband and who should not be asked to take on the additional burden of speaking in English to a stranger at such a time. Also, you may have other professionals, such as psychologists, administer tests to gain certain knowledge. These tests may be oral or written. Psychologists often use projective techniques, which allow the respondents to impose their own frame of reference on some stimulus, such as a picture. Or to have two sources of information, you may ask a psychiatrist or perhaps your supervisor to interview the client.

Along with questioning, you will use observation as a way of gathering data. Though we all use observation of others in daily interactions, much will be lost unless you learn to make deliberate planned use of the technique. As with verbal questions, observation can be structured or unstructured, and you can be a totally uninvolved observer, a participant observer, or a leader-and-initiator observer. For example, you may give a group of children a game to play and then observe and record their actions without being in any way involved in the game. Or you may be a committee member, both involved and observing. Or you may serve as a committee chairperson while trying to observe the interactions of the members. This last possibility will probably cause many to ask how effectively a chairperson can observe the interactions of other committee members. This is an example of questions that are often raised about the use of observations. What about the bias and the selectivity of the observer? No one can possibly observe all the interactions of a group, or even all the facial expressions and changes in posture of one person, in an interview. Observation requires sensitivity to others and the capacity to see small changes. In addition, it requires that you know yourself and your biases. It requires you to have given thought to what you want to learn through this process and to how you do it. Since you cannot collect all the data on any one transaction, you must recognize that you collect only certain information and are therefore selective. You must know what framework guides this selectivity.

The last general way to collect information is from existing written material not gathered specifically for the present situation. Often you may find that the agency or some other place has records of previous contacts with the client system. Usually it is wise to know the contents of such records and to discuss them with the client. Otherwise the client may waste valuable time and trouble in worrying over what you may know. If previous written materials are available, they can be a very efficient means of data collection. Their use places little demand on the client system and is within your control. But therein lies a seductive danger: such records can easily be used without the client's knowledge. There is another danger: when something is read, there is a tendency to feel that it is really known. For these reasons we especially caution you against the indiscriminate use of such material. You must question written material as you do a human informant. Does it give the facts? Are the facts documented? Or does the material merely reflect another person's judgments? You must also recognize that such material deals with the past, that it may not bear on the present problem and may even confuse the issue if it was written or gathered for a purpose unconnected with it, and (to repeat) that it may reflect the biases and selective perceptions and evaluations of the persons who collected it. Often there is a tendency to see written material as holding more of the truth than the practitioner's present experiences. This tendency should be strongly resisted. On the other hand, appropriate written material can be an effective source of data.

Skills in the Contact Phase

Most of this chapter has been devoted to answering the "what" question of the activities in the contact phase. We shall now try to answer the "how" question. Once again we must say that it is difficult to be specific and concrete. It is difficult to be sure that our words communicate to you what we are trying to communicate. This difficulty stems from two factors: words are the symbols of human interaction that carry meaning only within some context, and the same words often mean different things to different people, so that a common meaning can be established only by the sender accurately hearing the feedback from the system receiving the communication. Written communication can be put together in such a way that the writer believes that it establishes a context and a meaning, but one can be sure about that only through feedback. Thus we are dreadfully handicapped in communicating with you, particularly about some matters such as self-awareness.

If you are to carry through effectively on the tasks of the contact phase, you must engage the feelings and the thinking of the client in the process. We are not saying that a relationship must be developed, and especially we are not saying that a good relationship must be developed. What we are saying is that the client and you must engage with each other (interact with each other in a way that has meaning to the client system as a beginning of what will later become a working relationship). The first requirement for this engagement is certain types of knowledge, including knowledge of self—of the way you feel and think about the type of problem and the client—and cognitive knowledge of the resources available in both the change agent system and other community systems.

Let us go back for a moment to Mrs. C's case in which her son James has just stolen a car. There are a constellation of factors that may trap people into defining the problem as Mrs. C's overprotection of her son:

1. An immediate identification with the son as the "victim" of what has happened.

2. An emotional readiness to blame parents for their children's pain and trouble.

3. A belief in the personal-deficit concept of deviant behavior.

4. A belief that children's behavior is usually caused by parents' treatment of them.

5. An emotional and intellectual commitment to wanting to find "the real problem," which leads to the mistake of defining "cause" as "problem." (You may want to go back and read the quotations from Johnson in Chapter 2 on problem solving.)

6. The fact that you are presented with an upper-middle-class client who has internalized points 1 through 4 in her own thinking and who is so upset over this crisis (following upon another crisis that she may still not have mastered) that she is ready to fix blame on herself and spare her son. So you may define the problem as hers rather than her son's and help her beat herself into a further sense of inadequacy while you give the son a nice way of beginning to blame others for his actions.

Please note that this is not to say that there is no relationship between the mother's treatment of her son and his actions, nor is it to say that that connection and the mother's spontaneously suggesting it are ignored in setting the problem for work. One further comment: if you are seeking the "real problem," maybe it lies in the father's death, which is responsible for the mother's feelings and actions, which in turn are responsible for the son's behavior. Should those feelings be the problem for work? What would happen to the mother's sense of adequacy and her ability to develop different ways of treating her son if the problem for work was defined as her reaction to her husband's death and that reaction was assessed as a normal response to overwhelming stress and crisis? And what about her son's reaction to his father's death? These questions must be thought about by you and considered thoughtfully with the client system (mother and son). Data will be collected on all these life stresses that may have led to the problem behavior. The work of considering their impact, integrating them into some meaningful assessment of the situation, and planning the work together is a part of the next several chapters. What we are trying to make clear here is the importance of not confusing the presenting problem with the cause.

If you will go back to the factors listed earlier, you will note that some of these factors are cognitive, some are emotional, and some are both. Perhaps the most severe handicap in problem solving is our tendency to need a consistent frame of reference both intellectually and emotionally. This results in a tendency to define problems within our usual working notion of the human condition—to view clients' problems, as it were, from within our frame of reference. We may explain our clients' insistence that we look at the problem from their point of view as their resistance to seeing things accurately, and thus in itself proof of the correctness of our formulations. To make this clear, connect the dots in Figure 10-1 as directed.

Connect these dots by four
straight lines without lifting
the pencil from the paper

After you have tried to solve the problem, turn to the end of the chapter for the solution. Are you surprised? The thing that leads many people to failure in solving this problem is the fact that the first time people try it, they almost invariably make an assumption that the dots compose a square and that the problem must be defined as falling within the boundaries of that system. Thus, the failure to solve the problem does not lie with the difficulty of the problem or incapacity to do the necessary tasks. Rather it lies with self-imposed assumptions that nowhere are given as a part of the problem. This exercise demonstrates how important our unconscious assumptions can be to problem solving. You must be aware of your assumptions and make initial contact within the potential client's frame of reference.

Some further cautions before we move on to some specifics in the use of self in the contact phase. (1) The questions asked determine the answers given, and it is your responsibility to determine the questions. (2) Any behavior in the presence of another communicates a view of the nature of one's relationship with that person, and this principle applies to you as well as to the client. (3) An important part of human communication takes place through silence or lack of communication as well as through what is said and how it is said. Therefore, you must be aware of what is not being dealt with by the client as well as what is and must recognize that the client will interpret your silence in his or her own way. (4) Dependency and lack of responsibility for a person's actions are caused by someone else taking responsibility for that person's own thinking, feeling, and planning and are not caused by others giving too much or doing things for the person. The greatest causes of emotional dependency (as distinguished from the "normal" dependency of not being able to deal with concrete tasks because of handicaps of knowledge, skill, or other capacity) is the taking over of feelings, thinking, and decision-making responsibility. In fact, not doing *appropriate* things for clients may further break down their coping skills and result in further apathy.

The skills required in this phase are those described in Chapters 8 and 9, on relationship and communication, especially the ability to communicate empathy, genuineness, concern, trustworthiness, respect, and the conditions of service. Listening and attending skills are very important, as is attending both physically (in posture and body language) and psychologically to what the client is trying to communicate. It is important to listen both with ears to the words and with eyes to the body language and with the third ear to some total messages such as how clients feel and think about themselves, the world, significant others, and people in general; how clients perceive others related to them; and what clients' ambitions, goals, and aspirations are.

To be sure that you are interpreting the client's words and feelings accurately, you will have from time to time to check this out with the clients. This may be done by restating the basic messages that you think you hear in similar but fewer words, in submitting a tentative summary of what you made of the client's discussion, by connecting things that the client leaves unconnected but that you think may be connected. You will, of course, need skill in questioning, which is discussed in Chapter 9, on communication. There are times when you may use some tentative interpretation: "is it possible that what you are telling me means . . .?" Often you will be tempted to use reassurance: "I understand . . . " "That is hard . . . " "Most people would be upset. . . ." If you feel with the client, it is natural to want to do away with the pain and to try to help and support by an expression of understanding. However, you should be careful in the use of such phrases. They often serve to cut off the client's further exploration of the difficulty.

Many workers who feel the client's pain and have the impulse to help are greatly tempted to overuse reassurance. They want to remove the client's pain. But the purpose for which the clients come to them is not for the removal of the pain but for doing something about it. To help others, you must understand what the problem is that brings the client to you, and often this includes great pain for the client. However, help requires empathy, not pity or sympathy, which too early and too often communicates reassurance. Pain is a signal that there is trouble, and understanding the pain will help you to understand and define the problem as the client perceives it.

Emanuel Tropp (1984, p. 29) has developed an important set of statements related to the worker's presentation of self to the group. We see this as not limited to the group but as summing up in a very impressive way the necessary elements of the worker's presentation of self to the potential client system both at the initial contact and during the work together.

1. Compassion—I deeply care about you.

2. Mutuality—We are here on a common human level; let's agree on a plan, and then let's walk the path together.

3. Humility—Please help me to understand.

4. Respect—I consider you as having worth. I treat your ideas and feeling with consideration. I do not intrude upon your person.

5. Openness—I offer myself to you as you see me; real, genuine, and authentic.

6. Empathy—I am trying to feel what you are feeling.

7. Involvement—I am trying to share and help in your efforts.

8. Support—I will lend my conviction and back up your progress.

9. Expectation—I have confidence that you can achieve your goals.

10. Limitation—I must remind you of your agreed-upon obligations.

11. Confrontation—I must ask you to look at yourself.

12. Planning—I will always bring proposals, but I would rather have yours.

13. Enabling—I am here to help you become more able, more powerful.

14. Spontaneity and control—I will be as open as possible, yet I must recognize that in your behalf I need to exercise some self-control.

15. Role and person—I am both a human being like you and a representation of an agency, with a special function to perform.

16. Science and art—I hope to bring you a professional skill which must be based on organized knowledge, but I am dealing with people, and my humanity must lend art to grace the science.

Assessment

As we begin our discussion on assessment, we are once again reminded of the fact that the problem-solving process is not a linear but a spiral one. Although we list the steps of the process from problem definition to termination and evaluation in an orderly manner on a typeset page, the process does not move in clearly defined ways. This becomes particularly evident when we start to discuss assessment. Although assessment is a step in our outline, any assessment of a situation, problem, or client and the impact of the micro-, meso-, and macroenvironment is almost a continuous process from the time the worker enters a situation until termination.

Purpose and Process of Assessment The purpose of assessment is to reach an understanding of problem, client, and situation so that you can construct a plan to solve or alleviate the problem. Assessment is not conducted for the express purpose of understanding the client, although this is necessary to the extent that it relates to the problem, because you cannot help with a problem unless you understand it. Thus the ultimate purpose of assessment is to contribute understanding necessary for appropriate planning. We think this conceptualization is important because we believe there is a fine difference between seeking information simply to understand what motivates a person and seeking information for the purpose of action.

The process of assessment is an attempt (1) to comprehend the key elements in the problem situation, (2) to understand the meaning of the problem to the client in his or her situation, (3) to use all the client's understanding, (4) to direct all your professional knowledge in an active thinking process aimed at identifying what needs to be altered in the situation, and (5) to plan how these desired changes may be achieved. *Actually, the identified problem is likely to be an abstraction extracted from or teased out of a complex, uncertain, troubled situation by worker-client analysis and assessment.*

In many situations it is through the struggle to come to some agreement on what needs to be changed (what problem needs to be solved) and to trust, believe, and hope enough to engage in the work of problem solving that the client achieves for the first time an understanding of the problem and a belief in its manageability. Through the struggle toward the assessment that leads to problem definition, the client is enabled to comprehend the situation in a different way and if the client is a true participant in the process, to gain a sense of what a solution can mean.

Doing Assessment   Assessment involves an active thinking and testing process on the part of you and the client that results in the integration of understanding and knowledge in such a way that the problem becomes comprehensible and appears manageable enough to be converted into client actions and professional services. The test of a sound assessment is the contribution it makes to satisfactory problem resolution and to guiding the client's and your actions. It is probably best guided by a series of questions you pose both to yourself and to the client. The questions are generated from the material the client shares, from your professional knowledge of human beings and the way they grow and function, from the genesis and course of the problem, and from the effect of certain common or usual responses to the problem situation. The knowledge base that you bring to assessment consists of knowledge about critical issues that usually are found as key variables in situations similar to the one the client presents—for example, knowledge of the meaning of loss when a client speaks of losing a spouse or knowledge of the stress of transition when the client retires from a satisfying position to the role of senior citizen.

What must be determined in assessment is the applicability of this generalized knowledge to the particular situation of individual clients in their unique situations and environments. The questions that you ask should be focused on gaining an understanding of how this particular client's situation differs from the situation that would be constructed from generalized knowledge. Thus, with the client who has lost a husband, your generalized knowledge tells you something about the tasks necessary to pick up life after such a crisis and something about the feelings that usually accompany such an experience. You want to know if the tasks and the feelings are problematic for the client and how she is coping with them. At this point a comment is in order, based on your understanding as detailed above and designed to elicit a response from the client that will help you understand where she is with the problem: "It must be difficult to pick up the pieces and do all the things that have to be done around a house." Or if it seems more appropriate, ask a question: "Has it been hard to do all the things that have to be done around the house since your husband's death?" Or you may ask, "Most of the time when two people live together they share a lot of household tasks. Has it been difficult for you to have to do all these things by yourself?" We suggest asking about tasks rather than feelings because it is usually easier for the client to talk about facts than feelings. You should try to ask these questions and make these comments in a way that conveys to the client the message that you care and would like to help. You are hoping that as she answers these questions, she will of her own choice talk about feelings. If she doesn't, you will of course make a more direct comment about feelings, and you may wonder to yourself why she did not touch on feelings but rather gave a very factual answer.

There are many ways a client may answer these questions. Some examples are listed below. Try to decide what, if you were the worker, these responses might tell you.

1. "Oh, I haven't really done anything since he left me. The house is in a terrible mess and I don't have anything in the kitchen except some casseroles the neighbors brought over before the funeral. I feel awful when I look around my house, but we always did things together and I just can't get up the courage to tackle it by myself. I just sit and feel lost and cry."

2. "Well, you know, Tom never was very good about helping me with the house or other things. He went off to work and I did the rest. So I have kept busy doing things I usually do. Somehow I seem to miss him less if I keep busy. It's at night, when we used to watch TV together and discuss the programs, that I really feel so alone."

3. "Oh, my daughter lives down the street, and she comes up and keeps things going for me. I guess that I just sit. Somehow I don't want to do anything."

4. "Oh, my kids live close, and my daughter comes about three times a week and helps me. She brings groceries that she knows I need. When she can, she stays for supper and we talk about Dad. It is so good to talk to someone about all the things we did together and meant to each other. Somehow it's like he is there with us. My son comes maybe a couple of times a week and the three of us have supper and talk. It makes me feel so much better to remember all we had together and to know that the kids still remember and always will."

Exploring the Problem The long form of the problem-solving model at the end of Chapter 2, point I, A, c, 1, asks you to consider the "length of existence, previous occurrences, precipitating factors" of the problem. We think this is important to consider in assessment, because our knowledge base tells us that it is generally more difficult to solve a problem that has persisted for a long time. Clients usually form some pattern of adjustment to a long-standing problem and may find it hard to think of trying a new approach. The factors influencing a recent problem are much easier to understand, and the client will not be so debilitated in trying to deal with it. So if the client sighs a deep sigh and says the problem seems to have gone on forever, you may wonder about the energy that may be free to deal with it and the sense the client may have that it is unmanageable. How defeated is the client? These are important points to consider in assessment. What you must determine is whether these generalized assumptions abstracted from general knowledge are true for this particular client in his or her situation.

You also must understand why the client made the choice to come ask for help today. The answer to this question will tell you a lot about the individual client in the situation. Something must be different now, or why would he or she have come in today? So ask why, if the situation has gone on so long, he or she chose to come to now. It is important to know if the situation has simply reached the point where the client feels that unless there is some sort of relief he or she can't go on. Or did something happen just now that gave new hope or new urgency to the attempt at solution? If the problem has persisted for a long time and there is a serious and sudden event, perhaps you should explore with the client an immediate intervention.

You also need to know about previous occurrences of the problem and the client's prior attempts to change it. From the answers to these questions you can make some estimate of the capacity of the client to plan, to look forward and predict outcome, to invest energy. You also will have some evidence of the client's social skills and knowledge of social situations. Your knowledge base tells you that there are certain skills necessary to dealing with problems effectively, and you want to know if the client possesses these or is able to use them. You also want to know what the situation in which client and problem are embedded has contributed to the inability to solve the problem. You want to know how much sustained action the client was able to invest.

Putting Meaning to Situation While trying to collect facts on the problem and its existence, you should also be actively trying to relate your professional knowledge about people and situations in a way that helps you to understand the client's coping skills (or ego strength—refer to the discussion of the function of the ego in Chapter 4) and the environment of which the client and the situation are a part. What does the client's account of the attempts at solution tell you about the situational and environmental support and resources the client has available and what does it say about the obstacles in the environment? (Reread the material on systems theory and the discussion about levels of environment in Chapter 4.)

Feeling and Facts At the same time, you should use all your empathic skills to understand the meaning carried by the client's words and all your observational skills to read the body language. (Refer to Chapters 8 and 9.) You should add these understandings and observations to the other information we have collected. You should try to estimate whether the feeling the client is expressing is appropriate to the seriousness of the problem. If the problem is overwhelming but the client appears very placid or smiles a great deal, what theory will explain what is happening or its meaning? What knowledge can you draw on if there appears to be severe incongruence between the feeling and the information being shared? If these theoretical propositions are correct and it is appropriate to apply them to this individual client, what do they tell you about the client and perhaps about the appropriate plans for intervention?

As an aid to understanding assessment, reread the assessment statement in Mr. H's case (Appendix, A-3). Here, under the statement on motivation, the worker brings to bear her knowledge about the general course of human development and functioning when a person is confronted with constant pain. Yet in the next paragraph the worker talks about the individual strength of this man and about his supportive situation, which bears on the opportunities the worker saw to help the client manage the pain. We would prefer for the worker to have made a more detailed assessment of the client's strengths and their source. Here is an extremely strong man who copes extraordinarily well and who has strong ego defenses in dealing with the terrible situation in which he finds himself. The knowledge about the way people generally react to constant pain must be added to or integrated with the fact that this man is able to cope superbly with the problem.

Assessing the Keene Situation   As an example of how we may go about assessment, let us return to Mr. Keene's situation as outlined earlier in this chapter. Assume for a moment that at the point of the last recording the worker left the agency and you were assigned the Keene situation. You are going to see Mr. Keene tomorrow and inform him of the change in workers. You have two tasks: to make a brief assessment of the situation as you see it from the information and approach of the last worker and to plan for the interview, which will include testing your tentative assessment and considering the possibility of a different treatment plan.

In making the assessment you will want to note the previous worker's definition of the problem and her assessment of the situation. It appears that the worker concentrated totally on Mr. K's level of functioning compared with some notion of how an ideal father might be expected to relate to his children in a benign situation. There was no attempt on the part of the first worker to assess the systemic transactions of Mr. K's situation and Mr. K's development of parenting skills. Obviously the children have to have adequate care, but do you agree with the previous worker's concentration on this as solely Mr. K's responsibility, with no consideration of the impact of the situation on him and the family? The previous worker appeared to see Mr. K as a rather impulsive, dependent man who was inconsistent in his relationship with the children and impulsive in his relationship with his wife. But there is no evaluation of the meaning of the situation to Mr. K, the knowledge he had of the problem, or his social skills in dealing with the interaction of all the systems he suddenly had to interact with. Do you think there is a relationship between the worker's concentration on child care and at least some of Mr. K's continuing problem? In attempting to develop a tentative assessment of the situation, you will want to go back to precipitating factors of the problem. Let's see what knowledge you have of the situation and of the general meaning of such a situation to an individual.

The problem began as a crisis for Mr. K. Suddenly his wife was out of contact with reality and had to be hospitalized. What do you know about the impact of crisis on people and their ability to cope? Would Mr. K have functioned better if the worker had given some attention to what the crisis meant to him? The worker appears to ignore both what generalized crisis theory could tell her and what Mr. K's individual response to crisis might have been. A wife is more than just a child-care person or a homemaker. What do you know about the relationship between Mr. K and his wife? And what do you know about the meaning of sudden loss of a spouse? Would the loss of his wife have been more difficult for Mr. K because of the relationship between them? How does he cope with this? Would he be able to be a better father if he had some help with coping with the loss of his wife and with her meaning to him? What is the meaning of Mr. K's dependency? Does the dependency come out of the crisis and the loss of his wife as someone on whom he could depend? Does your understanding of loss and crisis lead you to make tentative plans for some interventions to help assess Mr. K's ability to cope and to offer him support?

Would all the inconsistencies and problems Mr. K had with his wife and children have been prevented if at the beginning the worker had assessed the situation differently? Suppose the worker had requested a homemaker with the personality and skills of the last homemaker and had offered Mr. K support and help in dealing with his and the children's loss of Mrs. K. Did the first worker see the children or the K home? What would it have meant to Mr. K if the worker had visited? What would it have meant to the homemaker?

Mr. K talks a good deal about his lack of knowledge of his wife's illness. What do you think this means? How much accurate knowledge does the average lay person have of the onset, course, and prognosis of mental illness? Did the hospital offer Mr. K any information about the cause of his wife's illness or the course of treatment? Can we expect clients to deal effectively with a problem when they do not have the facts of the situation? Mr. K continually makes remarks about his lack of knowledge. What is your responsibility to hear this and to understand from your knowledge of systems that the course of his wife's illness is a part of his situation?

Your knowledge base should inform you that in many instances of death and illness family members feel remorseful, angry, or deserted. How do we deal with remorse? Is it possible that Mr. K's inconsistent relationship with the children and his wife comes from remorse and anger? What will the level of feeling have to do with his ability to absorb the information you share? Our theories tell us (see Chapter 4) that high feeling restricts the ability to hear, understand, and use factual knowledge, that when feeling is high, you may have to act to reduce it before it can be expected that the client will hear what you say or be able to participate in planning. Does knowledge of the effect of feeling on ability to hear and understand facts give some guidance about whether to begin with information or with exploration of feeling? Does it seem possible that you should explore this as a way of helping Mr. K to develop a more consistent pattern of behavior?

Although there were signs of Mrs. K's growing illness, Mr. K seemed unaware of them until the illness reached a crisis. Is this unusual behavior, or is it common for family members to be oblivious to changes in close family members? What does Mr. K understand about his wife's illness and prognosis? About mental illness in general? How much contact has the hospital staff had with him? What are their observations of his behavior and relationship with his wife? Would Mr. K like you to contact the hospital staff? Would he like you to visit his wife? Would he want to go with you? What would your visit to his wife and the hospital contribute to your planning with Mr. K?

In the chapters on knowledge and theory we discussed the importance of understanding the situation from an ecosystems perspective. In this case the worker failed to consider Mr. K's situation or microenvironment and concentrated solely on his responsibility to care for the children from the standpoint of what might be expected of an ideal father in the ordinary course of living in a benign environment. In this situation the importance of looking at and understanding the total system is critical to the assessment of Mr. K's functioning. Assessment must be from a systems perspective and must be guided by knowledge of transactions and interactions between and among systems if you want to understand this situation and plan soundly for the children's welfare. There are further questions that may be important. What is Mr. K's notion of the role of the husband and father in a family? Does the macrosystem from which he comes set forth the role in ways that conflict with the worker's and housekeeper's notions? Does Mr. K have an extended family support system? Does he have neighbors he can turn to?

As you think about the plan for the first interview with Mr. K, what do you identify as the most helpful way to approach him? Your plan might look something like this:

A. Problems that will need to be explored
   1. Reactions to change in workers
   2. Problems of grief and loss
   3. Problem of transition to single parent
   4. Care of children
B. Climate of the interview
   1. An attempt to convey a caring for Mr. Keene and his feelings
   2. Acceptance and support
   3. Empathic and responsive; convey recognition of value of his statements
C. Pace of interview
   1. Relaxed—try to match Mr. Keene's tempo
D. Data collection
   1. Be alert to clues; attempt to expand, amplify, and clarify client's meaning
   2. Ask Mr. Keene to amplify and expand meaning
   3. Within this climate, interview to explore support networks and hospital contacts, knowledge of mental illness, and child care
E. Plan of interview
   1. Establish a beginning contact with Mr. Keene
   2. Learn more of Mr. Keene's struggles, worries, stresses
   3. Offer help to Mr. Keene in understanding his wife's illness
   4. Offer appropriate support to Mr. Keene
   5. Recognize Mr. Keene's struggles
F. Goal of interview
   1. A beginning understanding of the problems to be worked
   2. A beginning engagement with Mr. Keene that allows for working on the problem

In reading this plan for the interview, can you see how the questions related to assessment have been used to guide the interview? Notice how assessment of the loss, remorse, and pain of Mr. Keene over the illness of his wife affects the plan for the climate of the interview and its pace.

Recapitulation

In this chapter we have discussed the contact phase of the problem-solving process. We have pointed out that this phase involves nine essential tasks that can be summarized as follows:

1. The initial contact
2. The determination of the problem for work
3. Goal clarification
4. The clarification of service limits
5. The clarification of what will be asked of the client system
6. The development of appropriate relationships
7. The emergence of a commitment to work together
8. Data collection
9. Assessment

Note that these tasks demand the activity of the worker as well as the client.

This beginning part of the problem-solving process is extremely important because it sets the pattern for the phases of work that follow. We have suggested that given the limits of any specific situation, you collect information about at least three elements of the client system: the hope-discomfort balance that the client brings to the first encounter; the opportunities that the client sees and that you can bring to bear; and factors within the client system and in its relationships to the world around it.

One further caution. It is perhaps a misunderstanding of the level and magnitude of problem definition and goal setting that leads some professionals to view the problem-solving model as of value only to the client capable of highly rational functioning. It is our view that every human being has wants (if only to get rid of the worker) and that these wants can be translated into wishes and wishes into goals. The meaning and value of the goals have nothing to do with the worker's evaluation of their value; rather, they relate to the client's wishes. Practitioners often see the only goals worth setting as those that seem to the practitioner to involve a generally better life. However, for many clients the securing of essential survival needs and life supports are the only goals worth setting, at least when they have no reason to trust either the practitioner or life itself. If the problem that the client sees is the lack of certain concrete essentials of life, this can become the problem to be worked. Client and worker can agree that the securing of these essentials is the first and most important goal at the moment, and the plan can well be that the worker will find a way to supply this resource. In this situation, the worker may have done a good deal of the initial work in defining the problem, and the achievement of the goal may have come from the worker's concrete giving. The essential factor here is not the level of goal or who works toward the goal but that the client was involved in the thinking and planning that was done and that what was given was related to the client's wishes and not something that the worker unilaterally thought was needed. The inability to see small concrete goals as important objectives and the assumption that supplying concrete needs to apathetic, withdrawn, depressed, or angry people need not involve mutual problem definition and goal setting (no matter how primitive the level) are built on certain unconscious, or not so unconscious, practitioner assumptions about what is meaningful professional interaction. These assumptions should be seriously examined.

Summary of Problem Identification Activity

1. Define the problem as client sees it.
2. Feed back what you hear; paraphrase; clarify to be sure you really hear correctly.
3. Identify the significance of problem (objectively and subjectively) to the client.
4. What do you see as the problem?
5. Be aware of client feelings about problem and about asking for help. Discuss these or relate to them in other ways as seems helpful, supportive, and clarifying. What are your feelings about problem? Client?
6. Identify the duration, previous occurrences, and precipitating factors contributing to the present problem.

7. Determine how the client has dealt with this or similar problems before.
8. Determine why the client has come for help now.
9. Partialize the problem. Be specific. Maintain focus on one part of the problem at a time.
10. Get an understanding of how other systems relate to the client system and the problem (that is, with whom does the client interact and share the problem? How does the client think others see the problem?).
11. Determine the nature and source of the problem. Where does client locate it? Where do you locate it? Do not assume that the problem lies with the client system.
12. Try to reach a mutually acceptable statement of the problem. (Identify parts of the problem on which you and the client system agree that change is possible.)
13. Identify strengths in dealing with situation; ask what the client sees as strengths or successes in dealing with aspects of problem.
14. Summarize your perception of the problem and its impact on the client system.
15. Agree on a problem (or part of a problem) for work. This may be selected on the basis of
    a. The problem or part of problem that the client system thinks is most important or is most important or is a good beginning place.
    b. The problem that seems most urgent to you.
    c. The problem or part of the problem you believe yields most readily to help.
    d. The problem or part of the problem that falls within the action parameters of the helping system.

Summary of Goal-Setting Activity

1. Find out how client would like problem to be solved.
2. What does client think is needed for solution of problem?
3. Find out what the client system wants from you and how this is related to (1). (Are these expectations realistic?)
4. Discuss meaning of goals with client.
5. State the help you and your agency can offer, giving realistic hope for change. Discuss reasons for any limits on help directly, clearly, simply. Check out how the client feels about these limits and reasons for them.
6. From the partialized statement of the problem, partialize goals (long- and short-term). Be specific. Get feedback.
7. State your commitment to work with client and give hope for change over time.

Summary of Beginning Assessment Activity

1. How does client tell story? Is focus maintained on central issues and feelings? What side issues are brought in?
2. Does client seem to relate actions to outcome or to others' reactions?
3. Is client consistent in account of feelings?
4. How does client seem to relate to you as worker?

5. From discussions of situation, what kind of relationships does client have with others?
6. What account does client give of personal support networks?
7. What account does client give of use of institutional resources?
8. If you pick up on a cue and make a transition, does client follow?
9. If you comment on seeming inconsistencies, how does client respond?
10. How uncomfortable is client? Is this related to problems? Asking for help? Everything in life?
11. Does client seem to have hope of solving problems? Alone? With you? With others? Does client relate to your hope?
12. Observe and begin to assess meaning of patterns of behavior you observe.

Summary of Preliminary Contract

1. Make a preliminary contract regarding initial goals, problem for work, meetings, times, and length of the contract.
   a. Be clear about what is realistic.
   b. State that change takes time.
   c. State that the contract can change.
   d. State that together you will evaluate change as you progress.
   e. Consider the advisability of a written contract.
   f. State what you are prepared and able to do.
2. Based on your initial goals, plan with client for the next session as appropriate.

A Look Forward   We believe that your understanding of assessment will be furthered by careful study of the Gilgun article that follows this chapter. After finishing this chapter and the article, go back to the cases in the Appendix once again. Do a comparative assessment of the coping resources of Miss Smith, Mr. H, and Mrs. Stover (Readings A-1, A-3, and A-6). What devices or resources does each client use to deal with the situation? How does the macrosystem within which they live affect the plan you would develop for Mr. H and Ms. Xiong? Draw an ecomap of each client situation. In the next chapter we will deal in detail with treatment planning and contracting.

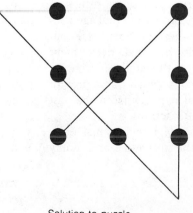

Solution to puzzle

Reading 10-1   *An Ecosystemic Approach to Assessment**

Jane F. Gilgun

A defining characteristic of social work practice is its focus on the person-environment interaction. Such a focus requires an assessment and an intervention plan that encompasses the person, the environment, and the interactions between them. An ecosystemic approach to assessment involves understanding the "interrelated, complex reality in people's lives" (Meyer, 1983, p. 30). When a practitioner does an ecosystemic assessment, as many as possible of the forces that affect the client system are examined. The starting point for an ecosystemic assessment is the client's perception of the environment. This type of assessment, then, starts where the client is and it is based on the principle that how a person thinks, feels, and behaves is based on the person's perceptions. The ecosystems approach places a major emphasis on observation of the client's interaction with members of the interpersonal environment, usually the family. Thus, practitioners with an ecosystemic perspective prefer to work with couples and families. It is possible, however, to work within an ecosystemic framework with individual clients.

The environment can be sliced into several categories. The client's most immediate environment is interpersonal, composed of individuals with whom the client interacts. This slice of the environment frequently is called the micro level (Bronfenbrenner, 1979; Garbarino, 1982). The family, friendship networks, and relationships in schools, the workplace, and governmental agencies are examples of settings where interpersonal connections are made. The interpersonal environment also can be historical, such as the family of origin or the death or birth of persons which affect present interactions. Interpersonal patterns from the past often influence present interactions.

Another dimension of the interpersonal environment is the stage of the individual and family life cycle. Interactions change depending on developmental stage. For example, parents are doomed to frustration when they attempt to force a 2-year-old to share toys happily. Sharing is not characteristic of a child at this age. The family with three young children under 5 will have far different issues and interactions with each other than they will when the children are between the ages of 10 and 15, although there also will be continuities. Looking at interpersonal interactions, then, requires an understanding of the dimension of time. Interactions can be understood as they are in the present, and as they are in the present given the family's and the individual's developmental stage.

A person's environment is also physical, as for example the presence or absence of businesses or other facilities that can offer employment. Access to schools, job training programs, grocery stores, playgrounds, and recreation all are part of the person's environment. They can have an enormous impact on the person's quality of life and opportunity. The relationship that exists between two micro level settings is called the meso level by Bronfenbrenner (1979) and Garbarino (1982). The school-home, church-home, and work-home relationships are examples. An isolated family has few meso level relationships, while a socially integrated family is characterized by numerous rich and supportive micro level relationships.

Persons often are affected by environments with which they do not come into direct contact but which may have profound impact on their interpersonal interactions. The environment of the workplace can affect family life; actions of the federal government can affect taxation and thus the individual and the family; the county welfare office can change policy, deeply affecting many individuals who have no contact with the county office. This is the exo level of the environment (Bronfenbrenner, 1979; Garbarino, 1982).

Even more nebulous than the effects of the exo level of the person's environment is the macro

---

*An original article prepared for this text.

level. Here, aspects of the environment are shaped by customs, norms, and practices which can be and often are fair to most people but which can be racist, sexist, and ageist. These aspects of the environment can be thought of as part of a stratification system where opportunity, power, privilege, and prestige are allocated along the dimensions of age, sex, social class, race, and sexual orientation, to name just a few. The consequences of stratification systems are experienced through social, economic, and political policy and practice, which often are exo level influences, as well as by the daily micro level interactions. These interpersonal interactions give individuals feedback on their social standing and either open or close opportunity for education, income, and social and political power.

Individuals usually are not aware of how profoundly macro level forces affect the course of their lives. Thus, a 27-year-old divorced mother of three children under age 10 may believe that her personal inadequacies are causing the family's financial troubles. She may become depressed and isolated. When she does seek opportunities for education and job advancement, there may be nothing available for her, resulting in more depression, feelings of inadequacy, and isolation. In fact, more than her individual choice has led to her poverty status and discouragement. Through public policy as well as more individualized micro level actions, many women live in poverty because of lack of encouragement, opportunity, and sometimes outright negation of their potential to develop a well-paying and meaningful career. The status that most persons have achieved results largely from socialization practices, opportunity structures, and beliefs, all macro level forces, over which individuals have little control and of which they usually are unaware.

This reading provides an example of how to do an ecosystemic assessment. Guidelines for doing this assessment will be developed out of case material. Thus, the approach to discussing an ecosystemic assessment is grounded in case data and is presented as it would be experienced by the practitioner: from the assignment of the case to gathering and organizing assessment data to thinking about the data and finally to developing an initial intervention plan. The reader, in effect, will be looking over the shoulder of an experienced practitioner as he or she does an ecosystemic assessment. The reader will be privy to the practitioner's self-talk.

AN INITIAL ASSESSMENT

You are a social work practitioner in a family service agency. Your supervisor gives you a face sheet and a file folder, which is empty except for a few lines recording a phone intake. Your supervisor says, "I'd like you to take this case." The face sheet tells you the initial contact was made by Mary Smith, 23, married to John Smith, 23, for five years. They have a 2½-year-old son, Billy, and a 1½-year-old daughter, Kelly. Mary is at home with the children, although prior to the birth of Kelly she worked as a computer operator. John is a diesel mechanic earning $32,000 a year. He has a side tow-truck business that provides a net income of $15,000 a year. Both are white and high school graduates. They went to the same high school. Their last names are Anglo-Saxon, and their religion is Catholic. Mary's parents are alive, and she has two older sisters and one younger sister. John's mother died when he was 14, and he left his father's home at 16 to live with an aunt and uncle. He has one younger brother. John's father has not remarried.

The intake note states that Mary has requested help in dealing with John's physical violence. She left the family home three times in the last six months. Twice she left without the children, and she feels guilty about that. One time she left home with slippers on, and it was December and cold outside. She told the intake worker that John would not come in for consultation.

KNOWLEDGE OF CONTENT AREA IS ESSENTIAL

Trained in ecosystemic thinking, you also have some knowledge of domestic abuse. Your first thought is whether Mary has a protection plan, which is a preplanned set of actions she will take in the event of an abusive episode. When you phone to make an appointment, you will check on the protection plan. You also intend to make an early appointment because in domestic abuse situations a person's life may be in danger. If the case had involved an area with which you weren't familiar, you would have discussed the case in depth with your supervisor before making the appointment, and you also would have gone to the agency library to educate yourself about the subject area. Accurate knowledge of the content area of a case is essential for effective practice. You are, in fact, knowledgeable about domestic abuse, and through experience you have gained confidence in your ability to deal effectively with such cases. When any practitioner does an ecosystemic assessment, knowledge in a content area goes hand in hand with doing the assessment. You would not have known about the centrality of a protection plan had you not had knowledge of domestic abuse as a content area.

You phone Mary, and she answers with a soft "Hello." You hear children crying in the background. You identify yourself and tell her you've called to schedule a time when she can come into the office for an appointment. Mary says, "I'm so glad it's you. I've been walking on eggs around here. John's tow business has been slow, and he's been so touchy. The kids are driving me crazy. I can't get Billy to play with Kelly, and they fight all day long. Just a few minutes ago Billy hit Kelly with a toy truck. I'm afraid he's going to be just like his father." The softness is gone from her voice. She sounds hoarse and distraught.

You negotiate a mutually agreeable time to meet with Mary. You check to see if she is willing to ask John to come in too, and she says, she doesn't want him there this time. "I need to see someone all by myself," she says. For most forms of work with married persons, the agency has a strict policy that the couples are seen together. An exception can be made for domestic abuse situations. If after a few sessions it appears that the husband and wife both want to remain together, the policy is to involve the other spouse in treatment. The rationale for involving both spouses is related to the idea that each spouse is a significant part of the interpersonal environment of the other. Each spouse mutually influences the behavior of the other, although there are a host of possible mediating variables that influence the couple's interaction. When a spouse in a domestic abuse situation is seen alone, the purposes are (1) to develop a protection plan, (2) to establish that responsibility for stopping the abuse lies with the batterer, and (3) to clarify whether the spouse wants to remain with the batterer. Thus there are very good reasons to see a married person alone in such cases. The agency has a similar policy when the presenting problem is alcohol or drug abuse, compulsive gambling, and compulsive sexual acting out.

You ask her if she would like to take a few minutes to talk about ways of protecting herself from battering. She says she would. You give her an example of a typical protection plan: having the names and phone numbers of shelters and friends and family she can go to if she finds herself in physical danger, keeping a spare car key and some money where she can get to them in an emergency, and not hesitating to call the police if she finds herself in danger. She listens intently and tells you she hadn't thought of calling the police and she doesn't know the names and phone numbers of any shelters. You encourage her to call the police, and you provide her with information on the shelters. You tell her she can phone the shelter at any time to get some advice and support. You also tell her that the shelters have ongoing groups for women in battering relationships. She expresses a great deal of gratitude for the information and for your interest in her well-being. She cries just a little. When she has left the home during episodes of violence in the past, she has gone to stay at her parents. "They let me stay, but they don't understand. It gets tense there after a while, and I go home," she said.

INITIAL ASSESSMENT OF ENVIRONMENTAL SUPPORTS
Because you think in terms of systems, you are able within a few minutes to assess Mary's environmental supports. She does have her parents' home as a safe environment during the violent periods, but she had no knowledge of shelters and the police as resources. When you discover this, you provide her with the necessary information. Thus, when doing ecosystemic assessments, the interventions can follow immediately, as they did in this case. Mary

did not know about some key resources, and the practitioner immediately provided her with the information.

Before you ask about the children's safety during the battering episodes, Mary tells you that John does not hit the children. A few times he has thrown objects at Mary and just missed the tops of the children's heads, but that is the extent of his physical violence toward them. Mary says that when she has left the home only to return within an hour or two, John has fed the children, bathed them, and read them bedtime stories. "He loves the kids," she says, "and he says he loves me. I don't know if he really loves me, but he works on being a good father."

As you hang up the phone, you realize that you have an ideal case. Mary is bright and articulate. Despite being in a battering situation, she has her wits about her. Although she is speaking for John, even through her eyes he has some strengths—he states his love for Mary and the children and apparently he enjoys parenting his children. You are not clear about the strengths of the marital relationship. That Mary is not saying she wants to leave John suggests that the marriage may provide a degree of satisfaction despite the serious issue of wife battering.

The face sheet, the intake data, and your initial phone call have provided you with the beginnings of an ecosystemic assessment. This type of assessment involves the generation of a great deal of data. The genogram and the ecomap are two ways of organizing data.

THE GENOGRAM

A genogram is a diagram of the family's generational configuration (Guerin & Pendagast, 1976; Hartman, 1978). It helps organize both historical and contemporary data on the major figures in the client's interpersonal environment. Thus it helps the social worker understand how family patterns are affecting the current situation. Births, deaths, mental illness, alcoholism, divorce, separation, adoption, incest, and family occupation are examples of types of family data present on genograms, which provide a concise means for organizing complex and significant information helpful to

intervention planning. The following symbols signify family events and relationships.

◯ = Female   □ = Male
▽ = Pregnancy   _ _ _ = Marital Separation
x = Death   . . . . . = Divorce

Names and ages customarily are placed on the genogram. Exhibit 10-1 is a genogram of the Smith family, based on the information the practitioner has gathered so far. As work with the family proceeds, information will be added to the genogram. The genogram provides a representation of the family generational structure. The initial information suggests John might have issues related to his mother's death, and his reasons for leaving his father's home at age 16 might be important. Neither set of grandparents were divorced, and John's father did not remarry. This, along with the couple's Catholicism, suggests the possibility that divorce is discouraged by family tradition. On the basis of the genogram information, the worker hypothesizes that John and Mary may be committed to staying together and that John may need to do some family of origin work; that is, work out his thoughts and feelings regarding his mother's death and possible cutoff from his father. Mary is likely to have family of origin issues related to her parents, but there are no data to support or disconfirm this yet.

THE ECOMAP

An ecomap is a diagram of the family within its social context, and it includes the genogram (Hartman, 1978; Seabury, 1985). The purpose of the ecomap is to organize and clarify data on the supports and stresses in the family's environment. The major meso level and exo level social systems which affect the family are placed within circles. The family genogram is placed within the center circle. The symbols for the ecomap are

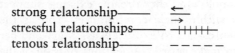

strong relationship———
stressful relationships———
tenous relationship———

No line at all means no relationships. Exhibit 10-2 is an initial ecomap of the Smith family. Many of

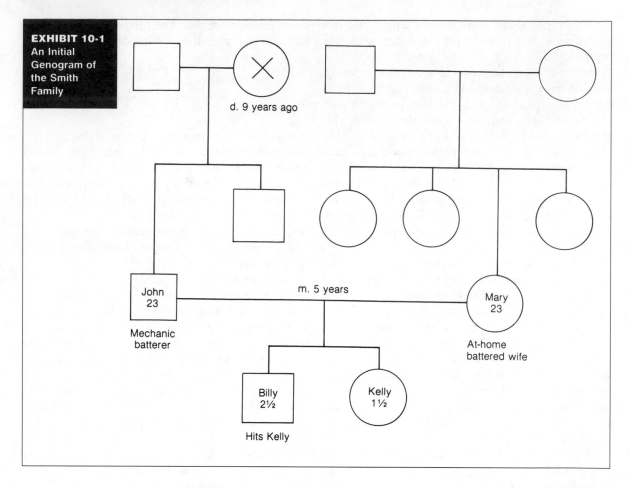

EXHIBIT 10-1
An Initial Genogram of the Smith Family

d. 9 years ago

m. 5 years

John
23

Mechanic
batterer

Mary
23

At-home
battered wife

Billy
2½

Hits Kelly

Kelly
1½

the possible community groups, support groups, and friendship networks are not known at this time. During your first interview with Mary, you intend to explore some of the other environmental supports she might have. The only two types of outside relationships that are known to you are John's with his work and Mary's with her parents. Chances are good that there are a few more relationships outside the family. Typically in families who come in for treatment, however, a major task is helping families hook into the already existing support networks within their communities. You as the practitioner expect to explore ways Mary and her family can make more connections outside of the nuclear family.

THE STRATIFICATION ASSESSMENT

The face sheet information also provides you with a set of facts which will help you do a stratification assessment. A stratification assessment involves looking at the family's and the individual family members' place in the social structure. Race, age, social class, sex, and sex role issues all are involved in a stratification assessment. These attributes greatly influence a person's access to opportunities, power, and prestige. Mary and John are both white Anglo-Saxons, and they thus are not likely to have suffered from racism. They are Catholic, and the area in which they live is predominantly Catholic. Religious prejudice also might not be an issue for them. They are a working-class couple, and they

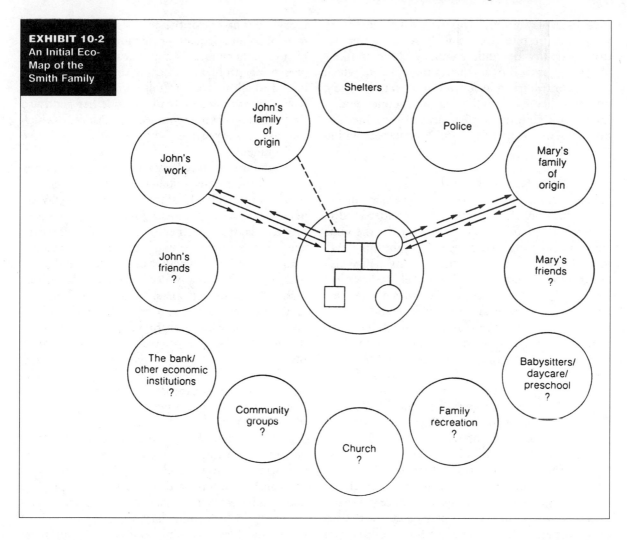

EXHIBIT 10-2
An Initial Eco-Map of the Smith Family

have a good income. They therefore are not suffering from economic deprivation. Given these data, they are not likely to be leaders and policy-makers in their communities or on a wider level. Their social power, therefore, is likely to be limited.

Sex roles issues in this family, however, may be significant. John has two jobs, while Mary appears to have almost sole responsibility for the children. This suggests an imbalance in parenting and bread-winner roles which may be a source of stress in the family. Mary's report that the kids are driving her crazy and your hearing the children screaming at each other while you talked with Mary by phone provide some support for hypothesizing an imbal-ance in parenting and breadwinner roles. John may be overworking, and you wonder what motivates him to work two jobs when his income from one job appears adequate. You wonder if Mary would like to go back to work. You know that in families where battering occurs, the battering spouse often has traditional sex role expectations. You plan to explore this at some time if it appears to be contributing to the battering. You also wonder if child care is available in the neighborhood or if there is a play group. This would provide Mary with some respite from child care and offer her the possibility of adult company. John is likely to have control over the family assets, which would contribute to his power in the family. Mary, on the other hand, is not earning money and is home with children a great deal of the time. She may experience herself as quite powerless within the family.

DEVELOPMENTAL ASSESSMENT

Stages of individual and family development are other areas which are important to understand in assessing this family. John and Mary are the same age, and they married at age 18, right after high school graduation. Thus, they are in a high-risk group for divorce, and they are likely to have had to struggle with late adolescent issues at the same time they were adapting to marriage and then to parenthood. They were married for about two years before Mary became pregnant with Billy, giving them some opportunity to establish themselves as a couple before becoming parents. Identity issues, which are salient in adolescence, might continue to be issues into the present. The form of these issues might, in part, be related to sex role practices, as discussed above. They have two very young children, which might be stressful to both parents for different reasons. John might be worried about financial support, and Mary might be overburdened with parenting. The children are not at an age where they would play quietly with each other. If they are cooped up in a house all day with each other, and if Mary is also there, the stress level of the mother-children interaction might be quite high. John's working two jobs would contribute to this stress. He would provide Mary with minimal companionship, and he would not be available to share child care responsibilities. They are likely to be in a tough spot developmentally, as individuals and as members of a family.

PLANNING FOR THE FIRST INTERVIEW

After doing the genogram, the ecomap, and the stratification and developmental assessments, and after thinking about the data you've gathered so far, you make a plan for your initial interview with Mary. Your first priority is to assess whether she has developed an adequate protection plan. Then you plan to gather more data on her perception of the presenting problem, which is the battering. You intend to allow Mary to tell her story in her own words, but you also intend to guide her gently so that you can continue to assess the extent to which she has a supportive or potentially supportive environment.

As you do the initial assessment, you are hoping that the process itself will help Mary to see her own situation more clearly. If this happens, she may, on her own, discover some action plans that could protect her from further violence. You intend to keep yourself open to many possibilities. You are taking no stand on whether or not she should stay with John. You simply don't have enough information on which to make a judgment. You also don't know how strongly Mary feels about working on her relationship with John. Out of respect for the client and because you truly want to start where Mary is, you plan not to make premature judgments about what you think she should do. If she or the children are in danger of serious physical injury, you will recommend physical separation from John until she and the children are safe.

As you listen to Mary and draw her out, you will be on the alert for data on environmental supports and stresses. How much time does John spend working? How might this affect the couple and family interactions? What kinds of friendship networks do John and Mary have? What kinds of recreation does the family enjoy? Is the interpersonal environment outside the nuclear family supportive or is it a source of additional stress? As Mary tells you about the presenting problem and family interaction, you are confident that much of these data will be part of her narrative. If there are some blanks, such as information on friendship networks or recreation, you intend to ask about these.

You also will be interested in understanding how stratification and sex role issues work themselves in the family. Who makes decisions for the family? Is there conflict over family roles? Does Mary wish she were back at work? Does she want John to work less and spend more time with her and the children?

You expect to gather a lot of information about these issues as Mary tells you her story.

As Mary describes the presenting problem, you plan to observe her account of her interactions with John. Interactions include such issues as hearing the other out vs. interrupting; asking for clarification and drawing the other out vs. assuming knowledge of what the other is thinking and feeling; the ability to express a range of thoughts and feelings vs. being able to express a limited range; self-centeredness vs. other-centeredness; taking responsibility for one's self vs. blaming; patterns of pushing the other around vs. cooperation; and the extent of problem-solving behavior vs. premature closure of discussion, unilateral actions, and high-handedness. These interactions are part of the interpersonal environment, and they are a significant part of an ecosystemic assessment.

You also realize that much of what you will learn from Mary's description will be self-report data. If Mary decides that she would like to work on the marital relationship and if John comes in for marital therapy, then you will have an opportunity to observe their interactions firsthand. However, Mary will be reporting her perceptions of the interactions, and it is on the basis of her perceptions that she thinks, feels, and acts.

THE FIRST INTERVIEW

Your intercom buzzes. "Mary Smith is here," the receptionist announces. You walk to the waiting room. Sitting on the edge of the red vinyl chair and biting her lower lip is a fair-skinned, freckled young woman with full, dark hair. "Mrs. Smith?" you say. You introduce yourself and exchange the usual pleasantries as you walk to your office. "No," she said, "I had no trouble finding the office. The kids' pediatrician is right across the street." You note that she takes the children to a pediatrician and the environment of the agency is familiar to her.

Mary quickly unburdens herself. She loves her husband, but he flares up and hits her. He gets mad at the drop of a hat. You ask her to describe a recent incident when he became angry and hit her. She said, "John always has two of his buddies over. They sit around and drink beer, eat chips, and watch football on TV. I'm the maid. John orders me around. I fetch the beer and fill up the chip bowls." You wonder if John wants to show his friends that he has a wife who is willing to wait on him. Is having such a wife some kind of proof that he is a competent male? Why does Mary wait on the men? Does she think that is her role? These kinds of thoughts relate to the stratification section of the assessment. You are trying to understand the sex role structure of the couple. Often traditional sex roles work very well for couples, but when the partners each have different ideas of appropriate sex role behavior, or if partners are being exploited, the scene is set for conflict.

Mary reports that all three of the men make fun of her—tell her she's got a fat can, ought to smile more, and why doesn't she keep the kids quiet. Last Saturday she got angry and told them to leave her alone. She refused to wait on them. "I slammed the door of the bedroom shut, and Kelly started to cry and banged on the door. Then Billy cried. John yelled at the kids to be quiet. I took the kids to the playground." Mary says that when she got home, John was alone. "He started yelling at me for humiliating him in front of his friends. I yelled back demanding that he apologize for treating me like a maid and for letting his friends make fun of me. He yelled that they were only kidding. I started swearing, and then he did. He hit me on the side of the head, and I swore some more. He started punching. I ran out of the house. I remember hearing the kids cry. I walked around for about an hour. When I came home, John was calmly feeding the kids. We didn't talk about the fight. In bed that night, he wanted to make love. I didn't feel like it. He got mad again, but we didn't fight. After a while we went to sleep." The next day was Sunday. They hardly spoke, and John was out all day and night towing cars with his two buddies. Mary was alone with the children.

ASSESSING THE CONTENT OF THE PRESENTING PROBLEM

When doing an ecosystemic assessment, asking for a description of a recent incident related to the presenting problem is an efficient way of obtaining data on which to base your continuing assessment. You've learned that Mary's father is an alcoholic and is verbally abusive, that John's father also was verbally abusive and beat his wife but not the children, and that John defended his mother against his father. You will place that information on the genogram when the interview is over.

The material for the ecomap, the stratification assessment, and the interactional assessment is plentiful. John has two close friends with whom he spends a lot of time. Certainly these men provide John with companionship, but they also might be a wedge between John and Mary if indeed they are "always" at the house. Mary feels rejected by them. Whether or not their teasing is intended to be good-natured, she feels put down by their remarks. These men also seem to think that it is appropriate for Mary to serve them beer and chips and to keep the children quiet. If Mary wanted to protest these assigned roles, John would be able to cite the rightness of the roles because he and his two friends all think they are appropriate. Thus on the ecomap Mary's relationship to these two men would be characterized as stressful, while John's relationship to them would be strong. That Mary did not call on anyone else when she left the home suggests that she has a tenuous support system during times of domestic strife. No new lines showing social support for Mary can be drawn. The presence of a playground is a positive aspect of the environment, and it should be indicated on the ecomap.

The material for the stratification assessment is quite rich. Mary and John are not in agreement about roles when John has friends over. Mary does not want to wait on them, while John expects her to. John also expects her to go along with teasing, which Mary doesn't like and wants stopped. The disagreement over appropriate roles was the reason Mary went to her room and then left the home to take the children on an outing. That she took the children instead of leaving them in John's care suggests that she considers child care her responsibility. John did not object when she took the children. Thus he is likely to agree that the children are largely her responsibility. Drinking beer, eating chips, and watching football on television also are activities strongly associated with the male sex role. It is possible that John is a traditional male, behaving in ways the culture suggests males ought

to behave. His emphasis on work, also, where he has two jobs, leads to the speculation that somehow work is highly valued by John. Some men believe their value lies in their wallets—meaning that the more money they earn, the more valued they are and the more proof they have that they are competent men. You wonder what Mary's and John's beliefs are about this.

The interactional assessment leads to the hypotheses that John and Mary apparently have few problem-solving skills, they are not able to draw each other out and hear each other's point of view, they appear to have a restricted range of expressiveness of thoughts and feelings, much of their behavior is unilateral, and each becomes frustrated. After a cooling-out period, they are not able to discuss or resolve conflict. They deal with frustration by swearing, yelling, and leaving the field. John has one additional and dangerous behavior: he beats his wife.

ASSESSING STRENGTHS

You decide, as you are listening to Mary and making your assessment, that you need a clearer picture of what the couple's strengths might be. You ask Mary to describe a recent incident in which things went smoothly between her and John. She says, "Three weeks ago on a Saturday morning, before John went off on his towing business, I suggested we go on a picnic next to a lake where we could swim. I know he likes picnics and swimming. His mother used to take him and his brother swimming a lot. I like picnics, and so do the kids. John wanted to go. He agreed to be home by noon. He got home by 12:30, and we were off by 12:45. We had a great day. John cooked; I set the table and cleaned up. He played with the kids in the water. I did, too. The kids fell asleep on the way home. We both unloaded the car and put the kids to bed. We made love that night." This story shows that the couple does share some recreation. Again the tasks performed generally fall along sex-typed lines, but there was a great deal of cooperative effort also. The couple apparently can take great pleasure in shared activities. The story also provides further data on the amount of time John spends at work and Mary spends with the children. Further data gathering will clarify the reasons for the amount of time the couple spends apart. You hypothesize that staying away is a means of avoiding conflict, a way for John to earn extra money, and an opportunity for John to be with his friends.

Without much pause, Mary's story about the happy family outing spills into her telling you how much John wanted a family when they were going out. His father used to beat his mother. One time John drew a knife on his father to stop the beating. His father didn't beat John, but he used to make fun of him and had little time for him. John sees his father once a year at Christmas. She says her own father was not a batterer, but he was an alcoholic and was verbally abusive.

DEVELOPMENTAL AND HISTORICAL ASSESSMENT

Mary's narrative provides a great deal of developmental and historical information. As a young family, they are able to participate in appropriate family activities. A picnic outing at a lake is something both the children and the adults enjoy, and they were able to interact with each other in mutually pleasurable ways. Some of the information, however, was Mary's interpretation of John's history, and you would prefer hearing John's story from John. Since, however, you have the data, it does help you to formulate additional hypotheses about the wife battering and the future of the marital relationship. John may well have had a close relationship with his mother. Her death may have been a serious and difficult loss. That his father used to beat his mother suggests that John had very poor modeling for problem solving and conflict management and resolution. He may well be bringing what he knows into his marriage. John, like all of us, would carry his earlier environment with him. If he had a close relationship with his mother, that might provide a basis for building a nonviolent relationship with Mary. Mary's report of her father's verbal abuse and drinking behavior suggests that she, too, came from a family with poor interpersonal skills of problem solving and conflict management and resolution.

These developmental and historical data provide you with a context in which to understand Mary and John. That there is a dovetailing of the family histories of each spouse does not surprise you. Commonalities in background, particularly emotional constellations, are the rule rather than the exception in couples work. The dovetailing makes the job of intervention much simpler. Each spouse has a part to play in clearing up communication difficulties. John, of course, has the additional task of coming to terms with his physical violence and learning and using alternatives to the violence. Mary will have the task of forgiving John for the violence, when and if he begins to use alternative means of expressing his strong negative emotions. The interview has given you some rich data, and you add information to the genogram and the ecomap. Exhibits 10-3 and 10-4 show how they look now.

PLANNING INTERVENTIONS

Your initial assessment with Mary has provided you with multiple intervention points. If she were a computer, you could easily reprogram her: hook her up to day care, play groups, a battered women's group, a job, a host of supportive friends, and the entire gamut of interpersonal skills. If John were a computer, you could teach Mary to program him to come in for marital therapy, and you could hook him up to a group for battering men, some friends who would help him to foster his relationship with Mary, the entire gamut of interpersonal skills, and some motivation to work less and spend more time with Mary and the children. Neither, of course, is a computer, nor are they programmable. The above lists of changes you would like to make, however, are based on your ecosystemic assessment. These changes are, in fact, the recommendations you intend to make to the couple over the course of your work with them. Exhibit 10-5 shows how you would like the family ecomap to look. The ecomap, then, helps you visualize treatment goals.

Your assessment, of course, is not complete. As you continue your work with Mary and possibly John, you will gather further data which will suggest further possible points of intervention. The data you have thus far, however, do touch on all the levels of ecosystemic assessment. From this point on your assessment will continue, but the balance of your work will tip toward ecosystemic interven-

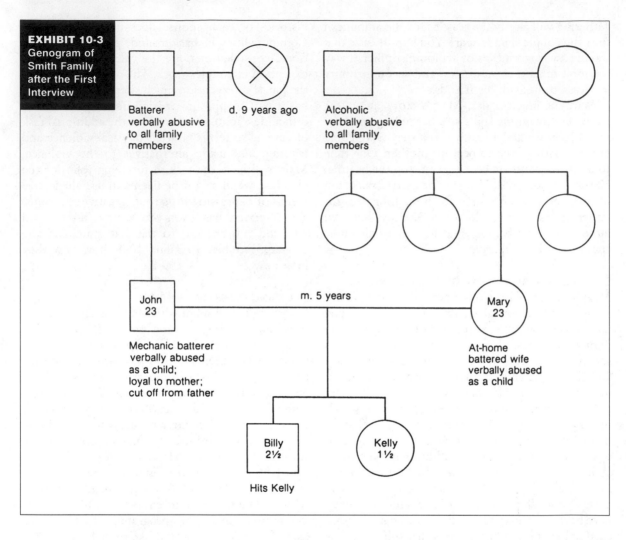

EXHIBIT 10-3
Genogram of Smith Family after the First Interview

Batterer verbally abusive to all family members

d. 9 years ago

Alcoholic verbally abusive to all family members

John 23

m. 5 years

Mary 23

Mechanic batterer verbally abused as a child; loyal to mother; cut off from father

At-home battered wife verbally abused as a child

Billy 2½

Kelly 1½

Hits Kelly

tions and evaluation of the effectiveness of the interventions.

You start the intervention planning where the client is. Mary is the client you have in your office, and it is with her you plan the interventions. What she wants and experiences as most pressing will be the focus of the intervention planning. The most pressing issues for her are likely to be (1) stopping the battering, (2) improving communication, and (3) redistribution of breadwinner and parenting roles. As you continue to work with her, she is likely to be ready to look at and change other aspects of her interpersonal environment. John may come

into treatment also. This is likely to facilitate more change in the couple's ecosystem.

The work you do with the family will proceed in microsteps, building on the foundation the clients provide. Your ecosystemic assessment will prove a blueprint for how you would like the family to be. The assessment will help you keep your focus as you work on small pieces of the couple's ecosystem. The couple, however, is ultimately in charge of the directions taken. Client self-determination is a fundamental right, superseded only by the right to protection of life. It is also a therapeutic necessity. Your assessment and intervention planning may be

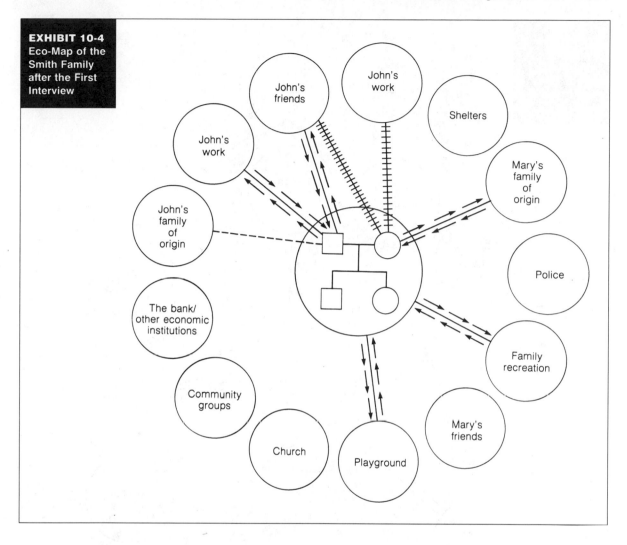

EXHIBIT 10-4
Eco-Map of the Smith Family after the First Interview

first-rate, but careful, respectful, and empathic work with clients to help them define their goals is the means by which you will achieve some of the goals suggested by the ecosystemic assessment.

In doing ecosystemic interventions, the practitioner has a great many choices. You will be working on more than one level. Often major issues are on the micro or interpersonal, interactional level, but the micro-level issues often are supported by, affected by, and affect meso-level, exo-level, and macro-level issues. In short, interactional, stratification, developmental, historical, exo- and meso-level issues are in dynamic and reciprocal interac-

tion. Concurrent interventions at two or more systems levels appear to be more effective than interventions on one level alone. Advocacy, lobbying for legislative change, working toward policy changes in your own agency, and setting up special community service programs may develop from your micro-level work with individual client systems.

SUMMARY AND DISCUSSION

In doing an ecosystemic assessment, the practitioner is gathering data on mutually interacting environmental systems. The genogram is a tool

EXHIBIT 10-5
The Smith Family Eco-Map as You Would Like It to Be

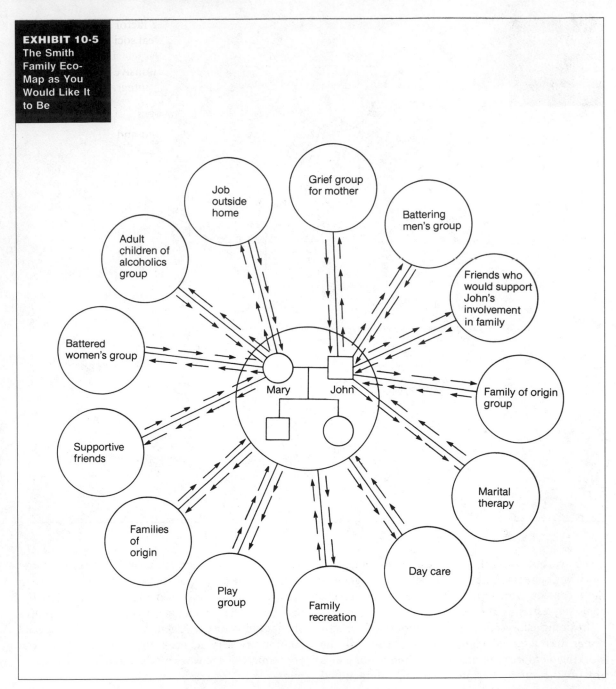

which helps to organize some of the historical and developmental data that influence present interactions. The ecomap helps organize meso-level and exo-level environmental contingencies which are part of the client's ecosystem. The interactional assessment provides information on the micro level. The stratification assessment helps organize data on sex roles, distribution of power such as in decision making, and the family's and the individual's place in the social structure as determined by age, sex, race, ethnicity, social class, sexual orientation, and occupation, to name a few. The influence of the macro level is seen in all four types of assessments.

The starting point for the ecosystemic assessment is the client's perception of the environment. Observation often is an important source of assessment data, but an ecosystemic assessment can be done with an individual client. An ecosystemic assessment provides many possible points of intervention. Where to start the intervention is determined by where the client is, meaning what the client wants and experiences as most pressing.

In involuntary situations, where a client is court-ordered into treatment, an ecosystemic assessment is especially desirable because the client might experience many aspects of the environment as painful. If the practitioner begins where the client is and contracts to facilitate changes which the client requests, the client may be more likely to work to change behavior which is harmful and illegal. For example, abusive parents often are court-ordered into treatment. By definition they are not choosing to work with a practitioner, and they may be quite reluctant to set treatment goals. An ecosystemic assessment might help client and practitioner to discover environmental contingencies which support the abusive behavior. Some of these contingencies might be experienced by the client as noxious. Feelings of isolation are common among abusive parents and often are both a source

of pain and a contributing factor to the abuse. An ecomap quickly would reveal social isolation. If the client would like to decrease social isolation, then this goal would be responsive to the client's request. Increased social integration might also decrease the likelihood of the parent abusing again. Many other mutually agreed-on ecosystemic goals would need to be developed and pursued in order to deal with the complex problem of child abuse. The ecosystemic assessment is a solid foundation on which to plan intervention into such complex situations.

Ecosystemic assessments and interventions respond to the heart of the definition of social work direct practice. As social workers, we are enjoined to treat the person-environment interface and we are enjoined to start where the client is. The ecosystemic approach helps us do this. In involuntary situations this approach has a great deal of promise in bringing about change in the client's interactions with the myriad aspects of an environment which the client undoubtedly experiences as painful. Finally, the ecosystems approach can also help us accept that there are some situations which we, together with our clients, may not be able to change. Sometimes the effects of racism, sexism, ageism, and classism have been so devastating on an individual client or family that we are fairly helpless in altering their effects. Widespread change in the social structure is the intervention that would facilitate solving the client's presenting problem. Social workers have a part to play in changing the social structure through research, client advocacy, lobbying legislators, and writing model laws and policy and by becoming planners, policymakers, or managers in human service agencies. The ecosystems approach, then, opens up many possibilities for intervention on the micro, meso, and macro levels both for direct practitioners and for social work planners, managers, policymakers, researchers, and educators.

For Further Reading

Bartlett, H. (1970). *The common base of social work practice*. New York: National Association of Social Workers.

Handiker, P., & Carnock, K. (1984). Social work assessment processes in work with ethnic minorities—the Doshi family. *British Journal of Social Work, 14*(1), 23–47.

McGoldrick, M., & Gerson, R. (1985). *Genograms in family assessment*. New York: W. W. Norton.

Monkman, M., & Allen-Meares, P. (1985). The TIE framework: A conceptual map for social work assessment. *Areté, 10*(1), 41–49.

Seabury, B. A. (1985). The beginning phase: Engagement, initial assessment, and contracting. In J. Laird & A. Hartman (Eds.), *A handbook of child welfare* (pp. 335–359). New York: Free Press.

Specht, H., & Specht, R. (1986a). Social work assessment: Route to clienthood, part I. *Social Casework, 67,* 525–532.

Specht, H., & Specht, R. (1986b). Social work assessment: Route to clienthood, part II. *Social Casework, 67,* 587–593.

The Contract Phase: Joint Assessment, Goal Setting, and Planning

This chapter is about participatory decision making—how decisions are made concerning the nature of the problem to be solved, desired goals or outcomes, and how the goals will be achieved. The chapter will define the contract phase of the problem-solving model, present an outline of the process by which you and your client will jointly arrive at the contract, and enumerate a set of principles to guide your participation in this process.

Definition of the Service Contract

In our discussions of the problem-solving process, identification of the problem, and data collection and assessment, we have maintained a consistent emphasis on the partnership nature of the interaction between you and the applicant. The partnership is working together to define and explore a common task. Mutuality between applicant and worker must be established at the very outset and continue through all their associations. In the service contract, however, the partnership concept is fully developed and made explicit. Anthony Maluccio and Wilma Marlow (1974, p. 30) have described contracting in social work and note:

> For the purposes of social work, the contract may be defined as the explicit agreement between the worker and the client concerning the target problems, the goals, and the strategies of social work intervention, and the roles and tasks of the participants. Its major features are mutual agreement, differential participation in the intervention process, reciprocal accountability, and explicitness. In practice these features are closely inter-related.

When considering the importance of mutuality in the partnership and in the joint understandings and operating principles that are involved in the concept of contract, do not lose sight of an equally important notion of difference. The concept of partnership does not mean that client and worker bring the same knowledge, understanding, feeling, and doing to the business of working together. Partnership and contract highlight the differences that worker and client can contribute to the process. "The contract is a tool for such delineation, and for both client and worker it is an ongoing reminder of their collaborative relationship and different responsibilities" (Maluccio & Marlow, 1974, p. 30).

The service contract involves input, decision making, planning, and commitment from both the client and the social worker. The process of arriving at a service contract protects the client's individuality and maximizes opportunities for the exercise of self-determination. In discussions, negotiations, and choosing among available alternatives or in making commitments to engage in developing new alternatives, the client's opportunities for meaningful decisions about self and situation are greatly increased.

In this chapter we describe what goes into the process of arriving at a service contract, and we go on to make explicit a number of principles that are implicit in the process. In many respects the process may appear similar to that described in Chapter 10 on the beginning phase of working together. The similarity exists partly because of the spiral nature of work with clients (a process that will be made more explicit in Chapter 16) and partly because the concept of contract also appears in the initial contact phase. An initial or exploratory contract is developed to facilitate the process of collecting data—a prerequisite for joint worker and client decision making concerning the problem to be worked, the desired goals, and the means or interventive efforts to be used in achieving those outcomes. Exhibit 11-1 identifies ingredients of a contract and distinguishes between an exploratory and a working contract.

Arriving at a service contract involves a series of applicant-worker negotiations directed to answering these questions: Is the problem we want to work on the one that was identified when we began work together? Why has the problem persisted despite earlier attempts to solve it? What is the desired solution (that is, what outcomes or goals should the interventive effort be directed toward achieving in relation to the problem)? How will this solution be achieved? Remember that the

EXHIBIT 11-1 Ingredients of a Contract	A working contract is essentially an agreement between at least two people and should cover:

1. The goals or ends (the what) toward which each party shall work. These goals or terminal behaviors should be specific, discrete, and whenever feasible, observable.
2. The specific responsibilities of each party to the contract in terms of rights and obligations.
3. The technique or means (the how) to be used in achieving the goals.
4. The administrative procedures to be involved—when to meet, where to meet, time, and so on.

These four ingredients cover the essential terms of a contract and should be sufficiently explicit and detailed so that each party knows clearly what is expected of them in the contract.

It is possible to specify at least two types of contracts: *initial,* or *exploratory,* and *working.*

1. An exploratory contract is an agreement to explore and negotiate the terms of working contract and no necessary commitment from either party is involved.
2. A working contract may or may not grow out of the initial contract; this will be dependent upon the negotiation that takes place.

Therefore, it is possible to specify the following kind of sequence:

1. Working on an exploratory type of contract.
2. The development of a working contract.
3. Review and evaluation of the accomplishments of the working contract.
4. Renegotiation resulting in a new working contract or termination (this stage is essentially a repeat of stage 1).

SOURCE: Joe Hudson, Professor, Faculty of Social Work, University of Calgary (Edmonton Division), Edmonton, Canada.

applicant may be an individual, a family, a group, or an organization and that you may be interacting with applicants in a variety of settings.

Joint Assessment and Decision Making

Joint assessment and decision making are at the very heart of the development of the service contract. In the contact phase worker and client have arrived at an initial definition of the problem to be worked. They have set initial goals, collected some data, and together explored the identified problem and goals. Now they must put these data together to determine what the problem is, what can be done about it (a reworking of the goal), and how they are going to do it. This process involves the ordering and organizing of the information, intuition, and knowledge on the part of both client and worker. The pieces should come together into some pattern that makes sense in the here and now, explains the problem, and relates this explanation to alternative solutions. There is movement from what is observed, inferred, or deduced from knowledge and experience to some conclusive explanation of what we make of it and thence to a determination of goals and how they can be implemented. Such assessments evolve not from one person's head or from the simple addition of one item to another but rather from a combination of data in relevant ways. They evolve from viewing the relationships of all elements to one another as client and worker appraise the client-in-situation and from the assessment of their total significance to the client in light of what the client wants to accomplish. Harriett Bartlett (1970, p. 144) refers to these processes as "analysis of a situation to identify the major factors operating within it" and "identification of those factors which appear most critical, definition of their interrelationships, and selection of those to be dealt with." At its best the processes involve both client and worker in assembling and ordering all information and in making judgments about their meaning for the work together.

Social workers often mistakenly assume that only the worker engages in these tasks. Both the worker and the client must do hard and independent thinking (for the worker this is a professional obligation). The test of the soundness of such thinking is how well their thinking fits together. Sometimes the culmination of this process is erroneously seen as putting the client in a category or affixing a label. That is emphatically not the purpose of the process. The process is not focused on the client alone; it is focused on the client, the problem, and the situation in a systematic interaction. In work with human beings, thinking and action cannot move in a straight line from cause to effect. Systems theory teaches us that problems are the result of complicated interactions among all system variables and that to seek a single ultimate cause or reason is to doom oneself and one's client to frustration and failure. So our aim is not to come up with an answer in labels or categories but to order the understanding of the client-situation-problem for purposes of deciding goals and actions.

Sometimes this process is called *diagnosis*. We dislike this term for several reasons. First, the primary definition of the term in *Webster's Ninth New Collegiate Dictionary* is "The art or act of identifying a disease from its signs and symptoms." Thus the term carries the implication that there is something wrong with the client. Second, it implies that the decision about what is wrong is made by the professional person through an examination. There is no inkling of dynamic interaction and joint responsibility. Finally, diagnosis is often seen as a process by which a professional arrives at a label for something. After all, that is what happens when doctors diagnose. They assign labels signifying what is wrong. This is their assessment as the knowing authority, and at even greater variance with the notions of the contract, doctors usually tell their patients what they have determined to be the most satisfactory form of treatment. The process of assessment and decision making in social work is quite different from diagnosis. The phrase *process of assessment* is used because assessment must be regarded as an ongoing, joint process, a shared endeavour.

Consistent with the approach outlined in Chapter 1, the problem for work may be defined as residing with the client, as outside the client but experienced by him or her, or as the result of the client-situation interaction. The target of change may or may not be the client. After client and worker have jointly defined the problem for work, which may or may not be the same as the presenting problem, the next decision is to define goals—what is to be done?

Setting Goals

What are the desired goals of the joint work? What is perceived as the appropriate solution for the problem? What are the goals of our actions? Essentially the same process is used in arriving at an answer to these questions as in developing a definition of the problem for work. Your first responsibility is to use interviewing skills to elicit from clients their views of desired outcomes. You may also have developed a view of the desired outcome that is shared with the client. If the two views are not congruent, this difference must be negotiated, just as incongruent perceptions of the problem were negotiated. Unless you and your client can arrive at mutually agreeable goals, there is no sense in proceeding because you will be working in opposed directions.

Research into outcomes of social work practice has accumulated evidence that social work is often not helpful because worker and client are not working toward the same purposes (Lerner, 1972; Mayer & Timms, 1969; Polansky, Bergman, & de Saix, 1973). When clients approach an agency expecting a certain kind of help toward a certain kind of goal, they will be confused and perhaps will feel even more inadequate if you offer something they do not understand and were not aware they wanted. In such situations clients often leave the agency in frustration and disappointment.

Thomas Kenemore (1987) conducted a qualitative study of workers' initial contact with clients and found that workers often have to negotiate with clients in regard to the nature of the services being provided. Many workers, however, were uncomfortable with this because explicit practice theory regarding negotiation of client preferences ran counter to the workers or agencies. Kenemore concludes that "practice theory should encourage workers to intervene in ways that respond to client expectations first, rather than after failure to get client compliance. Development of practice principles that instruct workers to resolve differences with clients by adapting to client preferences would be expected to enhance continuance in many instances and to alter the worker's reference for evaluation of performance" (pp. 132–143).

In setting goals, as in defining the problem for work, you will be working with your client to find a common area of agreement. Some authors (Kenemore, 1987; Murdach, 1982; Seabury, 1976, 1979) note the likelihood of worker-client conflict in negotiating a contract. This is an issue to which we will return later in this chapter. We suggest, however, that you enter your initial work with clients as a partner in problem solving. Your task as the worker is to find a common ground and a common goal to which you and your client can direct your change efforts. This may not be what you consider the most important or even the most urgent goal. But if it is important for the client and is a goal that you can appropriately work toward, begin at that point. Opportunities to define other goals will occur as you work together.

Consider the case of Mrs. Troy in Exhibit 11-2. The Troy family presents an example of what Germain and Gitterman refer to as "problems and needs associated with tasks involved in life transitions" (1980, p. 32). This worker may have been interested in goals such as helping Mrs. Troy develop skill at managing all her children and assisting Mrs. Troy in managing stress. After some further exploration and negotiation, however, the worker agreed to work with Mrs. Troy toward the goal of getting John out of the house. Working toward this goal, even though it was not the worker's first choice, provided an opportunity for the worker to provide immediate assistance and for Mrs. Troy and the worker to negotiate for other goals. The goal also meets two tests for a useful goal—specificity and attainability.

Specifying goals is a crucial element of the service contract. You must pay attention to two characteristics of the goals. First, they should be sufficiently specific and concrete to be measurable. Only in this way can the client and you know whether the goals have been accomplished, and only in this way can the profession of social work establish its accountability. Broadly stated goals, such as helping a person feel better, increasing opportunities for socializing experiences, and improving parent-child relationships, are meaningless. This topic will be discussed further in Chapter 16, on evaluation. The establishment of measurable goals is necessary to integrate social work practice with research and evaluation (Greene, 1989).

EXHIBIT 11-2
Getting John
Out of the
House

Mrs. Troy was referred to this agency for help in coping with her children. She was referred by a Welfare Department social worker who is providing brief individual counseling for Margaret, the 16-year-old daughter, regarding plans for her 2-month-old baby. The family consists of Mrs. Troy, age 42; John, age 19; Joe, age 17; Margaret, age 16; Robert, age 2 months (Margaret's baby); Marcel, age 14; and Raymond, age 12.

The social worker who made the referral thought Mrs. Troy needed help in handling the kids, especially the oldest boy, John. Before I saw Mrs. Troy, a second referral was made by the nurse who is working with Mrs. Troy, who is diabetic. The nurse stated that Mrs. Troy would become so upset with the kids, John in particular, that she would forget to take her medication. She thought that Mrs. Troy was at her wit's end and was threatening to leave the kids and disappear.

Mrs. Troy was not so desperate when I interviewed her two days later. She did, however, make it clear that she wanted some help to get John out of the house. She also wanted the other kids to do what they were told. Mrs. Troy saw John as the main problem. He deliberately aggravated the other kids, ordered them around, would sit around the house all day and have his friends over, refused to obey her, and called her profane names. Mrs. Troy's boyfriend moved out a few months ago because of the frequent arguments he had with John. She also felt that John's bad example was causing her to lose control of the other kids.

Mrs. Troy's primary request was for help in getting John to move out of the house, but she didn't seem to feel there was much hope of doing it. She had tried putting his clothes out, locking him out, and changing the locks. Each time, John persisted in his efforts to get back in by shouting and pounding on the doors and windows. Mrs. Troy, feeling powerless and seeing no alternative, would let him in. On one occasion, when John became belligerent after coming home drunk, she called the police. They simply drove him a few blocks away and released him.

Second, there should be a reasonable chance of attaining the goals. You and your applicants, as you work together to establish goals, will consider such variables as the degree of interest in attaining goals, abilities, and the available resources. Ripple and Alexander (1956) and others have referred to these considerations as motivation, capacity, and opportunity. Goals may be established in any of these areas. Legitimate outcomes of client-worker activity may be to increase motivation, abilities, or opportunities in defined areas. Regardless of the areas in which goals are established, consider the variables of motivation, capacity, and opportunity with a view toward establishing goals with a reasonable chance of attainment.

Planning for Intervention

Given a mutually determined definition of the problem and its solution, the task of planning a way to move from problem to solution remains. The development of an intervention plan consists of decisions, again jointly made by the applicant and you, about the steps each of you will be taking to solve the problem, that is, to reach the goals. The steps taken in making these decisions parallel those taken in defining the problem and arriving at goals. You will first discover from the client what he or she would like to do to reach the solution and what the client expects you to do. You must also establish your expectation of the client as well as what you expect to do to accomplish the goals, and again, any differences in these expectations are to be negotiated and resolved.

Systems theory suggests that there are many routes to any goal. A common temptation (and error) in social work is to offer an intervention plan without considering alternatives with your client. Consider, for example, this excerpt from the Stover case in the Appendix.

> Mrs. Stover brought up a further problem in connection with running the household. She is now getting more interested in housework and cooking. She is realizing how little she knows about cooking. She attempted to cook a goose for the family, but due to improper cleaning of the goose beforehand, spoiled it. She claims the food that she knows how to prepare is plain and unattractive and she feels she is lacking in knowledge of skill in cooking. The children do some complaining about the food, George recently pointing out that other children he knows get more variety than he does. It was arranged that I will bring a recipe file for Mrs. Stover containing a large variety of recipes and some instructions on food preparation and menus.

There appears to be agreement that the problem is Mrs. Stover's lack of knowledge about cooking, and the goal is for her to be able to prepare more attractive and varied meals. This worker then precipitously develops the intervention plan of providing Mrs. Stover with a recipe file. A better process would have been to involve Mrs. Stover in discussion of steps that might be taken to enable her to improve her cooking skills. Perhaps she knows of friends, relatives, or neighbors from whom she could request recipes; perhaps she could make use of the public library; perhaps there is a county Extension office or some other organization to provide the services of a home economist to Mrs. Stover.

Offering an intervention plan too quickly creates two problems. First, this action will deny clients' opportunities to plan and work toward solutions to their own problems, thus denying clients' involvement in their own problem-solving effort. Second, premature assumption of responsibility for an intervention plan may blind us to client strengths that may be brought to bear on the problem and accomplishment of the goal. Such a premature suggestion also denies the client the satisfying experience of exercising his or her own planning skills and the opportunity to develop self-esteem through making contributions to the process. With our orientation toward problems, we may at times fail to identify and mobilize the many strengths of our clients. To compensate for this danger, we suggest that development of an intervention plan include a systematic review of client strengths. You may find it useful to develop a list of client strengths and then to consider with your client how these might be used to accomplish each goal. Strengths, of course, include the personal resources of the client as well as the resources of family, friends, neighbors, and ethnic groups to which the client is attached. Possible strengths for Mrs. Stover might have included statements like "talks at least once a week with her mother," "occasionally has coffee with the neighbor," and "has visited the local public library."

The service contract, including the intervention plan, may be oral or written. Reducing agreements to written form may appear cumbersome, but it has some clear advantages. Barker (1987) argues that written agreements are effective tools for explicating goals and mutual expectations but are underused in social work. A written contract will help identify ambiguities and improve the specificity of the plan. It will reduce the likelihood of misunderstanding and aid evaluation. Putting plans in written form is also an aid to learning, especially in your early work at developing contracting skills. Exhibit 11-3 provides an illustration of what a written plan might have looked like for the Stover case. Note that this example also contains time limits for completion of the various tasks. Setting time limits helps maintain progress toward completion of goals and provides a basis for client-worker evaluation of their progress.

EXHIBIT 11-3
A Service Agreement for the Stover Case

Date: February 3 (Monday)
Problem: Mrs. Stover is unable to prepare an attractive variety of meals for her family.
Goal: Mrs. Stover will develop ability to prepare additional dishes.
Specific goal: By February 10, Mrs. Stover will be able to prepare and serve her family a dish she has not previously prepared.

Intervention plan:

1. On February 4 Mrs. Stover will invite her neighbor to coffee and make inquiries about recipes for preparation of low-cost main dishes.
2. By February 5 Mrs. Stover will call at the public library and check cookbooks for two or three new recipes.
3. Worker will contact the county Extension office to determine if: (a) the service of a home economist consultant is available; and (b) the agency has recipes available for low-cost main dishes.
4. Friday, February 7, worker will telephone Mrs. Stover to review progress on securing recipes. We expect that Mrs. Stover will be able to select a recipe to try over the weekend.
5. February 8 or 9 Mrs. Stover will prepare a new dish for her family.
6. February 10 Mrs. Stover and worker will meet at 10 a.m. to evaluate the plan and to decide about next steps.

Think back now to the Troy case (Exhibit 11-2). Mrs. Troy and the worker reached agreement on the goal of getting John out of the house, but no intervention plan was developed. Clearly there are several ways by which the worker and Mrs. Troy might proceed to accomplish this goal. Put yourself in the place of a worker and think a bit about possible intervention plans. What are the possible strengths that you might explore with Mrs. Troy? What are alternative ways to accomplish the goal? To help sharpen your thinking, draft out a possible service agreement. To keep this from becoming a one-sided effort, which of course is quite inconsistent with the thrust of social work practice we have been presenting, you might team up with a classmate, with one of you playing the role of Mrs. Stover and the other the social worker. When you do this, pay particular attention to your ability to identify and focus the client's strengths in relation to the goal (remember, all people have strengths) and your ability to explore with your client alternative courses of action that might be used to reach the goal. Also, recall the material we presented in Chapter 9, on communication. First, secure your client's views, and then you may discuss your own experience when it is related to the problem at hand.

Work with a client may involve a series of sequential agreements as you move step by step in decision making. Often these agreements will be oral (although we think

---

EXHIBIT 11-4
Goals and Intervention Plans with a Spouse Abuse Client

Jackie called the Geneva Women's Center early one morning and left a message on the answering machine saying she needed help and would like to meet with someone after work. Later that afternoon she came to the center. I met with Jackie, who said that she had to come in because she couldn't take it anymore. "It" consisted of repeated physical, verbal, and emotional assaults by Joe, her husband of three years. Jackie detailed numerous incidents of abuse in the last two years of their marriage. The last incident occurred over the weekend. Joe came home drunk, found her sleeping, and flipped their double bed over with her in it. He then began screaming and shouting at her, calling her names, and saying that she was no good, lazy, and that he "ought to take care of her." The episode ended when Joe literally threw her out of the bedroom and slammed the door. Jackie eventually slept on the couch but decided she had to leave. She believes that Joe will come after her if he knows she is trying to leave, which is why she waited until he would be working to take any action. Jackie heard about the center from a woman at work and wants help finding a place to stay until she can decide what to do.

I explained to Jackie about the shelter in Bluegrass (60 miles away) and the safe-house network here in Geneva. Jackie felt she wanted to stay in Geneva so she could keep working. She was pretty sure Joe would not bother her at work. I told her that a safehouse could be arranged. After determining Jackie's particular needs (smoker, not allergic to animals, no children, no personal items), I excused myself and alerted other staff, who began to make the arrangements. It was necessary to begin work on this immediately due to the lateness of the hour.

When I returned to the room, Jackie was crying. She said she didn't really want to leave, that she loved Joe, but she couldn't handle getting beat up all the time. She just didn't know what to do. I asked Jackie if she had thought about different things to do. Her list of possibilities included help for Joe, reconciliation and salvaging their marriage, and divorce. She hadn't made a decision as to which she should pursue. Jackie said she thought Joe would be mad if she didn't come home but that she didn't feel she could return there until things changed.

We discussed the resources she had available to her through the center: emotional support, assistance with filing an order for protection (OFP), legal advocacy, and assistance with financial and housing needs. I also mentioned the counseling program for abusive men offered by the mental

written agreements are appropriate and recommend that you work at getting your agreements with clients in written form). In Exhibit 11-1, Joe Hudson distinguishes between exploratory and working agreements. Exhibit 11-4 is a case example of a worker developing service agreements at the very earliest stages of work; these may be consistent with Hudson's exploratory agreements. As you read this example, try to identify the two agreements, the goals for each, and the intervention plans. Take a few minutes and put these into written form.

Most of our illustrations have dealt with developing service agreements with individual clients. You will also be defining problems, setting goals, and developing plans with groups. Working with groups introduces some additional complexities because of the group dynamics. Exhibit 11-5 offers some things you can do to help a group reach a decision.

Limitations on Worker Activity When negotiating interventive means, you are responsible for considering four important limitations on worker activity. These limitations are time, skill, ethics, and agency function. No worker can make unlimited time available to a specific client. Time constraints must always be considered in entering into a service contract. You cannot responsibly commit yourself to activities

---

health center. We talked at length about an OFP and the functions it provides: removing an abuser from the home, ordering counseling or treatment, ordering financial support, preventing the abuser from further assaults or threats of assault, and so on. I explained that two of the primary functions of the order were to provide safety for the victim and to provide up to one year for decision making.

After further review of the process of obtaining an OFP, Jackie thought she would like to file but wanted to think about it for a while. I said that would be fine. Our discussion was interrupted by a staff person, who related that a safe house had been arranged. I asked Jackie if she was ready to go. She was and I drove her to the safehouse. After getting Jackie settled, I gave her written information about the things we talked about and assured her that the woman she was staying with could answer any questions she might have. We then made arrangements to meet at the center the next day when she got off work to see if she'd made any decisions.

Jackie and I met the next day. She reported that she hadn't slept very well the night before, but that the woman she was staying with was very nice. Jackie also said she called Joe, who was wondering where she was and asked her repeatedly to come home. He said he loved her, that he was sorry, and that they could work things out. Jackie said she wanted to believe him but couldn't and that she told him she needed some time to think about things. Jackie went on to tell me that she thought the OFP was a good idea and that she wanted to file. She thinks that Joe might get help if the court orders him to, and maybe things would work out. She wanted to include exclusive occupancy in the order until Joe shows that he's really willing to change.

Jackie and I filled out an OFP form before she returned to the safehouse. We agreed that the following day she would get off work early and file, with my assistance. I would call the court administrator's office and let them know we were coming and pick Jackie up after work. In the event the order could not be served to Joe that same day, Jackie would arrange to stay at the safehouse one more night.

SOURCE: Case material was prepared by Ellen Holmgren, M.S.W. student, University of Minnesota School of Social Work.

EXHIBIT 11-5
Helping a
Group Reach
a Decision

1. State the problem clearly.
   Examples: The purpose of this meeting . . .
   Our job for today is . . .
2. If the problem or a given statement is not clear, ask for clarification.
   Examples: I'm not sure I understand the purpose of this meeting. Would you mind restating it?
   I'm sorry, I missed that point. Will you say it again?
3. Stay on the beam and help others to do so.
   Examples: I don't quite see how that relates to our problem.
   It seems to me we're digressing.
4. Summarize.
   Examples: Here are the points we have made so far . . .
   Thus far we have agreed . . .
5. Test workability of proposals
   Examples: Do you think the members would support that proposal?
   Where would we get the money to do that?
6. Test willingness to carry out the proposal.
   Examples: Would you be willing to . . .
   Who can take this responsibility?
7. Test readiness for decision.
   Examples: Are we agreed, then, that . . . ?
   Well, are we ready to make that decision?
8. Call for the decision.
   Examples: I move that . . .
   Will someone put this into a motion?

---

that extend beyond the time you have available; conversely, a client can reasonably expect you to do what you say you will do. Consider this incident. A social worker recently placed a 14-year-old boy in a foster home. The worker was cognizant of the fact that the youth might have some initial adjustment problems and indicated they would be visiting together on a weekly basis to talk about any placement problems. This worker, however, was employed in a large agency with a heavy caseload and because of the pressure of time was unable to visit with the boy until four weeks after the placement was made. By this time, the boy had justifiably become disillusioned and angry with the worker and rejected efforts by the worker to become jointly involved in problems that were occurring in the placement. The youth ran away and eventually was institutionalized. Had this worker made a realistic contract—to see the boy once a month instead of once a week—the client and worker might have been able to maintain their communication and to engage in more effective problem solving. A common misconception held by many new workers is to confuse intensity of service with quality of service. Poor-quality service is provided when workers make commitments that they cannot meet, and conversely, frequent contacts between worker and client do not necessarily imply high-quality service. The Stover case in the Appendix is a good example of quality but largely nonintensive service. You must plan your time so you will not make commitments beyond the time available.

Second, you should not enter into service contracts that call for activity on your part that exceeds your skills. It is a professional's responsibility to be aware of strengths and weaknesses and not to enter into agreements that exceed his or her ability. When a client requires a specialized skill that you do not possess, such as marriage counseling or bargaining with a large bureaucracy, the negotiated intervention plan will include involvement of an expert or specialist to assist with this aspect of the intervention. Our example of a service plan for the Stover case had the worker checking about the service of a home economist. We do not expect most social workers to be experts in cooking or nutrition. If a client and worker decide these skills and knowledge are necessary, the worker should arrange for a specialist to assist with this aspect of the work. In "The House on Sixth Street," one of the cases in the Appendix, the worker and tenants made use of specialists in city planning and law.

Third, you will avoid involvement in intervention plans that commit you to unethical behavior. An obvious example would be the securing of economic resources through illegal means. An economic crisis might be alleviated by a burglary, but it would not be appropriate for you to participate in planning or executing such an action. You must also not agree to participate in a plan that involves exploitation of others or furthers patterns of racial, ethnic, or sex discrimination.

Murdach (1982) notes that the organizational context provides a limitation on problem solving. We discussed this issue in Chapter 6, but we note again that agency function provides a further limitation for worker-client contracts. This limitation derives from the tendency to organize social services around functions rather than to provide generic services (Wilensky & Lebeaux, 1958, pp. 233–282). You can, however, seek to define agency function broadly, consider the possibility of requesting exceptions to agency limitations, and work within your agency to secure a broader definition of its functions. Some ways to accomplish such changes are discussed further in Chapter 6. But as long as agencies have community-sanctioned functions, you must be cognizant of this source of limitation when making commitments to clients.

Worker/ Client Differences of View

Criticisms of contracting   Some controversy has emerged about the use of the concept of contracting in social work practice (Rojek & Collins, 1987, 1988; Croxton, 1988; Miller, 1990). The criticisms are that the concept of contracting is misleading because the worker has the more powerful position, the client cannot clearly negotiate for his or her needs, there is no way the client can hold the worker accountable, and the process may trivialize the complexity of work with some clients. George Hoshino eloquently summarizes the concerns in Exhibit 11-6.

We believe these concerns are legitimate but constitute a misuse of the concept of contracting rather than grounds for abandoning the notion. The partnership concept that we have been stressing involves power sharing on the part of the worker, and respect for self-determination requires you to assist the client in articulating his or her own position. The antithesis of the concept of contracting in social work—and a practice that some of the critics may have in mind—is behavioral contracting as sometimes practiced in correction agencies and schools. Under these kinds of practice youth are often told what they must do and the consequences for failure to comply without any negotiation at all. Contracting does tend to focus and partialize the work with a client, but as we have noted previously, partialization has been a part of social

EXHIBIT 11-6
Contracting in
Social Work
Practice:
Another Fad?

In the literature and in my conversations with fellow social work professionals of late, I read and hear a great deal about contracting in social work practice; that is, the so-called client and his or her social worker enter into a contract in which both worker and client state what each is supposed to do and when. I have been puzzled by the choice of the term *contracting* by professionals when speaking of the relationship between professional and client. Although I have not surveyed other fields, my guess is that social workers are the only service professionals who use the term (as opposed to contractors like plumbers and electricians, who contract in writing to perform certain activities or repairs on one's house, like putting on a new roof, painting, or repairing the kitchen sink).

As I understand the concept of contract, it means a legally accepted and binding agreement between two contractable parties in which both parties state the terms of the agreement in explicit detail—for example, the roofer will remove and replace the existing roof, patch any needed spots, and replace the roofing with a new roof of specified material, which he guarantees for a certain period under certain terms (warranty), and that the work will be performed within a specified period. In turn, the home owner agrees to certain conditions of payment—for example, a partial payment when work begins and a final payment when the work is completed. This contract implies that both parties, the contractor and customer, are competent to enter into the contract—the contractor has the necessary knowledge, skill and equipment; the customer is legally competent (for example, children cannot enter into contracts) and financially able to pay for the services rendered under the terms of the contract. Moreover, both parties have the means to enforce the terms of the contract on each other, if necessary in the courts. The law of contracts is well established in both statutory and case law. There are also remedies available to each party, usually in the form of financial recovery for any damages or failure to carry out the terms of the contract. There also are invalid or illegal contracts; for example, one cannot legally contract with somebody to do something that is illegal, like murdering an enemy or embezzlement, or even perhaps, installing an electrical system that the contractor knows violates codes. Nor can a contractor enter into a contract that clearly is not possible to perform.

The main things are that both parties know what they want and have the capacity to do what is expected of them in the contract, and each has the means to compel the other to do what the contract calls for or recover damages.

I don't see these conditions applying in what social workers call contracts between worker—or-agency—and client. In the first place, a contract assumes that each party is freely entering into the agreement, knows what he or she wants or needs, and knows what to expect from the contractor. I think we all recognize that not very many social work clients are truly voluntary. Most are involuntary in various degrees, ranging from being under court order, on probation, committed as a mental patient to being recipients of public assistance or referred to the school social worker by the teacher or principal or into the new minor mothers service programs. In all these cases

work practice for years. We do not think this constitutes trivializing the work; indeed clients are more likely to be helped if they succeed in dealing with one matter at a time.

The matter of clients holding social workers accountable is one to which we will return in Chapter 16. We think this is a problem. Workers are more likely to be conscientious in following through on their commitments when these commitments are made very explicit in a contract. We also believe the profession should strengthen the channels by which clients may file complaints against workers who have not competently followed through on their commitments. Agency appeals are one way to handle this; consumer services involving the possibility of worker-client mediation are another. The third is for clients to file professional malpractice complaints against sanctioning is specifically prescribed for failure to follow steps in the case plan. I fail to see a fundamental characteristic of a true contract under these circumstances.

Can the client know what he or she needs or wants, as the home buyer or homeowner knows, at least in a general sort of way, what he or she wants in the way of a house or what kind and quality of new roofing to replace the present leaky one? Is there a meeting of minds of what the outcome should be; the homeowner knows, at least in a general way, what he or she wants in the way of a roof—or can ask around—and the contractor knows what he or she can deliver. The owner can make a judgment about his or her part, namely, what he or she can afford, given his financial circumstances. Is there a meeting of minds between social worker and client as to what is to come out of the relationship? Not very often. In the current push to reduce the number of children in out-of-home placements, the emphasis is on preventing placement in the first place through intensive home-based services. In contrast to court-ordered placements such as for child neglect or abuse, many out-of-home placements are voluntary, that is, initiated or demanded by the parent. If the worker refuses to go along, what then? On whose side is the worker? Certainly, what social workers call client advocacy is challengeable; for whom is the worker advocating?

To what extent does the client set or agree to the terms of the contract? I haven't seen any studies of client understanding of or agreement to the terms of these so-called contracts, but I daresay they would not stand up under the usual definition of contract either in its strict legal sense or in the man-on-the-street definition.

Finally, do both parties to the contract—that is, worker and client—have the means to compel the other party to comply with the terms of the contract as parties to the usual contract have? Certainly the client of the social worker has no way of compelling compliance with the contract beyond complaining or filing a grievance. The terms of the contracts between worker and client I've looked at aren't specific enough to hold anybody to much of anything. Legally regulated professions—doctors and lawyers—can be sued for malpractice or a complaint can be lodged in a professional complaints committee, but those are for generally gross or illegal activities like using a client's money for personal use or sexual relationship between therapist and patient. As I see it, the cards are all stacked in favor of the worker and against the client. That's not a contract as I understand the term and concept. Even plumbers and electricians can be sued for failure to perform the terms of the contract to do work or for not doing it properly. Obviously, the social worker's client can't even do that.

I conclude that adoption of the term contracting by social workers is simply another one of those fads through which the profession goes; picking up a nice-sounding phrase or even the idea but not really understanding it or implementing it in its true meaning.

SOURCE: George Hoshino, Professor Emeritus, School of Social Work, University of Minnesota.

workers. We believe that failure on the part of a worker to follow through on an agreed-upon intervention plan constitutes professional malpractice.

Confronting Differences in Worker and Client Views   The process of contracting that we are advocating clearly means that worker and client will be confronting differences of view that must be resolved. Murdach (1982) and Seabury (1979) both note the likelihood of worker and client conflict in contracting and the problem-solving model. We expect worker-client differences to be a regular occurrence. Further, such differences are likely to be desirable. When human beings come together, perceptions, thinking, and world views may be quite different. However, the process of working and sharing, bargaining and negotiating, will result in growth and change.

You should not expect to find your relationship with clients free from differences and conflict. Rather, hope for commitment and expect to work hard to find a common ground from which you and the client can move. We agree with Seabury (1979) that efforts to avoid conflict are counterproductive and result in corrupt contracts in which the worker and client are working toward different goals:

> Corrupt contracting will not take place if, during the early stages of contract negotiation, all parties conscientiously and explicitly state their thoughts, desires, and expectations. In many cases, however, corrupt contracting does occur because one or several parties fear that being explicit may cause conflict; this conflict will not be resolvable and therefore service will terminate even before it has begun. This logic is faulty, of course. Deceit serves no purpose, and honesty is always the appropriate strategy. There is nothing inherently bad about conflict, and attempts to avoid it during contracting are naive. Working out differences early in the contract process means that each party has a better chance to do some true negotiating of contract terms. In fact, when contracting goes too smoothly, it is often a sign that one side is selling out to the other.

An important principle in contracting is that conflict should not be avoided, differences must be teased out and negotiated, and the sooner differences are revealed, the better for the service process. Even if the conflict cannot be resolved and no contract is agreed on at the beginning, at least no time or energy will have been wasted on the corrupt contract. An agreement between worker and client not to pursue service because of recognized differences or conflict is in fact a contract.

If you are to be helpful, you and your client must find a common ground regarding problem definition, goals, and intervention plan. Much of this effort will involve bargaining and negotiating. Often you will have to persevere in the effort. The worker who comes back to a supervisor after a single contact with the client and announces that he or she is closing the case because an agreement could not be reached does not understand the nature of negotiation. Contrast this with the efforts of the worker in the Stover case (see Appendix), who spent several weeks and much effort to maintain contact with Mrs. Stover before a common goal could be developed.

Recapitulation   The service contract is a plan jointly negotiated by you and a client that defines the problem for work, specifies the goals, and provides an intervention plan designed to move from the problem to the goals. The process of negotiating the service contract culminates in a commitment on the part of both you and a client to implement the plan. Once negotiated, the service contract is binding on both the worker and the client and is not subject to unilateral changes. Changes can, of course, be jointly negotiated. Four principles in this chapter can be stated explicitly:

1. Joint negotiation of the service contract means precisely what the words imply. The contract involves input from both worker and client. We indicated disagreement with the concept of diagnosis because of a lack of client input in the decision making that leads to a diagnosis. But frequently workers also err in the other direction—in failing to provide their own input for fear that it might hamper the client's right to self-determination. A worker's professional judgment, experience, and background are all sources of knowledge and

information that should be available to the client in joint decision making. The key is to arrive at a service contract that is truly joint and representing the best collective judgment of both you and client.

2. The worker is expected to bring a broad knowledge base to the process of arriving at a service contract. This base will include knowledge of human functioning, of the social environment, and of the interaction of the two. The worker will be expected to draw on the sources of knowledge identified in Chapters 3, 4, and 5 and to apply those sources to the specific client situation under consideration.

3. The focus of the service contract and the intervention plan will be consistent with the concept of person-in-situation. This means that the worker and the client must be alert to the widest possible range of goals and interventive approaches. The target of change may be the client, forces in the environment, or the interaction of the two. Although no worker can be expected to master all change strategies, you can be expected to be aware of the broad repertoire of change strategies available to the profession and to be able to select jointly with the client the strategy most appropriate for the client. If you cannot provide that service, you must be able to locate it elsewhere in the community. Method specialties may be necessary, but they cannot be justified as blinders.

4. The development of a service contract is a cognitive process involving thinking, reasoning, and decision making. Feelings are important, but planning should be done on a rational basis. The planning may, of course, involve plans to deal with feelings. Further, rational planning precedes interventive activities. This does not deny the spiral concept of practice, which was identified in earlier chapters and will be made more explicit in Chapter 16, on evaluation. But whenever you are engaged in interventive efforts, those efforts should be based on a deliberate rational service contract negotiated with the client.

A Look Forward

This chapter has described a crucial component of social work processes—joint client-worker development of a rational plan to define the problem for work, establish objectives, and specify an interventive plan is a prerequisite to intervention. Chapters 12 and 13 contain material on worker intervention activities; teamwork is considered in Chapter 14. Ending services is discussed in Chapter 15 and evaluation in Chapter 16. Evaluation is an essential part of work with clients; it shows social work processes to be more dynamic and continuous than has been implied in the linear description of the problem-solving process.

Reading 11-1, by Edith Fine and Irene Staff, provides a process for goal setting with birth parents of children in care. The service planning involves identifying and stating goals, building on strengths and resources, and creating action plans. They offer useful guidelines for setting goals and creating case plans as well as some suggested formats. The application is to a particular type of client situation, but we believe you will find the concepts and suggestions useful for work with most client situations and encourage you to study and consider the material in Reading 11-1.

In the next chapter worker activity to move from problem to solution will be discussed in terms of interventive roles. Before these roles are used, however, a service contract must be developed to specify the nature of both worker and client activity.

As in the definition of the problem and of goals, any differences between worker and client in these areas are to be resolved before implementing any intervention plan.

Goal-Setting with Biological Families*

Edith Fein and Ilene Staff

"Goal-setting is one of the critical tasks of the social work problem-solving process" (Anderson, 1989). Goal-setting encourages procedures that give a clear picture of problems, support treatment planning and assessment of progress, and facilitate review and evaluation of outcomes.

This chapter presents policy and practice in setting goals with biological families whose children have been removed because of abuse or neglect. Using the experience of a demonstration program in operation since 1989 as illustration, the authors examine guidelines for the goal-setting process; set forth tools for helping workers in assessment, decision-making, and treatment- planning; discuss policy and practice aspects; and consider the application of results and conclusions from this example to family reunification practice in general.

THE FAMILY REUNIFICATION PROJECT

Casey Family Services is a voluntary long-term foster care and permanency planning agency founded in 1976 in Connecticut, currently serving over 200 children in six New England states. This chapter draws from the agency's experience with its Family Reunification Project, which assists families whose children are in foster care primarily because of abuse or neglect and who need a broad range of intensive or special services if the family is ever to be reunited. The program offers families case management and clinical intervention services in their own homes. Unlike most time-limited,

crisis-oriented family preservation programs, family reunification services may be provided for periods as long as two years. Professionals assigned to the families have low caseloads and are able to give sustained attention to the families.

Each family is assigned to a reunification team consisting of a social worker and a family support worker. The team provides such services as training in parenting skills; mental health counseling; respite care; group support; and assistance with housing, job training, transportation, and legal problems. Services begin before the child returns home, when the reunification team and the biological family create a service agreement setting forth treatment goals and plans, and continue after reunification for as long as needed, up to a two-year total.

Referrals to the program come from state agency workers who determine that reunification should be the permanent plan for an abused or neglected youngster, but who are not optimistic that it can be achieved unless intensive services are provided. The biological family must be willing and able to participate in formulating a service agreement and to work with the reunification team. In addition, the foster parents or residential care facility staff must be willing to work with the team, and the child must have been removed from the home within the previous 18 months. To protect children and ensure the safety of workers, cases are not accepted if a sibling has died because of abuse or neglect or if life-threatening abuse has taken place in the past; if the child's safety would be jeopardized by reunification; if sexual abuse has taken place and the perpetrator lives in the home or is an active member of the family; if violence has taken place (or a potential for violence exists) toward people outside the family; or if caregivers are substance abusers with no willingness to participate in treatment.

GOAL-SETTING IN CHILD WELFARE

Since the 1970s, goal-setting has found expression in several areas of practice, including the development of task-oriented casework (Reid & Epstein, 1972), time-limited therapy (Mann, 1973), and goal-attainment scaling (Garwick & Lampman, 1972). The child welfare field has benefited from this emphasis on goals. Permanency planning—the mainstream movement in delivering child welfare services—stresses explicit formulation of problems, treatment planning, identification of permanent placement options, case management, review of plans, and timely decision-making based on the implementation of service agreements (Maluccio et al., 1986). Permanency planning thus epitomizes goal-setting.

Functions

Service planning for family reunification using a goal and plan orientation, as Maluccio et al.(1986) suggest, fulfills the following functions:

- Encourages systematic thinking about many areas of family needs;
- Structures service delivery activity so workers, supervisors, and clients are fully aware of what is occurring;
- Aids in case planning and management, allowing for timely decision-making and corrective action when necessary;
- Helps clients participate in what is happening to their families in achieving reunification;
- Ensures program accountability; and
- Documents case progress for possible court testimony.

In the child welfare field, intensive family preservation programs have given further impetus to the goal-setting orientation. Intensive family preservation programs typically are in-home, time-limited, crisis-oriented services, and are designed to prevent foster care placement of children at risk of removal from their homes [Whittaker et al. 1990].

Various family preservation training courses and handbooks underscore the usefulness of focus and goal-setting in delivering these services (Lloyd & Bryce, 1985; Tracy et al., 1991; Whittaker et al., 1990).

Some family preservation program advocates believe the family preservation model might make family reunification efforts more timely and more successful than they are at present [Maluccio et al. 1991; Nelson 1990]. Many family reunification programs are superficially similar to family preservation services, having developed from the same roots. However, there are important differences. Most important, in intensive family preservation programs a family's motivation to develop and achieve goals and to work with service providers is tied to the fear that children will be removed from the home—a strong authoritative mandate. Families of children already in foster care, however, have different concerns.

First, family reunification readily occurs two-thirds to three-fourths of the time in the course of normal service delivery by state agencies [Fein et al. 1983; Tatara 1989]; parental motivation is not necessarily an issue. Second, those children not reunified with their families are typically victims of one or more unfortunate circumstances: the state agency may not be able to deliver the kind or depth of services the family needs; the children present almost insurmountable problems in adjusting to family life; or the families are too troubled to make use of the services available. Third, even children who are quickly reunited with their families face difficulties (Turner, 1984). When children stay out of the home for long periods, families achieve a new equilibrium without them, and parents may feel ambivalent about having the children return. As a result, reunification programs, which by their nature work with many families in situations such as those described above, are forced to deliver services without the motivation and authoritative mandate that family preservation programs command.

For all these reasons, goal-planning is an essential feature of family reunification practice and was made an integral part of the Casey program model. Family members and social workers alike can use the focus and structure that goal-planning provides, particularly when reunification aims at a level of reconnection short of living in the same household. In those cases, the goal-planning process enables the family and the social worker to identify the appropriate level of reconnection and achieve some success in attaining the selected level despite the family's inability to live together.

THE SERVICE PLANNING PROCESS

The process of service planning requires that workers and clients together (1) identify appropriate goals, (2) build on existing strengths and resources, and (3) create action plans to help the clients' progress toward the goals. Of the three, identifying and explicitly stating the goals is probably the most difficult, but all are crucial for a successful case plan.

Identifying and Stating Goals

To create a goal statement, the worker must consider what problems the family is facing (see figure 11-1), what must change about the family's functioning to allow reunification to take place, and what the family will be like if the goals are achieved. Goals are statements of positive family functioning, as illustrated in figure 11-2.

Building on Strengths and Resources

While goals are positive statements about changes the family can achieve, strengths and resources are abilities, ways of functioning, personal characteristics, environmental conditioning, social connections, or any positive aspects of the family's life that are present or that can be found or mobilized in behalf of the family (see figure 11-2).

Creating Action Plans

Particular actions must be taken by the reunification team and the family, separately and together, to achieve progress toward the family's goals. The plans should be specific, indicate a date by when they will be accomplished, and identify who will be working on each plan. For example, consider goal #1 in figure 11-2: Ms. Parker and Mr. Vega will not abuse drugs or alcohol. Plans for them might include the following actions:

- Ms. Parker will no longer associate with the drug dealers she knew in the past, beginning immediately. *Responsibility:* Ms. Parker.
- Weekly until May 1, Ms. Parker and the social worker will discuss Ms. Parker's drug cravings, how she feels about herself, and how she is managing her new life. *Responsibility:* Social worker and Ms. Parker.
- Mr. Vega will continue attending AA meetings. *Responsibility:* Mr. Vega.

GUIDELINES FOR SETTING GOALS AND CREATING CASE PLANS

The following guidelines should be applied in developing an effective service plan.

Goals

A. A goal should state how the family situation will be different, not what the reunification team or family will do to make it happen.

Confusing goals and plans is the problem most frequently encountered in writing goal statements. The goal is the end-state that is sought; details of the work that needs to be done will be written in the plans. They are related as strategy and tactics are related.

Not a goal: Mother will visit with her two sons.
Goal: Mother will give her children the affection and attention they need.

B. Each goal should be explicit and germane to the family's functioning and ability to cope. The language should be direct and informal.

To participate productively in their plans, client families have to understand the concepts and language of their goal statements. Technical jargon is not helpful. The goals should define what the clients' life situation must be to have their children live with them.

Unclear goal: Mother will have a responsive support network.
Clear goal: Mother will be close to other people she can talk to and get help from them when she needs it.

C. Goals should be formulated to balance explicit and assessable expectations with the family's social and emotional needs.

FIGURE 11-1 Problem Areas	*In creating goals and plans, each of the following problem areas should be considered for families whose children are in care because of abuse or neglect:*

1. Parents' feelings toward selves
2. Parents' relationship, including sexual relations
3. Parents' recognition of problems
4. Parents' capacity for child care
5. Parents' approval of children
6. Discipline of children
7. Supervision of children
8. Incidence of sexual abuse
9. Child's behavior
10. Relationship between parents and child
11. Child's relationship to family
12. Child's feelings toward self
13. Child's disabling condition
14. Child's developmental lags
15. Child's relationship to peers
16. Child's relationship to foster family
17. Child's educational needs
18. Health care
19. Home management (nutrition, clothing, sanitation, hygiene, physical safety)
20. Money management
21. Housing and transportation needs
22. Employment needs
23. Social networks

FIGURE 11-2
Goals and Strengths

Goals	*Strengths and Resources*
Ms. Parker and Mr. Vega will not abuse drugs or alcohol.	Mr. Vega has enrolled in a drug rehabilitation program. Ms. Parker has already completed Phase 1 of day treatment and has been regularly attending AA meetings.
Ms. Parker and Mr. Vega will have enough money to pay for the basic needs of life, including housing, clothing, food, and utilities, and will manage their money carefully.	Ms. Parker currently has a stable job. Mr. Vega is actively looking for a job.
Ms. Parker and Mr. Vega will set limits and teach Jacob right from wrong.	Ms. Parker and Mr. Vega want very much to learn better ways to be good parents.
Ms. Parker and Mr. Vega will have a good understanding of Jacob's needs.	Ms. Parker and Mr. Vega intend to visit Jacob regularly and will provide their own transportation.
Ms. Parker and Mr. Vega will develop a good relationship, free from abuse.	Mr. Vega and Ms. Parker are involved in counseling to improve their communication with each other.

The goals must specify the changes necessary for the family to attain reunification. Goals that define a better state but are irrelevant to the original reason for placement should not be identified.

Irrelevant goal: Mother should volunteer her time to help others.

Relevant goal: Mother will locate and use community resources.

D. Family members should be able to make progress on some goals in a fairly short time period so that a feeling of success can emerge from their interactions with the worker.

Long-term goals should include more easily attainable short-term goals, to encourage the confidence that family members must have to work toward their larger achievements.

Long-term goal: Mother will earn sufficient money from employment to support her children on her own.

Short-term goal: Mother will obtain services to have enough to pay for such basic needs as housing, clothing, food, and utilities.

E. Goals should be stated in such a way that progress toward their achievement can be assessed.

Progress toward a goal is an important concept. Some of the goals will never be fully reached—improvement is always possible in such areas as understanding a child's needs or providing needed affection. Goal achievement, moreover, is not always easily measured. Sufficient progress toward the goal, however, can be evaluated through the social worker's observation of parent-child interactions.

Limited goal: Mother will interact with her children.

Assessable goal: Mother will give her children more of the affection and attention they need.

Strengths and Resources

F. Family strengths and resources should be articulated so workers and family members begin to think positively about the family's potential.

Strengths may be dispositional attributes such as motivation, biological predispositions such as intellectual capacity, or positive events. They should always be the focus when formulating goals. Strengths should be germane to the particular case and explicitly stated.

Strength: Mother has had her own apartment in the past. Mother has begun to look at classified ads for affordable housing.

Goal #1: Mother will provide a home with space, furnishings, appliances, utilities, and so forth, adequate for essential household functions and for meeting the personal needs of family members.

Strength: Mother already receives food stamps and has dealt with state and local welfare offices.

Goal #2: Mother will have enough money to pay for basic needs, such as housing, clothing, food, and utilities, and will manage her money carefully.

Action Plans

G. Each action plan should be explicit, doable in a specified time period, and assessable.

The plans proposed to achieve each goal, that is, the work to be done, should be reasonable and specific enough so that the worker's and the family's actions can be monitored and measured.

Goal: Mother will give her children more of the affection and attention they need.

Plans: (A) Mother will visit children once a week at the agency office; (B) Social worker will bring children to mother's home once a week starting June 1st; (C) Mother will attend parent support group.

SUPPORTIVE RECORDKEEPING

Effective goal-planning requires a systematic recordkeeping procedure that is consonant with a program's philosophy and practice. The procedures suggested here are based on earlier work in goal-planning (Jones and Biesecker, 1980; Miller et al., 1984; Maluccio et al., 1986), and incorporate concepts and techniques developed in permanency planning work in child welfare. The recordkeeping system is a logical extension of the service-planning process and guidelines discussed above, and was developed by the staff of the project on which this chapter is based.

The recordkeeping system uses a variety of forms to establish goals with the family, outline the plan of action, define responsibilities, document case activity, and monitor and evaluate case progress. The forms are described briefly below, and in the following section their use is illustrated with a case example.

The Case Plan Form

The case plan form (figure 11-3) is the central document upon which most of the others depend. It defines what the case is about and what planning will lead to progress toward specified goals. The case plan requires that workers consider a multitude of potential problems, define applicable goals with the client, delineate resources and strengths that may be brought to bear, create plans that will help the client progress toward the goals, and identify responsibility for completion of the plans.

The Monthly Goal and Plan Rating Form

The monthly goal and plan rating form (figure 11-4) allows for monthly review of goal and plan progress. It tracks changes in the amount of effort expended, monitors continuance or completion of the plan, and evaluates the past month's efforts. The form is completed by the reunification team and reviewed with the family. The monthly evaluation enables both team and family to be supported in the successes they have had and to be aware of the work that remains.

Other Forms

Additional forms include a referral sheet (see figure 11-5), containing information provided by the state agency; a face sheet, with full demographic information; an assessment, using the Family Risk Scales (Magura et al., 1987), at several key points in case progress; a status change form, documenting milestones in case progress; narrative recordings, comprising an intake summary, periodic case updates, and case notes; an expense form; and the service agreement described above. The following

case example illustrates the use of some of these forms for service planning and goal setting and for case documentation.

> Five-year-old Josh has been in family foster care for the past three months. Months before, he was admitted to a hospital clinic along with his two-year-old brother, Philip. Both had bruises, head lice, and scabbed sores around the hairline severe enough for the clinic to refer them to state care. Josh was not yet toilet trained, Philip seemed to be developmentally delayed, and both boys were poorly socialized.
>
> This was not the first time the two boys had been removed from their family. Earlier in the year they had been placed in family foster care and later returned home. But now their mother was not keeping medical appointments and was known to be associating with drug dealers. In light of this information, social workers from the public child welfare agency were pessimistic about the outcome of a second effort to reunite the family, but they referred the family to a private agency for intensive reunification services.

Josh and Philip's case plan contained seven goals, three of which are illustrated in figure 11-3. The mother was involved in the creation of the goals and for each goal, family strengths were defined and plans made. The case plan identifies the date each goal and plan was established, as well as who is responsible for the plan. Note that for goals 1 and 3, additional plans were made a month after the original plans.

The Monthly Goal and Plan Rating Form (figure 11-4) illustrates the first month's rating of progress on goal 1. (A rating form is normally completed for each goal.) The social worker and family support worker team complete the form together. This form is shared with the mother or can be completed with her participation. The rating form charts progress, shows where more work needs to be done, and keeps the goals and plans in everyone's consciousness.

PROGRAM AND PRACTICE ISSUES

As discussed above, the goal-setting process is a familiar, if not completely comfortable, procedure for social workers. When it is used systematically,

FIGURE 11-3
Sample Case Plan

Family Name:	Smith	Case #: 01
Workers:	J. Jones	

Use as many pages as needed to identify all goals and plans to be worked on. Add new goals and plans as they emerge. In the right-hand columns, please indicate the date each goal and plan was identified and who will be working on each.

GOAL #: _____1_____

	Date	Who
Mother will give her children the affection and attention they need.	2/10/90	

Strengths and Resources

	Date	Who
Mother loves to play with the boys when they visit.	2/10/90	1
Mother likes to read magazine articles about child care.	2/10/90	1

Plan A.

	Date	Who
Mother will visit children once a week at the agency office.	2/10/90	1

Plan B.

	Date	Who
Worker will discuss discipline and other child-rearing problems at each home visit.	2/10/90	2

Plan C.

	Date	Who
Social worker will bring children to mother's home at each home visit.	3/10/90	3

Plan D.

	Date	Who
Mother will attend parent support group.	3/10/90	1

Codes: 1—Family, 2—Family Support Worker, 3—Social Worker, 4—Other (specify)

FIGURE 11-3
(continued)

Family Name: Smith   Case #:   01

Workers: J. Jones

Use as many pages as needed to identify all goals and plans to be worked on. Add new goals and plans as they emerge. In the right-hand columns, please indicate the date each goal and plan was identified and who will be working on each.

GOAL #:   _____3_____   Date   Who

Mother will not abuse drugs or alcohol.   2/10/90   _____

_____   _____   _____

_____   _____   _____

_____   _____   _____

_____   _____   _____

Strengths and Resources

Mother has been free of drugs for extended periods in the past.   _____   _____

Mother is determined to stay clean in the future.   _____   _____

_____   _____   _____

_____   _____   _____

Plan A.

Mother will no longer associate with the drug dealers she knew   2/10/90   1

in the past.   _____   _____

_____   _____   _____

_____   _____   _____

Plan B.

Mother will attend AA meetings each Wednesday evening.   2/10/90   1

_____   _____   _____

_____   _____   _____

Plan C.

Mother and social worker will discuss mother's cravings,   2/10/90   1, 3

how she feels about herself, and how she is managing her new life. _____   _____

_____   _____   _____

Plan D.

Mother will attend parent support group at the agency.   3/10/90   1

_____   _____   _____

_____   _____   _____

Codes: 1—Family, 2—Family Support Worker, 3—Social Worker, 4—Other (specify)

(continued)

FIGURE 11-3 (continued)

Family Name: Smith   Case #:   01

Workers: J. Jones

Use as many pages as needed to identify all goals and plans to be worked on. Add new goals and plans as they emerge. In the right-hand columns, please indicate the date each goal and plan was identified and who will be working on each.

	Date	Who
GOAL #: 2		
Mother will have enough money to pay for the basic needs of life,	2/10/90	
including housing, clothing, food, and utilities, and will manage her		
money carefully.		

Strengths and Resources

Mother already receives food stamps and has dealt with state and local welfare offices.

Plan A.

Worker will help mother draw up a budget.   2/10/90   2

Plan B.

Worker will go with mother to open a bank account.   2/10/90   1, 2

Plan C.

Mother will not buy anything on layaway or credit.   2/10/90   1

Plan D.

Worker will help mother with shopping to take advantage of coupons, sales and bargains.   2/10/90   1, 2

Codes: 1—Family, 2—Family Support Worker, 3—Social Worker, 4—Other (specify)

FIGURE 11-4 Sample Monthly Goal and Plan Rating Form	*Family Name:* Smith	*Case #:* 01	
	Workers: J. Jones, O. Doe	*Rating Date* 2/28/90	

INSTRUCTIONS: At month's end, list all goals and plans by describing them briefly in the space provided. Rate goals and plans on focus and status; indicate this month's progress for goals, and an evaluation for plans, in the third column. The codes and scales are listed on the bottom of the form.

GOAL #: 1	Focus	Status	Goal Progress
Mother will give her children the attention and	1	C	2
affection they need.			

Plan	Focus	Status	Eval.
A. Mother will visit.	1	C	3
B. Worker will discuss discipline, etc.	1	C	2
C.			
D.			
E.			
F.			
G.			
H.			
I.			
J.			
K.			
L.			

Codes:

Focus:
Over the past month, how much time has been spent by the family or the team on this plan? Toward achieving this goal?
1. A major amount of time.
2. A minor amount of time.
3. Goal or plan not worked on this month.

Goal Progress:
How much progress, if any, has there been this month in approaching this goal?

Status:
At this time this goal or plan is:
C. Continued
D. Discontinued

Plan Evaluation:
Over the past month, how well was this plan working?
1. Not at all.
2. Working a little.
3. Working very well.

0	1	2	3	4	5
Regress from goal	None	A little progress	Moderate progress	A lot of progress	Goal achieved

FIGURE 11-5
Sample
Referral Form

Case # _____ Referral Date _____ Taken by _____ Team Assigned _____

State Worker _____ Phone # _____

Child Information
Name _____ DOB _____

Current Placement: Type _____ Name _____ Removal Date _____

Address _____

_____ Phone # _____

Sex _____ Race _____ Grade _____ School _____

Previous Placements: ☐ No   ☐ Yes   How many? _____

To be reunified with
Name _____ Relationship to child _____

Address _____

_____ Phone # _____

Biological Parents   Mother   Father

   Name   _____   _____

   Address   _____   _____

               _____   _____

   Phone #   _____   _____

Comments (mention siblings to be reunified)

_____

_____

_____

_____

_____

_____

_____

_____

_____

_____

_____

_____

_____

_____

_____

benefits for clients and staff members are well documented (Klier et al., 1984; Miller et al., 1984). Agency reunification programs, however, have not generally directed themselves to the particular fit between their reunification objectives and a goal-setting orientation. For goal-setting (or goal-oriented service planning) to be an integral feature of family reunification programs, a number of factors must be considered.

WORKERS' SKILLS AND ATTITUDES

Social workers are often uncomfortable at first with formulating goals and plans. "We were struck by the meager reporting we found in most of the case records about the social worker's definition of clinical tasks and description of ongoing therapeutic work. A well-articulated service plan was often not present in the records" (Fanshel et al., 1989, p. 477). Indeed, many programs are not clear about their continuum of goals (Videka-Sherman, 1989). Even training courses designed to teach the procedure can add to the confusion—some define goals as the most general of the plans, others equate goals with mission statements, and still others confuse the workers' efforts with the clients' needs (Anderson, 1989).

Despite training and the availability of written guidelines, staff members may vary widely in their ability to articulate goals. Some workers may write goals that are action-oriented, rather than ones that describe new situations for the client. Consensus may not exist on the degree of specificity that differentiates a goal from a plan. Moreover, in some cases goals may correctly describe an improved family situation but their relationship to reunification may not be clear. A client's goal, for example, might be to become self-supporting, but having a job might not result in managing money well enough to achieve reunification.

To assist workers in the goal-setting process—in effect, to come to agreement on the proper scope for goals in relation to plans—the authors examined all the early goals and plans in the family reunification project being presented in this chapter. These goals and plans fell into fairly clear categories, addressing financial stability, child care, substance abuse treatment, and educational and vocational attainment. These categories were congruent with factors in the Family Risk Scales (Magura et al., 1987), already used in the project to assess families at intake, reunification, and case closing.

From this examination, a list of representative goals was created, amalgamating the workers' experience and the Family Risk Scale factors (see figure 11-6). Workers and family members can select a pertinent goal from the list or use one as a guide or model. This procedure, used in other goal-oriented programs (McCroskey & Nelson, 1989), can smooth out variations in specificity of goals and plans, and help to create goals that are germane to the reunification effort.

Role of Supervisor

The supervisor's importance in formulating, documenting, and monitoring goals and service delivery plans cannot be overestimated. Although an evaluation component within a program can help with monitoring and assuring consistency, it does not replace the supervisor. Service quality and oversight are managed by monitoring responsibility. For example, the case plan sets forth a clear overview of expected action for each case, indicates who is responsible for the action, and often provides a timeline. The supervisor can use the case plan to determine whether appropriate planning is taking place.

Supervisors also can use the Monthly Goal and Plan Rating form (figure 11-4) as a summary of progress and a basis for case conferences with workers and families. The goal concentration minimizes the sometimes rambling nature of presentations based on narrative recordings.

Number of Goals

As discussed elsewhere by Fein and Staff (1991), various issues arise in goal-oriented reunification services that are not readily dealt with by extra effort or training. In particular, how many goals should be set at the beginning of service? Some workers believe that it is most respectful of families if family members know from the beginning of service all they will need to do to have their families reunited. These workers advocate start-

> **FIGURE 11-6**
> Representative
> Goals
>
> The (parents) (family):
>
> 1. Will have and keep a clean, safe home, without physical dangers.
> 2. Will provide a home with space, furnishings, appliances, utilities, and so forth, adequate for essential household functions and meeting the personal needs of family members.
> 3. Will have enough money to pay for the basic needs of life, including housing, clothing, food, and utilities, and will manage their money carefully.
> 4. Will keep themselves and their children healthy by eating healthy, balanced meals and by getting medical and dental care when needed.
> 5. Will be close to other people they can talk to and get some help from when they need it.
> 6. Will get and use community services.
> 7. Will have a good relationship, free of abuse, with other adults in the home.
> 8. Will each feel that he or she is a good person and deserves to be treated well.
> 9. Will not abuse drugs or alcohol.
> 10. Will give their children the affection and attention that they need.
> 11. Will make sure that their children are safe from harm at all times, and that they are not left alone or left with someone who is not able to take care of them.
> 12. Will set limits and teach their children right from wrong without hurting them physically or with words.
> 13. Will have a good understanding of their children's needs.
> 14. Will make sure their children attend school regularly.

ing with as complete a list of goals as is necessary to effect reunification, with the understanding that other goals can be added if the situation changes during the course of the case. They reason that beginning with only a few goals and then adding others as early successes occur makes families feel they will never achieve the ultimate reunification.

Other workers fear that a complete list of goals will dishearten a family, that a few goals will lead to early successes, and that the original goals can easily be amended because the family will have had that understanding from the beginning. Some writers suggest that developing a complete list of goals is important; clients then rank goals and the most pressing receive attention first (Pomerantz et al., 1990).

No evidence documents that one method is superior to the others. Examination of various questions about goal-setting as a client motivator is sorely needed, particularly for neglectful families [Videka-Sherman 1989].

CONCLUSION

The project described in this chapter is part of a small, financially healthy, voluntary agency that can afford the small caseloads, specialized programs, and individualization of clients good case management and effective casework for reunification require. How well would the method apply to large, publicly funded reunification services in public agencies? If a public agency has the resources, it can implement a goal-oriented intensive service. Alternatively, it can contract for such services from voluntary agencies. The principles of goal orientation and careful and systematic documentation, however, can be used to support any agency's reunification efforts.

For Further Reading

Barker, R. L. (1987). Spelling out the rules and goals: The written worker-client contract. *Journal of Independent Social Work, 1*(2), 67–77.

Cordon, J., & Preston-Shoot, M. (1988). Contract or con trick? A postscript. *British Journal of Social Work, 18,* 623–624.

Cordon, J., & Preston-Shoot, M. (1987). *Contracts in social work.* Hants, England: Gower.

Estes, R., & Henry, S. (1976). The therapeutic contract in work with groups: A formal analysis. *Social Service Review, 50,* 611–622.

Fusco, L. J. (1991). Public assistance contracts with minors. *The Social Worker/Le Travailleur Social, 59*(1), 37–41.

Greene, G. J. (1989). Using the written contract for evaluating and enhancing practice effectiveness. *Journal of Independent Social Work, 4,* 135–155.

Kenemore, T. (1987). Negotiating with clients: A study of clinical practice experience. *Social Service Review, 61,* 132–144.

Maluccio, A., & Marlow, W. (1974). The case for the contract. *Social Work, 19,* 28–36.

Miller, P. (1990). Covenant model for professional relationships: An alternative to the contract model. *Social Work, 35,* 121–125.

Pinderhughes, E. B. (1983). Empowerment for our clients and ourselves. *Social Casework: Journal of Contemporary Social Work, 64,* 331–337.

Reid, William. (1992). *Task strategies: An empirical approach to clinical social work.* New York: Columbia University Press.

Reid, W. (1985). *Family problem solving.* New York: Columbia University Press.

Rhodes, S. (1977). Contract negotiation in the initial stage of casework service. *Social Service Review, 51,* 125–140.

Rojek, C., & Collins, S. (1988). Contract or con trick revisited: Comments on the reply by Gordon and Preston-Shoot. *British Journal of Social Work, 18*(6), 611–622.

Rojek, C., & Collins, S. A. (1987). Contract or con trick? *British Journal of Social Work, 17,* 199–211.

Zayas, L., & Katch, M. (1989). Contracting with adolescents: An ego-psychological approach. *Social Casework, 70,* 3–9.

PART

III

Tools for Doing the Decided

Interventive Roles: Implementation of the Plan

The service contract has been negotiated, agreement is achieved, and the client and you are now prepared for the hard business of intervention. You are confronted with the challenge of using abilities, skills, knowledge, and contacts to assist the client in reaching mutually defined goals. Your activity in this area will be discussed as interventive roles. The concept of interventive roles will be defined, and five such roles—broker, enabler, teacher, mediator, and advocate—will be discussed. Some general considerations about thinking of intervention as roles will be noted, and finally a configuration of interventive roles appropriate for the generalist worker will be presented.

Reading 12-1 by David Harrison and Miriam Johnson illustrates the social work process of social care provision. According to the reading, social care "involves responses to dependency and helping to provide the normal socialization, developmental, and counseling services that virtually everyone needs to live in today's complex societies." They illustrate social work as social care provision with the Milton-Clay extended family care later in this chapter. We suggest that you read this article now and make a list of all the actions undertaken by the social worker. This will assist you to understand intervention as the use of one of several different roles by a social worker. This care also illustrates social work as an unfolding problem solving process. Note that in the problem-solving work in this case, the worker and client move from problem to problem; the problems unfold as the interactions continue. Although many problems surfaced and were given attention in the process of social care provision, the worker in this case did not move to intervene until the problem and intervention were discussed with the client, alternatives considered, and an intervention decision was jointly made. Note further how carefully this worker involved the client in decision making.

The Concept of Interventive Roles

A more explicit statement of the concept of interventive roles can be developed by examining meanings for the terms *intervention* and *roles*. Throughout this book we have been using the term *intervention* in a more restricted and narrower sense than do many of our social work colleagues. Our usage of the term refers to activities undertaken subsequent to the development of a service contract and directed toward the achievement of goals specified in the service contract. Some social work scholars and practitioners use the term in a more global way to refer to all social work activities, including data collection and assessment as well as change efforts. This wider concept is often expressed by the statement that treatment begins at the opening of the first contact between worker and client.

We agree with the notion that patterns of relationship and communication begin to develop when the client and the practitioner first meet, but we differentiate exploration of problem and possible goals on the part of both worker and client from goal-directed, jointly planned change efforts. We prefer a more limited use of the concept of intervention to maintain the focus on activities directed toward goal attainment and to minimize the danger of making the concept of contracting secondary, or perhaps losing it, in efforts to produce change. We see danger in the desire of workers and sometimes clients to produce change quickly and move ahead with change activities without first developing a plan for accomplishing the objectives. We acknowledge the unfolding nature of problem solving as illustrated by the Harrison article. Addressing one problem may lead to others, but interventions, as also illustrated in this article, do not occur except as based on an agreement with the client. Maintaining a narrower definition of intervention and also stressing the functions of data collection and contracting will tend to keep these three aspects of social work processes in a more balanced perspective. Intervention in our usage therefore refers to social work processes that occur after a service contract has been developed and are directed specifically to the achievement of goals specified in that contract.

Role is a global concept with wide usage in the sociological, social-psychological, and psychological literature; but the term is not always used consistently (Biddle & Thomas, 1966, pp. 1–50; Gross, Masson, & McEachern, 1958 pp., 21–47; Neiman & Hughes, 1959). For our purposes *role* refers to the behaviors expected of a person. *Role enactment* will refer to the actual translation of these expectations into behavior. In a global sense people's roles can be conceived as comprising the total universe of expectations that they hold for their own behaviors as well as the expectations of their behaviors that are held by others. Our focus is much narrower. *Interventive role* will refer to the behavior by means of which both client (individual, family, group, or community) and you expect you to help accomplish goals specified in the service contract. One of the central points stressed in Chapter 11 was that intervention, along with all other social work processes, is undertaken jointly by you and your client. This chapter, however, focuses specifically on worker interventive activity.

Discussion will center on five interventive roles—those of social broker, enabler, teacher, mediator, and advocate. This is not an exhaustive listing. Some authors conceptualize social worker roles differently or add other roles. Charles Grosser (1965) has discussed the roles of broker, enabler, advocate, and activist in relation to community development work. The literature also includes references to such additional roles as therapist (Briar, 1967b, pp. 19–33), encourager (Biddle & Biddle, 1965, p. 82), ombudsman (Payne, 1972), bargainer (Brager & Jorcin, 1969), lobbyist (Mahaffey, 1972), and validator (Tobias, 1990). Bisno's (1969) description of nine social work methods appears very similar to our concept of role. The interventive roles of broker, enabler, teacher, mediator, and advocate provide a useful framework for the beginning social work practitioner to use in thinking about interventive activity. The value of the framework is further enhanced because, as is true of the concept of contract, it is not limited by the size of the relational system; you can use these interventive roles while working with individuals, small groups, or larger systems.

Our limiting the definition of intervention and our organization of this chapter around the concept of interventive roles is not meant to deny or ignore the importance of specific change modalities. Rather than attempt to catalog change modalities (many of which wax and wane as the culture and the profession emphasize different approaches), we choose to conceptualize intervention in a way that transcends specific modalities. Several authors have assembled lists of interventive modalities (Roberts & Nee, 1970; Rothman & Tropman, 1987, pp. 3–26; Tropp, 1968; Whittaker, 1974, pp. 200–451). The concept of interventive roles provides a framework for the analysis of interventive activity that is independent of the change modalities currently in vogue. Chapter 13 will discuss some change methods and processes that are generic to social work, are useful for the beginning practitioner, and have withstood the test of time for social work.

The Role of Social Broker

How will you enact the role of social broker? Analogies from other fields may be useful. How is the role of stockbroker enacted? Presumably a stockbroker assists clients in defining their resources and developing investment objectives. Once this has been accomplished, brokers use their contacts and knowledge of the market to select stocks that will assist clients in reaching the defined investment objectives. How about the real estate broker? Again, they assist clients in analyzing their resources and needs to define objectives in the type of home the client wishes to buy. Then, using their knowledge of the available resources, they will assist in matching the client's needs to the available housing. And so it is in the enactment of the social broker role. The worker serves as a link between the client and other community resources. Harold McPheeters and Robert Ryan (1971, p. 18), writing for the Southern Regional Education Board, note that the primary function of the broker is linkage, which they describe as follows:

> The primary objective is to steer people toward the existing services that can be of benefit to them. Its focus is on enabling or helping people to use the system and to negotiate its pathways. A further objective is to link elements of the service system with one another. The essential benefit of this objective is the physical hook-up of the person with the source of help and the physical connection of elements of the service system with one another.

The activities of the worker are directed toward making connections between the client and the community to accomplish the objectives specified in the service contract. Serving as a social broker requires a broad knowledge of community resources as well as a knowledge of the operating procedures of agencies so that effective connections can be made.

What are some examples of social brokering? The worker who arranges for a client to receive marital counseling, for job placement of an unemployed person, or for improved housing is acting as a broker if these activities involve connecting the client to other resources. The worker who brings outside experts to provide valuable information to groups is functioning as a social broker. Or when working with a community group, the worker may assist the group by identifying sources of funding for programs or additional outside expertise that can assist the organization in moving toward defined goals. What other examples of the broker role did you identify in the

EXHIBIT 12-1
Community
Guides

Effective guides tend to incorporate at least five elements in their work:
- They focus on the gifts and capacities of excluded people.
- They are well connected in associational life.
- The paths they walk into community life are based on relationships of trust rather than the authority of systems.
- They believe strongly that the community is filled with hospitality for strangers.
- They learn to leave the person they guide so that the community can surround them and become responsible for their lives.

SOURCE: McKnight, J. (1992). Redefining Community. *Social Policy*, 23 (Fall/Winter), 56–62.

Milton-Clay case in Reading 12-1? A common element in all these examples is making a referral to connect the client to another resource. Referral is a basic activity of the social broker role. Assisting a client to find and use a needed resource is frequently the most important service a worker can provide. The process of making a referral will be reintroduced in the concluding portions of this section as we discuss the integration of the roles of broker, enabler, teacher, mediator, and advocate and will be further developed in Chapter 15.

Serving as a social broker goes well beyond assisting clients to identify and access formal social agencies and programs in a community. At least as important is helping clients identify clubs, organizations, and associations in which they may wish to participate. McKnight (1992) has suggested that much of professional intervention may isolate people from their informal communities, associations, and groups. He suggests the need for community guides to help people to be introduced to and attached to individuals and groups within communities. Can a social worker serve as a community guide? McKnight is skeptical, as he believes the guide must be well established in the community in which the client is living or being introduced. However you might give some thought as to how you might perform this function or as a social broker how to help clients become connected with other neighborhood people who can serve as a community guide.

The Role of Enabler

You take an enabler role when intervention activities are directed toward assisting clients to find the coping strengths and resources within themselves to produce changes necessary for accomplishing objectives of the service contract. The major distinguishing element of the enabler role is that change occurs because of client efforts; the responsibility of the worker is to facilitate or enable the client's accomplishment of a defined change. A common misconception in discussing the enabler role is to see it only as a change that occurs within the client or in the client's pattern of relating to others or the environment. However, the enabler role can also be used to help the client find ways of altering the environment. In Reading 12-2 Barbara Solomon (1985) discusses an empowerment approach for work with families and identifies four empowerment strategies—enabling, linking, catalyzing, and priming. Another example is provided by Exhibit 12-2. The distinguishing feature of the enabler role is that the client effects the change, with the worker performing a supporting and empowering function for the client.

EXHIBIT 12-2
Gaining Use of
the Community
Room

Several men in the Riverview Senior Apartments desire to have access to the community room for cribbage games. The caretaker objects to the use of the community room for the men, as he is fearful that the men will interfere with other activities. Also, the caretaker does not believe that the men will clean up after themselves.

The worker meets with the men to plan a strategy in approaching the caretaker. A delegation of three is selected by the group and the caretaker is approached about a meeting. The men come to the meeting with a plan for scheduling activities in the room as well as an arrangement for the cleanup following activities. The caretaker is impressed with the men's plan and is relieved that someone is finally using the room responsibly.

The worker who assists a group of neighborhood residents in thinking through the need for a new day-care center, in identifying factors that must be considered in establishing the center, and in planning the steps that may be taken to provide day care is serving as an enabler to a community group. The worker who helps a group to identify sources of internal conflict as well as influences that are blocking the group from moving toward its defined goals and then to discover ways of dealing with these difficulties is serving as an enabler in relation to the group. Likewise, the worker who assists a mother in identifying problems in her relationship with her child and in identifying and selecting alternative courses of action to improve that relationship is also serving as an enabler. In what ways did you see the worker in the Harrison article serve as an enabler?

Encouraging verbalization, providing for ventilation of feelings, examining the pattern of relationships, offering encouragement and reassurance, and engaging in logical discussion and rational decision making are also avenues by which the enabler role can be enacted. What Tobias (1990) calls the validator role may also be an aspect of enabling. He writes that "the function of the validator is to confirm, legitimize, substantiate, or verify the feelings, ideas, values, or beliefs of the client as well-grounded, correct, or genuine within the client's system" (p. 357). The role is particularly important, according to Tobias, for work with the mentally ill," . . . who from the onset of their illness have experienced confusing and painful feelings and ideas, distorted perceptions, and impaired judgement . . . compounded by years of institutional delegitimation, disqualification, and negation" (p. 358). Using enabling as the interventive role will involve the worker primarily in contacts with the client system rather than with external systems. Note that the worker in Exhibit 12-2 meets with the seniors to plan a strategy that they then carried out. The enabler role can be used whether the client system be an individual, a group, or a community.

Some social workers are hesitant to refer to themselves as enablers because of the negative connotation given to this word by some people in the various addiction treatment industries. We think it useful to think in terms of positive and negative enabling. Justifying excessive use of alcohol because of stress; delinquency or crime because of unemployment; and spouse battering because of harassment are all examples of negative enabling, inappropriate in social work. We believe people must be responsible for the decisions they make and that part of our responsibility is to help clients sort through these decisions and their possible implications. We will not be involved in carrying out plans with clients that hurt other people. On the other hand, enabling can also be of a positive nature. This occurs when we assist individuals and groups to rally their strengths and respond to the problems they are experiencing in themselves or their environment. Stress, for example, may be handled through exercise, meditation, or joining a stress management group rather than drinking. Positive enabling is assisting people to mobilize their strengths to solve problems they are experiencing within themselves or within their environment in a way which does not harm others.

The Role of Teacher

Teaching is another interventive role available to you and your client. You may provide clients with new information necessary for coping with problem situations, assist clients in practising new behaviors or skills, and may teach through modeling alternative behavior patterns. Exhibit 12-3 illustrates use of role playing to assist a client deal with neighbors. When you supply low-income parents with shopping and nutritional information or provide parents with information regarding child development for coping with children, you are performing a teacher role. As you use role playing to transmit different ways of responding to the authority of teachers and principals to an adolescent, you will be using the teaching role. Or a neighborhood group desiring to influence a city council to secure more frequent refuse services may need to be taught through role playing or other approaches how to make the request to the city council. And you are teaching when you carefully check out the meaning of words and phrases and through modeling teach clients how to communicate. The teaching role has many similarities to the enabling role inasmuch as it is directed primarily to strengthening clients' abilities to cope with and solve their problems. The role is sufficiently important and useful in social work, however, that it warrants separation from enabling. Although the two roles may overlap, we perceive the enabling role as involving efforts to help clients mobilize existing resources within client systems and the teaching role as introducing additional resources into client systems.

Teaching is an important aspect of social work practice. Frequently you will provide clients with information necessary for decision making; in some situations information may be all that a client needs to accomplish the defined goals. Giving information must be clearly distinguished, however, from giving advice. Giving information implies supplying clients with data, input, or knowledge that clients are free to use or not to use on their own behalf. Giving advice implies that you know what is best for the client. You will rarely give advice, but providing information is an important service for clients.

One of the five tasks of the social work function as identified by Schwartz is the contribution of data that may help the client cope with social reality and the problem

EXHIBIT 12-3
Dealing with a Drop In Neighbor

Mary Maki is a resident of a local high-rise. Other residents of the apartments are constantly dropping in on her. Mrs. Maki feels her privacy is being violated. On several occasions Mary has become angry with other residents. She is concerned with balancing her privacy with maintaining friendships. The worker and Mary agree that alternative responses to anger are needed. Thus Mary and the worker role-play situations in which Mary can learn to deal with her drop-in neighbor without harming a friendship.

that is being worked. Schwartz (1961, pp. 146–171) also offers three important warnings: (1) Workers must recognize that the information they offer is only a small part of the available social experience. (2) The information should be related to the problem that bring the client and worker together. (3) Opinions should be clearly labeled as opinions and not represented as facts.

The Role of Mediator

Mediation involves efforts to resolve disputes between the client system and other persons or organizations. You may use the role of mediator when resolving disputes as an important step in accomplishing the service goals. If a young person has been expelled from school and the service contract has the goal of getting the student back into school, you may have to serve as a mediator between the young person and the school authorities. Or perhaps a neighborhood group wants a playground but is unable to mount sufficient political clout to do so because of rivalries with another neighborhood organization; such a situation may call for you to serve as a mediator between the two organizations. Exhibit 12-4 is an illustration of mediating between a client and the operator of a board and lodging home.

Mediation has many applications for social workers and clients, including divorce mediation to assist couples to work out child custody and property settlement conflicts (Boyer, 1991; Emery & Wyler, 1987; Hanney, 1989; Knuppel, 1991; Koopman & Hunt, 1988); mediation of neighborhood disputes (Beer, 1985; Shonholtz, 1984; Tomassic & Feeley, 1982); mediation between crime victims and offenders (Galaway & Hudson, 1990; Galaway, 1988; Umbreit, 1986; Wright & Galaway, 1988); and mediation of parent adolescent conflicts (Arthur & Foster, 1989; Lemmon, 1985; Haynes, 1992; Morris, 1983; Phear, 1985; Shaw, 1985; Zetzel & Wixted, 1984); and mediation of domestic violence disputes (Chandler, 1990; Corcoran & Melamed, 1990; Erickson & McKnight, 1990; Kilpatrick & Pippin, 1987; Marthaler, 1989; Yellott, 1990). Reading 12-3 by Marg Huber develops a model of mediation for use by Aboriginal urban communities. Social workers have always done mediation, especially in work with groups or families where disputes often occur; we are now seeing the development of specialists to provide mediation services (Chandler, 1985). In your work with clients, you may at times perform the role of mediator; at other times you may serve as a worker to assist your client to secure the services of a mediator specialist.

The mediator role will involve you in efforts to assist the clients and the other party to the dispute to find a common ground on which they can reach a resolution to the conflict. You will be called on to engage in a series of actions directed toward

---

EXHIBIT 12-4
Mediating Conflict in a Board and Lodging Home

Ida Wick lives in a board-and-lodging home. She enjoys keeping mementoes she accumulates in her day-to-day living situation. Additionally, she keeps old newspapers. The board-and-lodging operator has asked Ida to have some of the items moved because of fire regulations. Ida and the operator become irritated with one another. The social worker, acting as a mediator, first discusses the problem with Ida. Henceforth a request for a joint meeting with the operator is made. In the meeting the worker negotiates a settlement by which the fire safety standards can be met while allowing Ida to keep her more important mementoes by affording her a storage cabinet. Furthermore, she is provided with a scrapbook in which to keep newspaper clippings.

constructive conflict resolution. There is burgeoning literature regarding mediation and conflict resolution procedures (Moore, 1986; Deutsch, 1973; Jandt, 1973; Miller & Simons, 1974; Smith, 1971; Tedeschi, Schlenker & Bonoma, 1973; Walton, 1969).

In serving as a mediator, you will use techniques to bring about a convergence of the perceived values of both parties to the conflict; help each party recognize the legitimacy of the other's interests; assist the parties in identifying common interests in a successful outcome; avoid a situation in which issues of winning and losing are paramount; localize the conflict to specific issues, times, and places; break the conflict down to separate issues; and help parties realize that they have more at stake in continuing a relationship than the issue of the specific conflict. You will work at facilitating communication between the parties by encouraging them to talk to each other; sharing information and persuasion procedures may also be used.

We have identified the use of the mediator role in resolving disputes between the client system and external systems. You will also use some of the same procedures to resolve disputes within the client system as may occur when a social worker is working with groups or families. While this is mediation, settling intraclient system disputes can also be considered use of the enabling role inasmuch as resolving these intrasystem disputes is essential in enabling the client system to mobilize resources to move toward the accomplishment of the goals in the service contract. A debate about when mediation is mediation and when is it enabling is not particularly useful, although this illustrates that the boundaries separating the various interventive roles may not be fixed.

The Role of Advocate

Advocacy is a concept that social work has borrowed from the legal profession. As advocate, the social worker becomes the speaker for the client, presenting and arguing the client's case when it is necessary to accomplish the objectives of the contract. Charles Grosser (1965) notes that the advocate in social work is not neutral but like the advocate in law is a partisan representative for the client. Michael Sosin and Sharon Caulum (1983, p. 12) reviewed concepts of advocacy in social work, argue for more precision in definition, and offer this definition:

> An attempt, having a greater than zero probability of success, by an individual or group to influence another individual or group to make a decision that would not have been made otherwise and that concerns the welfare or interests of a third party who is in a less powerful status than the decision makers.

The advocate will argue, debate, bargain, negotiate, and manipulate the environment on behalf of the client. Advocacy differs from mediation; in mediation the effort is to secure resolution to a dispute through give and take on both sides. In advocacy the effort is to win for the client; advocacy is frequently directed toward securing benefits to which the client is entitled such as illustrated by Exhibit 12-5. Advocacy, like the other roles, can be used with client systems of various sizes.

Advocacy is a common role for social workers. Unlike the broker, enabler, teacher, and mediator roles, however, advocacy can be used without the direct involvement of the client. This creates a danger of falling to the temptation of serving as a client's representative without having a clear contract with the client to do so. Lawyers do not represent clients until clients have retained them and authorized them to extend

EXHIBIT 12-5 Advocacy with Social Security	Hullie Mutton's benefits from the Social Security office have been summarily decreased. The reason given by Social Security is that an overpayment was made by them to her. The Social Security office admits the error was theirs. The social worker discusses the decrease with the client and offers to contact the Social Security office in Mrs. Mutton's behalf. The worker contacts the Social Security representative, Miss Jones, to argue the client's position. The worker stresses that the error was not the client's, that the reduction in SSI is taxing to Mrs. Mutton. Further, the worker requests information on the appeal process and indicates that the client wishes to begin the proceedings. Miss Jones agrees to take a further look at Mrs. Mutton's situation and says she will talk to her supervisor and ask for an exception.

this service; likewise, social workers should be sure they have an explicit contract with the client before engaging in advocacy activities.

Roles and Specializing

The discussion of social work intervention roles as discrete entities may lead to the view that roles may serve as a basis for specialization in social work. Some of the roles, such as mediator, may be developed as a specialty practice, but we think a generalist worker must be able to serve as broker, enabler, teacher, mediator, or advocate. To specialize will limit your ability to be of service to a client. Rather than a specialty you will require abilities in all roles so that you and the client can select the most appropriate interventive role for each situation. Each of the roles may be used in some situations; this provides you and the client with alternative approaches to use in achieving goals.

Consider Exhibit 12-6, an excerpt from a report made by a social worker in a Head Start program. At the request of Mrs. B the worker came to her home to take an application to enroll the child in the program. The discussion described in Exhibit 12-6 occurred right after the application was completed. Note the development of a preliminary service contract. There is agreement that Mrs. B is having difficulty in the way she is handling Jimmy, and the goal is for her to learn new ways of handling him. The intervention proposed by the worker is to talk with Mrs. B about her parenting of Jimmy. The worker is proposing the enabler and possibly the teacher role, but in this situation the roles of broker, mediator, and perhaps advocate might have been used. Had this worker explored the situation more completely with Mrs. B, the intervention plan might have been different. For example, further exploration about what happened at the child guidance center, about Mrs. B's perceptions of what the doctor said, about her thinking and feelings concerning the experience, and about her willingness to return to the clinic might have led to an intervention plan involving the worker's serving as a broker and linking Mrs. B and the clinic. If there was a problem with the manner in which the clinic related to Mrs. B, the worker might have used a mediator role to resolve these disputes or advocate role to serve as Mrs. B's representative at the clinic. The objective remains the same—to help alter Mrs. B's way of relating to her son—but the intervention plan to accomplish this objective may involve counseling with Mrs. B, serving as the link between Mrs. B and the clinic, mediating differences between Mrs. B and the clinic, or acting as Mrs. B's advocate and representing her interests to the clinic. Consideration of all these alternatives is not likely to occur unless the worker is both willing and able to use all the roles and

EXHIBIT 12-6
How to Discipline Jimmy

The last question was, "Why do you want your child in Head Start?" Mrs. B answered by saying that he had to learn to behave better and he needed to be around other children more than he was. Putting the form aside, I asked her what sort of problems she was having with Jimmy. He had been sitting at her side, surprisingly quiet for a 3-year-old. In response to my question Mrs. B told me about taking Jimmy to the child guidance center and what the doctor told her. Apparently the doctor tested Jimmy and then talked to Mrs. B. She had complained of his bad behavior and said she didn't know how to discipline him. Apparently the doctor told her that the problem might be hers and not Jimmy's. He said that she was lonely and insecure and maybe needed some guidance in handling her children. She discussed this freely and admitted that this might be true. I asked her whether she would like to have me come over to talk to her about ways to handle Jimmy. She said definitely yes, that she couldn't do a thing with him.

is prepared to explore the client situation adequately before arriving at an intervention plan.

A second misconception that can grow out of a discussion of roles is that a worker will use only one role with each client. To the contrary, as illustrated by the Milton-Clay case in the Harrison and Johnson reading, an intervention plan may combine elements of various roles. This can be further illustrated by discussing the referral process—a major part of the social broker role. Three distinct subsequent steps are involved when a contract calls for referral to achieve its objectives. These are preparation of the client, preparation of the referral organization, and follow-up. Preparation of the client includes discussion of what the referral will involve and what the referral agency expects, and requires enabling and teaching roles. At this stage you are enabling a client to make effective use of the referral agency. Ethel Panter (1966) offers a useful discussion of client preparation and its ego-building potential for clients. Referral also generates feelings and reactions to loss on the part of both client and you; this aspect of referral will be discussed further in Chapter 15. Enabling skills are used to help clients deal with their reactions to new agencies or workers and are necessary to successful completion of a referral.

Preparation of the referral agency involves the sharing of information about the client (with the client's full knowledge and usually with the client's consent). In some situations an agency may be reluctant to accept a referral and to provide a service that it is mandated to provide. When this happens, you may have to use either mediation or advocacy. After the actual referral has been made (that is, after the client makes initial contact with the referral organization), you will follow up with both the client and the organization. Ideally, follow-up should be a part of the planning. As a result of follow-up, you may learn about client resistance to continuing the service or the referral organization's resistance to continuing with the client, which may again require use of enabling, teaching, mediation, and/or advocacy.

This model of social brokerage supplemented by the other roles to help a client secure services is one that will frequently be used by you and is central to the social care notion discussed by Harrison. If you are skilled at involving the client in developing a service contract, and skilled at helping the client to find and use the resources necessary to meet the objectives of the contract, you will provide a useful, largely unavailable service to clients. Such an approach requires the ability to use skills to humanize the ways in which services are delivered and to assist agencies in meeting their responsibilities to clients. This may be the essence of intervention derived from an assessment of the person-situation interaction.

Recapitulation   Intervention has been defined as the social worker's activity directed toward achieving the objectives of a service contract. Five interventive roles have been discussed — social broker, enabler, teacher, mediator, and advocate. Any of these roles may be used to reach the same contract objectives; this provides client and worker with alternative approaches to intervention. In addition, the roles may be used in conjunction with one another to reach the same objectives. A focus on social brokerage in which enabling and teaching are used to assist the client in using community resources and in which mediation and advocacy are used to influence the way the resources are delivered to the client may be a major part of the services provided by the generalist social worker.

A Look   Forward   We have already made use of the case included in the Harrison and Johnson reading. In addition, the Stover case in the Appendix illustrates use of all the interventive roles in work with a family. As you read this case, try to identify when the worker is a broker, enabler, teacher, mediator, and advocate. Also note the persistence and patience with which the worker engages Mrs. Stover. Many workers would have closed this case as one in which a problem could not be identified and a contract developed. This worker's willingness to remain available and to extend herself set the stage for a very helpful series of interventions. Although the contracts in this case are not as explicit as we recommend, clearly the worker has not moved ahead with interventive efforts without an agreement between worker and client. Reading 12-2 by Barbara Solomon offers some useful strategies for work with families, most of which are aspects of the enabler and teaching roles. The strategies are directed toward helping families be more effective in relation to their environment.

In Reading 1-1 Lyle Longclaws introduced you to the medicine wheel and discussed the meaning and significance of this framework for working with American Indian and Canadian Aboriginal peoples. In Reading 12-3 Marg Huber also makes use of the medicine wheel framework to develop a model of mediation that might be useful in urban Native communities.

In the next chapter we further develop some of these ideas in terms of helping clients maintain and develop competence. Subsequent chapters discuss teamwork, termination, and evaluation.

The Social Work Process of Social Care Planning*

W. David Harrison and Miriam Johnson

A great and growing proportion of social work involves helping people to take care of one another. At various points in the human life cycle we all must be cared for by others to some degree, and we must in turn care for others. The need for social care is universal. Most social care occurs in the community. In fact, mutual caring is one of the essential foundations of human community (Bulmer, 1987; Dokecki, 1992). Many social work students and practitioners, for example, make use of social care services to help look after their children or to help care for aging parents or other relatives. Often these services are integral parts of plans that allow us to go to school or work outside the home while fulfilling our roles as caring family members. On the job, social workers use problem-solving processes to help others make plans and to structure services to fit their wants and needs as well as possible. Social workers also help people to deal with the problems of their social roles as relatives and neighbors, with issues of dependence and independence, and with loss. Often social workers work to make the social processes of the community more functional in these universal human situations (Hadley, Cooper, Dale, & Stacy, 1987). In this paper we look at the basic ideas of social care planning and counseling as an application of the problem-solving model. This model is used extensively in the many settings that involve the use of practical care and related treatment services. To begin to grasp the sorts of human needs and problems involved in social care planning and counselling, consider the following excerpts from the interviews of a social worker in a rural setting.

Adolescent residing in a group home: "I've been here over a month and I still hate it. The counselors treat us like children. . . . My mom says it's not right. I'll go live with Ray; he's got a van . . . or you can move me to a better place."

Considerations for the social worker: Developmental stage of adolescence compounded by disrupted family structure; issues of separation from family and attachment to new people; conflict about family system and care-providing system.

Tasks for the social worker: Developing goals for care with youngster and family; resolving dilemmas about the most desirable placement versus the available placements; developing a cooperative plan of care.

Middle-aged man moving from a state mental hospital to a board-and-care home: "Do I really have to have a job when I leave here? I don't think I ever had a real job. I'd like to get a truck and do some light hauling. . . . MacDonald's is hiring. . . . I hope Ms. Coleman will come to see me. She'll help me with my medicine."

Considerations for the social worker: Basic security; the need for a home; continuity of relationships; preparation and training for employment; establishing realistic, meaningful goals; social influences on medical treatment and maintenance; how the people in the various communities see this man and others with similar disabilities.

Tasks for the social worker: Planning with the client in terms that are comprehensible and meaningful; coordinating services; providing long-term support; finding common ground between the individual and the communities he might become part of.

Young mother of two children in foster care because of abusive attempts at discipline: "You don't think I'm an unfit mother, do you? I spanked my kids to correct them. I love them, even if they drive me up a wall. I want my kids. . . . You're not like some of those other caseworkers. . . . Help me figure out how to get them back."

Considerations for the social worker: Ambivalence and inconsistency in the parent role; probably parental immaturity, but with genuine attempts to use support; appropriate use of the social work

---

*An original article prepared for this volume.

relationship; probable isolation from community resources.

Tasks for the social worker: Integrating child care with parental plans for change; making use of legal and professional planning processes to achieve client goals and sound permanent homes for children; combating isolation and alienation.

Sixty-year-old father of developmentally disabled adult daughter: "We always did what we were supposed to. You don't know what it's like to try to raise a girl who won't grow. . . . I don't see how a social worker can help now. . . . Why did God do this to us? . . . It's always so good to talk to you."

Considerations for the social worker: Long-term grief and sorrow; motivational picture of little hope and considerable discomfort; strain in fulfilling roles of two generations at once; need for respite for care givers; search for spiritual understanding of unanswerable questions.

Tasks for the social worker: Long-term support and cooperative planning; providing concrete services.

Day-care center owner: "You want me to take care of a boy who's hard of hearing? You people keep referring more and more difficult children to me. Sometimes I don't know what to do with them. What do you expect of me?"

Considerations for the care provider and social worker: Probable prejudice and lack of understanding of disability; increased expectations of care that call for specialized skills; need for the care provider to be part of a team in difficult care situations.

Tasks for the social worker: Encourage cooperative decision making and planning with relatives and care providers; apply a variety of social work roles, including educator.

These examples illustrate some of the situations in which social work processes take form. Services such as foster family and group care, community care of people with mental handicaps, and other social work jobs involve what Morris (1977) calls caring for as well as caring about people. Social work of this sort is a central part of the field known as the personal social services, which bring into focus social work's central role in social care (Kahn & Kamerman, 1982; Harrison & Hoshino, 1984). Social care in the personal social services means helping to provide the normal and extraordinary socializing, developmental, and counseling services

and resources that people need to live in today's complex societies. Demographic trends in Western societies strongly suggest that the need for social care will grow at a very fast rate; already in many parts of the world social care and social work are virtually synonymous terms.

In almost every case social care involves integrated planning and counseling. When it is done well, social care planning is truly social: it involves cooperation between individuals and their communities (Harrison, 1989, 1991; Harrison, Smale, & Hearn, 1992; Johnson, 1992; Martinez-Brawley, 1990; Smale, Tuson, Cooper, Wardle, & Crosbie, 1988; Specht, 1990). The best terminology for this kind of social work has not yet been agreed upon. Sometimes it is referred to as *case management.* Case managers often provide very helpful integration of services and a supportive relationship (Johnson, 1985). However, the term is problematic because of its implication that people are relatively passive and inanimate, "cases" to be managed by someone else, rather than being active, feeling, self-determining human beings. Unfortunately, there are examples of people being treated without respect for their dignity when case managers did not have the professional values and skills to do this extraordinarily complex work (see Netting, 1992). Instead of *case management* a good alternative is the British term *social care planning* (Barclay, 1982). This term is not limited to the development of concrete plans; in practice it also encompasses the emotional, informational, and decision-making aspects of counseling as well as the many levels of planning that most social workers are engaged in. Regardless of the terminology, it is crucial to recognize the ethical and pragmatic importance of partnership in planning. Keith-Lucas's (1973) concept of *coplanning* is particularly valuable because cooperative planning is ethically right for social work and because it is far more productive than planning that is done to or for people.

Care refers to the physically and emotionally necessary and nourishing activity, the doing for and interactive doing with that all human beings need at various times in their lives. The most important human relationships involve doing for and protecting, and they therefore involve also caring in the sense of a deep concern and wish for happiness and fulfillment. Think of the infant's nearly total need to be cared for by others. While we all receive care, almost everyone is also a care provider at some time. We recognize parent-child relations, for example, to be extremely important, whether the child is young or a grown child is caring for an aging or sick parent. These bonds often become life's most fulfilling, most difficult, most meaningful, and most problematic as the life cycle of care evolves. When the way we live forces us to change social care patterns, when care breaks down, or when especially difficult needs for care emerge, we often call on specialists, institutions, neighbors and relatives, or special training for the "natural" carers. Social care planning involves helping people to make use of these resources and to come to grips with the difficulties their lives present, while improving the quality of individual and social arrangements for care. It encompasses very practical, concrete arrangements as well as basic issues of emotion and finding meaning in life.

Not limited to work with individuals and families, social care planning includes projects such as adult day care, Meals on Wheels, and mobility programs to help with collective social care problems. Changing societal patterns and attitudes affect social workers' efforts with others. Particularly important are the new opportunities available to women, many of whom have been limited to finding meaningful work in the care of their families and others. With new opportunities have come needs to find new ways to fulfill caring functions. Likewise many people now face greatly expanded demands simultaneously to fulfill roles as family care providers and workers in other occupations. Social work processes can help individuals, families, communities, and even larger systems adapt to and shape these social forces.

In addition to assisting with people's normal social care arrangements, social workers often deal with severe care problems such as the inability to fulfill the parental roles that children need or the difficulty of providing sound socialization and humane care when there are serious physical or mental disabilities. Especially in these difficult situations, social care work involves a therapeutic dimension. Highly skilled social workers integrate cooperative social care planning and counseling with treatment and socialization in this respected professional role.

PROBLEM-SOLVING CONCEPTS IN SOCIAL CARE

Good social care work uses the problem-solving model of practice. The concepts and theories that make up the model can be extremely valuable to social workers in difficult situations. The model offers direction as you focus on providing quality care and helping people cope with associated difficulties and feelings.

Researchers from social work and the social science disciplines help us understand how people try to solve and to cope with problems. Usually the researchers' observations are not surprising to practitioners, but that makes them no less useful. For example, cognitive psychologists have found that successful human problem solving usually involves two processes. First, people must achieve some understanding of the problem. Understanding is a personally meaningful idea of the current situation and of another preferred way for things to be — that is, of some goal. The situation may be one in which things are getting worse, and the goal may be simply to halt the trend. Defining and coming to grips with reality are matters of great importance and difficulty that involve assuming responsibility for dealing with the situation, at least in some small way. It is often difficult to see a predicament clearly and to envision something else without a good deal of skilled and patient help. Clearly, there is a role for skilled social workers in the area of helping people define complex social care problems and goals.

Second, researchers have found that humans solving problems invoke some kind of plan, deliberate or haphazard, to reduce the discrepancy between the way things are and the preferred state of affairs (Anderson, 1980; Hayes, 1978; Newell & Simon, 1972; Rubinstein, 1975). Often what appears to be irrational or self-defeating behavior is the result of trying to deal with problems without some plan or attempting to reduce anxiety without addressing problems directly. A plan is an organized way of working toward solutions. It involves a set of actions and responsibilities, usually with some sequential order. In social care planning it is important to recognize the joint nature of this planning. Almost all problems that social workers and their clients face are complex and subject to a variety of definitions and possible plans of action. Emotions may cloud planning, just as they complicate problem definition. "As problems become less well defined, greater importance is attached to activities such as interpreting the problem, generating solution possibilities that are minimally suggested by the information given, and evaluating solution attempts" (Bourne, Dominowski, Loftus, & Healy, 1986, p. 237). Social care planning is an application of these principles and others in a deliberate way to situations that require some kind of interpersonal care.

It is also important to understand the roles of creativity and expertise in problem solving. When a problem is dealt with in a new and effective way, we say that it is dealt with creatively (Hayes, 1978). When social workers help people achieve a better understanding of their situations and plans that fit the unique situation very well and that lead to desirable results, then they have been creative. We value creativity, especially in problematic situations in which people face serious difficulties. Hayes suggests that creativity is most likely to occur when there is a large knowledge base, when there is an atmosphere that encourages new and more effective ways to deal with problems, and when there is a deliberate search for analogies between the current situation and others. These conditions describe some of the most important aspects of problem solving that a social worker can bring to a social care task to supplement the client's problem-solving abilities. Usually this process is truly a partnership in creativity between client and social worker.

In the following example many aspects of the problem-solving model of social work are put into practice by a family and the social workers who work to help them. See which aspects you can identify, and consider what creative steps you might have taken as the social worker.

THE MILTON-CLAY FAMILY

James Milton was 71 years old when he decided that things could not go on this way any longer. It had been hard for him and his wife, Mildred, to see their 35-year old daughter, Sharon Clay, struggle so long to rear her children. When the Miltons retired two years ago, they made a major decision to leave the small community where they had lived for years and move to a larger town some 30 miles away. One of the main reasons for moving was to put some space between themselves and Sharon and the children, who still lived out in the country. The Miltons knew that they complicated matters and that Ms. Clay was having trouble being a responsible adult as long as they were around. She still seemed more an adolescent than an adult much of the time, and the Miltons found it hard not to step into the picture when their grandchildren were unsupervised, the home was a wreck, and Sharon came to borrow rent money.

The Miltons had no really close friends or family members other than Sharon and the grandchildren. Dr. Milton was a retired veterinarian. He was still active in a black professional men's club, and when the weather was good, Mrs. Milton still liked to make the trip to church in the old community. These were their only important voluntary contacts. It was always awkward and painful to them to get close to people because their daughter and grandchildren's situation inevitably became a point for discussion. They would have preferred not to stay by themselves so much, but that was the pattern they had found easiest.

Dr. Milton went to Northwood Family Services, a voluntary agency that he knew had a group home program. He spoke to the family care unit worker, Kathleen Arthur, in very precise words and diction, his chin held high. His professional manner helped him contain the pain revealed in his story. Ms. Arthur could not help feeling for him in his turmoil. Dr. Milton had tried to be supportive and helpful, but he was afraid that he had actually made matters worse. He said he thought that he and his wife might have worked themselves into the position of being part of the problem rather than part of the solution. He explained to Ms. Arthur that his daughter had been a single parent for ten years, since she and her husband divorced. For a while Hank Clay tried to pay support regularly, but it was not enough, and then he disappeared about four years ago after saying that he was going to work in Saudi Arabia. Now Sharon Clay was left with a 14-year-old son, Henry, and a 12-year-old daughter, Tina. The Miltons opposed the marriage, but Sharon was insistent, and later, when she got pregnant, they still thought of her as a reckless teenager, even though she was 21.

After Henry's birth Sharon spent about six weeks in the state psychiatric hospital suffering from postpartum depression. That was when the Miltons started taking on parental duties for their grandchildren, and there had been little relief in the past 14 years. They were glad to do their part, Dr. Milton stressed, but things had gotten out of hand, and they couldn't keep driving back and forth whenever the neighbors called to complain that the children were left without supervision for as much as two days at a time.

Ms. Arthur acknowledged that things seemed to have been getting worse for some time, that it was understandable that children were much more difficult to care for when they became willful adolescents, and that it seemed a great strain on the Miltons to feel they ought to be parents of two generations. She thought that eventually she might be able to help the family sort things out and to make a plan. She asked what Dr. Milton meant about things getting out of hand lately.

Dr. Milton said he was afraid that his daughter was again suffering from a serious bout of depression but that it was such a surprise because she had been doing so well for several months, until a few weeks ago. He said she had finally put her mind to practical matters and had "practically taken the town by storm." She had gotten a job and worked eight to ten hours a day at an auto parts shop with great enthusiasm and get-up-and-go. She had apparently enjoyed a relationship with a young man who sounded relatively stable and kind. She was at one night spot or another every night, almost going without sleep, the children said. Dr. Milton changed the subject, almost as if he had said more than he was comfortable with. He said that now Mrs. Milton was very uncomfortable, since arthritis

affected her neck and she had great trouble getting around more often than not. In the most measured of tones Dr. Milton said that he and his wife wondered whether or not their daughter had become a drug addict.

Ms. Arthur said that it was, of course, a possibility but that it was important not to jump to conclusions. They discussed the situation further, and Dr. Milton said that he had never seen or heard anything specific about drug use in his daughter's home. He just saw these variations in her mood and feared that it might be caused by drugs. He had asked the children if they saw drugs very much at school and the neighborhood, and he had the feeling that they were appalled at the idea of drug abuse and that they were not involved. He assumed that their mother must have used drugs discreetly or when she was on one of her extended trips away from the children and the Miltons. He just had not been able to find the words to confront the issue directly with Sharon.

"Is this not the sort of situation your homes are designed for?" asked Dr. Milton. Ms. Arthur said that sometimes a plan involving group care could be helpful, but unlike what often happened in veterinary medicine, it was hard to find the remedy in these situations based solely on the symptoms and a diagnosis. She said that usually it was very important to discuss these matters with everyone involved, not to jump to a plan before the various ways of looking at the situation had been covered. She said that for example there were fairly common psychiatric problems other than drug abuse that led to the symptoms the Miltons noted and that these might be amenable to treatment. Dr. Milton did not think that his daughter had had a mental health consultation. He said he was willing to listen to Ms. Arthur's advice.

Ms. Arthur wondered whether it might be useful for Ms. Clay to talk together with the Miltons and with her about the situation. Dr. Milton thought she would be willing but probably would not want to drive so far to a strange place without a better idea of whether it would be helpful or not, and she was so depressed now that he was afraid she would see the situation as hopeless. Just what did Henry and Tina think of the situation, Ms. Arthur wondered. She asked whether anyone knew that Dr. Milton was making this contact with the agency. He said that Henry and Tina did not know about this specifically but that they talked very openly about their mother's condition and that it might be good to talk with them as soon as possible because they often felt like they had to tell their mother what to do anyway. They usually got angry when action was taken without their knowing about it, and they often responded by disappearing for a day or two at a time. Even the Social Service Department workers had been looking for them once after the neighbors called to say that something was wrong.

Ms. Arthur said that there was a legal responsibility to inform the Social Service Department if there was reason to believe that children might have been neglected. She suggested that it might be worthwhile for Dr. Milton to talk to Mr. Bowen from that department. She worked fairly often with him in helping people arrange child care, and it might be good to let him know that she and her agency might be getting involved and to make sure that he knew about the children's situation. Dr. Milton was a bit surprised at this, but he agreed to make the call, saying that he was afraid everyone was going to know about the situation before they were through. He learned on the telephone that a social worker from the Social Services Department had been assigned to the family but that he had to move on to more pressing situations when Henry and Tina last came home. Mr. Bowen suggested that Ms. Arthur try to meet with Ms. Clay and get back in touch with him afterward to see whether there were roles for the two agencies. He said the only program they had that might be helpful was Home Options. This program sent workers into the home for intensive work when the placement of the child was imminent. However, the apparent mental health problems and the backlog of cases made it difficult to plan for this service at this point.

Ms. Arthur suggested that Dr. Milton discuss today's conference with his daughter. She asked whether there were any other people in the community who "naturally" helped Ms. Clay or even others to look after children. Dr. Milton said he had often discussed this with his wife and

daughter but that Sharon seemed completely isolated. Ms. Arthur said that she would be available to meet with them all or with Ms. Clay alone but that it was not possible to jump in and intervene in Ms. Clay's affairs; that would probably belittle her all the more and lead to more confusion and friction. Ms. Arthur could go to Ms. Clay's home or to the Miltons if Ms. Clay preferred not to come to the agency at this point. Ms. Arthur said that she could contact Ms. Clay if necessary. Since Dr. Milton had made the first move, though, it might be best to let him work things out, assuming he still thought it would be helpful to work with the agency after more thought and discussion.

They talked at some length about how it felt to be a potential client and how Northwood Family Services worked with its clients. They discussed how the agency tried to work with the whole family and the fact that sometimes group home care was part of a plan but that often they were able to work out problems involving child care without anyone having to move. When a placement was worked out as part of a plan, though, they worked very hard on both long-term solutions and the immediate needs and interests of the youngsters. They worked carefully with the Social Service Department, which now had a Permanency Planning Program to make sure that no youngsters got lost in the system without the prospect of a permanent stable home. Ms. Arthur reassured Dr. Milton that she was not putting down his idea that his grandchildren might benefit from a group home but said instead that experience and research showed that it was most useful to get everyone together working on the same problems if possible. He decided to consider what he had learned and agreed to call back no matter what they decided.

Three days later Dr. Milton telephoned Ms. Arthur to say that he had indeed discussed the situation with his wife and his daughter. Since Ms. Arthur had taken some of the fear out of mentioning drug abuse, he had found it possible even to discuss the subject with Ms. Clay. She said that she had had nothing to do with drugs, but she became rather defensive concerning whether she was drinking herself into an increasingly miserable situation. She did agree to talk with Ms. Arthur. The Miltons and Ms. Clay wondered whether Ms. Arthur could come to the Miltons' home for a conference during school hours, not worrying Henry and Tina about a move unless it seemed a real possibility. Ms. Arthur agreed, saying that she would have to involve them as soon as possible if their mother became actively involved in working on her difficulties with Ms. Arthur.

The meeting occurred as planned. Almost immediately Ms. Arthur noted that Ms. Clay was seriously depressed. She talked very little at first, and when she did, she expressed almost complete hopelessness. She did confirm that she had severe ups and downs and had even been tempted to drive off the side of the road at times. She had not consulted any mental health professionals at any time since her hospitalization years ago. She said that she had often wondered if the children would be better off somewhere else, but she really had not thought beyond the possibility of her ex-husband returning out of the blue to do his duty for a while.

Ms. Arthur saw that there was probably a serious cyclic mood disorder present and that the Miltons' decreasing ability and willingness to provide direct care for increasingly demanding adolescents was indeed straining the coping patterns of the family. She had long ago learned that it was important to share her observations in a deliberate, honest way so that they could really be used by the family, and she had not yet even met Henry and Tina. Ms. Arthur suggested that she could probably help develop a plan to support the family now that they were under such stress. She discussed all of the ways that the family had adopted over the years to cope with whatever happened to them and said she hoped she and the agency might be seen as a new source of support as they worked things out. She wondered whether the adults thought it would be helpful for Henry and Tina to talk with her, and, after some initial uncertainty it was agreed that it probably would. Ms. Clay said she would tell her children what was being discussed, and she agreed to telephone Ms. Arthur the next morning. Given the level of concern Ms. Arthur felt over Ms. Clay's depression, she was glad to gain this commitment.

Ms. Clay called as she agreed to. Henry and Tina had huffed and complained about talking to a social worker and possibly going to a group home, but Ms. Clay said they would probably have done that if you had offered them a trip to Disneyland. Her ironic statement sounded peculiar in contrast to her dismal mood. They arranged to talk at Ms. Clay's home about an hour before Tina and Henry were to come home from school and then to meet the children.

Dr. Milton telephoned Ms. Arthur to thank her for her time and to say that he and his wife approved of the way she had dealt with them. He said he and his wife had made the contact but now they wanted to pull out of the process insofar as they could. He said they would do whatever was helpful, but they knew that sometimes their involvement might hold back Ms. Arthur and their daughter. Ms. Arthur thought that would probably be a good way to proceed, letting Ms. Clay take as much responsibility for herself as she could. Dr. Milton did wonder whether Ms. Arthur thought Sharon should see a psychiatrist, and Ms. Arthur said that she was going to suggest a consultation, since she was not an expert on mental disorders and psychotherapy.

The contrast between the Milton home and the Clay home was dramatic. Images of rock stars were on most of the walls, and Henry's many collected salt and pepper shakers and beer cans were prominently displayed on the shelves in the living room. Tina's records and tapes were piled high on the floor near the stereo. Ms. Arthur found the physical environment much like that in one of the group homes. It appeared reasonably orderly, certainly clean, and definitely inspired by the world of popular music. Ms. Clay had a large pile of papers on the kitchen table when Ms. Arthur arrived. Ms. Clay said that she would have to do something about all these bills and tax returns, but she had spent all day just getting them together. She went on to say that she had been looking for her will when she found all this, and she did not know whether to give it all to her father to sort out. She hated to do that, but she probably would have to eventually. After asking direct, tactful questions about Ms. Clay's previous reference to driving off the road and now her comment about the will, Ms. Arthur learned that the first thing Ms. Clay wanted to do was go to the hospital for some rest. She said she was worn out and did not see how she could continue. Yes, she had wondered sometimes if everyone would be better off if she were dead. Ms. Arthur was concerned that Ms. Clay was working on a suicide plan. She shared some of her concern by reflecting how grim the situation seemed to look to Ms. Clay and offered, rather insistently, to take Ms. Clay to the mental health center that afternoon. Ms. Clay thought that it probably would neither hurt nor help but volunteered that the children had been trying to get her to talk to the pastor, whom she did not want to see.

Ms. Clay said she had mentioned going to live with the Miltons to Tina and Henry, but they all know that that plan would not work for long. Henry had been the first to mention a group home, not really very seriously. He did know someone who lived in a group home who was actually allowed to drive the agency car sometimes, and this was a matter of real interest to him. Ms. Clay wondered if the children could be cared for in a group home, at least for the time she was in the hospital. She had told her children that Ms. Arthur was coming, but she said they seemed not to pay much attention.

Ms. Clay went on to say that she did not really think she could handle the job of parent anymore, that the children were beyond her, and that she was not able to supervise them. They had stopped listening to her and acted as if she were not there much of the time. Now they were starting to get into trouble at school. Nothing serious, just constant hassles and the teacher wanting her to come in for a meeting about it. The guidance counselor had sent home a note asking her permission to test Tina to see if she had a learning disability; Ms. Clay had given her an OK but she had not learned the results nor, for that matter, whether they had done the test yet.

The school bus stopped out front and Henry burst in. Far from being uninterested, he was extremely curious about Ms. Arthur's visit. He asked a number of questions about where she came from and what she knew about him. He wondered if she knew that his sister had threatened to run

away before they "put her away" somewhere. Before he could finish, Tina arrived. Ms. Arthur introduced herself. Tina mumbled her name but when Ms. Arthur asked if she had any questions about what they were discussing, all she would say was, "I don't know."

For the benefit of the children as well as to make sure that Ms. Clay understood, Ms. Arthur decided to summarize the discussion to that point. She said that there were several people, including their grandparents, concerned about how the family was managing. The children's suggestion that their mother talk to the pastor showed that they knew outside help was needed. Ms. Clay had been trying very hard, but she was feeling overwhelmed, and something had to be done.

Tina pointed to her mother and said, "She's what's wrong. She sick, sick, sick!" Ms. Clay started to cry. She said Tina was right, and then she said that Tina was cruel and ungrateful.

Ms. Arthur explained that the situation wasn't anybody's fault, not Ms. Clay's and not the kids' and not the grandparents'. But they would all have to work together to figure out what to do next because Ms. Clay needed to go into the hospital for some tests and to get a rest and to see if some medicine would help her.

Ms. Clay told the children that they would have to go to the Miltons for the night. The children actually seemed quite happy about this idea and Henry asked if whether they could rent a video on the way. Ms. Arthur detected both relief and a sense of relationship with the children, who she thought might have begun to see her as someone who would listen and act in a sensible way.

Ms. Clay called her parents, who agreed to pick up the children. Ms. Arthur suggested that Ms. Clay phone the mental health center to see if someone could be prepared for their coming, but Ms. Clay asked Ms. Arthur to call for her. This done, Henry asked about what life in a group home might be like. Ms. Arthur reminded him that no solution had been selected from the several alternatives available; they hadn't even decided yet how long the children would need a place to stay. But just as their mother and grandfather had done, the children protested vigorously when Ms. Arthur brought up the possibility of talking with others who might care for them in their own neighborhood.

Ms. Arthur cautioned them that often a foster family was selected, especially for younger children, but that a final placement choice depended on current vacancies. She was at least happy that they were not actively opposing the idea of placement, as many parents and children did, unable to see the possible options. They would have to work toward some idea of what problems they were up against and whether a plan for living in a group home would be helpful. Ms. Arthur assured the children that if they did need to live somewhere other than with their grandparents, they would be encouraged to visit the place first and to meet the adults and some of the children who lived there.

Ms. Arthur agreed to contact the children the following morning at the Miltons. Her overwhelming impression was that they were eager to have someone to help them bring order to their unhappy and sometimes frightening situation. The ambivalence of the children toward their mother was clear, with both love and anger being apparent.

After Dr. Milton picked up the children, Ms. Arthur and Ms. Clay went to the mental health center. The social worker and psychiatrist there saw Ms. Clay as seriously depressed and suicidal, probably suffering from a kind of bipolar affective disorder that would respond well to medication. Hospitalization was recommended to stabilize her condition for now and to begin medical treatment. Ms. Arthur told Mr. Bowen of the situation and said that she would be in touch if the children were in need of more attention or if a plan of care was arrived at. Ms. Arthur drove Ms. Clay to the hospital.

Over the next week Ms. Arthur had almost daily contact with the hospital staff, Henry and Tina, the Miltons, and Sharon Clay. The driving back and forth to the rural schools was unpleasant for Dr. Milton, but he thought that an end might be in sight. He and his wife were happy that Sharon was getting started on a medicine that held promise for her, and Ms. Arthur seemed to be a steadying influence. Dr. Milton thought that while things were apparently going to be better for Sharon and

that it had been remarkably smooth working with Ms. Arthur, Sharon would not be able to care for the children right away, and he and his wife could not do it much longer. As he considered the whole situation, many old incidents and feelings went through his mind, and he choked up with the intense memories of pleasure and disappointment when Sharon was a young girl.

After a second week it appeared that Ms. Clay would soon be ready to leave the hospital. A conference was held in which she discussed her situation with the hospital staff, Ms. Arthur, and at Ms. Clay's request, Dr. Milton. She might need to come to the outpatient day program for a few weeks. Ms. Clay asked if the group home placement could be worked out while she got a fresh start. She wanted to stabilize her medicine and get herself organized to get a new job and to take care of the paperwork she had left behind. It was agreed that Ms. Arthur would work with Ms. Clay, Tina, and Henry to pursue this alternative.

At the first family conference it was decided that there was indeed a good possibility that the group home would be part of a realistic goal-directed plan. It was decided to arrange for the Clays to meet the counselors and see the facilities that had space available. Ms. Arthur would also have to have permission to talk over the school situation with the principal and teachers and to have them share the planning with the school near the group home. Ms. Clay agreed to go along, but she wanted Ms. Arthur to do the talking. Henry and Tina seemed reassured to learn that even though the boys and girls were in different homes, they were almost next door to one another. Ms. Arthur suggested that all three of the Clays should be prepared to discuss why they thought the homes might be useful when they visited. As usual in arranging such visits, Ms. Arthur thought of her own leaving home to go to college and how much easier it had been on her, since she knew the campus well, than it had been on some others who had never even seen where they were headed.

On the way to the group home Ms. Arthur told the Clays to think about questions they wanted to ask. She had already talked about how many staff and other children lived there and had given Henry and Tina a copy of the house rules. She reminded all of them that most families feel anxious and awkward during these visits and that the group home staff understood that.

The visit went quite smoothly. The children were asked what they were interested in, how they might adapt to some rules and routines, and what specific things they might want to achieve or change. Neither Henry nor Tina had thought about things in quite this way before, but it seemed like something of a challenge, especially when they considered some of the privileges that went with living in the home. Henry was taken on a tour of the boys' home with his mother, and Tina saw the girls' home with Ms. Arthur. Each child had an opportunity to ask questions of the other children, who reported that they got tired of some of the rules but that generally things were OK and sometimes even fun. The counselors told Tina she could bring an inexpensive tape player and told Henry he could put up some posters in his room. The Clays hadn't felt comfortable asking about the racial composition of the homes and were relieved to see that there were some blacks among both the children and staff.

Ms. Clay and the children were surprised and reassured to learn that ordinarily there were no restrictions on family visits and telephone calls; in fact, a specific section of family contact would be included in the written care plan.

Later Ms. Arthur said it seemed that the decision had been reached by Ms. Clay and Henry and Tina that group care would help them take charge of their lives. They agreed, and Ms. Arthur said it would be important to come to an agreement about their situation and put together a formal plan, a sort of contract to help everyone know what was happening and what they were trying to do. Ms. Arthur said that the agency and the families had found written plans to be particularly helpful. After a good deal of discussion and deciding which points to focus on and which to leave out, a formal plan was drawn up. Most of it was in the Clays' own words, the product of their own discussions and various views. It was hard to imagine just how much work had gone into such a simple document, but Henry and Tina learned that most of the other residents had been through the same process.

This plan was not a complete solution to the Clays' problems of getting along with one another and providing social care. It did become an important part in their successful work on many fronts with Ms. Arthur and a variety of others to make things work out reasonably well. A great deal of work had to be done with Henry over the separation from his mother, who he feared would not be safe without him nearby. Eventually he overcame both the realistic aspects of this fear and the fantasies involved, through a great deal of support and reassurance.

Ms. Clay benefited greatly from her lithium medication, and she participated in no additional psychotherapy. Once a month at the mental health center she saw a psychiatrist who monitored her medication. She met weekly with Ms. Arthur, usually about specific plans for child care and practical things she could do to take control of her life and to become more independent. She became acquainted with relatives of children in the agency's care during parent support group meetings. Together with some other mothers she worked out plans to make treats for the children for special occasions. She decided to return to school, where she earned a certificate as an auto service technician. She remained skeptical of close attachments to new people, but she did seem to enjoy some of her co-workers when she obtained a job at an auto dealership. After a year in care, Henry and Tina returned to live with her on a full-time basis. Each maintained contact with some of the adults and teenagers they had grown close to at Northwood. Henry went back for a short-term aftercare counseling group and Tina continued to see the Big Sister who had been assigned to her. One of the clearest changes was that now the entire family seemed able to make use of some of the community supports that were available. While Ms. Clay's relations with the Miltons improved, she never felt free from the prospect of their intervening and taking over her affairs. The Miltons discussed their own sense of failure and their hopes in several meetings with a student social worker from Northwood who visited their home.

Six months after Tina and Henry returned to her home, Ms. Clay and Ms. Arthur had their last interview concerning putting her house in order to deal with her children. They went back and reviewed the entire agency file, and especially the progress detailed in the plans. The last contact of any sort they had was about three months later, when Ms. Clay called to ask whether Ms. Arthur knew how to sign people up for Meals on Wheels and homemaker services, because her parents seemed to be having more and more trouble with their daily cooking and cleaning and they were too proud to call for themselves. Ms. Arthur referred her to a colleague at the Northwood Family Services Office on Aging.

FOR DISCUSSION

The case presents many elements of the problem-solving model. Consider the personal and professional qualities that are necessary to put the model into place as well as the specific characteristics of the model itself.

1. Which characteristics of the problem-solving model do you identify?

2. What might Ms. Arthur have done better in making use of the model?

3. How do you think that each of the Miltons and Clays would have described the family situation before and after they worked with Mrs. Arthur? Write a pair of before and after sentences for each person.

4. Do you think the Miltons should have been involved in the written plan? Why or why not?

5. A great deal of work was done with each of the Clays after the move to the group home. This is not documented in the material presented. What do you think Ms. Arthur's roles and activities might have been? How might the subsequent plans have looked?

6. Assume that the situation at the beginning of this case example was the same except that Dr. Milton had come to the agency requesting help in caring for his wife, who had become almost immobile, and that he saw his problem as stemming from the decrease in help that his daughter was able to provide. How do you think that the social care planning and counseling process might have evolved? What do you think would have happened had he approached a psychiatrist? A mental health center?

7. Do you think that Ms. Arthur should have pursued neighborhood, church, or other local resources more vigorously?

8. Consider a situation you have known of personally in which social care planning and counseling might have been appropriate. Were any principles from the problem-solving model used? If so, how would you evaluate them?

9. Which aspects of social care planning work do you think would be the most rewarding for you, and which the most challenging?

CONCLUSION

The value of creative problem solving in social care situations is widely recognized by professionals and the general public. Beginning with the problem-solving model of practice, social workers have an excellent opportunity to make other people's lives more fulfilling and to have a meaningful, satisfying professional career.

FIGURE 1
Northwood
Family
Services
Family Plan of
Care

This is a family plan of care developed by Northwood Family Services and Sharon, Henry, and Tina Clay, with the support of the Social Services Department Permanency Planning Program. *The problem* leading to this plan is that Ms. Clay is for now unable to provide the care she wants for her children. Henry and Tina agree that they were reacting to their mother's condition in a way that was unsatisfactory to them and to her. Ms. Clay is stabilizing her condition. The Clays do not want to be depending on the Miltons so much in the future.

The goals developed by the Clay family are as follows:

1. Pleasant, productive living arrangements for Henry and Tina for the next six months (when the plan may be extended) at the Northwood group homes
2. A return to the Clays living independently as a family
3. Ms. Clay stabilizing her condition and obtaining employment
4. Less friction and conflict between Henry, Tina, and Ms. Clay than in the recent past
5. Better academic attendance and grades for both Henry and Tina Clay

Responsibilities include the following:

1. *Northwood Family Services* agrees to provide ongoing group care services, planning, and counseling. The agency agrees to develop individualized plans with Henry and Tina to find interests they want to pursue and needs they may have and to find ways to achieve their goals while living in the homes.
2. Northwood agrees to work with community resources (for example, schools, employers, neighbors) as much as possible to support reunion of the Clay family.
3. *Sharon Clay* agrees to continue her medical treatment, to search for a job, and to work with Ms. Arthur on planning for the return of Henry and Tina to her care. Ms. Clay agrees to contact her children by telephone at least twice per week and to visit at least once a week, working out the details with the Northwood staff. Ms. Clay agrees to pay $56 per week to the agency toward the cost of care for her children. Ms. Clay agrees to work with the Department of Social Services as required by law in order to allow for their financial support of the children's care and in documenting her plans and progress.
4. *Henry Clay* agrees to work with his counselors on his goals and needs while living in the home, to continue to work with Ms. Arthur and Ms. Clay on the goal of returning home, and to attend school. Henry has identified his hot temper and outbursts aimed at his mother as the main things he would like to learn to change.
5. *Tina Clay* agrees to work with her counselors on her goals and needs while living in the home, to continue to work with Ms. Arthur and Ms. Clay on the goal of returning home, to attend school, and to take new tests to help the school staff figure out the best ways to teach her arithmetic and reading.
6. *The Department of Social Services* agrees to provide an outside review of this planning process at the end of six months and to provide financial and medical support for the children while they are living in the group homes.

A review of this plan can be asked for by anyone involved at any time. At the end of six months a conference will be held to review the plan jointly and to evaluate it and to plan ahead. Everyone involved will have a copy, and the plan will guide everyone's efforts to achieve their goals.

Signed:

K. Archer

R. Bowen

B. Bloom (Group Care Counselor)

R. Maple (Group Care Counselor)

S. Clay

T. Clay

H. Clay

Date:

| Reading 12-2 | *How Do We Really Empower Families? New Strategies for Social Work Practitioners* * |

Barbara Bryant Solomon

This decade of the 1980s may in some future time be referred to as the "Decade of the Family." The need for our nation to place more emphasis on the family has been identified as a priority on the national agenda by diverse groups.

At the same time that there is evidence of marital breakdown, an increasing number of children born to unmarried teenagers, and family violence, there is also a growing effort to identify the strengths that characterize the majority of American families and to bring other families together into supportive, self-help networks.

There has been a great concern about whether or not the nation needs family policy initiated at the federal level. Conservatives are strongly opposed to such a policy which they consider an invitation for government intervention in family matters. Liberals have called for increased governmental support for programs that, in their opinion, support family functioning such as comprehensive child care. Some of the most innovative programs emphasize families helping each other rather than government subsidy.

It is my view that government has a clear responsibility to provide opportunities for families to meet their basic survival needs, e.g., to ensure that there will be adequate employment and educational opportunities, and health care. When these are not available to all in society, government intervention to assist those who are disadvantaged is an absolute necessity.

An empowerment strategy recognizes that the relationship between the families who need assistance and the service delivery systems that provide the assistance is critical if dependency is to be avoided and independent social functioning is to be enhanced. Moreover, efforts to assist families

should focus on the relationship between the family and these systems at least as often as on the internal relationships among the various family members.

A CHANGING PERSPECTIVE ON PROFESSIONAL ASSISTANCE TO FAMILIES

The irony of all this for social work practitioners is, that despite a history of concern within the profession for families and programs aimed at strengthening family life, they are more frequently perceived as associated with the creation of problems for families than with the solutions to those problems. For example, George Gilder, whose book, *Wealth and Poverty,* provides the ideological base for many of the current administration's social welfare policies, has suggested that the most serious threat to independent, social functioning of individuals and families is the army of welfare workers who seek to provide them with welfare programs rather than economic opportunity.

Professional social workers are quick to point out that welfare workers are not, for the most part, trained social workers and the welfare system in the U.S. is a creation of politicians, not professional social workers. Families have complained, however, that in many instances, professionally trained social workers have attempted to utilize a psychodynamic medical model to help families deal more effectively with their problems. This model focuses on family relationships as the source of family dysfunction and gives relatively little attention to the direct and indirect influences of social institutions. Therefore, many families—particularly those with considerable strengths despite difficulties they may be encountering—are likely to reject that kind of "help" which blames the victims.

Fortunately, there are some more recent developments of practice theory within the social work profession which should provide a more acceptable basis for professional assistance to families. Em-

---

*From "How Do We Really Empower Families? New Strategies for Social Work Practitioners," by B. B. Solomon, *Family Resource Coalition Report,* 4(3), pp. 2–3. Copyright 1985. Reprinted by permission.

powerment in general, and family empowerment in particular, represents one such development.

One of the basic tenets of an empowerment approach to assisting families is that different families may need different solutions to the same problems. Bureaucracies tend to develop stereotyped ways of addressing problems. Thus, if a family has an unemployed father, eligibility for assistance is most often based on employment status, and the rights to service of all families with unemployed fathers are the same.

Yet, the actual circumstances of the family might cry out for differential responses. For example, one unemployed father may have a history of successful employment and recent depletion of resources. His family might need basic financial assistance, but the father's greatest need is for a decent job that utilizes his skills and makes it possible for him to support his family without public assistance.

On the other hand, another unemployed father with limited skills and an erratic job history may need to be assisted in improving his skills through a training program while his family will need intensive financial support to sustain them during the training period. Both families may be offered a minimum of financial assistance and a modicum of employment or educational counseling in a manner which is likely to prevent the former father from applying at all, and to reinforce the latter father's feelings of powerlessness and dependency. In this sense, differential assessment and intervention is sacrificed to the notion of "equity" which too often means equally inadequate responses.

How is it possible to develop an approach to helping families which does not foster dependency, recognizes and/or promotes the development of family strengths, and utilizes a mix of family and professional resources to develop the family's capacities for independent, social functioning? This empowerment approach is based on four principles detailed in my book, *Black Empowerment* (1976).

EMPOWERMENT APPROACH PROMOTES DEVELOPMENT OF FAMILY STRENGTHS

A social worker who is utilizing an empowerment model of practice will be able to help families who are experiencing problems recognize that (1) they may not be entirely or even primarily responsible for their problems but they will have to take responsibility for their solution; (2) helping professionals have expertise which can be put at the family's disposal to use in the problem-solving process; (3) in order to resolve the problem, it will require the collaboration of the family and the "helpers" as peers. The family brings unique knowledge and perspective on its problems, and the helper brings specialized knowledge usually gained from training and experience with many families with similar problems; (4) their relationship to many external social institutions may influence the etiology and maintenance of their problems, e.g., their relationships with the police department, public housing authority, hospital or neighborhood health clinic, schools, probation department, etc.; and (5) the "system" is not monolithic but made up of many sub-systems as indicated above; furthermore, effective ways of relating to these external systems can be learned in the same way that relationships with individuals can be learned.

In a three-year research and demonstration project conducted in Los Angeles's inner city, specific empowerment strategies were employed to help families become more effective in their encounters with such institutions as schools, police, welfare departments, health agencies, the courts, and other community agencies. The families had come for counseling at inner-city church sites; however, counseling was not focused solely on family relationships or relationships with the counselor, but rather on the social network in which the families interacted. A description of the strategies utilized by the counselors may be instructive.

ENABLING

This strategy assumes that a family may have considerable resources that are not always recognized as useful in obtaining from a system what the family needs. Enabling refers to actions on the part of the social worker to provide information or contacts which will enable the family to utilize its own resources more effectively.

A family attempting to obtain special support services for a child who was failing in school was frustrated until the counselor made the parents aware of the legal remedies available to them in this situation. Given this new knowledge, the parents were able to confront the school authorities and obtain the services.

A single parent who could read only at a fifth grade level often experienced crisis situations due to the difficulty she encountered in reading utility bills, rental agreements, etc. The parent was helped to see that her teenage daughter could be a useful resource in interpreting written materials until the time that she could master basic reading and writing skills herself. The teenager viewed this request for consultation as an acknowledgement of her own growing maturity.

LINKING

This strategy assumes that families can augment their own strengths by linking with others who can provide new perceptions and/or opportunities. Families may link with others to provide a collective power which can be more successful in confronting a system than that available to any individual family.

Linking, then, refers to actions taken by the social worker to connect families to other families, groups, or networks. In the case of the single, illiterate parent above, she was also helped to join a support group of single parents, many of whom were enrolled in adult education classes. It was their influence which helped her to decide to increase her reading skills.

CATALYZING

This strategy assumes that families have resources, but additional resources may be needed before their own can be fully utilized. For example, if a parent has job skills, he or she will need an actual job before those skills can be used. Catalyzing refers to those actions taken by the social worker to obtain resources which are prerequisite to the family fully utilizing their existing resources.

One family had a relative who lived in another city but was willing to move in with the family and provide child care which the family could not otherwise afford. However, the family's apartment was too small to accommodate another adult and they had been unsuccessful in finding appropriate

yet affordable housing. By finding a room for the relative in the same neighborhood, the social worker was able to provide a resource that made it possible for the family to use their own extended family more effectively to meet their needs.

PRIMING

This strategy assumes that many of the systems with which families have negative encounters can respond more positively, but only under conditions which would not be perceived as a "cost" to the system, e.g., any suggestion that the system was not adhering to its own policies and procedures or that the system was "caving in" to some external pressure.

A family was experiencing a great deal of conflict. Their junior high school–age son had become angry and even assaultive with his siblings and parents when he was feeling particularly stressed. The social worker pointed out to the parents that although he had not exhibited the behavior at school, he might do so at any time and the school would very likely suspend him. The mother was able, therefore, to discuss her son's reactions to the stress situation at home with the school counselor and homeroom teacher, indicating that in the case of any unacceptable behavior she could be called to school to handle it. Thus, the social worker assisted the parent in priming the system so that it would respond differently and more positively than it would have otherwise.

CONCLUSION

An empowerment approach to families who are encountering problems in living is based essentially on assumptions of family strengths. At the same time, it does not equate a need for assistance as a sign of weakness or dependency. Perhaps most importantly, the assistance provided is more often directed toward increasing the family's capacity to use its own resources more effectively, particularly in encounters with external social institutions. The importance of this latter fact is due to the major role played by these institutions in the development of excessive stress on individuals and on whole families which may contribute to an array of family problems.

The next page to be written in the social history of the American people will probably document the emphasis placed on the family in the decades of the 80s. There is considerable promise that it will also recount a transformation of a significant number of families from powerless, unstable collectivities to strong, well-functioning centers of identity for its members. If so, it will be because there has been a fine balance achieved between the responsibility accepted and effectively implemented by government and the responsibility taken by family members for each other. In addition, those professionals sanctioned by society to provide assistance to families will have understood the difference between assisting problem families and empowering families to solve their problems.

Mediation Around the Medicine Wheel*
Marg Huber

Many Aboriginal people seek to learn mediation skills of the dominant culture as one source of information on suitable dispute resolution processes for their communities. The cooperative aspect of mediation is congruent with values of traditional cultures and has been practiced by Aboriginal peoples in many forms for centuries.

However, like adjudication, mediation as it is widely practiced in the dominant culture is oriented to individuals and the assertion of individual needs rather than to the individual-in-community. Moreover, mediation involves culturally bound assumptions about what is of procedural interest to the parties—that is, roles and characteristics of the intervenor and goals of the process. Aboriginal participants in generic mediation training must translate dominant culture mediation processes into their own vastly differing contexts. This encumbers and substantially impedes their learning and produces questionable benefits to their communities.

For management of Aboriginal organizations involved in education, administration of justice, employment training, or healing—there are over sixty such organizations in the Vancouver, Canada, area—the situation is exacerbated. The Aboriginal population in urban locations is comprised of those from diverse Aboriginal cultures, many of whom continue to identify themselves in terms of their community and the wide family network of which they are a part. Individuals vary in their degree of assimilation to the dominant culture and their aboriginal status. With such a diverse population, how does one respond in a culturally appropriate way to conflict?

According to Census Canada Statistics 1986, 4.4 percent of the population of British Columbia (B.C.) consists of Aboriginal people, approximately 20 percent of whom live in urban settings. It is a widely held view among Aboriginal service providers that many of these Aboriginal people are in personal and cultural identity crisis. Programs or services that kindle in individuals the desire to reconnect with their culture are the only ones that effectively strengthen identity and facilitate personal growth and healing.

PROCESS DESIGN

The development of an Aboriginal mediation model began as a process of inquiry: What would it take to make the process of mediation culturally relevant for Aboriginal people living in urban settings? The question arose as a result of mediation training for Native Courtworkers in B.C. in 1989 that utilized a dominant-culture mediation process. Feedback had indicated that the process was culturally inappropriate. The trainer of these participants sought out the opinions of an Aboriginal

*I acknowledge the contributors to the Aboriginal Mediation Process: M. Cantryn-White, A. Carroll, D. Kelly, G. Nicolson, L. Redwood, and C. White. Without the generosity of spirit on the part of the contributors to this project, the design process and subsequent model would not have been possible.
Source: *Mediation Quarterly*, vol. 10, no. 4, Summer 1993. © Jossey-Bass Publishers.

community leader to whom she was referred. Through his initiative and interest, a working group was formed to examine questions relating to mediation for Aboriginal people in urban settings. The group was comprised of six urban community leaders in management positions with four different organizations in Vancouver. They were members of five different Aboriginal nations within B.C. Those who chose to be involved in this informal process of exploration and subsequent model development did so because of their commitment to assisting their people in the urban community to find more respectful and effective means for resolving differences. The facilitator, a mediator in private practice, was a middle-class woman of English/Scottish descent whose family had lived in Canada for approximately 100 years.

All contributors and the facilitator volunteered their time. The exploration project consisted of weekly meetings over a three-month period. None of the contributors had prior experience using dominant-culture models of dispute resolution. They began with basic trust in one another and respect for each other's competencies.

The group examined motivations for involvement and objectives for the project. These focused on the creation of a suitable and helpful mediation process for urban Aboriginal individuals, and training in such a process, so that culturally appropriate mediation services could be provided. No research on Aboriginal mediation practices existed other than oral knowledge to guide our project.

The working group surfaced interest with respect to process through a series of questions to elicit beliefs and values common among Aboriginal peoples as they related to communication, conflict, the resolution of disputes, and the practice of mediation. In this way, the resulting model was grounded in culture, rather than modified from a dominant-culture process to accommodate for culture.

They recognized that value generalizations can often be meaningless and are not necessarily held by any specific individual. However, an urban community includes a mix of Aboriginal cultures. To accommodate this mix, they identified widely held Aboriginal values, in the belief that by adapting a culturally based model mediators would achieve greater relevance for the individuals in question.

Identified values important in dealing with conflict included cooperation, sharing, equality among people, harmony, consensus decision making, noninterference in individual matters, privacy, patience, and modesty. Values inherent in communications included moderation in speech, careful listening, physical communication (nonverbal), and quietness. Other values important in the Aboriginal way of life included family and community, cultural heritage, self-determination, respect for elders, a holistic approach to life, relativity of time, and spiritual connectedness.

From these values, the following procedural needs flowed: provisions for personal safety, honesty, and respect and dignity of the person; opportunity for personal growth and healing; enhancement of belongingness and personal identity; holistic and spiritual orientation; restoration of harmonious relationships for parties and their respective families and communities; and outcomes congruent with the values of those communities. The contributors unequivocally agreed that if a mediation process were to be successful in helping people make and manage change, it would need to be grounded in Aboriginal spirituality. The spiritual focus would enable participants to heal through understanding and make decisions based on dignity and respect.

The group decided that the intervenor needed to be someone both parties could trust, who is respected in the urban Aboriginal community (possibly a community leader, a professional person, or someone in a management position), familiar with community resources, competent with respect to process, impartial in the dispute in question, and nonjudgmental in attitude.

Potential roles of the intervenor included guiding the parties through the process, assisting them in their communication with one another, extracting the benefits to the parties from the discussion, encouraging the parties to take responsibility for their feelings, providing information on options, and urging them to find a realistic way of solving their own problems.

THE FOUR DIRECTIONS OF THE MEDIATION PROCESS
The resulting model is based on the above criteria.
It is conceptualized using the Four Directions of the
Medicine Wheel, an ancient symbol used to explain
many diverse and complex concepts. While this
symbol originates with Plains Nations, the cosmol-
ogy of the Four Directions is well known in
Aboriginal communities in general, and the Medicine Wheel is used for healing and self-knowledge
in many Aboriginal organizations in Vancouver. It
facilitates understanding of many aspects of life
that can be talked about in sets of four: the four
grandfathers, the four winds, the four stages of life,
the four seasons, and the four parts of the whole
person—the spiritual, emotional, physical, and
intellectual. These sets of four are located at the
four directions of the Wheel.

It is perplexing to describe in written form the
sacred symbol of the Medicine Wheel. How does
one write about the Medicine Wheel when it is part
of an oral tradition? Which is the most accurate
interpretation or description to use for this ancient
symbol? How can one explain the many meanings
and teachings of the Medicine Wheel in a limited
way, since for many people, they consume a lifetime
of study and practice? The Medicine Wheel is more
than just a tool. For many Aboriginal people, it
involves a transmission of ancient knowledge and
tradition from one generation to another.

The Sacred Tree, a Four Worlds Development
project, is frequently the reference of choice for
urban Aboriginal organizations in Vancouver that
use the Medicine Wheel. This book represents the
collaborative work of elders, cultural leaders, and
professionals from various communities across
North America, and as such it has broad applicability.

The authors of *The Sacred Tree* (1988, p. 37)
explain how the Wheel functions: "The medicine
wheel can be used as a model of what human beings
could become if they decided and acted to develop
their full potential. Each person who looks deeply
into the medicine wheel will see things in a slightly
different way.... Yet everyone who looks deeply
will see the tree of their unique lives with its roots
buried deep in the soil of universal truths. Many
tribes and peoples have used the medicine wheel to
look at themselves, and there are many different
ways of explaining those universal truths that
human beings share."

To conceptualize the mediation process using
the Wheel, the working group mapped the four
stages of the process at the four direction points.
In this way, the Wheel served as a visual and
spiritual map to orient clients to the process. Both
person and process are then in alignment and
harmony.

The mediation process follows the sacred Four
Directions of the Medicine Wheel, beginning in the
East and moving around the circle to the South, the
West, and the North.

The East: Setting the Climate
The place of the East—the spiritual—is associated
with opening and orientation. The gifts of the East
include concentration on the here and now, faith,
truthfulness, warmth of spirit, the ability to see
clearly through complex situations, uncritical acceptance of others, and clear speech.

It is here that the mediators *touch the spirit*
through opening prayer and possibly smudging, a
process of washing and cleansing the body, mind,
and spirit with the smoke of sweetgrass, sage, cedar,
or other spiritual plants. This establishes a peaceful
presence that is conducive to heartfelt, honest
discussion. Spiritual rituals decrease anxiety, dif-
fuse strong emotions, and clear minds. Smudging
serves further to offer protection and clear negativity. The effect on the parties of this spiritual
beginning is carried throughout the mediation.
Grounding the process in the spiritual makes
emotional expression safer and eases the discussion
of difficult issues.

Other tasks of this stage include conducting an
opening circle to bring everyone to the present,
establishing the purpose of the mediation, and
describing roles and process. The mediators attempt to set people at ease and to spiritually
connect as they speak with the parties. They may
ask the parties where they currently see themselves
on the Wheel.

Parties are inclined to expect the mediators to
explain the process from a personal perspective.
Examples of the mediators' own personal conflict

experiences normalize conflict and humanize the mediators. In the eyes of the parties, mediators then are more likely to understand the personal difficulty associated not only with the conflict itself but also with the process. Self-disclosure assists in building rapport and establishing trust.

The South: Telling the Story

The South is the place of the heart, the emotional aspect of one's being; it is associated with the ability to express feelings openly without hurting others, sensitivity to feelings of others, loyalty, and flexibility.

Emotional expression is encouraged. Parties are invited to speak openly of their perspective; listeners are encouraged to really understand what the other is saying, feeling, and experiencing. Until feelings are understood and released, they continue to block capabilities for genuine love and warmth, clear thinking, and effectiveness. Each party speaks fully without interruption. Mediators may ask questions to clarify what is underlying the situation, summarize what they have heard, and assist the parties in seeing their commonality.

The West: Discovering What Is Important

The expression of the South is naturally followed by reflection and introspection—gifts of the West, which is the home of the physical. Here one listens to one's inner voice, going to the center of one's being to experience the connection between the human spirit and the Creator. It is the place of testing. The nearer one draws toward a goal, the more difficult the journey becomes. The capacity to stick to a hard and painful challenge is an important lesson of the West. The West is also a place of honesty, humility, and sacrifice, where one learns to accept both spiritual and physical aspects of oneself, to give and take, to understand oneself in terms of others, and to respect the vision of elders. It is the place to learn how to correctly use power: power to heal, power to protect, power to see and know. Here the traveler must learn to manage power in harmony with the great universal teachings.

The tasks of the mediators are to help the parties focus inward, to understand not only their own values and needs with respect to the situation but those of their family and community, and to extend understanding and compassion to the other party.

The North: Creating Solutions

The North—intellect—is the place of wisdom and farsightedness, and its gifts include the capacity to solve problems, think and imagine, synthesize, discriminate, and organize. Here one learns the lessons of balance and justice and completes what one has begun. The gift of detachment bestows on the traveler the ability to see the past, the present, and the future as one.

Detachment also means standing apart from strong feelings and beliefs to see them in a different light. This enables one to appreciate the experience of others and find resolution to differences.

When the parties reach this stage of their journey, the mediators symbolically take them to the center of the Wheel for a holistic perspective on the situation. As they generate ideas for resolution in the North, mediators can provide information on options and encourage consultation with elders. The parties select the best way of resolving the conflict—a solution congruent with their respective communities' values. Family or community representatives may participate in this part of the process. Parties may choose to record and sign their agreement. They are then returned to the center of the Wheel, the place of volition from where they can move their decisions forward into action. A closing circle and prayer complete the process.

FEATURES OF THE PROCESS

The Medicine Wheel mediation model does not include delineation of issues and agenda formation early in the process. Such concepts are sequential and less natural for many Aboriginal people. The Medicine Wheel provides a framework that is flexible and yet holistic. Issues are extracted from the storytelling and become clarified in the process of moving around the Wheel. If the parties are having difficulty understanding each other, the mediators can assess where on the Wheel they are speaking from and why the other party is having trouble understanding: the other may be speaking from a different place on the Wheel. The emphasis throughout is on how one feels rather than on how one thinks—a more natural focus for many Aboriginal people. By interpreting parties' behavior in terms of the places on the Wheel, the mediators are in a stronger position to assess where the mediation may be blocked and determine the appropriate response, either in session or by referral outside of mediation.

A regard for the whole is reinforced by the treatment of past, present, and future as one, with a natural flow emerging from expression, through reflection, to clarification and resolution. Parties need to visit all the places on the Wheel to have truly understood each other and for the process to feel complete. They can then more readily see their experience in mediation as analogous to their ongoing life experiences: life is a process of revisiting all the places on the Wheel.

Premediation Assessment

A premediation assessment is an integral part of the mediation process. During a premediation phase, separate meetings with the parties take place and provide an opportunity for the mediators to determine the emotional state of the parties and the suitability of the case for mediation. This could include assessment for spiritual or emotional blocks which may impair participation in the process, abusive relationships, drug and/or alcohol problems, stress, and power imbalances, as well as the level of family or community support available to the individual. At this time, mediators familiarize the parties with the process in general and discuss how the model may be adapted to be relevant to their own particular situation.

Through such a discussion, safety measures are built into the process, and referral to appropriate community resources (for example, spiritual counselor, grief counselor, drug and/or alcohol treatment) precedes or accompanies the mediation.

The presession meeting is an opportunity to begin to develop trust in the process and the service providers and encourage openness in a safe environment without the other party. Information is provided and an evaluation conducted through informal conversation and specific questioning.

Procedural Suggestions

Comediation is preferred to balance for gender, specific Aboriginal culture, or other factors and to allow the responsibility for the process to rest on more than one individual.

The safety and comfort of the parties is enhanced if the sessions take place in an Aboriginal organization facility. A native education center or community hall might serve as such a location. The tone should be informal and as relaxed as possible. One might wish to design a *talking room* as a safe place for mediation to occur. Possibly, an Aboriginal community mediation center could be created. Mediators may consider holding the discussion outside in a natural setting.

Mediators should expect the length of the session to extend up to four hours. It may take a long time in session before the parties are individually ready to address the situation in question; they may need to talk at some length on unrelated matters to develop comfort with the process. The spiritual opening in itself may take up to one hour. Time is geared to the activity at hand. The parties must be allowed to tell their stories, however long that may take. At times, when emotions are high, it may be necessary to go around the circle to draw in everyone's experience of what is happening.

The mediation process is easier to understand and follow when it is experienced in a meaningful context. Living examples and associations with natural images are culturally relevant expressions by which one enhances understanding. Sometimes a whole set of ideas and feelings can be conveyed by the use of one symbol. Parties can be encouraged to develop their own examples and choice of symbols to associate with a concept. Metaphors are preferred to definitions. Stories clarify complex ideas and can convey messages in less direct or confrontational ways. Diagrams assist in making concepts visual. Aboriginal cultures are rich in imagery which can be incorporated into the mediation process.

Additional Participants in the Mediation

Elders can make valuable contributions to a mediation, both in terms of their wisdom and their presence. There are several potential ways to include them in the process. One or more elders present as silent process observers add a spiritual quality to the discussions; their very presence makes communications more respectful. An elder could be called on as a resource, especially in emotional matters (in this case, the elder needs to be told ahead of time what the expectations are of him or her and be familiarized with the mediation process). The elder may appoint a spokesperson to speak on financial matters. It is important that the right elders be included. Elders who are aware of what is happening in the Aboriginal community or those who use the talking stick are most helpful. The choice of elder may also depend on the issue being discussed.

One of the two mediators could be an elder, either acting as a silent mediator or making observations while the other mediator manages the process more actively.

Elders need to be provided with time to reflect. They are disinclined to respond with an answer right away; it is rare for them to say anything unless asked. They are respectful of the process and will not interfere but will allow it to unfold. Their comments may be included in the opening stage if they are seated as part of a circle which includes all the people in the room. At this time, everyone has an opportunity to talk and express the reason for their presence. The elder is the appropriate person to conduct an opening prayer, when one is used.

In addition to elders, one or more family members in attendance at the mediation session may make a party feel more protected in a process that could otherwise seem threatening and isolating. Family members may be silent process observers and part of the circle comprised of those in attendance. Depending on the nature of the dispute, their active involvement may be necessary; the needs and values of the family may well have to be factored into the discussion. Decisions may require their approval.

The Circle

The mediation session is held with everyone present seated in a circle. Face-to-face discussion, especially in front of strangers, of private or sensitive matters is often difficult for parties; a circular seating arrangement eases their discomfort.

The Mediation Circle is a symbol of wholeness, unity, oneness. All are equal around the circle. Everyone can see everyone else. Everyone has a voice. There is no beginning and no end. Mediators are separated across the circle for greater balance. The circle symbolizes that all present are necessary for successful resolution: if anyone leaves the circle, it is no longer complete and they are missed.

The circle is sacred; if one is using the circle, one must be prepared to honor its rules. While they may vary somewhat among Aboriginal cultures, the rules provide a powerful way of managing the process. The *problem* is symbolically located in the center of the circle for all to work on. When talking around the circle, people speak one at a time and in turn. One may choose not to speak, in which case one's space is filled with silence. People can take the time they need to think and speak without fear of interruptions. The mediation process is not time bound.

Protection from interruptions can be reinforced if a rock, feather, or talking stick is used to designate the speaker. This person holds the item, and no one else speaks until the item is relinquished to the next in turn. Other speakers must await their turn in the circle before addressing the point in question. In the meantime, they are provided with time to reflect and also consider subsequent comments from other participants. In then addressing what has been said, they may not pass judgment but only clarify or express their own point of view. Thus, talking around the circle is a primary way of maintaining respectful discussion and including all who are present.

Not all dialogue will necessarily transpire around the circle. However, at moments when emotions are high, this method of sequencing speakers provides a way of diffusing strong feelings and including additional perspectives. The circle contains the discussion and provides a sense of boundary. If a person has developed patterns of shutting down, blocking, or fading out on sensitive topics as a way of protection or self-preservation, procedural safety is of primary interest.

An opening circle brings everyone to the

present; a closing circle provides a sense of completion.

Process Management

The presence of elders, the spiritual tone established at the beginning of the session, the rules and practices of the circle, and the use of the Medicine Wheel as a framework for the mediation process itself all help the mediators to manage the process and maintain a productive working climate. Understanding is improved, negativity and defensiveness are reduced, and communications are respectful. These components of process decrease the need for mediators to use communication skills to shape the discussion and allow them to play a less directive role.

INTERCULTURAL APPLICATIONS OF THE MODEL

Although the model was conceptualized for conflict between and among Aboriginal people in urban settings, members of the dominant culture have expressed considerable interest in using this model in intercultural disputes. Many mediators in urban settings across Canada and the United States comment on the need for processes to address the individual in a more holistic way, and they see in this model the potential for doing so. Some community members currently engaged in multiparty processes believe that a culturally relevant model can more fully engage, include, and empower Aboriginal parties at the table. While all these views are driven by a sincere and compelling desire to move forward in addressing the deep conflicts of the times, potential negative effects could result from intercultural use of a model based in aboriginal spirituality. The use of the Aboriginal mediation model at the initiative of the non-Aboriginal party in an intercultural context could constitute a disrespectful appropriation of cultural heritage.

Granted, for centuries, First Nation peoples have borrowed each other's traditions and rituals for the betterment of their community. But this practice is viewed differently from the non-Aboriginal use of the same tradition.

All urban Aboriginal people must consider intercultural contexts when they consider dispute resolution processes. Urban life inevitably contains daily interfaces with non-Aboriginal people of many different cultures. Many of aboriginal descent have found that their survival depends on their ability to be bicultural. However, if an Aboriginal mediation process were to be considered for intercultural purposes, its use would need to be determined by and acceptable to the Aboriginal party. Those involved in the process would be required to have great respect for the spirituality associated with it and be willing and able to use it as a spiritual process.

MODIFICATION OF THE PROCESS

Those from Aboriginal cultures who wish to maintain the spiritual aspect of the Aboriginal mediation process but whose particular culture does not use the Medicine Wheel concepts may eliminate references to the Wheel and refer only to the Four Directions, conceptualizing the process as the Mediation Circle. The symbolism of both the Four Directions and the Circle is more universal and less associated with particular Aboriginal nations. Used as healing circles and respectful consensus-based approaches, these concepts are also viewed as sacred to Aboriginal people. If the Mediation Circle model were to be used for intercultural purposes, one would need to show respect for the rules of the circle, which determine its appropriate use.

CONCLUSION

This model represents the first step in the development of an Aboriginal mediation process that is culturally grounded and sufficiently flexible to allow for cultural differences between individuals in the urban aboriginal community. It can be tailored to address the needs of the presenting situation, while continuing to provide a framework that enables individuals to participate in the procedure with respect, dignity, and integrity. Whether it will prove useful in intercultural disputes or will contribute to dominant-culture processes will be determined by ongoing exploration.

REFERENCE

The Sacred Tree. (2nd ed.) Lethbridge, Alberta, Canada: Four Worlds Development Project, University of Lethbridge, 1988.

For Further Reading

Barber, J. G. (1986). The promise and the pitfalls of learned helplessness theory for social work practice. *British Journal of Social Work, 16,* 557–570.

Chandler, S. (1985). Mediation: Conjoint problem solving. *Social Work, 30,* 346–349.

Epstein, L. (1981). Advocates on advocacy: An exploratory study. *Social Work Research and Abstracts, 17*(2), 5–12.

Friedman, R., Duchnowski, A., & Henderson, E. (1989). *Advocacy on behalf of children with serious emotional problems.* Springfield, IL: Charles C. Thomas.

Friedman, S., & Taylor-Fanger, M. (1991). *Expanding therapeutic possibilities: Getting results in brief psychotherapy.* New York, Lexington Books.

Glassman, U., & Kates, L. (1986). Techniques of social group work: A framework for practice. *Social Work with Groups, 9*(I), 9–38.

McIntyre, E. L. G. (1986). Social networks: Potential for practice. *Social Work, 31,* 42–46.

McKnight, J. (1992). Redefining Community. *Social Policy 23* (Fall/Winter), 56–62.

Moore, C. W. (1986). *The mediation process.* San Francisco: Jossey-Bass.

National Institute (England) for Social Work. (1982). *Social workers: Their role and tasks.* London: Bedford Square Press.

O'Connell, M. (1988). *The gift of hospitality: Opening the doors of community life to people with disabilities.* Evaston, IL: Center for Urban Affairs and Policy Research, Northwestern University.

Parsons, R. J. (1991). The mediator role in social work practice. *Social Work, 36*(6), 483–487.

Proctor, E., & Rosen, A. (1983). A problem formulation and its relation to treatment planning. *Social Work Research and Abstracts, 19*(3), 22–28.

Rose, S. M., & Black, B. L. (1985). *Advocacy and empowerment: Mental health care in the community.* Boston: Routledge & Kegan Paul.

Schilling, R. F. 11. (1987). Limitations of social support. *Social Service Review, 61*(I), 19–31.

Solomon, B. (1976). *Black empowerment: Social work in oppressed communities.* New York: Columbia University Press.

Specht, H. (1986). Social support, social networks, social exchange, and social work practice. *Social Service Review, 60*(2), 218–240.

Umbrecht, M. (1994). *Mediation and social work.* Newbury Park, CA: Sage.

Whittaker, J., & Garbarino, J. (Eds.). (1983). *Social support networks: Informal helping in the human services.* New York: Aldine.

Chapter 13

Interventive Methods: Implementation of Roles

In the last chapter we discussed interventive roles, meaning the clusters of behaviors used by the worker in helping to accomplish the desired changes in client or situation. This chapter continues that discussion with an examination of some techniques and methods you may use in carrying out selected interventive roles. We will attempt to do this by listing and describing some of the methods commonly found in each role and by examining some of the worker-client activity detailed in the case examples found in the Appendix and in some of the case examples in the other readings.

The planning for change, the selection of roles and methods for carrying out the plan, and the specific way you use self in the activities of role and method are very complex. Even the most accurate and careful assessment and the most careful plan can be rendered useless by the manner in which you use self and other resources in helping to carry out the plan. There are four significant factors that impact on the selection and carrying out of roles. One factor, of course, is the client. We hope that by this time you are committed to the importance of understanding client wants and goals. Thus the client and the situational context of the client are critical factors to consider. Excellent examples of careful consideration of the situational context in planning are found in the "Pain Clinic Evaluation" (Appendix, A-3) and in the discussion of the Milton-Clay family in Reading 12-1. In addition to the factors involving the client, you need a breadth of understanding of your own context. You need to know the resources that agency and community may offer for helping the client, including your own resources of time and skill. Offering the client guidance in selecting among alternative sources of assistance is a complex business that involves what you know about resources available in the community; what you know about the agencies that control access to these resources; how comfortable you may feel in working with the professionals in these agencies; how you believe the agencies may treat the client; what assistance the client will need, given his or her social functioning, to approach the agency and secure the help sought; and what time, skill, and knowledge you will need to ensure that the service of others is usable for this particular client. The other two factors involve content of your activity with the client and with other resources (what you do) and the climate that you seek to establish for the work (the how).

As we discuss planning and use of roles and methods, it all sounds so rational and so well organized that we feel we must point out that your unspoken values and beliefs and your confidence in being able to use certain resources as well as the values, beliefs, fears, anxieties, and preferences of the client will influence these processes. Study Reading 12-1 again. It is quite obvious that Harrison and Johnson believe the problem-solving process is an appropriate model for social care planning. Can you determine their beliefs about the nature of people and how they can best handle difficulties? What beliefs and values underlie the careful exploration of the request for placement of the children?

Our discussion of methods to be used in the various roles and the way they may be used obviously rests on our values and beliefs about the nature of human beings, about appropriate actions in building a working relationship, and about what is involved in change. Having read the preceding chapters in this book, you may already feel that you know a great deal about our view of people and the nature and genesis of their troubles. Nevertheless, to be clear, we will develop a brief summary of selected values and beliefs that influence our view of the helping process so that you can put this discussion in context.

Struggle for Competence and Control Over Own Life

We believe in the inherent struggle of human beings toward competence and control of their own life. In fact, we feel that this is the central issue for all persons. Much of the basic anxiety and pain of people is caused by their fear of failure in this struggle, their perception of failure and the ensuing damage to self-esteem, their anger at discovering that the life situation in which they find themselves consistently denies them the resources and the power to shape their lives, their ambivalence over whether this failure is their personal failure or the problem of the environment, and their sense of hopelessness and despair when they conclude that their actions have no part in determining what happens to them. The belief in the importance of client participation in the work of problem solving, in the importance of understanding client goals, and in the concept of client-worker partnership stems from our belief in the importance of the client's struggle for competence. This belief demands that the worker have a deep respect for all people and for their struggle to control their destiny in ways congruent with what they feel is best for them.

We believe in the importance of social context in shaping people's lives. Social context rests on the assumption that people's ability to solve their problems in living is to a significant extent based on their ability to secure from their environment the resources they need or the power to change the negative impact of certain environmental conditions. This is what we mean by a match between the coping abilities of people and their environment. This seems such a simple statement. Most social workers would agree with it, but in much of our practice there is a tendency to look within the client for the cause of the problem and to concentrate on client pathology rather than to consider the efforts that could be directed to changing the environment, increasing the client's capacity to deal with environmental blocks, and reducing the negative response to the client by important others in his or her situation.

An important concept in planning action toward problem solution is a consideration of the concept of motivation. As we have previously stated, *motivation* may be defined as what one wants and how much one wants it. If you accept this definition, you must accept that you cannot expect the client to be motivated without making some contact with his or her goals. You cannot expect the client to be motivated to work toward imposed goals or your goals. None of us will move toward change unless we have some discomfort with our present situation. But of greater importance to social workers is the fact that people will not move toward change without hope that the situation can be improved. People tend to use offers of help more effectively if you address the hope-discomfort balance early in the contact. While you cannot promise particular outcomes, you can impart a certain optimistic stance that something helpful can be done. You should also use the client's goal to focus the discomfort on what can be changed rather than allowing discomfort to continue as a generalized feeling.

The suggestion that workers be active in aiding clients to use resources, in doing for and with clients, almost always raises questions about the creation of dependency. It seems to us that we are far more likely to produce dependency by doing people's thinking and planning for them and then assigning the task to the client than we are by involving clients in making decisions about what should be done and who should do it, and then offering our active help if there is client-worker agreement that this decision making is sound.

The notion that we should never do anything for people that they can do for themselves seems to us to be very destructive of the nurturing relationships that are necessary between human beings. We are socially interdependent beings, not totally independent ones. What better way to express concern for another than to help in a concrete, easily understood way by offering to relieve him or her of a dreaded task? The condition of total independence without the ability to take from others or the impulse to give to them is pathological. All of us who function well in life do so because we have multiple sources of dependency satisfaction and because we have learned to use each source appropriately. None of us could grow up an effective person without long years of very personal dependency. For far too long we have equated asking for help with dependency. We need to learn how to assess the sources available to clients for meeting dependency needs. Most have pitifully few sources. We need to understand two principles in considering the question of dependency. (1) We cannot be independent without knowledge and social skills. Dependency caused by lack of knowledge and social skills must not be confused with pathological dependence. (2) While there is such a thing as infantile dependency, this is furthered by making decisions for the client, by assuming the stance of knower and authority, by withholding active help from those who need it, and by assigning clients tasks that they do not understand or cannot carry out. Active involvement in the life space of the client in doing things as the client's agent cuts down significantly on transference elements and thus may actually serve to reduce pathological dependency.

Carrying Out Helping Roles Appropriate for Social Work

With this very brief summary of our basic notions about helping others, we will now examine ways of carrying out selected helping roles appropriate to social work practice. First, we will examine the relationship that supports these various social work roles. As the purpose of the relationship is to support the partnership for work, it is based in current reality. However, the climate you seek to build will differ even within the same role, so we cannot discuss a particular relationship as a requirement of any particular role. The quality of the relationship will be determined by your differential assessment of the amount of support and active help the client will need if he or she is to find and sustain the courage needed to work on the problem. With clients who have good ego strength, social skills in coping with ordinary tasks of life, and the power to do so, the primary stance of the worker is that of a concerned collateral resource. The relationship, while warm, supporting, and respectful, is also strongly task oriented and leaves the control in the hands of the client. You should stand beside, support, and comment but not seek to instill a nurturing quality. Good examples of this type of relationship are found in the "Pain Clinic Evaluation" (Appendix, A-3), the Lee family (Appendix, A-5) and in Ms. Arthur's work with Mr. Milton (Reading 12-1). With clients who have low self-esteem because of their life experiences and present social context, who have experienced poor parenting and who have had no models of sound social functioning, the climate for work must have a nurturing quality (a feeling of warmth, caring, concern, and desire to help). With clients whose situation is similar but who come in contact with you through the demand of others, it becomes more critical that you exercise exceeding care as to how you cross the boundaries of the referent client system as an uninvited intruder. With these clients you have the burden not only of communicating to the client a sense of caring and nurture but of establishing a sense of trust with a system that usually actively mistrusts. You must demonstrate complete concern for the system, but paradoxically, you may also have to take a firm positive stance within most of these situations. You need to be strong and active in your involvement with the referent. You are not standing by as a collateral resource but rather must be a part of the action. In such situations you should come across as a knowing person with considerable power. This must be connected with the communication of a commitment to using the power on behalf of the client and communication of the belief that the client is someone special. You must understand and accept that you do not have the right to demand liking or trust from the client. The limits to your ability to act totally as an agent of the client system must be recognized and discussed.

You should encourage such clients to be as dependent as necessary in the interest of protecting them from further damage and in the interest of building the necessary relationship. You must be strong and courageous, willing to risk a great deal without expecting a return. This relationship requires unconditional caring and giving while leaving the client free to fail without recriminations. In all relationships, even the most giving and nurturing ones, it is expected that the client will participate appropriately in the problem-solving work. This is critical to the client's growth. However, this expectation, just like the amount of nurturing offered, is paced to the client's level of social functioning. The acceptance will continue even if clients find it difficult to work on their part of the tasks. "Within the relationship, there is a lending of the worker's strength to supplement areas where the client cannot function. To be effective this must be a loan freely given, but it is a loan, not a gift, for while the loan need not be repaid and carries no interest payments, there is the implication that this loan is made for the purposes of the client's development of strength" (see Compton, Reading 13-1). The relationship developed between worker and client in the Smith case (Appendix, A-1) and the Stover case (Appendix, A-6) is much more nurturing and involves much more worker activity than does the relationship offered the client in Appendix Readings A-3 and A-5 and Reading 12-1.

We discussed the forming of a relationship earlier, but we want to repeat that careful listening, being sure you understand the client's communication, communicating this understanding to the client, pacing the interview to the client's need, and being concerned with client goals all help to build sound working relationships. Reassurance, the expression of approval of the client's capacities, achievements, feelings, and wants, is a common method to increase the positive climate of the interview and to increase the self-esteem of the client. With clients such as Mr. H

(Appendix, A-3), this is usually a passive technique in which you approve feelings, thoughts, and actions that the client shares. However, with clients such as Mrs. Stover (Appendix, A-6) and Debbie Smith (Appendix, A-1), this method is broadened into an active search for client strengths—a search for areas in which the system is able to cope adequately. When these areas are identified, you must take an active part in identifying them with the client to convey your active concern and partnership. An example of this is the worker's identification of Debbie's intellectual ability. Given this support, Debbie was willing to be tested and make plans to undertake further education. We remember one client, whose life had been lived in a hostile environment, as had Debbie's, who said he thought that an important part of the relationship with a good social worker was that he or she expected you to achieve more than you ever thought you could. You must make clear that this is an expectation based on a careful assessment of client skills. It is quite different from assigning the client tasks to carry out.

Providing Information An important part of acting as broker, enabler, advocate, and educator is to increase the client's knowledge about aspects of the problem that he or she may not know about. Information may include suggesting alternatives to the client's previous coping efforts and discussing how these alternatives can be used. It may also include information about important aspects of the problem or its possible solution and information about community resources, how to use them, what to expect from them; information about the client's entitlement to such services; and information about how you can act to aid the client's use of resources. Ms. Arthur provided information in all these areas in Reading 12-1, as did the worker in the pain clinic (Appendix, A-3).

Teaching Coping Skills This technique is central to the role of educator. In many instances it is closely allied to the method of information giving but often goes beyond simple giving of information to teaching clients coping skills to manipulate their environment to achieve desired outcomes. It may involve teaching clients how to claim their rights and entitlements. It requires a careful and painstaking consideration of the small details of daily living. It involves carefully helping the client to collect facts, to assess them, and to consider in careful detail alternative ways to secure what the client wants. This is a time-consuming method that demands great patience on your part. Some workers find it difficult to use this method without talking down to the client or moving at too rapid a pace, because the relationship that supports such work often resembles the worker's relationship to his or her own parents and results in worker discomfort. Yet this is a critical method to use with clients who seem hopeless and powerless because of the lack of nurture and deprivation in their environment.

Rehearsal This involves a detailed consideration during the interview of the exact details of how the client will carry out a specific task. Clients may be encouraged to role-play the way they intend to cope with the real situation. They can be encouraged to think of any obstacles that may appear in actually carrying out the task and how they may cope with them. This technique can be a part of the role of educator, broker, advocate, and enabler. It is a part of the enabler role if you encourage the client to role-model what he or she thinks can be done. It is a part of the educator role when you must role-play for the client and ask for a reaction.

Advice and Guidance   This method involves giving the client direct suggestions for actions. Social workers often resist this method because of their reluctance to tell the client what to do. They are much more comfortable with an enabling role, which attempts to help clients determine what to do for themselves. But if clients have had no experience in coping with this situation, it only damages them to expect them to find something within themselves that they do not have available. It is important that advice and guidance be given tentatively so that it may be rejected by the client if he or she does not approve. But a tentative offering of advice and guidance may help the client husband energy and assure him or her of your concern and willingness to join in the change effort.

Modeling and Identification   Closely related to advice and guidance is your presentation of self as a model for the client's consideration. In using this procedure you do not, as in advice and guidance, present yourself as an authority. Rather, you present yourself as an active partner who might behave in this particular way if confronted with the problem. Also, if you find it necessary to act on behalf of the client in brokering, advocating, or mediating, this method is helpful in teaching the client to consider how these actions are used to solve problems. When you act on behalf of the client, you must immediately discuss the actions taken with the client, both to keep the client informed and to solicit his or her response to what was done and to model an effective way to cope with the situation.

Logical Discussion   If the client has certain strengths in methods of problem solving and is able to make an accurate appraisal of reality, seeing and considering alternatives and consequences, then logical discussion can be used as a method for purposes of education or of utilization of resources.

Ventilation   This is a method that may be central to the role of enabler in that the client's expression of feelings about what may be happening to him or her releases energy that can be used to increase the client's capacity to cope. It also can further the development of the relationship and increase the client's sense of hope and worth.

Enhancing Awareness of Own Behavior

Enhancing awareness of the system's own behavior is used primarily with a system that does not understand just what it may be contributing to the problem. Behavior as used here includes both feelings and thinking. The useful techniques are outlined in the following discussion. The system may be helped to see itself more clearly if you paraphrase what the system has said.

Paraphrasing   This means that you restate the basic message in similar but usually fewer words—both as a test of your understanding and so that the system can hear its own productions. To do this you must listen very carefully for the basic message. Then you, in what is communicated to the client, must remain very close to what is being expressed, simplifying to make clear and synthesizing what the content, feelings, thinking, or behavior mean to you. Always be tentative in your synthesis when submitting it for the system's approval, amendment, or rejection. While sharing how you heard the system's message, watch carefully for clues that either confirm or deny the accuracy and helpfulness of the rephrasing.

Clarifying and Reflecting Clarifying and reflecting are other techniques that are helpful in improving awareness of behavior. These go beyond paraphrasing, which expresses only what is implied by the system. Clarifying and reflecting connect islands of feelings, experiences, and thinking that the system left unconnected or may not see as connected. Thus your communication will be seen by the client system as something very different from paraphrasing. Reflecting carries the feeling of trying to understand the world as the target system does. It is a sharing of the way you read the total message. You select and pull together the best mix of context, feelings, and action from the productions of the target system to advance the understanding of the system and thus bring change from new understanding. Clarifying summarizes core material and brings vague material into sharper focus. It identifies themes that seem to run throughout the behavior of the client system, drawing conclusions from the material presented. In clarifying, you make a guess regarding the system's basic meaning and offer it, along with an admission of your confusion, for consideration, or you may admit confusion about meaning and try to restate what the client has said. You may also ask for clarification, repetition, or illustration from the client system if it appears that the clients might understand the situation better if they tried to clarify it for you.

Checking Perception and Focusing Perception checking is a way of helping the system realize what it has just produced. You paraphrase what you believe was said and ask for confirmation or further clarification. Focusing is helpful in that it can be used to emphasize a feeling or idea from a vast array of verbalization and to reduce confusions, diffusion, and vagueness. Thus you assist the system in focusing on assumptions, ways of thinking, notions, or feelings that may be hidden in the discussion. You should use your own feelings of confusion and sense of the system's direction as a guide to decide when to focus appropriate questionings also helpful in clarifying for a system the effect of its behavior. Questions can be used to lead the system to clarify information, feelings, experiences and can serve to encourage the system to explore feelings and thinking or to elaborate on those already discussed.

Summarizing and Interpreting Along with questioning, summarizing can be used for many purposes, but in this cluster it is used to check your understanding and to encourage the clients to explore the material more completely. Interpreting is an active process of explaining the meaning of events to clients so that they are able to see their problems in a new way. You may interpret events presented from three perspectives: the client's own frame of reference, your frame of reference, and the frame of reference of another system. This last is often done in the brokering or mediating role, when you may present the target system with the frame of reference of the client system for the target systems' consideration and hopefully for its understanding. Or the process may be reversed, and the client system may be presented with the target system's frame of reference. You also may offer alternative frames of reference by relabeling the material presented. An example of relabeling is found in the old story of the pessimist as one who sees the glass of water as half empty;

the optimist, or worker, points out that it is half full. Another example is found in the behavior of Tom Sawyer, who labeled the work of whitewashing the fence for his Aunt Polly as a privilege rather than drudgery. As a result he promoted himself from worker to supervisor and collected considerable treasure as his friends bid for the privilege of becoming his workers.

In interpreting, you introduce your understanding of what you think the message or behavior means from your theory of human growth and behavior. This requires considerable skill, and the following rules must be observed. Keep the language simple and close to the system's message. Offer notions in a very, very tentative way as a possible contribution. Always solicit the client system's evaluation of just what the contribution is. In face of the client's denial that the contribution is pertinent, do not hold to it as correct but also do not negate it entirely. Say, for example, "It may not be a helpful idea, but I would like to do some more thinking about it."

Informing   Another technique useful in increasing the client's awareness of his or her own behavior is informing, which involves giving information, suggestions, or advice. Informing is probably underused by many workers because they assume that the system has certain knowledge and skills that they may not possess. If when you inform, the client indicates that he or she already has such information, you can apologize for the repetition. Generally workers give information, suggestions, or advice about four aspects of the situation. You may use informing and checking to establish a common understanding about the situation between you and the client. Informing is also used to share with the client your view of the situation—how you add it up. Informing may involve suggesting actions the client may want to try or it may involve the straight communication of new knowledge about the situation.

Actions   Clients may be encouraged to try a new way of responding to others or of handling their transactions with others followed by evaluation of the results of the changed action. In this way clients gain an understanding that their behavior influences the behavior of others as well as learning new social skills.

Confrontation   This technique is discussed last because it is probably the most difficult to use correctly. Confrontation is always hard for the client to accept or consider because it always involves some unmasking of distortions in the client's feelings, experiences, or behavior. You identify certain patterns that lie buried, hidden, or beyond the immediate knowledge of the client. It is something the client never thought about and/or was unwilling to accept before. Acceptance of confrontation is difficult also because it carries some challenge to do something about these things that have not yet even been acknowledged. It must be used as a mode of caring and involvement and not as punishment or discipline. Possibly no other technique offers such a tempting avenue for you to act out unacknowledged feelings about either yourself or the other system than the use of this technique. It is so easy to say that the system needs to face honestly what it is doing, that it needs to be shocked out of an unwillingness to work, and so on. These comments may cover your anger or frustration with the client, may cover your punitiveness toward the client, or may reveal your own hidden need to appear powerful or all-knowing in interaction with the client.

To be used effectively the confrontation must be based on a deep understanding of the implication for the client of being presented with this material. You must always keep in mind the question of how this action helps the client to move toward desired change or to cope with the situation's demands. Proper confrontation is always given tentatively with a motivation to help and as a part of the involvement with the client. Done poorly with a vulnerable system, it can result in a quick accommodation to your views or in the client's withdrawal from contact with perhaps considerable anger, either of which are ineffective ways of trying to solve problems. A problem of using confrontation with a target other than the client system is that the target may take out its anger and hurt at your activity on the client system and punish that system, since you are not so vulnerable. Finally, confrontation should be used only after a careful evaluation of the relationship and what such information will mean to the client within the already established climate of working together.

You will find an example of confrontation in the Debbie Smith case. The worker confronts Debbie with the inadequacy of her care of her children. Note how carefully the worker goes about this and how she ties the problem of the care of the children to Debbie's own goal to be a good mother. Use of confrontation at this point in the Smith situation serves another important function. Until this point the worker had not identified the reason for her intervention into Debbie's life. Note how much more productive the work became once the problem had been clearly identified. Sometimes when we approach a referent and must state the reason for our contact, we are engaging in a kind of confrontation.

Relationship   In using this group of techniques to enhance the client's awareness of his or her own behavior, your primary stance is that of a concerned collateral resource. Use such techniques when there is considerable expectation that the system is capable of taking the lead in problem solving with a little help. The relationship, while warm and supporting, is also strongly task oriented and leaves the control for the action in the hands of the client. You stand beside, support, and comment on the action toward solving the problem but do not become actively involved in the doing. This stance on your part is also important for the next group of techniques. You may be more active in contributing information and perspective in the type of work discussed in the next section.

Enhancing the Client's Awareness of Others' Behavior   In working to enhance the system's awareness of the meaning of other ways of behaving, you may use all the techniques described earlier but will be much more active in informing the client about the perspective of other systems. You may be much more active in simply giving knowledge about the expected norms of behavior. As an example of this, it is often found that parents who are experiencing trouble in their interaction with their children may have no notions of what kind of behavior to expect from their children. Or the school system may be very punitive toward a child for certain behavior that is a part of the culture from which the child comes. Or a group of male professors may be totally unaware of why the group's climate changed after the men referred to the middle-aged woman professor who was chairing the group and two other women members as "the girls." In these situations, when client systems are ignorant of the values or needs of the other systems, new information alone may be extremely helpful.

However, to accept and use new information often requires that the client change cherished ways of viewing human relationships and transactions. This may result in resistances that should be worked through.

Allowing the client to ventilate feelings and to think about expectations and norms of others is helpful and may prepare the way for some reframing of what is expressed. If a client can express anger or frustration with you, he or she will be better able either to listen to new information or to engage in logical discussions, which may be helpful. Perhaps two of the most helpful techniques in this area are the prediction of events and the discussion about how they may be handled differently than the client's usual way of responding. Thus the client may consider alternate ways of behaving to achieve a different relationship with others. Or the client system may be supported in discussing the problem with others. In either of these approaches the client system may be encouraged to rehearse how these new actions will be carried out and ways of evaluating the results.

The feeling tone of the relationship will vary in this situation largely in relation to the client's investment in the meaning he or she attaches to the behavior of others. The relationship offered may vary all the way from that of a concerned collateral resource to a strong supportive relationship (see Reading 13-1).

Supporting Client Role Performance

Active Supplying of Resources Since in many of these situations the goals that are important to the client involve concrete survival needs, your activities in supplying such concrete resources are extremely important in solving some very critical problems of the client. In the securing of such resources, you are usually actively involved in the work of physically getting the things. Do not act as broker or mediator for the client, expecting the client to carry through on most of the action alone. In attempting to help an individual to cope with role demands that have not been met previously, you also will have to be skilled in the use of advice, guidance, and encouragement. In addition, you will have to use the skills of helping the client in gradually being able to understand the others' position.

How active and firm you are in the use of these techniques will be based on the clients' motivation, ability, resources within their own control, and how they see the problem and goal. One of the important techniques is your active securing of resources for the client. You do the work of securing the material things rather than acting as a broker or mediator for the clients' activities.

Direct Intervention You also intervene directly in the living situation of the client and act for the client in the transactions with many systems, such as discussing a child's problems with the school system. In such situations you wish to impose minimal demands on the client. However, in all of this, the goal is to help the client toward better role performance. Therefore, you must be scrupulous about reporting what is being done and using this as teaching-learning material. You will also use modeling and identification, set appropriate limits for client behavior, and require clients to be as active on their own behalf as they can be. You will use all the minute particular details of life as material for teaching appropriate role behavior.

Action Perhaps one of the most effective ways to socialize a client system into effective role performance is through involving the client in planning necessary actions to reach desired goals and in taking responsibility for carrying out such necessary tasks within their ability to do so. Be cautious with such clients; do not involve them in planning actions that are beyond their ability to complete satisfactorily. In the case of client systems just beginning to take tentative steps to act on their own behalf, failure at planned tasks can discourage them from any future attempt and may convince them of their inability to cope. However, involving the client in careful consideration of tasks they seem able to perform can serve to enhance their self-image and further their sense of growth and competence. To participate with the client in planning and engaging in successful task completion requires that you identify, mobilize, and ally with the client's potential abilities and ways of coping. It further demands that you be able to engage in consideration of the minute particulars in planning and rehearsing actions. You must be available to support and encourage. (For further discussion of use of action, see Reading 13-2.)

Recapitulation

In this chapter we have discussed certain methods that are appropriate in carrying out certain roles. We have also recognized that interventive plans may require the use of several roles. In summary, we would like to discuss the roles used in some of the case material we have included in the book and ask you to see if you can identify the methods used and the relationship established in carrying out these roles.

Probably the best example of advocacy and the worker's active supplying of resources is found in Reading 13-3, "Helping Children with AIDS." Read this case carefully and see if you can identify methods of advocacy.

A good example of mediation is found in the Lee case (Reading A-5). In this family people were in trouble because of misunderstandings of the motivations of others, because they felt that they were not receiving the satisfactions to which they were entitled, and because they did not have appropriate information about how to cope with certain problems in a new culture.

There are a number of examples of the worker engaging in enabling work. These examples are found in work with Mr. H (Appendix, A-3), in the work in the Milton-Clay case (Reading 12-1), and in the work with Debbie Smith (Appendix, A-1).

There are also a number of cases in which the worker acted as broker. This is perhaps one of the most commonly used roles in social work. In fact, all the cases mentioned above involve examples of use of the role of broker. Probably the only case in which there was no use of it was in the case of Mrs. Z (Appendix, A-4), who never really became a client. If Mrs. Z could have accepted the client role, there might have been considerable use of brokering.

The two examples that most clearly show the work of the educator are found in the Smith (A-1) and the Stover (A-6) cases. You will note that these two clients were the persons who had the least effective coping skills and who had lived their lives in the most difficult social contexts.

A Look Forward

In the next chapter we will focus on another important helping process, the use of teamwork. One of the central social work activities is the mobilization of resources that are needed to solve the client's problems. This is often done through collaborative work with colleagues from other disciplines or with social workers in other agencies. Collaborative efforts and teamwork date to the earliest days of social work practice, yet we have not developed a very extensive literature detailing the methods by which such work can be successfully carried out. You will find that much of your time as a social worker is taken up with collaborative planning and action. We hope that this next chapter is of help to you as you engage in such tasks.

An Attempt to Examine the Use of Support in Social Work Practice*

Beulah Roberts Compton

The concept of support in human interaction is much older than social work practice. Social work as a profession grew out of the concern of individuals in an urban society of ever-growing complexity to find a way of assisting their fellow men and women in distress. Early social workers were "friendly visitors" attempting to sustain and encourage those who had fallen on evil days by environmental manipulation, direct advice and guidance, and expressions of concern and encouragement. These early visitors became the forerunners of a profession, and the techniques they used became, along with other techniques, a part of the methods of support and environmental manipulation.

PRACTICE WITH THE INDIVIDUAL

In the early 1940s with the appearance in casework of attempts to define and describe the major treatment methods and to organize and structure these methods into a system of practice theory, supportive treatment was first given recognition as a major helping approach, although it was still considered a simple one (Selby, 1956, pp. 400–414). All attempts to develop concepts of differential treatment methods that have appeared in the literature of the profession from 1940 until the present have included a group of techniques that have been called "supportive" or "sustaining." Just as the method has constantly appeared in the classification system, the techniques grouped together to make up the method have also been consistent. The commonly mentioned techniques

are (1) direct guidance and advice in practical matters, (2) environmental modification with the provision of specific and tangible services as needed, (3) the provision of opportunity for clients to discuss freely their troubling problems and their feelings about them, (4) expressions of understanding by the helper, along with assurance of interest in and concern for the client, (5) encouragement and praise implying confidence in the client's worth and abilities, and (6) protective action and exercise of professional authority when needed. The commonly listed supportive techniques suggest that the worker provide a therapeutic environment, based on understanding, concern, and acceptance in which clients can feel free to talk about their worries and concerns. The helper must take an active rather than a passive role in helping the individual to focus on the problem, in giving pertinent advice and suggestion, in reassuring, encouraging, and helping with specific practical planning. The worker should also be willing and able to enter into planning for everyday problems.

With the exception of Hollis's work (1964, pp. 52–63), the classification systems in casework have tried to label the therapeutic methods according to "level" or "depth" of help given. Support has been considered a "simple" method on the lower end of the scale of casework treatment; the aim or goal of this method was seen as helping the clients to feel more comfortable and to assist them in calling on existing strengths and resources. Support was thought to bring about relief of symptoms and better adaptive functioning through making the client feel more secure, reassured, accepted, protected, safe, and less anxious and less alone. This

---

*An original article prepared for this text.

method was considered appropriate for (1) the person who was too weak to tolerate work toward change and (2) the well-integrated person who was temporarily threatened by an overwhelming external crisis (Selby, 1956, pp. 400–414). It was assumed that the help offered by this method would not lead to personality change. Through environmental change and increased internal comfort, the individual might be enabled to maintain present functioning or to function at a somewhat improved level, but this was not assumed to represent basic change.

It might be well to consider that the early attempts to identify treatment methods and goals in casework practice came only a few years after the theory of the unconscious and the theory of psychic determinism as developed by Freud and other psychoanalytic writers and teachers had become widely available to social workers. These insights into human motivation and the increased understanding of human behavior that they offered were eagerly sought by caseworkers as such knowledge offered a new understanding of and seemed to hold the answers to questions that previously seemed unanswerable. In the light of the impact of this new knowledge on social casework practice and of the limits of the knowledge available (at this time only Freud's early writings about the ego were available in America), it is perhaps understandable that caseworkers tended to see internal structural conflict as the primary factor that brought people to grief in the business of living. In the excitement at the promise of this new understanding, it is perhaps also understandable that early caseworkers did not differentiate between using psychoanalytic theory to advance the aims and understanding of their own professional practice and the taking over of aims of psychoanalytic practice for themselves. Thus there grew within the profession a tendency to allot the highest status and value to those activities that seemed aimed at the resolution of internal conflict by helping the clients to develop "insight" into their conflicts whose genesis was to be found in early life experience (Simon, 1964).

In recent years social work has perhaps become more sophisticated about the use of borrowed concepts and certainly psychoanalytic researches

into the development and functioning of the ego have extended knowledge about personality structure and its interrelationship with social reality. However, these developments do not seem to have had the same impact upon social casework practice theory as did the earlier materials. Casework has used the knowledge of defense mechanisms provided by ego psychology, but it has not been as active in attempting to extend other concepts from ego psychology (except in certain fragmented instances, such as the development of crisis theory or in certain family counseling practices) to the reciprocal relationships between individuals and their situation.

PRACTICE WITH THE GROUP

Group work practice grew from different roots and at a different time. At the time when social caseworkers were struggling with the new knowledge of intrapersonal structure and functioning, group work was only beginning to be conscious of itself as a movement. Group work did not begin as a method of helping people in trouble to solve their problems but as a way of organizing individuals into groups for purposes of self-help toward a better way of life. The insights and concepts used by the early group workers did not come from the psychoanalytic theory with which caseworkers were struggling. Rather they came from education, especially from John Dewey, and from sociologists who were active in the self-help movements. As the years passed and group work became a part of the social work profession, its practitioners still were primarily engaged in helping groups of essentially normal individuals toward an increased self-development.

At the present time, however, the utilization of group work as a way of dealing with the individual's problems of social functioning is growing at a fast pace, and group work practitioners are becoming increasingly involved in attempts to use the insights from psychoanalysis and from group dynamics in developing practice theory for use with "treatment groups." There is also evidence of borrowing from casework practice theory; for example, Louise Frey (1962, pp. 35–42) took the list of treatment techniques considered "supportive" in casework literature and attempted to apply them to group work practice. She accepted the casework theory that support is "generally regarded as beneficial to people with weak egos and to the usually well-functioning person who is in a crisis that has impaired integrative capacity to some extent." This makes support seem safe enough, yet it does leave a question about the people served in groups who do not belong in these categories and who may actually be harmed in such a group and kept from treatment (more intensive?) sorely needed.

Frey's effort is the only example we could find in group work literature of a consideration of the interrelationship of certain group work techniques and the concept of support. In her consideration she seems to have borrowed the concept whole from casework including the dictum regarding the limits of its usefulness. Yet, the group worker's experience in work with developmental groups should be able to make a very large contribution to the concept of the ways in which the client system is supported in its efforts toward growth. At the other end of the continuum, Redl and Wineman's efforts (1957) with the aggressive and disturbed child in a group or life-space situation offer much material that workers need to consider in building a common theory of supportive practice with client systems for the totality of social work practice.

It would be hoped that in borrowing personality theory as a basis for a further development of work with groups, group work would not attempt to apply the older theory that casework borrowed at a particular point in time in its development of practice theory to group work practice in the present. Rather the two methods should join in attempting to see what both the older and the more recent theories of the nature of human beings mean for the totality of social work practice theory with any size of client system and for the specifics of method and technique.

There is a growing literature of ego psychology and of the nature of human learning that challenges the earlier Freudian psychoanalytic view of human beings as primarily seeking homeostasis as the most desirable state of human life. Rather the human need for goal-directed growth is seen as being a

basic need. The ego analysts give increased importance to situational events and to the learning of adaptive behaviors for reasons other than to discharge or control instinctual psychological energies. They emphasize that people select and control their own behaviors to achieve particular consequences which have meaning to them quite apart from innate psychological energies. People give evidence of response patterns learned independently from the reduction of instinctive drives. There is a growing push to integrate knowledge of the cognitive and affective aspects of the individual; a growing recognition that one cannot separate the need to learn and grow from the need to understand and control feelings so that an individual can grow. Social rules and individual behavior are seen as reciprocal influences, with society making possible the existence of the person and the full expression of innate characteristics other than the instinctive psychological energies (Erickson, 1950, 1959; White, 1963).

> The implicit model, at least for many psychiatrists, if not for social workers, is psychoanalysis. The ideal model, I believe, is life itself, the natural processes of growth and development and the rich trajectory of the life span. . . .
>
> The more we learn about the optimal conditions for human growth—the psychophysiology of health, the normal methods of satisfying needs, ways of learning to achieve sublimations and problems—and conflict solving—the more we shall be able to utilize the knowledge as a model for our psychotherapy. . . .

There are two assumptions underlining my argument which should be made explicitly. The first is that there are two major tendencies in all people from birth to death which are ceaselessly in opposition. These might be termed the progressive trends . . . in human nature. Our lives are circumscribed by these polarities. The second assumption is that, other things being equal, progressive forces are the stronger. Growing up, all education and that special form of education known as psychotherapy are based on such forces. Viewed in this framework, mental illness would then be an expression of blocks, obstructions, interferences, arrests and fixations of the progressive forces, which leads to and results in a strengthening and reinforcement of the regressive trends. Our therapeutic task, then, is twofold. First we must identify and help remove the blocks and obstacles; with our typical orientation to pathology this is often the major focus of many psychotherapists. Second, we must identify the progressive forces with which we can ally ourselves and which at the appropriate time, we can help mobilize. This aspect of our therapeutic task tends to be relatively neglected. Yet it may be the most effective instrument for the removal of obstacles. Of all these forces, love is the most effective antidote to anxiety (Bandler, 1963).

SUPPORTIVE PRACTICE WITH DIFFERENT-SIZE CLIENT SYSTEMS

If we as social workers may borrow Dr. Bandler's suggestion that we model our helping processes on life itself and the natural processes of growth and development, we essentially have two tasks in helping people: (1) to identify obstacles and blocks to the system's growth and to become a partner with the strength of the client to remove or ameliorate them and (2) to identify the progressive forces of the client system with which we can ally ourselves at the appropriate time. Given this position, all our efforts with client systems in social work practice are supportive as the focus is on development and is aimed at increasing ability to cope with life pressures.

Given this way of regarding social work practice, we have moved beyond the earlier concept of support as a way of maintaining the status quo to the concept of support as growth-producing. We could perhaps borrow further from the Bandler article and identify two large classifications of direct treatment methods: (1) those methods aimed at sustaining or restoring previous capacities now buried under crisis and stress and (2) those aimed at progressive growth, at developing new and different capacities and strengths.

Louis Towley is quoted by Frank Bruno (1957, p. 422) as saying "Social work's secret tool is the infinite untapped, unused, unsuspected capacity for growth in the sovereign individual person-

ality . . . of all types and breeds of social worker, the group worker most consciously accepts this democratic premise in his work." We do not want to do violence to Towley, but in the light of the greater understanding of the ego that is available to us today, it seems that it might be possible to rephrase the statement somewhat; for example, in the attempt to help people with problems of social functioning, social work must be primarily concerned with the infinite untapped, unused, unsuspected capacity for growth in the sovereign individual personality . . . all social workers should be most concerned with this principle of ego psychology.

If one is to operationalize the concept of ego-support, it is perhaps necessary that one state the functions of the ego, the techniques that support each function, and the way that such techniques are held to be useful. This task needs to be done but is beyond the scope of this paper. However, perhaps we can examine it in light of how we might move from the broad idea that all social work techniques may be considered to have this broad purpose to the examination of the specifics of treatment.

The provision of needed concrete resources, the therapeutic relationship, and the problem-solving process (in other words, the work on the task) are the elements of social work and must be worked within any size client system. Perhaps these elements might be examined in relation to the concept of the two classifications of social practice. The provision of resources to clients in need is as old as social work itself. Early social workers often felt that they could help people solve their problems by doing things to them—by rearranging their life situations for them. This often proved totally ineffective and, with the advance of the Freudian view that people come to grief because of internal conflict, often came to be viewed as a lesser part of the social work process. There were times when it appeared as though environmental manipulation was something done for the client quite apart from the rest of the "treatment" effort, and the client could be made to feel as though the need of concrete aid was an obstacle in the path of more elegant treatment.

USE OF RESOURCES

In supportive practice the worker is active in securing necessary concrete aids for the clients so that their energies may be saved for the problem-solving work and life made more comfortable — a human value of some worth in itself. It is recognized that the workers' willingness to involve themselves freely in the active seeking out and utilizing of concrete aids may not only help the client deal with obstacles and so preserve or restore system functioning, but it may also serve to build a sense of worth that is important in system growth. It is recognized that doing things for the clients even when they could possibly do them for themselves is not necessarily dependency producing but rather may be strengthening when the client is fully engaged in the decision-making process and allocation of problem-solving tasks that should precede any action of a professional person on behalf of the client system. The considerations of concrete resources and their selection for use, the considerations of how one uses such resources and to what end, the growth of a feeling of responsibility as one participates in decisions about one's life — all serve to support the progressive forces of the client system. If clients are able then to actively seek out and utilize resources on their own, so much the better, but to require them to do this at the expense of greatly heightened anxiety or possible failure feeds the regressive forces of the personality.

USE OF RELATIONSHIP

In supportive social work, the quality of the relationship that the worker seeks to create, regardless of system size, is that of a partnership for work. It is based in current reality as a good working relationship needs to be. The relationship has both a nurturing quality and an expectation that the client or group will participate appropriately in the problem-solving process. However, the expectation is paced to the client's capacity, and the acceptance will continue even if clients find it difficult to work on their part(s) of the task. Within the relationship, there is a lending of the worker's strength to supplement areas where the client is weak. To be effective this must be a loan freely given, but it is a loan, not a gift, for while the loan need not be repaid and carries no interest payments, there is the implication that this loan is made for the purposes of the system's development of its own strength. Elements of concern and respect have a major place in such a relationship. There is a recognition that both the client and the worker bring something of value to the working together. We believe that there is a common quality in the development and use of the relationship in supportive work whatever the size of client system that lies in the climate for work and in the attitude of the worker toward the clients — attitudes of attentiveness, receptivity, acceptance, and expectation.

USE OF SUPPORTIVE METHODS

The problem-solving methods themselves do not lend themselves as well to the global approach as does the discussion of the relationship and the provision of resources. Whatever may be said about the commonness of methods of offering service to different-sized client systems, when things get to the point of the worker across the desk from an individual or a worker in a circle with a group we see that they are doing different things, and workers need to develop somewhat different skills for different-sized client systems. However, it would seem possible to consider some common techniques of support and examine what these mean for what one does with any system. In the first place, we suspect that no one technique of problem-solving can be considered supportive in and of itself. It is supportive within the context of the relationship and within a pattern of techniques. In other words, we do not use any one technique in grand isolation but rather techniques are used in patterns and within a relationship. Let us attempt to examine some common techniques to see how these are used differentially in the one-to-one and in the one-to-group situation.

Reassurance

Reassurance, the expression of recognition and approval of the client's capacities, achievements, feelings, and needs, is a common procedure of supportive treatment. It is usually seen as a passive technique in which the worker approves an expression of the client. It could well be broadened into an active search for the strengths of the client—for the areas in which the system is able to cope successfully. When these areas are identified, the worker needs to take an active part in identifying them with the client. It might be well to keep reassurance as it is now understood and add "active recognition of the coping strengths of the client" to the list. The active component of the search for strengths seems to convey the worker's active concern and partnership to the client. Reassurance is primarily used as a technique of sustaining or restoring system capacity, but when used in conjunction with other techniques, it can be a part of help aimed at growth. In the one-to-one situation workers carry the burden of doing the reassuring. However, this depends upon a positive, warm relationship and the client's acceptance of the worker's authority to make the technique a helpful one. In the group situation group members may carry the burden of this with any particular member. The group members' discussion of their common problems and the member's growing awareness that feelings and needs are shared by others is reassuring.

Educational Methods

It is important in this consideration of the techniques of support that thought be given to the position of the worker as a teacher. One of the contributions of ego-psychology has been the recognition that the ego operates by means of its cognitive processes as well as its affective energies. Problem-solving in our complicated society requires not only that feelings and impulses be controlled but that the ego have at its disposal the knowledge and skills necessary to problem-solving. We often make the tragic mistake of confusing lack of cognitive and/or social skills for resistance or low motivation. We must remember that the client without cognitive or social skills in our society is as vulnerable as the emotionally ill. This technique demands that the worker give careful, painstaking consideration to the small details of daily living. It

requires a careful examination of reality with the worker actively supplying the knowledge the client does not possess. In work with groups, the group members may supply much of this direct teaching. The use of program media to provide opportunities for mastery and achievement and the development of structure and democratic organizational procedures are important ways that the group work may implement this technique. Workers may also use the members' involvement in decision making and conflict resolution as education in social skills as well as finding this technique useful for developing the ability to control feelings and to express oneself in a disciplined way that is an important part of personality growth. In the one-to-one situation the worker teaches decision making by carefully helping the client to collect the facts, to weigh them, to make considered judgments, to consider consequences of choices made, and to plan to implement the choice. The technique of education in cognitive and social skills is primarily one directed at growth rather than ego-sustaining. It is time-consuming and demands patience on the part of the worker. It has been used more extensively in work with client groups rather than in one-to-one work and has been used most extensively in work with groups of children, but it needs to become a better-understood part of practice with any size client system.

Rehearsal

In working with groups the worker may use the group interaction so that the individual has a specifically structured experience in a protected social environment in which social learning may take place and within which the client may practice carrying out a task. There is a somewhat similar technique called "rehearsal" that may be used in work with individuals. This is a detailed consideration in the interview situation of the exact details of how the client will carry out a specific task. In either situation the clients may be encouraged to "role play" the way they intend to carry out the action later in the real situation. They can be encouraged to think of any obstacles that may appear in actually attempting the task and to consider why they may come up and how they can meet them. This technique is used as either a sustaining or a growth technique. Its purpose is determined by whether it is used to help the clients accomplish tasks that they have previously been able to handle but are now unable to cope with or whether it is used to help clients carry out new methods of coping with problems.

Advice and Guidance

Advice and guidance are appropriate parts of the supportive treatment method. Here the worker uses professional knowledge and authority to express to the client, individual group member, or group an opinion about a course of action. As a rule this procedure is only used at a time when the clients are unable to find their own solution or when they need permissive authority to pursue a course of action. In the group the members often offer each other this type of support, or they may become auxiliary helpers of the worker in this regard. This technique is usually considered a sustaining technique—a way of rescuing a faltering system in an emergency—with the hope of helping the client through a crisis situation. However, one of the most remarkable facts of the helping process is that a gain in one area of functioning can release the progressive forces of the system and effect a redistribution of energies which is reflected in an improvement of functioning in many areas not directly touched on. Thus advice and guidance, if it helps a client deal successfully with an overwhelming situation, may be a growth-producing technique.

Modeling and Identification

Closely related to advice and guidance is the worker's presentation of self as an ego-ideal for the client's consideration. In using this procedure the workers do not, as in advice and guidance, present themselves as authorities. Rather they present themselves as active partners who might act this particular way if confronted with this problem. They attempt to leave the client free to adopt or reject this particular pattern, but they present it as a possible model that might be examined if the client were interested. In work with the group, one or several group members

may assume this role with any other member. This fact allows greater use of this technique in work with groups, where other members may support or reject any model offered, than in individual work where, unless the client recognizes the need of help, is ready to use it, and is secure in the worker's concern, it may be impossible to resist the inherent authority of the worker and reject the model that does not fit. This technique is used primarily in situations where one is hoping for ego-growth through identification with the strength of another.

Logical Discussion

The system's capacity for rational behavior is used in the technique of logical discussion. If the client or the group has certain strengths in the methods of problem-solving, if there are skills and knowledge to make appraisals of reality, if there is the ability to see alternatives and consequences, then logical discussion can serve to both sustain the system and to support its growth as it appeals to the capacity for rational behavior. However, if the client system had no opportunity in the life situation to approach the problem-solving process in this manner, this technique may be totally beyond it and may lead to further frustration and the destruction of motivation. Again, this is a technique that can be used with a client group with less concern as the group members can support each other in expressing openly the group frustration with such expectations. In the individual situation the client, alone with the worker, often does not have this strength and so must internalize frustration as a discouragement with self and functioning that cannot meet the expectations of the worker.

Ventilation

The worker often needs to elicit the client systems' expression of feelings about what may be happening to them. This technique releases energy that was bound up in the management and repression of the feeling and so acts to increase the capacity of the client system. It also serves to increase the client's sense of worth and thus the sense of hope. In the group the program activities may be used to increase the individual's acting out of feelings in an appropriate way and may thus increase the individual's capacity to handle emotions appropriately without excessive denial or repression.

Use of Limits

The use of limits appropriately is often another neglected technique of the supportive method. Workers so often think of treatment in terms of the liberation of the ego of the client from maladaptive restrictions that we do not consider carefully enough that limits set within a nurturing relationship may also be a need and may contribute to the support and growth of the client system. The appropriate use of limits may serve to help the client gain control of the impulses, but in addition it may build a sense of worth within the client system in that we care enough to risk hostility by such action, and that we believe the client is strong enough to accept the limits set. In work with groups the worker does not have to carry the entire burden of this technique. Group members will often set limits for each other either by a direct limit-setting in relationship to the behavior of one or a number of members, or by setting rules for the entire group. In fact, the preoccupation of certain groups with rules is indicative of the importance of such limits for the growth of the system.

Confrontation

Confrontation may be used two ways in supportive help. It is used to identify stereotyped or patterned behavior or ways of feeling and thinking in order that the clients' or system members' capacity to see themselves more accurately is increased. It may also be used with certain clients in order that they may better see and understand the way they are seen by others. This is the first step in helping the clients or members consider whether in light of new awareness they want to change their behavior or learn ways of accepting the judgment of others if they do not change. In working with a group the worker may do this with the entire group or in relation to a particular member. However, members often engage in this kind of activity in relation to each other. As the member's relationship to other members does not carry the authority aspects of the worker's relationship, this can be used with a greater freedom and less precaution in the group than in the worker-to-client relationship. This technique is used primarily when the goal is the growth of the client system.

SUMMARY

There are other techniques that need examination in light of their use to support the functioning of the client system. It is hoped that this brief list will serve as only a beginning. Certainly the use of ego-supportive techniques differentially with proper attention to the diagnosis of the clients or members with their problems in their situations is a challenge worthy of the highest knowledge and skill of the worker. It demands a unique combination of mind and heart and hand from the worker who would practice it in the interest of the client.

Reading 13-2 *Action as a Tool in Casework Practice** *

Anthony N. Maluccio

In casework practice there is extensive use of action—active doing, performing, or experiencing. Yet, action as a concept has received very little attention in the literature. There are various

*Reprinted by permission of Families International, Inc., from *Social Casework* 55:1 (January 1974), pp. 30 35.

reasons for this omission. An important one is the emphasis on the person as a sentient being and on the primacy of clinical dialogue. Perhaps a more crucial reason is the lack of a theoretical framework capable of providing an adequate rationale for the use of action and stimulating the emergence of pertinent practice principles.

Theorists have long recognized the significance

of action and have alluded to its theoretical underpinnings,[1] but the conceptual development of action has been so limited and fragmented that it appears to be a tool in search of a theory. An appropriate framework is necessary to give meaning and substance to action as a tool and to further its integration into the processes of casework.

This article examines the use of action in casework largely within the context of ego psychology. The central aim here is to clarify the purposes of action, its rationale, and the conditions necessary for its effective use in practice. The reason for choosing the context of ego psychology is that it offers a promising approach, especially through its recent emphasis on the autonomous development and functioning of the ego, the dynamic transaction between the person and the environment, and the crucial role played by a person's activities in adapting and coping efforts and in the ongoing struggle to achieve autonomy, competence, and identity. The formulations of such theorists as Erik H. Erikson (1959), Heinz Hartmann (1958), and Robert W. White (1963) counteract the classical Freudian emphasis on instinctual forces and tension reduction as the determinants of behavior. At the same time, they underline the notion of the human organism as an active rather than merely reactive participant in life.

POSITIVE PURPOSES OF ACTION

Action has been viewed as appropriate in social work primarily with such clients as hard-to-reach or nonverbal persons, severely deprived or disorganized families, and psychiatric patients in resocialization programs. Increasingly, however, empirical evidence supports the validity of the use of action as an integral feature of casework with a wider range of clients. Crisis intervention, behavior modification, Gestalt therapy, family treatment, and milieu therapy emphasize experiential learning

and the use of activities in the here-and-now situation of the person.

In family therapy, practitioners introduce role-playing and other activities in order to develop the client's capacity to cope with life challenges through involvement in concrete experiences. In residential treatment of disturbed children, workers arrange for children and parents to participate in social and cultural activities as a means of enhancing their competence and promoting a positive sense of self. In crisis intervention, quick involvement in life activities by the client is viewed as an essential step in resolution of the problem. In play therapy with children, activities constitute a basic medium of communication and interaction.

Ego psychology highlights the value of using action for such broad purposes as enhancement of the client's self-image, development of autonomy and competence, flowering of latent potentialities and innate creativity, and provision of opportunities for growth and mastery. Action can also serve as a means of facilitating and making alive in practice the expression of such basic elusive professional tenets as client participation and self-determination.

The utilization of action for these purposes is especially pertinent within the context of an expanded conception of casework, one encompassing not only clinical treatment but help through a variety of resources, services, and practice modalities. Such a conception underscores the worker's responsibility to identify, mobilize, and ally with the client's potentialities, natural life processes, and adaptive patterns. The purposes of action thus are consonant with a revitalized casework method patterned after life itself. In her formulation of a life model of practice, Carel B. Germain (1973) stresses the use of purposive activity as a major means of stimulating the client's growth, adaptation, and progressive forces.

Many case situations typically encountered by social workers may be imaginatively redefined to generate opportunities for the productive use of coping, striving, and goal-directed action. For example, activities may help a young unmarried mother to gain competence as a new parent, when her situation is defined as one involving a problem

---

[1] See Austin (1948); Hamilton (1951, pp. 246–249); and Oxley (1971). Austin and Hamilton point to the use of action in restructuring the environment and providing the client with positive reality experiences and opportunities for growth. Oxley highlights action as a major feature of a proposed life-model approach to casework treatment and suggests its significance in varied social work contexts.

in role transition rather than an underlying personality conflict. A crisis such as the death of a father in a young family may be approached as a challenge to the mother, suggesting multiple action strategies for helping her to call on her own resources and to enhance her skills in bringing up the children. A disorganized, multiproblem family may be helped to engage in an active struggle toward fulfillment, as well as survival, through involvement in meaningful activities and growth-producing experiences.

Action may be employed differentially in casework practice: as a diagnostic tool, to assess a person's special areas of aptitude and competence, quality of interaction with others, and so on; as an instrument of treatment, to provide a client with an opportunity to test him- or herself or to develop social skills; as the culmination of treatment, by facilitating a course of action, such as obtaining a job; as a measurement of the outcome of casework, by evaluating the results of particular client and worker activities; and as a means of mobilizing other people, instrumentalities, and resources in the client's ecological context.

ARTIFICIAL AND NATURAL ACTIVITIES

A distinction should be made between artificial activities that are provided for a client and natural activity or action that arises out of the life situation.

Artificial activities include role-playing, play therapy, and participation in activity groups. These activities are appropriately used as vehicles for learning, as media of communication, or as opportunities to practice desired behaviors. Often, the client's participation in one or more of them is necessary as preparation for engagement in life itself. Thus, there can be a complementary use of artificial and natural activities. For example, a school social worker found that, following participation in a discussion group of mothers with similar needs, an inner-city mother was able to go successfully through the experience of conferring with school personnel on behalf of her under-achieving child. She then felt a real sense of satisfaction as she shared her experience with other mothers in the group.

In contrast to activities that are artificially introduced into the helping situation, action involves real experiences (such as work, or play, or social interaction) emerging from life. Natural activities can be more meaningful and potentially more effective, since they are more closely related to the person's natural life processes of growth and adaptation.

A family service agency worker had tried to involve Mr. A, an isolated elderly man, in social activities at a neighborhood center. These efforts were unsuccessful, as Mr. A seemed disinterested in contact with his peers or in leaving his home. Eventually, he was faced with the need to relocate owing to redevelopment. As the worker accompanied him on various apartment-hunting trips in different parts of the city, Mr. A began to reminisce about his life experiences, showed much interest in the ways the city had changed, and expressed his desire to move into a setting with opportunity for companionship.

RATIONALE FOR THE USE OF ACTION

In an earlier era of casework, insight or self-understanding was idealized as the preferred goal of treatment. More recently has come the realization that insight is not enough and may not even be necessary. It has been recognized that, with or without self-understanding, a person's activities play a critical role in personality growth, adaptation, and social functioning.

An individual's active participation in successful transactions with the environment appears to be a prerequisite for growth, mastery, and identity. White (1963, p. 150) postulates that human behavior is motivated by an innate, autonomous drive to deal with the environment, which he terms *effectance* or *competence motivation*. He also stresses that the ego is strengthened through the person's successful action upon the environment, resulting feelings of efficacy, and the cumulative development of a sense of competence. The individual changes and grows through involvement in activities providing opportunities for need satisfaction, task fulfillment, crisis resolution, and learning of social skills (Cumming & Cumming, 1962, pp. 213–218).

Engagement in purposive, goal-directed activities can stimulate the person's coping efforts and strengthen the adaptive capacities. The experience of success in meaningful life activities can serve to improve coping skills, enhance personal well-being, and encourage new attempts. In his discussion of extratherapeutic experiences in psychoanalysis, Franz Alexander (1946, p. 40) notes that

> successful attempts at productive work, love, self-assertion, or competition will change the vicious cycle to a benign one; as they are repeated, they become habitual and thus eventually bring about complete change in the personality.[2]

In her extensive research on child development, Lois B. Murphy (1962, pp. 354–355) observes that there is a significant correlation between a child's activity and the capacity to cope with the environment; although excessive degrees of activity can lead to destructive consequences, in general it seems that active children are more successful in achieving mastery partly because they come in contact with more aspects of the environment, are confronted with more choices, and have more opportunities to practice and develop different skills. A child's successful completion of activities is closely related to the sense of adequacy and self-worth and the capacity to gain respect from others.

With adults as with children, doing can lead to feelings of worth and satisfaction, to fuller awareness of one's self and one's impact upon the world, and to greater understanding of one's environment. In many important ways, action constitutes an essential instrument for learning, for development of one's reality-testing, and for self-actualization.

Many of the people who come to the attention of social workers reveal a limited capacity for reality-testing, a seeming inability to learn, a sense of helplessness and frustration in their efforts to act upon their environment, and a low degree of self-esteem. Often, their life situations and environmental pressures have launched them onto a path of despair and frustration leading to cumula-

tive failures and the dulling of their innate potentialities and creative strivings. In Bruno Bettelheim's terms (1971, pp. 68–78), they are human beings whose autonomy or ability to govern themselves has withered away through excessive external management of their affairs in a mass age.

In casework practice, it is with these persons in particular that action can be utilized as a means of providing opportunities for developing their identity, for exercising their often atrophied drive toward competence, and for turning the trajectory of their ego development toward a positive direction. In an increasingly mass-oriented society, human beings increasingly need to be meaningfully involved in purposeful activities in their own behalf.

Every social worker encounters cases in which opportunities for constructive action evolve naturally out of the client's situation.

> An institutionalized man in a psychiatric hospital finds that he can perform well in a work experience. An adolescent in a correctional setting is given the opportunity to channel leadership qualities into organizing leisure activities with peers. A troubled child in a public school experiences delight in completing a difficult assignment. An unwed pregnant woman plans temporary living and working experiences which keep her in the mainstream of active life rather than passively awaiting confinement.

CONDITIONS NECESSARY FOR EFFECTIVE ACTION

Action does not necessarily lead to constructive change; there is no simple, linear connection between engagement in action and achievement of desired results. The eventual outcome is dependent upon a variety of interacting variables or conditions.

Client's Readiness to Change

The worker needs to consider the client's readiness to undertake certain activities. Beyond the capacity to perform a given action, there must be some tension needing release and some motivation toward an objective of importance to the person. The tension and motivation can be expressed in different forms, such as anxiety, dissatisfaction with life,

---

[2] For an extensive analysis of the role of action from a psychoanalytic perspective, see Wheelis (1950).

guilt, or even a hopeless dream or a fanciful ambition.

The quantity and quality of the client's tension influence the timing of the activity. In some situations, an impulse-ridden person may need help in delaying action. In general, however, the timing of the activity should be geared to the person's spontaneity. Henry A. Murray and Clyde Kluckhohn (1953, p. 19) point out that human beings in our society are typically required by social commitments and role responsibilities to act, even when they are not truly ready, in order to integrate their actions with those of others. Although this pattern is functional in terms of survival and role relationships, it results in a loss or reduction of spontaneity.

Choice of Alternatives

Another necessary condition in the effective use of action is the opportunity for client consideration of alternative courses. This opportunity can help people to evaluate various possibilities, to test their readiness, and to choose the most appropriate alternative. Furthermore, the deliberative process can stimulate people's cognitive growth and mastery, mobilize their decision-making functions, and reinforce the sense of autonomy that comes from involvement in purposive activities consonant with their needs as well as societal requirements. The worker plays an important role through provision of information concerning the potential effects of the action, of feedback heightening the client's awareness of reality, and of support in taking a risk. Client-worker interaction becomes more meaningful and productive as both parties go through the process of reaching agreement on specific goals, tasks, and procedures.[3]

In considering alternative courses of action, it is useful to keep in mind the principle of equifinality derived from systems theory or the notion that the same result can be achieved through following diverse pathways. The provision of diverse opportunities for action may tap the individuals' potential to look at the world in novel ways and facilitate

the selection of the activity most suited to their personal method of coping and their particular drive for competence. People cope differently with similar life crises, and if workers understand the person's unique ways of coping and adapting, they will be better able to perceive prospective opportunities for action that may maximize the effective outcome of the client's struggle toward mastery.

> A child welfare practitioner described a pertinent experience with Jean, a blind 12-year-old girl placed in foster care following the death of her parents. When Jean was confronted with the impending demolition of her natural family's home owing to urban renewal, she urged the worker to take her on a final tour of the house. During this visit, Jean methodically touched everything in each room, climbed into the attic, played the piano, and ran repeatedly around the backyard. While alternately crying, laughing, talking, and pausing in silence, Jean recalled innumerable family experiences and vividly traced her family's history and her own development. In reliving the past in a spontaneous and active manner at a crucial point in her life, Jean was courageously bracing herself for the future.

Relevance

The relevance of the proposed activity to the client's life situation is a further determinant of its effectiveness. The action should be meaningfully related to the person's goal or problem as defined. In addition, it should be consonant with natural growth processes, lifestyle, significant life events, and developmental stage in the life cycle. Good opportunities for action are often missed because of excessive reliance on artificial or formal procedures such as the office interview. Practice could become more meaningful and rewarding if social workers would function more spontaneously in the natural surroundings of clients and thus discover and encourage their often dormant potentialities.

In this regard, Esther E. Twente (1965) poignantly describes the strengths and creativity shown by older clients in their own home or group activities: the retired farmer who gains pride and pleasure in seeing others enjoy his singing; the elderly woman who takes music lessons by correspondence and derives satisfaction from entertain-

---

[3] The client-worker contract can serve as a dynamic tool in the process of considering and selecting appropriate courses of action. See Maluccio and Marlow (1974).

ing her fellow residents of a nursing home; the 90-year-old widow who seeks fulfillment in her embroidery, gardening, and vase collection; and the many others in whom the creative urge finds rich expression as life draws to a close.

In a life-oriented model of practice, the worker need not carry the entire or even major responsibility in direct work with the client. A fundamental function of the worker is to identify and mobilize the energies of people and systems that are more directly and significantly involved in the client's own life space, such as resources in the immediate family, in the social network, or in the school or work settings. In some situations, the client-worker relationship will appropriately be the primary vehicle of help. In others, however, the effective use of action will occur through other people, with the worker playing indirect roles. The emphasis will be on utilizing the environment itself as a basic means of helping (Germain, 1973, p. 326).

Client's Participation

Another important condition for effective use of action is maximum participation by the client in the activity. Through its focus on the role of one's own action in personality development, ego psychology underscores the primacy of client tasks and reinforces the hierarchy of interventive strategies, which has served as a guiding principle in casework practice: Doing *for* the client → Doing *with* the client → Doing *by* the client.

Availability of Support Systems

Finally, a prerequisite for action is the availability of appropriate social systems and supports, of an environmental climate with varied opportunities for success and achievement. Following an extensive review of clinical and experimental findings in situations of social isolation and extreme stress, Stuart C. Miller (1962, p. 8) concluded that the maintenance of ego autonomy is strongly dependent on appropriate inputs or "stimulus nutriments" from the environment. In social work there is an increasing awareness of the validity of this conclusion and of the urgent need to develop social institutions and systems more conducive to human growth. There is emphasis on the importance of the worker's (and the profession's) participation in action designed to "socialize" services, to restructure inadequate or detrimental societal systems, and to contribute to the development of environmental conditions providing maximum opportunity for each person to grow, to establish identity, and to achieve an increasingly satisfying level of competence (Meyer, 1970). Action is one of the basic tools through which the client and worker can seek to modify and humanize the environment.

CONCLUSION

Action, informed by the insights of ego psychology, can become one of the more promising and fundamental features of a life-oriented casework practice. However, to exploit the potential inherent in its use, social workers need to devote more deliberate attention to action. Their rich experiences should be gathered and examined, so that more specific guidelines and principles can be derived and action can be moved closer to becoming an explicit component of practice theory.

Action should not be viewed as an exclusive or separate mode of treatment. In life there is normally no rigid dichotomy between action and thought or feeling and talking. Action is an integral part of the complex whole representing human behavior and social interaction. To be effectively used in casework practice, it must be creatively integrated with the emotional, cognitive, and perceptual components in each client's experiences.

*Helping Children with AIDS: The Role of the Child Welfare Worker**

Mary G. Boland, Mary Tasker, Patricia M. Evans, and Judith S. Keresztes

Tony seems to have everything going for him. Excellent job. Good marriage. Lovely wife. A smiling, energetic son, Andrew, now eighteen months old. His wife, Rita, is expecting their second child in just a month.

As he watches his son play, Tony's forehead shows worry lines. Andrew suffers frequent bouts of illness including pneumonia, diarrhea, and oral thrush. He has been treated and has recovered from each episode, but the illnesses recur.

Tony is a former heroin addict, and his life is about to be shattered when tests show Andrew has AIDS. He will not yet have recovered from the shock when he learns that both he and his wife are human immunodeficiency virus (HIV) positive.

A few months later he will find out his new baby daughter also is infected with the virus that causes AIDS.

Since the first cases of acquired immune deficiency syndrome (AIDS) in children were reported in 1983, over 349 cases like Andrew's have been diagnosed. Stunned and desperate for help, their parents are turning to every possible resource for help. Often they are being met with resistance, fear, and even rejection. As the number of pediatric AIDS cases grows, service providers will be challenged not only to meet the increased demands of such children and their families but also to muster the resources to provide help; to educate staff as well as clients about the disease; and to counter the ignorance, fear, and discrimination that can block the delivery of badly needed services.

Most cases of pediatric AIDS are due to perinatal transmission, and approximately 80 percent of the children come from families where one or both parents have AIDS or are at risk of contracting the disease. The majority of the mothers of children with AIDS have a history of intravenous drug use or sexual contact with drug users or bisexuals. (While the Centers for Disease Control holds that additional studies are needed to delineate the risk of transmission from an infected pregnant woman to the fetus, it is believed that the fetus contracts AIDS while in the womb.) The diagnosis of AIDS in a child automatically implies a positive antibody test result in the mother, and it is not uncommon to discover that both parents are HIV positive.

Sometimes more than one child is infected. In nearly all of the cases reported to date, the children have been diagnosed before they reached one year of age, with the average case discovered by the time the child is six months old. In New Jersey, where the incidence of AIDS in adults has been significant, infants who are frequently sick, have repeated infections, or who are not growing at a rate consistent with their age are now routinely tested for AIDS.

While testing infants for AIDS admittedly is an emotional and controversial issue, medical experts say the benefits outweigh the disadvantages. Because most parents of children with AIDS are asymptomatic, the experts note, early diagnosis can encourage doctors to treat the disease more aggressively. Families adopting children with AIDS need to be aware of the diagnosis as well. From the perspective of a placement agency, however, a diagnosis of AIDS can make it difficult, if not impossible, to place a child in a foster home or with adoptive parents.

FOSTER CARE

Approximately 25 percent of all children here in the Children's Hospital program are already in foster care prior to diagnosis of AIDS. In a few cases, parents are unable or unwilling to care for the child after a diagnosis is made, so the child must be placed in a foster care home. Identifying appropri-

*From "Helping Children with AIDS: The Role of the Child Welfare Worker," by M. G. Boland, M. Tasker, P. M. Evans, and J. S. Keresztes, 1987, *Public Welfare*, Winter, pp. 23-28. Copyright 1987 by the American Public Welfare Association. Reprinted by permission.

EXHIBIT Commonly Used Terms	AIDS (acquired immune deficiency syndrome)—an illness caused by the retrovirus HIV and characterized by one or more opportunistic infections that indicate underlying cellular immunodeficiency. ARC (AIDS-related complex)—a combination of physical problems, existing over time, that indicates infection of a person with HIV. Symptoms include fatigue, fever, weight loss, diarrhea, night sweats, and swollen lymph nodes. HIV (human immunodeficiency virus)—virus that causes AIDS. Previously called human T-lymphotropic virus type III (HTLV-III) or lymphadenopathy-associated virus (LAV).

---

ate foster care homes for these children is a problem that will only continue to grow as the number of children with AIDS increases. Seeking out and training parents willing to take them will require an aggressive approach on the part of agencies. Child welfare personnel who make placements need to be knowledgeable about transmission of the disease as well as understanding of the need to obtain homes for children. Their attitudes—positive and negative—can influence the eventual placements and their outcomes.

Foster parents require special assistance in dealing with all the issues surrounding AIDS. While the severity of HIV infection can vary, all children with AIDS require ongoing medical care. Foster parents need help in complying with the demands of medical care and assistance in navigating the health care system. The response of the community to the foster family must also be considered. A family may be willing to care for a child but be severely stressed by the ostracism and stigmatization that occur when the diagnosis becomes known. School entry is particularly difficult since it is almost impossible to keep the child's health information confidential. The agency needs to be able to provide a variety of supports to the family if the placement is to be successful.

OBTAINING SERVICES

The challenges of caring for children with AIDS and for their families are as complex as the disease itself. The illness forces both families and professionals to confront feelings regarding issues, such as drug use, lifestyle choices, civil liberties, discrimination, confidentiality, and care of the terminally ill. Resources are often limited, and professionals

must be well informed about services in their community. It is unrealistic to expect a family to travel one or two hours to a program that accepts AIDS clients because a similar program within their own community refuses to provide care. If agencies refuse to provide services, human services workers must be assertive and advocate for the client.

Unfortunately, discrimination against potential clients does occur. Public agencies as well as private companies have refused to assist children with AIDS; and laws, though being considered in some states, have not yet been passed to prevent such discrimination. Private ambulance companies, schools, and notably early intervention programs have been especially reluctant to accept AIDS victims. In these cases, an aggressive educational program can help overcome service providers' fears. Concealing the diagnosis may obtain short-term service for the individual child, but it does nothing to improve the accessibility of services for other children with AIDS.

Oftentimes, staff members have never been in contact with AIDS patients before and are not even aware of how the disease is transmitted. In these instances, the battle is against ignorance and fear; and it becomes the responsibility of the referring agency to help and support providers in order to gain their cooperation and ensure that services are properly delivered. Many providers are aware of their responsibility but are unsure of how to proceed. They often respond well to education and support. Ideally, such education should be offered *before* service providers are faced with their first AIDS client; but this usually is not the case.

Workers must ensure that clients continue to

receive those services they require, including health care, education, and transportation. It cannot be assumed that whenever referrals are made services are being provided. It is important to follow up and maintain contact with the referral agency. When cases are managed inappropriately, it is usually due to poor understanding of the disease process and unrealistic expectations regarding the child's cognitive and motor abilities. Everyone involved in the care of the child therefore needs to have a clear understanding of the social and medical needs. Cases need to be reviewed regularly to be sure that problems and care needs are not minimized because of real or perceived difficulties in obtaining services. Despite the implications of the diagnosis, the welfare of the child must remain the primary concern of the agency.

DEMANDS ON WORKERS

Workers also need to be aware of their own behavior as they deal with the child and family. Are they treating this family differently than others in their caseload? Taking longer than usual to make the first home visit? Managing the case through telephone contact? Minimizing the problems? These are signs that workers are finding AIDS a difficult issue to handle.

To be of assistance to the family, workers must be aware of their own feelings regarding the disease. Training and support must be available to all levels of staff regarding AIDS service delivery and the demands that involvement with AIDS clients will place on them.

Efforts that may help include:
education of managers and supervisors in ways to support their staffs,
formal training programs for staff members,
programs to identify staff at all levels who are willing to work with families with AIDS,
programs to train designated staff to serve as AIDS experts at all levels within the agency,
readily available written resource materials,
use of consultants with expertise in the health care for children with AIDS,
recruitment and training of foster parents willing to care for children with AIDS, and
support groups for workers and foster parents.

Workers' concerns regarding transmission of the virus are normal and should be expressed. They should not expect to be comfortable the first time a child with AIDS is added to their caseload. But they can take comfort from the fact that the only recorded means of HIV transmission is through blood, sexual contact, and perinatally from mother to infant; that an individual cannot contract the disease by being in the same room, using a telephone, transporting the patient, and so forth; and that, during routine contact in the office or home, there is no need to take any special precautions. If basic training on AIDS is not provided to human services workers, up-to-date resource material should be obtained for their review.

Once concerns over transmission have been resolved, workers may find that families require intervention in various areas. The uncertain outcome and high mortality rate of the disease, for instance, place stress on the family. The need for complex medical care requires that the worker contact health care providers and establish a relationship with them. This relationship should be ongoing and provide a source of information on how the family is dealing with the medical issues. Workers also may need to be present when the treatment plan is discussed. Often workers can function as advocates and assist parents in obtaining information and clarifying medical jargon. The social worker or nurse can be helpful in explaining the implications of medical information for home care. They also may be aware of what services are available in the community.

Because of the chronic nature of the disease, AIDS cases can remain active for years. In the absence of extended family supports, case workers and medical personnel often become surrogate family for the client. The family looks to workers not only for assistance in crises but also for help in solving the daily problems that occur in any family. Frequently, it is impossible to do all that is asked; yet, because of the stigmatization that has occurred in the past, workers may feel that they are responsible for solving all the family's problems. It is helpful to regularly evaluate the status of the relationship with the family to prevent overinvolvement by workers and loss of the therapeutic relationship.

Workers may have to be persistent to obtain services, such as transportation, respite care, babysitting, and home care. Because it is not unusual for an agency to refuse service to an AIDS client once the diagnosis is known, workers can feel frustrated, isolated, and even stigmatized themselves. If these feelings occur, it is important to remember this is a normal response and to seek support from colleagues—especially those who have worked with AIDS clients. Medical personnel are familiar with these feelings, and discussing them with the social worker of an AIDS treatment program may help.

FAMILY RESPONSE TO DIAGNOSIS

It is difficult to think of any other word that can produce the fear, panic, and shock that AIDS evokes. Hearing the diagnosis of AIDS in a child can precipitate such feelings of shock, disbelief, and grief as to initially immobilize parents' capacity to respond. Varying degrees of denial are almost universally experienced. Initial reactions of disbelief and a feeling that a mistake has been made are defense mechanisms frequently employed to cope with deeper feelings of grief and fear. The words of one parent, as she spoke of hearing her child's diagnosis for the first time, illustrate this point: "When the doctor told me my baby had AIDS, I couldn't seem to hear anything after he said that word. I knew he was still talking, but the words just couldn't get inside me."

The feelings of disbelief—of becoming impenetrable—act as a buffer, a kind of emotional time-out from the grief experience. Feelings of grief are closely associated with loss. Parents experience anticipatory grieving not only for feared loss of the child but also for the loss of hopes and dreams for the family's future. These feelings are compounded if other members of the family are later diagnosed as having AIDS.

Denial in one form or another by parents is a common response. It arises from the need to keep the effects within bearable limits during sudden life crises. It can be viewed normatively or pathologically depending on the extent to which it helps or hinders parents' ability to cope with the reality of the diagnosis.

The task of workers during this initial phase in dealing with the affective responses of parents is to communicate a sense of understanding, acceptance, and support for the family. During the period following the diagnosis, parents need time to readjust and regain their equilibrium before moving on to a more task-oriented phase. While feelings of disbelief, grief, guilt, and anger are common normative reactions to the diagnosis, parents also may develop anxieties that cause them to block out important information regarding their child's needs. Workers can help alleviate this anxiety by reassuring parents that they are not expected to retain all the information being given to them at this time and that there will be many opportunities to discuss the diagnosis and related issues.

Workers also can expect to see parents experiencing guilt when transmission occurs due to parental intravenous drug use. It may come as a surprise to workers, however, that these parents are not the only ones to feel guilt. A parent whose child contracted the disease due to a maternal blood transfusion related the following story:

> I once thought about becoming a Jehovah's Witness, but changed my mind because I thought their position of not believing in blood transfusions was foolish. Now I wish I had listened to their ideas; I would have saved my baby from all this.

Workers can help parents reduce guilt feelings by clarifying what the parent has or has not done. The experience with one particular mother may serve as an example.

Alan is a four-year-old child with a diagnosis of AIDS related complex (ARC), acquired perinatally from his mother, a former intravenous drug user. Following a lung biopsy, the child was transferred to the intensive care unit for monitoring and specialized care. After visiting the child, his mother was visibly shaken and began to sob. She expressed her deep sorrow and guilt that she "did this to him" by her past drug abuse. After allowing parents time to express these guilt feelings, workers can help them differentiate between causality and intention-ality. For example, workers can point out that, while past drug abuse led to being infected, it was never the *intent* of the parent to cause harm. At a later time, Alan's mother was able to tell the worker that this kind of reasoning had helped her to overcome almost debilitating guilt feelings:

> I know that this happened because of me, but I'm working hard at not blaming myself. If I'd known that doing drugs could have hurt my son, I'm sure I would never have done it. I have done a lot of bad things in my life, but I've always tried to be the best I could for my child. If I let myself get too down with guilt, I won't have enough energy to help my son now.

Though guilt feelings need to be expressed freely, the task for workers is to assist parents in going beyond these feelings, which, if not mastered, would become debilitating and foster feelings of powerlessness. In helping parents to resolve these internal conflicts, workers can strengthen parents' coping capacities and move clients in a constructive direction. If parents get locked into guilt and self-blame, conflict resolution can become destructive and lead to depression, renewed substance abuse, or emotional breakdown.

Though not all families handle crises in the same manner, it is important for workers to bear in mind that initial intervention efforts with such families will necessarily focus on alleviating the impact of this crisis-inducing stress and on helping to mobilize resources, both inner and outer, of those affected.

The major challenge will center on helping families develop coping strategies for daily living. Tasks for workers include counseling family members and linking them to needed resources and services.

As the initial shock and blocking-out responses give way to restored equilibrium and newly learned coping behaviors, parents will seek information about the etiology of the disease, risk factors, and treatment plans. It is at this point that workers should begin to offer skills, knowledge, and services to the parents in order to begin the process of crisis resolution.

In most cases of chronic illness, families may reasonably expect that loving and concerned support will be forthcoming from immediate family and close friends. Due to the fear and panic provoked by AIDS in the community at large, however, many parents opt not to disclose the diagnosis, thus limiting potential sources of emotional and concrete assistance. With regard to concrete services, workers will need to identify and assess the resource needs of the families.

CARE DEMANDS

The stress of medical care demands on families cannot be overstated, so there is a critical need for workers to actively intervene on behalf of families to achieve a good working relationship with medical personnel. Workers efforts should center on helping parents to master the health care system, perhaps beginning by encouraging parents to tell what they understand concerning the diagnosis and treatment regimen. In this way, workers often gain insights into parents' understanding of the diagnosis and their expectations concerning their child. Teaching parents to plan for future encounters with doctors when their own concerns can be raised is an invaluable way to have them establish an active, participatory relationship. Often workers will find that the barrage of information parents have tried to absorb is perceived as overwhelming. Workers can best help parents by breaking down the information into manageable units so that they do not develop feelings of powerlessness and inadequacy. Activity is a valuable weapon against feelings of powerlessness, which can lead to depression.

Parents often are unable to transport their children to services, yet private transportation companies may refuse to transport a child with AIDS. In these instances, the worker may need to identify physicians willing to give a secondary diagnosis so that such services may be obtained. Concurrently, workers need to actively communicate with alternative providers and volunteer groups that are sympathetic to the needs of AIDS patients in order to supplement these services.

Children with AIDS may be eligible for benefits under the Supplemental Security Income (SSI) program. Obtaining benefits can be made easier if

---

EXHIBIT Resources on AIDS and Children	*The Child with HIV Infection: A Guide for Parents* by Mary G. Boland *Diet Guidelines for the Child with Aids* by Mary G. Boland *The Chronically Ill Child: A Guide for Parents and Children* by Audrey T. McCollum *Special Rights for Special Children* by Education Law Center Also see "Explaining AIDS to Your Children" by Tom Shealey in the Spring 1986 issue of *Children,* published by Rodale Press.

---

parents are given a simple fact sheet outlining the step-by-step process for application. In addition, if workers assist parents in obtaining a letter confirming the diagnosis, submission of such documentation at the time of application may result in the granting of "presumptive" disability benefits. This would shorten the waiting time between the application and receipt of benefits.

Families who qualify for Aid to Families with Dependent Children (AFDC) or SSI can also qualify for the special supplemental food program for women, infants, and children (WIC). Since many WIC programs now operate from a hospital setting, workers can help families coordinate medical and WIC appointments on the same day.

In addition to meeting a child's therapy needs, early intervention programs usually offer parent support groups. These programs also give children the opportunity for peer group play. Where these programs are not available, workers may help families obtain needed therapy services in the home through the local Visiting Nurse Association.

TELLING THE CHILD

Parents may be at a loss to know what, how, and even whether to tell their child anything about the disease. Many parents believe the child is too young to understand and would only become anxious if they divulged too much information. Unfortunately for the child, this attitude all too frequently results in parents not telling the child anything at all. Not surprisingly, then, a child is subjected to the rigors of aggressive medical intervention with little more explanation than "It's to help you not get sick." The bewilderment, anger, and fear a child can experience in this situation can become a literal and metaphorical nightmare, as illustrated in the case of Charlie.

Charlie is a six year old who was hospitalized for chronic respiratory infections that were unresponsive to standard medications. His past medical history and recently obtained information concerning parental risk factors—a mother who is an active intravenous drug user—raised suspicions of possible HIV infection. Initial tests confirmed a positive antibody, and the child was worked up to determine the extent of his infection. Blood samples were drawn frequently from the child who became alternately fearful and withdrawn. During conversations with a social worker, the child revealed a nightmare: "Last night I dreamed I escaped from my [hospital] room and got out down the hall. Just then, I met the doctor and she turned into Dracula."

The Dracula dream was a clear indication of the child's fear of having blood taken from him. His use of the term "escaped" indicates not only a wish fantasy but also his sense of being trapped, imprisoned, and, conceivably, punished. Subsequent conversations with his aunt, his legal guardian, revealed that while the child was told he was sick, he was given little explanation of why his blood was being taken.

Workers can help parents in these situations by modeling ways of communicating information to the child in order to reduce the child's anxiety. The child's emotional and cognitive state of development must be taken into consideration when explanations are given. Experts in child development can be asked for advice regarding the amount and quality of information to be given to the child. These efforts are best facilitated by discussing the need for this kind of interchange, first with parents or caregivers and then with the child's medical team. Sharing knowledge in this way can help children cope better with their questions and fears and develop deeper trust with the adults responsible for their care and well-being.

Talking to children about their conditions and anticipating their questions can reduce their anxiety. For young children, words alone are not effective in helping them deal with the stresses of related medical care. Because words are abstract substitutes for physical behavior, they tend to be less meaningful to children than are actions. Providing children with the opportunity to act out the fears that adults master through verbal expression is a critical part of intervention.

Play is the most natural method of self-healing that childhood affords, and play-therapy permits children to act out unconscious conflicts and fantasies. Toy medical kits, male and female dolls that can represent parents, nurse and doctor dolls, baby dolls with bottles and diapers, and toy baby blankets and cribs are useful to children in reconstructing real situations. Thus, in play, children can begin expressing the very real fears and hurts of stressful treatment. In addition to giving children a way to work through unconscious feelings, the play-therapy setting may encourage them to act out more conscious fears or angers that are often imitative of adults. This activity can provide workers with insights into areas where intervention efforts may be necessary.

DEALING WITH DEATH AND DYING

Because of the extremely high mortality rate associated with AIDS, workers will need to deal with issues of death and dying. Throughout the course of the illness, workers' primary focus will be on helping families develop coping strategies for daily living. When the family becomes aware that a child's death is imminent, feelings of anger, guilt, and grief will occur—and again, perhaps more strongly, feelings of denial. It should be remembered that not all families will experience all of these reactions in the same order or to the same degree. There is a danger that workers will try to "march" families through these stages and fail to see each family as individual and unique. Families will respond to workers who deal calmly and clearly with events as they happen and who help them to focus on problems as they arise.

A primary concern of many parents is that their child be free from pain. Workers can facilitate communication between parents and medical care providers so that these concerns can be expressed and responded to. Parents need to feel that they have input in decisions affecting the final stage of the child's life. If the child is hospitalized, every effort should be made to arrange for parents to be with the child at the time of death. If death occurs suddenly and the parents are not present, their two main concerns will most likely be "Was my child in pain?" and "Was my child afraid?"

After the child has died, the worker will need to help the family through the grieving process. It is important to remember that families often need concrete assistance, such as making funeral arrangements, in addition to emotional support and counseling. In the months after death, follow-up visits and regular telephone calls let families know help is still available. Referrals to bereaved parent support groups and counseling services can help parents deal with their grief.

Children with AIDS and their families present tremendous challenges to human services agencies and workers. While dealing with these children can be stressful, successfully meeting the emotional and concrete service needs of these families can be rewarding. The multiple problems produced by AIDS require a high degree of collaborative and cooperative efforts among agencies, workers, and families. These efforts can create a climate of common cause and purpose that in turn can generate feelings of mutual regard, trust, and intimacy between worker and family. Ultimately, these feelings of standing together before a common foe can sustain the worker-family relationship throughout the course of the illness and beyond.

Rural Social Work Practice: Clinical Quality*

M. Ellen Walsh

The literature on rural mental health practice is replete with descriptions of community values, techniques for community outreach and program development, and delineations of barriers to effective service delivery. According to a recent literature review done for the National Institute of Mental Health, however, "There is little especially pertinent to rural settings on the specifics of treatment apart from total program description" (Flax et al., 1979, p. 50).

This article will describe several characteristics of a model for delivery of clinical service to rural clientele. The effectiveness of these qualities of clinical practice is based upon the author's personal experience as a therapist in several rural communities, discussions with other rural-based clinical practitioners in the area, and the literature. By and large, generalizations drawn relate to a rural clientele at local mental health center outstations in five rural communities in Washington. Requests for service were self-initiated, frequently following a word-of-mouth referral from a former mental health center client. Local employment in these communities is primarily in the logging industry or in agriculture, although in other respects (size, availability of services, remoteness) the communities varied widely. There were slightly more female than male clients. Extensive prior footwork, including public relations work and relationship building, had been undertaken by the mental health center for the past five years.

There are many difficulties inherent in initiating mental health services in a rural area; however, they will not be addressed at length in this article (Cedar & Salasin, 1979). A successful program development strategy is a necessary prelude to the kind of clinical intervention delineated here. This article does not intend to propose specific techniques or modalities, but will characterize a practice stance or clinical style that can be adapted to fit a broad range of intervention modalities. A style that reflects authenticity, attention to the subtleties of hierarchy in the treatment relationship, and frank respect for the client is particularly well-suited to a rural population.

ELEMENTS OF CLINICAL STYLE

There is no question that an attempt to apply certain treatment modalities to a rural population will involve stretching the classical models to some extent. Successful social work practitioners in rural areas are both versatile and flexible in clinical treatment and do not tend to be rigid adherents of any specific treatment modality. Rural clinical treatment requires a clinician whose practice stance does not rule out transparency as a concept (Rogers, 1961, p. 67). Lack of anonymity for the professional in a rural area has been documented repeatedly (Bischoff, 1976, p. 8; Solomon, 1980), and clients who encounter their therapist at the cafe, the post office, and community gatherings of various sorts are apt to be acutely sensitive to differences in personal style between these gatherings and the treatment session. A clinician's willingness to behave in an authentically personal way with clients during the treatment session is an especially useful quality of practice in communities that place a high value on integrity and self-sufficiency. The clinician whose personal maturity and self-understanding does not lead him or her to have any large investment in identifying with the "mystique" of the "therapist" will, therefore, fare better in rural practice. The flavor of some of the literature on community organization for social workers in rural areas is reflected in this statement by Jim Morrison: "Other characteristics that rural community organizers would do well to possess are the ability to reject ideology, a sense of humor . . . and the capacity to work authentically" (Morrison, 1976, p. 60).

*Reprinted with permission of author and Families International, Inc., from Social Casework, October 1981.

The oft-described emphasis on self-sufficiency, personal responsibility, and self-determination in the rural community value system lends a certain bonus to the work of the clinical practitioner in these areas (Cedar & Salasin, 1979). That is, unlike many of their urban counterparts who are looking for a wizard/witch doctor in their therapist, rural clients are more likely to accept the concept of personal responsibility for change, and are more prepared for that inevitable moment in treatment when a client is faced with the realization that there is no magic dust at the therapist's fingertips. Although these are generalizations about client value systems and sensitivity to particular qualities of treatment, it is important to keep in mind that these are modal characteristics. As in any large population, there is great variation in individual makeup and flavor, and every rural client will not embody the self-reliance and sensitivity to inauthenticity reported here.

DANGERS OF CLASSISM

There are dangers of classism, real or perceived, on the part of the therapist in rural settings; and it is helpful to develop a perspective for understanding class sensitivity. Richard Sennett and Jonathan Cobb refer to class prejudice as "inferring a man's dignity from his social standing," and propose that "lower" or "working" class persons experience a "subordination in social position . . . as the result of circumstances of birth and class" (Sennett & Cobb, 1972, pp. 251, 119). Milton Mazer differentiates between values of middle-class American life and rural values, which tend to be more traditional (Mazer, 1976, p. 25). Mazer describes a dilemma faced by rural populations which he dubs "value-inconsistency." That is, a population with a deeply felt traditional value system is confronted daily with an alternate (often oppositional) set of assumed values via the media. Most television, radio, and advertising reflect an urban value stance that is a far cry from the principles rural communities hold dear (Mazer, 1976, p. 25). Hence, there is a preestablished "we versus them" (Reul, 1974) notion in the minds of rural dwellers. Sennett and Cobb perceive this dynamic as a byproduct of a "contest for dignity." "If you are a working class

person, if you have had to spend year after year being treated by people of a higher class as though there probably is little unusual or special about you to catch their attention . . . then to try to impugn the dignity of persons in a higher class becomes . . . an affirmation of your own claims for respect." (Sennett & Cobb, 1972, p. 148).

These reflections on urban class conflict shed some light on rural dwellers' perceptions of formally educated "city slickers," a stereotype that all too frequently includes mental health professionals. Perhaps in view of this backdrop, the rural clientele's acute sensitivity to classism will begin to make sense.

A therapist in a rural area will be more quickly effective, and will be more apt to reduce the likelihood of perceived classism, if he or she is particularly careful to use the client's own clichés and stock phrases in treatment, with perhaps a parenthetical "as you call it," or "as you say." Using even minimal professional jargon may ruin an otherwise potentially significant educational intervention technique. Translating sophisticated models into rural idiom requires a sound conceptual familiarity with the material being presented. Also, rural people are by and large people of few words. Their use of language is sparse, and frequently short phrases or single words suffice to communicate. In the interests of presenting the client with a style of communication that is familiar, rural clinicians should follow suit.

PACING

Pacing is another interesting variable of rural clinical work. Rural clients are apt to offer highly charged new information almost in passing, as though there is nothing special about this material. It is particularly important that the therapist not "jump" on these new hints, but rather to note the revelations and allow several minutes to pass before alluding to them. In so doing the therapist may gather more peripheral information than would have been revealed had he or she explored it immediately. It is difficult to analyze the rural client's apparent preference for a moderate pace to explore sensitive data, but it may correspond to the slower pace of rural life. The therapist should allow several minutes to pass before responding to this new information. The rural client places a high value on the time the therapist spent in reflection on the new information and is more convinced of acceptance than if he or she had hurried.

AUTHENTIC PRESENTATION

A willingness to present oneself authentically has many implications for rural treatment. Most rural clients have a fine-tuned sensitivity to dishonesty and incongruency. New rural practitioners should ask themselves throughout the treatment session, "Do I really mean it? Am I telling the truth?" For example, when presented with a complex monologue by a client, a rural practitioner needs to be especially careful not to feign understanding to "facilitate the flow." Even a less-simulated assumed "understanding" has its dangers. Rural clients are, at some level, acutely aware of the particularly unique, rich, and complex nature of their personal experience. Making evident the struggle to comprehend posture and facial expression is frequently a potent intervention. This obvious attention bespeaks a basic awareness of the uniqueness of the client and mitigates against a self-perception (by the therapist) of professional omnipotence (which a rural client is apt to regard as one-upmanship in any event).

ATTENTION TO PARAPHRASING

Rural clients are likely to react to a perceived conventionalization of emotions in paraphrasing and attempted normalization of client behavior and experience. For example, in the following situation Maggie, the client, says "We've been through this kind of thing before, Jim and I, three or four times. The other women are always much younger, and I imagine they're very beautiful. I'm working all day harvesting and canning — putting up the apricots this week — and he's being seduced by these women who actually have time to file their nails and wear shiny polish! He mentioned that last week, that she'd been wearing polish. How can I compete with that? Yeah, he's always sorry, and he always tells me about it, and it's always a one-shot deal, but I'm beginning to feel like a tired old rag."

The therapist would be ill-advised to respond with such a phrase as: "It sounds like you're experiencing some jealousy, Maggie." Special attention needs to be paid to avoid use of jargon and the subsuming of reported emotion into a stock word or phrase (other than that of the client). There is a price to be paid for such "tidying up" of material presented by the rural client.

POINTING OUT AMBIVALENCE

Another general characteristic of the rural client is that he or she is more apt than the generally better-educated, more well-read urban client to present to the therapist a one-dimensional picture of him- or herself. That is, this kind of client is more apt to disown the alternate side of the ambivalence when experiencing conflicting feelings in a given area. Therefore, with rural clients therapists must be particularly careful to avoid referring to or presenting the missing side of the ambivalence. For example, if a rural client is currently denying his concerns about the effect his aging will have on continued employment in the logging industry, it may be better for the therapist to lean *with* him toward his described *lack* of concern, adding a millimeter of emphasis in that direction, and wait for the client to balance the scales for himself. Thus, the therapist, rather than parading his or her intuitive prowess and mobilizing an already cautious defense system, gives the client an opportunity to portray the other side of the ambivalence himself. For example:

Client: I've always been a good breadwinner. Colleen and the kids have never wanted for anything important.

Therapist: Your family sounds like it's always been able to count on you, George.

Client: And it has. It has counted on me. Been dependable that way. [Silence.] And the company's been a good place to work. Boss knows what I'm worth to 'im. Paycheck's always on time. I work as fast as I ever did. Be hard for 'em to replace somebody who knows as much about the business as I do. Good company it is.

Therapist: Your family relies on you and you rely on the company. Sounds like the company is an excellent place to be working, George. Sounds like they always stick by their workers, never let you down. You know that's unusual these days, workin' a place that holds to its own every time like that. Must make you real comfortable being there.

Client: Yeah. Good job. [Silence.] I've always said.

Therapist: Good to hear about, George. A place everybody can feel fine about.

Client: Well now, it's not perfect, though. Tom Rutger got the ax a couple years back.

Although not always effective, this technique frequently hits paydirt with rural clients. They do not want to leave the therapist with *too* much of a misimpression.

CAREFUL INTERPRETATION

Another helpful attitude in rural practice is tentativeness in material presented to the client relating to assessment. Rural clients will more likely than not regard interpretation as infringement. As previously stated, they are very alert to issues of classism and one-upmanship on the part of the therapist, and, correspondingly, are very responsive to perceived respect and genuine appreciation of them by the therapist. When it is impossible to resist sharing a potentially accurate assessment or explanation of behavior with a rural client, the therapist can state it with hesitant carefulness. For example, "Hey, you know, this notion just flew across the back of my mind, and I guess I may as well check it out with you . . . " or "I'm just fishing here, and I know it, but . . . Do you suppose that's a possibility?"

A variation on this sensitivity to disrespect is many a rural client's quick reaction to overnurturance by a therapist. They will not comment on this, but at some level aware of the ultimately patronizing quality of overinvolvement by a professional, they simply will not return for treatment. To harbor vestiges of an "under-my-wing" attitude toward a client is a message that the therapist does not view the client as a whole, complete person with adequate resources and capabilities to deal with the struggles at hand. To comment on such a

basic tenet of social work practice may appear superfluous, yet clinical work in rural areas can lead one to an awareness of more and more subtle indices of underlying attitudes on the part of therapists. Absolute separateness on the part of the therapist portrays a respect for the client's aloneness which is invaluable in work with a rural population.

Therapists must take special care to avoid the temptation to steer the interview with rural clients, unless the therapist has elicited a clear indication from the clients that they are indeed willing to explore a given area in greater depth. This permission can be in the form of an informal contract, and may be a simple "Would it be all right with you, Louise, if we talked a little further about your mom's illness?" or, "Can we slow down and look at that a moment, Ralph?" Rural clients will usually tell the therapist if they do not care to do so, and should this be the case, the therapist has at least indicated a willingness to tackle a sensitive area at such time as the client is prepared to do so. Steering without contracting, then, becomes an acceptance issue in work with rural clients.

OWNING

As an overall stylistic emphasis in rural work, there is perhaps nothing as powerful as authenticity, as previously mentioned. "Owning" is magic with most of these clients, and a therapist who easily acknowledges his or her momentary confusion, ambivalence, or lack of familiarity with the subject at hand quickly wins the respect of a client population which places a high value on individual rights and self-assuredness. Nondefensive "owning," besides being an accurate representation of oneself at a given moment, is good modeling. This style is especially helpful to the professional new to a particular rural community, who will be encountering many references to a community history with which he or she is as yet unfamiliar.

Leon Ginsberg (1976) states, "Many of the things that happen may be based upon little remembered but enduringly important family conflicts, church schisms, and crimes. It may require months of investigation before a newcomer in a rural area fully understands" (p. 6).

"Owning" extends as well to the area of clinical faux pas. Should a client's storytelling send a therapist into a couple of minutes of personal reflection, it is recommended that he or she admit this interruption to the client. For example, "Excuse me, Frank. What you were saying made me think of something else that's going on, and I haven't been paying close attention for a minute, here. Can you go over that again? I was with you up to the point where you said Jan had no business interfering with the kids."

Despite most therapists' fears of revealing such incidents, rural clients are probably aware of these lapses anyhow, and the admission wins respect for its honesty and may relieve the client to some degree ("Hmm. Everyone's attention flags from time to time. But *this* person is actually going to let me know when that happens! They don't want to miss anything. They are genuinely interested in me.")

Comfort with self-revelation of this type can be acquired, and a willingness to expose oneself personally can have far-reaching effects on the treatment process with rural clients. One of the more obvious indicators of its efficacy is the apparent influence it has on duration of treatment; perhaps as a result of the increased trust that such styles of "leveling" can elicit. Attention to this point has led to a practice stance with rural clients which involves the therapist divulging personal internalized processes at selected moments during the session, either to check out an intuitive perception, or to highlight a treatment issue. For example, "Carol, there's something I want to tell you. I notice that whenever you talk about your huge fights with Marv—the big ones, where you're afraid he might fire you, when you're telling me what you say to him, I get this uneasy feeling inside. Like part of me just finds itself wondering if you're really telling me the whole story, or something. Not that I believe you're lying, I just get a strange feeling in the back of my mind, so I guess I should ask you if you know what I might be reacting to."

If a client in this type of interaction does not acknowledge awareness of peripheral issues influencing such an experience, the therapist can say something like, "Well, perhaps it's got more to do with me than it does with you. I just wanted to let you know about it. I don't like having things like that going across my mind without checking them out."

TRADITIONAL VALUES AND ROLES

Expressing Emotions

A final area of comment on rural clinical practice is related to traditional family values and role orientations. The rural male client, for example, will tend to have a negative self-outlook on crying, while other means of discharging strongly felt emotions (that is, chopping wood, shouting) are seen as both allowable and occasionally necessary. Male clients are used here with the awareness that tears are not thought to be "manly," however, this flavor of tears fiercely held in (and self-respect linked somehow to this restraint) can be found in rural females as well. Perhaps it bespeaks a "strong people don't cry," or a "grownups don't cry" value that overlays the more obvious sex-role identification.

Therapists in rural areas must develop some style of practice to use during those moments when a rural male client is close to tears. It may be preferable to discuss this issue at some time early in treatment when tears are not close to the surface. The subject of crying can be framed as a natural healing process which discharges distress. This reframing can be done in a casual manner with few words. For instance, if a rural client is feeling the therapist out with a teaser on the subject while recounting history: " . . . and Ted shed a tear over that incident, I can tell you." The therapist can reply, "Well, you know, they say you *see* things more clearly after a good cry." If a man is close to tears the therapist can give him concerned attention, and occasionally hand him a tissue by way of encouragement. Tears are a delicate matter with the rural man because too *much* focus will tend to close him up in the interest of self-protection. It is necessary for the therapist to maintain a clear and well-conveyed respect for the client throughout the period of strong emotion, and to avoid anything that looks like overnurturance. A simple "Go ahead, Frank, it's a good idea," or "Go on, Frank, it's good for you," is all the therapist need say. After a crying incident there are generally opportunities to address the subject further:

Client: I'm sorry. I'm sorry. Hate to cry. Damn kid.

Therapist: Ah, Frank. Way I look at it, we need a good cry, time to time. Keeps us from exploding.

Client: Makes me feel so goddamn weak.

Therapist: Makes all of us feel kind of tired and open, after a cry. But you know, Frank, they say it's a good idea to let it out, now and then. And they say when you're all through crying, if you go back and look at what started you off to begin with, you'll see it clearer, somehow. Look at it a little different, more accurately.

Exaggerated Verbal Anger

The verbal expression of anger by rural male clients will also fit the classic sex-role stereotype of the aggressive male. A combative, aggressive, intimidating verbal expression ("I'm going to shoot that so and so if he comes into the store again!" or "I'll burn the place down before I let him get it!") is the norm, and is usually merely a style of communication. Generally speaking, it is not to be taken literally. It is a means of communicating how upset the client is. It is not, however, out of line for a therapist to check on the matter. There is usually no need for subjective alarm on the part of the therapist; the appropriate move is toward the feeling content of the expression rather than to literal interpretation of it.

Using Familiar Terms

One clinical advantage of traditional family role orientation is illustrated by the female client who takes care of a husband and family wholeheartedly while ignoring many of her own personal needs and refusing to look at her own vulnerability. Whatever the presenting problem, should this kind of picture appear, the therapist need not go into any sophisticated, intellectualized rationales for self-care. The preexisting role orientation gives the therapist a whole language with which to access the resources and capabilities within the client. For example:

Therapist: Ah, Marilyn, sounds to me like you're being an excellent mother to everyone but Marilyn.

Client: What do you mean?

Therapist: I mean it seems like everyone around you except you has someone being a real good mother to them. You could use a little of that yourself, Marilyn.

Client: Think I need someone like a mother to take care of me?

Therapist: Marilyn, what if you were your own mother right now? Not your real mom. I mean, the part of *you* that is a mom. The mother inside of you. And this other part of you, the part that's been hurting so much lately, needed some comfort and some words of wisdom. What would you tell yourself?

Client: I don't usually think of it that way.

Therapist: You mean, think of being your own kid, like that?

This approach can work very effectively with rural clients. Although usually taken aback by the notion of being a "good mother" to themselves (that is, initiating self-care behaviors), they are familiar with the concept through *family* terminology, and they know where to look for those resources and skills. Therapists should try to use family terminology to get their point across, whenever it fits, with rural clientele.

EXCELLENCE THE KEYSTONE

Clinical work is an aspect of rural social work practice that is inextricably linked to other areas of practice such as community development, program planning, outreach, and consultation. It is the keystone of rural practice. One's professional reputation, referrals, and perceived dependability and expertise flow from high-quality clinical work. When a practitioner is making a fund raising plea to a town council, and is linked clinically in various ways with several members of the council (for example, the wife of one an ex-client, an adolescent son of another a current client), clinical excellence will come into play in fund raising. If the town is very small, a clinician will find that reputable citizens discuss the quality of their clinical interventions and listen closely to friends who have had reason to develop an opinion about them.

The flavor of rural America is distinctive enough to point toward some uniquely applicable qualities of clinical work. Clinical models derived from rural practice transfer well into urban work, although, the converse generally is not true. Rural practice grooms a therapist for increased authenticity, attention to subtleties of hierarchy in the treatment relationship, and genuine respect for the client. These qualities fare well in any area of clinical practice. Although he was not referring to it,

Sheldon Kopp captured the crux of rural clinical work very well: "The humanistic therapist meets the man he tries to help as one risking human being to another" (Kopp, 1971, p. 15).

Rural clients expect that kind of bareness between themselves and anyone to whom they reveal themselves intimately, including a therapist. They are not overly fond of affection, even if it be in the interests of maintaining a "professional" facade. One's professionalism becomes evident in the integrity with which one behaves, rather than in any more classic role enactment.

For Further Reading

Allen-Meares, P., & Lane, B. A. (1987). Grounding social work practice in theory. *Social Casework,* 515–521.

Attneave, C. L. (1979). Therapy in tribal settings and urban network intervention. *Family Processes, 8*(2), 192–210.

Martinez-Brawley, E. E. (1986). Beyond cracker-barrel images: The rural social work speciality. *Social Casework, 67*(2), 101–107.

McGowan, B. G. (1973). *Case advocacy: A study of the interventive process in child advocacy.* New York: Columbia University School of Social Work.

Chapter 14

Teamwork for Social Work Practice

This chapter moves from a focus on the client system and the change agent system that have been the center of the discussion throughout most of this book to consider other systems that involve the social worker. The focus is now on the principles of constructing and working within a particular type of action system—the professional team. You will be involved in many other types of action systems, but teams are such an important part of social work that we believe a chapter should be devoted to the principles of building and using teams.

You will often become aware that members of a client system are also being served by other helping institutions of the community. In the role of broker (see Chapter 12), you become aware of the need to link clients with various services they may require but cannot supply. A service you are able to offer, such as the care of children away from their homes, may require you to become part of a team to supply that service effectively. John Compher, in Reading 14-1, identifies some of the harmful effects on individuals and families when social workers from different agencies do not work together as a team. One important skill of social work practice is the capacity to operate as a productive member of a service team with members from different agencies and/or different professions.

There is another aspect of teamwork that may be even more difficult to understand. This involves teams composed of individual social workers representing a wide variety of agencies, who are brought together on an ad hoc basis to operate cooperatively in the interests of a particular client system. The members of this type of team can also be considered as making up an action system. These teams differ from others in that there is no one sanctioning authority to make assignments or evaluate performance. Instead each member represents and is responsible to a different authority. Time allocated for defining the problem, establishing working relationships, and performing the tasks may be extremely brief, and pressures to come up with a quick and simple answer are often great.

Types of Teams

Your work to implement intervention plans may involve you in working jointly as a member or leader of several different types of teams. You may be meeting and working collaboratively with social workers from your own agency, you may be meeting to coordinate services with social workers from other agencies, you may be working with members of other disciplines, and you may be working with what we call *indigenous helpers* (some use the term *paraprofessionals*). Exhibit 14-1 presents a typology of the different types of teams in which you may be functioning.

EXHIBIT 14-1 A Typology of Teams	WITHIN YOUR ORGANIZATION (INTRAAGENCY)	WITH OTHER ORGANIZATION (INTERAGENCY)
Social Work Team	**Type A** *Example:* Foster care worker and adoption worker from the same agency work together to develop and implement permanent plan for child in foster care.	**Type B** *Example:* Child protection worker, school social worker, and probation officer meet regularly to coordinate services for a family in which youth behavior problems relate to a pattern of intrafamily abuse.
Interdisciplinary	**Type C** *Example*: Hospital social worker, nurse, doctor, and physical therapist meet to coordinate discharge plan for a client-patient.	**Type D** *Example:* Public health nurse, adult protection worker, and senior citizen center worker meet to develop a protection and activity plan for a vulnerable older person living alone.
With Indigenous Helper	**Type E** *Example:* Social worker and foster parent develop service plan for youth in care.	**Type F** *Example:* Social worker and Parents Anonymous mutual aid group work to provide mutual aid and support to parents who under stress may abuse their children.

When we think of teams, we often think of interdisciplinary teams such as those formed in a hospital when members of different professions meet to coordinate services for a client-patient. Or we may think of teams as consisting of members of the same profession, as when social workers representing different agencies meet to coordinate services to a family. We will be broadening the team concept to include two additional types of teams. Exhibit 14-1 identifies the type E team as the team in which a social worker is working within his or her own agency with indigenous helpers, or paraprofessionals. Examples of this are the social worker working with the foster parent or working collaboratively with agency volunteers. Another type of team, type F, involves collaboration between the social worker and self-help or mutual aid groups. The emergence of thousands of mutual aid groups creates an unusual opportunity for social work collaboration with these organizations. In this chapter we will be examining the strengths and problems for the social worker functioning as a member of interdisciplinary (types A and B) and multidisciplinary (types C and D) teams; we will be looking at ways in which you can function effectively in work with indigenous helpers; and we will be examining the potential for cooperative arrangements between social workers and mutual aid groups. Our look at teamwork will include discussion of the problem of competition, the problem of professional and agency culture, the problem solving approach to teamwork, and methods of planning and sharing.

**Intrapro-
fessional and
Interdisci-
plinary
Teams**

For much of its history social work has been concerned with the fragmentation of helping services. Usually this concern has focused on the costliness of such fragmentation to the community rather than on the problems such service creates for the client. There have been periodic efforts to establish methods of collaboration between the various social agencies of the community. In the early 1900s, with Cabot's employment of social workers in the hospital setting, the problem of collaboration across professional lines was introduced. One of the authors, as a part of a community effort to examine the impact on clients of the fragmentation of social work services, asked a client whether it would be easier for her if she had to deal with only one practitioner rather than several. The client thought a moment and said, "I don't know. I think maybe I can use more than one because they are there for different purposes; for example, the county welfare worker is there to tell me how to spend money and the Catholic Social Services to console me." This client had reconciled a difference between services into a consistent pattern of living that we professionals often have not been able or willing to attain.

In spite of periodic efforts to establish better collaboration, relatively little progress has been made in understanding the ways in which professionals do or do not work together. As a social worker, you may spend as much as 25% or 30% of your time in dealing with other professions, not counting lunch and coffee breaks. John Compher points out (Reading 14-1) that without effective teamwork and collaboration, clients and families in the social service system are caught in a nightmarish fragmentation of care. Multiple talents and inputs, no matter how skillful from the view of the professional, become burdensome rather than helpful when families and clients are left alone to resolve professional conflicts, reconcile incongruities, and deal with contradictory advice.

Obstacles to Effective Teamwork   Teamwork is essential, yet we are often reluctant to get involved in learning teamwork skills. A story is told about a man who was crossing the street and was hit by a truck; some people passing by rushed over to see if they could help. Lo and behold, they saw the man crawling away as fast as he could on hands and one knee, dragging one leg helplessly. They said, "Where are you going? Don't you realize that you have just been hit by a truck? You need help."

The man replied, "Please leave me alone. I don't want to get involved."

Like the man, social workers are often reluctant to get involved in teamwork and interdisciplinary collaboration. Social workers are active players. The sense of satisfaction with what we do as well as our frustrations will be affected by how well we are able to participate. Our participation in helping each other to deliver services is as important as direct contact with our clients. In fact, our direct contact with clients will be helpful only if we can effectively use teamwork. If all these things are true, why is it that we have such trouble in working across professional lines? What are some obstacles to effective collaboration?

The first obstacle is the myth that all that is required is a spirit of cooperation. Who will define himself or herself as uncooperative? We may naively assume that since we are friendly, outgoing, and thoughtful of others that good interdisciplinary collaboration will follow us all the days of our lives and we will dwell in peaceful work situations the rest of our professional lives. There are two erroneous notions that feed this. One is that anyone can get along with others, and thus this is not a professional skill. The second is that teamwork rests totally on personality variables, and thus there is no need to pay attention to specific knowledge or skills. While personality dimensions are important, we are lost if we reduce the collaborative processes to psychological dimensions alone. We must resist the tendency, only too prevalent among the psychologically sophisticated, to handle our frustrations in dealing with others by assigning unconscious malevolent motivations to those others. That is too easy and leaves us too pure. However, there is one psychological factor that we may have to take into consideration. That factor is the tendency to resist difference, to see and evaluate difference in terms of right and wrong, to assume that if something is different from something else, then one must be preferable to the other. If this is so, the right must be of more value than the wrong. There is a further tendency, when the difference is among individuals, to assign less valuable qualities to the different one, such as impulsiveness, softness, and so forth. Teamwork requires an openness to difference of view and opinion, ease with conflict, and a willingness to enter into negotiations to resolve the differences or structure working relationships that accept the legitimacy of differences.

A second obstacle to effective collaboration is the feeling of helplessness in the face of the authority of another person or profession. Social workers complain of this in almost all secondary settings in which they work. The central message in such complaints is that there is nothing to be done to influence the course of things with such limited power. You must come to grips with your conception of power and authority if you are to work collaboratively. First, remember that if you see yourself as powerless, you are truly without power. If you say you can't do something, you can't. You can effectively carry out only something that you believe possible. Also remember that there are two types of authority—the authority of position and the authority of competence. The authority of competence is granted by your colleagues, by those with whom you interact each day. Thus, when you see a colleague as having more authority than you do, remember that you have given him or her a part of this authority. Allot yourself a certain authority. All professionals need power and authority—the power and authority to help—for effective helping requires these qualities. You must be willing to allocate to other professionals the authority that is necessary to carry out the responsibilities that are allocated to them, but you must retain the authority and power you need to carry out your job. Social workers may tend to underestimate their power vis-à-vis other professions. One reason may be, paradoxically, the desire to be omnipotent. Some social workers, unable to solve a problem that has plagued people for a generation, feel like failures. Your expectations should be more realistic.

The third obstacle has to do with the definition of the parameters of the profession. It is inevitable that professionals charged with working with individuals and their relationships will have areas of overlap, certain tasks that either professional could do. These areas may have to be negotiated around individuals' situations and can be effectively handled in this way. However, conflict over who does what often causes bitter feelings and raises barriers to collaboration. There is a tendency for the representatives of each profession to see their turf as being the village green and other professions as occupying only individual plots of ground. This has been a problem for social work: having poorly defined parameters, social workers often tend to see their function as all-encompassing. And there are some professionals who deny difference altogether, saying, "Any member of the staff can deal effectively with any problems." Workers should work on defining areas of overlap as well as areas of special competence. A dimension of collaborative skill for social workers, as well as for members of other professions, is the ability to engage in role negotiation: to be able to identify what the social worker has and does not have sanction for, to broaden the sanction appropriately, and to bargain for turf, especially when other professionals may have some claim to some of the same territory.

A fourth obstacle to working in a focused way on collaboration has to do with the nature of a profession. Knowledge of human beings, of the nature of growth and development, of the genesis of human problems, of the forces that keep problems in place is overwhelming and sometimes contradictory. Most of it is not generated by professionals but is borrowed from the more basic disciplines. Each profession borrows the knowledge most closely related to its function and best supporting the methods of practice that it has developed. Such knowledge is then integrated into a usable whole. The result of such a process is that each professional is educated to operate from a different conception of human nature, of human conduct, with different beliefs, assumptions, and expectations about people, what and how they act and conduct their human relationships. Each profession develops different styles of communication and methods of problem solving, especially data collection. Each profession has a different notion of what is effective outcome. Thus the rivalry and conflicts that arise between professionals are not totally a struggle for power or control or the desire to be acknowledged as right. Much of the problem comes from these very different beliefs and expectations, these specialized conceptions of how people act, or should act, how people change, and how they should be treated, guided, and helped when in need. Parker (1987), for example, analyzes the confusion that can result when an interdisciplinary team serving children in a psychiatric setting has staff who seek an internal causal approach to the problems and those with a conceptual perspective provided by systems theory and a relational formulation of conflict.

Different professions, however, should not see things from the same perspective. In difference there is strength. I do not want a physician at the scene of my accident putting his primary effort into trying to help me understand my pain. The physician is to act as necessary to deal with the physical damage first and foremost. But if injuries are extensive and handicapping, I expect the physician to explore the possibility of social work help. Professionals, because they are called on to act, have to believe that their approach is right. If we are to be helpful, we have to believe in what we are doing and our way of doing it. The ability to endure the ambiguity of acting on uncertain knowledge as though it were certainty, while recognizing that there is no certainty, is difficult for all professionals. Physicians seek cure. Social workers seek more social competence and expanded ways of coping with social life. These goals are not incongruent, but they often generate conflict over which is of more value. Thus you must recognize the inevitability of conflict and difference and learn to negotiate it in the interests of effective help to clients and their families. Abandon the notion that difference is wrong, that absolute agreement is possible, and that if you cannot agree with someone, then something is wrong—usually with the other person.

The Problem of Competition   Helping persons, groups, or organizations work together on a problem of a common client system raises both cooperative and competitive elements in the relationship among the helpers. Cooperative work requires disclosing the relationship with the client to other helping authorities who are valuable because they bring different knowledge, roles, and functions to the helping process. This means you must be willing to cross barriers of difference. This is not easy. We are continually amazed at the subtle—and sometimes not so subtle—ways practitioners compete in professional interaction whose stated purpose is cooperation. In most agencies and professional associations there are infinite possibilities of competitive behavior: "I understand the needs of those children better than the foster mother or the teacher"; "my work is more central to the client's welfare than yours"; "my supervisor knows more than your supervisor"; "my agency or my job is where the action really is."

The prevalence of competition in areas in which it is inappropriate or even destructive to the rational interests of the competing individuals has been highlighted by experiments in game theory. Game theory is a discipline that seeks to obtain understanding of the problems of human interaction and decision making by studying human exchange from the perspective of strategic games. One game that game theorists use in many different forms is the non–zero-sum game. Its purpose is to determine under what conditions players will cooperate. In contrast to win-lose games, these games are so structured as to make it absurd to play uncooperatively. A player who fails to cooperate has no chance of gaining and considerable chance of losing ground. Nevertheless, researchers in the area of human cooperation are always struck by the frequency with which uncooperative play predominates and by the frequency with which the play becomes more competitive as the games go on and players experience the full negative effects of competition. It is almost as though once caught in a win-lose situation, the players cannot extricate themselves even though it is demonstrated that it is a destructive situation. In social work practice the most unfortunate aspect of competitive interrelationships of practitioners is that it is the client who is damaged by them. Perhaps social workers are especially vulnerable to competitiveness because it is their status and authority that are involved and the client's welfare that is at stake.

Game theorists have sought to explain this behavior and to isolate variables that will determine how a player will behave. They find that players fall into these categories: (1) *maximizers,* who are interested only in their own payoffs; (2) *rivalists,* who are interested only in defeating other players and are not concerned with the result of the game itself; and (3) *cooperators,* who are interested in helping both themselves and their partners. There have been studies of non–zero-sum games in which communication between players was impossible and in which it was encouraged. Improved communication seemed to increase cooperation only in the case of the cooperators, who were already interested in bettering the results for both sides. It failed to change the behavior of the maximizers or the rivalists (David, 1970).

You can work toward changing a maximizer (interested only in personal gain) or a rivalist (interested only in being one up or in putting others down) into a cooperator (interested in helping all sides to aid the client) by the kind of climate you establish in professional conferences and associations. For example, you can actively recognize the importance of each team member in the execution of a task. Child-care staff, who often carry the heaviest burden of the daily stress of living with and loving disturbed and deviant children, often find their efforts go unrewarded by the professional staff, who may assume that they themselves are the only ones who really know what the child is like or what the child needs. Are helping people who risk proposing a change in a particular way of working rewarded for having attempted something worthwhile, or are their suggestions seen as something for someone else to top or negate? Rivalists often spend a great deal of time developing verbal ability and skill in the use of professional language and use this ability to make the point that anyone who risks a new suggestion really does not understand the underlying dynamics, or the person would not be so naive as to make the proposal. This is a cheap way to be one up and is of low cost to the rivalist because the one who is put down seldom challenges the negative predictions. Rivalists especially difficult to contend with when they use elegant professional language a knowing air. In such a situation the cost is borne by the person who risks making a proposal and by the client system involved.

When members fall into competitive rather than cooperative roles, the resulting situation is devastating to the purpose of teamwork. Members' ego involvement with their own professional orientation may completely block their ability to consider the opinions or perspectives of others (Mouzakitis & Goldstein, 1985). The degree and quality of communication and cooperation among people is vital—they must work to maintain relationships that foster trust and mutual respect (Mouzakitis & Goldstein, 1985). A team must also be clearly focused on the reason for coming together; the purpose is not to prove one's rightness but to use the expertise of individual members to solve a problem. It may be necessary to remind the team of this common goal. Rivalry must be avoided; cooperation is a key element of successful teamwork. But cooperation does not mean competition.

Diverse practitioners bring to the team different value systems, principles, frames of reference, moral language, and definitions of what makes good practice (Abramson, 1984). Strong disagreements about such things as client involvement in treatment planning can surface. Conflict may arise when team members disagree about whom to advocate for (for example, child versus parent, victim versus offender). These conditions can lead to outcomes born out of compromise rather than consensus, even though all members of a group are held responsible. The issue of confidentiality also becomes more complicated when several people are working on a case. How do you handle a request from a client to withhold information from the team? Sands, Stafford, and McClelland (1990) studied interdisciplinary teams in conflict and found that team members see themselves primarily as representatives of their own discipline rather than as members of a team; the different values and theoretical perspectives lead to a divergence of opinion. They identify a need for a common value base, language, and conceptual framework for teams.

Abramson (1984) provides guidelines for enhancing collective responsibility in interdisciplinary collaboration. Team members must establish shared meanings of important ethical concepts such as confidentiality and autonomy. Values and ethical principles should be put in priority order by individuals as well as by the group. The development of a regular procedure for analyzing complex ethical dilemmas when they arise gives direction to these processes and saves time. The ethics committees of one's professional organization and agency are resources for this purpose. If one or more members still cannot agree with the rest of the group, they can record their dissent and the reasons for it and be excused from that particular case (Abramson, 1984). Team members must be aware of their responsibility for group decisions and be informed that silent disagreement will not excuse them from this responsibility.

People sometimes become committed to the smoothness of team functioning to the point where disagreement is avoided at all costs. When this happens there is the danger of the group-think phenomenon. Shared responsibility sometimes leads to individuals feeling less accountable for what happens and consequently becoming less thorough. An example of this is the 1986 disaster with the *Challenger* space shuttle. Apparently the NASA team was so swept up in achieving the launch that they failed to see signs of risk, and no one felt the responsibility fully enough to make certain that conditions were optimal. Group think may be avoided by assigning rotating team members to the role of devil's advocate. Assigning a duty to challenge decisions reduces the chances of overlooking potential problems.

The Problem of Professional and Agency Culture Effective collaboration requires that helping persons demonstrate respect and trust, expectation, and acceptance in their interactions. The discussion of how respect and trust are demonstrated in the helping relationships also has relevance to professional working relationships. All social workers are taught the importance of accepting and respecting clients, but few examine what this means when applied to colleagues.

To work effectively together, to have meaningful exchange, you must respect the position from which the other acts. The worker who is involved in work across professional agency lines must be perceptive and understanding about the point of view of the other organizations and their professional staff. One mark of a profession is its value system. An important part of all professional education and staff development is the attempt to socialize workers to their agency and their profession (see Chapter 6). By this we mean working toward internalizing the values and culture of the profession so that you are constrained to work in certain ways and to take certain positions. This is critically important as protection to the client system, since in the helping process workers must use themselves and their judgment. There is no way another can dictate to the worker exactly how to use the self to carry out any specific action in any specific situation. Therefore the only assurance that a professional person really can be trusted with professional tasks is that action is based on deeply internalized feelings and judgments that stem from professional values and knowledge. This is the only meaningful protection in using a professional's services. However, internalization of professional values and culture is an unconscious process. Internalization can cause tremendous problems in interagency collaboration unless you become aware of your values and culture and learn to recognize that others have their values and their culture.

In addition to undergoing a process of professional socialization and identification, professional social workers (and members of other professions as well) usually work within established institutional settings. The machinery through which you work sets boundaries for practical purposes to the ways in which you will define the problems for work. Also, within these institutional settings a professional subculture grows up, and like all cultures it has its own value system and accepted ways of operating. As you are engaged in collaborative work with persons outside your agency, you must be a part of your agency and yet have the capacity to step out of

EXHIBIT 14-2 Trained Incapacity of Specialists	For example, a family may in its varied contacts receive professional care, advice, and services from a physician, a nurse, a social worker, a nutritionist, a home economist, a probation officer, a lawyer or judge, a minister, a psychologist, a teacher, a guidance counselor, an industrial relations advisor, a banker, a group worker, and so on, each of whom may give that family irreconcilable advice and treatment, guidance in how to live, keep healthy, maintain a home and family, care for and rear children, resolve family discord, and all other aspects of living, especially human relations. The family is expected to resolve these professional conflicts, to reconcile these incongruities, and often mutually contradictory advices into a coherent, consistent pattern of living, a reconciliation which the professionals will not or cannot attain.

Thus students in medical school, nursing, social work, law, engineering, business, architecture, public administration and the graduate departments of the social sciences and humanities are being inculcated each with a different conception of human nature, of human conduct, with different beliefs, assumptions, expectations about people, what and how they act and carry on their human relations. All of these students are going out to practice in our communities, with what Veblen once called the "trained incapacity of specialists" unable to communicate or collaborate in their practice or even to recognize what other specialists see and do. Indeed, we often find bitter rivalry and open conflicts arising not entirely from professional competition but from these very different beliefs and expectations, these specialized conceptions of how people act, or should act, and how they should be treated, guided and helped when in need.

NOTE: From "The Interdisciplinary frontiers in human relations studies" by L. Frank, 1954, *Journal of Human Relations, 7*, p. 89. Copyright 1954 by Central State University, Wilberforce, Ohio. Reprinted by permission.

its culture and be analytical about it. You must understand what is going on in your own agency and yet not be trapped within a particular way of approaching problems. Other workers have an equal identification with their agencies and an equal need to protect the functioning of those agencies. The social and helping services in the community, their organizations, and ways of working must be understood if you are to use other services effectively in working with your clients. Specialized and different conceptions of how people in need act or should act and how they should be helped, guided, or treated can result in bitter rivalry and conflict. Exhibit 14-2 presents an illustration of this.

Team interaction allows a very intimate view of one's colleagues. The questionable competence of a team member's performance can be a very touchy issue, especially if the offending person has more power and authority (Abramson, 1984). Many social workers stress the need for skill building in this area—all participants need to understand the basics of effective teamwork. It does little good for one profession to be dedicated to creating an atmosphere of mutual respect if other professions assume roles of self-appointed authority. The smoothness with which a team functions will reflect the degree to which the power base of the institution supports the teaming process (Nason, 1983). This support can be demonstrated by training on enhancing group problem solving and team building.

Teamwork and Advocacy   Exhibit 14-3 is a case illustration that may help you consider some of the challenges of teamwork. The social worker on this interdisciplinary (type C) team feels caught between the views of the team and the view of the client about an appropriate discharge plan. What do you think this worker should do? What is her

EXHIBIT 14-3
Tom and the
Discharge
Plan*

Tom is a 22-year-old single African-American man who entered the regional treatment center about six months ago. The admission was through a district court commitment for mental illness. At the time of hospitalization Tom was in a decompensated state, with significant disorganization of thought. Early treatment was complicated by difficulties in adjusting medications. There were severe side effects, and Tom was found to have both an unusual sensitivity and narrow range of medication tolerance. Tom is consistent in denying the mental illness and will either state no memory of dysfunctional and potentiality dangerous behavior or offers a different interpretation of events. Tom's family support is strong, and he was living with his mother at the time of the hospitalization. The family includes the patient's mother, an infant grandchild in her care, and an adult daughter who lives outside of this home. Since their arrival in the state about two years ago the family has experienced severe trauma with the murder of a daughter and two grandchildren and her son's serious illness and resulting hospitalizations. The treatment team perceives the family as mistrustful; interactions with treatment team members have been abrupt and conflict-filled. Discharge planning was under way at the time the case was assigned to me.

Tom's condition is considered stabilized on what is proving to be an effective medication regime. Tom is participating in selected group programs, his mood is generally consonant with the situation, his thinking is organized and lucid, and he is responsible in providing for his basic needs. Tom has had no significant experience with independent living and has been supported by others to varying degrees. Tom has been unable to specify goals beyond his desire to leave the treatment center. Tom is compliant with the medications, but he verbalizes no insight into the need or benefits of the medication. He will talk about undesirable side effects, which he agrees have been worse in the past. The team is recommending discharge to a group home because of Tom's history of poor medication compliance and need for monitoring for side effects. Tom is in agreement with discharge but disagrees with the team's plan.

I am responsible for implementation of the discharge plan and have had four interviews with Tom on the subject of discharge. Tom expressed many negative ideas about group homes and believed them to be undesirable places to live. Tom agreed to visit a group home to expand his information and clarify perceptions about group homes; he and I accomplished the visit together, and although Tom's apprehensions seemed to be reduced, his determination to return to his mother's home did not change. The significant difference between Tom and his family and the discharge team regarding discharge planning is resulting in conflict and alienation between the treatment team and Tom and his family.

*Case material prepared by Paulette Anderson, M.S.W. student, University of Minnesota School of Social Work, Minneapolis.

obligation to the client? How might she respond to her team? Mailick and Ashley (1981) discuss conflict between advocacy and teamwork and offer some suggestions for integrating these two aspects of social work practice. They suggest three guidelines that may help social workers resolve tension between interdisciplinary team collaboration and the obligation to serve as an advocate on behalf of a client. First is to be comfortable with the area of competency you bring to the team; this means recognizing that all team members bring competencies, that these differ, that no one team member is omnipotent, and that you should feel comfortable advocating on behalf of clients when the advocacy is consistent with your area of competence. Second is the timing of advocacy. This involves a sense of political acumen and setting priorities to guide you as to which matters you will advocate and which ones you will defer. Third is to learn how to advocate. Advocacy skills used in an interdisciplinary team, essentially the same as those used in other settings, include skill at presenting a well-reasoned position without anger and without attacking other positions.

The Social Worker and the Indigenous Helper Team

As a social worker you will also be working with what we call *indigenous helper* (some would say paraprofessional) *teams* as well as the more commonly considered interdisciplinary and intraprofessional teams. We see two quite different types of indigenous helper teams. One works within your own agency and includes volunteers, child-care workers, foster parents, and so forth, all of whom bring expertise and make unique contributions to the service plan. Second is mutual aid (or self-help) groups.

Working with Indigenous Helpers within Your Agency All of the ideas we discussed in relation to interdisciplinary and intraprofessional teams apply to work with an indigenous helper team within your agency. Working with these teams is difficult for some social workers because it involves the sharing of power and authority, often vested with the social worker, with other team members (Hazel, 1989; Hazel & Fenyo, 1993; Blüml et al, 1989). You as a social worker will probably be responsible for facilitating a team that includes, for example, a foster parent, a volunteer, or a child-care staff person. Exhibit 11-5 provides several suggestions for helping a group reach a decision. We introduced this material in Chapter 11 as an aid to a group reaching a decision about a problem and a goal as a part of developing a service contract, but we recommend that you again review this material because the same ideas will apply to your work as the facilitator of a team. A team is a task-centered group; your job as the facilitator will be to assist the team to come to a decision and to carry it out.

Exhibit 14-4 contains a set of principles we have found to be important and helpful in working cooperatively with an indigenous helper team within the agency. These seven principles provide for a degree of egalitarianism in the team functioning, the recognition of joint and differing expertise, an openness to a variety of suggestions and input, recognition that differences must be resolved through negotiation rather than arbitrary decision making by you as the authority, and an expectation of responsible behavior from all team members.

Let's examine the application of this set of principles in two situations involving a social worker and foster parent team.

Rose, age 16, was placed in a foster home because of sexual assaults by her stepfather. She has been in the home about six months and is making a good adjustment to the home and school. Recently she has been showing signs of depression and withdrawal. She was

EXHIBIT 14-4 Principles for Facilitating an Indigenous Helper Team	1. Recognition of different expertise 2. Sharing of all information 3. All team members involved in all phases of planning 4. Team members free to express differing opinions 5. Differences of opinions considered and action plans negotiated 6. Responsible behavior required of all team members 7. Performance problems discussed openly

evaluated by a psychologist who recommended family therapy with her and the foster parents. The foster parents want therapy for Rose but believe family therapy with them is unnecessary.

How would you handle this situation with your team members, the foster parents? Would you expect them to undergo therapy with Rose and attempt to enforce it as a condition of their service? If not, how would you handle the matter with the psychologist? In our opinion this request by the psychologist for the foster parents to undergo therapy with Rose is inappropriate; we should not expect members of a service team to enter therapy with their clients. Certainly members of a team can be expected to receive and consider feedback and suggestions from other professionals and to consider how these suggestions can be incorporated into their work with clients. And if there are performance problems on the part of a team member, these are to be discussed openly as a part of a team meeting and a plan developed for their resolution.

Here's another example of a difference that developed between a social worker and a foster parent.

> Jack, age 16, has been in foster family care for about two months. He is making a reasonably good adjustment to the foster home. Jack's mother, whom he sees irregularly, promised to visit him over the weekend. On Thursday she telephoned to say she would not be able to visit, and on Friday Jack skipped school. The social worker believes that Jack's skipping school was because of his disappointment about his mother's not visiting and that no disciplinary action is necessary. The foster parents, however, have told Jack that he must spend all day Saturday in the house studying.

How would you, as the social worker, respond to this difference? To what extent does the notion of differing expertise play a role in your decision? Do you respect the decision of your team member or overrule it? In our opinion this is the type of situation in which the social worker, even though disagreeing with the decision of the member of the team, should probably respect the decision; being grounded a day and required to study does not seem to be an unreasonable response to skipping school for a day, even though the skipping may well have been related to the disappointment relating to the canceled visit. There are, of course, other ways to handle disappointment, and this might well become the focus for some of the immediate work with Jack. The worker might also, in future team meetings, discuss this issue and attempt to negotiate an agreement among the team about how this type of problem will be dealt with in the future.

The Social Worker and Mutual Aid Groups People with good access to supportive human relationships are more effectively cushioned from adverse impacts of stressful life events and chronic hardships than those with few or poor-quality social ties (Cassel, 1974). The emergence of thousands of mutual aid groups provides social workers and clients access to network of supportive human relationships as a part of the service planning. Mutual aid groups are composed of people who come together for an extended period to share a common concern and to help one another cope or resolve problems related to their concern (Toseland & Hacker, 1985). Mutual aid groups coalesce around common issues such as recovery from alcoholism, mental health concerns, parenting concerns, coping with the stress of specific illnesses, and so forth. Most mutual aid groups provide a supportive function for members, but some begin with these functions of mutual support and then move outward to take on social action directed toward changing environment. Mutual aid groups provide a referral source for the social worker and client in developing a service plan and provide an opportunity to empower clients. Some mutual aid groups provide opportunities for social workers in an advisory, facilitating role.

As a social worker, you may have to understand the internal workings and ethos of mutual aid and understand its occurrence in the larger social and political structure to overcome professional biases and help clients tap this valuable resource. Rappaport (1985) suggests that we may have to speak in a new language, a language of empowerment, to enter into collaboration with the mutual aid movement. The language of medical terminology creates an unintentional split between the sick and the well, between us and them, and imposes artificial barriers between professionals and clients.

Toseland and Hacker (1985) investigated how social workers use mutual aid groups and what factors influenced the use of these groups. Most social workers had a positive view of mutual aid groups and found the attributes of peer support, sharing of practical ideas for coping, long-term support, and lack of stigma attached to group membership as very important reasons for the helpfulness of mutual aid groups. However, 60% of the social workers surveyed thought that mutual aid groups were biased against professional help and that the groups discouraged members from seeking additional help. Most of the social service agencies of the respondents did not have policies that encouraged the use of mutual aid groups in practice, and 80% of the respondents thought that mutual aid groups were underused by professional social workers. Toseland and Hacker concluded that there is a need to educate social workers regarding the availability and potential use of mutual aid groups and that lines of communication between social workers and mutual aid groups should be developed and strengthened.

Silverman (1986) notes that social workers can work effectively with mutual aid groups through making referrals, serving on advisory boards, providing consultation to groups who ask for assistance, and initiating efforts that lead to the establishment of new mutual aid groups. Gartner and Reissman (1984) found extensive social work involvement with mutual aid groups, and Coplon and Strull (1983), in a study of mutual aid groups, found several roles, including educator, resource provider, referral source, link to the greater community, consultant, and group facilitator, being played by social workers in the groups.

The Problem-Solving Approach to Teamwork

Teamwork as Providing a Resource for Clients The *American Heritage Dictionary* defines teamwork as the "cooperative effort by the members of a group or team to achieve a common goal." The definition refers to some of the concepts of problem solving. It requires that team members see the payoff in the honest attempt to identify the most appropriate actions and resources that they can supply to help the client. Thus, the purpose of coming together as a team is not to win your way or prove your rightness but to use the different capacities brought by the different members of the team to expand your knowledge and range of skills so that you can offer the client the best service in the direction that the client wishes to go. Teamwork requires that you keep this direction clearly before you as the reason you are together. In teamwork it is essential to recognize that you are trying to build interagency organizations and professional teams that function effectively in the interest of the client and the desired goals. You must function in the interests of the job to be done. Teams need a problem-solving focus to communicate around a defined task. Problems of communication and relationship must be worked out so that you can offer the client the most effective help possible.

In working with the client system you may have come to the conclusion that you cannot offer all the service a client needs or wants. What do you do? One thing is to discuss it with your supervisor to check out his or her thinking and knowledge of where you and the client can turn for help. Another important step is to talk with the client about how the client sees this notion. You may present this to the client as something that must be done in light of the nature of the problem, the goals sought, and the limits of service; for example, you may tell parents who have to place a child about foster home services and the necessary work with the foster parents. Or you may present it as something on which you and the client can come to a decision; for example, you may say that your understanding and assessment of the situation may be helped if the client can discuss the problem with the psychiatrist on the agency staff.

In beginning a working relationship with other helping persons to offer clients better service, you have the choice of asking clients whether they want to join in the conferences and planning or whether they prefer for you to carry this role alone. Practitioners working jointly with a client sometimes develop a pattern of meeting privately to pool observations and knowledge of the problem and to come to some understanding of how to proceed. Sometimes clients are told about this meeting, and sometimes they are not. Perhaps the possibility of such a meeting is used as a threat to clients. We think clients should be actively involved in consideration of the way different professionals can be used to help with their problems and that clients must be told about all professional consultations involving them. We much prefer to offer our clients the opportunity to come with us to meetings with other professionals and to participate in the deliberations so that they may understand what is involved and may speak for themselves (Williams, 1985).

Involving the Client in Teams and Decision Making   Before using another resource, the worker should talk with the client about that resource, how it may be used, what it can offer, why it is suggested at this point, and what is involved in using it. The client should understand what will have to be shared with the other agency. The street gang that the practitioner has been working with as an outreach worker may be very anxious when the practitioner suggests that an organized agency can offer a meeting place and opportunities for recreation. What is the worker going to tell the agency about the gang? Will the agency invite them in if it knows about their behavioral history? Is the agency going to try to control them? The parents of an angry, acting-out daughter will have similar questions if foster home placement is suggested as a temporary measure to help both child and parents think things out. Will the foster parents have to be told that the girl steals? What will the foster parents expect of them? Under what conditions will they be able to see their daughter? To take her home? How can foster parents help when they, her own parents, have failed? The client and the worker will have to discuss how the new service will be contacted and involved in their affairs. The expectations and requirements of the new service vis-à-vis the client will have to be carefully discussed and understood. What will be revealed about the client must be considered. It is usually helpful to ask clients what they think the agency will need to know or should be told about them.

What should you tell another agency about your client? Tell team members what they need to know to work with the client toward solution of the problem in the way the client and you have decided it will need to be worked out. The problem of sharing information with others is not a simple one. You inevitably will be confronted with the question of how the other person will use the information in the interests of the client. Social workers who place children in foster homes often face conflicts about what to tell foster parents about the children placed with them. And what should they say about the natural parents? We prefer to present clients in a positive light — yet how much information can be kept secret when foster parents and children live intimately as a family? There is no ideal answer to this question. However, one essential principle is to keep the client system aware of what is being told and why and whenever possible to involve the client system directly in the telling. In planning for foster care placement, for example, the birth parents and foster parents may meet to exchange information.

The case conference is a good device for joint planning and joint monitoring of work when more than one worker is involved with the client system. The client should be told about these conferences and their outcomes or invited to attend and participate. The questions you must ask in deciding this are these: Will attending the conference help clients analyze the problem? Will it help give clients a sense of being in control of their own destiny? Or is the conference likely to make them feel overwhelmed by professionals and by the problems they see in the situation? Will the decisions being made demand specific behavior of the client, or are they primarily decisions related to agency policies and parameters of service? Is it possible for the client to provide meaningful input into the conference?

The Team Leader Practitioners have to meet at least once to work successfully with a client. There is no substitute for this meeting, and lack of time is no excuse. Having served as practitioners in large public agencies and carried large case loads, we admit to violations of this principle. But the fact that something is not done does not negate its importance. We hope that you will adopt this as a desirable way of working even if you cannot follow through in all cases. Letters and telephone calls are an unsatisfactory substitute for at least one face-to-face planning session for a particular case.

In each case conference someone must take the position of leader. The leader takes the responsibility for seeing that all agencies and persons involved in the case are included in the conference, for defining the purpose and focus of the conference, for seeing that everyone present is heard, for clarifying the plans of action and who is to do what and when, and for helping to resolve any conflicts. The conference should result in group acceptance of the part each agency is to play. This agreement is facilitated by recording the conclusions of the conference before its termination. Thus everyone has a chance to correct the common plan and everyone is to receive a copy. Each agency then carries the responsibility for following through on the plan (which can be seen as a design for coordination) or for pointing out the necessity of changing it. The leader should also have the responsibility of seeing that the plan is implemented by each agency involved. The leader becomes the captain of the service team. Who is to serve in this role and how the leader is to be selected should be decided before the team actually begins the action phase of the work with the client. The assignment of this responsibility is an allotment of power and authority. The problems involved in accepting such a position must be considered in this light. There should be a clear focus on the purpose of the conference, and drifting away from that focus should be limited. Any problems of working relationships among the members of the team must be worked through to some acceptable conclusion, or they will distort the team's relationship to the client.

Some Disadvantages of Teamwork Teamwork has some distinct advantages, bringing shared expertise to the client and providing a mechanism for the coordination of services. But there are also some disadvantages that should be considered before making a decision regarding the use of teams. A poorly functioning team that leaves unresolved differences among the professionals may lead to confusion and be destructive rather than helpful for the client (Huslage & Stein, 1985; Parker, 1987). Another clear disadvantage is the cost. Team meetings requiring the time of several professionals can be a costly use of resources. For example, if the function is coordination of services, you should carefully consider whether coordination can come about more efficiently through careful case management (Kane, 1982). Schmitt, Farrell, and Heinemann (1989) found that studies of the effectiveness of geriatric interdisciplinary teams are rare despite frequent claims that they provide care superior to that of other approaches. On the other hand, if there are legitimate differences of view that must be resolved, a meeting with a careful airing of differences may be necessary. A third disadvantage is that often clients are excluded from the process. We perceive this as inconsistent with social work practice and believe that one of the functions of a social worker should be to ensure that if possible the client is present at the team meeting or at least has the opportunity to be present. If this is not possible, then the client is to be fully informed and advised of the team meeting and a systematic way to ensure input of client views into the team decision making is to be developed.

Recapitulation

In this chapter we have discussed teamwork in the interests of offering the client system better help in problem solving. Teams may be made up of members from within your agency or may be interagency. Teams may be interdisciplinary. Much of your work is likely to involve teaming with indigenous helpers and mutual aid groups. The aspects of competition have been discussed, as have the problem of professional and agency culture and how teamwork relates to problem solving.

A Look Forward

John Compher, in Reading 14-1, identifies four types of interactional modes among agencies and social workers that interfere with family work and suggests the need for collaboration to solve these problems. In the next chapter we discuss endings in social work and in Chapter 16, evaluation of your practice.

| Reading 14-1 | *The Dance Beyond the Family System** |

John Victor Compher

To recast the roles of the family therapist and the social worker in a way that makes it "difficult [for one] to separate the specialist in 'emotional' problems from the specialist in 'community' problems" is not a new challenge (Auerswald, 1968; Hoffman & Long, 1969). Since this bold admonition over 18 years ago, systems thinking has revolutionized clinical therapy, creating a flourishing literature and numerous family-therapy schools. However, the broader vision of the family in community and the systematic entanglements of these multisystems have produced only a sparse (yet growing) body of knowledge. The family's dependence on helping-agent networks is especially evident in the child welfare realm. Family-centered services have developed as a concept and as a means to strengthen the family's internal functioning as well as the family's ability to relate effectively to powerful public agents (Bryce & Maybanks, 1979; Hartmann & Laird, 1983).

However, social agencies (which often refer families for clinical treatment), children and family services, courts, schools, mental hospitals, and day programs often unwittingly create negatively charged triangulated relationships requiring direct and conjoint communication and case treatment planning (Compher, 1984; Jarkevic & Carl, 1983). For example, internal conflict among the helping agents of delinquency control is believed to be a contributing factor to the maintenance or exacerbation of delinquent patterns (Emerson, 1969; Miller, Baum, & McNeil, 1968; Miller, 1958). Similarly, the child's dual environments of family and school create contextual and relational dissonances that at times necessitate intervention into the adult relationships of both settings in order to promote the child's development (Aponte, 1976; Compher, 1982; Tucker & Dyson, 1976).

A full-systems therapeutic approach, therefore, widens the lens of assessment and intervention beyond the family system to the interactive patterns of the family's immediate community and service systems. The dance of the various parties is clearly observable and demonstrates that the service-community network relationships clearly have an impact on treatment outcomes. Because the dysfunctional extrafamilial processes may serve to maintain, exacerbate, or create symptomatic behaviors, it seems neither helpful nor accurate to characterize these interchanges as outgrowths of family pathology but rather to understand them as interdependent contributions.

Assessment characteristics of the interactional process of the family in community suggest at least four rather common dysfunctional modes. The blind, or dispersed, system operates in a vacuum of disengagement, abdicating responsibility and control. The conflicted interinstitutional system usually sets up a pattern of triangulation in which the family suffers setbacks. The rejecting system is characterized by ideological bias, struggles for reimbursement, or overwhelmed states of operation that create discontinuity and provoke a family's feelings of being cast about. Finally, the underdeveloped system affords the practitioner an opportunity to create optimal, reliable referrals that are coordinated through active conference work.

"BLIND" SERVICE NETWORK

The seemingly "blind" service network is composed of dispersed service entities that deal with the client in a manner that demonstrates little or no knowledge of other's involvements. The client controls the information flow and finds that he or she can reduce factors that might produce change by misinforming or not informing the network of various behaviors. Some important service or monitoring parties will have very little contact with the client because they feel overwhelmed by large caseloads. The more active service participants will feel impotent and wonder why their well-intended work is not favorably influencing the client. An illusion that there is no substantial problem may also operate. The client's defense mechanisms will exploit the service network's detachment, until at some point of desperation, symptomatic behavior will escalate. In sum, the professionals have allowed their own distraction or seduction.

The O family demonstrates classic roles of child and spouse abuse: The suspicious alcoholic husband, after gaining control over his parenting conduct, became increasingly prone toward violence with his wife. Mrs. O's lack of differentiation and threatened position seemed to cripple her from taking sufficient protective action for herself. Perhaps she also feared the engagement of protective services, which could remove the child. Because the father's original attack on the child had been life threatening, criminal charges led to his prosecution and to three years of reporting probation. The abused child was moved for six months to the grandparents' home in another city.

During the first year of probation, Mr. O told his probation officer and the child protective school worker that he was faithfully attending a counseling program and that he was no longer drinking. He was proud that he had two part-time jobs and that his wife was employed. His wife, however, was frightened and intimidated by him and believed that the therapy was making him worse. Indeed, on those days for which Mr. O alleged attendance, he returned home more agitated and more threatening than ever, which led Mrs. O to place a secret call to the child protective worker indicating that she was contemplating a move into a women's shelter because of her husband's direct threats.

The alarm of the child protective worker and her supervisor over the wife's fear of danger prompted an urgent case meeting with the probation officer, the therapist, the child protective worker, the supervisor, and subsequently with Mr. O. It became quite clear to all the professionals at their first meeting that indeed their own lack of communication with each other had contributed to the illusion that the client was improving. The therapist had accepted the client's cordiality and persistent denial of drinking and other problems and had agreed to hold monthly rather than weekly meetings. Until the spousal crisis occurred, the child protective worker had believed that there was little reason to be in contact with the therapist. The probation officer, with a caseload of nearly 250 clients, had not taken time to monitor the client closely or to verify his claims of keeping his appointments for treatment. In short, each of the parties had operated in a vacuum with little knowledge of the others' existence and without an understanding of each other's professional role in relation to the client family. Indeed, involvement with the family had in general been sporadic and minimal.

As a result of the case meeting, clinical therapeutic goals and service objectives were developed by the interagency representatives to include (1) strengthening the wife's status and concept of self, (2) enabling the wife to be in frequent communication with the support system, (3) regular reporting by the therapist to the probation officer, (4) further psychological testing and use of a new, intensive group for battering husbands, and (5) ongoing case conferences at about six-week intervals to assess progress and further interventions, including consideration of a detoxification program and marital counseling.

Although there had been some initial concern that Mr. O might react to the professional system's tighter controls through spousal violence or threats to his wife, it became clear that instead his symptomatic behavior was for the first time decreasing. Indeed, a correlation was evident in this case between the presence of acting out behavior on the part of the family and the professional community's ability to coordinate its own communication and intervention in an effective way.

CONFLICTED SERVICE NETWORK

The conflicted service network is characterized by overt, often intransigent, ideological battles and battles among service agencies in relation to the client. The client will experience varying degrees of triangulation by the parties who direct or support the client toward divergent goals. The splitting of service participants among themselves or by the client effectively eliminates the achievement of change and maintains the status quo. Differing values concerning maintaining family life versus placement or institutionalization frequently arouse such systemic conflict. In court-related matters, such as child-protection cases, an adversarial position may be unavoidable. When opposing parties are in a fiscal contract with each other, higher executive intervention may help resolve problems. If problem-solving efforts fail, a new and more compatible configuration of service participants will be necessary, along with a period of time to overcome setbacks and psychological damage to the family.

In the W family case, a single-parent mother demonstrated behaviors toward her son that fluctuated from angry physical assaults to extreme disengagement and depression. Mrs. W demanded that the boy, age 13, change his problem-filled behaviors—in this instance, stealing at home, acting out at school, and running away. Her practice of overwhelming him with orders and ultimatums and punishment through withdrawal and emotional distancing contributed to the maintenance of his chaotic and volatile behaviors. For the sake of her own coping, she demanded, within the family system and service system, the absolute right to engage or disengage at will. This behavior expressed itself particularly around placement issues.

Over a period of several years, the mother, with her son intermittently in placement, participated in a number of therapeutic attempts with a range of separate therapists who were invited to operate quite independently with the family, apart from the service and legal network. The mother sought constantly to bring her son back home from placement at the times he demonstrated the most progress away from home. She asserted that because he had improved and seemed well, she could manage him. A recommendation from her therapist coupled with a plea from her attorney completed the triangulation in regard to the placement facility and the child protective agency, setting in motion a judicial system that awarded the mother custody of her child with little consideration for whether or not the mother's relationship with him had actually changed.

A systems treatment modality was then instituted to bring together service planning in the context of family treatment. The child would remain in placement while the family attended biweekly sessions. At least monthly, key service personnel or legal representatives would be brought into sessions to monitor progress and to work cooperatively, if possible, toward the timing of another reunification attempt. The approach was embraced by the family's legal representatives and the current placement social worker; the family therapist and systems case manager from the child protective agency did the choreography.

A major setback to this new and positive momentum occurred, however, when the original social worker from the placement agency left the agency and was replaced by a new and quite inexperienced worker who promoted an agenda of his own. The new worker observed the newly emerging strengths of the family. To meet his administrator's strong demands for another bed in the short-term placement center, the worker operated outside the framework of the treatment team, allying himself with the mother's and the son's desire for a highly premature placement discharge and a temporary return home. Opposing the recommendations of the therapist and child protective case manager, Mrs. W seized the opportunity for an extended visit, which set in motion again the negative dynamics, resulting in one more failed attempt by the mother to discipline her son. Higher level administrative intervention was not available, and the team sustained a prolonged and serious setback in relationship to this mother and son and the original treatment goals.

When such a split occurs in the interagency team effort, the family's original maladaptive dynamics will prevail. The family, having been challenged either through its voluntary or involuntary involvement to try new, constructive behaviors, finds that it is now able to exploit or to be exploited by the irrational dynamics of the service system that had been defined as "helper." The family's inherent difficulties are thus reinforced, making future treatment efforts all the more difficult.

REJECTION BY SERVICE SYSTEMS

When a system is first and foremost responsive to its own operational needs and unresponsive to a client's specific concerns, the client not surprisingly feels rejected. The service system may be overwhelmed with too high a volume of work or it may be anxious about the possibility of not being paid, either by the client or by the client's insurance plan. In the large public sector, considerable case turnover—for example, movement of a case from intake to a series of other specialized services or from worker to worker—disallows sufficient opportunity for meaningful relationships to develop between the counselor and client. Gaps in service may also exist during transfers of staff. These factors contribute to the maintenance of behaviors and hold the client in the system for extended periods. If the client family demonstrates considerable emotional distress, the discontinuous transactions will usually cause an escalation of problems to emergency situations as the client seeks to reengage rejecting parties or elements of the service. Poorly planned discharges from mental health institutions provide tragic examples, on a massive scale, of rejected, deteriorating patients. Similar phenomena are occurring all too frequently with children's services, health care, aging, and other services.

In the M family's case, a single-parent mother who was a former drug abuser suffering from acquired immune deficiency syndrome (AIDS) was denied readmittance to a large metropolitan hospital because of an enormous outstanding bill that was not yet covered by medical assistance. The hospital argued that her condition was chronic, not acute, and that although she was slowly dying, so were many other patients, including cancer patients who could not be maintained at the hospital. Further, the hospital recommended nursing home care because Ms. M was too frail to care for her own needs. No private nursing home in the city was found that would admit her, however. High-level executive intervention was needed to gain her admission into the single public nursing home facility. The employees' union then balked, refusing to provide care to her out of fear of contagion. Because she contracted pneumonia during this

time, she was finally readmitted to the original hospital as an acutely ill patient.

After her pneumonia subsided, she was abruptly discharged without adequate community discharge planning and was delivered by ambulance to the yet unoccupied and unfurnished house of a supportive friend. Two days later, the newly assigned community nurse was appalled to find her in a hot, fly-infested vacant room lying near her own unemptied bedpan. Because of the acting-out behaviors exhibited by her young children in this traumatic context and allegations of child abuse from a caretaker aunt, child protective service and counseling for the family were provided.

The family's grief extended not only to the mother's misery and imminent death, but to the rejecting treatment of this modern health care system. Counseling was effective in large part because it acknowledged the service system's dysfunction as a key element of the traumatic and tragic circumstances. The practitioner intervened to help organize case conferences with hospital personnel, the community nursing system, a community-based AIDS task force, and a homemaker service. Stabilization of the turbulent system enabled the family to better focus on Ms. M's and their own needs and to appropriately grieve her death when it occurred several months later.

In summary, the rejecting nature and disarray of the original service system greatly contributed to an increase of stress and dysfunction in the M family. The original health problem was exacerbated as another family member became abusive and two of the children then tried to run away. This escalation likewise provided another signal for help by the extended family after their earlier, more rational protestations had fallen on deaf ears. An empathic professional response developed finally out of the reorganized service community. This development led to a rather rapid, yet lasting, amelioration of the problems of the extended family members. The health needs of the mother and the caretaking needs of the children were jointly resolved by the multiple professional parties, who had now begun to communicate with each other on behalf of the entire family. The formal joint meetings of the various services that were organized by the social worker provided a setting for public accountability and advocacy, which reduced the rejecting tendency of the original services.

UNDERDEVELOPED SYSTEM

It is not uncommon to discover in socially isolated families or in families new to the service system significant cultural deprivation, including an absence of key service providers. A careful therapeutic intake process that is systems-oriented will, therefore, determine the client's current range and degree of involvement within the service community. This service community may include schools, health centers, doctors, legal personnel, and religious institutions.

Because the inexperienced client may also feel insecure around professionals and be easily overwhelmed, he or she needs a good deal of support in establishing an effective network and in following through after professional contacts have begun. There is nothing more unhelpful to such a client than to refer him or her to unresponsive or inappropriate sources. It is therefore essential that the systems practitioner know the referral resources. Making a personal call, accompanying the client, or inviting the other professionals into sessions provides a clear, visible means of establishing interagency team relationships. Careful preparation, including role play and agenda settings, prepares the client for successful relationships within the network. Crisis points may be the best times to establish the coordinated services of a network.

Ms. R, a mother in her early 20s, entered the service network involuntarily through a child protective report and investigation. Her relative isolation had been a contributing factor to her frustration and to the physical abuse of her 6-year-old son, Timmy. She was also burdened by the demands of an active 4-year-old daughter. Although she felt at first quite defensive toward the protective service agency, claiming that she was being harrassed, she responded with interest and a sense of relief when advocacy was offered around Timmy's acknowledged school problems. She had had several unsuccessful encounters with a punitive principal and was understandably distressed that

Timmy was so frequently suspended from school. The school, she believed, was not dealing with Timmy or his problems, and it thus had alienated her as well. Although she was illiterate and was quite simple in her speech and manner, Ms. R was nevertheless ready to redress Timmy's school problems (with the assistance of an advocate).

The development of new and functioning relationships within the school system also provided opportunities for building trust and rapport between the client and the worker. Based on this relationship with the client, a second referral was initiated, this time to a clinical therapist and educational treatment program. In this instance, the systems worker selected a personally known source and attended the initial session to introduce the client to the new therapist and to clarify treatment goals. The clinical intake process revealed that Timmy had been conceived by a rape, which had contributed to his mother's negative, vindictive attitude toward him.

While the therapist-client relationship developed, the social worker, operating as a team member with the therapist, linked the client's family to additional services as needs were identified. These services included a day care program for the 4-year-old girl and, later, a family shelter for the mother and her children when she moved out of her own home to avoid abuse from her mate. The therapist also extended the network by arranging for an educational specialist to work with each child and for a case conference with Timmy's teacher. Joint efforts of the therapist and social worker promoted the client's emotional development and a system of tangible supports in the community. In summary, the client's isolation and abusive behaviors were mitigated through the client's engagement with an evolving supportive treatment and an evolving service community.

EXPLORING JOINT PRACTICE

From an ecological-systems perspective, the behavioral patterns of the family may be linked directly with those of the service-system providers. This linkage may be profound, particularly in cases in which the family's acting out violates social norms in a way that requires powerful interventions from society—for example, in the adult criminal justice, child welfare, juvenile justice, and mental health systems—or in cases in which a family member may be exceedingly vulnerable, as in the health-care context. The client, as if dealing with a series of powerful parental figures after the initial intervention, must reckon with the accountable presence, for better or worse, of various service personnel. Further dysfunctional family behavior may be correlated with the patterns, often irrational, of the complex service system itself.

How well the service community network recognizes the joint involvement and influence in relationship to the family will have a great impact on treatment and service effectiveness. The blind, triangulated, and rejecting service configurations are particularly apt to invite from certain families an escalation and reenforcement of presenting difficulties, but awareness by service staff of the potential to be part of a supportive community can provide an essential context for positive change.

Finally, although there has been some cross-fertilization among the related service fields and some broadening of clinical social work roles, in particular, in recent years, the frontier that combines individual, family, and social-systems assessment and operations into a sophisticated joint practice continues to remain open for active exploration. Families with serious problems, also intertwined in the dysfunctional social web, can only benefit from such expansionary approaches.

For Further Reading

Abramson, J. S. (1989). Making teams work. *Social Work With Groups, 12*(4), 45–63.

Abramson, M. (1984). Collective responsibility in interdisciplinary collaboration: An ethical perspective for social workers. *Social Work in Health Care, 10*(l), 35–43.

Blüml, H., Gudat, U., Langreuter, J., Martin, B., Schettner, H., & Schumann, M. (1989). Changing concepts of social work in foster family care. *Community Alternatives: International Journal of Family Care, 1*(1), 11–22.

Coplon, J., & Strull, J. (1983). Roles of the professional in mutual aid groups. *Social Casework: The Journal of Contemporary Social Work, 64,* 259–266.

Hazel, N., & Fenyo, A. (1993). *Free to be myself: The development of teenage fostering.* St. Paul: Human Service Associates.

Hazel, N. (1989). Adolescent fostering as a community resource. *Community Alternatives: International Journal of Family Care, 1*(1), 1–10.

Huslage, S., & Stein, F. (1985). A systems approach for the child study team. *Social Work in Education, 7,* 114–123.

Kane, R. A. (1982). Teams: Thoughts from the bleachers. *Health and Social Work, 7*(l), 2–4.

Lister, L. (1982). Role training for interdisciplinary health teams. *Health and Social Work, 7*(l), 19–25.

Mailick, M., & Ashley, A. (1981). Politics of interprofessional collaboration: Challenge to advocacy. *Social Casework: The Journal of Contemporary Social Work, 62,* 131–137.

Mouzakitis, C., & Goldstein, S. (1985). A multidisciplinary approach to treating child neglect. *Social Casework: The Journal of Contemporary Social Work, 66,* 218–224.

Parker, T. (1987). Dilemmas resulting from the application of extemporaneous ethics in interdisciplinary team decision making. *Family Therapy, 14,* 201–211.

Sands, R. G., Stafford, J., & McClelland, M. (1990). I beg to differ: Conflict in the interdisciplinary team. *Social Work in Health Care, 26,* 55–72.

Schmitt, M. H., Farrell, M. P., & Heinemann, G. D. (1988). Conceptual and methodological problems in studying the effects of interdisciplinary geriatric terms. *The Gerontologist, 28*(6), 753–764.

Smith, P. (1984). Social service teams and their managers. *British Journal of Social Work 14,* 601–613.

Toseland, R. W., & Hacker, L. (1985). Social workers' use of self-help groups as a resource for clients. *Social Work, 30,* 232–237.

Williams, B. C. (1988). Parents and patients: Members of an interdisciplinary team on an adolescent inpatient unit. *Clinical Social Work Journal, 16,* 78–91.

Chapter 15

Endings in Social Work Practice

This chapter will deal with three endings of the client-worker relationship: referral, transfer, and termination. So often workers are deeply concerned about clients only as long as they are involved in the interaction, but when they are no longer the primary professional, they may leave the clients to find their own way. It should be recognized that how a client-worker relationship ends may be crucial to what clients take with them in gains. In situations involving nonvoluntary adolescent clients, we cannot help being struck at the way in which we make ourselves indispensable at the beginning of our contacts with clients. And when clients feel they need workers most, which often is at the time of termination or transfer, the worker is often so preoccupied with new beginnings, either with other clients or with a new setting, that he or she is unavailable to the client. Referral, transfer, and termination have three factors in common: (1) some kind of problem identification has brought the worker and the client together for a greater or a lesser period of time; (2) the client is being sent on to a new phase, a new experience, another source of help, leaving the worker behind or being left behind by the worker; and (3) more is involved than simply saying good-bye and wishing everyone well. However, as each of the three tasks is different, they will be discussed separately in this chapter. We will begin with referral.

Referral Referral is a process that comes into play whenever a client or a service instigator requests your involvement in a situation that falls outside the parameters of your agency's defined services or whenever you define a problem as beyond your expertise or your agency's parameters of service. In its simplest terms referral means that rather than explore the situation yourself, you suggest that someone who has come to you for help should go to another source. Since the request for help has been defined as falling outside the agency's service responsibilities, it is often tempting to see your responsibility as ending when you state this fact to the person who requested your involvement. This is perhaps the end of your responsibility as an agent of a particular bureaucracy, but it is not the end of the professional responsibility. Professional commitment requires workers to assume responsibility not only for judgments and actions but for the results of judgments and actions. If you hold yourself out as a person concerned with the struggles of others, with problems of coping, you must be concerned not only with offering adequate service in connection with those problems that lie on your defined turf but also with offering the same skilled help to enable persons to reach the proper source of help. The first step in developing skills in referral is to know what it means to an individual to ask for help, either for oneself or for others. (The subject of asking for help was discussed in Chapter 10.) That knowledge is crucial in considering referral.

As a way of thinking about referrals, let's examine Reading A-7, "The House on Sixth Street," discussed in several earlier chapters. You will remember that Mrs. Smith came to the neighborhood center to request help with her housing situation. Fortunately, she came to an agency that could offer help not only to her but to all the tenants who shared her problem. Thus Mrs. Smith's original request came within the agency's parameters of service, and in the process of exploring her request, the practitioner was able to redefine the problem so that it became a community organization problem. This resulted in more effective action than would have been taken if the worker had defined the problem as only Mrs. Smith's. But suppose that Mrs. Smith turned to her Aid to Families with Dependent Children (AFDC) worker (as the only worker she knew) to talk about her problem. Suppose that the worker pointed out to her that the welfare board already had knowledge of the situation and had reduced the rent it was paying the landlord, and that was all it could do. What would have happened? Or suppose that Mrs. Smith felt that her AFDC worker really cared very little about her troubles, so she then went to a family agency she had heard about and the worker there pointed out that the agency could not offer help in a situation that was primarily between her, the welfare board, and the landlord. Is it not conceivable that Mrs. Smith would decide that there was no help for a person in her situation and that all the tenants would have gone on living in the same situation?

Now suppose instead that the worker at the private agency told Mrs. Smith that the agency could not help with the problem but that she would help find someone who could. Three days later the private agency worker reaches the welfare worker, who says he or she has done all he or she can and does not know what else can be done. Two days later the worker at the private agency finds out about the service center. The first of the next week she calls Mrs. Smith and tells her about the center, urging her to go there. By now Mrs. Smith and her children have endured another uncomfortable week, two social workers have said they cannot help, and she has been told that another worker might. How likely is it that Mrs. Smith will again bundle her four children up and trudge out to seek help at this new place?

But suppose that the family worker tells Mrs. Smith that she cannot help directly but that this does seem to be a very difficult situation for her and her children, so she would like to find out who could help. The family worker calls the welfare worker while Mrs. Smith is in the office and learns that the welfare worker cannot help. She asks the welfare worker whether she knows where such help can be sought. She looks up the agencies listed in the agency directory that most communities publish. While Mrs. Smith is still in the office, she finds out about the service center and calls to see whether it can help and what Mrs. Smith has to do to get its help. She asks Mrs. Smith whether and when she wants to go there and arranges an interview time with a worker whose name she gives Mrs. Smith. This information is shared with Mrs. Smith (often writing down names and addresses is helpful), being sure Mrs. Smith understands how to get in touch with the center worker and what the center worker will need to know about her situation. She expresses interest in seeing that Mrs. Smith gets some help and shows her understanding that it is hard to be shuffled around from agency to agency before finding anyone who will really listen. She expresses concern that Mrs. Smith get help and urges Mrs. Smith to get in touch again if this particular plan does not work out. In this case Mrs. Smith will probably get to the service center. She will also approach the new worker with some confidence in herself and her judgment in seeking help. Because of the experience she had with the family worker, she will expect to be met by a center worker who is concerned. Her quest for help has been met in a way that has furthered her confidence in her capacity to manage her life in a manner more satisfying for her.

Suppose you are driving in a strange city, thoroughly lost but hoping to work the problem out rather than having to stop and ask someone for directions, which is a common experience. What happens if you stop and ask someone who reels off complicated, generalized, and vague directions? When you ask for an estimate of how far away the destination is, the person says, "Quite a ways," and looks put off by the question. How do you feel? Do you decide that you were better off trying it on your own? You have taken the trouble to ask but are no further ahead now than before. In fact, you may be worse off because you have now wasted another half hour and feel more confused and less adequate than before.

This example illustrates the problems and principles in referrals. First, it is necessary to recognize that asking for help for yourself or others is not a simple process. Second, it is necessary to understand that when you decide to talk the situation over with someone else, the time of that decision and the move to implement it is a vulnerable period. It has taken effort to get to this point. This short vulnerable period in which the client is open to consideration of the work to be done is all too often followed by despair if something positive and forward moving is not offered.[1]

Most people wait until long after they have become aware of a problem before they seek help. They try to solve the problem alone until they become convinced of their inability to do so, so that their sense of capacity to cope has already had enough blows without the worker's telling them that they have again made a mistake by approaching the wrong resource.

The more threatening a problem is to the people asking help and the more disorganized and confused they are, the less able they are to follow through on complicated directions or to gather up the strength to retell their problem. Anyone who has experienced certain difficulties and been sent to several places before reaching the person who could help (even if the problem was only getting approval to drop one course and add another) can well understand the feelings of frustration or discouragement or anger that come with the demand that one explain the situation over and over again only to be referred somewhere else each time. Maybe the problem was finally straightened out satisfactorily, but at the cost of considerable time and effort. What would it have meant to have someone pick up the telephone and find out the right place to go and what to do?

Social agencies and the help they offer are complex businesses. It is a testimony to most people's competence that they are able to approach the appropriate agency most of the time. Rather than expect all clients to be able to handle the original request appropriately, workers should be surprised that any do so. The worker should treat

---

[1] This principle is the basis of crisis theory and other emergency services that the reader may want to explore but that cannot be developed here.

client confusion and uncertainty as a natural effect of the confusing pattern in which we seem to work.

A generalized goal for practice should be that if you cannot offer active help toward solving a problem, you at least leave clients as well prepared to deal with it as they were when you met them. You should recognize that by holding yourself out as a helping person and by being in a position that invites or allows the client to approach you, you have engaged in an interaction that places a responsibility upon you. Such responsibility is not discharged by a simple statement that the client has come to the wrong place.

Transfer

Transfer is the process by which the client is referred to another worker, usually in the same agency, after the initial worker has been working with the client on the problem. Although the transfer is sometimes made because the worker has difficulty in working with the problem or the client, usually it occurs because the initial worker is leaving the agency to take a job elsewhere.

In transfer three entities are involved: the present worker, the client, and the new worker. When clients learn that a practitioner is soon to leave the agency or that for any other reason the worker cannot continue with them, they may feel deserted and resent an ending that is imposed prematurely. They may feel that in leaving the worker is breaking the contract in which they were offered service and may resent what appears to be the worker's irresponsibility and lack of concern. Many factors may interact to determine the client's reaction. The most important will be the type of client system, the problem, and the type of relationship developed between the worker and the client. For the client whose problem involves internal system changes and who has had life experiences involving painful separations, the worker's departure may evoke all the accumulated pain of the other separations. A task-centered adult group working toward change in the community may also feel a sense of betrayal and desertion but may be more actively concerned about the competence of the new worker who will be involved with them in their work. Unexpected endings are a part of life, and if the experience is to be as positive as possible for the clients, workers who have made a decision that forces an ending to their association with clients must be aware of their own feelings, the worker who will replace them, and the possible reactions of clients.

Workers may have difficulty with their own feelings. They may feel that they are indeed betraying the client and violating the contract. They may feel that no other worker can really take their place with their clients and may subtly impart this judgment to the clients in ways that increase the clients' feelings of uncertainty. Leaving the agency can evoke painful feelings of separation in the worker. Workers may also be anxious about the demands of the new job or so deeply absorbed in these new demands that they do not give the problems of transfer their full attention. Or all these feelings may churn within them in some complex, interrelated struggle.

Perhaps the problems of transfer receive so little attention because of the difficulty of sorting out and resolving personal feelings about transfer. We once knew of a situation in which a worker shared with his client the fact that he was leaving the agency in six weeks. He promised the client that he would introduce him to his new probation officer and help him to get started with the new person. The client was an adolescent who had a long history of theft and assault. He was a young man who had never had a trusting relationship with anyone in his short life until he met the worker. However, through his relationship to the worker, he had made tremendous changes in his behavior over the year they had worked together. There had been no new offenses during this time. Thus the worker was surprised to hear from the police the next week that his client had stolen a car and resisted arrest when apprehended. When the two met to discuss the problem, the client greeted the worker by saying, "Now you can't leave. I am in a new mess and you can't leave until you go to court with me and get me straightened out again." This young man had acted out his pain of separation. What happens to the client's ability to form trusting relationships when the worker explains to him that he must go regardless of the client's sense of need? What can the worker do to ease the pain and to support the ability to trust?

The transfer may also pose some problems for the new workers. They may wonder whether they can offer as effective help as did the first worker and may meet clients with a kind of defensiveness and a determination to prove themselves rather than continue the work together. They may therefore move out too rapidly with new ideas that clients are not ready for. Clients may be angry and hurt about the transfer, and because of this as well as their feelings of loyalty and trust for the first worker it is often necessary for them to mark some time and do some testing before they are willing to move on. It is to be expected that certain clients will lose much of their trust in the worker and be afraid to risk establishing a new relationship with another person who may also leave. The new worker must recognize all these things, especially the right of the clients to have their feelings and take the time they need to deal with them.

A transfer is less hurtful and destructive to the work being done when there is time for both client and worker to deal with it and for the new worker to get involved in an orderly manner. When a transfer is necessitated by the first worker's leaving the agency, clients often regard it as a desertion. They may feel that if they were important to the worker or worse yet if they were a good and satisfying client, the worker would stay with them. Clients should be told as soon as possible about the worker's leaving, and they need to participate with the worker in the planning for transfer to another worker or possibly to terminate their contact with the agency. The client's feelings about the change should be recognized by the worker. The worker can invite the client to discuss these feelings. At times, particularly in group situations, clients can be encouraged to role-play the transfer, from their concern about the first worker's departure through their beginning with a new worker. They can discuss or role-play their fantasies about the new worker.

Clients need opportunities to meet with the new worker. The first time, the new worker may just stop in for a minute to be introduced by the old worker and say hello. After the new worker leaves, the old worker may discuss with clients their feelings and thoughts about the new worker from just this introduction.

The second time, if the client system is a group, the new worker may attend a meeting as an observer, or if the client system is an individual or a family, may sit in on an interview. The old worker remains in charge, so to speak, and the new worker is just there to get acquainted. At the third encounter the two workers operate as a team, with the new worker gradually assuming the primary professional role. At this encounter the two workers can talk together, trying to assess where they are and how the new worker understands and evaluates the contract, with the client as observer. This helps the client to understand very clearly what the new worker is told and what the new worker's commitment is. There may be a fourth formal session at which the new worker is in charge, but there should be a time at the end of the session for the client and the old worker to meet in the absence of the new worker for good-byes and for assessment, both of what has been accomplished by the first worker and of the client's expectations of the second.

If the transfer is being brought about because the client feels that there is a problem between the client and the first worker, the situation is different in that it is the client who is leaving the worker. In this situation workers should carefully examine their own feelings and to be sure that the client is left totally free to move on to another relationship.

Termination

Social work intervention is always time-centered. At its best it is directed toward the realization of goals that are specific enough for progress to be measured in relation to them. In *Social Work with Groups,* Helen Northen (1969, p. 222) makes a statement about termination with groups that is applicable to all sizes and types of systems:

> The purposeful nature of social work implies that from time to time it is necessary to assess the desirability of continuing service to the members. The judgment may be that there has been progress toward the achievement of goals and there is potential for further improvement, in which case the service should be continued. Another decision may be that little, if any, progress has been made; if this is combined with little potential for changing the situation, the service should be discontinued. Still another evaluation may be that progress toward the achievement of goals has been sufficient, and the service should be terminated. Social workers have undoubtedly anticipated termination from the beginning of their work with the group and have clarified with the members its possible duration, so that the goals and means toward their achievement have been related to the plans for both individuals and the group. Nevertheless, there comes a time when the worker and the members must face the fact of separation from each other and often, also, the end of the group itself.

Evaluation, the appraisal of the progress that the worker and client system as a working partnership have achieved is an ongoing process. The ultimate test of the effectiveness of social work practice is the extent to which positive movement toward the goals set has been accomplished. Thus the goals as initially developed between client and worker, as periodically evaluated, and as modified periodically by joint agreement become the criteria for evaluating progress. Whenever termination is being considered, a thorough review and evaluation of what has or has not been accomplished and of the processes by which these gains were made or failed to be made is imperative. In their own unilateral evaluation workers may begin to wonder whether the goals are in sight, and they may be the ones to introduce the matter of termination. Or clients may indicate that they are beginning to believe they are ready to move on to a new experience and leave the worker behind. This is often communicated to the worker by the client's behavior rather than by verbal discussion. Clients begin to miss appointments or indicate with pride that they took some unilateral action toward the goal. These are ways of saying that they can go it alone.

In talking about the indications for termination in the group, Helen Northen (1969, p. 225) says much the same thing:

As the group moves toward readiness for termination, there are clues to guide practitioners in their activities with the group. The goals that members have for themselves and each other have been partially achieved, at least, although movement in the group may have been faster for some than for others. Members come to talk about some of the changes that have taken place in them and in the group. Attendance becomes irregular unless the worker makes special efforts to motivate members to continue until the final meeting. . . . The structure tends to become more flexible; for example, by giving up official roles within the membership or by changes in time, place, and frequency of meetings. . . . Cohesiveness weakens as the members find satisfactions and new relationships outside the group.

The need for termination, whether introduced by the client or the worker, should be discussed well in advance of the termination date to allow sufficient time for this aspect of worker and client experience with each other to be as productive as other parts of work together. To quote Helen Northen (1969, p. 228) once again:

The time span between the initial information about termination and the final meeting of the group will vary with many factors, including the group's purpose, the length of time the group has been together, the problems and progress of the members, their anticipated reactions to termination, and the press of the environment on them.

These elements should be considered in working with individuals or families. In general the tasks of termination are (1) working out the conflict for both worker and client between the acknowledgment of improvement and goal achievement and the movement away from help, (2) working out the fear of loss of the relationship and of the support of a concerned person, (3) examining the experience and recognizing the progress made, (4) considering how this experience can be transferred to other problems as they come along, (5) examining what is involved in stabilizing the gains made, and (6) clarifying the worker's continuing position.

Termination of a relationship has great meaning, and a great investment of emotions and feelings of one person with another entails grief at such a loss. This grief may involve the following typical reactions: (1) the denial of termination (clients refuse to accept the notion of termination and behave as though it were not going to happen), (2) a return to patterns of earlier behavior or a reintroduction as problems of situations and tasks that have been taken care of long ago, (3) explosive behavior in which the client says that the worker was wrong when the worker thought that the client could go it alone, and (4) a precipitate break in the relationship by the client as though to say that the client will leave the worker before the worker leaves the client.

For social workers, termination stirs up emotions about both their professional activities and their feelings for their clients. They will undoubtedly feel pleased about the progress that has been made, but like the client will feel a sense of loss and grief in the parting. They may find that termination stirs up mixed feelings about the quality of their work; guilt about not having been able to do better; and fear of the client's efforts to go ahead independently.

In the final disengagement, workers make it clear that the door is open, that they will be available for future problem solving if this falls within their agency's services, and if it does not, that they will help find an agency that is appropriate. They assure their clients of their continued interest in them and of their belief in their ability to move onto other goals and other efforts. It is often well to mark the last contact by some symbol. With a family, group, or organization a party can be helpful. In some instances a formal letter of accomplishment of goals may be very meaningful.

Recapitulation

This chapter's discussion has focused on three special tasks in social work — referral, transfer, and termination. These are situations in which workers terminate their relationship with clients. In referral the client's request is considered to be beyond the parameters of the agency's services and the client is referred to others before any significant work on the problem is done. In transfer and termination the client and the worker have established a relationship over time. We have urged that these three special tasks are important aspects of the social work process and that you see them as involving significant skills.

Unfortunately, these tasks have not received appropriate attention in social work literature. Few articles develop the detailed statements about the methods of transfer or termination. We urge that you go back and read the Debbie Smith case (Reading A-1) and the Stover case (Reading A-6). In the Smith case the worker recorded that the client was now able to grow on her own, so she had no more use for the worker. There is no recorded material about how Miss Smith reacted to the closing. Do you think the worker helped Miss Smith to evaluate their work together? Did Miss Smith feel confident that she could go it alone? Should the worker have suggested that Miss Smith feel free to call if she needed more help? If you close a case with the statement that the client is now able to handle things alone, what do you think it means to the client if he or she is unable to do so in the face of new emergencies? To help to preserve the client's sense of competence, the worker must recognize with the client that new stresses sometimes can result in the need for some help once again. The worker was a student who was leaving the agency. Do you think this influenced the time and the way she ended the case?

Now read the Stover case. How much time elapsed between the time that the worker suggested closing Mrs. Stover's case and the time it was closed for regular work? Note the process that was a part of the closing. What do you think was accomplished by the worker's engaging the client in an evaluation of what had been accomplished? Note that the client was encouraged to reach out again to the agency if she felt it was necessary and that she did so. How helpful do you think this was in preserving the gains that Mrs. Stover had made?

A Look Forward

Because of the difficulty in finding articles on termination, we asked two social workers who have had an interest in this process to write a special article for this book. We hope you find it as helpful as we think it is. We have also included a brief list of articles and books that are available.

| Reading 15-1 | *Termination in Context** |

Howard Hess and Peg McCartt Hess

One of the distinctive characteristics of social work process is its temporary nature. Thus, termination is a natural conclusion, whether worker-client interaction has entailed a single interview for the purpose of assessment and referral or a series of interviews over time in the context of the therapeutic relationship. Once termination has begun, issues of separation and self-sufficiency are central. Interaction is dominated by recognition that at some point the process will cease and both client and social worker will make a determination about the value of their work together. Because of the potency of the issues of separation and evaluation, the ending is broadly recognized as a difficult phase for both client and practitioner (Fox, Nelson, & Bolman, 1969, p. 63; Shulman, 1992, pp. 173–174; Siebold, 1991; Siporin, 1975, p. 337; Webb, 1985). In many instances ambivalence about the ending causes both to vacillate in their judgments about the appropriate conclusion to their work. The capacity to bring resolution to this ambivalence determines the quality of the termination experience.

During termination clients must accomplish two general tasks: first, they must confront and begin to accept the impending separation from their helper, and second, they must come to terms with the outcome of the helping process. Client awareness of both loss and outcome is stimulated by the encroaching time limit of termination. At no other phase in the process is time such a powerful influence. The press of time requires client and practitioner to confront both the limits of their relationship and the importance of client self-responsibility and autonomy.

Because clients and practitioners often form close attachments, termination typically requires working through the grief resulting from a break in these ties. Movement through the grief process involves a giving up, or decathexis, of the lost object. This process is supported by the clear

evaluation or review of accomplishments. The termination phase thus demands an intricate management of both loss and evaluation of gain. The presence of one theme stimulates the other, ultimately allowing termination to occur. If the goals of working together have been accomplished, clients can be helped to acknowledge the appropriateness of ending. Conversely, if the goals have not been accomplished, the client can be helped to determine whether the goals were realistic and how problem solving can continue after the end point with the practitioner. When the helping process is disrupted, the termination work should clarify the nature of the necessary referral or transfer. As the work is reviewed, clients often experience a blend of pride in accomplished change, hope for the future, and sorrow about the loss of a valued resource. As the themes of loss and evaluation resonate against one another, the client moves toward either a resumption of living exclusive of the helping process or continuation of the process with another helping person.

The following vignette taken from student process recording of a final interview captures the interrelationship between loss and evaluation during the ending phase. The social work student and client both struggle with bringing closure to an experience which is somewhat new for both of them:

Student: I was wondering if we could talk a little bit about . . . We haven't talked very much about the fact that this is my last visit to you. I just wanted to hear how you're feeling about that.

Client: I'd rather you'd stay on . . . and still come . . . In a way I hated for you even to come today because I said I won't see her from now on . . . I said, well maybe I'll just leave the house and that way she might have to come back . . . I said no, I'll just wait.

Student: Endings are hard, C, and it's hard for me, too, because you've been a very important person to me these last months.

---

*An original paper written for this text.

Client: You've helped me a lot when nobody else could, just sitting down and talking. Other people say you're wrong, you're wrong. You're crazy. You think you are crazy. What's wrong with you? That's all I ever hear from B. I can't talk to B about nothing.

Student: It feels good to be able to talk and to say what's on your mind and not be judged. I'm glad that it has been helpful to you to have someone to talk to. I think you've done some things for yourself, too, C. That's kind of what I'd like to pay attention to just now.

Client: What?

Student: I'd like to talk about what you've been doing for yourself that has been helping.

Client: Yeah, but you know I just started almost not wanting to go back to the doctor's and the only thing that made me really want to go back was that I started bleeding yesterday.

Student: Uh huh.

Client: Cause I really started feeling again like I just didn't care no more.

Student: I wonder . . .

Client: Easy let down . . . It's easy for me to feel let down like that. Very easy.

Student: I wondered . . . I was thinking about what you had said last time. That you didn't want to be dependent on anybody and so forth. If that might have something to do with the fact that you had grown dependent on me over these past few months and that I was going to let you down just like everybody else has.

Client: I was thinking about how I'll feel about that other social worker. I don't know if I'll be able to talk to her like I've been able to talk to you. I might feel angry toward her. I've been thinking about that and feeling if maybe I'd feel angry because she's trying to take S's place. [Note: This is the first time C has referred to me in an interview by name. It impressed me as a way to touch as closely as it is possible for her to.] And it won't be the same.

In this instance client and social work student have worked together to resolve problems of a life-threatening nature. Although both agree that the treatment should continue with another social worker, the exploration of the client's ambivalence, of feelings of loss and anger, as well as of evaluation of gains made thus far facilitate closure and an effective transfer.

THE CONTEXT OF TERMINATION

Although the termination phase is unique, it cannot be accurately understood outside of the context of an entire course of treatment. Decisions made early about focus and goals directly determine the potential for review during termination. One of the major integrative dimensions that can be traced throughout the entire treatment process is the attachment that develops during early and middle phases between client and helper. Consequently, the practitioner's awareness of differential relationship patterns becomes crucial in the planning and management of termination. In addition, termination always occurs within a specified social context, including the organization which both sponsors and shapes the helping process. The practitioner must be able to relate the ending of treatment conceptually to each of these factors.

PROBLEM DEFINITION

Clarity about the focus of the helping process is a necessary prerequisite to successful termination. Specification of client problems and agreement about goals leads naturally to determination of how long the treatment will continue and how activities will be structured. Goals are established and reworked throughout the helping process and reflected in the specific termination plan. In this respect the quality of termination review can be directly correlated with the clarity of formulated treatment goals. Lack of precision in the early and middle phases of the work creates difficulty in measuring the extent to which the goals have been achieved (see Chapter 16, on evaluation). The point of termination then becomes more difficult to fix and relationship may become the focus of the work together rather than a vehicle.

If client problems are developmental or life transitional in nature, the termination may well be designed to allow periodic return, or checking in with the practitioner as the developmental progression continues (Golan, 1981, p. 269). On the other hand, if the client problems are related to specific material or physical difficulties, a fixed end point may be appropriate. When the expectations of the outcome of the helping process are shared and based upon a skillful assessment, the format of termination will have already been suggested.

Remember, clients' expectations concerning what will be derived from the helping process are maintained by hopes for specific change as well as the subjective meaning or value of the helping relationship. As the work progresses, the practitioner must monitor and maintain the appropriate balance between goal achievement and relationship gratification. Termination decisions should reflect awareness of client uniqueness in this regard.

THE HELPING RELATIONSHIP

The attachment between client and social worker is the source of both the pain experienced in termination and the support helpful in the ending period. The impending separation is a violation of the wish intrinsic in most meaningful attachments for the relationship to remain permanently active. For this reason termination may be approached with ambivalence by both client and practitioner. This ambivalence in a sense recapitulates the ambivalence about the beginning of the work together. Knowledge about the separation and individuation process verifies the presence of strongly felt, often contradictory feelings and ideas about leaving valued others (Kauff, 1977, pp. 3–18). Mastery of termination necessarily requires both client and practitioner to experience and share a variety of reactions to the ending.

One way that social workers can prepare for and guide termination is to teach clients about the predictable reactions to loss and to aid them in identifying those reactions when either directly or indirectly expressed. Various authors have written about the predictable stages of the grief process: denial, anger, sadness, acceptance, and disengagement (Germain & Gitterman, 1980; Kubler-Ross, 1969; Lindemann, 1956, pp. 7–21; Webb, 1985). For example, clients who have previously experienced multiple or traumatic losses may react with sadness and feelings of abandonment. On the other hand, clients who have succeeded in achieving

desired gains in treatment may be particularly proud and self-confident during the termination phase (Fortune, 1987). Exercise caution not to assume that all clients uniformly transverse these stages in lockstep fashion or that all clients react to termination with the same intensity. However, it is generally recognized that both clients and practitioners are prone to deal with termination initially with denial. The expression of this denial may take many forms varying from general detachment to premature discontinuation of sessions. Initially denial may provide the client with space for adaptation. Appropriate focus by the practitioner often aids in surmounting the denial and allows open exchange about the pain and confusion associated with loss. Practitioners may experience uncertainty about their own capacity to deal with the ending and encourage clients to remain in a state of denial as a form of self-protection. As noted earlier, separation and ending inevitably evoke self-examination regarding competence and accomplishment. Social workers and clients alike are forced to confront their own limitations. Denial may become a protection from self-doubt.

It is the responsibility of the practitioner to guide the ending process through appropriate timing of interventions and use of self-disclosure. The honest expression of the practitioners' own reactions during the termination phase facilitates the client's experience and expression of feelings and ideas stimulated by termination. Through this mutual exchange or sharing of responses, the reality of the ending is verified.

One of the major tasks of termination is to construct a bridge between treatment and the clients' subsequent problem-solving efforts. In part this may be accomplished through a synthesis of termination evaluation and planning. Clients should be empowered through the termination process to embark upon a self-directed course of action based upon a realistic assessment of their problem solving strengths. The mastery of termination issues supports client self-esteem and reinforces the client's hope that ongoing progress can be achieved. The work of the ending also frees the client to reinvest energy in appropriate life tasks and ongoing relationships that support problem solving.

Differential Patterns of Attachment

In the forgoing discussion the open-ended helping relationship between an individual client and practitioner was utilized as the vehicle for discussing feelings related to loss in termination. However, individual counseling is but one variation of the social work helping process. Many clients present problems related to either inadequate resources or information and have limited interest in or need for counseling. In addition, many clients are best helped within their families or in small groups.

Variations both in client problems and goals and the modality used are associated with important qualitative differences in the nature of the ending or termination of the helping process. In different types of work the nature of the client-practitioner attachment varies, as does the kind of focus and length of time required for successful mastery of the termination phase. The two-dimensional typology in Figure 15-1 represents variations in termination related to the social worker's primary treatment activities and system size. Variations considered relate to the attachment typically developed and resultant implications for the termination process.

Counseling

Individual counseling often allows for the development of a high degree of mutual attachment. The longer the duration of the process the more pronounced the intimate tie may become. Termination of individual counseling is quite likely to prompt elements of the grieving process for client and practitioner in response to loss. The termination of a predominantly counseling individual relationship may be time consuming and is typically discussed in the literature as requiring focused attention throughout the last sixth of the helping process. For example, in treatment of a year's duration, the last eight weeks should be utilized for ending, as would two of the last 8 to 12 interviews in short-term treatment (Reid & Epstein, 1972, pp. 22–23; Shulman, 1992, p. 176; Webb (1985), p. 338). Inattention to termination or prolonged use of denial may provoke regression and circumvent solidification of gains. The practitioner's role is to monitor and persistently call attention to the dynamics inherent in the ending phase.

Counseling with families and small groups can also entail a high degree of relationship intensity between clients and practitioner. The major distinction between family or group and individual treatment is that any single client's attachment is to several others. In fact, one of the practitioner's major goals in work with families and small groups is to facilitate individuals' communication with others as well as to solidify members' attachments with one another. The attachment between the individual client and practitioner is diffused throughout the client system. Although a family's termination with the practitioner may be painful to

FIGURE 15-1 Variations in Termination of the Helping Process		System Size		
	Primary Activities	**Individual**	**Group**	**Family**
	Counseling			
	Education			
	Resource mobilization (referral, mediation, advocacy, brokerage)			

individual family members, the experience of loss is often modified by the reality that the family is likely to remain intact and members can turn to one another for support. The practitioner's role during termination is to underscore the family's interpersonal resources. Loss of the practitioner is moderated by the attachments shared by family members and by review of the system's shared treatment accomplishments.

In the group, several phenomena may be present (Shulman, 1992, p. 573). If the group is ongoing or naturally formed, as is a neighborhood group, classroom, or cottage unit, individual group members may turn to one another for assistance during and following termination. Therefore, loss of the practitioner may stimulate a different reaction from that which occurs in a formed group that disbands at termination. Such a termination can be quite emotionally charged due to the members' loss of several objects, including the group as a whole, other group members, and the group worker. The group practitioner must facilitate the members' ability to detach from and dissolve the group. The loss theme resonates throughout the small group and is reworked in relationships not necessarily directly involving the group worker. In this instance the practitioner places major emphasis upon the group members' efforts to deal with the loss of one another and acts as a catalyst, encouraging member interactions.

Educational Interventions

Educational interventions tend to maintain a focus upon cognitive processes with new learning rather than emotional change or stabilization the major goal. Although intimate relationships certainly can develop when the helping goals and supporting interventions are educational, the attachment between client and practitioner may be less intense than described above. The point of termination is often preset by the specific nature and amount of material to be learned. There is typically less client concern that termination will endanger the maintenance of that which has been learned and more of an emphasis upon continued practice and utilization of new skills beyond the context of treatment. The practitioner's educational interventions en-

courage generalization of learning through rehearsal and practice in the client's natural environment. A clear focus upon evidence of the client's learning and self-sufficiency is the most effective method of reinforcing gains during the ending period. Educational interventions with families (family life education) or groups (parent education groups) are not likely to result in intense attachments between clients and practitioners. Feelings of loss are typically limited by the lesser degree of dependency encouraged by the educational focus.

Resource Mobilization

Interventions focused upon resource mobilization may include referral, mediation, brokerage, and/or advocacy. The relationship in these instances is often experienced intensely, with a rapidly developing attachment occurring between client and practitioner. This is likely either because of the urgency of the identified problem or the closely shared mobilization effort directed toward an outside source. However, in spite of the intensity of the effort, the worker's position is transitional: a way station to an additional helping resource somewhere else. Consequently, termination is focused heavily upon the success of resource mobilization and less upon the attendant interaction between client and practitioner. Resource mobilization with families such as foster families and groups such as community or neighborhood groups is also highly task focused. Termination is expected when the resource is activated but may include a provision for additional contact should resource problems reappear. Although attachments may be strong throughout a specific period, the relationship expectations are clearly delimited. Therefore, termination may be less affectively charged and may require differential emphasis upon evaluation of outcomes rather than upon issues of loss or grief.

Certain general statements can be made about the presence of differential helping relationships based both upon the primary activities and the system size with which interventions occur:

1. The more exclusive the relationship between client and practitioner, the more intense the attachment between them is likely to be. Greater intensity of attachments typically necessitates greater attention to the grieving process. Generally family and group system sizes allow multiple resources for resolution of grief. Feelings of loss are diffused and shared with other clients.

2. The greater or more pervasive the dependency and/or attachment developed between client and practitioner, the more emotionally charged the termination is likely to be. The ending phase of such relationships will require sensitive support and encouragement toward self-sufficiency. Certain interventions as discussed above more typically result in client dependency upon the practitioner than do others.

3. The greater the extent to which clients can continue in relationships that were a part of the helping process, the more limited will be their reactions to the loss of the practitioner. Clients in families and ongoing groups are more likely to be able to substitute one another for the lost practitioner and thereby more readily resolve the grieving process.

4. Themes of both loss and evaluation can be expected to be present in the termination of each helping relationship, and therefore clients' ideas and feelings with regard to each theme should be recognized and explored.

In summary, the differential character of relationship patterns contributes to the balance of these themes. For example, counseling relationships must include a time for grief work in order to progress through termination. Educational interventions, focused upon the efficacy of the learned content and rehearsal for its use suggest an ending phase linked to learning transfer and opportunity for clients to participate in problem-solving efforts beyond the treatment situation. Successful treatment using educational interventions will therefore be less exclusively shared by client and worker and require considerably less focus upon their relationship. In the area of resource mobilization the attachment may be temporarily strong but is soon offset by the fulfillment of a need or a linkage to another helping resource. The theme of termination may be expected to be upon the success of resource linkage rather than the dimension of losing the helper.

The typology in Figure 15-2 is presented to illustrate the central points in the above discussion.

While the above guidelines provide a framework for anticipating the balance of loss and evaluation themes in termination, it is recognized that each case is unique. Practitioners often engage in multiple intervention activities throughout the helping process; thus termination may be a blend of the characteristics described. In addition, individual clients' sensitivity to loss will further influence the balance of these themes in the ending process.

Organizational Influences upon the Ending Phase

Even as termination is defined by the client's problem and the nature of the helping relationship, it is shaped by the organizational context within which social work intervention occurs. The organizational mission delineates boundaries both for the nature of the client problems addressed and the typical or preferred treatment modalities utilized. Intra- and interorganizational factors may also affect the timing and process of termination.

The impact of the organizational mission upon the process of termination is most evident in settings that provide social work services as a secondary service, such as hospitals, schools, emergency shelters, and the workplace. In such settings typically clients are eligible for the practitioner's assistance only for the duration of their involvement with the primary service. Thus, when patients are discharged from the hospital, children reach the end of the school year, clients leave an emergency shelter, or employees experience a change in employment, their relationship with a social worker employed by the organization is most likely terminated. While such setting-specific endings are planned for and anticipated openly by the client and practitioner together, the ending itself may be experienced as an unnatural or premature closure. A social worker in a children's hospital noted: "Each morning when I come in to work, the first thing I do is check the census to see who's missing." Such abrupt endings may be accompanied by a brief follow-up period for attention to termination issues or by referral of the client for continuing services. However, provision of time to accomplish the tasks of termination is crucial both for clients, whether or

FIGURE 15-2 Variations in Termination of the Helping Process	Primary Activities	System Size		
		Individual	**Group**	**Family**
	Counseling	Attachment may be intense. Loss in termination may include considerable grief; must be openly managed and processed in mutual interaction.	Attachment may be intense but shared with group worker, group as a whole and other members. Grief may be considerable; when formed groups terminate, focus must be maintained upon ending and multiple separations. In natural groups loss moderated by ongoing ties between members. Termination should include support of groups' ongoing motivation to support members.	Attachment may be intense but is shared with other family members. Loss moderated by family's continuation. Termination focus upon improved attachments and communication within family system.
	Education	Attachment may be of moderate intensity. Ending often preset in original plan and focuses upon success in learning and generalization beyond treatment setting.	Attachment usually more moderate in intensity. Differences persist between formed and natural groups, but have less impact upon the nature of termination. Emphasis in both groups upon evaluation of learning. Some formed groups may continue after treatment ends.	Attachment often more moderate in intensity. As family is usually ongoing, termination includes focus upon members' mutual support and application of learning that has occurred.

(continued)

FIGURE 15-2 (continued)		System Size		
	Primary Activities	**Individual**	**Group**	**Family**
	Resource mobilization (referral, brokerage, mediation, advocacy)	Attachment may be intense, but transitional and/or intermittent.	Attachment may be intense but present between multiple group members.	Attachment may be intense and may have resulted in strengthening family relationships.
		Loss moderated by attachment to new resource and/or need satisfaction. Focus is upon evaluation of mobilization with door open for return. Loss not usually theme in termination discussion.	Termination should enhance groups' capacity to locate and utilize resources independently. During this phase some formed groups will develop into natural groups maintaining their ties.	Termination should enhance the family's capacity to locate and utilize resources independently. Specific skills regarding use of resources learned by family members may be consolidated during termination.

not they seek services elsewhere, and for practitioners, who must begin with other clients necessarily anticipating the likelihood of premature closure.

Settings in which social services are the primary organizational mission also structure beginnings and endings of client-practitioner relationships through available program options and preferred treatment modalities. For example, clients may be referred within the agency following problem definition and assessment to a six- or eight-week divorce adjustment group. Public agencies mandated to serve all persons requesting services in a geographic area, such as a community mental health center, may develop guidelines limiting the length of time client services are available or designating the modalities to be utilized, such as crisis intervention, planned short-term treatment, or group treatment. In the process of contracting with clients, such agency guidelines should be openly shared. This minimizes the client's personal rejection at the time of ending and maximizes the realistic definition of treatment goals.

Other organizational factors also impact upon the progression of the helping process. For example, requirements for practitioners' productivity or for third-party reimbursement for agency services may contribute to subtle or explicit pressures upon practitioners. There may be expectations that social workers continue with clients beyond contracted services to maintain a percentage of direct service time or terminate prematurely because of the exhaustion of reimbursement benefits by the client. Practitioners may also be asked to terminate with clients prematurely in order to serve growing numbers of persons on the waiting list. Such pressures regarding the treatment process present ethical dilemmas for the individual social worker as well as for the organization and inevitably impact upon the practitioners' feelings about the employing agency and about beginnings and endings with clients.

Interorganizational pressures may also occur when clients have been referred involuntarily by the courts or other systems, such as the workplace and schools. Potential difficulties in the ending phase are presented for client and practitioner alike when the problem definition and/or length of treatment are determined externally and as a condition for an event such as a child's return home from foster care, an employee's return to work, or a continuation of probation.

Organizational commitments to professional training also shape the termination process. An exploratory study of students' termination of individual clinical work at the end of an academic year found that students in the sample appeared to learn about termination primarily from their agency supervisors (Gould, 1978, pp. 235–269). Students' first-year field agency supervisors as well as several of the second-year supervisors encouraged students not to discuss the predictable training-related ending of treatment with their clients until the latter part of treatment (Gould, 1978, pp. 235–251, 260–261).

The approach encouraged with these students places both student practitioners and clients in a compromising position. While the organization's desire to present students as employees may be benign in intent, the potential destructive impact of this misrepresentation upon the helping process, particularly in the termination phase, is a matter of concern. "Where agencies are open and direct about their training function, and present their students as supervised learners, termination is less complicated by guilt and resentment. Clients expect the student's departure at the end of the academic year and termination and transfer are most likely to be viewed as legitimate" (Germain & Gitterman, 1980, p. 257).

Thus the organizational context, even as do the clients' problems and the differential nature of the client-practitioner relationship, influences the nature of the help offered and received. Therefore it is crucial that inter- and intraorganizational factors be fully and openly weighed early in the process as the client and practitioner explore goals, options, and tasks together, and in the ending phase as feelings and content regarding loss and evaluation emerge. Any other stance jeopardizes the productive completion of the ending phase and the positive evaluation of work together.

THE ROLE OF SELF-AWARENESS IN TERMINATION

The nature of the tasks presented during the ending phase demands openness on the part of the worker to a range of intense feelings and reactions from the client, including sadness, anger, and negative evaluation of their work together. Clients may also express relief, increased self esteem, and diminished need for the worker's assistance. The predictable themes of the ending phase frame important areas for social worker's introspection and action.

Competent use of the professional self relies upon practitioners' continuing self-examination and self-awareness. Social workers necessarily explore their own attitudes, values, experiences, and feelings in order that the interaction between worker and client be guided by the client's rather than the worker's needs and concerns. In the termination phase these include the worker's life-long experiences with and feelings about separations generally; feelings and concerns about the worker's competence as a helping person; and feelings about a specific client system and the ending of work together.

The predictable stirring of memories and feelings associated with separation for both client and worker is the major consistent theme in the description of the process of termination: "The ending process in a helping relationship can trigger feelings of the deepest kind in both worker and client. This is the reason why there is potential for powerful work during this phase as well as ineffective work if the feelings are not dealt with" (Shulman, 1992, p. 174). The social worker's ability to deal with these feelings in the helping interaction builds upon awareness of the personal meaning of separation. Therefore, the practitioner's own experiences with separation and assumptions about clients' feelings emerge as areas for reflection. Thus, practitioners' experiences, whether with death, divorce, geographic moves, or other losses or transitions, may affect their ability to individualize the meaning of the ending to specific clients. Painful or recent separation experiences may prompt a practitioner to deny the importance of the ending to the client in order to avoid remembering or reexperiencing painful feelings.

When the termination is based upon the practitioner's own timetable and needs rather than those of the clients, self-awareness of own feelings is particularly important. For example, practitioners leaving an agency or students completing a semester of agency-based practicum training (Gould, 1978, pp. 235–269; Moss & Moss, 1967, pp.

433–437; Siebold, 1991) may experience conflict because they are acting in their own interest rather than concern for the client. A second-year social work student described her reactions to termination: "I haven't yet had any real terminations with clients—all my cases have ended when the placement is over—I feel so guilty to quit working with my clients because my time is over, not because we're through. I have offered to volunteer here at the agency when the placement is over." Persons completing professional training are also typically in the process of separating from the university, from the student role, from practicum agency and field instructor, and from classmates. Therefore, client terminations become part of a broader current separation experience. It is important that the multifaceted nature of this transition period be explored and understood by the student practitioner (Husband & Scheunemann, 1972, pp. 505–513).

A second area in which practitioners must be self-aware is that of confidence in their own competence. Inevitably the evaluative component of ending raises the questions, "Have I done well by this client? Could I have done more to be helpful?" It is not possible to evaluate and review client goal accomplishment without scrutiny of the practitioner's sensitive and skilled use of self in the process. While it has been concluded that the major reason for professional inattention to termination as a phase of treatment "seems to be the general sensitivity to loss and separation" (Fox, Nelson, & Bolman, 1969, p. 62), another contributing factor may be the profession's general sensitivity to accountability and evaluation. Germain and Gitterman (1980, p. 278), emphasize, however, "Endings can be particularly valuable to workers' efforts to build professional knowledge and to refine their skills. Careful assessment of outcomes with clients, identifying what was helpful and what was not helpful, and why, can gradually be generalized to the level of practice principles." Objective evaluation and conceptualization of one's practice is preceded by self-examination and acknowledgement of the practitioner's level of training and experience and the professional expectation of continued growth. Each termination provides fur-

ther information regarding the practitioner's strengths and professional learning needs.

However, feelings of inadequacy or guilt about the failure to help a particular client should be shared and examined with one's supervisor, consultant, or colleagues to determine the reality of this assessment and to prevent transmission of the message that the client should either reassure the practitioner of his or her worth or confirm lack of worth.

The specific meaning for the practitioner of a particular client and of that client's termination also merits self-examination. For example, has this client been particularly gratifying? Or ungratifying? Is this client terminating with little accomplished? Has the client's success or lack of success taken on a special meaning for the practitioner personally or within the organization? Does the practitioner have fantasies of a continuing relationship with the client? Is there relief at the idea of terminating with this client? Have organizational pressures become an issue in the treatment and termination? Levinson writes, "During treatment the therapist has an opportunity to participate in a creative process in which a new or modified self emerges. . . . Saying good-bye to the patient by the therapist can be akin to saying good-bye to a part of himself" (Levinson, 1977, p. 483). The meanings of termination are personal to the practitioner as well as to the client. Anticipating these meanings is an important aspect of preparation for the disciplined and conscious use of self in attending to the meaning of the ending for the client.

Practitioners anticipate the ending in part through exploring their personal reactions to separation, feelings of professional worth and adequacy, and reactions to each unique ending. Self-awareness in these areas enables the worker to help the client express feelings and skillfully to assist the client throughout the ending phase.

SUMMARY

Whether brief or long-term, the intent of the helping process is to make a positive difference in the life of the client. It is through the process of termination that this difference can be understood, evaluated, and maintained. The major task of the practitioner during the ending phase is to help the client move from denial of the inevitable ending point to exploration of ideas and feelings related both to outcome of the helping process and to the termination of the helping relationship. The practitioner's ability to accomplish this task will depend upon his or her self-awareness and skills as well as his or her own conceptual grasp of the multifaceted context within which termination occurs: the client's problems and goals, the differential nature of the helping relationship, and the sponsoring organization. Thus each termination can be uniquely anticipated and sensitively completed.

For Further Reading

Fortune, A. (1987). Grief only? Client and social worker reactions to termination. *Clinical Social Work Journal, 15,* 159–171.

Fortune, A., Pearlingi, B., and Rochelle, C. (1991). Criteria for terminating treatment. *Families in Society: The Journal of Contemporary Human Services, 72,* 366–370.

Fox, E., Nelson, M., & Bolman, W. (1963). The termination process: A neglected dimension in social work. *Social Work, 14,* 53–63.

Golan, N. (1981). *Passing through transitions.* New York: Free Press.

Gould, R. (1978). Students' experience with the termination phase of treatment. *Smith College Studies in Social Work, 48,* 235–269.

Husband , D., & Scheunemann, H. (1972). The use of group process in teaching termination. *Child Welfare, 51,* 505–513.

Kauff, P. (1977). The termination process: Its relationship to the separation individuation phase of development. *International Journal of Group Psychiatry, 27(7),* 3–18.

Levinson, H. (1977). Termination of psychotherapy: Some salient issues. *Social Casework, 58,* 480–498.

Moss, S., & Moss, M. (1967). When a caseworker leaves an agency: The impact on worker and client. *Social Casework, 48(7),* 433–437.

Shulman, L. (1992). *The skills of helping individuals, families, and groups* (3rd ed). Itasca, IL: F.E. Peacock.

Siebold, C. (1991). Termination: When the therapist leaves. *Clinical Social Work Journal, 19,* 191–204.

Webb, N.B. (1985). A crisis intervention perspective on the termination process. *Clinical Social Work Journal, 13(4),* 329–340.

Evaluation

Social workers, along with other human service professionals, are called on to justify the efficiency and effectiveness of their services and intervention plans. *Effectiveness* refers to answering the question of whether the services or intervention plans are accomplishing their intended goals. *Efficiency* refers to the cost of services and intervention plans in money, time, and other resources. As a social worker, you will be involved in several different types of evaluation activities, including the following:

1. Evaluating with your clients the efficiency and effectiveness of the specific intervention plan you are following.
2. Working jointly with colleagues to evaluate the programs and services offered by your agency.
3. Using knowledge generated by program evaluation to assist you and your clients in selecting approaches to intervention that are likely to achieve the agreed on goals. In Chapters 3 and 4 we identified our responsibilities to contribute to knowledge development and to bring knowledge to the client-worker relationship as an aid in decision making. One important area of knowledge is the effectiveness and efficiency of various approaches to intervention that you can make available to your client and yourself in deciding about the intervention plan.
4. Being aware of and sensitive to the possibilities of unintended consequences and taking reasonable steps to guard against harmful effects of intervention.

Program Evaluation and Practice Evaluation

Some social workers and schools of social work make a sharp distinction between program evaluation and practice evaluation. Program evaluation refers to efforts to measure the effectiveness or efficiency of programs, such as family counseling, case management, foster family care, and so forth. Practice evaluations are carried out by individual social work practitioners and their clients to measure the efficiency and effectiveness of a specific intervention plan in relation to a specific client problem and set of objectives. Hudson and Grinnell (1989) have identified five categories of program evaluation—front-end analysis including needs assessment, process analysis, evaluability assessment, outcome analysis including cost-benefit analysis, and program monitoring; they provide definitions and discussions of each of these five categories, including their application to specific worker-client intervention plans as well as at the program level. The procedures for conducting evaluations and the problems likely to be encountered in the process are essentially the same whether the evaluation addresses a program or a specific intervention plan. Therefore, in our view a sharp distinction between program evaluation and social work practice evaluation is not warranted. In this chapter we will first present a framework for thinking about evaluation that is applicable at either the program or practice level. We'll move to a discussion of evaluation conducted by the social worker and the client, including a discussion of confrontation and feedback skills that often are required at this point. We'll return to a discussion of our responsibilities to contribute to knowledge development through participation in program-level evaluation as well as the use of knowledge to guide decision making. We'll conclude with a consideration of unintended consequences.

Evaluation is the application of scientific methods to measure both change processes and the results or outcomes of change efforts. As in any good research, the evaluation is directed toward measuring the outcomes (dependent variables) of programs or specific interventions, toward measuring the change processes or the nature of the interventions themselves (the independent variables), and toward doing so with a research design that will permit you to attribute the outcome to the change processes. The terms *summative* and *formative* may be used to refer to two types of evaluations. Summative evaluation is the study of program or intervention outcomes or effectiveness; formative evaluation is the study of program processes.

Both types of evaluation will occur on two levels. At the program level social workers are asked to measure the impact and the nature of programs such as child protection, family counseling, community development, and so on. This may be referred to as program evaluation research. But evaluation research will also occur at the level of individual worker and client relationships. Just as you can ask about the nature of human service programs, their outcomes, and what leads anyone to believe that the programs lead to the outcomes, so too may you ask about the nature of individual intervention by social workers and clients, their presumed outcomes, and what leads anyone to believe that the interventions led to the outcomes.

An Evaluation Model   Hudson and Grinnell (1989) offer a useful model. They call it "Elements of Program Structure and Logic," and we reproduce it here as Exhibit 16-1. The structure of an evaluation—either a program or a practice evaluation—will involve four elements or sets of variables: inputs, activities, outputs, and outcomes. Social workers sometimes have difficulty with the program evaluation literature until

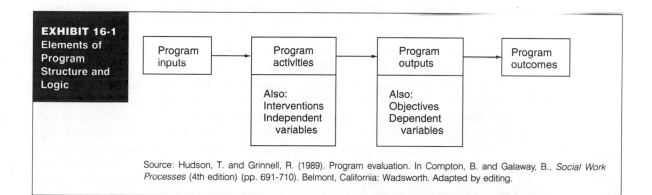

EXHIBIT 16-1
Elements of Program Structure and Logic

Program inputs → Program activities → Program outputs → Program outcomes

Program activities
Also:
Interventions
Independent
variables

Program outputs
Also:
Objectives
Dependent
variables

Source: Hudson, T. and Grinnell, R. (1989). Program evaluation. In Compton, B. and Galaway, B., *Social Work Processes* (4th edition) (pp. 691-710). Belmont, California: Wadsworth. Adapted by editing.

they recognize that the problem may be one of nomenclature—different words may be used for the same concept. Once this recognition occurs, it becomes relatively clear that the same conceptual framework can be used when referring to either program or practice evaluation. We will try to clarify this matter.

Inputs in Exhibit 16-1 are the resources necessary to implement the program or the intervention. At the program level resources may include things like money, particular types of staff such as licensed social workers, and of course clients for the service. At the social worker–client level resources will include things like worker time, skill, and access to information and resources necessary to carry out the intervention plan.

At the program level activities are the things that agencies do to try to produce changes. At times we may refer to these as the services provided. At the program level activities may include things like intake interviewing, counseling, referral, and so forth. At the worker-client level, activities are the process of intervention—the things you and your client will do to implement the intervention plan. Thus we perceive the concept of program activities and interventive activities to be synonymous, although program activities may be used to refer to the program level and interventive activities to refer to the client–social worker level. This matter may be further elaborated by pointing out that the term *activities* in this model also corresponds to the concept of independent variables that you were taught in your research courses. Program activities or interventive activities are the things we do to produce change; we believe they are the cause of the change and thus the independent variables.

Outputs and outcomes are a bit more confusing. Output is the immediate result of the program or intervention plan. For example, the output of an intervention plan designed to assist an unemployed person secure employment might be securing a job. But the securing of a job may also have longer-term benefits, such as increasing self-esteem, self-support, financial independence, and so forth. We refer to these longer-term benefits as outcomes. The difference between outputs and outcomes is at times fuzzy, but there are two distinguishing characteristics. Outputs are immediate results of a program or intervention, and outcomes are longer-term benefits. Second, outcomes provide the socially justifying reason for the intervention or program. The outcomes stand on their own and do not require any further justification, but outputs are generally viewed as stepping stones to some further benefit. For example, at the program level an intervention designed to increase the availability of day care in a particular community might have as an output an increase in the number of child-days of day care provided. But this may not be a sufficient justification for the program unless it is linked to longer-term benefits such as providing opportunities for self-support for mothers, improved employment opportunities for parents, or improved child care for preschool children.

As another example, Exhibit 16-2 presents an intervention plan. The desired output of this intervention plan is a decision on the part of the client to proceed in one direction or another, whereas an outcome might well be an improvement in parent-child relations, stable living arrangements for the adolescent, and so forth. What are referred to as outputs in the program evaluation literature correspond to our concept of the objectives of intervention. Thus they are the dependent variables, or what we believe will be the result of the intervention. The concept of outputs and outcomes also leads us to the notion of causal chain. A variable may be both

EXHIBIT 16-2 An Initial Service Plan	BACKGROUND: Richard is the 12-year-old son of Jon and Bonita Jasper. Jon is a merchant seaman and is at sea for extended periods of time, leaving Bonita as the primary provider of child care. Richard has been staying out late at night, is refusing to do household chores, and recently was gone from home overnight. Bonita, in her efforts to control Richard, has used harsh discipline including beating him with a belt that left welts. The school made a referral to child protection; the child protection agency is holding the case open because Bonita has asked for services from the family service unit of the Maritime Union. This initial plan was developed by Bonita and Sally Harlow, the worker, during a home visit.

DATE: March 5

PROBLEM: Bonita is having difficulty managing Richard without anger or resorting to harsh punishment and is considering requesting an out-of-home placement.

OBJECTIVE: Bonita will be able to make a decision between requesting placement for Richard and developing a service plan to retain Richard at home.

SERVICE PLAN:

Task	*Who Will Do?*	*To Be Completed by:*
1. Meet twice in Bonita's home to discuss the choices available and the pros and cons of each choice.	Bonita & Sally; Sally will visit Bonita at her home for these meetings	1st meeting on March 12; 2nd meeting on March 19.
2. Bonita will make a decision among: (*a*) requesting placement, (*b*) developing a service plan for retaining Richard in the home, and (*c*) discontinuing service.	Bonita	March 23
3. Telephone conference to discuss the decision and schedule another meeting if Bonita decides for (*a*) or for (*b*).	Worker will call Bonita	March 24

independent and dependent, depending on where it lies in the chain of events. In our earlier example, getting a job was a dependent variable for the interventive efforts but was an independent variable in relation to increasing self-support. In the illustration in Exhibit 16-2, a decision by Bonita is a dependent variable of the worker-client meetings (the interventions or independent variables) but is an independent variable of what may follow in the planning for Bonita and Richard. In Chapter 11 we said that the objectives of intervention should be specific, concrete, and proximate. Thus, the objectives of a social worker's intervention will correspond to the concept of outputs in the model in Exhibit 16-1, although clearly these outputs will also be connected to things clients desire for a less stressful and more comfortable life.

The Linking Logic Finally, we need linking logic to connect the set of concepts— inputs, activities, outputs, and outcomes. What is the reason for believing that if the resources are provided, the activities will occur? Or if the activities occur, that the outputs will result? Or if the outputs occur, that the outcomes will result? For example, day care is often promoted necessary to reduce the number of persons on the AFDC caseload, and federal financial support is often cited as a resource (input) necessary to develop day care. The linking logic, however, must explain why increased federal appropriations for day care will extend the number of day-care facilities available for low-income families. Second, we must answer the question of how increasing day-care facilities for low-income families will result in a reduction in the AFDC caseload. And of course we should make the further connection to some socially justifying outcome: what is the reason for believing that reducing the AFDC caseload will bring about any improvement in social conditions or the quality of life for low-income persons?

As another example, intensive family intervention is often promoted as reducing the need for out-of-home placement of children and youth, and professionally trained social workers are often thought to be necessary to carry out the intensive home intervention programs. In this example the professionally trained social worker is an input; the intensive family intervention program is the activity, or independent variable; and the reduction of out-of-home placement is the output, or dependent variable. The linking logic must explain why a professionally trained social worker is necessary for intensive family home intervention and why intensive family intervention will reduce out-of-home care. Again, we should draw a connection between the output (reduction of out-of-home care) and some socially justifying outcome presumably having something to do with the quality of care and meeting the developmental needs of children and youth. The linking logic constitutes the intervention or program theory—it explains the connections. You may not think much about the linking logic, but as you develop in your responsibility to be a scholar-researcher-practitioner, you will be able to explain more explicitly the linking logic or theories behind your work.

For many the term *program evaluation* carries the connotation of a summative program evaluation—an attempt to assess the extent to which a program is reaching its goals, either outputs or outcomes. While summative evaluations are useful in making judgments about the worth of a program, they have little use unless the program or interventions used are well conceptualized and understood. Knowing that goals are being accomplished is of little use unless you also know how they are being accomplished. Likewise, knowing that goals are not being accomplished is not useful unless you are clear about what interventions were used and failed to accomplish the desired goals. For example, if you find a reduction in child abuse after a parent skills training program, a laudable goal may well have been accomplished. But unless you understand clearly the nature of the parent-training program that presumably led to the reduction in child abuse, the finding is of little practical value. Not knowing the nature of the program, you are not in a position to replicate it in the future. Or assume that you are working with a senior citizens group toward securing better police protection in their neighborhood. Even if the goal is accomplished—say more foot patrols are assigned to the neighborhood at hours when senior citizens would like to be on the streets—unless you can document how this goal was accomplished, the finding is of limited value and will not contribute to the developing knowledge base of the profession.

The Social Worker as Practitioner-Researcher

Evaluation as a Client Service   As part of the services provided to each client, you will be called on to be a researcher, to apply sound scientific method to an understanding of the nature of interventions and the measurement of impacts. You and clients will ask, What are our activities (independent variables)? What are our goals (dependent variables)? How can we relate activities to the goals? In Chapter 3 we talked about testing our assumptive knowledge and the commitment to the scientific method as a response to the discomfort that occurs in the poor light of incomplete knowledge. As we carry out our obligations to be competent researchers with our clients, we test our assumptive knowledge, contribute to knowledge development for the profession, and use program evaluation concepts in our practice.

In much of social work our independent variables (the program or intervention methods used) are poorly conceptualized. Thus efforts to measure outputs and outcomes may be premature unless workers are also simultaneously engaging in formative evaluations directed toward conceptualizing and measuring the nature of the intervention used. Studies and program and interventive processes are essential to the development of the knowledge base of the profession and are an essential prerequisite to summative evaluations. Before talking about program or intervention effectiveness (that is, summative evaluations), we must first answer a series of questions about the program or intervention itself:

1. What am I attempting to accomplish? What are the objectives that have been set for the program or the intervention by the individual worker and client? Clarity about objectives is essential for either type of evaluation.
2. What is the population for which these objectives are to be accomplished? In some cases this may be an individual, a group of clients, a neighborhood, or an even larger population.
3. What are the components or parts of the program or intervention plan that are necessary to accomplish the objectives for the defined population or client? You should be able to specify all of the program components or interventions that will go toward accomplishing the objectives.
4. How do these components or parts fit together? Should some precede others? Do some occur concurrently? How do the parts of the program or intervention fit together into an integrated plan to accomplish the desired objectives? At this point you may draw flowcharts to illustrate relationships among the various intervention strategies and how they relate to accomplishing the final goals.
5. What are the reasons for believing that if the intervention strategies are carried out, the objectives will be accomplished? This, of course, moves into the area of the linking logic or intervention theory. Workers must have some ideas or hypotheses that will lead them to predict that objectives will be accomplished if they complete the intervention plan. Part of evaluation is to test these hypotheses—to test assumptive knowledge and expand the knowledge base of the profession.

Perhaps an illustration of this process will be helpful. Let's go back to the senior citizens group that is working with a social worker to increase public safety in its neighborhood. These seniors like to be out visiting during the late afternoon and early evening hours; however, they feel unsafe in their immediate neighborhood because of concern about muggings, purse snatchings, and so on. Let us assume that they have decided on an immediate objective of having a pair of police officers assigned to patrol the neighborhood on foot during the 3 to 11 p.m. shift to supplement the regular squad car patrols; the objective is clear. The next step is to develop an intervention plan that will lead to the objectives. In thinking through ways of accomplishing the objective, the seniors and their social worker decide that first they must influence the chief of police to secure support for the notion of a foot patrol for their neighborhood, and second they must influence the city council to secure some additional resources for the neighborhood. They decide that in the process of implementing this plan, they will have to bring two kinds of pressure to bear—factual and political. They will have to assemble facts concerning the number of crimes against the elderly that are occurring in the neighborhood as well as the extent to which activities of the seniors may be limited by fear of being out at night. Second, even with the knowledge, they will have to mobilize a show of political support to convince the city council members that this is an important issue for their attention. After considerable brainstorming and planning, the social worker and clients may well have developed an intervention plan similar to that represented in Exhibit 16-3.

Exhibit 16-3 is a simplified flowchart of an intervention plan that indicates the various components (activities or independent variables) of the effort to produce change and shows their relationship. Formative evaluation is directed at monitoring the extent to which each of these activities occurs. If the persons responsible for gathering the evidence fail to do so and the group fails to influence the police chief,

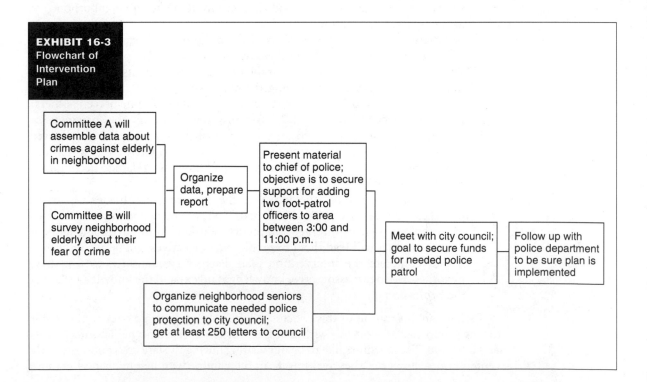

EXHIBIT 16-3
Flowchart of Intervention Plan

Committee A will assemble data about crimes against elderly in neighborhood

Committee B will survey neighborhood elderly about their fear of crime

Organize data, prepare report

Present material to chief of police; objective is to secure support for adding two foot-patrol officers to area between 3:00 and 11:00 p.m.

Organize neighborhood seniors to communicate needed police protection to city council; get at least 250 letters to council

Meet with city council; goal to secure funds for needed police patrol

Follow up with police department to be sure plan is implemented the worker and clients have a clearer understanding of what went wrong in accomplishing their objectives. Or the plan may be perfectly implemented but still the objectives not accomplished. If this should happen, you may well do a summative evaluation and be able to make a judgment that the plan itself was not appropriate. Client and worker in this situation may then consider alternative plans and strategies for accomplishing their objectives. Perhaps they will work to unseat some city council members or perhaps form coalitions with other organizations to bring additional political pressure to bear to secure the desired objective.

This example also further illustrates the distinction between outputs and outcomes. The output of the intervention was the assignment of a team of foot patrol officers to the neighborhood, and the desired outcome was a reduction in crime against senior citizens. Whether the output, the two patrol officers, will actually lead to the outcome is of course a separate research question that will be of critical interest to this social worker and the group of clients. Thus you may ask, do the interventions (program activities) lead to the objectives (outputs) and do the outputs lead to the outcomes?

Confronting Formative evaluations address the following key question: Is the program activity or intervention plan being implemented as designed? Focus for a moment on intervention plans, although the same procedures hold true for programs. Think of two levels, the conceptual and the operational. The conceptual level is the intervention plan itself—what did you agree to do? It is the concept, the plan you are going to follow to accomplish the objectives, and it is often in written form. The operational level is the intervention activities themselves—what do you actually do, in what activities do you and the client engage to accomplish the objectives? Formative evaluation addresses this question: Did you do what you said you were going to do?

Many of your evaluation activities with clients will be of this nature: Was the intervention plan to which you agreed carried out? Sometimes it is not; clients may not follow through and do what they have agreed to do, and workers may not be able to follow through and do what they have agreed to do. For example, a formative evaluation of the intervention plan represented in Exhibit 16-3 may result in the discovery that the committee designated with responsibility to collect evidence of the need for police protection did not collect the evidence or did not collect it in a timely fashion. Or perhaps the intervention in Exhibit 16-2 was not implemented because the worker was unable to schedule the second visit with Bonita. If the client-worker evaluation reveals that the plan has not been implemented as scheduled, you must decide together how to deal with this implementation issue.

Consider this example. Tom, age 16, has burglarized a small owner-operated business and in the course of burglary did about $480 of vandalism. He and the social worker have agreed, as a part of the service plan, to meet with the victim so that Tom can negotiate a mutually satisfactory way that he can make amends to the victim. This portion of the service plan is presented as Exhibit 16-4. The social worker follows through on his portion of the plan by contacting the victim. He learns that the victim is willing to meet with Tom, schedules a meeting, and communicates this to Tom by telephone. Tom, however, fails to appear for the meeting with the social worker to prepare for negotiation with the victim and

<table>
<tr><td>**EXHIBIT 16-4**
Service Plan
for Tom</td><td colspan="3">DATE: January 20.
PROBLEM: Tom has committed a burglary and has been told by the judge that he will be
               expected to make restitution to the victim.
OBJECTIVE: To develop and present to the court a restitution plan that is acceptable to both
               the victim and Tom.
SERVICE PLAN:</td></tr>
</table>

What Is to Be Done?	*By Whom?*	*When?*
1. Meet with Mr. Higby (victim) to determine if he is willing to meet with Tom to work out a restitution plan. Try to secure his agreement to meet.	1. Mr. Garcia (social worker)	1. February 1
2. Telephone Tom to let him know results of meeting with Mr. Higby and to schedule meetings 3 and 4.	2. Mr. Garcia	2. February 2
3. Meet at office to prepare for meeting with Mr. Higby.	3. Tom and Mr. Garcia	3. February 7
4. Meet with Mr. Higby to develop restitution plan; Mr. Garcia to serve as mediator.	4. Tom and Mr. Garcia	4. February 15
5. Present restitution plan to judge at disposition hearing.	5. Tom with assistance from Mr. Garcia as needed	5. February 20

fails to appear for the meeting with the victim. The plan has not been implemented as agreed. What should be done?

Formative evaluations will lead you to confront clients who do not follow through on their agreements. In Chapter 9 we talked about feedback in communications; confrontation is a specialized form of feedback that addresses discrepancies between statements and actions. In Reading 9-1, Cournoyer discusses and gives examples of the use of confrontation in groups. We also discussed confronting in Chapter 13.

Confronting comprises skills that you will also use when you note discrepancies in the implementation of an intervention plan. In Exhibit 16-5 we offer some guidelines for use in confrontation. Essentially confronting is a gentle but firm process that is limited to the discrepancy between words and actions under consideration. Confronting is nonjudgmental; do not go beyond the immediate discrepancy to make any type of judgment about the client. The purpose of confronting is to identify the discrepancy as a problem for resolution in the worker-client relationship; it is not an expression of anger or judgment toward the client. Once the discrepancy is noted and discussed, the client is to be involved in the resolution of this problem, just as clients have been involved in all previous problem statements and planning. You as a social worker do have responsibility to follow up on situations in which the intervention plan is not being followed, and generally you should not ignore these discrepancies.

In Tom's case the social worker telephoned the following day after school and made arrangements to stop by his home. Tom met the worker at the door and showed him to the kitchen table, where this conversation ensued.

<table>
<tr><td>

EXHIBIT 16-5
Guidelines for
Confronting
</td><td>

1. The purpose of confronting is to involve the client in solving a problem of a discrepancy between a verbal commitment and behavior.
2. Confronting is *not* an expression of worker anger or frustration.
3. Confronting relates to specific behavior.
4. Limit confronting to the behavioral discrepancy; do *not* transcend the specific discrepancy to any judgment about the person.
5. Do not offer answers or explanations for the discrepancy.
6. Explore and whenever possible use the client's solution to the discrepancy as the basis for reinstituting or revising the plan.
</td></tr>
</table>

Worker: Tom, I thought we ought to talk a bit about what happened that you didn't show up for the meeting with me and with Mr. Higby.

Tom: Okay.

Worker: Can you tell me what happened?

Tom: I don't know, I just didn't make it. [Silence.]

Worker: Tom, are you a little uncomfortable with the idea of talking with Mr. Higby?

Tom: Not really; I can handle it.

Worker: How would you like to proceed from here?

Tom: I'll meet with the guy.

Worker: Tom, there are at least two ways that we can proceed with this. We can go ahead and try to arrange for a meeting so you can see if you can negotiate an arrangement with Mr. Higby, or we can ask the judge to decide what would be fair in terms of restitution in this situation.

Tom: I'd rather meet with him.

This led to some further exploration of how such a meeting might go, how Tom handles himself in an unpleasant situation, and some work to prepare him for how he should conduct himself in a meeting with the victim. The meeting was held the following week with both Tom and his mother attending. Tom was able to participate in conversations with the victim, and together they developed a plan whereby Tom would provide 45 hours of labor to the business as payment for his share of the damages.

This case illustrates some of the important elements of confronting. The worker did not allow the situation to be ignored. The focus was on the specific behavior. The discrepancy itself became the focus of a problem that led to work with the boy in terms of how he handled these situations, and in this situation the confronting resulted in implementation of the plan. In some situations, however, the confronting may result in a revision in the plan because the discrepancy can be resolved either by bringing behavior into conformance with a plan or by changing the plan itself. Tom, for example, might well have decided to allow the judge to make a decision regarding restitution and have avoided the whole matter of a meeting with the victim. Had he chosen this course of action, the focus of work would have shifted to preparing Tom for a meeting with the judge and for thinking through the kind of proposal he would like to make to the court.

Evaluation is Continuous All social workers have a responsibility to be researchers with their clients. An appropriate beginning place for your research efforts will be in conceptualizing and measuring the nature and extent of your intervention activities. Before you do this, you need a clear picture of how you are going to go about intervening and why you believe that the interventions, if accomplished, will lead to the objectives you and your client have established. If this is done, you can begin thinking about summative evaluation or measuring the extent of goal attainment. Research and evaluation are a continual process providing a flow of data in which you can reassess objectives, intervention plans, and even the definition of the problem.

Exhibit 16-6 is a representation of the problem-solving process, showing evaluation as providing feedback loops permitting clients and workers to reassess continually the problem they have defined for work, the objectives they have selected, and the intervention plan they have formulated. Client and worker are continually involved in an evaluation of their experiences in trying to produce change. Their evaluation may indicate a need to redefine the problem (or define an entirely new problem), to reassess objectives (or develop new objectives), or to alter the intervention plan. The impact of evaluation and feedback loops is to reduce the linearity of the problem-solving model and to permit the model to take on a dynamic, systemic, constantly changing quality. The opportunity to change problem definition, goals, and intervention plan does not, however, remove from you the responsibility of being sure that any changes are negotiated with the client and that any intervention activities are based on a clearly specified service agreement. Experience with interventive activities may indicate a need for a change in the contract, but changes in contracts cannot be made unilaterally.

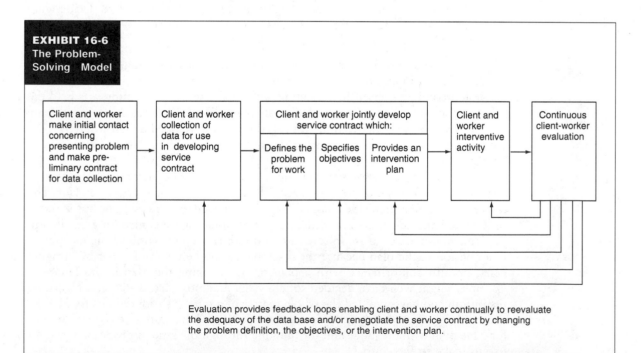

EXHIBIT 16-6
The Problem-Solving Model

Client and worker make initial contact concerning presenting problem and make preliminary contract for data collection → Client and worker collection of data for use in developing service contract → Client and worker jointly develop service contract which: Defines the problem for work | Specifies objectives | Provides an intervention plan → Client and worker interventive activity → Continuous client-worker evaluation

Evaluation provides feedback loops enabling client and worker continually to reevaluate the adequacy of the data base and/or renegotiate the service contract by changing the problem definition, the objectives, or the intervention plan.

In Chapter 11 we stressed the importance of clearly specifying goals. This is a prerequisite to evaluation. Without clarity about goals, the evaluation of progress toward the accomplishment of goals is impossible. Likewise, a clear specification of the intervention plan is necessary to assess whether client and worker activities are appropriate for reaching the desired goals. Without a clear specification of the intervention plan, client and worker cannot evaluate whether what is happening leads or fails to lead to goal accomplishment.

Goal Attainment Scaling The specification of measurable concrete objectives is one of the more difficult tasks of the social work practitioner. Goal attainment scaling was developed in 1968 (Kiresuk & Sherman, 1968) as a tool to evaluate patient progress in mental health programs; the procedures can be used in any situation in which goal setting is a part of the process, including measuring client progress toward service objectives, student progress toward learning goals, and agency progress toward organizational objectives. Goal attainment scaling is particularly useful to the social work practitioner because it permits the individualization of objectives; there is no effort to impose predetermined standardized objectives. Rather, client and worker work toward objectives individually tailored to a particular situation. The procedures, however, measure only the extent of attainment of the goal or objective. They do not in any way measure the importance or significance of the objectives themselves, nor do they determine the intervention methods. How objectives are achieved is not a part of goal attainment scaling.

The grid used in goal attainment scaling is reproduced in Exhibit 16-7. It provides for the development of scale—one for each objective—with five levels of predicted attainment for a specified period of time; the levels range from the most unfavorable to the most favorable result thought likely, with the expected level of result at the midpoint on each scale. You should develop at least one scale for each problem area and write a heading for each scale. Develop as many scales as are necessary. Once the scale headings are in place, set a follow-up date and

EXHIBIT 16-7
Goal
Attainment
Follow-Up Grid

Program using goal attainment scaling	Date of scale construction _____ Follow-up date _____			
Levels of Predicted Attainments	Scale Headings and Scale Weights			
	Scale 1: ($w_1 = \ $)	Scale 2: ($w_2 = \ $)	Scale 3: ($w_3 = \ $)	Scale 4: ($w_4 = \ $)
Most unfavorable results thought likely				
Less than expected success				
Expected level of success				
More than expected success				
Most favorable results thought likely				

indicate the predicted level of achievement for each scale as of the follow-up date.

Where do the client and you expect to be at the specified follow-up date? The entire objective may not be attained by that time; the task, therefore, is to indicate the expected level of accomplishment by the follow-up date. The next steps are to indicate the most unfavorable result and the most favorable result you think likely by the follow-up date. Then the intermediate levels of less than expected success and more than expected success can be completed. The levels of predicted attainment are to be specified objectively enough to be reliably scored on the follow-up date. Whenever possible quantification is desirable, but it is not absolutely essential in establishing the scale levels.

Be sure that each scale is both exhaustive and mutually exclusive. None of the five levels of success should overlap (each should be mutually exclusive), and the scale levels should account for all outcome possibilities thought likely (be exhaustive). The scales, once developed, can be set aside until the designated follow-up date. Scoring consists of checking what has been accomplished on each scale at the designated follow-up date. Kiresuk and Garwick (1974) present a formula for calculating an overall goal attainment scale score and discuss procedures for weighting scales if some are thought more important than others.

Exhibit 16-8 illustrates a completed set of goal attainment scales that might have been developed with Mrs. B in the situation described in Exhibit 12-6. After study of this example, begin experimenting with goal attainment scaling. The procedures can be used whenever objectives are set; thus, goal attainment scaling can be learned without actually working with clients. Personal learning objectives can be set. How many books will you read next month? How many articles? What are your objectives in grades this term? What percent of written assignments will you complete on time? Your own learning plans will provide ample opportunity to begin work with goal attainment scaling.

Single-Subject Design   The type of practitioner research we have been discussing in this section is often referred to in the social work literature as the *single-subject design*. The single-subject design involves a research sample of one rather than the more common groups of subjects. The single-subject design is a particularly useful concept as we think of social work practitioners engaged in the evaluation of their own practice and as we develop the notion of the social worker as a researcher-practitioner. Sharon Berlin (1983) reviews some of the literature on the single subject design and the debate about its appropriateness, and she offers another example of the use of this design by a social work practitioner-researcher working with a client with symptoms of depression. Robert Weinbach discusses use of the single-subject design in Reading 16-1.

Assisting with Program Evaluation   In addition to systematic evaluation of your own practice as a part of the service you provide to clients, you will likely be involved in working with your agency to engage in program evaluation. Earlier in this chapter we made the argument that the approach to program evaluation and the approach to practice evaluation are essentially the same, the only difference being that one effort is to conduct studies of a program and the other is an evaluation of a specific intervention plan.

EXHIBIT 16-8 Goal Attainment Follow-Up Grid (examples of scales that might have been developed with Mrs. B)				
Program using GAS Head Start Client Mrs. B	Intercity		Date of scale construction August 1 Follow-up date September 1	

Levels of Predicted Attainments	Scale Headings and Scale Weights			
	Scale 1: ($w_1 = $)	Scale 2: ($w_2 = $)	Scale 3: ($w_3 = $)	Scale 4: ($w_4 = $)
Most unfavorable results thought likely	Mrs. B reports angrily yelling at Jimmy daily or oftener during last week in August.	No action or discussion of Mrs. B's loneliness.	No discussion or action about returning to clinic.	
Less than expected success	Mrs. B reports angrily yelling at Jimmy more than three times but less than daily during last week in August.	Mrs. B discusses her loneliness but can not make plans to deal with it.	Mrs. B is discussing her reaction to the clinic but has not formulated plans to return.	
Expected level of success	Mrs. B reports angrily yelling at Jimmy no more than three times during last week in August.	Mrs. B is discussing her loneliness and making plans to join a group.	Mrs. B has discussed her reaction to the clinic and plans to secure a return appointment.	
More than expected success	Mrs. B has discontinued angrily yelling at Jimmy but has not discovered another way to discipline him.	Mrs. B has initiated contacts with a group.	Mrs. B has telephoned the clinic for a return appointment.	
Most favorable results thought likely	Above, and Mrs. B is using another form of discipline before becoming angry with Jimmy.	Mrs. B has attended one group meeting.	Mrs. B has been to the clinic for a return appointment.	

As a practitioner, you will be involved in program evaluation in several ways. You will be requested to provide data for the program evaluation effort, usually by completing forms necessary to provide the data for a program evaluation. Beyond this, however, we expect that you may also be involved in the process of thinking through the questions to be addressed by a program evaluation and in being a user of the program evaluation results. Program evaluation is conducted to provide information to key decision makers; practitioners are key decision makers in determining, along with their clients, the most appropriate intervention in a given set of circumstances. Exhibit 16-9 provides an example of a program evaluation policy developed by an agency. We suggest that you read through this brief policy statement and think about the implications it could have if you were a social worker practicing in that agency.

In addition to being a user of the evaluation efforts of your agency, you will be using the research and evaluation findings reported in the literature. This is one source of knowledge that you bring to the client-worker relationship—knowledge that you

---

EXHIBIT 16-9
An Agency
Program
Evaluation
Policy

What is Program Evaluation? Program evaluation amounts to systematically collecting, assessing and using information about programs and services, and using this information to improve our practice. In other words, program evaluation research is a *practice tool* that is based on the assumption that the feedback of information is a necessary condition for good practice.

Why Do Program Evaluation? One of the hallmarks of a professional is that they are trying to improve their practice. This means they need to be constantly collecting, assessing, and using information about their practice so as to make necessary improvements. HSA is made up of professionals who aim to deliver the very best services to the children and families with whom we work. This means HSA must do program evaluation.

What Kind of Program Evaluation? HSA is committed to carrying out two types of program evaluation research. One type takes the form of an information system providing continuous streams of information about agency activities. This will amount to producing a quarterly information report on agency activities available to board members, administrative staff, social workers, and foster parents. A second type of evaluation research to be carried out in the agency will be planning and conducting special evaluation studies on particular agency activities. These special studies will again be reported to the different sets of interested users—foster parents, social workers, administrative staff and board.

Who Should Be Involved? The intended clients or users of *both* types of agency evaluation activities are board members, administrative staff, social workers, and foster parents. All parties will have opportunities to participate by identifying and suggesting the specific kind of information they need to better carry out their work, the specific kind of evaluations that should be done to produce the needed information and, as well, opportunities to participate in collecting the needed information, reviewing the results of completed evaluations, and identifying the actions that should be taken as a result of the reported findings. In short, all members of the agency will have opportunities to participate in the program evaluation work planned and undertaken as well as opportunities to make use of the findings produced. Program evaluation in HSA is intended to be a collaborative effort that produces useful information used to improve service.

SOURCE: Policy Statement from Human Service Associates, Inc., St. Paul, Minnesota.

can contribute to your joint decision making. Thus, in addition to a continuous evaluation of your own practice and involvement in agency-level program evaluation, you have responsibility to remain current in the literature and to bring information regarding the effectiveness and efficiency of various types of social work interventions to your clients for consideration in your and their decision making.

Unintended Consequences

Our evaluation efforts, whether evaluations of our own practice or program evaluations, are often directed only toward determining if we accomplish our objectives—do the good that we intend to do. Seldom do social workers consciously consider the possibility and seek evidence that the work may have unintended, perhaps harmful, consequences. All summative evaluations, both practitioner and program, should move beyond simply asking the question of whether you accomplish your objectives and should seriously examine the question of whether there are unintended harmful consequences flowing from the intervention. It may be more important to know whether you are causing harm than whether you are doing good.

Sieber (1981) offers a useful framework for considering the problem of unintended consequences. He argues that in addition to the intended effects, you must be aware that any social intervention may have unintended effects that may be of two natures—either side effects or regressive effects. Side effects are effects that result from the intervention but that have no direct bearing on the problem itself. We are familiar with the concept of side effects in medicine; for example, some chemotherapies for cancer may cause loss of hair, dizziness, nausea, or other reactions that do not relate directly to the cancer itself. Side effects may be classified as positive, neutral, or negative. It is possible that some side effects result in benefits to the client, although they may not directly address the problem to which the intervention was focused. Others may be neutral in that they neither benefit nor harm, and still others may be harmful to the client. Regressive effects, contrasted with side effects, have a direct bearing on the problem the intervention was designed to resolve inasmuch as they actually make the condition worse. Thus, regressive effects occur when the results of an intervention are the opposite of what was intended; that is, rather than being solved, the problem has become worse.

Exhibit 16-10 contains an interesting example of unintended regressive effects. This exhibit is from a well-designed study involving random selection of a group of juvenile offenders to three types of intervention—restitution, probation supervision, and mental health counseling. Before and after data on delinquent behavior were collected for each group of offenders and then standardized to provide a measure of the rate of delinquent incidents per 100 youths over a period of one year. The results of this program evaluation research indicate that the delinquent behavior of the group of youths who received mental health treatment actually increased after treatment (a regressive effect), whereas the delinquent behavior of youths in the other groups decreased or remained unchanged. A single study does not, of course, provide justification for discontinuing providing mental health treatment to delinquent youth, but studies such as this do suggest that interventions may have harmful regressive effects.

There was another problem with this research to which we have alluded throughout this chapter. The independent variable, mental health treatment, was never operationalized. This is such a common problem in program evaluation that we

EXHBIT 16-10 Example of Regressive Effects	This study involved random assignment of youth adjudicated delinquent to four treatment strategies-restitution either to community or victim, mental health counseling for a diagnostic session followed by therapy, probation supervision and mental health counseling, and probation supervision alone. The outcome goal for all the treatment strategies was to reduce the incidence of delinquent behavior. Here are the results. What evidence do you see of regressive effects?

| | Group | | | |
	Restitution Only	Restitution & Mental Health Counseling	Mental Health Counseling	Probation Only
Rate of delinquent incidents per 100 youth for year before intervention.	101	55	64	75
Rate of delinquent incidents per 100 youth for one year beginning with intervention.	74	47	84	75

NOTE: From ''Restitution and Recidivism Rates of Juvenile Offenders: Results from Four Experimental Studies'' by A. Schneider, 1986, *Criminology, 24*, pp. 533-552. Copyright 1986 by American Society of Criminology. Reprinted by permission. Findings presented in this exhibit are from the Clayton County, Georgia, Juvenile Restitution Program.

think it's essential to point out again: that you must be able to describe very clearly what the treatment is. The term *mental health treatment* covers a large number of quite different types of interventions; it is possible, of course, that some of these will have harmful effects and others, helpful ones.

Social work often involves dealing with people who are under stress, with social workers and clients often discussing intimate details of clients' lives. Our work as practitioners is frequently with vulnerable people and has the potential for intruding into people's social systems. We believe that any intrusive service has the potential for harm and that we as practitioners must be aware of this possibility, consciously think about the potential for negative side effects or regressive effects, and take reasonable steps to try to prevent these from happening. We believe there are two reasonable steps that can help us move along in this direction. The first step is to move as close as is possible to the ideal of the partnership arrangement we have been discussing throughout this book. The more the client is involved in decision making and the more you function within the framework of what the client wants, the less likely you are to be imposing intrusive procedures from the outside that may have harmful effects. But this is not an absolute assurance that harmful effects will not occur. Therefore, as a second step, our commitment at least to consider and consciously think about the possibility of doing harm is necessary to reduce the likelihood that regressive and negative side effects will occur.

Recapitulation

Your involvement with evaluation efforts will occur at two levels. You and your client will be involved in a continuous process of evaluating the extent to which the goals of the service contract are being accomplished. This evaluation provides feedback loops and an opportunity continually to renegotiate the problem for work, objective, and interventive means in relation to the problem. You will also be called on to cooperate and assist with broader agency program evaluation. Such efforts will provide feedback concerning the interventive approaches that appear to be most effective in given circumstances. Evaluation at both levels requires an explicit statement of goals and conceptualization of interventive means or program inputs. One model for measuring goal attainment—goal attainment scaling—was discussed in relation to the measurement of client progress.

A Look Forward Two readings are included with this chapter. The reading by Robert Weinbach (Reading 16-1) further discusses practitioner evaluation of practice through use of single-case designs. John McKnight in Reading 16-2 provides additional insight into the importance of considering the possibility of negative unintended consequences.

Reading 16-1 *Evaluating Individual Practice Effectiveness: Single Subject Research**

Robert Weinbach

A relatively small number of social workers have the opportunity to design and implement program evaluations. A larger percentage participate in them. But *all* social workers can and should evaluate whether their individual practice is achieving its objectives. The most common method for doing this is single-subject research, also referred to as N = 1 research, single-system design, single-case experiment, and idiographic research.

TOWARD ACCOUNTABLE PRACTICE
The impetus for social work practitioners to evaluate the effectiveness and efficiency of their practice comes from a variety of sources. Over the past 30 years many interrelated phenomena have contributed to a need for accountability in both programs and individual services. Those most responsible for an increased emphasis on single subject research are the following:

• Conservative political leadership that spotlighted the "failures" of human service programs (especially public assistance) and demanded proof that tax dollars were being used productively

• A reduction in resources for human services that led to government and charitable emphasis on funding only programs and services that can demonstrate that they "work" and withdrawal of funding from those that cannot

• Priority setting by human service professionals who are faced with funding cutbacks and so seek to identify services that if cut out would represent the least loss to client groups

• The consumer movement, which argued that clients had a right to expect that they would be involved in planning for services and that they had a right to expect that programs and services would accomplish their objectives

• Increased incidence of litigation in which consumers of services sought compensation not only for professional malpractice but also for promised results that were not achieved

• Skepticism within the profession of social work that examined studies of casework effectiveness and suggested that it may be less effective than previously believed

• More than a decade of emphasis by professional organizations on the utilization of research by practitioners (Grasso and Epstein, 1992)

*An original paper prepared for this edition.

Recent action by the Council on Social Work Education, the accrediting body for social work professional education programs, now ensures that future social workers will have at least a beginning understanding of methods for evaluating the effectiveness of their own practice (Council on Social Work Education, 1992a, p. 8; 1992b, p. 9). These methods employ many of the established procedures of scientific inquiry, but they also may differ markedly from more traditional research in a number of ways, most dramatically in their objectives. Traditional group research studies seek to study a sample or portion of the research universe or population and to identify relationships between variables within it. Statistical methods are used to determine whether the relationships within the sample are also likely to be true of the population. In this way general knowledge is developed. However, both program evaluation and single-subject research are less concerned with developing general knowledge than with determining whether a given program is working within a given organization or (in the case of single-subject research) whether a given treatment is effective with a given case. The *external validity,* or generalizability, of findings from a program evaluation, whether those findings may be true of similar or identical programs, is assumed to be low (Rubin and Babbie, 1993, pp. 286–288). No two programs are exactly alike. What we learn about one may not be true of another. Similarly and for the same reason, the results of a single-subject study are assumed to have little or no external validity (Marlow, 1993, p. 168).

RESEARCH FOR AND BY THE PRACTITIONER

With single-subject research the generalizability of findings is relatively unimportant. What the social worker wants to know is whether the intervention method appears to be making a difference in this work with *this* client or client group. Single-subject research is conducted by the responsible practitioner. It is research conducted by social workers primarily for their own use. Also, unlike some group research, there is rarely any point in decep-

tion. Clients participate in identifying and setting treatment goals. They are aware that research is occurring and participate in collecting and reporting data.

There is little reason for a client or client group to object to single-subject research. It involves doing what a good social worker wants to do anyway—conscientiously monitor the client's progress—but in a more organized and objective manner than he or she might ordinarily do it.

In many ways single-subject research is more like good practice than like research as we usually think about it. The similarities to traditional designs for research on groups are all quite superficial (Yegidis and Weinbach, 1991, p. 126–128). It uses a small number of research subjects (one), but that's about the only similarity to the exploratory, qualitative research design that researchers call a case study. It makes repeated, ongoing measurements of the same variable (client behavior, attitude, and so on) that the social worker is seeking to influence. That's a characteristic of all forms of longitudinal research. But longitudinal studies usually have a slightly different purpose, to learn when in general certain changes occur. As I have noted, single-subject research is not in the business of making generalizations. Single-subject research does make some effort to have a quasi–control group (the behavior of the client or client group when the treatment is *not* being offered), but it falls far short of other requirements for classic experimental research. For example, the case studied is not selected randomly; it is purposefully sampled because it seems especially appropriate for a single-subject research study.

Usually the term *single-subject research* brings to mind a social worker's research with one individual person (client), but it can and is used with all client systems. While it is probably employed most with individual clients, it is equally well suited to examining practice effectiveness in with work with couples, families, groups, organizations, and communities (Thyer, 1993, p. 95). So long as a social worker can specify his or her client system, can specify the intervention method being used, and can accurately measure the behavior, attitude, or other problem that he or she is attempting to influence, it can be used.

Single-subject research is not designed for use with every case that a social worker may be carrying. It is used most frequently with cases that show a clear pattern in the target problem (the dependent, or criterion, variable in research terminology). That pattern can be rising, falling, steady, or even fluctuating, but in some consistent way over time. The target problem is most often behavior, but it may be some other attribute like an attitude or a perception that can be measured repeatedly and with accuracy. It can be measured over time in different ways—for example, its frequency, duration, magnitude or the length of the interval between its occurrences. Which of these measurements should a social worker choose for research? The answer to this question is one that is used frequently in designing single subject research—it depends on the goals for the social worker's intervention that have been agreed upon in a participatory process involving the client. The social worker and the client have formed a partnership in order to change something. What is it that they want to change? What is a realistic treatment goal on which they have agreed?

What are some of the target problems that a social worker may select as the dependent variable in single subject research? The possibilities are almost endless, but they include these:

• Frequency of practice of safe sex by a client at high risk for contracting the HIV virus
• Number of hours that an AFDC mother spends helping her child with homework
• Number of positive comments by a verbally abusive parent
• Number of times that disagreements between spouses are settled through discussion rather than verbal or physical abuse
• Number of meals eaten with all family members present
• Duration of discussions about child-rearing issues between parents
• Percent of members who verbally participate in a treatment group

• Number of participants in a group who have worked actively to seek employment
• Number of times that legislators request the opinions of social workers on pending social legislation
• Number of minority candidates elected to office in a community

Note that the target problems above are expressed in positive terms. While this is not always feasible, it is desirable because it is consistent with social work values and processes. We seek to build on strengths rather than focusing on the negative aspects of problems. Also note that most of the above examples address behavior that is easily measured. With single-subject research, simple is almost always better.

Often the intervention in single subject research is an innovative treatment of a problem about which little has been learned. Or it may be an intervention generally believed to be effective with one problem or client but not yet tried with another one. Single-subject research is exploratory. It asks, "I wonder if I can document that this is associated with a difference?" It often is the precursor to replication with other similar clients who have the same target problem or ultimately to various forms of group research designed to have more external validity.

SINGLE-SUBJECT RESEARCH: GOOD SOCIAL WORK PRACTICE

The question of whether a good social worker evaluates his or her practice using single subject research or whether single subject research is really just a refinement of good social work practice is really an academic one. The truth is, single-subject research methods are quite consistent with good practice. Much of what is done in the process of conducting single-subject research is what a good practitioner would do anyway, only perhaps single subject research helps us to do it better. For example, it has been suggested in Chapters 11 and 16 that in social work practice the independent, or predictor, variable (the intervention) often is poorly conceptualized. One of the most important steps in planning for single-subject research (see planning model below) is to develop a clear conceptualization and specification of the intervention. It is not enough merely to conduct research that asks, "Did it make a difference?" We want to know exactly *what* made a difference or did not make it. That is the only way that we can learn from our efforts.

Similarly, the process of measuring the dependent variable forces the social worker clearly to define and specify the treatment goal and to develop or find objective ways of measuring it. This is also consistent with sound social work practice. For example, if alcohol abuse is the general problem, is the treatment goal total abstinence, not drinking on the job, drinking that is not associated with abuse of family members, or some other type of alcohol-related behavior? In the participatory planning process, what do the social worker and the client conclude is a realistic objective? Would the substitution of another substance be indicative of success or failure? Should the dependent variable be amount of alcohol consumed over a period, the

frequency of bouts of drinking, their duration, their magnitude, or the length of time between them? "What is the goal we agreed on?" is a question that inevitably is factored in to the specification and measurement of the dependent variable. It also is an important component of any good treatment planning. Note the other similarities between the steps in planning for single research in Figure 16-1 and the usual questions asked in good social work assessment and treatment planning.

Step six in Figure 16-1 alludes to ethical concerns. Whenever single-subject research is conducted, strict adherence to professional ethical standards is essential. Consistent with professional values, the specific intervention method that the social worker is evaluating is often offered as an adjunct to usual treatment or intervention. It is not usually a replacement for it, as it sometimes is in group research. For example, a patient in an inpatient psychiatric facility continues occupational therapy, group treatment, physical therapy, medication therapy, and so on, while a social worker may alternate periods of access to television

---

FIGURE 16-1
Planning for Single Subject Research

1. Briefly descibe the client's problem, or at least its manifestation.
2. Specify the target behavior, attitude, and so on (the dependent variable) and how you propose to measure it. It may be just a symptom of an underlying problem if that symptom is problematic enough to merit concern.
3. Identify the pattern of the dependent variable (stable, rising, falling).
4. In 50 words or (preferrably) less, specify the treatment or intervention to be used (the independent variable), and how it will relate to other ongoing services to the client.
5. Locate and identify research studies or professional literature suggesting that your treatment may produce the desired results.
6. Select from among the various single-subject designs the one that you will use to examine the relationship between the independent and dependent variables. Justify why it is best, given such factors as time and ethical constraints.
7. Determine which pattern of the dependent variable indicates that your intervention may be related to a desired effect with your client, that is, the goal of treatment that you and the client have agreed on?
8. Determine what patterns suggest the possibility that your intervention has promoted unhealthful dependency or some other unintended consequence.
9. Conduct the research, carefully graphing the fluctuations in the dependent variable.
10. Carefully analyze the results of the research relative to steps 7 and 8. If the pattern in step 7 is observed, speculate on which other clients may find the intervention helpful.
11. Replicate the research with similar clients or with other clients who may benefit from the intervention.

with no access to see whether the intervention (access to TV) seems to be related to a decline in violent acts toward other patients. In this way the withdrawal of the intervention (a requirement of the research design) is less of an ethical problem. The patient is not denied treatment; sometimes he or she merely is not given the *specific* intervention that is being evaluated.

Consistent with social work values, research must always take a back seat to the interest of clients and their welfare. Single-subject research can (and sometimes should) be terminated prior to its completion for ethical reasons. If, for example, you conclude that an intervention is associated with an undesirable fluctuation in the target problem, you should not reintroduce it, even if the research design calls for its reintroduction. Conversely, you may decide that it is in the client's best interests to continue indefinitely an intervention that appears to be highly effective even though the research design calls for a period of not offering it.

Step 6 refers to various research designs. They are all in a sense variations on a theme. In all single-subject research the target problem is subjected to alternate periods when the specific intervention is offered (B phases) and periods when it is not (A phases), and a chart is kept of its fluctuations. The simplest of designs, known as AB, consists of one period of observation during which the dependent variable is measured and recorded but the intervention (independent variable) is not offered (A) followed by another period in which it is measured and recorded with intervention present (B). This design is used most frequently when the social worker believes that the desired effects of the intervention are likely to be permanent. For example, an intervention believed to increase assertiveness may be tested with an AB design because it is believed that assertiveness, once learned, is self-reinforcing.

Other designs add one or more A or B phases to see if there is a pattern to the dependent variable when the intervention is withdrawn or reintroduced. An ABA design adds a second A phase after intervention to see if the dependent variable changes when treatment is withdrawn. An ABAB (reversal) design adds both second baseline and

second intervention (B) phases to see what happens to the dependent variable when the intervention is withdrawn and then reintroduced. Other examples of designs have specialized uses. For example, ABCBC monitors the effects of twice introducing two different interventions on a single dependent variable; the multiple baseline designs "measure outcomes across clients, across settings, and across clients' multiple target problems" (Thyer, 1993, pp. 110–113). Others are more complicated. They are various creative attempts to assure that any difference in the dependent variable is a function of an intervention, not of something else; that is, they try to increase the research's internal validity (Rubin and Babbie, 1993, p. 263–264). The more complex designs probably produce more definitive answers about a social worker's practice effectiveness. However, the price paid for this is loss of simplicity. Use of the more complex designs may require advanced research training and more time than you are willing or able to spend.

Ideally, research begins in an A (also called *baseline*) phase of observation (when the dependent variable is measured but no intervention is given) so that a baseline (what is typical when the intervention is not present) can be established. Long A phases are desirable because they "contain enough points to establish the unlikelihood that extraneous events affecting the target problem will coincide only with the onset of intervention" (Rubin and Babbie, p. 307). But again, ethical concerns must prevail. What if the dependent variable is a behavior that represents a serious problem for the client? Maybe it is even life threatening, such as the practice of unsafe sex. Sometimes a valid retrospective baseline can be based on an historical recollection of the recent past. If this is impossible, can the social worker ethically deny an intervention that may be effective during a period of observation, merely to establish a baseline? Of course not. Instead, select one of the alternative research designs (such as BAB) that begins in an intervention (B) phase, even though it may not be the design of choice from a purely research perspective. The best interests of the client must be given top priority.

INTERPRETING FINDINGS

Once a design is selected and implemented, you should record and plot the target problem's frequency, duration, and so on at regular intervals and make note of patterns of the behavior. Changes in the dependent variable are displayed graphically. The time dimension (which can be hours, days, weeks, months, number of interviews, and so on) is recorded along the horizontal axis, and the repeated measurements of the dependent variable are displayed along the vertical axis. Make every effort to adhere to the research design while remaining consistent with professional values and ethics. But you should also use the chart for ongoing feedback, and constantly seek to interpret it. The client, as a partner in the treatment process, discusses progress, perhaps using the graph or chart used in the research as a focus for discussion. For example, you may ask both yourself and the client if the client (a recovering stroke patient) seems to be falling into a pattern of spending more time in performing activities of daily living when the intervention (a form of bibliotherapy) is present than during periods when it is not. You may also examine together the degree of consistency of any pattern. When the time allotted for the research has been completed, look at the entire pattern of the dependent variable over the course of the research and ask many questions. They have their origins in practice knowledge, values and skills. For example, for the stroke sufferer:

• What else was going on in the life of the patient during the research?

• What other components of the treatment package (besides the independent variable) may have contributed to changes in the dependent variable?

• How may normal physical recuperation (time) have influenced the dependent variable?

• How much dependency on the social worker is reflected in the fluctuations in the dependent variable that occurred, and is this desirable?

• How efficient (costly) is the use of the intervention, given the results documented?

• How likely is the pattern to continue if the intervention is permanently discontinued?

• Overall, how consistent are the results with treatment goals and objectives?

AN EXAMPLE: INTERVENTION IN A SUPPORT GROUP

Other examples of the use of single-subject research in evaluating the effectiveness of work with individual clients abound in the social work research literature. But what about the use of it with a different client system? Look at an example from group services to clients:

Rhoda was a social worker in a large general hospital. She was leading one Tuesday support group for ten juvenile type I (insulin-dependent) diabetics who were having trouble controlling their blood sugar and was about to start a new group. In reading about the problem of juvenile diabetes and talking to colleagues she learned that despite the hazards to their health, many children continue to eat sugary foods because they think they won't like the taste of foods prepared with sugar substitutes. She wanted to see if regular exposure to a pleasant-tasting snack made with sugar substitutes and other low-calorie ingredients might contribute to better blood glucose control among her group members. She defined her intervention as "bringing in a home-cooked sugar-free snack and spending five minutes of each group session with all group members tasting it and discussing it." Her dependent variable was the results of the children's blood test taken three days after each group session, a measurement already in use and available. At the time of testing clinic staff recorded for each child whether he or she was or was not within the optimum blood glucose range.

Rhoda selected ABAB design for her research. Since the target problem was not immediately life-threatening for the children, she felt that she could ethically begin her research in a nonintervention (A) phase. She also believed that ABAB with its four phases should provide enough opportunity for a pattern of relationship between the dependent and independent variables to develop if one existed. She recognized the major limitations of the research. She knew that the glucose reading taken on Fridays in the hospital may not have been typical for any or all of the children. She also could not control the other two major influences on blood

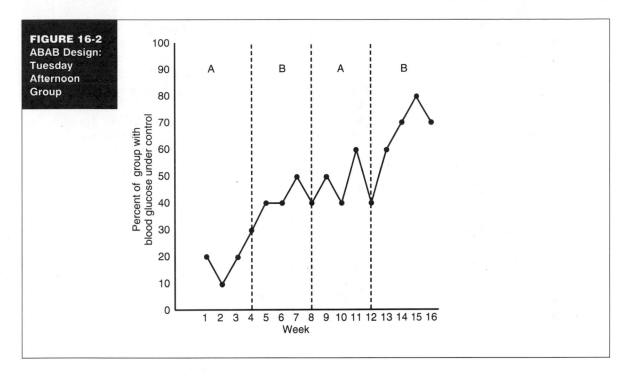

FIGURE 16-2
ABAB Design: Tuesday Afternoon Group

glucose level (besides diet), insulin intake and exercise. But she knew that single-subject research is exploratory at best. It seeks association between variables and rarely claims to uncover relationships of pure cause and effect. Rhoda implemented her research and kept a chart of the results.

After the 16 weeks of her research elapsed, Rhoda tried to make some sense of her findings. Was her intervention effective? As with most single-source research efforts, there were few conclusive findings. But she made three important observations that influenced her practice as a group leader:

1. Overall the children showed a desirable change in the dependent variable over the course of the research.
2. There were no dramatic differences when the intervention was introduced or withdrawn in weeks five, nine or thirteen.
3. The verbal participation by group members increased dramatically over the course of the research. By week sixteen, all children were active participants.

There were many questions that were suggested to Rhoda by these findings. They included these:

• Should the intervention be regarded as successful, since the percentage of children with their blood glucose level in control consistently and dramatically improved over the 16 weeks?
• If so, does the research suggest that the periodic reinforcement method used is the ideal method for employing the intervention?
• Does the lack of a decline in the dependent variable when the treatment was withdrawn indicate that the treatment was ineffective or that it had a healthy carryover effect?
• Would a decline at these points have been consistent with treatment goals of independent blood sugar management?
• Would the changes in the dependent variable have occurred even without the intervention just because of experience, learning, time, or some other factor?

• How much did the increased verbal interaction within the group contribute to change in the dependent variable?

• Did the intervention contribute to the increased verbal participation in the group, perhaps even more so than it did to changes in the dependent variable? If so, what are the treatment implications of this?

Using the ABAB design, Rhoda could not isolate any cause and effect relationships of her intervention, but the group's improved blood glucose level and an unintended change, the increase in their verbal participation, left her pleased with her research findings. The intervention had been associated with *two* desirable changes, both of which in her experience with similar groups did not usually occur until the groups had been in existence longer. Did it matter exactly how and why these desirable changes occurred? Probably not, at least not in this early stage of her inquiry. She decided to replicate her research with her next new diabetic support group.

SUMMARIZING: STRENGTHS AND WEAKNESSES

Single-subject research will never replace group research for generalized knowledge building for the social work profession, but it is a valuable partner of it. Its findings have limited external validity; only through replication with similar clients can more generalized knowledge regarding practice effectiveness be generated. It also is vulnerable to charges that it lacks internal validity (Marlow, 1993, p. 168) in that it is virtually impossible to determine whether any changes in the dependent variable resulted from something other than the presence or absence of the intervention. Single-subject research also is difficult to use to evaluate intervention effectiveness in working with some problems, especially those that are not easily measured. It is most suitable when one behavior or attitude stands out as problematic for the client system as opposed to situations in which the client system has a multitude of equally severe problems or symptoms.

Single-subject research requires administrative support and encouragement. The results should be used only for candid feedback to the social worker himself or herself. They should never be used for administrative evaluation of one's work by a supervisor. This must be understood if the right organizational climate for single subject research is to exist.

The limitations of single-subject research are also common to social work practice. Practice often must depend on the self-report of clients for data, particularly for the measurement of the dependent variable. The social worker must assume that the information thus received is truthful. Also, clients may substitute one problem for another (for example, cocaine dependency for alcohol dependency), thereby confounding interpretation of the success of an intervention. Defining the dependent variable broadly rather than narrowly (for example, substance abuse) will help to alleviate this potential difficulty. The issue of withdrawing an intervention and its ethical implications also must be addressed. Research may have to be scrapped if its continuation might prove harmful to the client. And of course the problem of undesirable dependency of the client on the social worker must be considered in interpreting the desirability of any identifiable patterns in the dependent variable. But addressing all of these issues is just part of good social work practice.

The advantages of single-subject research clearly outweigh its limitations and demands. It is inexpensive, both in dollars and in the time demanded of the social worker. The basics of it are easily taught and understood in a one-day workshop. There is not the ethical issue associated with the use of true control groups seen in experimental research, which sometimes requires denial of treatment to those in need of help. Utilization of findings, unlike many group research studies, is virtually guaranteed. Findings, while always tentative, can provide good early feedback on the effectiveness of a new approach to intervention. The intervention can be discarded if it appears that it makes no difference or it can be reevaluated through replication.

Single-subject research is well suited to task-centered problem-solving methods of practice. It is consistent with a wide variety of methods and social work processes that stress the importance of sound, accountable social work practice. It also is well suited to the client participatory methods of social work practice described elsewhere in this book.

Reading 16-2 *Do No Harm: Policy Options that Meet Human Needs**

John McKnight

The medical profession has long understood that its interventions have the potential to hurt as well as to help. The Hippocratic oath, repeated by physicians to this day, concludes with the primary mandate. "This above all, do no harm." The harmful capacity of medicine is recognized in what current medical language calls iatrogenic disease—doctor-created maladies.

Much of the positive reputation of the medical profession flows from the ethic that assumes a good doctor, before undertaking any intervention, always asks: "Will this initiative help more than hurt?" Responsible professionals are bound by Hippocrates to consider the balance before acting. Indeed, in the most ethical practice, the burden of proof for efficacy is upon the physician.

The traditional ethical code that prominently displays the Hippocratic principle in the foreground of the medical profession stands in stark contrast to the theory, research, and practice of most other "human service" professions. In the fields of social work, developmental disabilities, physical disability, or care of the elderly, no tradition of routinely analyzing possible negative side-effects exists. Instead, evaluation usually focuses on whether an intervention "made a difference." The intervention is presumed to help if it has any effect at all, and if it has no measurable effect, it is assumed not to have hurt.

Some observers suggest the lack of accounting for negative effects in the human services is a consequence of those interventions not being "powerful" ones when compared to the chemicals and scalpels of medicine. Instead, there is an unstated assumption that these non-medical professions are searching for something that "works" within fields characterized by effective, neutral or abandoned initiatives, none of which could have basically injured their clients. It is this naive assumption that has degraded the nonmedical human service professions and contributed to popular impressions that many of the clients of these professions are not worth a public investment. Indeed, we now hear the constant claim that the clients of human service professionals—the poor, disadvantaged, disabled, young and old—have not been helped by "pouring money on the problem." The client is usually blamed for not blooming under this "rain of dollars." What has actually happened, however, is that money has been "poured" into the programs of human service professionals,[1] and we have no knowledge of whether the effects of their ministrations have been iatrogenic. Instead, the labelled and vulnerable in our society are blamed. From this perspective, the regressive public policies of the last decade can be understood as an era of blaming the client for many of the iatrogenic practices of human service professionals. Regressive policymakers and human service professionals have made unintended common cause because the profession is unable to analyze the negative effects its interventions have had as the potential cause of failed policy.

If we are to recover the potential of public policy as an asset for those who are labelled, exploited and

---

Source: Social Policy, Summer 1989, 5–15.

[1] *Up from Dependency,* Supplement 1, Volume 1, Executive Office of the President (1986) reports the major increases between 1960 and 1985 in public allocations to service systems for low-income populations.

excluded, it is critical that we begin to understand the iatrogenic aspects of the major agent of public policy—the human service professions. When we can conceptualize the structurally negative effects of their interventions, we can begin a reasoned decision-making process regarding the two basic questions that should determine social policy:

- "Which of the competing human service solutions have more efficacy than negative side effects?"
- "Is there a less iatrogenic solution that does not involve human service methods?"

This latter question is a critical element of the policymaking process. We often forget that a human service is only one response to a human condition. There are always many other possibilities that do not involve paid experts and therapeutic concepts.

Mark Twain reminds us that "If your only tool is a hammer, all problems look like nails." While the human service tool has undoubted efficacy in particular situations, like the hammer, it can also do great harm when used inappropriately. All the problems of those who are vulnerable, exploited, excluded, or labelled are not nails. They do not always "need" human services. More often, they may "need" justice, income, and community.

This paper is an attempt to formulate a conceptual framework to assess the iatrogenic effects of the tool called human services. What structurally negative effects does it incorporate? When is it inappropriately used? And what methods might test the iatrogenic potential?

There are at least four structurally negative characteristics of the human service tool.[2]

The first is the consequence of seeing individuals primarily in terms of their "needs." Each of us can be conceived as a half-glass of water.

We are partly empty. We have deficiencies.

We are also partly full. We have capacities.

Human service professionals focus on deficiencies, call them "needs," and have expert skills in giving each perceived deficiency a label. The

negative effects of this diagnostic process have been thoroughly explored in the literature regarding labelling theory (Wolfensberger, 1975). As a result, we are generally aware that to be diagnosed and labelled as "mentally ill" or "disadvantaged" carries a heavy negative social consequence.

What is less well understood is the fact that the labelling professions force us, structurally, to focus on the empty half when the appropriate focus may be the full half. For example, many people labelled "developmentally disabled" or "physically disabled" are never going to be "fixed" by the service professions. Nonetheless, they are frequently subjected to years of "training" to write their name or tie their shoes. These same people may have many capacities that are unused and unshared while their lives are surrounded by special services that will demonstrably fail to fix the deficiency. Denying opportunities to express capacities is often the structurally iatrogenic effect of the use of ineffective therapeutic tools.

For those whose "emptiness" cannot be filled by human services, the most obvious "need" is the opportunity to express and share their gifts, skills, capacities, and abilities with friends, neighbors, and fellow citizens in the community. As deficiency-oriented service systems obscure this fact, they inevitably harm their client and the community by preempting the relationship between them.[3]

The second structurally negative effect of the use of the human service tool is its effect on public budgets. It is clear to every elected official that the public purse is limited. Contemporary legislative process is mainly about the division of that purse. To give more to one activity (defense) usually means giving less to another (agriculture or education). Therefore, a realistic approach to public policy and expenditure always requires an understanding of trade-offs—who or what gets less as something else gets more.

This process occurs between major expenditure categories such as education, highways, defense,

---

[2] For the seminal analysis of modern therapeutic counter-productivity, see Ivan Illich, *Medical Nemesis* (New York: Pantheon, 1976).

[3] Mary O'Connell, *The Gift of Hospitality,* Center for Urban Affairs and Policy Research, Northwestern University, Evanston, IL (1988) is a report of local initiatives designed to counteract this iatrogenic effect in the lives of people labelled developmentally disabled.

medicine, and agriculture. Trade-offs also take place within each of these categories. We understand this trade-off, for example, as it is publicly debated about the defense budget. Should we have more land-based bombers or more missiles? There is a choice to be made.

The same process occurs within the human service budget. Here, however, it is less well understood because the basic competition for the limited funds available for the "disadvantaged" is between the human service system and cash income for labelled people. Service system lobbyists and advocates see the competition for limited public resources as a jockeying between various service providers and systems. They rarely recognize or acknowledge, however, that the net effect of their lobbying is to limit cash income for those they call "needy" and increase the budget and incomes of service programs and providers.

As a recent federal study showed, between 1960 and 1985 federal and state cash assistance programs grew 105 percent in real terms, while non-cash programs for services and commodities grew 1,760 percent. By 1985, cash income programs amounted to $32.3 billion, while commodity[4] and service programs received $99.7 billion.[5]

The service system's preemption of public wealth designated for the "disadvantaged" is also demonstrated by recent studies of poverty allocations in New York City and Chicago.[6] Both studies demonstrate that over 60 percent of all public funds allocated in those cities for low-income people are allocated for services rather than for income.

The effect of trading cash for human services is devastating for people whose lives cannot be "fixed" by service intervention. Nonetheless, we have no effective measures that allow legislators or policymakers to assess whether public investments

for services would be more enabling as cash income. As a consequence, most legislative debate surrounding labelled people is about which services to fund, and for how much.

The third structurally negative effect of the human service tool is its impact upon community and associational life. The community, a social space where citizens turn to solve problems, may be displaced by the intervention of human service professionals as an alternative method of problem solving. Human service professionals with special expertise, technique, and technology push out the problem-solving knowledge and action of friend, neighbor, citizen, and association. As the power of profession and service system ascends, the legitimacy, authority, and capacity of citizens and community descend (Illich et al., 1977). The *citizen* retreats. The *client* advances. The power of community action weakens. The authority of the service system strengthens. And as human service tools prevail, the tools of citizenship, association, and community rust. Their uses are even forgotten. Many local people come to believe that the service tool is the only tool, and that their task as good citizens is to support taxes and charities for more services.

The consequence of this professional persuasion is devastating for those labelled people whose primary "need" is to be incorporated in community life and empowered through citizenship. These people include those frequently labelled as developmentally disabled, physically disabled, elderly, ex-convicts. They desperately "need" incorporation into community life but the community of citizens and associations has often been persuaded by human service advocates that vulnerable people:

. . . need to be surrounded by professional services in order to survive;

. . . are therefore appropriately removed from community life in order to receive these special service programs in special places;

. . . cannot be incorporated into community life because citizens don't know how to deal with these special people.

The result of this professional pedagogy is a disabled citizenry and impotent community associations, unable to remember or understand how

---

[4] While commodity programs and vouchers such as food stamps and housing vouchers represent a minority of these dollars, they are often preferable to human service allocations because they provide a greater range of choice and are appropriated for more basic life requirements.

[5] *Up From Dependency,* pp. 12–14.

[6] David Grossman and Geraldine Smolka, *New York City's Poverty Budget,* Community Service Society of New York, NY (1984); Diane Kallenback and Arthur Lyons, *Government Spending for the Poor in Cook County, Illinois: Can We Do Better?,* Center for Urban Affairs and Policy Research, Northwestern University, Evanston, IL (1989).

labelled people were or can be included in community life.

Instead of recognizing the crucial need most labelled people have for the empowerment of joining community life as a citizen, expressing capacities and making choices, many good-willed citizens volunteer to assist service systems free of charge. In this simple act, citizen volunteers trade off their unique potential to bring a labelled person into their life and the associational life of community in exchange for the use of their time as an unpaid agent for a service system. The community group that might ask a disabled or vulnerable person to join as a member decides, instead, to raise money for wheelchairs and rehabilitation centers. The associations of community life are led to support segregated, professionally controlled athletic events rather than incorporating a labelled person into a church bowling league.

In working to meet this need for incorporation, it is necessary to recognize that the human service tool typically limits, weakens or replaces community, associational and citizen tools. This is in the nature of any approach built on the premise that vulnerable people will be better because an expert knows better.

The fourth structurally negative consequence of using human service programs is that they can create, in the aggregate, environments that contradict the potential positive effect of any one program. When enough programs surround a client, they may combine to create a new environment in which none of the programs will be efficacious.

This particular iatrogenic effect is difficult to comprehend because it grows from the use of programs, any one of which might seem reasonable standing alone. Indeed, most individual service programs appear reasonable and "needed" when presented to legislators. What is invisible is the effect of the program when it is joined by many other service programs as they surround a labelled person. With enough services surrounding a life, a new environment emerges that has its own peculiar system of incentives, rewards, and penalties.

The process is analogous to an aggregation of trees. In an urban neighborhood there are usually trees in yards and parkways. We would not say, however, that people in that neighborhood live in a forest, even though the trees in a forest may be of the same kind. We would not call an area a forest until it has enough trees to create a new environment that does not exist in the neighborhood. In the forest, the shade and fallen leaves kill off grasses. In their place appear new wild flowers and bushes. The grassland animals are replaced by those that live in trees. Prairie birds are replaced by forest birds. The forest flora and fauna create a different world; most people even act differently in a forest, even though it is a place comprised of trees familiar from their neighborhood.

By way of analogy, each individual service program is like a tree. But when enough service programs surround people, they come to live in a forest of services. The environment is different from the neighborhood or community. And people who have to live in the service forest will act differently than those people whose lives are principally defined by neighborhood relationships.

We all recognize the forests of services that are called institutions. They are places where people live wholly surrounded by service professionals, programs, and plans. The uniqueness of this environment is emphasized by large buildings, walls, fences, and so on. Nonetheless, forests of services can be created without walls or large buildings. Places called group homes, halfway houses, and convalescent homes are usually service forests. Also, some labelled individuals who live with their families can be so fully served by professionals that their life is lived in a forest although their residence is in a neighborhood.

There are also low-income neighborhoods where so many people live lives surrounded by services that the neighborhood itself becomes a forest. People who live in this neighborhood forest are now called the "underclass." This is an obvious misnomer. Instead, we should say that the neighborhood is a place where citizens act as anyone else would if their lives were similarly surrounded and controlled by paid service professionals. A more accurate label than "underclass" would be "dependent on human service systems." A more accurate differentiation of status

EXHIBIT Four Struc- turally Negative Effects of Human Services	1. Human services emphasize deficiencies. →	1. Undermines the sense of capacity and self worth of a client.
	2. Human services create a demand on public budgets. →	2. Reduces the cash income and market choices of the client.
	3. Human services focus on problem solving by experts and systems. →	3. Decreases participation in community life by the client.
	4. A dense environment of services surrounds individuals and communities on all sides. →	4. Intensifies dependency, stimulates deviance, and neutralizes the positive potential of individual programs of service intervention.

would be to say the residents are "clients" rather than "citizens."

When the services grow dense enough around the lives of people, a circular process develops. A different environment is created for these individuals. The result of a non-community environment is that those who experience it necessarily act in unusual and deviant ways. These new ways, called inappropriate behavior, are then cited by service professionals as proof of the need for separation in a forest of services and the need for more services.

The disabling effect of this circular process is devastating to the client and to our communities. The public is understandably mystified. Each individual program appears to be reasonably needed and appropriate. However, in the aggregate, each program has become ineffective and often harmful. The situation is analogous to a person who dies of taking 20 different pills, any one of which might have been helpful.

Physicians have long recognized this interactive iatrogenic effect. Service systems have not. Instead, human service systems nearly always prescribe more programs, more services, more "targeting," and larger forests. The result is predictably counterproductive. Costs increase. Programs proliferate. Forests grow. Clients multiply. People adapt their behavior to the forest and are called maladaptive. The cycle spirals downward and the failures are blamed on the victims.

In summary, these iatrogenic effects tell us that policymakers and practitioners should be constantly aware that the use of human service tools places a person at risk of: a reduced sense of self worth; poverty; segregation from community life;

and disempowerment as a citizen. The risks demand the most serious reevaluation of policies that empower human service professionals and systems to intervene in the lives of labelled and vulnerable people.

A practical framework for this policy reevaluation would begin by placing the burden of proof upon those who propose a human service intervention as a means of helping a person with a particular condition. This "burden" is analogous to that understood by the Food and Drug Administration as it evaluates the use of various medical interventions. The intervenor has the responsibility to identify the negative side effects and to prove the benefits are greater.

This is an excellent model for evaluating proposed human service interventions. The service advocate should be required to identify the negative effects, present evidence of the benefits, and demonstrate that the benefits outweigh the negative effects. The effect of such a rigorous evaluation would create a positive new force in the lives of labelled people. The service agency, department, or professional would be asked by legislators, public executives, boards of directors, foundations, or groups of labelled people to specify the negative effects of their proposals. This wholesome new discipline placed upon the service advocates would often create a revolutionary reexamination of their assumptions and practices.

In addition to the burden of proof regarding negative effects and benefits of a particular service intervention, the service advocate should also be required to present evidence that the intervention will not be used cumulatively, creating a service forest. Just as the ethical medical professional recognizes and protects against the negative effects of the interaction among many drugs, the human service professional should be required to identify the negative effect of aggregating programs around a person's life and define the safeguards that will be used to protect against the dependency and deviance that so frequently result from a "forest" of services.

Once both requirements are met by service advocates and the particular and interactive negative effects are clarified, policymakers should quickly recognize that the use of a particular human service tool is not necessarily good or even neutral. They should see that a service is a potentially injurious tool and begin to ask whether other kinds of non-service resources, activities, or opportunities might be appropriate for the person said to be in need of a service. They could begin to ask, "Is there a different kind of approach that doesn't involve a human service that might be more effective and have less negative effect?"

Here again, the medical analogy is helpful. While the Food and Drug Administration may approve a medicine as being more beneficial than harmful, an ethical physician does not assume that it should therefore be prescribed. Instead, the physician asks whether there are other, more effective ways of dealing with the condition that do not involve use of the drug and its negative effects.

The current protocol for high blood pressure provides a good example. All the approved medicines have some significant negative effects. Therefore, ethical physicians first seek non-medical alternatives before risking use of the medicine. This often involves advising clients to undertake an exercise program, reduce their weight, and decrease their salt intake. Similarly, a review of policy options to address conditions of vulnerable and labelled people should systematically examine non-human service responses that might provide the same or better results with fewer or no negative side effects.

This policy-options review requires that policymakers have a set of alternatives to test against proposed human service interventions. Fortunately, there are at least three alternatives that have historically proven effective in addressing the conditions of many who are vulnerable, labelable, or said to be in need.

The first option is to identify the capacities, skills, or potential contributions of the persons said to be in need. What policies, resources, or activities could result in the exercise, expression, visibility, and magnification of those assets? For example, many people labelled "developmentally disabled" have been found to thrive and flourish when they escape a "forest" of professional services and are provided community opportunities to express their unique gifts.[7] Similarly, low-income people, neighborhoods, and public housing developments experience regeneration when they focus on their capacities rather than an exclusive emphasis upon problems, deficiencies, and needs (McKnight, 1987). However, in the case of both groups of people, the files of the local human service agencies and authorities are filled with descriptions of their needs, deficiencies, diagnoses, and problems. Therefore, those agencies are not useful as a resource for capacity-oriented development. Policymakers will need to find other activities and supports if the assets and capacities of people and communities are to be viewed as the basic problem-solving tools.

The second option is to provide cash income in lieu of access to prepaid or vouchered human services. This option provides an opening to many new opportunities and even creates better services. The advantages of income over services include:

. . . providing empowering choices in a free market;

. . . providing choices between services, thus creating a competitive market that should improve services;

. . . creating a market in low-income areas where mainline enterprises will have an incentive to reach out to low-income people.

There is, of course, the stereotypic concern that "disadvantaged" people might not use their income wisely. However, there is no evidence that, as a group, these people are less wise in the use of their money than doctors, psychologists, social workers,

---

[7] *The Gift of Hospitality.*

or other professionals who are now the primary beneficiaries of dollars appropriated for low-income and other labelled people.

The third option is to seek participation in community life and citizenship activities instead of human service interventions. This option flows from the fact that many vulnerable people are primarily disabled by their segregation from community life in institutions, "special" programs, or service ghettos (Rothman, 1971). Paradoxically, their lives often improve significantly when they leave service systems and become effectively incorporated in community life (Woodson, 1981). Therefore, the challenge is to create policies that stimulate the hospitality of citizen associations and community groups so that they will incorporate and share the capacities and gifts of those who have been excluded because of their labels.

My purpose in this analysis has been to establish two basic premises:

1. Human service interventions have negative effects as well as benefits.
2. Human service interventions are only one of many ways to address the condition of people who are labelled.

Many of our failed reforms and programs during the last two decades are the result of our failure to recognize these two realities. When policymakers begin to evaluate human service proposals from the perspective of these two premises, we will create much more effective means of problem solving. Making these premises operational is reasonably simple. They can be expressed in five basic questions that can be asked by any person responsible for policies affecting those citizens who are especially vulnerable, disadvantaged, or exploited:

1. What are the negative effects of the human service proposed to help the class of people?
2. What are the situations where the proposed service may be applied with many other services and what interactive negative effects will result?
3. Will a focus on the capacities of the class of people be more effective than a service program's focus on deficiencies and needs?
4. Will providing the dollars proposed for funding the human service provide greater benefits if given to the clients as cash income?
5. Will incorporation into community life be more beneficial than special, separating service treatments?

The last three questions incorporate the central values of a free and democratic society. They recognize that the greatest "service" our society provides is the opportunity to express our unique capacities, to have a decent income and join with our fellow citizens in creating productive communities. No human service professional or program will ever equal the healing and empowering effect of those three democratic opportunities. Therefore, policies that support citizen capacity, income, and community should have preference over other forms of intervention that are necessarily second-rate and second-best responses. Effective democratic policy is guided by three powerful principles: citizenship, income, and community.

For Further Reading

Blythe, B., & Tripodi, T. (1989). *Measurement in direct practice*. Newbury Park, CA: Sage.

Brekke, J. S. (1986). Scientific imperatives in social work research: Pluralism is not scepticism. *Social Service Review, 60*, 538–554.

Cheetham, J., Fuller, R., McIvor, G., & Petch, A. (1992). *Evaluating social work effectiveness*. Buckingham, England, and Philadelphia: Open University Press.

Gibbs, L. (1991). *Scientific reasoning for social workers: Bridging the gap between research and practice*. New York: Merrill/Macmillan.

Grinnell, R. M. Jr. (Ed.). (1988). *Social work research and evaluation* (3rd ed.). Itasca, IL: F. E. Peacock.

Howitt, D. (1993). *Child abuse errors: When good intentions go wrong*. New Brunswick, NJ: Rutgers University Press.

Hudson, J., & Grinnell, R. (1989). Program evaluation. In B. Compton & B. Galaway (Eds.), *Social Work Processes* (4th ed.). Belmont, CA: Wadsworth.

Kiresuk, T., & Sherman, R. E. (1968). Goal attainment scaling: A general method for evaluating comprehensive community health programs. *Community Mental Health Journal, 4,* 443–453.

Mager, R. F. (1972). *Goal analysis.* Belmont, CA: Fearon.

Patten, M. (1986). *Utilization-focused evaluation* (2nd ed.). Beverly Hills, CA: Sage.

Pleper, M. H. (1985). The future of social work research. *Social Work Research and Abstracts, 21*(4), 12–20.

Rosenthal, B. S. (1992). Does the social work profession value research based knowledge as a basis for social policy? *Areté, 17*(1), 38–46.

Rubin, A. (1985). Practice effectiveness: More grounds for optimism. *Social Work, 30,* 469–476.

Rutman, L. (Ed.). (1984). *Evaluation research methods: A basic guide* (2nd ed.). Beverly Hills, CA: Sage.

Chapter 17

On Becoming a Social Worker

So you want to be a social worker? We assume you do, or you would have abandoned this book long before you reached this last chapter. We hope that the book has been helpful in your effort to learn about social work. However, reading this book is only the beginning of your journey to becoming a social worker. The material in the book is more complex than it may appear. It will demand some thought, study, and experimentation to achieve mastery of the content. In addition, we assume that by now you are aware that this book does not tell it all. That is one of the exciting things about social work. It is a never-ending learning experience. We have not tried to tell it all. Rather, we have tried to present some of the basic core knowledge of social work practice, to introduce you to the time-tested knowledge, and to select and present ideas that will establish a foundation on which you can build the special knowledge you will need for your practice.

We hope you are seeking to learn and to serve, that you find problem solving involving the complexity and interdependence of human relationships and processes both challenging and satisfying. We hope you care deeply about the pains and troubles of others and have the strength and courage to stand with your clients as they struggle to solve their problems in living, with respect for their wisdom and courage as they seek to grow through crisis and difficulties. We hope you recognize that all of us have much yet to learn about the process of human growth, development, and change and that you are willing to take on some of the responsibility to engage in constant inquiry so that you can add to professional understanding of this complex process.

We hope that you believe firmly in the impulse for growth and development in human beings and in their capacity to continue to grow and change throughout their lives. We hope you have a deep respect for each individual and for his or her understanding of his or her own life, his or her own pain, and his or her own goals. We hope you recognize that the social context of each life and the meaning it has for the individual are critical; that you recognize the critical roles of the various levels of environment in denying the individual the power necessary to develop the competence he or she seeks to develop life in the desired way.

By now we assume you are aware that social work as a profession is not free of conflict and that as a social worker you will face certain stresses and feel certain tensions. We would like to discuss some of these stresses with you for several reasons. If you understand some of the problems that will confront you as a worker before you find yourself in the middle of them, you may be able to deal with them more successfully and with more comfort. At least they will not be a surprise. In addition, it may be helpful to realize that certain stresses seem to come with the job. Every job has its conflicts. It may be helpful to realize that these stresses and the feelings they bring are not yours alone. They come with the territory, so you are not at fault for feeling them. The question for you is to find a way to recognize and deal with them. Since you know that they are common problems, you may find that one way of lessening stress is to explore the possibility of finding or establishing a support group that will be helpful to everyone.

Social workers need to cultivate self-awareness. It is one of the most valuable qualities we can seek to develop, and it is something that we may work at all our professional lives. We must work at knowing and accepting ourselves, at knowing what we can do and accepting what we can't. We need to know our particular vulnerabilities so we can find ways to deal with them. While it is essential to feel empathy for our client, it is dangerous to both our welfare and that of the clients when we take on the client's pain as being the same as our pain and when we think the client can use our successful solution. We must be aware of it when we identify so closely with the client that we cannot make objective assessments of the problems. We can be particularly vulnerable to overidentification with the client when the problem the client presents is similar to one with which we have struggled. An example of a worker's struggle to separate her feelings from those expressed by the client is found in the worker's account of her response to Mrs. Manley's ambivalence about returning to work (Appendix, A-2).

Social workers often demand too much of themselves. Let's go back a minute to the case of Mrs. Z (Appendix, A-4). The worker in that case was suffering because she could not establish a helping relationship with Mrs. Z, as both she and the hospital expected that she should. It would have been helpful to the worker to recognize several things. First, she needed to accept the fact that she could not create a good helping relationship all by herself. As we have stated earlier in this text, the client has a part in establishing relationships. It is true that the worker was not approaching the task appropriately, but she was too stressed from accepting the total responsibility to establish contact with Mrs. Z to step back and consider what she knew about building relationships. Second, it was probably impossible for her to establish a relationship with Mrs. Z as long as she did not recognize her own anger and frustration with the client. Mrs. Z was behaving in a way designed to provoke, and her methods were successful. If the worker had been consciously aware of the feelings toward Mrs. Z and treated them as a problem to be understood and resolved, she could have asked Mrs. Z directly about her behavior, clearly sharing with Mrs. Z the results of such behavior. Our responses to clients do not come out of nowhere. They develop from our relationships with important people in our life and from our interactions with other clients. We should not be afraid to examine them, nor should we blame ourselves if they seem inappropriate. The task is to analyze the interaction, assess the problem, and attempt to do something about it. It may be helpful to remember that if we find our clients' behavior irritating, it is probable that other people respond to the client's behavior in similar ways. It may be important to help the client become aware of the impact of this on his or her patterns of relationships with others.

In our struggle to develop self-awareness, we need to examine our expectations for ourselves, our clients, and for the outcome of our work. We need to learn to accept that clients' problems are usually products of complex social interaction over some period of years during which many hurtful things may have happened. We cannot undo what has been done, nor can we engage in blaming those involved. We need to accept what happened as reality, help the client accept it as reality, and confront the question of where we go from here. None of us can solve in a few days problems that have developed over a lifetime. In fact, the problem can be solved only when the client is able to participate in the actions to be taken. This may take considerable time. We cannot remake lives, but we can help people deal in more satisfying ways with the life they now have.

We need to work at accepting the fact that the pace of human change is very slow. We often expect far too much of ourselves, assuming that we ought to be able to change things overnight. Life does not move that way. Look at the amount of time that the worker invested in Mrs. Stover (Appendix A-6) and at the pace of the gains. As is very common in work with clients, Mrs. Stover was not actively appreciative of the time the worker invested. Yet she was very much aware of change, and the school noted significant change in the children. As the worker assessed what had been accomplished in the case, it may have seemed to be very simple, but the impact of the work on helping Mrs. Stover and her children solve their problems in living was tremendous.

Obviously, you seek to obtain satisfaction from your work with clients. We all want to feel professionally competent, and one source of this feeling is our awareness that the clients find us helpful. Ask yourself whether you expect the clients themselves to be a source of satisfaction or whether you seek satisfaction from competent problem solving. You may not consciously desire to use the clients toward your ends, but you may want to be liked and appreciated by your clients. Unfortunately, the clients who need the most help are likely to be those who find taking responsibility for themselves the most difficult and who are likely to reject your offers to help in solving their problems. It may be helpful to recognize that their anger and rejection are not necessarily aimed at you personally but are a response to the social context in which they find themselves and the interactions that are a part of such context. Work at separating personal from professional needs, at recognizing your ambivalent feelings toward clients who reject you. But you should not feel a failure just because you have these very natural responses to certain situations. These feelings simply present you with a problem to solve. You will find these easier to confront if you can define them as problems to work and share them with a support group.

Once again, expecting too much of yourself, which leads you to consider any negative feelings or problems you can't seem to solve as weaknesses or as an indication you are bad or incompetent, may result in reluctance to ask for appropriate professional help or colleague support. You may also have difficulty in accepting the importance of being able to impose some limitations on client demands when such demands take time you need to meet your own and your family's legitimate needs. If you are to have resources to give to others, you need time to care for yourself. You also must be able to discuss agency limitations and policies with clients without apology. They are there; you may wish we could change them, and indeed you may be working to do just that, but it is not helpful to join the client in anger or resistance. Of course, if policies or limits are truly hurtful to people and involve the welfare of several clients, you may wish to help them form an advocacy group to protest the situation and attempt to make a change. This is different from simply joining the client in impotent anger.

It may be that your expectations for yourself are related to your need to control. The need to control is a very subtle and very risky business for both you and the client. It is a widespread problem in human service professions. Helping is often regarded as first cousin to controlling. The fact that the client wants help and has to seek it from a worker who through access to agency and community resources has the power to help also means that the client to a greater or lesser degree must submit to the control of the worker. If you feel you know how a problem should be solved, it is easy to use your power position to influence or coerce the client into acting in the way that you think is correct. If it is important to be successful with a problem, you will be pushed to control the client to ensure that you know the outcome.

One of the best ways we know to accept oneself is to write a careful statement of the client's problem, goal, assessment, and plan. Carefully done with careful consideration of realistic limits, such written plans can keep you from expecting too much. You may come back from seeing Mrs. X, who seems to be functioning no better or more comfortably than she was three interviews ago, and feel frustrated and defeated. But if you look at your plan and see that in calmer times you recognized that you could expect only slow change in Mrs. X's situation, you may feel a real sense of satisfaction with the gains that you know have been made.

You have an overwhelming caseload. You feel defeated and discouraged because you know you can't help all these people. You need to remember that you never promised to help all of them to the maximum. To scurry breathlessly from interview to interview with no time to relax and listen to the client or to make careful plans is going to help no one. Again, accept the limits of reality without self-blame (you didn't create the reality) and make realistic plans to do what you can do. Sit down with your supervisor and decide how many cases you can serve to your fullest, how many will absolutely explode without regular visits, and how many can get along with fewer. Select from this caseload two groups of clients to serve to the maximum possible: the people who just have to be seen and some clients whom you would like to work with for your own learning and satisfaction. These you should plan to see regularly. Plan to see other clients and offer only the minimum service they need or the agency mandates. You should, however, make a plan for those clients too, and record what you plan to do and why. We do need to work toward lower caseloads, but at this point the size of the caseload is beyond our control. In the meantime, all you can do is do what you can. And if you want to continue to find satisfaction in your work, you must have opportunities to learn, so you need time and situations that can contribute to learning.

One of the problems that we often see in agencies is the constant focusing on the weaknesses and pathology of clients. Workers tend not to deal much with their strengths. Maybe it would help to search a bit more for client strengths. Also, ask your clients for feedback about how things are going with them. Perhaps every six months or so you should sit down with your clients and evaluate gains made and battles lost. This usually results in positive feedback from the clients, who may be more aware of the change in the situation than you are. It is helpful to know how clients think things are going. It is often helpful to ask clients about their pleasures in life. What are the things they enjoy? It is good social work to know the clients' situations and how they find pleasures in life. It helps you to understand them, and perhaps it helps you to set realistic goals for them and for yourself in the struggle to make life better for as many people as possible.

As a worker in an agency, you may have only limited influence on the structure of supervision and colleague relationships. However, we have found that one of the most helpful devices for guarding against becoming exhausted and defeated is to have regular colleague group meetings. These are not for the direct benefit of either agency or client but for that of the workers. Such meetings are informal, with only loose agendas, and are a time for workers to talk with other workers about their feelings, their defeats, their successes, and the new things they have tried. They help you to understand that you are not alone in either succeeding or failing. They build a structure of group support.

Another helpful exercise is to use some evenings and weekends to read in the literature of the history and biography of social work and social workers. You are in danger of feeling defeated if you are unable to take a long view of the profession. You need to understand the struggles of those who have gone before us, of the gains they made. You may often feel frustrated and helpless at the sexism and racism in the profession, but if you read the reaction of white men senators 60 years ago to the proposal of women social workers for an act to support maternal and child health, you will marvel at the women's courage and at the changes that have been made. Social workers have indeed made great strides in the interests of better and safer lives for many vulnerable people. We should be proud of our profession. But more important, we need to understand that these gains did not come overnight.

To make one more addition to what it means to be a social worker, we would like to quote from a tape recording of a group of clients who were originally respondents talking about how they came to see their social workers. One client said:

"I think a social worker is—could be put in the same class as a doctor or a priest. It's a vocation, not just a job. It has a very definite calling to them, and I don't know how you would class them that makes them special, but it is just the one thing they would pick to do. Of course, there are some that should never have gone into it—it is just a job to them, and they might as well stay home" (Compton, 1959, p. 59).

Another client in the same group said:

"It's a person who in your first acquaintance lets you know by his or her expression that he's in your home to be of service to you if possible; and to show trust because most people are trustworthy if one shows trust in them; to be able to understand reasonably well problems concerning the family as a whole; not to criticize but to analyze why a person or a family is in unfavorable circumstances; to give helpful advice in a way that isn't demanding but that lets a person feel that it's his own idea; one who has a sincere desire to help people feeling that it might have been her as well as they but for the grace of God; one who encourages you to go beyond the capabilities you thought you possessed; one who guides you and makes the way possible but who insists that you do for yourself what you are capable of doing." (Compton, 1959, p. 53)

A final word. As a social worker, you need relationships outside work and other things to do that will bring satisfaction. Do not build your whole life around your profession. Remember, you must be more than your profession if you are to serve it well.

So we come to the end of our book. We urge you once again to look forward to the reading that follows this chapter. It focuses on burnout and how social workers deal with exhaustion and defeat. We hope that this final word, which asks you to look to your own welfare and ways to help yourself, truly serves that function.

Reading 17-1	*Burnout: An Occupational Hazard for Social Workers?**

Jan L. Hagen

Over the past decade a great deal of attention has been given to burnout. The topic is of particular concern to social work because in general social workers are regarded as being at high risk for it. Many social workers enter the profession with an idealized sense of mission or calling to help others and work within demanding bureaucratic constraints. These factors contribute to social workers' vulnerability to burnout. The risk of burnout may be particularly high during the initial years of practice, as social workers confront the realities of their jobs, their clients, and their own competence as practitioners (Cherniss, 1980; Edelwich & Brodsky, 1980). Burnout is expressed in a variety of ways with diverse consequences:

> I am only 31 years old and feel that my job has stifled my ability and drive. I hope to get a job which will bring my old self out, where I can think for myself, plan, use my brain again. It is hard to recover from burnout, but I plan to.
>
> Workers here are unappreciated. Administrators do not care about their people and it filters down from there. Only failures are noted, so morale is very low. The goal of 100% excellence is impossible to reach. Therefore, some stop trying while others get ulcers trying to stay afloat.

As these quotations illustrate, burnout is costly to practitioners, to organizations, and to clients. For the individual practitioner, there is physical and emotional exhaustion; depression and general malaise; feelings of helplessness and hopelessness;

the potential for physical problems such as headaches, ulcers, hypertension, fatigue, and backaches; and possibly the development of personal problems such as marital conflict and drug and alcohol abuse (Maslach 1982, 1976; Pines, Aronson & Kafry, 1981). For the organization, burnout results in ineffective and inefficient workers, low morale, absenteeism, and high turnover. For clients, burnout among service providers results in impersonal, dehumanized, and uncaring services.

Burnout is not yet a clearly defined concept, nor has a clearly articulated theoretical model been developed. This article reviews definitions of burnout, specifies variables contributing to it, and examines strategies for prevention and intervention by both individuals and agencies. If they know the personal, organizational, and societal variables that contribute to burnout, practitioners will be better prepared to prevent and alleviate it.

DEFINING BURNOUT

Freudenberger, a psychoanalyst, is credited with coining the term *burnout* to refer to emotional and physical exhaustion brought about by conditions at work. In exploring burnout, Freudenberger (1974) focused on individual psychology and identified types of personalities prone to burnout: the dedicated worker who takes on too much work with an excess of intensity; the overcommitted worker whose outside life is unsatisfactory; and the authoritarian worker who needs extensive control in his or her job (Karger, 1981). While highlighting the role of individual characteristics, Freudenberger's conceptualization of burnout excludes the

---

*Paper prepared for this edition.

interactions between people and their environments.

A broader approach to burnout has been developed by Maslach and Pines (Pines & Maslach, 1978; Maslach, 1978; Maslach, 1982; Pines, Aronson & Kafry, 1981). They propose a social-psychological perspective of burnout that examines the relationship between individuals and their work environments. Based on her numerous investigations, Maslach has concluded that

> burn-out is best understood (and modified) in terms of the social and situation sources of job-related stresses. Although personality variables are certainly relevant in the overall analysis, the prevalence of the phenomenon and the range of seemingly disparate staff people who are affected by it suggest that the search for causes is better directed away from identifying the bad people and toward uncovering the characteristics of the bad situations where many good people function. (1978, p. 114)

For Maslach, burnout is

> a syndrome of emotional exhaustion, depersonalization, and reduced personal accomplishment that can occur among individuals who do "people work" of some kind. It is a response to the chronic emotional strain of dealing extensively with other human beings, particularly when they are troubled or having problems.(1982, p. 3)

The variables to consider in this formulation of burnout include (1) personal characteristics of the practitioner; (2) the job setting in terms of supervisory and peer support as well as agency rules and regulations; and (3) the actual work with individual clients.

On a societal level Karger (1981) argues that professional burnout is very similar to industrial alienation as defined by Marx. In Marxian theory burnout and dissatisfaction are logical outgrowths of a capitalist system in which workers become alienated from their work. Burnout and dissatisfaction are "reactions to the fragmentation of work, to competition within the workplace, and to the loss of worker autonomy" (Farber, 1983, p. 8). By broadening the frame of reference for burnout to include larger societal issues of how work is structured and valued in society, a Marxist analysis

is helpful in conceptualizing burnout among human service providers. However, as Farber (1983) has noted, the helping professions are unique in numerous ways, and a class analysis of the role of the helping professions within society is inadequate.

These various approaches to burnout highlight the lack of consensus about the specific nature of burnout and its causes. All seem to agree, however, that the symptoms of burnout include attitudinal, physical, and emotional components.

It is most useful to think of burnout as a work-related strain, the "outcomes of experienced stress-emotions and behaviors that deviate from the individual's normal response" (Jayaratne, Tripodi, & Chess, 1983). Job dissatisfaction is another work-related strain, but it is a concept distinct from, although not unrelated to, burnout. As a strain, burnout produces at least three outcomes. The first is emotional exhaustion, a lack of emotional energy to use and invest in others. The second outcome of burnout is depersonalization, responding to others in callous, detached, emotionally hardened, and dehumanizing ways. Responses to others become increasingly negative, and there is a loss of caring. The third outcome is a reduced sense of personal accomplishment: "Providers have a gnawing sense of inadequacy about their ability to relate to recipients, and this may result in a self-imposed verdict of "failure" (Maslach, 1982, p. 3–6).

While consensus about burnout as a concept is developing, there is little agreement about the key factors or stressors that contribute to burnout. These stressors include variables related to the individual, the helping relationship, the work environment, and society.

THE INDIVIDUAL

The initial work on burnout focused on individual psychology and personality structures. While these are not the only factors, who we are as people, our needs, and our sense of ourselves play a role in burnout. Excessive emotional demands in a work situation place anyone at risk for burnout. However, characteristics of some individuals make them especially vulnerable to burnout. Low self-esteem and lack of confidence increase vulnerability to burnout, as does a lack of understanding of one's limitations, strengths, and weaknesses. As Maslach notes,

> The failure to recognize personal limits is especially critical in helping professions, where people are dealing with other people's lives. All too often providers feel completely responsible for whether a client succeeds or fails, lives or dies—and are emotionally overwhelmed by this heavy burden. This unwarranted sense of responsibility is usually tied to feelings of omnipotence . . .As a result, there will be discrepancies between aspirations and actual achievement—and feelings of failure will be sure to follow. (Maslach, 1982, p. 65)

When asked why they entered social work, practitioners often note the desire to help others, to make a contribution to the betterment of others, to create a just world. The loftiness of these ideals has repeatedly been noted as contributing to burnout (Cherniss, 1980a, 1980b; Edelwich & Brodsky, 1980). If these ideals generate unrealistic goals and expectations, practitioners quickly become disillusioned with both themselves and their clients. Unrealistic goals and expectations include notions that clients' problems require only simple solutions, that problems will be solved quickly, that it is possible to work effectively with anyone, and that the practitioner's work with clients will drastically alter their lives, for which clients will show the utmost appreciation (Edelwich & Brodsky, 1980, pp. 52–58).

Other reasons for entering social work are personal needs such as recognition, approval, affection, power and control, and intimacy. In and of themselves these needs neither help nor hinder work with clients. The risk of burnout increases, however, if practitioners expect clients to fulfill these personal needs. While helping professionals need satisfaction and a sense of accomplishment from their jobs, emphasis on deriving affection, respect, self-esteem, and personal identity from clients generates emotional stress for the practitioner and fosters burnout.

Maslach's research has highlighted certain demographic characteristics of those most vulnerable to burnout. In general, men and women experience burnout similarly, although some gender differences have been noted. Women are more likely to experience emotional exhaustion and to experience it more intensely. Depersonalization, characterized by callousness toward clients, is more common among men (Maslach, 1982, pp. 57–62; Jayaratne, Tripodi, & Chess, 1983, pp. 19–27).

The few studies that have included ethnicity as a variable indicate that burnout among whites and Asian-Americans is similar. However, blacks are less vulnerable to burnout than whites. Maslach attributes this to the fact that blacks are more experienced in dealing directly with people, including emotionally charged situations, and to their being more prepared to

> deal with problems and pain, since it is likely that they have experienced them more in their own lives (because of discrimination and poverty) than whites have. The troubles they have already seen may give them a more balanced and realistic perspective on the ones yet to come for them and those they work with. Knowing already that the world cannot be changed overnight, they will be less disillusioned the next morning when it has not. (Maslach, 1982, p. 59)

Vulnerability to burnout appears to be related to age—younger workers are more likely to burn out than older workers, who not only have more time on the job but also tend to have a more balanced and realistic perspective on life (Maslach, 1982, p. 59–60).

Education plays a complex role in burnout. In Maslach's (1982, pp. 61–62) studies, those with some college who did not graduate were at lower risk for burnout than those with four years of college or postgraduate education. Of the three groups, those with four years of college were at highest risk for burnout. This, too, may be related to age as well as practitioners' unrealistic expectations of themselves and their work with clients.

Relationships with family members and friends also influence burnout. As part of the practitioner's social support system, family and friends can buffer the stresses of work. Research indicates that the more positive these personal relationships are, the less likely a person is to burn out (Pines, Aronsen, & Kafry, 1981, p. 132). But if relationships with family members and friends are stressful, they may contribute to job stress and burnout by creating additional demands and obligations that conflict with work roles (Cherniss, 1980b, p. 138).

THE HELPING RELATIONSHIP

The helping relationship plays a key role in burnout. In fact, burnout has been defined as the "result of constant or repeated emotional pressure associated with an intense involvement with people over long periods of time" (Pines, Aronsen & Kafry, 1981, p. 15). The helping relationship exists primarily for the benefit of the client, and the emotional giving in the helping relationship is one-way from the practitioner to the client. The constant demand for emotional giving and sharing the intense feelings of others may result in emotional depletion. Some client problems are more emotionally draining than others. Incest, child abuse, wife battering, and rape are all examples of highly charged situations that place tremendous demands on the emotional reserves of the practitioner. While some problems and situations are initially emotionally stressful to all helping professionals, what is emotionally stressful and depleting for one person may not be for another. Emotionally charged situations will vary according to experience with similar situations and personal life experiences. Without an adequate knowledge base, a commitment to individualization, and sufficient awareness of personal responses, the practitioner may respond to emotionally charged situations presented by clients with hostility and callous attitudes toward them. Additionally, practitioners may lose their objectivity and become ineffective, getting caught up in clients' emotions or overidentifying with them.

Clients come for services not when they are functioning at their optimal and healthiest level but when they are encountering difficulties. Often, by the time clients reach a social worker, they have exhausted their own resources, including informal social supports, in trying to solve their problems. They may be at their wit's end, with a sense of failure and hopelessness. Many times, work focuses exclusively on client problems and deficiencies, with little or no attention to the more positive aspects of their lives. Clients' strengths, abilities, and resources are ignored. This not only limits the ability to work effectively with clients but also fosters a cynical notion of clients resulting in depersonalization. A tendency among social work practitioners is to focus on unsuccessful interventions with clients. To the extent that a careful examination of work with clients helps build further knowledge and skills, evaluation of failed interventions is helpful. But successes should be evaluated as well. Exclusive focus on either successes or failures distorts the picture of practice effectiveness. The likelihood of burnout is reduced when feedback is received from clients (Pines & Kafry, 1978, p. 503). Practitioners run the risk of receiving only negative feedback and focusing exclusively on the negative components of working with others if they fail to build on ongoing evaluation and systematic approaches to practice evaluation.

THE WORK ENVIRONMENT

Numerous factors in the work environment contribute to the development of burnout. Three factors are central: workload, role ambiguity, and role conflict. Other critical factors include co-workers, supervisors, and agency goals and procedures.

An early study by Pines and Kafry (1978) on burnout among social service workers identified caseload size as being related to burnout, particularly the development of negative attitudes toward clients. Maslach (1982, pp. 38–40) also identifies demands of too many clients as resulting in emotional withdrawal and impersonal service to clients. More recent studies indicate that the relationship between workload and burnout is not so clear-cut. The actual size of the workload is not crucial; rather, the important issue is the workers' perception of the workload; that is, do they regard it as too large? Additionally, the role workload dissatisfaction plays in burnout seems to vary by the type of setting; for example, child welfare services or family services (Jayaratne & Chess, 1984).

Both role ambiguity and role conflict have been identified as important stressors in the work environment. As defined by Farber, "*Role ambiguity* is associated with a lack of clarity regarding a worker's rights, responsibilities, methods, goals, status, or accountability. . . . *Role conflict* occurs when inconsistent, incompatible, or inappropriate demands are placed upon an individual (Jayaratne & Chess, 1983, p. 6).

Role ambiguity and role conflict contribute to burnout by reducing the clarity of goals and expectations in work with clients. They also hinder the development of positive relationships with co-workers and supervisors by contributing to confusion regarding work responsibilities.

Using job satisfaction as an indirect indicator of burnout, Harrison (1980) found high levels of role ambiguity and role conflict related to low levels of job satisfaction among child protective workers. However, in studies on social workers generally, Jayaratne and Chess found that role conflict and role ambiguity "do not play a significant role in either the assessment of job satisfaction or in the reporting of burnout" (1983, p. 137). Again, however, the importance of role ambiguity and role conflict in the development of burnout may vary by job position and setting (Jayaratne & Chess, 1984).

Relationships with co-workers and supervisor also have a bearing on burnout. The relationships themselves may be an additional source of stress if they are competitive or conflicted. However, co-workers and supervisors are an important source of social support, playing vital roles in helping practitioners learn new skills, evaluate the effectiveness of their work, develop competence in their positions, and understand the purpose and function of the agency. A study of social service workers found that workers having positive relationships with co-workers, having someone to discuss work problems with, and receiving feedback from both co-workers and supervisors were less likely to burn out (Pines & Kafry, 1978).

Agency goals and procedures also may foster burnout. If the agency's goals are unclear or ambiguous, role ambiguity or role conflict results. Ambiguous goals contribute to difficulties in measuring effectiveness of interventions and hinder the provision of helpful feedback from co-workers and supervisors. Agency procedures such as mandating the collection of certain data on all clients regardless of its relevance to the clients' problems also interfere with the client-worker relationship and worker effectiveness.

The work environment may be constrained by a lack of sufficient resources to fulfill agency responsibilities. Inadequate funding results in insufficient resources and support for agency staff to meet demands for service. While staff may be reduced, the workload of the agency seldom is, which results in increased and often inappropriately large workloads.

Societal Factors

Although numerous factors in society may be identified as contributing to burnout, three are particularly relevant to social work: process and implementation of social welfare policy, changing expectations of work, and sexism.

The development of social welfare policy in the United States is primarily a political process. Although this is one of the strengths of a democratic society, this process of policy development frequently results in vaguely stated policy directions and ambiguous program goals, which contribute to the conflicting, ambiguous, and overextended role demands on social workers. Legislation may be symbolic and ambitious, with objectives exceeding its funding. As a consequence, service providers must negotiate high consumer expectations with inadequate resources. Or legislation may fragment services, which reduces resources and generates role ambiguity and conflict for workers. Ambiguous legislation results in a lack of job specificity, lack of program structure, and excessive paperwork in an attempt to build in accountability (Dresser, 1982).

Cherniss has identified unfulfilled expectations as a major source of burnout among human service providers. Contributing to this has been "the growing belief during the last 40 years that . . . a job had to be a vehicle for self-actualization as well as economic security" (Cherniss, 1980b, p. 150). Seeking self-actualization through work and only through work fosters the development of burnout by creating unrealistic expectations for the work setting.

Discrimination based on gender has been well documented in society and in social work. By influencing salary levels, promotions, organizational influence and power, job assignments, and role expectations in fulfilling assignments, sexism contributes to burnout among women (Edelwich & Brodsky, 1980, p. 18). For women, sexism in the workplace may foster a sense of helplessness and powerlessness, decrease the availability of vital feedback on performance, and interfere with social support from co-workers and supervisors.

PREVENTING AND ALLEVIATING BURNOUT

Much popular as well as scholarly literature has focused on techniques for stress management and stress reduction. Often recommended are relaxation techniques, physical exercise, proper nutrition and rest, and the reduction of coffee, cigarette, drug, and alcohol consumption. These are all important techniques for health promotion and well-being. As methods of preventing or alleviating burnout, however, they address the symptoms, not the causes. Strategies for addressing the causes of burnout must parallel the sources of those stressors at both the individual level, including the client-worker relationship, and the organizational and societal levels.

Individual Strategies

While organizational factors are key contributors to burnout, individual practitioners must assume some responsibility for vulnerability to it. For new practitioners early in their career, the search for overidealized notions of professional performance may lead to a "crisis of competence" (Cherniss, 1980a, pp. 21–37). Building on White's theory that a sense of competence develops when a person affects the environment and meets its challenges, Harrison (1980, p. 42) suggests that "workers are able to develop positive affective responses to their jobs only if there is some certainty that what they do is valuable and makes a difference in the lives of clients." One aspect of being able to achieve the goal of helping competence is "the worker's skill, including techniques judgment, and the ability to

use him or herself effectively" (Harrison, 1983, p. 32). In this area the individual has the greatest control over creating a positive work experience rather than one leading to burnout.

Building and expanding one's knowledge base is an ongoing responsibility. This includes keeping up on the professional literature, receiving additional education through in-service training and continuing education programs, and learning from clients, peers, and supervisors. A lifelong challenge, the openness to continual learning is critical in developing professional competence. A strong knowledge base is vital for understanding the client's current situation and designing appropriate practice interventions in keeping with the client's goals. Particular attention must be given to developing an awareness of and sensitivity to the influence of cultural variables on the client's situation. A deficiency in this area can only foster inappropriate work with the client.

Also crucial to the development of competence is the setting of realistic goals, both for the practitioner in the overall work environment and in direct work with clients. Establishing realistic goals for the work environment will enable the practitioner to measure progress, to have a sense of accomplishment, and to feel mastery over the environment. While noble ideals of fighting injustice or providing happiness and well-being to all may be motivators for work with others, progress toward those goals is difficult to measure without more specific and realistic indicators along the way. Work with clients must stem from mutual definitions of realistic goals accompanied by specific subgoals to mark progress. If work with clients is based on notions of partnership and mutual work, the practitioner is less likely to set inappropriate or unrealistic goals that result in a sense of failure for both the worker and the client. Clarity of both goals and expectations greatly facilitates the joint efforts of the practitioner and the client. Using models based on worker-practitioner partnership also reduces the inappropriate sense of total responsibility for clients' well-being that many beginning practitioners develop.

Focusing on clients' strengths, abilities, and resources reduces the risk of burnout. With an understanding of these assets, the practitioner develops a more complete and realistic perspective of clients as well as of realistic interventions. A focus solely on the problems and the deficiencies in client situations limits the ability to design effective interventions and leads to negative ideas of clients generally.

Self-awareness, commonly expressed in the dictum "know thyself," also reduces the likelihood of burnout. First, self-awareness contributes to an understanding of personal limitations so that responsibility is not accepted inappropriately, achievable goals are set, and work expectations are realistic. Second, self-awareness allows for understanding personal needs and the extent to which they interfere with work with clients. If you are aware that personal needs are being inappropriately met in work with clients, you can develop other resources for fulfilling these needs. Third, self-awareness allows for recognizing and dealing with subjective reactions to clients, which hinder effective work. Because the use of self is critical in work with clients, awareness of personal emotional responses is vital for the well-being of both the client and the practitioner.

To develop competence and to avoid burnout, feedback on performance is necessary. Practitioners must actively seek feedback and evaluation about their work with clients. This includes direct feedback through systematic and continual evaluation with clients of progress towards goals. The progress in clinical research has facilitated the practitioner's ability to gather information about effectiveness. Additionally, feedback may be gathered indirectly by evaluation of the clients' movement and progress in treatment. Colleagues and supervisors are also sources of feedback, and continual, systematic evaluation from them should be cultivated.

Building a social support system at work is critical in reducing the likelihood of burnout. Co-workers and supervisors are not only important sources of feedback on effectiveness. They also fulfill a number of other social support functions, including listening without judgment, technical support, technical challenge, emotional support, emotional challenge, and sharing social reality (Pines, 1983). In part, the development of a support system in the work environment is the practitioner's responsibility, and the energy invested in developing relationships with others at work is repaid many times over through access to their expertise and support.

Research indicates that having a fulfilling and enriching personal life contributes to positive attitudes toward work. As Maslach (1982, p. 104) notes, "When your whole world is your work and little else, then your whole world is more likely to fall apart when problems arise on the job. Your sense of competence, your self-esteem, and your personal identity are all based on what you do in life, and they will be far more shaky and insecure if that base is a narrow one."

Placing boundaries on your work is often the first step in building an enriching and fulfilling personal life (Maslach, 1982). Setting aside personal time is not enough, however; it must be used for meaningful and personally rewarding activities. This includes developing and fostering personal relationships and exploring personal interests during leisure time. Developing a rich and fulfilling life in both personal and professional spheres contributes to self-actualization.

Organizational and Societal Strategies

Although the individual worker has a major influence on vulnerability to burnout, agencies must assume responsibility for creating work environments that decrease vulnerability. A strategy frequently suggested is the development of training programs. Particularly important is training devoted not to stress or time management but to programs designed to increase practitioners' skills and knowledge so they may fulfill the jobs demanded of them. This includes not only the development and refinement of interpersonal skills but also information about the clients served, realistic goals for that population, and practice models appropriate for intervention. Additionally, practitioners need information about evaluating the effectiveness of their interventions. This type of training serves to enhance the practitioner's sense of competence.

Agency policies can help reduce burnout in four significant ways. First, agency policies and procedures should be designed to be responsive to client needs. The needs for data collection, documentation, and other processing procedures as well as mandated procedures for intervention should be carefully examined. To the extent that they interfere with the helping relationship, they contribute to burnout. Second, agency policies and procedures, both formal and informal, must provide clarity of job function and tasks. Without such clarity, role ambiguity and conflict will result for both supervisors and practitioners. Third, the importance of social support from co-workers and supervisors indicates that agency policy that fosters the development of these relationships will contribute to a reduction in burnout. Fourth, agency policies and procedures, both formal and informal, should be nonsexist. All workers, regardless of gender, expect to be treated equally and equitably in the work environment. A nonsexist orientation by the agency will facilitate workers' belief that promotions, pay increases, and work assignments are handled fairly by the administration.

Specific strategies have been proposed to deal with the emotional energy that work with clients demands (Daley, 1979; Pines & Kafry, 1978; Zastrow, 1984). One possibility is to rotate assignments, allowing practitioners some variety and perhaps challenge in their work. This must be used with caution, however, in order not to undermine beginning development of competency. A more useful alternative is to balance each practitioner's case assignment, so situations that may be particularly emotionally exhausting are distributed among the staff. Work assignments should be flexible to allow for individual practitioner needs based on caseload composition. Providing a variety of case assignments reduces the risk of burnout. Another alternative is time-outs, allowing practitioners to assume less stressful work assignments for a period. Reduction in caseload size is an intervention agencies can undertake to reduce burnout. Inappropriately large caseloads have been documented as contributors to burnout—a costly consequence for agencies in terms of absenteeism, worker inefficiency and ineffectiveness, and turnover.

At the societal level involvement in the political process is appropriate for both agency representatives and individual practitioners. Action in this area may be addressed to designing social welfare legislation responsive to the needs of clients with realistic program goals and adequate funding to meet those goals. Since pursuing this goal as an individual is beyond the reach of most people, joining an organized group is more effective. For social workers, the National Association of Social Workers actively lobbies on both the state and federal levels in support of legislation in keeping with the principles and goals of the profession.

CONCLUSION

Social workers are at risk for burnout by virtue of who they are, the work they do, and the environments in which they work. Once burnout has developed, it is extremely difficult to reverse. And the costs of burnout are a burden for the client, the practitioner, and the agency. Prevention is a more successful strategy for reducing the intensity of job stress and eliminating burnout. Although burnout stems from numerous stressors, the individual practitioner is able to reduce the risk of burnout by awareness of these stressors and implementing strategies for reducing their potency.

Appendix

*The Debbie Smith Case**

Debbie Smith was a disgusting hunk of humanity—that was clear. At least it was clear to all of the previous caseworkers, who didn't hesitate to moralize at length about her in the case record.

A 22-year-old woman who had dropped out of school in the tenth grade, Miss Smith had gotten pregnant twice by men old enough to be her father. She was receiving AFDC for her two children, Angelia, 5, and Tommy, 3. She was described as a poor housekeeper, a negligent mother, and a person without any motivation. She had been active with protective services for some time because of concern about neglect of her children.

On the first visit, I went to her apartment and knocked several times without receiving an answer. As I was leaving, a woman came out of the house in front and said in a disgusted voice: "She's in there—you just have to pound and pound." She directed me back to the apartment, a partially converted garage, and knocked loudly and shouted. After a while an obese woman came to the door wrapped in a dirty robe. She looked much older than 22 years old and her skin was crusted over with eczema sores. She acted sleepy but warmly invited me in. The other woman left after having made a snide remark to the client and having told me to tell Miss Smith to clean up her house. The front room served as a living room and a bedroom for Miss S; it was small, dreary, and dirty. The

shades were drawn and the temperature of the room was in the high 80s with a heater still going full blast. It was a beautiful, bright afternoon outside but everything in the room led one to believe otherwise. The first interview consisted of my introducing myself and attempting to establish rapport. No mention was made of the condition of the house nor of the fact that the children could not be adequately supervised by her when she was asleep. Fortunately the second point was not of immediate importance since the woman in the "big house" in front, as it was called, was Miss S's aunt and was "keeping an eye" on them. The client went to get the children, at her own initiative, to introduce them to me, and they were brought back with a display of affection. She talked with pride of their accomplishments. Angelia seemed to be an alert, bright child but somewhat shy. Tommy seemed quite affectionate and outgoing but mentally slow.

My initial impression was not of disgust as it had been with previous workers. It was more one of pity. I felt Miss S was extremely bright and articulate and had a great deal of affection for her children. I was impressed by the fact that she felt it was important that I meet them and with the obvious interest she had in them. She seemed to have so little meaning in her life other than the children.

THE PRELIMINARY ASSESSMENT
Weekly visits were made for five more weeks, during which time information was gathered for assessing the needs and strengths of the family and

---

* This is a case carried and recorded by a student at Indiana University School of Social Work.

rapport was established. I tried to go about understanding Miss Smith's view of her problems and collecting data in such a way as to establish a relationship of trust which could be utilized in bringing about changes once the client saw the need and was ready to take the necessary steps.

My assessment was based on the three members of the S family as the person side of the transaction. Biogenetically there were several problems. Miss S had medical problems, the most noticeable of which were her obesity and eczema. I strongly suspected that she had metabolism problems, which possibly contributed to obesity and which were perhaps responsible for her desire for extremely warm temperatures and for her lethargy. There were indications that the children were not receiving balanced, nutritious meals partly due to the lack of attention they received during the day.

Cognitively, Miss S showed her greatest strength. She was not only quite bright and articulate in discussing ideas but she was easily motivated in this area. Angelia appeared to share her talents, but Tommy appeared to be quite slow for his age.

Psychosocially this was a poorly adjusted family. Miss S had spent a short time as a child with her mother, who had grown up in a middle-class family and was the so-called black sheep of the family. All the other members of the family had gone to college and had been successful, but Miss S's mother had shocked the family by becoming pregnant repeatedly by men whom the family classed as undesirable. An aunt who had been unsuccessful in her attempts to have children of her own had offered to take Miss S and raise her. The mother, already under financial strain, could see the benefits of this arrangement for both her daughter and herself and agreed to this. Miss S was raised by her aunt and uncle in a city quite distant from her mother; they provided material support but gave her little emotional support. The aunt always felt that Miss S was stigmatized by the fact that she was illegitimate. Her personality was cold and punitive and her attitude toward sex was prudish to the point of unhealthiness.

The aunt and I had several contacts which helped me to substantiate what Miss S told me of her. She lectured to me at length about how Debbie was worthless and would end up in the gutter. These were lectures to which Miss S was subjected daily. Miss S disliked her aunt but felt that she was dependent upon her and that she had a moral obligation to be thankful for everything her aunt did. Miss S blamed her mother for having rejected her and for having given her to an aunt who was so devoid of human emotion.

Miss S wanted to provide more warmth and love for her children than she had experienced but the inadequate model of successful family functioning made it difficult for her to see what she would have to do to meet the children's needs. In addition, her own problems interfered with her ability to adequately nurture the children. She gave them sincere, showy affection at times but was inconsistent in her behavior with them. Because of the long hours of sleeping each day she mainly avoided them, but at other times she would express her frustration by shouting at them; then she would feel guilty and hug and kiss them. She did not show preference toward either of them. This was in spite of Angelia's obvious superior intelligence. She recognized that they had different areas of strength and encouraged them in these areas.

The environment in which Miss S lived was overwhelmingly a hostile one. Her aunt was constantly nagging her about what she should do (get out of bed and clean the house), what she was (a no-good tramp), and what she should not do (get into trouble again). This advice had been reinforced by a long series of social workers. She had no positive social experience and indeed had become a total recluse. She spent large portions of her time in bed, seemingly as an escape. Her children had few experiences. The great-aunt occasionally took them someplace.

The situation is a good example of a mismatch of coping patterns and impinging environment which results in feedback that creates further mismatching. It is a vicious circle which involves an increasingly large number of people (basically offspring) and which contributes to an ever greater dysfunctioning. The strengths consisted of Miss S's hopes and aspirations for her children and her desire to do more for them. The fact that she was bright and articulate and enjoyed discussing her situation was also seen as a great positive.

I hoped by use of a strategy of intervention to break the circle of mismatchings, but I had to decide the most effective point of intervention. Alleviation of medical problems seemed a logical starting point. My efforts in finding medical resources and providing access to them would be a concrete example of nurturing and supporting. If medical problems could be overcome, then it was hoped the family members would be able to function at maximum physical strength and would be able to cope more effectively with their other problems. It would also provide an opportunity to assess how much motivation Miss S would be able to muster and whether she would be willing to follow through on a plan mutually conceived.

I decided I would explore with Miss S the necessity of seeking treatment and suggest the possible treatment resources. With her permission I would make a referral to the visiting public health nurse, who could help her with explaining health problems and be able to give her advice on how to minimize them. She would also be able to help Miss S plan balanced diets. Although I was fairly sure that Tommy was not mentally retarded, there was a special fund available for a work-up to rule out mental retardation. I felt that this should be explored so that planning could be made before he began school.

The community had two nursery schools. I felt that one of these could be utilized to give the children a wider range of experiences. I hope to interest Miss S in the cooperative school because this would involve her in an activity and would help her to develop techniques of child care.

THE WORKING ASSESSMENT

At the next interview I had hoped to explore all of the above suggestions with Miss S. But when I arrived, I was so appalled by the condition of the house that it changed my plans. The living room-bedroom had debris piled four or five inches thick over the entire floor. In order to sit down, I had to remove a pile of records and clothing from a chair and then clear off a section of the floor on which to set the chair. Miss S was lying in between sheets that

were so incredibly filthy that it was hard to believe they had ever been gray, much less white; they must not have been washed in weeks. I felt that the condition of the apartment represented a health and safety hazard to the children and Miss S and that a confrontation was necessary. I did not want to lecture her on her failures or to put things in terms of right and wrong. I decided instead to focus on the children's welfare, a matter with which she was concerned. I was direct and firm in my approach and pointed out that it was unfair to subject the children to these kinds of conditions and that rats and cockroaches were inevitable if things did not improve. She listened attentively and then admitted that she had not considered the effect it might have on the children nor the health and safety hazards which were presented. It seemed to make an impression on her that I discussed it in a rational, unemotional way and did not couch the discussion in terms of how evil she was to live this way. I tried to show her that I respected her in spite of the fact that I did not like her behavior in this instance. Her reaction was to promise to clean up the house if I would return in a week to see it. Far more important, however, was the fact that the incident presented an opportunity for her to unleash her feelings about herself.

She was surprised that I did not understand why she did not keep her house clean and informed me that her apartment was like herself—dirty. Having her aunt nag at her constantly and making the connection between her evil behavior and her dirty house only served to reinforce this. When I explored with her why she felt she was dirty, she was rather surprised that it was not immediately obvious to me that I had to ask. This appeared to be her first feedback that others might not agree with her self-perception. (Generally, they probably did.) She explained that having had three illegitimate pregnancies, having dropped out of school and having to depend on welfare support certainly were indications of the fact that she was dirty. In fact, everything she did she felt was an indication that she was a worthless, dirty person.

This was the first time that I had known of a third child. It was her first child, whom her aunt had arranged to be given to a friend. Debbie had no choice in the matter, just as she had no choice when her aunt declared that she was to keep the second child as punishment for having gotten into trouble again. This left her with unresolved feelings about her first child. She had a desire to see the child and is fearful that the child will feel rejected by her when she grows up. Unavoidably she has feelings that Angelia is a source of punishment, even though she loves her very much.

The incident and the new knowledge I now had of Miss S changed my assessment and my strategy of intervention. I decided that I could expect little movement from her until her self-image was improved and that this would have to take priority over the other goals. I knew she would have to feel that a change in self-esteem was necessary and possible and that this would have to be incorporated into her value system. Since the topic had arisen and she seemed receptive to discussing her feelings, I felt that we should begin immediately. We discussed on a very intellectual plane how one develops a self-image and the philosophical idea of the basic worth of man.

She was then able to apply the abstract ideas to her own life experiences and to examine how she came to have a negative self-image. She recalled how miserable she had been as a teenager. Her aunt continually lectured to her on the evils of sex. These ideas were in contradiction to those of her peers. Sex was an area in which she could most threaten her aunt, and in retrospect she sees her actions as a way of punishing her aunt. In addition, she felt that she was searching for the kind of relationship which she had never received from her mother or aunt and uncle—one that provided warmth and love. She did not find this type of relationship, however. All three children were the result of casual affairs with older men whom she saw as socially undesirable. She felt unworthy of any other man, however. The parallel between her actions and those of her mother hardly seem accidental. In a sense it was a self-fulfilling prophecy—many times her aunt had accused her of being like her mother, and it was small wonder that she chose this way in which to rebel.

As a result of the second pregnancy she was moved into her present apartment, which was fashioned out of one half of a garage. The other half housed the latest-model Cadillac. Miss S was able to verbalize the feeling that she shared the affection as well as living quarters with the car and that moving from the "big house" was both punishment and rejection. She offered to show the worker the apartment and for the first time it became apparent that Angelia did not live with her. This was discussed and Miss S said that Angelia had a room in the "big house" (and by implication, room in the aunt's heart) but ate with Tommy and her. The relationship between Angelia and the aunt was explored, and it was obvious that a complex situation existed. The aunt had special affection for Angelia and had strongly hinted that Angelia should stay with her if Miss S were ever to break the ties and move from her present situation. Miss S had been partly convinced that this would be the best situation for her daughter, since she had so little to offer Angelia.

At this point I felt that we had made a beginning toward definition and prioritizing of problems and a more adequate assessment of Miss S's situation. She had expressed awareness of problems and the desire for change. With the relationship which had already been established, it appeared that a plan of action could be mutually worked out and first steps at redirection taken.

Our plan was to begin by helping Miss S to become independent from her aunt. Separation from the hostile environment was valuable in itself but in addition it would prove to Miss S that she was capable of managing on her own and was able to be self-sufficient. It would also mean leaving the dreary surroundings, hopefully for more pleasant ones. Separation presented a financial problem, however, because the public welfare grant only provided $46 per month housing allowance and this was inadequate to pay the rent anywhere else. Closely connected to this problem of separation was the problem of helping her to see that she was creating the same situation with her daughter as she had undergone and helping her to realize that she had a real contribution to make to her daughter. Separation would bring the problem into the open and the situation would have to be dealt with.

The original goals of getting medical treatment for her and the children could be incorporated into the self-image building attempts. Improving her body image could serve to help boost her self-esteem.

On the next few visits rapid movement was evident. We began to explore alternative ways to the goals we had set. Miss S had made great strides toward cleaning her house and I praised her. But I looked forward to a day when she would do it for herself, not for me. We discussed her situation and I shared with her what I saw as her strengths. She was flattered by my feeling that she was bright and enthusiastically agreed to be tested by Oakland City College. Our interview served to strengthen her self-esteem.

Our plans took shape, and Miss S began to make actual change efforts in the next three months. During this time I was able to share some of the results of her testing at the City College. She had a high I.Q. and her aptitude scores for college subjects was so good that the school was willing to accept her as a freshman without her having a high school diploma. She went for counseling and decided to take a review course and get her General Educational Development diploma before going to college. She felt that it would give her more security to have it. She was showing a great deal of maturity in her decisions. She got psychology and philosophy books from the library to enlighten herself (and to impress me) on the things we had been discussing. She was able to understand Freud's concepts of id, ego, and superego with little difficulty. Health problems had been explored. It was discovered that her teeth needed extracting and after having this done her general state of health improved. The gum disease had resulted in a general weakening of her health.

Tommy was found to have an average I.Q. but was found to be behind his age group developmentally due to a very severe hearing loss. He was referred to the Crippled Children's Society, which sponsored corrective surgery.

The public health nurse came weekly to help with planning a balanced diet for the children and a weight reduction one for Miss S. I coordinated my efforts with the nurse and she reinforced my efforts to build her self-esteem.

It was a process of continual upward climb, but there were periods of regression. I had to get her out of bed on many occasions. More often, however, the house was cleaner, the shades were up and the heat was reasonable. I could see improvement in her skin, and she seemed happier.

The children were taken with her to the library and finally were enrolled in the nursery school. The children would run up to tell me what they had been doing, and when I got in the apartment I got the same kind of excited reaction from Miss S.

Each success Miss S achieved helped to convince her that she could build a satisfying life. Each successful accomplishment helped to lay the groundwork for further gains. Once the fear of failure was overcome, she could look hopefully toward experiencing success.

THE CONTINUING REASSESSMENT

A point came at which I felt that a greater level of functioning could be aspired to and hopefully obtained. I felt we were ready to begin the generalization and stabilization of change. Two major considerations marked this period. One was a fortunate decision on the part of Miss S's aunt to tear down the garage and build several apartment units instead. This meant that Miss S would be forced by circumstances to make the desired separation. The second was the necessity to counteract Miss S's attempts at structuring our relationship into a friendship rather than a professional relationship. It was felt that the present relationship had been useful in helping to modify Miss S's behavior. The relationship had been used purposefully to motivate Miss S to follow through on proposed projects. Although the relationship would remain a warm one, it had been necessary to resist attempts to let discussions become book review sessions or to become social calls. In a sense, she was resisting attempts to go further and to utilize the knowledge she had gained to help herself. It was a tactic to resist change. It was necessary to clarify the nature of the relationship and to set a new goal—that of widening social contacts so that others in the community could provide the friendship relationship she so much desired.

Successful separation from her aunt and successful establishment of social contacts became goals during this period. She used agency policy to give her support in moving Angelia with her. She explained to her aunt that the public welfare agency could not give her money for a child which was not living with her. She had become convinced by this time that she had more to offer Angelia but was still finding it difficult to directly confront her aunt.

The new apartment was larger and more cheerful and the neighbors were friendly. She thrived in the new environment and this helped her to follow through on some of the worker's suggestions for broadening her social contacts. She began going to church fellowship meetings and did volunteer work for a civil rights group during the hours the children were in the nursery school. She was so efficient that she soon became an officer in the group. She made a good child-care arrangement with a neighbor for the evenings she had to go to the GED review course. At Christmas she got a job as a gift wrapper at a large department store.

She developed enough friends that she was happy to use our relationship in a professional way. She discussed her feelings toward people visiting in the home. She became anxious and did not want people in her apartment for too long a period of time. She had the feeling of being invaded, as if they were encroaching on her private world. She had used her apartment as a protective womb for such a long time that she was threatened by friends coming there. We worked through many such fears, or at least relieved her anxiety about holding such beliefs.

Her apartment was consistently clean, partly because she knew guests might drop around at any time. Her eczema was rapidly disappearing and she bragged of having lost 50 pounds. Her change of attitude was reflected in the behavior of the children and in her care of them. She was more consistent in her discipline and they were more responsive.

She took the children on a bus trip to visit her mother. It was a very good experience. Her mother was glad to see her and the children and Miss S was able to satisfy herself that she was loved by her mother. She felt she had made peace with her mother after all these years.

Soon afterward she began dating a man who was a college graduate, an accountant. After several months she became engaged to him and was extremely happy. Problems began arising, however. His parents were unhappy that he had chosen someone who had illegitimate children and who was a high school dropout. Their pressure was sufficient to break up the relationship. As soon as I learned of the broken engagement, I made a home visit. I was sure that this would result in a great regression and I wanted to head it off. I could visualize a dirty apartment, drawn shades, and extreme temperature. When I arrived the apartment was spotless and she was smiling. I told her of what I had expected and she laughed. "The relationship was a good one for me. I know now that someone who is handsome, intelligent and well-educated can love me. But I wouldn't touch Robert with a ten-foot pole; he's a momma's boy. Any man who can't make decisions for himself isn't worth having. I'm going to college next year and will have the opportunity to meet all kinds of men. I'm not going to settle for a weak man; I want one that will think of me first." It appeared we were ready to terminate our relationship. Debbie Smith no longer needed me. She had the inner strength to make her own decisions and to motivate herself.

SUMMARY

Debbie Smith's case is a rare success. She represented a mismatching of coping patterns and impinging environment. Although Debbie was very intelligent, she was unable to use this intelligence to solve any of her problems because she was so immobilized by her lack of confidence in herself. Her childhood was devoid of warmth and love, which prevented her from functioning affectively as a mother and which led her to seek love in casual sexual relationships that only added to her troubles. She had the idea that she was dirty, and her aunt only added to this image. Everything in the environment reinforced her feelings of dirtiness and she began structuring her environment to reflect this dirtiness. She retreated into a warm, dark bed, which did not solve her problems and only created more for her children, who were not cared for properly during those long hours in which she slept.

The worker hoped to intervene to help to break the cycle of the environment reinforcing her negative feelings about herself and help her to use her environment in a constructive way. Changes were attempted with the client system and with the environment.

The casework relationship was a warm and meaningful one. It provided the client with an opportunity to express her feelings in a nonhostile relationship and demonstrated to the client that she could establish a meaningful relationship with someone. It was not only a source of satisfaction to the client but the relationship could be used effectively to gain movement in other areas. She was encouraged to remove herself from the stressful environment, namely living in close proximity to her aunt.

Several elements were added to her environment. She was challenged intellectually, which motivated her to use the library facilities. The public health nurse began visiting her on a regular basis and served as another interested person. Health care was provided for both the client and her children, and she became associated with groups through which she could find satisfaction (church, neighbors, and civil rights groups).

Stresses in the environment were modified by developing her sense of self-esteem and by having two professionals whose attitudes of respect towards her helped to increase her ability to deal with the stressful environment.

Many interviews were directed at helping her to understand her instinctual needs and how to channel them in appropriate ways. Since illicit sexual relationships contributed toward her feelings of dirtiness, it was necessary to discuss sex with her to help her overcome her misconceptions and to develop a normal, healthy attitude toward such relationships.

A great deal of time was devoted toward improving ego functioning, both in terms of helping the ego to manage impulses and feelings and in terms of developing skills of coping with environment. It was felt in fact, that ego development was necessary before any other changes could take place. Miss S was avoiding self-appraisal by escaping into her bed. It was too painful for her to face the self-image she had developed, and so she avoided it. She was helped to trace the connections between her past experiences and the effect that these had on her current behavior. Fortunately, she was able to use the information gained by an intellectual study of the processes to understand her current behavior and was able therefore to modify the behavior.

Many resources and opportunities were provided to help her develop skills, which resulted in an increased sense of competency and ultimately in the ability to take on more difficult tasks with confidence. The goals were structured so that she was not overwhelmed with a large number of expectations. They were developed in such a way that they became increasingly more difficult as her expertise in handling them was developed.

In the beginning demands placed on the ego were restricted, but later it was felt that she was able to cope with the demands. She was helped to see that she was getting into the situation of giving her daughter to her aunt and that she had far more to give her daughter (emotional security) than the aunt (who only had material goods to give). She was helped to choose between these demands. She was moved into a more supportive environment by moving away from her aunt. In general the demands were not reduced; instead one demand at a time was considered and dealt with. Although the demand was overlooked for the time being, it was not totally discarded. The worker attempted to work with the aunt to help her have greater understanding of Miss S's needs and to help utilize her in the treatment process, but this was unsuccessful.

Work with Mrs. Manley*

Mrs. Manley was referred to our outpatient clinic by Dr. S for evaluation as a candidate for admission to a stress management program conducted by Dr. A at General Hospital. Her appointment had been made by her husband. Mrs. Manley and I were both aware that this 1½-hour interview was likely to be our only face-to-face contact. (As this was my first interview at the clinic, I was mildly nervous; I soothed myself by viewing the situation as likely to require only a confirmation of already formulated therapeutic plans.) Mrs. Manley presented herself as a poised, well-dressed, attractive 48-year-old white woman who settled easily into the chair next to my desk. I introduced myself and my position at the agency and continued, "I know you've filled out a data base sheet and I've had a chance to look it over, but I think it'll be most helpful if we start from scratch even if we cover some of the same material." (I was focused on my own concerns here: worry that I would not obtain all of the required information.) "Can you give me some idea of what brought you here today?"

Mrs. Manley [very smoothly]: I've been under a lot of stress lately—I've never handled stress very well—and Dr. A and I thought it might be a good idea for me to try the stress management program at General Hospital. If health insurance is to cover the costs, they need a second outside recommendation, so that's why I'm here.

The client has presented me with both a problem, the stress, and a solution, the program, in the same breath, and I'm beginning to feel both superfluous and a bit relieved. I make two erroneous assumptions that persist throughout the interview: (1) that Dr. A is thoroughly familiar with Mrs. Manley and her family and with the program recommended; and (2) that Mrs. Manley and her physician have explored the possibility

of other alternatives together and have selected this program as the most suitable for her needs.

Worker: I'm not familiar with that program. Do you know what it involves?
Mrs. Manley: Well, I think it's a group program that teaches relaxation and breathing techniques and that sort of thing.
Worker [nodding]: Can you give me some idea of why such a program might be helpful? What kind of stress you've been under?

Mrs. Manley explained that she had accepted a position teaching German in a private junior high school after a 25-year absence from the field. The offer was unexpected; she had little time to prepare and is using a teaching method unfamiliar to her. She has been surprised by the difficulties she has had in coping with the new job. The position is temporary until June; she is not sure she wants to continue after that—coping with seventh and eighth graders all day is really tough—but it's very important to her to uphold the commitment she made to finish out the year. (I am struck by the similarities between Mrs. Manley's position and my own in returning to school after 20 years. I don't mention this because I don't think the "me, too" revelation would have any significance for her at this point and I am reluctant to reveal my own inexperience.)

Worker: Stress is kind of a vague word. I'd like to get a better idea of what it means to you, what kind of problems you're having.

Mrs. Manley explained that she has always had a lot of premenstrual tension, mainly insomnia, but considered the sleeping problem manageable with medication. She has had a prescription for Valium for premenstrual tension and was accustomed to taking one a night for two or three nights at a time as needed. She dislikes using medication and "wants to find a better way." Lack of sleep gives her

---

* Case disguised and prepared by Beulah R. Compton from a process recording of a student placed in a comprehensive mental health center.

"headachy" symptoms. She describes herself as premenopausal, her periods as irregular. Now she feels stress nearly every day: she cries a lot, sometimes loses her appetite and feels nauseous, sometimes feels "paralyzed, falling apart and shaky inside." For the first time Mrs. Manley seemed ill at ease; she occasionally punctuated her descriptions with a nervous laugh as if to belittle the severity of her symptoms.

Worker: Have you missed any workdays because of your stress?

Mrs. Manley: No, not at all. Mostly I just can't leave the job behind when I get home. I worry about doing a good job—all out of proportion, Jim says. Those parents are paying a lot of money for their kids' education [laughs].

Worker: And that makes you feel very responsible?

Mrs. Manley: Of course [laughs again].

Worker: Is there any way of making your job easier, less of a strain?

Mrs. Manley: Well, I did have my schedule changed. First I had six classes at four different levels. That was impossible. So I had it changed to four classes at three levels.

Worker: Did it bother you to ask for that change?

Mrs. Manley: No, not at all. The people at school have been very helpful and supportive.

Worker: What about at home?

Mrs. Manley: Well, we just have one boy at home now, Paul—he's 16—so there isn't that much to do. And my family is pretty understanding about late meals and dust. I don't know. I go to bed a lot right after dinner. Jim says I'm my own worst enemy—I worry that I'm going to either cheat my family or the kids at school.

Worker: Have there been any changes at home since you started to work, any jobs taken over by Jim or Paul?

Mrs. Manley: No, it's really my problem. Jim left the decision to go to work totally up to me. Sometimes he plays devil's advocate, but it's my decision really—something I wanted to do for myself. He's really concerned about my being so upset. It isn't good to fall apart. He worries about me and he wants me to learn to handle it. It's my stress, not his.

I think Mrs. Manley is assuming too much responsibility for the situation, but I don't voice my opinion.

Worker: I believe you when you say Jim is concerned, but has this problem caused any difficulties in your relationship with him?

Mrs. Manley: Well, of course our sex life isn't too great when I go to bed at eight o'clock [laughs]. I really have no interest in sex now. And the crying is really upsetting to Jim—he was sympathetic at first, but now he doesn't know how to handle it. He thinks I'm making such a big deal out of everything. He tries to reason with me, but it doesn't do much good.

Worker: How does that make you feel?

Mrs. Manley: What?

Worker: Is it annoying to be "reasoned with" when you're upset?

Mrs. Manley: Oh, I don't know. When the stress is there I don't listen to anybody about anything anyway.

(I'm interested in Mrs. Manley's relationship with her husband, but I don't know quite how to pursue it, so I change the topic.)

Worker: Is there anything else in your life besides the job that's worrying you now?

Mrs. Manley: Well, my father-in-law. He's in poor health and will probably die soon or have to go into a nursing home. And he'll fight it. Some decision will have to be made. Jim copes with uncertainty better than I do. He's so busy he doesn't think about it, I guess. I think we should be looking into nursing homes or something.

Worker: Do you feel this is more your responsibility than you would like it to be?

Mrs. Manley: Yes, I think so. I have a better feel for my own parents. I would know better what to do for them. I could accept their death, I think, maybe better than the other alternatives.

(I'm interested in what Mrs. Manley is saying, but I'm very much aware again of having to cover other material.)

Worker: I'd like to talk a little bit more about your own family.

Mrs. Manley described her family of origin history, her own and family medical history. She received a degree in language from State College, where she taught until her marriage. She and her husband studied in Germany as Fulbright scholars.

Since that time her husband has done graduate work and held university teaching positions, including the position at Central College. Their first son is 22, the second 20, and the third 19. She described her early married life as sheltered. "Jim was doing the adjusting; I wasn't." She recalled her husband as not only earning a living but as sharing parenting responsibilities, being there when the kids needed him.

Worker: You've mentioned several times that you don't handle stress well. Can you think of a time like that?

Mrs. Manley: Well, there was one time with our son, Ted—the middle one. When he was 17 he was hospitalized for what they called a "thinking disorder"—it was drug-related. We just lived through it on a day-to-day basis. But Jim and I handled that together; it brought us closer together. We saw a counselor at Ted's school for a while afterwards.

Worker: Was that helpful?

Mrs. Manley: Well, Ted wouldn't always go, but Jim and I went anyway.

Worker: Do you see any similarities to your problem now?

Mrs. Manley: Well, it was a traumatic time, but there was a valid reason for the stress and it was over pretty quickly.

Worker: Is your present stress "valid"?

Mrs. Manley: Well, *I* think so.

Worker: I think so, too. I think returning to work after 25 years would be very, very difficult. But you *are* here doing something about it.

(Again I think about sharing with her some of my feelings about being in a similar situation, but I don't.) I have some questions now that are a little bit different from the ones I've asked before.

I proceeded with a mental status exam. Mrs. Manley was oriented to person, place, and time. Her remote memory, recent memory, and recall were good. Her immediate memory—ability to repeat a series of digits forward and backward was poor, as was her ability to do simple calculations "in the head." She said she felt nervous about this part of the interview and expressed relief when it was over.

(I was feeling anxious now about winding up the interview. I could see no harm in the stress management program for Mrs. Manley, but I had other ideas for treatment that I thought might be more effective. I was just not sure of myself, so I asked.)

Worker: Do you have any objections to my talking to Dr. A and Dr. S? I would like to do that—to find out more about the program and how it might be useful for you. I also will be discussing our interview with Dr. K [the director of our clinic].

Mrs. Manley had no objections, and we agreed that I would call her the following week to let her know our recommendation. I was surprised to learn from Dr. A that there was no group stress management program at General Hospital at that time. I called Dr. S and learned that he had only a very sketchy knowledge of the patient, her family, and the problem situation, that the program had been her suggestion (or perhaps her husband's?), and that he had not discussed other alternatives with her. I told Dr. S we were recommending time-limited marital or family therapy as helpful in coping with some of the issues underlying Mrs. Manley's situational stress. Dr. S had no objections to this change in service, especially as such services were available to Mrs. Manley at the clinic. After discussing our recommendations with me and with Dr. S, Mrs. Manley elected to begin a combination of individual and couple therapy. She was desirous that I make the necessary referral to the clinic and gave me permission to share our interview with the practitioner at the clinic. I called Mrs. J, intake worker, and was able to arrange an appointment for Wednesday at a time convenient for Mrs. Manley.

A. STUDY DATA

1. Problem and Goal Identification

Mrs. Manley perceived the problem as the stress she was experiencing upon returning to work after a 25-year absence—the crying spells, insomnia, the nauseous and shaky feelings, the constant worry that she was not performing her job adequately. She strongly identified precipitating factors contributing to the problem as lying totally within herself and she was reinforced by her husband in defining as a suitable goal—beneficial, not only in the present situation but in the future as well—a change in self: better self-control of her stressful symptoms. Mrs. Manley sought from the service system instruction in stress management as a means to reach her goal. She sought from our agency a recommendation which would permit her group health plan to cover the cost of this instruction.

As recommending worker, I agreed with Mrs. Manley's identification of her stress as the presenting problem. I believed, however, that there were precipitating factors outside of the client that she was not taking sufficiently into account—most particularly, interactions between herself and others within the family system. I saw the client's goal of symptom control as an acceptable short-term goal, but I also saw, as a possibly more challenging long-term goal, elimination rather than simple management of much of her stress through changes in perception of self and changes in her interactions with others in the family system. Specifically, our problem for work was to agree upon goals and an appropriate service modality.

2. The Client

a. Motivation. Someone's discomfort with the present situation was high; whether it was Mrs. Manley's or her husband's or both was unclear. He had made the appointment for her; she related, "Jim wants me to learn to handle stress better." At the same time, though she made an effort to keep our interview on almost a social level, at times embarrassed to describe her depressive symptoms, her descriptions of an emotional state seriously interfering with her daily functioning were plain. She was determined to finish out her school year commitment, had mobilized herself very quickly— within a month of beginning to experience difficulties—to seek professional help, and had already devised one means of dealing with the problem—the stress management program.

b. Opportunity. Although Mrs. Manley repeatedly labeled herself "poor at handling stress," when asked to give specific examples, she identified only a two- or three-year history of premenstrual tension, which had been adequately controlled by minimal use of medication and an episode involving her son which, along with her husband, she had handled quite well. In the present situation she had promptly sought assistance from an outside institution—the health care system—was readily able to identify need for change and use support resources in one interpersonal system—the school environment—but either was reluctant to use or was unable to find these same kinds of support resources in the marital or nuclear family system.

c. Capacity. Mrs. Manley presented herself as a warm, physically attractive woman who related to the interviewer in a friendly, egalitarian manner. Her energy level was high, and as a former college teacher and Fulbright scholar, she was obviously intelligent. She had fulfilled the demanding social roles of wife to a college professor and mother to three boys for many years. Yet the long absence from the teaching field was a tremendous liability to overcome in a matter of weeks—her memory and concentration were not as efficient as she would like, and she was finding the work emotionally and physically exhausting. Mrs. Manley was aware of her own tendency to set exceedingly high standards for herself but seemed unable to let up—to her already existing tasks of teaching and homemaking she had now added a third—stress managing.

B. PSYCHOSOCIAL ASSESSMENT

Social role theory provides one way of conceptualizing Mrs. Manley's problem. Social roles are learned and can reflect personal needs and drives as well as sociocultural and family system expectations. Though Mrs. Manley and her husband had entered their marriage as professional equals, within a very few years she had exchanged her career for the traditional feminine occupation of domestic work and child care, and her husband had assumed both the responsibility and the power of being the family's sole economic support. Mrs. Manley's return to work was a significant role change that neither she nor her family seemed quite willing to acknowledge. It is almost impossible to change the role of one family member without changing the role of another, yet the Manley family seemed determined to do just that. Now employed full-time, Mrs. Manley was experiencing a great deal of interpositional role conflict, as there had been no reduction of her work load at home. Part of the responsibility may lie with her own anxiety about departing from the familiar patterns of wife and mother or guilt about not fulfilling traditional duties or reluctance to give up some of the power associated with being central in the family. Part of the responsibility may lie with other family members still expecting total availability for their needs. We can only speculate, too, about the significance of her husband's refusal to comment about her new work role. Surely he must have some opinion about an extra $10,000+ yearly income or about his wife being out of the home 40 hours a week or about her reentry into their shared professional field. Why the reluctance to reveal his thoughts, to make the decision a shared one?

The idea of resistance to change can be found as well in general systems theory. The Manley family can be viewed as a living unit which though inherently subject to change and conflict, also has developed unique and stable ways of functioning which are resistant to change. Individual behavioral deviations—Mrs. Manley's reactions to stress—which seem at first to be wholly dysfunctional may serve to protect the stability of the system itself. What, for example, would happen to Mr. Manley in his long-standing position as the rational, strong protector if his wife should learn to "handle her stress" as he has directed her to do?

Mrs. Manley's return to work was not prompted by economic concerns. Both she and her husband may have been influenced by a social variable, current "feminist" thinking about the oppressiveness of traditional feminine roles and the desirability of women seeking satisfactions outside the home. Mrs. Manley's depressive symptoms may be attributed less to guilt at indulging in self-fulfillment as to shock at realization that her dual work status is not the fun-filled challenge she envisioned it to be. Mr. Manley in turn may be hesitant to voice objections to her working for fear of denying her right to an enhancing experience.

C. POLICY IMPLICATIONS
1. Working Wives
The Manley family is not unique. The employment of the majority of American women has not yet released them from primary responsibility in the home. Wives who work still expect and are expected to be totally responsive to the family's needs. The job itself frequently does not contain the same benefits that it might for a man—respect, high earnings, opportunities to develop personal capabilities. Until this is a reality and until domestic work is shared equally or based on personal preferences and individual talents rather than upon sex-prescribed roles, blanket encouragement of wives to work irrespective of economic needs may be more punitive than rewarding.

2. Family Developmental Stages
A developmental orientation can be useful in working with families like the Manley family. Families, like individuals, can be viewed as going through stages and facing different developmental tasks over their life spans. A change in work role for a family member is a predictable crisis point for both the individual and the family system. A particularly stressful stage in the life of a marriage is that beginning with the exit of the first child and ending with the exit of the last—a time of marital reassessment of expectations and responsibilities in preparation for the "empty nest." Families can be helped to anticipate such stress points and to maintain adequate functioning.

D. CONTRACT GOALS AND INTERVENTIONS
It was certainly not "by accident" that Mrs. Manley chose to talk about the family's experience in dealing with her son's hospitalization. I think that regardless of her insistence that the present problem was hers alone, she was feeling quite isolated in her struggles and welcomed the interpretation that this was a suitable problem for the entire family unit to work on. If I had continued working with her, I would have suggested working with the entire family directed toward the achievement of two goals: (1) examination of the meaning to her and the family of her commitment to teach until the end of the school year; and (2) a decision, based on

assessment of that experience, of whether or not she should continue working. Some specific directions with the family could include setting less demanding expectations of Mrs. Manley's participation in home tasks, trying out new schedules of household chores which would examine the possibility of assigning some responsibility to father and son, frank exploration of the meaning of Mrs. Manley's return to work for each family member and for the family system as a whole, and attention to related issues involving marital power and responsibility—for example, concerns about the Manleys' aging parents' health and ability to live alone.

E. BARRIERS TO UNDERSTANDING AND APPROPRIATE ACTION

Mrs. Manley was so similar to me in age, education, social class, family composition, and life experience and her problem situation so closely allied to my own in returning to school after a long absence that while I could readily understand her problem cognitively and emotionally, I also greatly feared inaccurate projection of thinking and feeling about myself. This prevented me from relating to her as directly and freely as I could have. In addition, during our interview I was consistently under the impression that someone "wiser than I" had already made a therapeutic plan, and I allowed this to inhibit my discussing what I judged to be a better alternative. In effect the client and I were given another opportunity: there was no stress management program available; consultation with Dr. K gave me the confidence to present the alternatives of marital or family therapy with assurance; and almost in spite of the vagaries of the health care system, the client ended up with what I believe was a more suitable therapeutic choice.

Reading A-3   *Pain Clinic Evaluation**

Mr. H was seen in the pain clinic of General Hospital on 10/02/87 with a history of stomach, groin, hand, and leg pain resulting from 12 amputations (including both legs, several fingers, and a penectomy) due to complications of his juvenile-onset diabetes. Mr. H came to the hospital seeking evaluation of his pain and some recommendations concerning pain management. He also has difficulty with vision, hearing, and pain in his eyes. Mr. H's pain is accompanied by sleep disturbance, depression, and anxiety. Mr. H is a 51-year-old white divorced male with one son.

Mr. H was accompanied to the evaluation by his 17-year-old son, with whom he lives, and his mother. The family appeared concerned throughout the interview about his pain problem, welcoming suggestions from myself, and later from the rest of the team—the physicians, psychologists, and clinical social worker—in their subsequent interviews.

Worker: Mr. H, could you explain the exact nature of the pain you experience? For example, where it occurs, what happens to provoke it, what it feels like?

Mr. H: Yes, well I'm diabetic, you know, and because of the complications arising from my condition, I've had 12 amputations. They were to remove the gangrene. However, I still have gangrene throughout various parts of my body, and the pain is excruciating. The worst thing is that my body is progressively deteriorating, and the pain is getting progressively worse, increasingly unbearable.

Worker: Where exactly do you feel the pain, Mr. H?

Mr. H: All over, really, but especially at the points where I've been amputated. It feels like there's so much pressure there. I have horrible pain in both my hands. (His hands were swollen, red, and quite grotesque looking, from his numerous amputations.) I also have pain across my stomach, or midline, but the distressing pain is in my groin. It feels like someone is kicking me there for up to 12–14 hours a day. My penis was partly amputated twice. I had a stroke, too, just recently and it has caused me to have quite a bit of pain on the left side of my body. My eyes have started to hurt quite a

---
* Case material prepared for this book.

bit. Also, I have unbearable stomach cramps. Lately, I've awakened screaming in pain. The pain seems to be more violent when awakening, for about 30 minutes.

Worker: Mr. H, I noticed on your questionnaire that you only get 2 or 3 hours of sleep a night.

Mr. H: Yes, that's a big problem. I have a terrible time getting to sleep at night. Last night, for instance, I only got 2 hours of sleep.

Worker: How did you know that it was only 2 hours?

Mr. H: I kept watching the clock. The last time I saw it it was 5:00 a.m., and my alarm went off at 7:00 a.m.

Worker: How do you know other nights, the amount of sleep you get?

Mr. H: Well, I have the TV on at night and sometimes I'll drop off to sleep and wake up, and the same person will be in dialogue as when I drifted off. That's how I know that I haven't slept much. It'll seem like I've been asleep for hours, but really it'll only be a few minutes.

Worker: Do you ever lie down and turn off the lights to try to sleep?

Mr. H: No, that does no good at all for me. I'm just too anxious, and concentrating on the pain.

Worker: The reason I'm asking these questions, Mr. H, is that sometimes a preoccupation with time and the amount of sleep one gets at night can inhibit sleep. Clock-watching, etc., can become an obsession, and trying so hard to sleep can almost make sleep impossible. We have found, however, from other patients who have trouble sleeping at night, that it is better to read or watch TV in order to fall asleep, because they are distracted. Lying in bed is sometimes the worst thing a person can do. It sounds like you are not doing that, however, which is probably a good thing.

Mr. H: No, no. I've learned the same thing. I can't lie down and think about how I have to sleep. It just doesn't work.

Worker: But you are very preoccupied with the amount you sleep and watching the clock, is that correct? At least, that's what I've picked up from what you've said about keeping track of times and all.

Mr. H: You could be right there. I just can't relax.

Worker: Is part of the problem knowing how you'll feel when you wake up? You said that that was when it was most painful.

Mr. H: Exactly. I'm worried about falling asleep because of the anticipation of the pain I'll experience in the morning. It's absolutely horrible.

Worker: However, you do fall asleep every night regardless, and wake up in the morning with pain. You'd probably feel much better if you had eight hours rather than two or three, yet you'd feel no more pain with eight hours, would you?

Mr. H: You're right. It's just a matter of being able to relax. Not only am I in pain, but I can't stop worrying about things. What do you suggest I do?

Worker: You might be helped by some relaxation training and exercises. Possibly stress-management classes could benefit you.

Mr. H: Oh, exercises. I'm good at exercises! [Mr. H was smiling.] I jump off my wheelchair and on to my bed and then jump up and down on the bed.

Mother: He's not kidding, either. He really does this. Last year he flew off his wheelchair onto the bed and flew off the other side. He couldn't stop. He broke three ribs and his collarbone. [Everyone was laughing, including myself. Mr. H was quite proud of the fact that he exercised like this.]

Worker: Well, what I meant by relaxation exercises would be different than the kind you've been doing, but we'll explain this later, when we come up with your recommendation. I've gotten sidetracked from your pain problem. It sounds like it's quite extensive, all over your body, and a very intense kind of pain. Mr. H, when did you begin experiencing so much pain? Have you had it for a long time, or did it begin just recently?

Mr. H: I was doing pretty well, despite my diabetes, until about two years ago. I suffered a complete renal shutdown. After my kidney transplant I had increasing neuropathy and stomach cramping. Shortly after the transplant I had the stroke, which affected my left side. And then came all the amputations. Everything seemed to strike all at once. It's really only been one year that I've been disabled. The pain has gotten bad just this year. I just had a second transplant this past year, too. That's two kidney transplants in two years. I've been in the hospital a tremendous amount of time, in about every station, too.

Worker: So it's really been just this past year that the pain has become unbearable. [He nods.] Mr. H, what kinds of things lessen your pain, or at least keep you from thinking about it so much?

Mr. H: Probably heat, massage, rest, and distraction.

Worker: What types of distraction help, Mr. H?

Mr. H: Well, I am much better when I'm in a conversation or even a good fight or argument with someone. But you can't fight with someone all the time. My ex-wife, for example, a few times when I've talked to her on the phone, she gets me so riled up—but after I hang up, I notice that I hadn't even thought of my pain.

Mother: But H, you do enjoy talking to people, and that helps. [Turning to me] I had a dinner party last week for his birthday. It was a huge Chinese dinner, so there were lots of courses, you know. H was so busy talking the whole time, he never once mentioned his pain.

Worker: What other types of distractions help, Mr. H?

Mr. H: Well, I enjoy reading tremendously. And writing, too. I hope to write a book about myself and my battle against diabetes. It would be in a humorous way, of course. That's the only way I could do it. I've already started the book. But with my hands it's getting extremely difficult to write. I used to create quite a bit of poetry. But with some of my fingers amputated, it's very difficult, plus it can be painful holding a pen at times. I enjoy music, too. And of course TV. My reading used to be a great source of pleasure for myself, but my eyesight has gotten so bad that it takes me all morning just to get through part of the paper. I can hardly read at all any more. And with my loss of hearing, I don't enjoy music as much as I used to, either. It just seems like there is less and less I can do all the time. Without being able to walk, a lot of my previous sources of enjoyment have stopped, also.

Worker: It sounds like your life has changed considerably due to increases in pain and with the impact of your illness. And you've suffered considerable loss within the past two years. [Mr. H nods.] Mr. H, if you did not have pain, what things would you do that you cannot do now because of the pain?

Mr. H: I'd be more active in social events, and of course do more reading, studying, and writing.

Worker: What about medications, Mr. H? Are you currently taking any drugs for your pain?

Mr. H: Yes, I'm taking methadone.

Worker: How often do you take methadone?

Mr. H: Four times a day.

Worker: Would you say that you experience much relief from the drug?

Mr. H: Not really. I still have a great deal of pain. It doesn't really provide any relief from pain.

Worker: Mr. H, the methadone you've been taking could actually be increasing your pain; do you realize that? Not infrequently, chronic pain patients become addicted to pain medications. In addition, after they withdraw from the drug, many find that their pain is greatly *diminished*. [I go on to explain the dangers of addiction and also the fact that often in chronic pain patients who take medication, the body elicits greater pain in order to obtain the much wanted medication.]

Mr. H: Yes, I have heard that, and I have tried to stop taking the methadone. But I've felt excruciating pain and then had to resume the medication.

Worker: Yes, that's to be expected. The body wants the medication, and is used to having it. Often the body experiences great pain shortly after withdrawal, but later on the pain is greatly reduced. Often, it is better to gradually reduce the medication intake because a sudden cessation can cause this pain, and cause the person in pain to go back on the medication.

Mr. H: Well, I suppose I could give it a try. I just don't know if it'll do any good.

Worker: It's up to you, Mr. H. I don't know what kind of relief you are actually getting from the medication. You are the best judge at this point. I'm just trying to make you aware of some things we have found here at the clinic, and possible implications they have for you and your situation.

Mr. H: I see.

Worker: What is your living situation at this time, Mr. H?

Mr. H: I live with my son. We just moved in together last month. He was living with his mother, but we decided to try it this way for a while. I wanted to encourage my son with his schooling. He had dropped out, and now he's back in.

Worker: Mr. H, how is this working out?

Mr. H: Oh, pretty well. We're getting along fine. And I think it's helping my son also with his schoolwork. I was very concerned earlier. And he helps me get around, too.

Worker: Where did you live before?

Mr. H: The past four years I've lived with my mother. Before that with my wife, but after she was out of the picture and I began having some problems, I went to live with my mother.

Mother: He's welcome home again any time he wants. I wish he were still there. I worry about his having an insulin shock and no one being home. Adam [son] is gone to school all day.

Mr. H: Mother, I thought it was a good idea for me to leave for a while. I'm a grown man and should be able to have my own place. And I haven't gone into insulin shock for over a year now. I can feel it coming on and do something about it.

Worker: Mr. H, what was it that precipitated your move?

Mr. H: Well, like I said, part of it was to be with Adam [his son] and help him with his schooling. Plus we just wanted to live together for a while. And I wanted to be more independent.

Worker: Adam, what is it like for you, living with your father?

Adam: Fine. It's going OK. He has really helped me become more motivated in school. Of course, sometimes it bugs me when he tells me what to do all the time. When I was with my mother, I pretty much could do what I wanted. But I screwed up more then.

Worker: Is it restricting for you at all, as far as taking care of your father?

Adam: No, it really isn't. I go out at night sometimes if I want to. I'm doing as much as I ever did before. [We talk some about the living situation.]

Worker: Mr. H, what is a typical day for you?

Mr. H: I usually get up at about 7:00 a.m. and have breakfast. Between 8:00 a.m. and 9:00 a.m. I straighten up the bedroom and kitchen. Then I take a bath for about an hour, shave, try to read the newspaper. By 11:00 a.m. I prepare lunch, eat, and clean up. In the afternoon I read or telephone people. I phone my mother daily. I try to nap some in the afternoon and maybe write a little bit. At 5:00 p.m. I prepare dinner. In the evening I read, watch TV, talk to Adam, listen to music. I'm typically up until 4:00 a.m. reading or watching TV. I just can't fall asleep.

Worker: It sounds like you're alone pretty much, Mr. H.

Mr. H: Yes, and its quite a switch from what my life used to be like. I used to be personnel manager at the XYZ Company. I have an MBA, but much of my time at the company was spent counseling employees. I've always loved to be around people and enjoy conversation tremendously.

Mother: Yes, that's what's kept H going all this time. Just his love of life and people. He's almost given up a few times.

Worker: Well, Mr. H, it sounds as though your illness has very significantly affected your lifestyle. Your life has changed considerably due to increases in pain and disability, is that right?

Mr. H: Very much.

Worker: Would you consider yourself depressed much of the time?

Mr. H: Yes, sometimes I have uncontrollable crying spells. But I come out of them OK. It just disturbs me that I have had to curtail activities that I used to enjoy so much. Pain and difficulty with my eyesight have caused me to have to stop reading and writing as much. And I can't concentrate due to the pain, and that makes me more depressed. Then I think about my pain more and get even more depressed than before. Sometimes I just don't know what to do about it. And I guess I have a lot of resentment toward the hospital. I can't hear as well because of some anesthesia I was given before an operation. It was too much. And then when I was operated on [amputated], my legs were healing just fine until a couple of nurses dropped me on the stub. So they had to amputate it even further because it blackened. And then I was overdosed twice in the hospital. I guess I really blame them for a lot of my problems. I know its not all their fault, but I sometimes am depressed about what didn't have to happen.

Worker: Have you thought about committing suicide, Mr. H?

Mr. H: Well, I did at one point. But I decided that I still have a lot to live for. I did make one decision, however. When the kidney I have now stops functioning (it's a cadaver kidney) I will not have another kidney transplant, nor will I go on dialysis. I've just decided to let fate take its course. [Mr. H will live a few weeks after his renal shutdown, if this is what he chooses to do. We talk a little about this.]

Worker: Back to the pain problem. Mrs. H and Adam this will be directed at you. How can you tell when Mr. H is in pain?

Mother: Well, he will verbalize his pain sometimes. Or else I'll see him grimacing. He'll groan sometimes, too.

Worker: Adam?

Adam: About the same thing. Or else he'll be lying down.

Worker: What kinds of things do you do in response to the pain?

Mother: Well, I usually try to do something to make him feel better. But you know there's not really much that I can do. He just has to live with it. Sometimes I just pretend I don't notice it.

Worker: What do you do, Adam?

Adam: I try to make him more comfortable or ask how he feels. I don't know. I guess he really doesn't complain very much.

Mr. H: I think that I used to verbalize my pain more than I do now. I have come to realize that it's my problem and that I have to live with it.

Worker: What about your conversations on the phone Mrs. H? Does pain enter into the conversation?

Mother: Well, yes. I ask him how he's feeling every day, and he'll tell me about the pain.

Adam: Sometimes we talk about his pain. But we talk about other things, too. Mostly about cars. That's what I want to do after school, do some work in auto mechanics.

[I go further in finding out what the family members do in response to Mr. H's pain and how much it is entrenched in the relationships they have.]

Worker: One thing that we have found here in the pain clinic is that focus on pain does not help the patient or person experiencing the pain, but rather it makes it worse. Chronic pain is not like acute pain at all. It's not the same as when a person is sick for a short time. You pamper them, etc. With chronic pain, the more attention that is paid to the pain problem, the greater the pain. Here in the pain clinic we teach families of the patient to ignore the pain behaviors. By pain behaviors, I mean the things you've just mentioned: verbal complaints, grimacing, holding the area that hurts, lying down, etc. When the person does these pain behaviors, its better for the family to *ignore* them. Mr. H, you've mentioned yourself that distraction is one of the things that relieves your pain, at least to some degree.

Mother: You know, it's really good to hear that, because for a while I think we did let H's pain problem consume us all. And even now I do ignore his complaints sometimes because I know that I can't really do anything about the pain—anything to alleviate it. But I do feel guilty when I do this because I know he is in pain and feel that I should not be ignoring him. At the same time I know he would be better off not focusing on the problem. It's really good to have permission to do that. I really am convinced that it's the best thing and am glad to hear you say that, really relieved in a way.

Worker: Yes, focus on pain can strain family relationships in many ways. In our pain program we have the family draw up a contract as far as retraining goes. The patient needs to give the family explicit permission to ignore pain behavior in the future; they must all understand that the patient will not be able to stop the pain behaviors immediately and that the patient will no doubt become angry when pain behaviors are ignored. The patient and family must learn to view the usually unacceptable behavior of ignoring illness and concern with body functioning as in this case an act of love and caring. It's important that all other significant persons with whom Mr. H comes in contact know about this concept and will cooperate with the plan. Adam, do you understand this?

Adam: Yeah.

Worker: Mr. H, how does this make you feel?

Mr. H: Well, I know that it's the best thing. I really do. I agree that when I am distracted and don't concentrate on my pain, I do feel better. I don't think I really do talk about the pain much.

Worker: Well, that's a positive thing, but it sounds as though there is *some* concentration and some focus on the pain, and that's what we are concerned with. We're talking about eliminating virtually *all* talk about the pain. However, along with that there needs to be some positive reinforcement and distraction also. Mr. H, I guess I see that as one concern—the fact that you are alone so much and don't have much conversation and activity to distract you. How often do you see other people?

Mr. H: Well, I have a home health nurse assistant that comes to see me three times a week. Believe me, she is a godsend. I just love having her come around. And by the way, she does ignore my complaints. She gets me right out of bed if I'm still there. And we have some wonderful conversations. I really do enjoy having her come over. I see my mother weekly and talk to her daily on the phone. And my son is there many evenings. But I guess for the most part I am home alone.

Worker: I think that one thing that would help tremendously would be for you to be in contact with people more often, just from what you have said about loving being around others, engaging in conversation, and doing things. And you seem to be in less pain then.

Mr. H: Yes, I know. I keep telling myself that, but I always say that I'll wait until I feel better to do something. But I guess that just getting out would make me feel better. It's hard to break that cycle, though.

Worker: How easy is it for you to get out, Mr. H?

Mr. H: That's another problem. I can only go somewhere when my son's home. That's in the evenings. We have a van that I can be transported in, so that's a help. But I can't go anywhere during the day very easily. If I could only get out, even to the mall. Then I could go and bother all the shopkeepers. I know a lot of them, and it's fun talking with some of them.

Worker: Well, maybe we can explore some alternatives this week before we meet with you again with our recommendations. I think that more social activity would be very beneficial.

Mr. H: Yes, I'd like that. Maybe skateboarding every Tuesday? [He chuckles.]

At this point I sum up the main points of the interview and some of the recommendations made already. Then Mr. H and the family members with him have interviews with a physician, psychologist and counseling psychologist. MMPIs are administered, and an appointment is scheduled next week, when the team will have made some recommendations for pain management.

THE PROBLEM

I. Contact phase

   A. Problem as the client system sees it: Mr. H saw the problem as his pain primarily. Other complicating factors were his diabetes, renal failure, gangrene due to poor circulation, loss of eyesight, loss of hearing, loss of body parts, sleep disturbance, depression, and anxiety. He stated that his difficulties with pain significantly affected his lifestyle . . . and this factor was what brought him to the pain clinic for some recommendations.

   B. Problem as defined by significant systems in contact with client:

     Mr. H's family saw the problem as the pain as well as the medical problems involved. Mr. H's pain affected them as well as Mr. H. Chronic pain, defined as at least four months' duration, is increasingly seen as a disease entity with far-reaching consequences for the family and society. Ultimately pain may become the larger part of a person's identity, and all interactions with the environment may be couched in words or actions that involve pain. Family members begin to go about their daily lives without the patient or stay home with them and feel resentful. The pain may consume the family (as Mrs. H mentioned) and eventually become an integral yet detrimental factor in the family relationships. Others step in to perform tasks formerly done by the patients.

   C. Problem as the worker sees it:

     The pain, and medical problems and how they have affected/changed Mr. H's life. I was concerned with the whole theme of loss that was prevalent in Mr. H's life. Loss of his marriage; loss of his kidney, spleen; loss of eyesight; loss of hearing; loss of his legs, penis, fingers; loss of his job; loss of independence; loss of mobility; loss of a pain-free body; loss of recreational activity; loss of an active social life; etc. It was evident that pain and disability had significantly affected his lifestyle. The psychological and emotional effects of this would appear to be overwhelming, as was evident in Mr. H's statement that he had become depressed, anxiety-ridden, and unable to sleep well during the past year. Mr. H reported that pain interfered with all aspects of his life. In addition, Mr. H had to deal with a dependence upon methadone.

   D. Problem for work

     The problem for work here was to come up with some recommendations concerning pain management and for some suggestions in dealing with what at first appeared to be a hopeless situation, especially since Mr. H's disease is getting progressively worse.

II. Goal identification

   A. How the client system sees (or wants) the problem to be worked out:

     Mr. H may have been looking for some relief of pain by coming to the pain clinic. However, the clinic is a last resort for those who have exhausted all medical efforts. The program is geared toward living with the pain, and this was explained. With this understanding, Mr. H probably hoped for some recommendations regarding his pain problem and its effect on his life. He sought some suggestions for pain management.

   B. What the client system thinks is needed for a solution of the problem:

     There is no "solution" in this case. However, I believe that Mr. H was searching for help in living/coping with his problem, living a life that was somewhat higher in quality. He probably would accept concrete resources, specific assistance, and advice or guidance.

   C. What the client system seeks and/or expects from the agency as a means to a solution: I believe that Mr. H and his family are seeking specific assistance and recommendations. Concrete services would be helpful in enabling Mr. H to get around. The social systems involving Mr. H, mainly his family, were in some need of change, in that the pain was of great significance in family interactions. Getting pain out of the family relationships was one suggestion already made. Advice/instruction was sought by Mr. H; probably some degree of support or reassurance also; however, it would have to be short-term, as the pain clinic structure was such.

III. Assessment

  A. Motivation

    1. Discomfort—It was fairly obvious that Mr. H's discomfort was very extensive. As discussed before, not only was Mr. H disabled, but he was in constant pain and his body progressively deteriorating. His disease was not limited to one area of his body but rather of comprehensive scope. There was no hope for any of his problems getting any better but rather only worse. The discomfort is generalized to his total life situation. And it is both a physical and emotional problem with far-reaching implications. Setting aside the health problems and the physical disability, the pain alone was a big problem. Research indicates that persons with chronic pain become isolated and lonely, unable to attend to any stimulus other than the pain experience. They become anxious, depressed, fearful, untrusting, and obsessed with body functions or problems; they feel utterly useless. They often begin to avoid intimacy and responsibility for their own lives. Sexual relationships change, and patient or partner withdraws, fearful of being hurt or hurting the other or being rejected. Ultimately pain may become the larger part of the patients' identities, and all interactions with the environment may be couched in words or actions that involve pain. One plus here is that Mr. H wasn't uncomfortable with the help-seeking role; rather he was extremely eager to hear our suggestions and seemed to enjoy the interviews.

    2. Hope—For his present situation, Mr. H possesses an enormous amount of hope, not for improvement in his condition but rather for an improved life situation. Although his hope is realistic, he is still somewhat optimistic, as could be seen throughout his interview in his humor. He seems to have an extensive history of successful coping. Even his mother stated in the interview that Mr. H appears to have a fierce love of life . . . he'd have to, to keep going as he is. She also mentioned that the doctors continue to be amazed that Mr. H is still alive. They'd considered him a goner many times. Mr. H prides himself on being able to keep going (to cope) and also on his counseling abilities. However, he does seem at present to be caught in a vicious cycle of being in pain, so not keeping actively involved physically and socially, and therefore being more focused on pain, and therefore experiencing even more pain, and so on. During the interview this was dealt with. Mr. H appears to understand this process and agree that it is operating in his situation.

  B. Opportunity

    Opportunities for solution of problem as the worker sees it:

    Although there is no "solution," I believe that there are at least five recommendations to help Mr. H cope with his problems of pain and disability.

    1. Mr. H's family should ignore and discourage talking about pain with the patient, as focusing on pain results in increases in perception of pain.

    2. Since he reports that he receives no benefits from methadone, Mr. H should attempt to decrease or discontinue his use of analgesic medication.

    3. Opportunities for increasing Mr. H's social network through utilization of community resources should be pursued

so that he can become more involved socially, as this appears to result in decreases in pain.

4. Relaxation training, biofeedback, and/or hypnosis might be helpful for Mr. H in managing his pain.

5. Mr. H should attempt to make use of Dictaphone and other equipment designed to help him carry on with those activities that he finds personally enjoyable rather than curtail his pursuit of these activities.

C. Capacity of the client system:

1. Physical and intellectual—Physically, Mr. H is very ill and disabled. His appearance is rather grotesque, and his energy level somewhat cut down by pain. However, he is nevertheless energetic and very animated while talking. His intellectual level appears very high. Mr. H is a very articulate and well-read person. He appears to have a good grasp on his surroundings and is an expert on his condition. He has read much on the biological factors involved and various treatments, etc. He seems very able to reason and focus on a particular area.

2. Socioeconomic factors—Mr. H is living on Social Security benefits, as he is unable to work at all. Fortunately, his entire medical treatment of kidney failure is covered by Medical Assistance. Although his Social Security benefits allow Mr. H a modest living, he is restricted in what he can do. The fact that he once held a job (personnel manager) and is now unable to work is a problem which I'm sure affects his sense of adequacy and self-worth. He mentioned this while telling me he thought it was very ironic that at one time he had been on the giving end of counseling, and now he was on the receiving end. Mr. H apparently has no strong ethnic identification (he is white) but has what he describes as strong family ties with his mother and son. He doesn't appear to be strongly religious.

D. Natural interpersonal systems:
The two family members most involved with Mr. H are his mother and his son. He continues to have limited contact with his ex-wife, but she is not very involved in his life. Mr. H's son was given an MMPI as part of his father's pain evaluation. He approached the test items in an honest and candid fashion. His MMPI profile was within normal limits, suggesting no significant psychopathology. He is an energetic young man with a positive outlook and a variety of aesthetic interests. He is an outgoing individual who perceives himself as being able to cope adequately with the demands of day-to-day living. Mr. H was unable to take the MMPI because of severe visual problems. Mrs. H, his mother, took the test but approached the test items in an extremely defensive and guarded manner, attempting to present herself in a highly favorable light. Thus, her profile must be interpreted as invalid, and no inferences concerning her current style of functioning can be made on the basis of her MMPI.

Both Mr. H's mother and son agreed to ignore and discourage talking about pain with the patient, as focusing on his pain would only result in increases in his perception of the pain. They are both very supportive and concerned for his well-being.

A public health nurse is another person closely involved with Mr. H and whom he views as a strong support system. She engages him in conversation and "brightens up his day" when she is there.

E. Institution systems:
The health system is very involved, as Mr. H is in the hospital very often. He also receives Medical Assistance and Social Security. He seems adept in dealing with these institutions. However, he did have some bitterness toward the hospital, for reasons that he explained during the interview. We

do not know what the whole story was on this, but it was beyond our scope and purpose to explore this. We did, however, explore Metro Mobility because of Mr. H's complaint that he could not get around very well except after 4:00 p.m., when son would be home from school. I talked to the organization and was told that all Mr. H had to do was fill out an application, send in a doctor's statement that the applicant is in fact disabled. Metro Mobility would then provide transportation within the Twin Cities area with two hours' advance notice. However, when I presented this to Mr. H, he stated that he had had very bad experiences with Metro Mobility. At times they'd never show up; other times they'd be eight hours late. In addition, since he'd moved, they would not come to his side of the street. We are still exploring this system with Mr. H. We're going to find out ourselves what the problem is.

F. Environmental context:

Mr. H's life seems to be adequate in the area of income, although Mr. H had said that it is somewhat restrictive as far as what he can do. Obviously, his health status is not good, which is very restrictive. Nutritionally Mr. H is well off. He enjoys cooking and says that having his son with him inspires him to make good meals. Mr. H also seems to be an expert on his diet and intake; he has to be with his renal failure and cadaver kidney. Meaningfulness of work is one problem Mr. H has. He has had trouble reading and writing, due to pain. In addition, he has been unable to be employed for several years. He mentioned that he wanted to get into some setting where he could do counseling. We put him in touch with several agencies where he might be able to explore this.

G. Worker barriers involved:

1. Emotional barriers—There is something about the client's problem situation that is reminiscent of one of my own life's experiences, although not nearly to the degree Mr. H was experiencing. I had to go to Mayo Clinic for a health problem about one year ago. I can remember both my fear for my health and the frustration of not being able to do anything myself. The hospital setting was also somewhat frightening. I think the worst part of the whole experience was not knowing what was ahead. Mr. H lives with this fear from day to day. Not only does he not know what may happen with his body tomorrow—another kidney rejection, amputation, further loss of sight or hearing—he also knows that things are not going to be getting any better or easier in the future. All of these things compounded would have to cause some anxiety and depression. This was one aspect of Mr. H's situation that I could relate to, although the full extent of his situation I could only imagine. The loss of limbs, sight, hearing, renal function, job, independence; all of these things I will never be able to understand emotionally, to the fullest.

2. Cognitive barriers—One cognitive barrier that is quite wide is the gap in age. Mr. H is 30 years older than myself, so I am unfamiliar with the feelings that go along with his age. His divorce is another issue that I would not be able to relate to, although I have experienced a few painful break-ups. His medical condition, diabetes and renal failure, was one that I have become very familiar with this past year, as my other placement has been in kidney transplants. I found that with this experience working with diabetics and transplant patients helped me understand to a much greater extent what Mr. H was going through and how the whole family is affected. (I have been running a support group for kidney patients, diabetics, and patients on dialysis and their families.)

H. Resources:

The resources I had available were both my supervisors from the pain clinic and the kidney transplant ward, the clinical psychologist in the pain clinic, two social workers in the rehabilitation center who informed me of resources suitable for Mr. H, the Kidney Foundation, the Diabetes Association, and various books and journals I found in the pain clinic.

RECOMMENDATIONS

It was the consensus of the team that pain has significantly affected Mr. H's lifestyle. He enjoys writing and reading. Pain, difficulty with his eyesight, and difficulty with concentration have forced him to curtail these activities somewhat. Increases in depression also apparently affect his ability to concentrate, resulting in more pain and increases in depression. His current living situation and difficulty with mobility result in him spending a great deal of time alone and may have contributed to increases in pain and depression.

Dr. L, clinical psychologist, recommended that Mr. H be referred to Dr. G, who specializes in hypnosis, for possible management of his pain. Biofeedback was also recommended. Dr. L contacted Dr. G and arranged for Mr. H to visit. Mr. H emphasized that he wanted to pursue hypnosis.

As the social worker, I investigated possible resources for increases in Mr. H's social activities:

1. *Metro Mobility* (which was already mentioned)
2. *Diabetes Association*—There was a branch located very near Mr. H's home. They have weekly diabetic support group sessions. There is no wheelchair ramp, but after contacting Mrs. W, she stated that if Mr. H would call ahead and let them know he was coming, they would hold the meeting on the first floor, which is accessible by wheelchair. Meetings are facilitated by a family life educator and a diabetes spokesman. Diabetics and their families are invited. Through this support group it would be possible for Mr. H to become acquainted with other members and activities of the Diabetes Association. A branch of this association meets at the hospital. The meetings are the third Thursday of every month. They also offer educational classes in series groups. There is one currently going on, which Mr. H could become involved in. They offer lectures dealing with different aspects of diabetes, dealing with stress, trends, diet, etc. Doctors, other medical professionals, social workers, etc. lead the classes and discussions.
3. *Rehabilitation center*—The Courage Center offers many group activities—swimming, games, etc.—for the handicapped. They take the participants to a wide variety of functions, provide many activities.
4. *The rehabilitation institute*—Has an adult day-care center, an intensive program where the participants are there all day. They provide many activities throughout the whole day. (This was felt to be unsuitable for Mr. H, so it was not recommended after exploration.)

A feedback conference was arranged for Mr. H, his son, his mother, myself, the clinical psychologist, and Mr. H's public health nurse. We went through all of the above recommendations, and I gave him my list of resources and contact persons. Mr. H was especially interested in the support group that met near his home, although he said it seemed funny to think that he would be going there himself to participate in a support group, when a few years ago he was asked to be president of it. In addition we went over the other recommendations:

1. Mr. H's family should ignore and discourage talking about pain with the patient, as focusing on pain results in increasing perception of pain. We inquired if the family had been doing this since our initial interview, and they stated that they had and that it had really helped, although it was sometimes hard to do. We assured them that it takes a lot of practice and that changed behaviors cannot take place over night.
2. Since he reports that he receives no benefits from methadone, Mr. H should attempt to

decrease or discontinue his use of analgesic medication. Mr. H had not been successful in doing this yet, and Dr. L went over some specific recommendations and advice on how to go about this. He did a lot of coaching and showed a lot of support.

3. Opportunities for increasing Mr. H's social network through utilization of community resources were presented so that he could become more involved socially, as this appears to result in decreases in pain. I went through my list of resources and talked with him about these possibilities. Mr. H stated that he kept telling himself that when he felt better he would start to pursue social interests, but then he'd stay home and concentrate on the pain and feel even worse. We talked some about breaking this cycle.

4. Relaxation training was recommended as a possibility for helping Mr. H manage his pain.

5. Mr. H should attempt to make use of Dictaphones and other equipment designed to help him carry on with those activities that he finds personally enjoyable rather than curtail his pursuit of these activities. Mr. H was very receptive to this idea and talked some about the book he was in the process of writing.

6. We mentioned that we were working on progress with Metro Mobility.

These recommendations were communicated to Mr. H's physician. In addition, a care conference with Mr. H's physician and the public health team involved in his care was arranged to discuss our findings and recommendations.

Reading A-4 *Mrs. Z**

PREFACE

Social work in a hospital is in a secondary setting and it is usually up to the worker to initiate the relationship, which may or may not be reciprocated, depending on the patient's or family member's level of need. Services may be concrete—that is, arranging for transportation or equipment, help in discharge planning like nursing home placements, or arranging of public health nurse, etc. Or services may be more psychosocially oriented, such as counseling with people about emotional problems for themselves or family, helping them to problem-solve more effectively during a time of crisis, aiding in facilitating communication within the family, interpreting family's position to other hospital staff, and playing a supportive role in helping patients cope and deal with the problems they face physically and emotionally.

---

* Case material prepared for this book.

ASSESSMENT

Mrs. Z is a woman in her mid 50s who has lymphoma and was being treated for progression of her disease. While in the hospital, her physical problems were many. Besides the serious degree to which her cancer had advanced, she also had phlebitis in her leg. This caused her leg to swell to nearly twice its normal size and also caused partial paralysis of it. In addition, she had a doxorubicin infiltrate to her hand (this is a condition of the chemotherapy drug being administered through an IV infiltrated directly under her skin rather than in the vein). This is toxic to the system and causes literally a very severe burn, which caused the entire arm and hand to swell and was intensely painful. A large area of her hand was "gutted" (eaten away), and surgery for a skin graft was necessary. This was not very successful; because of the lymphoma the healing process was extremely poor. To further complicate these physical problems, Mrs. Z was allergic to many of the narcotics used for pain control, which made pain management a problem in itself.

Besides the physical problems described above, it was also known that Mrs. Z had been divorced for about eight years. She had three sons that were married and not very close to her. She lived in a small town 200 miles away from the hospital, and consequently there was little family involvement or friends available to provide support for this woman.

Another problem was that Mrs. Z was viewed as a problem by the medical staff (doctors and nurses) because she was extremely demanding and impatient. There were many conflicts between her and the nurses, which caused problems of alienation and resentment. Mrs. Z would turn her call light on almost continuously, and no matter what the nurses did, she would complain—they didn't come soon enough, she didn't like the way they did what she asked them to do, etc. Frustration was high for Mrs. Z as well as the medical staff.

Because of these various problems, it was decided that I would follow Mrs. Z and act partially as a support system during this stressful period of hospitalization. In doing so, I had hoped to penetrate the angry behavior Mrs. Z exhibited toward the staff and encourage her to vent these angry feelings as well as other thoughts and fears that might be affecting her and immobilizing her at this point, through all that had taken place. I felt perhaps the basis of her anger really had more to do about the cancer itself rather than treatment by staff. She had been a very independent woman, very active and very concerned about her appearance. She had always made a meticulous effort on her part to look her best. I felt the physical changes in her appearance induced by her cancerous condition were extremely difficult for her to accept and adversely affected her feelings of self-worth; also, the frustrating limitations of her treatment affected her own autonomy and sense of control of her life. This was even more devastating for her because of the lack of other support systems to help buffer her through these crises. I had hoped with her expression of these greater thoughts and fears, she might gain more insight into her own behavior and therefore be able to better deal with the root of her anger and regain her coping capacity to endure all this in a more satisfying way. Also, I would be acting as a liaison between her and the hospital staff so they might better understand each other's needs and desires and thereby facilitate more effective interactions between them.

I had visited Mrs. Z on several occasions before and tried to be as supportive as possible, allowing her to express her anger toward the staff and her treatment and sorrow over her physical condition as much as she could at the time. I felt it especially necessary to acknowledge her statements without challenging them to the least degree initially because I felt it the best way to establish a relationship of trust and gain her confidence in the beginning without threatening her. I felt that underneath that stern, demanding, and controlling exterior she portrayed to others there was a very fearful, lonely, hurting, and fragile woman who coped by keeping her guard up and acting strong. By rushing in, I felt I would only alienate her, so I tolerated much of her acting out behavior.

I might add at this point that it was also very frustrating working with her because at times she was experiencing a high degree of pain and I don't think always could hear what was being said because she was so preoccupied by her uncomfortableness, yet other times she would be so doped up with pain medications that that also interfered with meaningful interactions. I am not faulting her; it was a reality of her physical condition which was not always conducive to clear communication but rather created some barriers in our interactions. I oftentimes had to reorient her to our past discussions, and I'm pretty sure from her perception our talks did seem to be intermittent, and one could not really get a sense of progression in resolving certain issues. For my part, I'll say it another way. It was like at some points our discussions would begin to break through her more superficial anger at the staff and I could be more confrontive and help her look at the greater implications of her disease, yet the next time I might see her, she would be in so much pain that I would feel the need to be much more supportive and try not to confront her, but I now think I may have been reinforcing the behavior I was hoping to help change. It is still hard for me to assess that, but at any rate I too at times felt I was not being consistent. Yet with the complicating circumstances of her physical pain and my not wanting to add to her discomfort, I wasn't sure how to proceed.

In the beginning I felt our discussions were helpful, but as her pain became more in control through pain medications which were effective, I got the impression that she disliked my being there to discuss her feelings and thoughts. At times she viewed me as an intruder. I was very confused. I thought perhaps on one hand she might be associating me with the other medical staff that she had so much resentment for. I think her resentment was especially high because she couldn't control them. (By this I mean she would become very indignant that they wouldn't answer her call light *immediately* and give her the attention she seemed to demand from them). Or was it that our talking about cancer and the changes it caused in her life and greater fears of death were too painful for her to acknowledge, so she was distancing herself from me? Or was it because I was younger than she and she in her need to be in control didn't want me to have any power over her and felt she was too much more mature, older, and wiser to accept what I had to say? (I did get the feeling at times she tried to put me down as if to say she knew all this, yet I don't think she really was aware of how this was affecting her in totality. It was as if any concession of what I had to say made her feel "less than," although that was never my intention.

It was a real dilemma because on one hand, I felt it necessary to hang in there because I realized what a hurting person she really was, physically and emotionally, and wanted to be of some support, since she was lacking in her own support systems of family and friends, yet I recognized the client's right to self-determination, and she certainly didn't ask for my involvement. Was this an assumption that she needed and wanted help? Or did she really want help but didn't know how to handle it?

PROCESS OF INTERVENTION

Finally, through my frustration, I talked with my supervisor and told her I felt Mrs. Z did not want my involvement and felt it futile that she and I continue to maintain this relationship, which did not appear to be helpful to her. I knew she was in discomfort, but what right did I have to pursue something that she might not want any part of? It was decided I should confront Mrs. Z with this to know how I should proceed with her.

I was prepared to accept that she might not want my involvement and didn't want to force myself on her. But also she was due to be discharged, and the doctors were very concerned about her discharge plans, knowing that she would require a great deal of care. We as a staff felt she was underestimating what this would involve. It seemed she was so angry and eager to be released that she didn't give much consideration to planning adequately for her discharge. She had an older cousin who was going to let her stay with her but didn't know if this cousin realized how much care and attention Mrs. Z required and if this would be a problem for her. Mrs. Z wanted to be independent, but the reality was that she would be very dependent on another for physical care.

As a hospital social worker, it is also part of my responsibility to try to assist in discharge plans and hopefully work out plans that are feasible. In this case I was concerned because I knew Mrs. Z had a lot of problems, and I wanted things to go as smoothly as possible for her. The following is the process recording of our interaction that day.

As I walked in the room, Mrs. Z was yelling at the nurse. Apparently she had wanted her walker and the nurse had not come immediately to get it.

Nurse: Jo, they didn't know you needed your walker.
Mrs. Z: Yes they did! They just wouldn't answer the light.

The nurse was helping her back into bed and was being pleasant and understanding. Jo seemed very angry and upset, almost like she was pouting in the way she spoke. I believe this woman is in a great deal of pain but also feel it is difficult to cope with her attitude. Because she is always complaining, it is hard to discern what complaints are really justified. To Mrs. Z her discomfort and unhappiness is very real. She has a great deal of anger. To continue:

K: Hi, Jo. You don't look like you feel very well right now.

Mrs. Z: No, I don't.

K: I'm really sorry to hear that. I know this hasn't been easy for you.

Mrs. Z: No, it's not! Would you get me my ice [said it very demanding. I got it for her.] Will you put water in it? I want water in it! [Sounded very demanding and frustrated.]

K: Sure I will. [I did so, and she heard me in the bathroom filling up the water and yelled.]

Mrs. Z: Not too much! You're putting too much in!

K: [I returned and showed her how much I had put in and asked her if that was all right. She seemed upset, anxious in pain and angry.] "Jo, is this OK for you?"

Mrs. Z: Yes! Now put it on the table [I did]. Well, push it closer to me. I can't get it over there! [She did not give me any time even to get a chance to do so before she said this.]

It was clear to me she was in pain and was angry and this is what at least some of her anger was about. I wanted to sympathize with her and acknowledge her pain and also make sure what she was bothered about. In doing so, I thought she might calm down a little bit and reassure her that I knew how difficult this was for her. Hopefully it would encourage conversation.

K: Jo, are you in a lot of pain right now?

Mrs. Z: Yes I am [defiantly]. I've been in pain all morning, and everyone takes their sweet old time around here, but I finally got my pain shot.

K: Jo, I'm sure that must really be difficult to take. You've had to put up with so much pain, and I think I myself would be so terribly frustrated in having to endure that besides having to *wait* for someone to come with your pain shot so you can get some relief. I think it's easy for people to forget how hard it is to lie there, unable to do the things you want to do for yourself, and be in such pain.

Mrs. Z: Yes, they don't know what it's like for us. [She is whimpering this and looking out the window. I paused so to see what else she might say. There was a moment of silence.] I've got some good news, though.

K: You do? Can you tell me what it is?

Mrs. Z: Yes, they are going to discharge me on Saturday, and I finally got my pain shot a little while ago, and my niece bought me this wig [she had it on]. I guess it looks OK until I can get my own.

She was very pleased about the discharge news. She had been looking forward to this for weeks, and I was glad she brought it up because I wanted to explore what her plans were with her. Also, the remark about the wig was very significant. Jo's hair had always been important to her. Apparently her other relatives had always commented on how beautiful Jo's hair always looked and she took great pride in this. I remember from the first time I met Mrs. Z, she was most concerned about her hair and wanted me to arrange for a hairdresser for her while in the hospital. Also, she wanted to go through such extreme measures through her chemotherapy as packing her head in ice so that she would be less likely to lose her hair (evidently she had read about such experiments). Thus I saw Jo's hair as being very reinforcing to her and the social reinforcement she got had been important to her self-worth. I felt she was looking for reassurance about her appearance at this time, especially in anticipation of going out in public again and how others might view her in light of the changes she's gone through in her physical appearance. I thought it would be ego-building and reassuring to comment positively about this and discuss it a bit, because I think she was feeling a little anxious about it.

K: Wow, that is all good news! I think your wig looks lovely on you—it really matches your hair well. [We discussed that for a while, and I felt this very productive because I felt she was mourning the loss of her hair and physical changes for that matter, and it was helpful for her to feel assured. After this she was really beginning to act very drowsy. Her eyes were half-closed and I think the pain medication was taking effect at this point.] That is also really good news about your being discharged. Before, you mentioned staying with your cousin. Is that where you'll be going?

Mrs. Z: Well yes, but the doctors here are sending me to the Rehabilitation Hospital near River City [where she lives] for a couple of days.

K: Do you know why they will be transferring you there?

Mrs. Z: No. [I wanted her to understand what was going on, because the uncertainty of why things are being done to a patient may create unnecessary added fear.]

K: Well it's my understanding you need to get some more chemotherapy, but you'll be able to get it there, where it's closer to home and where you'd rather be.

Mrs. Z: Yes. [Eyes closed, looks as if resting more comfortably, didn't respond further.]

K: So then after your stay in the hospital will your cousin be picking you up then?

Mrs. Z: Yes. [Didn't elaborate.]

K: Have you had a chance to talk with your cousin about your staying there and the kinds of things you'll be needing? [I was a little more specific and described different equipment she might require and also help in and out of bed, etc.]

Mrs. Z: No! [Responded very angrily.] What are you getting at?

At this point, there became a marked change in her behavior again. She became highly aroused and seemed suspicious, as if she were being threatened, so I tried to explain why I was asking that question.

K: I don't mean to alarm you. I guess I asked that because I'm wondering how you think things might go for you at your cousin's home, and if you think you'll both be able to manage by yourselves all right. I guess I see you being in a lot of pain and discomfort here and was hoping going back home would go smoothly and as comfortably as possible for you. [I paused, but there was no response from her, so I continued.] Sometimes it can be helpful to have a public health nurse available to check in on you and see how you are doing. I'm not sure how much experience your cousin has in dealing with the physical aspects of care that you'll likely be requiring, and a public health nurse might be a helpful resource person to help you and your cousin manage with different needs that might arise. I was just wondering if you and she had considered anything like this?

Mrs. Z: No! [Exploded—very angry now] But yes, she can manage!! She invited me to stay with her and she'll take care of me, just like you would take care of someone if you asked them to stay with you. I'm tired of this. Why do you keep coming in here and talking about these things that have no bearing on you? I can take care of myself and make my own arrangements.

K: Jo, I really don't mean to be bothering you, and I'm sorry you feel that way. I guess I'm concerned about you and just wanted to sort of check things out with you about how you're feeling here in the hospital, because I know it can be pretty stressful, especially with all the setbacks and pain you've been through. I know getting along with the nurses and staff has been a problem for you and would like to help in any way I can in clarifying any communication problems. And as far as arrangements to go home, I guess I'd just like things to go as smoothly as possible for you so that you don't have to worry about all those things by yourself when you might not feel up to it.

At this time I was totally shocked and didn't know how to react for sure. I had never before had a client react so violently and felt unprepared as to how to deal with it. In retrospect I think it would have been more reorienting for Jo if I had again described the role of the social worker in this setting and then explained why I felt it important to be involved, but at the time, I didn't think of it, and ended up somewhat defending myself. I felt angry because I felt we had talked about some of these issues before and forgot at the time she had had a lot of disorienting experiences, being on the pain medications etc. I also thought she was very angry at the nurses again today and this was her way of controlling me and expressing that anger. My feelings of anger lasted only momentarily because I realized the degree of pain physically and emotionally she had endured, and I found myself feeling very sorry for her again. To continue:

Mrs. Z: Well I don't need you to be concerned for me. I never asked you to be concerned and as far as getting along with the nurses, you should have been here two months ago!

K: [I tried to speak softly and comfortingly because I didn't want to cause her any more discomfort. I did not want to be confrontive in a punishing way. I just didn't understand all that she was saying to me at the time. I will elaborate on this later.] Jo, right now I feel that you're angry and upset, and it doesn't appear from what I've heard you say today about the nurses that you feel good about their service. I think I have tried to talk with you about that on several occasions and we have discussed it. There have been several times that you tell me things and we have discussed it. There have been several times that you tell me things are going OK and that you understand that they are busy and say you don't need to talk about it. Do you remember talking about that?

Mrs. Z: Well I don't know, I don't remember. [She is quieter again. I don't know if this is because she doesn't want to talk or because of the pain medication.]

K: Well, I guess I think we have. You know, lately, I get the impression you don't always want to talk with me. Maybe I'm not being helpful to you. Is that how you feel? [Silence; her eyes are rolling up. I think she hears me, but the pain medication has really made her dopy by now.] Jo, can you hear me? [I'm speaking very softly and trying to be more supportive.]

Mrs. Z: Yes, but I don't feel well. I need to rest.

K: So is it that you don't want to talk anymore right now?

Mrs. Z: Yes, I want to rest.

K: Would you like me to come back so we can finish talking about this later when you feel better?

Mrs. Z: Well, if *you* want to.

K: Jo, I would like to come, but only if you would like me to come. If this is not helpful to you, perhaps it would be best if I didn't.

Mrs. Z: Well, you can visit me if you want, but you don't have to come because you're concerned about what I'm going to do. I can take care of myself.

K: OK, Jo, I'm glad to hear that but I would like you to rest now, I'll be back later. Take care now.

FURTHER ASSESSMENT AND EVALUATION

I would like to talk further about my feelings during and after this interview because this awareness has a significant bearing on how I handled the current situation as well as what I learned from it and what might be more helpful in the future as far as dealing with similar situations as a result of this learning experience. This was my first experience with an angry client, and I felt unprepared in handling it.

To begin, during the conversation I felt myself reacting to her anger and becoming angry myself and feeling hurt because I took it personally, like I had failed at what I wanted to do and frustrated at how hard I had tried to accommodate her controlling behavior. I do not mean to imply I tried to do something to her, because I realize that is not consistent with social work philosophy. I tried to stick with what I felt going on with her. When she told me at times she was satisfied with the care she was getting, I tried to pursue it because I felt she was saying things to appease me, yet she denied this, so I didn't feel it was in my place to force an issue that she didn't care to discuss. Yet I allowed myself to get caught up in the hostility she demonstrated at the moment, rather than looking beyond to what greater implications this anger might have been about. I think that was my big mistake in this discussion, because it kept us locked into secondary issues rather than what I believe were the underlying problems of this situation. Unfortunately, I was then in the position of defending myself, when in reality I don't think that was really what the issue was at all about.

First, I forgot two important factors. I knew we had discussed the nursing issues before, and there had also been times I tried to talk about it and she didn't want to discuss it, and now I was hearing from her that I should have done so, which made me angry because I felt I had. Part of my anger might have been from the fact that at the moment I had lost sight of the fact that our conversations were erratic and vague at times because she was on medications, which would inhibit her ability to recall all that had been discussed. But beyond this I was defending my position and recalling her attention to discussions we had had, when in actuality I don't think that was what she was really angry about, which contributed to the misfocus of our conversation. Now, I don't believe she was attacking me; there was much more going on, and yet at the time I was caught up in her anger and took it for that.

Also, I think it would've been more helpful for Mrs. Z if I had reoriented her as to the role of the social worker. I think she was resentful that I was checking into her life so to speak, and she didn't want this. What I thought was concern she took as pity, which she did not want. I think she would have accepted concrete services I might have been able to offer instead.

In reflecting back, I don't believe her anger was really about me or the nursing staff, but rather at her predicament itself. I think Mrs. Z had been a very independent woman for the most part, and I think this hospitalization with all its complications and difficulties, physically and emotionally, had really taken its toll on her. She had had multiple losses and was grieving those losses, and I believe her anger was more about not being able to return to her previous lifestyle and instead having to go to someone's home and be dependent. I think she is suffering the loss of her own independence, her mobility, and the physical distortions of her body, (hair, hand, leg, etc.).

She had a great need to control others. This may have been a pattern she developed out of her own anger at having to be put in the position of being almost totally dependent on others. She enjoys ordering others, but I think this is mainly out of preservation of retaining her own autonomy.

She thrives on the attention she can get from others from her demanding behavior and becomes angry when she doesn't receive the attention and this way is very dependent on others. Yet I think this is what also contributes to her sense of low self-esteem, suffering from a loss of her physical self-image and also having to be put in the position where she is dependent upon others, which is contrary for her.

I would also imagine that her loss of independence is a devastating thing, especially at her young age. She needs time to work through her feelings about it and look at ways to begin to cope. The adaptive mechanism she has assumed is not a helpful one, that is, being demanding and critical of others.

I would have been more helpful if I could have focused more specifically on what is really causing the emotional pain for her, the losses, and not focusing on the nurses—that really only reinforced her use of them as scapegoats for her anger. The anger needs to be focused on the appropriate object. I think anger and hostility are common reactions during a grief period, and I took it more personally than would have been appropriate.

Another factor I think was very important would be that I felt she had a great deal of fear about the future and the uncertainty that affords, and it would have been helpful if this could be addressed. I think she needs to verbalize her *real* fears so that she can begin to cope with them.

My concern for her came out of my empathy for her because I too have been in a hospitalization where I felt demeaned and demoralized as a person because my own personal body I felt was being violated. Not being able to be independent, having

to rely on others to perform functions which I normally had done for myself, and having to do them at someone else's convenience rather than mine was very frustrating. I felt no one really cared about how it felt to me, and I was just another body to tend to. The total lack of privacy I felt, and the feeling that the medical staff were more intruders into my life and I had to subject myself on their conditions was painful, physically and emotionally.

Because of this, I felt I identified in some ways with Mrs. Z, and also felt even more concerned because the pain she endured and also the whole issue of a bleak future was much more extensive than I experienced. (I must also remember that my feelings are my own and may not necessarily be accurate in her case. It only provided me with something I could relate to her and one must try to constantly check it out with the patient and not put words in their mouth.)

Although my intentions might have been well intended, I think she interpreted my concern as pity and it was a reminder to her of all the things she couldn't do for herself, which was not what she needed.

Perhaps it would have been more helpful if I could have reassured her and supported her more in the planning she had done, so that she would have felt more reinforced for her capabilities, despite her limitations. And yet, my conflict was that I didn't feel her plans were realistic, and that she was so anxious to be discharged, that she didn't really consider what limitations she might encounter, no matter how much she wanted to be independent. (This was not only my feeling, but was shared by doctors and nurses and the clergy as well.) I guess sometimes I really don't know where I would have come out differently in this situation, because it seemed unless you accepted everything verbatim as to what she said, she wouldn't accept another outlook on the situation that didn't support what she was saying. It seemed she only heard what she wanted to hear and I wasn't able to get her to look beyond. I think she must have had a lot of anger and was also very much afraid about her future, that actually the hard core wall she put up around herself was a protective device to sustain a very fragile person.

In a way I don't really consider this a failure on my part, although certainly there may have been some things I could have done differently. I tried to give her all the support I could. Still, it is up to the individual as to what they can hear and accept, and I think in her case, she wasn't able to do this. I believe her distancing from me at times and others was her way of coping the way she knew how.

I realize I can't possibly be all things to all people—that there are going to be some people I can relate to and some not. Still, I want to always be open enough to critical review and not just accept the attitude "you win some; you lose some," because I need to be responsible for my own actions and try to be as facilitative as possible in my interventions with people, because I feel if I'm only serving my needs and not theirs, I don't belong there at all.

This leads me to another point that I struggled with in this case. Medical social work as discussed in the beginning can be very complicating. Mrs. Z did not request my intervention, and yet she was considered at risk, with all the forces going on against her, so in another way, it also seemed a very responsible effort in the least to maintain some type of contact with her on a periodic basis to reassess what needs there might be.

On one hand, I felt she didn't always want me to be there, and on the other, felt also somewhat of an obligation to stay in touch under the circumstances. After all, the patient may likely say they don't want any involvement, yet perhaps really it is that they don't know how to ask for help. It is a very undefined line, which is why I felt I had some problems with Mrs. Z. The boundaries of our relationship were very vague, and despite the fact that I felt her reasoning might have been inappropriate at times, she also had every right to behave as she did, because she didn't ask for my help. I felt there were some definite issues there to deal with, yet I didn't feel I had the right to force these issues either. It was very complex.

Also, I think her statement that she wouldn't mind if I came back to visit but she didn't want me asking questions about her plans or life was significant. I think this reflected the fact she was lonely and enjoyed the emotional support of having someone come in to say hi. Seeing and listening to how she was doing that day was therapeutic, and she appreciated this from me. But, it seemed when I was asking about her plans for the future, or delaying with certain other issues, this was very threatening to her and she withdrew, and I felt reluctant to force this, because not only did she not ask me for this, but also, this woman was in such tremendous pain at times, who was I to make her feel worse? That is not my role, and yet there was somewhat of a conflict for me in consideration of my social work role in the hospital and trying to act as a liaison with the patient and staff when she wasn't willing to discuss it with me, and also in solidifying appropriate planning for discharge. It is still confusing to me and difficult to try and capture all that I mean on paper at this time. I would appreciate any thoughts you might have and maybe we could discuss this sometime.

In this setting, my interventions are mainly supportive as well as encouraging verbalization of people's thoughts and feelings and venting feelings of anger, frustration or joy also. Another factor is my mediator role and patient advocate with the medical team in trying to provide consistent and facilitative care for the patient during their hospital stay which for the most part is very stressful.

Oftentimes it is helpful to help encourage and expand on problem-solving skills in the midst of a period characterized as a crisis state and help people develop coping skills and expand on problem solving capacities in a time they may be feeling immobilized by the overwhelming facts of all that is happening to them, beyond even the diagnosis of cancer. There are many physical and psychological adjustments to be made, and this often means adapting to a new lifestyle because of the demands living with cancer creates on the individual.

For most people this is a time of a high degree of discomfort and they need to redefine who they are and what goals they have in the future. Many feel hopeless in this time of despair and disorganization, and need to reorganize their coping capacities in order to regain a sense of control over their life.

With Mrs. Z, I felt our relationship was therapeutic in the sense that my presence allowed her to ventilate a lot of her feelings of anger and pain at the time. Many times I saw her she seemed relieved to have someone to talk to, and this way I felt I gave her a lot of support and validated her feelings.

However, in trying to explore these feelings further and trying to discuss with her what implications the diagnosis of cancer had on her future, and in consideration of how this related to other systems, such as financial and emotional support from her family (or lack of it I should say), work-related restrictions, and a changed lifestyle altogether, I don't know how effective our relationship was. I tried to address these areas, but whether they were too painful for her to deal with at the time and she closed off, or whether she didn't want to discuss it with me period, I don't know. I was confused as to what extent to pursue this in light of the factor of client self-determination. After all, it may have been my feeling that it would have been helpful to deal with some of these issues in the long run, but it may have not been hers, so one must ask the question—whose need is it, the patient's or the worker's?

On the other hand, I felt that I respected her not wanting to talk about this and yet also addressed them in a supportive superficial way, so maybe I planted a few seeds for thought. Although she overtly seemed to resent this, possibly in preservation of her own autonomy, perhaps she will think about these things on her own. At any rate, I do not know how to assess the impact I had on her, and this was especially hindered by her poor physical state and erratic visits with her. I do believe I tried very hard to extend feelings of genuineness, warmth and understanding to her and felt she appreciated this to the extent she could. Yet, she was not able to discuss more painful issues and used a lot of anger and could be very demanding at times in an effort perhaps to demonstrate the control she wanted over her life.

As for my outlook on Mrs. Z, I would have to say I'm very concerned about her adjustment to this crisis situation. She does not appear to be willing to look at the more intensive aspects of what this situation means. Or perhaps it would be more accurate to say that if she does, she keeps it to herself and does not discuss it at a high rate with others. This may be OK if she is able to handle it, but so far, with her critical and demanding behaviors, it doesn't appear she is coping as well as she might be. This is especially a concern in light of the fact that she at least at this time has such limited support systems available to her and how this will affect her ability to cope with her situation.

On the other hand, perhaps she will deal with it, but for now, it is too painful for her to discuss. I only hope when the time comes, there will be someone who can be helpful in doing so.

There are many issues I don't know about, because she would not discuss them with me, so it is hard to speculate on what things may be like for her in the future. I do hope she is able to resolve some of these things, because at the moment, I don't think she is in a very good place with herself, and she needs to be reassured she is a worthwhile person and perhaps talk about her hopes for the future as well as her fears to find the peace of mind that will allow her to deal with her present life situation as well as her anticipated death.

I tried to incorporate my theoretical notions within this last portion, but to briefly reiterate what these are I will say that cancer constitutes a crisis in the individual and family's life, and thereby upsets the equilibrium of their steady state.

In medical social work, I rely mainly on principles of crisis intervention and problem solving techniques. This is also utilized within the context of systems approach in looking at the different systems this affects and helping expand coping and adaptive capacities to the situation.

The use of relationship and trying to encourage the client's verbal feelings is important especially in this time of high discomfort in order to regain a feeling of hope and maximizing and building on ego strengths to recover a sense of balance and equilibrium. I try to do this in a supportive and reinforcing manner, in narrowing the gap of unrealistic perceptions and reality. This is especially helpful in aiding the individual or family to cope with potential problems in the future through the skills and support they receive, yet this should be done in a manner which supports the premise of client self-determination and allow them to retain as much autonomy as possible.

Allowing a person to ventilate their feelings and accepting and reassuring them validates them as a person and facilitates coping capacities.

The Lee Family*

In the Lao-Hmong family the service unit is an extended family consisting of a husband, wife, three children, and an elderly mother. The husband is 45; the wife, 43; two sons, ages 15 and 13; a daughter, 8; and the mother, 69. Another son, the eldest in the family, was left behind in their home country.

In Laos the husband's family was a member of the upper class, representing established wealth with family prestige. Chong Lee, the head of the family, was the chief of service of a government agency in Laos. At intake Mr. Lee was working as a janitor in a hospital and was the identified client. Mrs. Lee came from a well-known family in Laos. She was a high school graduate. Over the course of her marriage, she was a successful teacher in the family's town. At the moment she was not working because she did not speak English. Mang Xiong, mother of Mr. Lee, is a member of a wealthy family in Laos. She lived with her oldest son and daughter-in-law before she came to this country. At the time of evacuation, Mr. Lee, her youngest son, was able to leave Laos due to his government association. The grandmother joined him and his family to come to the refugee camps in Thailand. They stayed in the refugee camps for nearly four years and then decided to come to the United States.

Mr. Lee was referred for counseling to the Refugee Social Adjustment Program (RSAP) by his sponsor, Mr. Smith. Mr. Smith was concerned that Mr. Lee looked depressed and unhappy with his family. Mr. Smith didn't know what was the matter with Mr. Lee. However, he understood that Mr. Lee was concerned about his son who was left behind, but it was difficult to discuss because Mr. Lee did not speak much English. It also seemed to

him that the mother and Mrs. Lee didn't get along very well. Mr. Smith wanted the family to get help they needed.

Based on the referral information, Vu, a RSAP social worker, telephoned the family. Mr. Vu told Mr. Lee that his sponsor indicated that there might be some area in which the family could use help that the sponsor couldn't provide due to the language barriers. Over the phone Vu introduced himself as a worker from an agency which helped refugees who have emotional and social adjustment problems from the resettlement process. He asked Mr. Lee general questions about his family, what they were doing in Laos, where they were living, and how many family members were left behind. Mr. Vu made sure Mr. Lee understood that this program was funded by the local and federal governments, and there would be no charge for the services. He then arranged an initial meeting with the family and let Mr. Lee know that he could call any time to cancel the appointment if he wished. Vu told Mr. Lee that he was concerned about the family situation at home.

Vu, the social worker, made a home visit to Mr. Lee's house and reintroduced himself as a social worker from an agency to help refugees in the resettlement process. Most of the conversation was directed to Mr. Lee, with few general questions directed to both husband and wife. The family had a large portrait exhibited on the wall, and this family portrait served as a topic of the conversation and opened up the whole area of the family's breakup during the evacuation.

One of the issues which emerged in the initial interview involved a misunderstanding between the sponsor and the client's family. Mr. Lee said that he felt constrained by a sense of obligation and loyalty to the sponsor and avoided talking about some

---

* Case material prepared for this book.

issues with him for fear that the sponsor would see him as not grateful. The family felt that they should not be a burden on the sponsor's family. Consequently, the Lees avoided imposing on the sponsor's family. The sponsor didn't understand why. Vu commented about some of the same difficulties that many refugee families have encountered with their sponsors. Mr. Lee became more relaxed and started to bring up additional problems.

Employment was another difficult area. Mr. Smith had been instrumental in helping Mr. Lee get a job, but the menial nature of janitorial work was hard for him to accept. This job was a major source of frustration. Mr. Lee didn't feel he could express his feelings to Mr. Smith about the job, for fear that the sponsor would believe him to be not grateful. Because of this, he didn't feel comfortable making inquiries about other types of work. He saw no future in this type of work, which compounded his sense of despair and hopelessness. In addition, he had a feeling that he could make more money to support his family by receiving public assistance. But that alternative was precluded by his unwillingness to receive such money.

Vu mentioned that in this country people were not likely to feel the same kind of loyalty as did Mr. Lee. That is, his job seeking would not necessarily be viewed as disloyal. It would be more likely to say that it was as an individual trying to help himself and his family. Vu explained that the sponsor found him a job as a janitor, in the hopes that it would be temporary until Mr. Lee was able to find a more suitable job. The initial interview concluded with Mr. Vu's indication to the client that through job training and English classes, new job opportunities might develop.

In the next interview Vu found that Mr. Lee was concerned about his family remaining in Laos, especially the welfare of his eldest son. He said his eldest brother was also in Laos. His mother had been living with this elder brother until the evacuation, when she had decided to come to this country with Mr. Lee and his family. Vu remarked that such a change often caused family difficulties because the daughter-in-law was not used to a mother-in-law's presence in the home. Mr. Lee stated that he felt caught in the middle with the

difficulties between his wife and mother. He felt torn between his role as a husband and his role as a son. He could not make a decision in this problem area. Mrs. Lee viewed Mr. Lee's reluctance to take any action as an indication that he was supporting his mother against her. She had recently begun to talk about separation and divorce. The wife felt that the mother-in-law was expecting too much from her, especially since they were in America, not in Laos. In America the daughter-in-law's position was not the same as in Laos. She did not have to do everything the mother-in-law expected of her. Mr. Vu arranged a private session with Mr. Lee at the counseling agency for the following day. The purpose of the session would be to more fully detail the marital and family difficulties evident in the client's home.

The following day Mr. Lee and Vu met for a private session to discuss the family problems further. Vu was able to determine that the major problem derived from his mother's criticism of the wife's behavior as a mother, wife, and daughter-in-law. The older woman felt that the daughter-in-law was a poor housekeeper, since she didn't pay sufficient attention to the needs of her children and she behaved in a disrespectful way to her mother-in-law. Mr. Lee explained that his mother also believed that his wife was stingy, because the wife had been handling the family's finances. The mother's SSI check had become a necessary part of the family income needed to buy food and clothes and to pay rent. Because she didn't fully understand the change in the family's fortunes, the mother assumed that this action was due to unnecessary saving on the part of her daughter-in-law. Mr. Lee's opinion of his wife was that she was not behaving in a good daughter-in-law fashion and that she should have been more understanding and respectful of her mother-in-law.

Mr. Lee had strong moral obligation to provide a home for his elderly mother but also a strong loyalty to his wife for many years. The result of this conflict was apparent in the man's decision regarding what steps might be taken to solve the family difficulties. Sometimes Mr. Lee seemed to favor the wife's resolution to move the grandmother out into her own home. But economic factors eliminated this solution, since the family could not afford to support Mrs. Lee in separate residence. At other times he felt that his obligation to his mother should take precedence over his wife and that the grandmother should remain with the family.

The worker expressed concern that the actors in this situation not take any hasty action which would be later regretted. Mr. Lee was advised to continue in his role as family mediator for a while longer and to indicate to his wife that a solution acceptable to all parties would be forthcoming. Mr. Vu commented to Mr. Lee concerning his difficult position in the family. He also gave Mr. Lee his telephone number, inviting him to call should things become difficult at home. Plans were made for the worker to see the wife in private session at the office. The husband approved of the plan, since it was portrayed as a necessary intermediate step in working toward a solution.

Vu asked Mr. Lee to explain to his wife the role of the worker in respect to the family. He again mentioned that he was there to help them in adjustment difficulties the family was having in America. This allowed the worker to discuss more directly with Mrs. Lee the difficulties in the family situation. Because the worker is a male, a private meeting with Mrs. Lee would have to be approved and sanctioned by the husband to conform to traditional rules governing behavior between a man's wife and another man not related by kinship.

ACTION PHASE

At the office Vu greeted Mrs. Lee and introduced himself as a worker from an agency that helps with the Indochinese resettlement. He explained that his conversations with her husband led him to understand that the family was having some difficulties. Vu acknowledged to Mrs. Lee that he understood that these problems might be sensitive and possibly embarrassing. Vu also explained that it was necessary to be frank, because the situation could become more serious if it was allowed to continue. The wife initially responded to the explanation with some anger, since she wondered what negative statement her husband may have made about her.

Vu reassured Mrs. Lee that her husband had not made negative remarks about her, but he was very concerned about the family situation. Vu mentioned that one of her husband's concerns was that she and her mother-in-law were not getting along. The wife believed there were some tensions involving her mother-in-law, but her major concern centered around her husband. The wife said that she understood role expectations, but her husband's loyalty to her seemed less than his loyalty to his mother. Vu commented that it might appear that way, but he reminded the wife that a relationship between a man and his wife and a man and his mother are quite different. She had been worried about this matter for some time and felt the only solution was for either her or the mother-in-law to leave. The worker remarked that although that may seem like the only solution available, he would like to help the family to identify as many alternatives as possible. He also suggested that her preferred solution might be hasty because if she left her husband, she would be very miserable and depressed. It would also be hard on the children not to have a mother. But if the mother-in-law left, it would be very difficult for her husband, who would feel ashamed at his treatment of his mother. The wife agreed that her solution might not be the best answer. Vu told Mrs. Lee that he would like to have a joint discussion with her and her husband.

In the joint session the worker brought up the issue of the mother-in-law and Mrs. Lee's concern regarding her relationship with her mother-in-law. Vu asked for time to outline the domestic situation as he had come to understand it based on his interviews with both marital partners. He outlined the current situation and asked for opinions from husband and wife as to how well this description fit their situation. The wife felt that her role in the situation was exaggerated and that she did not show disrespect to her husband's mother or do things to purposely upset the older woman. This statement was another example of her husband's giving support to his mother and not to her. Vu intervened at this point and suggested that this sort of blaming would not help the situation. He encouraged both husband and wife to try to work together to find a solution. Vu stated that they needed to talk about this at some length to identify possible solutions for the home situation. To this, Mrs. Lee remarked that nothing would help except moving her mother-in-law into her own place. The worker asked the husband if he felt comfortable with such a solution. He said that he had already considered it. This decision might have to be accepted as a last resort but he didn't believe that his mother would be able to live on her own. He felt a strong obligation to care for her in their own home, since she had come to the United States because of this promise that she would live with them. He said, however, that his mother wanted to move out, too, because of her feeling of tension at home and her perception of her daughter-in-law's hostility toward her.

Vu proceeded to examine this alternative with the family members. After going through the family's income it became clear to the family that they could not afford to establish a separate residence for Mr. Lee's mother. Vu suggested that Mrs. Lee might feel better about the home situation if she were involved in some activities outside the house. Vu asked the husband if he would mind if his wife enrolled in a training program in preparation for finding a job. He added that in the new land, due to the loss of family fortunes, many women had to work to help support their families. Besides, he continued, the wife was a professional and had contributed to the family in those days in Laos. This situation was different than if she were to work in the United States, most likely as a menial worker like her husband. Vu asked Mrs. Lee if she would be interested in such an opportunity. She said she would be, since a chance to financially help her family might help change her mother-in-law's view of her.

The worker suggested that the couple seriously consider this option, which would include the grandmother to help out around the home with some of the things she had already begun to do, such as cooking and taking care of the children. The couple agreed that this might be helpful.

In the initial phases of marital counseling, it is generally a good policy for the RSAP to see the husband and the wife separately. The worker acts as a mediator and helps both parties to better understand each other. Oftentimes, neither spouse may be aware of the consequences of complicated actions in America. This is especially true when considering such issues as the rearing of the children, economic survival, social life, and basic self-image. It is important that both parties understand the positive and negative consequences of such action. It is the worker's responsibility to develop additional alternatives to minimize the family conflicts. By minimizing the emphasis on negative feelings and accusations, the worker reduces the potential for losing face by all parties.

Once a viable solution has been developed, the worker should take an active role in assuring that the client is able to implement the indicated solutions or changes. The worker should actively make necessary resources available. Generally speaking, once the worker has assisted the client to admit that there is a problem, he assumes an active direct approach to problem-solving.

The preceding case illustrates several of the cultural themes that many refugees approached. Mr. and Mrs. Lee were experiencing a successful marriage until their move to the United States. In addition to this move which involved the need for the adjustment to the culture in the United States, the family experienced a change in economic circumstances. From the position of wealth in Laos, the family was relegated to poverty with the move to the new land. With the addition of Mr. Lee's mother to the household, the family experienced another dramatic change.

For Mrs. Xiong, the mother, the change in residence is equally important. From a longstanding residence with her eldest son and his family, she moved into the home of her youngest son, who was married to a woman that Mrs. Xiong opposed as a marriage choice. This change in living, both in residence and lifestyle, posed serious difficulties for her. With inadequate understanding of her son's reduced income, Mrs. Xiong felt that her daughter-in-law's stinginess was disrespect rather than a necessity required for family survival.

In the fifth session Vu had brought both husband and wife together in a joint session. Until that time, he had been seeing them separately and had been acting as a go-between who attempted to explain the one spouse's feelings to the other. In this conjoint session Vu continued his work as a mediator in that he attempted to keep both parties engaged in the problems at hand and make certain that both husband and wife had a chance to express their opinions and position. A central focus of the worker's task was to engage the couple in mutual problem-solving behavior and to assist the couple in examining various possible solutions. The worker met with both Mr. and Mrs. Lee. Based on Mrs. Lee's request, her husband has spoken with his mother regarding her criticism of his wife. He emphasized the need to get in the United States because of the hardships that everyone was experiencing. In addition, Mr. Lee had openly discussed with his mother the family's financial position. He pointed out that because of the family's poverty, all family income had to be used for support. Mr. Lee also indicated to his mother that should his wife find work as a result of her involvement in a training program, the family's financial situation would greatly improve, and the grandmother would get some money for her own needs.

Vu praised Mr. Lee for this discussion with his mother. Mr. Lee also indicated that he and his mother had discussed her daughter-in-law's behavior as a wife for the past several years. The grandmother accepted the fact that he had no reasons for complaints, since she had indeed been a very good wife and mother. Vu supported Mrs. Lee for her patience with her mother-in-law. He also raised the issues of her enormous adjustment that the grandmother was making to both living in the new country and also living with another son's family. The couple felt that this was important because they sometimes forgot that Mr. Lee's mother was also having to make a very difficult change in her life.

The worker terminated the sessions, giving both spouses a lot of praise for their work and also for patiently understanding the need to work out difficulties before making rash decisions. Vu arranged the follow-up meeting to see Mrs. Lee through the process of enrolling in a job training program, and to ensure that the family's adjustment was proceeding well.

Vu was able to enroll Mrs. Lee in a training program from which she graduated. She was placed in a job and was able to supplement the family income. The grandmother gradually took over many of the household chores and child-rearing duties. The problems between husband, wife, and mother-in-law were drastically reduced and the family was able to continue in their difficult but healthy adjustment to their new life in the new country.

Reading A-6   *Stover Family**

This family was referred to Family Service Agency from the child protection unit of the County Department of Public Welfare. The family at time of referral included Earl (husband and father) age 43, June (wife and mother) age 39, and three children. The two oldest children (George, age 12 and Larie, age 5) are June Stover's children by a previous marriage; Eileen, age 4, is of this marriage.

Mr. and Mrs. Stover had been active with 22 social agencies during the past 15 years. Mrs. Stover has had three marriages, the first after she became pregnant while in high school. She never lived with her first husband. Her second husband was a seriously developmentally disabled ward of the state. She had four children by him, three of whom were placed for adoption. She became involved with Mr. Stover while still married to her second husband, her first child by Mr. Stover arriving four months after their marriage. Mrs. Stover has shown other signs of instability and attempted suicide eight years ago.

Mr. Stover has been known to the Veterans Administration since his army discharge 10 years ago as a psychoneurotic. He is reportedly alcoholic.

* A case study prepared for this text.

During contacts with Family Service three years ago, Mrs. Stover reported a number of episodes of physical abuse of herself and the children by Mr. Stover.

Since the present marriage there have been six complaints of neglect of the children. These have originated from Mrs. Stover's relatives, her former husband and his relatives, the school nurse, and the minister. The Child Protection Unit has found insufficient evidence to proceed on these charges. Workers have found it difficult to work with Mrs. Stover; when contacted by a worker, she has been superficially cooperative but then avoids workers whenever possible. If an appointment is made in advance, she is never home. Family Service was reluctant to reopen the case, as indications were that this woman couldn't use help. However, on plea from the Public Welfare Department, we decided to make another attempt to provide service.

Eileen Stover, the 4-year-old, has had a condition believed to be muscular dystrophy. Previous workers have found Mrs. Stover unrealistic in her attitude toward this.

MARCH 20 TO APRIL 15

I have tried to contact the Stover family since Family Services accepted the case without any success. The Public Welfare worker says it is impossible to find Mrs. Stover at home if she knows who is coming and that Mrs. Stover is not to be trusted at all. She agrees to everything and does nothing. On April 13, I sent a note saying I would call on April 15; this time Mrs. Stover was home.

The Stovers have two rooms on the second floor of a large house, the ground floor of which is in the process of being remodeled. Though I had previously sent a note advising of my plan to call, Mrs. Stover indicated that she couldn't talk to me, since her husband was sleeping. Mrs. Stover is a woman of medium height, quite dirty in appearance with old slacks, a man's shirt hanging out, and bare feet. She is in her seventh month of pregnancy. I referred to the previous contacts of Family Services and other agencies and explained we had decided to come to see Mrs. Stover as we knew about a number of problems which she might be continuing to have. I indicated that I was aware of her previous marital difficulties and the fact that she had temporarily left her husband last March, we knew that this resulted in difficulties for the family as a whole. Mrs. Stover's immediate reaction to this was to say that the situation has cleared up and she feels that the marital relationship is now OK. She did, however, appear responsive to interest in her problems and accepted an office interview for April 23. She intends to go to General Hospital in the morning of that date in connection with Eileen's muscular dystrophy, mentioning that she finds these trips to the hospital clinic very wearisome and dislikes the long waiting period. She thinks that Eileen is improving, however.

APRIL 23

Mrs. Stover did not keep appointment. On repeated calls in person I did not find her home. I made two appointments by telephone, neither of which she kept.

JUNE 24

Worker finally located Stover family when welfare called to say they had moved to Jonesville. On this date I found them both home. The present housing of the Stover family is a four-room shack raised about five feet from the ground on stilts beside the river. The home was flooded out in the floods two years ago. There is no foundation. The beams and supporting joists in the house were seriously weakened by the flood. The sides and interior partitions are still caked with dirt from the flood.

There is no sign of paint on the interior or exterior of the house and all in all the house is barely habitable. The front door has a drop of about four feet to the ground with only a crude ladder. The home has two bedrooms, a living room, and kitchen. These are adequate in size. Toilet facilities are of the outdoor variety. The shack was previously owned by an elderly bachelor who died. The house was in estate when the Stovers moved in, and they are paying $125 a month which may be applied toward a purchase price if the Stovers decide to stay.

Mr. and Mrs. Stover were both present. Mr. Stover is a small-built man neatly dressed, unshaven, and quiet. Mrs. Stover had made him aware of the fact that I had seen her earlier. He indicated in reply to my inquiry that he knew what it was about. He said that they were getting on well now outside of the fact that he is unemployed at the present. He said that the previous difficulties between himself and Mrs. Stover had been due largely to his alcoholic problem. Quarrels occurred usually when he was drinking. He would get angry and has a strong temper. He indicated that he thought welfare workers knew about these episodes in the past. He said that there have been no such happenings now for the last 10 months. I asked him to what did he attribute the change. He feels that difficulties arose because of his nervousness and unemployment. When he is nervous he starts drinking and they go round and round again. He said that he had been employed pretty steady during the last summer and fall, mostly on temporary labor jobs. The reason he can't get employment now as a carpenter is that the employer must insure him and in order to do this he must pass a physical examination. Thus, he finds himself confined largely to odd jobs and casual labor jobs. Another thing which bothers him about employment is the fact that he gets nervous working too close to too many people and that he dislikes working for other people. Small things bother him, he is easily irritated and has a quick temper. He would prefer to work for himself. He prefers country life to the city life. His ambition would be to get a small farm of his own where he could grow vegetables and so on for the market. The problem here is lack of capital and he doubts if he will get a chance to do this. Mr. Stover seemed to be feeling that they are getting on well at this time. They appear to present a united front to the world. Mrs. Stover neither nodded nor spoke in support of much of what her husband said. She also made a point of saying in his presence that she felt his drinking had improved.

JULY 17
Again, I failed to find the Stovers at home on visits I made by appointment. On a visit, July 15, it appeared as though they had moved again. Public Welfare Department had no new address. But, on this date, to my surprise Mrs. Stover came into the office. She was neatly dressed in a clean dress and had her hair done up; this was the first time I have seen her where she had obviously given some attention to her appearance. She seemed uneasy about the story she had to tell and was trying to be placating. She said she had decided to leave her husband, because he has been drinking heavily, mostly wine, and has been beating her and the kids. She is afraid of what will happen. She can't talk to him because he is sensitive and trying to find out what is wrong merely antagonizes him more. He was on the wagon up to June but started drinking again. Mrs. Stover felt this had something to do with the troubles with housing and also that Mr. Stover had picked up with a neighbor man who drinks and they have been going out together. Mr. Stover, she said, "gets nervous and edgy." He orders the kids and Mrs. Stover around. Nothing she does pleases him. She is called all sorts of names by him when he gets drunk. Mr. Stover pushed Eileen down in the yard because she got in his way.

Mrs. Stover hasn't notified Public Welfare of the change in circumstances. She is out of money and the baby is due shortly. I gave her a check for immediate needs and advised her to go immediately to the Welfare Board and get things straightened out with them. She was obviously attempting to charm me into helping her with this as she says the Welfare Board won't do anything for her. I agreed to talk to AFDC about her application there.

JULY 18 TO SEPTEMBER 1
Together Mrs. Stover and I made application for AFDC and arranged for care of the children during her confinement. I visited with her twice in the hospital. After the baby's birth Mrs. Stover moved in with her sister without notifying Public Welfare. I pointed out to her that this was why she had trouble with AFDC. She complained they couldn't trust her but this behavior certainly seemed to prove their point. Mrs. Stover said she was planning on moving again. She promised to notify AFDC and workers of her new address; this time she did.

SEPTEMBER 15. AFDC VISIT TO MRS. STOVER

Mrs. Stover, Eileen, and Peter, the baby, were at home; the two children played happily in the apartment: Eileen has come to know me. The apartment consists of three good-sized rooms in a row in an old apartment building. Mrs. Stover has the apartment neat and clean. She was dressed in slacks and noticeably cleaner and paying more attention to her appearance herself. Mrs. Stover mentioned she has bought winter clothes for the children. But, not all she needs yet. She showed me her AFDC budget which totals $345 per month, of which $180 has to be signed over by Mr. Stover from his disability pension. Mr. Stover held up signing the documents which would permit this to be done, but instead gave Mrs. Stover some money himself in September, and is offering to do this every month. Mrs. Stover refused this offer and reported the whole matter to the VA office and they will contact him. By law she feels he will be required to sign the document since part of his disability pension is for his wife and children. She feels Mr. Stover is still trying to spoil her plans or to get back and live with her. I raised the question of Mrs. Stover's plans regarding the marriage. Mrs. Stover seems quite sure at this point that she wants a permanent separation. She would want a rule that Mr. Stover would visit the children, but only when sober and could only visit his two children; that is, Peter and Eileen. Mrs. Stover again admitted ambivalent feelings about Mr. Stover. She has always felt she needed him, couldn't get along without him. She was ready to put up with his drinking to some extent. She was always afraid of being alone in the world. On the other hand she regards him as an intelligent man, who is not at all hard to get along with when not drinking. However, she now feels his drinking has got to the point where he can't control it and he won't admit it. She is risking her own safety and realizes now that staying with Mr. Stover may cost her the family. The children could be harmed or it might be necessary for an agency to place them. At the present time Mrs. Stover doesn't know where Mr. Stover is.

SEPTEMBER 22

I suggested that Mrs. Stover make her need for a stove known to her AFDC worker. She doesn't wish to tell them. I pointed out that she could be cheating herself since it is my understanding that AFDC can assist with a need of this kind. I indicated that her reluctance to approach them regarding this matter seemed to indicate that all was not yet well in her relationship to AFDC or her feeling about the agency and asked what did she feel was the trouble. Mrs. Stover again said she doesn't trust them. You never know what they'll do behind your back. Checks have been held up when she didn't fully appreciate the reason. She has been given to understand that she is a babysitter for her own children. AFDC, she feels, are paying her in that capacity and have given her to understand that they may fire her at any time. I brought up incidents indicating that there had been reasons for concern about the children in the past. I interpreted that it seemed to me that dangers seemed to lie more in Mrs. Stover's disturbed marriages. That I have observed that she has feeling for the children, she has indicated clearly to me that she wants to keep them, and it appears to me that she is capable of caring for the children as well. On the other hand, we had to consider the emotional effect on the children as well as possible physical dangers in the violence that had occurred in her marriages. Mrs. Stover again said she knows I'm there because of the children. She indicated that she doesn't resent this from me because she knows I'm out to support her effort to get out of the tangled marital situation. She does resent this from AFDC workers; however, on the other hand, she recognizes that she has given AFDC workers reason for concern because of her avoidance of them. I pointed out that Mrs. Stover can improve and is improving her relationship with AFDC by going out of the way to inform them of changes and needs. Mrs. Stover pointed out that lately she has been phoning her AFDC worker about every change and circumstance. We decided that Mrs. Stover would explore the possibility of getting the stove from her landlord and failing this will think further about approaching AFDC. The difficulty as she sees it, is that she doesn't want to ask for extra things for fear that she will be thought too demanding. She has considerable doubt about explanation that a request of this kind might even help to convince AFDC that she wants to meet the needs of her family.

Mrs. Stover says that she thinks perhaps they regard her as lacking in intelligence. I challenged this by pointing out that AFDC records actually show her to be of very superior intelligence (reported IQ is 142). Mrs. Stover indicated in response to this that she knows about her own high intelligence, recalls going with a sister to have IQ test. Mrs. Stover went with the sister mainly to reassure her, since the sister was unwilling to go on her own. Mrs. Stover knows that her IQ is 142 though she doesn't recall who told her this. I explained this placed her within the upper 1 percent of the population in intelligence whereupon Mrs. Stover demanded "Where has it got me?" She went on to say, "My life is a complete mess," pointing out her three unhappy marriages at 39, the fact that she has been all confused, recognizes she has brains but has never been able to use them properly. Here she mentions that she didn't do as well in school as she should have, always had her nose in a book, has always had a liking for books but cannot use this information in her own life. Her dream of what a proper job for her would be is that of a librarian. At times, she thinks that after five years or so when Peter is older and in school, she would like to have some kind of training for work, and her first choice would be library work. Her future plans she thinks are in terms of working and supporting her children and she stressed that she wants *no more men*.

Mrs. Stover further raised the question of how could she have made such a mess of her life. I then discussed the importance of feelings, that these are often as important as brains in determining what we do and suggested that she has to work on the problem of how her experiences and life and her feelings have landed her where she is. She can still use books to acquire knowledge and training, but this is not enough by itself. Mrs. Stover seemed very taken by this and said she should think more about how she gets her life in such a mess. I agreed that this was a good time to do it while immediate pressures are less.

OCTOBER 13

Mrs. Stover volunteered that she is not feeling well, has been cranky lately. This she attributes to her current concern about her husband. At times she feels lonely and that she needs him. Most of the time, however, she is contented to stay apart from him, but gets restless and starts to move things around in the apartment. I commented that the children are cleaner and better clothed, that I had noticed her in several situations giving instructions to the children and that they seemed to obey her well and willingly. Mrs. Stover feels this is a gain she has made (particularly with regard to housework) since the change in her marital situation. Her housing is much improved over what she has had in the past, she also feels that here she has less on her mind, is less confused and knows what she is after, and there is more satisfaction for her in doing housework. She used to depend largely on her family for this sort of thing and there is a certain satisfaction for her in being able to make some decisions on her own or with the support of the agency without having to turn to her mother.

OCTOBER 20

Discussed with Mrs. Stover that Public Welfare had requested a conference so that we might work together better. I told her what material I would be sharing with them. I invited her comments but she was upset and angry, as she was sure they wanted to discontinue AFDC.

OCTOBER 26. CONFERENCE WITH PUBLIC WELFARE

Public Welfare is concerned about Mrs. Stover's record of unstable marriages, the fact that they have often been unable to keep in touch with her or to keep up with her changes of address, is prepared to keep AFDC in cash, but is concerned about a possibility of repetition of her unsatisfactory mental experience and can she really keep Mr. Stover at arm's length? A review of developments in the case by Family Service indicates that Mrs. Stover is presently trying to free herself of concern regarding the situation she has got herself into. A decision was made because Mrs. Stover shows good feeling for the children and capacity to meet their needs, that AFDC will be continued in cash subject to further period of time which will be spent on working out Mrs. Stover's problems in relation to men and her marriages. Question of Mrs. Stover's distrust of AFDC was discussed in some detail, and it was felt that AFDC worker will try to create an opportunity to discuss this at some length with Mrs. Stover and thus reassure her of their interest and frankness with her.

NOVEMBER 3. VISIT TO MRS. STOVER
BY APPOINTMENT

At this time Eileen and Peter were taking their regular afternoon sleep and the other children were in school. Mrs. Stover now seems to have the household well organized, and the children are regular in sleeping habits, and there is a marked improvement in the appearance of the apartment, with all floors swept and the dust off the furniture and the kitchen in good order. Mrs. Stover was dressed in blue denims for housework, but was neat and clean apparently paying more attention to her personal appearance. The interview began with a discussion of the meeting with Public Welfare. Much of this was a review of the reasons for concern of both our agency and AFDC about the children and Mrs. Stover's marital relationships. Mrs. Stover brought up that she had had considerable apprehension about the meeting, being concerned that there might be plans on the way to cancel her allowance again. Since the last interview, her AFDC worker visited and spent an hour with her. Mrs. Stover felt this interview helped a great deal, she is now more satisfied that AFDC is on her side and anxious to support her efforts to do better. She was greatly relieved, she indicated, by assurance that her allowance would not be arbitrarily cut off unless the AFDC worker was unaware of her whereabouts. Mrs. Stover brought up a further problem in connection with running the household. She is now getting more interested in housework and cooking. She is realizing how little she knows about cooking. She attempted to cook a goose for the family, but due to improper cleaning of the goose beforehand, spoiled it. She claims the food that she knows how to prepare is plain and unattractive and she feels she is lacking in knowledge of skill in cooking. The children do some

complaining about the food, George recently pointing out that other children he knows get more variety than he does. It was arranged that I will bring a recipe file for Mrs. Stover containing a large variety of recipes and some instructions on food preparation and menus. Mrs. Stover is also interested in tackling her budget problems in a more organized fashion, and felt she would use budget envelopes from the agency in which she would keep track of her expenses for two months, to gain a more accurate idea of where her money is going.

NOVEMBER 10. VISIT TO MRS. STOVER
BY APPOINTMENT

She indicated that since starting divorce action she has been feeling edgy and had trouble sleeping last night. Mrs. Stover feels she has a need to get married. After divorce it is open season, and there is some danger that she would make another mistake, although she reiterates that she is through with men. Mrs. Stover feels that the first step is one of getting used to living without a man in the household. She feels that possibly she picks husbands of the kind she does because she feels sorry for them. Her father was a man who needed reforming. At this point I relayed information that I had from her family's record regarding her father, to the effect that he was a smooth dapper man who was openly unfaithful to his wife and had an alcoholic problem. Then Mrs. Stover said this described him to a T. She realizes also that her mother was trying to reform her father and perhaps Mrs. Stover is doing the same thing. She expressed considerable hostility toward her father, pointing out that it was all take on his part and no give. Her mother played right into this attitude since she rushed around doing everything for him without too much protest and never drew the line. Mrs. Stover has had the attitude too, that a man is someone who bosses you around and she feels she expects this from men and obeys them. She feels that she catered to her husband, did everything possible to pacify, didn't complain about his drinking, didn't draw the line for him beyond which he couldn't go or she would terminate the marriage. Instead of this she let the abuse go on without really facing him with it until she finally ran out on the situation. She related this again to her mother, pointing out that her mother was just as much at fault as her father. She indicated she realized this as an adolescent. She became aware that her mother needn't take everything she took from the father, but in fact was encouraging him in his behavior by being too forgiving. Mrs. Stover is sure that this has been her pattern in relation to men also.

She brought up that realizing all these things about herself makes her feel guilty, edgy, and anxious. This morning she feels better but didn't sleep very well last night. At least she is now not as doubtful as before about what she wants to do. I pointed out that her anxiety is a natural part of finding out things about herself. Mrs. Stover then brought up that she still has ambivalent periods about her husband being away. She describes this as a feeling of loneliness and realization that by just saying the words she could have him back, and at times she is tempted to do this. However, she has held the line firmly, and as she accomplished a little more on her own and the care of the children, she has less of this feeling of wanting him back. At the moment she realizes the need for larger housing since there is no privacy for George. She handles periods of anxiety by getting busy in the apartment, housecleaning, preparing meals, or sewing. Time doesn't hang heavily on her hands especially with her young children. She feels that she is now giving them more attention than ever and maybe giving Peter too much attention. During the period at his grandmother's he got used to having somebody playing frequently and interrupts her housework to do this. Mrs. Stover's own tendency with the children has been to do too much for them. Larie hasn't yet fully learned how to dress herself and Mrs. Stover recognizes this is because Mrs. Stover has taken too much responsibility for this herself.

I posed for Mrs. Stover the question of what she has been looking for in the husband, what does she feel she wants. Mrs. Stover feels she has been wanting someone to look after her, who would in a sense be a good father for her. She laughed about this, recognizing how far she had deviated from that in her actual choice of husbands.

NOVEMBER 25. HOME VISIT TO MRS. STOVER BY APPOINTMENT

Mrs. Stover was in the middle of moving, was up high on a ladder installing curtains and so I did not prolong the interview. Mrs. Stover, however, wanted to tell me about a new angle that has occurred to her. She pointed out that this is the first time that she has lived alone with her children following disruptions of her marriages. Before that she always went home to mother and from mother's home she picked up with another man. When Mrs. Stover came to the present building where she was living, her mother told her that she would be lonely living by herself, that she would never make a go of it, that she ought to stay in the mother's home. Mrs. Stover realized that this was typical of her mother's attitude. There is some tendency here for her mother to keep her tied to her, and Mrs. Stover recognized that she was a willing participant in this. She has never felt capable of managing her own life or making decisions on her own and has had to turn to her mother all through her life for even small decisions. She made moving to her present apartment a sort of test case, since she took the decision herself and made a point of not telling anybody about it until after she had rented the larger apartment. After doing this she acted as if she had really taken a step on her own and accomplished something. She then described how she was "the good little girl" at the home all her life. From an early age her mother seemed to expect her to take a lot of responsibility for caring for her younger brother and later her sister. She changed, dressed, and bathed them when they were toddlers, though at the time she was only 9 or 10 herself. Part of this was due to the fact that her mother was frequently sick. When Mrs. Stover was in grade 10, her mother was ill in the hospital for a considerable time, during which she left Mrs. Stover, who was then 15, with the total responsibility for the household. The father also expected her to function as the mistress of the home. This situation was intolerable for her, and it was at this time that she got involved with her first husband and became pregnant by him. He was an older man who offered her companionship. He seemed to take it for granted that she would sleep with him and she did. At the time, she felt she acted largely on impulse, meeting her needs or the man's needs without much thought given to it. Her first marriage was a runaway marriage and only lasted for a few days. The mother had been in bed around this time for one year with "bad legs." Mrs. Stover recalls at this time trying to cook the meals and run the house and hating to come home from school every day. Whenever she got a chance she stuck her nose in a book. She recognizes that reading has always been an escape to her. Now she doesn't read for this purpose as much, however. Her first husband seemed at first to offer her affection and wouldn't endlessly criticize her as the father did.

DECEMBER 8. VISIT WITH MRS. STOVER
BY APPOINTMENT

I suggested during a telephone conversation that we review where we had got to date; Mrs. Stover had accepted this.

On my arrival for the interview she started by pointing out her new apartment which has a large living room, kitchen, and two bedrooms, and will permit George to have his own room where he can be later on joined by Peter. Mrs. Stover deliberately made the decision without advance consultation with her mother, which she used to always do, or with myself. She felt this was something of a gain in itself since she used to have so much trouble making decisions.

Mrs. Stover also mentioned that the children are getting more attention than they used to. In fact she feels they may be getting too much attention, particularly Peter who she probably spoils. I didn't at this point pick up on this, but inquired in what other ways did Mrs. Stover feel that changes had occurred.

Mrs. Stover said that she feels more secure with herself. This is the first time she has ever had her own place. When her marriages failed in the past, she always went back to mother.

I raised the question with Mrs. Stover of how she felt she had been able to change this. Mrs. Stover mentioned first the fact that she has nice neighbors. They are friendly, cooperate with her, and she gets a real feeling of support from them. For example, the family across the hall, who have a car, take her shopping in order to permit her to buy her things at a supermarket, since there is no supermarket in the immediate area.

Along this same line Mrs. Stover brought up the fact that she had some activity with the school. Mrs. Stover laughingly commented "I'm all tangled up with the school around planning parties." The school had asked the assistance of some parents to act as "party room mothers" to help look after the children. Mrs. Stover and a neighbor, Mrs. Kirby, had gone to the school to do this and have been asked by the school to recruit 11 more mothers to act in this capacity. Mrs. Stover has been on the phone a lot about this. While it is a chore and a nuisance, she enjoys it, and she has a lot of respect for the school principal. It makes her feel good to know the school trusts her with such a job.

In response to my further questions as to why Mrs. Stover feels she is functioning differently, Mrs. Stover mentioned her increased self-confidence. She related this to her contact with Family Service and AFDC branch, since the two agencies have demonstrated a lot of confidence with her. She said, "You must have this confidence in me or you wouldn't have spent as much time helping me as you did." This, Mrs. Stover states, has raised her own self-confidence and her feeling of being able to do things. She also used to lie awake at night worrying about whether her AFDC check was going to come. Now she doesn't do this. She described also, in relation to Family Service, a feeling of having someone available to her if things did go wrong or get difficult.

Mrs. Stover also brought up some negatives. She said for one thing thinking about herself makes her feel like "she is peeking inside other people." At times it makes her edgy and nervous. She sees other people making the same mistakes and having the same problems she did. This sometimes makes her uncomfortable. Then she either wants to leave such people or doesn't feel relaxed with them.

Mrs. Stover went on to discuss her concern about Eileen who next fall will be old enough to start school. Mrs. Stover doubts if this will be possible, however, because of Eileen's clinging to her mother. Mrs. Stover said that Eileen simply can't keep up with the other children nor can she follow their games.

In response to my question, Mrs. Stover clarified that her concern at this point is not with Eileen's present behavior so much as the fact that it may be difficult to get her started in any kind of educational program next fall. She hopes to use the time between now and next fall to foster a little independence in Eileen. I supported this idea pointing out several ways in which Mrs. Stover could achieve this; through encouraging Eileen in outdoor play, deliberately conditioning her to stay with the neighbor for short periods of time at first which could be lengthened later, provided the neighbor was willing to help with this plan. I also suggested giving Eileen a good deal of encouragement for anything she can accomplish, since she is aware of her inability to keep up with the other children.

I suggested that over the next few months plans be worked out to have Eileen get an aptitude test at the school's Guidance Office, and if necessary, disclose the possibility of Eileen's enrolling in the nursery school for retarded children. Mrs. Stover was skeptical about this plan. She wasn't sure she wanted to ask the school about this. Worker pointed out that this was the way she felt about AFDC too, and things worked out better when she bared her problems with them.

JANUARY 16
Telephone call from Mrs. Stover inquiring whether I thought she should move. She has been offered an apartment in the same building a floor above her existing apartment, that is cleaner, with more closet space and would have more privacy for George and more living space in general. Mrs. Stover wound up by wondering if I ought to look at it and approve the new apartment that she was considering. I indicated willingness to do this but said that I was quite willing to trust her own decision on the matter.

JANUARY 19
Mrs. Stover announced that she had thought over the decision about moving and decided against it. The thing that had decided her against it had been the fact that as soon as she talked it over with the children she noticed that they became very anxious and edgy. She noticed this in all of the children except Peter. This made her realize the extent to which the children had been upset by the moves she had in the past, together with her other troubles, and she said, "I figured I'd be losing more than I gained by moving now." Mrs. Stover had also been concerned about the fire hazard about living on the third floor, had recently heard an opinion quoted by the fire marshal to the effect that the old building is a big firetrap and would burn rapidly. This is a special problem for Mrs. Stover since she has not only Peter but Eileen to be treated like a baby in a situation of this kind.

JANUARY 25. HOME VISIT BY APPOINTMENT
Mrs. Stover at this point was involved in washing, explaining that she has been borrowing the neighbor's washing machine and taking it whenever she can get it.

I explained to Mrs. Stover her eligibility for supplementary assistance from AFDC for a washing machine and outlined the procedure. Mrs. Stover was initially lukewarm to this idea. I raised the question with her as to why she was reluctant. Mrs. Stover expressed ideas which she had also expressed at an earlier time, that is, that it wasn't smart to ask AFDC worker for too much, the less you ask them for the better off you are and so on. I took issue with this, pointing out that this seems to be part of a larger problem; AFDC is aimed at enabling her to bring up children, and its purpose can be frustrated unless she takes responsibility for letting AFDC worker know of needs. The latter cannot anticipate everybody's needs in advance. Mrs. Stover accepted this, brought up that she is expecting a visit from the AFDC worker and will let me know result of this.

Mrs. Stover brought out that she enjoys the job of calling the parents for the school party. This makes her feel that she is helping the school out.

I mentioned PTA as an aid to any feelings of isolation which Mrs. Stover might have as a result of being tied down, new in the district, and so forth. Mrs. Stover said she liked the idea of PTA or something which will "broaden my life out a little bit," but at the same time her family keeps her busy; time if anything goes too fast. She does have considerable association with adults through the immediate neighbors. She didn't really know about PTA.

FEBRUARY 8

Mrs. Stover had had a visit from AFDC worker, who according to Mrs. Stover didn't like the apartment because of the lack of play space for the children. Mrs. Stover had raised problem of washing machine and bedding with the AFDC worker who said to make arrangements to get the bedding on time payments if necessary, paying for it out of her household allowance included in the AFDC budget. Mrs. Stover has gone ahead and done this. She is awaiting a chance to get the three estimates on the washing machine which I had discussed with her and which had been confirmed by AFDC worker.

Mr. Stover had sent toys for the children in a surprise move. He had sent them through his mother, who had delivered them. Mrs. Stover had accepted them without question because she thought the mother-in-law possibly didn't know from Mr. Stover that Mrs. Stover was averse to taking anything from him. Mrs. Stover was very angry that Mr. Stover had used deception in this manner. I wondered if Mrs. Stover could explain her attitude in this matter of fact manner as soon as possible to the mother-in-law to prevent the latter from being used as a go-between in the future. Mrs. Stover accepted this idea. She is on good terms with the mother-in-law and feels she could explain the whole situation to her quite readily.

MARCH 15

Mrs. Stover says she has again been troubled by Mr. Stover phoning the lady upstairs. I made a suggestion to Mrs. Stover for handling these calls as follows: Ask the person calling to leave his name and number. If he calls again, that she encourage the neighbor to tell him that she is not taking any more calls for Mrs. Stover. Mrs. Stover seemed pleased at this plan.

MARCH 22

Mrs. Stover said that Eileen is starting to go outside on her own without being urged by Mrs. Stover. Mrs. Stover since our recent clarification had felt

more relaxed about this and is letting Eileen also go out on the back porch. She formerly had done this, but kept running out every few minutes. I brought out again that I thought there was an intermediate stage between school and home; that is, a stage in which Eileen would have a place to go to develop a range of activity beyond the home and be able to play with the other children.

Mrs. Stover said she feels more confident that this sort of thing can be done now and that much of the problem was probably her own attitude toward Eileen. She brought up the possibility of East School summer program for prekindergarten children which she had heard about last year. The idea of this program as Mrs. Stover understands it is to give the children some experience of being away from their parents and getting used to the school building. This has been discussed at the last PTA meeting that Mrs. Stover had attended. These meetings take place in the afternoons at the school. At the next meeting Mrs. Stover is planning to go 15 minutes early to see the teacher about Larie's progress in kindergarten. The plan is that she will take Eileen with her, and during the interview with the teacher, Eileen will play with the group of other children at the school.

George is continuing to get good school reports but does not like school work in some of its aspects. He doesn't like writing stuff down.

I asked how she handles this and she said she tries to encourage George to recognize that school can't be all pleasurable activities, nor will he necessarily like all of his teachers. The thing for him to do is to try to cultivate an attitude of putting up with these unpleasant aspects, because there are so many things about school he likes. I supported Mrs. Stover in this, pointing out the desirability of consistently encouraging George in responsible attitudes.

APRIL 12

Mrs. Stover discussed the Easter party at school and her taking Eileen. The teacher had noticed that Eileen was attached to her mother. Eileen nonetheless went cheerfully to play with the other children and allowed Mrs. Stover to go in and see the teacher by herself. The teacher had said also that from talking to Eileen she feels that Eileen should be able to start with the others in kindergarten. The teacher had apparently liked Eileen and felt she would be very glad to have her in the class. She had indicated to Mrs. Stover that at the end of the kindergarten year a decision could be made regarding a special class for Eileen.

Mrs. Stover wanted to tell me also that there has been some good development regarding her AFDC. Her AFDC worker had said that "the welfare had found Mrs. Stover could be relied on." Mrs. Stover was very pleased about this. The welfare also got her a washing machine, Mrs. Stover having finally got the three estimates.

APRIL 15

Psychological report received regarding Eileen. Eileen scored at the borderline defective intelligence level in this examination, with an IQ of 74.

APRIL 18. VISIT TO MRS. STOVER BY APPOINTMENT

This interview was taken up with a discussion of a report from the psychologist which I had brought with me. In going over the report it became evident that Mrs. Stover was having a good deal of difficulty accepting the report that Eileen is developmentally disabled.

In relation to planning a school program based on the report, Mrs. Stover felt that she would like to take the teacher up on her statement that she felt Eileen could do well and the teacher could do well with Eileen in the kindergarten group the first year, followed by an evaluation of progress and the probability of a special class or school after that. Mrs. Stover prefers this class to possible use of the nursery for developmentally disabled children.

MAY 3. HOME VISIT BY APPOINTMENT

Mrs. Stover began the interview by some further remarks regarding Eileen. She felt the last two discussions had helped clarify her own thinking regarding this problem. She said she feels more relaxed with Eileen and Eileen is continuing to play outside a good deal with other children.

I raised the problem of her plans about the divorce. How does she feel about this at this point? Mrs. Stover said that she still feels that it

may as well sit. She had not had much recent trouble with Mr. Stover and is hoping that he had decided not to bother her. She would take divorce action only if she had more trouble with Mr. Stover at least for the present. In the meantime, she is keeping her mind closed on the whole subject.

Mrs. Stover went on to say that she would like some further help in future interviews with the problem of raising her kids. At the moment she is concerned about George, who is having problems in school. He comes home at noon hour crying. She and one of George's teachers don't get along either. Mrs. Stover feels that this teacher is extremely punitive in her attitude toward George. She is rapping George over the knuckles with a ruler. On Monday of this week George had been ill and Mrs. Stover phoned the school explaining this, leaving word in the office. It had been arranged that Mrs. Stover would phone back when George was ready to return. She did this Tuesday morning as George returned to school. Later in the morning Mrs. Stover received a call from the teacher claiming that George was playing hookey, though it was subsequently verified that George was in school. George didn't even have a class with the teacher that morning. Mrs. Stover argued that it was none of her business. George had recently made a mistake on his arithmetic calculations and the teacher made him stay after school and do them over 200 times each. Shortly after this she had sent home a paper to Mrs. Stover which she had refused to mark because the writing was too faint. Mrs. Stover showed the paper to me and the writing was quite legible and clear. As a result of this George had had to do these calculations a total of 600 times. George says that when he gets out of school "he feels like killing somebody." As a result of what Mrs. Stover believes is the punitive treatment of George by the teacher, George is now taking the attitude "to heck with school." Mrs. Stover says that George really knows he has no choice in the matter of attending school, nor is he at all likely to truant.

I picked up on this offering to visit the school and to review the problem with the principal and the school social worker, with Mrs. Stover present or not as she desired. In advance of this we could work how best to present the problem to the school in such a way as not to make it strictly as a complaint against the teacher but put it on the basis of concern about George and his discouragement about the school situation. Mrs. Stover said she liked this idea except that she felt she wanted to try this out on her own; she felt she could use the approach which I had suggested and do it herself.

This led to a discussion of how she should handle this with George. To this point Mrs. Stover had been very careful not to side completely with George and point the teacher up as the villian. When he comes home crying she puts her arm around him and comforts him. On the other hand she has tried to help him see that he is likely to meet other teachers like this one, that this is part of going to school. George has wanted a transfer to another school but at this point she thinks it is too late in the year. I supported Mrs. Stover in her stand with George and her plan to go to the school to discuss it.

MAY 10

Mrs. Stover was quite angry at Public Welfare, bringing out that her budget has been reduced by $15 a month. She talked in terms of going off AFDC and going to work. I asked her to examine this carefully in terms of what it would mean to her to try to manage the children and work at the same time, and what it would mean also of her relationship with the children, how much she could give them, and so on. I concurred in the idea of her working as a long-term goal but suggested very careful consideration of this as something she could do soon. After this Mrs. Stover calmed down and said she realized this was not a constructive thing to do. I thereupon brought up the possibility of using a home economist as a consultant to help Mrs. Stover get the most out of her present budget. Mrs. Stover said, "I'm all for that," but added that she felt she is managing pretty economically at present. She doesn't see where she is going to manage with a $15 decrease.

I later saw the home economist briefly and a joint visit with home economist was planned for May 24.

MAY 25

Brief home visit, taking clothing supplied by home economist, including a dress for Mrs. Stover, three small comforters for the younger children, a jacket for Eileen.

JUNE 6. VISIT TO MRS. STOVER BY APPOINTMENT

We initially discussed Mrs. Stover's arrangements with the home economist regarding the budget. Mrs. Stover said, "She showed me how I could cover all my expenses and a little extra." She added that she hoped this could be done, but she remained somewhat skeptical. She currently planned, however, to give this a try and to confer further with the home economist on any difficulties that come up.

She has recently heard indirectly that Mr. Stover is planning to get married. His son by an earlier marriage lives just a short distance down the street from Mrs. Stover's present location. I inquired what Mrs. Stover's reaction to this information was and she said she feels greatly relieved. It had made her feel that she was free of him, and had also made her realize the extent to which she still had a feeling of protectiveness toward him, and a feeling of responsibility of him. She felt she had come to realize that it was this more than anything else that had been a barrier to her taking divorce action. This latest news takes the decision out of her hands, and she agreed with my comment that she feels that it gets her off the hook. She had always had some sort of feeling that it was her duty to stay with Mr. Stover no matter what he did, since he needed to be looked after.

I asked where does Mrs. Stover feel she is at with this problem at the moment. Mrs. Stover went on to talk in terms of her former pattern of running away from one situation into a worse one. She wouldn't allow anybody to help her or to get close enough to her to help her. She feels now she understands more why she got into this series of messes and is less apt to jump before she looks. She cites her impulse to throw over AFDC as an example of how she used to operate, but now she stops and thinks before she makes a decision of this kind.

Mrs. Stover went on to talk about her present feeling of having something of her own and the fact that she is not afraid any more of losing it. She feels comfortable also in her attitude toward men of not having anything to do with them. She said, "My way of looking at a man now is in terms of what can he give me as a husband that is better than what I've got now. So far I haven't met anybody who I thought could measure up to this." She is not going to feel any responsibility to save a man.

Here she went on to add that she continues in her former attitude that she and men just don't mix, that basically she has no use for men and this would prevent her ever having a productive relationship with a man. On the other hand, she does worry about the effects of her extreme dislike of men and her frank prejudices toward men on the children; she doesn't want the girls to be prejudiced against men, and she has an adolescent boy.

I introduced the idea of discussing in the future interviews the specific methods she may use in teaching the children about such matters and in cultivating attitudes toward men.

JUNE 14

I further raised with Mrs. Stover the question of her instruction of the children. I went over some material abstracted from a recent book dealing with attitudes of adolescents toward the opposite sex. This was done by way of introducing Mrs. Stover to the book and the possibility of her using it with George. Mrs. Stover said that she felt the book would be useful to her. The children do not volunteer much in this area nor do they ask many questions. She tried to deal with these on a factual basis as they come up.

Mrs. Stover indicated that she feels it is her own attitudes that are important. Nonetheless, she can perhaps avoid giving the children a biased attitude toward men. I suggested presenting Mr. Stover and his problems in as favorable a light as possible to the children, attempting to avoid running him down. Mrs. Stover thought this would be quite possible for her. The children speak little of Mr. Stover but seem settled in the attitude that he doesn't want to be with the family. George shows some resentment, occasionally commenting that they are better off now than they were when Mr. Stover was in the family. Mrs. Stover felt she could make use of my suggestion of using occasions when George makes

remarks of this kind to point out that Mr. Stover has his problems too, but also has his good points, and it was more a matter of can't rather than didn't want to be a father to the family.

JUNE 28. VISIT TO MRS. STOVER BY APPOINTMENT

Mrs. Stover was flying around in a complete dither and made the remark, "I ain't going to talk to you long." To my inquiry as to what had happened Mrs. Stover said that the other day her AFDC worker had informed Mrs. Stover that her apartment is not a fit place for the children to live. She had told Mrs. Stover to go to the housing project and to apply for an apartment. Mrs. Stover had done this and had been told that there was an apartment available and that she should be prepared to move in three days. Mrs. Stover talked at first as though she hadn't been given any choice in the matter. When I inquired about this, however, she agreed that it is her decision as to whether or not she goes to the housing project. She clarified that she feels that it is circumstances that are forcing her into moving so quickly. By this she means that she has to take an apartment while it can be got.

Later Mrs. Stover phoned again, wanting to know if I had any information as to why the county might have held up her check since she did not receive it. Later Mrs. Stover found out that the check had been sent to her new address by the county, but since Mrs. Stover's name was not on the mailbox, the check had been returned. It will now be sent back to her again and it will likely be two or three days before Mrs. Stover receives it. Mrs. Stover is angry at AFDC again as she says the workers told her that she couldn't say when this would be since it takes a variable amount of time, and had advised Mrs. Stover not to get too excited about it, that to make such a big fuss over a check being late was neurotic.

JULY 6. HOME VISIT TO MRS. STOVER'S NEW APARTMENT IN THE HOUSING PROJECTS

The family has a two-bedroom unit, Mrs. Stover and the girls having one room and the boys having the other.

The interview consisted of a review of Mrs. Stover's current difficulties with AFDC and a discussion of future plans around vacation and possible termination.

The most recent incident has aroused considerable fresh hostility in Mrs. Stover toward the AFDC, since she stoutly maintains that she told the worker that the check should be mailed to her new address. Mrs. Stover said, "I can't do anything with the Welfare." Whatever they try to plan together, hitches develop. At this point she was making a joke about having been called neurotic, explaining that the previous day she and her mother and sisters and the children had gone on an outing, and the joke of the day amongst her mother and sisters had been don't go near June, she's neurotic. A further difficulty that developed was the fact that when the family got to the apartment the electricity was not connected. Two days later the company had come out and connected it on the date of deposit.

We then tried to analyze the difficulties with AFDC from the point of view of Mrs. Stover's part in them. I pointed out that with her dealings with our agency she showed good capacity to plan, and why was there this difference? Mrs. Stover, in thinking about it felt that it might be a matter that she has greater feeling about the AFDC and that in her doings with AFDC she is tense and more apt to fly off the handle, partly from past conflict with the welfare and partly from the fact that the AFDC is in a sense a more authoritative position with her than is Family Service, since they have what she feels is absolute control over the purse strings. Mrs. Stover agrees that being in this frame of mind, she is especially likely to have misunderstanding or antagonism with the AFDC. On the other hand, she feels that the agency contributes to this itself by the hurried manner in which everything is handled, the fact that AFDC workers come to her place unexpectedly to see her, often catching her off guard, and come up with things such as the order to move to the new apartment, which seemed to come out of the blue. On top of this, Mrs. Stover feels pushed around by AFDC, maintaining she was told that she would have to move to public housing development. Mrs. Stover sees no solution at present, of feeling that she never hit it off with welfare and finds it difficult to visualize the time when she ever

will. Her current attitude is that the best thing is to do what they tell her, try to avoid breaking any regulations, and keep out of trouble.

Mrs. Stover said she guessed the main thing in her dealings with AFDC would be to try to keep from getting excited and losing her head, realizing that she is more prone to do this by virtue of the past relationship with AFDC. The remainder of the interview consisted of a discussion of future plans and goals. Mrs. Stover was aware of coming vacation plan and the possibility of termination we had discussed several times earlier. Mrs. Stover gave some evaluation at this point of what she thought the relationship with Family Service means to her. She sees it largely as a control on impulsive behavior. Before acting she phones me and I help her think the thing through so that she acts in a more planned way and not on the spur of the moment. Despite her recent difficulties with the AFDC, she feels there has been real improvement to the point where they at least have greater trust in her and she some greater trust in them. Then, too, she has had less difficulty with her husband for a long time, and has a feeling of having made some progress in getting Eileen ready for a more wholesome school experience when the time comes. In the light of all this she feels that objectively considered, her situation is better and she can probably handle it more easily than she could before. The vacation could be a kind of planned period to see how she manages, and tentative appointment was set for follow-up visit in August.

AUGUST 30

The interview consisted of a review of the earlier plan of termination. Mrs. Stover obviously had mixed feelings about it. On the one hand she reiterates her former sentiments about having fewer problems, being better able to manage with them at this point. She is now meeting things that she had difficulty in handling or that threw her. On the other hand, her tie to the agency implies some security for her, inasmuch as she knows that if things do take a downturn, she can always turn to the agency. I explained that she could do this in any case, but she is wanting us to hold it open, and it was agreed that this would be done at least for the present.

SEPTEMBER 18
The school social worker telephoned regarding Eileen. Mrs. Stover started Eileen in kindergarten at the beginning of this month. It was noted that the school's health record shows that Eileen has muscular dystrophy, and the teacher had spoken to the social worker about this, wanting further clarification of it. It was also the teacher's observation that Eileen showed no ability to relate to other children in her group. Eileen is, after all, only four to begin with and won't be five until October, but Mrs. Stover had, during her visits to the school last May and June, talked the problem over with the school staff, and they had agreed to start Eileen.

I clarified the medical diagnosis with the social worker. The school social worker felt that continuing Eileen in kindergarten might also be good in view of the problem of the mother's overprotection of Eileen and the fact that the mother is trying to overcome this and has been working on it for some months. If Eileen's limitations are accepted in the group and not much is expected of her in way of either skills or sociability for the present, it is quite likely that she will be able to make some kind of an adjustment to the kindergarten situation. Failing this, the possibility of Eileen's admission to a school for retarded children should be considered. Matters were left that the school social worker will call us further in about six weeks, and that period will be used to see how Eileen gets along.

Later in the day I dropped in on Mrs. Stover to discuss the school's report. Mrs. Stover said that she recognized Eileen is behind the group in sociability, and we briefly reviewed the report which we had obtained in April regarding her intellectual state.

At the same time, Mrs. Stover was pleased Eileen had been able to separate herself from the mother and also from Larie without apparent difficulty. Her immediate reaction is that she wants to visit the school soon and see the teacher and get more information on it for herself.

A further visit will be planned for a month's time after Mrs. Stover has had a chance to visit the school. Despite the previous plan to terminate, both Mrs. Stover and the school are at this time wanting the agency to stay at least until the matter of Eileen's problem has been worked out.

SUMMARY. OCTOBER 18 THROUGH DECEMBER 1
Mrs. Stover had visited the school in October and got a very favorable report on Eileen. Mrs. Stover said the teacher told her that Eileen cannot comprehend things with the rest of the children, but her behavior is not abnormal nor does it in any way hamper the class or harm the other children. Eileen plays very little with the other children though she is beginning to make some tentative overtures to them according to Mrs. Stover. On the other hand the teacher was reassuring and talked to Mrs. Stover about this, pointing out that lots of children play by themselves in the classroom situation. On November 16 a further brief report was received from the school social worker which confirmed the information that came from Mrs. Stover.

SUMMARY. DECEMBER 1 THROUGH JANUARY 8
The two interviews during this period with Mrs. Stover were concerned largely with working through her feelings about the agency closing its case.

In the midst of her conflict about worker's leaving, another incident reactivated Mrs. Stover's hostilities toward the AFDC. This led to a lengthy discussion of how Mrs. Stover has been in a family which has been on welfare as far back as she can remember and had built up certain more or less fixed attitudes toward the welfare agency. These included a feeling of being pushed around, worthless, and not treated as an individual. She heartily agreed with my point that partly this stemmed from being chronically on the receiving end and never having a feeling of being able to give to others. In addition Mrs. Stover's belief in the welfare agency as an almost all-powerful agency, which is apt to do anything without any explanation, seems unshakable at this point.

FEBRUARY 15. LAST VISIT

In this termination interview Mrs. Stover summed up her feelings as follows: "We've changed in the fact that we are more settled, more of a family instead of five people. Each is different, that is to be expected, but we are more united, kind of. That's the biggest change, more secure in ourselves as a family. Larie and George and I each worried about ourselves instead of all of us. Now it isn't so much a personal worry as how is this family going to get along. We think of the good of the family rather than for each one. It's not so much what you've said and done as what you've listened to. I could talk things over and sort them out, kind of. I could bring up things that I wouldn't ordinarily be able to tell people. If I told these things to others, they would get all mixed up in my problem, but you don't.

I think too, I've found out there is always a reason for the way welfare acts. And, if I try I can usually find out what it is. And the school is so much help to me with Eileen. They trust me."

ENTRY FOR RECORD

April 23

Call received from Mrs. Stover and telephone referral done to Miss Bithy, social worker at the school for retarded regarding Eileen.

ENTRY FOR RECORD

June 17

Call from school social worker to report on the family. The school has been asking, "What kind of casework did Mrs. Stover receive?" There has been remarkable change in the children. Physical care greatly improved. Larie is described as "top girl in her class." Eileen has made a great deal of progress in relating to other children. School wondering what has happened to account for the change. The social worker and I agreed that it is a cumulation of things over two years rather than anything recent and dramatic. She will talk further to the teachers. Later telephoned Mrs. Stover and relayed the school's message. She was very pleased and said that she herself notices a big change in Eileen. Application is pending for Eileen's admission to the School for Retarded Children.

ENTRY FOR RECORD

September 11

Mrs. Stover called to say Eileen enrolled at the School for Retarded Children and enjoying the experience. She is very tired when she gets home. She leaves the home readily, however, in the morning, much to the surprise of Mrs. Stover.

Reading A-7 *The House on Sixth Street**

Francis P. Purcell and Harry Specht

The extent to which social work can affect the course of social problems has not received the full consideration it deserves.[1] For some time the social

* Copyright 1965, National Association of Social Workers, Inc. Reprinted with permission, from *Social Work,* vol. 10, no. 4 (October 1965), pp. 69–76.

[1] Social work practitioners sometimes use the term *social problem* to mean "environmental problem." The sense in which it is used here corresponds to the definition developed by the social sciences. That is, a social problem is a disturbance, deviation, or breakdown in social behavior that (1) involves a considerable number of people and (2) is of serious concern to many in the society. It is social in origin and effect, and is a social responsibility. It represents a discrepancy between social standards and social reality. Also, such socially perceived variations must be viewed as corrigible (see Merton & Nisbet, 1961, pp. 6, 701).

work profession has taken account of social problems only as they have become manifest in behavioral pathology. Yet it is becoming increasingly apparent that, even allowing for this limitation, it is often necessary for the same agency or worker to intervene by various methods at various points.

In this paper, the case history of a tenement house in New York City is used to illustrate some of the factors that should be considered in selecting intervention methods. Like all first attempts, the approach described can be found wanting in conceptual clarity and systematization. Yet the vital quality of the effort and its implications for social work practice seem clear.

THE PROBLEM

"The House on Sixth Street" became a case when Mrs. Smith came to an MFY Neighborhood Service Center to complain that there had been no gas, electricity, heat, or hot water in her apartment house for more than four weeks. She asked the agency for help. Mrs. Smith was 23 years old, black, and the mother of four children, three of whom had been born out of wedlock. At the time she was unmarried and receiving Aid to Families with Dependent Children. She came to the center in desperation because she was unable to run her household without utilities. Her financial resources were exhausted—but not her courage. The Neighborhood Service Center worker decided that in this case the building—the tenants, the landlord, and circumstances affecting their relationships—was of central concern.

A social worker then visited the Sixth Street building with Mrs. Smith and a community worker. Community workers are members of the community organization staff in a program that attempts to encourage residents to take independent social action. Like many members in other MFY programs, community workers are residents of the particular neighborhood. Most of them have little formal education, their special contribution being their ability to relate to and communicate with other residents. Because some of the tenants were Puerto Rican, a Spanish-speaking community worker was chosen to accompany the social worker. His easy manner and knowledge of the neighborhood enabled him and the worker to become involved quickly with the tenants.

Their first visits confirmed Mrs. Smith's charge that the house had been without utilities for more than four weeks. Several months before, the city Rent and Rehabilitation Administration had reduced the rent for each apartment to one dollar a month because the landlord was not providing services. However, this agency was slow to take further action. Eleven families were still living in the building, which had twenty-eight apartments. The landlord owed the electric company several

thousand dollars. Therefore, the meters had been removed from the house. Because most of the tenants were welfare clients, the Department of Welfare had "reimbursed" the landlord directly for much of the unpaid electric bill and refused to pay any more money to the electric company. The Department of Welfare was slow in meeting the emergency needs of the tenants. Most of the children (forty-eight from the eleven families in the building) had not been to school for a month because they were ill or lacked proper clothing.

The mothers were tired and demoralized. Dirt and disorganization were increasing daily. The tenants were afraid to sleep at night because the building was infested with rats. There was danger of fire because the tenants had to use candles for light. The seventeen abandoned apartments had been invaded by homeless men and drug addicts. Petty thievery is common in such situations. However, the mothers did not want to seek protection from the police for fear that they would chase away all men who were not part of the families in the building (some of the unmarried mothers had men living with them—one of the few means of protection from physical danger available to these women—even though mothers on public assistance are threatened with loss of income if they are not legally married). The anxiety created by these conditions was intense and disabling.

The workers noted that the mothers were not only anxious but "fighting mad"; not only did they seek immediate relief from their physical dangers and discomforts but they were eager to express their fury at the landlord and the public agencies, which they felt had let them down.

The effect of such hardships on children is obvious. Of even greater significance is the sense of powerlessness generated when families go into these struggles barehanded. It is this sense of helplessness in the face of adversity that induces pathological anxiety, intergenerational alienation, and social retreatism. Actual physical impoverishment alone is not nearly so debilitating as poverty attended by a sense of unrelieved impotence that becomes generalized and internalized. The poor then regard much social learning as irrelevant, since they do not believe it can effect any environmental change (Purcell, 1964, p. 432).

INTERVENTION AND THE SOCIAL SYSTEMS

Selecting a point of intervention in dealing with this problem would have been simpler if the target of change were Mrs. Smith alone, or Mrs. Smith and her co-tenants, the clients in whose behalf intervention was planned. Too often, the client system presenting the problem becomes the major target for intervention, and the intervention method is limited to the one most suitable for that client system. However, Mrs. Smith and the other tenants had a multitude of problems emanating from many sources, any one of which would have warranted the attention of a social agency. The circumstantial fact that an individual contacts an agency that offers services to individuals and families should not be a major factor in determining the method of intervention. Identification of the client merely helps the agency to define goals; other variables are involved in the selection of method. As Burns and Glasser (1963) have suggested:

> It may be helpful to consider the primary target of change as distinct from the persons who may be the primary clients. . . . The primary target of change then becomes the human or physical environment toward which professional efforts via direct intervention are aimed in order to facilitate change. (p. 423)

The three major factors that determined MFY's approach to the problem were (1) knowledge of the various social systems within which the social problem was located (i.e., social systems assessment), (2) knowledge of the various methods (including non-social work methods) appropriate for intervention in these different social systems, and (3) the resources available to the agency (Specht & Reissman, 1963).

The difficulties of the families in the building were intricately connected with other elements of the social system related to the housing problem. For example, seven different public agencies were involved in maintenance of building services. Later other agencies were involved in relocating the tenants. There is no one agency in New York City that handles all housing problems. Therefore, tenants have little hope of getting help on their own. In order to redress a grievance relating to water supply (which was only one of the building's many problems) it is necessary to know precisely which city department to contact. The following is only a partial listing:

1. No water—Health Department
2. Not enough water—Department of Water Supply
3. No hot water—Buildings Department
4. Water leaks—Buildings Department
5. Large water leaks—Department of Water Supply
6. Water overflowing from apartment above—Police Department
7. Water sewage in the cellar—Sanitation Department

The task of determining which agencies are responsible for code enforcement in various areas is not simple, and in addition one must know that the benefits and services available for tenants and for the community vary with the course of action chosen. For example, if the building were taken over by the Rent and Rehabilitation Administration under the receivership law, it would be several weeks before services would be re-established, and the tenants would have to remain in the building during its rehabilitation. There would be, however, some compensations: tenants could remain in the neighborhood—indeed, in the same building—and their children would not have to change schools. If, on the other hand, the house were condemned by the Buildings Department, the tenants would have to move, but they would be moved quickly and would receive top relocation priorities and maximum relocation benefits. But once the tenants had been relocated—at city expense—the building could be renovated by the landlord as middle-income housing. In the Sixth Street house, it was suspected that this was the motivation behind the landlord's actions. If the building were condemned and renovated, there would be twenty-eight fewer low-income housing units in the neighborhood.

It is obvious, even limiting analysis to the social systems of one tenement, that the problem is enormous. Although the tenants were the clients in this case, Mrs. Smith, the tenant group, and other community groups were all served at one point or another. It is even conceivable that the landlord might have been selected as the most appropriate recipient of service. Rehabilitation of many slum tenements is at present nearly impossible. Many landlords regard such property purely as an investment. With profit the prime motive, needs of low-income tenants are often overlooked. Under present conditions it is financially impossible for many landlords to correct all the violations in their buildings even if they wanted to. If the social worker chose to intervene at this level of the problem, he might apply to the Municipal Loan Fund, make arrangements with unions for the use of non-union labor in limited rehabilitation projects, or provide expert consultants on reconstruction. These tasks would require social workers to have knowledge similar to that of city planners. If the problems of landlords were not selected as a major point of intervention, they would still have to be considered at some time since they are an integral part of the social context within which this problem exists.

A correct definition of interacting social systems or of the social worker's choice of methods and points of intervention is not the prime concern here. What is to be emphasized is what this case so clearly demonstrates: that although the needs of the client system enable the agency to define its goals, the points and methods of intervention cannot be selected properly without an awareness and substantial knowledge of the social systems within which the problem is rooted.

DEALING WITH THE PROBLEM
The social worker remained with the building throughout a four-month period. In order to deal effectively with the problem, he had to make use of all the social work methods as well as the special talents of a community worker, lawyer, city planner, and various civil rights organizations. The social worker and the community worker functioned as generalists with both individuals and

families calling on caseworkers as needed for specialized services or at especially trying times, such as during the first week and when the families were relocated. Because of the division of labor in the agency, much of the social work with individuals was done with the help of a caseworker. Group work, administration, and community organization were handled by the social worker, who had been trained in community organization. In many instances he also dealt with the mothers as individuals, as they encountered one stressful situation after another. Agency caseworkers also provided immediate and concrete assistance to individual families, such as small financial grants, medical care, homemaking services, baby-sitting services, and transportation. This reduced the intensity of pressures on these families. Caseworkers were especially helpful in dealing with some of the knotty and highly technical problems connected with public agencies.

With a caseworker and a lawyer experienced in handling tenement cases, the social worker began to help the families organize their demands for the services and utilities to which they were legally entitled but which the public agencies had consistently failed to provide for them.

The ability of the mothers to take concerted group action was evident from the beginning, and Mrs. Smith proved to be a natural and competent leader. With support, encouragement, and assistance from the staff, the mothers became articulate and effective in negotiating with the various agencies involved. In turn, the interest and concern of the agencies increased markedly when the mothers began to visit them, make frequent telephone calls, and send letters and telegrams to them and to politicians demanding action.

With the lawyer and a city planner (an agency consultant), the mothers and staff members explored various possible solutions to the housing problem. For example, the Department of Welfare had offered to move the families to shelters or hotels. Neither alternative was acceptable to the mothers. Shelters were ruled out because they would not consider splitting up their families, and they rejected hotels because they had discovered from previous experience that many of the "hotels" selected were flop-houses or were inhabited by prostitutes.

The following is taken from the social worker's record during the first week:

> Met with the remaining tenants, several black men from the block, and [the city planner]. . . . Three of the mothers said that they would sooner sleep out on the street than go the Welfare shelter. If nothing else, they felt that this would be a way of protesting their plight . . . One of the mothers said that they couldn't very well do this with most of the children having colds. Mrs. Brown thought that they might do better to ask Reverend Jones if they could move into the cellar of his church temporarily. . . . The other mothers got quite excited about this idea because they thought that the church basement would make excellent living quarters.

After a discussion as to whether the mothers would benefit from embarrassing the public agencies by dramatically exposing their inadequacies, the mothers decided to move into the nearby church. They asked the worker to attempt to have their building condemned. At another meeting, attended by tenants from neighboring buildings and representatives of other local groups, it was concluded that what had happened to the Sixth Street building was a result of discrimination against the tenants as Puerto Ricans and blacks. The group—which had now become an organization—sent the following telegram to city, state, and federal officials:

> We are voters and Puerto Rican and black mothers asking for equal rights, for decent housing and enough room. Building has broken windows, no gas or electricity for four weeks, no heat or hot water, holes in floors, loose wiring. Twelve of forty-eight children in building sick. Welfare doctors refuse to walk up dark stairs. Are we human or what? Should innocent children suffer for landlords' brutality and city and state neglect? We are tired of being told to wait with children ill and unable to attend school. Black and Puerto Rican tenants are forced out while buildings next door are renovated at high rents. We are not being treated as human beings.

For the most part, the lawyer and city planner stayed in the background, acting only as consultants. But as the tenants and worker became more involved with the courts, and as other organizations entered the fight, the lawyer and city planner played a more active and direct role.

RESULTANT SIDE-EFFECTS

During this process, tenants in other buildings on the block became more alert to similar problems in their buildings. With the help of the community development staff and the housing consultant, local groups and organizations such as tenants' councils and the local chapter of the Congress of Racial Equality were enlisted to support and work with the mothers.

Some of the city agencies behaved as though MFY had engineered the entire scheme to embarrass them—steadfastly disregarding the fact that the building had been unlivable for many months. Needless to say, the public agencies are overloaded and have inadequate resources. As has been documented, many such bureaucracies develop an amazing insensitivity to the needs of their clients (Bendix, 1952, pp. 114–134). In this case, the MFY social worker believed that the tenants—and other people in their plight—should make their needs known to the agencies and to the public at large. He knew that when these expressions of need are backed by power—either in numbers or in political knowledge—they are far more likely to have some effect.

By the time the families had been relocated, several things had been accomplished. Some of the public agencies had been sufficiently moved by the actions of the families and the local organizations to provide better services for them. When the families refused to relocate in a shelter and moved into a neighborhood church instead, one of the television networks picked up their story. Officials in the housing agencies came to investigate and several local politicians lent the tenants their support. Most important, several weeks after the tenants moved into the church, a bill was passed by the city council designed to prevent some of the abuses that the landlord had practiced with impunity. The councilman who sponsored the new law referred to the house on Sixth Street to support his argument.

Nevertheless, the problems that remain far outweigh the accomplishments. A disappointing epilogue to the story is that in court, two months later, the tenants' case against the landlord was dismissed by the judge on a legal technicality. The judge ruled that because the electric company had removed the meters from the building it was impossible for the landlord to provide services.

Some of the tenants were relocated out of the neighborhood and some in housing almost as poor as that they had left. The organization that began to develop in the neighborhood has continued to grow, but it is a painstaking job. The fact that the poor have the strength to continue to struggle for better living conditions is something to wonder at and admire.

IMPLICATIONS FOR PRACTICE

Social work helping methods as currently classified are so inextricably interwoven in practice that it no longer seems valid to think of a generic practice as consisting of the application of casework, group work, or community organization skills as the nature of the problem demands. Nor does it seem feasible to adapt group methods for traditional casework problems or to use group work skills in community organization or community organization method in casework. Such suggestions—when they appear in the literature—either reflect confusion or, what is worse, suggest that no clear-cut method exists apart from the auspices that support it.

In this case it is a manifestation of a social problem—housing—that was the major point around which social services were organized. The social worker's major intellectual task was to select the points at which the agency could intervene in the problem and the appropriate methods to use. It seems abundantly clear that in order to select appropriate points of intervention the social worker need not only understand individual patterns of response, but the nature of the social conditions that are the context in which behavior occurs. As this case makes evident, the social system that might be called the "poverty system" is enduring and persistent. Its parts intermesh with precision and disturbing complementarity. Intentionally or not, a function is thereby maintained that produces severe social and economic deprivation. Certain groups profit enormously from the maintenance of this system, but larger groups suffer. Social welfare—and, in particular, its central profession, social work— must examine the part it plays in either maintaining or undermining this socially pernicious poverty system. It is important that the social work profession no longer regard social conditions as immutable and a social reality to be accommodated as service is provided to deprived persons with an ever increasing refinement of technique. Means should be developed whereby agencies can affect social problems more directly, especially through institutional (organizational) change.

The idea advanced by MFY is that the social worker should fulfill his professional function and agency responsibility by seeking a solution to social problems through institutional change rather than by focusing on individual problems in social functioning. This is not to say that individual expressions of a given social problem should be left unattended. On the contrary, this approach is predicated on the belief that individual problems in social functioning are to varying degrees both cause and effect. It rejects the notion that individuals are afflicted with social pathologies, holding, rather, that the same social environment that generates conformity makes payment by the deviance that emerges. As Nisbet points out ". . . socially prized arrangements and values in society can produce socially condemned results" (Merton & Nisbet, 1961, p. 7). This should direct social work's attention to institutional arrangements and their consequences. This approach does not lose sight of the individual or group, since the social system is composed of various statuses, roles, and classes. It takes cognizance of the systemic relationship of the various parts of the social system, including the client. It recognizes that efforts to deal with one social problem frequently generate others with debilitating results.

References

Abramson, J., & Terry, M. (1986). Strategies for enhancing collaboration between social workers and physicians. *Social Work in Health Care, 12*(1), 1–20.

Abramson, J. S. (1989). Making teams work. *Social Work with Groups, 12*(4), 45–63.

Abramson, M. (1984). Collective responsibility in interdisciplinary collaboration: An ethical perspective for social workers. *Social Work in Health Care, 10*(1), 35–43.

Addams, J. (1964). Ann F. Scott (Ed.), *Democracy and social ethics.* Cambridge, MA: Harvard University Press.

Ad Hoc Committee on Advocacy. (1969). The social worker as advocate: Champion of social workers. *Social Work, 14*(2), 16–22.

Akers, R. L. (1964). Socio-economic status and delinquent behavior: A retest. *Journal of Research on Crime and Delinquency, 1*(1), 38–46.

Alcabes, A., & Jones, T. A. (1985). Structural determinants of clienthood. *Social Work, 30*(1), 49–53.

Alexander, F. (1946). Extratherapeutic experiences. In F. Alexander & T. M. French (Eds.), *Psychoanalytic therapy: Principles and applications.* New York: Ronald Press.

Alinsky, Saul. (1946). *Reveille for radicals.* New York: Random House.

American Psychological Association. (1983). Publication Manual of the American Psychological Association (3rd ed.). Washington, DC: Author.

Anderson, J. R. (1980). *Cognitive psychology and its implications.* San Francisco: W. H. Freeman and Company.

Anderson, S. C. (1989, October). *Goal Setting in Social Work Practice.* Paper presented at the annual meeting of the National Association of Social Workers, San Francisco.

Antonovsky, A. (1980). *Health, stress, and coping.* San Francisco: Jossey-Bass.

Aponte, H. J. (1976). The family-school interview: An ecostructural approach. *Family Process, 15*(3), 303–311.

Aponte, H. J. (1985). The negotiation of values in therapy. *Family Process, 24*(3), 323–338.

Aponte, H. J. (1986). If I don't get simple, I cry. *Family Process, 25*(4), 531–548.

Arthur, R., & Foster, S. (1989). *Negotiating Parent Adolescent Conflict.* New York: Guilford Press.

Auerswald, E. H. (1968). Interdisciplinary versus ecological approach. *Family Process, 7*(2), 202–215.

Auerswald, E. H. (1987). Epistemological confusion in family therapy and research. *Family Process, 26,* 317–330.

Austin, L. N. (1948). Trends in differential treatment in social casework. *Social Casework, 29*(6), 203–211.

Austin, M. J., Kopp, J., & Smith, P. L. (1986). *Delivering human services* (2nd ed.). New York: Longman.

Axelrod, R. (1970). *Conflict of interest.* Chicago: Markham.

Baer, B. L., & Federico, R. C. (1978). *Educating the baccalaureate social worker.* Cambridge, MA: Ballinger.

Badding, N. C. (1989). Client involvement in case recording. *Social Casework, 70,* 539–548.

Baier, A. (1986). Trust and Antitrust. *Ethics, 96*(2), 325.

Baline, M. (1957). *The doctor, his patient and the illness.* New York: International Universities Press.

Bandler, B. (1963). The concept of ego-supportive psychotherapy. In H. J. Parad & R. R. Miller (Eds.), *Ego-oriented casework: Problems and perspectives.* New York: Family Service Association of America.

Bandler, R., & Grinder, J. (1979). *Frogs into princes: Neurolinguistic programming.* Moab, UT: Real People Press.

Barber, B. (1961). Social-class differences in educational life chances. *Teachers College Record, 63*(2), 102–113.

Barclay, P. M. (Chair) (1982). *Social workers: Their roles & tasks.* London: National Institute for Social Work/Bedford Square Press.

Barghi, J. H. (1968). Premature termination of psychotherapy and patient-therapist expectations. *American Journal of Orthopsychiatry, 22.*

Barker, R. (1988). Just whose code of ethics should the independent practitioner follow? *Journal of Independent Social Work, 2*(2), 1–5.

Barker, R. L. (1987a). Spelling out the rules and goals: The written worker-client contract. *Journal of Independent Social Work, 1*(2), 67–77.

Barker, R. L. (1987b). Private and Proprietary Services. In A. Minehan (Ed.), *Encyclopedia of Social Work* (18th ed.) (pp. 324–329). Silver Spring, MD: National Association of Social Workers.

Barker, R. L. (1987c). *The social work dictionary.* Silver Spring, MD: National Association of Social Workers.

Bartlett, H. (1958). Toward clarification and improvement of social work practice. *Social Work, 3*(2), 3–9.

Bartlett, H. M. (1970). *The common base of social work practice.* New York: National Association of Social Workers.

Bateson, G., Jackson, D., Haley, J., & Weekland, J. (1963). A note on the double bind. *Family Processes, 2*(1), 154–161.

Beard, G. (1881). *American Nervousness.* New York: G. P. Putnam.

Beaver, J. W. (1979). *To Have What Is One's Own.* Ottawa: The National Indian Socio-Economic Development Committee. (Available through the Department of Indian and Northern Affairs.)

Beck, D. F. (1988). *Counselor characteristics: How they affect outcomes.* Milwaukee: Family Service America.

Becker, H. (1963). *The outsiders: Studies in the sociology of deviance.* New York: Free Press.

Beer, J. (1985). *Peacemaking in your neighborhood: Reflections on an experiment in community mediation.* Santa Cruz, CA: New Society Publishers.

Behavior Associates. (1976). *Parents anonymous self-help for child-abusing parents: Project evaluation report.* Tucson, AZ.

Beinecke, R. H. (1984). PORK, SOAP, STRAP, and SAP. *Social Casework, 65,* 554–558.

Bendix, R. (1952). Bureaucracy and the problem of power. In R. K. Merton, A. Gray, B. Hockey, & H. C. Sebrin (Eds.), *Reader in bureaucracy.* New York: Free Press.

Benjamin, A. (1987). *The helping interview: With case illustrations.* Boston: Houghton Mifflin.

Bennis, W. (1969). Post-bureaucratic leadership. *Transaction, 6*(9), 44–52.

Bennis, W., Benne, K., & Chin, R. (Eds.). (1969). *The planning of change.* New York: Holt, Rinehart & Winston.

Bennis, W., & Sheppard, H. (1956). A theory of group development. *Human Relations, 9*(4), 415–537.

Berelson, B., & Steiner, G. A. (1964). *Human behavior: An inventory of scientific findings.* New York: Harcourt Brace Jovanovich.

Berger, R. (1986). Social work practice models: A better recipe. *Social Casework: The Journal of Contemporary Social Work, 67*(1), 45–54.

Berkeley Planning Associates. (1978). Evaluation of child abuse and neglect demonstration projects 1974–1977. Final Report.

Berkowitz, S. J. (1969). Curriculum models for social work education. In *Modes of professional education,* Tulane Studies in Social Welfare. New Orleans: New Orleans School of Social Work, Tulane University.

Berlin, S. (1980). Cognitive-behavioral interventions for problems of self-criticism among women. *Social Work Research and Abstracts, 16*(4), 191–28.

Berlin, S. (1983). Single-case evaluation: Another version. *Social Work Research and Abstracts, 19*(1), 3–11.

Berlin, S. B. (1982). Cognitive-behavioral interventions for social work practice. *Social Work, 27,* 218–226.

Berman-Rossi, T., & Rossi, P. (1990). Confidentiality and informed consent in school social work. *Social Work in Education, 12*(3), 195–207.

Bertcher, H. J. (1979). *Group participation: Techniques for leaders and members.* Beverly Hills, CA: Sage Publications.

Bettelheim, B. (1971). *The informed heart.* New York: Avon.

Beutler, L. E., Crago, M., & Arizmendi, T. G. (1986). Therapist variables in psychotherapy process and outcome. In S. L. Garfield & A. E. Bergin (Eds.), *Handbook of psychotherapy and behavior change* (3rd ed.), (pp. 257–301). New York: John Wiley.

Biddle, B. J., & Thomas, E. J. (1966). *Role theory: Concepts and research.* New York: John Wiley & Sons.

Biddle, W. W., & Biddle, L. J. (1965). *The community development process: The rediscovery of local initiative.* New York: Holt, Rinehart & Winston.

Biestek, F. (1957). *The casework relationship.* Chicago: Loyola University Press.

Biestek, F., & Gehrig, C. (1978). *Client self determination in social work: A fifty year history.* Chicago: Loyola University Press.

Bischoff, H. G. W. (1976). Rural settings: A new frontier in mental health. Paper presented at Summer Study Program on Rural Mental Health Services. University of Wisconsin, Madison, WI.

Bisno, H. (1969). A theoretical framework for teaching social work methods and skills with particular reference to undergraduate social welfare education. *Journal of Education for Social Work, 5*(2), 5–17.

Blair, G. M., Jones, R. S., & Simpson, R. H. (1954). *Educational psychology.* New York: Macmillan.

Blau, P. M. (1963). *The dynamics of bureaucracy* (rev. ed.) Chicago: University of Chicago Press.

Blishen, B. R., Lockhard, A., Craib, P., & Lockhard, E. (1979). *Socio-economic impact model for northern development.* Ottawa: Research Branch, Policy, Research and Evaluation Group, Department of Indian and Northern Affairs.

Block, J., & Breger, B. (1983). *Mediation: An alternative for PINS.* New York: Children's Aid Society.

Bloom, A. (1980). Social work and the English language. *Social Casework, 61*(6), 332–338.

Bloom, M. (1978). Challenges to the helping profession and the responses of scientific practice. *Social Service Review, 52*(4), 584–596.

Bloom, M., & Fischer, J. (1982). *Evaluating practice: Guidelines for the accountable professional.* Englewood Cliffs, NJ: Prentice-Hall.

Bloom, S. W., & Wilson, R. N. (1979). Patient-practitioner relationships. In H. E. Freeman, S. Levine, & L. G. Reeder (Eds.), *Handbook of Medical Sociology* (pp. 285–288). Englewood Cliffs, NJ: Prentice-Hall.

Blüml, H., Gudat, U., Langreuter, F., Martin, B., Permion, H., Rummel, C., Schettner, H., & Schumann, M. (1989). Changing concepts of social work in foster family care. *Community Alternatives: International Journal of Family Care, 1*(1), 11–22.

Boehm, W. W. (1958). The nature of social work. *Social Work, 3*(2), 10–19.

Boehm, W. W. (Ed.) (1959a). *Social work curriculum study* (12 Vols.). New York: Council on Social Work Education.

Boehm, W. W. (1959b). *The social casework method in social work education: The comprehensive report of the curriculum study* (Vol. 10). New York: Council on Social Work Education.

Bogdan, R. C., & Biklen, S. K. (1982). *Qualitative research for education.* Boston: Allyn & Bacon.

Bogo, M., & Herington, W. (1986). The universality of western social work's knowledge base in the international context: Myth or reality? *Social Development Issues, 10*(2), 56–65.

Bok, S. (1978). *Lying: Moral choice in public and private life.* New York: Pantheon Books.

Bok, S. (1980). Whistle blowing and professional responsibility. *New York University Education Quarterly, 2*(4), 2–10.

Borenzweig, H. (1981, May). Agency vs. private practice: Similarities and differences. *Social Work, 26,* 239–44.

Borkman, T. (1976). Experiential knowledge: A new concept for the analysis of self-help groups. *Social Service Review, 50*(3), 445–446.

Borowski, A. (1988). Social dimensions of research. In R. M. Grinnell, Jr. (Ed.), *Social work research and evaluation* (3rd ed.). Itasca, IL: Peacock.

Bosanquet, B. (1916). The philosophy of case work. *Charity Organization Bulletin, 7,* 121–131.

Bosk, C. L. (1979). *Forgive and remember.* Chicago: University of Chicago Press.

Bostwick, G. J., & Kyte, N. S. (1988). Validity and reliability. In R. M. Grinnell, Jr. (Ed.), *Social work research and evaluation* (3rd ed.). Itasca, IL: Peacock.

Bott, E. (1957). *Family and social network.* London: Tavistock Publications.

Bourne, L. E., Dominowski, R. L., Loftus, E. F., & Healy, A. F. (1986). *Cognitive processes* (2nd ed.). Englewood Cliffs, NJ: Prentice-Hall.

Boyer, L. L. (1991). Family mediation: A way to humanize divorce, a service to the family. *The Social Worker, 57*(4), 186–189.

Brager, G. (1963). Organizing the unaffiliated in a low-income area. *Social Work, 8*(2), 34–40.

Brager, G. (1968). Advocacy and political behavior. *Social Work, 13*(2), 5–15.

Brager, G. (1975). Helping vs. influencing: Some political elements of organizational change. Paper presented at the National Conference on Social Welfare, San Francisco.

Brager, G. A., & Jorcin, V. (1969). Bargaining: A method in community change. *Social Work, 14*(4), 73–83.

Brenner, C. (1955). *An elementary textbook in psychoanalysis.* New York: Doubleday.

Briar, S. (1967a). The social worker's responsibility for the civil rights of clients. *New Perspectives, 1*(1), 89–92.

Briar, S. (1967b). The current crisis in social casework. In National Conference on Social Welfare (Ed.), *Social Work Practice.* New York: Columbia University Press.

Briar, S. (1968). The casework predicament. *Social Work, 13*(1), 5–12.

Briar, S. (1973). Effective social work intervention in direct practice: Implications for education. In S. Briar, W. B. Cannon, L. H. Ginsberg, S. Horn, & R. C. Sarri, *Facing the*

Challenge: Plenary Session from the 19th Annual Program Meeting. New York: Council on Social Work Education, 17–30.

Briar, S., & Miller, H. (1971). *Problems and issues in social casework.* New York: Columbia University Press.

Bridgman, P. W. (1945). The prospect for intelligence. *Yale Review, 34*(3), 444–461.

Brilliant, E. L. (1986). Community planning and community problem solving: Past, present, and future. *Social Service Review, 60*(4), 568–589.

Bristol, M. C. (1936). *Handbook of social case recording.* Chicago: University of Chicago Press.

Brody, R. (1982). *Problem solving: concepts and methods for community organizations.* New York: Human Sciences Press.

Bronfenbrenner, V. (1979). *The ecology of human development.* Cambridge, MA: Harvard University Press.

Brower, Aaron M. (1988). Can the ecological model guide social work practice? *Social Service Review, 62,* 411–429.

Brown, R. A. (1973). Feedback in family interviewing. *Social Work, 18*(5), 52–59.

Bruner, J. S., Goodnow, J., & Austin, J. A. (1962). *A study of thinking* (Vol. 7). New York: John Wiley & Sons.

Bruno, F. J. (1957). *Trends in social work, 1874–1958.* New York: Columbia University Press.

Bryant, B. (1981). Special foster care: A history and rationale. *Journal of Clinical Child Psychology, 10*(1), 8–20.

Bryant, C. (1980). Introducing students to the treatment of inner-city families. *Social Casework, 61,* 629–636.

Bryce, M., & Maybanks, S. (1979). *Home-based services for children and families.* Springfield, IL: Charles C. Thomas.

Buckley, W. (1967). *Sociology and modern systems theory.* Englewood Cliffs, NJ: Prentice-Hall.

Bulmer, M. (1987). *The social basis of community care.* London: Allen & Unwin.

Burgess, E. W. (1928). What social case records should contain to be useful for sociological interpretation. *Social Forces, 6,* 524–532.

Burns, M. E., & Glasser, P. H. (1963). Similarities and differences in casework and group work practice. *Social Service Review, 37*(4), 416–428.

Buros, O. K. (Ed.). (1972). *The seventh mental measurement yearbook* (2 vol.). Highland Park, NJ: Gryphon Press.

Bush, S. (1977). A family-help program that really works. *Psychology Today, 10*(12), 48–50, 84–88.

Butz, R. (1985). Reporting child abuse and confidentiality in counselling. *Social Casework, 66*(2), 83–90.

Canda, E. R. (1988). Conceptualizing spirituality for social work: Insights from diverse perspectives. *Social Thought, 14,* 30–46.

Carew, R. (1979). The place of knowledge in social work activity. *British Journal of Social Work, 9,* 349–363.

Carkhuff, R. R., & Anthony, W. A. (1979). *The skills of helping.* Amherst, MA: Human Resource Development Press.

Carnegie, D. (1936). *How to win friends and influence people.* New York: Simon & Schuster.

Cassel, J. (1974). Psychosocial processes and stress: Theoretical formulations. *International Journal of Health Services, 4*(3), 471–482.

Cedar, T., & Salasin, J. (1979). *Research directions for rural mental health.* McClean: MITRE Corporation.

Chaiklin, H. (1974). Honesty in casework treatment. In National Conference on Social Welfare (Ed.), *Social Welfare Forum 1973.* New York: Columbia University Press.

Challis, D., & Chesterman, J. (1985). A system for monitoring social work activity with the frail elderly. *British Journal of Social Work, 15,* 115–132.

Chandler, D. B. (1990). Violence, fear and communication: The variable impact of domestic violence on mediation. *Mediation Quarterly, 7*(4), 331–346.

Chandler, S. (1985). Mediation: Conjoint problem solving. *Social Work, 31*(4), 346–349.

Cherniss, C. (1980a). *Professional burnout in human service organizations.* New York: Praeger.

Cherniss, C. (1980b). *Staff burnout.* Beverly Hills: Sage.

Chess, W. A., & Norlin, J. M. (1988). *Human behavior and the social environment: A social systems model.* Boston: Allyn & Bacon, Inc.

Cicourel, A. V. (1968). *The social organization of juvenile justice.* New York: John Wiley & Sons.

Clapp, R. F. (1966). Spanish Americans of the Southwest. *Welfare in Review, 4*(1), 1–12.

Cohen, B. Z. (1986). Written communication in social work: The report. *Child Welfare, 65*(4), 399–407.

Cole, S., Gendreau, M., & Lehman, S. (1979). *Orthopsychiatry Report.*

Collins, B. G. (1986). Definining feminist social work. *Social Work, 31,* 214–219.

Collins, J. (1977). The contractual approach to social work intervention. *Social Work Today, 8*(18), 13–15.

Comfort, L. K. (1982). Goals and means: The problem of specifications in the development of effective public policy. *Administration and Society, 13,* 77–108.

Commission on Social Work Practice, National Association of Social Workers. (1958, April). Working definition of social work practice. *Social Work, 3*(4), 5–8.

Compher, J. V. (1982). Parent, school, child systems: Triadic assessment and intervention. *Social Casework, Journal of Contemporary Social Work, 63*(7), 415–423.

Compher, J. V. (1984). The case conference revisited: A systems view. *Child Welfare, 63*(5), 411–418.

Compton, B. R. (1959). *Learning from our clients.* St. Paul, MN: Greater St. Paul Community Chest and Councils.

Compton, B. R. (1979). Family-centered project revisited. Minneapolis: University of Minnesota.

Compton, B. R., & Galaway, B. (1979). *Social work processes* (3rd ed.). Homewood, IL: Dorsey Press.

Connaway, R. S. (1975). Teamwork and social work advocacy: Conflicts and possibilities. *Community Mental Health Journal, 11*(4), 381–388.

Connor, T. M., & Gilgun, J. F. (1987). *Isolation and the adult male perpetrator of child sexual abuse.* Minneapolis: University of Minnesota.

Constable, R. C. (1983). Values, religion, and social work practice. *Social Thought, 9*(4), 29–41.

Coogler, J. (1978). *Structured mediation in divorce settlement.* Lexington, MA: D. C. Heath/Lexington Books.

Cooper, S. (1978). A look at the effect of racism on clinical work. *Social Casework, 54*(2), 76–84.

Coplin, W. D. (1971). *Introduction to international politics.* Chicago: Markham.

Coplon, J., & Strull, J. (1983). Roles of the professional in mutual aid groups. *Social Casework: The Journal of Contemporary Social Work, 64*(5), 259–266.

Corcoran, K., & Melamed, J. (1990). From coercion to empowerment: Spousal abuse and mediation. *Mediation Quarterly, 7*(4), 303–316.

Corcoran, K. J. (1988). Selecting a measuring instrument. In R. M. Grinnell, Jr. (Ed.), *Social work research and evaluation* (3rd ed.). Itasca, IL: Peacock.

Corcoran, K. J., & Fischer, J. (1987). *Measures for clinical practice.* New York: Free Press.

Cordon, J., & Preston-Shoot, M. (1988). Contract or con trick? A postscript. *British Journal of Social Work, 18*(6), 623–624.

Cordon, J., & Preston-Shoot, M. (1987). *Contracts in social work.* Hants, England: Gower.

Cormican, J. D. (1978). Linguistic issues in interviewing. *Social Casework, 59*(3), 145–152.

Coulton, C. J., & Solomon, P. L. (1977). Measuring outcomes of intervention. *Social Work Research and Abstracts, 13*(4), 3–9.

Council on Social Work Education (1992a). Curriculum policy statement for Baccalaureate degree programs. Washington, D.C.: Author.

Council on Social Work Education (1992b). Curriculum policy statement for master's degree programs. Washington, D.C.: Author.

Council on Social Work Education. (1993). *Curriculum Policy Statement.* Washington, DC: Author.

Cournoyer, B. (1991). *The social work skills workbook.* Belmont, CA: Wadsworth.

Cross, T. L. (1986). Drawing on cultural tradition in Indian child welfare practices. *Social Casework, 67*(5), 283–289.

Coyle, G. L. (1948). *Group work with American youth.* New York: Harper & Row.

Cronbach, L. (1954). *Educational psychology.* New York: Harcourt Brace Jovanovich.

Croxton, T. A. (1974). The therapeutic contract in social treatment. In P. Glasser, R. Sari, & R. Vinter (Eds.), *Individual change through small groups.* New York: Free Press.

CSWE. (1988). *Handbook of accreditation standards and procedures.* Washington, DC: Council on Social Work Education.

Cullen, J. B. (1978). *The structure of professionals: A quantitative examination.* New York: PBI.

Cumming, J., & Cumming, E. (1962). *Ego and milieu: Theory and practice of environmental therapy.* New York: Atherton Press.

Curtis, P., & Lutkus, A. (1985). Client confidentiality in policy social work settings. *Social Work, 34*(1), 33–38.

Daley, M. R. (1979). Burnout: Smoldering problem in the protective services. *Social Work, 24*(5), 375–379.

Dalton, G. W. (1970). Influence and organizational change. In G. W. Dalton, P. R. Lawrence, & L. E. Greiner (Eds.), *Organizational change and development* (pp. 250–258). Homewood, IL: Richard D. Irwin.

Davenport, J., & Reims, N. (1978). Theoretical orientation and attitudes toward women. *Social Work, 23*(4), 306–311.

David, M. (1970). *Game theory.* New York: Basic Books.

Davidson, W., & Rapp, C. (1976). Child advocacy in the justice system. *Social Work, 21*(3), 225–232.

Davis, J. D. (1971). *The interview as arena.* Stanford, CA: Stanford University Press.

Davis, L. V. (1985). Female and male voices in social work. *Social Work, 30,* 106–113.

DeMartini, J. R., & Whitbeck, L. B. (1987). Sources of knowledge for practice. *Journal of Applied Behavioral Science, 23,* 219–231.

DeHoyos, G., & Jensen, C. (1985). The systems approach in American social work. *Social Casework: The Journal of Contemporary Social Work, 66*(8), 490–497.

Denito, D. M., & Dye, T. R. (1983). *Social welfare politics and public policy.* Englewood Cliffs, NJ: Prentice-Hall.

De Schweinitz, K., & de Schweinitz, E. (1962). *Interviewing in the social services.* London: National Institute for Social Work Training.

Deutsch, K. W. (1968). Toward a cybernetic model of man and society. In W. Buckley (Ed.), *Modern system and research for the behavioral scientist.* Hawthorne, NY: Aldine.

Deutsch, M. (1973). *The resolution of conflict.* New Haven, CT: Yale University Press.

Dewey, J. (1933). *How we think* (rev. ed.). New York: Heath.

Dillman, D. A. (1978). *Mail and telephone surveys: The total design method.* New York: John Wiley & Sons.

Doel, M., & Lawson, B. (1986). Open records: The client's right to partnership. *British Journal of Social Work, 16*(4), 407–430.

Dokecki, P. R. (1992). On knowing the community of caring persons: A methodological basis for the reflective-generative practice of community psychology. *Journal of Community Psychology, 20,* 26–35.

Douglas, C., & Jurkovic, G. J. (1983). Agency triangles: Problems in agency-family relationships. *Family Process, 22*(4), 441–451.

Downs, A. (1977). *Inside bureaucracy.* Boston: Little, Brown.

Dressel, P. L. (1982). Policy sources of work dissatisfaction: The case of human services in aging. *Social Service Review, 56*(3), 406–423.

Drezner, S. M. (1973). The emerging art of decision making. *Social Casework, 54*(1), 5–12.

Duehn, W. D. (1981). The process of social work practice and research. In R. M. Grinnell, Jr. (Ed.), *Social work research and evaluation.* Itasca, IL: Peacock.

Duehn, W. D. (1985). Practice and research. In R. M. Grinnell, Jr. (Ed.), *Social work research and evaluation* (2nd ed.). Itasca, IL: Peacock.

Duhl, F. (1969). Intervention, therapy, and change. In W. Gray, F. Duhl, & N. D. Rizzo (Eds.), *General systems theory and psychiatry.* Boston: Little, Brown.

Dumont, M. (1968). *The absurd healer.* New York: Viking Press.

Edelwich, J., & Brodsky, A. (1980). *Burn-out.* New York: Human Services Press.

Edwards, R. E., & Reid, W. J. (1989). Structured care recording in child welfare: An assessment of social workers' reactions. *Social Work, 34,* 49–52.

Egan, G. (1986). *The skilled helper* (3rd ed.). Monterey, CA: Brooks/Cole.

Eiduson, B. (1964). Intellectual inbreeding in the clinic? *American Journal of Orthopsychiatry, 34*(4), 714–721.

Elashoff, J., & Thoresen, C. (1978). Choosing a statistical method for analysis of an intensive experiment. In T. R. Kratochwill (Ed.), *Single subject research: Strategies for evaluating change.* New York: Academic Press.

Eliot, T. (1928). Objectivity and subjectivity in the case record. *Social Forces, 6,* 539–544.

Emerson, R. (1969). *Judging delinquents: Context and process in juvenile court.* Chicago: Aldine.

Emery, R. E., & Wyer, M. M. (1987). Child custody mediation and litigation: An experimental evaluation of the experience of parents. *Journal of Consulting and Clinical Psychology, 55*(2), 179–186.

Emmet, D. (1962). Ethics and the social worker. *British Journal of Psychiatric Social Work, 6*(6), 165–172.

Empey, L., & Erickson, M. L. (1966). Hidden delinquency and social status. *Social Forces, 44*(4), 546–554.

England, H. (1986). *Social work as art.* London: Allen & Unwin.

Epstein, I. (1968). Social workers and social action. *Social Work, 13*(2), 101–108.

Epstein, I. (1970). Professional role orientations and conflict strategies. *Social Work, 15*(4), 87–92.

Epstein, I. (1988). Quantitative and qualitative methods. In R. M. Grinnell, Jr. (Ed.), *Social work research and evaluation* (3rd ed.). Itasca, IL: Peacock.

Epstein, L. (1985). *Talking and listening: A guide to the helping interview.* St. Louis: Times Mirror/Meghy.

Epstein, L. (1988). *Helping people, the task-centered approach.* Columbus, OH: Merrill.

Epstein, W. M. (1986). Science and social work. *Social Service Review, 60*(1), 145–160.

Erickson, S., & McKnight, M. (1990). Mediating spousal abuse divorces. *Mediation Quarterly, 7*(4), 377–388.

Etzioni, A. (1986). Mixed scanning revisited. *Public Administration Review, 46,* 8–14.

Erikson, E. H. (1950). *Childhood and society.* New York: Norton.

Erikson, E. H. (1959). *Identity and the life cycle: Psychological issues.* Monograph No. 1. New York: International Universities Press.

Estes, R., & Henry, S. (1976). The therapeutic contract in work with groups: A formal analysis. *Social Service Review, 50*(4), 611–622.

Etzioni, A. (1964). *Modern Organizations.* Englewood Cliffs, NJ: Prentice-Hall.

Evaluation Research Society. (1982). Evaluation Research Society standards for program evaluation. In P. H. Rossi (Ed.), *New directions for program evaluation: Standards for evaluation practice.* San Francisco, CA: Jossey-Bass.

Evans, D. R., Hearn, M. T., Uhlemann, M. R., & Ivey, A. E. (1984). *Essential interviewing: A programmed approach to effective communication* (2nd ed.). Monterey, CA: Brooks/Cole.

Executive Office of the President. (1986). *Up From Dependency.* Report of the major increases between 1960 and 1985 in public allocations to service systems for low-income populations. Supplement 1, Volume 1.

Fanshel, D., Finch, S. J., & Grundy, J. F. (1989). Foster Children in Life-Course Perspective: The Casey Family Program Experience. *Child Welfare 68*(5), 467–478.

Farber, B. A. (1983). Introduction: A critical perspective on burnout. In B. A. Farber (Ed.), *Stress and burnout in the human service professions.* New York: Pergamon Press.

Fein, E., Maluccio, A. N., Hamilton, V. J., & Ward, D. (1983). After foster care: Outcomes of permanency planning. *Child Welfare 62*(6), 485–558.

Fein, E., & Staff, I. (1991). Implementing reunification services. *Families in Society 72*(6), 335–343.

Feyerabend, P. K. (1975). *Against method.* London: New Left Books.

Fischer, J. (1978). *Effective casework practice: An eclectic approach.* New York: McGraw-Hill.

Fischer, J. (1981). The social work revolution. *Social Work, 26*(3), 201–202.

Fisher, R. (1969). *International conflict for beginners.* New York: Harper & Row.

Fisher, R., & Ury, W. (1983). *Getting to yes: Negotiating agreement without giving in.* New York: Penguin Books.

Flax, J. W., et al. (1979). *Mental health and rural America: An overview and annotated bibliography.* Washington, DC: U.S. Department of Health, Education, and Welfare.

Flexner, A. (1915). Is social work a profession? *Proceedings of National Conference on Charities and Corrections,* 575–590.

Fordor, A. (1976). Social work and system theory. *British Journal of Social Work, 6,* 13–42.

Fosdick, H. E. (1926). *Adventurous religion.* New York: Harper.

Foster, A. (1979). Who has the right to know? *Public Welfare, 37,* 34–37.

Fox, E., Nelson, M., & Bolman, W. (1969). The termination process: A neglected dimension in social work. *Social Work, 14*(4), 53–63.

Fox, R. (1987). Short-term, goal oriented family therapy. *Social Casework, 68,* 494–499.

Fox, R. C. (1957). Training for uncertainty. In R. K. Merton, G. G. Reader & P. L. Kendall (Eds.), *The student-physician* (pp. 207–241). Cambridge, MA.

Fraley, Y. L. (1969). A role model for practice. *Social Service Review, 43*(2), 145–154.

Frank, J. D. (1967). The dynamics of the psychotherapeutic relationship. In T. J. Scheff (Ed.), *Mental illness and social process* (pp. 168–206). New York: Harper & Row.

Frank, J. D. (1978). Expectation and therapeutic outcome—The placebo effect and the role induction interview. In J. D. Frank (Ed.), *Effective ingredients of successful psychotherapy.* New York: Bruner/Mazel.

Frank, L. (1954). The interdisciplinary frontiers in human relations studies. *Journal of Human Relations, 7*(2), 89–92.

Frankena, W. (1973). *Ethics* (2nd ed.). Englewood Cliffs, NJ: Prentice-Hall.

Frankenstein, R. (1982). Agency and client resistance. *Social Casework, 52*(1), 24–28.

Freed, A. O. (1978). Clients' rights and casework records. *Social Casework, 59,* 458–164.

Freedberg, S. (1989). Self-determination: Historical perspectives and effects on current practice. *Social Work, 34,* 33–38.

Freidson, E. (1961). *Patient's views of medical practice* (chap. 9). New York: Russell Sage Foundation.

French, T. M. (1952). *The integrating behavior: Basic postulates.* Chicago: University of Chicago Press.

Frese, M., & Sabini, J. (Eds.). (1985). *Goal directed behavior: The concept of action in psychology.* Hillsdale, NJ: Lawrence Erlbaum Associates.

Freud, S. (1963). On psychotherapy. In P. Rieff (Ed.), *Collected papers.* New York: Collier Books.

Freudenberger, H. J. (1974). Staff burn-out. *Journal of Social Issues, 30*(1), 159–165.

Frey, L. (1962). Support and the group. *Social Work, 7*(4), 35–42.

Friedman, R., Duchnowski, A., & Henderson, E. (1989). *Advocacy on behalf of children with serious emotional problems.* Springfield, IL: Charles C. Thomas.

Friedman, S., & Taylor-Fanger, M. (1991). *Expanding therapeutic possibilities: Getting results in brief psychotherapy.* Lexington Books.

Friedson, E. (1970). Dominant professions, bureaucracy and client services. In W. R. Rosengren & M. Lefton, *Organizations and clients.* Columbus, OH: Charles E. Merrill.

Fromm, E. (1956). *The art of loving.* New York: Harper & Row.

Fuller, L. (1961). The adversary system. In J. Berman (Ed.), *Talks on American law.* New York: Vintage Trade Books.

Fusco, C. J. (1991). Public assistance contracts with minors. *The Social Worker/Le Travailleur Social, 59*(1), 37–41.

Gadamer, H. G. (1981). *Truth and method.* London: Sheed & Ward.

Galaway, B. (1981). Social services and criminal justice. In N. Gilbert & H. Specht (Eds.), *Handbook of the social services* (pp. 250–280). Englewood Cliffs, NJ: Prentice Hall.

Galaway, B. (1988). Crime victim offender mediation as a social work strategy. *Social Service Review, 62*(4).

Galaway, B., & Hudson, J. (Eds.) (1990). *Criminal Justice, Restitution, and Reconciliation.* Monsey, NY: Criminal Justice Press.

Galaway, B., & Hudson, J. (Eds.) (1994). *Community Economic Development: Social and Economic Perspectives in Research and Policy.* Toronto: Thompson Educational Publishing.

Gambrill, E. (1983). *Casework: A competency-based approach.* Englewood Cliffs, NJ: Prentice-Hall.

Gambrill, E., & Barth, R. (1980). Single-case study designs revisited. *Social Work Research and Abstracts, 16*(3), 15–19.

Gamson, W. (1968). *Power and discontent.* Homewood, IL: Dorsey Press.

Garbarino, J. (1982). *Children and families in the social environment.* New York: Aldine.

Garland, J. A., Jones, H. E., & Kolodny, R. L. (1968). A model for stages of development in social work groups. In Saul Bernstein (Ed.), *Explorations in group work* (pp. 12–53). Boston: Boston University School of Social Work.

Garrett, A. (1972). *Interviewing: Its principles and methods* (2nd ed.). New York: Family Service Assn. of America.

Gartner, A., & Reissman, F. (Eds.) (1984). *The self-help revolution.* New York: Human Sciences Press.

Garvin, C. D. (1981). Research-related roles for social workers. In R. M. Grinnell, Jr. (Ed.), *Social work research and evaluation.* Itasca, IL: Peacock.

Garvin, C. D., & Seabury, B. A. (1984). *Interpersonal practice in social work.* Englewood Cliffs, NJ: Prentice-Hall.

Garwick, G., & Lampman, S. (1972). Typical problems bring patients to a mental health clinic. *Community Mental Health Journal 8*(4), 271–280.

Gazzaniga, M. S. (1988). *Mind matters.* Boston: Houghton Mifflin.

Gaylin, W., Glasser, I., Marcus, S., & Rothman, D. J. (1978). *Doing good: The limits of benevolence.* New York: Pantheon Books.

Gergen, K. J. (1982). *Toward transformation in social knowledge.* New York: Springer-Verlag.

Germain, C. B. (1968). Social study: Past and future. *Social Casework, 49*(7), 403–409.

Germain, C. B. (1971). Casework and science: An historical encounter. In R. W. Roberts & R. Nee (Eds.), *Theories of casework.* Chicago: University of Chicago Press.

Germain, C. B. (1973). An ecological perspective in casework practice, *Social Casework, 54*(June 1972), 326.

Germain, C. B. (1979). Ecology in social work. In *Social work practice: People and environments.* New York: Columbia University Press.

Germain, C. B. (1981). The ecological approach to people – environmental transactions. *Social Casework, 62*(6), 323–331.

Germain, C. B., & Gitterman, A. (1980). *The life model of social work practice.* New York: Columbia University Press.

Gilchrist, L. D., & Schinke, S. P. (1988). Research ethics. In R. M. Grinnell, Jr. (Ed.), *Social work research and evaluation* (3rd ed.). Itasca, IL: Peacock.

Gilder, G. (1981). *Wealth and Poverty.* New York: Basic Books.

Gilgun, J. F. (1984a). A non-coercive method of helping children discuss their own sexual abuse. Unpublished manuscript. University of Minnesota School of Social Work, Minneapolis.

Gilgun, J. F. (1984b). Does the mother always know? Alternatives to blaming mothers of child sexual abuse victims. *Response, 7*(4), 2–4.

Gilgun, J. F. (1984c). The sexual abuse of the young female in life course perspective (Doctoral dissertation, Syracuse University, 1983). *Dissertation Abstracts International, 44,* 3058.

Gilgun, J. F. (1986). Sexually abused girls' knowledge of sexual abuse and sexuality. *Journal of Interpersonal Violence, 1*(3), 209–225.

Gilgun, J. F. (1988). Why children don't tell: Fear of separation and loss and the disclosure of child sexual abuse. *New Designs in Youth Development, 7.*

Gilgun, J. F., & Connor, T. M. (1987a). Children as objects of sexual gratification: A grounded theory approach. Minneapolis: University of Minnesota School of Social Work.

Gilgun, J. F., & Connor, T. M. (1987b, May). *Childhood maltreatment and the development of sexually abusive behaviors.* Paper presented at the annual meeting of the American Association of Sex Educators, Counselors, and Therapists, New York, New York.

Ginsberg, L. (1976). An overview of social work education for rural areas. In L. Ginsberg (Ed.), *Social work in rural communities.* New York: Council on Social Work Education.

Gitterman, A. (1971) Group work in the public schools. In W. Schwartz & S. Zalba (Eds.), *The practice of group work* (pp. 45–56). New York: Columbia University Press.

Gitterman, A., & Schaeffer, A. (1972). The white professional and the black client. *Social Casework, 53*(5), 280–291.

Glaser, B., & Strauss, A. L. (1967). *The discovery of grounded theory.* Chicago: Aldine.

Gochros, H. L. (1988). Research interviewing. In R. M. Grinnell, Jr. (Ed.), *Social work research and evaluation* (3rd ed.). Itasca, IL: Peacock.

Goff, R. M. (1954). Some educational implications of rejection on aspiration levels of minority group children. *Journal of Experimental Education, 23*(2), 179–183.

Goffman, E. (1961). The medical model and mental hospitalization. *Asylums.* Garden City, NY: Anchor Books.

Goffman, E. (1969). *Strategic interaction.* Philadelphia: University of Pennsylvania Press.

Golan, N. (1969). How caseworkers decide. *Social Service Review, 43*(3), 286–296.

Golan, N. (1981). *Passing through transitions.* New York: Free Press.

Goldberg, G., & Middleman, R. (1974). *Social service delivery: A structural approach to social work practice.* New York: Columbia University Press.

Goldstein, H. (1973). *Social work practice: A unitary approach.* Columbia: University of South Carolina.

Goldstein, H. (1981a). *Social learning and change: A cognitive approach to human services.* Columbia, SC: University of South Carolina Press.

Goldstein, H. (1981b). Generalist social work practice. In N. Gilbert & H. Specht (Eds.), *Handbook of the social services* (pp. 413–433). Englewood Cliffs, NJ: Prentice-Hall.

Goldstein, H. (1983). Starting where the client is. *Social Casework: The Journal of Contemporary Social Work, 64*(5), 267–275.

Goldstein, H. (1984). *Creative change: A cognitive-humanistic approach to social work practice.* New York: Tavistock.

Goldstein, H. (1986). Toward the integration of theory and practice: A humanistic approach. *Social Work, 31*(5), 352–357.

Goldstein, H. (1987). The neglected moral link in social work practice. *Social Work, 32*(3), 181–186.

Goldstein, H. (1990). Strength or pathology: Ethical and rhetorical contrasts in approaches to practice. *Families in Society, 71,* 267–275.

Goode, W. J. (1964). *The family.* Englewood Cliffs, NJ: Prentice-Hall.

Goode, W. J. (1969). The Theoretical Limits of Professionalism. In A. Etzioni (Ed.), *The Semi-professions and their organization: Teachers, nurses, social workers* (pp. 266–313).

Goodman, J. A. (1974). Preface. In James A. Goodman (Ed.). *Dynamics of racism.* Washington, DC: National Association of Social Workers.

Googins, B., & Davidson, B. (1993). The organization as client: Broadening the concept of employee assistance programs. *Social Work, 38*(4), 477–484.

Gordon, R. (1992). *Basic interviewing skills.* Itasca, IL: Peacock.

Gordon, W. E. (1962). A critique of the working definition. *Social Work, 7*(4), 3–13.

Gordon, W. E. (1965). Knowledge and value: Their distinction and relationship in clarifying social work practice. *Social Work, 10*(4), 32–39.

Gordon, W. E. (1969). Basic concepts for an integrative and generative conception of social work. In Gordon Hearn (Ed.), *The general systems approach: Contributions toward an holistic conception of social work.* New York: Council on Social Work Education.

Gottlieb, B. H., & Farquharson, A. (1985). Blueprint for a curriculum on social support. *Social Policy, 15*(3), 31–34.

Gottlieb, N. (1974). *The welfare bind.* New York: Columbia University Press.

Gottman, J. M., & Leiblum, S. R. (1974). *How to do psychotherapy and how to evaluate it.* New York: Holt, Rinehart and Winston.

Gottschalk, L. (1973). A study of prediction and outcome in a mental health crisis clinic. *American Journal of Psychiatry, 130,* 1107–1111.

Gould, R. (1978). Students' experience with the termination phase of individual treatment. *Smith College Studies in Social Work, 48*(3), 235–269.

Gouldner, A. (1954). *Patterns of industrial bureaucracy.* New York: Free Press.

Gouldner, A. (1960). *The norm of reciprocity.* American Sociological Review, 25(2), 161–178.

Grasso, A., & Epstein, I. (1992). *Research utilization in the social services.* New York: Haworth Press.

Green, A. D. (1966). The professional worker in the bureaucracy. *Social Service Review, 40*(1), 71–83.

Greene, G. J. (1989). Using the written contract for evaluating and enhancing practice effectiveness. *Journal of Independent Social Work, 4*(2), 135–155.

Greer, J. H., Davidson, G. C., & Gatchel, R. I. (1970). Reduction of stress in humans through non-veridical perceived control of aversive stimulation. *Journal of Personality and Social Psychology, 16*(4), 731–738.

Grinnell, R. M., Jr. (1981a). Becoming a knowledge-based social worker. In R. M. Grinnell, Jr. (Ed.), *Social work research and evaluation.* Itasca, IL: Peacock.

Grinnell, R. M., Jr. (Ed.). (1981b). *Social work research and evaluation.* Itasca, IL: Peacock.

Grinnell, R. M., Jr. (1983). Quantitative articles in social work journals: A research note. *Areté, 8*(1), 33–38.

Grinnell, R. M., Jr. (1985a). Becoming a practitioner-researcher. In R. M. Grinnell, Jr. (Ed.), *Social work research and evaluation* (2nd ed.). Itasca, IL: Peacock.

Grinnell, R. M., Jr. (Ed.). (1985b). *Social work research and evaluation* (2nd ed.). Itasca, IL: Peacock.

Grinnell, R. M., Jr. (Ed.). (1988). *Social work research and evaluation* (3rd ed.). Itasca, IL: Peacock.

Grinnell, R. M., Jr., & Kyte, N. S. (1977). A model for bridging the gap between undergraduate research and practice. *Journal of Education for Social Work, 13*(2), 30–36.

Grinnell, R. M., Jr., & Siegel, D. H. (1988). The place of research in social work. In R. M. Grinnell, Jr. (Ed.), *Social work research and evaluation* (3rd ed.). Itasca, IL: Peacock.

Grinnell, R. M., Jr., & Stothers, M. (1988). Utilizing research designs. In R. M. Grinnell, Jr. (Ed.), *Social work research and evaluation* (3rd ed.). Itasca, IL: Peacock.

Grob, G. N. (1985). *The inner world of American psychiatry, 1890–1940.* New Brunswick, NJ: Rutgers University Press, p. 10.

Gross, N., Masson, W., & McEachern, A. W. (1958). *Explorations in role analysis.* New York: John Wiley & Sons.

Grosser, C. (1965). Community development programs serving the urban poor. *Social Work, 10*(3), 15–21.

Grossman, D., & Smolka, G. (1984). *New York City's poverty budget.* New York: Community Services Society of New York.

Guerin, P. J., & Pendagast, E. G. (1976). Evaluation of family system and genogram. In P. J. Guerin (Ed.), *Family therapy theory and practice* (pp. 450–464). New York: Gardner.

Guttentag, M. (1970). Group cohesiveness, ethnic organization and poverty. *Journal of Social Issues, 26*(2), 105–132.

Hadley, R., Cooper, M., Dale, P., & Stacy, G. (1987). *A community social worker's handbook.* London: Tavistock.

Hahn, N., Bellah, R. N., Rabinow, P., & Sullivan, W. (Eds.). (1983). *Social science as moral inquiry.* New York: Columbia University Press.

Haley, J. (1959). An interactional description of schizophrenia. *Psychiatry, 22*(4), 321–332.

Haley, J. (1963). *Strategies of psychotherapy.* New York: Grune and Stratton.

Hallowell, A. I. (1975). Ojibway ontology, behavior, and worldview. In D. Tedlock and B. Tedlock (Eds.), *Teachings from the American earth* (pp. 141–178).

Halmos, P. (1966). *Faith of the counselors.* New York: Schocken.

Hamilton, G. (1946). *Principles of social case recording.* New York: Columbia University Press.

Hamilton, G. (1949). Helping people—the growth of a profession. In *Social work as human relations: Anniversary papers of the New York School of Social Work and the Community Service Society of New York* (pp. 3–18). New York: Columbia University Press.

Hamilton, G. (1950). The underlying philosophy of social casework. In C. Casius (Ed.), *Principles and techniques in social casework: Selected articles,* 21. New York: Family Service Association of America.

Hamilton, G. (1951). *Theory and practice of social casework* (2nd ed.). New York: Columbia University Press.

Hammond, D. C., Hepworth, D. H., & Smith, V. G. (1977). *Improving therapeutic communication.* San Francisco: Jossey-Bass.

Handiker, P., & Carnock, K. (1984). Social work assessment processes in work with ethnic minorities—the Doshi family. *British Journal of Social Work, 14*(1), 23–47.

Hanlan, A. (1967). Counteracting problems of bureaucracy. *Social Work, 12*(3), 88–94.

Hanlan, A. (1971). Casework beyond bureaucracy. *Social Casework, 52*(4), 195–196.

Hanney, R. M. (1989). The leading edge: In the best interest of the family: A rationale for mandatory entry into divorce mediation. *The Social Worker, 57*(2), 101–102.

Harding, S., & Hintikka, M. (Eds.). (1983). *Discovering reality: Feminist perspectives on epistemology, methodology, and philosophy of science.* Boston: Dordrecht, Reidel.

Hardman, D. (1960). The constructive use of authority. *Crime and Delinquency, 6*(3), 245–254.

Harrison, B. (1972). Education and underemployment in the urban ghetto. *American Economic Review, 62*(5), 796–812.

Harrison, W. D. (1980). Role strain and burnout in child protective service workers. *Social Service Review, 54*(1), 31–44.

Harrison, W. D. (1983). A social competence model of burnout. In B. A. Farber (Ed.), *Stress and burnout in the human service professions.* New York: Pergamon.

Harrison, W. D. (1987). Reflective practice in social care. *Social Service Review, 61,* 393–404.

Harrison, W. D. (1989). Social work and the search for postindustrial community. *Social Work, 34,* 73–75.

Harrison, W. D. (1991). *Seeking common ground: A theory of social work in social care.* Aldershot, UK: Avebury; Brookfield, VT: Gower.

Harrison, W. D., & Hoshino, G. (1984). Britain's Barclay report: Lessons for the United States. *Social Work, 29*(3), 213–218.

Harrison, W. D., Smale, G. G., & Hearn, B. (1992, March). Toward a practice theory for community social work: Britain's Practice and Development Exchange. Paper presented at the Council on Social Work Education Annual Program Meeting, Kansas City, MO.

Hartman, A. (1970). To think about the unthinkable. *Social Casework, 51*(8), 467–474.

Hartman, A. (1974). The generic stance of the family agency. *Social Casework, 55*(4), 199–208.

Hartman, A. (1978). Diagrammatic assessment of family relationships. *Social Casework, 59*(8).

Hartman, A. (1979). The extended family as a resource for change: An ecological approach to family-centered practice. In Germain, C. B. (Ed.), *Social work practice: People and environments: An ecological perspective* (pp 239–265). New York: Columbia University Press.

Hartman, A., & Laird, J. (1983). *Family centered social work practice.* New York: Free Press.

Hartman, B. L., & Wickey, J. M. (1978). The person-oriented record in treatment. *Social Work, 23,* 296–299.

Hartman, S. (1983). A self-help group for women in abuse relationships. In B. G. Reed & C. D. Garvin (Eds.), *Groupwork with women/groupwork with men.* New York: Haworth Press.

Hartman, S. (1986). The therapeutic self-help group: A process of empowerment for women in abusive relationships. In C. M. Brody (Ed.), *Women in groups.* New York: Springer.

Hartmann, H. (1958). *Ego psychology and the problem of adaptation.* New York: International Universities Press.

Hartsock, N. (1983). The feminist standpoint: A specifically feminist historical materialism. In S. Harding & M. Hintikka (Eds.), *Discovering reality: Feminist perspectives on epistemology, methodology, and philosophy of science.* Boston: Dordrecht and Reidel.

Hatcher, H. A. (1978). *Correctional casework and counseling.* Englewood Cliffs, NJ: Prentice-Hall.

Haworth, G. O. (1984). Social work research practice and paradigms. *Social Service Review, 58*(3), 355.

Hayes, J. R. (1978). *Cognitive psychology: Thinking and creating.* Homewood, IL: Dorsey Press.

Hayes, S. (1981). Single case experimental design and empirical clinical practice. *Journal of Consulting and Clinical Psychology, 49*(2), 193–211.

Haynes, J. M. (1992). Mediation and therapy: An alternative view. *Mediation Quarterly, 10,* 21–33.

Haynes, S. M., & Wilson, C. C. (1979). *Behavioral assessments: Recent advances in methods, concepts, and application.* San Francisco: Jossey-Bass.

Hazel, N. (1989). Adolescent fostering as a community resource. *Community Alternatives: International Journal of Family Care, 1*(1), 1–10.

Hazel, N., & Fenyo, A. (1993). *Free to be myself: The development of teenage fostering.* St. Paul, MN: Human Service Associates.

Healy, W. (1917). The bearings of psychology on social case work. *Proceedings of National Conference of Social Work,* 104–112.

Hearn, G. (Ed.). (1969). *The general systems approach: Contributions toward a wholistic conception of social work.* New York: Council on Social Work Education.

Hearn, G. (1974). General systems theory and social work. In Francis Turner (Ed.), *Social work treatment.* New York: Free Press.

Heineman, M. B. (1981). The obsolete scientific imperative in social work research. *Social Service Review, 55*(3), 371–397.

Herbruck, C. (1979). *Breaking the cycle of child abuse.* Minneapolis: Winston Press.

Herstein, N. (1969). The latent dimensions of social work research. *Social Casework, 50,* 269–275.

Heus, M., & Pincus, A. (1986). *The creative generalist: A guide to social work practice.* Barneveld, WIS: Micamar.

Holbrook, F. (1983). Notes on policy and practice: Case records: Fact or fiction? *Social Service Review, 57,* 645–658.

Hoffman, L., & Long, L. (1969). A systems dilemma. *Family Process, 8*(3), 211–234.

Holland, T. P. (1989). Values, faith and professional practice. *Social Thought, 15,* 28–40.

Hollingshead, A. M. (1950). Class differences in family stability. *Annals of the American Academy of Political and Social Science, 272,* 39–46.

Hollis, F., & Woods, M. (1981). *Casework: A psychosocial therapy* (3rd ed.). New York: Random House.

Holmes, S. (1978). Parents anonymous: A treatment method for child abuse. *Social Work, 23*(3), 245–247.

Hooker, C. E. (1976). Learned helplessness. *Social Work, 21*(3), 194–98.

Horejsi, J., Walz, T., & Connolly, P. (1977). *Working in welfare: Survival through positive action.* Iowa City: University of Iowa Press.

Hornick, J. P., & Burrows, B. (1988). Program evaluation. In R. M. Grinnell, Jr. (Ed.), *Social work research and evaluation* (3rd ed.). Itasca, IL: Peacock.

Hosch, D. (1973). *Use of the contract approach in public social services.* Los Angeles: Regional Research Institute in Social Welfare, University of Southern California.

Hoshino, G. (1971). The public welfare worker: Advocate or adversary? *Public Welfare, 29*(1), 35–41.

Houghkirk, E. (1977). Everything you've always wanted your clients to know but have been afraid to tell them. *Journal of Marriage and Family Counselling, 3,* 27–33.

Howard, J. H. (1977, reprint). *The Plains-Ojibwa or Bunji.* Lincoln, Nebraska: J. & L. Reprint Co.

Hudson, J., & McRoberts, H. A. (1984). Auditing evaluation activities. In L. Rutman (Ed.), *Evaluation research & methods: A basic guide* (2nd ed.). Beverly Hills, CA: Sage.

Hudson, W. W. (1982). *The clinical measurement package: A field manual.* Homewood, IL: Dorsey Press.

Husband, D., & Scheunemann, H. (1972). The use of group process in teaching termination. *Child Welfare, 51*(8), 505–513.

Huslage, S., & Stein, J. (1985). A systems approach for the child study team. *Social Work in Education, 7*(2), 114–123.

Hyman, H. H. (1953). The value systems of different classes: A social psychological contribution to the analysis of stratification. In R. Bendix & S. M. Lipset (Eds.), *Class, status, and power.* New York: Free Press.

Hyman, I., & Schreiber, K. (1974). The school psychologist as child advocate. *Children Today, 3*(2), 21–33, 36.

Illich, I. (1976). *Medical nemesis.* New York: Pantheon.

Illich, I. et al. (1977). *Disabling professions.* London: Marion Boyars.

Imre, R. W. (1971). A theological view of social casework. *Social Casework, 52,* 578–585.

Imre, R. W. (1982). *Knowing and caring: Philosophical issues in social work.* Washington, DC: University Press of America.

Imre, R. W. (1985, February 19). *Understanding practice wisdom: Clues from the humanities.* Revision of paper presented at the Annual Program Meeting of the Council on Social Work Education, Washington, D.C.

Imre, R. W. (1989). Moral theory for social work. *Social Work, 15,* 18–27.

Irving, H. (1981). *Divorce mediation: The rational alternative.* Toronto: Personal Library Publishers.

Irwin, J. (1970). *The felon.* Englewood Cliffs, NJ: Prentice-Hall.

Jacobs, P. (1968). *Prelude to riot.* New York: Vintage Books.

Jahn, K. (1986). The usefulness of DSM-III and systematic interviews in treatment planning. *Women and Therapy, 5*(1), 91–99.

James, W. (1942). *The varieties of religious experience.* New York: Modern Library.

Jampala, V. C., Sierles, F. S., & Taylor, M. A. (1986). Consumers' views of DSM-III: Attitudes and practices of U.S. psychiatrists and 1984 graduating psychiatric residents. *American Journal of Psychiatry, 43,* 148–153.

Jandt, F. (1973). *Conflict resolution through communication.* New York: Harper & Row.

Jayarantne, S. (1978). Analytic procedures for single-subject designs. *Social Work Research and Abstracts, 14*(3), 30–35.

Jayaratne, S., & Chess, W. A. (1983). Job satisfaction and burnout in social work. In B. A. Farber (Ed.), *Stress and burnout in the human service professions.* New York: Pergamon.

Jayaratne, S., & Chess, W. A. (1984). Job satisfaction, burnout, and turnover: A national study. *Social Work, 29*(5), 451.

Jayarantne, S., & Levy, R. (1979). *Empirical clinical practice.* New York: Columbia University Press.

Jayaratne, S., Tripodi, T., & Chess, W. A. (1983). Perceptions of emotional support, stress, and strain by male and female social workers. *Social Work Research and Abstracts, 19*(2), 19–27.

Jelinek, E. C. (Ed.). (1980). *Women's autobiography.* Bloomington, IN: University of Indiana Press.

Johnson, H. C. (1978). Integration of the problem-oriented record with a systems approach to case assessment. *Journal of Education for Social Work, 14*(3), 71–77.

Johnson, M. (1992). Describing the population we serve: Viewing children in a family context. *R & D: Research and Evaluation in Group Care, 2*(1), 18–21.

Johnson, P. J. (1985). Social workers as case managers: A combined methods approach. In A. E. Fink, J. H. Pfouts, and A. Dobelstein (Eds.), *The field of social work* (8th ed.), Hollywood, CA: Sage.

Johnson, W. (1951). Being understanding and understood: Or how to find a wandered horse. *ETC, 8*(1), 161–179.

Johnston, N. (1956). Sources of distortion and deception in prison interviewing. *Federal Probation, 20*(1), 43–48.

Jones, M., & Biesecker, J. (1980). *Goal planning in children and youth services.* DHHS Publication No. (OHDS) 81-30295. Washington, DC: US Government Printing Office.

Joseph, M. V. (1988). Religion and social work practice. *Social Casework, 69,* 443–452.

Kadushin, A. (1959). The knowledge base of social work. In A. Kahn (Ed.), *Issues in American social work.* New York: Columbia University Press.

Kadushin, A. (1972). *The social work interview.* New York: Columbia University Press.

Kagle, J. D. (1984a). Restoring the clinical record. *Social Work, 29,* 49–50.

Kagle, J. D. (1984b). *Social work records.* Homewood, IL: Dorsey Press.

Kagle, J. D. (1988). Recording in direct practice. *Encyclopedia of social work, 2*(18th ed.) (pp. 463–467). Washington, DC: National Association of Social Workers.

Kahn, A. H., & Kamerman, S. B. (1982). *Helping America's families.* Philadelphia: Temple University Press.

Kahn, A. J. (1954). The nature of social work knowledge. In C. Kasius (Ed.), *New directions in social work.* New York: Harper & Row.

Kahn, R., & Connell, C. (1957). *The dynamics of interviewing.* New York: John Wiley & Sons.

Kallenbach, D., & Lyons, A. (1989). *Government spending for the poor in Cook County, Illinois: Can we do better?* Evanston, IL: Center for Urban Affairs and Policy Research, Northwestern University.

Kamerman, S. B., Dolgoff, R., Getzel, G., & Nelson, J. (1973). Knowledge for practice: Social science in social work. In A. J. Kahn (Ed.), *Shaping the new social work.* New York: Columbia University Press.

Kane, R. (1975). The interprofessional team as a small group. *Social Work in Health Care, 1*(1), 19–32.

Kane, R. (1982). Teams: Thoughts from the bleachers. *Health and Social Work, 7*(1), 19–25.

Kane, R. A. (1974). Look to the record. *Social Work, 19,* 412–419.

Kanter, J. S. (1983). Reevaluation of task-centered social work practice. *Clinical Social Work Journal, 11,* 228–244.

Kaplan, A. (1964). *The conduct of inquiry: Methodology for behavior science.* San Francisco: Chandler.

Kaplan, L. (1986). *Working with multiproblem families.* Lexington, MA: Lexington Books.

Karger, H. J. (1981). Burnout as alienation. *Social Service Review, 55*(2), 270–283.

Katz, A., & Bender, E. (Eds.) (1976). *The strength in us: Self-help groups in the modern world.* New York: Franklin-Watts.

Kauff, P. (1977). The termination process: Its relationship to the separation individuation phase of development. *International Journal of Group Psychotherapy, 27*(1), 3–18.

Kazdin, A. E. (1974). Reactive self-monitoring: The effects of response desirability, goal setting, and feedback. *Journal of Consulting and Clinical Psychology, 42*(5), 704–716.

Kazdin, A. E. (1981). Drawing valid inferences from case studies. *Journal of Consulting and Clinical Psychology, 49*(2), 183–192.

Kiefer, C. W. (1988). *The mantle of maturity: A history of ideas about character development.* Albany, NY: State University of New York Press.

Keith-Lucas, A. (1957). *Decisions about people in need.* Chapel Hill: University of North Carolina Press.

Keith-Lucas, A. (1972). *Giving and taking help.* Chapel Hill: University of North Carolina Press.

Keith-Lucas, A. (1973, Winter). Philosophies of public social service. *Public Welfare, 31*(1), 21–24.

Keller, S. (1963). The social world of the slum child: Some early findings. *American Journal of Orthopsychiatry, 33*(5), 823–831.

Kenemore, T. (1987). Negotiating with clients: A study of clinical practice experience. *Social Service Review, 61*(1), 132–144.

Kidneigh, H. C. (1969). A note on organizing knowledge. In *Modes of professional organization: Vol. II. Tulane Studies in Social Welfare.* New Orleans: School of Social Work, Tulane University.

Kilpatrick, A., & Pippin, J. (1987). Families in crisis: A structured mediation method for peaceful solution. *International Social Worker, 30*(2), 159–169.

Kirk, S., & Kutchins, H. (1992). *Selling of DSW-III: The rhetoric of science in psychiatry.* Hawthorne, NY: Aldine de Gruyter.

Kirsh, S., & Maidman, F. (1984). Child welfare problems and practice: An ecological approach. In F. Maidman (Ed.) *Child welfare: A source book of knowledge and practice.* New York: Child Welfare League of America.

Kinsey, A. C. (1948). *Sexual behavior in the human male.* Philadelphia: W. B. Saunders.

Kiresuk, T., & Garwick, G. (1974). Basic goal attainment scaling procedures. *Project Evaluation Report* (chap. 1). Minneapolis: Program Evaluation Project.

Kiresuk, T., & Sherman, R. (1968). *Community Mental Health Journal, 4*(6), 443–453.

Kirk, S., Osmalov, M., & Fischer, J. (1976). Social worker's involvement in research. *Social Work, 21*(2), 121–131.

Klenk, R. W., & Ryan, R. M. (1974). *The practice of social work,* (2nd ed.). Belmont, CA: Wadsworth.

Klier, J., Fein, E., & Genero, C. (1984). Are written or verbal contracts more effective in family therapy? *Social Work 29*(3), 298–299.

Klockars, C. B. (1972). A theory of probation supervision. *The Journal of Criminal Law, Criminology and Police Science, 63*(4), 550–557.

Kolevzon, M. S., & Maykranz, J. (1982). Theoretical orientation and clinical practice: Uniformity versus eclecticism. *Social Service Review, 56,* 120–129.

Konopka, G. (1958). *Edward C. Lindemann and social work philosophy.* Minneapolis: University of Minnesota Press.

Konopka, G. (1963). *Social group work: A helping process.* Englewood Cliffs, NJ: Prentice-Hall.

Koopman, E. J., & Hunt, E. J. (1988). Child custody mediation: an interdisciplinary synthesis. *American Journal of Orthopsychiatry, 58*(3), 379–386.

Kopp, S. (1971). *Guru-metaphors from a psychotherapist.* Palo Alto, CA: Science and Behavior Books.

Knuppel, S. K. (1991). Promise and compromise in divorce mediation. *Journal of Dispute Resolution, 1991*(1), 127–135.

Kubler-Ross, E. (1969). *On death and dying.* New York: Macmillan.

Kunin, R. (1985). *A study of clients' self-reports of their experience of personal change in direct practice.* Unpublished doctoral dissertation. Cleveland, OH: Case Western University.

Kutchins, H., & Kirk, S. (1987). DSM-III and social work malpractice. *Social Work, 32*(3), 205–211.

Laird, J., & Allen, J. (1989, March). *The quest for meaning in social work interview: New theories, new metaphors.* Paper presented at the Annual Program Meeting of the Council on Social Work Education, Chicago.

Lantz, J. E. (1986). Integration of reflexive and task-oriented techniques in family treatment. *Child Welfare, 65,* 261–270.

Lazare, A. (Ed.). (1979). *Outpatient psychiatry: Diagnosis and treatment* (chaps. 7 & 8). Baltimore: Williams & Wilkins.

Lazare, A., Eisenthal, S., Frank, A., & Stoeckle. (1976). Studies on a negotiated approach to patienthood. In E. Gallagher (Ed.), *The doctor-patient relationship in the changing health scene*. Washington, DC: U.S. Department of Health, Education and Welfare.

Lederer, W. J., & Jackson, D. D. (1968). *The mirages of marriage*. New York: W. W. Norton.

Lee, P. R. (1929). Social work: Cause or function. In National Conference on Social Welfare, *Proceedings of the National Conference of Social Work* (pp. 3–20). NY: Columbia University Press.

Lefcourt, H. M. (1966). Belief in personal control: Research and implications. *Journal of Individual Psychology, 22*(2), 185–195.

Lemert, E. (1967). The juvenile court—quest and realities. In President's Commission on Law Enforcement and Administration of Justice, *Task force report: Juvenile delinquency and youth crime*. Washington, DC: U.S. Government Printing Office.

Lemmon, J. A. (1985). *Family mediation practice*. New York: The Free Press.

Lerner, B. (1972). *Therapy in the ghetto*. Baltimore: Johns Hopkins Press.

Levenson, B. (1961). Bureaucratic succession. In A. Elzioni (Ed.), *Complex organizations*. New York: Holt, Rinehart & Winston.

Levinson, D. J. (1978). *The seasons of a man's life*. New York: Alfred A. Knopf.

Levinson, H. (1977). Termination of psychotherapy: Some salient issues. *Social Casework, 58*(8), 480–489.

Levitt, J. L., & Reid, W. J. (1981). Rapid assessment instruments for practice. *Social Work Research and Abstracts, 17*(1), 13–20.

Levy, C. S. (1972). Values and planned change. *Social Casework, 53*(8), 488–493.

Levy, C. S. (1973). The value base of social work. *Journal of Education for Social Work, 9*(1), 34–42.

Levy, C. S. (1976). *Social work ethics*. New York: Human Sciences Press.

Levy, C. S. (1983). Client self-determination. In A. Rosenblatt & D. Waldfogel (Eds.), *Handbook of clinical social work*. New York: Academic Press.

Lewis, H. (1972). Morality and the politics of practice. *Social Casework, 53*(6), 404–417.

Lewis, H. (1984). Self-determination: The aged client's autonomy in service encounters. *Journal of Gerontological Social Work, 7*(3), 41–63.

Lewis, O. (1966). *La vida: A Puerto Rican family in the culture of poverty*. New York: Random House.

Lewis, R. G., & Ho, M. K. (1975). Social work with native Americans. *Social Work, 20*(5), 379–382.

Lewis, W. W. (1984). Ecological change: A necessary condition for residential treatment. *Child Care Quarterly, 13*(1), 21–29.

Libassi, M. (1988). The chronically mentally ill: A practice approach. *Social Casework, 69*(2), 88–96.

Liberman, B. (1978). The role of mastery in psychotherapy: Maintenance of improvement and prescriptive change. In J. Frank, R. Hoehn-Saric, S. Imber, B. Liberman, & A. Stone (Eds.), *Effective ingredients in successful psychotherapy* (pp. 35–72). New York: Bruner/Mazel.

Lieberman, M., & Borman, L. (1979). *Self-help groups for coping with crisis*. San Francisco.

Liebman, J. L. (1946). *Peace of mind*. New York: Simon & Schuster.

Lindbergh, A. M. (1975). *Gift from the sea*. New York: Random House.

Linblom, C. E. (1977). *Politics and markets*. New York: Basic Books.

Linblom, C. E. (1980). *The policy making process*. Englewood Cliffs, NJ: Prentice-Hall.

Lindblom, C. E. (1970). The science of muddling through. In F. Cox, J. Erlich, J. Rothman, & J. Tropman (Eds.), *Strategies of community organization*. Itasca, IL: Peacock.

Lindeman, E. C. (1949). Science and philosophy: Sources of human faith. In *Social work as human relations: Anniversary papers of the New York School of Social Work and Community Service Society of New York* (pp. 207–211). New York: Columbia University Press.

Lindemann, E. (1956). Symptomatology and management of acute grief. In H. Parad (Ed.), *Crisis intervention: Selected readings.* New York: Family Service Association.

Lindenthal, J., Jordan, T., Lentz, J., & Thomas, C. (1988). Social workers' management of confidentiality. *Social Work, 33*(2), 157–159.

Lindsey, D. (1981). Data analysis with the computer. In R. M. Grinnell, Jr. (Ed.), *Social work research and evaluation.* Itasca, IL: Peacock.

Lister, L. (1982). Role training for interdisciplinary health teams. *Health and Social Work, 7*(1), 19–25.

Lloyd, J. C., & Bryce, M. E. (1985). *Placement prevention and family reunification: A handbook for the family-centered service practitioner.* Iowa City, IA: The University of Iowa National Resource Center on Family Based Services.

Locke, E. A., Saari, L. M., Shaw, K. N., & Latham, G. P. (1981). Goal setting and task performance: 1969–1980. *Psychological Bulletin, 90*(1), 125–152.

Loewenberg, F., & Dolgoff, R. (1988). *Ethical decisions for social work practice* (3rd cd.). Itasca, IL: Peacock.

London, P. (1986). *The modes and morals of psychotherapy* (2nd ed.). New York: Hemisphere.

Lonsdale, S., Webb, A., & Briggs, T. (Eds.) (1980). *Teamwork in the personal social services and health care: British and American perspectives.* London: Croom Helm.

Luft, L., Smith, K., & Kace, M. (1978). Therapists', patients', and inpatient staff's views of treatment modes and outcomes. *Hospital and Community Psychiatry, 29*(8), 505–511.

Lugones, M. C., & Spelman, E. V. (1983). Have we got a theory for you! Feminist theory, cultural imperialism and the demand for "the woman's voice." *Women's Studies International Forum, 6*(6), 576.

Lurie, N. O. (1976). The will-o-wisp of Indian unity. *Indian History, 9*(3), 19–24.

Lutz, W. A. (1956). *Concepts and principles underlying social casework practice: Social work practice in medical care and rehabilitation settings* (Monograph 3). Washington, DC: National Association of Social Workers.

Maas, H. S. (1954). The role of numbers in clubs of lower-class and middle-class adolescents. *Child Development, 25*(4), 241–251.

Maas, H. S. (1955). Socio-cultural factors in psychiatric services for children. *Smith College Studies in Social Work, 25*(2), 1–90.

Maas, H. S. (1963). Group Research Project (Hectograph). Berkeley: School of Social Welfare, University of California.

MacBride, D. (1969). *Power and process: A commentary on eminent domain.* Washington, DC: American Society of Appraisers.

Macht, M., & Quam, J. (1986). *Social work, an introduction.* Columbus, OH: Merrill.

Magnusson, D., & Allen, V. L. (1983a). *Human development: An interactional perspective.* New York: Academic Press.

Magnusson, D., & Allen, V. L. (1983b). An interactional perspective for human development. In D. Magnusson & V. L. Allen (Eds.), *Human development: An interactional perspective.* New York: Academic Press.

Magura, S., Moses, B. S., & Jones, M. A. (1987). *Assessing risk and measuring change in families.* Washington, DC: The Child Welfare League of America.

Mahaffey, M. (1972). Lobbying and social work. *Social Work, 17*(1), 3–11.

Maher, T. F. (1974). Freedom of speech in public agencies. *Social Work, 19*(6), 698–703.

Mailick, M., & Ashley, A. (1981). Politics of interprofessional collaboration: Challenge to advocacy. *Social Casework: The Journal of Contemporary Social Work, 62*(3), 131–137.

Maluccio, A., & Marlow, W. (1974). The case for the contract. *Social Work, 19*(1), 28–36.

Maluccio, A. N. (1979). *Learning from clients: Interpersonal helping as viewed by clients and social workers*. New York: Free Press.

Maluccio, A. N., Fein, E., & Olmstead, K. (1986). *Permanency planning for children: Concepts and methods*. London and New York: Routledge, Chapman and Hall.

Maluccio, A. N., Kreiger, R., & Pine, B. A. (1991). Preserving families through reunification. In E. M. Tracy, D. A. Haapala, J. Kinney, & P. J. Pecora (Eds.), *Intensive family preservation services: An instructional sourcebook* (pp. 215–235). Cleveland, OH: Mandel School of Applied Social Sciences, Case Western Reserve University.

Mann, J. (1973). *Time-limited psychotherapy*. Cambridge, MA: Harvard University Press.

Manocchio, A. J., & Dunn, J. (1970). *The time game*. New York: Dell Publishing Company, Inc.

Manor, O. (1986). The preliminary interview in social group work: Finding the spiral steps. *Social Work with Groups, 9*(2), 21–39.

March, J., & Simon, H. (1958). *Organizations*. New York: John Wiley & Sons.

Marcus, G. F. (1939). The statute of social case work today. In *M. Van Waters (Ed.), Readings in social casework, 1920–1938* (pp. 122–135). New York: Columbia University Press.

Marlatt, G. A. (1980). *Relapse prevention: A self-control program for the treatment of addictive behaviors*. Seattle: University of Washington Alcoholism and Drug Abuse Institute.

Marthaler, D. (1989). Successful mediation with abusive couples. *Mediation Quarterly, 23*, 53–66.

Martin, C. (1971). Beyond bureaucracy. *Child Welfare, 50*(7), 384–388.

Martin, M. A., & Nayowith, S. A. (1988). Creating community: Groupwork to develop social support networks with homeless mentally ill. *Social Work with Groups, 11*(4).

Martinez-Brawley, E. E. (1990). *Perspectives on the small community: Humanistic views for practitioners*. Silver Spring, MD: National Association of Social Workers.

Marlow, C. (1993). *Research Methods for Generalist Social Work*. Pacific Grove, CA: Brooks/Cole.

Maslach, C. (1978). The client role in staff burn-out. *Journal of Social Issues, 34*(4), 111–124.

Maslach, C. (1982). *Burnout: The cost of caring*. Englewood Cliffs, NJ: Prentice-Hall.

Maslach, C. (1976). Burned-out. *Human Behavior, 5*(9), 16–22.

Mayer, J. E., & Timms, N. (1969). Clash in perspective between worker and client. *Social Casework, 50*(1), 32–40.

Mayer, J. E., & Timms, N. (1970). *The client speaks: Working class impressions of casework*. New York: Atherton Press.

Maynard-Moody, S., & McClintock, C. C. (1981). Square pegs in round holes: Program evaluation and organizational uncertainty. *Policy Studies Journal, 9*(5), 644–666.

Mazer, M. (1976). *People and predicaments*. Cambridge: Harvard University Press.

McCall, G. J., & Simmons, J. L. (1966). *Identities and interactions* (chap. 6). New York: The Free Press.

McClelland, D. C. (1961). *The achieving society*. New York: Van Nostrand Rheinhold.

McClelland, D. C. (1969). *Motivating economic achievement*. New York: Free Press.

McCormick, M. (1970). Social work advocacy: A new dimension in social work. *Social Casework, 51*(1), 3–11.

McCroskey, J., & Nelson, J. (1989). Practice-based research in the family support program: The family connection project example. *Child Welfare 63*(6), 573–587.

McDermott, F. E. (Ed.) (1975). *Self-determination in social work*. London: Routledge & Kegan Paul.

McDonald, C. C. (1988). Social work interviewing and feminism. *Australian Journal of Social Work, 41*(2), 13–16.

McDonald, J. M. (1950). *Strategy in poker, business and war*. New York: W. W. Norton.

McFadden, E. J. (1992). The inner world of children and youth in care. *Community Alternatives: International Journal of Family Care, 4*(1), 1–17.

McKnight, J. (1987). *The future of low-income neighborhoods and the people who reside there.* Evanston, IL: Center for Urban Affairs and Policy Research, Northwestern University.

McKnight, J. (1992). Redefining community. *Social Policy, 23,* 56–62.

McPheeters, H., & Ryan, R. (1971). *A core of competence for baccalaureate social welfare and curricular implications.* Atlanta, GA: Southern Regional Education Board.

Meador, B. D., & Rogers, C. R. (1984). Person-centered therapy. In R. J. Corsini (Ed.), *Current psychotherapies* (pp. 142–195). Itasca, IL: Peacock.

Meehl, P. F., & McClosky, H. (1947). Ethical and political aspects of applied psychology. *Journal of Abnormal and Social Psychology, 42*(1), 91–98.

Menninger, K. (1968). *The crime of punishment.* New York: Viking Press.

Menninger, K. (1964). *Theory of psychoanalytic technique.* New York: Harper & Row.

Menninger, W. C. (1948). *Psychiatry: Its evolution and present status* (p. 33). Ithaca, NY: Cornell University Press.

Merton, R. K. (1968). *Social theory and social structure* (4th ed.). New York: Free Press.

Merton, R. K., & Nisbet, R. A. (Eds.). (1961). *Contemporary social problems.* New York: Harcourt Brace Jovanovich.

Meyer, C. H. (1970). *Social work practice: A response to the urban crisis.* New York: Free Press.

Meyer, C. H. (1973). Direct services in old and new concepts. In A. J. Kahn (Ed.), *Shaping the new social work.* New York: Columbia University Press.

Meyer, C. H. (1983). The search for coherence. In C. H. Meyer, (Ed.), *Clinical social work in the eco-systems perspective* (pp. 5–34). New York: Columbia University Press.

Meyer, D. (1988). *The positive thinkers: Popular religious psychology from Mary Baker Eddy to Norman Vincent Peale and Ronald Reagan* (rev. ed.). Middletown, CT: Wesleyan University Press.

Meyerhoff, H. L., & Meyerhoff, B. (1964). Field observations of middle-class gangs. *Social Forces, 42*(3), 328–336.

Miller, D. R. (1963). The study of social relationships: Situation identity and social interaction. In S. Koch (Ed.), *Psychology: A study of science.* New York: McGraw-Hill.

Miller, G., & Simons, H. (Eds.) (1974). *Perspectives on communication in social conflict.* Englewood Cliffs, NJ: Prentice-Hall.

Miller, H. (1968). Value dilemmas in social casework. *Social Work, 13*(1), 27–33.

Miller, K., Fein, E., Howe, G., Claudio, C., & Bishop, G. (1984). Time-limited, goal-focused parent aide services. *Social Casework 68*(8), 472–477.

Miller, P. (1990). Covenant model for professional relationships: An alternative to the contract model. *Social Work, 35*(2), 121–125.

Miller, S. C. (1962). Ego autonomy in sensory deprivation, isolation, and stress. *The International Journal of Psychoanalysis, 43*(1), 1–20.

Miller, W. B. (1958). Inter-institutional conflict as a major impediment to delinquency prevention. *Human Organization, 17*(3), 20–23.

Miller, W. B. (1959). Implications of urban lower-class culture for social work. *Social Service Review, 33*(3), 219–236.

Miller, W. B., Baum, R. C., & McNeil, R. (1968). Delinquency prevention and organizational relations. In S. Wheeler (Ed.), *Controlling delinquents.* New York: John Wiley & Sons.

Milner, J. (1987). An ecological perspective on duration of foster care. *Child Welfare, 66*(2), 113–123.

Mindel, C. H., & McDonald, L. (1988). Survey research. In R. M. Grinnell, Jr. (Ed.), *Social work research and evaluation* (3rd ed.). Itasca, IL: Peacock.

Miranda, M. R. (1976). *Psychotherapy with the Spanish-speaking: Issues in research and service delivery.* Los Angeles: Spanish-Speaking Mental Health Center.

Mitchell, W. C. (1973). Bargaining and public choice. In H. J. Leavitt & L. R. Pondy (Ed.), *Readings in managerial psychology* (2nd Ed.) (pp. 583–594). Chicago: University of Chicago Press.

Monkman, M., & Allen-Meares, P. (1985). The TIE framework: A conceptual map for social work assessment. *Areté, 10*(1), 41–49.

Moore, C. W. (1986). *The mediation process.* San Francisco: Jossey-Bass.

Mowrer, O. H. (1961). *The crisis in psychiatry and religion.* Princeton, NJ: Van Nostrand.

Morgan, R. (1962). Role performance in a bureaucracy. In National Conference on Social Welfare (Ed.), *Social work practice.* New York: Columbia University Press.

Morrell, C. (1987). Cause in function. *Social Service Review, 61*(1), 144–155.

Morris, M. (1983). *Parent-child mediation: An alternative that works.* New York: Children's Aid Society.

Morris, R. (1977). Caring for versus caring about people. *Social Work, 22*(5), 353–359.

Morrison, J. (1976). Community organization in rural areas. In L. Ginsberg (Ed.), *Social work in rural communities.* New York: Council on Social Work Education.

Moss, K. E. (1988). Writing research proposals. In R. M. Grinnell, Jr. (Ed.), *Social work research and evaluation* (3rd ed.). Itasca, IL: Peacock.

Moss, S., & Moss, M. (1967). When a caseworker leaves an agency: The impact on worker and client. *Social Casework, 48*(7), 433–437.

Mouzakitis, C., & Goldstein, S. (1985). A multidisciplinary approach to treating child neglect. *Social Casework: The Journal of Contemporary Social Work, 66*(4), 218–224.

Mullen, E., & Dumpson, J. (1972). *Evaluation of social intervention.* San Francisco: Jossey-Bass.

Mullen, E. J. (1985). Methodological dilemmas in social work research. *Social Work Research and Abstracts, 21*(4), 12–20.

Mullen, E. J. (1988). Constructing personal practice models. In R. M. Grinnell, Jr. (Ed.), *Social work research and evaluation.* (3rd ed.). Itasca, IL: Peacock.

Murdach, A. (1982). A political perspective in problem solving. *Social Work, 27*(5), 417–421.

Murdach, A. D. (1980). Bargaining and persuasion with nonvoluntary clients. *Social Work, 25*(6), 458–461.

Murphy, L. B. (1962). *The widening world of childhood.* New York: Basic Books.

Murray, H. A., & Kluckhohn, C. (1953). Outline of a conception of personality. In C. Kluckhohn & H. A. Murphy (Eds.), *Personality in nature, society and culture.* New York: Alfred A. Knopf.

Mutschler, E., & Hasenfeld, Y. (1986). Integrated information systems for social work practice. *Social Work, 31,* 345–349.

Myrdal, G. (1948). *An American dilemma.* New York: Harper & Row.

Nader, R., Petkas, P. J., & Blackwell, K. (1972). *Whistle-blowing.* New York: Grossman Publishers.

Nason, F. (1983). Diagnosing the hospital team. *Social Work in Health Care, 9*(2), 25–45.

NASW. (1980). *Code of ethics of the National Association of Social Workers.* Silver Spring, MD: National Association of Social Workers.

Needleman, M. L., & Needleman, C. E. (1974). *Guerrillas in the bureaucracy.* New York: John Wiley & Sons.

Neiman, L. J., & Hughes, J. W. (1959). The problem of the concept of role—A re-survey of the literature. In H. D. Stein and R. A. Cloward (Eds.), *Social perspectives on behavior.* New York: Free Press.

Nelsen, J. C. (1988). Single subject research. In R. M. Grinnell, Jr. (Ed.), *Social work research and evaluation* (3rd ed.). Itasca, IL: Peacock.

Nelson, D. (1990). Recognizing and realizing the potential of family preservation. In J. K. Whittaker, J. Kinney, E. M. Tracy, & C. Booth, (Eds.), *Reaching high-risk families: Intensive family preservation in human services* (pp. 13–30). Hawthorne, NY: Aldine de Gruyler.

Nelson, R. O. (1981). Realistic dependent measures for clinical use. *Journal of Consulting and Clinical Psychology, 49*(2), 168–182.

Netting, F. E. (1992). Case management: Service or symptom? *Social Work, 37,* 160–164.

Newell, A., & Simon, H. A. (1972). *Human problem-solving.* Englewood Cliffs, NJ: Prentice-Hall.

Nicholson, B., & Matross, G. (1989). Facing reduced decision-making capacity in health care: Method for maintaining client self-determination. *Social Work, 25*(3), 234–238.

Nierenberg, G. I. (1980). *The art of negotiating.* New York: Cornerstone Library.

Northen, H. (1969). *Social work with groups.* New York: Columbia University Press.

O'Connell, M. (1988). *The gift of hospitality: Opening the doors of community life to people with disabilities.* Evanston, IL: Center for Urban Affairs and Policy Research, Northwestern University.

O'Connell, P. (1972). Developmental tasks of the family. *Smith College Studies in Social Work, 42*(3), 203–210.

O'Connor, G. (1972). Toward a new policy in adult correction. *Social Service Review, 46*(4), 581–596.

Ogg, E. (1978). Partners in coping groups for self and mutual help. *Public Affairs Pamphlet.*

Orback, S. (1978). *Fat is a feminist issue: A self-help guide for compulsive eaters.* New York: Berkley Medallion Books.

Orlinsky, D. E., & Howard, K. I. (1986). Process and outcome in psychotherapy. In S. L. Garfield & A. E. Bergin (Eds.), *Handbook of psychotherapy and behavior change* (3rd ed.), (pp. 311–376). New York: John Wiley & Sons.

Ornstein, R. (1986). Social work method: A review of the past decade. *Social Work, 10,* 166–178.

O'Regan, P., & O'Connor, T. (1989). *Community: Give it a go.* Wellington, New Zealand: Allen & Unwin.

Overton, A. (1965). Establishing the relationship. *Crime and Delinquency, 11*(3), 229–238.

Overton, A., & Tinker, K. (1957). *Casework notebook.* St. Paul, MN: Greater St. Paul Community Chest and Councils.

Oxley, G. (1971). A life-model approach to change. *Social Casework, 52*(10), 627–633.

Oxley, G. B. (1966). The caseworker's expectations in client motivation. *Social Casework, 47*(7), 432–437.

Panter, E. (1966). Ego building procedures that foster social functioning. *Social Casework, 47*(3), 139–145.

Paradis, B. (1987). An integrated team approach to community mental health. *Social Work, 32*(2), 101–104.

Parker, T. (1987). Dilemmas resulting from the application of extemporaneous ethnics in interdisciplinary team decision making. *Family Therapy, 14*(3), 201–211.

Parloff, M. B., Iflund, B., & Goldstein, N. (1957). *Communication of "therapy values" between therapist and schizophrenic patients.* Paper presented before American Psychiatric Association, Chicago.

Parsons, R., Hernandez, S., & Jorgensen, J. (1988). Integrated practice: A framework for problem solving. *Social Work, 33*(5), 417–421.

Parsons, R. J. (1991). The mediator role in social work practice. *Social Work, 36*(6), 483–487.

Paster, O. S. (1986). A social action model of intervention for difficult to reach populations. *American Journal of Orthopsychiatry, 56*(4), 625–629.

Patti, R. (1974). Limitations and prospectives of internal advocacy. *Social Casework, 55*(9), 537–545.

Patti, R. J. (1974). Organizational resistance and change: The view from below. *Social Service Review, 48*(3), 367–383.

Patti, R. J., & Resnick, H. (1972). Changing the agency from within. *Social Work, 17*(4), 48–57.

Patton, M. Q. (1986). *Utilization-focused evaluation* (2nd ed.). Beverly Hills, CA: Sage.

Pawlak, E. J. (1976). Organizational tinkering. *Social Work, 21*(5), 376–380.

Payne, J. E. (1972). Ombudsman roles for social workers. *Social Work, 17*(1), 94–100.

Peale, N. V. (1952). *The power of positive thinking.* New York: Prentice-Hall.

Pearson, J., & Thoennes, M. (1982). Mediation and divorce: The benefits outweigh the costs. *Family Advocate, 4*(3), 26–32.

Pecora, P., & Austin, M. J. (1983). Declassification of social service jobs: Issues and strategies. *Social Work, 28,* 421–426.

Perlman, H. H. (1957). *Social casework: A problem solving process.* Chicago: University of Chicago Press.

Perlman, H. H. (1961). The role concept and social casework: Some explorations. *Social Service Review, 35*(4), 370–381.

Perlman, H. H. (1962). The role concept and social casework: Some explorations, II. *Social Service Review, 36*(1), 17–31.

Perlman, H. H. (1965). Social work method: A review of the decade 1955-1965. *Social Work 10*(October 1965), 166–179.

Perlman, H. H. (1968). *Persona: Social role and personality.* Chicago: University of Chicago Press.

Perlman, H. H. (1971). *Perspectives on social casework.* Philadelphia: Temple University Press.

Perlman, H. H. (1972). The problem solving model in social casework. In R. W. Roberts, & R. H. Nee (Eds.), *Theories of social casework.* Chicago: University of Chicago Press.

Perlman, H. H. (1975). In quest of coping. *Social Casework, 56*(4), 213–225.

Perlman, R. (1975). *Consumers and social services* (Chap. 5). New York: John Wiley & Sons.

Perrow, C. (1972). *Complex organizations: A critical essay.* Glenview, IL: Scott Foresman.

Peterson, K. J. (1979). Assessment in the life model: A historical perspective. *Social Casework, 60*(10), 586–596.

Phear, P. (1985). Parent child mediation: Four states, four models. *Mediation Quarterly, 7,* 35–45.

Pieper, M. H. (1985). The future of social work research. *Social Work Research and Abstracts, 21*(4), 3–11.

Piliavin, I. (1968). Restructuring the provision of social services. *Social Work, 13*(1), 34–41.

Pincus, A., & Minahan, A. (1973). *Social work practice: Model and method.* Itasca, IL: Peacock.

Pinderhughes, E. B. (1983) Empowerment for our clients and ourselves. *Social Casework: Journal of Contemporary Social Work, 64*(6), 331–337.

Pines, A. (1983). On burnout and the buffering effects of social supports. In B. A. Farber (Ed.), *Stress and burnout in the human service professions* (pp. 158–160). Elmsford, NY: Pergamon Press.

Pines, A., Aronson, E., & Kafry, D. (1981). *Burnout: From tedium to personal growth.* New York: Free Press.

Pines, A., & Kafry, D. (1978). Occupational tedium in the social services. *Social Work, 23*(6), 499–507.

Pines, A., & Maslach, C. (1978). Characteristics of staff burnout in mental health settings. *Hospital and Community Psychiatry, 29*(4), 233–237.

Pinker, R. (1979). *The idea of welfare.* London: William Heinemann.

Piven, F., & Cloward, R. (1977). *Poor peoples movements: Why they succeed, how they fail.* New York: Pantheon Books.

Platt, A. (1977). *The child savers: The invention of delinquency* (2nd ed.). Chicago: University of Chicago Press.

Podell, L., & Miller, R. (1974). *Professionalism in public social services,* (Vol. 1, No. 2 Study Series). New York: Human Resources Administration.

Polansky, N. A., Borgman, R. D., & de Saix, C. (1973). *Child neglect: Understanding and reading the parent.* New York: Child Welfare League.

Polkinhorne, D. E. (1988). *Narrative knowing and the human sciences.* Albany, NY: State University of New York Press.

Polster, R. A., & Collins, D. (1988). Measuring variables by direct observations. In R. M. Grinnell, Jr. (Ed.), *Social work research and evaluation* (3rd ed.). Itasca, IL: Peacock.

Polya, G. (1957). *How to solve it.* Princeton: Princeton University Press.

Pomerantz, B. (1984). Collaborative interviewing: A family centered approach to pediatric care. *Health and Social Work, 9*(1), 66–73.

Pomerantz, P., Pomerantz, D. J., & Colca, I. A. (1990). A case study: Service delivery and parents with disabilities. *Child Welfare 69*(1), 65–73.

Posavac, E. J., & Carey, R. G. (1985). *Program evaluation: Methods and case studies* (2nd ed.). Englewood Cliffs, NJ: Prentice-Hall.

Powers, E., & Witmer, H. (1951). *An experiment in the prevention of delinquency: The Cambridge-Sommerville youth study.* New York: Columbia University Press.

Pratt, G. (1974). The demonstration grant is probably counter productive. *Social Work, 19*(4), 486–489.

Proceedings of the First Conference of Charities and Correction. (1875). Boston: Press of George H. Ellis.

Proctor, E., Vosler, N., & Sirles, E. (1993). The social-environmental context of child clients: An empirical exploration. *Social Work, 38*(3), 256–261.

Pruger, R. (1973). The good bureaucrat. *Social Work, 18*(4), 26–32.

Pruger, R. (1978). Bureaucratic functioning as a social work skill. In B. L. Baer & R. C. Federico (Eds.), *Educating the baccalaureate social worker.* Cambridge, MA: Ballinger.

Pumphrey, M. (1959). *The teaching of values and ethics in social work education.* New York: Council on Social Work Education.

Pumphrey, M. (1991). Mary Richmond—the practitioner. *Social Casework, 42*(10), 375–385.

Pumphrey, R., & Pumphrey, M. (1961). *The heritage of American social work.* New York: Columbia University Press.

Purcell, F. P. (1964). The helping professions and problems of the brief contact. In F. Reissman, J. Cohen, & A. Pearl (Eds.), *Mental health of the poor.* New York: Free Press.

Quam, J. K., & Austin, C. D. (1984). Coverage of women's issues in eight social work journals, 1970–1981. *Social Work, 29*(4), 360–364.

Rabinow, P., & Sullivan, W. M. (1987). The interpretive turn: A second look. In P. Rabinow & W. M. Sullivan (Eds.), *Interpretive social science: A second look* (pp. 1–30). Berkeley, CA: University of California Press.

Radloff, L. (1977). The CES-D scale: A self-report depression scale for research in the general population. *Journal of Applied Psychological Measurement, 1,* 385–401.

Rainwater, L. (1960). *And the poor get children.* Chicago: Quadrangle Books.

Ramos, R. (1985). Participant observation. In R. M. Grinnell, Jr. (Ed.), *Social work research and evaluation* (2nd ed.). Itasca, IL: Peacock.

Rapoport, L. (1959, June). In defense of social work: An examination of the stress of the profession. Lecture, at School of Social Welfare, University of California at Berkeley.

Rappaport, J. (1985). The power of empowerment language. *Social Policy, 16*(2), 15–21.

Raven, B. H., & Rubin, J. Z. (1976). *Social psychology.* New York: John Wiley & Sons.

Rawls, J. (1971). *A theory of justice.* Cambridge, MA: Harvard University Press.

Raymond, F. B. (1985). Program evaluation. In R. M. Grinnell, Jr. (Ed.), *Social work research and evaluation.* (2nd ed.). Itasca, IL: Peacock.

Raynor, P. (1985). *Social work, justice, and control.* Oxford, England: Basil Blackwell.

Reamer, F. (1979). Fundamental ethical issues in social work: An essay review. *Social Service Review, 53*(2), 229–243.

Reamer, F. (1980). Ethical contention social work. *Social Casework, 61*(9), 531–540.

Reamer, F. (1982a). *Ethical dilemmas in social service.* New York: Columbia University Press.

Reamer, F. (1982b). Conflicts of professional duty in social work. *Social Casework, 63*(10), 579–585.

Reamer, F. (1991). AIDS, social work, and the duty to protect. *Social Work, 36*(1), 56–59.

Reamer, F. (1993a). AIDS and social work: The ethics and civil liberties agenda. *Social Work, 38*(4), 412–419.

Reamer, F. (1993b). *The philosophical foundations of social work.* New York: Columbia University Press.

Reamer, F., & Abramson, M. (1982). *The teaching of social work ethics.* Hastings-on-Hudson, NY: Hastings Center.

Redhorse, J. G. (1980a). American Indian elders: Conference of Indian families. *Social Casework, 61*(8), 490–493.

Redhorse, J. G. (1980b). A family structure and value orientation in American Indians. *Social Casework, 61*(8), 462–467.

Redhorse, J. G., et al. (1978). Family behavior of urban American Indians. *Social Casework, 59*(2), 67–72.

Redl, F., & Wineman, D. (1957). *The aggressive child.* Glencoe: Free Press.

Redlich, F. C., & Freedman, D. K. (1966). *The theory and practice of psychiatry.* New York: Basic Books, p. 36.

Reid, W. J. (1975). A test of a task-centered approach. *Social Work, 20*(1), 3–9.

Reid, W. J. (1978). *The task-centered system.* New York: Columbia University Press.

Reid, W. J. (1980). Research strategies for improving individualized services. In D. F. (Ed.), *Future of social work research* (pp. 38–52). Washington: National Association of Social Workers.

Reid, W. J. (1985). *Family problem solving.* New York: Columbia University Press.

Reid, W. J. (1988). Writing research reports. In R. M. Grinnell, Jr. (Ed.), *Social work research and evaluation* (3rd ed.). Itasca, IL: Peacock.

Reid, W. J., & Epstein, L. (1977). *Task-centered practice.* New York: Columbia University Press.

Reid, W. J., & Epstein, L. (1972). *Task-centered casework.* New York: Columbia University Press.

Rein, M. (1970). Social work in search of a radical profession. *Social Work, 15*(2), 13–33.

Reisch, M., Wenocur, S., & Sherman, W. (1981). Empowerment, conscientization, and animation as core social work skills. *Social Development Issues, 5*(2).

Reul, M. R. (1974). *Territorial boundaries of rural poverty: Profiles of exploitation.* Lansing, MI: Michigan State University Cooperative Extension Service.

Reynolds, B. (1932). The role of the psychiatric social worker in therapy. In F. E. Williams (Ed.), *Proceedings of first international congress on mental hygiene* (pp. 668–685). New York: The International Committee for Mental Hygiene.

Reynolds, B. C. (1963). *Uncharted journey.* New York: Citadel Press.

Rhodes, M. (1986). *Ethical dilemmas in social work practice.* Boston: Routledge & Kegan Paul.

Rhodes, S. (1977). Contract negotiation in the initial stage of casework service. *Social Service Review, 51*(1), 125–140.

Rich, J. (1968). *Interviewing children and adolescents.* New York: St. Martin's Press.

Richey, C., Blythe, B., & Berlin, S. (1982). *A follow up study of the educational unit: Do our graduates evaluate their practice?* Paper presented at the Annual Program Meeting, Council on Social Work Education, New York, NY.

Richmond, M. (1920a). What are you thinking? *The Family, 1*(1), 1–3.

Richmond, M. (1920b). Some next steps in social treatment. *Proceedings of the National Conference of Social Work,* 1920. Chicago: University of Chicago Press, p. 254.

Richmond, M. E. (1899). *Friendly visiting among the poor: A handbook for charity workers.* New York: Macmillan.

Richmond, M. E. (1917). *Social diagnosis.* New York: Russell Sage Foundation.

Rieff, P. (1966). *The triumph of the therapeutic: Uses of faith after Freud.* New York: Harper & Row.

Riessman, F. (1962). *The culturally deprived child.* New York: Harper & Row.

Riessman, F. (1976). How does self-help work? *Social Policy, 7*(2), 41–45.

Ripple, L., & Alexander, E. (1956). Motivation, capacity and opportunity as related to casework service: Nature of the client's problem. *Social Service Review, 30*(1), 38–54.

Ripple, L., Alexander, E., & Polemis, B. (1964). *Motivation, capacity and opportunity: Studies in casework theory and practice.* Chicago: School of Social Service Administration, University of Chicago.

Roberts, H. (1979). *Community development: Learning and action.* Toronto: University of Toronto Press.

Roberts, R. W. (1980). The relationship between social work research and practice: Toward dissolution or consummation. *Hong Kong Journal of Social Work, 14,* 2–12.

Roberts, R. W., & Nee, R. H. (Eds.). (1970). *Theories of social casework.* Chicago: University of Chicago Press.

Robinson, J. P., & Shaver, P. R. (1973). *Measures of social psychological attitudes* (rev. ed.). Ann Arbor, MI: Survey Research Center, Institute for Social Research.

Robinson, V. (1930). *A changing psychology in social case work.* Chapel Hill, NC: University of North Carolina Press.

Robinson, V., & Taft, J. (1944). *A functional approach to family casework.* Philadelphia: University of Pennsylvania Press.

Rogers, C. (1968). Some personal learnings about interpersonal relationships [Film].

Rogers, C. (1966). Client-centered therapy. In C. H. Patterson (Ed.), *Theories of counseling and psychotherapy.* New York: Harper & Row.

Rogers, C. R. (1951). *Client-centered therapy.* Boston: Houghton Mifflin.

Rogers, C. R. (1961). *On becoming a person.* Boston: Houghton Mifflin.

Rogers, C. R. (1967). Carl R. Rogers. In E. G. Boring & G. Lindzey (Eds.), *History of psychology in autobiography, 5,* 343–383. New York: Appleton, Century,Crofts.

Rogers, C. R. (1974). In retrospect: Forty-six years. *American Psychologist, 29,* 46–69.

Rojek, C., & Collins, S. A. (1987). Contract or con trick? *British Journal of Social Work, 17*(2), 199–211.

Rojek, C., & Collins, S. (1988). Contract or con trick revisited: Comments on the reply by Gordon and Preston-Shoot. *British Journal of Social Work, 18*(6), 611–622.

Rooney, R. (1988). Socialization strategies for involuntary clients. *Social Casework: Journal of Contemporary Social Work, 69*(3), 131–140.

Rooney, R. (1989). *Strategies for work with involuntary clients.* New York: Columbia University Press.

Rose, A. M. (Ed.). (1962). *Human behavior and social processes.* Boston: Houghton Mifflin.

Rose, S. M., & Black, B. L. (1985). *Advocacy and empowerment: Mental health care in the community.* Boston: Routledge & Kegan Paul.

Rose, S. (Ed.) (1992). *Case Management and Social Work Practice.* White Plains, NY: Longman.

Rosen, A., & Lieberman, D. (1972). The experimental evaluation of interview performance of social workers. *Social Science Review, 46*(3), 395–412.

Rosenthal, D. (1955). Changes in some moral values following psychotherapy. *Journal of Consulting Psychology, 19*(6), 431–436.

Ross, H., & Johnson, A. M. (1950). The Growing Science of Casework. In C. Kasius (Ed.), *Principles and Techniques in Social Casework: Selected Articles, 1940–50* (p. 53). New York: Family Service Association of America.

Rossi, P. H. (1979). *Evaluation: A systematic approach.* Beverly Hills, CA: Sage.

Roth, J. A. (1962). The treatment of tuberculosis as a bargaining process. In A. M. Rose (Ed.), *Human behavior and social processes* (pp. 575–588). Boston: Houghton Mifflin.

Roth, J. A. (1963). *Timetables.* Indianapolis: Bobbs-Merrill.

Rothman, D. J. (1971). *The discovery of the asylum.* Boston: Little, Brown.

Rothman, J., & Tropman, J. (1987). Models of community organization and macro practice perspectives: Their mixing and phasing. In F. Cox, J. Erlich, J. Rothman, & J. Tropman (Eds.), *Strategies of community organization* (4th ed.) (pp. 3–26). Itasca, IL: Peacock.

Rubin, A. (1988). Secondary analyses. In Richard M. Grinnell, Jr. (Ed.), *Social work research and evaluation* (3rd ed.). Itasca, IL: Peacock.

Rubin, A., & Babbie, E. (1993). *Research methods for social work* (2nd ed.). Pacific Grove, CA: Brooks/Cole.

Rubin, A., & Johnson, P. (1984). Direct practice interests of entering MSW students. *Journal of Social Work Education, 20.*

Rubin, J. Z., & Brown, B. R. (1975). *The social psychology of bargaining and negotiation.* New York: Academic Press.

Rubington, E., & Weinberg, M. S. (1968). *Deviance: The Interactionist Perspective.* New York: Macmillan.

Rubinstein, M. A. (1975). *Patterns of problem-solving.* Englewood Cliffs, NJ: Prentice-Hall.

Ruckdeschel, R. A., & Farris, B. E. (1981). Assessing practice: A critical look at the single case design. *Social Casework, 62*(7), 413–419.

Ruesch, J. (1961). *Therapeutic communication.* New York: W. W. Norton.

Russell, P. A., Lankford, M. W., & Grinnell, R. M., Jr. (1983). Attitudes toward supervisors in a human service agency. *The Clinical Supervisor, 1*(1), 57–71.

Russell, P. A., Lankford, M. W., & Grinnell, R. M., Jr. (1985). Administrative styles of social work supervisors in a human service agency. In Simon Slavin (Ed.), *Introduction to human services administration.* New York: Haworth.

Rutman, L. (1977). *Evaluation research methods: A basic guide.* Beverly Hills, CA: Sage.

Rutman, L. (1980). *Planning useful evaluations: Evaluability assessment.* Beverly Hills, CA: Sage.

Rutman, L. (1984). Evaluability assessment. In Leonard Rutman (Ed.), *Evaluation research & methods: A basic guide* (2nd ed.). Beverly Hills, CA: Sage.

Rutman, L., & Hudson, J. (1984). Evaluation research in human services. In B. R. Compton, & B. Galaway (Eds.), *Social work processes* (3rd ed.). Homewood, IL: Dorsey.

Ryan, W. (1971). *Blaming the victim.* New York: Vintage Press.

Sainsbury, E. (1980). Research and reflection on the social work task. *Social Work Service, 23,* 13.

Saleebey, D. (1988). *Theory and the generation and subversion of knowledge.* School of Social Work, University of Kansas.

Saleebey, D. (1990). Philosophical disputes in social work: Social justice denied. *Journal of Sociology and Social Welfare, 17*(2), 29–40.

Salomon, E. L. (1967). Humanistic values and social casework. *Social Casework, 48*(1), 26–33.

Saltzman, A. (1986). Reporting child abusers and protecting substance abusers. *Social Work, 31*(6), 474–475.

Sancier, B. (Ed.) (1984). Ethics and values. *Practice Digest, 6*(4), entire issue.

Sander, F. (1982, June). Keynote address at the first American Bar Association Conference on Alternative Means of Family Dispute Resolution, Washington, D.C.

Sanders, M. K. (1957, March). Social work: A profession chasing its tail. *Harpers, 56–62.*

Sands, R. G. (1988). Sociolinguistic analysis of a mental health interview. *Social Work, 33*(2), 149–154.

Sands, R. G., Stafford, T., & McClelland, M. (1990). I beg to differ: Conflict in the interdisciplinary team. *Social Work in Health Care, 26*(4).

Saxon, W. (1979). Behavioral contracting: Theory and design. *Child Welfare, 63*(8), 523–529.

Schafer, R. (1968). Interpersonal dynamics in the test situation. In A. Z. Guiora and M. A. Brandwin (Eds.), *Perspectives in clinical psychology* (pp. 13–44). Princeton, NJ: D. Van Nostrand.

Schafler, M. (1980). Individualized educational programs in a school for the handicapped. *Social Work in Education, 3*(1), 32–43.

Schelling, T. C. (1960). *The strategy of conflict* (chap. 2). London: Oxford University Press.

Scherrer, J. (1976). How social workers help lawyers. *Social Work, 21*(4), 279–283.

Schon, D. A. (1983). *The reflective practitioner: How professionals think in action.* New York: Basic Books.

Schrier, C. J. (1980). Guidelines for recordkeeping under privacy and open-access laws. *Social Work, 25,* 452–457.

Schmitt, M. H., Farrell, M. P., & Heinemann, G. D. (1988). Conceptual and methodological problems in studying the effects of interdisciplinary geriatric teams. *The Gerontologist, 28*(6), 753–764.

Schubert, M. (1982). *Interviewing in social work practice* (2nd ed.). New York: Council on Social Work Education.

Schuler, H. (1982). *Ethical problems in psychological research* (M. S. Woodruff & R. A. Wicklund, trans.). New York: Academic Press.

Schur, E. (1973). *Radical non-intervention: Rethinking the delinquency problem.* Englewood Cliffs, NJ: Prentice-Hall.

Schwartz, G. (1989). Confidentiality revisited. *Social Work, 34*(3), 223–226.

Schwartz, W. (1961). Social worker in the group. In National Conference on Social Welfare (Ed.), *Social Welfare Forum.* New York: Columbia University Press.

Schwartz, W. (1971). Social group work: The interactionist approach. In R. Morris (Ed.), *Encyclopedia of social work.* New York: National Association of Social Workers.

Scott, D. C. (1989). Meaning construction and social work practice. *Social Service Review, 63*(1), 39–51.

Seaberg, J. R. (1988). Utilizing sampling procedures. In R. M. Grinnell, Jr. (Ed.), *Social work research and evaluation* (3rd ed.). Itasca, IL: Peacock.

Seabury, B. (1971). Arrangement of physical space in social work settings. *Social Work, 16*(4), 43–49.

Seabury, B. (1976). The contract: Uses, abuses and limitations. *Social Work, 21*(1), 16–21.

Seabury, B. (1979). Negotiating sound contracts with clients. *Public Welfare, 37*(2).

Seabury, B. (1980). *Successful case advocacy: A prescriptive model.* Paper presented at the Annual Program Meeting, Council on Social Work Education, Los Angeles, CA.

Seabury, B. A. (1985). The beginning phase: Engagement, initial assessment, and contracting. In J. Laird & A. Hartman (Eds.), *A handbook of child welfare* (pp. 335–359). New York: Free Press.

Seagull, A. A., & Noll, R. B. (1982). Beyond informed consent: Ethical and philosophical considerations in using behavior modification or play therapy in the treatment of enuresis. *The Journal of Clinical Child Psychology, 11*(1), 44–49.

Seidel, J. V., Kjolseth, R., & Clark, J. A. (1985). *The Ethnograph.* Littleton, CO: Qualis Research Associates.

Selby, L. G. (1956). Supportive treatment: The development of a concept and a helping method. *Social Service Review, 30*(4), 400–414.

Seligman, M. E. P. (1974). Depression and learned helplessness. In R. J. Friedman & M. M. Katz (Eds.), *The psychology of depression: Contemporary theory and research.* New York: Halstead Press.

Seligman, M. E. P. (1975). *Helplessness: On depression, development and death.* San Francisco: W. H. Freeman.

Senna, J. J. (1974). Changes in due process of law. *Social Work, 19*(3), 319–324.

Sennett, R., & Cobb, J. (1972). *The hidden injuries of class.* New York: Random House.

Shaw, M. (1985). Parent child mediation: A challenge and a promise. *Mediation Quarterly, 7,* 23–33.

Sheafor, B. W., Horejsi, C. R., & Horejsi, G. A. (1988). *Techniques and guidelines for social work practice.* Boston: Allyn and Bacon.

Sheffield, A. E. (1920). *The social case history: Its construction and content.* New York: Russell Sage Foundation.

Sheldon, B. (1978). Theory and practice in social work: A re-examination of a tenuous relationship. *British Journal of Social Work, 8,* 1–25.

Shireman, C. H., & Reamer, F. (1986).*Rehabilitating juvenile justice.* New York: Columbia University Press.

Shonholtz, R. (1984). Neighborhood justice systems: Work, structure, and guiding principles. *Mediation Quarterly, 3.*

Short, J. S., & Nye, F. I. (1957). Reported behavior as a criterion of deviant behavior. *Social Problems, 5*(3), 207–213.

Shulman, L. (1967). Scapegoats, group workers and pre-emptive intervention. *Social Work, 12*(2), 37–43.

Shulman, L. (1979). *The skills of helping.* Itasca, IL: Peacock.

Shulman, L. (1984). *The skills of helping individuals and groups* (2nd ed.). Itasca, IL: Peacock.

Sieber, S. (1981). *Fatal remedies.* New York: Plenum Press.

Siegel, D. H. (1988). Integrating data gathering techniques and practice activities. In R. M. Grinnell, Jr. (Ed.), *Social work research and evaluation* (3rd ed.). Itasca, IL: Peacock.

Siegel, D. H., & Reamer, F. G. (1988). Integrating research findings, concepts, and logic into practice. In R. M. Grinnell, Jr. (Ed.), *Social work research and evaluation* (3rd ed.). Itasca, IL: Peacock.

Silbert, M. H., & Pines, A. M. (1983). Early sexual exploitation and an influence in prostitution. *Social Work, 28*(4), 285–289.

Silverman, M. (1977). Children's rights and social work. *Social Service Review, 51*(1), 171–178.

Silverman, P. R. (1986). The perils of borrowing: Role of the professional in mutual help groups. *The Journal for Specialists in Group Work, 11*(2), 68–73.

Simmons, J. L. (1969). *Deviants.* Berkeley, CA: Glendessary Press.

Simmons, R. L. (1982). Strategies for exercising influence. *Social Work, 27*(3), 268–274.

Simmons, R. L. (1985). Inducement as an approach to exercising influence. *Social Work, 30*(1), 56–62.

Simon, B. (1964, April). *Borrowed concepts. Problems and issues for curriculum planning, health and disability concepts in social work education* (pp. 31–42). Proceedings of a workshop conference, School of Social Work, University of Minnesota, Minneapolis.

Simon, H. (1952). Comments on the theory of organization. *American Political Science Review, 46*(4), 1130–1139.

Simon, H. (1957). *Administrative behavior* (2nd ed.). New York: Macmillan.

Simons, R. L., & Aigner, S. M. (1985). *Practice principles: A problem-solving approach to social work*. New York: Macmillan.

Simpson, R. L. (1978). Is research utilization for social workers? *Journal of Social Service Research, 2*(2), 143–158.

Siporin, M. (1975). *Introduction to social work practice*. New York: Macmillan.

Siporin, M. (1978). Practice theory and vested interests. *Social Service Review, 52,* 418–436.

Siporin, M. (1983). Morality and immorality in working with clients. *Social Thought, 9*(4), 10–18.

Siporin, M. (1985). Current social work perspectives on clinical practice. *Clinical Social Work Journal, 13,* 198–217.

Sklar, K. K. (1985). Hull House in the 1890s: A community of women reformers. *Signs: Journal of Women in Culture and Society, 10,* 658–677.

Slavin, S. (1969). Concepts of social conflict: Use in social work curriculum. *Journal of Education for Social Work, 5*(2), 47–60.

Sloan, D. (1979). The teaching of ethics in American undergraduate curriculum, 1876–1976. *Hastings Center Report, 9.*

Smale, G., Tuson, G., Cooper, M., Wardle, M., & Crosbie, D. (1988). *Community social work: A paradigm for change*. London: National Institute for Social Work.

Smart, J. J. C., & Williams, B. (1973). *Utilitarianism: For and against*. Cambridge, England: Cambridge University Press.

Smith, C. (1971). *Conflict resolution: Contributions of the behavior sciences*. Notre Dame, IN: University of Notre Dame Press.

Smith, N. J. (1988). Formulating research goals and problems. In R. M. Grinnell, Jr. (Ed.), *Social work research and evaluation* (3rd ed.). Itasca, IL: Peacock.

Smith, P. (1984). Social service teams and their managers. *British Journal of Social Work, 14*(6), 601–613.

Snyder, G. H., & Diesing, P. (1977). *Conflict among nations* (Chap. 2). Princeton, NJ: Princeton University Press.

Solomon, B. (1976). *Black empowerment: Social work in oppressed communities*. New York: Columbia University Press.

Solomon, B. (1985). How do we really empower families? New strategies for social work practitioners. *Family Resource Coalition Report, 4*(3), 2–3.

Solomon, G. (1980). *Problems and issues in rural community mental health: A review*. Lubbock: Department of Psychology, Texas Technical University.

Sosin, M., & Caulum, S. (1983). Advocacy: A conceptualization for social work practice. *Social Work, 28*(1), 12–17.

Southard, E. E. (1919). The individual versus the family as a unit of interest in social work. *Proceedings of National Conference of Social Work,* 582–587.

Specht, H. (1968). Casework practice and social policy formulation. *Social Work, 13*(1), 42–52.

Specht, H. (1988). *New Directions for Social Work Practice* (pp. 49–56). Englewood Cliffs, NJ: Prentice-Hall.

Specht, H. (1990). Social work and the popular psychotherapies. *Social Service Review, 64,* 345–358.

Specht, H., & Riessman, F. (1963, June). Some notes on a model for an integrated social work approach to social problems (Mimeo). New York: Mobilization for Youth.

Specht, H., & Specht, R. (1986a). Social work assessment: Route to clienthood, part I. *Social Casework, 67*(9), 525–532.

Specht, H., & Specht, R. (1986b). Social work assessment: Route to clienthood, part II. *Social Casework, 67*(10), 587–593.

Speck, R. F. (1967a). *Psychotherapy of family social networks.* Paper presented at the Family Therapy Symposium, Medical College of Virginia, Richmond.

Speck, R. F. (1967b). *The politics and psychotherapy of mini-and micro-groups.* Paper presented at Congress on Dialectics of Liberation, London.

Sprout, H., & Sprout, M. (1961). Environmental factors in the study of international politics. In J. N. Rosenau (Ed.), *International politics and foreign policy* (pp. 106–119). New York: The Free Press of Glencoe.

Stace, W. (1975). Ethical absolutism and ethical relativism. In K. J. Strutil & P. Rothenberg (Eds.), *Ethics in Perspective* (pp. 51–60). New York: Random House.

Stein, T., & Gambrill, E. (1977). Facilitating decision making in foster care: The Alameda project. *Social Service Review, 51*(3), 502–513.

Stein, T., Gambrill, E., & Wiltse, K. (1974). Foster care: Use of contracts. *Public Welfare, 32*(4), 20–25.

Strauss, A. (1978). *Negotiations.* San Francisco: Jossey-Bass.

Strauss, A., Schatzman, L., Bucher, R., Ehrlich, D., & Sabshin, M. (1964). *Psychiatric ideologies and institutions.* New York: Free Press.

Strauss, A., Schatzman, L., Ehrlich, D., Bucher, R., & Sabshin, M. (1963). The hospital and its negotiated order. In E. Freidson (Ed.), *The hospital in modern society* (pp. 147–169). New York: Free Press.

Strauss, A. L. (1987). *Qualitative analysis for social scientists.* New York: Cambridge University Press.

Streat, Y. (1987). Case recording in children's protective services. *Social Casework, 68,* 553–560.

Stretch, J. J. (1967). Existentialism: A proposed philosophical orientation for social work. *Social Work, 12*(4), 97–103.

Stroup, H. (1960). Social work's new era. In *Social welfare forum, 1960* (pp. 67–78). New York: Columbia University Press.

Strupp, H. H., & Hadley, S. (1977, March). A tripartite model of mental health and therapeutic outcomes. *American Psychologist, 32,* 187–196.

Stuart, P. (1988). Historical research. In R. M. Grinnell, Jr. (Ed.), *Social work research and evaluation* (3rd ed.). Itasca, IL: Peacock.

Studt, E. (1968). Social work theory and implications for the practice of methods. *Social Work Education Reporter, 16*(2), 22–24, 42–46.

Suchman, E. A. (1967). *Evaluative research: Principles and practice in public service and social action programs.* New York: Russell Sage Foundation.

Sullivan, H. S. (1954). *The psychiatric interview.* New York: Norton.

Sullivan, H. S. (1970). *The psychiatric interview.* New York: Norton.

Swift, L. B. (1928). Can the sociologist and social worker agree on the content of case records? *Social Forces, 6,* 535–538.

Sytz, F. (1949). Teaching recording. *Journal of Social Casework, 30,* 399–405.

Taber, M., & Shapiro, I. (1965). Social work and its knowledge base: A content analysis of the periodical literature. *Social Work, 10*(4), 100–106.

Taber, M. A., & Vattano, A. J. (1970). Clinical and social orientations in social work: An empirical study. *Social Service Review, 44*(1), 34–43.

Taber, R. H. (1969). *Providing mental health services to a low socio-economic black community without requiring that people perceive themselves as patients: An ecological system approach to a community group.* Paper presented at 46th Annual Meeting of the American Orthopsychiatric Association, New York.

Taft, J. (1920). The Social Worker's Opportunity. *Proceedings of the National Conference of Social Work, 1920,* 374–375. Chicago: University of Chicago Press.

Taft, J. (1935). *The dynamics of therapy in a controlled relationship.* New York: Macmillan.

Tannenbaum, F. (1951). *Crime and community* (2nd ed.). New York: Columbia University Press.

Tatara, T. (1989). Characteristics of children in foster care. *Division of Child, Youth, and Family Services Newsletter* (American Psychological Association) *12*(3), 16–17.

Teare, R. J. (1983). Reclassification and Licensing. In S. Briar (Ed.), *1983–84 Supplement to the Encyclopedia of Social Work* (17th ed.), (pp. 120–27).

Tedeschi, J., Schlenker, B., & Bonoma, T. (1973). *Conflict, power and games: The experimental study of interpersonal relations.* Hawthorne, NY: Aldine.

Teicher, M. I. (1967). Social casework: Science or art? *Child Welfare, 46,* 393–396.

Terrell, P. (1967). The social worker as radical: Roles of advocacy. *New Perspectives, 1*(1), 83–88.

Thomas, E. J. (1975). Use of research methods in interpersonal practice. In N. P. (Ed.), *Social work research: Methods for the helping professions* (rev. ed.) (pp. 254–288). Chicago: University of Chicago Press.

Thomas, E. J. (1978). Research and service in single-case experimentation: Conflicts and choices. *Social Work Research and Abstracts, 14*(4), 20–31.

Thomas, G. (1978). Final report of the temporary foster care project (Mimeograph). Lansing, MI: Division of Youth Services, Department of Social Services.

Thompson, J. D. (1967). *Organizations in action.* New York: McGraw-Hill.

Thyer, B. A. (1987). Contingency analysis: Toward a unified theory for social work practice. *Social Work, 32*(2), 150–158.

Thyer, B. A. (1993). Single system research designs. In Richard M. Grinnell, Jr. (Ed.), *Social Work Research and Evaluation* (4th ed.). Itasca, IL: Peacock.

Tillich, P. (1962). The philosophy of social work. *Social Service Review, 36*(1), 12–16.

Timms, N. (1972). *Recording in social work.* London: Routledge & Kegan Paul.

Tobias, M. (1990). Validator: A key role in empowering the chronically mentally ill. *Social Work, 35*(4), 357–359.

Toch, H. (1970). The care and feeding of typologies and labels. *Federal Probation, 34*(3), 15–19.

Tomassic, R., & Feeley, M. (Eds.). (1982). *Neighborhood justice: An assessment of an emerging idea.* New York: Longman.

Toseland, R. W. (1985). Research methods. In R. M. Grinnell, Jr. (Ed.), *Social work research and evaluation* (2nd ed.). Itasca, IL: Peacock.

Toseland, R. W., & Hacker, L. (1985). Social workers' use of self-help groups as a resource for clients. *Social Work, 30*(3), 232–237.

Towle, C. (1965). *Common human needs.* New York: National Association of Social Workers (Original work published 1945).

Tracy, E. M., Haapala, D. A., Kinney, J., & Pecora, P. J. (Eds.). (1991). *Intensive family preservation services: An instructional sourcebook.* Cleveland, OH: Mandel School of Applied Social Sciences, Case Western Reserve University.

Trader, H. (1977). Survival strategies for oppressed minorities. *Social Work, 22*(1), 10–13.

Tripodi, T. (1983). *Evaluative research for social workers.* Englewood Cliffs, NJ: Prentice-Hall.

Tripodi, T. (1985). Research designs. In R. M. Grinnell, Jr. (Ed.), *Social work research and evaluation* (2nd ed.). Itasca, IL: Peacock.

Tropp, E. (1968). The group: In life and in social work. *Social Casework, 49*(5), 267–274.

Tropp, E. (1976). *Theories of social work with groups.* New York: Columbia University Press.

Tropp, E. (1984). Three problematic concepts: Client, help, and worker. *Social Casework, 55*(1), 19–29.

Truax, C., & Mitchell, K. (1971). Research on certain interpersonal skills in relation to process and outcome. In A. Bergin & S. Garfield (Eds.), *Handbook for psychotherapy and behavior*. New York: John Wiley & Sons.

Truax, C. B., & Carkhuff, R. (1967). *Toward effective counseling and psychotherapy: Training and practice*. Hawthorne, NY: Aldine.

Tucker, B. Z., & Dyson, E. (1976). The family and the school: Utilizing human resources to promote learning. *Family Process, 15*(1), 125–141.

Turner, F. J. (Ed.). (1986). *Social work treatment: Interlocking theoretical approaches* (3rd ed.). New York: Free Press.

Turner, J. (1984). Reuniting children in foster care with their biological families. *Social Work, 29*(6), 501–505.

Twente, E. S. (1965). Aging, strength and creativity. *Social Work, 10*(3), 105–110.

Udry, J. R. (1966). *The social context of marriage*. Philadelphia: J. B. Lippincott.

Ullman, M. (1969). A unifying concept linking therapeutic and community process. In F. Duhl & N. Rizzo (Eds.). *General systems theory and psychiatry*. Boston: Little, Brown.

Umbrecht, M. (1994). *Mediation and Social Work*. Newbury Park, California: Sage.

Umbreit, M. (1986). Victim offender mediation: A national survey. *Federal Probation, 50*(4), 53–56.

Veroff, J., Kulka, R. A., & Douvan, E. (1976). *Mental health in America: Patterns of help-seeking from 1957 to 1976*.

Videka-Sherman, L. (1989). Intervention for child neglect: The empirical knowledge base. Paper presented at the National Centre on Child Abuse and Neglect Research Symposium on Child Neglect, Washington, DC.

Videka-Sherman, L., & Reid, W. J. (1985). The structured clinical record: A clinical education tool. *The Clinical Supervisor, 3*(1), 45–62.

Vogel, E., and Bell, N. (1968). The emotionally disturbed child as the family scapegoat. In E. Vogel & N. Bell (Eds.), *A Modern Introduction to the Family* (pp. 382–397). New York: Free Press.

Voss, H. L. (1966). Socio-economic status and reported delinquent behavior. *Social Problems, 13*(3), 314–324.

Waelder, R. (1950). The scientific approach to casework with special emphasis on psychoanalysis. In C. Kasius, (Ed.), *Principles and techniques in social casework: Selected articles, 1940–50* (p. 35). New York: Family Service Association of America.

Wakefield, J. C. (1988a). Psychotherapy, Distributive Justice, and Social Work (pt. 1). *Social Services Review, 62*(2), 187–210.

Wakefield, J. C. (1988b). Distributive justice as a conceptual framework for social work (pt. 2). *Social Services Review, 62*(3), 353–382.

Walsh, M. E. (1981). Rural social work practice: Clinical quality. *Social Casework: The Journal of Contemporary Social Work, 62*(8), 458–464.

Walton, R. (1969). *Interpersonal peace making*. Reading, MA: Addison-Wesley.

Wasserman, H. (1970). Early careers of professional workers in a public child welfare agency. *Social Work, 15*(3), 98–101.

Wasserstrom, R. (1975). The obligation to obey the law. In R. Wasserstrom (Ed.), *Today's moral problems* (pp. 358–384). New York: Macmillan.

Watkins, S. (1989). Confidentiality and privileged communications: Legal dilemma for family therapists. *Social Work, 34*(2), 133–136.

Weber, M. (1947). *The theory of social and economic organization*. New York: Free Press.

Weber, R. E., & Polansky, N. A. Evaluation. In N. A. Polansky (Ed.), *Social work research: Methods for the helping professions* (rev. ed.). Chicago: University of Chicago Press.

Weber, T., McKeever, J. E., & McDaniel, S. H. (1985). A beginner's guide to the problem-oriented first family interview. *Family Process, 24*(23), 357–364.

Webster's Ninth New Collegiate Dictionary. (1988). Springfield, MA: Merriam-Webster.

Weed, L. L. (1969). *Medical records, medical education, and patient care.* Cleveland, OH: Case Western Reserve University.

Weick, A. (1983). Issues in overturning a model of social work practice. *Social Work, 28*(6), 467–471.

Weick, A. (1987). Reconceptualizing the philosophical perspective of social work. *Social Service Review, 61,* 218–230.

Weick, A., & Pope, L. (1988). Knowing what's best: A new look at self-determination. *Social Casework, 69*(1), 10–16.

Weick, A., Ropp, C., Sullivan, W., & Kishardt, W. (1989). A strengths perspective for social work practice. *Social Work, 31,* 332–337.

Weinbach, R. W. (1988). Agency and professional contexts of research. In R. M. Grinnell, Jr. (Ed.), *Social work research and evaluation* (3rd ed.). Itasca, IL: Peacock.

Weinbach, R. W., & Grinnell, R. M., Jr. (1987). *Statistics for social workers.* White Plains, NY: Longman.

Weiner, H. (1979, February). *Knowledge and skills for collaborative care.* Paper presented at the Institute on Collaborative Practice in Health Care, Long Island Jewish-Hillside Medical Center, New Hyde Park, New York.

Weisband, E., & Franck, T. M. (1975). *Resignation in protest.* New York: Grossman.

Weisman, M., & Lockes, B. (1975). *Comparison of a self-report symptom rating scale (CES-D) with standardized depression rating scales in a psychiatric population: A preliminary report.* Paper presented at the Society for Epidemiological Research, Albany, NY.

Weiss, C. H. (Ed.). (1972a). *Evaluating action programs: Readings in social action.* Boston: Allyn & Bacon.

Weiss, C. H. (1972b). *Evaluation research: Methods of assessing program effectiveness.* Englewood Cliffs, NJ: Prentice-Hall.

Weissman, H. H. (1973). *Overcoming mismanagement in the human services.* San Francisco: Jossey-Bass.

Werner, H. D. (1982). *Cognitive therapy: A humanistic approach.* New York: Free Press.

Werner, H. D. (1986). Cognitive theory. In F. J. Turner (Ed.), *Social work treatment* (pp. 91–130). New York: Free Press.

Wetzel, J. W. (1986). A feminist world view conceptual framework. *Social Casework, 67,* 166–173.

Whan, M. W. (1979). Accounts, narrative, and case history. *British Journal of Social Work, 9,* 489–499.

Wheelis, A. (1950). The place of action in personality change. *Psychiatry, 13*(2), 135–148.

White, A. (1971). *The apperceptive mass of foreigners as applied to Americanization: The Mexican group, 1923.* Berkeley: University of California.

White, R. W. (1959). Motivation reconsidered: The concept of competence. *Psychological Review, 66*(5), 297–334.

White, R. W. (1963). *Ego and reality in psychoanalytic theory.* New York: International Universities Press.

Whittaker, J. K. (1974). *Social treatment: An approach to interpersonal helping.* Hawthorne, NY: Aldine.

Whittaker, J. K., Kinney, J., Tracy, E. M., & Booth, C. (Eds.). *Reaching high-risk families: Intensive family preservation in human services.* Hawthorne, NY: Aldine de Gruyter.

Whittaker, J. K., Schinke, S. P., & Gilchrist, L. D. (1986). The ecological paradigm in child, youth and family services: Implications for policy and practice. *Social Service Review, 60*(4), 483–503.

Wilczynski, B. L. (1981). New life for recording: Involving the client. *Social Work, 26,* 313–317.

Wilensky, H. L., & Lebeaux, C. N. (1958). *Industrial society and social welfare.* New York: Russel Sage Foundation.

Williams, B. C. (1988). Parents and patients: Members of an interdisciplinary team on an adolescent inpatient unit. *Clinical Social Work Journal, 16*(1), 78–91.

Williams, J. B. W. (1981). DSM-III: A comprehensive approach to diagnosis. *Social Work, 26*(2), 101–107.

Williams, L., & Hopps, J. (1988). On the nature of professional communication: Publication for practitioners. *Social Work, 33*(5), 453–459.

Wills, T. A. (1978). Perceptions of clients by professional helpers. *Psychological Bulletin, 85*(5), 968–1000.

Wilson, S. (1978). *Confidentiality in social work: Issues and principles.* New York: Free Press.

Wilson, S. J. (1980). *Recording: Guidelines for social workers.* New York: Free Press.

Wiseman, J. P. (1970). *Stations of the lost* (chap. 9). Englewood Cliffs, NJ: Prentice-Hall.

Witkin, S. L. (1982). Cognitive processes in clinical practice. *Social Work, 27,* 389–395.

Witkin, S. L. (1989, March). *The implications of social constructionism for social work education.* Paper presented at the Annual Program Meeting of the Council on Social Work Education, Chicago.

Wolfensberger, W. (1975). *The origin and nature of our institutional models.* Syracuse, NY: Human Policy Press.

Wood, K. (1978, November). Casework effectiveness: A new look at the research evidence. *Social Work, 23*(6), 437–459.

Woodson, R. (1981). *A summons to life.* Cambridge, Mass: Ballinger.

Wright, M., & Galaway, B. (Eds.). (1988). *Mediation in criminal justice: Victims, offenders, and communities practice.* London: Sage.

Wrobel, A. (Ed.). (1987). *Pseudo-science and society in nineteenth-century America.* Lexington: University Press of Kentucky.

Yalom, I. D. (1985). *The theory and practice of group psychotherapy* (3rd ed.). New York: Basic Books.

Yegidis, B., & Weinbach, R. (1991). *Research Methods for Social Work.* White Plains, NY: Longman.

Yellot, A. W. (1990). Mediation and domestic violence: A call for collaboration. *Mediation Quarterly, 8*(1), 39–50.

Young, I. M. (1986). Impartiality and the civic public: Some implications of feminist critiques of moral and political theory. *Praxis International, 5*(4), 381–401.

Zastrow, C. (1984). Understanding and preventing burn-out. *British Journal of Social Work, 14*(2), 141–155.

Zayas, L., & Katch, M. (1989). Contracting with adolescents: An ego-psychological approach. *Social Casework, 70*(1), 3–9.

Zehr, Howard. (1990). *Changing Lenses.* Scottdale, PA: Herald Press.

Zeilinger, R. (1979). The need vs. the right to know. *Public Welfare, 37*(3), 44–47.

Zetzel, G. (1985). In and out of the family crucible: Reflections on parent-child mediation. *Mediation Quarterly, 7,* 47–67.

Zetzel, G., & Wixted, S. (1984). *Parent child mediation.* Cambridge, MA: Children's Hearings Project.

Index

TO THE OWNER OF THIS BOOK:

We hope that you have found *Social Work Processes*, Fifth Edition, useful. So that this book can be improved in a future edition, would you take the time to complete this sheet and return it? Thank you.

School and address: _____

Department: _____

Instructor's name: _____

1. What I like most about this book is: _____

_____

_____

2. What I like least about this book is: _____

_____

_____

3. My general reaction to this book is: _____

_____

4. The name of the course in which I used this book is: _____

_____

5. Were all of the chapters of the book assigned for you to read? _____

   If not, which ones weren't? _____

 6. In the space below, or on a separate sheet of paper, please write specific suggestions for improving this book and anything else you'd care to share about your experience in using the book.

_____

_____

_____

_____

_____

Optional:

Your name: _____ Date: _____

May Brooks/Cole quote you, either in promotion for *Social Work Processes*, Fifth Edition, or in future publishing ventures?

Yes: _____ No: _____

Sincerely,

Beulah R. Compton
Burt Galaway

FOLD HERE

FOLD HERE

Brooks/Cole is dedicated to publishing quality publications for education in the human services fields. If you are interested in learning more about our publications, please fill in your name and address and request our latest catalogue, using this prepaid mailer.

Name: _____

Street Address: _____

City, State, and Zip: _____

FOLD HERE

FOLD HERE